IMPORTANT

HERE IS YOUR REGISTRATION CODE TO ACCE[SS]
PREMIUM CONTENT AND MCGRAW-HILL ONLI[NE]

For key premium online resources you need THIS CODE to gain access. Once the code is entered, you will be able to use the web resources for the length of your course.

Access is provided only if you have purchased a new book.

If the registration code is missing from this book, the registration screen on our website, and within your WebCT or Blackboard course will tell you how to obtain your new code. Your registration code can be used only once to establish access. It is not transferable

To gain access to these online resources

1. USE your web browser to go to: **www.mhhe.com/stanford**

2. CLICK on "First Time User"

3. ENTER the Registration Code printed on the tear-off bookmark on the right

4. After you have entered your registration code, click on "Register"

5. FOLLOW the instructions to setup your personal UserID and Password

6. WRITE your UserID and Password down for future reference. Keep it in a safe place.

If your course is using WebCT or Blackboard, you'll be able to use this code to access the McGraw-Hill content within your instructor's online course.

To gain access to the McGraw-Hill content in your instructor's WebCT or Blackboard course simply log into the course with the user ID and Password provided by your instructor. Enter the registration code exactly as it appears to the right when prompted by the system. You will only need to use this code the first time you click on McGraw-Hill content.

These instructions are specifically for student access. Instructors are not required to register via the above instructions.

The McGraw-Hill Companies
Mc Graw Hill **Higher Education**

Thank you, and welcome to your McGraw-Hill Online Resources.

0-07-321283-0 t/a
Stanford
Responding to Literature: Stories, Poems, Plays, and Essays, 5/e

PNY1-4KWV-6I8X-FAS

REGISTRATION CODE
REGISTRATION CODE

D0586176

on yellow slips:
pages: 5, 11

all of chap 2: 13-56
esp:
p 101
143

also worthwhile (in add'l
to yellow slip 164/65, 170/71

Responding to Literature

Responding to Literature
Stories, Poems, Plays, and Essays

FIFTH EDITION

Judith A. Stanford
Rivier College

Boston   Burr Ridge, IL   Dubuque, IA   Madison, WI   New York
San Francisco   St. Louis   Bangkok   Bogotá   Caracas   Kuala Lumpur
Lisbon   London   Madrid   Mexico City   Milan   Montreal   New Delhi
Santiago   Seoul   Singapore   Sydney   Taipei   Toronto

The McGraw·Hill Companies

Higher Education

Published by McGraw-Hill, an imprint of The McGraw-Hill Companies, Inc., 1221 Avenue of the Americas, New York, NY 10020. Copyright © 2006, 2003, 1999, 1992. All rights reserved. No part of this publication may be reproduced or distributed in any form or by any means, or stored in a database or retrieval system, without the prior written consent of The McGraw-Hill Companies, Inc., including, but not limited to, in any network or other electronic storage or transmission, or broadcast for distance learning.

This book is printed on acid-free paper.

1 2 3 4 5 6 7 8 9 0 DOC/DOC 0 9 8 7 6 5

ISBN 0-07-296278-X

Editor in Chief: *Emily Barrosse;* Publisher: *Lisa Moore;* Director of Development: *Carla Kay Samodulski;* Marketing Manager: *Lori DeShazo;* Senior Media Producer: *Todd Vaccaro;* Managing Editor: *Melissa Williams;* Senior Project Manager: *Christina Gimlin;* Manuscript Editor: *Patricia Ohlenroth;* Art Director: *Jeanne Schreiber;* Senior Design Manager: *Cassandra Chu;* Text Designer: *Linda Robertson;* Cover Designer: *Cassandra Chu;* Associate Art Editor: *Ayelet Arbel;* Senior Photo Research Coordinator: *Nora Agbayani;* Senior Production Supervisor: *Tandra Jorgensen;* Lead Media Project Manager: *Marc Mattson*

Composition: 10.5/12 Bembo by Thompson Type
Printing: 29# Opaque, RR Donnelley, Crawfordsville

Cover art: *Lou Beach*

Credits: The credits section for this book begins on page C-1 and is considered an extension of the copyright page.

Library of Congress Cataloging-in-Publication Data
Responding to literature : stories, poems, plays, and essays / [edited by] Judith A. Stanford.—5th ed.
    p. cm.
  Includes bibliographical references and index.
  ISBN 0-07-296278-X
    1. College readers. 2. English language—Rhetoric—Problems, exercises, etc. 3. Report writing—Problems, exercises, etc. 4. Literature—Collections. I. Stanford, Judith Dupras, 1941–
PE1417.R4745 2005
808'.0668—dc22

2005040888

The Internet addresses listed in the text were accurate at the time of publication. The inclusion of a website does not indicate an endorsement by the authors or McGraw-Hill, and McGraw-Hill does not guarantee the accuracy of the information presented at these sites.

www.mhhe.com

For Lisa Moore and Carla Samodulski

Preface

The first chapter in *Responding to Literature* asks "Why Read Literature?" That chapter, as well as every chapter throughout the book, addresses this question by inviting readers to value, to explore, and to broaden their own ways of responding to poetry, fiction, drama, and nonfiction.

I started on the path toward understanding and appreciating the importance of the reader's response to literature only after several years as a college English instructor. I had been working diligently to teach my students the art of close reading, carefully instructing them—as I had been taught during my own undergraduate and graduate study—to value objective thinking and to reject subjective response.

As my students used this approach, however, I saw that they often remained disengaged from the literature they were reading. They wrote dutifully about what they read, but many of them saw both reading and writing as joyless, uninspired processes. Finally, I began to recognize that there had to be a connection between what I thought of as "public" reading (which I believed must always remain objective) and "private" reading (which I believed could combine objective and subjective responses). I had come to think of the literature I taught in classes as connecting only to the life of intellect. On the other hand, poems, fiction, and plays I read for my own pleasure connected to my intellect, but also to my emotions, experiences, judgments, and moral choices.

I discussed my classroom experiences with colleagues, both on my own campus and at conferences, and they offered recommendations. As I read Louise Rosenblatt, Robert Bleich, and Nancie Atwell—as well as Wolfgang Iser, Robert Probst and so many others—I began to see that the emotions, moral beliefs, and personal experiences of readers are, in fact, legitimate and valuable parts of the process of understanding and connecting to literature, not only in private life but also in the classroom.

wou flew on pp on to more critical exploration.

As I integrated these ideas into my courses, I noticed that both the students and I became engaged with the literature and joined together as a community of readers and writers much earlier in the semester than with my old approach. The close reading strategies I learned to value during my own college and graduate school years remained as an anchor for each course. Now, however, the responses of readers (both mine and my students') served as a way into each work we read and as a way to continually reassess and reevaluate initial judgments as we discussed, reread, and wrote about a work.

I not only modified my classroom process, but I also grew more confident about introducing students to the many authors who were not part of the traditional literary canon. Poets who published mainly in small press magazines—such as Kristine Batey, Neal Bowers, and David Huddle—found their way into the minds (and often the hearts) of my students. They read the fiction of Hemingway and Faulkner, but also short stories I had just discovered by writers like Louise Erdrich, José Armas, and Rita Dove.

Another change in my teaching came as I pondered the many ways I could use the study of literature to promote the critical thinking so essential to the students' academic life and, of course, to their lives after graduation. While analyzing and explicating literary works requires careful study and thought, more and more I saw the importance of learning how to make intriguing and thoughtful comparisons. From this observation came my decision to organize the teaching of literary works thematically, asking students to talk, think, and write about significant issues and ideas related to themes most of them found thought-provoking and important such as "Families," "Roots, Culture, and Identity," and "War and Power."

From this evolving experience as a reader and teacher came the inspiration for the first edition of *Responding to Literature*. During the fourteen years since this book was first published, I have been fortunate to receive many letters and e-mails from students. Among my favorites are those from students who ask me to suggest other works by an author they've come to appreciate or from students who tell me they've decided to keep their copy of *Responding* because they want to read more of the works than were assigned in class. One of my primary goals, both as a teacher and as a textbook author, is to interest students so much that as they close the book after the final classroom assignment, their desire to continue exploring the world of literature opens.

PROVEN FEATURES

Through its four previous editions, the following features have provided instructors and students with many ways to read, think about, discuss, and write about literature and—it is my most sincere hope—to find the deep joy that comes both from intellectual challenge and academic rigor, as well as from personal identification and connection.

• **An emphasis on making connections among works.** As noted, one advantage the thematic organization of the text provides is the way it helps students make thoughtful connections to their own lives. Throughout the book, thought-provoking "Considerations" and "Connections" questions about the works provide ways of thinking and writing about the selections that lead readers away from a single "correct" interpretation and, instead, suggest multiple possibilities—always, of course, to be supported by evidence in the work itself.

• **Strong coverage of the writing process.** Chapter 4 devotes special attention to the writing process, including strategies for discovering and exploring ideas, considering the audience, drafting, revising, and editing. This chapter provides five examples of students writing in different ways as they respond to Dylan Thomas's "Do Not Go Gentle into That Good Night" and Joan Aleshire's "Slipping." The five papers—a personal response, a comparison, an analysis, an explication, and an evaluation—are accompanied by clear and thorough explanations of each student's process. Set off from the text throughout this chapter are summaries of many flexible, yet precisely described, guidelines for writing about literature.

• **Enhanced coverage of argument and research.** For those instructors who emphasize the importance of writing strong arguments about literary works, the coverage of argument has been expanded and moved to a new chapter. Chapter 5 also provides detailed coverage of the research process. An extended example demonstrates one student's process through the stages of writing a researched argument. In addition, this chapter explains MLA documentation and provides numerous illustrations of the most recent MLA guidelines.

• **Plenty of topics for writing and discussion.** These topics invite students to think about the important issues inherent in each chapter's theme.

• **Opportunities for collaborative work.** Sharing ideas and writings with other students can often enrich each student's experience of a literary work. Therefore, at the end of each thematic chapter, at least one collaborative project is included in the "Connections" for writing and discussion. In addition, Chapter 4 includes "Strategies for Collaborative Work."

• **An approach grounded in personal response.** As noted, to invite students to become more engaged with the literary works they are studying, the text stresses the importance of the reader's interaction with and response to what he or she reads. Chapter 1 explores the relationship between reading as a choice and reading as a requirement; this emphasis on the reader's engagement with the literary work is reflected throughout the text.

• **A thorough introduction to literary terms.** Chapter 2 invites students to become part of the literary conversation by showing how literary terms relate to ideas and concepts with which they are already familiar.

• **A thorough introduction to genres and approaches to literary criticism.** Chapter 3 provides clear definitions and short historical overviews of short fiction, poetry, drama, and nonfiction, thus providing students with the background information that will help them form their responses. In addition, students are introduced to five approaches to scholarly criticism.

  • **Literature and art.** Encouraging students to relate literature to other art forms, a full-color chapter (14) invites students to make connections between sixteen poems and the works of art that inspired them (or vice versa).

  • **Thematic chapter photos.** Each thematic chapter is introduced by a carefully selected photograph intended as a way to open a discussion of the theme the picture represents.

  • **Exceptionally thorough support for instructors.** The Instructor's Manual provides sections on teaching the first class and encouraging collaborative interaction in the classroom. The manual includes suggested responses for each discussion or writing topic in *Responding to Literature*. In addition, practical examples of students preparing for and participating in conferences with the instructor as well as with a writing center tutor are included in Chapter 4.

  • **Alternative tables of contents.** To facilitate flexibility in course planning, two alternative Tables of Contents are provided.

  • **Alternative Themes:** The alternative thematic table of contents expands the number of themes an instructor might address and demonstrates how selections from various thematic chapters might be grouped or paired to address a "theme within a theme."

  • **Genre:** Arranging selections by genre and, within each genre, by chronological order by the date of publication (which is provided), this table of contents provides instructors with an easy way to balance selections from various historical and literary periods, should they so desire.

NEW FOR THIS EDITION

Acting on the advice of reviewers who have shared their students' responses to the text, as well as their own suggestions, I have made the following revisions to the fifth edition:

  • **Over 50 new selections.** The new selections in the fifth edition include works by Naomi Shihab Nye, Sherman Alexie, N. Scott Momaday, W. S. Merwin, Gish Jen, Kate Chopin, Leslie Marmon Silko, Annie Dillard, and Bharati Mukherjee. Margaret Edson's play *Wit,* which won the Pulitzer Prize in 1999, raises controversial issues related to technology and ethics. In addition, a seldom-anthologized, edgy play by Langston Hughes, "Soul Gone Home," powerfully addresses American cultural issues that remain current. Finally, the "Nature" chapter now offers "Riders to the Sea," a one-act play by Irish playwright John Millington Synge, which addresses the all-too-relevant theme of the way nature (and the sea in particular) dominates the lives of those whose work and culture require that they live on the shore.

• **A new chapter on writing a researched paper and writing an argument.** As noted earlier, Chapter 5, "Argument, Critical Thinking, and Research," gives students guidelines for writing a paper that argues for a particular interpretation of a literary work, along with advice on locating evidence outside the work to back up an argumentative thesis and guidelines for citing sources using the MLA system of documentation.

• **Expanded American Poets Section.** Chapter 14, "Four Poets: Then and Now," includes works by Emily Dickinson and Robert Frost (with critical studies of his work) as well as by the contemporary poets Billy Collins and Rita Dove. This chapter highlights the associations between these four poets, providing a sample of themes that are considered quintessentially American and giving students more possibilities for response.

• **Integrated support on CD-ROM and on the Web.** To enrich students' experience of literature even further, boxes throughout the text indicate where they can find additional resources on *ARIEL,* McGraw-Hill's new fully interactive literature CD-ROM, and on the book's Online Learning Center (www.mhhe.com/stanford). Available for packaging free with *Responding to Literature, ARIEL* contains 28 author casebooks, annotated texts, video and audio clips, critical essays, essay topics, an extensive glossary of literary terms, and more. The Online Learning Center features casebooks for 20 authors along with glossaries of literary terms, advice on avoiding plagiarism, and help with online research.

• **New theme: Technology and Ethics.** Dealing with a topic that has an enormous impact on students' everyday lives and will continue to have an impact on their futures, this new chapter includes "The Birthmark" by Nathaniel Hawthorne; "Videotape" by Don DeLillo; poems by Emily Dickinson, Walt Whitman, Cathy Song, and Rita Dove; and *Wit,* the Pulitzer–prize-winning play by Margaret Edson.

• **Increased emphasis on visual texts: Then and Now photo essays.** Three new photo essays offer visual texts that complement and enrich the selections in three of the thematic chapters. Chapter 6, "Innocence and Experience," includes a photo essay with pictures of Hamlet as portrayed by different actors in different eras. The photo essays in Chapter 9, "Families," and Chapter 11, "War and Power," consist of compelling images—both photographs and fine art—that connect with other works within the chapter and offer additional opportunities for discussion and topics for writing.

• **"Art and Poetry" as a separate chapter.** The 16 works of art and accompanying poems in this color chapter offer a rich variety of opportunities for response, with four new pairings added for this edition.

• **A focus on film as a dramatic genre.** Because students respond enthusiastically to the medium of film, new Film Connection boxes in the text discuss three films and offer exercises that prompt students to react to them: *Hamlet* (the version released in 2000, starring Ethan Hawke), *Wit,* and

Three Kings. Each of these films offers expanded teaching opportunities. The Ethan Hawke *Hamlet,* set in current-day New York, gives students and instructors the opportunity to discuss themes in the play as they relate to modern culture. Emma Thompson's stunning portrayal of the dying Vivian Bearing in *Wit* brings to life the challenges, controversies, and questions raised by this play. Finally, *Three Kings,* a film set in the first Gulf War, provides a recent historical context for the current war in Iraq, addressing issues and moral choices that concern us all as we hear each new report from the Middle East. McGraw-Hill will offer DVDs for these three films to instructors who adopt the Fifth Edition of *Responding to Literature,* thus expanding the selections from which instructors may choose.

• **New Web Connections questions.** At the end of each thematic chapter, new "Web Connections" questions encourage students to explore issues using the enormous resources available on the World Wide Web.

SUPPLEMENTS ACCOMPANYING *RESPONDING TO LITERATURE*

Supplements for Students

ARIEL **(A Resource for the Interactive Exploration of Literature) CD-ROM:** *ARIEL,* McGraw-Hill English's fully interactive CD-ROM, is an exciting new tool that introduces students to the pleasures of studying literature. The CD features nearly thirty casebooks on authors ranging from Sophocles to Rita Dove. Each casebook offers a rich array of resources, including hyperlinked texts; video and audio clips; critical essays; a biography, bibliography, and webliography; essay questions, quizzes, and visuals. General resources include a robust glossary and more.

Online Learning Center to Accompany *Responding to Literature* **(www.mhhe.com/stanford):** This rich online learning center offers complete texts of selected classic works with embedded links to relevant sites; a linked table of contents; a linked timeline offering historical and cultural contexts for all anthologized works; author biographies; a complete glossary; literature-specific Web links; guidelines for library and Internet research; a tutorial on avoiding plagiarism; a writing tutor for an interpretive paper; and interactive quizzes, Web exercises, and writing prompts offering students additional practice in literary response, interpretation, and evaluation.

Trade books: A number of modern and classic works of fiction and nonfiction are available at a substantial discount when packaged with Stanford's *Responding to Literature:*

Abbey, *The Monkey Wrench Gang*
Achebe, *Things Fall Apart*
Alexie, *The Lone Ranger and Tonto Fistfight in Heaven*

Angelou, *I Know Why the Caged Bird Sings*
Bissinger, *Friday Night Lights,* Second Edition
Cisneros, *The House on Mango Street*
Conrad, *Heart of Darkness*
Dillard, *Pilgrim at Tinker Creek*
Erdrich, *Love Medicine*
Esquivel, *Like Water for Chocolate*
Ha Jin, *Waiting*
Hurston, *Their Eyes Were Watching God*
Jenkins, *A Walk across America*
Kingston, *Woman Warrior*
Momaday, *House Made of Dawn*
Morrison, *Beloved*
Nafisi, *Reading Lolita in Tehran*
Spiegelman, *Maus, Vol. 1*
Tan, *Joy Luck Club*
White, *Essays of E. B. White*

Poetry to My Ear (0-07-229543-0): This is the first CD-ROM to cover
the formal components of poetry (rhyme, rhythm, line, and form), to define
and illustrate concepts, and to enable students to try their own hands at some
of the techniques in the interactive studio. By offering students the opportunity to hear a recitation of each anthologized poem (in some cases by the author), this groundbreaking teaching tool engages students with poetry, poetic
language, and poets at a truly inspirational level. *Poetry to My Ear* is available at
a discount when packaged with *Responding to Literature.*

Supplements for Instructors

Instructor's Manual to accompany *Responding to Literature:* Available online at www.mhhe.com/stanford, the Instructor's Manual includes
suggested responses for each discussion or writing topic in the book and provides sections on teaching the first class and encouraging interaction in the
classroom.

In Their Own Voices: A Century of Recorded Poetry (0-07-242404-4): An
audio CD collection of classic and contemporary poems in the voices of the
poets who wrote them.

Online Learning Center to Accompany *Responding to Literature*
(www.mhhe.com/stanford): In addition to offering the complete Instructor's Manual (see above) as a downloadable document, the Online Learning
Center offers links of interest to instructors of literature as well as the student
resources listed on page xii.

PageOut, WebCT, and More! The online content of *Responding to
Literature* is supported by WebCT, eCollege.com, and Blackboard. Additionally,
our PageOut service is available to get you and your course up and running

online in a matter of hours—at no cost! To find out more, contact your local McGraw-Hill representative or visit http://www.pageout.net.

Teaching Composition Faculty Listserv at <www.mhhe.com/ tcomp>. Moderated by Chris Anson at North Carolina State University and offered by McGraw-Hill as a service to the composition community, this listserv brings together senior members of the college composition community with newer members—junior faculty, adjuncts, and teaching assistants— through an online newsletter and accompanying discussion group to address issues of pedagogy, both in theory and in practice.

Please contact your local McGraw-Hill representative for details concerning policies, prices, and availability of these supplements.

ACKNOWLEDGMENTS

My own teaching and the inspiration for this text owe much to the writing of Louise Rosenblatt, Robert Scholes, Robert DiYanni, Nancie Atwell, and Mike Rose. Rebecca Burnett, master teacher, researcher, and writer, continues as a role model and true friend. For many years, Lynn Quitman Troyka has inspired me, both as a teacher and a writer. I thank my husband, Don, and my sons, David and Aaron, for being people who enjoy reading and who share with me their thoughts about what they read. My mother, Arline Dupras, earns praise not only for the endless support she gives in helping me to proofread each new edition, but also for being the person who first taught me that reading is joyful.

I extend special thanks and gratitude to all students whose writing and discussion contributed to this book. These students include not only those whom I have taught in the classroom, but also the many students who have read various editions of *Responding to Literature* and who have taken the time to e-mail me their thoughts and suggestions. I believe the fifth edition has benefited greatly from the many conversations I have had with students and with their instructors.

The reviewers of this edition as well as those of the first four editions offered helpful and wise suggestions, which I greatly appreciate. Reviewers for the first edition include Thomas Dukes, University of Akron; Cynthia A. Eby, James Madison University; Leonard Engel, Quinnipiac College; Jennifer W. Thompson, University of Kansas; James Wanless, Henry Ford Community College. Reviewers for the second edition include Elizabeth Addison, Western Carolina University; Melissa E. Barth, Appalachian State University; Denise David, Niagara County Community College; Ruth Elowitz, Chabot College; Anita R. Guynn, University of South Carolina, Columbia; John Heyda, Miami University; Anna Jackson, Southern Illinois University, Carbondale; Pansy J.

Jackson, Virginia State University; Maggy Lindgren, University of Cincinnati; Elizabeth C. Mitchell, Ocean County College; Alan B. Shaw, Monroe Community College; Camille Taylor, College of Lake County; Cyrilla Vessey, Northern Virginia Community College; and Bertha L. Wise, Oklahoma City Community College. Reviewers for the third edition include Margaret Lindren, University of Cincinnati; Zack Miller, Brookhaven College; David Norlin, Cloud County Community College; William Provost, University of Georgia; Mark Richardson, Georgia Southern University; Jacquelynn Sorensen, University of Nebraska-Lincoln; Ann Tippett, Monroe Community College; William Tomory, Southwestern Michigan College; and Bertha Wise, Oklahoma City Community College. Reviewers for the fourth edition include: Mark Vernier, Blinn College; Karen Blomain, Kutztown University; Charles Coleman, CUNY-York College; Laurie Lopez Coleman, San Antonio College; Kirsten Day, University of Arkansas; Rick Kempa, Western Wyoming Community College; Mary Ann Klein, Quincy University; Ron Kyhos, U.S. Naval Academy; Robert Myers, Lock Haven University; David Norland, Cloud County Community College; Joe Popson, Macon State College; Elaine Razzano, Lyndon State College; Lucille M. Schulta, University of Cincinnati; Lolly Smith, Everett Community College; William Tomory, Southwestern Michigan College; Lisa Williams, Jacksonville State University; Bertha Wise, Oklahoma City Community College. For the fifth edition, I am indebted to the following reviewers:

> Lindsay Pentolfe Aegerter, Lakeside School
> Thomas Austenfeld, North Georgia College and State University
> Mary Anne Bernal, San Antonio College
> Tina S. Blue, University of Kansas
> Vince Brewton, University of North Alabama
> Carol Ann Britt, San Antonio College
> George Cheatham, Greensboro College
> Alan P. Church, University of Texas at Brownsville
> Stacy M. Clanton, Southern Arkansas University
> Timothy R. Cramer, Santa Monica College
> Rose Day, Albuquerque TVI Community College
> Eduardo del Rio, University of Texas at Brownsville
> John Dudley, University of South Dakota
> Patty Keefe Durso, Montclair State University
> Lisa Edmunds, Miami Dade Community College
> Janis Greve, Western New England College
> Susan Hudson Grimland, Collin County Community College
> Stephanie Downie Hummer, University of Georgia
> Eric Hibbison, J. Sargeant Reynolds Community College
> John M. Krafft, Miami University Hamilton

Harriet Masembe, Norfolk State University
Donna Mayes, Blue Ridge Community College
Dennis McDonald, Iowa Lakes Community College
Kelly A. O'Connor-Salomon, Black Hills State University
Brian L. Olson, Kalamazoo Valley Community College
Carole Clark Papper, Ball State University
Pennie Pflueger, Southeast Missouri State University
Michael L. Richmond, Nova Southeastern University
Guinevere Shaw, Passaic County Community College
Mark Spalding, Manchester College
Kelly Stanley, Ball State University
Pamela Stout, Oklahoma City Community College
James G. Van Belle, Edmonds Community College
Jessica Lyn Van Slooten, State University of West Georgia
Kenneth Womack, Penn State Altoona
Sara B. Wood, Mississippi State University

Bertha Wise, Chair of the Department of English at Oklahoma City Community College, devised outstanding writing topics for those selections new to the third edition and in addition has offered valuable suggestions for the fourth and fifth editions. Leslie Van Wagner, Director of the Rivier College Writing Center, made helpful contributions to the third edition of the Instructor's Guide. Susan Van Schuyver, of the Department of English at Oklahoma City Community College, made several useful suggestions for teaching the "Art and Poetry" section, which are now included in the Instructors Guide. Barbara Armentrout researched and wrote detailed and intriguing author biographies for the third and fourth editions. For the fourth edition and for this edition, I owe great thanks to Lorraine Lordi, my friend and colleague at Rivier College, not only for her support and encouragement, but also for providing thoughtful and inspiring writing topics. In addition, she has ably tackled the task of writing entries for the new selections for the Instructor's Guide for the fourth and fifth editions. In doing so, she draws on the wit and wisdom developed during her many years of remarkably successful classroom experience. I would also like to thank Emily Lordi for her lively and literate contributions to the "Art and Poetry" section of the Instructors Guide.

This book began its journey at Mayfield Publishing Company. I owe a great debt to Mayfield, and I extend special thanks to Jan Beatty, the editor who first invited me to publish with Mayfield and who saw *Responding* through its initial publication and two revisions. The transition to McGraw-Hill was made smooth by many people. Steve DeBow, who listened, encouraged, and generally made me feel welcome and supported deserves particular mention, as does Sarah Touborg, who was then executive editor at McGraw-Hill. Sarah gracefully assumed direction of the revision process for the fourth edition and turned what might have been a daunting task into a great pleasure. Christina Gimlin, production editor, ably focused the production of the fourth and fifth editions with grace, energy, and efficiency. Marty Granahan, once again, attended to the difficult task of obtaining permissions. I am also grateful to Cassandra Chu for her creative vision in working with the design of this edition. Patricia Ohlenroth, as copy editor, offered valuable suggestions that were always right on target. I also wish to thank the English Field publishers Byron Hopkins, Ray Kelley, Paula Radosevich, and Jason Dewey and the McGraw-Hill sales representatives for their hard work on behalf of this book.

My deepest thanks go to Lisa Moore, English Publisher; Carla Samodulski, Director of Development, English and New Media; and Lori DeShazo, Marketing Manager. Lisa Moore's vision and commitment to this project have provided great inspiration and affirmation. Carla Samodulski has offered wise editorial advice at every stage of development of this edition, providing constant support and much appreciated communication during this journey to the fifth edition. In addition, her editing suggestions have not only made the book stronger, but have also helped me to grow as a writer. Marketing Manager Lori DeShazo and I first met when she was a Field Publisher. I deeply appreciate her understanding of the underlying values and pedagogy of this text, as well as her enthusiasm and consummate skill in helping to put *Responding to Literature* in the hands of professors and students.

—Judith Stanford

Responding to Literature

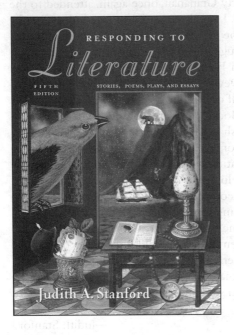

RESPONDING TO *LITERATURE* IS ABOUT MAKING CONNECTIONS

Welcome! The following pages will serve as a map of sorts to using this book. To get the most out of *Responding to Literature,* spend a few minutes getting to know its organization and features.

Chapter 1 encourages you to make **personal connections to the literary works** you will be reading—to bring your own knowledge and values to bear on the reading experience. Chapters 2 and 3 introduce you to **literary terms, genres, and approaches to literature.**

1

Why Read Literature?

At the first meeting of a course called "Literature and Writing," a professor asked students to respond to a question written on the forms she distributed to them. She explained that some students would receive Form A and some, Form B. The question on each form was different, although the two questions differed by only one word.

Form A asked students, "Why do *you* read literature? (For the purposes of this response, please consider 'literature' to mean any and all fiction, poetry, drama, and essays.)"

Form B asked students, "Why do *we* read literature? (For the purposes of this response, please consider 'literature' to mean any and all fiction, poetry, drama, and essays.)"

Exercise

Before you read further, consider the two questions. Do you see any real difference between them? How would you respond to each question? Take a few minutes to jot down your thoughts. Then compare your responses with those that follow.

WHY DO YOU READ LITERATURE?

Students responded to this question in a wide variety of ways. The following comments are representative:

> I read mostly fiction for pleasure. Poetry and drama I don't read much. When I read, I like to escape—to get away from all the

1

Chapter 4 gives you **guidelines for and student models of five different approaches to writing about literature:** a personal response, a comparison, an analysis, an explication, and an evaluation.

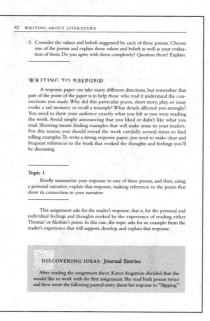

> 92 WRITING ABOUT LITERATURE
>
> 5. Consider the values and beliefs suggested by each of these poems. Choose one of the poems and explain those values and beliefs as well as your evaluation of them. Do you agree with them completely? Question them? Explain.
>
> **WRITING TO RESPOND**
>
> A response paper can take many different directions, but remember that part of the point of the paper is to help those who read it understand the connections you made. Why did this particular poem, short story, play, or essay evoke a sad memory or recall a triumph? What details affected you strongly? You need to show your audience exactly what you felt as you were reading the work. Avoid simply announcing that you liked or didn't like what you read. Showing means finding examples that will make sense to your readers. For this reason, you should reread the work carefully several times to find telling examples. To write a strong response paper, you need to make clear and frequent references to the work that evoked the thoughts and feelings you'll be discussing.
>
> **Topic 1**
>
> Briefly summarize your response to one of these poems, and then, using a personal narrative, explain that response, making references to the poem that show its connection to your narrative.
>
> This assignment asks for the reader's response, that is, for the personal and individual feelings and thoughts evoked by the experience of reading either Thomas' or Aleshire's poem. In this case, the topic asks for an example from the reader's experience that will support, develop, and explain that response.
>
> **DISCOVERING IDEAS: Journal Entries**
>
> After reading the assignment sheet, Karen Angstrom decided that she would like to work with the first assignment. She read both poems twice and then wrote the following journal entry about her response to "Slipping."

5

Argument, Critical Thinking, and Research

ARGUMENT AND CRITICAL THINKING

Throughout this text, you will find various discussions on the process of critical thinking. For instance, Chapter 4 discusses ways in which writing encourages critical thinking (page 87–88). Chapter 6 suggests ways in which reading various works of literature comparatively and in relationship to specific themes leads to thinking critically (page 193). This chapter considers the process of developing an argument through critical thinking. For instance, to build a thoughtful argument you need to evaluate carefully the details you plan to use as evidence. In addition, to think critically about a controversial issue you need to be willing to entertain multiple points of view and to sort through those viewpoints to arrive at the thesis for an argument you believe you can logically develop and support.

Definition of Argument

To many people, the word "argument" brings to mind images of anger and bitter conflict. Sometimes it seems as if the world is filled with argument, in this sense of the word. Talk show hosts invite guests and audience members to disagree heatedly with each other, sometimes to the point of physical violence. Sports fans, players, and coaches (and even Little League parents) contest referees' and umpires' decisions with what can, at best, be called colorful language and energetic gestures. Politicians appearing on television panels take turns calling each other "incompetent," "dishonest," or "unpatriotic."

Another definition of argument, however, calls for a different kind of response to the situations described in the previous paragraph. According to this

147

New to this edition, Chapter 5 offers **guidelines for writing a researched argument** about a literary work and includes a **sample student paper** as well as detailed information on how to cite information from sources using **MLA style.**

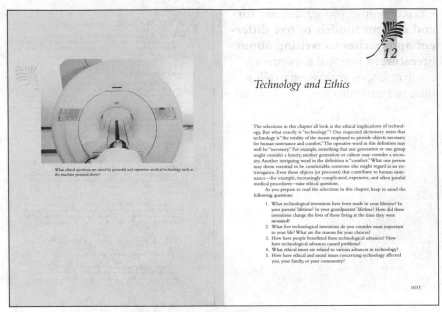

12

Technology and Ethics

The selections in this chapter all look at the ethical implications of technology. But what exactly is "technology"? One respected dictionary states that technology is "the totality of the means employed to provide objects necessary for human sustenance and comfort." The operative word in this definition may well be "necessary." For example, something that one generation or one group might consider a luxury, another generation or culture may consider a necessity. Another intriguing word in the definition is "comfort." What one person may deem essential to be comfortable, someone else might regard as an extravagance. Even those objects (or processes) that contribute to human sustenance—for example, increasingly complicated, expensive, and often painful medical procedures—raise ethical questions.

As you prepare to read the selections in this chapter, keep in mind the following questions:

1. What technological inventions have been made in your lifetime? In your parents' lifetime? In your grandparents' lifetime? How did these inventions change the lives of those living at the time they were invented?
2. What five technological inventions do you consider most important to your life? What are the reasons for your choices?
3. How have people benefited from technological advances? How have technological advances caused problems?
4. What ethical issues are related to various advances in technology?
5. How have ethical and moral issues concerning technology affected you, your family, or your community?

What ethical questions are raised by powerful and expensive medical technology such as the machine pictured above?

1033

Chapters 6–13 provide **fiction, poetry, drama, and essays on thought-provoking themes** that you can connect to your own experience, such as "Families," "Roots, Culture, and Identity," and "War and Power." **New** to this edition, **Chapter 12, "Technology and Ethics,"** deals with a topic that has an enormous impact on everyday life.

Boxes throughout the text indicate where you can find **additional resources on** *ARIEL,* McGraw-Hill's new fully interactive literature CD-ROM, and on the book's **Online Learning Center (www.mhhe.com/stanford).**

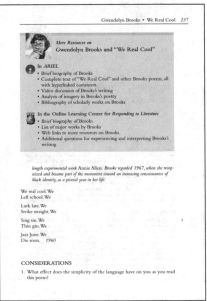

Gwendolyn Brooks • We Real Cool 237

More Resources on
Gwendolyn Brooks and "We Real Cool"

In *ARIEL*
• Brief biography of Brooks
• Complete text of "We Real Cool" and other Brooks poems, all with hyperlinked comments
• Video discussion of Brooks's writing
• Analysis of imagery in Brooks's poetry
• Bibliography of scholarly works on Brooks

In the Online Learning Center for *Responding to Literature*
• Brief biography of Brooks
• List of major works by Brooks
• Web links to more resources on Brooks
• Additional questions for experiencing and interpreting Brooks's writing

length experimental work Annie Allen. Brooks regarded 1967, when she recognized and became part of the movement toward an increasing consciousness of black identity, as a pivotal year in her life.

We real cool. We
Left school. We

Lurk late. We
Strike straight. We

Sing sin. We
Thin gin. We

Jazz June. We
Die soon. *1960*

CONSIDERATIONS

1. What effect does the simplicity of the language have on you as you read this poem?

The **16 works of art, in color, and accompanying poems in Chapter 14** offer you a rich variety of opportunities to make—and write about—connections between these two art forms.

Henri Matisse (French, 1869–1954). *Dance* (first version). Paris (March 1909). Oil on canvas, 8 ft. 6½ in. × 12 ft. 9½ in. (259.7 × 390.1 cm). Gift of Nelson A. Rockefeller in honor of Alfred H. Barr, Jr. Photograph © The Museum of Modern Art/Licensed by Scala/Art Resource, New York. © 2002 Successors H. Matisse, Paris/Artists Rights Society (ARS), New York.

NATALIE SAFIR (1935–)
Matisse's Dance

A break in the circle dance of naked women,
dropped stitch between the hands
of the slender figure stretching too hard
to reach her joyful sisters.

Spirals of glee sail from the arms
of the tallest woman. She pulls
the circle around with her fire.
What has she found that she doesn't
keep losing, her torso
a green-burning torch?

Grass mounds curve ripely beneath
two others who dance beyond the blue.
Breasts swell and multiply and
rhythms rise to a gallop.

Hurry, frightened one and grab on—before
the stitch is forever lost, before the dance
unravels and a black sun swirls from that space. *1990*

CONNECTIONS • Art and Poetry *17*

Billy Collins *1267*

will fall into itself, an image that recurs throughout Frost's poetry.[4] Thus the child's grave predicts the dissolution of household, a movement towards the open cellar of "The Generations of Men," almost a literal "home burial."

The husband seems about to learn what the husband learns in "The Hill Wife"—"of finalities / Besides the grave"—but he will learn the lesson *because of* the grave of his son, the once and future rival for his wife's attention.... *1987*

BILLY COLLINS (1941–)

Born in New York City in 1941, Billy Collins developed an early interest in poetry. His father, who was working as an electrician when Collins was born and who later became the vice president of an insurance company, was a vibrant, passionate individual with a wide variety of avocations, ranging from playing golf to reading poetry. As a high school student, Collins worked as a caddy at his father's golf club, where he learned a great deal about himself and about social class in America. In an interview with James Dodson, Collins noted, "When you're a caddy, you're basically invisible. People talk as if you aren't even there . . . [and] you gain a valuable new insight into people." These insights later contributed to an essential aspect of Collins's poetry: The creation of a speaker, whose voice sounds throughout the body of his work. In an interview with Elizabeth Lund, Collins observed, "A novelist invents many characters . . . but the poet's job is to create one character, one distinctive voice." Collins believes that his poetic voice "attempts to blend humor and seriousness, to balance those two realms."

Collins remembers his father commuting to Wall Street, then returning in the evening with reading material such as Poetry magazine. Intrigued by his father's interest in poetry, Collins began to read widely in the magazines he brought home, and by the time he entered his freshman year at the College of the Holy Cross in Worcester, Massachusetts, he was also writing and publishing his own poems. Reading poetry, however, continued to be central and essential to his life. He remembers, for example, that he and his roommates circumvented the strict 10:00 P.M. lights out policy in his dorm by stuffing the cracks of their door with towels and tin foil so that they could keep their lamps burning—and the pages of books turning—late into the night. The writers he remembers most from that

[*]See, for example, "The Census Taker," where the rotting and abandoned house never held women; "The Black Cottage," where the boards are warping and bees live in the walls; "A Fountain, a Bottle, A Donkey's Ears, and Some Books," where the doors still hold but the broken windows allow easy entry; and "The Thatch," where a hundred-year-old cottage opens itself to the rain at the dissolution of the marriage within.

Chapter 15, "Four Poets: Then and Now" highlights the connections between two classic American poets, Robert Frost and Emily Dickinson, and two contemporary poets, Billy Collins and Rita Dove, providing a sample of themes that are considered quintessentially American and giving you more possibilities for response.

Three new photo essays offer visual texts that complement and enrich the selections in three thematic chapters. Chapter 6, Innocence and Experience, includes a photo essay on Hamlet as portrayed by different actors in different eras. The photo essays in Chapter 9, Families, and Chapter 11, War and Power, consist of photographs and fine art that connect with other works within the chapters and offer additional opportunities for discussion and topics for writing.

Because film is a genre that you probably have already enjoyed—and responded to—**new Film Connection boxes** in the text discuss three films related to works or themes within the text and offer guidelines for developing your response: *Hamlet* (the version starring Ethan Hawke), *Wit,* and *Three Kings.*

1130 TECHNOLOGY AND ETHICS

■■■ Film Connection: *Wit*

While film and other genres of literature share certain elements, such as word choice and plot development, there are some elements unique to film. Of course, it is obvious that a film, unlike a written work, offers visual images that can be seen with the eye rather than imagined in the mind. These visual aspects contribute to the viewers' response, to their pleasure, and to their ability to analyze and evaluate the film.

Consider, as an example, the HBO production of *Wit* (2001), directed by Mike Nichols and with Emma Thompson playing the lead role of Vivian Bearing. In this film, the role of technology in healthcare and the ethical issues related to it raise questions that are at the core of this chapter's theme.

Color and Light In *Wit*, bright, harsh light contributes much to the tone of the main setting, a large teaching hospital. In the hospital, even at night, the patients cannot escape the lights that illuminate their beds, their rooms, and even parts of their bodies for examination and testing by various medical professionals. In addition, the bright light that frequently focuses on Vivian Bearing ironically suggests that she is in the spotlight, forced by her illness to play the central role in a terrifying drama.

Exercise Notice the color of various objects that are part of the hospital setting. In what ways do these colors contrast with the washed out whites and pastels of the patient's room, her regulation hospital garments, and even the uniforms of the medical staff? How does the emphasis on these objects relate to the theme of the film?

Camera Angles and Movement In several scenes, the camera pulls away and up, looking straight down on Vivian Bearing as she struggles with various stages of her illness and treatment. The viewer experiences a sense of distance and separation from the character, yet remains acutely aware of the suffering human being at the distant focus of this shot. Through the camera work, Bearing's isolation and loneliness are emphasized, as well as her loss of power. No longer is she in the center of the action, controlling her life, her subject matter, and her students. Now she is at the mercy of the hospital, the medical professionals, and the technology used to pursue the research study to which she has agreed.

Exercises

1. Note the extreme close-up shots, and choose one or two to discuss. How do the shots you chose contribute to the development of character, conflict, or theme? For instance, consider the opening shot of Dr. Kelekian when he delivers the diagnosis of advanced ovarian cancer.

SUGGESTION FOR COLLABORATIVE LEARNING

Working in groups of three or four, choose four selections from the various genres in this chapter. As a group, choose three or four good, open-ended questions that address the topics of love, marriage, men, and women. After the questions and selections have been agreed on, each member of the group then chooses one selection to analyze in terms of how the character or narrator in the piece would answer the given questions. Collectively, the group then synthesizes their responses and creates a screenplay or script of sorts in which four different characters/speakers answer the question and respond to one another. If you like, you can set this up as a popular talk show panel and perform it for the class when you are ready.

WEB CONNECTIONS

1. In many of the selections in this chapter, human emotions play an integral part in the major conflicts within and among the characters. How does an individual control an emotion, and how is that emotion born in the first place? What happens when emotions end up controlling people instead of the other way around? Are there distinct differences between men and women when it comes to emotions? If so, are these differences based on genetic predisposition or on social expectation? To consider the complexity of emotions and the role they play in our lives, visit the *Great Ideas in Personality* Web site at http://personalityresearch.org. This site links to student and professional essays on emotions, as well as modern gender roles. Under "Personality Research Programs," click on "Basic Emotions" for links. The link for the "Emotions Home Page" leads to more links to scholarly publications.

2. In what ways are our expectations and views on emotions shaped by the early literature we read as well as the fictional characters we celebrate both in the United States and around the world? In order to gain a better understanding of gender roles and stereotyping in children's literature, go to *Children's*

At the end of each thematic chapter, **new Web Connections questions** encourage you to explore issues using the vast amount of resources available on the World Wide Web.

We hope that you will come away from *Responding to Literature* having found new ways to read, think about, discuss, write about—and enjoy—literature.

Contents

Works with an asterisk are new to this edition.

Alternate Contents by Genre

Works with an asterisk are new to this edition.

Poetry

Alternate Contents by Theme

★Works with an asterisk are new to this edition.

Identification and Alienation

Learning and Teaching

Poetry

Drama

Essays

Journeys

Fiction

American Conflicts and Crises

Why Read Literature?

At the first meeting of a course called "Literature and Writing," a professor asked students to respond to a question written on the forms she distributed to them. She explained that some students would receive Form A and some, Form B. The question on each form was different, although the two questions differed by only one word.

Form A asked students, "Why do you read literature? (For the purposes of this response, please consider 'literature' to mean any and all fiction, poetry, drama, and essays.)"

Form B asked students, "Why do we read literature? (For the purposes of this response, please consider 'literature' to mean any and all fiction, poetry, drama, and essays.)"

Exercise

Before you read further, consider the two questions. Do you see any real difference between them? How would you respond to each question? Take a few minutes to jot down your thoughts. Then compare your responses with those that follow.

WHY DO YOU READ LITERATURE?

Students responded to this question in a wide variety of ways. The following comments are representative:

> I read mostly fiction for pleasure. Poetry and drama I don't read much. When I read, I like to escape—to get away from all the

pressures of everyday life. So, I don't want to read about a lot of the same troubles I have. And no unhappy endings.

—KARIN ESTES

I don't read what you call literature except that you said "any and all fiction, poetry, drama, or essays." So, if "any and all" can mean Stephen King (which a teacher I had said was not literature), then that's what I read. And the reason is his books always hold my interest because I get interested in the characters' lives. Then, when they get into totally weird situations, it's like I can really believe that. I don't know why I like to read stuff that scares me, but I do. I also like this kind of movie.

—JEFF PEDINO

Literature to me has always meant a place to find someone else who goes through the same things I do. But seeing them and their problems or situations more in an objective way. When I was in middle school, I read a lot of Judy Blume's novels. I liked that she was honest and wrote about real feelings people have instead of what was some fantasy of how people should feel. She wasn't always teaching a lesson. Also, in high school I read *Tess of the D'Urbervilles* by Thomas Hardy. I thought Hardy was really honest, too, and Tess is not just the perfect little heroine. Then I read three more novels by Hardy because I liked how he wrote. I do that. Read a lot of one author when I find someone I like.

—KATE ANSTROM

I read literature for two reasons: (1) it's assigned by a teacher, and (2) it's something that interests me. Most of the time these are not the same thing. Forget poetry, which is always a big puzzle to me. I don't want to have to figure out hidden meanings. I don't read drama because who buys drama in a bookstore? I like novels or short stories in some magazines. Adventures that move fast and have a good plot really keep my interest (mysteries are sometimes good, too, when you don't figure out on the second page who the killer was).

—DAVE WILLETTE

WHY DO WE READ LITERATURE?

The responses to this question were not so widely varied, but they were very different from the responses to the first question. Here are two samples; nearly all students gave a variation on one of these two themes:

We read literature to find the beauty of words of great writers. Literature teaches us the truth about our lives. We learn good values from literature like Shakespeare.

—ELAYNE MERCIER

Literature is very important to read, because those writers have lasted
through a lot of years, and so what they say must be important.
Otherwise they would have been forgotten. We read literature
because it is an important part of our education. Like history is one
part and math is one part and literature is one part.

—RICK MCDOUGAL

BRIDGING THE GAP

The differences students saw between personal reading (and the reasons
for it) and "school reading" (and the reasons for it) show up clearly in these
different responses. When answering the universally phrased question "Why
do we read literature?" students dutifully answered with language that echoed
pat textbook phrases, such as "beauty of words," "truth about our lives," and
"lasted through . . . years." Few students mentioned whether they themselves
found literature beautiful; few wondered why literature had "lasted through
the years." Almost no one commented on any personal, individual reading
choices. The only author consistently mentioned by name was Shakespeare.

By contrast, students' responses to the more individual question ("Why
do you read literature?") varied widely and showed that literature was important to them for many different reasons. In addition, they noted some of the
problems they encountered with traditionally defined "literature." For example, when Jeff Pedino comments that a teacher did not consider Stephen King's
writing literature, he's beginning to search for a definition. In essence, Jeff is
asking, "What makes a story, novel, poem, play, or essay 'literature'?"

Note, also, Dave Willette's comment that he doesn't enjoy poetry because he doesn't like reading that is a "puzzle." Dave cuts right to the heart of
an issue that had always bothered him—the feeling that reading literature (and
especially poetry) was basically a grueling search through a maze of difficult
words to find a hidden meaning.

Some students made observations about their reading patterns. For instance, Kate Anstrom likes to read many novels by the same author (she mentions Judy Blume and Thomas Hardy). Kate's response is interesting because
she bridges the gap between literature that is read in school and outside school.
She read *Tess of the D'Urbervilles* for a class and liked the novel because she
thought Hardy was honest. He created a heroine who was far from perfect.

So, Kate makes a connection between her values (it's clear that truth, honesty, and realism are important to her) and the literature she reads. She looks at
assigned books in a personal way and thus makes them part of her world. Of
course, there's a reciprocal exchange involved, too. Hardy and his characters become part of Kate's world, but she also becomes part of theirs. When she reads
Hardy's novels, she sees, senses, and experiences nineteenth-century England in
a direct and detailed way. She doesn't read with detachment but instead becomes deeply involved with Hardy's creation.

This text invites you to make personal connections with various selections of literature that other readers have found important to their lives. A work of literature exists on the printed page, but it gains life and meaning only when individual readers bring their knowledge, beliefs, feelings, and values to the reading experience. You are not expected to like or to enjoy everything you read in this text (or everything that you read anywhere): no reader could honestly claim to do that. But you should be able to *respond* to every work that you read. Having a genuine response—and being willing to explore that response—is the key to opening new possibilities in whatever you read, in or out of class, both now and in the future.

RESPONDING TO WHAT YOU READ

The great thing about responding to literature is that there are no absolute answers. A response is a beginning point. You read a work through, keeping your mind and spirit open, and then jot down what you thought and felt as you read it. An initial response might include any of the following:

- A question (about the meaning of a word or sentence, the choice of a word, the reason a particular character appears in the work, the reason the author chose to begin or end as he or she did)

- A comment on what you think the work is about and why you are interested or not interested in that idea

- An observation about a particular description, or line, or sentence to which you had a strong reaction (you liked it; you disliked it; it made you angry, happy, sad, puzzled, uncomfortable)

- A connection between this work and something else you have read, experienced, or observed in your own life

Remember that a response is a place to begin. Just as we often change our first impressions of a person or situation, readers often revise initial responses to a work of literature.

Exercise

Read the following poem by Robert Frost, and then write down your responses. You don't have to interpret the poem (although interpretation can certainly be one part of response). Don't worry about what you are "supposed to get" from the reading. Just notice your reactions and then write them down. When you are finished, compare your responses to the students' comments that follow Frost's poem. If possible, compare your comments to those of students in your class.

ROBERT FROST (1874–1963)

The Road Not Taken

Two roads diverged in a yellow wood,
And sorry I could not travel both
And be one traveler, long I stood
And looked down one as far as I could
To where it bent in the undergrowth;   5

Then took the other, as just as fair,
And having perhaps the better claim,
Because it was grassy and wanted wear;
Though as for that the passing there
Had worn them really about the same,   10

And both that morning equally lay
In leaves no step had trodden black.
Oh, I kept the first for another day!
Yet knowing how way leads on to way,
I doubted if I should ever come back.   15

I shall be telling this with a sigh
Somewhere ages and ages hence:
Two roads diverged in a wood, and I—
I took the one less traveled by,
And that has made all the difference.   *1915*   20

Sample Student Responses to "The Road Not Taken"

> This person is standing in the woods, and it's probably fall, because the
> leaves are yellow. This is a nice time to take a walk, and it's a question
> which way he wants to go, because he would like to see all of the
> woods. He can go on only one path today. But I can't figure out why
> he says in lines 14 and 15 that he couldn't come back. Why does he
> doubt he'll come back, if he wants to see what's on the other path?
>
> —JANICE ANGSTROM

> This is not a poem about Frost just taking some walk in the woods.
> It's about him making a choice to be a poet. Then in the last stanza
> he is glad he made that choice, and he says it has made all the
> difference in his life.
>
> —GILBERT BROWN

> I see this as a poem about choices. The poet might be thinking
> about one choice, but I think it could mean many different possible
> decisions. I don't think the choice seems too big at first, because I
> notice lines 9 and 10 say that the paths really had been traveled

almost the same amount. To me, this is like a lot of life decisions. They may seem small at the time, but as Frost says, one way leads on to another, and you can't go back and relive your life.

—ANITA JUAREZ

In the poem, the poet is sorry he made a certain choice in his life. He calls the poem "The Road Not Taken," so he is looking at the choice he didn't make and thinking about it for some reason. Maybe wondering what life would be like if he took that other road. And that is why he sighs in the last stanza. He is regretting what he lost out on. I can understand this because I do this, too. I look back and see some choices I made—like dropping out of school and going into the army—and I can see what I missed.

—DAVID FURMAN

Commentary

You may find one or more of these responses similar to yours, or they all may be very different. Some of the observations may have surprised you. And certainly you noticed that two of the student writers had reactions that were nearly opposite. Gilbert Brown thinks that the speaker in the poem is glad he made a certain choice, whereas David Furman thinks that the speaker regrets the choice.

Suppose those two students compared their responses to Frost's poem. Noticing the difference in their reactions, they might reread "The Road Not Taken." David Furman has already offered some evidence to back up what he says: he notes that the title focuses on the path that was not followed, and he reads the sigh as sad. But Gilbert Brown might well ask whether a sigh is always sad. A sigh might show pleasure, contentment, relief, or any number of other emotions. How can these two commentators resolve their differences?

The answer is that they don't have to find a single resolution. Both readings of this poem are possible. By listening to a number of responses and then rereading the work to see what evoked those responses, readers often discover multiple possibilities, new ways of looking at the work that they had not previously considered.

Of course, there is always the chance that returning to the work will cause a reader to rethink an initial reaction. For instance, how would Gilbert Brown support his idea that the poem is about Frost's decision to be a poet? Nothing in the poem directly backs up this reading; to the contrary, lines 9 and 10 suggest that the choice involves two rather similar alternatives. Nevertheless, nothing in the poem definitely rules out the possibility that the choice relates to careers. Gilbert Brown might decide, however, to broaden the scope of his initial reaction.

Notice that David Furman relates strongly to what he sees as the speaker's regret. David's response shows that he regrets several life choices he made, and so he believes that the speaker in the poem must be experiencing this emotion, too. Even if David Furman modifies his reading to include other possibilities (for example, that the speaker in the poem might be proud of or pleased with his choice), that revision does not lessen the importance of the personal connection David has made with the poem. His reading remains a possibility, but now he also sees a fuller context than he did at first.

And what about Janice Angstrom? She sees the poem as basically about taking a walk in the woods. Is she wrong or imperceptive? No. Her reading is a very useful first step. She sees clearly the picture the poet paints and, in addition, she sees that part of the picture is puzzling. In lines 14 and 15, Janice recognizes an element of contradiction. If the speaker in the poem were simply talking about a woodland walk, he would not be so concerned about being unable to back-track and explore another path. Janice, then, uses her literal first response to raise questions that lead to a nonliteral reading of the poem. Janice shows that she is perceptive by recognizing those questions and by being willing to pursue them.

Anita Juarez makes an intriguing observation when she notes that lines 9 and 10 suggest that the choice is not between extreme opposites. The paths are almost equally worn, so the choice is probably not between, for instance, non-conformity and conformity. Because of her own experiences, Anita sees a valuable insight in Frost's poem: it's frequently the apparently minor decisions in life that end up making "all the difference." Because of her initial reaction to "The Road Not Taken," she decided to read the poem more closely and to use it for the following assignment:

> Choose a poem to which you have a strong personal response. Then reread the poem and come to class prepared with notes to help you explain your response. Be sure to refer to specific lines and stanzas in the poem as you explain your thoughts and feelings.

Exercise

After reading the discussion and example that follow, choose a poem from any of the thematic chapters of this text (Chapters 6 through 13), and take notes as though you were preparing for the assignment given to Anita.

CONSIDERING EVIDENCE TO SUPPORT YOUR RESPONSE

As you read the commentary that follows the four students' responses to Frost's poem, you may have noticed that none of them is described as being the "right" response. That is because each student provides details and examples to show what led to the response. Each student moved from simply stating a response, such as "I see this as a poem about choices," to providing information so that someone else can see why he or she had this response. Offering details and examples from the literary work to support your response is one of the first steps in learning to think critically about what you read.

Although many responses can provide great starting places for discussing literature, writing about literature requires a careful consideration of how you are going to convincingly convey your views about a poem, a story, or a play to your audience. How can you most effectively use evidence from the work to explain to your readers the points you want to make? Sometimes an initial reading or response will seem quite plausible, yet as you ask yourself, "What is it in this work that makes me think in this way?" you may find the question very difficult to answer. It is tempting sometimes to respond to this difficulty by bending the evidence and insisting on your original reading. For example, suppose I read "The Road Not Taken" and then wrote a paper stating, "This poem is about someone who got lost in the woods and is waiting to be rescued by forest rangers." How could I answer a questioner who asked, "Well, I can see how, perhaps, the traveler's trouble with making a decision could be interpreted as being 'lost' in some way, but where do you get the idea about forest rangers?" I might stick with my original idea and simply insist that the speaker in the poem is sighing in the final stanza because he is still lost and that he is waiting for forest rangers to show up and rescue him. However, the evidence in the poem really does not support the forest ranger interpretation, and it's unlikely that I would be able to make a very convincing case for my reading.

The example here, of course, is very far-fetched. However, I've included it at the request of a number of students and instructors who have used earlier editions of the text and who asked that I address the concept of "convincing" and "unconvincing" readings. Thoughtful readers frequently find they need to modify or develop their initial responses when they begin writing because they recognize that their first ideas no longer make sense to them. If the response no longer makes sense to the reader, it's certainly not going to make sense to the audience for whom that reader might be writing a paper. Therefore, it's important for all readers and writers to distinguish between the immediate response and the considered response and, when writing papers, to work toward shaping a convincing reading to present to the audience.

CLOSE ACTIVE READING

Once you've read a work of literature—poem, story, novel, or play—and noted your initial response, you may decide (or be asked) to read more closely. As you read, you analyze your first reactions, and you consider the reactions you've heard others express. Close active reading always means reading with a

pen or pencil (rather than a highlighter) in your hand. You might use a highlighter during your first reading to mark passages that impress, puzzle, delight,
or outrage you, but a close reading requires actually interacting with the
work—writing down your questions and observations as you go
Here is how Anita Juarez marked "The Road Not Taken":

The Road (Not) Taken

Why not "The Road Taken"?

Two roads diverged in a (yellow wood,) — *Why yellow? Could be fall or spring New beginnings?*
And sorry I could not travel both
And be one traveler, long I stood
And looked down one as far as I could
To where it bent in the undergrowth; — *maybe hard to get past.*   5

Then took the other, as just as fair, — *are they the same?*
And having perhaps the better claim,
Because it was grassy and wanted wear;
Though as for that the passing there
Had worn them really about the same. *Again— seems similar*   10

And both that morning equally lay
In leaves no step had trodden black.
Oh, I kept the first for another day!
Yet knowing how way leads on to way, / *Like a lot of choices in life – lead you in many directions.*
I doubted if I should ever come back. /   15

Happy or Sad About Choices? //

I shall be telling this with a sigh
Somewhere ages and ages hence:
Two roads diverged in a wood, and I—
I took the one less traveled by,
And that has made all the difference.   20

Sample Oral Response to "The Road Not Taken"

Using these notes as a guide, Anita Juarez gave the following informal
oral response in class:

When I read this poem, I thought right away of the choice I made in
high school not to study foreign languages. In the poem, the speaker
makes his choice in either fall or spring—when the woods are
yellow. I see both these seasons as times of new beginnings. In spring,
everything new is growing. In fall (at least for students), it's the start
of a new school year. I made my choice one fall when a guidance
director told me I was not "college material" and recommended that
I drop my French class. September should have been a beginning, but

I saw it as an end to my dream for college. It's only now that I can begin to think it was—in a way—a beginning, too.

Dropping French was desirable because I didn't do well in languages, but taking a language was also desirable because you had to take a language to get into college. So, like the speaker in the poem, I made a choice between two possibilities—and just as the poem says, both these two choices had been made before by many people. As Frost says, "the passing there / Had worn them really about the same."

What really interested me about the poem is the way it says that "way leads on to way." Because I decided not to take a language, I knew I couldn't go to college—back then you had to have a language to get into college. So, after high school, I went to work at Sears, and at work I met my husband. So, working at Sears was what got me to meet that particular man. And then, marrying him, I had children (that were of course different from those I might have had if I married somebody else). I could keep going on, but you get the idea about how "way led on to way" in my life.

In the poem the person doubts that he will "ever come back." Well, at first when I read this, I thought that in a way I have come back because now I am starting college, which I couldn't do out of high school. But I really know it's still not the same, because I am a different person than I was then. All those "ways that lead to other ways" have made me—or maybe helped me to become—somebody new. So, this is not about going back to an old fork in the road but being at a new one.

You can't really tell whether in the last stanza the speaker is entirely happy, entirely sad, or some mixture. But you can see he knows now how important life's choices can be. He knows he'll think back over one particular choice even when he is an old man ("somewhere ages and ages hence"). I feel the same way. Reading this poem has made me look at some of the choices I've made, and I know I'll still be looking at them years from now. And, whether for better or worse, those choices will have "made all the difference."

Commentary

Anita Juarez read "The Road Not Taken" carefully and related the speaker's experience to her own choices in life. Her observations show that she became genuinely interested in Frost's theme and was able to appreciate his poem more fully by bringing something of herself to her reading. You may think her commentary is very different from what you have previously thought of as "literary analysis." Certainly, her ideas are expressed informally and personally, yet she has indeed "analyzed" the poem (looked at how parts of it work to create the whole).

In the next four chapters, we will look at some ways you can develop such a personal analysis in more detail. Chapter 2 introduces and explains terms that are useful when you talk or write about literature, Chapter 3 suggests two ways of extending the conversation about literature, Chapter 4 demonstrates and explains five ways of writing about literature, and Chapter 5 shows how to write an argument that requires research. As you read Chapters 2, 3, 4, and 5, remember that all real enjoyment and understanding of literature begin with your engagement as a reader and your willingness to discover and explore the kinds of responses introduced in this chapter.

Exercise

Using the notes you took for the exercise on page 4, plan an oral response similar to the one you just read. Remember to refer to specific parts of the poem to explain why you had the responses you describe.

KEEPING A READING JOURNAL

In addition to taking notes, keeping a reading journal is one of the best ways to explore your responses to literature as well as to discover ideas for papers you may write. The comments on pages 1, 2 and 3 come from students' journals, as do the paragraphs that introduce each new section in Chapter 2 (see pages 26, 27, 32, 33, 41, 42, 47, 48, 53, 54).

There are many different ways of keeping such a journal. If you write a journal for your class, the instructor may ask you to write a certain number of entries each week and may specify how long those entries should be. The instructor may also suggest topics or approaches to help you determine the focus of some or all of the entries.

For journal entries that you plan yourself, consider the possibilities presented in the Guidelines box.

GUIDELINES

Keeping a Reading Journal

1. After you read a work, jot down several questions that come to mind. Then choose one question and explore it more fully.
2. List the emotions (anger, pity, envy, admiration, astonishment, and so on) the work evoked. Then explain the reasons you think you felt these emotions.

(continued)

GUIDELINES, continued

3. Copy one sentence, one line, or one phrase that struck you as especially beautiful, puzzling, enlightening, and so on. Then discuss how and why the sentence, line, or phrase evoked this response.
4. Write a letter to the author asking questions or making observations about the work.
5. Write a letter to one of the characters (or to the speaker in a poem) describing your response to a choice or decision he or she made.
6. Explain why you could—or couldn't—identify with a particular character or situation in the work.
7. Jot down your initial impression of a work. Then reread and write another entry describing new or changed impressions.
8. Make notes during class discussion of a particular work. Then respond to a comment made either by your instructor or by another student.

More Resources on

Robert Frost and "The Road Not Taken"

In *ARIEL*

- Brief biography of Frost
- Complete text of "The Road Not Taken," "Mending Wall," and "Stopping by Woods on a Snowy Evening," all with hyperlinked comments
- Audio reading of "The Road Not Taken" and of "Stopping by Woods on a Snowy Evening"
- Analysis of symbol in "The Road Not Taken"
- Bibliography of scholarly works on Frost

In the Online Learning Center for *Responding to Literature*

- Brief biography of Frost
- List of major works by Frost
- Web links to more resources on Frost
- Additional questions for experiencing and interpreting Frost's writing

2

Joining the Conversation: Ways of Talking about Literature

People who start a new job or pursue a new sport often find themselves surrounded by unfamiliar language. "Byte," "hard disk," and "system error" may not mean much to a newly hired office worker, but the new employee soon learns the terminology along with the practical steps required to use the office computer. Saying "monitor" instead of "the thing that looks like a TV" simplifies communication. The novice skier is in a similar situation. Someone who has never skied probably doesn't know or care about the difference between "new powder" and "packed, granular snow." As soon as a person rents skis and takes the first lesson, however, understanding the words that describe the condition of the ski slopes becomes important. It's much easier to warn a fellow skier of danger on the slopes by mentioning "moguls" than by describing "bumps and ridges with hard, icy coverings." In addition, learning new words to describe kinds of snow makes skiers more conscious of the natural world around them. They become aware of subtle distinctions they might not have noticed before.

Like computer users and skiers, many people who talk and write about literature use specialized terminology. Understanding the terms that describe various aspects of literature enriches the reader's experience. This vocabulary not only provides a shortcut for talking or writing about literature but also often suggests new ways of looking at poetry, fiction, drama, and nonfiction and at the connections between our lives and the literary works we read.

To begin learning about the language of literature, read the following selections. Each represents one genre of literature: fiction, poetry, drama, or nonfiction. As you read, make notes in the margins to keep track of your responses to each selection. (For note-taking suggestions, see Chapter 1, page 4.) Following each selection are suggestions for writing to develop your responses further.

PATRICIA GRACE (1937–)

Butterflies

The grandmother plaited her granddaughter's hair and then she said, "Get your lunch. Put it in your bag. Get your apple. You come straight back after school, straight home here. Listen to the teacher," she said. "Do what she say."

Her grandfather was out on the step. He walked down the path with her and out onto the footpath. He said to a neighbor, "Our granddaughter goes to school. She lives with us now."

"She's fine," the neighbor said. "She's terrific with her two plaits in her hair."

"And clever," the grandfather said. "Writes every day in her book."

5   "She's fine," the neighbor said.

The grandfather waited with his granddaughter by the crossing and then he said, "Go to school. Listen to the teacher. Do what she say."

When the granddaughter came home from school her grandfather was hoeing around the cabbages. Her grandmother was picking beans. They stopped their work.

"You bring your book home?" the grandmother asked.

"Yes."

10   "You write your story?"

"Yes."

"What's your story?"

"About the butterflies."

"Get your book then. Read your story."

15   The granddaughter took her book from her schoolbag and opened it.

"I killed all the butterflies," she read. "This is me and this is all the butterflies."

"And your teacher like your story, did she?"

"I don't know."

"What your teacher say?"

20   "She said butterflies are beautiful creatures. They hatch out and fly in the sun. The butterflies visit all the pretty flowers, she said. They lay their eggs and then they die. You don't kill butterflies, that's what she said."

The grandmother and the grandfather were quiet for a long time, and their granddaughter, holding the book, stood quite still in the warm garden.

"Because you see," the grandfather said, "your teacher, she buy all her cabbages from the supermarket and that's why."   *1988*

Responding to "Butterflies"

1. Describe the relationship between the granddaughter and grandparents. Compare it to your own relationship to your grandparents or to other grandchild-grandparent relationships you know of.

2. What can you tell about the place where these people live? Can you make any guesses about the time period in which they live?

3. Even though the schoolteacher does not appear in the story, can you tell anything about her? What kind of a person do you think she is? How effective do you think she is as a teacher? Why?

4. What is your response to the advice the grandfather gives the granddaughter as she sets out for school? Do you think the grandfather might change his advice in response to his granddaughter's experience? Explain.

5. What was your response to the connection the grandfather makes between cabbages and butterflies? Explain.

 LANGSTON HUGHES (1902–1967)

Theme for English B

The instructor said,

> Go home and write
> a page tonight.

> And let that page come out of you—
> Then, it will be true.   5

I wonder if it's that simple?

I am twenty-two, colored, born in Winston-Salem.
I went to school there, then Durham, then here
to this college on the hill above Harlem.
I am the only colored student in my class.   10
The steps from the hill lead down to Harlem,
through a park, then I cross St. Nicholas,
Eighth Avenue, Seventh, and I come to the Y,
the Harlem Branch Y, where I take the elevator
up to my room, sit down, and write this page: 15

It's not easy to know what is true for you or me
at twenty-two, my age. But I guess I'm what
I feel and see and hear. Harlem, I hear you:
hear you, hear me—we two—you, me talk on this page.
(I hear New York, too.) Me—who?   20
Well, I like to eat, sleep, drink, and be in love.
I like to work, read, learn, and understand life.
I like a pipe for a Christmas present,
or records—Bessie, bop, or Bach.

25   I guess being colored doesn't make me not like
         the same things other folks like who are other races.
         So will my page be colored that I write?
         Being me, it will not be white.
         But it will be
30   a part of you, instructor.
         You are white—
         yet a part of me, as I am a part of you.
         That's American.
         Sometimes perhaps you don't want to be a part of me.
35   Nor do I often want to be a part of you.
         But we are, that's true!
         As I learn from you,
         I guess you learn from me—
         although you're older—and white—
40   and somewhat more free.

         This is my page for English B.   *1951*

Responding to "Theme for English B"

1. Describe the thoughts and feelings that run through the speaker's mind as he considers the assignment for his English course. Does his process in any way remind you of the way you think about course assignments? Or do you work entirely differently? Explain.

2. What places seem significant to the speaker? How are they significant? For example, what differences does he suggest between the places he has lived (and the place he now lives) and the place he attends his classes? What comparisons can you make between places where you have lived and places where you have attended school?

3. What does the poem tell you about the speaker? Make two lists, one describing what might be called external facts (the speaker's age, for example) and the other describing the inner speaker (his hopes, fears, motivations, personality traits, and so on).

4. What do you make of the question "So will my page be colored that I write?" (line 27)? What is the speaker's answer to his own question? What is your response to this answer?

5. If you were the instructor and received this poem in response to the assignment suggested in lines 2–5, how would you grade the paper? What comments would you write to explain your thoughts and feelings to the student?

More Resources on
Langston Hughes and "Theme for English B"

In *ARIEL*
- Brief biography of Hughes
- Audio reading of "Theme for English B"
- Complete text of "Theme for English B," as well as texts of other Hughes poems such as "I, Too" and "Dream Deferred"
- Analysis of figurative writing in Hughes's poetry
- Bibliography of scholarly works on Hughes

In the Online Learning Center for *Responding to Literature*
- Brief biography of Hughes
- List of major works by Hughes
- Web links to more resources on Hughes
- Additional questions for experiencing and interpreting Hughes's writing

WENDY WASSERSTEIN (1950–   )
The Man in a Case

Characters
BYELINKOV
VARINKA

Scene *A small garden in the village of Mironitski. 1898.*

(BYELINKOV *is pacing. Enter* VARINKA *out of breath.*)

BYELINKOV: You are ten minutes late.

VARINKA: The most amazing thing happened on my way over here. You know the woman who runs the grocery store down the road. She wears a black wig during the week, and a blond wig on Saturday nights. And she has the daughter who married an engineer in Moscow who is doing very well thank you and is living, God bless them, in a three-room apartment. But he really is the most boring man in the world. All he talks about is his future and his station in life. Well, she heard we were to be married and she gave me this basket of apricots to give to you.

BYELINKOV: That is a most amazing thing!

VARINKA: She said to me, "Varinka, you are marrying the most honorable man in the entire village. In this village he is the only man fit to speak with my son-in-law."

5 BYELINKOV: I don't care for apricots. They give me hives.

VARINKA: I can return them. I'm sure if I told her they give you hives she would give me a basket of raisins or a cake.

BYELINKOV: I don't know this woman or her pompous son-in-law. Why would she give me her cakes?

VARINKA: She adores you!

BYELINKOV: She is emotionally loose.

10 VARINKA: She adores you by reputation. Everyone adores you by reputation. I tell everyone I am to marry Byelinkov, the finest teacher in the county.

BYELINKOV: You tell them this?

VARINKA: If they don't tell me first.

BYELINKOV: Pride can be an imperfect value.

VARINKA: It isn't pride. It is the truth. You are a great man!

15 BYELINKOV: I am the master of Greek and Latin at a local school at the end of the village of Mironitski.

(VARINKA *kisses him.*)

VARINKA: And I am to be the master of Greek and Latin's wife!

BYELINKOV: Being married requires a great deal of responsibility. I hope I am able to provide you with all that a married man must properly provide a wife.

VARINKA: We will be very happy.

BYELINKOV: Happiness is for children. We are entering into a social contract, an amicable agreement to provide us with a secure and satisfying future.

20 VARINKA: You are so sweet! You are the sweetest man in the world!

BYELINKOV: I'm a man set in his ways who saw a chance to provide himself with a small challenge.

VARINKA: Look at you! Look at you! Your sweet round spectacles, your dear collar always starched, always raised, your perfectly pressed pants always creasing at right angles perpendicular to the floor, and my most favorite part, the sweet little galoshes, rain or shine, just in case. My Byelinkov, never taken by surprise. Except by me.

BYELINKOV: You speak about me as if I were your pet.

VARINKA: You are my pet! My little school mouse.

25 BYELINKOV: A mouse?

VARINKA: My sweetest dancing bear with galoshes, my little stale babka.

BYELINKOV: A stale babka?

VARINKA: I am not Pushkin.°

Pushkin: A Russian poet and prose writer (1799–1837).

BYELINKOV *(Laughs)*: That depends what you think of Pushkin.

VARINKA: You're smiling. I knew I could make you smile today.   *30*

BYELINKOV: I am a responsible man. Every day I have for breakfast black bread, fruit, hot tea, and every day I smile three times. I am halfway into my translation of the *Aeneid*° from classical Greek hexameter° into Russian alexandrines.° In twenty years I have never been late to school. I am a responsible man, but no dancing bear.

VARINKA: Dance with me.

BYELINKOV: Now? It is nearly four weeks before the wedding!

VARINKA: It's a beautiful afternoon. We are in your garden. The roses are in full bloom.

BYELINKOV: The roses have beetles.   *35*

VARINKA: Dance with me!

BYELINKOV: You are a demanding woman.

VARINKA: You chose me. And right. And left. And turn. And right. And left.

BYELINKOV: And turn. Give me your hand. You dance like a school mouse. It's a beautiful afternoon! We are in my garden. The roses are in full bloom! And turn. And turn. *(Twirls* VARINKA *around)*

VARINKA: I am the luckiest woman!   *40*

*(*BYELINKOV *stops dancing.)*

Why are you stopping?

BYELINKOV: To place a lilac in your hair. Every year on this day I will place a lilac in your hair.

VARINKA: Will you remember?

BYELINKOV: I will write it down. *(Takes a notebook from his pocket)* Dear Byelinkov, don't forget the day a young lady, your bride, entered your garden, your peace, and danced on the roses. On that day every year you are to place a lilac in her hair.

VARINKA: I love you.

BYELINKOV: It is convenient we met.   *45*

VARINKA: I love you.

BYELINKOV: You are a girl.

VARINKA: I am thirty.

BYELINKOV: But you think like a girl. That is an attractive attribute.

VARINKA: Do you love me?   *50*

BYELINKOV: We've never spoken about housekeeping.

VARINKA: I am an excellent housekeeper. I kept house for my family on the farm in Gadyatchsky. I can make a beetroot soup with tomatoes and aubergines which is so nice. Awfully, awfully nice.

BYELINKOV: You are fond of expletives.

Aeneid: Epic poem written by Vergil (70–19 B.C.). *hexameter:* A line of verse having six metric units. *alexandrine:* A line of verse having six metric units.

VARINKA: My beet soup, sir, is excellent!

55   BYELINKOV: Please don't be cross. I too am an excellent housekeeper. I have a place for everything in the house. A shelf for each pot, a cubby for every spoon, a folder for favorite recipes. I have cooked for myself for twenty years. Though my beet soup is not outstanding, it is sufficient.

VARINKA: I'm sure it's very good.

BYELINKOV: No. It is awfully, awfully not. What I am outstanding in, however, what gives me greatest pleasure, is preserving those things which are left over. I wrap each tomato slice I haven't used in a wet cloth and place it in the coolest corner of the house. I have had my shoes for seven years because I wrap them in the galoshes you are so fond of. And every night before I go to sleep I wrap my bed in quilts and curtains so I never catch a draft.

VARINKA: You sleep with curtains on your bed?

BYELINKOV: I like to keep warm.

60   VARINKA: I will make you a new quilt.

BYELINKOV: No. No new quilt. That would be hazardous.

VARINKA: It is hazardous to sleep under curtains.

BYELINKOV: Varinka, I don't like change very much. If one works out the arithmetic, the final fraction of improvement is at best less than an eighth of value over the total damage caused by disruption. I never thought of marrying till I saw your eyes dancing among the familiar faces at the headmaster's tea. I assumed I would grow old preserved like those which are left over, wrapped suitably in my case of curtains and quilts.

VARINKA: Byelinkov, I want us to have dinners with friends and summer country visits. I want people to say, "Have you spent time with Varinka and Byelinkov? He is so happy now that they are married. She is just what he needed."

65   BYELINKOV: You have already brought me some happiness. But I never was a sad man. Don't ever think I thought I was a sad man.

VARINKA: My sweetest darling, you can be whatever you want! If you are sad, they'll say she talks all the time, and he is soft-spoken and kind.

BYELINKOV: And if I am difficult?

VARINKA: Oh, they'll say he is difficult because he is highly intelligent. All great men are difficult. Look at Lermontov, Tchaikovsky, Peter the Great.

BYELINKOV: Ivan the Terrible.

70   VARINKA: Yes, him too.

BYELINKOV: Why are you marrying me? I am none of these things.

VARINKA: To me you are.

BYELINKOV: You have imagined this. You have constructed an elaborate romance for yourself. Perhaps you are the great one. You are the one with the great imagination.

VARINKA: Byelinkov, I am a pretty girl of thirty. You're right, I am not a woman. I have not made myself into a woman because I do not deserve that honor.

Until I came to this town to visit my brother I lived on my family's farm. As the years passed I became younger and younger in fear that I would never marry. And it wasn't that I wasn't pretty enough or sweet enough, it was just that no man ever looked at me and saw a wife. I was not the woman who would be there when he came home. Until I met you I thought I would lie all my life and say I never married because I never met a man I loved. I will love you, Byelinkov. And I will help you to love me. We deserve the life everyone else has. We deserve not to be different.

BYELINKOV: Yes. We are the same as everyone else.   75

VARINKA: Tell me you love me.

BYELINKOV: I love you.

VARINKA *(Takes his hands)*: We will be very happy. I am very strong. *(Pauses)* It is time for tea.

BYELINKOV: It is too early for tea. Tea is at half past the hour.

VARINKA: Do you have heavy cream? It will be awfully nice with apricots.   80

BYELINKOV: Heavy cream is too rich for teatime.

VARINKA: But today is special. Today you placed a lilac in my hair. Write in your note pad. Every year we will celebrate with apricots and heavy cream. I will go to my brother's house and get some.

BYELINKOV: But your brother's house is a mile from here.

VARINKA: Today it is much shorter. Today my brother gave me his bicycle to ride. I will be back very soon.

BYELINKOV: You rode to my house by bicycle! Did anyone see you?   85

VARINKA: Of course. I had such fun. I told you I saw the grocery store lady with the son-in-law who is doing very well thank you in Moscow, and the headmaster's wife.

BYELINKOV: You saw the headmaster's wife!

VARINKA: She smiled at me.

BYELINKOV: Did she laugh or smile?

VARINKA: She laughed a little. She said, "My dear, you are very progressive to   90 ride a bicycle." She said, "You and your fiancé Byelinkov must ride together sometime. I wonder if he'll take off his galoshes when he rides a bicycle."

BYELINKOV: She said that?

VARINKA: She adores you. We had a good giggle.

BYELINKOV: A woman can be arrested for riding a bicycle. That is not progressive, it is a premeditated revolutionary act. Your brother must be awfully, awfully careful on behalf of your behavior. He has been careless—oh so careless—in giving you the bicycle.

VARINKA: Dearest Byelinkov, you are wrapping yourself under curtains and quilts! I made friends on the bicycle.

BYELINKOV: You saw more than the headmaster's wife and the idiot grocery   95 woman.

VARINKA: She is not an idiot.

BYELINKOV: She is a potato-vending, sausage-armed fool!

VARINKA: Shhhh! My school mouse. Shhh!

BYELINKOV: What other friends did you make on this bicycle?

100 VARINKA: I saw students from my brother's classes. They waved and shouted, "Anthropos in love! Anthropos in love!!"

BYELINKOV: Where is that bicycle?

VARINKA: I left it outside the gate. Where are you going?

BYELINKOV *(Muttering as he exits)*: Anthropos in love, anthropos in love.

VARINKA: They were cheering me on. Careful, you'll trample the roses.

105 BYELINKOV *(Returning with the bicycle)*: Anthropos is the Greek singular for man. Anthropos in love translates as the Greek and Latin master in love. Of course they cheered you. Their instructor, who teaches them the discipline and contained beauty of the classics, is in love with a sprite on a bicycle. It is a good giggle, isn't it? A very good giggle! I am returning this bicycle to your brother.

VARINKA: But it is teatime.

BYELINKOV: Today we will not have tea.

VARINKA: But you will have to walk back a mile.

BYELINKOV: I have my galoshes on. *(Gets on the bicycle)* Varinka, we deserve not to be different. *(Begins to pedal. The bicycle doesn't move.)*

110 VARINKA: Put the kickstand up.

BYELINKOV: I beg your pardon.

VARINKA *(Giggling)*: Byelinkov, to make the bicycle move, you must put the kickstand up.

(BYELINKOV *puts it up and awkwardly falls off the bicycle as it moves.*)

(Laughing) Ha ha ha. My little school mouse. You look so funny! You are the sweetest dearest man in the world. Ha ha ha!

(Pause)

BYELINKOV: Please help me up. I'm afraid my galosh is caught.

VARINKA *(Trying not to laugh)*: Your galosh is caught! *(Explodes in laughter again)* Oh, you are so funny! I do love you so. *(Helps* BYELINKOV *up)* You were right, my pet, as always. We don't need heavy cream for tea. The fraction of improvement isn't worth the damage caused by the disruption.

115 BYELINKOV: Varinka, it is still too early for tea. I must complete two stanzas of my translation before late afternoon. That is my regular schedule.

VARINKA: Then I will watch while you work.

BYELINKOV: No. You had a good giggle. That is enough.

VARINKA: Then while you work I will work too. I will make lists of guests for our wedding.

BYELINKOV: I can concentrate only when I am alone in my house. Please take your bicycle home to your brother.

120 VARINKA: But I don't want to leave you. You look so sad.

BYELINKOV: I never was a sad man. Don't ever think I was a sad man.

VARINKA: Byelinkov, it's a beautiful day, we are in your garden. The roses are in bloom.

BYELINKOV: Allow me to help you on to your bicycle. *(Takes* VARINKA's *hand as she gets on the bike)*

VARINKA: You are such a gentleman. We will be very happy.

BYELINKOV: You are very strong. Good day, Varinka.

125

(VARINKA pedals off. BYELINKOV, *alone in the garden, takes out his pad and rips up the note about the lilac, strews it over the garden, then carefully picks up each piece of paper and places them all in a small envelope as lights fade to black.)* 1986

Responding to *The Man in a Case*

1. Describe the relationship between the man and woman in the play. What seems important to each of them? Do any things seem important to them both? Explain. Does their relationship remind you of any relationships you know about? Describe the differences and similarities you see.

2. Did you find it important to know that this play takes place in 1898? Where do you think the village of Mironitski is located? Was knowing the location in any way connected to your response to the play?

3. Were you more sympathetic to one of the characters than to the other? Or did you find them both equally appealing (or lacking in appeal)? Explain.

4. What did you make of the bicycle episode? Why is Byelinkov so upset about Varinka's riding the bicycle? What is her response? How does this episode relate to other episodes in the play?

5. Write a short scene that takes place between Varinka and Byelinkov two weeks after the day of the play's action. What future do you predict for them? Why?

More Resources on

Wendy Wasserstein

 In the Online Learning Center for *Responding to Literature*

- Brief biography of Wasserstein
- List of major works by Wasserstein
- Web links to more resources on Wasserstein
- Additional questions for experiencing and interpreting Wasserstein's writing

E. B. WHITE (1899–1985)

Education

I have an increasing admiration for the teacher in the country school where we have a third-grade scholar in attendance. She not only undertakes to instruct her charges in all the subjects of the first three grades, but she manages to function quietly and effectively as a guardian of their health, their clothes, their habits, their mothers, and their snowball engagements. She has been doing this sort of Augean task° for twenty years, and is both kind and wise. She cooks for the children on the stove that heats the room, and she can cool their passions or warm their soup with equal competence. She conceives their costumes, cleans up their messes, and shares their confidences. My boy already regards his teacher as his great friend, and I think tells her a great deal more than he tells us.

The shift from city school to country school was something we worried about quietly all last summer. I have always rather favored public school over private school, if only because in public school you meet a greater variety of children. This bias of mine, I suspect, is partly an attempt to justify my own past (I never knew anything but public schools) and partly an involuntary defense against getting kicked in the shins by a young ceramist on his way to the kiln. My wife was unacquainted with public schools, never having been exposed (in her early life) to anything more public than the washroom of Miss Winsor's. Regardless of our backgrounds, we both knew that the change in schools was something that concerned not us but the scholar himself. We hoped it would work out all right. In New York our son went to a medium-priced private institution with semi-progressive ideas of education, and modern plumbing. He learned fast, kept well, and we were satisfied. It was an electric, colorful, regimented existence with moments of pleasurable pause and giddy incident. The day the Christmas angel fainted and had to be carried out by one of the Wise Men was educational in the highest sense of the term. Our scholar gave imitations of it around the house for weeks afterward, and I doubt if it ever goes completely out of his mind.

His days were rich in formal experience. Wearing overalls and an old sweater (the accepted uniform of the private seminary), he sallied forth at morn accompanied by a nurse or a parent and walked (or was pulled) two blocks to a corner where the school bus made a flag stop. This flashy vehicle was as punctual as death: seeing us waiting at the cold curb, it would sweep to a halt, open its mouth, suck the boy in, and spring away with an angry growl. It was a good deal like a train picking up a bag of mail. At school the scholar

---

Augean task: A very difficult task. (King Augeas of Elis set the Greek hero Hercules to the task of cleaning the royal stables, which had been neglected for thirty years.)

was worked on for six or seven hours by a half a dozen teachers and a nurse, and was revived on orange juice in mid-morning. In a cinder court he played games supervised by an athletic instructor, and in a cafeteria he ate lunch worked out by a dietitian. He soon learned to read with gratifying facility and discernment and to make Indian weapons of a semi-deadly nature. Whenever one of his classmates fell low of a fever the news was put on the wires and there were breathless phone calls to physicians, discussing periods of incubation and allied magic.

In the country all one can say is that the situation is different, and somehow more casual. Dressed in corduroys, sweatshirt, and short rubber boots, and carrying a tin dinner-pail, our scholar departs at crack of dawn for the village school, two and a half miles down the road, next to the cemetery. When the road is open and the car will start, he makes the journey by motor, courtesy of his old man. When the snow is deep or the motor is dead or both, he makes it on the hoof. In the afternoons he walks or hitches all or part of the way home in fair weather, gets transported in foul. The schoolhouse is a two-room frame building, bungalow type, shingles stained a burnt brown with weather-resistant stain. It has a chemical toilet in the basement and two teachers above stairs. One takes the first three grades, the other the fourth, fifth, and sixth. They have little or no time for individual instruction, and no time at all for the esoteric. They teach what they know themselves, just as fast and as hard as they can manage. The pupils sit still at their desks in class, and do their milling around outdoors during recess.

There is no supervised play. They play cops and robbers (only they call it "Jail") and throw things at one another—snowballs in winter, rose hips in fall. It seems to satisfy them. They also construct darts, pinwheels, and "pick-up sticks" (jackstraws), and the school itself does a brisk trade in penny candy, which is for sale right in the classroom and which contains "surprises." The most highly prized surprise is a fake cigarette, made of cardboard, fiendishly lifelike.

The memory of how apprehensive we were at the beginning is still strong. The boy was nervous about the change too. The tension, on that first fair morning in September when we drove him to school, almost blew the windows out of the sedan. And when later we picked him up on the road, wandering along with his little blue lunch-pail, and got his laconic report "All right" in answer to our inquiry about how the day had gone, our relief was vast. Now, after almost a year of it, the only difference we can discover in the two school experiences is that in the country he sleeps better at night—and *that* probably is more the air than the education. When grilled on the subject of school-in-country *vs.* school-in-city, he replied that the chief difference is that the day seems to go so much quicker in the country. "Just like lightning," he reported.   *1939*

Responding to "Education"

1. Make a list of the details the speaker provides to explain why he has "an increasing admiration for the teacher in the country school." Do you agree that these qualities are admirable? Explain.

2. How do the physical facilities of the city school compare with those of the country school? Which school would you prefer to attend (or to teach in)? Discuss your reasons.

3. Read paragraph 3 carefully and explain your response to the speaker's description of the school bus that takes his son to the city school.

4. In the final paragraph, the speaker says, "Now, after almost a year of it, the only difference we can discover in the two school experiences is that in the country he sleeps better at night—and *that* probably is more the air than the education." To what extent do the details in the rest of the essay suggest that the speaker does or does not favor one school over the other? Do you find evidence to suggest that the "third-grade scholar" prefers one school to the other?

5. The speaker says that he "always rather favored public school over private school." What is your response to this judgment? Have you attended private schools? Public schools? Both? What differences do you believe exist between public and private schools?

THE VOCABULARY OF LITERATURE

As you look at your own responses to the four selections you've just read, you'll almost certainly find comments about actions and events, about people and places, about ideas and values. In addition, you'll probably note questions about the significance of particular objects, about the choice of certain words, or about references to people, places, and events outside the work itself.

Each of the following sections begins with observations, evaluations, or questions written by students—mostly freshmen and sophomores—who had just read the same selections you have. The commentary following their responses suggests how these students have provided insights both into the works themselves and into ways of reading, writing, thinking, and talking about literature.

ACTIONS AND EVENTS

In "Butterflies," the granddaughter is at a big point in her life—starting school. You can tell it's near the beginning because she writes a story in only two sentences. Also, you get the impression she has drawn a picture when she says, "This is me." Usually you only draw pictures like that very early in your school years. You can see she is not in agreement with her teacher, because of the killing of the butterflies, which the teacher didn't understand. And I don't understand this, really. Why would the granddaughter want to kill butterflies?

—LISA TISICO

I think the student in this poem ["Theme for English B"] is walking all the time that he is talking. In the lines where he talks about the steps that lead down the hill and "through a park" and then he even shows taking the elevator. Well, I guess once he's off the elevator and in his room, he's not walking then. But I liked the verse where he is walking, because I could picture this. Probably because this is how I do a lot of my planning for classes and other things. I walk a lot, and I am always putting my mind in gear and thinking while I do this.

—JIM BELANGER

At first I thought that *The Man in a Case* was just all talking, but when I went back to read again, it was full of action. I love the way Varinka gets Byelinkov to dance. He is so stuffy and talks about how he is "a responsible man, but no dancing bear." Then two minutes later, he is dancing (and I could picture him like a dancing bear because Varinka counts off the steps like a bear trainer). This shows you that they really do seem to have fun together. But later the action with the bicycle makes everything fall apart. He is so jealous of her because she is free and not afraid to do things like riding a bicycle when she could be arrested or when other people might not approve.

—BONNIE DEDERIAN

I can really understand the feelings of the third-grade kid that the father talks about [in E. B. White's essay]. Changing schools is hard because you're the new kid and you have to get to know everything, like the teacher, the other kids, and how things are done, all over again. My father is in the military, so we moved all the time. The best part of the essay for me was when the father tells that the kid thinks his day goes by "just like lightning." You can tell he must like that school because time usually goes by very slowly in school, and especially when you're young.

—RYAN BERKER

When readers react to literature, among the first aspects they notice are actions and events. You can see how natural this response is when you think about talking to a friend who recommends a new film. You'd almost certainly ask some version of this question: "What's it about?" And your friend would almost certainly respond by giving you a brief summary of what happens in the film or perhaps (like Bonnie Dederian in her response to *The Man in a Case*) by singling out particular actions that seemed especially interesting, entertaining, moving, frightening, or significant in some way.

Plot

When you tell what happens in a film or in a work of literature, you are describing the **plot,** the sequence of events that take place. Most readers begin by describing *external* actions, those that, through the writer's description, we can see and hear. For instance, in her response to "Butterflies," Lisa Tisico begins by writing about the granddaughter's starting school and the drawing she includes in her story of killing butterflies. These are external plot actions. But Lisa also asks questions that indicate her interest in *internal* actions, those events that take place inside the mind and heart. For example, she sees that the granddaughter does not agree with the teacher; in addition, Lisa wonders why the child would want to kill butterflies. So, looking at the external actions carefully led Lisa to think about the internal changes that might be happening.

Structure

The sequence of external and internal actions and events in a literary work creates its **structure,** the pattern the plot follows. In most traditional plays and works of fiction, the plot structure is something like this:

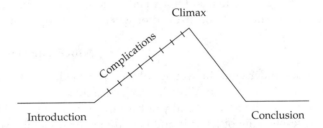

The work usually opens with an **introduction** that lets us know whom the action will concern and where the action will take place. Next, we are given a **complication** or a series of complications (small or large problems, sometimes comic, sometimes serious). For instance, in *The Man in a Case,* after Byelinkov and Varinka greet each other, they almost immediately have a series of small disagreements. He claims not to like the apricots she has received as a gift for him. She offers to return the apricots and try to exchange them for a different gift. He responds by disparaging the character of the woman who gave Varinka the apricots.

It's easy to see that these two are not an entirely compatible couple, and most readers begin to wonder about the wisdom of their engagement. These early complications are revealed primarily through conversation, but, as Bonnie Dederian notes in her comment on this play, their incompatibility becomes even more obvious through two key actions in the play. The first action is the dance. Byelinkov protests that he is not a dancing bear, yet Varinka is able to lead him into a romantic, gently humorous noonday waltz in the garden. Now the two characters seem to come together, yet almost immediately they get into another squabble, this time over housekeeping styles. As Varinka talks about her fantasy of a marriage in which she and her husband will have "the life everyone has," Byelinkov appears to agree with her. So far in this play, the complications seem to follow a pattern of disagreement followed by reconciliation followed by new disagreement and further reconciliation.

The episode of the bicycle, however—which Bonnie Dederian sees as the action "that makes everything fall apart"—takes the play beyond complications and to the **climax** (the point of greatest tension or the turning point). Varinka has braved the law against women riding bicycles as well as the possible bad opinion of people who might see her. Byelinkov is shocked and particularly upset that some of his students have seen Varinka; he fears that they will laugh at him for being engaged to such a free-spirited woman. The turning point comes when Byelinkov tries to take charge by riding the bicycle back to the house of Varinka's brother. However, Byelinkov simply embarrasses himself by showing that he has no idea how to ride the bicycle. When Varinka first laughs and then rushes to help in response to his pleas, Byelinkov sends her away. Whether they will marry or not remains to be seen; however, the **conclusion,** the ending of the play, shows him ripping up and scattering the pieces of the note reminding him to put lilacs in Varinka's hair. Byelinkov must wonder if he will ever again be able to feel totally in control of his life or whether he'll be able to rely so completely on his carefully kept lists and notes.

Conflict

As you read a literary work and think about the structure of the plot—and particularly as you focus on the complications and climax—keep in mind that nearly all fiction and drama, and many poems, focus on a **conflict,** a struggle between opposing forces. The conflict or conflicts in a literary work are usually reflected or accompanied by the external and internal action. For instance, in Langston Hughes's poem "Theme for English B," the speaker starts by introducing a complication: he has been assigned a topic for a theme. As Jim Belanger notes in his response to the poem, the first verse shows the speaker walking and thinking as he struggles to decide how to write this theme. The external actions (walking and taking the elevator) suggest the internal action (thoughts moving along and then suddenly upward with the idea of what to write in response to the assignment). The conflict here takes place *within the speaker's mind*. The speaker wonders what he can write that will fulfill the assignment, that his instructor will understand, and that will allow him to still remain true to himself.

In addition to conflicts inside the mind, literary works may focus on conflicts *between individuals* (as with Varinka and Byelinkov), *between an individual and a social force* (a community, school, church, workplace), and *between an individual and a natural force* (disease, fire, flood, cold, famine). It's important to note that conflicts do not necessarily belong in just one category. For instance, in "Theme for English B," the speaker is definitely experiencing an internal conflict, yet he also demonstrates the conflicts he feels between himself and various social forces (for example, the discrepancy between his world and the world of his white instructor).

Sometimes you find conflict even in works of nonfiction, where you might not expect it. For example, Ryan Berker's comment on E. B. White's "Education" suggests some of the conflicts the third-grader might face as he changes schools. And, of course, the essay focuses on the conflict between the values and procedures of the public school and the values and procedures of the private school.

Whatever the nature of the conflict, it often forces characters to make a decision: to act or not to act, to behave according to a personal moral code or an external moral code, to compromise or to refuse to compromise, to grow and change or to remain more or less the same. The point at which characters make these choices is usually the climactic moment of the story, poem, or play. The effects or implications of this choice usually represent the conclusion of the literary work.

Irony of Situation

The actions and events in a work may generate a sense of irony. **Irony of situation** is a difference between what a character says and what that character does. For example, Bonnie Dederian notes that Byelinkov claims he is not a dancing bear yet a minute later is, in fact, performing just like the animal he claims to disdain. The discrepancy between what Byelinkov says and what he does is ironic. In this case, the irony is comic, but sometimes the ironic discrepancy can be sad or tragic. If a character claims to be brave, for instance, yet fails to act bravely in a crucial moment, that discrepancy is ironic. This irony, however, might well shock or sadden readers rather than amuse them.

Irony of situation also occurs when a character expects one thing to happen and instead something else happens. For instance, in "Butterflies," the granddaughter expected that her story of the butterflies would please her teacher. The teacher's reaction, however, was very different from the one the child expected. The grandfather's final comment, "Because you see, your teacher, she buy all her cabbages from the supermarket and that's why," underlines the irony. To the child, the butterflies are pests whose eggs will hatch into worms that destroy the cabbage crop. When she kills butterflies in her grandfather's garden, she is acting practically and usefully. To the teacher, who does not have to grow her own food, the butterflies are simply beautiful creatures of nature.

Terms Related to Actions and Events

plot: The sequence of events and actions in a literary work.

structure: The pattern formed by the events and actions in a literary work. Traditional elements of structure are introduction, complications, climax, and conclusion.

introduction: The beginning of a work, which usually suggests the setting (time and place) and shows one or more of the main characters.

complications: Events or actions that establish the conflict in a literary work.

climax: The turning point, often signified by a character's making a significant decision or taking action to resolve a conflict.

conclusion: The ending of a work, which often shows the effects of the climactic action or decision.

conflict: A struggle between internal and external forces in a literary work.

irony of situation: A discrepancy between what is said and what is done or between what is expected and what actually happens.

Exercises: Actions and Events

1. Think about a television program or a film you have seen recently that shows a character facing a conflict. Describe the conflict, its resolution, and your response to that resolution. For instance, would you have made the same choice or choices as the character? Why? Do you find the character's reaction to the conflict realistic? Explain.

2. Think of an ironic situation you have observed or experienced. Briefly describe the situation, and then explain why you see it as ironic. Do you consider this ironic situation comic, sad, annoying, enlightening? Explain. Remember that irony always requires a discrepancy between two things (what is said and what is done, for instance).

3. Read any one of the following works from this book.

"Graduation in Stamps," page 385

"Telephone Conversation," page 466

Trifles, page 666

"The Bass, the River, and Sheila Mant," page 227

"Traveling through the Dark," page 872

Then describe the complications that lead one character or speaker to the climactic action or decision. Explain your response to each complication. Do you see one particular complication as more important than any others? Why? Speculate on what might have happened if the character or speaker had responded differently than he or she did to any of the complications you identified.

PEOPLE

The grandfather and grandmother [in "Butterflies"] seem like very wise people to me even though they don't speak correct English. They try to give their granddaughter good advice, and I noticed that both of them tell her to do what the teacher says. What's really good and what makes me say they are wise is that when the granddaughter comes home, they ask her about school and they really listen. They are quiet with her when they find out what the teacher said about the butterflies. I think this is because they know she must feel bad or at least confused. What's also good, and shows the grandfather to be wise, is that in the end he makes a comment about why the teacher said what she did. You get the feeling that maybe he will be thinking hard about his advice to "listen to the teacher."

—MARK JAMES

You think about this poem ["Theme for English B"] and you don't right away think about a person or character because it's like the poet, Langston Hughes, is describing something that happened. But when you think about it, this could be something that happened to Hughes or not. Because a poem can be made up—and I think a lot of them are—just like the story we read about the butterflies, which didn't necessarily happen to the author. So when I stopped thinking about just the poet, I started to think about the person that was created in the poem. And you know a lot about him. He is black (but he says "colored," which isn't a word I'd expect him to use), he is 22 years old, and he is taking a class called "English B" that sounds to me like a freshman course from the assignment. So, he's a little old to be starting college, and he mentions his age again in line 17, so maybe he thinks about it a lot. He's on his own, too. Lives at the "Y"—not at home or in a dorm. Maybe being older and on your own would make you especially think about being free, which he talks about. But he doesn't feel completely free—you can see that in line 40 when he says his English instructor is "more free" than he is.

—CARLENE INDREASANO

At first I was totally sympathetic with Varinka [in the play *The Man in a Case*]. If I ask myself who I would rather spend the afternoon with, there's no contest. Varinka has a good sense of humor and a spirit of adventure (she's not afraid to ride the bicycle, even though it's illegal). Also, she seems to love life—she wants to enjoy apricots and dancing and flowers. Byelinkov, on the other hand, is just depressing. He is too concerned with what his students think—too uptight, not liking to have fun. But then I thought about some of the questions he asks Varinka about why she is marrying him. She sees him one way, and he sees himself another way. He may be boring, but he has a right to be himself, so by the end I have some sympathy for Byelinkov and I can see why he rips up the note—but I did wonder why he picked up the pieces again—maybe just he's so concerned with neatness?

—NATHALIE LAROCHELLE

The father in "Education" has a good sense of humor, and you can see that he laughs at himself as well as at other people. He makes fun of the way parents in New York got on the telephone to each other and to the doctor whenever one of the children in the school got sick. But he also is sort of making fun of himself because he tells about things like picking his son up after his first day at the new school and being deeply relieved when he said his day had been "all right." Underneath almost every sentence, you can feel a father who cares a lot and thinks a lot about his son.

—DORA DIFONZO

Most of us are interested in other people. When we meet someone for the first time, we notice certain things: how the person looks, speaks, and acts, for example. We make judgments according to what we notice. Sometimes, as we get to know the person better, those evaluations are affirmed. Sometimes they are challenged. Interest in other people is more than just idle curiosity. We base our most important life decisions—whom we will be friends with, whom we will live with, whom we will love—on what we learn from observing, talking with, and interacting with other people.

It's not surprising, then, that when we watch television programs, see movies, or read literature, most of us pay close attention to the people—the

characters—whose lives unfold before us. To stay interested in a film, a novel, a short story, or a play, we must find the characters interesting in some way. Some characters fascinate us by being very different—by living in a distant place or a time long past or by being wildly glamorous or consummately evil. Sometimes characters may capture our minds and hearts because they are people we can relate to. They may face circumstances similar to our own or may act in ways that make us feel as though we are looking in a mirror. Frequently a character intrigues us by displaying a special quality or style: a unique sense of humor, a gift for the absurd, or a profoundly wise way of looking at the world.

Characters: Listening and Observing

Just as we respond to the people in our lives according to what we notice when we look at them and listen to them, readers respond to the speech, actions, and appearance of literary characters.

Listening Sometimes characters speak with others **(dialogue).** For example, as Mark James observes, the grandparents in "Butterflies" speak kindly to their granddaughter. They show they want the best for her by encouraging her to do well in school. And they ask questions that indicate their concern when she returns from school. We learn a great deal about the grandparents from listening to what they say. It is also interesting to note Mark's comment that the grandparents "don't speak correct English." Debates about what is and is not "correct" English have been going on for centuries and will continue to go on, but, nonetheless, Mark has noticed something important. The grandparents speak a **dialect,** a language that is different from the form taught in school. Noticing the grandparents' speech patterns leads to seeing a gentle irony in their wisdom. They may not know how to speak the "proper" English of the schools, but unlike the schoolteacher, who buys "all her cabbages from the supermarket," they understand the point of their granddaughter's story. Further, they grasp the reason behind the teacher's different interpretation.

When characters speak to each other, they reveal certain qualities about themselves and about their relationships with the characters to whom they speak. The conversation between the grandparents and granddaughter provides one example; the dialogue between Varinka and Byelinkov provides another. He speaks primarily in an orderly, controlled manner, whereas she tends to be as extravagant in her language as she is in her behavior: to Varinka everything is "the sweetest in the world" or "awfully, awfully nice." We can learn a great deal about Varinka's and Byelinkov's personalities just by noticing how they speak to each other; understanding their personalities leads to questions about their relationship, their conflicts, their hopes for the future.

In addition to speaking to others, characters sometimes talk to an absent or unspeaking listener **(monologue).** In a play, a character may address thoughts directly to the audience, or the character may speak thoughts aloud without any acknowledgment that an audience is there **(soliloquy).** Such a strategy gives the audience a chance to hear the uncensored thoughts of the character, thoughts that are shaped by the interaction with another character in the play.

The character in "Theme for English B" reveals everything we know about him through a monologue: musings that he addresses to his instructor. The reader has a chance to "hear" the thoughts of this character (sometimes called the *persona* or *speaker*) and to learn certain things about him. Carlene Indreasano notices that the speaker mentions twice that he is twenty-two. Wondering why age might be important to him, she links his age with his concern for freedom. You may have noticed other details that the speaker reveals through his monologue, and you may have had a response quite different from Carlene's. For instance, many readers note the questions of race and of nationality that the speaker raises in lines 25–40. The point here is not that everyone should notice the same details—or that some details are necessarily more important than others—but rather that "listening" carefully to what the speaker says leads to learning more about him, to asking questions, and to speculating on the significance of the experience he describes.

Observing   Hearing what characters say leads to insights into who they are: what they believe, what they fear, what they hope for, and how they think about themselves and others. Observing characters provides further information. Just as you notice certain external characteristics about a person you meet, readers notice those qualities about a literary character. We know, for instance, that the granddaughter in "Butterflies" wears her hair in "two plaits" (braids) and that she carries a schoolbag, so we can create a picture of her in our minds. We know from Varinka's description that Byelinkov wears round spectacles, perfectly pressed pants, and galoshes (whether or not it's raining). These details allow us not only to visualize Byelinkov but also to make some inferences about his personality.

If you've ever indulged in "people watching" (perhaps at an airport or in a supermarket), you are probably an expert at noticing characteristics (such as age, hair color, manner of dress) and at observing gestures, body movements, and other actions. Nathalie LaRochelle notes two significant actions in *The Man in a Case.* Varinka rides a bicycle (suggesting to Nathalie that Varinka has "a spirit of adventure"), and Byelinkov rips up the note he has written to remind himself to place lilacs in Varinka's hair. Byelinkov's action raises a question for Nathalie and leads her to think further about his **motivation** (the reason behind the action).

Seeing a play is like people watching. Your understanding of the characters is enriched by seeing their dress, gestures, and so on. When you read plays, it's important not to skip the **stage directions** (parenthetical notes by the playwright, at the beginning of the play or just before or just after a speech). These directions indicate what the characters are doing, describe their significant gestures and tone of voice, and often tell as much about the characters as do their words.

Although it may seem easier to notice gestures and movements of characters in plays or in works of fiction than in poetry, the speaker's words often indicate actions. In "Theme for English B," for example, the speaker's walk from the college "on the hill above Harlem" to his room at "the Harlem Branch Y" suggests the physical distance he must travel each day and may hint at the distance he feels between himself and his white instructor.

Another way to learn about literary characters is to pay attention to the *names* given them by the author. For example, in "Young Goodman Brown" (p. 194), Nathaniel Hawthorne gives the title character's wife the name Faith. If you read this story, you will see that the name was carefully chosen and relates to the main conflict faced by Goodman Brown. Another example occurs in the story "A Worn Path" (p. 844). The main character's name is Phoenix Jackson. The phoenix is a legendary bird depicted by the ancient Egyptians as being completely consumed by fire yet rising again in perfect condition from its own ashes. Knowing this reference to Phoenix Jackson's name provides another dimension to understanding what her character accomplishes. Although not all literary characters have names that are important to their identities, many do. It is worth your time to consider this aspect as you read and think about the characters you meet in fiction, poetry, and drama.

By observing literary characters astutely and listening carefully to their words and thoughts, we bring them closer to our own lives. In much the same way, getting to know a person better may bring joy, pain, complication, challenge, frustration, and fulfillment.

Characters: Growing and Changing

In life, all of us grow and change every day. We often don't notice day-to-day changes because they are so small, but if we haven't seen someone for a while—for a year or two or even a few months—we usually notice differences, both in physical appearance and in the way the person thinks, speaks, and acts. To observe changes accurately, and to speculate on what brought about those changes, we have to know a person fairly well.

So it is with literary characters. Many times, a story, play, or poem shows a character who changes—a **dynamic character.** To be interested in the change, we need to know the character fairly well. He or she must come alive for us. To capture our interest, the author must create a **round** (well-developed) **character** rather than a **flat character** who shows only one or two characteristics. When Mark James talks about the grandparents in "Butterflies," he focuses on the qualities he observes: they try to give their granddaughter good advice; they listen to her; they show they are sensitive to her feelings by being quiet with her. Finally, Mark notes that the grandparents, particularly the grandfather, change at the end of the story. The grandfather sees that the teacher does not necessarily have all the right answers, or at least the only right answers. She does not know that butterflies can be harmful to cabbages, so she misunderstands the granddaughter's story. As Mark suggests, the grandfather's final comment strongly suggests that he will rethink his advice to "listen to the teacher."

Although "Butterflies" is a very short story, the grandfather comes alive as a round, dynamic character. The teacher, by contrast, is a flat character. She shows herself only in her single, rather rigid comment to the granddaughter. Flat characters are nearly always **static;** that is, they do not change. Round characters, however, may be either static or dynamic. And noting whether a round character changes or remains the same can lead you to ask significant questions about the work you are reading.

For example, consider Nathalie LaRochelle's observations about Byelinkov. She notices some negative qualities about Byelinkov, but she is also sympathetic to the questions he asks about Varinka's reasons for marrying him. She sees that Byelinkov is more than just a stereotypical fussy old schoolmaster; he shows more than one side to his character. When Nathalie comments on Byelinkov's action at the end of the play—ripping up the note and scattering the pieces—she wonders why he picks the pieces up again. She pushes the question further, speculating that the gathering up might reflect nothing more than Byelinkov's concern with neatness. According to this reading, Byelinkov has not been changed by the events of the afternoon. Now suppose the gathering up indicates that he wants to save the note, that he regrets his rejection both of Varinka and of the romantic gesture the note represents. If so, Byelinkov has grown and developed, and your response to him and to the play might be quite different from your response during the first reading.

As you read literature, there are two other important terms to keep in mind for describing people: **protagonist** and **antagonist.** The protagonist is the major character with whom we generally sympathize, while the antagonist is the character with whom the protagonist is in conflict. The antagonist is generally not sympathetic. In "Butterflies," the granddaughter could be seen as the protagonist and the teacher as the antagonist.

As with our readings of the comments and actions of people we meet in everyday life, no single reading of literary characters' words or gestures is necessarily "correct." No single observation represents the "final answer." Instead, multiple possibilities exist. The important thing to remember is that all those possibilities must be suggested—and supported—by details in the text. Obviously we draw on our own life experiences and observations when we think about literary characters, but it's essential to keep in mind that the information that leads to our responses comes from what the work itself offers.

Characters: Point of View

Suppose you hear a friend talk angrily about an argument with a roommate and later hear the roommate describe the same disagreement. What are the chances that the two reports will be the same? Almost none. Accounts such as these are bound to be very different, primarily because they are being told from two distinct **points of view.** What information is offered? What is withheld? Which words are repeated? Which are suppressed? What significance is the incident given? The answers to all these questions depend on who is describing the argument. When you form your own opinion about the disagreement, you take into account who is recounting the incident. In much the same way, readers think carefully about point of view in literary works.

Author and Speaker Distinguishing author from speaker in a literary work is essential. Unlike roommates describing an argument, poets, playwrights, writers of fiction, and sometimes even writers of nonfiction are not necessarily telling personal stories. Although **authors** often do write about incidents or people from their own lives, they write through a created voice that is not necessarily identical to their own.

Carlene Indreasano points out this distinction between author and speaker. In her comment on "Theme for English B," she says that the events in the poem "could be something that happened to Hughes [the poet] or not." Carlene is absolutely right. In fact, Hughes did attend Columbia University (which does sit "on the hill above Harlem"), but it does not matter whether or not he received the assignment described and responded to it in the way described. What matters is that Hughes has created a **speaker (persona)** who describes receiving and responding to an assignment that asks students to "Go home and write / a page tonight. / And let that page come out of you— / Then, it will be true."

Narrator Just as the voice in a poem is called the speaker, the voice that tells a story (in a novel or short fiction) is called the **narrator.** (Sometimes a play has a narrator. Usually, however, a play unfolds directly from the characters' dialogue, along with the playwright's stage directions.)

In fiction, the narrator is sometimes **omniscient** (all-knowing), moving freely into the minds of all the characters. An omniscient narrator can report not only what characters look like, what they do, and what they say but also what they think. A variation is the **limited omniscient** narrator, who sees into the mind of only one character. Obviously, when the thoughts of only one character are reported, readers know more about that character than any other and see the events of the story—as well as the other characters—through that character's eyes.

Sometimes the narrator is also a character in the story. In this case, the narrator uses the **first person** ("I" or "we"). First-person narrators can, of course, report only what is in their own minds or what they see or hear. Omniscient, limited omniscient, and first-person narrators may also make evaluations—for example, they may state that a character is brave or silly or that an action was wise or foolhardy. As readers, we must consider the source of such judgments. Is the narrator **reliable** or **unreliable?** Is there reason to think that the narrator is suppressing information, is lying outright, or is simply incapable of seeing and understanding certain facts? Even if the narrator is reliable, keep in mind that the events are reported from that person's point of view—a different viewpoint might lead to a very different story. Consider, for example, how different the episode in "Butterflies" would be if it were told from the point of view of the teacher.

Sometimes the narrator is **objective,** like a sound camera that reports what it sees and hears. This point of view is used in the story "Butterflies." We are told what the characters do and say, but we are not taken inside their minds. Objective point of view leaves all evaluation and judgment to the reader. Even so, the narrator still has a great deal of power. This particular objective narrator, for example, shows us only the girl and her grandparents; we do not get to see the teacher and to observe for ourselves her response to the girl's story. It's always essential, then, to recognize that the speaker in a poem and the narrator (or characters) in a work of fiction or in drama show us only one way of looking at an experience, an object, a person, or an emotion. There are many other ways—left unexplored except in our own imaginations—of looking at that same experience, object, person, or emotion.

People in Nonfiction Nonfiction—essays, articles, letters, journals, documents—does not usually have fictional characters, yet in every work of nonfiction there is at least one very important point of view: the author's. Identifying and understanding the author's point of view help suggest the work's meaning. For instance, Dora DiFonzo notes that the father who talks about his son in "Education" uses humor. Yet behind the humor, Dora thinks, lie deep concern and—perhaps—a serious comment about the effect of school experiences not only on the child but also on the parents.

Terms Related to People

characters: The fictional people who are part of the action of a literary work.
dialogue: A conversation between two or more fictional characters.
dialect: A variety of a language different from that generally taught in school; may include distinctive pronunciations of words, original vocabulary, or grammatical constructions that are not considered standard.
monologue: A speech by one character addressed to a silent or absent listener.

(continued)

(continued)

soliloquy: A speech by one character in a play, given while the character is alone on the stage or standing apart from other characters and intended to represent the inner thoughts of the character.

motivation: The reason or reasons that cause a character to think, act, or speak in a certain way.

stage directions: Comments by the playwright to provide actors (or readers) with information about actions and ways of speaking specific lines.

dynamic character: A character who changes in some significant way during the course of the work.

round character: A character who shows many different facets; often presented in depth and with great detail.

flat character: A character who usually has only one outstanding trait or feature.

static character: A character who does not change in any significant way during the course of the work.

protagonist: The major character with whom we generally sympathize.

antagonist: The character with whom the protagonist is in conflict, generally not a sympathetic character.

point of view: The position from which the details of the work are reported or described.

author/speaker/persona/narrator: The author is the person who writes the literary work. Do not confuse the author with the speaker or persona, the voice that is heard in a poem, or the narrator, the voice that tells a work of fiction (or sometimes frames a play).

omniscient narrator: A narrator who knows everything and can report both external actions and conversations as well as the internal thoughts of all characters and who often provides evaluations and judgments of characters and events.

limited omniscient narrator: A narrator who can report external actions and conversations but who can describe the internal thoughts of only one character. A limited omniscient narrator may offer evaluations and judgments of characters and events.

first-person narrator: A narrator who is also a character in the work and who uses "I" or "we" to tell the story. First-person narrators can report their own thoughts but not the thoughts of others. They may offer evaluations and judgments of characters and events.

reliable/unreliable narrators: A reliable narrator convinces readers that he or she is reporting events, actions, and conversations accurately and without prejudice. An unreliable narrator raises suspicions in the minds of readers that events, actions, and conversations may be reported inaccurately and that evaluations may reflect intentional or unintentional prejudice.

objective narrator: A narrator who, like a camera, shows external events and conversations but cannot look inside the minds of characters or offer evaluations and judgments.

Exercises: People

1. Describe your first impressions of a person you now know well, noting what caused you to have these impressions. Then explain your current view of this person. Discuss what events, conversations, actions, or interactions either confirmed or changed your initial impression.

2. Think of a film you have seen or a book you have read in which the characters changed significantly. Explain what the characters were like both before and after the change. What motivated the change? What was your response to the change?

3. Read (or reread) any of the works listed in Exercise 3, page 32. Think about how the point of view of the speaker, narrator, or characters affects your response to that work. Try rewriting one section of the work from a different point of view. For example, if the poem or story uses the first-person point of view, try changing every instance of "I" to "he" or "she." Or, if the story or poem is told from an omniscient point of view, try retelling it through the eyes of one of the characters (consider minor characters as well as major characters). Explain how you think the work would change if it were told from this new point of view.

PLACES AND TIMES

This story ["Butterflies"] makes me very confused. I can see the grandparents are farmers who probably grow their own food or maybe sell food, so it seems like they are in an isolated place. Also, I thought maybe this happened a long time ago because in some ways it sounds like a fairy tale or any story that might start like: "In a far-away place, long ago. . . ." But then they talk about the supermarket, so it's got to be modern and not too isolated. And I don't get the part about the teacher buying her cabbages in supermarkets. What does that have to do with the butterflies?

—LARA ZOUFALLY

First I look at the introductory sentence under "Scene" [in *The Man in a Case*], and I see "1898" which, right away, makes me know I am not going to like this play because I like to read modern things. Then, I don't know where Mironitski is (but I figure that out from "Moscow" in the first speech of Varinka—Russia). So now I am totally turned off because it's also a country I don't know much about and am not really interested in. What is funny is that as I read even though there are things I don't know—like "little stale babka"—basically, Byelinkov and Varinka could be this couple I know! She is really crazy and does things that are wild and slightly illegal (driving too fast, etc.). He is—I know this is unbelievable—just like B. Even to the round glasses and the "being neat" stuff. But these people are still together, so maybe there's hope for V and B at the end. (He *could* learn to ride a bike!!!) So how much difference is there between love in Russia (1898) and love in the U.S. (2002)?

—TANYA ELIZAH

Places and Times in "Theme for English B": I would say the time is both past and present. You start in the present, jump to the past, then back to the present. Places? Well, the speaker is in one place—walking from his college to his room at the Harlem Branch Y—but, on the other hand, there is another place, too, which is inside his mind when he thinks back to the past. I looked up Winston-Salem and it's in the South, and there is also a Durham, N.C., so Durham could be (and probably is) south, too. I think this is important—the North and the South all together because the speaker seems to come to a point about being American and having all the parts (people and parts of the country, I think he means) connected. They have to interact whether they want to or not.

—PAUL MEDINO

This essay ["Education"] must have been written quite a few years ago because I don't think that now even way out in the country they have schools where the teachers have to cook on a stove in the classroom (except for homemaking classes, I mean). And I think it would be a fire hazard to heat a school with a stove. But other than those things, both of the schools seemed like places that could exist today. I liked the way the author seemed to make the point that it didn't matter that the city school had all this fancy equipment. The country school was better because of the people. I think that's true now. There's too much push for more money to build schools and to make the *place* better, but what needs more attention is the people.

—RAY CONOVER

"Where do you come from?" You can expect new acquaintances to ask this question. Learning where others were born or grew up or discovering where they have lived or traveled helps us understand them better. In some cases, a new friend comes from a place where customs and values are different from ours. For instance, most people in the United States believe that not looking another person in the eye indicates shame or deceit. In some cultures, however, looking directly at another individual is a sign of boldness and lack of respect.

Time can be as important as place in determining the way a person thinks and acts. Consider the way people from different generations characteristically think about circumstances and ideas. For instance, many people who lived through the Great Depression of the 1930s attach more importance to saving money and achieving job security than people who have not experienced widespread poverty and unemployment. Although not all people who live in a particular time think exactly the same way, recognizing the influence of time helps us understand and appreciate the differences we observe in our daily lives.

In reading literature, it is just as important as it is in daily life to think about time and place, the **setting** of the work.

Time and Place: The Cultures of the Work, the Writer, and the Reader

Your reading of a work will be richer when you consider more than just the literal time and place of the work. Of course, the time and the place of the work's action are important. As you look at Paul Medino's response to "Theme for English B," you'll note that he has begun to explore the importance of the speaker's southern roots as they relate to his current northern experience. Various clues in the poem might lead the reader to research the New York setting of the poem further and to learn what was happening at the time. The reference to Harlem, for example, might lead to learning about the Harlem Renaissance, a time when original African-American music, art, and literature flourished.

In addition, a reader might seek to understand the time and the place in which the writer was living when he or she wrote the work. In the instance of this writer, Langston Hughes, a biography is provided on page 382 of this text. The fact that Hughes himself was a student at Columbia University in New York does not necessarily guarantee that the poem was written about an incident that actually happened, but having this information does provide a richer context within which to read the poem.

Finally, a reader brings to the poem his or her own setting. For example, we usually read works differently at different times in our lives. For instance, a reader who is seventeen and has left high school with no intention of going to college will almost certainly relate differently to Hughes's poem than will the same reader who, five years later, has returned to college and has lived through the experience of receiving a challenging writing assignment from an instructor of freshman English.

Remaining open and alert to the cultures of the work, of the writer, and of ourselves as readers raises complex questions and challenges yet also increases the richness of nearly any work we read.

Place

Lara Zoufally raises important questions about the setting of "Butterflies." She notices that the grandparents seem to live in a somewhat isolated place where they farm and grow their own vegetables. But, Lara notes, they can't be too isolated because the grandfather talks about supermarkets. When Lara read this journal entry aloud in class, another student, Rolf Jensen, responded to her final question, "What does that have to do with the butterflies?" He explained that certain butterflies lay eggs on cabbages. The eggs hatch into caterpillars that eat the cabbages. For a farm family, killing the butterflies is a useful—even necessary—act. Like the teacher in the story, Lara (and many other readers) may not immediately see the irony in the teacher's response to the granddaughter's story. Rolf, who grew up in a family that farmed, was able to provide the information, related to the setting, that made the story meaningful for Lara.

In addition to talking with others, readers can sometimes uncover information about setting by finding out something about the author's background. Reference books, such as *Contemporary Authors, Dictionary of Literary Biography,* and *American Authors, 1600–1900,* are useful resources. For instance, if you knew that Patricia Grace, the author of "Butterflies," is a Maori New Zealander, you could read about the Maori population. Although you can't assume that Grace is definitely writing about the Maori culture, you might find details that suggest a larger context for the grandparents' way of speaking, for the value they place on education, and for their relationship with their granddaughter.

So, as you read "Butterflies," it's helpful to think about the location—a somewhat isolated farm—and it's interesting to speculate that the farm may be part of a Maori village in New Zealand. Smaller details of setting are also important. For instance, in "Theme for English B," the speaker describes "the steps from the hill" that lead to the Harlem Y, where he takes the elevator (another detail of setting) and goes to his room (yet another setting). Paul Medino also notes an intriguing aspect of the setting in "Theme for English B." Much of the setting is inside the speaker's mind. The speaker recalls the Southern cities where he was born and went to school. Later, he talks directly to Harlem (lines 18 and 19) as though it were a person. The **exterior** (outside) **setting** in this poem in many ways reflects and enhances our understanding of the **interior setting:** the setting inside the speaker's mind and heart.

Sometimes place is the main focus of a work. For example, in E. B. White's "Education," the two schools and their surroundings are central. Details of setting fill the essay. The "cold curbs" and "cinder court" in the city contrast sharply with the country roads and unsupervised playground in the country. The settings imply the more important spiritual difference suggested by the author's final paragraph: his son now sleeps better, and his school day goes by "like lightning."

Time

Tanya Elizah was disappointed when she read the **scenic directions** at the beginning of *The Man in a Case* and discovered that the play took place not only in a location she had never heard of but also during a time that she believed would not interest her. She discovered, however, that the conversations, conflicts, and actions of the characters transcended their own time. Varinka and Byelinkov reminded her of people she knew, leading her to ask how much difference there is between love in 1898 Russia and love in the present-day United States.

If Tanya had pursued this question, she might have noticed that, in spite of the many similarities, there are also real differences. In the United States today, a woman would hardly be regarded as revolutionary for riding a bicycle—and even if she were, there are few laws today that forbid to women actions allowed to men. Also, although there are certainly women today who are eager to marry, few of them would spend their twenties living on their parents' farm, apparently engaged in no occupation other than hoping that some man would finally look at them and "see a wife." Varinka's passive way of living seems to contradict her lively, unconventional spirit unless we remember that, in 1898, women of the upper and middle classes had very limited options. Most either married or were dependents of any male relative who would take them in.

The scenic directions often provide details of setting; you can learn other details from the comments and observations the characters make. For example, Varinka and Byelinkov both talk about the lilacs and roses in bloom in the garden, so we can infer that the play takes place in the spring. How might this point be significant? Consider, for example, how the drama would change if it took place in a cavernous, dark, wood-paneled living room lit only by the flames in a large fireplace and if Byelinkov placed a sprig of holly instead of lilacs in Varinka's hair.

Writers understand the power of time and often use time in special ways. For instance, Paul Medino says that the time in "Theme for English B" is "both past and present," noting that the poem begins "in the present, jump[s] to the past, then back to the present." The events in the poem do not take place in chronological order, with the speaker telling us about his birth, his early education, and then his present education. Instead, the poem begins in the present, with the instructor's assignment; then there is a **flashback,** a description of events that occurred earlier. Whenever a writer chooses to change time sequence—to work with a structure other than chronological order—the reader should ask why. How is my response affected by the way time is used in this work? For instance, what if the instructor's words (and the question in line 6) were not given until after line 10?

Terms Related to Places and Times

setting: The time and place of a literary work. Setting includes social, political, and economic background as well as geographic and physical locations.

exterior setting: Aspects of setting that exist outside the characters.

interior setting: Aspects of setting that exist inside the minds and hearts of the characters.

scenic directions: Comments by the playwright to provide actors (or readers) with information about the times and places in which the play or different scenes of the play are set.

flashback: An interruption in the chronological order of a work by description of earlier occurrences.

Exercises: Places and Times

1. Write a paragraph or two about an event that took place before you were born (for example, the passage of the Nineteenth Amendment, which gave women the right to vote; the Vietnam War; President Kennedy's assassination). Then interview someone who was alive then and remembers the event. After the interview, write another paragraph indicating anything new that you have learned, explaining which of your ideas and impressions were confirmed and which were changed.

2. Think about films and television programs you have seen recently. Then discuss one whose setting strikes you as especially important. First, explain the place and the time, and then describe how the setting relates to the characters and their actions. What would happen if these characters and their story were transported to another time or place?

3. Read (or reread) any of the works listed in Exercise 3, page 32. Explain when and where the work takes place. How can you identify times and locations? Think about how the setting affects your response to that work.

What aspects of the work would be greatly changed if the setting were changed? Do any aspects seem "timeless" and "placeless" (aspects that would be meaningful and important in nearly any place or time)? Explain.

WORDS AND IMAGES, SOUNDS AND PATTERNS

You [the instructor] said "Theme for English B" is a poem, but it seems more like a speech or maybe a journal entry to me. The assignment from the speaker's teacher (lines 2–5) is like a poem with rhyme words at the end of lines. Also, I noticed a few other rhymes like "write"/"white" (lines 27–28), "true"/"you" (lines 36–37), and "me"/"free"/"B" (line 38 and lines 40–41). But most of this "Theme," when you read it out loud and don't look at the way the lines are set up on the page, could be just a regular paragraph. So why is it a poem? Because it begins and ends with the rhyming lines?

—TERENCE SULLIVAN

The butterflies mean one thing to the grandparents and the granddaughter and something else to the teacher. Now, I think I am supposed to sympathize with the granddaughter, and I do feel sorry for her that her teacher didn't like her story. But the teacher's view of butterflies is more like my own. I think they are beautiful, and I was really shocked to think about the granddaughter drawing a picture of killing them. When she said that, it really gave me a strange feeling because I thought it was very odd and not what I expected. So to the granddaughter the butterflies are one thing and to the teacher another (and I feel more or less like the teacher, but I see the granddaughter's reason). So who is right here about butterflies? This is something to think about.

—NAOMI ROUSSEAU

Just look at the way Byelinkov and Varinka talk, and you know they are two opposite people. Varinka just goes on and on and uses lots of cute expressions, like calling Byelinkov a "little school mouse" and talking about his "perfectly pressed pants" and his "sweet little galoshes." Byelinkov tells her, "You are fond of expletives" (which according to my dictionary means a word or phrase that is not needed for the sense of a sentence). Byelinkov likes to talk in short sentences and to give advice: "Pride can be an imperfect value" and "Being married requires a great deal of responsibility." Varinka likes to compare Byelinkov to things, like a mouse, a dancing bear, and a stale babka and to famous people in Russian history, like Lermontov, Tchaikovsky, and Peter the Great. She sees that the roses are beautiful, but he sees beetles in the roses. To my mind, he talks about translating

Greek and Latin poetry—which he probably thinks is beautiful—but Varinka sees things around her as beautiful and special, and Byelinkov doesn't even really seem to look at those things.

—MAUREEN WIMSELSKI

The absolute best thing in this essay [E. B. White's "Education"] is the school bus in the city. It's hilarious but it also shows a kind of terror. First White says the bus is "punctual as death." Then the school bus proceeds to "open its mouth" and apparently eat up the boy. Then it takes off like a vicious animal "with an angry growl." To me this says it all. Going to that school is like death—or like getting eaten up by a beast. You can just feel the dread of the kid (or maybe it's the father's dread, maybe he remembers his own school days).

—GERALD STRYKER

One of the things that gives life to a fictional character is the way that character speaks. We come to identify certain words and expressions with that particular character.

Style

A character's style is established by the way that character speaks and acts. Of course, authors choose the words and phrases that make up their characters' speech, describe their actions, and create the setting in which they speak and act. We need to keep this in mind when we consider exactly what it is that distinguishes the **style** of one writer from that of another. And, of course, it's essential to ask how a writer's style affects your response to that person's literary work. Why do you like one style better than another? Why does one style bore, puzzle, or annoy you, whereas another delights, informs, and makes you want to read on? How does the author's style relate to the meaning or meanings you discover in the work or to the questions the work raises?

Tone

Tone, the attitude of the author to the characters and situations in the work, is closely related to style. For example, Gerald Stryker notes that, in "Education," E. B. White uses humorous images that are tinged with seriousness (even terror). The yellow city school bus that "swallows" the child in the story is funny, but White's words also suggest that a child can be overwhelmed by the trappings and demands of certain kinds of schooling. The tone here is complex, and it suggests the complexity the author sees in his subject.

Diction

Diction (choice of words) helps to establish a writer's style and tone. Some writers, for example, choose to use many descriptive words, whereas some use almost none. Consider the contrast between the speeches Wendy

Wasserstein gives her characters in *The Man in a Case* and the language of the narrator and characters in Patricia Grace's "Butterflies." Wasserstein's play is filled with language that appeals to all the senses **(imagery);** we can easily conjure up the scent of the lilacs and roses, the anticipated delicious apricots and cream, the picture of Byelinkov wrapped in his "quilts and curtains" as he retires for the night. In contrast, Grace's story focuses on only one image: that of the butterflies. The description is spare and, as Lara Zoufally (page 41) notes, the story "sounds like a fairy tale or any story that might start like: 'In a faraway place, long ago. . . .'" Lara notices, then, that the language of "Butterflies" makes it sound like one of those childhood tales, perhaps a fable. The story's language raises questions about its meaning. Does it have a simple moral—or lesson—as a fable does? Or is Patricia Grace's story more complex than that?

Syntax

Syntax is the arrangement of words in phrases or sentences and the arrangement of phrases or sentences in paragraphs (fiction), speeches (plays), or lines and stanzas (poetry). Choices related to syntax are aspects of a writer's style. Terence Sullivan raises an important question when he notes that much of "Theme for English B" sounds like a paragraph of regular prose. Unless you look at the arrangement of the sentences and phrases into lines and stanzas, you might not be aware that you are reading a poem. Why does Langston Hughes choose this syntax to write about this experience? The speaker, after all, describes an assignment to which most students would respond by writing a carefully planned essay with an opening paragraph, thesis statement, body, and conclusion. Why, then, does he respond with a poem?

Rhythm and Rhyme

Closely connected to the syntax of a work—and also part of a writer's style—are **rhythm** (the pattern of sound) and **rhyme** (the matching of final sounds in two or more words). The rhythms of many parts of "Theme for English B," for example, are the rhythms of everyday prose speech. Yet, as Terence Sullivan notes, the instructor's assignment at the beginning sounds like a traditional poem. You can read these lines aloud in an exaggerated way to hear the regular beat:

> Go home and write
> a page tonight.
> And let that page come out of you—
> Then, it will be true.

It's intriguing that the instructor's words have such a regular pattern, seeming to lead logically to the speaker/student's otherwise unconventional essay poem.

Perhaps this student sees and hears the world in terms of poetic sound and patterns?

Terence Sullivan also comments on rhyme; he wonders if a poem that doesn't rhyme in a regular pattern is really a poem, raising the question of how to distinguish between poetry and prose. Terence notes that the poem begins and ends with rhyming lines, creating, in a sense, bookends of strong end rhymes to frame the rest of the poem. In addition to using end rhymes, the poet also uses internal rhyme. Look at lines 16 and 17, for instance.

> It's not easy to know what is **true** for **you** or me
> at twenty-**two**, my age.

And the next three lines have seven one-syllable words that rhyme with "you"; the repetition of these words and, of course, the fact that they rhyme contribute to a subtle, insistent poetic rhythm even while the speaker seems simply to be conversing in everyday speech.

Notice also, in line 24, the list of records the speaker likes: "Bessie, bop, or Bach." These choices represent a wide range of musical taste, and notice also that the words sound musical as you pronounce them. The identical initial sounds create **alliteration.**

Of course, alliteration is not a device used strictly by poets: the romantic Varinka, as Maureen Wimselski notes, describes Byelinkov's "perfectly pressed pants." The rhythmic sound of the initial *p*'s underlines the extravagance of her speech and makes many readers smile in sympathy at Byelinkov's complaint that she is "fond of expletives."

Figurative Language

As they work, writers choose whether and when to use **figurative language:** words or expressions that carry more than their literal meaning. Wendy Wasserstein, for instance, fills Varinka's speeches with **metaphors** (comparisons of unlike objects). Varinka calls Byelinkov "my little school mouse," "my sweetest dancing bear," and "my little stale babka." Byelinkov also makes comparisons, but his are less direct; he uses **similes** (comparisons of unlike things using the words "like" or "as"), such as "You speak about me as if I were your pet" and "You dance like a school mouse."

Sometimes the writer's figurative language allows a reader to see an object in a new way. For example, in "Theme for English B," the speaker uses an **apostrophe** (he speaks directly to an inanimate object or place) when he says: "I feel and see and hear. Harlem, I hear you." The apostrophe seems to show that he feels connected to Harlem, perhaps as he would feel connected to a close friend or relative. During class discussion of this work, Terence Sullivan (whose response to the poem appears on page 47) wondered why, when the speaker says he also hears New York, he does not choose to speak directly to that city as he does to Harlem.

Personification means giving an inanimate object the characteristics of a person or animal. E. B. White's beastlike school bus is an excellent example of this kind of figurative language. We can see the bus bearing down on its innocent victim, and we certainly get the impression that city schooling, for White, has more to do with being a helpless captive than a willing participant.

A writer sometimes repeats a word or image so many times in a literary work that you begin to wonder why. Why, for instance, does Patricia Grace call her story "Butterflies" and use butterflies as the central image? Naomi Rousseau writes that the "butterflies mean one thing to the grandparents and the granddaughter and something else to the teacher." And, to the reader, the butterflies may come to have a meaning different from either of those two. The butterflies, then, become a **symbol,** standing for more than just winged creatures that lay eggs on cabbages. The butterflies may indicate the great diversity of ways to look at the world around us; they may suggest the need not to limit ourselves, but to stay open to many possibilities.

Verbal Irony

Just as there can be discrepancies between what a character says and what that character does, or between what a character believes to be true and what the reader knows to be true (irony of situation, page 30), so, too, can there be discrepancies between what a character or author says and what he or she means **(verbal irony).** For example, when Varinka compares Byelinkov to Lermontov, Tchaikovsky, and Peter the Great (all respected Russian men), Byelinkov adds, "Ivan the Terrible." Of course, Byelinkov does not really mean he is like the merciless tyrant; he is being ironic. But Varinka either doesn't pick up on the irony or replies with an ironic statement of her own, "Yes, him too." Whether Varinka is intentionally ironic or not, the discrepancies underline the enormous differences between these two would-be lovers.

Allusions

To understand the irony just described, you have to know that Lermontov, Tchaikovsky, and Peter the Great are all admired figures from Russian history and that Ivan the Terrible (whose name should give him away) was a ruthless czar. When writers use **allusions** (references to events, people, and places outside the work itself), you can usually figure out what is going on from the context. However, if you are interested in adding an extra dimension to your reading, it's easy enough to find the references in a dictionary or encyclopedia. *Webster's New World Dictionary,* for instance, would let you know that Lermontov was a Russian poet and novelist, Tchaikovsky a composer, and Peter the Great a czar. Knowing these specific definitions underlines the extent of Varinka's exaggerations; she considers—or perhaps wishes—her fiancé to be the equal of the most outstanding writers, composers, and rulers of their country.

Terms Related to Words and Images, Sounds and Patterns

style: The way an author chooses words; arranges them in lines, sentences, paragraphs, or stanzas; and conveys meaning through the use of imagery, rhythm, rhyme, figurative language, irony, and other devices.

tone: The attitude of the author toward the subject of the work.

diction: Choice of words.

imagery: Words that appeal to the five senses: touch, taste, sight, hearing, and smell.

syntax: The way words are arranged in phrases or sentences and the way phrases or sentences are arranged in paragraphs (fiction), speeches (plays), or lines and stanzas (poetry).

rhythm: Pattern of sound.

rhyme: The matching of final sounds in two or more words.

alliteration: The repetition of identical initial sounds in neighboring words or syllables.

figurative language: Words or expressions that carry more than their literal meaning.

metaphor: Comparison of two unlike things.

simile: Comparison of two unlike things, using the words "like" or "as."

apostrophe: Addressing an inanimate object or place as if it were alive.

personification: Giving an inanimate object the qualities of a person or animal.

symbol: In a literary work, an object, action, person, or animal that stands for something more than its literal meaning.

verbal irony: A discrepancy between what is said and what is meant or between what is said and what the reader knows to be true.

allusion: A reference to a person, place, object, or event outside the work itself.

Exercises: Words and Images, Sounds and Patterns

1. Think of three friends or acquaintances who speak in a distinctive way. Imagine a conversation between these three people (even though they may not know each other). Write the conversation, and then explain briefly what special qualities you notice in the way these three people speak. What would make you recognize these people if you could hear but not see them?

2. For one day, carry a small notebook with you and write down every example of figurative language you see or hear. Keep your mind open to all kinds of possibilities: explanations in textbooks, the language of sports reporters, the speeches of politicians, the exaggerations of advertising. And, of course,

stay alert to overheard conversations as well as to your own speech. At the end of the day, write a brief comment describing your discoveries and your response to those discoveries.

3. Read, reread, or reconsider any of the works listed in Exercise 3, page 32. Try reading a section (a stanza, a paragraph or two) aloud and (if possible) have someone else read the same section aloud so that you can listen. What do you notice about sounds, images, words, patterns? Describe your response to the author's (or a character's) diction, to a particularly striking or strange image, to an intriguing use of figurative language, or to the rhythm (or rhyme) of a work.

IDEAS

The following excerpts from journal entries show the ideas students discovered as they read, discussed, and thought about "Butterflies," *The Man in a Case,* and "Theme for English B." The italicized sentences represent general statements that could apply beyond the work itself.

"Butterflies" shows how easy—and how dangerous—it is to look at the world around you in just one way. The teacher sees only the beauty in the butterfly and doesn't even consider any other possibility. Because she doesn't know about, or try to find out about, another possibility, her student goes home very puzzled and unhappy.

—LARA ZOUFALLY

The butterflies symbolize destruction to the grandparents and beauty to the teacher. Who is right? Neither. *People see things according to their own perspective, and sometimes this causes problems in communication.* Sure, maybe the teacher should have asked the granddaughter about her picture without making such a judgment. But, on the other hand, the grandparents maybe need to look more carefully and see that even though the butterflies cause problems, they are also beautiful.

—NAOMI ROUSSEAU

"Theme for English B" has ideas both of separation and of connection. The speaker is physically apart from his instructor. The instructor is at the college on the hill in NYC, and the speaker is back in his room in Harlem. But the speaker is writing an assignment for the instructor, so even though there's separation, there's connection. And I think this is very important and what is meant by "As I learn from you, / I guess you learn from me." The instructor learns from the student while the student learns from the teacher because both have different experiences and knowledge to give. *What is meant here is that everyone can gain from listening to someone else who is different from themselves.*

—PAUL MEDINO

As the speaker walks and walks to his room in Harlem, it seems like his thoughts are walking, too. And you get the impression that those thoughts walk all over America. He's looking at what it means to be a black person in America, and he's arguing that white people have to see that black people are just as American as they are. Even for people who may not like it. As he says, the instructor is "a part of me, as I am a part of you." *Whites had better realize that blacks are part of America too, and that there has to be some kind of connection between the two parts.*

—MARK JAMES

Varinka makes fun of Byelinkov for being so stuffy and wearing galoshes all the time. True, he has a rather rigid way of looking at things, but Varinka is also rigid. For instance, she wants to get married to have "the life everyone else has" and to "not be different." And she wants Byelinkov to fit into one specific role—a hero, like Peter the Great. *To me, people have to let others be themselves. Love doesn't come from trying to change someone. You have to accept people as they are.*

—NATHALIE LAROCHELLE

I kept thinking and thinking about the title: *The Man in a Case.* I saw the line where Byelinkov says that he thought he "would grow old preserved like those which are left over, wrapped suitably in my case of curtains and quilts." I realized that later Varinka tells him, "You are wrapping yourself under curtains and quilts." So, to me, some of the curtains and quilts were the real ones on his bed, but they were also a metaphor. Those curtains and quilts are like a cocoon, an outer case, that Byelinkov has to protect himself against experiences of the world. But you get the impression that Byelinkov will never "hatch" out into maturity. *Protection like that has a cost. Insulation against experiences of the world—even something simple like eating peaches and cream for lunch—means that a person may lose the chance of human connection (of love, in this case).*

—MAUREEN WIMSELSKI

White may say that the only difference he sees in the two schools is that his son "sleeps better at night." It's clear to me, however, that he's really saying something quite different. *A simple and uncomplicated schooling is better in every way than a school that has too many trend-setting new programs.* In the city, his son gets "worked on," but in the country it seems to be the boy who does the work and the teacher is just there to help. She gives him food for his body and food for his mind. It's simple and direct—not planned by a dietitian or other fancy experts.

—MARIANNE BACHMANN

After reading a work carefully, with mind and spirit fully open to actions, events, people, places, times, sounds, images, words, and patterns, a reader may well feel overwhelmed. "What does it all mean?" "What's the point?" "What am I supposed to get from this?" "What's the lesson here?" "What's the author trying to say?" These questions—and others—often nag insistently at us, giving us the sense that even though the work evoked a definite response, something more has been left undiscovered.

These questions lead you to consider **theme,** the central idea you seek as you read a work and think about it. The theme of a work is a generalization: an idea that can be broadly applied both to the work itself and to real-life situations outside the work. For example, consider Maureen Wimselski's statement: *"Protection like that has a cost. Insulation against experiences of the world— even something simple like eating peaches and cream for lunch—means that a person may lose the chance of human connection (of love, in this case)."* The italicized words represent a general statement of theme that could apply to people and circumstances very different from those in Wasserstein's play. The details from the play are examples that demonstrate how Maureen arrived at her larger idea, her statement of theme.

It's important to understand that "meaning" is not fixed in literature. Two people reading the same work may see different themes. One person reading a work at age twenty and the same work at age thirty or forty-five may see different themes. Literary scholars reading the same work frequently see different themes. So, questions such as "What am I supposed to get from this?" do not have a specific, easily defined answer. Although it's interesting— and often helpful—to know what others think about a work, their ideas should not define what any other reader is "supposed to get" from the work.

Some literary works, such as fables and biblical parables, do have a lesson or a moral that is directly stated by the writer. Most works, however, convey their meaning indirectly. Whether or not there is something to be learned— and what that something is—depends on what the reader discovers in the work and on how those discoveries interact with what the reader already knows, thinks, or feels about the subject of the work. Sometimes a work of literature causes us to think differently about something; sometimes it reinforces what we already believe, adding new details to support our current beliefs and emotions; sometimes we encounter a work whose main idea offends or angers us. A reader who is affronted by a work is likely to see a very different theme than the reader whose values are reaffirmed by the same work.

What a writer intended to say is not necessarily what the work "says" to various readers. So the question "What is the writer trying to say?" is not really very helpful. For example, a writer may convey one thing to an audience from her or his own time and something quite different to an audience reading the same work a century later. The reader—not the author—defines the theme, although, of course, the reader's ideas relate directly to what the author has written.

As you read the students' responses at the beginning of this section, you almost certainly noticed that those who commented on the same works had quite different views. For instance, Lara Zoufally focused on the teacher's narrow view in "Butterflies," whereas Naomi Rousseau thought that both the grandparents and the teacher lacked something in the way they looked at butterflies. As you read the story, you might have discovered still another theme. Notice that both Lara and Naomi use specific details and examples from the story to support their generalization (their statement of theme). Because they offer evidence from their reading, it's easy to see how they arrived at their ideas. Direct references to the work make these statements of theme convincing and thought-provoking.

As you think about a work and the main idea it conveys to you, remember to support your observations with specific references to the work. Don't be intimidated by the thought that the theme must be some hidden secret. Instead, look at what you know about the work, what you have felt, what you have observed as you read. Work from the strength of what you do know rather than assuming that you are faced with a mysterious puzzle.

Exercises: Ideas

1. Choose a film that you have seen more than once and that you think is worth seeing again. Write a paragraph or two explaining why you feel so strongly about this film. As part of your explanation, include a brief discussion of the film's theme.

2. Write a response to one of the students' comments at the beginning of this section. Explain why you agree or disagree with the way that student sees the work in question.

3. Read, reread, or rethink any of the selections listed in Exercise 3, page 32. Write a response that includes your view of the work's theme. Be sure to make specific references to the work to explain what you say.

3

Continuing the Conversation: Considering Genre and Listening to Other Voices

Chapter 2 introduces terms people use to talk about literature. This chapter suggests two other useful ways to expand the conversation about literature. First, four short sections describe the major literary genres: fiction, poetry, drama, and the essay. Next, the text introduces ways of listening to the voices of other people who have read and commented on literary works in which you have an interest.

Genre is a French term used in literary criticism to indicate a type or form of literature. Understanding the history of the four major literary genres and considering various strategies for reading them should add to your pleasure as well as your understanding of fiction, poetry, drama, and essays. Understanding genre also provides you with new ways to talk and write about literature.

EXPECTATIONS: SHORT FICTION, POETRY, DRAMA, NONFICTION

Chapter 2 encourages you to look at the similarities between everyday conversation and conversation about literature. In each section of Chapter 2, the specialized language of literary conversations is introduced as it applies to the sample selections representing four literary genres: a short story, a poem, a play, and an essay. Thus, the similarities among the four genres are stressed. Yet there are also important distinctions among the genres. The expectations with which readers approach a short story, for example, differ from the expectations with which readers approach a play. Each genre has unique powers and conveys unique pleasures.

Distinctions: Short Fiction and Drama

Consider, for example, the short story "A Jury of Her Peers" (page 558) and the play *Trifles* (page 666), both written by Susan Glaspell. While these works share the same general setting (a Midwestern farming community in the late 1800's) and the same characters, the theme unrolls differently in the two works. The central idea of both the short story and the play might be stated in this way: Communication between men and women can often be complicated, and, in some cases, disastrous.

In the short story, we learn about events and actions that are filtered through the eyes of Mrs. Hale. The story begins in her kitchen, which she must leave in disarray because she is suddenly called to accompany her husband to the scene of a neighbor's death. The only character whose inner thoughts and observations we see is Mrs. Hale. Her voice and her point of view provide us with all the details that make up the plot. While not all short stories have a limited narrative point of view, the device of seeing into the thoughts of one or more characters is much more common in fiction than it is in drama. As we read a short story, we usually notice carefully who is telling the story (whether in the first or third person) and how the story's conflicts and characterizations might be affected by this point of view. In reading a play, on the other hand, we are much more likely to transform the written action into scenes that play out in our minds as they might be acted on a stage. We feel a more direct connection with the characters, their dialogue, and their actions because we imagine that we are experiencing them firsthand, not through the eyes of a narrator.

With the story "A Jury of Her Peers," Mrs. Hale becomes, in a way, the forewoman of the jury. She is the one who observes the details of the interrupted daily activities in Minnie Foster's kitchen. And because we know she was concerned about leaving her own kitchen in disorder, we can easily understand how she makes the leap to tie the details at the Foster's house together into a neat package of evidence. In the play *Trifles,* we see the two characters, Mrs. Hale and Mrs. Peters, together discovering the uncleaned kitchen, the erratic sewing, and, finally, the dead bird. In the play, the women seem to play quite equal roles, whereas in the short story, it is Mrs. Hale who seems to lead the way to the unofficial verdict the women finally reach. Because the short story shows us Mrs. Hale's inner thoughts, we see clearly that she is convinced first and that she must then subtly influence Mrs. Peters to also recognize the harsh justice Minnie Foster has dealt her husband. In addition, Mrs. Hale conveys her support and understanding of Minnie and her actions. In the play, the actors' expressions and the gestures, as well as the directors' instructions would take the place of the interior view the fiction provides of Mrs. Hale's thoughts. Depending on the cast and the director's vision, the play might take several different directions.

Distinctions: Poetry

While short stories and plays encourage us to hear voices of narrators and of characters, the pleasure of reading poetry comes even more fully from the sense of sound. Originally, poetry was entirely an oral form passed from a speaker to a listener (who often then became a speaker for new listeners). As we read poems, the rhythms and sound devices (such as rhyme and alliteration) should create songs in our minds, sometimes harmonious, sometimes discordant. These "mental songs" help to create and emphasize the poem's themes and ideas. In addition to the importance of sound, poetry is also distinct from other genres because of its compact form. Of course, the writers of plays and short stories use figurative language, images, similes, metaphors, and symbols. But poets make use of these devices much more often because they seek to convey feelings, experiences, pleasures, and sorrows in far fewer words. In poetry, then, the richness of the language, along with its music are the distinctions to watch for. Consider, for example, the following poem, which looks at a theme similar to that of the short story "A Jury of Her Peers" and the play *Trifles*.

MARGARET ATWOOD (1939–   )

you fit into me

you fit into me
like a hook into an eye

a fish hook
an open eye

Here the repetition of the words "hook" and "eye" command the readers' attention and ask them to note carefully what is being said. The image in the first stanza suggests a perfect, somewhat sensual, relationship. The two people apparently fit together as smoothly and closely as the fastener on a dress. Yet the second stanza uses repetition of sound to transform that image into something sharply discordant and ironic. Now the reader experiences only the acute pain of a fishhook in a human eye. Here the anguish of a destructive relationship is conveyed, not through the tale of narrator or through dialogue and stage action, but rather through the powerful and economic use of sound and image.

Distinctions: Nonfiction

There are many forms of nonfiction that may be considered literature—for example, the essay, the letter, the journal, speeches, and certain kinds of documents. By definition, nonfiction uses as its subject matter events that actually happened and people who actually lived or are living. Fiction, drama, and poetry often integrate references to actual people and events or reflect imaginative versions of real individuals and experiences, yet the subject matter of these genres originates primarily in the fertile minds and hearts of the writers.

While nonfiction may be written in the form of narrative, the purpose of most nonfiction is not simply to tell a story or to create dramatic action. Nonfiction can have many purposes—for example, to entertain, to inform, or to argue. The nonfiction writer often seeks to convey information. For example, instead of writing a short story or play like Susan Glaspell's works or a poem like "you fit into me," a nonfiction writer might compose an essay about gender and communication.

As you read the more detailed discussions of fiction, drama, poetry, and nonfiction in this chapter, keep in mind that you are developing your own set of expectations for each of these genres.

AN INTRODUCTION TO SHORT FICTION

Cave paintings showing the outcome of a hunting expedition or the imagined exploits of a fantastic beast testify to the ancient roots of the human love for stories. From the time when people first discovered how to communicate through spoken words or written symbols, they have instructed, amazed, warned, and entertained each other with tales both true and fictional.

Early Forms of Fiction

Allegory **Allegories** are stories in which each character, action, and setting stands for one specific meaning. For example, in John Bunyan's allegory *A Pilgrim's Progress* (1678/1684), a character named Christian represents the virtues associated with the ideal member of that faith. In the allegory, Christian passes through a landscape of temptations and dangers with areas symbolically named the "Slough of Despond," the "City of Destruction," and the "Valley of Humiliation" before he reaches the "Celestial City." Allegories, which are intended to teach moral lessons, may also be written as poetry and drama.

Myth **Myths** often tell the stories of ancient deities, sometimes describing their exploits, sometimes explaining how a particular god or goddess came into being. Other myths address the mysteries of nature, including the creation of the universe and its diverse inhabitants. Ancient people probably invented myths as a way to make sense of the world in which they lived. For instance, gods and goddesses were described as experiencing human emotions—hate, jealousy, love, passion, despair—and as facing the human conflicts these feelings create.

Legend **Legends** recount the amazing achievements of fictional characters or exaggerate the exploits of people who actually lived. For example, the story of Paul Bunyan is apparently based on a real man, but his size, his blue ox (Babe), and his astounding feats are inventions of those who told and retold tales of the resourceful lumberjack. Legends—which often include the entertaining tall tale—frequently praise and confirm traits that a society particularly values. For instance, Paul Bunyan works hard, never backs down from a fight, and knows how to enjoy a party—all qualities that were greatly admired during the early years of the American westward expansion.

Fairy Tale Like myths, **fairy tales** focus on supernatural beings and events. They are not peopled by gods and goddesses, however, but by giants, trolls, fairy godmothers, and talking animals who happily coexist with humans—both royalty and common folk. Fairy tales do not attempt to explain the natural world or to affirm national values but instead focus on the struggle between clearly defined good and evil. In fairy tales, good always prevails over evil, although—in those that have not been censored to suit modern sensibilities—the "good" is often achieved by rather terrifying means. Figures of evil drop into pots of boiling oil, are flayed alive, or are cooked into (evidently tasty) pies.

Fable The best-known **fables** are those that were told by the Greek slave Aesop. Fables usually feature animals who can talk and, in general, act just as rationally (and just as irrationally) as humans. Unlike myths, legends, and fairy tales—but like allegories—fables state an explicit lesson. For instance, nearly everyone knows the story of the race between the boastful Hare, who runs quickly ahead of the plodding Tortoise, stops for a rest, and is beaten to the finish line by his slow yet determined rival. "Slow but steady wins the race," Aesop told his listeners, stating specifically the moral he wished to teach.

Parable Like fables, **parables** teach a lesson or explain a complex spiritual concept. Unlike a fable, which tells a story that demonstrates the stated moral, a parable is a narrative that serves as an analogy for the principle being taught. For example, the New Testament contains many parables that suggest the relationship between God and humans. In one parable, God is depicted as a Good Shepherd who looks for one lost sheep in a flock of one hundred. In another parable, God is compared to a father who rejoices at the return of a son who has strayed.

Modern Short Fiction

All of these early forms of short fiction still exist today. In the nineteenth century, however, a new form evolved. It was exemplified by the work of writers such as Guy de Maupassant in France; Anton Chekhov in Russia; George Eliot and Thomas Hardy in Great Britain; and Edgar Allan Poe, Nathaniel Hawthorne, Herman Melville, Mary Wilkins Freeman, and Sarah Orne Jewett in the United States.

The Realistic Short Story   The nineteenth-century **realistic short story** differed from early forms of fiction in many ways. Nineteenth-century realistic short stories focused on scenes and events of everyday life. Ordinary men, women, and children—not fabulous gods, powerful giants, and talking animals—inhabited these stories. Characters were developed more fully; rather than representing one primary trait, the central figures of short stories exhibited the complexities and contradictions of real people. Plots became more intricate to suggest the workings of characters' souls and minds and to depict their external actions. Settings became more than briefly sketched backdrops; times and places were described in vivid detail. Most important, realistic short stories moved away from teaching one particular moral or lesson. Although the theme of a short story often suggested certain values, readers were expected to find meaning for themselves. The author no longer served up a moral or a lesson in a direct and obvious way.

The realistic short story, as it evolved from the nineteenth century to the twentieth, usually focuses on a conflict experienced by a character or group of characters. Often, by facing that conflict, the characters come to know themselves (and other people) more fully. A short story that shows a young person moving from innocence to experience is called a **story of initiation.** A related form is the **story of epiphany,** in which a character experiences a conflict that leads to a sudden insight or profound understanding. (The word "epiphany" comes from the name of the Christian feast day celebrating the revelation of the infant Jesus to the Magi. These wise men, who had traveled from the East, returned to their own countries deeply moved and changed by what they had seen in Bethlehem.)

The Nonrealistic Short Story   The nineteenth century also saw the development of the **nonrealistic short story.** For example, many of Nathaniel Hawthorne's stories introduced supernatural beings, strange settings, or plot events that could not be explained by the traditional laws of nature. (See, for example, "Young Goodman Brown," page 194.) Although these nonrealistic stories often incorporated elements of earlier forms of short fiction (for instance, characters—human or animal—with unusual powers), they shared certain qualities with the realistic short story. Their characters were more fully developed and had spiritual and psychological depth, their plots were more complex, and their settings were more fully described. Most important, their themes often led the reader to speculate, wonder, and question rather than to accept a directly stated moral or lesson.

In the twentieth century, writers such as Leslie Marmon Silko ("The Man to Send Rain Clouds," page 854) continue the tradition of the nonrealistic short story. Unbound by realistic dimensions of time and space, unfettered by the laws of physics or even by the conventions of human psychology, these writers push their own imaginations—and the imaginations of their readers—in new and sometimes unsettling directions. Reading nonrealistic fiction requires what the nineteenth-century poet Samuel Taylor Coleridge called "the willing suspension of disbelief"—the willingness to read, enjoy, and ponder settings, plots, and characters that seem strange and unconventional. Even more so than realistic fiction, nonrealistic stories lead in many diverse directions rather than toward a single theme.

A Word about Fiction and Truth

What distinguishes true stories from fiction? An easy answer is that true stories tell about events that actually happened to people who actually lived, whereas fiction tells about events and people who are imaginary. It's often difficult, however, to make such neat distinctions clearly. For example, consider a short story set during a recent time in a familiar city. As you read, you may recognize the names of streets and remember some of the events of the era. Although most of the characters who inhabit this familiar city are imagined, occasionally one of those fictional characters meets—or refers to—a person who was alive at the time the story takes place. To what extent, then, is this story true? Are only the parts that can be verified by your own observation (street names, for example) or through historical reports (assassinations, wars, economic upheavals) true? Or are the created characters—their actions, their conflicts, their emotions—also true in some sense? And what about stories that take place entirely outside the realm of what we currently recognize as reality—for example, stories set in the future or in an imagined country with no familiar patterns or rules? In what ways might such stories tell the "truth"? Consider such possibilities as human emotions, conflicts, and interactions that the story portrays.

As you read the short stories in this anthology, think about the people you meet, the places they live, the conflicts they face. Sort out for yourself what truths these people, places, and conflicts have to offer. Consider how those truths fit—or do not fit—with your life, your hopes, your fears, your values.

GUIDELINES

Short Fiction

These considerations provide guidelines for reading, thinking about, and writing about short fiction. Although not every consideration applies to every story, these guidelines can help you read more deeply and experience the story more fully.

1. Read the opening paragraphs carefully several times. Jot down questions, predictions, and expectations for the rest of the story. After you finish reading the story, look back at your early responses. To what extent were your questions answered and your predictions and expectations fulfilled

2. As you read, list the conflicts in the story (consider major as well as minor characters). Note how the characters face and resolve (or do not resolve) those conflicts. Then discuss the implications of the characters' actions (or inaction).

3. To continue thinking about conflict, identify a character who faces a difficult choice, perhaps a moral decision. What would you do under the same or similar circumstances? Compare your imagined response to the character's response.

4. Describe the setting of the story in detail. Remember to consider the following: (a) large elements of place (city, state, section of country, nation); (b) small elements of place (a bedroom, a business office, a battlefield); (c) large elements of time (century, part of century); (d) small elements of time (day, night, season of the year, holiday). How important is setting to the meaning you find in the story? How would the story be changed if any (or several) of the elements of setting were changed?

5. Consider the viewpoint from which the story is told. How would the story change if that viewpoint were different? Try retelling any part of the story through the eyes of a different character or through the eyes of an objective observer.

6. Read the story once quickly, and then jot down your responses, impressions, and questions. Wait several days, and then reread the story slowly and carefully. Return to your original responses, impressions, and questions to consider what you now have to add or to change. Note the reasons for making these changes and additions.

7. Note any objects, animals, physical gestures, or aspects of nature that are mentioned repeatedly or receive unusual emphasis. What do these

GUIDELINES, continued

elements contribute to your experience of the story? In what ways might they add to the meaning(s) you see?

8. Think about the comparisons and contrasts you see in the story. For example, are there two characters who face the same situation yet act very differently? Consider also comparisons you can make between the characters, setting, conflicts, and action in two different stories. What significance can you see in the differences and similarities you've discovered?

9. Compare any situation, character, choice, or decision in the story to some aspect of your own life. Explain how the story is different from or similar to your own experience.

10. Write a continuation of the story. For example, imagine what will happen immediately after the ending scene. Or project what one or more of the characters might be like in five or ten years. Explain the thinking that led you to your speculations.

AN INTRODUCTION TO POETRY

Long before humans could read or write, they created, understood, and valued poetry. Historic events, natural catastrophes, and dramatic predictions were remembered and embellished in the verses of song-makers, court poets, and minstrels, who also invented ballads recording the universal emotions evoked by lovers' quarrels, forbidden romance, and family fights.

The works of early poets were recited or sung; the audience gathered in groups and listened. These ancient settings suggest the important connection between the sound of a poem and the meaning it creates. More than any other qualities, rhythm and structural patterns distinguish poetry from prose. Today, most poetry is read silently and alone. To bring poetry to life, however, we must reach back into the past to revive its music.

Suggestions for Reading Poetry

When you first approach a poem, try reading it aloud. Stay alert to the ways the words sound as you pronounce them. You may notice rhyme or alliteration (see page 49), although not every poem uses these sound devices.

Enjambment Listen carefully to how the lines flow together. Be aware of **enjambment:** the carrying over of meaning and sound from one line to the next with no pause between lines. Consider this example from Sappho's "To me he seems like a god":

> To me he seems like a god
> as he sits facing you and
> hears you near as you speak
> softly and laugh
> in a sweet echo that jolts
> the heart in my ribs.

Although there are six lines, there is only one sentence. If you come to a full stop at the end of each line as you read, the poem will sound disjointed and the meaning will be obscured. Do *not* read these lines like this:

> To me he seems like a god *(long pause)*
> as he sits facing you and *(long pause)*
> hears you near as you speak *(long pause)*

Rather, read them like this:

> To me he seems like a god *(very brief pause)* as he sits facing you and *(very brief pause)* hears you near as you speak *(very brief pause)* softly and laugh *(very brief pause)* in a sweet echo that jolts *(very brief pause)* the heart in my ribs.

Notice that when you pay attention to the enjambment, the lines flow together and become more coherent. The sound and meaning work together rather than against each other.

At this point you may well wonder why poets bother to write lines rather than standard sentences and paragraphs. Often, poets use enjambed lines because they want the reader to pause (but only for an instant) so that the next words (those that begin the next line) will be particularly noticed.

Enjambment, then, lets the poet emphasize a phrase or idea or (sometimes) surprise the reader with the thought on the next line. Look at enjambed lines with aroused curiosity and read them with a sense of discovery. Try to discover why the poet chose to end the line at this particular point rather than at another.

Once you understand how enjambment works, you'll be able to read poetry aloud smoothly and with enjoyment. Try, also, to keep it in mind as you read poetry silently. Learn to "hear" with your mind so that every experience with poetry, whether actually voiced or not, combines sound and meaning.

Syntax The **syntax** (the arrangement of words in a sentence) of poetry is sometimes different from the syntax of prose. Consider, for example, these lines from W. H. Auden's "The Unknown Citizen":

Except for the War till the day he retired
He worked in a factory and never got fired

Most speakers would use this word order:

Except for the War, he worked in a factory till the day he retired and never got fired.

The poet inverts the expected order of the phrases and clauses within the sentence to focus our attention both on the length of the citizen's working time ("till the day he retired") and on his steadiness ("never got fired"). In addition, the inversion allows for the rhyme of "retired" and "fired," which further emphasizes the length of the citizen's work life.

Pay attention to the syntax as you read, especially if you are pondering the meaning of some lines. Often, experimenting with ways to rearrange the words and phrases will lead you to see meanings you had not noticed before.

Structure   Although poetry was originally a strictly oral art form, for centuries it has also been a visual form. When asked how they differentiate prose from poetry, many readers say, "The way it looks on the page" or "The way the lines are arranged."

Closed Form   In many traditional forms of poetry, the lines and stanzas must be arranged according to established patterns. Japanese **haiku** is one example. Each haiku must have seventeen syllables (in the original Japanese), generally divided into three lines. Here is a haiku:

The piercing chill I feel:
my dead wife's comb, in our bedroom,
under my heel . . .

—TANIGUCHI BUSCON
(translated by Harold G. Henderson)

Other examples of traditional poetic forms are the ode and the sonnet. When you read **closed-form** poetry, ask yourself why the poet chose this form and how the form contributes to the meaning the work conveys to you.

Open Form   Many readers think of closed form as an inherent part of poetry. And, indeed, for centuries poems from all cultures and in all languages conformed to set rules of line, stanza, and/or syllable length and often had set rhyme patterns. In the nineteenth century, however, poets began to experiment, resisting the limitations they believed were imposed by traditional poetic forms.

These poets determined the length of their own lines and stanzas, used unexpected rhythms and rhymes, and frequently did away with rhyme entirely.

For an example of **open-form** poetry, read e.e. cummings's "Buffalo Bill's" (page 1191).

When you read such a poem, ask yourself why the poet chose not to use a traditional form. How would the meaning of the poem be changed if the same images and themes were set in a carefully rhymed sonnet, for example, rather than in an unrhymed series of lines that are uniquely arranged?

Types of Poetry

Although not all poems fit neatly into categories, the two major types of poems are **narrative** and **lyric.** Narrative poems tell stories. They often present a significant episode or series of episodes in the life of one primary character (or, sometimes, two primary characters). Lyric poems express the feelings, musings, or emotions of a single character (the speaker).

Narrative Poetry Examples of narrative poems include long **epics** (such as Homer's *Iliad* or Milton's *Paradise Lost*) as well as short **ballads.** Nearly all narrative poems stress action and suggest a conflict. Many focus on a moral choice or difficult decision. For examples of modern narrative poems, see William Stafford's "Traveling through the Dark" (page 872), Seamus Heaney's "Mid-Term Break" (page 239), and Denise Levertov's "During a Son's Dangerous Illness" (page 1195).

Lyric Poetry The word "lyric" comes from the lyre, the Greek instrument used for musical accompaniment of poetry, which was often sung or chanted. Although a lyric poem may depict an outward action, it generally focuses on inward reactions, insights, or responses. Lyric poems are written in many forms, including the following:

Italian (or Petrarchan) Sonnet The **Italian sonnet** is divided into two parts, an **octave** (eight lines) with the rhyme scheme *abbaabba* and a **sestet** (six lines) with the rhyme scheme *cdecde* (or some variation). The octave usually develops an idea or image, and the sestet comments on this idea or image.

English (or Shakespearean) Sonnet The **English sonnet** falls into three **quatrains** (four lines) and a concluding **couplet** (two lines). The rhyme scheme is *abab cdcd efef gg.* The first three quatrains usually develop an idea or image, and the closing couplet comments on this idea or image. For an example, see Shakespeare's "Let me not to the marriage of true minds" (page 592).

Open Form Open-form lyric poems do not follow any particular pattern or structure.

GUIDELINES

Poetry

These considerations provide guidelines for reading, thinking about, and writing about poetry. Although not every consideration applies to every poem, these guidelines can help you read more deeply and experience the poem more fully.

1. After reading and thinking about a poem, read it aloud several times to an audience (at least two or three people). With each reading, use a different tone of voice and emphasize different lines and words. Discuss with your audience how the different readings changed the poem for them. Explain your discoveries about the possible ways to read this poem.

2. Write a brief character sketch of the speaker in the poem. What values do you think the speaker holds? What is your response to these values? Refer to specific details in the poem to support your evaluation.

3. Using Christopher Marlowe's "The Passionate Shepherd to His Love" (page 598) and Sir Walter Raleigh's "The Nymph's Reply to the Shepherd" (page 599) as models, write your own "reply" to any of the poems in this anthology. Reply in poetry or in prose.

4. Consider two or three poems that treat the same theme (perhaps in one of the thematic anthology sections). Compare and explain the significant differences and similarities you see in your responses to these poems.

5. Consider a poem in which the speaker describes or addresses another person. Imagine how that person might respond to the poem. For example, consider how the man described in Sappho's "To me he seems like a god" (page 591) might react to his deification or how the mother might respond to her daughter's description of her in "The Youngest Daughter" (page 469).

6. Find a poem with figures of speech (metaphors, similes, personifications) you find particularly intriguing, puzzling, moving, affirming (or whatever) and explain your response. As you write, focus specifically on one or two figures of speech. Explain the meanings they suggest as well as the emotions they evoke.

(continued)

GUIDELINES, continued

7. Read a poem whose title caught your attention. Discuss the connection you see between the poem and its title. Were you disappointed, surprised, pleased by the relationship between the poem and its title? Explain whether and why your expectations were fulfilled, disappointed, or exceeded.
8. Consider the final stanza or lines of a poem carefully. Then suggest an alternative ending. Explain why you would make the changes you have indicated or how they would diminish the poem.
9. Discover a poem that describes a character, place, action, conflict, or decision that relates in some way to a person, place, action, conflict, or decision in your own life. Compare your experience to the experience described in the poem.
10. After reading the works of several poets, choose one you would like to know more about. Read biographical information as well as more of the poet's works. Then choose *one* aspect of the poet's life that particularly intrigues you and that you see reflected in the poet's work. Write a paper explaining what you have discovered.

AN INTRODUCTION TO DRAMA

Since the days of ancient Greece, people have created, watched, and participated in drama. Drama makes events and emotions—whether realistic or fantastic—come to life before the eyes of the audience. More than any other literary form, drama is a visual experience. Whether we read it or see it on-stage, a play leaves pictures in our minds. These pictures, along with the echoes of the characters' (and, of course, the playwright's) words, create the emotions and ideas that together make up that play's themes.

Suggestions for Reading Drama

Reading drama, of course, is not exactly the same as seeing a play performed. Some qualities are lost—yet others are gained—when you read the playwright's descriptions and dialogue without the intervening interpretation of directors and actors.

Dialogue For some people, reading plays is difficult because they find the structure of the dialogue (the characters' conversations with others, with themselves, or with the audience) hard to follow. Although it may seem artificial to have the character's name at the beginning of each speech, it is obviously essential to know who is talking.

With a little practice, you can adjust to this distraction by training yourself to "read through" the characters' names. Try simply to note the name, rather than actually reading it as part of the speech. Consider the name almost as you would a mark of punctuation. It's there to guide you, but you don't consciously think about it any more than you consciously note a period, apostrophe, or comma when you come across those guides to meaning.

If you find this strategy unworkable, try providing your own transitional words to link the name to the speech. For instance, consider these speeches from *Antigone:*

> ISMENE: Why do you speak so strangely?
> ANTIGONE: Listen, Ismene:
> > Kreon buried our brother Eteocles
> > With military honors.

To get rid of the artificial introductory names, read the speeches this way:

> Ismene *says,* "Why do you speak so strangely?"
> Antigone *answers,* "Listen, Ismene . . ."

Using this strategy, you create a bridge from the name of the character to the words the character says.

Stage Directions Playwrights provide stage directions that explain details of setting and give information about the way characters speak and move. For some readers, stage directions divert attention from the dialogue, causing them to lose their train of thought. Yet it is necessary to be aware of stage directions to understand fully how the playwright envisioned both setting and action.

Some people read a play at least twice, once paying close attention to the stage directions and once simply noting the stage directions as brief guides but not stopping to read them in detail. They try to hold the information in their minds from the first reading, and, during the second reading, they use the stage directions to start "creating" or "directing" their own version of the play.

Some students read the play in short sections—by scenes or parts of scenes. They read the stage directions for a scene first (without paying much attention to the dialogue). Then they return to read the dialogue, this time integrating what they learned about setting and action from their reading of the stage directions.

List of Characters At the beginning of most plays, the playwright gives a list of characters and often a brief description of each. Read this list before you start reading the play; you'll get a head start on understanding the relationships and dynamics between characters. Reading the list of characters also alerts you to watch for the entrance of each individual and helps you become aware of the role—however important or minor—each plays in the drama.

Traditional Forms of Drama

Traditional forms of drama are still performed and enjoyed. In addition, modern playwrights often adapt, incorporate, or rebel against elements of traditional drama as they write today's plays.

Greek Drama Formal competitions among Greek playwrights began in approximately 530 B.C. These competitions continued to be held for several centuries, always in connection with religious celebrations dedicated to Dionysus, the god of wine, who symbolized life-giving power. Greek plays were performed in large, outdoor, semicircular **amphitheaters** that held as many as 15,000 people.

These audiences, of course, understood the conventions of Greek theater. For example, the **chorus** (usually representing the voice of the community) danced and sang in the **orchestra** (a round area at the foot of the amphitheater). On an elevated stage behind the orchestra, the actors—wearing masks that symbolized their primary characteristics and, in addition, amplified their voices—performed their roles. Although Greek theaters did not have elaborate sets, they did have one rather spectacular stage device, the **deus ex machina** (god from the machine). By means of elaborate mechanisms, actors were lowered from above to the stage to play the role of gods meting out punishments or rewards to the human characters.

Scenes end with the dances and songs of the chorus (the **ode**), which sometimes comment on the action of the scene or provide background information clarifying the action of the scene. As the chorus sang one part of their observation (the **strophe**), they moved from right to left on the stage; as they sang another part (the **antistrophe**), they moved to the right.

Greek plays are short in comparison to five-act Shakespearean plays or modern three-act plays. Because the audience was familiar with the myths and legends on which most of the plays are based, the playwrights did not have to spend time explaining many of the background circumstances. Most Greek plays can be acted in about an hour and a half.

For an example of a Greek tragedy, read Sophocles' *Antigone* (page 978) or *Oedipus Rex* (page 748).

Elizabethan Drama William Shakespeare's plays exemplify the drama written during the reign of Queen Elizabeth I of England (1558–1603). Shakespeare wrote tragedy, comedy, and history; he captured the large, spectacular actions of kings, queens, and other highborn characters (and the people who serve them) as well as the romances and intrigues that were part of their lives.

Elizabethans followed Greek tradition by barring women from the stage. Adolescent boys played the parts of young heroines such as Juliet, and male character actors eagerly sought the parts of older women.

Although currently there is much speculation about the design of Elizabethan theaters, most scholars agree that early Elizabethan plays were performed in makeshift locations such as inn yards or open spaces between buildings such as the Inns of Court, which was a London law college. When theaters were built, they were usually octagonal on the outside. Inside, they were circular. The audience sat on both sides as well as in front of the raised stage. As in the Greek theater, there was little scenery or stage setting, except for the booms and machinery used to lower actors who came on as messengers or agents of supernatural forces. Unlike Greek theaters, however, Elizabethan theaters had a second-level balcony, doors at the back for entrances and exits, a curtained alcove, and a trapdoor in the stage floor for surprise entrances of ghosts and spirits. Although the huge Greek amphitheaters could accommodate many thousands of theatergoers, most Elizabethan theaters could house no more than about 1,000 to 2,000, including 500 to 800 **groundlings** (common folk who could not afford seats and thus stood at the foot of the stage). The composition of the Elizabethan audiences—ranging from the illiterate groundlings to the highly educated nobility—presented a challenge to the playwright. Successful plays usually melded action, humor, and violence with philosophical insights and evocative poetry. For an example of such a play, read *Hamlet* (page 244).

Modern Forms of Drama

Following the flourishing drama during the Elizabethan period, playwrights—particularly in England and in France—focused on comedy as well as tragedy. These eighteenth- and nineteenth-century playwrights frequently satirized the failings and foibles of society in witty dramas depicting romantic intrigues and entanglements. During this same time in the United States, playwrights developed the tradition of **melodrama,** plays with stereotyped villains and heroes representing extremes of good and evil.

Realistic Drama Reacting against both stylized comedy and exaggerated melodrama, some late nineteenth- and early twentieth-century dramatists began to develop a new form: the **realistic drama.** These dramatists worked to present everyday life—crises, conflicts, and emotional responses to which ordinary people could relate.

Dramatists writing in the realistic tradition depict problems with work, with family relationships, with community politics. Ghosts do not pop up from the floor of the realistic stage to introduce problems into the characters' lives, nor do gods descend from above to solve those problems. Instead, the difficulties the characters face seem to follow logically from events and decisions with which most members of the audience can identify. Most can also relate to—if not agree with—the responses characters have to the conflicts in their lives.

Settings and props in the realistic theater are more important than in earlier forms of drama, because the dramatist seeks to create the illusion of real life. Often the stage is like a room with the fourth wall removed. The audience is invited to watch ordinary people and listen to them conversing in ordinary language rather than in polished poetry, stylized witty exchanges, or highly dramatic pronouncements.

Examples of realistic drama in this anthology include Ibsen's *A Doll's House* (page 608), Glaspell's *Trifles* (page 666), and Fugard's *"Master Harold" . . . and the Boys* (page 474).

Theater of the Absurd In the second half of the twentieth century, a number of playwrights rejected the conventions of realistic drama. Instead of a sequence of logically connected events, absurdist drama offers actions that lead in no predictable direction. The motivations of characters are contradictory or absent altogether. Conversations and speeches ramble disjointedly, leaping first one way and then another for no apparent reason.

Rather than suggesting coherent themes, absurdist dramas invite the audience to ask questions about the world in which we live. Martin Esslin, who first called these dramas **"theater of the absurd,"** offers the following insights:

> The Theater of the Absurd shows the world as an incomprehensible place. The spectators see the happenings on the stage entirely from the outside, without ever understanding the full meaning of these strange patterns of events, as newly arrived visitors might watch life in a country of which they have not yet mastered the language.
>
> (*The Theater of the Absurd,* New York: Doubleday, 1969)

Types of Drama

Whether ancient or modern, plays represent a wide range of emotions and views of the world. Although most plays contain both serious and comic elements, they usually fit into one of two major dramatic categories: **tragedy,** which focuses on life's sorrows and serious problems, and **comedy,** which focuses on life's joys and humorous absurdities.

Tragedy Traditionally, the tragic play looks at the life of a royal figure or highly respected official. During the course of the drama, this character's fortunes change drastically from good to bad. Having enjoyed high status in society, the **tragic hero** meets his or her downfall for one (or a combination) of these three reasons: fate or coincidence beyond the control of the character, a flaw in character, or a mistake in judgment.

Because the traditional tragic hero is a noble character, his or her fall has been regarded as particularly moving to the audience. After all, if someone as brave, stalwart, wise (and so on) as the tragic hero can fall prey to random accidents, character flaws, or poor judgment, how much more vulnerable must we ordinary mortals be? In the *Poetics,* Aristotle suggested that watching the tragic hero's downfall (the **catastrophe,** which generally involves the death not only of the hero but also of other, often innocent, individuals) inspires in us the emotions of pity and terror. By watching the tragic hero move steadily toward disaster, and by seeing the drama's **resolution** (the conclusion, in which order is generally restored to the society at large), we viewers may experience **catharsis** (profound relief from the tension of the play and a sense that we have gained insight and enlightenment, rather than simply entertainment, from the drama). For classic examples of traditional tragic heroes, consider the title characters in Sophocles' *Antigone* or Shakespeare's *Hamlet.*

Modern plays that are sometimes termed tragedies do not always strictly follow the conventions of traditional tragedy. For instance, the main character may not be highborn but may instead be a rather ordinary person, like Nora in Ibsen's *A Doll's House.* Also, as in *A Doll's House,* a modern tragedy may not end with the main character's physical death but rather with the death of a way of life. Some scholars argue that these modern plays are not true tragedies and that their main characters are not true tragic heroes. *A Doll's House* (page 608) provides an opportunity to consider the nature of modern tragic drama and modern tragic characters.

Comedy Unlike traditional tragic drama, which focuses on the lives of noble, highborn characters, comic drama shows us the lives of ordinary people. Like the characters in tragedies, these people encounter conflicts, challenges, and difficulties. Yet their problems are seldom deeply serious—or if they are serious, they are treated in a lighthearted way.

The humor in comic plots has many sources. **Satiric comedy** exposes the foibles and shortcomings of humanity, inviting us not only to laugh at the often-exaggerated stage examples but also to pay attention to our own idiosyncrasies and follies. Satiric comedy may be light and witty, but often its humor is rather dark and biting. We laugh at the characters, yet we cannot help but see the selfishness and egotism in their plights. The source of satiric humor is often both verbal and visual. Writers of satiric comedy use sharp words and cutting phrases as well as pratfalls and fisticuffs to inspire laughter in their audience.

In **romantic comedy,** by contrast, the source of humor is frequently mistaken identity and unexpected discoveries as well as romping stage chases, mock fistfights, and other physical action. Unlike satiric comedy, romantic comedy aims not at chastising and improving human behavior but rather at inviting the gentle laughter of self-recognition. Romantic comedy seeks to delight the audience rather than to teach a lesson. Shakespeare's comedies, such as *As You Like It,* typify romantic comedy.

Whether the comic drama is satiric or romantic, it differs in major ways from tragedy. Whereas tragedy moves toward the main characters' downfall, comedy moves toward the improvement of the main characters' fortunes. Tragedy usually ends with death and then with restoration of order; comedy concludes with reconciliation, often through the marriage of the main characters as well as the marriage of minor or supporting characters.

Tragicomedy More common among modern dramas than the comedy is the **tragicomedy:** a play that mixes elements of comedy and tragedy. For instance, Glaspell's *Trifles* (page 666) focuses on a tragedy, a woman's murder of her husband. Yet the bumbling sheriff and his male cohorts become darkly comic figures as they make fun of the two women who manage to solve the crime that stumps all the men. Other plays in this anthology that combine comedy and tragedy include Fugard's *"Master Harold" . . . and the Boys* (page 474).

Tragicomedy takes many forms. Sometimes, as with *Trifles,* the play is primarily tragic yet is relieved by moments of humor. Sometimes humor dominates the play, yet serious themes lie behind the comic words and actions. Consider, for example, Fierstein's *On Tidy Endings* (page 1203) with its witty exchanges between the characters yet with underlying themes relating to loss and death.

GUIDELINES

Drama

These considerations provide guidelines for reading, thinking about, and writing about drama. Although not every consideration applies to every play, these guidelines can help you read more deeply and experience the play more fully.

1. Find one scene (or part of one scene) that you find particularly strange, intriguing, puzzling, powerful, or moving. Briefly summarize the scene and explain your response. As you explain, indicate

GUIDELINES, continued

the relationship between the scene you are discussing and the rest of the play.

2. Compare the primary qualities of two characters in the play. Explain why you find their similarities and differences significant.

3. Describe your initial response to one of the play's main characters (after reading the first act or scene); then explain your response after you finished reading (and rereading) the entire play. Evaluate the events, actions, and speeches in the play that either confirmed your first response or caused you to change it.

4. List all the conflicts you see in the play, whether they are experienced by major or minor characters. Then consider how these conflicts might be related. How are they similar? How are they different? How does the characters' resolution of conflicts contribute to the play's resolution?

5. Rewrite a significant scene (or part of a scene) from the play in short story form. Provide detailed descriptions of the characters' inner feelings and thoughts as well as the setting in which the action takes place.

6. Watch a live or filmed performance of one of the plays (or a film based on the play). Compare your responses as you read it to your responses as you viewed the stage or film version. Notice particularly aspects the stage or film directors have chosen to change. For example, are any characters eliminated? Added? Are scenes omitted? Added? Evaluate the effect of these decisions.

7. Explicate the opening dialogue of any of the plays. Consider each line—and the language within each line—very carefully. What tone does this dialogue establish? What expectations do these lines raise concerning the play's conflicts and themes?

8. Consider the conflicts and choices of any character. Explain your response to the way the character deals with conflict. Draw on your own experiences and observations as you evaluate this character's decisions and actions (or failure to decide or to act).

9. Write either an alternative ending for one of the plays or an additional scene to take place at a specified time after the current final scene. Explain the reasons for your changes or for your speculation concerning the futures of the characters. Refer to specific details in the play as you make this explanation.

(continued)

> **GUIDELINES, continued**
>
> 10. Read biographical background on the playwright, reviews of performances, or critical essays analyzing and evaluating the play. Choose one or two new insights about the play that you have gained from your reading, and explain them. How has your research changed, challenged, affirmed, or enriched your initial reading?

AN INTRODUCTION TO NONFICTION

Nonfiction is often defined as prose works that are factual. Under this definition, all prose works other than imaginative literature (novels, short stories, poetry, and drama) are considered nonfiction. Essays, transcriptions of speeches, letters, documents, and journals are nonfiction. So are recipes, corporate reports, and grant proposals. But are all of these forms literature?

For centuries, most readers and scholars have agreed that one particular type of essay—referred to as **belles-lettres** (French for "fine letters")—deserves to be called literature. These essays often pursue philosophical subjects using language with the figures of speech we traditionally think of as literary, such as metaphor, simile, and personification. C. S. Lewis's "We Have No 'Right' to Happiness" (page 678) exemplifies the belletristic essay.

While the term "belles-lettres" is rarely used today, works such as personal essays, memoirs, and descriptive reflections echo roots in the belletristic tradition. These works, called **creative nonfiction,** frequently use narration and description to meditate on, analyze, evaluate, or reflect on various subjects and experiences. While a creative nonfiction essay may seek to inform or to persuade, it may also serve primarily as a vehicle for self-reflection, as the author ponders experiences, encounters, and observations. Both Langston Hughes's "Salvation" (page 382) and Maya Angelou's "Graduation in Stamps" (page 385) provide examples of the **memoir,** a sub-genre of creative nonfiction that uses as its subject matter events from the writer's past. Barbara Huttman's "A Crime of Compassion" (page 1230) incorporates personal narrative that leads to analysis and persuasion. C. S. Lewis's essay "We Have No 'Right' to Happiness" serves as an example of the tradition of belles-lettres with a strong emphasis on argument and persuasion.

But what about other forms of nonfiction? Most people would immediately reject recipes, corporate reports, and grant proposals as examples of literature, perhaps because these forms of writing are meant simply to convey information rather than to intrigue both the minds and emotions of readers;

perhaps because these forms deal primarily with facts rather than ideas, ideals, and emotions; perhaps because the language of these forms is usually literal rather than figurative; perhaps because these forms tend to avoid ambiguity and complication rather than suggest them; perhaps because these forms generally provide answers and certainties rather than raising questions and possibilities.

These "perhapses," then, suggests a possible definition for literary works:

1. They deal with ideas, ideals, and emotions.
2. Their language is often figurative.
3. They suggest ambiguity and complication.
4. They raise questions and possibilities.

It is important to realize that readers and scholars have proposed many different definitions of literature. (During your lifetime of reading, you may develop your own definition of literature, and it may be different both from the one suggested here and from those of other readers.) Many forms that have not traditionally been called literary meet the four criteria in the preceding list. Certain transcriptions of speeches, letters, documents, and journals may be read as literature.

Consider, for example, Lincoln's Gettysburg address or John F. Kennedy's inaugural address. What makes these speeches memorable and important? (Consider not only their original audiences but also those who hear them repeated or who read transcripts.) The answer is complex: certainly the sensitive and striking choice of language (Lincoln, for example, begins with "Fourscore and seven years ago" rather than with the more common "eighty-seven years ago"); certainly the powerful rhythm (both Lincoln and Kennedy make use of parallel structure: "Government of the people, by the people, for the people shall not perish from the earth" and "Ask not what your country can do for you; ask what you can do for your country"); certainly the thought-provoking themes offered and the complex questions raised. We might say, then, that these speeches can be called literature.

Suggestions for Reading Speeches

When you read speeches, try to picture the original audience. How has the speech-giver chosen his or her words to reach that audience? Imagine the possible responses of that audience to the speech. Consider, too, that many speakers are aware that their speeches will be reported by the press or—at the very least—repeated by those who have heard them. What elements of the speech might appeal to an even wider audience than that originally addressed? Keep in mind, too, that one of the best ways to appreciate a transcript of a speech is to read it aloud—or to listen to it being read aloud. Chief Seattle's "My People" (page 517) is an example of a speech.

Suggestions for Reading Letters

Like speeches, letters are addressed to an audience. When you read letters, keep in mind the original audience. Some letters were intended to be read by only one other person. Others were written for a far larger audience. Consider how the different audiences affect how the writer treats his or her subject.

Suggestions for Reading Documents

As you read a document—for example, the Declaration of Independence—consider its purpose. Consider also how effective you think the document might have been in accomplishing that purpose.

Ask yourself, also, how responses to the document may have changed from the time it was written to the present. Consider why and how readers' responses might have changed (or stayed nearly the same).

Suggestions for Reading Journals and Diaries

Unlike most other writings, journals and diaries were usually originally composed for an audience of only one: the writer. Journals may jump from subject to subject without any clear connection because the writer is not trying to communicate ideas or emotions to a group of readers but, instead, is exploring those ideas or emotions for personal reasons.

Reading journals and diaries gives us the opportunity to look directly into the hearts and minds of writers; to observe the ideas, images, and emotions they treasure for themselves; and to see the early stages of the creative process. Frederick Douglass's "Learning to Read and Write" (page 520) was originally part of a journal that Douglass later revised to become his autobiography.

Suggestions for Reading Essays

As you respond to an essay, consider what its central purpose seems to be. Is it written primarily to describe a person or place? Or does it, perhaps, tell a true story (a **narrative**)? What significance do you see in the description or in the narrative? How does that description or narrative relate to your own observations and experiences?

An essay may make significant comparisons or contrasts; it may explain the reasons something happened or explore the effects of a particular event or action. Some essays contemplate or speculate on an idea, exploring many possibilities without insisting on one final conclusion. Many other essays, in one way or another, argue for or against a point of view, a solution to a problem, or a new way of thinking about the world.

Whatever the essay's purpose, look carefully at the writer's choice of words as well as the way he or she structures both the essay itself and its sentences and paragraphs. Then consider how well you believe the writer has fulfilled his or her purpose. Consider also the details, reasons, and examples the writer supplies to support generalizations. Do you find them convincing? Intriguing? Weak? Insufficient?

Notice the questions and complexities stated or implied by the writer as well as answers or solutions that are offered. Think carefully about your own response to these questions, complexities, answers, and solutions.

GUIDELINES

Nonfiction

These considerations provide guidelines for reading, thinking about, and writing about nonfiction. Although not every consideration applies to every nonfiction work, these guidelines can help you read more deeply and experience the work more fully.

Speeches

1. Imagine that you are an audience member first hearing the speech. Describe the setting, the speaker, and your response to the speech.
2. Write a speech in response to the one you have read. In yours, pose questions or suggest alternatives to the views you have read.

Letters

1. Assume that you are the person (or one of the persons) to whom the letter was originally addressed. Write a response to the writer. Refer to specific details in the letter as you plan your response.
2. Write a character sketch of the person who wrote the letter. What do the details of the letter (content as well as style) suggest to you about this person? Use specific examples from the letter to support your character analysis.

Documents

1. Imagine that you are one of the drafters of the document. Describe the process of planning and writing the document. Project the arguments and disagreements that might have been part of this process and explain how they were resolved. (You may want to research some of the historical background relating to the document.)

(continued)

GUIDELINES, continued

2. Write a document styled on the one you read but relating to a current political issue.

Journals

1. Write the entry (or series of entries) you imagine might follow the one(s) you have read. Try to capture the writer's style as you build on his or her ideas and emotions.
2. Write a letter to the journal's author explaining your responses to what you have read.

Essays

1. Explain what you see as the author's purpose in writing the essay. How effectively has the author accomplished that purpose? Explain.
2. Find a passage or sentence you find particularly thought-provoking. Copy the passage or sentence and then write your response to it.
3. Identify the point of view taken by the writer. Compose a response written from a different point of view.
4. Describe the values you believe are exemplified by the points raised, the questions asked, or the views asserted in the essay. Write an evaluation of those values, explaining how they compare to or contrast with your own.
5. Write a letter to the author of the essay explaining your response to specific parts of the essay (for instance, to specific examples or to a specific argument or proposal). Begin this assignment by making a list of five to ten questions you would like to ask the author if you could speak to him or her privately.

CONSIDERING OTHER VOICES

Listening to the voices of others who read, talk about, and write about literary works provides an opportunity to expand your enjoyment and understanding of these works. Some voices—professors and class members, friends and relatives—are close and easily accessible. Other voices must be sought out, usually from printed sources. Such voices include authors who have written about their own works or who have been interviewed about their works. Still other voices come from critical reviews of dramas or of collections of poetry, fiction, or essays and from scholarly journals or books in which professors of literature share their views of the literature they study and teach. In this text-book, each of the thematic chapters provides a "Commentary," a voice or voices that suggest new ways of looking at one of the works in that chapter.

Listening to the voices of others can enable you to develop your own literary conversation in ways you may not previously have considered. As you listen to various voices, you will notice that they do not always agree. For ex-ample, Ervin Beck (page 512) and Brian Sutton (page 514) offer opposing views of *"Master Harold"* . . . *and the Boys.* When you read voices that disagree with each other, you are confronted with the importance of your own ability to make judgments about the literature you read. Because even "experts" dis-agree, you need to develop strategies for reading their comments, returning to the text, and then making up your own mind.

Note that if you do consult other sources and refer to their views in your own writing, you must give proper documentation (see pages 169–91). Failure to acknowledge the use of other people's ideas, opinions, and judgments in your own writing constitutes plagiarism.

Authors' Commentaries and Interviews

Many authors write commentaries or provide interviews with insights about their works. Although one should not necessarily accept an author's statement about the meaning of his or her work without closely examining the evidence in the work itself (as W. K. Wimsatt warned in his 1964 book, *The Verbal Icon*), it is usually extremely interesting and helpful to hear what an author has to say. Sometimes authors discuss the origins of their ideas; some-times they address what they believe to be mistaken interpretations of their works; sometimes they explain points that many readers have found puzzling or difficult to understand. For authors who have been writing during the past seventy years or so, the *New York Times Index* and the *Humanities Index* (which indexes various literary magazines and scholarly journals) can provide sources for tracking down such commentaries and interviews. In this text, Gilman's "Why I Wrote 'The Yellow Wallpaper'" (page 546), Faulkner's "The Meaning of 'A Rose for Emily'" (page 1170), and Welty's "Is Phoenix Jackson's Grand-son Really Dead?" (page 852) provide examples of commentaries and inter-views that shed light on the author's work.

Reviews

Most major newspapers and many magazines offer reviews of newly pub-lished works, newly compiled anthologies, and new productions of plays. A highly useful source of such reviews is the *New York Times Index.* If you know the year in which a work was published or in which a new production of a play began, you can use this index to discover whether the *New York Times* published a review. These reviews are written for the general, educated reader and so will probably not use the highly specialized vocabulary of scholarly literary criticism. In this textbook, Lloyd Rose's Review of *Wit* (page 1085) provides an example of the voices you can discover through reading reviews.

Scholarly Criticism

Although scholars have been reading, thinking about, and writing about literature for hundreds of years, it is only in the twentieth century that such commentary has been divided into complex, separate schools. To locate scholarly criticism of works in which you are interested, consult the card catalogue of your library, the *Humanities Index,* and the *MLA International Bibliography.* (The indexes, especially the *MLA,* can be a bit complicated to use at first; you may need to ask a librarian for help. Once you know the process, however, you'll have easy access to an amazing number of new voices.)

As you continue with the study of literature, you'll hear references to various ways of reading texts, such as **formalist, reader response, sociological, psychoanalytic,** and **new historical.** Although these terms may seem daunting, they simply describe many different paths to follow in pursuit of the pleasure, revelation, illumination, and elevation of spirit and mind that come from reading deeply, fully, and well. Many of the most outstanding scholars who write about literature do not adhere to only one way of reading texts but rather consider the many possibilities. They draw from these many ways of reading literature to create the most sensible, helpful critical commentaries possible.

Brief definitions of these various approaches follow. The definitions are intended only as starting points, as ways to begin thinking about the study of literature. If you are interested in learning more, you might begin by consulting a literary handbook, such as *A Glossary of Literary Terms* by M. H. Abrams, which can help you find more extensive discussions about various aspects of literary criticism as well as bibliographies for further reading.

Formalist Criticism Formalist criticism, sometimes called new criticism, looks at a work as existing by itself. Formalists pay little attention to biographical or historical information; instead, they use a process called *close reading* to look at the various parts of the work in detail. Close reading, also called *explication,* requires a careful analysis of the various elements within a work. While explicating a work, a reader watches for ambiguities (apparent contradictions) within a text and works to explain how these ambiguities ultimately lead to the text's theme. David Huddle's analysis of Robert Hayden's "Those Winter Sundays" (page 742) provides an example of formalist criticism.

Reader-Response Criticism Reader-response criticism, as you might expect, focuses on the meaning that is created when a reader interacts with a text. This way of reading does not assume that there is one single "correct" reading of a text but rather that multiple readings, which are equally defensible, can be derived from any given work. One of the points made by reader-response theorists is that all written texts have what German critic Wolfgang Iser calls "gaps"—places where details or inferences are not provided by the writer but instead must come from the reader. How readers fill in those gaps may differ according to each reader's age, gender, socioeconomic background, occupation, religion, and so on.

Sociological Criticism Sociological criticism, in direct opposition to formalist criticism, argues that literature is profoundly affected both by the societal forces that surround authors and by the societal forces that surround readers. Sociological criticism is often divided into two schools: feminist and Marxist.

Feminist criticism notes that our civilization has been predominantly male-centered and that, therefore, literature reflects **patriarchal** (male-dominated) themes. Feminist critics read classics with an eye toward paying fair mind to female values, ideals, and points of view. In this textbook, Carolyn Heilbrun's essay "The Character of Hamlet's Mother" (page 361) demonstrates this approach to feminist criticism. Feminist criticism also addresses the omission of women writers from the **canon** (the standard group of works that have been accepted as great literature). Through the work of feminist critics, such writers as Charlotte Perkins Gilman (page 532), Susan Glaspell (page 558, 666), and Kate Chopin (page 153) have come to prominence. Their works, previously paid little attention and in some cases suppressed, are now widely anthologized and available to many readers.

Marxist criticism is named for social and economic reformer Karl Marx (1818–1883). Marx described the process by which, he believed, wealthy capitalists oppress the working classes and create an unfair distribution of power. Literary critics who subscribe to Marx's theories read literary texts to discover evidence of the way social, political, and economic forces have shaped not only the destinies of living people but also the themes of imaginative literature written by authors who were and are part of capitalist societies.

Psychoanalytic Criticism Psychoanalytic criticism views the themes, conflicts, and characterizations of a work primarily as a reflection of the needs, emotions, states of mind, and subconscious desires of the author. Psychoanalytic critics apply to characters in literary texts the principles established by Sigmund Freud (1856–1936) for understanding human behavior. For example, many psychoanalytic critics, beginning with Freud himself, have studied *Hamlet*. In *The Interpretation of Dreams,* you can see how Freud uses his theories of repression and the subconscious mind to explain why Oedipus kills his father, whereas Hamlet continually delays killing Claudius, even after he is convinced that the ghost of his father has correctly named Claudius as his killer.

New Historicism New-historicist criticism is related to sociological criticism and reader-response criticism in that its proponents point out the impact of the politics, ideologies, and social customs of the author's world on the themes, images, and characterizations of his or her work. The new-historicist view notes that an important element is omitted when we read a work as though it existed in a vacuum, completely unrelated to the conditions and influences of the historical events that were taking place when it was written. In addition to making this connection between history and literature, new historicists note that no historical event remains absolutely fixed; new discoveries and new interpretations change the way we look at and interpret history and, therefore, the way we look at history in relation to literary works. Laura Bohannan's "Shakespeare in the Bush" (page 367) provides an example of such criticism.

4

Writing about Literature

At first I hated that we have to keep journals for this class, but after a while what I noticed is that when I write about some poem or story that we've read, I find out ideas I didn't know I had.

—MAURINE BUCKLEY

For me reading has always been my best pleasure. Even when I was only five or six, people were always saying, "She's always got her nose in a book." Writing about what I read is not that hard for me. What I like best is starting a paper with what I think is a great idea and then finding out while I'm writing that a lot of other ideas are in my head, too. So it's a way to think about what I've read.

—NADINE NUÑEZ

No way will I ever "enjoy" writing a paper, but I do have to say that one thing that happens is this: When I start really thinking about an idea I have for a paper, and listening hard to class discussion, and pushing thoughts around in my brain and then trying out writing them, I sometimes find that I've changed my mind from my first reaction to the story, poem, or whatever. This is a big step because I don't usually change my mind. So for me, writing in this class has made me see that an idea might start out in one direction, but when you really think about it, it might take you some place entirely different.

—TIM JANNING

WRITING AND CRITICAL THINKING

Maurine, Nadine, and Tim, students in an introductory course called "Literature and Writing," reacted to writing about literature in different ways. Nadine found writing about what she read rather easy. Maurine and Tim at

87

first saw writing as an obstacle, a requirement to be dutifully carried out. As their comments show, however, during the semester they all discovered this important insight that Nadine suggests: Writing is a way of thinking critically. It's important to understand that thinking critically does not necessarily mean thinking in a negative way or looking for flaws in what one reads. Instead, it means thoughtfully examining and considering an author's words and ideas.

In the student journal entries that start this chapter, Maurine demonstrates her recognition of the way writing encourages critical thinking when she says that she discovered ideas she didn't know she had. Tim sees that the mental energy required to really think through a topic for a paper often leads him to modify his initial way of reading and responding to the work.

The value, then, of writing about literature is the same as the value of writing honestly and with emotional and intellectual vigor about any subject: the hard work brings new ways of understanding, of thinking and feeling. Both the process of writing and the final product provide the satisfaction of learning new ways to perceive, to speculate, to wonder, and to know.

This chapter explains strategies for and approaches to writing about literature by using samples of students' spoken and written responses to the following two poems. You'll find the samples of students' writing more meaningful if you take time now to read the poems and to respond to them through both discussion and writing.

DYLAN THOMAS (1914–1953)

Do Not Go Gentle into That Good Night

Do not go gentle into that good night,
Old age should burn and rave at close of day;
Rage, rage against the dying of the light.

Though wise men at their end know dark is right,
5   Because their words had forked no lightning they
Do not go gentle into that good night.

Good men, the last wave by, crying how bright
Their frail deeds might have danced in a green bay,
Rage, rage against the dying of the light.

10   Wild men who caught and sang the sun in flight,
And learn, too late, they grieved it on its way,
Do not go gentle into that good night.

Grave men, near death, who see with blinding sight
Blind eyes could blaze like meteors and be gay,
15   Rage, rage against the dying of the light.

And you, my father, there on the sad height,
Curse, bless, me now with your fierce tears, I pray,
Do not go gentle into that good night.
Rage, rage against the dying of the light.   *1952*

Responding to "Do Not Go Gentle into That Good Night"

1. Given the details of the poem, how do you picture the speaker in the poem? How do you picture his father?

2. What advice does the speaker in this poem give to his father? What is your response to this advice?

3. Imagine that you are the father, hearing this advice. What might you say in a letter answering your son?

4. Read the poem aloud and, if possible, listen to the poem being read aloud. Try using a different tone of voice or emphasizing different phrases. Notice whether—and how—your response to the poem changes with these variations.

JOAN ALESHIRE (1947–   )

Slipping

Age comes to my father as a slow
slipping: the leg that weakens, will
barely support him, the curtain of mist
that falls over one eye. Years, like
pickpockets, lift his concentration,   5
memory, fine sense of direction. The car,
as he drives, drifts from lane to lane
like a raft on a river, speeds and slows
for no reason, keeps missing turns.

As my mother says, "He's never liked   10
to talk about feelings," but tonight
out walking, as I slow to match his pace—
his left leg trailing a little like
a child who keeps pulling on your hand—he says,
"I love you so much." Darkness, and the sense   15
we always have that each visit may be
the last, have pushed away years of restraint.

A photograph taken of him teaching—
white coat, stethoscope like a pet snake
20   around his neck, chair tipped back
against the lecture-room wall—shows
a man talking, love of his work lighting
his face—in a way we seldom saw at home.
I answer that I love him, too, but
25   hardly knowing him, what I love
is the way reserve has slipped from
his feeling, like a screen suddenly
falling, exposing someone dressing or
washing: how wrinkles ring a bent neck,
30   how soft and mutable is the usually hidden flesh.   *1987*

Responding to "Slipping"

1. How did you respond to the description of the father in the first stanza? Was this response changed or reinforced after you finished reading the poem? Explain.

2. How do you imagine the relationships among the family members described in this poem? What facts about their lives do the details of the poem show? What can you infer from those details?

3. Explain your response to the speaker's attitude regarding the changes in her father.

4. Try writing this poem as though it were a prose paragraph. Copy the sentences and punctuation exactly as they appear, but arrange the sentences in a paragraph rather than in lines. Pay attention to the length of the sentences as you write them and to the way some of the sentences are punctuated with dashes. Does reading the new arrangement change your response to the poem? Explain.

PREPARING TO WRITE ABOUT LITERATURE

Understanding the Assignment

When you are writing about literature for a class, your writing assignments originate—at least to some extent—from your instructor. It's important to have a clear notion of what you are being asked to do. An assignment may be quite open ("Write an essay responding to any work we have read this semester"), or it may be structured in a number of ways. Read or listen to the assignment carefully before you begin planning how you will fulfill it.

Thinking about the Assignment

Keep in mind the following questions as you begin thinking about an assignment:

1. Does the assignment ask that your subject be a specific work or works?
2. Does the assignment ask that you focus on a specific genre (poetry, fiction, drama, nonfiction)?
3. Does the assignment ask that you focus on a particular aspect of the literary work or works (for example, on the images of war or on the concept of honor)?
4. Does the assignment specify an audience, real (for instance, will you be reading part or all of the paper to the class?) or imagined (for example, will you be writing a fictional letter from one character to another?)?
5. Does the assignment ask for a particular approach or organization? For example, are you being asked to compare? To explicate? To evaluate? (These approaches and methods of organization are explained and demonstrated on pages 92–146.)
6. Does the assignment specify a length? (The focus of a two-page paper will be quite different from that of a ten-page paper.)
7. Does the assignment ask for (or allow) research?
8. Does the assignment ask that you discover a topic for yourself?

Keeping these questions in mind, read the following assignment. The instructor wants students to write a paper of two to four pages (typewritten, double-spaced). When they submit their papers, students are to give a brief talk (three to five minutes) explaining the most significant point of the paper.

Assignment Topics (Choose One)

1. Briefly summarize your response to one of these poems and then, using a personal narrative, explain that response, making references to the poem that show its connection to your narrative.

2. Explore the similarities and differences you see between these poems. Then write a paper explaining what you discovered and what significance you find in these similarities and differences.

3. Explain how the figurative language in one of the poems suggests the relationship between the speaker and his or her father.

4. What, exactly, does the speaker say in each poem? And how does he or she say it? Look carefully at the language in the poems. Then choose one poem and explain how the central idea of the poem unfolds as you read from one stanza to the next.

5. Consider the values and beliefs suggested by each of these poems. Choose one of the poems and explain those values and beliefs as well as your evaluation of them. Do you agree with them completely? Question them? Explain.

WRITING TO RESPOND

A response paper can take many different directions, but remember that part of the point of the paper is to help those who read it understand the connections you made. Why did this particular poem, short story, play, or essay evoke a sad memory or recall a triumph? What details affected you strongly? You need to show your audience exactly what you felt as you were reading the work. Avoid simply announcing that you liked or didn't like what you read. Showing means finding examples that will make sense to your readers. For this reason, you should reread the work carefully several times to find telling examples. To write a strong response paper, you need to make clear and frequent references to the work that evoked the thoughts and feelings you'll be discussing.

Topic 1

Briefly summarize your response to one of these poems, and then, using a personal narrative, explain that response, making references to the poem that show its connection to your narrative.

This assignment asks for the reader's response, that is, for the personal and individual feelings and thoughts evoked by the experience of reading either Thomas' or Aleshire's poem. In this case, the topic asks for an example from the reader's experience that will support, develop, and explain that response.

DISCOVERING IDEAS: Journal Entries

After reading the assignment sheet, Karen Angstrom decided that she would like to work with the first assignment. She read both poems twice and then wrote the following journal entry about her response to "Slipping."

DISCOVERING IDEAS: Journal Entries *(continued)*

OK, first time through I kept thinking about this daughter who seems like she's glad her father is old and weak because now he tells her he loves her. I felt sympathy for the daughter. But the second time through, her response began to seem selfish to me. She seemed to me to be willing to have her father old and weak as long as he would say that he loved her. But what about how the father felt inside? Maybe he was acting the way he was because he was scared. The poem talks about the screen falling down, which seems to me like the person's protection against the world. That made me think about Mr. Gagnon and the way he was after his stroke—how he lost his protection. The poem looks from the daughter's point of view, and she sees the change as positive. But from the point of view of the person who is changing, losing part of what has been yourself has to be frightening. And I definitely see that as negative. So I see another side to this poem.

This journal entry shows Karen's changing response as she read "Slipping." In addition, she keeps the writing topic she has chosen in mind, remembering that she has to include a personal narrative to explain her response. As she thinks about her second reading, she focuses on one particular image (the screen suddenly falling) that triggered a strong memory for her and leads her to the observation that "losing part of what has been yourself has to be frightening."

Considering Audience

After deciding to write about Aleshire's poem and to use the story of Mr. Gagnon to illustrate her response, Karen thought about the audience for her paper (and for the oral response that was part of the assignment). Her instructor would be reading the paper; both the instructor and her classmates would be listening to her report. Everyone in this audience would be familiar with "Slipping," so Karen knew she wouldn't have to give a detailed summary of the poem.

No one in her audience, however, knew Mr. Gagnon, a man who had lived in Karen's neighborhood for as long as she could remember. She knew she would have to give some background information to help her audience understand why the changes in Mr. Gagnon after his surgery were so important to her and how having known Mr. Gagnon affected her response to the poem.

Karen also thought about the different views various classmates held. She knew that some would not share her response to "Slipping." She realized she would need to choose her words and examples carefully to express herself honestly without alienating readers or listeners whose responses to the poem were different from her own. Her purpose in writing the paper was not to challenge her audience but rather to show clearly her own thoughts and feelings.

Narrowing the Topic

Having decided on a general topic—the way the change in Mr. Gagnon related to her response to "Slipping"—Karen realized that she needed to find a more specific focus before she began drafting her paper. To explore possibilities, she made the following lists:

"Slipping"
   father used to be full of energy
   "love of work lighting his face"
   now losing physical abilities
      can't drive
      can't walk easily
   used to be reserved about emotions
   now exposes emotions
   can't (or doesn't) control feelings

Mr. Gagnon
   always full of energy and life
      never praised or said thanks
      brain tumor
      surgery not successful
      changing—every day worse
      exposing emotions he never would have
      pain from exposing
      no control over feelings

As Karen looked at these lists, she paid special attention to the idea of exposing emotions and to the sense of losing control. She then made another list, this time with possible subjects for her response essay.

   emotions and old age
   old age: changing emotions
   emotions, control, and self

Karen decided that the third topic best fit her response both to the poem and to her former neighbor, Mr. Gagnon. She knew that she wanted to explore a view of the changes brought by old age and illness that differed from the view suggested by Aleshire.

Devising a Preliminary Thesis Statement

Once Karen had a narrowed topic in mind, she thought about what she wanted to say about this subject. She came up with these possibilities. Remember that a **thesis statement** makes an assertion; it does not simply announce a subject but instead indicates what the writer plans to say about the subject. Remember also that a preliminary thesis statement is tentative. You may revise it or even change it completely during the drafting process. The benefit of having a preliminary thesis is that it provides the sense of a central idea as you begin writing.

> When a person's "reserve has slipped from feeling," the main emotion revealed may be fear.
> Losing control because of sickness or old age may make a person emotional because of fear.
> Losing control over your life is frightening.

The first thesis seemed strongest to Karen because it focuses specifically on what she wanted to say about her response to the poem. The assertion in the second statement is not as clear or as straightforward as the first, and the third thesis is too broad and general. Also, the first thesis is strengthened by the specific reference to the poem, which supports the central idea she proposes.

Planning and Organizing

While evaluating possible thesis statements, Karen saw what direction she wanted to take. Also, she'd made a list of ideas to discuss in her response to the poem and in the narrative about Mr. Gagnon that would explain her response. She now thought about how to organize her material, how to present it most effectively to her audience. The opening paragraph, she decided, would briefly describe her response to Aleshire's poem. The story of Mr. Gagnon's relationship with her and her brother Cory would follow. It seemed logical to give the details in chronological order, beginning with Mr. Gagnon before he became sick and then explaining the changes after his surgery.

To help keep this organization clearly in mind, Karen wrote an informal outline.

1. Introduction (My response to "Slipping"—details of what the father has lost—driving, work, etc.)
2. Mr. Gagnon
    When I was young—always there, welcoming us, but also grouchy; never saying thanks
    Mr. G's illness and surgery
    Visiting Mr. G—his change
3. Conclusion???

Drafting

After doing the preliminary reading, writing, and thinking described here, Karen realized that she knew how she wanted to start her paper and she had a plan for developing the narrative example. She did not, however, know how she was going to conclude.

At this point, writing a draft—putting her explorations together on paper—seemed the best strategy.

CHANGES
Karen Angstrom

The daughter in Joan Aleshire's poem "Slipping" is seeing her father become more open to expressing emotions as he becomes older. "Like a screen suddenly falling." The daughter sees this change as positive, and my first response was to agree with her view, then I thought about the changes the father has gone through. He can't do the things he loved anymore. Work as a teacher. Drive a car safely. Walk without limping. Everything that used to make up this man's self seems to be gone. Yes, he says words of love, but when a person's "reserve has slipped from feeling," because of old age or illness, the main emotion which is revealed may be fear.

There was a man in our neighborhood who reminds me of the father in "Slipping." He, too, loved to work. He sang at the top of his voice (usually off tune) whenever he worked outside and he was always demanding that we join in. Both in his songs and in his projects. "In the good old SUMMER-TI-IME," my brother Cory and I would bellow as we helped him rig up a pulley to lift stones over his garden fence. "Let me call you SWE-EE-THEART," we'd try to harmonize as we built a bird feeder designed to completely baffle squirrels. Mr. G was always busy and was always trying to figure out some new way to do something.

When Cory and I worked with him, he didn't have too much patience. There might be a tool that we'd drop or we'd put something together wrong, he'd have some sharp comment for us. Sometimes he'd send us home. Or even tell us to "get lost." There were many years, however, when we were fascinated by his strange inventions, and we'd always go back when we got one of his semi-grouchy invitations to "stop staring at me and get over here to help." As we got older, we really were able to help, but Mr. Gagnon never said thank you. I guess he never thought about it. Because Cory and I were always there, willing to come.

One day, when I was twelve years old, I realized I hadn't seen Mr. G for two or three days. I was told by my mother that he'd been sick.

A brain tumor was diagnosed by the doctors, they wanted to operate. I felt sick myself thinking about it. Mr. G didn't want the surgery because he was told all the things that could happen. His eyesight or his ability to walk could be lost. Not to mention his memory. Finally, however, he had the surgery.

When he came home, my mom, Cory, and I went to visit. It was horrible. Mr. G had been in the hospital for two weeks and he had lost lots of weight. Mrs. G said that he had bad dreams both when he was awake and when he was asleep. He just stared at us. He looked scared. Then he croaked in a little, tinny voice "Who's that? Who's that?" We said our names, and he called for me to come over. He grabbed at my hand and started to tell me how glad he was to see me; how much he liked Cory and me. He thanked us for coming to see him. And kept saying over and over to please come back.

Unlike the speaker in the poem, I didn't feel good about this change. There were times that I used to wish that Mr. G would at least acknowledge the good things Cory and I did. But, now as he talked, it just seemed that he didn't have any of himself left. I suppose, in a way, I was seeing behind a screen that suddenly fell away. I was seeing an intimate part of Mr. G, but I felt like he was forced into showing this part of himself. It wasn't like he just decided he wanted to express that he liked us. It seemed like he was forced into it by his sickness. It was the weakness and the fear of not being strong again. The fear that we wouldn't come to visit now that he was changed.

The speaker in "Slipping" says that what she loves about her aging father is "the way reserve has slipped from his feeling." But is emotion expressed under these circumstances really something to celebrate?

Revising Focus: Titles, Openings, Conclusions

After Karen had written her draft, she put it away for several days and then looked at it again with a fresh mind and "new eyes." As she read, Karen liked very much the way she had described Mr. Gagnon. For example, she saw that the specific details she had used—the songs he taught and the projects he worked on—showed the reader his life and energy.

But she was not happy with her title. She felt it was too general and did not really reflect what she hoped to say in the paper. Also, she thought the opening paragraph was somewhat confusing. She didn't explain the first quote she used; it just seemed to hang there without really making much sense. In addition, her tentative thesis needed added detail to make clear that the changing emotions she discussed resulted from the weakening that often accompanies aging and illness.

Karen also recognized that her conclusion was much too brief. Her question was a starting place, but she needed to develop her response more fully. Her list for revising looked like this:

1. Title—needs to be more specific
2. Opening paragraph
   Explain quote better
   Revise thesis
3. Conclusion—expand (maybe try answering question?)

Editing Focus: "To Be," Expletives, Passive Voice

As Karen reread her paper, she noticed that some of her sentences seemed awkward. They just didn't sound right as she read them aloud. With some help from a tutor at the writing center on her campus, she saw three problems she could correct:

1. Overuse of forms of the verb "to be." Karen replaced them with active verbs where possible.

   Mr. G. was always busy and was always trying to figure out some new way to do something.
   Edited: Mr. G. always kept busy trying to figure out some new way to do something.

2. Overuse of expletives such as "there is" and "there are."

   There was a man in our neighborhood who reminds me of the father in "Slipping."
   Edited: Mr. Gagnon, a man from our neighborhood, reminds me of the father in "Slipping."

3. Overuse of passive-voice constructions. (In passive-voice constructions, the subject of the sentence is acted on; in active voice, the subject acts.)

   A brain tumor was diagnosed by the doctors.
   Edited: The doctors had diagnosed a brain tumor.

Proofreading Focus: Fragments and Comma Splices

The tutor at the writing center also told Karen that some of her sentences were confusing because they were fragments or comma splices.

Fragment: Drive a car safely
Edited: He can't drive a car safely.

Comma splice: The daughter sees this change as positive, and my first response was to agree with her view, then I thought about the changes
the father has gone through.

Edited: The daughter sees this change as positive, and my first response
was to agree with her view. Then I thought about the changes the
father has gone through.

Exercise

Keeping in mind the revising, editing, and proofreading focuses just discussed, as well as your own evaluation of the draft, try rewriting Karen's paper.
Think carefully about the reasons for the changes you make. Then compare
your final version with the one that follows. Of course, each person's revision
of this paper will be different. The point is not to duplicate Karen's final paper
but to think about the differences and similarities between the choices she
made and the choices you made.

Final Copy: Writing to Respond

CHANGES: FOR BETTER OR WORSE?
Karen Angstrom

The daughter in Joan Aleshire's poem "Slipping" notices her father
becoming more open to expressing emotions as he becomes older.
She says his normal reserve is "like a screen suddenly falling." The
daughter sees this change as positive, and my first response was to
agree with her view. Then I thought about the changes the father has
gone through. He can't do the things he loved anymore. He can't
work as a teacher or drive a car safely or walk without limping.
Everything that used to make up this man's self seems to be gone.
Yes, he says words of love, but when a person's "reserve has slipped
from feeling" because of old age or illness, the main emotion revealed
may be fear.

Mr. Gagnon, a man from our neighborhood, reminds me of the
father in "Slipping." Like the father, Mr. G, too, loved to work. He
sang at the top of his voice (usually off tune) whenever he worked
outside, and he frequently demanded that my brother Cory and I
join him, both in his songs and in his projects. "In the good old
SUMMER-TI-IME," my brother and I would bellow as we helped
Mr. G rig up a pulley to lift stones over his garden fence. "Let me call
you SWE-EE-THEART," we'd try to harmonize as we built a bird

feeder designed to completely baffle squirrels. Mr. G always kept busy trying to figure out some new way to do something.

When Cory and I worked with him, he didn't have too much patience. If we dropped a tool or put something together wrong, he'd have some sharp comment for us. Sometimes he'd send us home or even tell us to "get lost." Nevertheless, for many years, we were fascinated by his strange inventions, and we'd always go back when we got one of his semi-grouchy invitations to "stop staring at me and get over here to help." As we got older, we really were able to help. We unloaded countless boxes of supplies from his old station wagon and picked up hundreds of scraps to store in what he called his "useful junk" pile. During all these years, Mr. Gagnon never said thank you or told us that we did a good job. He never told us he was glad to see us, either. I guess he never thought about it, since Cory and I were always there, willing to come.

One day, when I was twelve years old, I realized I hadn't seen Mr. G for two or three days. My mother told me that he'd been sick. The doctors diagnosed a brain tumor, and they wanted to operate. I felt sick myself thinking about it. When he was told all the possible side effects of the operation, Mr. G didn't want the surgery. He could have lost his eyesight or his ability to walk, not to mention his memory. Finally, however, he had the surgery.

When he came home, my mom, Cory, and I went to visit. It was horrible. Mr. G had been in the hospital for two weeks, and he had lost lots of weight. Mrs. G said that he had bad dreams both when he was awake and when he was asleep. He just stared at us, looking scared. Then he croaked in a little, tinny voice: "Who's that? Who's that?" We said our names, and he called for me to come over. He grabbed at my hand and started to tell me how glad he was to see me. He repeated several times how much he liked Cory and me. He thanked us for coming to see him and kept saying over and over to please come back.

Unlike the speaker in the poem, I didn't feel good about this change. Sometimes I used to wish that Mr. G would at least acknowledge the good things Cory and I did. But, now as he talked, it just seemed that he didn't have any of himself left. I suppose, in a way, like the daughter in "Slipping," I was seeing behind a screen that had suddenly fallen away. I was seeing an intimate part of Mr. G, but I felt like he was forced into showing this part of himself. He didn't have the chance to decide for himself that he wanted to express that he liked us. He seemed forced by his weakness, and the fear of not being strong again, to talk about his feelings. I believed he feared that we wouldn't come to visit now that he could no longer create intriguing projects or order us around.

The speaker in "Slipping" says that what she loves about her aging father is "the way reserve has slipped from his feeling." But is emotion expressed under these circumstances really something to celebrate? I don't think so. Yes, "years of restraint" may have been pushed away, yet the force that pushes them may be fear rather than love. The person who stands exposed like "someone dressing or washing" has lost all of his privacy and all of his personal power. That person has no more real self.

Exercise

Read a work from the anthology sections of this book and then, using the process demonstrated with Karen's paper, plan and write a response. Begin by briefly summarizing your response to the work, and then use a personal narrative to explain that response. Make references to the story, poem, play, or essay that show its connection to your narrative.

As you write your response, keep the following guidelines in mind.

GUIDELINES

Writing a Response

1. Read the work several times, making marginal notes and writing journal entries to explore your responses.
2. Focus on one response that seems particularly strong.
3. Explain that response, using examples from your own experience, but also make certain to refer to the work so that the connections between your experience and the work are clear.
4. Remember that a response asks for your own ideas and feelings, not simply a summary of the ideas and feelings in the work.

WRITING TO COMPARE

The second assignment topic asks the reader to make comparisons between "Slipping" and "Do Not Go Gentle."

Topic 2

Explore the similarities and differences you see between these poems. Then write a paper explaining what you discovered and what significance you find in these similarities and differences.

As Walter Johnson considered this topic, he thought that it was relatively simple to see several things that were the same about the two poems as well as several things that were different. But the topic also asked for an explanation of the significance of the similarities and differences. This step—making meaning from the comparisons and contrasts—seemed more difficult.

DISCOVERING IDEAS: Discussion and Collaboration

Walter read the poems several times and made these lists of similarities and differences to bring to a scheduled small-group discussion of paper topics.

	"Do Not Go Gentle"	"Slipping"
SUBJECT	old age of speaker's father	same
RHYME	regular rhyme pattern	no rhyme
IMAGES	mostly visual (lots about light)	visual and physical— leg weakens, walking slowly; screen falling
SETTING	on a mountain? ("sad height"?)	in familiar places; walking near home; thinking of photograph (probably at home)—picture shows father at work
IDEA	changes in father seen as negative; he should fight old age (the "good night")	changes in father positive; becomes more loving, less reserved

Walter's instructor assigned him to a group of four students; all of them were working on the comparison topic. Several had brought lists of their own. Everyone agreed that finding the significance was the most difficult part of the assignment. The following edited excerpt from a taped transcript of their discussion illustrates the way talking about literature can lead to discovering possibilities for writing.

> *Walter:* One poem—"Do Not Go Gentle"—says that the changes in old age are bad, but in "Slipping" the person seems to see those changes as good. So they're completely opposite.
>
> *Anna:* Well, I don't see—I don't think that—in "Do Not Go" what you have to look at is that he says "*good* night." Why is old age—or, I think it's death—a "good night" if it's bad? But I agree he wants his father to fight it.
>
> *Tomás:* Same thing to me about "Slipping." You can't—in my opinion, you can't just say that she—the person who's talking in the poem—is saying something like, "Old age is really great and it makes people change in a good way." I mean it's definitely under pretty awful circumstances. Like the guy—her father—is losing his memory and he can't even drive a car right. So I would say *some* changes in old age can be good.
>
> *Michelle:* But what Anna was saying, I think "good night" could be just like saying "good-bye." So that it would be: "Don't go without a fight into that last 'good-bye.'" Don't just go through these changes without resisting what you lose.
>
> *Walter:* Right. I can see what Anna says, but he says "rage, rage against the dying of the light" so many times. And like I wrote on the list here with the rhyme words—so many of them rhyme with "light"—it's like he really wants to emphasize that. To emphasize that the father should fight against the light going away—the light, I think, is like his life—his normal life. It's a metaphor or symbol—whatever—for life.
>
> *Anna:* I can agree—but what I'm just saying—it's not the opposite of what you're saying—it's just that you can't totally ignore the "good" part.
>
> *Tomás:* So does it matter whether this guy thinks that old age can be a little bit good or not? What I noticed was the way he was giving advice to his father. He's like really making a lot of decisions for his father, I think. Or trying to make them.
>
> *Walter:* The person in "Slipping," she's not telling her father what to do—she's just glad he is changed.
>
> *Michelle:* Right. The speaker in "Do Not Go Gentle" seems like he can't accept the changes in his father—or in anyone who gets old and is facing death. The daughter in "Slipping," you can see she's accepting the changes—and she even appreciates some of the changes.

GUIDELINES

Strategies for Collaborative Work

The preceding discussion is just one example of the way collaboration can work to enrich both discussing literature and writing about it. Working in groups can be extremely rewarding, and the following guidelines are intended as suggestions for helping that work to progress smoothly:

1. When the group first meets, someone should agree to take notes.
2. Group members should introduce themselves, and, if the group will be meeting outside the classroom, members should exchange telephone numbers and/or e-mail addresses. At the end of the meeting, it's helpful to set the date of the next meeting while all members of the group are available to coordinate their calendars. One person should volunteer to contact all members to remind them of the next meeting.
3. When the group first meets, members should discuss the task they are assigned so that everyone understands in the same way the goals toward which they are working.
4. If the assignment requires multiple tasks or is divided into multiple sections, the group may agree that each member will be responsible for a certain part or parts and should set deadlines for those parts to be available to other members for review and suggestions for revision.
5. To work well as a group member, try to think not only of your own contribution but also of what you can gain from others. Try to encourage quiet members to voice their ideas by giving them "space"; for example, ask, "What do you think about this, Paul?" or say, "I'd be interested to hear what you think about this, Jane."
6. Instead of challenging or disagreeing with someone's idea or comment immediately, try asking a question that indicates your concern. For example, "Could you explain more about your reasons for thinking that?" or "What kind of evidence can we give to support that point?"
7. Remember to set deadlines well ahead of the project's due date. With many people working together, there are multiple possibilities of personal emergencies that may delay progress.
8. Work actively and thoughtfully to complete any parts of the project you have agreed to do. Seek help from the professor, from the campus writing center, or from library professionals if you feel stuck on any part of your work.

GUIDELINES, continued

9. Keep an open mind! Notice not only what you learn about the subject you are pursuing, but also what you learn about the way people (including, of course, yourself) work together to complete collaborative assignments.
10. Remember that with collaborative work the project may seem to take longer at first, but when several minds work together on a project or problem, new ideas and possibilities often flow rapidly and in unexpected and enlightening ways.

Considering Audience, Narrowing the Topic, and Devising a Preliminary Thesis

After thinking about this discussion, Walter realized he needed to be careful not to make sweeping generalizations he couldn't support. For instance, he saw that Anna had a reasonable point about the ambiguity of the phrase "good night." To make what he said convincing to other students (and, of course, to the instructor), he could not simply say that one poem showed the changes of old age as bad and the other showed those changes as good.

The last part of the discussion printed here seemed particularly useful for discovering a specific topic and formulating a preliminary thesis. Walter thought about the speaker in "Do Not Go Gentle" giving advice to his father and compared that to the speaker in "Slipping" describing her thoughts. She seems to be much more accepting of the changes of old age than does the speaker in Thomas' poem.

This insight led to the following preliminary thesis:

> The speakers in Joan Aleshire's poem "Slipping" and Dylan Thomas'
> poem "Do Not Go Gentle into That Good Night" raise questions
> about the responses of those who must watch someone they love
> face the changes of old age.

Planning and Organizing

Walter now had a central idea to work with, and he had the list he'd made to bring to the group discussion. In addition, he had other notes written in the margins of the poem as well as notes taken in class and during and after the small-group discussion.

When he thought about organizing the information, he remembered from his composition course that there are two standard ways to write about comparisons and contrasts. He could talk about one poem first and then talk about the second, referring back to the first to note similarities and differences. Or he could talk about one point he wanted to make and discuss each poem in relationship to that point, then go on to a new point once again, discussing each poem in relationship to that point, and so on. Instead of deciding on one structure and then drafting, Walter decided to try writing two outlines to see which organization would work better with the ideas and information he had gathered.

RESPONSES
I. Introduction—responses of person watching a parent face the changes of old age
II. "Do Not Go Gentle"
   A. Speaker's tone—giving advice
   B. Rhyme and rhythm—emphasize pattern; speaker wants order; wants listener to do what speaker wants
   C. Setting—general, symbolic, applies to many "old men" (people?) in various circumstances
   D. Images—mostly visual; focus on seeing and on past actions
III. "Slipping"
   A. Speaker's tone—explaining, reassuring
   B. No rhyme—rhythm close to ordinary talking; not like planned speech
   C. Setting—real-life (a walk outside family house; a photo of the father in his classroom)
   D. Images—appeal to both sight and touch—more intimate
IV. Conclusion: Speakers' responses different; themes of poems go in different directions. Contradictory? Agreeing in any way?

RESPONSES
I. Introduction—responses of person watching a parent face the changes of old age
II. Speaker's tone
   A. "Do Not Go Gentle"—giving advice, resisting
   B. "Slipping"—accepting
III. Rhyme and rhythm
   A. "Do Not Go Gentle"—emphasizes pattern; speaker wants order; wants listener to do what speaker wants
   B. "Slipping"—no rhyme—rhythm seems close to ordinary talking—not like planned speech
IV. Setting
   A. "Do Not Go Gentle"—general, applies to many "old men" (people?) in various circumstances

B. "Slipping"—specific: one father; individual experiences (teaching, going for walks)
V. Images
   A. "Do Not Go Gentle"—mostly visual; focuses on seeing and on past actions
   B. "Slipping"—appeals to both sight and touch—more intimate
VI. Conclusion: Speakers' responses different; themes of poems go in different directions. Contradictory? Agreeing in any way?

Drafting

After thinking about both possibilities for organizing, Walter decided to try the first arrangement. Like most successful writers, he revised throughout the process of working on the assignment. For instance, looking at the two outlines convinced him that his title needed to be more specific. He needed to connect his idea of responses to the theme he was working with, and so he came up with "Responses: Raging versus Slipping."

Note, too, that he doesn't expect to resolve every question about his topic completely before he starts drafting. For example, his outlines show that he still has questions about the paper's conclusion.

RESPONSES: RAGING VERSUS SLIPPING
Walter Johnson

The speakers in Joan Aleshire's poem "Slipping" and Dylan Thomas' poem "Do Not Go Gentle into That Good Night" describe their responses as their fathers face the changes of old age. The speakers in these two poems look at their aging parents in very different ways.

In "Do Not Go Gentle" the speaker is talking to his father and is telling him to fight against "the dying of the light." The speaker sounds like he is giving a speech that is meant to convey the conviction to his father, and a larger audience would be informed as well, that it's important to "rage, rage" against the changes of old age. This is advice given to all old men, not just to one old man. Then each of the stanzas that follows talks about one category of old men and showed that no matter what they may have done in life, in the end they all fight the changes that lead to death. They did not give in easily.

The regular rhythm and rhyme in the poem contributes to making it sound like an argument. This repetition emphasizes the speaker's plea. It sounds like a carefully planned speech that is designed to be very convincing to anyone who hears it, not just the father who is not spoken to directly until the last stanza.

It's hard to tell where this speaker is. He isn't clearly in a house or a work place or any building. In the middle four stanzas, the men described are related to parts of nature but these seemed to be general and not specific places. The father in the final stanza is on a "sad height," which doesn't seem like a real mountain. Instead, it may be a metaphor for the final place humans reach just before they die. All these setting elements emphasized that the speaker was arguing for an approach to old age that he thinks is best for many men. Of course, it was also best for his father as well.

Most of the images in the poem are visual. They are things you see or think about. Things you feel or experience are not pictured. For example, the speaker talks about words that "forked no lightning" and deeds that "might have danced in a green bay." The speaker talked about past deeds rather than about the present experience of aging and (possibly) illness that these old men, and the speaker's father, now face.

The speaker's tone in "Slipping" is explanatory and accepting. The speaker is describing the changes in her father with understanding. She sympathizes with her father and understands what he is facing, but she doesn't wish him back the way he was. She expresses, instead, her love for his new way of expressing his emotions.

In "Slipping" there are no rhymes, and the rhythm seems like an ordinary conversation and not like a planned speech that is making an argument. The speaker even uses direct quotations, giving the exact words of her mother and father.

In "Slipping" the settings are from real life. The father is shown driving a car, taking a walk with his daughter, and there is a picture of him teaching in his classroom.

The images in "Slipping" are personal and appeal to both sight and touch. The father's leg "trailing a little" and the "curtain of mist" that obscures his sight make the changes he faces specific. He is compared to "a child who keeps pulling on your hand," and his feelings are exposed like someone who was dressing behind a screen that suddenly falls down.

The speakers, who clearly love the aging fathers, have very different responses to the changes they see. The speaker in "Do Not Go Gentle" takes the responsibility for his father's life on his own shoulders. He tells his father how to approach old age. It seems like the speaker just thinks about death as the ultimate enemy which everyone should fight. On the other hand, the speaker in "Slipping" sees both the negative aspects of the changes and also the positive aspects. The speaker in "Do Not Go Gentle" rages against accepting his father's changes. On the other hand, the speaker in Aleshire's poem just slips into this new phase of life.

Revising Focus: Transitions, Development of Ideas

When Walter read his paper to Anna, Tomás, and Michelle during an in-class workshop, he asked about the organization of his paper. As he reread his paper, the meaning didn't seem to flow smoothly from paragraph to paragraph. He wondered whether he should have used the organization shown in the second outline (pages 106–7). Here's an excerpt from an edited transcript of the tape made during the discussion that followed:

Anna: I don't know—to me, the other organization—where you discuss each little bit separately—that could be just as jumpy.

Tomás: The main thing for me was that when you got to the part on "Slipping," it seemed really like a surprise. I didn't really see where you led into it.

Michelle: We were talking the last time about similarities and differences— which is the subject or—well—the approach to the paper. But I don't see that.

Walter: Don't see what?

Michelle: Don't see that you are comparing. It's like two separate papers—except for the first paragraph and the conclusion.

After thinking about the comments of his writing group, Walter saw that he had not connected his thoughts clearly. He had not shown his readers how he got from one idea to the next. He knew that he needed to work on **transitions:** words, phrases, and sentences that provide a bridge from one paragraph to the next or from one section of the paper to the next. He had to show the relationship among his ideas and examples.

In addition, he noticed that some of his paragraphs seemed too short. As he read them, he saw that he needed to expand and explain his ideas more fully. He needed to be more specific: to give details, reasons, and examples that would convey his thoughts accurately to his audience.

Editing Focus: Nominalizations, Parallel Structure

The writing group also noticed several sentences that needed to be edited. Most of the sentences either used some form of the verb "to be" too much (see page 98) or relied too heavily on nouns that were formed from verbs (nominalizations). As an example, Tomás pointed out this sentence from the second paragraph:

The speaker sounds like he is giving a speech that is meant to convey the conviction to his father, and a larger audience would be informed as well, that it's important to "rage, rage" against the changes of old age.

Notice that Walter uses some form of the verb "to be" three times. When a sentence sounds wordy and plodding, you can often improve it by getting rid of excess "to be" verbs. In addition, this sentence uses the nominalization "convey the conviction" instead of the simpler, more direct, active form of the verb "convince." Here's the sentence as Walter edited it.

> The speaker sounds like he is giving a speech meant to convince his father, and a larger audience would be informed as well, to "rage, rage" against the changes of old age.

Walter can improve the structure of this sentence further by using parallel phrases instead of the awkward "his father, and a larger audience would be informed as well."

> The speaker sounds like he is giving a speech meant to convince not only his father but also a larger audience to "rage, rage" against the changes of old age.

Notice that the edited sentence is much leaner and sleeker than the original; the edited sentence uses thirty words, whereas the original uses forty.

Proofreading Focus: Subject–Verb Agreement, Tense Agreement

As the writing group gave final consideration to Walter's paper, Michelle suggested that he proofread for two other problems:

1. Problem with subject-verb agreement.

   Plural subject   *Singular verb*
   The regular *rhythm* and *rhyme* in the poem *contributes* to making it sound like an argument.

   Plural subject   *Plural verb*
   Edited: The regular *rhythm* and *rhyme* in the poem *contribute* to making it sound like an argument.

2. Problem with verb tense agreement. Verbs should all be in the same tense unless there is a reason to indicate a change to another time. Generally, papers about literature are written in present tense. In this sentence, "showed" marks an unneeded switch from present to past tense:

   Present
   Then each of the stanzas that follows *talks* about one category of

   Past
   old men and *showed* that no matter what they may have done in

   Present
   life in the end they all *fight* the changes that lead to death.

   Edited: Then each of the stanzas that follows *talks* about one category of old man and *shows* that, no matter what they may have done in life, in the end they all *fight* the changes that lead to death.

Exercise

Keeping in mind the revising, editing, and proofreading focuses just discussed as well as your own evaluation of the draft, try rewriting Walter's paper. Think carefully about the reasons for the changes you make. Then compare your final version with the one that follows. Of course, each person's revision of this paper will be different. The point is not to duplicate Walter's final paper but to think about the differences and similarities between the choices he made and the choices you made.

Final Copy: Writing to Compare

RESPONSES: RAGING VERSUS SLIPPING
Walter Johnson

The speakers in Joan Aleshire's poem "Slipping" and Dylan Thomas' poem "Do Not Go Gentle into That Good Night" describe their responses as their fathers experience the changes of old age. Thomas' speaker sees his father as representative of all men facing old age and urges his father to fight old age. Aleshire's speaker, on the other hand, looks at her father's changes in a more personal way and sees some of the changes as being in some ways positive.

In "Do Not Go Gentle," the speaker talks to his father and tells him to struggle against "the dying of the light." The speaker sounds like he is giving a speech meant to convince not only his father but also a larger audience to "rage, rage" against death. For instance, he says in the first stanza, "Old age should burn and rave at close of day." Here the speaker advises all old men, not just one old man. Then each stanza that follows talks about one category of old man and shows that, no matter what they may have done in life, in the end they all fight death. They do not give in easily.

The regular rhythm and rhyme in the poem contribute to making it sound like an argument. Of the nineteen lines in the poem, thirteen end either with the word "light" or "night" or with a word that rhymes with "light" or "night." This repetition emphasizes the speaker's plea. It sounds like a carefully planned speech designed to convince not just the father, who is not directly addressed until the last stanza, but anyone who hears it.

The setting of the poem also indicates a larger audience than just the father. It's hard to tell where this speaker is. He isn't clearly in a building or in a specific outdoor location. In the middle four stanzas, the men described relate to parts of nature (lightning, a green bay, the sun, meteors), but these seem to be general and not specific places. The father in the final stanza stands on a "sad height," which doesn't seem like a real mountain but instead like a metaphor for the final place humans reach just before they die. All these setting elements emphasize that the speaker argues for an approach to old age that he considers best for many men as well as for his father.

The speaker's approach to old age seems to be highly idealistic and philosophical. Most of the images in the poem are visual. They show things you see or think about rather than things you feel or experience, for example, words that "forked no lightning" and deeds that "might have danced in a green bay." The speaker talks about past deeds rather than about the present experience of aging and (possibly) illness that these old men, and the speaker's father, now face.

In contrast to the formal, arguing tone of "Do Not Go Gentle," the speaker's tone in "Slipping" explains and accepts. The speaker describes the changes in her father with understanding. She sees that his legs can "barely support him" and that he is losing his memory. These details show that she sympathizes with her father and recognizes what he is facing, but she doesn't wish him back the way he was. She expresses, instead, her love for his new way of expressing his emotions. She describes this openness with a gentle image, noting "how soft and mutable is the usually hidden flesh."

The rhyme and rhythm also contrast sharply with those of "Do Not Go Gentle." In Thomas' poem, the rhythm and rhyme are regular and repetitive. In "Slipping," there are no rhymes, and the rhythm seems like everyday speech and not like a planned formal argument. The speaker even uses direct quotations, giving the exact words of her mother ("He's never liked to talk about feelings") and her father ("I love you"). This dialogue gives an intimate view of a specific family rather than the formal picture conveyed by the language of "Do Not Go Gentle."

In "Do Not Go Gentle," there's no clear picture of the speaker's location, and his examples also have general, idealized settings. In "Slipping," however, the setting comes from real life. The father is shown driving a car, taking a walk with his daughter, and teaching in his classroom. Even the metaphor the daughter uses to describe his changes—the screen falling—gives a picture of a dressing room, like the ones in a doctor's office.

The images in "Slipping" also show the difference between this poem and "Do Not Go Gentle." While Thomas' images are visual and can be applied generally to large groups of men, the images in "Slipping" are personal and appeal to both sight and touch. The father's leg "trailing a little" and the "curtain of mist" that obscures his sight make the changes he faces specific. His trailing leg is compared to "a child who keeps pulling on your hand," and his feelings are exposed like someone who was dressing behind a screen that suddenly falls down. Both images give a physical sense of someone who has lost power.

The speakers, who clearly love their aging fathers, have very different responses to the changes they see. The speaker in "Do Not Go Gentle" takes the responsibility for his father's life on his own shoulders. He tells his father how to approach old age. It seems like the speaker just thinks about death as the ultimate enemy that everyone should fight. On the other hand, the speaker in "Slipping" sees both the negative and the positive aspects of the changes. The father no longer has the pleasure of his work, but he now has found a relationship with his family, which never seemed to be possible before. The speaker in "Do Not Go Gentle" rages against accepting his father's changes, whereas the speaker in Aleshire's poem seems, like her father, to slip gently into this new phase of life.

Exercise

Read several works from any one of the thematic chapters of this book (Chapters 6 through 13). Then, using the process demonstrated with Walter's paper, choose two works and plan and write a comparison. Keep in mind the principles presented in the following Guidelines box.

GUIDELINES

Writing a Comparison

1. As you plan the paper by doing preliminary reading, writing, and thinking, remember that listing and outlining are useful strategies for planning a comparison paper.
2. Remember that a comparison should be made for a purpose. A comparison should not simply list the similarities and differences discovered during planning sessions.

(continued)

GUIDELINES, continued

3. Note which similarities or differences seem most significant, and decide which you will emphasize.

4. Decide how you will organize your paper—for example, the "whole-subject" approach, the "point-by-point" approach, or a combination of these approaches.

5. Open with a paragraph that focuses on the purpose and point of the comparison. For example, do *not* say

   > In this paper "Slipping" will be compared to "Do Not Go Gentle into That Good Night."

   or

   > There are many similarities and differences between "Slipping" and "Do Not Go Gentle into That Good Night."

   Do say, for example,

   > The speakers in Joan Aleshire's poem "Slipping" and Dylan Thomas' poem "Do Not Go Gentle into That Good Night" describe their responses as their fathers face the changes of old age.

6. Develop each subject (or each point) in a separate paragraph (or a series of carefully related and logically linked paragraphs).

7. Make certain that transitions between paragraphs and between sections of the paper show the connections—the comparisons and contrasts—you want to make.

8. Develop a conclusion that offers an analysis, evaluates the evidence the body of your paper provides, or in some other way shows the significance of the comparison you have made.

WRITING TO ANALYZE

When you analyze, you look at parts (or at a part) in relationship to the whole to which they belong. For example, a United States history exam might ask you to discuss and explain the significance of the economic causes of the American Revolution. Such a question requires that you look at part (the economic causes) of a whole (the American Revolution) and that you explain how knowing about that part contributes to understanding the whole. When you analyze a work of literature, you look carefully at its parts—or at one particular part—to see what they contribute to the meaning the whole work holds for you. For instance, you might look carefully at the language of a poem, a particular character in a short story, or a significant scene in a play. The third assignment topic asks for such an approach.

Topic 3

Explain how the figurative language in one of the poems suggests the relationship between the speaker and his or her father.

As Catherine Hupel considered this topic, she noticed that "Slipping" was divided into three stanzas. She knew that she was being asked to look at one element—figurative language—and to talk about how that element worked to create the poem's meaning. Looking at the parts in relation to the whole called for analysis, so she decided to look at each stanza to see how the figurative language helped to develop the speaker's view of her father.

DISCOVERING IDEAS: Listing and Grouping

Catherine began by making the following lists:

Stanza 1:   Father's aging is like "Slow slipping"
             Eyes blinded "curtain of mist" (cataract?)
             Years (father's aging) like "pickpockets"
             Father drives car "like raft on river"
                        "drifts from lane to lane"

Stanza 2:   Father's leg "trails like a child"

Stanza 3:   Father in photo: "Stethoscope like a pet snake"
             Father's reserve has fallen "like a screen"

After making the list, Catherine saw that these figures of speech were all comparisons, either similes or metaphors. She noticed that several of the images suggested something hidden or stealthy. She noticed, too, that some had a negative connotation, whereas others were dreamlike. She grouped these images as follows:

hidden/stealthy	*negative*	*dreamlike*
curtain of mist	pickpockets	slow slipping
pickpockets	pet snake	curtain of mist
		drifts . . . like a raft
		screen

Catherine knew that dividing the images into these lists would help her to plan her paper. She also noted that not every image fit neatly. For instance, "curtain of mist" and "pickpockets" seemed to belong in two categories, whereas "like a child" did not seem to fit any category.

Considering Audience, Narrowing the Topic, and Devising a Preliminary Thesis

Catherine knew that other students in the class would be reading her draft as part of the revision process. She also knew that some of them might not see the similes as falling into the categories she had created. For instance, she knew that not everyone would see "pet snake" as negative, so she realized she had to convince her readers that her analysis was plausible, even though they might not agree with her conclusions. Considering her evaluation of her audience, Catherine decided to narrow her focus to the ambivalent feelings she believed the speaker's similes reveal. Catherine developed the following tentative thesis:

> Although the speaker in Joan Aleshire's poem "Slipping" clearly loves her father, some of the figurative language in the poem suggests a darker side to their new closeness.

Planning, Organizing, and Drafting

At first, Catherine thought she would organize her paper by going through the poem and discussing each stanza. However, as she thought about her thesis, she decided that the most effective way to convince her audience would be to discuss the speaker's positive feelings first and then to show that the figurative language also suggested negative aspects. Here is Catherine's next-to-final draft:

LOVE AND LOSS IN "SLIPPING"
Catherine Hupel

Joan Aleshire's poem demonstrates the strong emotions the speaker feels for her father. She describes with kind understanding the symptoms of his aging and indicates her pleasure at feeling closer to her father than she has in the past. Nevertheless, although the speaker clearly loves her father, some of the figurative language in the poem suggests a darker side to their new closeness.

It is easy to identify images and figures of speech that show the speaker's caring for her father. For example, in the first stanza, she describes her father's losses with such phrases as "slow slipping" and "curtain of mist." These phrases clearly show his changes, yet the words are also gentle, even dreamlike, suggesting her sympathy for him.

The speaker goes on to describe her father's weak leg. It drags behind "like / a child who keeps pulling on your hand." She also notes that her father is now more open to her and that he finds a sense of pleasure in visits where "years of restraint" have been "pushed away." In fact, she describes this change with a simile: The "reserve has slipped from / his feeling, like a screen suddenly / falling." Now they are able to say to each other the words "I love you."

In spite of the positive feelings expressed, much of the figurative language shows negative emotions that underlie the speaker's picture of her father. For example, even the title "Slipping" can mean so many things. "To slip" can mean to lose physical and mental health, which is what is literally meant. On the other hand, we also think of "to slip" as meaning to make a mistake. Perhaps the father has been "slipping" even before his old age. A simile that would confirm this interpretation is the comparison of his stethoscope (in his picture as a younger man) to "a pet snake." The snake is shown in the Bible as a tempter.

Other images that give a dark feeling to the poem include the comparison to the years as "pickpockets." The father has his strength stolen, but the daughter has also had something stolen from her by time—the chance to really know her father well. The comparison of the father's car when he drives to a "raft on a river" suggests a sense of moving away and a lack of direction. It seems that he missed some turns earlier in his life as well, when his face was lighted by "love of his work" in a way the narrator "seldom saw at home."

The image of the father's left leg "trailing a little like / a child who keeps pulling on your hand" may reflect the way the speaker believes her father saw her when she was a child. Finally, the simile that suggests that the father's uncustomary loss of restraint is "like a screen suddenly / falling" has ambiguous meaning. When a screen falls down, it reveals whatever is behind it. That may be good or it may be bad. The speaker says that she loves the fact that he is no longer so reserved. Yet she also is able to see all the wrinkles and flaws.

The figurative language of the poem suggests that the speaker has gained something positive from being with her aging father: she has had a small glimpse into his heart. On the other hand, she has also had to recognize and face up to all that she has lost because this moment of closeness has been so long coming.

Revising Focus: Using and Explaining Examples

As Catherine read her draft, she recognized that sometimes her ideas were not fully explained. For example, consider her second paragraph:

It is easy to identify images and figures of speech that show the speaker's caring for her father. For example, in the first stanza, she describes her father's losses with such phrases as "slow slipping" and "curtain of mist." These phrases clearly show his changes, yet the words are also gentle, even dreamlike, suggesting her sympathy for him.

In this paragraph, Catherine gives examples of images and figures of speech in her second sentence, but she doesn't really show how these examples relate to the statement in her first sentence. Here's how she revised this paragraph:

> It is easy to identify images and figures of speech that show the speaker's caring for her father. For example, in the first stanza, she shows the gradual losses that her father must endure. These losses include physical weakness in the legs, the ability to remember and to concentrate, and the ability to drive safely. She describes these losses with phrases like "slow slipping" and "curtain of mist." These phrases clearly show his changes, yet the words are also gentle, even dreamlike, suggesting her sympathy for him.

Exercise

Compare the rest of Catherine's next-to-final draft with the final paper (page 119). Identify places where she has amplified and explained her examples. Then explain why you think she made these choices. What has been gained by the revisions she made? Keep in mind the principles presented in the Guidelines box on page 121.

Editing Focus: Word Choice

In an earlier draft of her paper (not included here), Catherine had written the following sentences. As she read this draft, some of the words she had chosen did not sound quite right to her. These words are indicated in the examples that follow by boldface type. She checked with a dictionary and in a few cases asked her professor's advice, and then she replaced the word she had used with one that reflected the meaning she had intended.

1. *Original:* Joan Aleshire's poem **denotes** the strong emotions the speaker feels for her father.
   Edited: Joan Aleshire's poem **demonstrates** the strong emotions the speaker feels for her father.
2. *Original:* For example, in the first stanza, she shows the **graduated** losses that her father must endure.
   Edited: For example, in the first stanza, she shows the **gradual** losses that her father must endure.
3. *Original:* Finally, the simile that suggests that the father's **unaccustomary** loss of restraint is "like a screen suddenly / falling" has ambiguous meanings.
   Edited: Finally, the simile that suggests that the father's **uncustomary** loss of restraint is "like a screen suddenly / falling" has ambiguous meanings.

Exercise

Check the words in these examples in a dictionary, and explain why you think Catherine made the choices shown in the edited sentences.

Proofreading Focus: Misplaced Modifiers

In an early draft, not shown here, Catherine had written this sentence:

Although loving her father, the figurative language in the poem suggests a darker side to their new closeness.

As she read the sentence, she could see that something was wrong. After talking with a tutor at the campus writing center, Catherine saw that she had written a sentence with a misplaced modifier. The introductory phrase "although loving her father" should describe the word or phrase that follows it. Of course, "although loving her father" does not describe "the figurative language"; it describes the speaker. Catherine revised the sentence this way:

Nevertheless, although the speaker loves her father, some of the figurative language in the poem suggests a darker side to their new closeness.

Exercise

Identify and revise the misplaced modifiers in the following paragraph:

Driving his car in a dangerous way, the lives of the father and others could have been threatened. The daughter's thoughts only should have been about the safety of her father and others on the road with him. Instead, while continuing to drive erratically, the daughter seems to be doing nothing to keep her father off the road.

Final Copy: Writing to Analyze

After revising, editing, and proofreading, Catherine submitted to her professor the following draft of her paper.

LOVE AND LOSS IN "SLIPPING"
Catherine Hupel

Joan Aleshire's poem demonstrates the strong emotions the speaker feels for her father. She describes with kind understanding the symptoms of his aging and indicates her pleasure at feeling closer to her father than she has in the past. Nevertheless, although the speaker clearly loves her father, some of the figurative language in the poem suggests a darker side to their new closeness.

It is easy to identify images and figures of speech that show the speaker's caring for her father. For example, in the first stanza, she shows the gradual losses that her father must endure. These losses include physical weakness in the legs, the ability to remember and to concentrate, and the ability to drive safely. She describes these losses with such phrases as "slow slipping" and "curtain of mist." These phrases clearly show his changes, yet the words are also gentle, even dreamlike, suggesting her sympathy for him.

The speaker goes on to describe her father's weak leg in a somewhat playful way. It drags behind "like / a child who keeps pulling on your hand." She also notes that her father is now more open to her and that he finds a sense of pleasure in visits where "years of restraint" have been "pushed away." In fact, she describes this change with a simile: The "reserve has slipped from / his feeling, like a screen suddenly / falling." Now she is able to see her father more fully than ever before, and they are able to say to each other the words, "I love you."

In spite of the positive feelings expressed, much of the figurative language shows negative emotions that underlie the speaker's picture of her father. For example, even the title "Slipping" can mean so many things. "To slip" can mean to lose physical and mental health, which is what is literally meant. On the other hand, we also think of "to slip" as meaning to make a mistake. Perhaps the father has been "slipping" even before his old age. A simile that would confirm this interpretation is the comparison of his stethoscope (in his picture as a younger man) to "a pet snake." The snake is shown in the Bible as a tempter. Perhaps the father was always tempted by his work, which is represented by his stethoscope, to stay away from his family. He seems to have withheld any expressions of love toward them until now.

Other images that give a dark feeling to the poem include the comparison to the years as "pickpockets," that is, sneak thieves. Time has stolen the father's strength, but it has also stolen something from the daughter—the chance to know her father well. The comparison of the father's car to a "raft on a river" suggests a sense of moving away and a lack of direction. True, this is happening to the father now in his old age, but it seems that he missed some turns earlier in his life as well, when his face was lighted by "love of his work" in a way the narrator "seldom saw at home."

The image of the father's left leg "trailing a little like / a child who keeps pulling on your hand" may reflect the way the speaker believes her father saw her when she was a child. She may believe that he saw her as a force slowing him down and keeping him away from the work he loved. Finally, the simile that suggests that the father's uncustomary loss of restraint is "like a screen suddenly / falling" has ambiguous meaning. When a screen falls down, it reveals whatever is behind it. That may be good, or it may be bad. The speaker says that she loves the fact that he is no longer so reserved. Yet she also is able to see all the wrinkles and flaws.

The figurative language of the poem suggests that the speaker has gained something positive from being with her aging father: she has had a small glimpse into his heart. On the other hand, she has also had to recognize and face up to all that she has lost because this moment of closeness has been so long coming.

GUIDELINES

Writing an Analysis

1. An analysis looks at parts (or at a part) in relationship to the whole to which they belong.
2. A literary analysis often focuses on one or more elements of literature, including—but not limited to—the following:
   sound (rhyme and rhythm)
   structure (patterns of lines and stanzas; organization and structure of paragraphs and/or dialogue)
   figurative language (such as metaphors, similes, personification, symbols)
   development of characters
   development of plot and action (particularly conflict/ resolution)
   irony
3. An analysis shows how the element or elements being considered contribute to the whole meaning of the work; each part of the discussion, therefore, must relate to a clear, central idea.
4. An analysis is not a paraphrase (a restatement of the ideas of the work in your own words); instead, it is an explanation of the way a work communicates (see page 116).

WRITING TO EXPLICATE

Explication is one form of analysis. The word "explicate" comes from the Latin *explicare,* which means "to unfold." When you write a paper that unfolds the meaning of a work, you are writing an explication. The fourth assignment topic asks for such an approach.

Topic 4

What, exactly, does the speaker say in each poem? And how does he or she say it? Look carefully at the language of the poem. Then choose one poem and explain how the central idea of the poem unfolds as you read from one stanza to the next.

Matt Cejak chose to focus on the Dylan Thomas poem for this topic. He noticed that the first part of the topic seemed relatively easy; he didn't think he'd have much trouble describing what the speaker says. He also felt confident that he could talk about the central idea of the poem (as required by the last part of the topic). Explaining both how the speaker conveys his meaning and how each stanza relates to the central idea of the poem seemed more difficult.

DISCOVERING IDEAS: Paraphrasing

To make certain he had a sense of what was going on in each stanza, Matt decided to write a **paraphrase.** That is, he decided to write a series of short paragraphs, putting each stanza into his own words.

PARAPHRASE OF "DO NOT GO GENTLE" (BY DYLAN THOMAS)

1. People who are old should not be resigned to dying. They should fight against it.
2. People who are wise may know that death is the right thing, but (????something about lightning???not sure) they still resist dying.
3. People who are good (seems to mean morally upright?) realize that their time on earth is nearly through, but they think about the things they have done, and that makes them fight against death.
4. "Wild men" (outlaws? rebels? nonconformists? crazy people?) who did strange and brave things and acted like they didn't care if they were doing things that might kill them find out at the end of their lives that they regret having to give up life. They then fight against death.
5. Serious (sad?) men who are near death and nearly blind (with disease or old age?) realize (or think) they could still act in some special way (like meteors). These people fight death, too.

6. (Talks directly to his father) You are facing death. I want you to give me your blessing, even though you may curse me with your angry tears, so that you can fight against death.

As he read over the paraphrase, Matt saw that he had a place to begin. But he also saw that working on the explication was going to be harder than he had thought. The paraphrase of "Do Not Go Gentle" seemed matter-of-fact and overly simple. It had none of the energy of the original poem. In addition, the paraphrase raised questions: some of the stanzas were hard to put into prose. They didn't easily yield one thought or idea.

Matt looked closely again at the poem and compared it to his paraphrase. He made this list of what the paraphrase lacked:

1. sound—rhyme, rhythm
2. pattern—repetition, arrangement and number of lines in stanzas
3. figurative language—metaphors, symbols
4. many possible meanings to phrases and sentences

Matt decided to use this list as a guide when he drafted his explication. As he discussed each stanza, he would consider how each of the elements helped to convey meaning.

Considering Audience, Narrowing the Topic, and Devising a Preliminary Thesis

At this point, Matt thought about focusing his topic more clearly and about finding a preliminary thesis. Everything he came up with seemed too obvious. For example, here are some possibilities he tried:

Dylan Thomas' poem "Do Not Go Gentle into That Good Night" describes the words of a son pleading with his father to fight death.
The speaker in Dylan Thomas' poem "Do Not Go Gentle into That Good Night" urges his father to fight against the ending of his life.
In the poem "Do Not Go Gentle into That Good Night" by Dylan Thomas, the idea is given that death is a force to fight.

Matt liked the third possibility better than the other two because the idea seemed more widely applicable, but he was not really satisfied. Looking back at the topic he'd chosen for this paper, he realized that none of his possible theses really addressed the question of how the ideas and feelings in the poem were conveyed.

Thinking of his instructor as an important part of the audience for this paper, Matt realized that he needed to work on all parts of the topic. Although he was not happy with any of his possible theses, he decided to write a draft to see whether he could discover a clear focus during writing.

Planning and Organizing

Because Matt was still not sure where he was going, he had trouble planning the organization of the draft. He didn't have any idea how to write an opening paragraph because he still didn't have a clear preliminary thesis. He remembered, however, that an explication is an unfolding of the meaning of a work. So, he decided to start by discussing the first stanza and then move chronologically through the other five stanzas. He hoped this process would help him to discover how the poem "worked"; then he could return during the revision process to write an introduction.

Drafting

Matt began work on the draft, keeping in mind the four elements he'd listed as crucial to the way the poem conveys meaning.

EXPLICATION: "DO NOT GO GENTLE"
Matthew Cejak

In the first stanza, three lines give the speaker's plea to old people not to die easily. They should fight and be angry at "close of day." The first and third lines of the stanza rhyme—"night" and "light." The word "rage" is repeated twice. "Night" is a metaphor for death, and "day" or "light" are metaphors for life.

In the second stanza, there are three lines again. They have the same rhyme pattern as the first stanza. In this stanza, the speaker talks about wise men who "know dark is right." When they spoke during their lifetime maybe they didn't really get their message across. They didn't speak like lightning. So they don't want to die, they want to continue to live. The last line repeats the first line of the first stanza.

Revising Focus: Summarizing versus Analyzing

At this point, Matt stopped and reread what he had written. He was happy with some aspects and unhappy with others. He had gone beyond the paraphrase he had written earlier and was paying attention to the list he'd made of elements to consider, but the draft still didn't seem to address the "how" part of the assignment. At this point, Matt asked his instructor for a conference. To prepare for the office conference, Matt consulted the guidelines the instructor had distributed at the beginning of the term.

GUIDELINES

Preparing for a Writing Conference

1. Gather all preliminary work (notes, drafts, books with your annotations, and so on) to bring with you.
2. List the strong points of your paper.
3. List the weak points of your paper. Focus first on large issues, such as organization or use of examples, rather than finer points, such as word choice or punctuation.
4. List approaches you have considered to revise the weaknesses you see.
5. Make a list of questions about your writing project.
6. Make your questions precise.
     Not this: How can I get a better grade on this paper?
     But this: This statement, I know, is too general. How can I make my point more specific?

The following conversation is an edited transcript of Matt's conference with his instructor:

Matt: I can't get started—I know this is wrong.

Instructor: Well, actually, you have a good start here. You've got a lot on paper. Try reading what you've written in this draft out loud.

Matt: (After finishing reading) I know it's not—not enough—or, somehow, doesn't answer the "how" part. But—

Instructor: I think you're right—do you see why?

Matt: No! If I saw why—I would—If I saw why, I'd change it.

Instructor: (Laughs) Right—yes—I see your point. OK. This time, listen to me read what you've said. Tell me what you're learning—new insights into the poem—whatever. *(Reads the draft)*

Matt: What it sounds like to me is a summary of the notes—here—I did this paraphrase and then this list.

Instructor: Good stuff here, Matt. You've done a lot of work—but now you need to go further. You said the word yourself. You've got mostly summary—either summary of meaning or summary of various elements. Take this paragraph, for instance:

In the first stanza, three lines give the speaker's plea to old people not to die easily. They should fight and be angry at "close of day." The first and third lines of the stanza rhyme—"night" and "light." The word "rage" is repeated twice. "Night" is a metaphor for death, and "day" or "light" are metaphors for life.

What's the point here?

Matt: I guess—mmm—it's just to tell what the aspects of the poem are.

Instructor: Can you put any of these sentences together—work on them in a connected way? How do they relate?

Matt: Well, I talk about "night" and "day" or "light" being metaphors, and then there's this part about "night" and "light" rhyming and this part where I quote "close of day"—so—maybe—something about how they go together? Why they go together?

Instructor: Sounds like a good plan—let me hear you talk a little more about your idea.

Matt: Well, how about that "night" and "day" are really important to the poem and that this repeating—and the metaphor—and the rhyme—I would say maybe that's how Thomas makes you really notice the importance.

Instructor: See—now you're really getting away from summary and into the analysis—the explication. Good. See—you say "that's *how* Thomas makes you notice. . . ."

After talking with his instructor, Matt knew what direction he wanted his paper to take. He had to make the hard decision to discard most of the first draft. Keeping in mind the idea of making connections and of analyzing rather than summarizing, Matt wrote this second draft. He still was not sure of his central idea, so he again followed his plan of explicating each stanza in order, planning to go back and write an introductory paragraph later.

EXPLICATION: "DO NOT GO GENTLE"
Matthew Cejak

The first stanza begins with the speaker's plea, addressed to old people. They should fight against going "into that good night," a metaphor for death. The words in this stanza set a tone of heat and passion. Those who face death should "burn," "rave," and "rage." The repetition of the word "rage" emphasizes the importance the speaker places on this fight against death.

The second stanza gives the first of three examples demonstrating why the speaker believes old people should resist death. Wise men may know that "dark"—another metaphor for death—"is right." But when these wise men spoke during their lifetime maybe they didn't really get their message across. They didn't speak like lightning. So they don't want to die, they want to continue to live. "Lightning" relates to "light" in the first stanza; both indicate something powerful and good. The lightning may be powerful words, while the light represents life itself. In this stanza, the rhyme scheme of the poem begins to underline the speaker's insistence on life. Like in the first stanza, the first and third lines rhyme. And all four of these lines (1, 3, 4, and 6) rhyme, too. The rhyme emphasizes the relationship between "light" (life) and "night" (death) and the struggle between the two.

"Good men" serve as the example in stanza 3. They don't want to die because they think back on the actions of their lives, and they realize that these actions may not have been fully appreciated. These actions are described as "frail deeds." The word "frail" suggests the weakness often associated with old age, and the "good men" think about how those actions "might have danced in a green bay." This phrase shows the men's actions as lively and sparkling, like light on the water in a bay. Once again, the idea of light is emphasized as good and the idea of dark (death) as bad. The deeds could have been "bright," and so these "good men" fight against letting their light go out. The importance of life is stressed by the rhyming of "bright" and "light" at the ends of the first and last lines in the stanza.

"Wild men" are shown in the fourth stanza as the example of old people who fight death. They seem to be people who grabbed on to parts of life and yet also let those same parts of life go with no regrets. They "caught" the sun, which may be a metaphor for a very intense and beautiful part of life, but they sang "the sun in flight." This singing indicates that they were able to say good-bye to these intense, beautiful times with joy. But now they realize that they also feel sorrow. They feel the loss of these strong experiences. Once again, the image of light (the sun) is good. It represents power, energy, and life. Like the "wise men" wishing their words had been like lightning, and like the "good men" imagining their deeds dancing "in a green bay," the "wild men" seem to have a strong connection with the physical part of nature (in this case the sun). The final line repeats the ending line of the second stanza and the first line of the first stanza: "Do not go gentle into that good night." The repetition ties this example in with the others and shows that yet one more category of old people fight the ending of life.

The final example of those who "rage, rage against the dying of the light" are grave men. It's interesting to note that "grave" means serious, yet "grave" here could also maybe suggest the nearness to burial—the grave of the dead. These grave men may be nearly blind, but the speaker says they see with "blinding sight." This means that even though they might not have all their senses working in the same way as a younger person, they can still *see* meaning in life. Here again the imagery relates to a beautiful, strong, and spectacular part of nature—meteors. The blind eyes of the grave men could still "blaze" with commitment to the power of life.

The poem concludes with a stanza that returns to the plea of the first stanza. In the middle four stanzas that give examples, the lines "Rage, rage against the dying of the light" and "Do not go gentle into that good night" have been used to complete sentences of description. For example, "Good men rage against the dying of the light" or "Wild men do not go gentle into that good night." Now these lines are addressed directly to the speaker's father, so they would read more like this, "Father, I am asking you not to 'go gentle into that good night,'" or "Father, I am pleading with you to 'rage, rage against the dying of the light.'" The opening request is backed up by a series of examples, leading to a stronger plea (the only four-line stanza in the poem). The speaker builds an argument that he hopes will encourage his father to stay strong and brave even in the face of death. The frequent rhymes emphasize the opposing forces of "light"/"bright" (life) and "night" (death) and the repetition of the speaker's pleas ("Do not go . . ." and "Rage, rage . . .") underline the urgency of his message to his father.

Matt was much happier with this draft. He read it through and decided that what he talked about most was the repetition and the emphasis that repetition gave to the poem. He revised his title and—after several tries—wrote this opening paragraph to make the focus of his paper clear:

THE POWER OF SOUND AND SIGHT IN "DO NOT GO GENTLE"
Matthew Cejak

Dylan Thomas' poem "Do Not Go Gentle into That Good Night" gives a man's plea to his father to fight death. Images of strength, power, and life fill the poem, showing nature's beauty and energy and giving reasons for the father to fight death. The poem's rhythm and sound seem to oppose death, too. The rhymes and repetition of lines build a lively pattern to the speaker's final argument.

Editing Focus: Conciseness

One of the earlier versions of Matt's opening paragraph looked like this:

In Dylan Thomas' poem "Do Not Go Gentle into That Good Night," he writes about the plea a man is making to his father to mount a gallant battle against the trials and tribulations of the finality of death. The poem is filled with images of strength, power, and life. These images show to the reader the beauty and energy of nature and give reasons for the father to fight the grim reaper. As a matter of fact, the poem has a rhythm and sound that seem to oppose the ghastly specter of death, too. The rhymes and repetition of lines build a lively pattern to the speaker's final argument.

With his instructor's help, Matt identified the following problems. Matt edited to make certain that he conveyed his meaning as directly and clearly as possible.

1. Unneeded words and phrases.

   Wordy: As a matter of fact, the poem has a rhythm and sound that seem to oppose the ghastly specter of death, too.
   Edited: The poem's rhythm and sound seem to oppose death, too.

2. Unnecessary repetition. Matt combined sentences, trying to eliminate repetition.

   Wordy: The poem is filled with images of strength, power, and life. These images show to the reader the beauty and energy of nature and give reasons for the father to fight the grim reaper.
   Edited: Images of strength, power, and life fill the poem, showing nature's beauty and energy and giving reasons for the father to fight death.

3. Clichés and overused phrases.

   Wordy: fight the grim reaper
   Edited: fight death

4. Redundancy.

   Wordy: the finality of death.
   Edited: death. (Death is obviously final, so "finality of death" is ineffectively repetitious.)

Exercise

Compare the two versions of Matt's paragraph on pages 128–29. Then, editing for conciseness, revise the following early version of another paragraph from Matt's paper. When you have completed the revision, compare your editing decisions with the editing decisions demonstrated by the second paragraph of Matt's paper, page 126.

> The second stanza gives the first of three examples the speaker gives for the purpose of demonstrating why he believes old

people should resist death. Wise men may know that "dark is right." Like "night" in the first stanza, "dark" is a metaphor for death. But these wise men, when they spoke during their lifetime maybe they didn't really get their message across. They didn't speak like lightning. So they don't want to die. Instead, continuing in life is their heart's desire. "Lightning" relates to "light" in the first stanza. Good is implied by these words, and they also suggest strong power. The lightning may be powerful words. Light, on the other hand, represents the liveliness of life itself. In this stanza, the type of rhyme scheme of the poem begins to underline the insistence of the speaker on life. As in the first stanza, the first and third lines rhyme. And all four of these lines (1, 3, 4, and 6) rhyme, too. The rhyme emphasizes the relationship between "light" (life) and "night" (death) and the struggle that is continually going on between these two archenemies.

Proofreading Focus: Apostrophes, Quotation Marks to Indicate Words Used in a Special Way

As he completed his draft, Matt noticed that he had questions about the use of apostrophes. In addition, when he discussed a word from the poem, he was not certain whether to underline it, put it in quotation marks, or use no punctuation.

A quick check with a grammar handbook told him that apostrophes are required in the following situations:

- To form possessive nouns:

Singular: One author's opinion.
Plural: Two authors' opinions.

Note: Do not use apostrophes with possessive pronouns such as "his," "hers," "theirs," and "ours."

Note: When a word does not form the plural by adding "s" or "es," form the possessive simply by adding apostrophe "s."
No: The childrens' story.
Yes: The children's story.

- To form contractions:

"Were not" becomes "weren't."

Note: "It's" is the contraction for "it is"; "its" is a possessive pronoun. (The bird left its nest.)

Note: Do not use apostrophes with verbs that are not part of contractions.
  No: He read's well.
  Yes: He reads well.

The handbook gave the following rule for punctuating words used in special situations:

- Words referred to as words can be either underlined (italicized, in printed material) or enclosed in quotation marks.

"Light" is used as a metaphor for life.

or

Light is used as a metaphor for life.

Be consistent throughout the paper; use either quotation marks or underlining, not a combination.

Some instructors will want you to observe strict MLA (Modern Language Association) style, which calls for italics, not quotation marks. Be sure to check with your instructor and follow his or her requirements in your paper.

Exercises

1. Applying these rules, proofread and correct the following earlier versions of sentences from Matt's paper. Add apostrophes where needed; delete incorrectly used apostrophes. Add either quotation marks or underlining to words used as words (be consistent; use either quotation marks or underlining, not both).

    The first stanza begins with the speakers plea, addressed to old people.

    The repetition of the word rage emphasizes the importance the speaker places on this fight against death.

    They didnt speak like lightning.

    This phrase shows the mens' actions as lively and sparkling, like light on the water in a bay.

    It represent's power, energy, and life.

    Its interesting to note that grave means serious, yet "grave" here could also maybe suggest the nearness to burial.

    Now these lines are addressed directly to the speakers' father.

2. Keeping in mind the revising, editing, and proofreading strategies described in this chapter (as well as other strategies you know), combine Matt's first paragraph (page 128) with his draft (pages 126–27) to make a strong, unified essay. Be prepared to explain the choices you make as you revise, edit, and proofread. Compare your final copy with the version that follows. Of

course, each person's revision of this paper will be different. The point is not to duplicate Matt's final paper but to think about the differences and similarities between your version and his.

Final Copy: Writing to Explicate

THE POWER OF SOUND AND SIGHT IN "DO NOT GO GENTLE"
Matthew Cejak

Dylan Thomas' poem "Do Not Go Gentle into That Good Night" is a man's plea to his father to fight death. Images of strength, power, and life fill the poem, showing nature's beauty and energy and giving reasons for the father to fight death. The poem's rhythm and sound seem to oppose death, too. The rhymes and repetition of lines build a lively pattern to the speaker's final argument.

The first stanza begins with the speaker's plea, addressed to old people. He urges them to fight against going "into that good night," a metaphor for death. The words in this stanza set a tone of heat and passion. Those who face death should "burn," "rave," and "rage." The repetition of the word "rage" emphasizes the importance the speaker places on this fight against death.

The second stanza gives the first of three examples demonstrating why the speaker believes old people should resist death. Wise men may know that "dark"—another metaphor for death—"is right." But when these wise men spoke during their lifetime, maybe they didn't really get their message across. They didn't speak like lightning. So they don't want to die; they want to continue to live. "Lightning" relates to "light" in the first stanza; both indicate something powerful and good. The lightning may refer to powerful words, whereas the light represents life itself. In this stanza, the rhyme scheme of the poem begins to underline the speaker's insistence on life. As in the first stanza, the first and third lines rhyme. And all four of these lines (1, 3, 4, and 6) rhyme, too. The rhyme emphasizes the relationship between "light" (life) and "night" (death) and the struggle between the two.

The phrase "Good men" serves as the example in stanza 3. They don't want to die, because as they think back on the actions of their lives they realize that these actions may not have been fully appreciated. These actions are described as "frail deeds." The word "frail" suggests the weakness often associated with old age, and the "good men" think about how those actions "might have danced in a green bay." This phrase shows the men's actions as lively and sparkling, like light on the water in a bay. Once again, the idea of light is emphasized as good, and the idea of dark (death) as bad. The deeds could have been "bright," and so these "good men" fight against letting their light go out. The importance of life is stressed by the rhyming of "bright" and "light" at the ends of the first and last lines in the stanza.

"Wild men" are shown in the fourth stanza as old people who fight death. They seem to be people who grabbed on to parts of life and yet also let those same parts of life go with no regrets. They "caught . . . the sun" (a metaphor for a very intense and beautiful part of life), but they sang "the sun in flight." This singing indicates that they were able to say good-bye with joy to these intense, beautiful times. Now, however, they realize that they also feel sorrow. They feel the loss of these strong experiences. Once again, the image of light (the sun) is good, representing power, energy, and life. Like the "wise men," wishing their words had been like lightning, and like the "good men," imagining their deeds dancing "in a green bay," the "wild men" seem to have a strong connection with the physical part of nature (in this case the sun). The final line repeats the ending line of the second stanza and the first line of the first stanza: "Do not go gentle into that good night." The repetition ties this example in with the others and shows yet one more category of old people who fight the ending of life.

The final example of those who "rage, rage against the dying of the light" is grave men. It's interesting to note that "grave" means "serious," yet "grave" here could also maybe suggest the nearness to burial—the grave of the dead. These grave men may be nearly blind, but the speaker says they see with "blinding sight." This means that even though they might not have all their senses working in the same way as a younger person, they can still *see* meaning in life. Here again the imagery relates to a beautiful, strong, and spectacular part of nature—meteors. The blind eyes of the grave men could still "blaze" with commitment to the power of life.

The poem concludes with a stanza that returns to the plea of the first stanza. In the middle four stanzas that give examples, the lines "Rage, rage against the dying of the light" and "Do not go gentle into that good night" have been used to complete sentences of description. For example, "Good men . . . rage against the dying of the light" or "Wild men . . . do not go gentle into that good night." Now these lines are addressed directly to the speaker's father, so they would read more like this: "Father, I am asking you not to 'go gentle into that good night,'" or "Father, I am pleading with you to 'rage, rage against the dying of the light.'" It is clear now that the opening request is backed up by a series of examples, leading to a stronger plea (the only four-line stanza in the poem). The speaker builds an argument that he hopes will encourage his father to stay strong and brave even in the face of death. The frequent rhymes emphasize the opposing forces of "light"/"bright" (life) and "night" (death) and the repetition of the speaker's pleas ("Do not go . . ." and "Rage, rage . . .") underline the urgency of his message to his father.

Exercise

Read several poems from any thematic section (Chapters 6–12) and then, using the process demonstrated with Matt's paper, plan and write an explication. Keep in mind the principles presented in the following Guidelines box.

GUIDELINES

Writing an Explication

1. An analysis, or explication, "unfolds" the poem (or section of a short story, novel, play, or essay). That is, it explains in detail how the work communicates to the reader.
2. An explication considers significant details and suggestions in the poem, including—but not limited to—these elements:
   sound (rhyme and rhythm)
   structure (patterns of lines and stanzas)
   figurative language (metaphors, similes, symbols)
   irony
   definitions of words
3. An explication shows how each part contributes to the whole meaning of the work; each part of the discussion, therefore, must relate to a clear central idea.
4. An explication is not a paraphrase (a restatement of the ideas of the work in your own words); instead, it is an explanation of the way a work communicates.
5. An explication is easy to organize; working sequentially from first to last stanza of a poem (or from beginning to end of a section from a short story, novel, essay, or play) makes the most sense.
6. An explication begins with an introduction indicating the main idea of the work and suggesting the direction of the explication.
7. An explication concludes with a paragraph that sums up the meaning that has been unfolded for the reader.

WRITING TO EVALUATE

A literary work can be judged in many ways. For instance, a reader may evaluate a work by asking questions such as these: "Is this poem beautiful?" "Are the motives of the characters in this short story convincing?" "Are the ideas in this play worthy of close, careful attention?" "What are the values supported by this work? And do I subscribe to those values?"

You are probably prompted to ask a question of your own: "According to what standards?" Any evaluation—whether of a literary work, a scientific theory, or a historical event—must be based on criteria. The next question, of course, is "Who sets these criteria?" The answers to these questions are not simple. Each reader must develop his or her own standards for evaluation, but where do these criteria come from? They come from what we have learned, what we have experienced, what we have observed or heard—not only in school but also at home, in our communities, in our religious institutions, at work.

A topic such as number 5 requires an evaluation of the values and beliefs expressed by the work, and—more importantly—asks the reader to examine his or her own values and beliefs as a means of judging the work.

Topic 5

Consider the values and beliefs suggested by each of these poems. Choose one of the poems, and explain those values and beliefs as well as your evaluation of them. Do you agree with them completely? Question them? Explain.

DISCOVERING IDEAS: Interviewing

After reading both poems, Joann Epstein wrote this journal entry:

> I read "Do Not Go Gentle" first, and I thought how much this son loved his father, that he didn't want him to just die with no fight. I was thinking right away that I would write the paper on the values in this poem which I can relate to—not so much my father, but my grandfather—I really want him to keep going even though he does have emphysema. I hate to see him slow down. Then I read "Slipping." This was a hard poem for me to read because you can see she loves her father, but she in some ways really likes seeing him slow down. Now, this to me is almost the exact opposite of the idea in

(continued)

> ## DISCOVERING IDEAS: Interviewing *(continued)*
>
> Thomas' poem. It's saying, "Don't fight the changes of old age, just accept them and look for the good." I didn't agree with this, because I think you should always fight for every bit of life. But the more I thought about it, the more I wondered which way I would want my relatives to think or act if I was the person who was getting old.

After writing this journal entry and thinking about the topic for a while, Joann still wasn't sure what her own criteria were for judging the values suggested by the two poems. She decided to work on "Slipping" because she saw that the poem supported the ideas of love and commitment (which she also believed in). But the means of showing love—accepting and even welcoming debilitating changes—was something she found difficult to understand.

To think further about the issues raised by the poem, Joann decided to interview Norma Heath, a nurse who worked with elderly patients and their families at the hospital where Joann held a part-time job. She chose Norma because in the past they'd had conversations about some patients in the hospital. Joann knew Norma believed that families often distressed hospitalized relatives by pushing for more treatment rather than accepting the changes brought on by illness. To prepare Norma for the interview, Joann asked her to read the poem. She also wrote a list of questions she wanted to ask. After asking permission, Joann taped the interview so that she could review it at home and make certain she was accurate if she decided to quote Norma. The following is a transcript of part of that tape:

> *Joann:* So, what did you think of the poem?
>
> *Norma:* I'm not a great one for poetry—but this one I liked—I kept reading it—especially the last lines.
>
> *Joann:* Why the last lines?
>
> *Norma:* I think—I guess—well, for me the screen seems like the ones we have in some of the exam rooms. And it falls, and you really see the whole truth about this man—who, I think, was a doctor in his professional life. So he was used to examining people and seeing— maybe "the truth" about them. But nobody saw him in that way.
>
> *Joann:* I see what you mean. But I still think it's weird that his daughter is, like, loving this change. Because, to me, what it shows is that her father is really not her father—I mean the way she always knew him. He's like weaker, but she likes that just because now he says he loves her.

Norma: To me it makes total sense—and I'm not sure what you mean by weaker. You mean the father is physically weak or emotionally weak because he says he loves her?

Joann: No, I—of course I don't mean to say "I love you" is emotionally weak, but it's because he's physically weak that he says it. I mean, would he say that if he still was totally well? I think the physical weakness has, sort of, broken him down.

Norma: I'm not sure I agree. Yes, his body is weak. But sometimes the inner change is not like breaking down. More like letting something go. Letting something go that has been preventing strength—hmm— preventing strong feelings. Like the poem says here "reserve has slipped" away from him. Now his loving of his daughter can be seen. And he is lucky she can accept that. And she's not just totally cynical about it.

Joann: What do you mean by totally cynical?

Norma: Well, some families, they just ignore changes like that because it's like they feel it's just another symptom of the person getting old. Or else they get angry with the person and it's like, "Well, it's too late!" I see a lot of bitterness.

Joann: But this daughter seems happy—she's not angry or bitter.

Norma: That's what I get—and I tell you, I wish we had more daughters like her who could say, "what I love" is this or that about some change they see in their parent—mother or father.

After the interview—and after spending more time rereading and rethinking the poem—Joann thought more about the speaker in the poem and about the implications of her responses to her father's changes. Norma's comment about the change showing strength rather than weakness really intrigued her.

Considering Audience, Narrowing the Topic, and Devising a Preliminary Thesis

Joann decided to focus on emotional strength as a central concept for evaluating the poem. She came up with this list of questions:

What does the poem say about emotional strength?
Who shows emotional strength?
Why is this person (or persons) showing emotional strength?
What is the definition of emotional strength in this poem?
What is my definition of emotional strength?
What does the poem say about the relationship between emotional strength and love?
What do I think about the relationship between emotional strength and love?

Joann knew that several people in the class had a strongly negative response to the values expressed in the poem. Just as she at first had questioned the daughter's motives for admiring the changes in her father, many students had seen her reaction as selfish. Joann realized that she was going to propose an alternative reading. She knew that she would have to work hard to find evidence that was convincing. She also knew she had to express her ideas so that people who did not share her views would not feel personally attacked.

Joann had no trouble coming up with a preliminary thesis. She knew she wanted to focus on the concept of emotional strength.

Both the speaker and the father in Joan Aleshire's poem "Slipping" show emotional strength and love as they face the changes brought by his aging.

Planning and Organizing

When she was ready to draft, Joann thought about how she wanted to start her essay and where she would go with it. She decided to focus on the questions she had listed and to use images and ideas from the poem to explore those questions. She rewrote the questions as statements and reordered the questions like this:

Introduction: focus on relationship of emotional strength and love.
1. Both father and daughter show emotional strength.
2. They show emotional strength in different ways and for a different reason.
    A. Father: physical changes cause him to drop his guard; wants to tell what has always been there.
    B. Daughter: accepts changes; does not act angry or judgmental.
3. Emotional strength means being able to change and to accept change.
4. Having the ability to change and accept change is a necessary part of loving and being loved.

Drafting

Using the notes she had taken during the interview, notes she had made on a copy of the poem, journal entries, and the outline, Joann wrote several drafts.

Revising Focus: Logic

While she was drafting, Joann saw that she needed to work on presenting her ideas logically. She isolated these particular problems in earlier drafts of the final copy, which begins on page 143.

1. Making **absolute statements** that could not be supported. For
    instance, she used words such as "all," "every," and "none" when she
    should have acknowledged exceptions.

    Illogical: All the images in the first two stanzas suggest the father's
    physical weakness. (Not every image in these stanzas suggests physical
    weakness; for example, the image of the darkness pushing "away years
    of restraint" suggests an emotional, not a physical, change.)
    Revised: Many of the images in the first two stanzas suggest the fa-
    ther's physical weakness.

2. Using a **question-begging approach,** that is, stating that
    something "is obvious" or that "everyone knows" something rather
    than providing evidence to support the point.

    Illogical: It's obvious that the daughter, too, shows emotional strength.
    She really understands her father and herself. (It's not obvious to the
    reader of the paper; evidence is needed to demonstrate the daughter's
    emotional strength and to demonstrate—rather than simply
    announce—her understanding of her father and herself.)
    Revised: The daughter, too, shows her emotional strength. She hon-
    estly describes the father she knew when she was growing up as
    someone who didn't show too much affection at home. However,
    she doesn't seem bitter and angry, which would show weakness. In-
    stead, she loves her father the way he is now. She doesn't berate him
    for what happened in the past. Also, even though it seems like her
    father didn't spend too much time with the family in the past, she is
    still willing to take walks with him and to talk to him. She doesn't
    hold a grudge or retaliate by rejecting him. (Here details and exam-
    ples provide evidence to show the reader the validity of the draft
    paragraph's initial sentence and to replace the broad generalization of
    the second sentence in the draft version.)

3. Using a **non sequitur.** This Latin term means "it does not follow"
    and describes conclusions drawn from evidence that cannot logically
    support them—for example, saying that a certain point in a work of
    literature is true because the speaker states that it is so. (Because some
    speakers are unreliable, their statements cannot be taken as truth.)

    Illogical: She honestly describes the father she knew when she was
    growing up as someone who didn't show too much affection at
    home. Of course, because he is her father, she knows that he really
    did love her, and she is not bitter or angry. (It is not necessarily true
    that "because he is her father" she would know that he loved her.
    The mere fact of parenthood does not ensure love.)

Revised: She honestly describes the father she knew when she was growing up as someone who didn't show too much affection at home. However, she doesn't seem bitter and angry, which would show weakness. Instead, she loves her father the way he is now. (Here the transitional sentence beginning with "however" shows the logical relationship between the ideas expressed in the sentences that precede and follow it.)

The three fallacies in the preceding list are examples of problems with logic that can make a paper unclear or undermine an essential point. For additional discussion of this issue, see pages 168–69.

Editing Focus: Integrating and Punctuating Quotations

As Joann read through an early draft of her paper, she realized that she had problems with the quotations she had used. She edited her paper to conform to the following rules:

1. Make clear whose ideas you are quoting and whom you are talking about:

   Unclear: The poem talks about slowing down "to match his pace" and being similar to "a child who keeps pulling on your hand."
   Edited: When the father takes a walk with his daughter, she has to slow down "to match his pace." She describes his leg as dragging like "a child who keeps pulling on your hand."

2. Use quotation marks around short quotations (four lines or fewer) that are combined with your own sentences.

   When he takes a walk with his daughter, she has to slow down "to match his pace."

3. When you cite three or fewer lines of poetry, run the words or phrases into your own sentences. Indicate line breaks with a slash (/), preceded and followed by a single space.

   Recalling her mother's observation that "[your father] never liked / to talk about feelings," the speaker honestly describes the father she knew when she was growing up as someone who didn't show too much affection at home.

4. Set off long quotations (four or more lines) in a separate block (called an extract) indented several spaces. Do not use quotation marks around the extract.

   His daughter explains that a familiar photograph of him, teaching with his

> chair tipped back
> against the lecture-room wall—shows
> a man talking, love of his work lighting
> his face—in a way we seldom saw at home.

5. Integrate quotations into your own sentences to show the relationship of the quotation to the point you are making.

   Unclear: Now, he puts his emotions into his family instead of his work. "I love you so much."
   Edited: Now instead of putting his emotions into his work, he freely tells his daughter, "I love you so much."

   Unclear: Another change relates to his work.

   > A photograph taken of him teaching—
   > white coat, stethoscope like a pet snake
   > around his neck, chair tipped back
   > against the lecture-room wall—shows
   > a man talking, love of his work lighting
   > his face—in a way we seldom saw at home.

   Edited: Another change that might be seen as weakening is the way he no longer keeps his feelings inside himself. For much of his life, this man has saved his emotional energy for his work. His daughter explains that a familiar photograph of him, teaching with his

   > chair tipped back
   > against the lecture-room wall—shows
   > a man talking, love of his work lighting
   > his face—in a way we seldom saw at home.

6. Use the ellipsis (three spaced periods) to show that words are omitted. (Example: Lincoln said that "government of the people . . . and by the people" should not be destroyed.)

7. Use brackets to indicate a minor change that makes a quotation grammatically compatible with the rest of your sentence.

   Original: As the daughter watches her father's changes, it's clear that "what I love / is the way reserve has slipped from / his feeling."
   Edited: As the daughter watches her father's changes, it's clear that "what [she loves] is the way reserve has slipped from / his feeling."

8. Check carefully to make certain that quotations are accurate.

9. To make your quotations effective, use them sparingly. Overly long quotations often obscure the meaning they are intended to convey.

Proofreading Focus: Pronoun Reference, Pronoun Agreement, Treatment of Titles

While proofreading, Joann realized she needed to work on revising pronoun references. For example, here's a sentence from an earlier draft of paragraph 4.

> Her mother says that her father "never liked / to talk about feelings." She honestly describes him as someone who didn't show too much affection at home.

To whom does "her" in the phrase "her father" refer? To the mother or to the daughter? Almost certainly it refers to the daughter, but the reference needs to be made clear.

> *Edited:* Recalling her mother's observation that "[your father] never liked / to talk about feelings," the speaker honestly describes the father she knew when she was growing up as someone who didn't show too much affection at home.

Of course, this sentence can also be revised in other ways—but the proofreading issue here is that a pronoun cannot convey its meaning accurately if the reader cannot tell who or what that pronoun represents.

Another problem with pronouns in the paper was their agreement with the nouns to which they referred.

> It's as if the weakening of the body has allowed his strong feelings to come out. It was simply trapped inside. ("It" is singular, and the word referred to, "feelings," is plural. Pronouns must agree in number with the words to which they refer.)
>
> *Edited:* It's as if the weakening of the body has allowed his strong feelings to come out. They were simply trapped inside.

As Joann proofread, she realized she wasn't sure how to treat titles, so she checked an English handbook and found these rules:

Treatment of Titles

1. When citing a poem, short story, or essay, put the title in quotation marks.

   In Joan Aleshire's poem "Slipping," a daughter describes the changes old age has brought to her father.

2. When citing a novel or a play, underline the title (or use italics).

   Dickens's novel <u>A Tale of Two Cities</u> is often required reading for high school sophomores.

or

Dickens's novel *A Tale of Two Cities* is often required reading for high school sophomores.

3. When writing the title of your own paper, do not underline it or put it in quotation marks.

   Love and Strength

4. Always capitalize the first and last word in a title as well as all other important words. Do not capitalize small, unimportant words such as "and," "the," "an," "a," "of," "to," "in," and other conjunctions and prepositions.

   Dylan Thomas published "Do Not Go Gentle into That Good Night" in 1952.

Final Copy: Writing to Evaluate

LOVE AND STRENGTH
Joann Epstein

In Joan Aleshire's poem "Slipping," a daughter describes the changes old age has brought to her father. The father gradually loses his physical abilities and, in addition, becomes less reserved. The daughter accepts the physical changes and welcomes her father's loss of restraint. Although both the speaker and the father are weak in some ways, they also show emotional strength and love as they face the changes brought by his aging.

Many images in the first two stanzas suggest the father's physical weakness: "the leg that weakens [. . .] the curtain of mist that falls over one eye"; the lost concentration and "fine sense of direction." In addition, he has become dependent on other family members. When he takes a walk with his daughter, she has to slow down "to match his pace." She describes him as being similar to "a child who keeps pulling on your hand."

Another change that might be seen as weakening is the way he no longer keeps his feelings inside himself. For much of his life, this man has saved his emotional energy for his work. His daughter explains that a familiar photograph of him, teaching with his

> chair tipped back
> against the lecture-room wall—shows
> a man talking, love of his work lighting
> his face—in a way we seldom saw at home.

Now instead of putting his emotions into his work, he freely tells his daughter, "I love you so much." So his ability to keep up his reserve with his family is no longer there. True, in a way he has weakened, but also he now shows real feelings for his daughter, which is a kind of emotional strength. It's as if the weakening of the body has allowed his strong feelings to come out. They were simply trapped inside.

The daughter, too, shows her emotional strength. Recalling her mother's observation that "[your father] never liked / to talk about feelings," the speaker honestly describes the father she knew when she was growing up as someone who didn't show too much affection at home. However, she doesn't seem bitter and angry, which would show weakness. Instead, she loves her father the way he is now. She doesn't berate him for what happened in the past. Also, even though it seems like her father didn't spend too much time with the family in the past, she is still willing to take walks with him and to talk to him. She doesn't hold a grudge or retaliate by rejecting him.

The father has grown stronger in family relationships even though his body has grown weaker. The daughter shows that she is strong because she accepts the love her father has begun to express. Both the father and the daughter use the emotional strength brought about by his aging to express the connection they feel to each other. Both say, "I love you," which are words they may not have spoken out loud before.

Exercise

Read several works from the anthology chapters (Chapters 6 through 12) and then, using the process demonstrated with Joann's paper, plan and write an evaluation of the beliefs and values expressed in one of the works. Keep the principles presented in the following Guidelines box in mind.

GUIDELINES

Writing an Evaluation of Beliefs and Values

1. Identify the beliefs and values expressed in the work, making note of specific details that demonstrate these beliefs and values.
2. Think about the criteria you will use to evaluate those beliefs and values.

GUIDELINES, continued

3. Consider what questions might be raised concerning those beliefs and values. (If you share those values, imagine the response of someone who does not.)
4. To expand your thinking, consider interviewing others who might be particularly interested in the values and beliefs expressed in the work.
5. Decide whether your evaluation will support or question (perhaps even refute) the values and beliefs expressed in the work.
6. List your reasons for supporting, questioning, or refuting these values and beliefs.
7. Remember to reread the work frequently to make certain you are responding to values and beliefs actually expressed there.
8. Make certain the opening section of the paper makes clear both the values and beliefs expressed in the work and the approach you are taking toward those values and beliefs.
9. Make certain the conclusion sums up the evaluation—the reasons you support and subscribe to (or do not support and subscribe to) the beliefs and values expressed in the work.

SUMMARY

Strategies for Discovering and Exploring Ideas

1. Write journal entries about the work (page 92).
2. Discuss the work with others (page 102).
3. Make lists of questions or observations about the work (page 115).
4. Write a paraphrase of a poem or of a complex section of a story, play, or essay (page 124).
5. Interview someone who has special interest or expertise in the theme or subject of the work (page 135).
6. Research the ideas of others on the work (pages 162–63).

Strategies for Evaluating Your Audience

1. Consider the readers' interests (page 93).
2. Consider the readers' knowledge (page 93).
3. Consider the readers' opinions (page 93).
4. Consider the readers' values (pages 116, 135).

Strategies for Revising

1. Give the paper an accurate, inviting title (page 93).
2. Open with a paragraph that indicates the paper's purpose and intrigues the reader (page 93).
3. Conclude with a paragraph that follows logically from the rest of the paper and that does more than summarize (page 93).
4. Use clear transitions to show the relationship between sections of the paper, between paragraphs, and between sentences (page 109).
5. Use evidence—details, reasons, and examples—from the work to support your ideas (pages 109, 117).
6. Keep summaries of works very short (no more than a few sentences at most). Know the difference between summarizing and discussing your own ideas (page 124).
7. Make sure your ideas are logically presented (pages 138–40).
8. Make sure the organization of your paper is clear (pages 105, 116, and 138).

Strategies for Editing

1. Avoid overuse of the verb "to be," expletives, passive voice, and nominalizations (pages 98, 109).
2. Use parallel structure effectively (page 109).
3. Make careful word choices (page 118).
4. Be concise (page 128).
5. Integrate quotations well and punctuate them accurately (pages 140–42).

Strategies for Proofreading

1. Rewrite fragments and comma splices as complete sentences (page 98).
2. Make subjects and verbs agree (page 110).
3. Make verb tenses agree (page 110).
4. Identify and revise misplaced modifiers (page 119).
5. Make sure that pronoun references are clear (page 142).
6. Make pronouns agree with the nouns to which they refer (pages 142–43).
7. Punctuate lines of poetry correctly (pages 140–41).
8. Use apostrophes correctly (page 130).
9. Use quotation marks correctly (pages 140–41).
10. Format titles correctly (pages 142–43).
11. Check for spelling and typographical errors.

Argument, Critical Thinking, and Research

ARGUMENT AND CRITICAL THINKING

Throughout this text, you will find various discussions on the process of critical thinking: For instance, Chapter 4 discusses ways in which writing encourages critical thinking (page 87–88). Chapter 6 suggests ways in which reading various works of literature comparatively and in relationship to specific themes leads to thinking critically (page 193). This chapter considers the process of developing an argument through critical thinking. For instance, to build a thoughtful argument you need to evaluate carefully the details you plan to use as evidence. In addition, to think critically about a controversial issue you need to be willing to entertain multiple points of view and to sort through those viewpoints to arrive at the thesis for an argument you believe you can logically develop and support.

Definition of Argument

To many people, the word "argument" brings to mind images of anger and bitter conflict. Sometimes it seems as if the world is filled with argument, in this sense of the word. Talk show hosts invite guests and audience members to disagree heatedly with each other, sometimes to the point of physical violence. Sports fans, players, and coaches (and even Little League parents) contest referees' and umpires' decisions with what can, at best, be called colorful language and energetic gestures. Politicians appearing on television panels take turns calling each other "incompetent," "dishonest," or "unpatriotic."

Another definition of argument, however, calls for a different kind of response to the situations described in the previous paragraph. According to this more formal definition, which applies to argument in academic settings, speakers or writers can address areas of disagreement or controversy without taking a negative or aggressive approach to a subject. Instead, in this context making a strong argument means learning how to think critically, to read closely, to observe carefully, and to research extensively in order to support a point of view. In addition, writing a strong argument requires considering points of view that might be different from your own and refuting those points. Through presenting carefully chosen evidence, writers strive to convince their audience that their view deserves consideration.

Purpose for Argument

Although some arguments are written to persuade others to change their minds about a view they already hold, many written arguments have a broader purpose. They seek primarily to demonstrate, through the use of well-chosen evidence, that the writer's main idea is reasonable. When a writer proposes a main idea that is subject to question, that idea is called a **claim**. In arguments related to literature, the main claim is usually proposed in the thesis statement. As the argument is developed, it is usually supported by a series of smaller claims. To arrive at a main claim, the writer often begins with a preliminary question, then investigates the question, and after having considered the evidence encountered through this search, formulates a thesis (claim). The smaller claims that support the main claim may include logical appeals (which are objectively verifiable) as well as emotional appeals (which attempt to reach an audience through appeals to values, needs, and feelings). There are many possible approaches to writing arguments about literature. In fact, all of the writing assignments described in Chapter 4 can be described as arguments because the primary purpose of each of those assignments is to convince the reader to accept the writer's thesis as reasonable. Here is a list of some of the most common topics for writing an argument about a literary work, illustrated by a preliminary question, a thesis statement (claim), and a possible approach to developing the argument and providing smaller claims to support the thesis.

Topics for Argument

> *Topics related to similarities and differences within or among works of literature.*

Example of preliminary question: What are the differences and similarities between Prince Hamlet and his father?

Example of thesis for argument: *Most readers see Hamlet and his stepfather, King Claudius, as opposites; however, they are alike in several significant ways.*

Here, the writer would probably begin by explaining why most readers see Hamlet and Claudius as different, briefly stating and giving evidence for those differences. Then the writer would argue why, in spite of these contrasts, the two characters actually have similarities that are significant in some way to the theme of the work. (For a detailed example of a paper that makes an argument through comparison and contrast, see pages 101–14, where student writer Walter Johnson argues that although the poems "Slipping" and "Do Not Go Gentle into That Good Night" both describe aging fathers, the two poems provide significantly different points of view.)

Topics related to evaluation of a character's moral or ethical choices and behaviors.

Example of preliminary question: Is Hamlet justified when he condemns his mother for her marriage to King Claudius?

Example of thesis for argument: *While Hamlet condemns his mother, Queen Gertrude, for her hasty marriage to King Claudius, there are convincing reasons to argue that she, in fact, made an ethically correct decision.*

To address this topic, the writer might first research beliefs about remarriage to a husband's brother in the Elizabethan era. Then the writer might explain why Hamlet believes his mother's decision to be unethical. The main body of the paper would be devoted to finding textual evidence from the play, in the form of direct quotations or paraphrases, to refute the reasons Hamlet (and Elizabethan society) might give for condemning Gertrude's remarriage. (For a detailed example of a paper that makes an argument through evaluation, see pages 135–45, where student writer Joann Epstein argues that the speaker and her father in the poem "Slipping," who may appear to be weak, in fact demonstrate considerable strength.)

Topics related to gender, class, or racial issues.

Example of preliminary question: Is Ophelia a passive victim to the actions and wishes of the other characters?

Example of thesis for argument: *Ophelia's responses to Hamlet, to her father, Polonius, and to her brother, Laertes, suggest that she is not simply a passive victim. In fact, in several instances she challenges the roles imposed on women of her time in surprising and witty ways.*

A writer might begin this argument by finding quotations from literary scholars who have seen Ophelia as a flat, somewhat stereotypical "discarded girlfriend" figure. In addition, the writer might find examples in the text of the play that seem to support this interpretation. The body of the paper would then be devoted to presenting reasons why Ophelia does not fit this stereotype and to refuting the reasons others have given that she does. (For further discussion of sociological approaches to literature that could lead to literary arguments, see "Sociological Criticism," page 85).

Topics related to the meaning of significant words, images, or phrases.

Example of preliminary question: What is the real significance of the advice "To Thine Ownself Be True?"

Example of thesis for argument: *One of the most frequently repeated quotations from* Hamlet *is "To Thine Ownself Be True." However, it can be argued that the meaning of this statement is highly ironic because it comes from a speech by Polonius, a character whose word cannot be trusted and who often appears to be foolish.*

In an argument about this topic, a writer would need to look closely at the character of Polonius, at his relationship with other characters, and at the nature of the advice he gives. In addition, the writer would closely examine the primary words in the command "To thine own self be true," considering possible definitions and applications to the situations within the play, as contrasted to the way the words might be understood outside the context of the play. (For a detailed example of a paper that makes an argument related to diction, consider the analysis written by Catherine Hupel, pages 119–21. Her thesis proposes that in Joan Aleshire's poem "Slipping," some of the figurative language in the poem indicates "a darker side" to the "new closeness" between the speaker and her father. She looks very carefully at the images and diction of the poem and makes her argument through her analysis of this language.)

Topics related to the theme of a work.

Example of preliminary question: What is the significance of the complicated family relationships in *Hamlet?*

Example of thesis for argument: *The theme of* Hamlet *cannot be stated easily. In fact, it can be argued that both* Hamlet, *the play, and* Hamlet, *the character, suggest a complex theme related to the intricacies of family relationships as well as to the nature of a true prince.*

A writer might develop this argument by citing examples from the text of *Hamlet* that suggest that his relationship to his mother, to his father, and to his uncle have both personal and public political implications. The conclusion of the argument—and its purpose—might be to argue for a specific way of stating the theme, making sure that this statement of the theme is supported by the evidence provided in the body of the paper. (For further discussion of theme in literary works, see "Ideas," pages 53–56).

Topics related to the comparison of a literary work to a work in another genre.

Example of preliminary question: Why did the director of the Miramax film decide to use present day New York City for the setting of his production of *Hamlet?*

Example for thesis of argument: *The Miramax film production of* Hamlet, *set in present-day New York City, suggests that human fears, hopes, and motivations have changed very little in the past 400 years.*

A writer working with this argument might begin by noting first the differences that are apparent between the play and the film and then, in the body of the paper, cite scenes from each work that suggest the similarities set forth in the thesis. (For a brief discussion of the Miramax film production of *Hamlet*, see page 378. Also, to see a paper that addresses comparisons and contrasts between a poem and a work of graphic art, see Janice Moore's argument that Death as depicted by Randall Jarrell's "Knight, Death, and the Devil" is significantly different from Death as depicted in Albrecht Dürer's engraving with the same name, insert page 4.)

Topics related to the setting of a literary work.

Example of preliminary question: Why is the coldness and bitterness of the weather stressed so much in the first act of *Hamlet?*

Example of thesis for argument: *The element of cold, which is a significant part of the setting of* Hamlet *beginning in act 1, scene 1, becomes even more significant as the play progresses.*

Close reading to gather evidence plays an important role in the development of nearly all literary arguments. A writer addressing this topic would need to read the play closely to gather as many references as possible to cold (whether temperature or a symbolic representation of the emotions of various characters). The writer might develop the argument by discussing, first, the physical elements of cold and then moving on to argue that this aspect of the setting reflects the actions and ethical choices of various characters in the play. (For further discussion of elements of setting, see "Places and Times," pages 41–47.)

Topics related to cultural and historical background.

Example of preliminary question: Who was the original audience for *Hamlet* and how did the expectation of this audience respond to the play?

Example of thesis for argument: *Although* Hamlet *is set in the royal court of early 16th-century Denmark, it was written and performed for an audience of Elizabethan English men and women from different classes and backgrounds. The cultures of both early 16th-century Denmark and of Elizabethan England must be considered in an evaluation of the play's theme.*

Developing this argument would require considerable research into the historical background of the play's setting and of Shakespeare's England. Because it would be impossible for a relatively short argument paper to address all the similarities and differences, the writer would probably choose two or three significant aspects of the culture to address. For instance, the intrigue behind the succession to the throne might be significant to both cultures and also to the play's theme. The writer might, then, decide to focus the argument on this particular historic detail. (For a discussion of historical criticism, see page 86.)

Topics related to interpretation.

Example of preliminary question: Does Hamlet have flaws of character, and if so, what are they?

Example of thesis for argument: *The flaws in Hamlet's character can be interpreted not only through his own speeches and actions, but also through the way other characters in the play describe him.*

Developing this argument requires close reading of the lines in the play where other characters are describing Hamlet. To understand these passages clearly, a writer might present an explication of a particularly challenging speech, looking at both the denotative and connotative meanings of the words. (For a detailed example of an argument made through explication, consider the paper written by Matthew Cejak, pages 132–34. His thesis proposes that in Dylan Thomas's poem "Do Not Go Gentle into That Good Night" the images and sound patterns in the poem reflect the theme of resistance to death.)

In addition, to develop the interpretation of Hamlet's character flaws, the writer would need to analyze what he or she discovered through close reading, perhaps looking for patterns in the way various characters describe Hamlet. The writer might look particularly closely at the differences in the way Hamlet is described, and might offer evidence to suggest that no one description provides a completely accurate view of this protagonist. (For a detailed example of a paper that makes an argument through analysis, consider the paper written by Catherine Hupel, pages 119–21.)

WRITING AN ARGUMENT: THE PROCESS

In some cases, an argument may be written to address a controversy related to literary texts. For instance, readers (including literary scholars) may disagree about the interpretation of a character as brave or cowardly. To argue for or against a particular interpretation requires close reading, critical thinking, and also, in many cases, research on the views others have of this controversy. To understand some of the many aspects to consider in writing an argument related to a controversy about literary texts, read the following story, "The Storm" by Kate Chopin. Later in this chapter, student writer Josh LaChance provides an example of the steps involved in writing an argument about a literary controversy. In addition, on page 186, you will find a copy of Josh's paper on a controversy related to "The Storm."

KATE CHOPIN (1851–1904)

The Storm

The leaves were so still that even Bibi thought it was going to rain. Bobinôt, who was accustomed to converse on terms of perfect equality with his little son, called the child's attention to certain sombre clouds that were rolling with sinister intention from the west, accompanied by a sullen, threatening roar. They were at Friedheimer's store and decided to remain there till the storm had passed. They sat within the door on two empty kegs. Bibi was four years old and looked very wise.

"Mama'll be 'fraid, yes," he suggested with blinking eyes.

"She'll shut the house. Maybe she got Sylvie helpin' her this evenin'," Bobinôt responded reassuringly.

"No; she ent got Sylvie. Sylvie was helpin' her yistiday," piped Bibi.

Bobinôt arose and going across to the counter purchased a can of   5
shrimps, of which Calixta was very fond. Then he returned to his perch on the keg and sat stolidly holding the can of shrimps while the storm burst. It shook the wooden store and seemed to be ripping great furrows in the distant field. Bibi laid his little hand on his father's knee and was not afraid.

II

Calixta, at home, felt no uneasiness for their safety. She sat at a side window sewing furiously on a sewing machine. She was greatly occupied and did not notice the approaching storm. But she felt very warm and often stopped to mop her face on which the perspiration gathered in beads. She unfastened her white sacque at the throat. It began to grow dark, and suddenly realizing the situation she got up hurriedly and went about closing windows and doors.

Out on the small front gallery she had hung Bobinôt's Sunday clothes to dry and she hastened out to gather them before the rain fell. As she stepped outside, Alcée Laballiere rode in at the gate. She had not seen him very often since her marriage, and never alone. She stood there with Bobinôt's coat in her hands, and the big rain drops began to fall. Alcée rode his horse under the shelter of a side projection where the chickens had huddled and there were plows and a harrow piled up in the corner.

"May I come and wait on your gallery till the storm is over, Calixta?" he asked.

Come 'long in, M'sieur Alcée."

His voice and her own startled her as if from a trance, and she seized   10
Bobinôt's vest. Alcée, mounting to the porch, grabbed the trousers and snatched Bibi's braided jacket that was about to be carried away by a sudden gust of wind. He expressed an intention to remain outside, but it was soon apparent

that he might as well have been out in the open: the water beat in upon the boards in driving sheets, and he went inside, closing the door after him. It was even necessary to put something beneath the door to keep the water out.

"My! What a rain! It's good two years sence it rain' like that," exclaimed Calixta as she rolled up a piece of bagging and Alcée helped her to thrust it beneath the crack.

She was a little fuller of figure than five years before when she married; but she had lost nothing of her vivacity. Her blue eyes still retained their melting quality; and her yellow hair, dishevelled by the wind and rain, kinked more stubbornly than ever about her ears and temples.

The rain beat upon the low, shingled roof with a force and clatter that threatened to break an entrance and deluge them there. They were in the dining room-the sitting room-the general utility room. Adjoining was her bed room, with Bibi's couch along side her own. The door stood open, and the room with its white, monumental bed, its closed shutters, looked dim and mysterious.

Alcée flung himself into a rocker and Calixta nervously began to gather up from the floor the lengths of a cotton sheet which she had been sewing.

15   "If this keeps up, Dieu sait° if the levees goin' to stan it!" she exclaimed.

"What have you got to do with the levees?"

"I got enough to do! An' there's Bobinôt with Bibi out in that storm—if he only didn' left Friedheimer's!"

"Let us hope, Calixta, that Bobinôt's got sense enough to come in out of a cyclone."

She went and stood at the window with a greatly disturbed look on her face. She wiped the frame that was clouded with moisture. It was stiflingly hot. Alcée got up and joined her at the window, looking over her shoulder. The rain was coming down in sheets obscuring the view of far-off cabins and enveloping the distant wood in a gray mist. The playing of the lightning was incessant. A bolt struck a tall chinaberry tree at the edge of the field. It filled all visible space with a blinding glare and the crash seemed to invade the very boards they stood upon.

20   Calixta put her hands to her eyes, and with a cry, staggered backward. Alcée's arm encircled her, and for an instant he drew her close and spasmodically to him.

"Bonte!"° she cried, releasing herself from his encircling arm and retreating from the window. "The house'll go next! If I only knew w'ere Bibi was!" She would not compose herself; she would not be seated. Alcée clasped her shoulders and looked into her face. The contact of her warm, palpitating body when he had unthinkingly drawn her into his arms, had aroused all the old-time infatuation and desire for her flesh.

"Calixta," he said, "don't be frightened. Nothing can happen. The house is too low to be struck, with so many tall trees standing about. There! aren't

Dieu sait: God knows. *Bonte:* Goodness.

you going to be quiet? Say, aren't you?" He pushed her hair back from her face that was warm and steaming. Her lips were as red and moist as pomegranate seed. Her white neck and a glimpse of her full, firm bosom disturbed him powerfully. As she glanced up at him the fear in her liquid blue eyes had given place to a drowsy gleam that unconsciously betrayed a sensuous desire. He looked down into her eyes and there was nothing for him to do but to gather her lips in a kiss. It reminded him of Assumption.

"Do you remember—in Assumption, Calixta?" he asked in a low voice broken by passion. Oh! she remembered; for in Assumption he had kissed her and kissed and kissed her; until his senses would well nigh fail, and to save her he would resort to a desperate flight. If she was not an immaculate dove in those days, she was still inviolate; a passionate creature whose very defenselessness had made her defense, against which his honor forbade him to prevail. Now—well, now—her lips seemed in a manner free to be tasted, as well as her round, white throat and her whiter breasts.

They did not heed the crashing torrents, and the roar of the elements made her laugh as she lay in his arms. She was a revelation in that dim, mysterious chamber; as white as the couch she lay upon. Her firm, elastic flesh that was knowing for the first time its birthright, was like a creamy lily that the sun invites to contribute its breath and perfume to the undying life of the world.

The generous abundance of her passion, without guile or trickery, was   25
like a white flame which penetrated and found response in depths of his own sensuous nature that had never yet been reached.

When he touched her breasts they gave themselves up in quivering ecstasy, inviting his lips. Her mouth was a fountain of delight. And when he possessed her, they seemed to swoon together at the very borderland of life's mystery.

He stayed cushioned upon her, breathless, dazed, enervated, with his heart beating like a hammer upon her. With one hand she clasped his head, her lips lightly touching his forehead. The other hand stroked with a soothing rhythm his muscular shoulders.

The growl of the thunder was distant and passing away. The rain beat softly upon the shingles, inviting them to drowsiness and sleep. But they dared not yield.

III

The rain was over; and the sun was turning the glistening green world into a palace of gems. Calixta, on the gallery, watched Alcée ride away. He turned and smiled at her with a beaming face; and she lifted her pretty chin in the air and laughed aloud.

Bobinôt and Bibi, trudging home, stopped without at the cistern to make   30
themselves presentable.

"My! Bibi, w'at will yo' mama say! You ought to be ashame'. You oughta' put on those good pants. Look at 'em! An' that mud on yo' collar! How you got that mud on yo' collar, Bibi? I never saw such a boy!" Bibi was the picture of pathetic resignation. Bobinôt was the embodiment of serious solicitude as he strove to remove from his own person and his son's the signs of their tramp over heavy roads and through wet fields. He scraped the mud off Bibi's bare legs and feet with a stick and carefully removed all traces from his heavy brogans. Then, prepared for the worst—the meeting with an over-scrupulous housewife, they entered cautiously at the back door.

Calixta was preparing supper. She had set the table and was dripping coffee at the hearth. She sprang up as they came in.

"Oh, Bobinôt! You back! My! But I was uneasy. W'ere you been during the rain? An' Bibi? He ain't wet? He ain't hurt?" She had clasped Bibi and was kissing him effusively. Bobinôt's explanations and apologies which he had been composing all along the way, died on his lips as Calixta felt him to see if he were dry, and seemed to express nothing but satisfaction at their safe return.

"I brought you some shrimps, Calixta," offered Bobinôt, hauling the can from his ample side pocket and laying it on the table.

35 "Shrimps! Oh, Bobinôt! You too good fo' anything!" And she gave him a smacking kiss on the cheek that resounded, "J'vous reponds,° we'll have a feas' to-night! umph-umph!"

Bobinôt and Bibi began to relax and enjoy themselves, and when the three seated themselves at table they laughed much and so loud that anyone might have heard them as far away as Laballiere's.

IV

Alcée Laballiere wrote to his wife, Clarisse, that night. It was a loving letter, full of tender solicitude. He told her not to hurry back, but if she and the babies liked it at Biloxi, to stay a month longer. He was getting on nicely; and though he missed them, he was willing to bear the separation a while longer—realizing that their health and pleasure were the first things to be considered.

V

As for Clarisse, she was charmed upon receiving her husband's letter. She and the babies were doing well. The society was agreeable; many of her old friends and acquaintances were at the bay. And the first free breath since her marriage seemed to restore the pleasant liberty of her maiden days. Devoted as she was to her husband, their intimate conjugal life was something which she was more than willing to forego for a while.

So the storm passed and everyone was happy. *1898*

J'vous reponds: I tell you.

More Resources on
Kate Chopin and "The Storm"

In *ARIEL*
- Brief biography of Chopin
- Complete texts of "The Storm" and "The Story of an Hour," both with hyperlinked comments, and the text of Chapters 1 to 3 of *The Awakening*
- Analysis of irony in "The Storm" and "The Story of an Hour"
- Bibliography of scholarly works on Chopin

In the **Online Learning Center** for *Responding to Literature*
- Brief biography on Chopin
- List of major works by Chopin
- Web links to more resources on Chopin
- Additional questions for experiencing and interpreting Chopin's writing

Argument and Controversy

Writing an essay that proposes an argument about a controversy in a literary text requires that a writer look at two views on an issue and consider both of them (and possibly additional views) carefully. Sometimes, the evidence to support the thesis of the argument comes entirely through close reading of the literary work (or works) that are the focus of the essay. Many times, however, a writer needs to do research to make the strongest argument possible. Through close reading and research—in addition, sometimes, to discussion with others—the writer formulates a thesis that he or she finds convincing, and then writes a paper trying to convince others that this point of view is worthy of consideration.

Determining a Thesis for Argument

The process of writing an argument, of course, does not usually proceed in a clean, direct path from point A to point B. For example, your initial response after reading a short story such as Kate Chopin's "The Storm" (page 153) may be to see a potential controversy for readers of Chopin's work. For instance, some readers respond negatively to the main characters and their actions, while other readers believe that these characters and their actions should not be condemned. Your immediate reaction may lead you to make statements and ask questions in class discussion. Formulating questions related to a work is espe-cially important since these questions may provide one path to formulating a tentative thesis. Often such questions also suggest a fruitful path for research. (For examples of preliminary questions leading to a thesis [claim], see pages 148–52).

In addition, the responses of the professor and other students to thought-provoking questions may move you to reconsider your initial reading, and you may return to the text to find support for your point of view. You may also look carefully to see what support there may be for those responses with which you disagreed.

After considering details discovered through your new close reading, you may change your mind or you may find your original point of view con-firmed. If you decided to pursue this controversy in a paper, you might then do research in books, journals, and online sources. Once again, the path proba-bly will not be completely straightforward. Each new article or chapter in a book may bring new evidence to your attention, and you may find yourself refining the thesis of your argument again.

One Student's Process for Writing an Argument about Literature

Choosing a Topic for Argument   Before deciding to research and write an argument on a question related to a literary text, it is important to remember that not all topics are appropriate for argument. Some matters of fact that can easily be checked through reliable sources are not legitimate argument topics. For instance, if someone in a class discussion says that Kate Chopin must have been writing in the later part of the twentieth century given the subject mat-ter of "The Storm," it is easy to refute this point by citing any number of reli-able sources that show she died in 1904. So it is not necessary to pursue this question through a thoughtfully developed written argument—one sentence (with documented evidence) proves the point.

While there are many ways to write arguments about literature, some of the most productive arguments are those that lead the writer to identify the theme or themes of the work. (For a detailed discussion of "theme" see pages 55–56). When Josh LaChance was in the early stages of writing an argument re-lated to Kate Chopin's story "The Storm," he worked with other members of his class to brainstorm possible thesis statements. They considered some of the topics for argument explained on pages 148–52, as well as some variations of those top-ics. As part of their initial prewriting, class members focused on the following possible topics and, in response, drafted these initial thesis statements (claims):

- Moral or ethical choices made by characters.

   Possible thesis: The moral choices made by Calixta and Alcée and the consequences of those choices suggest that judgment about such actions is not always simple.

- The significance of setting in establishing theme.

   Possible thesis: As many readers have noted, the elements of setting in "The Storm" suggest passion, but in addition they may also suggest ugliness and danger.

- The way literary devices, such as irony or symbolism, support or fail to support a particular way of reading the text.

   Possible thesis: While the final words of "The Storm" state that "everyone was happy," these words may be considered ironic.

- The relationship of the title to the theme (or themes) of the work.

   Possible thesis: The storm in Kate Chopin's short story by that title refers not only to the rain, thunder, and lightning of the setting, but also to the actions and conflicts of the characters.

- The way literary language, for instance metaphor or patterns of imagery, suggest the theme (or themes) of the work.

   Possible thesis: The images Kate Chopin chooses to describe Alcée and Calixta's love making suggest that this act is beautiful, not sinful.

- New insights that the theory of a particular school of criticism, for example, feminist or Marxist criticism (page 85), might bring to ways of reading the work.

   Possible thesis: In considering the relationship between Alcée and Calixta, it is important to explore the significance of the differences in the culture and class to which each belongs.

Exercise

Consider a short story, poem, play, or essay suggested by your instructor or chosen from the list below. Read this work and, individually or as a small group project, brainstorm possible preliminary questions and thesis statements (claims). Refer to the "Topics for Argument" on pages 148–52, as well as to the example of Josh LaChance's paper (page 153).

Short Stories:

"The Red Convertible"	Louise Erdrich	218
"Sonny's Blues"	James Baldwin	412
"Roman Fever"	Edith Wharton	547
"Hills Like White Elephants"	Ernest Hemingway	839
"The Things They Carried"	Tim O'Brien	934

Poems

Plays

Essays

Considering Audience   During the process of exploring a question leading to the thesis of an argument, it is important to think about the audience for whom you are writing. As Josh planned to write his argument, he kept these questions in mind:

- How diverse is the audience?

   For example, are your readers of widely differing ages? Do they seem to hold mainly the same ethical views? Do they come from different kinds of communities and from different parts of the country or the world? Or do they mainly come from comparable and geographically similar locations? For Josh's paper, the audience would be his professor and his fellow classmates, so he needed to think about the views and responses of these people.

- How much does the audience already know about the subject (see page 93)?

   For example, since Josh's class had read and discussed Kate Chopin's "The Storm," he knew he did not need to provide the details of the story's plot. However, when he later decided to include references to "At the 'Cadian Ball," the prequel to "The Storm," he knew that he would need to include a very brief summary.

- What are the values, opinions, assumptions, and moral or ethical views of the audience (see pages 137–38)?

- In considering this aspect of audience, you evaluate what your readers' values and ethical views might lead them to think about the point you are arguing. This consideration is particularly important when you are anticipating opposing points of view, which you must address to make your argument convincing. For example, Josh knew from class discussion that several people in his audience held strongly traditional views of marriage. So he knew he'd need to keep that in mind as he wrote about Calixta's, Alcée's, and Bobinôt's choices and actions.

Exploring Ways to Refine the Thesis and Support the Argument As suggested earlier, identifying a question that will lead to an argument about a literary text, proposing a thesis (claim) for the argument, and discovering support for the argument will not be a straightforward or simple task. The value of learning this process lies in the fact that it requires constant vigilance and critical thinking. Most important, the process requires an open mind and a willingness to refine and change the thesis of the argument when the evidence you are seeking does not fit your original point of view. As you explore your topic, consider the following strategies:

Close Reading   For nearly any formal argument, written or oral, in academic settings or in the workplace or community, close reading of original texts is essential. An example of using close, active reading to refine ideas and find evidence can be found in Chapter 1 (pages 8–11).

Discussion and Interviews   Discussions, either formal or informal, or interviews with someone knowledgeable about your topic can help you test your thesis and find new ways of thinking about your topic and your supporting evidence.

Library and Online Research   Many arguments, especially those written in an academic setting, will require the use of the library and of online research. Finding out what experts have to say about your topic can be one of the best ways to determine the approach you want to take and the way you want to frame your thesis. Research can also help you discover details, reasons, and examples to present as evidence that your thesis is reasonable and worthy of consideration.

ARGUMENT AND RESEARCH

The Research Question

Most research papers, written for all subject areas, begin with the writer identifying a question. For instance, in a history course the research question might be "Was President Lincoln a racist?" In a business course, the question might be "What impact has Internet crime had on small business?" These questions lead writers to investigate sources, both primary and secondary. For a literature paper beginning with a research question on Kate Chopin's fiction, the **primary source** might be the short story "The Storm" while **secondary sources** would include books and articles written about Kate Chopin and her works. The process of investigating the initial question may lead to a research paper that has primarily a **persuasive aim.**

The Persuasive Research Paper

The aim of a persuasive research paper is to develop an argument that will convince readers that a particular point of view is worthy of consideration. As we have seen, often the preliminary research question that begins the process addresses a controversy. For example, after reading the story "The Storm," Josh LaChance formulated a preliminary question: "Is Bobinôt just a simple and somewhat comic character?" The question itself implies that some readers would argue for this view of Bobinôt. By formulating a question, the writer keeps an open mind while gathering and evaluating information. Then the writer refines the question, develops and investigates a tentative thesis, and finally states it as a formal thesis (claim).

Exploring the Research Question

To gather information, Josh began by making an appointment with a reference librarian, David Bauer. With David's help, Josh discovered many possibilities within the four main categories of resources: reference works, such as specialized encyclopedias; monographs and other books; printed periodicals; and online resources.

Resources for Research: Reference Works   These valuable resources can provide background information for almost any research project. It's often a good idea to consult them as you begin your research. These books are usually kept in the library's reference room and often cannot be checked out; however, most libraries provide photocopiers, which students can use for a small fee. For example, for Josh's project, David suggested the *Annual Bibliography of English Language and Literature.* In addition, Josh was able to find useful background information in *The Dictionary of National Biography* and *American Women Writers: A Critical Reference Guide from Colonial Times to the Present.*

Monographs and Other Books   Josh was already familiar with this resource and knew how to use the library's **online catalogue** to find books relating to Chopin's work. He put in the key words "Kate Chopin," which produced a list of books by this author, as well as books written about her and her works. David provided Josh with more options, however, by explaining the process of **interlibrary loan** so that Josh could have access to books not held by his college's library. Most colleges and universities can provide this service. The only drawback to interlibrary loan is that it often takes several weeks to get the book, so you have to get an early start on research for the process to work.

Printed Periodicals   While many periodicals (journals and magazines) and some newspapers (like the *New York Times*) can be accessed directly through online databases such as *EBSCOhost* and *InfoTrac*, most college and university libraries maintain subscriptions to many of these resources in printed form. David explained to Josh how to use some of the online databases that provide citations but not full text articles. He also showed him how to use the *Reader's Guide to Periodical Literature*, which is available in both print and online form. In some cases, the library may have printed copies of a journal or magazine you need. If not, they can usually be accessed via the interlibrary loan process.

Online Resources   Josh used the **Internet** often and for many purposes, but when he tried to use his favorite **search engine** (program for finding information) to research his topic, he was frustrated with the number of hits—possible Web sites—he got. David explained to him how to limit the search effectively. (See Guidelines for Locating Online Resources, page 164.) In addition, David provided useful information on evaluating Internet resources (see Guidelines for Evaluating Internet Resources, page 165).

David also described to Josh the various **online databases** to which his library subscribed, noting that these databases had the advantage of being carefully reviewed so that by using them Josh had a better chance of quickly finding the reliable sources he would be seeking for his paper (see Guidelines for Using Online Resources, page 164). A source that is particularly useful to writers doing research on a literary topic is the *MLA International Bibliography of Books and Articles in the Modern Languages and Literatures*. As is true of many libraries, Josh's library offered the *MLA Bibliography* as an online resource (CD-ROM) as well as in print form. David helped Josh to understand the organization of the print form of this important research tool, which provides listing of books as well as articles in scholarly journals published in any specified year. The authors are grouped according to their nationality and according to the period in which they wrote. So, for instance, to find resources on Kate Chopin in the printed *MLA Bibliography* Josh searched the section on American Literature, in the subsection 1800–1899. If he were using the online version, he would be able to search directly by author, title, or topic. Once he found some promising citations, Josh searched in other online databases, such as *EBSCOhost*, and in the library's online catalog to locate them.

GUIDELINES

Locating Online Resources

1. Understand the **distinctive features** of each search engine or database you use. Read the help screens of each one to discover answers to the following questions:
   - Can you search by author's name? If so, do you need to reverse the author's first and last names? (Chopin, Kate instead of Kate Chopin)
   - Can you search by title?
   - Can you search for a phrase, or must you use a key word (an identifying word; for example, instead of using "the poetry of Kate Chopin" does this search engine or database require that you begin with the key word "Kate Chopin"?)
   - Can you organize the hits by date, so that you can find the most recent materials quickly?
   - Does the search engine or database arrange hits in order, with those most likely to be relevant appearing first?

2. Understand how to use **search terms**. (The use of search terms can vary according to the search engine or database you are using, but most allow you to use at least some of the following strategies. Consult the help screens for specific information on search terms.)
   - Enclose phrases in quotation marks: "Vietnam War"
   - Enclose proper names in quotation marks: "Flannery O'Connor"
   - Use the word AND or the plus sign (+) to make your search more specific:
     violence AND women
     violence AND women AND "New York"
     +violence+women
   - Use parentheses and the word OR to include common synonyms for your key terms:
     violence AND (women OR females)
   - Use the words AND NOT or the minus sign (–) (with no space after it) to avoid getting links to articles or Web sites that do not address your topic:
     vegans AND NOT vegetarians
     vegans –vegetarians
   - Use the asterisk ★ to *truncate* (shorten) terms in order to find variations of your search terms:
     mechan★ (will find mechanical, mechanic, mechanism)

Evaluating Sources

Once you have located sources, it is important to evaluate them for accuracy, reliability, timeliness, and possible bias. You must consider the expertise of the writer as well as the reputation of the publisher.

Print Sources An article appearing in *The New York Times* or *Harper's Magazine* would have credibility with most readers because these are well-established and highly respected publications that stand by the accuracy of their reporting. On the other hand, an article appearing in *The National Enquirer* might contain information that is questionable at best. Most readers would not consider a tabloid such as *The National Enquirer* to be a convincing source.

For most topics on which you are writing, you will want to find the most recent sources available. Even on a topic such as Kate Chopin, who lived in the nineteenth century, scholars are discovering new biographical information and insights every day.

You will also need to be aware of any biases (special interests) that a publication or author may have. Having a special interest does not mean that the publication is unreliable, but it does suggest a particular emphasis or point of view. For instance *The Journal of Women in Culture and Society* might look at gender issues in works of literature in great depth and might be particularly useful for topic related to gender issues.

Internet Resources Like print sources, Internet resources must be carefully evaluated. You need to be especially cautious, though, because anyone can post information on the Web. In addition, some search engines, such as Google, organize links according to their popularity, with the ones that are accessed most frequently appearing first. However, these are not always the most useful resources. To make your use of the Internet most effective, consider the following guidelines:

GUIDELINES

Evaluating Internet Resources

For each internet source that you consider, think about the following issues:

- **Authority:** What are the credentials of the individual or organization who has posted this information? For example, information posted by

(continued)

GUIDELINES, continued

a professor at a university is likely to be more accurate than a research paper written by a high-school student on the same topic.

- **Source:** What type of organization hosts the site on which the information appears? Is it from an academic institution, a business, a government organization, or an individual? The last part of the Web address (also called the *domain*) can help you determine where the information is coming from. Typical domain indicators are .com (a commercial or business site), .gov (a site maintained by a government agency), .org (a site maintained by a nonprofit organization), and .mil (a military site). A tilde (~) in a web address means that the page belongs to an individual. This person may have expertise in the area you are researching, or he or she may simply be expressing undocumented opinions. You need to be careful about using such sites to gather data for research papers because it is difficult to be sure of their accuracy.

- **Intent:** What is the intention of the Web site? Does it aim simply to give a brief overview of the topic you are covering? If so, it might not provide enough depth to be a truly useful resource. Does it aim to sell a product? (For example, is it selling a book on the author you are researching.) If so, the information about that product may be slanted.

- **Currency:** How recently has the site been posted or updated? Is it up-to-date? For many research topics, you need to have absolutely current information in order to make accurate judgments. To check the currency of a site, you should look for the posting or revision date at the beginning or end. You can also evaluate a site's currency by testing the *links* it provides. **Links** are words or phrases that are usually underlined or in bold print. When you click on these words or phrases, you should be able to get to other sites containing information relevant to the topic of the site you are currently visiting. If the links have become outdated and nonfunctional, it's a clue that the site you've found has not been updated recently and may not be current.

Planning an Argument and Formulating the Thesis

After he had gathered resources on "The Storm," Josh read through them, taking notes as he progressed (for details on note taking, see pages 170–73). He discovered that Kate Chopin had written another story, set five years earlier than "The Storm" and involving the same characters.

To explore his evaluation of Bobinôt, which was different from the evaluation of most students in his class, he decided to locate and read the earlier story, "At the 'Cadian Ball." After reading this additional primary source, Josh read several articles and chapters in books about the two stories in which Bobinôt appears as a character. He took notes from these sources and then reread and organized the notes (for details on note taking, see pages 170–73). He then returned to the two stories to find additional details that would support the thesis he had now formulated: "Many readers ignore Bobinôt or see him as a somewhat comic individual who is to be pitied. However, he is, in fact, a much more complex and significant character."

Drafting an Argument

As Josh drafted his argument, he kept in mind that he needed to do the following:

- Provide evidence from primary and secondary resources to support his claims.
- Consider and address points that would oppose his own claims.
- Remember the importance of thinking logically and of avoiding logical fallacies (see Guidelines on Rational Appeals, pages 167–69).

GUIDELINES

Rational Appeals

To evaluate the claims and the support for those claims in an argument, consider the following points:

- *Have you provided sufficient evidence?* Providing just one or two details from a literary work may not be enough to support a major claim. Make certain that you have offered the audience as much evidence as possible.
- *Have you used only relevant evidence?* For instance, in a paper about the character of Bobinôt, it may be tempting to talk about other Cajun characters in Kate Chopin's work, but unless a direct connection is made with her treatment of Bobinôt, this evidence would be irrelevant and off track.
- *Have you qualified statements where necessary?* Very seldom can words such as *all, every,* and *never* be used accurately. To be believable, statements

(continued)

GUIDELINES, continued

often require such qualifying words as *some, most,* or *in many cases.* For instance, saying that "Readers look at Bobinôt as a simple and somewhat stupid character" is almost certainly not accurate. To be more precise and convincing, say "Some readers look at Bobinôt . . ."

- *Have you successfully avoided* logical fallacies *(flaws in reasoning)?* Logical fallacies often sound reasonable, but to a critical reader they are a sign that the writer's thinking has gone astray. Sometimes, fallacies result from a writer's carelessness; other times a writer may purposely use fallacious reasoning, hoping to manipulate the unwary reader. In your own writing, avoid logical fallacies. When reading or listening to a speaker, be alert for these errors in reasoning. Logical fallacies include—but are not limited to—the following:

Logical Fallacies

- *Begging the Question (Circular Reasoning):* Making a statement in which the claim and the proof are actually variations of the same point.

  Example: We can see that Clarisse is a sly character because she is cunning.

  Explanation: "sly" and "cunning" mean the same thing, so this assertion just goes around in circles and does not provide convincing evidence.

- *Bandwagon:* Claiming that because a large number of people act or think in a certain way that action or way of thinking must be correct.

  Example: Except for Bobinôt, no one at the ball thought that Alcée's actions were suspect, so Bobinôt must have been wrong.

  Explanation: There could be other explanations. For instance, Bobinôt could be more perceptive than the rest of the people at the ball. The fact that a large number of people hold—or do not hold—an opinion does not necessarily prove it is right—or wrong.

- *Either-Or Fallacy (False Dilemma):* Suggesting that there are only two alternatives when, in fact, there are other possibilities.

  Example: Alcée had to make a choice. He had to marry either Calixta or Clarisse.

  Explanation: Alcée does not have to marry either woman. He could remain single, or marry someone else.

GUIDELINES, continued

- *False Cause*: Claiming that because one event happened before another, the first event caused the second to happen.

  Example: Bobinôt went into town with Bibi, which caused Calixta to have an affair with Alcée.

  Explanation: There is no evidence that Bobinôt's trip to town caused Calixta's sexual encounter with Alcée. Just because the trip to town happened first, does not mean it caused the event that followed.

- *Irrelevant Argument*: The Latin term for this fallacy is *non sequitur*, which means "it does not follow." An irrelevant argument occurs when a conclusion is based on evidence that cannot support it.

  Example: If Bobinôt just keeps bringing presents to Calixta, she will continue to be happy and in a good mood.

  Explanation: The reader knows that while Calixta may appreciate Bobinôt's gift, her happy mood almost certainly comes from her response to the sexual encounter with Alcée.

Revising an Argument

After writing his first draft, Josh took into consideration the various strategies for revising, editing, and proofreading introduced in Chapter 4 (see Revising Focus: pages 97, 109, 117, 124 and 138; Editing Focus: pages 98, 109, 118, 128, and 140; Proofreading Focus: pages 98, 110, 119, 130, and 142). In addition, because he was using multiple primary and secondary sources, as well as his own ideas, he paid special attention to the rules for documenting those sources correctly. (See Using and Documenting Sources on pages 169–75 and Using and Documenting Quotations From Literary Works on pages 175–85). In addition, he carefully checked the format of his "Works Cited" list (see Guidelines: Compiling a List of Works Cited," page 181).

USING AND DOCUMENTING SOURCES

As you do research, whether with traditional print sources or online sources, you'll find that taking notes is an essential strategy that enables you to keep track of all the information you discover. In some cases, a source may yield only a small amount of useful information, whereas other sources will contain a wealth of helpful material. Taking notes can help you to organize the material you have discovered.

Taking Notes

There are many ways to take and to store notes. Different writers and different writing tasks may call for a variety of strategies. For instance, some people prefer to use handwritten notecards; others type their notes on a computer, storing them in different files to organize the information they have gathered. Some writers photocopy or print out resources and then highlight or underline important information and make notes to themselves in the margin. If you use this method, you should keep the photocopies in an orderly folder (or set of folders), which will allow you to return to them easily during the writing process. Whatever method you choose, as you take notes, it is essential to remember four points:

- Organize carefully.
- Paraphrase and summarize to avoid copying long quotations.
- Paraphrase sparingly. It is preferable to summarize information briefly.
- Copy quotations that you believe to be essential carefully and accurately.

Organizing Your Notes Some useful strategies for staying organized include the following:

- Use a new note card or new page for each new piece of information.
- Arrange your notes after each note-taking session. You may find that your notes begin to fall into categories, for instance, arguments for your thesis and arguments against your thesis. Sorting your notes into categories may suggest ways to organize your paper. In addition, you will see more easily the parts of your paper that require more research.
- Be sure to identify your source on each page of your notes, so you will know where to give credit when you document the information. (For information on documenting sources, see pages 173–81.)
- Record all the information you will need to document each source on a separate card or page. It is essential to have a written record of this information so that you do not have to waste time retracing your steps when you write in-text citations and your "Works Cited" list (for detailed information on documenting sources, see pages 173–81.)

Summarizing and Paraphrasing In most cases, you will want to summarize or paraphrase potentially useful information that you find in your sources. When you **paraphrase,** you restate information from a source in your own words and using your own sentence structure. When you **summarize,** you reduce a large amount of information to its most essential points and restate them in your own words. Some useful strategies for summarizing and para-phrasing when you are taking notes include the following:

- Read each source you have discovered and decide whether or not that source has information that will support your thesis.
- For each useful source, begin by writing down on a separate card or page all of the information you will need to cite the source in your paper.   *card 1*
- Use a key word from the title of the source as an identifier at the top   *card 2* of the notecard or page.
- Number the cards or pages so that you will know the sequence in which you took the notes.
- Paraphrases or summaries should always be written in your own words, not the words of the source. When you are writing a paraphrase, you should also use your own sentence structure. In other words, you should express the source's ideas in your own way.
- Paraphrases or summaries should include only the ideas from the source, not your own reactions or responses to the source. These can be included on separate note cards or pages, or in the margin if you are working with photocopies or printouts.
- Enclose any phrases that come directly from the source in quotation marks. Then you will know to use quotation marks in your paper and thus avoid plagiarism. (For a detailed discussion of avoiding plagiarism, see pages 174–75).

Copying Quotations In an argument about a literary work you will usu-ally quote from the work itself to support your thesis. If you are consulting other sources of information about the work, you might want to copy phrases or sentences from the source that are especially striking—that would lose force if you were simply to paraphrase or summarize them. Such quotations should be used sparingly, but when used well they can strengthen your argument.

- Make a note to yourself to indicate the context of the quotation. For instance, is this quote suggesting a view that the author later challenges and argues against? If so, you need to remember that if you use that quotation, you need to indicate that the author disagrees with it.
- Copy all quotations accurately. Check to be sure that you have in-cluded all the words the author wrote. Check spelling and punctuation to be sure it is the same as the author's.
- Enclose the quotation in quotation marks so you will know it is a quo-tation and must be cited as such when you incorporate it into your paper (for more details on incorporating quotations, see pages 175–81).
- Use ellipses (three spaced periods) to indicate where you have omitted any of the author's words.

Sample Notecards Here are four sample note cards that show a bibliographic entry, a paraphrase, a summary, and a direct quotation. All four refer to the following paragraph:

When Chopin wrote "At the 'Cadian Ball" in 1892, did she envisage the denouement we find in "The Storm" of 1898? Did she have daring sequels in mind for such tales as "A Respectable Woman" and "Athenaise"? And, if she had such sequels in mind, what persuaded her to write this one when she did? It is my view that she did envisage daring sequels and, as Alcée's letter to his wife suggests, she may have had yet another story to tell about Calixta, Clarisse, Alcée and Bobinôt.

—from *The Real Kate Chopin,* p. 116, Lorraine Nye Eliot
Dorrance Publishing Company, Pittsburgh, PA, 2002

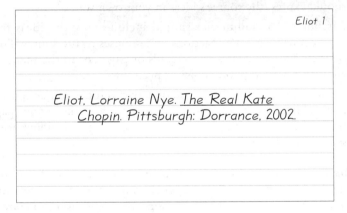

Figure 1. Bibliography note card.

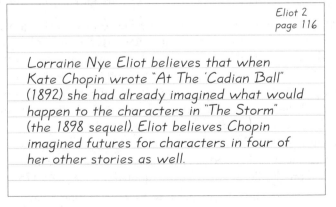

Figure 2. Paraphrase note card.

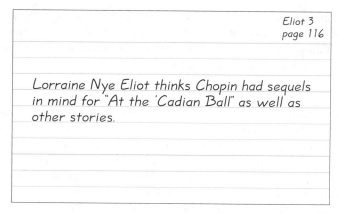

> Eliot 3
> page 116
>
> Lorraine Nye Eliot thinks Chopin had sequels in mind for "At the 'Cadian Ball" as well as other stories.

Figure 3. Summary note card.

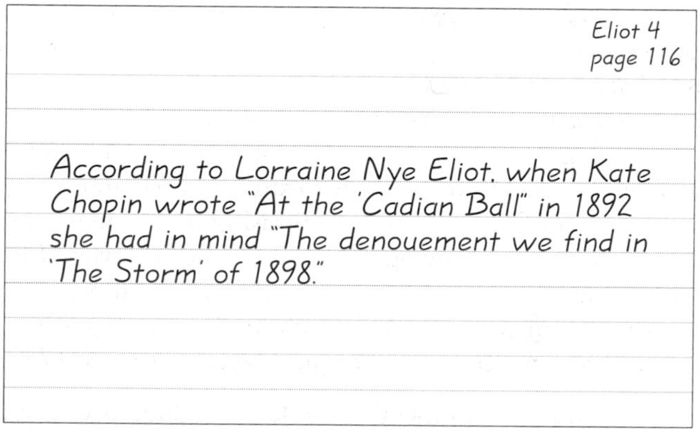

> Eliot 4
> page 116
>
> According to Lorraine Nye Eliot, when Kate Chopin wrote "At the 'Cadian Ball" in 1892 she had in mind "The denouement we find in 'The Storm' of 1898."

Figure 4. Quotation note card.

Determining What Needs to Be Documented

Whenever you use someone else's words or unique ideas, either by summarizing, paraphrasing or quoting directly, you must provide documentation to acknowledge your source. By providing documentation, you give credit to the sources you have consulted and enhance the credibility of your argument.

What Does Not Need to Be Documented In any research project, you will come across some information that nearly everyone, or at least everyone in a particular field, knows. That information—known as **common knowledge**—does not need to be documented. For example, most people in the United States know that Abraham Lincoln wrote the Gettysburg Address and delivered it on a Civil War battlefield, so that information would not need to be documented. In addition to commonly known facts, there are facts that not everyone in a general audience would know, but that are readily available in many sources. These do not need to be documented. For example, the fact that Kate Chopin was born in 1851 appears in hundreds of sources. So this date would not require documentation.

Avoiding Plagiarism In your writing, whether for college courses, for professional situations, or for personal purposes, you must respect your audience and the rights of other writers by providing documentation when you use work that is not your own and that is not common knowledge. **Plagiarism** may be defined as taking words or ideas written or originated by someone else and using them as your own. There are a number of systems for documenting quotations, paraphrases, and summaries of the work of others. In this chapter, the MLA system, which is widely used in the humanities, is demonstrated and explained.

It is important to understand that plagiarism occurs for different reasons. For instance, a writer who knowingly copies the work of another and tries to pass it off as her or his own work is guilty of an obvious and intentional form of plagiarism that is easy to avoid.

However, some inexperienced writers may not realize that even copying a few sentences or significant phrases from a source, without documentation, is also plagiarizing. Taking an original idea from a source and using it as your own is another form of plagiarism. Paraphrasing or summarizing a passage from another writer, without giving credit, is yet another type of plagiarizing.

The following examples will help you understand more clearly how to avoid plagiarism. All of the examples provided here refer to the paragraph taken from *The Real Kate Chopin* by Lorraine Nye Eliot (page 172).

> *Plagiarized:* It may be possible that while Kate Chopin was writing some of her stories, she was imagining lively sequels.
> *Reason:* The idea that Chopin had sequels in mind comes from Eliot's book and therefore, she must be given credit.
> *Correctly documented:* As Lorraine Nye Eliot suggests, it may be possible that while Kate Chopin was writing some of her stories, she was imagining lively sequels.

> *Plagiarized:* Lorraine Nye Eliot asks whether it is possible that when Kate Chopin wrote "At the 'Cadian Ball," she envisaged the denouement we find in "The Storm."
> *Reason:* While Eliot is mentioned here, the phrase "envisaged the denouement we find in 'The Storm'" is lifted almost exactly from Eliot's work. (The only difference is that the verb "envisage" has been changed to past tense.)
> *Correctly documented:* Lorraine Nye Eliot asks whether it is possible that when Kate Chopin wrote "At the 'Cadian Ball," "she envisage[d] the denouement we find in 'The Storm'" (116).

Note: Here the quoted words are enclosed in quotation marks; the past tense ending, a change made by the student, has been acknowledged by enclosing that change in brackets; and the title "The Storm" has been put within single quotation marks because it appears within a quotation. Finally, the ending parentheses with the page number have been added.

Exercise

Read the following sentence, from an article by Peggy Skaggs. Then read the sentences written by students who had read Skaggs' article. Decide whether each sentence is correctly documented or plagiarized. If a sentence is plagiarized, explain why and then revise so that it is correctly documented.

> Chopin views the question of human identity for everyone as a quest growing out of three often contradictory human drives—the drive for a sense of belonging, for love relationships with others, and for selfhood. (From *"The Boy's Quest in Kate Chopin's 'A Vocation and a Voice,'"* by Peggy Skaggs, *American Literature,* May 1979, p. 270.)

1. Kate Chopin sees characters who are seeking their identity as motivated by three forces: the desire to belong, the desire for romantic relationships, and the desire for an independent self.

2. As Angelo State Professor Peggy Skaggs suggests, Kate Chopin sees characters who are seeking their identity as motivated by three forces: the desire for a sense of belonging, for romantic relationships with others, and for selfhood.

3. As Angelo State Professor Peggy Skaggs suggests, Kate Chopin sees characters who are seeking their identity as motivated by three forces: "the desire for a sense of belonging, for love relationships with others, and for selfhood" (270).

USING AND DOCUMENTING QUOTATIONS FROM LITERARY WORKS: MLA STYLE

When you are ready to incorporate quotations from the literary work that you are writing about, as well as material from your sources, you should use the format established by the Modern Language Association.

Quoting from Poems

1. When you quote one line from a poem or a verse play, run the line in with your own words and enclose it in quotation marks:

> The narrator urges his father, "Do not go gentle into that good night."

2. When you quote two or three lines of poetry, you may either run them in with your own words or set them off separately. When you run them in with your own words, enclose the quotation in quotation marks, and indicate line breaks with a slash. Use a space before and after the slash.

> The narrator in "Slipping" tells us, "Age comes to my father as a slow / slipping: the leg that weakens, will / barely support him. . . ."

Note: The three dots at the end of the sentence (called an ellipsis) indicate that the line continues but that those words have been omitted here. The fourth dot is the period that would normally go at the end of the sentence.

3. When you quote more than three lines of poetry, you must set them apart from your own words by beginning a new line and indenting. Indent the quotation one inch or 10 character spaces. *Do not use quotation marks with an indented quotation.*

> The first stanza of Thomas's poem introduces its memorable images and rhythms:
>
> > Do not go gentle into that good night,
> >
> > Old age should burn and rave at close of day;
> >
> > Rage, rage against the dying of the light.
> >
> > Though wise men at their end know dark is right,
> >
> > Because their words had forked no lightning they
> >
> > Do not go gentle into that good night.

Quoting from Plays

1. When you are quoting from a verse play, follow the guidelines for quoting poems.
2. When you are quoting from a play that is divided into acts, scenes, and lines, you should indicate this information in parentheses following the quotation (see the example that follows item 3).
3. When you are quoting no more than three lines, run them in with your own words.

> Hamlet reminds the Queen, "I must be cruel only to be kind" (III.IV.182).

Note: The traditional format uses roman numerals for the act and scene and arabic numbers for the line or lines. Some instructors may prefer that you use arabic numbers for act, scene, and lines: (3.4.182).

Note also that the parenthetical information comes *after* the quotation marks but *before* the period.

4. When you are quoting more than three lines from a play, you must set them off from your own words by leaving an extra line of space and indenting. In this case, do not enclose the quotation in quotation marks, and place the parenthetical information *after* the period.

Example from a verse play

Hamlet reminds the Queen:

> I will bestow him, and will answer well
>
> The death I gave him. So again, good night.
>
> I must be cruel only to be kind
>
> Thus bad begins and worse remains behind. (III.IV.183–86)

Example from a prose play

In Fierstein's On Tidy Endings, Arthur tells Marion:

> His things are not yours to give away, they're mine! This death does not belong to you, it's mine! Bought and paid for outright. I suffered for it, I bled for it. I was the one who cooked his meals. I was the one who spoon-fed them. I pushed his wheel-chair. I carried and bathed him. (1100)

Note: Because this is a one–act play and does not have line designations, the citation is the page number on which the quotation appears in the book from which the play is taken.

Quoting from Fiction

1. When you are quoting no more than four lines, run them in with your own words.

    In Faulkner's "A Rose for Emily," the narrator calls Miss Emily "a fallen monument" (1051).

    Note: The citation is the page number on which the quotation appears in the book from which the story is taken. In a short paper that discusses only one or two stories, your instructor may not require this citation.

2. When you are quoting more than four lines from a work of fiction, you must set them off from your own words by beginning on a new line and indenting. Indent the quotation one inch or 10 character spaces. In this case, the quotation is not enclosed in quotation marks.

William Faulkner opens his short story "A Rose for Emily" with the narrator's description of the town's response to Miss Emily's death:

> When Miss Emily Grierson died, our whole town went to her funeral: the men through a sort of respectful affection for a fallen monument, the women mostly out of curiosity to see the inside of her house, which no one save an old manservant . . . had seen in at least ten years. (1051)

Note: The citation is the page number on which the quotation appears in the book from which the story was taken. The three dots are an ellipsis indicating that words are omitted from the original quotation.

3. When you quote a short passage from a work of fiction that contains dialogue, you must punctuate the dialogue as a quotation within a quotation.

Example of a short passage with dialogue

> The narrator explains the problem of confronting Miss Emily by describing the reaction of an important town official. " 'Dammit, sir,' Judge Stevens said, 'will you accuse a lady to her face of smelling bad?' " (1054).

Note: The quotation is set off by regular (double) quotation marks; the dialogue within the quotation is set off by single quotation marks. The page number citation appears after the question mark because the question mark, unlike the period, remains inside the quotation marks.

Example of a long passage (more than four lines) with dialogue

> The narrator's description of town gossip shows the difficulties Miss Emily faced in her new relationship with Homer:
>
> > At first we were glad that Miss Emily would have an interest, because the ladies all said, "Of course a Grierson would not think seriously of a Northerner, a day laborer." But there were still others, older people, who said that even grief could not cause a real lady to forget noblesse oblige—without calling it noblesse oblige. (1055)

Note: With a long passage, the quotation is indented but not enclosed in quotation marks. The dialogue, therefore, is set off by standard quotation marks rather than the single quotation marks. Note also that when you are indicating a range of numbers, MLA style omits the redundant digits in the hundreds and thousands; for example, 905–10, 1456–60 (rather than 905–910, 1456–1460).

Incorporating Material from Sources into Your Paper

The following list suggests some ways of incorporating someone else's words or ideas into the body of your paper. Items 1 through 4 illustrate these ways by referring to the following source material by Nancie Atwell:

> Like writing, reading becomes meaningful only when it involves the particular response of an individual—one's own ways of perceiving reality through the prism of written language. And, like writing, reading generates its most significant meanings when the reader engages in a process of discovery, weaving and circling among the complex of behaviors that characterizes genuine participation in written language. (From *In the Middle* by Nancie Atwell, Boynton-Cook Publishers, Portsmouth, N.H., 1987, p. 155.)

Item 5 in the list refers to another original source:

> New evidence suggests that at least two theaters used during Shakespeare's time may have been uncovered at a London construction site. One theater, the Swan, is believed to be at least 350 years old. (From "Shakespearean Theaters Reborn," *New York Times,* August 19, 1987, p. 56.)

1. A brief quotation, including the author's name:

   > Nancie Atwell believes that meaningful reading and writing both require "the particular response of an individual" (155).

   Because the author's name appears in the introduction to the quotation, document it simply by giving the page number where the original quotation appears. Place the page number in parentheses before the ending punctuation.

2. A brief quotation without the author's name:

   > "The particular response of an individual" gives meaning to both reading and writing (Atwell 155).

   Because the author's name does not appear in the text, you must provide it, along with the page number. Give the author's last name only. (However, if in your paper you cite two or more authors with the same last name, use both first and last name.) If you cite more than one source by the same author, use an abbreviated title (one or two significant words) to identify the work, for example, (Atwell, *Middle* 155).

3. A paraphrase or summary:

   > Nancie Atwell suggests that both reading and writing gain meaning only when they involve the unique reaction of one

person—an individual's special way of understanding his or her
world through the prism of literature (155).

Even though Atwell's sentences and phrases are not directly cited,
the writer uses this author's ideas. (Note particularly the use of the
prism image.) Therefore, the source must be documented. (For more
on documentation, see pages 169–75.) Because Atwell's name is mentioned, only the page number (in parentheses, before the final punctuation) is required. When the author's name is not mentioned, his or
her last name appears within the parentheses just before the page number, for example, (Atwell 155).

4. A long quotation:

> Those interested in the importance of the reader's response to
> literature should consider Nancie Atwell's thoughts:
>
> > Like writing, reading becomes meaningful only when it
> > involves the particular response of an individual—one's
> > own ways of perceiving reality through the prism of
> > written language. And, like writing, reading generates
> > its most significant meanings when the reader engages
> > in a process of discovery. . . . (155)

When you quote four or more typed lines, indent the quotation
one inch or 10 spaces from the left margin. Use the normal right margin. *Do not use quotation marks.* Provide documentation within parentheses *after* the final mark of punctuation.

If you do not cite the author's name in the introduction to the quotation, you must include it in the parenthetical documentation. If you do
cite the author's name in the introduction to the quotation, provide only
the page number.

5. A quotation from an unsigned source (for instance, an unsigned
newspaper article):

> The <u>New York Times</u> noted that a theater uncovered at a con-
> struction site in London "is believed to be at least 350 years old"
> ("Shakespearean" 56).

When the article has no author's byline, use an abbreviated title
(often the first word other than "a," "an," or "the") and the page number in parentheses.

6. A source written by two or more people:

If the source is written by two or three people, use all authors'
names. For instance, if your source is *No Man's Land* by Sandra Gilbert
and Susan Gubar, you could cite it in either of these ways:

> The writer's pen may be considered by some to be "a
> metaphorical pistol" (Gilbert and Gubar 3).

or

> Gilbert and Gubar note that some consider the writer's pen to
> be "a metaphorical pistol" (3).

If the source is written by four or more authors, give only the name of the first author, followed by "et al." Note that *et,* the Latin word for "and," is not an abbreviation and therefore requires no period. *Al.* is the abbreviation for the Latin *alia* (meaning "others") and does require a period. For instance, if the source is *Women's Ways of Knowing* by Mary Field Belenky, Blythe McVicker Clinchy, Nancy Rule Goldberger, and Jill Mattuck Tarule, you could cite it in either of these ways:

> Instructors should consider studies suggesting "that women
> cultivate their capacities for listening while encouraging men to
> speak" (Belenky et al. 45).

or

> As Belenky et al. remind us, instructors should consider studies
> suggesting "that women cultivate their capacities for listening
> while encouraging men to speak" (45).

Compiling a List of Works Cited

Documentation in the text of a paper and in parenthetical citations leads readers to a list of works cited. This list appears at the end of the paper and includes only those works that are actually paraphrased or quoted within your paper. Arrange entries in the list of works cited alphabetically so that the reader can find the full reference quickly.

The following list of sample entries illustrates the MLA bibliographic style. If you are using a type of source not included in this list, consult a more complete handbook or style guide.

Print Resources

1. Book by one author:

    Atwell, Nancie. <u>In the Middle</u>. Portsmouth: Boynton-Cook, 1987.

2. Book by two or three authors:

    Gilbert, Sandra M., and Susan Gubar. No Man's Land. New
        Haven: Yale UP, 1988.

3. Books by four or more authors:

    Belenky, Mary Field, et al. <u>Women's Ways of Knowing</u>. New
        York: Basic, 1986.

4. Book with an editor:

> Gill, Elaine, ed. Mountain Moving Day: Poems by Women. Tru-
> mansburg: Crossing, 1973.

5. Two or more books by the same authors (list in alphabetical order by title):

> Gilbert, Sandra M., and Susan Gubar. The Madwoman in the
> Attic. New Haven: Yale UP, 1979.
>
> ---. No Man's Land. New Haven: Yale UP, 1988.

6. Works in an anthology or collection:

> Atwood, Margaret. "Fishbowl." Mountain Moving Day: Poems by
> Women. Ed. Elaine Gill. Trumansburg: Crossing, 1973. 104–7.

7. Multiple works from the same collection or anthology:

Anthology

> Stanford, Judith, ed. Responding to Literature. 4th ed. New
> York: McGraw, 2002.

Works in the anthology

> Whitman, Walt. "The Dying Veteran." Stanford 982–83.
>
> Yeats, William Butler. "The Lake Isle of Innisfree." Stanford 544–45.

8. A later edition of a book:

> Coffin, Charles M. The Major Poets: English and American. 2nd
> ed. New York: Harcourt, 1959.

9. A reprint (for example, the paperback version of a hardcover book)

> Prejean, Sr. Helen. Dead Man Walking. 1993. New York: Vintage,
> 1994.

10. A translated book:

> Mann, Thomas. Death in Venice and Other Stories. Trans. David
> Luke. New York: Bantam, 1988.

11. An introduction, foreword, or afterword or other editorial apparatus:

> Bentley, Eric. Foreword. Collected Plays. By George Bernard
> Shaw. New York: New American Library, 1960.

12. An encyclopedia:

Signed article

> Camras, Marvin. "Acoustics." Funk and Wagnalls New
> Encyclopedia. 1986 ed.

Unsigned article:

"Acheans." Funk and Wagnalls New Encyclopedia. 1986 ed.

13. Multivolume work:

Graves, Robert. The Greek Myths. Vol. 2. New York: Braziller, 1967.

14. Article from a professional journal that paginates each issue separately (each new issue begins with page 1):

Johnson, Gale. "Ibsen's Tragic Comedies." The Center Magazine 12.2 (1979): 15–21.

15. Article from a professional journal that paginates issues continuously throughout the year: for instance, the first issue of 1991 might begin with page 1 and end with page 330. The second issue, then, would begin with page 331, and so on:

Heilman, Robert B. "Charlotte Brontë, Reason, and the Moon." Nineteenth-Century Fiction 14 (1960): 283–302.

16. Article in a newspaper:

Signed

Paulsen, Karen. "Poetry for the '90's." Boston Globe 12 Sept. 1990: A55.

Unsigned

"Shakespearean Theaters Reborn." New York Times 19 Aug. 1987, late ed., sec. A1: 56.

17. A book review:

Hackett, Joyce. "The Reawakening." Rev. of Kate Chopin: Complete Novels and Stories, ed. Sandra M. Gilbert. Harper's Magazine Oct. 2003: 82–86.

18. An article in a magazine:

McArdle, Elaine. "The Lost Boys." Boston Magazine Sept. 2003: 50–54.

Oral Communications

19. A personal interview:

Roth, Katherine. Personal Interview. 1 March 2004.

Media and Performance Sources

20. A television or radio program:

Masterpiece Theater. PBS. 5 Sept. 2004.

21. A film or videotape:

> <u>Tadpole</u>. Dir. Gary Winnick. Miramax, 2002.

22. A performance:

> <u>Down the Road</u>. By Lee Blessing. Dir. Wally Marzano. The Phil
> Bosakowski Theater, New York. 21 Jan. 2004.

Online Sources

23. Online book published independently:

> Austen. Jane. <u>Pride and Prejudice. Great Literature Online</u>.
> 1997–2004. 12 Sept. 2004
> <http//wwwclasicauthors.net/Austen/pandp/>.

24. Online book within a scholarly project:

> Austen, Jane. <u>Persuasion</u>. 1818. <u>Project Gutenburg</u>. Ed. Sharon
> Partridge. Feb. 1994. 23 Sep. 2004
> <http://wwwgutenburg.net/dirs/etext94/persu11.txt>.

25. Article in a scholarly journal, found online:

> McGrath, Sean. "Toward a Technology That Allows the Beauti-
> ful to Occur." <u>Animus</u> 8 (2003). 4 Sept. 2004 <http://
> www.swgc.mun.ca/animus/current/current.htm>.

26. Article in a magazine, found online:

> Flora, Carlin. "Opiate in a Minor: Pleasant Music Can Soothe
> Pain." <u>Psychology Today</u> Mar.–Apr. 2004. 4 Sept. 2004
> <http://www.findarticles.com/p/articles/mi_m1175/
> is_2_37/ai_1153444423>.

27. A review, found online:

> Millán, Naomi. Rev. of <u>Scorched Earth, Blighted Vision</u>, by Jerry
> Williams. <u>Gulf Coast: A Journal of Literature and Fine Arts</u>
> 16.1 (2004): 218–24. 4 Sept. 2004 <http://
> wwwgulfcoastmag.org/GCIssues/gcl_folder/
> 16.1%20Reviews/16.1Millan/9c16.1R.Milan.html>.

28. Work from an online subscription service:

> Westphal, Jonathan. "Thomas's 'Do Not Go Gentle into That
> Good Night.'" <u>Explicator</u> 52.2 (1994). EBSCOhost. Regina

Library, Rivier College, Nashua, NH. 1 July 2000
<http://ehostvgwl.com/>.

29. Work from a home page:

Shafer, Michael. HUX 543. Course home page. Sept. 1999–April
2000. Dept. of English, U. of California. 26 Sept. 1999
<http://www.csudh.edu/hux/syllabi/543/1html>.

Note: Additional information about documenting information from
the World Wide Web may be found at the following Web site:
<http://www.mla.org/>.

30. E-mail:

Colebrooke, Nancy. "Re: Divorced Parents." E-mail to Jean
Creeg. 23 Sept. 2003.

31. Listserv posting:

Wetzel, Karen A. "[LIBREF-L] ARL/OLMS Online Course: Measuring Library Service Quality (Oct. 12–Nov. 19, 2004)." Online posting. 8 Sep. 2004. Library Reference Issues. 23 Sep.
2003 <http://listserv.kent.edu/archives/libref-1.hmtl>.

32. Single-edition CD-ROMs:

"Dramatic Irony." Ariel: A Reader's Interactive Exploration of
Literature. CD-ROM. New York: McGraw, 2003.

GUIDELINES

Preparing the List of Works Cited

- Double-space entries.
- Double-space between entries.
- Begin the first line of each entry at the left margin.
- Indent the second and subsequent lines one-half inch or five spaces.
- Arrange entries in alphabetical order according to the first word of the
  entry (excluding "a," "an," or "the").

SAMPLE OF COMPLETED RESEARCHED ARGUMENT

Page number, preceded by student's name, in upper right corner.

Student's name and course information in upper left corner, double-spaced.

Josh LaChance

Professor Stanford

English 102

2 May 2005

Title centered.

A Closer Look at Bobinôt

Readers of Kate Chopin's short story "The Storm" often focus their attention mainly on the actions of Alcée and Calixta. The details of their love affair are powerful

Quotation from the story is integrated into sentence, with page number.

and the final words of the story, "So the storm passed and every one was happy" (156), lead many readers to look primarily at the actions of the two lovers. However, to really examine the conflict in this story, it is necessary to look at the character of Bobinôt, not only as he appears in "The Storm," but also as he appears in "At the 'Cadian Ball." As Peggy Skaggs, contributing editor to the *Heath*

Quotation from secondary source is presented, with the author's name in the introduction to the quotation.

Anthology of American Literature, notes, "'The Storm,' being a sequel to 'At the 'Cadian Ball' becomes much clearer in characterization and theme" when the two are read together. In fact, Bobinôt, whom readers may be tempted to ignore or look at as a somewhat comic, pitiful

Thesis statement.

individual, can be seen as a complex and significant character.

One view of Bobinôt is that he is weak and

Argument against alternate point of view about Bobinôt.

powerless. For instance, literary scholar Robert Wilson notes that when Calixta and Alcée begin gathering the clothes from the line because of the approaching storm, "Alcée grabs Bobinôt's pants, symbolically subverting the social and marital constraints that control Calixta." In addition, when Calixta worries that Bobinôt and their son,

LaChance 2

Bibi, may be harmed by the storm, Alcée replies, "Let us hope, Calixta, that Bobinôt's got sense enough to come in out of a cyclone" (Chopin, "Storm," 857). This comment suggests that Alcée sees Calixta's husband as just barely smart enough to get himself and his son out of a raging storm. Calixta does not reply, so we cannot tell if she agrees or disagrees. Perhaps her silence simply means that she is distracted by the storm and by the feelings she has for Alcée. However, it is important to note that, in this story, she never criticizes her husband directly to Alcée.

    In "At the 'Cadian Ball," which takes place five years earlier than the events in "The Storm," Bobinôt is shown as "good natured" (Chopin, "'Cadian," 223). Yet he also has deep feelings for Calixta, and when he learns that his rival, Alcée, has decided to attend the ball, Bobinôt makes a decision to attend also. Professor Bernard Koloski states that Bobinôt worries about Alcée's appearance because Alcée is of a higher social class than either Bobinôt or Calixta and thus threatens to "cut him off from Calixta and destroy his hopes" (56). So it might be easy to see Bobinôt's decision as just a way to benefit his own desires.

    However, the narrator tells us that Bobinôt believes that if Alcée has a "drink or two" it could "put the devil in his head" (224). Here it seems that Bobinôt is not just thinking of himself, but also of protecting Calixta against the intentions of Alcée. This thought process shows that Bobinôt can interpret the behavior of others, anticipate possible negative actions, and act to prevent them. He is not just a simple person, reacting to whatever happens at the moment. In addition, the narrator says that what Alcée "did not show outwardly was that he was in a mood for

Author's name, shortened title of story, and page number presented in parentheses.

Author's name, shortened title of second Chopin story, and page number in parentheses.

Support for view of Bobinôt as a complex character, taken from the earlier story.

ugly things tonight" (Chopin, "'Cadian," 223). The choice of the phrase "ugly things" indicates that his passion for Calixta may not be just a harmless fancy. And almost no one at the ball notices: "Poor Bobinôt alone felt it vaguely" (Chopin, "'Cadian," 223). So, even though a few minutes later Calixta taunts Bobinôt, claiming that he looks like an old cow, in fact, he is the only one who is smart enough to guess Alcée's intentions.

Later, when Alcée has deserted Calixta to follow Clarisse, a woman from his own social class, Bobinôt is the one who finds Calixta. Although he almost certainly suspects what has happened, Bobinôt does not say anything, except to warn Calixta to guard her dress against the wet weeds through which they walk. He knows Alcée has left her for another woman, but he is wise enough not to say anything. It is interesting that in "The Storm," it appears that Calixta has convinced herself that Alcée left her in order to protect her virtue. In this point, it would seem that it is Calixta who lacks perception and Bobinôt who has it.

When Calixta responds to her sadness and anger at Alcée's desertion by accepting Bobinôt's proposal, she refuses to kiss him. She looks at him with a face "that was almost ugly after the night's dissipation," (Chopin, "'Cadian," 227) yet he seems not to notice. When she demands to know if the acceptance of the proposal is not enough to satisfy him, he responds, "Oh, I'm satisfy, Calixta" (Chopin, "'Cadian," 227). He clearly understands that he is her second choice, but he loves Calixta and is happy to be her husband under any circumstances. His choice is made not out of stupidity, but with the knowledge of exactly where he stands.

LaChance 4

In "The Storm" Calixta seems in some ways to be the same person she was at the 'Cadian Ball, except that she is "a little fuller of figure" (856). She is still high spirited and wants her own way. Although she worries about Bobinôt and Bibi, it is Bobinôt who seems to take on many of the responsibilities of the household. Calixta may do the washing, but Bobinôt is the one who worries about keeping Bibi clean so that his mother will not be angry. He is the kind of father and husband who notices what will cause problems and tries to make things right. He also plans to bring Calixta some shrimp, her favorite food, hoping to please her with this treat. These details suggest that he is not stupid. Instead, he is perceptive. Although we know from the narrator's comment that Calixta's body knew "for the first time its birthright" (Chopin, "Storm," 858) when Alcée and she made love that the physical relationship between Calixta and Bobinôt is not ideal, Bobinôt keeps trying to build a family. He is persistent in following what he wants. It is also important to note that in "The Storm" Calixta does not taunt or mock Bobinôt. Instead she worries about his safety. She seems to have grown to recognize some of his good qualities.

So while Alcée may move in and out of Calixta's life, it is Bobinôt who is the steady anchor. At the end of "'Cadian Ball," Calixta grudgingly accepts Bobinôt's proposal. At the end of "The Storm," she seems to have become more accepting and caring of him, even before the sexual relationship with Alcée. Scholar Lorraine Nye Elliot believes that Chopin had in mind "daring sequels" and "may have had yet another story to tell about Calixta, Clarisse, Alcée, and Bobinôt" (116). If that is true, the sequel to "The Storm" may have shown Bobinôt

Additional support for thesis, taken from "The Storm."

Conclusion reinforces the view of Bobinôt as a complex character.

continuing to be loyal to his family, yet using his
perception to understand how complicated it is for that
family to be "happy." Bobinôt is an admirable and
somewhat complex character, not a simple buffoon.

LaChance 6

Works Cited

Chopin, Kate. "At the 'Cadian Ball." The Complete Works
    of Kate Chopin. Vol.1. Baton Rouge: Louisiana State
    UP, 1969. 222–27.

---. "The Storm." Responding to Literature. Ed. Judith
    Stanford. 4th ed. New York: McGraw, 2002, 853–59.

Eliot, Lorraine Nye. The Real Kate Chopin. Pittsburgh:
    Dorrance, 2002.

Koloski, Bernard. Kate Chopin: A Study of the Short
    Fiction. New York: Twayne, 1996.

Skaggs, Peggy. Heath Anthology of American Literature
    On-line. 12 Sept. 2003. <http://college.huco.com/
    english/heath/chopin.html>.

Wilson, Robert. "Feminine Sexuality and Passion: Kate
    Chopin's 'The Storm.'" The University of British
    Columbia, 22 Oct. 1992 <http://www.interchg.obc.ca/
    rw/eng304-1htm>.

*Works Cited begins a new
page. Title is centered.*

*Citation for second work
by Chopin begins with
three hyphens.*

Citations for books.

*Citation for an online
article.*

What lessons can experience teach? What gifts can innocence give?

not yet read

6

Innocence and Experience

ON READING LITERATURE
THEMATICALLY: CRITICAL THINKING

The first five chapters of this text have suggested many ways to read, think, talk, and write about individual works of literature. As you approach the selections in Chapters 6 through 15, your responses should be enhanced by keeping the suggestions from Chapters 1 to 5 in mind.

Chapters 6 through 15 invite you to go beyond considering the individual work; they provide an opportunity to explore stories, poems, plays, and essays that share thematic links. Looking for similarities and differences among the works that you read and, most important, considering the implications of the comparisons and contrasts you make constitute a highly sophisticated and complex way of thinking critically. For example, the selections in Chapter 6 lead the reader to consider the concepts of innocence and experience. Each selection in this chapter explores the passage from a relatively simple view of some aspect of the world to a more complicated and often puzzled view of the same aspect. As you read these selections, they should raise questions in your mind about the nature of this passage. In addition, by reading several selections that focus on this theme, you'll no doubt discover ambiguities, contrasts, and comparisons in the ways different authors have chosen to explore the two worlds of innocence and experience. The dialogues—spoken, written, or within your own mind—that result from such discoveries should lead you to see both the literary selections and the world in which you live differently and more fully.

By reading literature thematically, you move beyond analysis of individual works and, instead, consider broad and varied views of topics and ideas that are part of the literary world but that are also part of the historic as well as the present living world. The themes addressed in this text, in addition to Innocence and Experience, include Roots, Identity, and Culture; Love and Hate; Families; Nature; War and Power; Technology and Ethics; and Death. As you think about the titles of these thematic chapters, consider how you form your opinions and beliefs about these topics that are of such profound significance to everyone's life. Most people develop their beliefs and opinions through such sources as popular media, personal observation and experience, conversations with friends and relatives, and statements from authority figures (for example, government, religious leaders, and teachers). Literature provides another resource for investigating, exploring, and testing our beliefs and opinions about significant aspects of our world and our lives.

Most people can remember specific moments when a cherished idea was suddenly challenged, or when a friend or relative showed a particularly disillusioning weakness or unexpected strength. These are examples of the moments that move us from the comfortable and comforting world of innocence to the more challenging and complex world of experience.

As you read the selections in this chapter, keep in mind the following questions:

1. What are the events in life that move individuals from innocence to experience?
2. Do most of the events occur in childhood? In adolescence? In adulthood?
3. How does the movement from innocence to experience differ in these different stages of life?
4. What is lost or gained as individuals make the journey from innocence to experience?
5. How are the passages from innocence to experience affected by the various subcultures (socioeconomic, professional, gender, ethnic, religious) to which the individual belongs?

Fiction

 ## NATHANIEL HAWTHORNE (1804–1864)
Young Goodman Brown

After his sea captain father died while on a journey, Nathaniel Hawthorne was raised mainly by his mother, living in various family households in Maine and Massachusetts. From his earliest years, Hawthorne was fascinated with his ancestor William Hathorne, a magistrate in early Salem, Massachusetts, and with

William's son John, who was one of the three presiding judges at the witch trials of 1692. Many of his short stories, as well as two of his novels—The Scarlet Letter *and* The House of Seven Gables—*explore the moral complexities related to life in Puritan America.*

Young Goodman° Brown came forth, at sunset, into the street at Salem village; but put his head back, after crossing the threshold, to exchange a parting kiss with his young wife. And Faith, as the wife was aptly named, thrust her pretty head into the street, letting the wind play with the pink ribbons of her cap while she called to Goodman Brown.

"Dearest heart," whispered she, softly and rather sadly, when her lips were close to his ear, "prithee put off your journey until sunrise and sleep in your own bed to-night. A lone woman is troubled with such dreams and such thoughts that she's afeared of herself sometimes. Pray tarry with me this night, dear husband, of all nights in the year."

"My love and my Faith," replied young Goodman Brown, "of all nights in the year, this one night must I tarry away from thee. My journey, as thou callest it, forth and back again, must needs be done 'twixt now and sunrise. What, my sweet, pretty wife, dost thou doubt me already, and we but three months married?"

"Then God bless you!" said Faith, with the pink ribbons; "and may you find all well when you come back."

"Amen!" cried Goodman Brown. "Say thy prayers, dear Faith, and go to bed at dusk, and no harm will come to thee."   5

So they parted; and the young man pursued his way until, being about to turn the corner by the meeting-house, he looked back and saw the head of Faith still peeping after him with a melancholy air, in spite of her pink ribbons.

"Poor little Faith!" thought he, for his heart smote him. "What a wretch am I to leave her on such an errand! She talks of dreams, too. Methought as she spoke there was trouble in her face, as if a dream had warned her what work is to be done to-night. But no, no; 'twould kill her to think it. Well, she's a blessed angel on earth; and after this one night, I'll cling to her skirts and follow her to heaven."

With this excellent resolve for the future, Goodman Brown felt himself justified in making more haste on his present evil purpose. He had taken a dreary road, darkened by all the gloomiest trees of the forest, which barely stood aside to let the narrow path creep through, and closed immediately behind. It was all as lonely as could be; and there is this peculiarity in such a solitude, that the traveller knows not who may be concealed by the innumerable trunks and the thick boughs overhead; so that with lonely footsteps he may yet be passing through an unseen multitude.

Goodman: Polite term of address for a man who ranks below gentleman.

"There may be a devilish Indian behind every tree," said Goodman Brown, to himself and he glanced fearfully behind him as he added, "What if the devil himself should be at my very elbow!"

10   His head being turned back, he passed a crook of the road, and, looking forward again, beheld the figure of a man, in grave and decent attire, seated at the foot of an old tree. He arose at Goodman Brown's approach and walked onward side by side with him.

"You are late, Goodman Brown," said he. "The clock of the Old South was striking as I came through Boston, and that is full fifteen minutes agone."

"Faith kept me back a while," replied the young man, with a tremor in his voice, caused by the sudden appearance of his companion, though not wholly unexpected.

It was now deep dusk in the forest, and deepest in that part of it where these two were journeying. As nearly as could be discerned, the second traveller was about fifty years old, apparently in the same rank of life as Goodman Brown, and bearing a considerable resemblance to him, though perhaps more in expression than features. Still they might have been taken for father and son. And yet, though the elder person was as simply clad as the younger, and as simple in manner too, he had an indescribable air of one who knew the world, and who would not have felt abashed at the governor's dinner table, or in King William's° court, were it possible that his affairs should call him thither. But the only thing about him that could be fixed upon as remarkable was his staff, which bore the likeness of a great black snake, so curiously wrought that it might almost be seen to twist and wriggle itself like a living serpent. This, of course, must have been an ocular deception, assisted by the uncertain light.

"Come, Goodman Brown," cried his fellow-traveller, "this is a dull pace for the beginning of a journey. Take my staff, if you are so soon weary."

15   "Friend," said the other, exchanging his slow pace for a full stop, "having kept covenant by meeting thee here, it is my purpose now to return whence I came. I have scruples touching the matter thou wot'st° of."

"Sayest thou so?" replied he of the serpent, smiling apart. "Let us walk on, nevertheless, reasoning as we go; and if I convince thee not thou shalt turn back. We are but a little way in the forest yet."

"Too far! too far!" exclaimed the goodman, unconsciously resuming his walk. "My father never went into the woods on such an errand, nor his father before him. We have been a race of honest men and good Christians since the days of the martyrs; and shall I be the first of the name of Brown that ever took this path and kept—"

"Such company, thou wouldst say," observed the elder person, interpreting his pause. "Well said, Goodman Brown! I have been as well acquainted with your family as with ever a one among the Puritans; and that's no trifle to

---

King William: William III, king of England from 1689 to 1702. *wot'st:* Knowest.

say. I helped your grandfather, the constable, when he lashed the Quaker woman so smartly through the streets of Salem; and it was I that brought your father a pitch-pine knot, kindled at my own hearth, to set fire to an Indian village, in King Philip's war.° They were my good friends, both; and many a pleasant walk have we had along this path, and returned merrily after midnight. I would fain be friends with you for their sake."

"If it be as thou sayest," replied Goodman Brown, "I marvel they never spoke of these matters, or, verily, I marvel not, seeing that the least rumor of the sort would have driven them from New England. We are a people of prayer, and good works to boot, and abide no such wickedness."

"Wickedness or not," said the traveller with the twisted staff, "I have a   *20* very general acquaintance here in New England. The deacons of many a church have drunk the communion wine with me; the selectmen of divers towns make me their chairman; and a majority of the Great and General Court are firm supporters of my interest. The governor and I, too—But these are state secrets."

"Can this be so!" cried Goodman Brown, with a stare of amazement at his undisturbed companion. "Howbeit, I have nothing to do with the governor and council; they have their own ways, and are no rule for a simple husbandman° like me. But, were I to go on with thee, how should I meet the eye of that good old man, our minister at, Salem village? Oh, his voice would make me tremble both Sabbath day and lecture day!"

Thus far the elder traveller had listened with due gravity; but now burst into a fit of irrepressible mirth, shaking himself so violently that his snake-like staff actually seemed to wriggle in sympathy.

"Ha! ha! ha!" shouted he again and again; then composing himself, "Well, go on, Goodman Brown, go on; but, prithee, don't kill me with laughing."

"Well, then, to end the matter at once," said Goodman Brown, considerably nettled, "there is my wife, Faith. It would break her dear little heart; and I'd rather break my own."

"Nay, if that be the case," answered the other, "e'en go thy ways, Good-   *25* man Brown. I would not for twenty old women like the one hobbling before us that Faith should come to any harm."

As he spoke he pointed his staff at a female figure on the path, in whom Goodman Brown recognized a very pious and exemplary dame, who had taught him his catechism in youth, and was still his moral and spiritual adviser, jointly with the minister and Deacon Gookin.

"A marvel, truly, that Goody° Cloyse should be so far in the wilderness at night fall," said he. "But with your leave, friend, I shall take a cut through

---

King Philip's war: War waged between the Colonists (1675–1676) and the Wampanoag Indians, led by Metacomet, known as "King Philip." *husbandman:* A common man; sometimes, specifically, a farmer. *Goody:* Contraction of "Goodwife," a polite title for a married woman of humble rank.

the woods until we have left this Christian woman behind. Being a stranger to you, she might ask whom I was consorting with and whither I was going."

"Be it so," said his fellow-traveller. "Betake you the woods, and let me keep the path."

Accordingly the young man turned aside, but took care to watch his companion, who advanced softly along the road until he had come within a staff's length of the old dame. She, meanwhile, was making the best of her way, with singular speed for so aged a woman, and mumbling some indistinct words—a prayer, doubtless—as she went. The traveller put forth his staff and touched her withered neck with what seemed the serpent's tail.

30   "The devil!" screamed the pious old lady.

"Then Goody Cloyse knows her old friend?" observed the traveller, confronting her and leaning on his writhing stick.

"Ah, forsooth, and is it your worship indeed?" cried the good dame. "Yea, truly is it, and in the very image of my old gossip,° Goodman Brown, the grandfather of the silly fellow that now is. But—would your worship believe it?—my broomstick hath strangely disappeared, stolen, as I suspect, by that unhanged witch, Goody Cory, and that, too, when I was all anointed with the juice of smallage and cinquefoil and wolf's bane—"°

"Mingled with fine wheat and the fat of a new-born babe," said the shape of old Goodman Brown.

"Ah, your worship knows the recipe," cried the old lady, cackling aloud. "So, as I was saying, being all ready for the meeting, and no horse to ride on, I made up my mind to foot it; for they tell me there is a nice young man to be taken into communion to-night. But now your good worship will lend me your arm, and we shall be there in a twinkling."

35   "That can hardly be," answered her friend. "I may not spare you my arm, Goody Cloyse; but here is my staff, if you will."

So saying, he threw it down at her feet, where, perhaps, it assumed life, being one of the rods which its owner had formerly lent to the Egyptian magi. Of this fact, however, Goodman Brown could not take cognizance. He had cast up his eyes in astonishment, and, looking down again, beheld neither Goody Cloyse nor the serpentine staff but his fellow-traveller alone, who waited for him as calmly as if nothing had happened.

"That old woman taught me my catechism," said the young man; and there was a world of meaning in this simple comment.

They continued to walk onward, while the elder traveller exhorted his companion to make good speed and persevere in the path, discoursing so aptly that his arguments seemed rather to spring up in the bosom of his auditor than to be suggested by himself. As they went, he plucked a branch of maple to serve for a walking-stick, and began to strip it of the twigs and little boughs,

---

gossip: A close friend. *smallage, cinquefoil, wolf's bane:* Plants native to New England (possibly reputed to have been used in magical ceremonies).

which were wet with evening dew. The moment his fingers touched them they became strangely withered and dried up as with a week's sunshine. Thus the pair proceeded, at a good free pace, until suddenly, in a gloomy hollow of the road, Goodman Brown sat himself down on the stump of a tree and refused to go any farther.

"Friend," said he, stubbornly, "my mind is made up. Not another step will I budge on this errand. What if a wretched old woman do choose to go to the devil when I thought she was going to heaven: is that any reason why I should quit my dear Faith and go after her?"

"You will think better of this by and by," said his acquaintance, composedly. "Sit here and rest yourself a while; and when you feel like moving again, there is my staff to help you along."   40

Without more words, he threw his companion the maple stick, and was as speedily out of sight as if he had vanished into the deepening gloom. The young man sat a few moments by the roadside, applauding himself greatly, and thinking with how clear a conscience he should meet the minister in his morning walk, nor shrink from the eye of good old Deacon Gookin. And what calm sleep would be his that very night, which was to have been spent so wickedly, but so purely and sweetly now, in the arms of Faith! Amidst these pleasant and praiseworthy meditations, Goodman Brown heard the tramp of horses along the road, and deemed it advisable to conceal himself within the verge of the forest, conscious of the guilty purpose that had brought him thither, though now so happily turned from it.

On came the hoof-tramps and the voices of the riders, two grave old voices, conversing soberly as they drew near. These mingled sounds appeared to pass along the road, within a few yards of the young man's hiding-place; but, owing doubtless to the depth of the gloom at that particular spot, neither the travellers nor their steeds were visible. Though their figures brushed the small boughs by the wayside, it could not be seen that they intercepted, even for a moment, the faint gleam from the strip of bright sky athwart which they must have passed. Goodman Brown alternately crouched and stood on tiptoe, pulling aside the branches and thrusting forth his head as far as he durst without discerning so much as a shadow. It vexed him the more, because he could have sworn, were such a thing possible, that he recognized the voices of the minister and Deacon Gookin, jogging along quietly, as they were wont to do, when bound to some ordination or ecclesiastical council. While yet within hearing, one of the riders stopped to pluck a switch.

"Of the two, reverend sir," said the voice like the deacon's, "I had rather miss an ordination dinner than to-night's meeting. They tell me that some of our community are to be here from Falmouth and beyond, and others from Connecticut and Rhode Island, besides several of the Indian powwows,° who,

---

powwow: Here, a shaman or medicine man.

after their fashion, know almost as much deviltry as the best of us. Moreover, there is a goodly young woman to be taken into communion."

"Mighty well, Deacon Gookin!" replied the solemn old tones of the minister. "Spur up, or we shall be late. Nothing can be done, you know, until I get on the ground."

45   The hoofs clattered again; and the voices, talking so strangely in the empty air, passed on through the forest, where no church had ever been gathered or solitary Christian prayed. Whither, then, could these holy men be journeying so deep into the heathen wilderness? Young Goodman Brown caught hold of a tree for support, being ready to sink down on the ground, faint and overburdened with the heavy sickness of his heart. He looked up to the sky, doubting whether there really was a heaven above him. Yet, there was the blue arch, and the stars brightening in it.

"With heaven above, and Faith below, I will yet stand firm against the devil!" cried Goodman Brown.

While he still gazed upward into the deep arch of the firmament and had lifted his hands to pray, a cloud, though no wind was stirring, hurried across the zenith and hid the brightening stars. The blue sky was still visible, except directly overhead, where this black mass of cloud was sweeping swiftly northward. Aloft in the air, as if from the depths of the cloud, came a confused and doubtful sound of voices. Once the listener fancied that he could distinguish the accents of towns-people of his own, men and women, both pious and ungodly, many of whom he had met at the communion table, and had seen others rioting at the tavern. The next moment, so indistinct were the sounds, he doubted whether he had heard aught but the murmur of the old forest, whispering without a wind. Then came a stronger swell of those familiar tones, heard daily in the sunshine at Salem village, but never until now from a cloud of night. There was one voice, of a young woman, uttering lamentations, yet with an uncertain sorrow, and entreating for some favor, which, perhaps, it would grieve her to obtain; and all the unseen multitude, both saints and sinners, seemed to encourage her onward.

"Faith!" shouted Goodman Brown, in a voice of agony and desperation; and the echoes of the forest mocked him, crying, "Faith! Faith!" as if bewildered wretches were seeking her all through the wilderness.

The cry of grief, rage, and terror was yet piercing the night, when the unhappy husband held his breath for a response. There was a scream, drowned immediately in a louder murmur of voices, fading into far-off laughter, as the dark cloud swept away, leaving the clear and silent sky above Goodman Brown. But something fluttered lightly down through the air and caught on the branch of a tree. The young man seized it, and beheld a pink ribbon.

50   "My Faith is gone!" cried he, after one stupefied moment. "There is no good on earth; and sin is but a name. Come, devil; for to thee is this world given."

And, maddened with despair, so that he laughed loud and long, did Goodman Brown grasp his staff and set forth again, at such a rate that he seemed to fly along the forest path, rather than to walk or run. The road grew wilder and drearier and more faintly traced, and vanished at length, leaving him in the heart of the dark wilderness, still rushing onward with the instinct that guides mortal man to evil. The whole forest was peopled with frightful sounds—the creaking of the trees, the howling of wild beasts, and the yell of Indians; while sometimes the wind tolled like a distant church bell, and sometimes gave a broad roar around the traveller, as if all Nature were laughing him to scorn. But he was himself the chief horror of the scene, and shrank not from its other horrors.

"Ha! ha! ha!" roared Goodman Brown when the wind laughed at him. "Let us hear which will laugh loudest! Think not to frighten me with your deviltry! Come witch, come wizard, come Indian powwow, come devil himself, and here comes Goodman Brown. You may as well fear him as he fears you!"

In truth, all through the haunted forest there could be nothing more frightful than the figure of Goodman Brown. On he flew among the black pines, brandishing his staff with frenzied gestures, now giving vent to an inspiration of horrid blasphemy, and now shouting forth such laughter as set all the echoes of the forest laughing like demons around him. The fiend in his own shape is less hideous than when he rages in the breast of man. Thus sped the demoniac° on his course, until, quivering among the trees, he saw a red light before him, as when the felled trunks and branches of a clearing have been set on fire, and throw up their lurid blaze against the sky, at the hour of midnight. He paused, in a lull of the tempest that had driven him onward, and heard the swell of what seemed a hymn, rolling solemnly from a distance with the weight of many voices. He knew the tune; it was a familiar one in the choir of the village meeting-house. The verse died heavily away, and was lengthened by a chorus, not of human voices, but of all the sounds of the benighted wilderness pealing in awful harmony together. Goodman Brown cried out; and his cry was lost to his own ear by its unison with the cry of the desert.

In the interval of silence he stole forward until the light glared full upon his eyes. At one extremity of an open space, hemmed in by the dark wall of the forest, arose a rock, bearing some rude, natural resemblance either to an altar or a pulpit, and surrounded by four blazing pines, their tops aflame, their stems untouched, like candles at an evening meeting. The mass of foliage that had overgrown the summit of the rock was all on fire, blazing high into the night and fitfully illuminating the whole field. Each pendent twig and leafy festoon was in a blaze. As the red light arose and fell, a numerous congregation alternately shone forth, then disappeared in shadow, and again grew, as it were, out of the darkness, peopling the heart of the solitary woods at once.

"A grave and dark-clad company," quoth Goodman Brown.   55

In truth, they were such. Among them, quivering to-and-fro between gloom and splendor, appeared faces that would be seen next day at the council

---

demoniac: An evil spirit.

board of the province, and others which, Sabbath after Sabbath, looked devoutly heavenward, and benignantly over the crowded pews, from the holiest pulpits in the land. Some affirm that the lady of the governor was there. At least there were high dames well known to her, and wives of honored husbands, and widows, a great multitude, and ancient maidens, all of excellent repute, and fair young girls, who trembled lest their mothers should espy them. Either the sudden gleams of light flashing over the obscure field bedazzled Goodman Brown, or he recognized a score of the church-members of Salem village famous for their especial sanctity. Good old Deacon Gookin had arrived, and waited at the skirts of that venerable saint, his revered pastor. But, irreverently consorting with these grave, reputable, and pious people, these elders of the church, these chaste dames and dewy virgins, there were men of dissolute lives and women of spotted fame, wretches given over to all mean and filthy vice, and suspected even of horrid crimes. It was strange to see, that the good shrank not from the wicked, nor were the sinners abashed by the saints. Scattered also among their pale-faced enemies were the Indian priests, or pow-wows, who had often scared their native forest with more hideous incantations than any known to English witchcraft.

"But, where is Faith?" thought Goodman Brown; and, as hope came into his heart, he trembled.

Another verse of the hymn arose, a slow and mournful strain, such as the pious love, but joined to words which expressed all that our nature can conceive of sin, and darkly hinted at far more. Unfathomable to mere mortals is the lore of fiends. Verse after verse was sung; and still the chorus of the desert swelled between, like the deepest tone of a mighty organ; and, with the final peal of that dreadful anthem there came a sound, as if the roaring wind, the rushing streams, the howling beasts, and every other voice of the unconcerted wilderness were mingling and according with the voice of guilty man in homage to the prince of all. The four blazing pines threw up a loftier flame, and obscurely discovered shapes and visages of horror on the smoke wreaths above the impious assembly. At the same moment the fire on the rock shot redly forth and formed a glowing arch above its base, where now appeared a figure. With reverence be it spoken, the figure bore no slight similitude, both in garb and manner, to some grave divine of the New England churches.

"Bring forth the converts!" cried a voice that echoed through the field and rolled into the forest.

60   At the word, Goodman Brown stepped forth from the shadow of the trees and approached the congregation, with whom he felt a loathful brotherhood by the sympathy of all that was wicked in his heart. He could have well nigh sworn that the shape of his own dead father beckoned him to advance, looking downward from a smoke wreath, while a woman, with dim features of despair, threw out her hand to warn him back. Was it his mother? But he had no power to retreat one step, nor to resist, even in thought, when the minister

and good old Deacon Gookin seized his arms and led him to the blazing rock. Thither came also the slender form of a veiled female, led between Goody Cloyse, that pious teacher of the catechism, and Martha Carrier,° who had received the devil's promise to be queen of hell. A rampant hag was she. And there stood the proselytes beneath the canopy of fire.

"Welcome, my children," said the dark figure, "to the communion of your race. Ye have found thus young your nature and your destiny. My children, look behind you!"

They turned; and flashing forth, as it were, in a sheet of flame, the fiend worshippers were seen; the smile of welcome gleamed darkly on every visage.

"There," resumed the sable form, "are all whom ye have reverenced from youth. Ye deemed them holier than yourselves, and shrank from your own sin, contrasting it with their lives of righteousness and prayerful aspirations heavenward. Yet here are they all in my worshipping assembly. This night it shall be granted you to know their secret deeds: how hoary-bearded elders of the church have whispered wanton words to the young maids of their households; how many a woman, eager for widow's weeds, has given her husband a drink at bedtime, and let him sleep his last sleep in her bosom; how beardless youths have made haste to inherit their fathers' wealth; and how fair damsels—blush not, sweet ones—have dug little graves in the garden, and bidden me, the sole guest, to an infant's funeral. By the sympathy of your human hearts for sin ye shall scent out all the places—whether in church, bed-chamber, street, field, or forest—where crime has been committed, and shall exult to behold the whole earth one stain of guilt, one mighty blood spot. Far more than this. It shall be yours to penetrate, in every bosom, the deep mystery of sin, the fountain of all wicked arts, and which inexhaustibly supplies more evil impulses than human power—than my power at its utmost—can make manifest in deeds. And now, my children, look upon each other."

They did so; and, by the blaze of the hell-kindled torches, the wretched man beheld his Faith, and the wife her husband, trembling before that unhallowed altar.

"Lo, there ye stand, my children," said the figure, in a deep and solemn tone, almost sad with its despairing awfulness, as if his once angelic nature could yet mourn for our miserable race. "Depending upon one another's hearts, ye had still hoped that virtue were not all a dream. Now are ye undeceived. Evil is the nature of mankind. Evil must be your only happiness. Welcome, again, my children, to the communion of your race."

"Welcome," repeated the fiend worshippers, in one cry of despair and triumph.

And there they stood, the only pair, as it seemed, who were yet hesitating on the verge of wickedness in this dark world. A basin was hollowed,

65

Martha Carrier: One of the women hanged for witchcraft in Salem in 1697.

naturally, in the rock. Did it contain water, reddened by the lurid light? or was it blood? or, perchance, a liquid flame? Herein did the shape of evil dip his hand and prepare to lay the mark of baptism upon their foreheads, that they might be partakers of the mystery of sin, more conscious of the secret guilt of others, both in deed and thought, than they could now be of their own. The husband cast one look at his pale wife, and Faith at him. What polluted wretches would the next glance show them to each other, shuddering alike at what they disclosed and what they saw!

"Faith! Faith!" cried the husband, "look up to heaven, and resist the wicked one."

Whether Faith obeyed he knew not. Hardly had he spoken when he found himself amid calm night and solitude, listening to a roar of the wind which died heavily away through the forest. He staggered against the rock, and felt it chill and damp; while a hanging twig, that had been all on fire, besprinkled his cheek with the coldest dew.

70   The next morning young Goodman Brown came slowly into the street of Salem village, staring around him like a bewildered man. The good old minister was taking a walk along the graveyard to get an appetite for breakfast and meditate his sermon, and bestowed a blessing, as he passed, on Goodman Brown. He shrank from the venerable saint as if to avoid an anathema. Old Deacon Gookin was at domestic worship, and the holy words of his prayer were heard through the open window. "What God doth the wizard pray to?" quoth Goodman Brown. Goody Cloyse, that excellent old Christian, stood in the early sunshine at her own lattice, catechizing a little girl who had brought her a pint of morning's milk. Goodman Brown snatched away the child as from the grasp of the fiend himself. Turning the corner by the meeting-house, he spied the head of Faith, with the pink ribbons, gazing anxiously forth, and bursting into such joy at sight of him that she skipped along the street and almost kissed her husband before the whole village. But Goodman Brown looked sternly and sadly into her face, and passed on without a greeting.

Had Goodman Brown fallen asleep in the forest and only dreamed a wild dream of a witch-meeting?

Be it so, if you will; but, alas! it was a dream of evil omen for young Goodman Brown. A stern, a sad, a darkly meditative, a distrustful, if not a desperate man did he become from the night of that fearful dream. On the Sabbath day, when the congregation were singing a holy psalm, he could not listen because an anthem of sin rushed loudly upon his ear and drowned all the blessed strain. When the minister spoke from the pulpit with power and fervid eloquence, and, with his hand on the open Bible, of the sacred truths of our religion, and of saint-like lives and triumphant deaths, and of future bliss or misery unutterable, then did Goodman Brown turn pale, dreading lest the roof should thunder down upon the gray blasphemer and his hearers. Often, awakening suddenly at midnight, he shrank from the bosom of Faith; and at morning or eventide, when the family knelt down at prayer, he scowled and muttered to himself, and gazed sternly at his wife, and turned away. And when he had lived long, and was borne to his grave a hoary corpse, followed by Faith, an aged woman, and children and grandchildren, a goodly procession, besides neighbors, not a few, they carved no hopeful verse upon his tombstone, for his dying face was gloom.   *1835*

More Resources on
Nathaniel Hawthorne and "Young Goodman Brown"

In *ARIEL*

- Brief biography of Hawthorne
- Complete text of "Young Goodman Brown," with hyperlinked comments
- Video clip of dramatic production of "Young Goodman Brown"
- Analysis of nonrealistic fiction in "Young Goodman Brown"
- Bibliography of scholarly works on Hawthorne

CONSIDERATIONS

1. How is Faith's name significant to the story? What qualities does Faith represent to her husband? Contrast the way present-day readers might respond to her name with the way that Hawthorne's nineteenth-century audience—who were mostly middle- or upper-class, well-educated, white Protestants—might have responded.

2. How does Goodman Brown's journey into the forest relate to his relationship with his wife? How would you compare the second traveler to Faith? Who or what might the second traveler (who bears "a considerable resemblance" to Goodman Brown) represent?

3. Make a list of the other men and women whom Goodman Brown encounters. How does Hawthorne portray the men? The women? Do you see any significant similarities or differences?

4. Referring to evidence in the story, explain why you do or do not see the encounter in the forest as an actual event (as opposed to a dream or fantasy).

5. Read the final paragraph of the story carefully. Does Goodman Brown's lifelong depression seem justified? Or does the narrator seem critical of his response to his encounter with darkness? Explain.

JAMES JOYCE (1882–1941)
Araby

Born in a suburb of Dublin, Ireland, James Joyce received his early education at schools run by Jesuit priests. Joyce had a troubled childhood: his father's heavy drinking and resulting unemployment led the family into serious economic difficulties. Nevertheless, Joyce was able to attend University College in Dublin. After his graduation in 1902, he moved to Paris. Although he returned for a brief time to Ireland to stay with his mother during her final illness, he left again in 1904, believing that he had to leave his childhood home to examine his complex thoughts and responses to his native land and to find the freedom needed "to forge in the smithy of my soul the uncreated conscience of my race." He spent the rest of his life living in major European cities—Trieste, Zurich, and Paris— while writing Dubliners, *the collection of short stories in which "Araby" appears (written between 1904 and 1907; published in 1914);* Portrait of the Artist as a Young Man, *an autobiographical novel (1916);* Ulysses *(1922); and* Finnegans Wake *(1939).*

North Richmond Street, being blind, was a quiet street except at the hour when the Christian Brothers' School set the boys free. An uninhabited house of two stories stood at the blind end, detached from its neighbors in a square ground. The other houses of the street, conscious of decent lives within them, gazed at one another with brown imperturbable faces.

The former tenant of our house, a priest, had died in the back drawing-room. Air, musty from having been long enclosed, hung in all the rooms, and the waste room behind the kitchen was littered with old useless papers. Among these I found a few paper-covered books, the pages of which were curled and damp: *The Abbot,* by Walter Scott, *The Devout Communicant* and *The Memoirs of Vidoca.* I liked the last best because its leaves were yellow. The wild garden behind the house contained a central apple-tree and a few straggling bushes under one of which I found the late tenant's rusty bicycle-pump. He had been a very charitable priest: in his will he had left all his money to institutions and the furniture of his house to his sister.

When the short days of winter came dusk fell before we had well eaten our dinners. When we met in the street the houses had grown somber. The space of sky above us was the color of ever-changing violet and towards it the lamps of the street lifted their feeble lanterns. The cold air stung us and we played till our bodies glowed. Our shouts echoed in the silent street. The career of our play brought us through the dark muddy lanes behind the houses where we ran the gantlet of the rough tribes from the cottages, to the back doors of the dark dripping gardens where odors arose from the ashpits, to the dark odorous stables where a coachman smoothed and combed the horse or shook music from the buckled harness. When we returned to the street, light from the kitchen windows had filled the areas. If my uncle was seen turning the corner we hid in the shadow until we had seen him safely housed. Or if Mangan's sister came out on the doorstep to call her brother in to his tea we watched her from our shadow peer up and down the street. We waited to see whether she would remain or go in and, if she remained, we left our shadow and walked up to Mangan's steps resignedly. She was waiting for us, her figure defined by the light from the half-opened door. Her brother always teased her before he obeyed and I stood by the railings looking at her. Her dress swung as she moved her body and the soft rope of her hair tossed from side to side.

Every morning I lay on the floor in the front parlor watching her door. The blind was pulled down to within an inch of the sash so that I could not be seen. When she came out on the doorstep my heart leaped. I ran to the hall, seized my books and followed her. I kept her brown figure always in my eye and, when we came near the point at which our ways diverged, I quickened my pace and passed her. This happened morning after morning. I had never spoken to her, except for a few casual words, and yet her name was like a summons to all my foolish blood.

Her image accompanied me even in places the most hostile to romance.   5 On Saturday evenings when my aunt went marketing I had to go to carry some of the parcels. We walked through the flaring streets, jostled by drunken men and bargaining women, amid the curses of laborers, the shrill litanies of shop-boys who stood on guard by the barrels of pigs' cheeks, the nasal chanting of street-singers, who sang a *come-all-you°* about O'Donovan Rossa, or a ballad about the troubles in our native land. These noises converged in a single sensation of life for me: I imagined that I bore my chalice safely through a throng of foes. Her name sprang to my lips at moments in strange prayers and praises which I myself did not understand. My eyes were often full of tears (I could not tell why) and at times a flood from my heart seemed to pour itself out into my bosom. I thought little of the future. I did not know whether I would ever speak to her or not or, if I spoke to her, how I could tell her of my confused adoration. But my body was like a harp and her words and gestures were like fingers running upon the wires.

---

come-all-you: A ballad bginning with the familiar words "come all you," as in "Come all you, fair and tender maidens."

One evening I went into the back drawing-room in which the priest had died. It was a dark rainy evening and there was no sound in the house. Through one of the broken panes I heard the rain impinge upon the earth, the fine incessant needles of water playing in the sodden beds. Some distant lamp or lighted window gleamed below me. I was thankful that I could see so little. All my senses seemed to desire to veil themselves and, feeling that I was about to slip from them, I pressed the palms of my hands together until they trembled, murmuring: *O love! O love!* many times.

At last she spoke to me. When she addressed the first words to me I was so confused that I did not know what to answer. She asked me was I going to *Araby.* I forget whether I answered yes or no. It would be a splendid bazaar, she said; she would love to go.

—And why can't you? I asked.

While she spoke she turned a silver bracelet round and round her wrist. She could not go, she said, because there would be a retreat that week in her convent. Her brother and two other boys were fighting for their caps and I was alone at the railings. She held one of the spikes, bowing her head towards me. The light from the lamp opposite our door caught the white curve of a neck, lit up her hair that rested there and, falling, lit up the hand upon the railing. It fell over one side of her dress and caught the white border of a petticoat, just visible as she stood at ease.

10 —It's well for you, she said.

—If I go, I said, I will bring you something.

What innumerable follies laid waste my waking and sleeping thoughts after that evening! I wished to annihilate the tedious intervening days. I chafed against the work of school. At night in my bedroom and by day in the classroom her image came between me and the page I strove to read. The syllables of the word *Araby* were called to me through the silence in which my soul luxuriated and cast an Eastern enchantment over me. I asked for leave to go to the bazaar on Saturday night. My aunt was surprised and hoped it was not some Freemason affair. I answered few questions in class, I watched my master's face pass from amiability to sternness; he hoped I was not beginning to idle. I could not call my wandering thoughts together. I had hardly any patience with the serious work of life which, now that it stood between me and my desire, seemed to me child's play, ugly monotonous child's play.

On Saturday morning I reminded my uncle that I wished to go to the bazaar in the evening. He was fussing at the hall-stand, looking for the hat-brush, and answered me curtly:

—Yes, boy, I know.

15 As he was in the hall I could not go into the front parlor and lie at the window. I left the house in bad humor and walked slowly towards the school. The air was pitilessly raw and already my heart misgave me.

When I came home to dinner my uncle had not yet been home. Still it was early. I sat staring at the clock for some time and, when its ticking began to irritate me, I left the room. I mounted the staircase and gained the upper part of the house. The high cold empty gloomy rooms liberated me and I went from room to room singing. From the front window I saw my companions playing below in the street. Their cries reached me weakened and indistinct and, leaning my forehead against the cool glass, I looked over at the dark house where she lived. I may have stood there for an hour, seeing nothing but the brown-clad figure cast by my imagination, touched discreetly by the lamplight at the curved neck, at the hand upon the railings and at the border below the dress.

When I came downstairs again I found Mrs. Mercer sitting at the fire. She was an old garrulous woman, a pawnbroker's widow, who collected used stamps for some pious purpose. I had to endure the gossip of the tea-table. The meal was prolonged beyond an hour and still my uncle did not come. Mrs. Mercer stood up to go: she was sorry she couldn't wait any longer, but it was after eight o'clock and she did not like to be out late, as the night air was bad for her. When she had gone I began to walk up and down the room, clenching my fists. My aunt said:

—I'm afraid you may put off your bazaar for this night of Our Lord.

At nine o'clock I heard my uncle's latchkey in the halldoor. I heard him talking to himself and heard the hall-stand rocking when it had received the weight of his overcoat. I could interpret these signs. When he was midway through his dinner I asked him to give me the money to go to the bazaar. He had forgotten.

—The people are in bed and after their first sleep now, he said.   20

I did not smile. My aunt said to him energetically:

—Can't you give him the money and let him go? You've kept him late enough as it is.

My uncle said he was very sorry he had forgotten. He said he believed in the old saying: *All work and no play makes Jack a dull boy.* He asked me where I was going and, when I had told him a second time he asked me did I know *The Arab's Farewell to His Steed.* When I left the kitchen he was about to recite the opening lines of the piece to my aunt.

I held a florin tightly in my hand as I strode down Buckingham Street towards the station. The sight of the streets thronged with buyers and glaring with gas recalled to me the purpose of my journey. I took my seat in a third-class carriage of a deserted train. After an intolerable delay the train moved out of the station slowly. It crept onward among ruinous houses and over the twinkling river. At Westland Row Station a crowd of people pressed to the carriage doors; but the porters moved them back, saying that it was a special train for the bazaar. I remained alone in the bare carriage. In a few minutes the train drew up beside an improvised wooden platform. I passed out on to the road and saw by the lighted dial of a clock that it was ten minutes to ten. In front of me was a large building which displayed a magical name.

I could not find any sixpenny entrance and, fearing that the bazaar would   25
be closed, I passed in quickly through a turnstile, handing a shilling to a weary-

looking man. I found myself in a big hall girdled at half its height by a gallery. Nearly all the stalls were closed and the greater part of the hall was in darkness. I recognized a silence like that which pervades a church after a service. I walked into the center of the bazaar timidly. A few people were gathered about the stalls which were still open. Before a curtain, over which the words *Café Chantant* were written in colored lamps, two men were counting money on a salver. I listened to the fall of the coins.

Remembering with difficulty why I had come I went over to one of the stalls and examined porcelain vases and flowered tea-sets. At the door of the stall a young lady was talking and laughing with two young gentlemen. I remarked their English accents and listened vaguely to their conversation.

—O, I never said such a thing!

—O, but you did!

—O, but I didn't!

30 —Didn't she say that?

—Yes. I heard her.

—O, there's a . . . fib!

Observing me the young lady came over and asked me did I wish to buy anything. The tone of her voice was not encouraging; she seemed to have spoken to me out of a sense of duty. I looked humbly at the great jars that stood like eastern guards at either side of the dark entrance to the stall and murmered:

—No, thank you.

35 The young lady changed the position of one of the vases and went back to the two young men. They began to talk of the same subject. Once or twice the young lady glanced at me over her shoulder.

I lingered before her stall, though I knew my stay was useless, to make my interest in her wares seem the more real. Then I turned away slowly and walked down the middle of the bazaar. I allowed the two pennies to fall against the sixpence in my pocket. I heard a voice call from one end of the gallery that the light was out. The upper part of the hall was now completely dark.

Gazing up into the darkness I saw myself as a creature driven and derided by vanity; and my eyes burned with anguish and anger. *1914*

CONSIDERATIONS

1. Compare the adult narrator who tells the story with the younger self he describes. What differences do you see in the two? Similarities?
2. List several details relating to the story's setting, and consider how those details relate to the changes the narrator experiences.
3. What does the narrator expect to find at Araby? What drives him so intensely to the bazaar? Why is he so intensely disappointed?

4. What is your response to the final passage describing the narrator's experience when he finally arrives at Araby?

5. Describe an experience in which you anticipated an event with pleasure but found the actual event disappointing. Provide specific details that show what you hoped for and why those hopes were not realized. In addition, show the difference between the way you looked at this experience as a child and the way you look at it now.

More Resources on
James Joyce and "Araby"

In *ARIEL*
- Brief biography of Joyce
- Complete text of "Araby," with hyperlinked comments
- Audio reading of a section of "Araby"
- Analysis of theme in "Araby"
- Bibliography of scholarly works on Joyce

In the **Online Learning Center** for *Responding to Literature*
- Brief biography of Joyce
- List of major works by Joyce
- Complete text of "Araby"
- Web links to more resources on Joyce
- Additional questions for experiencing and interpreting Joyce's writing

WAKAKO YAMAUCHI (1924–   )
And the Soul Shall Dance

Wakako Yamauchi was born in Westmoreland, California, in 1924, to parents who had immigrated from Japan. While growing up on the family farm, Yamauchi spent every minute of leisure reading voraciously, imagining herself as part of the varied worlds created in the books she read. In 1942, Yamauchi and her family were interned in Arizona as a result of the United States government's World War II policy to "relocate" West Coast residents of Japanese ancestry. Although she met and became friends with the Japanese-American writer Hisaye Yamamoto during her time in the internment camp, she herself did not begin to write until several years later. Many of Yamauchi's stories, including "And the Soul Shall Dance," deal with the struggles between Japanese immigrant parents and their American-born children. Her published stories include "Songs My Mother Taught Me" (1977), "Boatmen on Toneh River" (1983), "Surviving the Wasteland Years" (1988), "Makapoo Bay" (1989), and "Maybe" (1990).

It's all right to talk about it now. Most of the principals are dead, except, of course, me and my younger brother, and possibly Kiyoko Oka, who might be near forty-five now, because, yes, I'm sure of it, she was fourteen then. I was nine, and my brother about four, so he hardly counts at all. Kiyoko's mother is dead, my father is dead, my mother is dead, and her father could not have lasted all these years with his tremendous appetite for alcohol and pickled chilies—those little yellow ones, so hot they could make your mouth hurt; he'd eat them like peanuts and tears would surge from his bulging thyroid eyes in great waves and stream down the dark coarse terrain of his face.

My father farmed then in the desert basin resolutely named Imperial Valley, in the township called Westmoreland; twenty acres of tomatoes, ten of summer squash, or vice versa, and the Okas lived maybe a mile, mile and a half, across an alkaline road, a stretch of greasewood, tumbleweed and white sand, to the south of us. We didn't hobnob much with them, because you see, they were a childless couple and we were a family: father, mother, daughter, and son, and we went to the Buddhist church on Sundays where my mother taught Japanese, and the Okas kept pretty much to themselves. I don't mean they were unfriendly; Mr. Oka would sometimes walk over (he rarely drove) on rainy days, all dripping wet, short and squat under a soggy newspaper, pretending to need a plow-blade or a file, and he would spend the afternoon in our kitchen drinking sake and eating chilies with my father. As he got progressively drunker, his large mouth would draw down and with the stream of tears, he looked like a kindly weeping bullfrog.

Not only were they childless, impractical in an area where large families were looked upon as labor potentials, but there was a certain strangeness about them. I became aware of it the summer our bathhouse burned down, and my father didn't get right down to building another, and a Japanese without a bathhouse . . . well, Mr. Oka offered us the use of his. So every night that summer we drove to the Okas for our bath, and we came in frequent contact with Mrs. Oka, and this is where I found the strangeness.

Mrs. Oka was small and spare. Her clothes hung on her like loose skin and when she walked, the skirt about her legs gave her a sort of webbed look. She was pretty in spite of the boniness and the dull calico and the barren look; I know now that she couldn't have been over thirty. Her eyes were large and a little vacant, although once I saw them fill with tears; the time I insisted we take the old Victrola over and we played our Japanese records for her. Some of the songs were sad, and I imagined the nostalgia she felt, but my mother said the tears were probably from yawning or from the smoke of her cigarettes. I thought my mother resented her for not being more hospitable; indeed, never a cup of tea appeared before us, and between them the conversation of women was totally absent: the rise and fall of gentle voices, the arched eyebrows, the croon of polite surprise. But more than this, Mrs. Oka was *different*.

Obviously she was shy, but some nights she disappeared altogether. She would see us drive into her yard and then lurch from sight. She was gone all evening. Where could she have hidden in that two-roomed house—where in that silent desert? Some nights she would wait out our visit with enormous forbearance, quietly pushing wisps of stray hair behind her ears and waving gnats away from her great moist eyes, and some nights she moved about with nervous agitation, her khaki canvas shoes slapping loudly as she walked. And sometimes there appeared to be welts and bruises on her usually smooth brown face, and she would sit solemnly, hands on lap, eyes large and intent on us. My mother hurried us home then: "Hurry, Masako, no need to wash well; hurry."

You see, being so poky, I was always last to bathe. I think the Okas bathed after we left because my mother often reminded me to keep the water clean. The routine was to lather outside the tub (there were buckets and pans and a small wooden stool), rinse off the soil and soap, and then soak in the tub of hot hot water and contemplate. Rivulets of perspiration would run down the scalp.

When my mother pushed me like this, I dispensed with ritual, rushed a bar of soap around me and splashed about a pan of water. So hastily toweled, my wet skin strapped the clothes to me, impeding my already clumsy progress. Outside, my mother would be murmuring her many apologies and my father, I knew, would be carrying my brother whose feet were already sandy. We would hurry home.

I thought Mrs. Oka might be insane and I asked my mother about it, but she shook her head and smiled with her mouth drawn down and said that Mrs. Oka loved her sake. This was unusual, yes, but there were other unusual women we knew. Mrs. Nagai was brought by her husband from a geisha house; Mrs. Tani was a militant Christian Scientist; Mrs. Abe, the midwife, was occult. My mother's statement explained much: sometimes Mrs. Oka was drunk and sometimes not. Her taste for liquor and cigarettes was a step in the realm of men; unusual for a Japanese wife, but at that time, in that place, and to me, Mrs. Oka loved her sake in the way my father loved his, in the way of Mr. Oka, and the way I loved my candy. That her psychology may have demanded this anesthetic, that she lived with something unendurable, did not occur to me. Nor did I perceive the violence of emotions that the purple welts indicated—or the masochism that permitted her to display these wounds to us.

In spite of her masculine habits, Mrs. Oka was never less than a woman. She was no lady in the area of social amenities; but the feminine in her was innate and never left her. Even in her disgrace, she was a small broken sparrow, slightly floppy, too slowly enunciating her few words, too carefully rolling her Bull Durham, cocking her small head and moistening the ocher tissue. Her aberration was a protest of the life assigned her; it was obstinate, but unobserved, alas, unheeded. "Strange" was the only concession we granted her.

10   Toward the end of summer, my mother said we couldn't continue bathing at the Okas'; when winter set in we'd all catch our death from the commuting and she'd always felt dreadful about our imposition on Mrs. Oka. So my father took the corrugated tin sheets he'd found on the highway and had been saving for some other use and built up our bathhouse again. Mr. Oka came to help.

While they raised the quivering tin walls, Mr. Oka began to talk. His voice was sharp and clear above the low thunder of the metal sheets.

He told my father he had been married in Japan previously to the present Mrs. Oka's older sister. He had a child by the marriage, Kiyoko, a girl. He had left the two to come to America intending to send for them soon, but shortly after his departure, his wife passed away from an obscure stomach ailment. At the time, the present Mrs. Oka was young and had foolishly become involved with a man of poor reputation. The family was anxious to part the lovers and conveniently arranged a marriage by proxy and sent him his dead wife's sister. Well that was all right, after all, they were kin, and it would be good for the child when she came to join them. But things didn't work out that way, year after year he postponed calling for his daughter, couldn't get the price of fare together, and the wife—ahhh, the wife, Mr. Oka's groan was lost in the rumble of his hammering.

He cleared his throat. The girl was now fourteen, he said, and begged to come to America to be with her own real family. Those relatives had forgotten the favor he'd done in accepting a slightly used bride, and now tormented his daughter for being forsaken. True, he'd not sent much money, but if they knew, if they only knew how it was here.

"Well," he sighed, "who could be blamed? It's only right she be with me anyway."

15   "That's right," my father said.

"Well, I sold the horse and some other things and managed to buy a third-class ticket on the Taiyo-Maru. Kiyoko will get here the first week of September." Mr. Oka glanced toward my father, but my father was peering into a bag of nails. "I'd be much obliged to you if your wife and little girl," he rolled his eyes toward me, "would take kindly to her. She'll be lonely."

Kiyoko-san came in September. I was surprised to see so very nearly a woman; short, robust, buxom: the female counterpart of her father; thyroid eyes and protruding teeth, straight black hair banded impudently into two bristly shucks, Cuban heels and white socks. Mr. Oka brought her proudly to us.

"Little Masako here," for the first time to my recollection, he touched me; he put his rough fat hand on the top of my head, "is very smart in school. She will help you with your school work, Kiyoko," he said.

I had so looked forward to Kiyoko-san's arrival. She would be my soul mate; in my mind I had conjured a girl of my own proportion: thin and tall, but with the refinement and beauty I didn't yet possess that would surely someday come to the fore. My disappointment was keen and apparent. Kiyoko-san stepped forward shyly, then retreated with a short bow and small giggle, her fingers pressed to her mouth.

My mother took her away. They talked for a long time—about Japan, about enrollment in American school, the clothes Kiyoko-san would need, and where to look for the best values. As I watched them, it occurred to me that I had been deceived: this was not a child, this was a woman. The smile pressed behind her fingers, the way of her nod, so brief, like my mother when father scolded her: the face was inscrutable, but something—maybe spirit— shrank visibly, like a piece of silk in water. I was disappointed; Kiyoko-san's soul was barricaded in her unenchanting appearance and the smile she fenced behind her fingers.

She started school from third grade, one below me, and as it turned out, she quickly passed me by. There wasn't much I could help her with except to drill her on pronunciation—the "L" and "R" sounds. Every morning walking to our rural school: land, leg, library, loan, lot; every afternoon returning home: ran, rabbit, rim, rinse, roll. That was the extent of our communication; friendly but uninteresting.

One particularly cold November night—the wind outside was icy; I was sitting on my bed, my brother's and mine, oiling the cracks in my chapped hands by lamplight—someone rapped urgently at our door. It was Kiyoko-san; she was hysterical, she wore no wrap, her teeth were chattering, and except for the thin straw zori, her feet were bare. My mother led her to the kitchen, started a pot of tea, and gestured to my brother and me to retire. I lay very still but because of my brother's restless tossing and my father's snoring, was unable to hear much. I was aware, though, that drunken and savage brawling had brought Kiyoko-san to us. Presently they came to the bedroom. I feigned sleep. My mother gave Kiyoko-san a gown and pushed me over to make room for her. My mother spoke firmly: "Tomorrow you will return to them; you must not leave them again. They are your people." I could almost feel Kiyoko-san's short nod.

All night long I lay cramped and still, afraid to intrude into her hulking back. Two or three times her icy feet jabbed into mine and quickly retreated. In the morning I found my mother's gown neatly folded on the spare pillow. Kiyoko-san's place in bed was cold.

She never came to weep at our house again but I know she cried: her eyes were often swollen and red. She stopped much of her giggling and routinely pressed her fingers to her mouth. Our daily pronunciation drill petered off from lack of interest. She walked silently with her shoulders hunched, grasping her books with both arms, and when I spoke to her in my halting Japanese, she absently corrected my prepositions.

Spring comes early in the Valley; in February the skies are clear though the air is still cold. By March, winds are vigorous and warm and wild flowers dot the desert floor, cockleburs are green and not yet tenacious, the sand is crusty underfoot, everywhere there is a smell of things growing and the first tomatoes are showing green and bald.

As the weather changed, Kiyoko-san became noticeably more cheerful. Mr. Oka, who hated so to drive, could often be seen steering his dusty old Ford over the road that passes our house, and Kiyoko-san sitting in front would sometimes wave gaily to us. Mrs. Oka was never with them. I thought of these trips as the westernizing of Kiyoko-san: with a permanent wave, her straight black hair became tangles of tiny frantic curls; between her textbooks she carried copies of *Modern Screen* and *Photoplay,* her clothes were gay with print and piping, and she bought a pair of brown suede shoes with alligator trim. I can see her now picking her way gingerly over the deceptive white peaks of alkaline crust.

At first my mother watched their coming and going with vicarious pleasure. "Probably off to a picture show; the stores are all closed at this hour," she might say. Later her eyes would get distant and she would muse, "They've left her home again; Mrs. Oka is alone again, the poor woman."

Now when Kiyoko-san passed by or came in with me on her way home, my mother would ask about Mrs. Oka—how is she, how does she occupy herself these rainy days, or these windy or warm or cool days. Often the answers were polite: "Thank you, we are fine," but sometimes Kiyoko-san's upper lip would pull over her teeth, and her voice would become very soft and she would say, "Drink, always drinking and fighting." And those times my mother would invariably say, "Endure, soon you will be marrying and going away."

Once a young truck driver delivered crates at the Oka farm and he dropped back to our place to tell my father that Mrs. Oka had lurched behind his truck while he was backing up, and very nearly let him kill her. Only the daughter pulling her away saved her, he said. Thoroughly unnerved, he stopped by to rest himself and talk about it. Never, never, he said in wide-eyed wonder, had he seen a drunken Japanese woman. My father nodded gravely, "Yes, it's unusual," he said and drummed his knee with his fingers.

30   Evenings were longer now, and when my mother's migraines drove me from the house in unbearable self-pity, I would take walks in the desert. One night with the warm wind against me, the dune primrose and yellow poppies closed and fluttering, the greasewood swaying in languid orbit, I lay on the white sand beneath a shrub and tried to disappear.

A voice sweet and clear cut through the half-dark of the evening:

> Red lips press against a glass
> Drink the purple wine
> And the soul shall dance

Mrs. Oka appeared to be gathering flowers. Bending, plucking, standing, searching, she added to a small bouquet she clasped. She held them away; looked at them slyly, lids lowered, demure, then in a sudden and sinuous movement, she broke into a stately dance. She stopped, gathered more flowers, and breathed deeply into them. Tossing her head, she laughed—softly, beautifully, from her dark throat. The picture of her imagined grandeur was lost to me, but the delusion that transformed the bouquet of tattered petals and sandy leaves, and the aloneness of a desert twilight into a fantasy that brought such joy and abandon made me stir with discomfort. The sound broke Mrs. Oka's dance. Her eyes grew large and her neck tense—like a cat on the prowl. She spied me in the bushes. A peculiar chill ran through me. Then abruptly and with childlike delight, she scattered the flowers around her and walked away singing:

> Falling, falling, petals on a wind . . .

That was the last time I saw Mrs. Oka. She died before the spring harvest. It was pneumonia. I didn't attend the funeral, but my mother said it was sad. Mrs. Oka looked peaceful, and the minister expressed the irony of the long separation of Mother and Child and the short-lived reunion; hardly a year together, she said. We went to help Kiyoko-san address and stamp those black-bordered acknowledgments.

When harvest was over, Mr. Oka and Kiyoko-san moved out of the Valley. We never heard from them or saw them again and I suppose in a large city, Mr. Oka found some sort of work, perhaps as a janitor or a dishwasher and Kiyoko-san grew up and found someone to marry.   *1974*

CONSIDERATIONS

1. Read the first paragraph, and write a brief prediction about the story's possible themes based only on the images and short character sketches you find there. Then read the story and explain how your initial responses changed or developed.
2. At the end of paragraph 4, the narrator characterizes Mrs. Oka as "*different.*" What effect is created by printing the word in italics? As you read the description of Mrs. Oka, what details suggest that she is or is not, in your own definition, "different"? From whom is she different? Do you see the narrator's designation of "different" as negative, positive, or neutral? Explain.
3. Describe the narrator's response to and interactions with Kiyoko-san. What is Kiyoko-san's role in the narrator's growth from innocence to experience?
4. Toward the end of the story, the narrator's mother advises Kiyoko-san, "Endure, soon you will be marrying and going away." How would you evaluate this advice? What advice would you have given Kiyoko-san, under the same circumstances? Suggest possible outcomes both for the advice of the narrator's mother and for the advice you would have given.

5. Read paragraph 32 carefully, and consider the possible themes for this story suggested by the images in the narrator's description and in the poem Mrs. Oka sings.

More Resources on
Wakako Yamauchi

 In the Online Learning Center for *Responding to Literature*
- Brief biography of Yamauchi
- List of major works by Yamauchi
- Web links to more resources on Yamauchi
- Additional questions for experiencing and interpreting Yamauchi's writing

LOUISE ERDRICH (1954–   )
The Red Convertible

Louise Erdrich is the daughter of a German-born father and a Chippewa mother, who were both working for the Bureau of Indian Affairs in North Dakota when she was born in 1954. During most of Erdrich's childhood, her maternal grandfather was tribal chair of the Turtle Mountain Band of Chippewa. Erdrich received her bachelor of arts from Dartmouth College and her master of arts from Johns Hopkins University. In addition to writing, she has taught in the Poetry in the Schools Program in North Dakota and has edited a Native American newspaper in Boston. She wrote a novel and two books of nonfiction with her late husband, Michael Dorris, who was a professor of Native American studies at Dartmouth. Among her solo-authored works, the best-known are the poetry collection Jacklight *(1984) and the four-novel series about several generations of a Native American family, which includes* The Beet Queen *(1986),* Tracks *(1988), and* The Bingo Palace *(1994). "The Red Convertible" is a chapter from the first book of the series,* Love Medicine, *which won the National Book Critics Circle Award in 1984.*

I was the first one to drive a convertible on my reservation. And of course it was red, a red Olds. I owned that car along with my brother Henry Junior.

We owned it together until his boots filled with water on a windy night and he bought out my share. Now Henry owns the whole car, and his youngest brother Lyman (that's myself), Lyman walks everywhere he goes.

How did I earn enough money to buy my share in the first place? My own talent was I could always make money. I had a touch for it, unusual in a Chippewa. From the first I was different that way, and everyone recognized it. I was the only kid they let in the American Legion Hall to shine shoes, for example, and one Christmas I sold spiritual bouquets for the mission door to door. The nuns let me keep a percentage. Once I started, it seemed the more money I made the easier the money came. Everyone encouraged it. When I was fifteen I got a job washing dishes at the Joliet Café, and that was where my first big break happened.

It wasn't long before I was promoted to busing tables, and then the short-order cook quit and I was hired to take her place. No sooner than you know it I was managing the Joliet. The rest is history. I went on managing. I soon became part owner, and of course there was no stopping me then. It wasn't long before the whole thing was mine.

After I'd owned the Joliet for one year, it blew over in the worst tornado ever seen around here. The whole operation was smashed to bits. A total loss. The fryalator was up in a tree, the grill torn in half like it was paper. I was only sixteen. I had it all in my mother's name, and I lost it quick, but before I lost it I had every one of my relatives, and their relatives, to dinner, and I also bought that red Olds I mentioned, along with Henry.

The first time we saw it! I'll tell you when we first saw it. We had gotten   5
a ride up to Winnipeg, and both of us had money. Don't ask me why, because we never mentioned a car or anything, we just had all our money. Mine was cash, a big bankroll from the Joliet's insurance. Henry had two checks—a week's extra pay for being laid off, and his regular check from the Jewel Bearing Plant.

We were walking down Portage anyway, seeing the sights, when we saw it. There it was, parked, large as life. Really as *if* it was alive. I thought of the word *repose,* because the car wasn't simply stopped, parked, or whatever. That car reposed, calm and gleaming, a FOR SALE sign in its left front window. Then, before we had thought it over at all, the car belonged to us and our pockets were empty. We had just enough money for gas back home.

We went places in that car, me and Henry. We took off driving all one whole summer. We started off toward the Little Knife River and Mandaree in Fort Berthold and then we found ourselves down in Wakpala somehow, and then suddenly we were over in Montana on the Rocky Boy, and yet the summer was not even half over. Some people hang on to details when they travel, but we didn't let them bother us and just lived our everyday lives here to there.

I do remember this one place with willows. I remember I laid under those trees and it was comfortable. So comfortable. The branches bent down all around me like a tent or a stable. And quiet, it was quiet, even though there was a powwow close enough so I could see it going on. The air was not too still, not too windy either. When the dust rises up and hangs in the air around the dancers like that, I feel good. Henry was asleep with his arms thrown wide. Later on, he woke up and we started driving again. We were somewhere in Montana, or maybe on the Blood Reserve—it could have been anywhere. Anyway it was where we met the girl.

All her hair was in buns around her ears, that's the first thing I noticed about her. She was posed alongside the road with her arm out, so we stopped. That girl was short, so short her lumber shirt looked comical on her, like a nightgown. She had jeans on and fancy moccasins and she carried a little suitcase.

10   "Hop on in," says Henry. So she climbs in between us.
"We'll take you home," I says. "Where do you live?"
"Chicken," she says.
"Where the hell's that?" I ask her.
"Alaska."
15   "Okay," says Henry, and we drive.
We got up there and never wanted to leave. The sun doesn't truly set there in summer, and the night is more a soft dusk. You might doze off, sometimes, but before you know it you're up again, like an animal in nature. You never feel like you have to sleep hard or put away the world. And things would grow up there. One day just dirt or moss, the next day flowers and long grass. The girl's name was Susy. Her family really took to us. They fed us and put us up. We had our own tent to live in by their house, and the kids would be in and out of there all day and night. They couldn't get over me and Henry being brothers, we looked so different. We told them we knew we had the same mother, anyway.

One night Susy came in to visit us. We sat around in the tent talking of this and that. The season was changing. It was getting darker by that time, and the cold was even getting just a little mean. I told her it was time for us to go. She stood up on a chair.

"You never seen my hair," Susy said.

That was true. She was standing on a chair, but still, when she unclipped her buns the hair reached all the way to the ground. Our eyes opened. You couldn't tell how much hair she had when it was rolled up so neatly. Then my brother Henry did something funny. He went up to the chair and said, "Jump on my shoulders." So she did that, and her hair reached down past his waist, and he started twirling, this way and that, so her hair was flung out from side to side.

20   "I always wondered what it was like to have long pretty hair," Henry says. Well we laughed. It was a funny sight, the way he did it. The next morning we got up and took leave of those people.

———

On to greener pastures, as they say. It was down through Spokane and across Idaho then Montana and very soon we were racing the weather right along under the Canadian border through Columbus, Des Lacs, and then we were in Bottineau County and soon home. We'd made most of the trip, that summer, without putting up the car hood at all. We got home just in time, it turned out, for the army to remember Henry had signed up to join it.

I don't wonder that the army was so glad to get my brother that they turned him into a Marine. He was built like a brick outhouse anyway. We liked to tease him that they really wanted him for his Indian nose. He had a nose big and sharp as a hatchet, like the nose on Red Tomahawk, the Indian who killed Sitting Bull, whose profile is on signs all along the North Dakota highways. Henry went off to training camp, came home once during Christmas, then the next thing you know we got an overseas letter from him. It was 1970, and he said he was stationed up in the northern hill country. Whereabouts I did not know. He wasn't such a hot letter writer, and only got off two before the enemy caught him. I could never keep it straight, which direction those good Vietnam soldiers were from.

I wrote him back several times, even though I didn't know if those letters would get through. I kept him informed all about the car. Most of the time I had it up on blocks in the yard or half taken apart, because that long trip did a hard job on it under the hood.

I always had good luck with numbers, and never worried about the draft myself. I never even had to think about what my number was. But Henry was never lucky in the same way as me. It was at least three years before Henry came home. By then I guess the whole war was solved in the government's mind, but for him it would keep on going. In those years I'd put his car into almost perfect shape. I always thought of it as his car while he was gone, even though when he left he said, "Now it's yours," and threw me his key.

"Thanks for the extra key," I'd said. "I'll put it up in your drawer just in case I need it." He laughed.   25

When he came home, though, Henry was very different, and I'll say this: the change was no good. You could hardly expect him to change for the better, I know. But he was quiet, so quiet, and never comfortable sitting still anywhere but always up and moving around. I thought back to times we'd sat still for whole afternoons, never moving a muscle, just shifting our weight along the ground, talking to whoever sat with us, watching things. He'd always had a joke, then, too, and now you couldn't get him to laugh, or when he did it was more the sound of a man choking, a sound that stopped up the throats of other people around him. They got to leaving him alone most of the time, and I didn't blame them. It was a fact: Henry was jumpy and mean.

I'd bought a color TV set for my mom and the rest of us while Henry was away. Money still came very easy. I was sorry I'd ever bought it though, because of Henry. I was also sorry I'd bought color, because with black-and-white the pictures seem older and farther away. But what are you going to do? He sat in front of it, watching it, and that was the only time he was completely still. But it was the kind of stillness that you see in a rabbit when it freezes and before it will bolt. He was not easy. He sat in his chair gripping the armrests with all his might, as if the chair itself was moving at a high speed and if he let go at all he would rocket forward and maybe crash right through the set.

Once I was in the room watching TV with Henry and I heard his teeth click at something. I looked over, and he'd bitten through his lip. Blood was going down his chin. I tell you right then I wanted to smash that tube to pieces. I went over to it but Henry must have known what I was up to. He rushed from his chair and shoved me out of the way, against the wall. I told myself he didn't know what he was doing.

My mom came in, turned the set off real quiet, and told us she had made something for supper. So we went and sat down. There was still blood going down Henry's chin, but he didn't notice it and no one said anything, even though every time he took a bite of his bread his blood fell onto it until he was eating his own blood mixed in with the food.

30   While Henry was not around we talked about what was going to happen to him. There were no Indian doctors on the reservation, and my mom couldn't come around to trusting the old man, Moses Pillager, because he courted her long ago and was jealous of her husbands. He might take revenge through her son. We were afraid that if we brought Henry to a regular hospital they would keep him.

"They don't fix them in those places," Mom said; "they just give them drugs."

"We wouldn't get him there in the first place," I agreed, "so let's just forget about it."

Then I thought about the car.

Henry had not even looked at the car since he'd gotten home, though like I said, it was in tip-top condition and ready to drive. I thought the car might bring the old Henry back somehow. So I bided my time and waited for my chance to interest him in the vehicle.

35   One night Henry was off somewhere. I took myself a hammer. I went out to that car and I did a number on its underside. Whacked it up. Bent the tail pipe double. Ripped the muffler loose. By the time I was done with the car it looked worse than any typical Indian car that has been driven all its life on reservation roads, which they always say are like government promises—full of holes. It just about hurt me, I'll tell you that! I threw dirt in the carburetor and I ripped all the electric tape off the seats. I made it look just as beat up as I could. Then I sat back and waited for Henry to find it.

Still, it took him over a month. That was all right, because it was just getting warm enough, not melting, but warm enough to work outside.

"Lyman," he says, walking in one day, "that red car looks like shit."

"Well it's old," I says. "You got to expect that."

"No way!" says Henry. "That car's a classic! But you went and ran the piss right out of it, Lyman, and you know it don't deserve that. I kept that car in A-one shape. You don't remember. You're too young. But when I left, that car was running like a watch. Now I don't even know if I can get it to start again, let alone get it anywhere near its old condition."

"Well you try," I said, like I was getting mad, "but I say it's a piece of junk." *40*

Then I walked out before he could realize I knew he'd strung together more than six words at once.

After that I thought he'd freeze himself to death working on that car. He was out there all day, and at night he rigged up a little lamp, ran a cord out the window, and had himself some light to see by while he worked. He was better than he had been before, but that's still not saying much. It was easier for him to do the things the rest of us did. He ate more slowly and didn't jump up and down during the meal to get this or that or look out the window. I put my hand in the back of the TV set, I admit, and fiddled around with it good, so that it was almost impossible now to get a clear picture. He didn't look at it very often anyway. He was always out with that car or going off to get parts for it. By the time it was really melting outside, he had it fixed.

I had been feeling down in the dumps about Henry around this time. We had always been together before. Henry and Lyman. But he was such a loner now that I didn't know how to take it. So I jumped at the chance one day when Henry seemed friendly. It's not that he smiled or anything. He just said, "Let's take that old shitbox for a spin." Just the way he said it made me think he could be coming around.

We went out to the car. It was spring. The sun was shining very bright. My only sister, Bonita, who was just eleven years old, came out and made us stand together for a picture. Henry leaned his elbow on the red car's windshield, and he took his other arm and put it over my shoulder, very carefully, as though it was heavy for him to lift and he didn't want to bring the weight down all at once.

"Smile," Bonita said, and he did. *45*

That picture. I never look at it anymore. A few months ago, I don't know why, I got his picture out and tacked it on the wall. I felt good about Henry at the time, close to him. I felt good having his picture on the wall, until one night when I was looking at television. I was a little drunk and stoned. I looked up at the wall and Henry was staring at me. I don't know what it was, but his smile had changed, or maybe it was gone. All I know is I couldn't stay in the same room with that picture. I was shaking. I got up, closed the door, and went into the kitchen. A little later my friend Ray came over and we both went back into that room. We put the picture in a brown bag, folded the bag over and over tightly, then put it way back in a closet.

I still see that picture now, as if it tugs at me, whenever I pass that closet door. The picture is very clear in my mind. It was so sunny that day Henry had to squint against the glare. Or maybe the camera Bonita held flashed like a mirror, blinding him, before she snapped the picture. My face is right out in the sun, big and round. But he might have drawn back, because the shadows on his face are deep as holes. There are two shadows curved like little hooks around the ends of his smile, as if to frame it and try to keep it there—that one, first smile that looked like it might have hurt his face. He has his field jacket on and the worn-in clothes he'd come back in and kept wearing ever since. After Bonita took the picture, she went into the house and we got into the car. There was a full cooler in the trunk. We started off, east, toward Pembina and the Red River because Henry said he wanted to see the high water.

The trip over there was beautiful. When everything starts changing, drying up, clearing off, you feel like your whole life is starting. Henry felt it, too. The top was down and the car hummed like a top. He'd really put it back in shape, even the tape on the seats was very carefully put down and glued back in layers. It's not that he smiled again or even joked, but his face looked to me as if it was clear, more peaceful. It looked as though he wasn't thinking of anything in particular except the bare fields and windbreaks and houses we were passing.

The river was high and full of winter trash when we got there. The sun was still out, but it was colder by the river. There were still little clumps of dirty snow here and there on the banks. The water hadn't gone over the banks yet, but it would, you could tell. It was just at its limit, hard swollen, glossy like an old gray scar. We made ourselves a fire, and we sat down and watched the current go. As I watched it I felt something squeezing inside me and tightening and trying to let go all at the same time. I knew I was not just feeling it myself; I knew I was feeling what Henry was going through at that moment. Except that I couldn't stand it, the closing and opening. I jumped to my feet. I took Henry by the shoulders and I started shaking him. "Wake up," I says, "wake up, wake up, wake up!" I didn't know what had come over me. I sat down beside him again.

50   His face was totally white and hard. Then it broke, like stones break all of a sudden when water boils up inside them.

"I know it," he says. "I know it. I can't help it. It's no use."

We start talking. He said he knew what I'd done with the car. It was obvious it had been whacked out of shape and not just neglected. He said he wanted to give the car to me for good now, it was no use. He said he'd fixed it just to give it back and I should take it.

"No way," I says. "I don't want it."

"That's okay," he says, "you take it."

"I don't want it, though," I says back to him, and then to emphasize, just to emphasize, you understand, I touch his shoulder. He slaps my hand off.   *55*

"Take that car," he says.

"No," I say. "Make me," I say, and then he grabs my jacket and rips the arm loose. That jacket is a class act, suede with tags and zippers. I push Henry backwards, off the log. He jumps up and bowls me over. We go down in a clinch and come up swinging hard, for all we're worth, with our fists. He socks my jaw so hard I feel like it swings loose. Then I'm at his rib cage and land a good one under his chin so his head snaps back. He's dazzled. He looks at me and I look at him and then his eyes are full of tears and blood and at first I think he's crying. But no, he's laughing. "Ha! Ha!" he says. "Ha! Ha! Take good care of it."

"Okay," I says. "Okay, no problem. Ha! Ha!"

I can't help it, and I start laughing, too. My face feels fat and strange, and after a while I get a beer from the cooler in the trunk, and when I hand it to Henry he takes his shirt and wipes my germs off. "Hoof-and-mouth disease," he says. For some reason this cracks me up, and so we're really laughing for a while, and then we drink all the rest of the beers one by one and throw them in the river and see how far, how fast, the current takes them before they fill up and sink.

"You want to go on back?" I ask after a while. "Maybe we could snag a   *60* couple nice Kashpaw girls."

He says nothing. But I can tell his mood is turning again.

"They're all crazy, the girls up here, every damn one of them."

"You're crazy too," I say, to jolly him up. "Crazy Lamartine boys!"

He looks as though he will take this wrong at first. His face twists, then clears, and he jumps up on his feet. "That's right!" he says. "Crazier 'n hell. Crazy Indians!"

I think it's the old Henry again. He throws off his jacket and starts spring-   *65* ing his legs up from the knees like a fancy dancer. He's down doing something between a grass dance and a bunny hop, no kind of dance I ever saw before, but neither has anyone else on all this green growing earth. He's wild. He wants to pitch whoopee! He's up and at me and all over. All this time I'm laughing so hard, so hard my belly is getting tied up in a knot.

"Got to cool me off!" he shouts all of a sudden. Then he runs over to the river and jumps in.

There's boards and other things in the current. It's so high. No sound comes from the river after the splash he makes, so I run right over. I look around. It's getting dark. I see he's halfway across the water already, and I know he didn't swim there but the current took him. It's far. I hear his voice, though, very clearly across it.

"My boots are filling," he says.

He says this in a normal voice, like he just noticed and he doesn't know what to think of it. Then he's gone. A branch comes by. Another branch. And I go in.

70   By the time I get out of the river, off the snag I pulled myself onto, the sun is down. I walk back to the car, turn on the high beams, and drive it up the bank. I put it in first gear and then I take my foot off the clutch. I get out, close the door, and watch it plow softly into the water. The headlights reach in as they go down, searching, still lighted even after the water swirls over the back end. I wait. The wires short out. It is all finally dark. And then there is only the water, the sound of it going and running and going and running and running.   *1984*

CONSIDERATIONS

1. As you read this story, make a list of at least ten phrases or sentences that give you insight into the character of the narrator, Lyman Lamartine. Then write a short essay describing Lyman. Use some (or all) of the phrases or sentences you listed as evidence to demonstrate the points you are making about Lyman.
2. In the final sentence of the opening paragraph, Lyman uses third person to describe himself. What effect does this choice of language create? How would the rest of the story be changed if it were told in third, rather than first, person?
3. Note the setting of each section of the story (time and place). How do the narrator's descriptions of time and place relate to the story's themes? For example, what is the effect of the jump ahead in time in paragraph 46, where the narrator describes his responses to the photograph taken by his sister?
4. What significance do you see in the fact that Lyman and Henry are Native Americans? Does this part of their background contribute to your own response to their actions and choices? Explain.
5. How does the red convertible serve as a symbol that relates to the story's central conflicts and resolutions (or lack of resolutions)?

W. D. WETHERELL (1948–   )

The Bass, the River, and Sheila Mant

*W. D. Wetherell is not only an accomplished writer of fiction; he is also an avid
fly-fisherman and has written three books on the subject:* Upland Stream
(1991), Vermont River *(1993), and* One More River *(1998). His most
recent book,* North of Now *(1998), is a celebration of western New Hampshire, where he has lived for many years. He has also written three novels and
two collections of short stories. The following story was first published in* The
Man Who Loved Levittown *(1985), which won the Drue Heinz Literature
Prize. He is also the recipient of a National Endowment for the Arts creative
writing fellowship.*

There was a summer in my life when the only creature that seemed lovelier to me than a largemouth bass was Sheila Mant. I was fourteen. The Mants
had rented the cottage next to ours on the river; with their parties, their frantic
games of softball, their constant comings and goings, they appeared to me
denizens of a brilliant existence. "Too noisy by half," my mother quickly decided,
but I would have given anything to be invited to one of their parties, and when
my parents went to bed I would sneak through the woods to their hedge and
stare enchanted at the candlelit swirl of white dresses and bright, paisley skirts.

Sheila was the middle daughter—at seventeen, all but out of reach. She
would spend her days sunbathing on a float my Uncle Sierbert had moored in
their cove, and before July was over I had learned all her moods. If she lay flat
on the diving board with her hand trailing idly in the water, she was pensive,
not to be disturbed. On her side, her head propped up by her arm, she was observant, considering those around her with a look that seemed queenly and
severe. Sitting up, arms tucked around her long, sun-tanned legs, she was ap-
proachable, but barely, and it was only in those glorious moments when she
stretched herself prior to entering the water that her various suitors found the
courage to come near.

These were many. The Dartmouth heavyweight crew would scull by her
house on their way upriver, and I think all eight of them must have been in
love with her at various times during the summer; the coxswain° would curse
them through his megaphone, but without effect—there was always a pause in
their pace when they passed Sheila's float. I suppose to these jaded twenty-
year-olds she seemed the incarnation of innocence and youth, while to me she
appeared unutterably suave, the epitome of sophistication. I was on the swim
team at school, and to win her attention would do endless laps between my

---

coxswain: The person who guides the crew and boat in a race.

house and the Vermont shore, hoping she would notice the beauty of my flutter kick, the power of my crawl. Finishing, I would boost myself up onto our
dock and glance casually over toward her, but she was never watching, and the
miraculous day she was, I immediately climbed the diving board and did my
best tuck and a half for her, and continued diving until she had left and the
sun went down and my longing was like a madness and I couldn't stop.

It was late August by the time I got up the nerve to ask her out. The tortured will-I's, won't-I's, the agonized indecision over what to say, the false starts
toward her house and embarrassed retreats—the details of these have been
seared from my memory, and the only part I remember clearly is emerging
from the woods toward dusk while they were playing softball on their lawn, as
bashful and frightened as a unicorn.

5   Sheila was stationed halfway between first and second, well outside the
infield. She didn't seem surprised to see me—as a matter of fact, she didn't
seem to see me at all.

"If you're playing second base, you should move closer," I said.

She turned—I took the full brunt of her long red hair and well-spaced
freckles.

"I'm playing outfield," she said, "I don't like the responsibility of having
a base."

"Yeah, I can understand that," I said, though I couldn't. "There's a band
in Dixford tomorrow night at nine. Want to go?"

10   One of her brothers sent the ball sailing over the leftfielder's head; she
stood and watched it disappear toward the river.

"You have a car?" she asked, without looking up.

I played my master stroke. "We'll go by canoe."

I spent all of the following day polishing it. I turned it upside down on
our lawn and rubbed every inch with Brillo, hosing off the dirt, wiping it with
chamois until it gleamed as bright as aluminum ever gleamed. About five, I slid
it into the water, arranging cushions near the bow so Sheila could lean on
them if she was in one of her pensive moods, propping up my father's transis-
tor radio by the middle thwart so we could have music when we came back.
Automatically, without thinking about it, I mounted my Mitchell reel on my
Pfleuger spinning rod and stuck it in the stern.

I say automatically, because I never went anywhere that summer without
a fishing rod. When I wasn't swimming laps to impress Sheila, I was back in
our driveway practicing casts, and when I wasn't practicing casts, I was tying
the line to Tosca, our springer spaniel, to test the reel's drag, and when I wasn't
doing any of those things, I was fishing the river for bass.

15   Too nervous to sit at home, I got in the canoe early and started paddling
in a huge circle that would get me to Sheila's dock around eight. As automatically as I brought along my rod, I tied on a big Rapala plug, let it down into
the water, let out some line and immediately forgot all about it.

It was already dark by the time I glided up to the Mants' dock. Even by day the river was quiet, most of the summer people preferring Sunapee or one of the other nearby lakes, and at night it was a solitude difficult to believe, a corridor of hidden life that ran between banks like a tunnel. Even the stars were part of it. They weren't as sharp anywhere else; they seemed to have chosen the river as a guide on their slow wheel toward morning, and in the course of the summer's fishing, I had learned all their names.

I was there ten minutes before Sheila appeared. I heard the slam of their screen door first, then saw her in the spotlight as she came slowly down the path. As beautiful as she was on the float, she was even lovelier now—her white dress went perfectly with her hair, and complimented her figure even more than her swimsuit.

It was her face that bothered me. It had on its delightful fullness a very dubious expression.

"Look," she said. "I can get Dad's car."

"It's faster this way," I lied. "Parking's tense up there. Hey, it's safe. I won't   20
tip it or anything."

She let herself down reluctantly into the bow. I was glad she wasn't facing me. When her eyes were on me, I felt like diving in the river again from agony and joy.

I pried the canoe away from the dock and started paddling upstream. There was an extra paddle in the bow, but Sheila made no move to pick it up. She took her shoes off, and dangled her feet over the side.

Ten minutes went by.

"What kind of band?" she said.

"It's sort of like folk music. You'll like it."   25

"Eric Caswell's going to be there. He strokes number four."

"No kidding?" I said. I had no idea who she meant.

"What's that sound?" she said, pointing toward the shore.

"Bass. That splashing sound?"

"Over there."   30

"Yeah, bass. They come into the shallows at night to chase frogs and moths and things. Big largemouths. *Micropetrus salmonides,*" I added, showing off.

"I think fishing's dumb," she said, making a face. "I mean, it's boring and all. Definitely dumb."

Now I have spent a great deal of time in the years since wondering why Sheila Mant should come down so hard on fishing. Was her father a fisherman? Her antipathy toward fishing nothing more than normal filial rebellion? Had she tried it once? A messy encounter with worms? It doesn't matter. What does, is that at that fragile moment in time I would have given anything not to appear dumb in Sheila's severe and unforgiving eyes.

She hadn't seen my equipment yet. What I *should* have done, of course, was push the canoe in closer to shore and carefully slide the rod into some branches where I could pick it up again in the morning. Failing that, I could have surreptitiously dumped the whole outfit overboard, written off the forty or so dollars as love's tribute. What I actually *did* do was gently lean forward, and slowly, ever so slowly, push the rod back through my legs toward the stern where it would be less conspicuous.

35   It must have been just exactly what the bass was waiting for. Fish will trail a lure sometimes, trying to make up their mind whether or not to attack, and the slight pause in the plug's speed caused by my adjustment was tantalizing enough to overcome the bass's inhibitions. My rod, safely out of sight at last, bent double. The line, tightly coiled, peeled off the spool with the shrill, tearing zip of a high-speed drill.

Four things occurred to me at once. One, that it was a bass. Two, that it was a big bass. Three, that it was the biggest bass I had ever hooked. Four, that Sheila Mant must not know.

"What was that?" she said, turning half around.

"Uh, what was what?"

"That buzzing noise."

40   "Bats."

She shuddered, quickly drew her feet back into the canoe. Every instinct I had told me to pick up the rod and strike back at the bass, but there was no need to—it was already solidly hooked. Downstream, an awesome distance downstream, it jumped clear of the water, landing with a concussion heavy enough to ripple the entire river. For a moment, I thought it was gone, but then the rod was bending again, the tip dancing into the water. Slowly, not making any motion that might alert Sheila, I reached down to tighten the drag.

While all this was going on, Sheila had begun talking and it was a few minutes before I was able to catch up with her train of thought.

"I went to a party there. These fraternity men. Katherine says I could get in there if I wanted. I'm thinking more of UVM or Bennington. Somewhere I can ski."

The bass was slanting toward the rocks on the New Hampshire side by the ruins of Donaldson's boathouse. It had to be an old bass—a young one probably wouldn't have known the rocks were there. I brought the canoe back into the middle of the river, hoping to head it off.

45   "That's neat," I mumbled. "Skiing. Yeah, I can see that."

"Eric said I have the figure to model, but I thought I should get an education first. I mean, it might be a while before I get started and all. I was thinking of getting my hair styled, more swept back? I mean, Ann-Margret? Like hers, only shorter?"

She hesitated. "Are we going backward?"

We were. I had managed to keep the bass in the middle of the river away from the rocks, but it had plenty of room there, and for the first time a chance to exert its full strength. I quickly computed the weight necessary to draw a fully loaded canoe backwards—the thought of it made me feel faint.

"It's just the current," I said hoarsely. "No sweat or anything."

I dug in deeper with my paddle. Reassured, Sheila began talking about   50
something else, but all my attention was taken up now with the fish. I could
feel its desperation as the water grew shallower. I could sense the extra strain
on the line, the frantic way it cut back and forth in the water. I could visualize
what it looked like—the gape of its mouth, the flared gills and thick, vertical
tail. The bass couldn't have encountered many forces in its long life that it
wasn't capable of handling, and the unrelenting tug at its mouth must have
been a source of great puzzlement and mounting panic.

Me, I had problems of my own. To get to Dixford, I had to paddle up a
sluggish stream that came into the river beneath a covered bridge. There was a
shallow sandbar at the mouth of this stream—weeds on one side, rocks on the
other. Without doubt, this is where I would lose the fish.

"I have to be careful with my complexion. I tan, but in segments. I can't
figure out if it's even worth it. I shouldn't even do it probably. I saw Jackie
Kennedy in Boston and she wasn't tan at all."

Taking a deep breath, I paddled as hard as I could for the middle, deepest
part of the bar. I could have threaded the eye of a needle with the canoe, but
the pull on the stern threw me off and I overcompensated—the canoe veered
left and scraped bottom. I pushed the paddle down and shoved. A moment of
hesitation . . . a moment more. . . . The canoe shot clear into the deeper water
of the stream. I immediately looked down at the rod. It was bent in the same,
tight arc—miraculously, the bass was still on.

The moon was out now. It was low and full enough that its beam shone
directly on Sheila there ahead of me in the canoe, washing her in a creamy, luminous glow. I could see the lithe, easy shape of her figure. I could see the way
her hair curled down off her shoulders, the proud, alert tilt of her head, and all
these things were as a tug on my heart. Not just Sheila, but the aura she carried about her of parties and casual touchings and grace. Behind me, I could
feel the strain of the bass, steadier now, growing weaker, and this was another
tug on my heart, not just the bass but the beat of the river and the slant of the
stars and the smell of the night, until finally it seemed I would be torn apart
between longings, split in half. Twenty yards ahead of us was the road, and
once I pulled the canoe up on shore, the bass would be gone, irretrievably
gone. If instead I stood up, grabbed the rod and started pumping, I would have
it—as tired as the bass was, there was no chance it could get away. I reached
down for the rod, hesitated, looked up to where Sheila was stretching herself
lazily toward the sky, her small breasts rising beneath the soft fabric of her
dress, and the tug was too much for me, and quicker than it takes to write
down, I pulled a penknife from my pocket and cut the line in half.

With a sick, nauseous feeling in my stomach, I saw the rod unbend.   55

"My legs are sore," Sheila whined. "Are we there yet?"

Through a superhuman effort of self-control, I was able to beach the
canoe and help Sheila off. The rest of the night is much foggier. We walked to

the fair—there was the smell of popcorn, the sound of guitars. I may have danced once or twice with her, but all I really remember is her coming over to me once the music was done to explain that she would be going home in Eric Caswell's Corvette.

"Okay," I mumbled.

For the first time that night she looked at me, really looked at me.

60   "You're a funny kid, you know that?"

Funny. Different. Dreamy. Odd. How many times was I to hear that in the years to come, all spoken with the same quizzical, half-accusatory tone Sheila used then. Poor Sheila! Before the month was over, the spell she cast over me was gone, but the memory of that lost bass haunted me all summer and haunts me still. There would be other Sheila Mants in my life, other fish, and though I came close once or twice, it was these secret, hidden tuggings in the night that claimed me, and I never made the same mistake again.   *1985*

CONSIDERATIONS

1. From the details in the opening paragraph, what do you learn about the narrator, and in what ways does this information hint at the central conflict within him?

2. How would you describe the narrator's tone in this story? Is he cynical, angry, indifferent—or something else? At what point in his life do you think the narrator is retelling his story? Explain.

3. Go back through the story, and list the specific words the narrator uses to describe Sheila Mant as well as what she reveals about herself. From this list what conclusions can you draw about Sheila? What conclusions can you draw about the narrator?

4. In what ways do the narrator's struggle and subsequent decision to let the bass go parallel typical adolescent experiences of falling in love?

5. In the last line of this story, the narrator says, "I never made the same mistake again." What, then, has he learned about himself and about love from this experience? What has he gained? What has he lost? According to your own experiences, is this story realistic? Explain.

Poetry

WILLIAM BLAKE (1757–1827)
London

> *William Blake wrote both short lyric poems and longer epic poems based on an elaborate mythology that he devised, but he was not recognized as a poet during his lifetime. He earned his living as an engraver and painter. As a working artisan, he experienced the inequities of socioeconomic conditions in late eighteenth- and early nineteenth-century England. "London" was first published in 1794 as part of Blake's* Songs of Experience.

I wander through each chartered street,
Near where the chartered Thames does flow,
And mark in every face I meet
Marks of weakness, marks of woe.

In every cry of every man,   5
In every Infant's cry of fear,
In every voice, in every ban,
The mind-forged manacles I hear.

How the Chimney-sweeper's cry
Every black'ning Church appalls;   10
And the hapless Soldier's sigh
Runs in blood down Palace walls.

But most through midnight streets I hear
How the youthful Harlot's curse
Blasts the new-born Infant's tear,   15
And blights with plagues the Marriage hearse.   *1794*

CONSIDERATIONS

1. According to the images in this poem, what might it be like to live in London at the time this poem was written?
2. Identify the symbols in the last two stanzas. Discuss how these symbols might suggest a central conflict between life and death, sin and absolution, innocence and experience.

GERARD MANLEY HOPKINS (1844–1889)

Spring and Fall

To a Young Child

> *Gerard Manley Hopkins, a convert to Roman Catholicism who became a Jesuit priest, wrote innovative poetry that experimented with rhythms and line patterns. His poems often celebrate the beauty of God's world, although his later poems, like "Spring and Fall" (1880), also show a sense both of darkness and of the fragility of human life.*

Márgarét, are you gríeving
Over Goldengrove unleaving?
Leáves, líke the things of man, you
With your fresh thoughts care for, can you?
5 Ah! ás the heart grows older
It will come to such sights colder
By and by, nor spare a sigh
Though worlds of wanwood leafmeal lie;
And yet you wíll weep and know why.
10 Now no matter, child, the name:
Sórrow's spríngs áre the same.
Nor mouth had, no nor mind, expressed
What heart heard of, ghost guessed:
It ís the blight man was born for,
15 It is Margaret you mourn for.   *1880*

CONSIDERATIONS

1. Although this poem is addressed to a young child, what does it reveal about the narrator?
2. According to the poem, what is the source of Margaret's suffering? What does the tone of the poem suggest about Hopkins's view of her sadness?

A. E. HOUSMAN (1859–1936)

When I was one-and-twenty

> *Although he failed his final examinations at Oxford in 1881, A. E. Housman was regarded as an excellent student. Later he earned a master of arts and became a professor of Latin at Cambridge University. Housman, who believed that*

*poetry should appeal more to the heart than to the mind, often wrote on themes
related to the transitory quality of youth and romantic love.*

When I was one-and-twenty
   I heard a wise man say,
"Give crowns and pounds and guineas
   But not your heart away;
Give pearls away and rubies   5
   But keep your fancy free."
But I was one-and-twenty,
   No use to talk to me.

When I was one-and-twenty
   I heard him say again,   10
"The heart out of the bosom
   Was never given in vain;
'Tis paid with sighs a plenty
   And sold for endless rue."
And I am two-and-twenty,   15
   And oh, 'tis true, 'tis true.   *1896*

CONSIDERATIONS

1. Compare the advice given by the wise man in stanza 1 to the advice he
   gives in stanza 2. Is he saying the same thing both times? Or do you see the
   meaning as different? What might he mean, for instance, by "keep your
   fancy free"?
2. How does the attitude of the speaker change from stanza 1 to stanza 2? Pay
   particular attention to the last two lines in each stanza. What are the implications of the change?
3. Imagine the speaker at thirty-two (or at forty or at sixty-five). To what extent and in what ways do you think this early lesson might affect his later
   life? Create several possible scenarios.

COUNTEE CULLEN (1903–1946)

Incident

*Along with Langston Hughes, Richard Wright, and Jean Toomer, Countee
Cullen was a major figure in the Harlem Renaissance of the 1920s. Most of
his work focuses on themes related to race and class structure. He published five*

volumes of poetry and a novel, One Way to Heaven *(1932), which is set in
Harlem in the 1920s and depicts conflicts and contrasts between wealthy and
poor African Americans.*

Once riding in old Baltimore,
   Heart-filled, head-filled with glee,
I saw a Baltimorean
   Keep looking straight at me.

5 Now I was eight and very small,
   And he was no whit bigger,
And so I smiled, but he poked out
   His tongue and called me, "Nigger."

I saw the whole of Baltimore
10   From May until December:
Of all the things that happened there
   That's all that I remember.   *1925*

CONSIDERATIONS

1. Read this poem aloud. How do the rhythm and rhyme in the poem relate
   to the picture given of the speaker and of his experience?
2. What is the significance of the final stanza? Why is this the only event that
   the speaker remembers about his eight-month stay in Baltimore?
3. Describe an incident from your past that you remember as vividly as the
   speaker remembers this one. Focus on one particular moment lasting no
   more than five or ten minutes. Explain both what happened and why it
   was so significant that you can still recall it in detail.

GWENDOLYN BROOKS (1917–2000)

We Real Cool
The Pool Players.
Seven at the Golden Shovel.

*Shortly after her birth in Kansas, Gwendolyn Brooks's family moved to
Bronzeville in Chicago's South Side. Living in this predominantly African-
American district provided Brooks with her sources, images, and direction as a
poet. In 1949, she was awarded the Pulitzer Prize for Poetry for her book-*

More Resources on
Gwendolyn Brooks and "We Real Cool"

In *ARIEL*
- Brief biography of Brooks
- Complete text of "We Real Cool" and other Brooks poems, all with hyperlinked comments
- Video discussion of Brooks's writing
- Analysis of imagery in Brooks's poetry
- Bibliography of scholarly works on Brooks

In the Online Learning Center for *Responding to Literature*
- Brief biography of Brooks
- List of major works by Brooks
- Web links to more resources on Brooks
- Additional questions for experiencing and interpreting Brooks's writing

length experimental work Annie Allen. *Brooks regarded 1967, when she recognized and became part of the movement toward an increasing consciousness of black identity, as a pivotal year in her life.*

We real cool. We
Left school. We

Lurk late. We
Strike straight. We

Sing sin. We   5
Thin gin. We

Jazz June. We
Die soon.   *1960*

CONSIDERATIONS

1. What effect does the simplicity of the language have on you as you read this poem?

2. What purpose does the repetition of "we" serve in this poem? What is missing from the first line, and why does this matter to the poem as a whole?

JOHN UPDIKE (1932–   )

Ex-Basketball Player

> *Although John Updike is best known for his novels and short stories, he has also*
> *published over two dozen books of poetry, including* The Carpentered Hen
> and Other Tame Creatures *(1958), the source of this poem. He began his*
> *career as a writer for* The New Yorker *from 1955 to 1957. But after he left*
> *that job, he devoted himself full-time to his own writing. During his career, he*
> *has won numerous awards, including two Pulitzer Prizes, first for his novel*
> Rabbit Is Rich *(1981) and second for its sequel,* Rabbit at Rest *(1990).*
> *Updike was born in a small town in Pennsylvania, the son of a teacher and an*
> *author, and much of his writing draws on that background. As one critic has*
> *noted, "he transmutes the stubborn banality of middle-class existence into*
> *tableaux that shiver with the hint of spiritual meaning."*

Pearl Avenue runs past the high-school lot,
Bends with the trolley tracks, and stops, cut off
Before it has a chance to go two blocks,
At Colonel McComsky Plaza. Berth's Garage
5   Is on the corner facing west, and there,
Most days, you'll find Flick Webb, who helps Berth out.

Flick stands tall among the idiot pumps—
Five on a side, the old bubble-head style,
Their rubber elbows hanging loose and low.
10   One's nostrils are two S's, and his eyes
An E and O. And one is squat, without
A head at all—more of a football type.

Once Flick played for the high-school team, the Wizards.
He was good: in fact, the best. In '46
15   He bucketed three hundred ninety points,
A county record still. The ball loved Flick.
I saw him rack up thirty-eight or forty
In one home game. His hands were like wild birds.

He never learned a trade, he just sells gas,
20   Checks oil, and changes flats. Once in a while,

As a gag, he dribbles an inner tube,
But most of us remember anyway.
His hands are fine and nervous on the lug wrench.
It makes no difference to the lug wrench, though.

Off work, he hangs around Mae's luncheonette.   25
Grease-gray and kind of coiled, he plays pinball,
Smokes those thin cigars, nurses lemon phosphates.
Flick seldom says a word to Mae, just nods
Beyond her face toward bright applauding tiers
Of Necco Wafers, Nibs, and Juju Beads.   *1958*   30

CONSIDERATIONS

1. Who is Flick Webb? Do you think his experience, as suggested by the images of the poem, is common among high school athletes?
2. What do you think the future holds for Flick Webb? Who or what is responsible for this future?

SEAMUS HEANEY (1939–   )

Mid-Term Break

> *Seamus Heaney's poetry is rooted both in his native Northern Ireland and in his own life experiences. His volumes of verse include* Door into the Dark *(1969),* North *(1975), and* Field Work *(1979). Many of his critical and autobiographical pieces in prose appear in the collection* Preoccupations *(1980). He was awarded the Nobel Prize for literature in 1995. In 1999 he published a highly regarded new verse translation of the Anglo-Saxon epic* Beowulf.

I sat all morning in the college sick bay
Counting bells knelling classes to a close.
At two o'clock our neighbors drove me home.

In the porch I met my father crying—
He had always taken funerals in his stride—   5
And Big Jim Evans saying it was a hard blow.

The baby cooed and laughed and rocked the pram
When I came in, and I was embarrassed
By old men standing up to shake my hand

10 And tell me they were "sorry for my trouble,"
 Whispers informed strangers I was the eldest,
 Away at school, as my mother held my hand

 In hers and coughed out angry tearless sighs.
 At ten o'clock the ambulance arrived
15 With the corpse, stanched and bandaged by the nurses.

 Next morning I went up into the room. Snowdrops
 And candles soothed the bedside; I saw him
 For the first time in six weeks. Paler now,

 Wearing a poppy bruise on his left temple,
20 He lay in the four foot box as in his cot.
 No gaudy scars, the bumper knocked him clear.

 A four foot box, a foot for every year. *1980*

CONSIDERATIONS

1. From the first stanza to the last, elements of time are clear and present. How does this attention to time serve the poem's theme? What do these time details reveal about the narrator?
2. What are the major differences between the narrator and the other mourners in this poem? What might Heaney be suggesting about life's stages?

GARY SOTO (1952–)

Oranges

> *Gary Soto grew up in Fresno in California's San Joaquin Valley; his grandparents had migrated there from Mexico in the 1930s to work as farm laborers. With degrees from California State University, Fresno, and the University of California at Irvine, he now teaches English at the University of California at Berkeley. Starting with his first book of poetry,* The Elements of San Joaquin *(1977), most of his writing is set in the Mexican-American neighborhoods of Fresno. In addition to several books of poetry, Soto has also published collections of autobiographical essays, including* Living Up the Street *(1984) and* Small Faces *(1986), and short stories, including* Baseball in April *(1990), as well as numerous books for children and adolescents. As in the poem "Oranges," his work often describes experiences of childhood and adolescence.*

The first time I walked
With a girl, I was twelve,
Cold, and weighted down
With two oranges in my jacket.
December. Frost cracking   *5*
Beneath my steps, my breath
Before me, then gone,
As I walked toward
Her house, the one whose
Porch light burned yellow   *10*
Night and day, in any weather.
A dog barked at me, until
She came out pulling
At her gloves, face bright
With rouge. I smiled,   *15*
Touched her shoulder, and led
Her down the street, across
A used car lot and a line
Of newly planted trees,
Until we were breathing   *20*
Before a drugstore. We
Entered, the tiny bell
Bringing a saleslady
Down a narrow aisle of goods.
I turned to the candies   *25*
Tiered like bleachers,
And asked what she wanted—
Light in her eyes, a smile
Starting at the corners
Of her mouth. I fingered   *30*
A nickel in my pocket,
And when she lifted a chocolate
That cost a dime,
I didn't say anything.
I took the nickel from   *35*
My pocket, then an orange,
And set them quietly on
The counter. When I looked up,
The lady's eyes met mine,
And held them, knowing   *40*
Very well what it was all
About.

Outside,
A few cars hissing past,
45 Fog hanging like old
Coats between the trees.
I took my girl's hand
In mine for two blocks,
Then released it to let
50 Her unwrap the chocolate.
I peeled my orange
That was so bright against
The gray of December
That, from some distance,
55 Someone might have thought
I was making a fire in my hands.   *1985*

CONSIDERATIONS

1. Describe the setting of the poem. What effect is produced by the contrasts of the cold December day and the images of heat and warmth? What else is the speaker trying to show? Look especially at the imagery in the last ten lines of the poem.
2. The title of the poem is "Oranges," and yet the poem is about young love. Explain the image of "Cold, and weighted down / With two oranges in my jacket." What is the speaker's intention in having two oranges? Besides the physical weight of the oranges in his pocket, is there anything else you might make of this?
3. It was once very common for a store's door to have a bell that would signal someone's entrance. Why is the sound of the tiny bell important in this poem? Is it just to allow the saleslady to be a part of the scene? Explain.
4. Why did the saleslady know "very well what it was all about"? Would you have empathized with the young man and accepted the orange in place of the money? Why? Why not?
5. What did the young man learn from this experience? Was he innocent? Explain the difference between his innocence and that of someone more mature in a similar situation.
6. Have you ever been on a date and had an experience similar to that of the young man in this poem, when your date chose something you could not afford? Describe your experience. What did you do? Do you think that the young man acted appropriately? What else could he have done?

NAOMI SHIHAB NYE (1952–   )

Rain

Born in St. Louis, Missouri, to an American mother and a Palestinian father,
Nye has traveled widely in Asia and the Middle East, representing the United
States Information Agency. She believes strongly that people from very different
cultures can find common ground in appreciation for the arts. She has published
several books of poetry and, in addition, has written children's books and edited
anthologies of prose.

A teacher asked Paul
what he would remember
from third grade, and he sat
a long time before writing
"this year sumbody tutched me   5
on the sholder"
and turned his paper in.
Later she showed it to me
as an example of her wasted life.
The words he wrote were large   10
as houses in a landscape.
He wanted to go inside them
and live, he could fill in
the windows of "o" and "d"
and be safe while outside   15
birds building nests in drainpipes
knew nothing of the coming rain.   *1986*

CONSIDERATIONS

1. Who or what is the poem mainly about? Explain.
2. Line 9 seems to be a dividing point between an objective observation and
   an analysis of the situation. Why might the author have structured the poem
   this way?

Drama

WILLIAM SHAKESPEARE (1564–1616)
Hamlet

Although there is little direct evidence relating to Shakespeare's childhood and adolescence, it is almost certain that he was educated at the free grammar school in his native Stratford-on-Avon, England. As Shakespeare entered his teens, his father experienced serious financial setbacks, and William apparently had to leave school to help support the family. At eighteen, he married Anne Hathaway, with whom he had three children. Sometime after the birth of his children, Shakespeare left Stratford-on-Avon and went to London, where he began his career as an actor and playwright. By 1594, he had gained both wealth and prestige, perform- ing at court for Queen Elizabeth I. During the 1590s, he wrote a series of son- nets, many of which address themes of love. His plays include comedies such as As You Like It (1599), A Midsummer Night's Dream (1595), and Twelfth Night (1599). Shakespeare's best-known tragedies are Hamlet (1602), Othello (1604), King Lear (1605), and Macbeth (1606). Richard III (1592) and Henry IV, Parts I and II (1590) are among his historical plays based on the political struggles of England's ruling families. In 1611, he retired to Stratford, where he lived until his death in 1616. After his burial, his grave was marked by a stone bearing an inscription (supposedly dictated by Shakespeare himself) that warns all who come "Bleste Be Ye Man Yt Spares Thes Stones / And Curst Be He Yt Moves My Bones."

Characters

CLAUDIUS, *King of Denmark*
HAMLET, *son of the late King Hamlet, and nephew to the present King*
POLONIUS, *Lord Chamberlain*
HORATIO, *friend to Hamlet*
LAERTES, *son to Polonius*
VOLTIMAND,
CORNELIUS,
ROSENCRANTZ, ⎫
GUILDENSTERN, ⎬ *courtiers*
OSRIC,
GENTLEMAN, ⎭
PRIEST, OR DOCTOR OF DIVINITY
MARCELLUS, ⎫ *officers*
BERNARDO, ⎭

FRANCISCO, *a soldier*
REYNALDO, *servant to Polonius*
PLAYERS
TWO CLOWNS, *grave-diggers*
FORTINBRAS, *Prince of Norway*
CAPTAIN
ENGLISH AMBASSADORS
GERTRUDE, *Queen of Denmark, mother to Hamlet*
OPHELIA, *daughter to Polonius*
LORDS, LADIES, OFFICERS, SOLDIERS, SAILORS, MESSENGERS, AND OTHER
    ATTENDANTS
GHOST *of Hamlet's father*

Scene *Denmark*

ACT I
SCENE I°

   (Enter BERNARDO *and* FRANCISCO, TWO SENTINELS, *[meeting].)*

BERNARDO: Who's there?
FRANCISCO: Nay, answer me.° Stand and unfold yourself.
BERNARDO: Long live the King!
FRANCISCO: Bernardo?
BERNARDO: He.   5
FRANCISCO: You come most carefully upon your hour.
BERNARDO: 'Tis now struck twelve. Get thee to bed, Francisco.
FRANCISCO: For this relief much thanks. 'Tis bitter cold,
    And I am sick at heart.
BERNARDO: Have you had quiet guard?
FRANCISCO: Not a mouse stirring.   10
BERNARDO: Well, good night.
    If you do meet Horatio and Marcellus,
    The rivals° of my watch, bid them make haste.

    (Enter HORATIO *and* MARCELLUS.)

FRANCISCO: I think I hear them. Stand, ho! Who is there?
HORATIO: Friends to this ground.
MARCELLUS: And liegemen to the Dane.°   15
FRANCISCO: Give you° good night.

ACT I, SCENE I. *Location:* Elsinore castle. A guard platform. 2 *me:* Francisco emphasizes that *he*
is the sentry currently on watch. 13 *rivals:* Partners. 15 *liegemen to the Dane:* Men sworn to serve
the Danish king. 16 *Give you:* God give you.

MARCELLUS: O, farewell, honest soldier.
    Who hath relieved you?
FRANCISCO: Bernardo hath my place.
    Give you good night.   *(Exit* FRANCISCO.*)*
MARCELLUS: Holla, Bernardo!
BERNARDO: Say,
    What, is Horatio there?
HORATIO: A piece of him.
20 BERNARDO: Welcome, Horatio. Welcome, good Marcellus.
HORATIO: What, has this thing appear'd again tonight?
BERNARDO: I have seen nothing.
MARCELLUS: Horatio says 'tis but our fantasy,
    And will not let belief take hold of him
25   Touching this dreaded sight, twice seen of us.
    Therefore I have entreated him along
    With us to watch the minutes of this night,
    That if again this apparition come
    He may approve° our eyes and speak to it.
HORATIO: Tush, tush, 'twill not appear.
30 BERNARDO: Sit down awhile,
    And let us once again assail your ears,
    That are so fortified against our story,
    What we have two nights seen.
HORATIO: Well, sit we down,
    And let us hear Bernardo speak of this.
35 BERNARDO: Last night of all,
    When yond same star that's westward from the pole°
    Had made his° course t' illume that part of heaven
    Where now it burns, Marcellus and myself,
    The bell then beating one—

    (Enter GHOST.*)*

40 MARCELLUS: Peace, break thee off! Look where it comes again!
BERNARDO: In the same figure, like the King that's dead.
MARCELLUS: Thou art a scholar.° Speak to it, Horatio.
BERNARDO: Looks 'a° not like the King? Mark it, Horatio.
HORATIO: Most like. It harrows me with fear and wonder.
BERNARDO: It would be spoke to.
45 MARCELLUS: Speak to it,° Horatio.
HORATIO: What art thou that usurp'st this time of night,
    Together with that fair and warlike form

---

29 *approve:* Corroborate. 36 *pole:* Polestar. 37 *his:* Its. 42 *scholar:* One learned in Latin and able
to address spirits. 43 *'a:* He. 45 *It . . . it:* A ghost could not speak until spoken to.

In which the majesty of buried Denmark°
Did sometimes° march? By heaven I charge thee, speak!
MARCELLUS: It is offended.
BERNARDO: See, it stalks away.   50
HORATIO: Stay! Speak, speak. I charge thee, speak.   *(Exit* GHOST.*)*
MARCELLUS: 'Tis gone, and will not answer.
BERNARDO: How now, Horatio? You tremble and look pale.
   Is not this something more than fantasy?
   What think you on 't?   55
HORATIO: Before my God, I might not this believe
   Without the sensible° and true avouch
   Of mine own eyes.
MARCELLUS: Is it not like the King?
HORATIO: As thou art to thyself.
   Such was the very armor he had on   60
   When he the ambitious Norway° combated.
   So frown'd he once when, in an angry parle,°
   He smote the sledded° Polacks on the ice.
   'Tis strange.
MARCELLUS: Thus twice before, and jump° at this dead hour,   65
   With martial stalk hath he gone by our watch.
HORATIO: In what particular thought to work I know not,
   But, in the gross and scope° of mine opinion,
   This bodes some strange eruption to our state.
MARCELLUS: Good now,° sit down, and tell me, he that knows,   70
   Why this same strict and most observant watch
   So nightly toils° the subject° of the land,
   And why such daily cast° of brazen cannon,
   And foreign mart° for implements of war,
   Why such impress° of shipwrights, whose sore task   75
   Does not divide the Sunday from the week.
   What might be toward,° that this sweaty haste
   Doth make the night joint-laborer with the day?
   What is 't that can inform me?
HORATIO: That can I,
   At least, the whisper goes so. Our last king,   80
   Whose image even but now appear'd to us,
   Was, as you know, by Fortinbras of Norway,

48 *buried Denmark:* The buried king of Denmark. 49 *sometimes:* Formerly. 57 *sensible:* Confirmed by the senses. 61 *Norway:* King of Norway. 62 *parle:* Parley. 63 *sledded:* Traveling on sleds; *Polacks:* Poles. 65 *jump:* Exactly. 68 *gross and scope:* General view. 70 *Good now:* An expression denoting entreaty or expostulation. 72 *toils:* Causes to toil; *subject:* Subjects. 73 *cast:* Casting. 74 *mart:* Buying and selling. 75 *impress:* Impressment, conscription. 77 *toward:* In preparation.

Thereto prick'd on° by a most emulate° pride,
Dar'd to the combat; in which our valiant Hamlet—
85   For so this side of our known world esteem'd him—
Did slay this Fortinbras; who, by a seal'd compact,
Well ratified by law and heraldry,
Did forfeit, with his life, all those his lands
Which he stood seiz'd° of, to the conqueror;
90   Against the° which a moi'ty competent°
Was gaged° by our king, which had return'd
To the inheritance of Fortinbras
Had he been vanquisher, as, by the same comart°
And carriage° of the article design'd,
95   His fell to Hamlet. Now, sir, young Fortinbras,
Of unimproved° mettle hot and full,
Hath in the skirts° of Norway here and there
Shark'd up° a list of lawless resolutes°
For food and diet° to some enterprise
100   That hath a stomach° in 't, which is no other—
As it doth well appear unto our state—
But to recover of us, by strong hand
And terms compulsatory, those foresaid lands
So by his father lost. And this, I take it,
105   Is the main motive of our preparations,
The source of this our watch, and the chief head°
Of this post-haste and romage° in the land.
BERNARDO: I think it be no other but e'en so.
Well may it sort° that this portentous figure
110   Comes armed through our watch so like the King
That was and is the question of these wars.
HORATIO: A mote° it is to trouble the mind's eye.
In the most high and palmy° state of Rome,
A little ere the mightiest Julius fell,
115   The graves stood tenantless and the sheeted° dead
Did squeak and gibber in the Roman streets;
As° stars with trains of fire and dews of blood,

---

83 *prick'd on:* Incited; *emulate:* Ambitious. 89 *seiz'd:* Possessed. 90 *Against the:* In return for; *moi'ty competent:* Sufficient portion. 91 *gaged:* Engaged, pledged. 93 *comart:* Joint bargain (?). 94 *carriage:* Import, bearing. 96 *unimproved:* Not turned to account (?) or untested (?). 97 *skirts:* Outlying regions, outskirts. 98 *Shark'd up:* Got together in haphazard fashion; *resolutes:* Desperadoes. 99 *food and diet:* No pay but their keep. 100 *stomach:* Relish of danger. 106 *head:* Source. 107 *romage:* Bustle, commotion. 109 *sort:* Suit. 112 *mote:* Speck of dust. 113 *palmy:* Flourishing. 115 *sheeted:* Shrouded. 117 *As:* This abrupt transition suggests that matter is possibly omitted between lines 116 and 117.

Disasters° in the sun; and the moist star°
Upon whose influence Neptune's° empire stands°
Was sick almost to doomsday° with eclipse.°   120
And even the like precurse° of fear'd events,
As harbingers° preceding still° the fates
And prologue to the omen° coming on,
Have heaven and earth together demonstrated
Unto our climatures° and countrymen.   125

(Enter GHOST.*)*

But soft, behold! Lo where it comes again!
I'll cross° it, though it blast me. Stay, illusion!
If thou hast any sound, or use of voice,
Speak to me!   *(It spreads his arms.)*
If there be any good thing to be done   130
That may to thee do ease and grace to me,
Speak to me!
If thou art privy to thy country's fate,
Which, happily,° foreknowing may avoid,
O, speak!   135
Or if thou hast uphoarded in thy life
Extorted treasure in the womb of earth,
For which, they say, you spirits oft walk in death,   *(The cock crows.)*
Speak of it. Stay, and speak! Stop it, Marcellus.
MARCELLUS: Shall I strike at it with my partisan?°   140
HORATIO: Do, if it will not stand.   *(They strike at it.)*
BERNARDO: 'Tis here!
HORATIO: 'Tis here!
MARCELLUS: 'Tis gone.   *(Exit* GHOST.*)*
     We do it wrong, being so majestical,
     To offer it the show of violence;
     For it is, as the air, invulnerable,   145
     And our vain blows malicious mockery.
BERNARDO: It was about to speak when the cock crew.
HORATIO: And then it started like a guilty thing
     Upon a fearful summons. I have heard,
     The cock, that is the trumpet to the morn,   150

---

118 *Disasters:* Unfavorable signs of aspects; *moist star:* Moon, governing tides. 119 *Neptune:* God of the sea; *stands:* Depends. 120 *sick . . . doomsday:* See Matt. 24:29 and Rev. 6:12. 121 *precurse:* Heralding, foreshadowing. 122 *harbingers:* Forerunners; *still:* Continually. 123 *omen:* Calamitous event. 125 *climatures:* Regions. 127 *cross:* Meet, face directly. 134 *happily:* Haply, perchance. 140 *partisan:* Long-handled spear.

   Doth with his lofty and shrill-sounding throat
   Awake the god of day, and, at his warning,
   Whether in sea or fire, in earth or air,
   Th' extravagant and erring° spirit hies
155   To his confine; and of the truth herein
   This present object made probation.°
MARCELLUS: It faded on the crowing of the cock.
   Some say that ever 'gainst° that season comes
   Wherein our Savior's birth is celebrated,
160   The bird of dawning singeth all night long,
   And then, they say, no spirit dare stir abroad;
   The nights are wholesome, then no planets strike,°
   No fairy takes,° nor witch hath power to charm,
   So hallowed and so gracious° is that time.
165   HORATIO: So have I heard and do in part believe it.
   But, look, the morn, in russet mantle clad,
   Walks o'er the dew of yon high eastward hill.
   Break we our watch up, and by my advice
   Let us impart what we have seen tonight
170   Unto young Hamlet; for, upon my life,
   This spirit, dumb to us, will speak to him.
   Do you consent we shall acquaint him with it,
   As needful in our loves, fitting our duty?
MARCELLUS: Let's do 't, I pray, and I this morning know
175   Where we shall find him most conveniently.   *(Exeunt.)*°

SCENE II°

   (Flourish. Enter CLAUDIUS, *King of Denmark,* GERTRUDE *the Queen,*
   COUNCILORS, POLONIUS *and his son* LAERTES, HAMLET, *cum aliis*° *[in-
   cluding* VOLTIMAND *and* CORNELIUS].)

KING: Though yet of Hamlet our dear brother's death
   The memory be green, and that it us befitted
   To bear our hearts in grief and our whole kingdom
   To be contracted in one brow of woe,
5   Yet so far hath discretion fought with nature
   That we with wisest sorrow think on him,
   Together with remembrance of ourselves.
   Therefore our sometime sister, now our queen,

---

154 *extravagant and erring:* Wandering. (The words have similar meaning.) 156 *probation:* Proof.
158 *'gainst:* Just before. 162 *strike:* Exert evil influence. 163 *takes:* Bewitches. 164 *gracious:* Full
of goodness. 175 s.d. *Exeunt:* Latin for "they go out." ACT I, SCENE II. *Location:* The castle; s.d.
cum aliis: With others.

Th' imperial jointress° to this warlike state,
Have we, as 'twere with a defeated joy—   10
With an auspicious and a dropping eye,
With mirth in funeral and with dirge in marriage,
In equal scale weighing delight and dole—
Taken to wife. Nor have we herein barr'd
Your better wisdoms, which have freely gone   15
With this affair along. For all, our thanks.
Now follows that you know° young Fortinbras,
Holding a weak supposal° of our worth,
Or thinking by our late dear brother's death
Our state to be disjoint and out of frame,   20
Colleagued with° this dream of his advantage,°
He hath not fail'd to pester us with message
Importing° the surrender of those lands
Lost by his father, with all bands° of law,
To our most valiant brother. So much for him.   25
Now for ourself and for this time of meeting.
Thus much the business is: we have here writ
To Norway, uncle of young Fortinbras—
Who, impotent and bed-rid, scarcely hears
Of this his nephew's purpose—to suppress   30
His° further gait herein, in that the levies,
The lists, and full proportions are all made
Out of his subject;° and we here dispatch
You, good Cornelius, and you, Voltimand,
For bearers of this greeting to old Norway,   35
Giving to you no further personal power
To business with the King, more than the scope
Of these delated° articles allow.   *(Gives a paper.)*
Farewell, and let your haste commend your duty.
CORNELIUS, VOLTIMAND: In that, and all things, will we show our duty.   40
KING: We doubt it nothing. Heartily farewell.
                              (Exit VOLTIMAND *and* CORNELIUS.*)*
And now, Laertes, what's the news with you?
You told us of some suit; what is 't, Laertes?
You cannot speak of reason to the Dane°

9 *jointress:* Woman possessed of a joint tenancy of an estate. 17 *know:* Be informed (that). 18 *weak supposal:* Low estimate. 21 *Colleagued with:* Joined to, allied with; *dream . . . advantage:* Illusory hope of success. 23 *Importing:* Pertaining to. 24 *bands:* Contracts. 31 *His:* Fortinbras's; *gait:* Proceeding. 31–33 *in that . . . subject:* Since the levying of troops and supplies is drawn entirely from the King of Norway's own subjects. 38 *delated:* Detailed. (Variant of "dilated.") 44 *the Dane:* The Danish King.

45   And lose your voice.° What wouldst thou beg, Laertes,
      That shall not be my offer, not thy asking?
      The head is not more native° to the heart,
      The hand more instrumental° to the mouth,
      Than is the throne of Denmark to thy father.
      What wouldst thou have, Laertes?
50 LAERTES: My dread lord,
      Your leave and favor to return to France,
      From whence though willingly I came to Denmark
      To show my duty in your coronation,
      Yet now I must confess, that duty done,
55   My thoughts and wishes bend again toward France
      And bow them to your gracious leave and pardon.°
    KING: Have you your father's leave? What says Polonius?
    POLONIUS: H'ath, my lord, wrung from me my slow leave
      By laborsome petition, and at last
60   Upon his will I seal'd my hard° consent.
      I do beseech you, give him leave to go.
    KING: Take thy fair hour, Laertes. Time be thine,
      And thy best graces spend it at thy will!
      But now, my cousin° Hamlet, and my son—
65 HAMLET: A little more than kin, and less than kind.°
    KING: How is it that the clouds still hang on you?
    HAMLET: Not so, my lord. I am too much in the sun.°
    QUEEN: Good Hamlet, cast thy nighted color off,
      And let thine eye look like a friend on Denmark.
70   Do not forever with thy vailed° lids
      Seek for thy noble father in the dust.
      Thou know'st 'tis common,° all that lives must die,
      Passing through nature to eternity.
    HAMLET: Ay, madam, it is common.
    QUEEN: If it be,
75   Why seems it so particular with thee?
    HAMLET: Seems, madam! Nay, it is. I know not "seems."
      'Tis not alone my inky cloak, good mother,
      Nor customary suits of solemn black,

---

45 *lose your voice:* Waste your speech. 47 *native:* Closely connected, related. 48 *instrumental:* Ser-
viceable. 56 *leave and pardon:* Permission to depart. 60 *hard:* Reluctant. 64 *cousin:* Any kin not
of the immediate family. 65 *A little . . . kind:* Closer than an ordinary nephew (since I am stepson), and yet more separated in natural feeling (with pun on "kind," meaning affectionate and
natural, lawful). (This line is often read as an aside, but it need not be.) 67 *sun:* The sunshine of
the King's royal favor (with pun on "son"). 70 *vailed:* Downcast. 72 *common:* Of universal occurrence. (But Hamlet plays on the sense of "vulgar" in line 74.)

Nor windy suspiration of forc'd breath,
No, nor the fruitful° river in the eye,   80
Nor the dejected havior of the visage,
Together with all forms, moods, shapes of grief,
That can denote me truly. These indeed seem,
For they are actions that a man might play.
But I have that within which passes show;   85
These but the trappings and the suits of woe.
KING: 'Tis sweet and commendable in your nature, Hamlet,
To give these mourning duties to your father.
But you must know your father lost a father,
That father lost, lost his, and the survivor bound   90
In filial obligation for some term
To do obsequious° sorrow. But to persever°
In obstinate condolement° is a course
Of impious stubbornness. 'Tis unmanly grief.
It shows a will most incorrect to heaven,   95
A heart unfortified, a mind impatient,
An understanding simple and unschool'd.
For what we know must be and is as common
As any the most vulgar thing to sense,°
Why should we in our peevish opposition   100
Take it to heart? Fie, 'tis a fault to heaven,
A fault against the dead, a fault to nature,
To reason most absurd, whose common theme
Is death of fathers, and who still hath cried,
From the first corse° till he that died today,   105
"This must be so." We pray you, throw to earth
This unprevailing° woe, and think of us
As of a father; for let the world take note,
You are the most immediate° to our throne,
And with no less nobility of love   110
Than that which dearest father bears his son
Do I impart toward you. For your intent
In going back to school in Wittenberg,°
It is most retrograde° to our desire,
And we beseech you, bend you° to remain   115
Here in the cheer and comfort of our eye,
Our chiefest courtier, cousin, and our son.

---

80 *fruitful:* Abundant. 92 *obsequious:* Suited to obsequies or funerals; *persever:* Persevere. 93 *condolement:* Sorrowing. 99 *As . . . sense:* As the most ordinary experience. 105 *corse:* Corpse. 107 *unprevailing:* Unavailing. 109 *most immediate:* Next in succession. 113 *Wittenberg:* Famous German university founded in 1502. 114 *retrograde:* Contrary. 115 *bend you:* Incline yourself.

QUEEN: Let not thy mother lose her prayers, Hamlet.
        I pray thee stay with us, go not to Wittenberg.
120 HAMLET: I shall in all my best obey you, madam.
    KING: Why, 'tis a loving and a fair reply.
        Be as ourself in Denmark. Madam, come.
        This gentle and unforc'd accord of Hamlet
        Sits smiling to my heart, in grace whereof
125   No jocund° health that Denmark drinks today
        But the great cannon to the clouds shall tell,
        And the King's rouse° the heaven shall bruit again,°
        Respeaking earthly thunder.° Come away.

                        (Flourish. Exeunt all but HAMLET.*)*

    HAMLET: O, that this too too sullied° flesh would melt,
130   Thaw, and resolve itself into a dew!
        Or that the Everlasting had not fix'd
        His canon° 'gainst self-slaughter! O God, God,
        How weary, stale, flat, and unprofitable
        Seem to me all the uses of this world!
135   Fie on 't, ah, fie! 'Tis an unweeded garden
        That grows to seed. Things rank and gross in nature
        Possess it merely.° That it should come to this!
        But two months dead—nay, not so much, not two.
        So excellent a king, that was to° this
140   Hyperion° to a satyr; so loving to my mother
        That he might not beteem° the winds of heaven
        Visit her face too roughly. Heaven and earth,
        Must I remember? Why, she would hang on him
        As if increase of appetite had grown
145   By what it fed on, and yet, within a month—
        Let me not think on 't. Frailty, thy name is woman!—
        A little month, or ere those shoes were old
        With which she followed my poor father's body,
        Like Niobe,° all tears, why she, even she—
150   O God, a beast, that wants discourse of reason,°
        Would have mourn'd longer—married with my uncle,
        My father's brother, but no more like my father

---

125 *jocund:* Merry. 127 *rouse:* Draft of liquor; *bruit again:* Loudly echo. 128 *thunder:* Of trumpet
and kettledrum, sounded when the King drinks; see I.iv.8–12. 129 *sullied:* Defiled. 132 *canon:*
Law. 137 *merely:* Completely. 139 *to:* In comparison to. 140 *Hyperion:* Titan sun-god, father of
Helios. 141 *beteem:* Allow. 149 *Niobe:* Tantalus's daughter, Queen of Thebes, who boasted that
she had more sons and daughters than Leto; for this, Apollo and Artemis, children of Leto, slew
her fourteen children. She was turned by Zeus into a stone that continually dropped tears. 150
wants . . . reason: Lacks the faculty of reason.

Than I to Hercules. Within a month,
Ere yet the salt of most unrighteous tears
Had left the flushing in her galled° eyes, 155
She married. O, most wicked speed, to post
With such dexterity to incestuous° sheets!
It is not nor it cannot come to good.
But break, my heart, for I must hold my tongue.

(Enter HORATIO, MARCELLUS, *and* BERNARDO.*)*

HORATIO: Hail to your lordship!
HAMLET: I am glad to see you well. 160
    Horatio!—or I do forget myself.
HORATIO: The same, my lord, and your poor servant ever.
HAMLET: Sir, my good friend; I'll change° that name with you.
    And what make° you from Wittenberg, Horatio?
    Marcellus? 165
MARCELLUS: My good lord.
HAMLET: I am very glad to see you. *(To* BERNARDO.*)* Good even, sir.—
    But what, in faith, make you from Wittenberg?
HORATIO: A truant disposition, good my lord.
HAMLET: I would not hear your enemy say so, 170
    Nor shall you do my ear that violence
    To make it truster of your own report
    Against yourself. I know you are no truant.
    But what is your affair in Elsinore?
    We'll teach you to drink deep ere you depart. 175
HORATIO: My lord, I came to see your father's funeral.
HAMLET: I prithee do not mock me, fellow student;
    I think it was to see my mother's wedding.
HORATIO: Indeed, my lord, it followed hard° upon.
HAMLET: Thrift, thrift, Horatio! The funeral bak'd meats 180
    Did coldly furnish forth the marriage tables.
    Would I had met my dearest° foe in heaven
    Or° ever I had seen that day, Horatio!
    My father!—Methinks I see my father.
HORATIO: Where, my lord?
HAMLET: In my mind's eye, Horatio. 185
HORATIO: I saw him once. 'A° was a goodly king.
HAMLET: 'A was a man, take him for all in all,

---

155 *galled:* Irritated, inflamed. 157 *incestuous:* In Shakespeare's day, the marriage of a man like
Claudius to his deceased brother's wife was considered incestuous. 163 *change:* Exchange (i.e.,
the name of friend). 164 *make:* Do. 179 *hard:* Close. 182 *dearest:* Direst. 183 *Or:* Ere, before.
186 *'A:* He.

I shall not look upon his like again.

HORATIO: My lord, I think I saw him yesternight.

190   HAMLET: Saw? Who?

HORATIO: My lord, the King your father.

HAMLET: The King my father.

HORATIO: Season your admiration° for a while
With an attent° ear, till I may deliver,
Upon the witness of these gentlemen,
This marvel to you.

195   HAMLET: For God's love, let me hear!

HORATIO: Two nights together had these gentlemen,
Marcellus and Bernardo, on their watch,
In the dead waste and middle of the night,
Been thus encount'red. A figure like your father,

200   Armed at point° exactly, cap-a-pe,°
Appears before them, and with solemn march
Goes slow and stately by them. Thrice he walk'd
By their oppress'd and fear-surprised eyes
Within his truncheon's° length, whilst they, distill'd

205   Almost to jelly with the act° of fear,
Stand dumb and speak not to him. This to me
In dreadful secrecy impart they did,
And I with them the third night kept the watch,
Where, as they had delivered, both in time,

210   Form of the thing, each word made true and good,
The apparition comes. I knew your father;
These hands are not more like.

HAMLET: But where was this?

MARCELLUS: My lord, upon the platform where we watch.

HAMLET: Did you not speak to it?

HORATIO: My lord, I did,

215   But answer made it none. Yet once methought
It lifted up it° head and did address
Itself to motion, like as it would speak;
But even then the morning cock crew loud,
And at the sound it shrunk in haste away,
And vanish'd from our sight.

220   HAMLET: 'Tis very strange.

HORATIO: As I do live, my honor'd lord, 'tis true,

---

192 *Season your admiration:* Restrain your astonishment. 193 *attent:* Attentive. 200 *at point:* Completely; *cap-a-pe:* From head to foot. 204 *truncheon:* Officer's staff. 205 *act:* Action, operation.
216 *it:* Its.

And we did think it writ down in our duty
    To let you know of it.
HAMLET: Indeed, indeed, sirs. But this troubles me.
    Hold you the watch tonight?
ALL: We do, my lord.   *225*
HAMLET: Arm'd, say you?
ALL: Arm'd, my lord.
HAMLET: From top to toe?
ALL: My lord, from head to foot.
HAMLET: Then saw you not his face?
HORATIO: O, yes, my lord. He wore his beaver° up.   *230*
HAMLET: What, looked he frowningly?
HORATIO: A countenance more
    In sorrow than in anger.
HAMLET: Pale or red?
HORATIO: Nay, very pale.
HAMLET: And fix'd his eyes upon you?
HORATIO: Most constantly.
HAMLET: I would I had been there.
HORATIO: It would have much amaz'd you.   *235*
HAMLET: Very like, very like. Stay'd it long?
HORATIO: While one with moderate haste might tell° a hundred.
MARCELLUS, BERNARDO: Longer, longer.
HORATIO: Not when I saw 't.
HAMLET: His beard was grizzl'd,—no?
HORATIO: It was, as I have seen it in his life,   *240*
    A sable silver'd.°
HAMLET: I will watch tonight.
    Perchance 'twill walk again.
HORATIO: I warr'nt it will.
HAMLET: If it assume my noble father's person,
    I'll speak to it, though hell itself should gape
    And bid me hold my peace. I pray you all,   *245*
    If you have hitherto conceal'd this sight,
    Let it be tenable° in your silence still,
    And whatsomever else shall hap tonight,
    Give it an understanding, but no tongue.
    I will requite your loves. So, fare you well.   *250*
    Upon the platform, 'twixt eleven and twelve,
    I'll visit you.

---

230 *beaver:* Visor on the helmet. 237 *tell:* Count. 241 *sable silver'd:* Black mixed with white.
247 *tenable:* Held tightly.

ALL: Our duty to your honor.

HAMLET: Your loves, as mine to you. Farewell.

(Exeunt [all but HAMLET*].)*

My father's spirit in arms! All is not well.

255   I doubt° some foul play. Would the night were come!

Till then sit still, my soul. Foul deeds will rise,

Though all the earth o'erwhelm them, to men's eyes.   *(Exit.)*

SCENE III°

(Enter LAERTES *and* OPHELIA, *his sister.)*

LAERTES: My necessaries are embark'd. Farewell.

And, sister, as the winds give benefit

And convoy is assistant,° do not sleep

But let me hear from you.

OPHELIA: Do you doubt that?

5   LAERTES: For Hamlet, and the trifling of his favor,

Hold it a fashion and a toy in blood,°

A violet in the youth of primy° nature,

Forward,° not permanent, sweet, not lasting,

The perfume and suppliance° of a minute—

No more.

OPHELIA: No more but so?

10   LAERTES: Think it no more.

For nature crescent° does not grow alone

In thews° and bulk, but, as this temple° waxes,

The inward service of the mind and soul

Grows wide withal.° Perhaps he loves you now,

15   And now no soil° nor cautel° doth besmirch

The virtue of his will;° but you must fear,

His greatness weigh'd,° his will is not his own.

For he himself is subject to his birth.

He may not, as unvalued persons do,

20   Carve° for himself; for on his choice depends

The safety and health of this whole state,

And therefore must his choice be circumscrib'd

---

255 *doubt:* Suspect. ACT I, SCENE III. *Location:* Polonius's chambers. 3 *convoy is assistant:* Means of conveyance are available. 6 *toy in blood:* Passing amorous fancy. 7 *primy:* In its prime, spring-time. 8 *Forward:* Precocious. 9 *suppliance:* Supply, filler. 11 *crescent:* Growing, waxing. 12 *thews:* Bodily strength; *temple:* Body. 14 *Grows wide withal:* Grows along with it. 15 *soil:* Blemish; *cautel:* Deceit. 16 *will:* Desire. 17 *greatness weigh'd:* High position considered. 20 *Carve:* Choose pleasure.

Unto the voice and yielding° of that body
Whereof he is the head. Then if he says he loves you,
It fits your wisdom so far to believe it   25
As he in his particular act and place
May give his saying deed,° which is no further
Than the main voice of Denmark goes withal.
Then weigh what loss your honor may sustain
If with too credent° ear you list° his songs,   30
Or lose your heart, or your chaste treasure open
To his unmaster'd importunity.
Fear it, Ophelia, fear it, my dear sister,
And keep you in the rear of your affection,
Out of the shot° and danger of desire.   35
The chariest° maid is prodigal enough
If she unmask her beauty to the moon.
Virtue itself scapes not calumnious strokes.
The canker galls° the infants of the spring
Too oft before their buttons° be disclos'd,°   40
And in the morn and liquid dew° of youth
Contagious blastments° are most imminent.
Be wary then; best safety lies in fear.
Youth to itself rebels, though none else near.

OPHELIA: I shall the effect of this good lesson keep   45
As watchman to my heart. But, good my brother,
Do not, as some ungracious pastors do,
Show me the steep and thorny way to heaven,
Whiles, like a puff'd° and reckless libertine,
Himself the primrose path of dalliance treads,   50
And recks° not his own rede.°

    (Enter POLONIUS.*)*

LAERTES: O, fear me not.
I stay too long. But here my father comes.
A double blessing is a double° grace;
Occasion° smiles upon a second leave.

POLONIUS: Yet here, Laertes? Aboard, aboard, for shame!   55
The wind sits in the shoulder of your sail,

---

23 *voice and yielding:* Assent, approval. 27 *deed:* Effect. 30 *credent:* Credulous; *list:* Listen to. 35
shot: Range. 36 *chariest:* Most scrupulously modest. 39 *canker galls:* Cankerworm destroys. 40
buttons: Buds; *disclos'd:* Opened. 41 *liquid dew:* Time when dew is fresh. 42 *blastments:* Blights.
49 *puff'd:* Bloated. 51 *recks:* Heeds; *rede:* Counsel. 53 *double:* I.e., Laertes has already bidden his
father good-bye. 54 *Occasion:* Opportunity.

And you are stay'd for. There—my blessing with thee!
And these few precepts in thy memory
Look thou character.° Give thy thoughts no tongue,
60 Nor any unproportion'd thought his° act.
Be thou familiar,° but by no means vulgar.°
Those friends thou hast, and their adoption tried,°
Grapple them to thy soul with hoops of steel,
But do not dull thy palm with entertainment
65 Of each new-hatch'd, unfledg'd courage.° Beware
Of entrance to a quarrel, but, being in,
Bear't that° th' opposed may beware of thee.
Give every man thy ear, but few thy voice;
Take each man's censure,° but reserve thy judgment.
70 Costly thy habit as thy purse can buy,
But not express'd in fancy; rich, not gaudy,
For the apparel oft proclaims the man,
And they in France of the best rank and station
Are of a most select and generous chief° in that.
75 Neither a borrower nor a lender be,
For loan oft loses both itself and friend,
And borrowing dulleth the edge of husbandry.°
This above all: to thine own self be true,
And it must follow, as the night the day,
80 Thou canst not then be false to any man.
Farewell. My blessing season° this in thee!
LAERTES: Most humbly do I take my leave, my lord.
POLONIUS: The time invests° you. Go, your servants tend.°
LAERTES: Farewell, Ophelia, and remember well
What I have said to you.
85 OPHELIA: 'Tis in my memory lock'd,
And you yourself shall keep the key of it.
LAERTES: Farewell.   *(Exit* LAERTES.*)*
POLONIUS: What is 't, Ophelia, he hath said to you?
OPHELIA: So please you, something touching the Lord Hamlet.
90 POLONIUS: Marry,° well bethought.
'Tis told me he hath very oft of late
Given private time to you, and you yourself
Have of your audience been most free and bounteous.

---

59 *character:* Inscribe. 60 *his:* Its. 61 *familiar:* Sociable; *vulgar:* Common. 62 *tried:* Tested. 65
courage: Young man of spirit. 67 *Bear't that:* Manage it so that. 69 *censure:* Opinion, judgment.
74 *generous chief:* Noble eminence (?). 77 *husbandry:* Thrift. 81 *season:* Mature. 83 *invests:* Be-
sieges; *tend:* Attend, wait. 90 *Marry:* By the Virgin Mary (a mild oath).

If it be so—as so 'tis put on° me,
And that in way of caution—I must tell you   95
You do not understand yourself so clearly
As it behooves my daughter and your honor.
What is between you? Give me up the truth.

OPHELIA: He hath, my lord, of late made many tenders°
Of his affection to me.   100

POLONIUS: Affection? Pooh! You speak like a green girl,
Unsifted° in such perilous circumstance.
Do you believe his tenders, as you call them?

OPHELIA: I do not know, my lord, what I should think.

POLONIUS: Marry, I will teach you. Think yourself a baby   105
That you have ta'en these tenders° for true pay,
Which are not sterling.° Tender° yourself more dearly,
Or—not to crack the wind° of the poor phrase,
Running it thus—you'll tender me a fool.°

OPHELIA: My lord, he hath importun'd me with love   110
In honorable fashion.

POLONIUS: Ay, fashion° you may call it. Go to, go to.

OPHELIA: And hath given countenance° to his speech, my lord,
With almost all the holy vows of heaven.

POLONIUS: Ay, springes° to catch woodcocks.° I do know,   115
When the blood burns, how prodigal the soul
Lends the tongue vows. These blazes, daughter,
Giving more light than heat, extinct in both
Even in their promise, as it is a-making,
You must not take for fire. From this time   120
Be something scanter of your maiden presence.
Set your entreatments° at a higher rate
Than a command to parle.° For Lord Hamlet,
Believe so much in him° that he is young,
And with a larger tether may he walk   125
Than may be given you. In few,° Ophelia,

94 *put on:* Impressed on, told to. 99 *tenders:* Offers. 102 *Unsifted:* Untried. 106 *tenders:* With added meaning here of "promises to pay." 107 *sterling:* Legal currency; *Tender:* Hold. 108 *crack the wind:* Run it until it is broken, winded. 109 *tender me a fool:* (1) Show yourself to me as a fool; (2) show me up as a fool; (3) present me with a grandchild ("fool" was a term of endearment for a child). 112 *fashion:* Mere form, pretense. 113 *countenance:* Credit, support. 115 *springes:* Snares; *woodcocks:* Birds easily caught; here used to connote gullibility. 122 *entreatments:* Negotiations for surrender (a military term). 123 *parle:* Discuss terms with the enemy. (Polonius urges his daughter, in the metaphor of military language, not to meet with Hamlet and consider giving in to him merely because he requests an interview.) 124 *so . . . him:* This much concerning him. 126 *In few:* Briefly.

Do not believe his vows, for they are brokers,°
Not of that dye° which their investments° show,
But mere implorators° of unholy suits,
130   Breathing° like sanctified and pious bawds,
The better to beguile. This is for all:
I would not, in plain terms, from this time forth
Have you so slander° any moment leisure
As to give words or talk with the Lord Hamlet.
135   Look to 't, I charge you. Come your ways.
OPHELIA: I shall obey, my lord.   *(Exeunt.)*

SCENE IV°

(Enter HAMLET, HORATIO, *and* MARCELLUS.*)*

HAMLET: The air bites shrewdly; it is very cold.
HORATIO: It is a nipping and an eager air.
HAMLET: What hour now?
HORATIO: I think it lacks of twelve.
MARCELLUS: No, it is struck.
HORATIO: Indeed? I heard it not.
5   It then draws near the season
Wherein the spirit held his wont to walk.
        (A flourish of trumpets, and two pieces° go off within.)
What does this mean, my lord?
HAMLET: The King doth wake° tonight and takes his rouse,°
Keeps wassail,° and the swagg'ring up-spring° reels;
10   And as he drains his draughts of Rhenish° down,
The kettle-drum and trumpet thus bray out
The triumph of his pledge.°
HORATIO: Is it a custom?
HAMLET: Ay, marry, is 't,
But to my mind, though I am native here
15   And to the manner° born, it is a custom
More honor'd in the breach than the observance.°
This heavy-headed revel east and west°

---

127 *brokers:* Go-betweens, procurers. 128 *dye:* Color or sort; *investments:* Clothes (i.e., they are not what they seem). 129 *mere implorators:* Out-and-out solicitors. 130 *Breathing:* Speaking. 133 *slander:* Bring disgrace or reproach upon. ACT I, SCENE IV. *Location:* The guard platform. 6 s.d. *pieces:* I.e., of ordnance, cannon. 8 *wake:* Stay awake and hold revel; *rouse:* Carouse, drinking bout. 9 *wassail:* Carousal; *up-spring:* Wild German dance. 10 *Rhenish:* Rhine wine. 12 *triumph . . . pledge:* His feat in draining the wine in a single draft. 15 *manner:* Custom (of drinking). 16 *More . . . observance:* Better neglected than followed. 17 *east and west:* I.e., everywhere.

Makes us traduc'd and tax'd of° other nations.
They clepe° us drunkards, and with swinish phrase°
Soil our addition;° and indeed it takes   20
From our achievements, though perform'd at height,°
The pith and marrow of our attribute.
So, oft it chances in particular men,
That for some vicious mole of nature° in them,
As in their birth—wherein they are not guilty,   25
Since nature cannot choose his° origin—
By the o'ergrowth of some complexion,°
Oft breaking down the pales° and forts of reason,
Or by some habit that too much o'er-leavens°
The form of plausive° manners, that these men,   30
Carrying, I say, the stamp of one defect,
Being nature's livery,° or fortune's star,°
Their virtues else, be they as pure as grace,
As infinite as man may undergo,
Shall in the general censure take corruption   35
From that particular fault. The dram of eale°
Doth all the noble substance of a doubt°
To his own scandal.°

(Enter GHOST.)

HORATIO: Look, my lord, it comes!
HAMLET: Angels and ministers of grace defend us!
    Be thou a spirit of health° or goblin damn'd,   40
    Bring with thee airs from heaven or blasts from hell,
    Be thy intents wicked or charitable,
    Thou com'st in such a questionable° shape
    That I will speak to thee. I'll call thee Hamlet,
    King, father, royal Dane. O, answer me!   45
    Let me not burst in ignorance; but tell
    Why thy canoniz'd° bones, hearsed° in death,

---

18 *tax'd of:* Censured by. 19 *clepe:* Call; *with swinish phrase:* By calling us swine. 20 *addition:* Reputation. 21 *at height:* Outstandingly. 24 *mole of nature:* Natural blemish in one's constitution. 26 *his:* Its. 27 *complexion:* Humor (i.e., one of the four humors or fluids thought to determine temperament). 28 *pales:* Palings, fences (as of a fortification). 29 *o'er-leavens:* Induces a change throughout (as yeast works in dough). 30 *plausive:* Pleasing. 32 *nature's livery:* Endowment from nature; *fortune's star:* Mark placed by fortune. 36 *dram of eale:* Small amount of evil (?). 37 *of a doubt:* A famous crux, sometimes emended to "oft about" or "often dout," i.e., often erase or do out, or to "antidote," counteract. 38 *To . . . scandal:* To the disgrace of the whole enterprise. 40 *of health:* Of spiritual good. 43 *questionable:* Inviting question or conversation. 47 *canoniz'd:* Buried according to the canons of the church; *hearsed:* Coffined.

Have burst their cerements;° why the sepulcher
Wherein we saw thee quietly interr'd
50   Hath op'd his ponderous and marble jaws
To cast thee up again. What may this mean,
That thou, dead corse, again in complete steel
Revisits thus the glimpses of the moon,°
Making night hideous, and we fools of nature°
55   So horridly to shake our disposition
With thoughts beyond the reaches of our souls?
Say, why is this? Wherefore? What should we do?

(GHOST beckons HAMLET.)

HORATIO: It beckons you to go away with it,
As if it some impartment° did desire
To you alone.
60   MARCELLUS: Look with what courteous action
It waves you to a more removed ground.
But do not go with it.
HORATIO: No, by no means.
HAMLET: It will not speak. Then I will follow it.
HORATIO: Do not, my lord.
HAMLET: Why, what should be the fear?
65   I do not set my life at a pin's fee,°
And for my soul, what can it do to that,
Being a thing immortal as itself?
It waves me forth again. I'll follow it.
HORATIO: What if it tempt you toward the flood, my lord,
70   Or to the dreadful summit of the cliff
That beetles o'er° his° base into the sea,
And there assume some other horrible form
Which might deprive your sovereignty of reason,°
And draw you into madness? Think of it.
75   The very place puts toys of desperation,°
Without more motive, into every brain
That looks so many fathoms to the sea
And hears it roar beneath.
HAMLET: It waves me still.
Go on, I'll follow thee.
MARCELLUS: You shall not go, my lord.   *(They try to stop him.)*

---

48 *cerements:* Grave-clothes. 53 *glimpses of the moon:* Earth by night. 54 *fools of nature:* Mere men, limited to natural knowledge. 59 *impartment:* Communication. 65 *fee:* Value. 71 *beetles o'er:* Overhangs threateningly; *his:* Its. 73 *deprive . . . reason:* Take away the rule of reason over your mind. 75 *toys of desperation:* Fancies of desperate acts, i.e., suicide.

HAMLET: Hold off your hands!   *80*
HORATIO: Be rul'd, you shall not go.
HAMLET: My fate cries out,
    And makes each petty artery° in this body
    As hardy as the Nemean lion's° nerve.°
    Still am I call'd. Unhand me, gentlemen.
    By heaven, I'll make a ghost of him that lets° me!   *85*
    I say, away! Go on. I'll follow thee.   *(Exeunt* GHOST *and* HAMLET.*)*
HORATIO: He waxes desperate with imagination.
MARCELLUS: Let's follow. 'Tis not fit thus to obey him.
HORATIO: Have after. To what issue° will this come?
MARCELLUS: Something is rotten in the state of Denmark.   *90*
HORATIO: Heaven will direct it.°
MARCELLUS: Nay, let's follow him.   *(Exeunt.)*

SCENE V°

    (Enter GHOST *and* HAMLET.*)*

HAMLET: Whither wilt thou lead me? Speak. I'll go no further.
GHOST: Mark me.
HAMLET: I will.
GHOST: My hour is almost come,
    When I to sulph'rous and tormenting flames
    Must render up myself.
HAMLET: Alas, poor ghost!
GHOST: Pity me not, but lend thy serious hearing   *5*
    To what I shall unfold.
HAMLET: Speak. I am bound to hear.
GHOST: So art thou to revenge, when thou shalt hear.
HAMLET: What?
GHOST: I am thy father's spirit,
    Doom'd for a certain term to walk the night,   *10*
    And for the day confin'd to fast° in fires,
    Till the foul crimes° done in my days of nature
    Are burnt and purg'd away. But that° I am forbid
    To tell the secrets of my prison-house,
    I could a tale unfold whose lightest word   *15*
    Would harrow up thy soul, freeze thy young blood,

---

82 *artery:* Sinew. 83 *Nemean lion:* One of the monsters slain by Hercules in his twelve labors; *nerve:* Sinew. 85 *lets:* Hinders. 89 *issue:* Outcome. 91 *it:* The outcome. ACT I, SCENE V. *Location:* The battlements of the castle. 11 *fast:* Do penance. 12 *crimes:* Sins. 13 *But that:* Were it not that.

Make thy two eyes, like stars, start from their spheres,°
Thy knotted and combined locks° to part,
And each particular hair to stand an end, °
20   Like quills upon the fearful porpentine.°
But this eternal blazon° must not be
To ears of flesh and blood. List, list, O, list!
If thou didst ever thy dear father love—
HAMLET: O God!
25   GHOST: Revenge his foul and most unnatural murder.
HAMLET: Murder?
GHOST: Murder most foul, as in the best it is,
But this most foul, strange, and unnatural.
HAMLET: Haste me to know 't, that I, with wings as swift
30   As meditation or the thoughts of love,
May sweep to my revenge.
GHOST: I find thee apt;
And duller shouldst thou be than the fat weed
That roots itself in ease on Lethe° wharf,°
Wouldst thou not stir in this. Now, Hamlet, hear.
35   'Tis given out that, sleeping in my orchard,
A serpent stung me. So the whole ear of Denmark
Is by a forged process° of my death
Rankly abus'd.° But know, thou noble youth,
The serpent that did sting thy father's life
Now wears his crown.
40   HAMLET: O my prophetic soul!
My uncle!
GHOST: Ay, that incestuous, that adulterate° beast,
With witchcraft of his wits, with traitorous gifts—
O wicked wit and gifts, that have the power
45   So to seduce!—won to his shameful lust
The will of my most seeming-virtuous queen.
O Hamlet, what a falling-off was there!
From me, whose love was of that dignity
That it went hand in hand even with the vow
50   I made to her in marriage, and to decline

---

17 *spheres:* Eye sockets, here compared to the orbits or transparent revolving spheres in which, according to Ptolemaic astronomy, the heavenly bodies were fixed. 18 *knotted . . . locks:* Hair neatly arranged and confined. 19 *an end:* On end. 20 *fearful porpentine:* Frightened porcupine. 21 *eternal blazon:* Revelation of the secrets of eternity. 33 *Lethe:* The river of forgetfulness in Hades; *wharf:* Bank. 37 *forged process:* Falsified account. 38 *abus'd:* Deceived. 42 *adulterate:* Adulterous.

Upon a wretch whose natural gifts were poor
To those of mine!
But virtue, as it never will be moved,
Though lewdness court it in a shape of heaven,°
So lust, though to a radiant angel link'd,   55
Will sate itself in a celestial bed,
And prey on garbage.
But, soft, methinks I scent the morning air.
Brief let me be. Sleeping within my orchard,
My custom always of the afternoon,   60
Upon my secure° hour thy uncle stole,
With juice of cursed hebona° in a vial,
And in the porches of my ears did pour
The leprous° distillment, whose effect
Holds such an enmity with blood of man   65
That swift as quicksilver it courses through
The natural gates and alleys of the body,
And with a sudden vigor it doth posset°
And curd, like eager° droppings into milk,
The thin and wholesome blood. So did it mine,   70
And a most instant tetter° bark'd° about,
Most lazar-like,° with vile and loathsome crust,
All my smooth body.
Thus was I, sleeping, by a brother's hand
Of life, of crown, of queen, at once dispatch'd,°   75
Cut off even in the blossoms of my sin,
Unhous'led,° disappointed,° unanel'd,°
No reck'ning made, but sent to my account
With all my imperfections on my head.
O, horrible! O, horrible, most horrible!   80
If thou hast nature° in thee, bear it not.
Let not the royal bed of Denmark be
A couch for luxury° and damned incest.
But, howsoever thou pursues this act,
Taint not thy mind, nor let thy soul contrive   85

---

54 *shape of heaven:* Heavenly form. 61 *secure:* Confident, unsuspicious. 62 *hebona:* Poison. (The word seems to be a form of "ebony," though it is perhaps thought to be related to "henbane," a poison, or to "ebenus," yew.) 64 *leprous:* Causing leprosy-like disfigurement. 68 *posset:* Coagulate, curdle. 69 *eager:* Sour, acid. 71 *tetter:* Eruption of scabs; *bark'd:* Covered with a rough covering, like bark on a tree. 72 *lazar-like:* Leper-like. 75 *dispatch'd:* Suddenly deprived. 77 *Unhous'led:* Without having received the sacrament of Holy Communion; *disappointed:* Unready (spiritually) for the last journey; *unanel'd:* Without having received extreme unction. 81 *nature:* The promptings of a son. 83 *luxury:* Lechery.

Against thy mother aught. Leave her to heaven
And to those thorns that in her bosom lodge,
To prick and sting her. Fare thee well at once.
The glow-worm shows the matin° to be near,
90   And 'gins to pale his uneffectual fire.°
Adieu, adieu, adieu! Remember me.   *(Exit.)*
HAMLET: O all you host of heaven! O earth! What else?
And shall I couple° hell? O fie! Hold, hold, my heart,
And you, my sinews, grow not instant old,
95   But bear me stiffly up. Remember thee!
Ay, thou poor ghost, whiles memory holds a seat
In this distracted globe.° Remember thee!
Yea, from the table° of my memory
I'll wipe away all trivial fond° records,
100   All saws° of books, all forms,° all pressures° past
That youth and observation copied there,
And thy commandment all alone shall live
Within the book and volume of my brain,
Unmix'd with baser matter. Yes, by heaven!
105   O most pernicious woman!
O villain, villain, smiling, damnèd villain!
My tables—meet it is I set it down,
That one may smile, and smile, and be a villain.
At least I am sure it may be so in Denmark.   *(Writing.)*
110   So, uncle, there you are. Now to my word;
It is "Adieu, adieu! Remember me."
I have sworn 't.

(Enter HORATIO *and* MARCELLUS.*)*

HORATIO: My lord, my lord!
MARCELLUS: Lord Hamlet!
HORATIO: Heavens secure him!
HAMLET: So be it!
115   MARCELLUS: Illo, ho, ho, my lord!
HAMLET: Hillo, ho, ho,° boy! Come, bird, come.
MARCELLUS: How is 't, my noble lord?
HORATIO: What news, my lord?
HAMLET: O, wonderful!

89 *matin:* Morning. 90 *uneffectual fire:* Cold light. 93 *couple:* Add. 97 *globe:* Head. 98 *table:* Writing tablet. 99 *fond:* Foolish. 100 *saws:* Wise sayings; *forms:* Images; *pressures:* Impressions stamped. 116 *Hillo, ho, ho:* A falconer's call to a hawk in air. Hamlet is playing upon Marcellus's "Illo," i.e., "halloo."

HORATIO: Good my lord, tell it.
HAMLET: No, you will reveal it.
HORATIO: Not I, my lord, by heaven.
MARCELLUS: Nor I, my lord.   120
HAMLET: How say you, then, would heart of man once think it?
    But you'll be secret?
HORATIO, MARCELLUS: Ay, by heaven, my lord.
HAMLET: There's never a villain dwelling in all Denmark
    But he's an arrant° knave.
HORATIO: There needs no ghost, my lord, come from the grave   125
    To tell us this.
HAMLET: Why, right, you are in the right.
    And so, without more circumstance° at all,
    I hold it fit that we shake hands and part,
    You, as your business and desire shall point you—
    For every man hath business and desire,   130
    Such as it is—and for my own poor part,
    Look you, I'll go pray.
HORATIO: These are but wild and whirling words, my lord.
HAMLET: I am sorry they offend you, heartily;
    Yes, faith, heartily.
HORATIO: There's no offense, my lord.   135
HAMLET: Yes, by Saint Patrick,° but there is, Horatio,
    And much offense too. Touching this vision here,
    It is an honest° ghost, that let me tell you.
    For your desire to know what is between us,
    O'ermaster 't as you may. And now, good friends,   140
    As you are friends, scholars, and soldiers,
    Give me one poor request.
HORATIO: What is 't, my lord? We will.
HAMLET: Never make known what you have seen tonight.
HORATIO, MARCELLUS: My lord, we will not.
HAMLET: Nay, but swear 't.
HORATIO: In faith,   145
    My lord, not I.
MARCELLUS: Nor I, my lord, in faith.
HAMLET: Upon my sword.°   *(Holds out his sword.)*
MARCELLUS: We have sworn, my lord, already.
HAMLET: Indeed, upon my sword, indeed.   *(GHOST cries under the stage.)*

124 *arrant:* Thoroughgoing. 127 *circumstance:* Ceremony. 136 *Saint Patrick:* The keeper of purgatory and patron saint of all blunders and confusion. 138 *honest:* I.e., a real ghost and not an evil spirit. 147 *sword:* The hilt in the form of a cross.

GHOST: Swear.

150   HAMLET: Ha, ha, boy, say'st thou so? Art thou there, truepenny? °
        Come on, you hear this fellow in the cellarage.
        Consent to swear.

HORATIO: Propose the oath, my lord.

HAMLET: Never to speak of this that you have seen,
        Swear by my sword.

155   GHOST *(beneath)*: Swear.

HAMLET: Hic et ubique?° Then we'll shift our ground.

                                            (He moves to another spot.)

        Come hither, gentlemen,
        And lay your hands again upon my sword.
        Swear by my sword
160   Never to speak of this that you have heard.

GHOST *(beneath)*: Swear by his sword.

HAMLET: Well said, old mole! Canst work i' th' earth so fast?
        A worthy pioner!° Once more remove, good friends.   *(Moves again.)*

HORATIO: O day and night, but this is wondrous strange!

165   HAMLET: And therefore as a stranger give it welcome.
        There are more things in heaven and earth, Horatio,
        Than are dreamt of in your philosophy.°
        But come;
        Here, as before, never, so help you mercy,
170   How strange or odd soe'er I bear myself—
        As I perchance hereafter shall think meet
        To put an antic° disposition on—
        That you, at such times seeing me, never shall,
        With arms encumb'red° thus, or this headshake,
175   Or by pronouncing of some doubtful phrase,
        As "Well, well, we know," or "We could, an if° we would,"
        Or "If we list° to speak," or "There be, an if they might,"
        Or such ambiguous giving out,° to note°
        That you know aught of me—this do swear,
180   So grace and mercy at your most need help you.

GHOST *(beneath)*: Swear.   *(They swear.)*

HAMLET: Rest, rest, perturbed spirit! So, gentlemen,
        With all my love I do commend me to you;
        And what so poor a man as Hamlet is

---

150 *truepenny:* Honest old fellow. 156 *Hic et ubique:* Here and everywhere (Latin). 163 *pioner:*
Pioneer, digger, miner. 167 *your philosophy:* This subject called "natural philosophy" or "science"
that people talk about. 172 *antic:* Fantastic. 174 *encumb'red:* Folded or entwined. 176 *an if:* If.
177 *list:* Were inclined. 178 *giving out:* Profession of knowledge; *note:* Give a sign, indicate.

May do, t' express his love and friending to you,   185
God willing, shall not lack. Let us go in together,
And still° your fingers on your lips, I pray.
The time is out of joint. O cursed spite,
That ever I was born to set it right!   *(They wait for him to leave first.)*
Nay, come, let's go together.   *(Exeunt.)*   190

ACT II
SCENE I°

(Enter old POLONIUS, *with his man [*REYNALDO*].)*

POLONIUS: Give him this money and these notes, Reynaldo.
REYNALDO: I will, my lord.
POLONIUS: You shall do marvel's° wisely, good Reynaldo,
   Before you visit him, to make inquire
   Of his behavior.
REYNALDO: My lord, I did intend it.   5
POLONIUS: Marry, well said, very well said. Look you, sir,
   Inquire me first what Danskers° are in Paris,
   And how, and who, what means,° and where they keep,°
   What company, at what expense; and finding
   By this encompassment° and drift° of question   10
   That they do know my son, come you more nearer
   Than your particular demands will touch it.°
   Take° you, as 'twere, some distant knowledge of him,
   As thus, "I know his father and his friends,
   And in part him." Do you mark this, Reynaldo?   15
REYNALDO: Ay, very well, my lord.
POLONIUS: "And in part him, but," you may say, "not well.
   But, if 't be he I mean, he's very wild,
   Addicted so and so," and there put on° him
   What forgeries° you please—marry, none so rank   20
   As may dishonor, him take heed of that,
   But, sir, such wanton,° wild, and usual slips,
   As are companions noted and most known
   To youth and liberty.
REYNALDO: As gaming, my lord.

---

187 *still:* Always. ACT II, SCENE I. *Location:* Polonius's chambers. 3 *marvel's:* Marvelous(ly).
7 *Danskers:* Danes. 8 *what means:* What wealth (they have); *keep:* Dwell. 10 *encompassment:*
Roundabout talking; *drift:* Gradual approach or course. 11–12 *come . . . it:* You will find out more
this way than by asking pointed questions (*particular demands*). 13 *Take:* Assume, pretend. 19 *put
on:* Impute to. 20 *forgeries:* Invented tales. 22 *wanton:* Sportive, unrestrained.

25 POLONIUS: Ay, or drinking, fencing, swearing,
    Quarreling, drabbing°—you may go so far.
REYNALDO: My lord, that would dishonor him.
POLONIUS: Faith, no, as you may season° it in the charge.
    You must not put another scandal on him
30   That he is open to incontinency;°
    That's not my meaning. But breathe his faults so quaintly°
    That they may seem the taints of liberty,°
    The flash and outbreak of a fiery mind,
    A savageness in unreclaimed° blood,
    Of general assault.°
35 REYNALDO: But, my good lord—
POLONIUS: Wherefore should you do this?
REYNALDO: Ay, my lord,
    I would know that.
POLONIUS: Marry, sir, here's my drift,
    And, I believe, it is a fetch of wit.°
    You laying these slight sullies on my son,
40   As 'twere a thing a little soil'd i' th' working,°
    Mark you,
    Your party in converse,° him you would sound,°
    Having ever° seen in the prenominate crimes°
    The youth you breathe° of guilty, be assur'd
45   He closes with you in this consequence:°
    "Good sir," or so, or "friend," or "gentleman,"
    According to the phrase or the addition°
    Of man and country.
REYNALDO: Very good, my lord.
POLONIUS: And then, sir, does 'a this—'a does—what was I about to say?
50   By the mass, I was about to say something.
    Where did I leave?
REYNALDO: At "closes in the consequence."
POLONIUS: At "closes in the consequence," ay, marry.
    He closes thus: "I know the gentleman;
    I saw him yesterday, or th' other day,

---

26 *drabbing:* Whoring. 28 *season:* Temper, soften. 30 *incontinency:* Habitual loose behavior. 31 *quaintly:* Delicately, ingeniously. 32 *taints of liberty:* Faults resulting from freedom. 34 *unreclaimed:* Untamed. 35 *general assault:* Tendency that assails all unrestrained youth. 38 *fetch of wit:* Clever trick. 40 *soil'd i' th' working:* Shopworn. 42 *converse:* Conversation; *sound:* Sound out. 43 *Having ever:* If he has ever; *prenominate crimes:* Before-mentioned offenses. 44 *breathe:* Speak. 45 *closes . . . consequence:* Follows your lead in some fashion as follows. 47 *addition:* Title.

Or then, or then, with such, or such, and, as you say,   55
There was 'a gaming, there o'ertook in 's rouse,°
There falling out° at tennis," or perchance,
"I saw him enter such a house of sale,"
Videlicet,° a brothel, or so forth. See you now,
Your bait of falsehood takes this carp° of truth;   60
And thus do we of wisdom and of reach,°
With windlasses° and with assays of bias,°
By indirections find directions° out.
So by my former lecture and advice
Shall you my son. You have me, have you not?   65
REYNALDO: My lord, I have.
POLONIUS: God buy ye; fare ye well.
REYNALDO: Good my lord.
POLONIUS: Observe his inclination in yourself.°
REYNALDO: I shall, my lord.
POLONIUS: And let him ply° his music.
REYNALDO: Well, my lord.   70
POLONIUS: Farewell.   *(Exit* REYNALDO.*)*

    (Enter OPHELIA.*)*

           How now, Ophelia, what's the matter?
OPHELIA: O, my lord, my lord, I have been so affrighted!
POLONIUS: With what, i' th' name of God?
OPHELIA: My lord, as I was sewing in my closet,°
    Lord Hamlet, with his doublet° all unbrac'd,°   75
    No hat upon his head, his stockings fouled,
    Ungart'red, and down-gyved to his ankle,°
    Pale as his shirt, his knees knocking each other,
    And with a look so piteous in purport
    As if he had been loosed out of hell   80
    To speak of horrors—he comes before me.
POLONIUS: Mad for thy love?
OPHELIA: My lord, I do not know,

---

56 *o'ertook in 's rouse:* Overcome by drink. 57 *falling out:* Quarreling. 59 *Videlicet:* Namely (Latin). 60 *carp:* A fish. 61 *reach:* Capacity, ability. 62 *windlasses:* Circuitous paths (literally, circuits made to head off the game in hunting); *assays of bias:* Attempts through indirection (like the curving path of the bowling ball which is biased or weighted to one side). 63 *directions:* The way things really are. 68 *in yourself:* In your own person (as well as by asking questions). 70 *let him ply:* See that he continues to study. 74 *closet:* Private chamber. 75 *doublet:* Close-fitting jacket; *unbrac'd:* Unfastened. 77 *down-gyved to his ankle:* Fallen to the ankles (like gyves or fetters).

But truly I do fear it.
POLONIUS: What said he?
OPHELIA: He took me by the wrist and held me hard.
85   Then goes he to the length of all his arm,
             And, with his other hand thus o'er his brow,
             He falls to such perusal of my face
             As 'a would draw it. Long stay'd he so.
             At last, a little shaking of mine arm
90   And thrice his head thus waving up and down,
             He rais'd a sigh so piteous and profound
             As it did seem to shatter all his bulk°
             And end his being. That done, he lets me go,
             And, with his head over his shoulder turn'd,
95   He seem'd to find his way without his eyes,
             For out o' doors he went without their helps,
             And, to the last, bended their light on me.
POLONIUS: Come, go with me. I will go seek the King.
             This is the very ecstasy° of love,
100   Whose violent property° fordoes° itself
             And leads the will to desperate undertakings
             As oft as any passion under heaven
             That does afflict our natures. I am sorry.
             What, have you given him any hard words of late?
105 OPHELIA: No, my good lord, but, as you did command,
             I did repel his letters and denied
             His access to me.
POLONIUS: That hath made him mad.
             I am sorry that with better heed and judgment
             I had not quoted° him. I fear'd he did but trifle
110   And meant to wrack thee; but, beshrew my jealousy!°
             By heaven, it is as proper to our age°
             To cast beyond° ourselves in our opinions
             As it is common for the younger sort
             To lack discretion. Come, go we to the King.
115   This must be known, which, being kept close,° might move
             More grief to hide than hate to utter love.°
             Come.   (*Exeunt.*)

---

92 *bulk:* Body. 99 *ecstasy:* Madness. 100 *property:* Nature; *fordoes:* Destroys. 109 *quoted:* Observed. 110 *beshrew my jealousy:* A plague upon my suspicious nature. 111 *proper . . . age:* Characteristic of us (old) men. 112 *cast beyond:* Overshoot, miscalculate. 115 *close:* Secret; 115–16 *might . . . love:* Might cause more grief (to others) by hiding the knowledge of Hamlet's strange behavior to Ophelia than hatred by telling it.

SCENE II°

(Flourish. Enter KING *and* QUEEN, ROSENCRANTZ, *and* GUILDENSTERN
[with others].)

KING: Welcome, dear Rosencrantz and Guildenstern.
    Moreover that° we much did long to see you,
    The need we have to use you did provoke
    Our hasty sending. Something have you heard
    Of Hamlet's transformation—so call it,   5
    Sith° nor th' exterior nor° the inward man
    Resembles that° it was. What it should be,
    More than his father's death, that thus hath put him
    So much from th' understanding of himself,
    I cannot dream of. I entreat you both   10
    That, being of so young days° brought up with him,
    And sith so neighbor'd to his youth and havior,
    That you vouchsafe your rest° here in our court
    Some little time, so by your companies
    To draw him on to pleasures, and to gather   15
    So much as from occasion you may glean,
    Whether aught to us unknown afflicts him thus,
    That, open'd,° lies within our remedy.
QUEEN: Good gentlemen, he hath much talk'd of you,
    And sure I am two men there is not living   20
    To whom he more adheres. If it will please you
    To show us so much gentry° and good will
    As to expend your time with us awhile
    For the supply and profit° of our hope,
    Your visitation shall receive such thanks   25
    As fits a king's remembrance.
ROSENCRANTZ: Both your Majesties
    Might, by the sovereign power you have of us,
    Put your dread pleasures more into command
    Than to entreaty.
GUILDENSTERN: But we both obey,
    And here give up ourselves in the full bent°   30
    To lay our service freely at your feet,
    To be commanded.

ACT II, SCENE II. *Location:* The castle. 2 *Moreover that:* Besides the fact that. 6 *Sith:* Since; *nor . . .
nor:* Neither . . . nor. 7 *that:* What. 11 *of . . . days:* From such early youth. 13 *vouchsafe your rest:*
Please to stay. 18 *open'd:* Revealed. 22 *gentry:* Courtesy. 24 *supply and profit:* Aid and successful
outcome. 30 *in . . . bent:* To the utmost degree of our capacity.

KING: Thanks, Rosencrantz and gentle Guildenstern.

QUEEN: Thanks, Guildenstern and gentle Rosencrantz.

35   And I beseech you instantly to visit

    My too much changed son. Go, some of you,

    And bring these gentlemen where Hamlet is.

GUILDENSTERN: Heavens make our presence and our practices

    Pleasant and helpful to him!

QUEEN: Ay, amen!

(Exeunt ROSENCRANTZ *and* GUILDENSTERN *with some* ATTENDANTS.*)*

(Enter POLONIUS.*)*

40 POLONIUS: Th' ambassadors from Norway, my good lord,

    Are joyfully return'd.

KING: Thou still° hast been the father of good news.

POLONIUS: Have I, my lord? I assure my good liege

    I hold my duty, as I hold my soul,

45   Both to my God and to my gracious king;

    And I do think, or else this brain of mine

    Hunts not the trail of policy so sure

    As it hath us'd to do, that I have found

    The very cause of Hamlet's lunacy.

50 KING: O, speak of that! That do I long to hear.

POLONIUS: Give first admittance to th' ambassadors.

    My news shall be the fruit° to that great feast.

KING: Thyself do grace to them, and bring them in.   *(Exit* POLONIUS.*)*

    He tells me, my dear Gertrude, he hath found

55   The head and source of all your son's distemper.

QUEEN: I doubt° it is no other but the main,°

    His father's death, and our o'erhasty marriage.

(Enter AMBASSADORS *[*VOLTIMAND *and* CORNELIUS, *with* POLONIUS*].)*

KING: Well, we shall sift him.—Welcome, my good friends!

    Say, Voltimand, what from our brother Norway?

60 VOLTIMAND: Most fair return of greetings and desires.

    Upon our first,° he sent out to suppress

    His nephew's levies, which to him appear'd

---

42 *still:* Always. 52 *fruit:* Dessert. 56 *doubt:* Fear, suspect; *main:* Chief point, principal concern.
61 *Upon our first:* At our first words on the business.

To be a preparation 'gainst the Polack,
But, better look'd into, he truly found
It was against your Highness. Whereat griev'd   65
That so his sickness, age, and impotence
Was falsely borne in hand,° sends out arrests
On Fortinbras, which he, in brief, obeys,
Receives rebuke from Norway, and in fine°
Makes vow before his uncle never more   70
To give th' assay° of arms against your Majesty.
Whereon old Norway, overcome with joy,
Gives him three score thousand crowns in annual fee,
And his commission to employ those soldiers,
So levied as before, against the Polack,   75
With an entreaty, herein further shown,   *(Giving a paper.)*
That it might please you to give quiet pass
Through your dominions for this enterprise,
On such regards of safety and allowance°
As therein are set down.

KING: It likes° us well;   80
And at our more consider'd° time we'll read,
Answer, and think upon this business.
Meantime we thank you for your well-took labor.
Go to your rest; at night we'll feast together.
Most welcome home!   *(Exeunt* AMBASSADORS.*)*

POLONIUS: This business is well ended.   85
My liege, and madam, to expostulate°
What majesty should be, what duty is,
Why day is day, night night, and time is time,
Were nothing but to waste night, day, and time.
Therefore, since brevity is the soul of wit,°   90
And tediousness the limbs and outward flourishes,
I will be brief. Your noble son is mad.
Mad call I it, for, to define true madness,
What is 't but to be nothing else but mad?
But let that go.

QUEEN: More matter, with less art.   95

POLONIUS: Madam, I swear I use no art at all.
That he is mad, 'tis true; 'tis true 'tis pity,

---

67 *borne in hand:* Deluded, taken advantage of.   69 *in fine:* In the end.   71 *assay:* Trial.   79 *On . . .
allowance:* With such pledges of safety and provisos.   80 *likes:* Pleases.   81 *consider'd:* Suitable for
deliberation.   86 *expostulate:* Expound.   90 *wit:* Sound sense or judgment.

And pity 'tis 'tis true—a foolish figure,°
But farewell it, for I will use no art.
100   Mad let us grant him, then, and now remains
That we find out the cause of this effect,
Or rather say, the cause of this defect,
For this effect defective comes by cause.°
Thus it remains, and the remainder thus.
105   Perpend.°
I have a daughter—have while she is mine—
Who, in her duty and obedience, mark,
Hath given me this. Now gather, and surmise.
(Reads the letter.) "To the celestial and my soul's idol,
110   the most beautified Ophelia"—
That's an ill phrase, a vile phrase; "beautified" is a vile
phrase. But you shall hear. Thus: *(Reads.)*
"In her excellent white bosom, these, etc."
QUEEN: Came this from Hamlet to her?
115   POLONIUS: Good madam, stay awhile; I will be faithful.   *(Reads.)*
"Doubt° thou the stars are fire,
    Doubt that the sun doth move,
Doubt truth to be a liar,
    But never doubt I love.
120   O dear Ophelia, I am ill at these numbers.° I have
not art to reckon° my groans. But that I love thee
best, O most best, believe it. Adieu.
            Thine evermore, most dear lady, whilst this
                machine° is to him, Hamlet."
125   This in obedience hath my daughter shown me,
And, more above,° hath his solicitings,
As they fell out° by time, by means, and place,
All given to mine ear.
    KING: But how hath she
    Receiv'd his love?
    POLONIUS: What do you think of me?
130   KING: As of a man faithful and honorable.
    POLONIUS: I would fain prove so. But what might you think,
        When I had seen this hot love on the wing—
        As I perceiv'd it, I must tell you that,

---

98 *figure:* Figure of speech. 103 *For . . . cause:* I.e., for this defective behavior, this madness has a
cause. 105 *Perpend:* Consider. 116 *Doubt:* Suspect, question. 120 *ill . . . numbers:* Unskilled at
writing verses. 121 *reckon:* (1) Count, (2) number metrically, scan. 124 *machine:* Body. 126 *more
above:* Moreover. 127 *fell out:* Occurred.

Before my daughter told me—what might you,
Or my dear Majesty your Queen here, think,   *135*
If I had play'd the desk or table-book,°
Or given my heart a winking,° mute and dumb,
Or look'd upon this love with idle sight?°
What might you think? No, I went round° to work,
And my young mistress thus I did bespeak:°   *140*
"Lord Hamlet is a prince, out of thy star;°
This must not be." And then I prescripts gave her,
That she should lock herself from his resort,
Admit no messengers, receive no tokens.
Which done, she took the fruits of my advice;   *145*
And he, repelled—a short tale to make—
Fell into a sadness, then into a fast,
Thence to a watch,° thence into a weakness,
Thence to a lightness,° and, by this declension,°
Into the madness wherein now he raves,   *150*
And all we mourn for.
KING: Do you think this?
QUEEN: It may be, very like.
POLONIUS: Hath there been such a time—I would fain know that—
    That I have positively said " 'Tis so,"
    When it prov'd otherwise?
KING: Not that I know.   *155*
POLONIUS *(pointing to his head and shoulder):* Take this from this, if this be
        otherwise.
    If circumstances lead me, I will find
    Where truth is hid, though it were hid indeed
    Within the center.°
KING: How may we try it further?
POLONIUS: You know, sometimes he walks four hours together   *160*
    Here in the lobby.
QUEEN: So he does indeed.
POLONIUS: At such a time I'll loose my daughter to him.
    Be you and I behind an arras° then.
    Mark the encounter. If he love her not

---

136 *play'd . . . table-book:* Remained shut up, concealing the information. 137 *winking:* Closing of
the eyes. 138 *with idle sight:* Complacently or uncomprehendingly. 139 *round:* Roundly, plainly.
140 *bespeak:* Address. 141 *out of thy star:* Above your sphere, position. 148 *watch:* State of sleep-
lessness. 149 *lightness:* Light-headedness; *declension:* Decline, deterioration. 159 *center:* Middle
point of the earth (which is also the center of the Ptolemaic universe). 163 *arras:* Hanging,
tapestry.

165   And be not from his reason fall'n thereon,°
        Let me be no assistant for a state,
        But keep a farm and carters.
KING: We will try it.

        (Enter HAMLET *reading on a book.)*

QUEEN: But look where sadly the poor wretch comes reading.
POLONIUS: Away, I do beseech you both, away.
        I'll board° him presently.
                                (Exeunt KING *and* QUEEN *with* ATTENDANTS.)*
170   O, give me leave.
        How does my good Lord Hamlet?
HAMLET: Well, God-a-mercy.°
POLONIUS: Do you know me, my lord?
HAMLET: Excellent well. You are a fishmonger.°
175 POLONIUS: Not I, my lord.
HAMLET: Then I would you were so honest a man.
POLONIUS: Honest, my lord?
HAMLET: Ay, sir. To be honest, as this world goes, is to be one man pick'd out
        of ten thousand.
180 POLONIUS: That's very true, my lord.
HAMLET: For if the sun breed maggots in a dead dog, being a good kissing
        carrion°—Have you a daughter?
POLONIUS: I have, my lord.
HAMLET: Let her not walk i' th' sun.° Conception° is a blessing, but as your
185   daughter may conceive, friend, look to 't.
POLONIUS *(aside)*: How say you by that? Still harping on my daughter. Yet he
        knew me not at first; 'a said I was a fishmonger. 'A is far gone. And truly
        in my youth I suff'red much extremity for love, very near this. I'll speak
        to him again.—What do you read, my lord?
190 HAMLET: Words, words, words.
POLONIUS: What is the matter,° my lord?
HAMLET: Between who?
POLONIUS: I mean, the matter that you read, my lord.
HAMLET: Slanders, sir; for the satirical rogue says here that old men have gray
195   beards, that their faces are wrinkled, their eyes purging° thick amber and
        plum-tree gum, and that they have a plentiful lack of wit, together with

---

165 *thereon:* On that account. 170 *board:* Accost. 172 *God-a-mercy:* Thank you. 174 *fishmonger:*
Fish merchant (with connotation of "bawd," "procurer"[?]). 181–82 *good kissing carrion:* A good
piece of flesh for kissing, or for the sun to kiss. 184 *i' th' sun:* With additional implication of the
sunshine of princely favors; *Conception:* (1) Understanding, (2) pregnancy. 191 *matter:* Substance
(but Hamlet plays on the sense of "basis for a dispute"). 195 *purging:* Discharging.

most weak hams. All which, sir, though I most powerfully and potently
believe, yet I hold it not honesty° to have it thus set down, for you yourself, sir, shall grow old as I am, if like a crab you could go backward.

POLONIUS *(aside)*: Though this be madness, yet there is method in 't.—Will   *200*
you walk out of the air, my lord?

HAMLET: Into my grave.

POLONIUS: Indeed, that's out of the air. *(Aside.)* How pregnant° sometimes
his replies are! A happiness° that often madness hits on, which reason
and sanity could not so prosperously° be deliver'd of. I will leave him,   *205*
and suddenly contrive the means of meeting between him and my
daughter.—My honorable lord, I will most humbly take my leave of you.

HAMLET: You cannot, sir, take from me any thing that I will more willingly
part withal—except my life, except my life, except my life.

(Enter GUILDENSTERN *and* ROSENCRANTZ.*)*

POLONIUS: Fare you well, my lord.   *210*

HAMLET: These tedious old fools!°

POLONIUS: You go to seek the Lord Hamlet; there he is.

ROSENCRANTZ *(to* POLONIUS*)*: God save you, sir!   *(Exit* POLONIUS.*)*

GUILDENSTERN: My honor'd lord!

ROSENCRANTZ: My most dear lord!   *215*

HAMLET: My excellent good friends! How dost thou, Guildenstern? Ah,
Rosencrantz! Good lads, how do you both?

ROSENCRANTZ: As the indifferent° children of the earth.

GUILDENSTERN: Happy in that we are not over-happy. On Fortune's cap we
are not the very button.   *220*

HAMLET: Nor the soles of her shoe?

ROSENCRANTZ: Neither, my lord.

HAMLET: Then you live about her waist, or in the middle of her favors?

GUILDENSTERN: Faith, her privates° we.

HAMLET: In the secret parts of Fortune? O, most true; she is a strumpet.°   *225*
What news?

ROSENCRANTZ: None, my lord, but the world's grown honest.

HAMLET: Then is doomsday near. But your news is not true. Let me question
more in particular. What have you, my good friends, deserv'd at the hands
of Fortune that she sends you to prison hither?   *230*

GUILDENSTERN: Prison, my lord?

HAMLET: Denmark's a prison.

---

198 *honesty:* Decency. 203 *pregnant:* Full of meaning. 204 *happiness:* Felicity of expression. 205
prosperously: Successfully. 211 *old fools:* I.e., old men like Polonius. 218 *indifferent:* Ordinary. 224
privates: Close acquaintances (with sexual pun on "private parts"). 225 *strumpet:* Prostitute (a
common epithet for indiscriminate Fortune).

ROSENCRANTZ: Then is the world one.

HAMLET: A goodly one, in which there are many confines,° wards,° and dun-
235   geons, Denmark being one o' th' worst.

ROSENCRANTZ: We think not so, my lord.

HAMLET: Why then 'tis none to you, for there is nothing either good or bad
    but thinking makes it so. To me it is a prison.

ROSENCRANTZ: Why then, your ambition makes it one. 'tis too narrow for
240   your mind.

HAMLET: O God, I could be bounded in a nutshell and count myself a king
    of infinite space, were it not that I have bad dreams.

GUILDENSTERN: Which dreams indeed are ambition, for the very substance
    of the ambitious° is merely the shadow of a dream.

245 HAMLET: A dream itself is but a shadow.

ROSENCRANTZ: Truly, and I hold ambition of so airy and light a quality that
    it is but a shadow's shadow.

HAMLET: Then are our beggars bodies,° and our monarchs and outstretch'd°
    heroes the beggars' shadows. Shall we to th' court? For, by my fay,° I can-
250   not reason.

ROSENCRANTZ, GUILDENSTERN: We'll wait upon° you.

HAMLET: No such matter. I will not sort° you with the rest of my servants,
    for, to speak to you like an honest man, I am most dreadfully attended.°
    But, in the beaten way° of friendship, what make° you at Elsinore?

255 ROSENCRANTZ: To visit you, my lord, no other occasion.

HAMLET: Beggar that I am, I am even poor in thanks; but I thank you, and
    sure, dear friends, my thanks are too dear a halfpenny.° Were you not
    sent for? Is it your own inclining? Is it a free visitation? Come, come,
    deal justly with me. Come, come; nay, speak.

260 GUILDENSTERN: What should we say, my lord?

HAMLET: Why, anything, but to th' purpose. You were sent for; and there is a
    kind of confession in your looks which your modesties have not craft
    enough to color. I know the good King and Queen have sent for you.

ROSENCRANTZ: To what end, my lord?

265 HAMLET: That you must teach me. But let me conjure° you, by the rights of
    our fellowship, by the consonancy of our youth,° by the obligation of
    our ever-preserv'd love, and by what more dear a better proposer° could

---

234 *confines:* Places of confinement; *wards:* Cells. 243–44 *the very . . . ambitious:* That seemingly
very substantial thing which the ambitious pursue. 248 *bodies:* Solid substances rather than shadows (since beggars are not ambitious); *outstretch'd:* (1) Far-reaching in their ambition, (2) elon-
gated as shadows. 249 *fay:* Faith. 251 *wait upon:* Accompany, attend. 252 *sort:* Class, associate.
253 *dreadfully attended:* Waited upon in slovenly fashion. 254 *beaten way:* Familiar path; *make:* Do.
257 *dear a halfpenny:* Expensive at the price of a halfpenny, i.e., of little worth. 265 *conjure:* Ad-
jure, entreat. 266 *consonancy of our youth:* The fact that we are of the same age. 267 *better proposer:*
More skillful propounder.

charge° you withal, be even° and direct with me, whether you were sent
    for, or no?

ROSENCRANTZ *(aside to* GUILDENSTERN*)*: What say you?   270

HAMLET *(aside)*: Nay then, I have an eye of° you.— If you love me, hold
    not off.

GUILDENSTERN: My lord, we were sent for.

HAMLET: I will tell you why; so shall my anticipation prevent your discov-
    ery,° and your secrecy to the King and Queen molt no feather.° I have   275
    of late—but wherefore I know not—lost all my mirth, forgone all custom
    of exercises; and indeed it goes so heavily with my disposition that this
    goodly frame, the earth, seems to me a sterile promontory; this most excel-
    lent canopy, the air, look you, this brave° o'erhanging firmament, this
    majestical roof fretted° with golden fire, why, it appeareth nothing to me   280
    but a foul and pestilent congregation of vapors. What a piece of work is a
    man! How noble in reason, how infinite in faculties, in form and moving
    how express° and admirable, in action how like an angel, in apprehension
    how like a god! The beauty of the world, the paragon of animals! And yet,
    to me, what is this quintessence° of dust? Man delights not me—no, nor   285
    woman neither, though by your smiling you seem to say so.

ROSENCRANTZ: My lord, there was no such stuff in my thoughts.

HAMLET: Why did you laugh then, when I said "man delights not me"?

ROSENCRANTZ: To think, my lord, if you delight not in man, what lenten
    entertainment° the players shall receive from you. We coted° them on   290
    the way, and hither are they coming, to offer you service.

HAMLET: He that plays the king shall be welcome; his Majesty shall have trib-
    ute of me. The adventurous knight shall use his foil and target,° the lover
    shall not sigh gratis, the humorous man° shall end his part in peace, the
    clown shall make those laugh whose lungs are tickle o' th' sere,° and the   295
    lady shall say her mind freely, or the blank verse shall halt° for 't. What
    players are they?

ROSENCRANTZ: Even those you were wont to take such delight in, the
    tragedians of the city.

HAMLET: How chances it they travel? Their residence,° both in reputation   300
    and profit, was better both ways.

---

268 *charge:* Urge; *even:* Straight, honest. 271 *of:* On. 274–75 *prevent your discovery:* Forestall your
disclosure. 275 *molt no feather:* Not diminish in the least. 279 *brave:* Splendid. 280 *fretted:*
Adorned (with fretwork, as in a vaulted ceiling). 283 *express:* Well-framed (?), exact (?). 285
quintessence: The fifth essence of ancient philosophy, beyond earth, water, air, and fire, supposed to
be the substance of the heavenly bodies and to be latent in all things. 289–90 *lenten entertainment:* Meager reception (appropriate to Lent). 290 *coted:* Overtook and passed beyond. 293 *foil
and target:* Sword and shield. 294 *humorous man:* Eccentric character, dominated by one trait or
"humor." 295 *tickle o' th' sere:* Easy on the trigger, ready to laugh easily. (*Sere* is part of a gun-
lock.) 296 *halt:* Limp. 300 *residence:* Remaining in one place, i.e., in the city.

ROSENCRANTZ: I think their inhibition° comes by the means of the innovation.°

HAMLET: Do they hold the same estimation they did when I was in the city?
305   Are they so follow'd?

ROSENCRANTZ: No, indeed, are they not.

HAMLET: How comes it? Do they grow rusty?

ROSENCRANTZ: Nay, their endeavor keeps in the wonted° pace. But there is, sir, an aery° of children, little eyases, that cry out on the top of ques-
310   tion,° and are most tyrannically° clapp'd for 't. These are now the fashion, and so berattle° the common stages°—so they call them—that many wearing rapiers° are afraid of goose-quills° and dare scarce come thither.

HAMLET: What, are they children? Who maintains 'em? How are they escoted?° Will they pursue the quality° no longer than they can sing?°
315   Will they not say afterwards, if they should grow themselves to common° players—as it is most like, if their means are no better—their writers do them wrong, to make them exclaim against their own succession?°

ROSENCRANTZ: Faith, there has been much to do° on both sides; and the nation holds it no sin to tarre° them to controversy. There was, for a
320   while, no money bid for argument° unless the poet and the player went to cuffs in the question.°

HAMLET: Is 't possible?

GUILDENSTERN: O, there has been much throwing about of brains.

HAMLET: Do the boys carry it away?°

325   ROSENCRANTZ: Ay, that they do, my lord—Hercules and his load° too.

HAMLET: It is not very strange; for my uncle is King of Denmark, and those that would make mouths° at him while my father liv'd, give twenty, forty, fifty, a hundred ducats° apiece for his picture in little. 'Sblood,° there is something in this more than natural, if philosophy could find it out.

(A flourish of trumpets within.)

330   GUILDENSTERN: There are the players.

---

302 *inhibition:* Formal prohibition (from acting plays in the city). 303 *innovation:* I.e., the new fashion in satirical plays performed by boy actors in the "private" theaters; or possibly a political uprising; or the strict limitations set on the theater in London in 1600. 308 *wonted:* Usual. 309 *aery:* Nest; *eyases:* Young hawks. 309–10 *cry . . . question:* Speak shrilly, dominating the controversy (in decrying the public theaters). 310 *tyrannically:* Outrageous. 311 *berattle:* Berate; *common stages:* Public theaters. 311–12 *many wearing rapiers:* Many men of fashion, who were afraid to patronize the common players for fear of being satirized by the poets who wrote for the children. 312 *goose-quills:* Pens of satirists. 314 *escoted:* Maintained; *quality:* (Acting) profession; *no longer . . . sing:* Only until their voices change. 315–16 *common:* Regular, adult. 317 *succession:* Future careers. 318 *to do:* Ado. 319 *tarre:* Set on (as dogs). 320 *argument:* Plot for a play. 320–21 *went . . . question:* Came to blows in the play itself. 324 *carry it away:* Win the day. 325 *Hercules . . . load:* Thought to be an allusion to the sign of the Globe Theatre, which was Hercules bearing the world on his shoulder. 327 *mouths:* Faces. 328 *ducats:* Gold coins; *in little:* In miniature; *'Sblood:* By His (God's, Christ's) blood.

HAMLET: Gentlemen, you are welcome to Elsinore. Your hands, come then. Th'
appurtenance of welcome is fashion and ceremony. Let me comply° with
you in this garb,° lest my extent° to the players, which, I tell you, must
show fairly outwards,° should more appear like entertainment° than yours.
You are welcome. But my uncle-father and aunt-mother are deceiv'd.   335
GUILDENSTERN: In what, my dear lord?
HAMLET: I am but mad north-north-west.° When the wind is southerly I
know a hawk from a handsaw.°

(Enter POLONIUS.*)*

POLONIUS: Well be with you, gentlemen!
HAMLET: Hark you, Guildenstern, and you too; at each ear a hearer. That   340
great baby you see there is not yet out of his swaddling-clouts.°
ROSENCRANTZ: Happily° he is the second time come to them; for they say
an old man is twice a child.
HAMLET: I will prophesy he comes to tell me of the players; mark it.—You
say right, sir, o' Monday morning, 'twas then indeed.   345
POLONIUS: My lord, I have news to tell you.
HAMLET: My lord, I have news to tell you. When Roscius° was an actor in
Rome—
POLONIUS: The actors are come hither, my lord.
HAMLET: Buzz,° buzz!   350
POLONIUS: Upon my honor—
HAMLET: Then came each actor on his ass—
POLONIUS: The best actors in the world, either for tragedy, comedy, history,
pastoral, pastoral-comical, historical-pastoral, tragical-historical, tragical-
comical-historical-pastoral, scene individable,° or poem unlimited.°   355
Seneca° cannot be too heavy, nor Plautus° too light. For the law of writ
and the liberty,° these are the only men.
HAMLET: O Jephthah, judge of Israel,° what a treasure hadst thou!
POLONIUS: What a treasure had he, my lord?
HAMLET: Why,   360

---

332 *comply:* Observe the formalities of courtesy. 333 *garb:* Manner; *my extent:* The extent of my
showing courtesy. 334 *show fairly outwards:* Look cordial to outward appearances; *entertainment:* A
(warm) reception. 337 *north-north-west:* Only partly, at times. 338 *hawk, handsaw:* Mattock (or
"hack") and a carpenter's cutting tool, respectively; also birds, with a play on "hernshaw" or
heron. 341 *swaddling-clouts:* Cloths in which to wrap a newborn baby. 342 *Happily:* Haply, perhaps. 347 *Roscius:* A famous Roman actor who died in 62 B.C. 350 *Buzz:* An interjection used
to denote stale news. 355 *scene individable:* A play observing the unity of place; *poem unlimited:* A
play disregarding the unities of time and place. 356 *Seneca:* Writer of Latin tragedies; *Plautus:*
Writer of Latin comedy. 356–57 *law . . . liberty:* Dramatic composition both according to rules
and without rules, i.e., "classical" and "romantic" dramas. 358 *Jephthah . . . Israel:* Jephthah had to
sacrifice his daughter; see Judges 11. Hamlet goes on to quote from a ballad on the theme.

"One fair daughter, and no more,
         The which he loved passing° well."

POLONIUS *(aside)*: Still on my daughter.

HAMLET: Am I not i' th' right, old Jephthah?

365   POLONIUS: If you call me Jephthah, my lord, I have a daughter that I love
         passing well.

HAMLET: Nay, that follows not.

POLONIUS: What follows, then, my lord?

HAMLET: Why,

370   "As by lot, God wot,"°
         and then, you know,
         "It came to pass, as most like° it was."
         The first row° of the pious chanson° will show you more, for look where
         my abridgement° comes.

         (Enter the PLAYERS.*)*

375   You are welcome, masters; welcome, all. I am glad to see thee well. Wel-
         come, good friends. O, old friend! Why, thy face is valanc'd° since I saw
         thee last. Com'st thou to beard° me in Denmark? What, my young lady°
         and mistress? By 'r lady, your ladyship is nearer to heaven than when I
         saw you last, by the altitude of a chopine.° Pray God your voice, like a
380   piece of uncurrent° gold, be not crack'd within the ring.° Masters, you
         are all welcome. We'll e'en to 't like French falconers, fly at anything we
         see. We'll have a speech straight.° Come, give us a taste of your quality;
         come, a passionate speech.

FIRST PLAYER: What speech, my good lord?

385   HAMLET: I heard thee speak me a speech once, but it was never acted, or, if it
         was, not above once, for the play, I remember, pleas'd not the million;
         'twas caviary to the general.° But it was—as I receiv'd it, and others,
         whose judgments in such matters cried in the top of° mine—an excel-
         lent play, well digested in the scenes, set down with as much modesty as
390   cunning.° I remember one said there were no sallets° in the lines to make
         the matter savory, nor no matter in the phrase that might indict° the au-
         thor of affectation, but call'd it an honest method, as wholesome as sweet,

362 *passing:* Surpassingly. 370 *wot:* Knows. 372 *like:* Likely, probable. 373 *row:* Stanza; *chanson:* Ballad, song. 374 *my abridgement:* Something that cuts short my conversation; also, a diversion. 376 *valanc'd:* Fringed (with a beard). 377 *beard:* Confront (with obvious pun); *young lady:* Boy playing women's parts. 379 *chopine:* Thick-soled shoe of Italian fashion. 380 *uncurrent:* Not pass- able as lawful coinage; *crack'd . . . ring:* Changed from adolescent to male voice, no longer suitable for women's roles. (Coins featured rings enclosing the sovereign's head; if the coin was cracked within this ring, it was unfit for currency.) 382 *straight:* At once. 387 *caviary to the general:* Caviar to the multitude, i.e., a choice dish too elegant for coarse tastes. 388 *cried in the top of:* Spoke with greater authority than. 390 *cunning:* Skill; *sallets:* Salad, i.e., spicy improprieties. 391 *indict:* Convict.

and by very much more handsome than fine.° One speech in 't I chiefly
lov'd: 'twas Aeneas' tale to Dido, and thereabout of it especially when he
speaks of Priam's slaughter.° If it live in your memory, begin at this line: *395*
let me see, let me see—
"The rugged Pyrrhus,° like th' Hyrcanian beast"°—
'Tis not so. It begins with Pyrrhus:
"The rugged Pyrrhus, he whose sable° arms,
Black as his purpose, did the night resemble   *400*
When he lay couched in the ominous horse,°
Hath now this dread and black complexion smear'd
With heraldry more dismal.° Head to foot
Now is he total gules,° horridly trick'd°
With blood of fathers, mothers, daughters, sons,   *405*
Bak'd and impasted° with the parching streets,°
That lend a tyrannous and a damned light
To their lord's° murder. Roasted in wrath and fire,
And thus o'er-sized° with coagulate gore,
With eyes like carbuncles, the hellish Pyrrhus   *410*
Old grandsire Priam seeks."
So proceed you.

POLONIUS: 'Fore God, my lord, well spoken, with good accent and good
discretion.

FIRST PLAYER: "Anon he finds him
Striking too short at Greeks. His antique sword,   *415*
Rebellious to his arm, lies where it falls,
Repugnant° to command. Unequal match'd,
Pyrrhus at Priam drives, in rage strikes wide,
But with the whiff and wind of his fell° sword
Th' unnerved father falls. Then senseless Ilium,°   *420*
Seeming to feel this blow, with flaming top
Stoops to his° base, and with a hideous crash
Takes prisoner Pyrrhus' ear. For, lo! His sword,
Which was declining on the milky head
Of reverend Priam, seem'd i' th' air to stick.   *425*
So as a painted° tyrant Pyrrhus stood,

---

393 *fine:* Elaborately ornamented, showy. 395 *Priam's slaughter:* The slaying of the ruler of Troy,
when the Greeks finally took the city. 397 *Pyrrhus:* A Greek hero in the Trojan War, also known
as Neoptolemus, son of Achilles; *Hyrcanian beast:* I.e., the tiger. 399 *sable:* Black (for reasons of
camouflage during the episode of the Trojan horse). 401 *ominous horse:* Trojan horse, by which
the Greeks gained access to Troy. 403 *dismal:* Ill-omened. 404 *gules:* Red (a heraldic term);
trick'd: Adorned, decorated. 406 *impasted:* Crusted, like a thick paste; *with . . . streets:* By the
parching heat of the streets (because of the fires everywhere). 408 *their lord's:* Priam's. 409 *o'er-
sized:* Covered as with size or glue. 417 *Repugnant:* Disobedient, resistant. 419 *fell:* Cruel. 420
senseless Ilium: Insensate Troy. 422 *his:* Its. 426 *painted:* Painted in a picture.

And, like a neutral to his will and matter,°
Did nothing.
But, as we often see, against° some storm,
430   A silence in the heavens, the rack° stand still,
The bold winds speechless, and the orb below
As hush as death, anon the dreadful thunder
Doth rend the region,° so, after Pyrrhus' pause,
Aroused vengeance sets him new a-work,
435   And never did the Cyclops'° hammers fall
On Mars's armor forg'd for proof eterne°
With less remorse than Pyrrhus' bleeding sword
Now falls on Priam.
Out, out, thou strumpet Fortune! All you gods,
440   In general synod,° take away her power!
Break all the spokes and fellies° from her wheel,
And bowl the round nave° down the hill of heaven,
As low as to the fiends!"
POLONIUS: This is too long.
445   HAMLET: It shall to the barber's with your beard.—Prithee say on. He's for a
jig° or a tale of bawdry, or he sleeps. Say on; come to Hecuba.°
FIRST PLAYER: "But who, ah woe! had seen the mobled° queen"—
HAMLET: "The mobled queen?"
POLONIUS: That's good. "Mobled queen" is good.
450   FIRST PLAYER: "Run barefoot up and down, threat'ning the flames
With bisson rheum,° a clout° upon that head
Where late the diadem stood, and for a robe,
About her lank and all o'er-teemed° loins,
A blanket, in the alarm of fear caught up—
455   Who this had seen, with tongue in venom steep'd,
'Gainst Fortune's state° would treason have pronounc'd.°
But if the gods themselves did see her then
When she saw Pyrrhus make malicious sport
In mincing with his sword her husband's limbs,
460   The instant burst of clamor that she made,
Unless things mortal move them not at all,
Would have made milch° the burning eyes of heaven,

427 *like . . . matter:* As though poised indecisively between his intention and its fulfillment. 429 *against:* Just before. 430 *rack:* Mass of clouds. 433 *region:* Sky. 435 *Cyclops:* Giant armor makers in the smithy of Vulcan. 436 *proof eterne:* Eternal resistance to assault. 440 *synod:* Assembly. 441 *fellies:* Pieces of wood forming the rim of a wheel. 442 *nave:* Hub. 446 *jig:* Comic song and dance often given at the end of a play; *Hecuba:* Wife of Priam. 447 *mobled:* Muffled. 451 *bisson rheum:* Blinding tears; *clout:* Cloth. 453 *o'er-teemed:* Worn out with bearing children. 456 *state:* Rule, managing; *pronounc'd:* Proclaimed. 462 *milch:* Milky, moist with tears.

And passion in the gods."

POLONIUS: Look whe'er° he has not turn'd his color and has tears in 's eyes.
Prithee, no more.   465

HAMLET: 'Tis well; I'll have thee speak out the rest of this soon. Good my lord,
will you see the players well bestow'd?° Do you hear, let them be well us'd,
for they are the abstract° and brief chronicles of the time. After your death
you were better have a bad epitaph than their ill report while you live.

POLONIUS: My lord, I will use them according to their desert.   470

HAMLET: God's bodkin,° man, much better! Use every man after his desert,
and who shall scape whipping? Use them after your own honor and dignity. The less they deserve, the more merit is in your bounty. Take them in.

POLONIUS: Come, sirs.

HAMLET: Follow him, friends. We'll hear a play tomorrow. *(As they start to*   475
leave, HAMLET *detains the* FIRST PLAYER.*)* Dost thou hear me, old friend?
Can you play the Murder of Gonzago?

FIRST PLAYER: Ay, my lord.

HAMLET: We'll ha 't tomorrow night. You could, for need, study a speech of
some dozen or sixteen lines, which I would set down and insert in 't,   480
could you not?

FIRST PLAYER: Ay, my lord.

HAMLET: Very well. Follow that lord, and look you mock him not.—My
good friends, I'll leave you till night. You are welcome to Elsinore.
(Exeunt POLONIUS *and* PLAYERS.*)*

ROSENCRANTZ: Good my lord!   485
(Exeunt ROSENCRANTZ *and* GUILDENSTERN.*)*

HAMLET: Ay, so, God buy you.—Now I am alone.
O, what a rogue and peasant slave am I!
Is it not monstrous that this player here,
But in a fiction, in a dream of passion,
Could force his soul so to his own conceit°   490
That from her working all his visage wann'd,°
Tears in his eyes, distraction in his aspect,
A broken voice, and his whole function suiting
With forms to his conceit?° And all for nothing!
For Hecuba!   495
What's Hecuba to him, or he to Hecuba,
That he should weep for her? What would he do,
Had he the motive and the cue for passion
That I have? He would drown the stage with tears

---

464 *whe'er:* Whether. 467 *bestow'd:* Lodged. 468 *abstract:* Summary account. 471 *God's bodkin:*
By God's (Christ's) little body, "bodykin" (not to be confused with "bodkin," dagger). 490 *conceit:* Conception. 491 *wann'd:* Grew pale. 493–94 *his whole . . . conceit:* His whole being responded with actions to suit his thought.

500   And cleave the general ear with horrid speech,
      Make mad the guilty and appall the free,°
      Confound the ignorant, and amaze indeed
      The very faculties of eyes and ears. Yet I,
      A dull and muddy-mettled° rascal, peak,°
505   Like John-a-dreams,° unpregnant of° my cause,
      And can say nothing—no, not for a king
      Upon whose property° and most dear life
      A damn'd defeat was made. Am I a coward?
      Who calls me villain? Breaks my pate across?
510   Plucks off my beard, and blows it in my face?
      Tweaks me by the nose? Gives me the lie° i' th' throat,
      As deep as to the lungs? Who does me this?
      Ha, 'swounds, I should take it; for it cannot be
      But I am pigeon-liver'd,° and lack gall
515   To make oppression bitter, or ere this
      I should have fatted all the region kites°
      With this slave's offal. Bloody, bawdy villain!
      Remorseless, treacherous, lecherous, kindless° villain!
      O, vengeance!
520   Why, what an ass am I! This is most brave,
      That I, the son of a dear father murder'd,
      Prompted to my revenge by heaven and hell,
      Must, like a whore, unpack my heart with words,
      And fall a-cursing, like a very drab,°
525   A stallion!° Fie upon 't, foh! About,° my brains!
      Hum, I have heard
      That guilty creatures sitting at a play
      Have by the very cunning of the scene
      Been struck so to the soul that presently°
530   They have proclaim'd their malefactions;
      For murder, though it have no tongue, will speak
      With most miraculous organ. I'll have these players
      Play something like the murder of my father
      Before mine uncle. I'll observe his looks;
535   I'll tent° him to the quick. If 'a do blench,°

---

501 *free:* Innocent.   504 *muddy-mettled:* Dull-spirited; *peak:* Mope, pine.   505 *John-a-dreams:* Sleepy dreaming idler; *unpregnant of:* Not quickened by.   507 *property:* The crown; perhaps also character, quality.   511 *Gives me the lie:* Calls me a liar.   514 *pigeon-liver'd:* The pigeon or dove was popularly supposed to be mild because it secreted no gall.   516 *region kites:* Kites (birds of prey) of the air, from the vicinity.   518 *kindless:* Unnatural.   524 *drab:* Prostitute.   525 *stallion:* Prostitute (male or female); *About:* About it, to work.   529 *presently:* At once.   535 *tent:* Probe; *blench:* Quail, flinch.

I know my course. The spirit that I have seen
May be the devil, and the devil hath power
T' assume a pleasing shape; yea, and perhaps
Out of my weakness and my melancholy,
As he is very potent with such spirits,°   *540*
Abuses° me to damn me. I'll have grounds
More relative° than this. The play's the thing
Wherein I'll catch the conscience of the King.   *(Exit.)*

ACT III
SCENE I°

(Enter KING, QUEEN, POLONIUS, OPHELIA, ROSENCRANTZ,
GUILDENSTERN, LORDS.*)*

KING: And can you, by no drift of conference,°
    Get from him why he puts on this confusion,
    Grating so harshly all his days of quiet
    With turbulent and dangerous lunacy?
ROSENCRANTZ: He does confess he feels himself distracted,   *5*
    But from what cause 'a will by no means speak.
GUILDENSTERN: Nor do we find him forward° to be sounded,°
    But with a crafty madness keeps aloof
    When we would bring him on to some confession
    Of his true state.
QUEEN: Did he receive you well?   *10*
ROSENCRANTZ: Most like a gentleman.
GUILDENSTERN: But with much forcing of his disposition.°
ROSENCRANTZ: Niggard of question,° but of our demands
    Most free in his reply.
QUEEN: Did you assay° him
    To any pastime?   *15*
ROSENCRANTZ: Madam, it so fell out that certain players
    We o'er-raught° on the way. Of these we told him,
    And there did seem in him a kind of joy
    To hear of it. They are here about the court,
    And, as I think, they have already order   *20*
    This night to play before him.
POLONIUS: 'Tis most true,

---

540 *spirits:* Humors (of melancholy). 541 *Abuses:* Deludes. 542 *relative:* Closely related, pertinent. ACT III, SCENE I. *Location:* The castle. 1 *drift of conference:* Direction of conversation.
7 *forward:* Willing; *sounded:* Tested deeply. 12 *disposition:* Inclination. 13 *question:* Conversation.
14 *assay:* Try to win. 17 *o'er-raught:* Overtook and passed.

And he beseech'd me to entreat your Majesties
To hear and see the matter.

KING: With all my heart, and it doth much content me
25   To hear him so inclin'd.
Good gentlemen, give him a further edge,°
And drive his purpose into these delights.

ROSENCRANTZ: We shall, my lord.

(Exeunt ROSENCRANTZ *and* GUILDENSTERN.*)*

KING: Sweet Gertrude, leave us too,
For we have closely° sent for Hamlet hither,
30   That he, as 'twere by accident, may here
Affront° Ophelia.
Her father and myself, lawful espials,°
Will so bestow ourselves that seeing, unseen,
We may of their encounter frankly judge,
35   And gather by him, as he is behav'd,
If 't be th' affliction of his love or no
That thus he suffers for.

QUEEN: I shall obey you.
And for your part, Ophelia, I do wish
That your good beauties be the happy cause
40   Of Hamlet's wildness. So shall I hope your virtues
Will bring him to his wonted way again,
To both your honors.

OPHELIA: Madam, I wish it may.   *(Exit* QUEEN.*)*

POLONIUS: Ophelia, walk you here.—Gracious,° so please you,
We will bestow ourselves. *(To* OPHELIA.*)* Read on this book,

(Gives her a book.)

45   That show of such an exercise° may color°
Your loneliness. We are oft to blame in this—
'Tis too much prov'd°—that with devotion's visage
And pious action we do sugar o'er
The devil himself.

KING *(aside)*:   O, 'tis too true!
50   How smart a lash that speech doth give my conscience!
The harlot's cheek, beautied with plast'ring art,
Is not more ugly to° the thing° that helps it

---

26 *edge:* Incitement. 29 *closely:* Privately. 31 *Affront:* Confront, meet. 32 *espials:* Spies. 43 *Gracious:* Your Grace (i.e., the King). 45 *exercise:* Act of devotion. (The book she reads is one of devotion.); *color:* Give a plausible appearance to. 47 *too much prov'd:* Too often shown to be true, too often practiced. 52 *to:* Compared to; *thing:* I.e., the cosmetic.

Than is my deed to my most painted word.
O heavy burden!
POLONIUS: I hear him coming. Let's withdraw, my lord.   *55*

(KING *and* POLONIUS *withdraw.*°)

(Enter HAMLET. OPHELIA *pretends to read a book.)*

HAMLET: To be, or not to be, that is the question:
    Whether 'tis nobler in the mind to suffer
    The slings and arrows of outrageous fortune,
    Or to take arms against a sea of troubles,
    And by opposing end them. To die, to sleep—   *60*
    No more—and by a sleep to say we end
    The heart-ache and the thousand natural shocks
    That flesh is heir to. 'Tis a consummation
    Devoutly to be wish'd. To die, to sleep;
    To sleep, perchance to dream. Ay, there's the rub,°   *65*
    For in that sleep of death what dreams may come
    When we have shuffled° off this mortal coil,°
    Must give us pause. There's the respect°
    That makes calamity of so long life.°
    For who would bear the whips and scorns of time,   *70*
    Th' oppressor's wrong, the proud man's contumely,°
    The pangs of despis'd° love, the law's delay,
    The insolence of office,° and the spurns°
    That patient merit of th' unworthy takes,
    When he himself might his quietus° make   *75*
    With a bare bodkin?° Who would fardels° bear,
    To grunt and sweat under a weary life,
    But that the dread of something after death,
    The undiscover'd country from whose bourn°
    No traveler returns, puzzles the will,   *80*
    And makes us rather bear those ills we have
    Than fly to others that we know not of?
    Thus conscience does make cowards of us all
    And thus the native hue° of resolution

---

56 s.d. *withdraw:* The King and Polonius may retire behind an arras. The stage directions specify that they "enter" again near the end of the scene. 65 *rub:* Literally, an obstacle in the game of bowls. 67 *shuffled:* Sloughed, cast; *coil:* Turmoil. 68 *respect:* Consideration. 69 *of . . . life:* So long-lived. 71 *contumely:* Insolent abuse. 72 *despis'd:* Rejected. 73 *office:* Officialdom; *spurns:* Insults. 75 *quietus:* Acquittance; here, death. 76 *bodkin:* Dagger; *fardels:* Burdens. 79 *bourn:* Boundary. 84 *native hue:* Natural color, complexion.

85   Is sicklied o'er with the pale cast° of thought,
        And enterprises of great pitch° and moment°
        With this regard° their currents° turn awry,
        And lose the name of action.—Soft you now,
        The fair Ophelia. Nymph, in thy orisons°
        Be all my sins rememb'red.
90   OPHELIA: Good my lord,
        How does your honor for this many a day?
     HAMLET: I humbly thank you; well, well, well.
     OPHELIA: My lord, I have remembrances of yours,
        That I have longed long to re-deliver.
        I pray you, now receive them.   *(Offers tokens.)*
95   HAMLET: No, not I,
        I never gave you aught.
     OPHELIA: My honor'd lord, you know right well you did,
        And with them words of so sweet breath compos'd
        As made these things more rich. Their perfume lost,
100   Take these again, for to the noble mind
        Rich gifts wax poor when givers prove unkind.
        There, my lord.   *(Gives tokens.)*
     HAMLET: Ha, ha! Are you honest?°
     OPHELIA: My lord?
105 HAMLET: Are you fair?°
     OPHELIA: What means your lordship?
     HAMLET: That if you be honest and fair, your honesty° should admit no dis-
        course° to your beauty.
     OPHELIA: Could beauty, my lord, have better commerce° than with honesty?
110 HAMLET: Ay, truly; for the power of beauty will sooner transform honesty
        from what it is to a bawd than the force of honesty can translate beauty
        into his likeness. This was sometime° a paradox,° but now the time° gives
        it proof. I did love you once.
     OPHELIA: Indeed, my lord, you made me believe so.
115 HAMLET: You should not have believ'd me, for virtue cannot so inoculate°
        our old stock but we shall relish of it.° I lov'd you not.
     OPHELIA: I was the more deceiv'd.

---

85 *cast:* Shade of color. 86 *pitch:* Height (as of a falcon's flight); *moment:* Importance. 87 *regard:*
Respect, consideration; *currents:* Courses. 89 *orisons:* Prayers. 103 *honest:* (1) Truthful, (2) chaste.
105 *fair:* (1) Beautiful, (2) just, honorable. 107 *your honesty:* Your chastity. 107–8 *discourse:* Familiar dealings. 109 *commerce:* Dealings. 112 *sometime:* Formerly; *paradox:* A view opposite to commonly held opinion; *the time:* The present age. 115 *inoculate:* Graft, be engrafted to. 116 *but . . .
it:* That we do not still have about us a taste of the old stock; i.e., retain our sinfulness.

HAMLET: Get thee to a nunn'ry.° Why wouldst thou be a breeder of sinners?
I am myself indifferent honest;° but yet I could accuse me of such things
that it were better my mother had not borne me: I am very proud, re-   *120*
vengeful, ambitious, with more offenses at my beck° than I have thoughts
to put them in, imagination to give them shape, or time to act them in.
What should such fellows as I do crawling between earth and heaven?
We are arrant knaves, all; believe none of us. Go thy ways to a nunn'ry.
Where's your father?   *125*

OPHELIA: At home, my lord.

HAMLET: Let the doors be shut upon him, that he may play the fool nowhere
but in 's own house. Farewell.

OPHELIA: O, help him, you sweet heavens!

HAMLET: If thou dost marry, I'll give thee this plague for thy dowry: be thou   *130*
as chaste as ice, as pure as snow, thou shalt not escape calumny. Get thee
to a nunn'ry, farewell. Or, if thou wilt needs marry, marry a fool, for wise
men know well enough what monsters° you° make of them. To a nunn'ry,
go, and quickly too. Farewell.

OPHELIA: Heavenly powers, restore him!   *135*

HAMLET: I have heard of your paintings too, well enough. God hath given
you one face, and you make yourselves another. You jig,° and amble, and
you lisp, you nickname God's creatures, and make your wantonness your
ignorance.° Go to, I'll no more on 't; it hath made me mad. I say, we will
have no more marriage. Those that are married already—all but one—   *140*
shall live. The rest shall keep as they are. To a nunn'ry, go.   *(Exit.)*

OPHELIA: O, what a noble mind is here o'erthrown!
The courtier's, soldier's, scholar's, eye, tongue, sword,
Th' expectancy and rose of the fair state,°
The glass of fashion and the mold of form,°   *145*
Th' observ'd of all observers,° quite, quite down!
And I, of ladies most deject and wretched,
That suck'd the honey of his music vows,
Now see that noble and most sovereign reason,
Like sweet bells jangled, out of time and harsh,   *150*
That unmatch'd form and feature of blown° youth

---

118 *nunn'ry:* (1) Convent, (2) brothel. 119 *indifferent honest:* Reasonably virtuous. 121 *beck:*
Command. 133 *monsters:* An allusion to the horns of a cuckold; *you:* You women. 137 *jig:* Dance
and sing affectedly and wantonly. 138–39 *make . . . ignorance:* Excuse your affection on the
grounds of your ignorance. 144 *Th' expectancy . . . state:* The hope and ornament of the kingdom
made fair (by him). 145 *The glass . . . form:* The mirror of fashion and the pattern of courtly behavior. 146 *observ'd . . . observers:* The center of attention and honor in the court. 151 *blown:*
Blooming.

Blasted with ecstasy.° O, woe is me,
T' have seen what I have seen, see what I see!

(Enter KING *and* POLONIUS.*)*

KING: Love? His affections do not that way tend;
155   Nor what he spake, though it lack'd form a little,
          Was not like madness. There's something in his soul,
          O'er which his melancholy sits on brood,
          And I do doubt° the hatch and the disclose°
          Will be some danger; which for to prevent,
160   I have in quick determination
          Thus set it down: he shall with speed to England,
          For the demand of° our neglected tribute.
          Haply the seas and countries different
          With variable° objects shall expel
165   This something-settled° matter in his heart,
          Whereon his brains still beating puts him thus
          From fashion of himself.° What think you on 't?
POLONIUS: It shall do well. But yet do I believe
          The origin and commencement of his grief
170   Sprung from neglected love.—How now, Ophelia?
          You need not tell us what Lord Hamlet said;
          We heard it all.—My lord, do as you please,
          But, if you hold it fit, after the play
          Let his queen mother all alone entreat him
175   To show his grief. Let her be round° with him;
          And I'll be plac'd, so please you, in the ear
          Of all their conference. If she find him not,
          To England send him, or confine him where
          Your wisdom best shall think.
KING: It shall be so.
180   Madness in great ones must not unwatch'd go.   *(Exeunt.)*

SCENE II°

(Enter HAMLET *and three of the* PLAYERS.*)*

HAMLET: Speak the speech, I pray you, as I pronounc'd it to you, trippingly
          on the tongue. But if you mouth it, as many of our players° do, I had as

152 *ecstasy:* Madness. 158 *doubt:* Fear; *disclose:* Disclosure. 162 *For . . . of:* To demand. 164 *variable:* Various. 165 *something-settled:* Somewhat settled. 167 *From . . . himself:* Out of his natural manner. 177 *round:* Blunt. ACT III, SCENE II. *Location:* The castle. 2 *our players:* Indefinite use; i.e., "players nowadays."

lief the town-crier spoke my lines. Nor do not saw the air too much with your hand, thus, but use all gently; for in the very torrent,tempest, and, as I may say, whirlwind of your passion, you must acquire and beget 5
a temperance that may give it smoothness. O, it offends me to the soul to hear a robustious° periwig-pated° fellow tear a passion to tatters, to very rags, to split the ears of the groundlings,° who for the most part are capable of° nothing but inexplicable dumb-shows and noise. I would have such a fellow whipp'd for o'er-doing Termagant.° It out-herods 10
Herod.° Pray you, avoid it.

FIRST PLAYER: I warrant your honor.

HAMLET: Be not too tame neither, but let your own discretion be your tutor. Suit the action to the word, the word to the action, with this special ob-servance, that you o'erstep not the modesty of nature. For anything so 15
o'erdone is from° the purpose of playing, whose end, both at the first and now, was and is, to hold, as 't were, the mirror up to nature, to show virtue her feature, scorn her own image, and the very age and body of the time his° form and pressure.° Now this overdone, or come tardy off,° though it makes the unskillful laugh, cannot but make the judicious 20
grieve, the censure of which one° must in your allowance o'erweigh a whole theater of others. O, there be players that I have seen play, and heard others praise, and that highly, not to speak it profanely, that, nei-ther having th' accent of Christians nor the gait of Christian, pagan, nor man, have so strutted and bellow'd that I have thought some of nature's 25
journeymen° had made men and not made them well, they imitated hu-manity so abominably.

FIRST PLAYER: I hope we have reform'd that indifferently° with us, sir.

HAMLET: O, reform it altogether. And let those that play your clowns speak no more than is set down for them; for there be of them° that will them- 30
selves laugh, to set on some quantity of barren° spectators to laugh too, though in the mean time some necessary question of the play be then to be consider'd. That's villainous, and shows a most pitiful ambition in the fool that uses it. Go, make you ready.   *(Exeunt* PLAYERS.*)*

(Enter POLONIUS, GUILDENSTERN, *and* ROSENCRANTZ.*)*

---

7 *robustious:* Violent, boisterous; *periwig-pated:* Wearing a wig. 8 *groundlings:* Spectators who paid least and stood in the yard of the theater. 9 *capable of:* Susceptible to being influenced by. 10 *Ter-magant:* A god of the Saracens; a character in the St. Nicholas play, wherein one of his worshipers, leaving him in charge of goods, returns to find them stolen; whereupon he beats the god or idol, which howls vociferously. 11 *Herod:* Herod of Jewry. (A character in *The Slaughter of the Innocents* and other cycle plays. The part was played with great noise and fury.) 16 *from:* Contrary to. 19 *his:* Its; *pressure:* Stamp, impressed character; *come tardy off:* Inadequately done. 21 *the censure . . . one:* The judgment of even one of whom. 26 *journeymen:* Laborers not yet masters in their trade. 28 *indifferently:* Tolerably. 30 *of them:* Some among them. 31 *barren:* I.e., of wit.

35   How now, my lord? Will the King hear this piece of work?

POLONIUS: And the Queen too, and that presently.°
HAMLET: Bid the players make haste.   *(Exit* POLONIUS.*)*
          Will you two help to hasten them?
ROSENCRANTZ: Ay, my lord.   *(Exeunt they two.)*
40   HAMLET: What ho, Horatio!

          (Enter HORATIO.*)*

HORATIO: Here, sweet lord, at your service.
HAMLET: Horatio, thou art e'en as just a man
          As e'er my conversation cop'd withal.°
HORATIO: O, my dear lord—
HAMLET: Nay, do not think I flatter;
45   For what advancement may I hope from thee
          That no revenue hast but thy good spirits,
          To feed and clothe thee? Why should the poor be flatter'd?
          No, let the candied° tongue lick absurd pomp,
          And crook the pregnant° hinges of the knee
50   Where thrift° may follow fawning. Dost thou hear?
          Since my dear soul was mistress of her choice
          And could of men distinguish her election,
          Sh' hath seal'd thee for herself, for thou hast been
          As one, in suff'ring all, that suffers nothing,
55   A man that Fortune's buffets and rewards
          Hast ta'en with equal thanks; and blest are those
          Whose blood° and judgment are so well commeddled°
          That they are not a pipe for Fortune's finger
          To sound what stop° she please. Give me that man
60   That is not passion's slave, and I will wear him
          In my heart's core, ay, in my heart of heart,
          As I do thee.—Something too much of this.—
          There is a play tonight before the King.
          One scene of it comes near the circumstance
65   Which I have told thee of my father's death.
          I prithee, when thou seest that act afoot,
          Even with the very comment of thy soul°
          Observe my uncle. If his occulted° guilt
          Do not itself unkennel in one speech,

36 *presently:* At once. 43 *my . . . withal:* My contact with people provided opportunity for encounter with. 48 *candied:* Sugared, flattering. 49 *pregnant:* Compliant. 50 *thrift:* Profit. 57 *blood:* Passion; *commeddled:* Commingled. 59 *stop:* Hole in a wind instrument for controlling the sound. 67 *very . . . soul:* Inward and sagacious criticism. 68 *occulted:* Hidden.

It is a damned° ghost that we have seen,   70
And my imaginations are as foul
As Vulcan's stithy.° Give him heedful note,
For I mine eyes will rivet to his face,
And after we will both our judgments join
In censure of his seeming.°

HORATIO: Well, my lord.   75
If 'a steal aught the whilst this play is playing,
And scape detecting, I will pay the theft.

(Flourish. Enter trumpets and kettledrums, KING, QUEEN, POLONIUS,
OPHELIA, ROSENCRANTZ, GUILDENSTERN, *and other* LORDS, *with*
GUARDS *carrying torches.)*

HAMLET: They are coming to the play. I must be idle. Get you a place.
                        (The KING, QUEEN, *and* COURTIERS *sit.)*

KING: How fares our cousin Hamlet?

HAMLET: Excellent, i' faith, of the chameleon's dish:° I eat the air, promise-   80
cramm'd. You cannot feed capons so.

KING: I have nothing with° this answer, Hamlet. These words are not mine.°

HAMLET: No, nor mine now. *(To* POLONIUS.) My lord, you played once i' th'
university, you say?

POLONIUS: That did I, my lord; and was accounted a good actor.   85

HAMLET: What did you enact?

POLONIUS: I did enact Julius Caesar. I was killed i' th' Capitol; Brutus kill'd me.

HAMLET: It was a brute part of him to kill so capital a calf there. Be the players ready?

ROSENCRANTZ: Ay, my lord; they stay upon your patience.   90

QUEEN: Come hither, my dear Hamlet, sit by me.

HAMLET: No, good mother, here's metal more attractive.

POLONIUS *(to the* KING): O, ho, do you mark that?

HAMLET: Lady, shall I lie in your lap?   *(Lying down at* OPHELIA'S *feet.)*

OPHELIA: No, my lord.   95

HAMLET: I mean, my head upon your lap?

OPHELIA: Ay, my lord.

HAMLET: Do you think I meant country° matters?

OPHELIA: I think nothing, my lord.

HAMLET: That's a fair thought to lie between maids' legs.   100

---

70 *damned:* In league with Satan. 72 *stithy:* Smithy, place of stiths (anvils). 75 *censure of his seem-*
ing: Judgment of his appearance or behavior. 80 *chameleon's dish:* Chameleons were supposed to
feed on air. Hamlet deliberately misinterprets the King's "fares" as "feeds." By his phrase *eat the air*
he also plays on the idea of feeding himself with the promise of succession, of being the "heir."
82 *have . . . with:* Make nothing of; *are not mine:* Do not respond to what I asked. 98 *country:*
With a bawdy pun.

OPHELIA: What is, my lord?

HAMLET: Nothing.

OPHELIA: You are merry, my lord.

HAMLET: Who, I?

105   OPHELIA: Ay, my lord.

HAMLET: O God, your only jig-maker.° What should a man do but be merry?
For look you how cheerfully my mother looks, and my father died
within 's° two hours.

OPHELIA: Nay, 'tis twice two months, my lord.

110   HAMLET: So long? Nay then, let the devil wear black, for I'll have a suit of
sables.° O heavens! Die two months ago, and not forgotten yet? Then
there's hope a great man's memory may outlive his life half a year. But,
by 'r lady, 'a must build churches, then, or else shall 'a suffer not thinking
on,° with the hobby-horse, whose epitaph is "For, O, for, O, the hobby-

115   horse is forgot."°

(The trumpets sound. Dumb show follows.)

Enter a KING *and a* QUEEN *very lovingly; the* QUEEN *embracing him, and
he her. She kneels and makes show of protestation unto him. He takes her up,
and declines his head upon her neck. He lies him down upon a bank of flowers.
She, seeing him asleep, leaves him. Anon comes in another man, takes off his
crown, kisses it, pours poison in the sleeper's ears, and leaves him. The* QUEEN
returns; finds the KING *dead, makes passionate action. The* POISONER, *with
some three or four, come in again, seem to condole with her. The dead body is
carried away. The* POISONER *woos the* QUEEN *with gifts; she seems harsh
awhile but in the end accepts love.*

(Exeunt.)

OPHELIA: What means this, my lord?

HAMLET: Marry, this' miching mallecho;° it means mischief.

OPHELIA: Belike° this show imports the argument° of the play.

(Enter PROLOGUE.*)*

HAMLET: We shall know by this fellow. The players cannot keep counsel;°

120   they'll tell all.

---

106 *only jig-maker:* Very best composer of jigs (song and dance).   108 *within 's:* Within this.
110–11 *suit of sables:* Garments trimmed with the fur of the sable and hence suited for a wealthy
person, not a mourner (with a pun on *sable*, black).   113–14 *suffer . . . on:* Undergo oblivion.
114–15 *"For . . . forgot":* Verse of a song occurring also in *Love's Labor's Lost*, III.1.30. The hobby-
horse was a character made up to resemble a horse, appearing in the Morris dance and such
May-game sports. This song laments the disappearance of such customs under pressure from the
Puritans.   117 *this' miching mallecho:* This is sneaking mischief.   118 *Belike:* Probably; *argument:*
Plot.   119 *counsel:* Secret.

OPHELIA: Will 'a tell us what this show meant?

HAMLET: Ay, or any show that you will show him. Be not you° asham'd to
    show, he'll not shame to tell you what it means.

OPHELIA: You are naught,° you are naught. I'll mark the play.

PROLOGUE: For us, and for our tragedy,   125
    Here stooping° to your clemency,
    We beg your hearing patiently.   *(Exit.)*

HAMLET: Is this a prologue, or the posy of a ring?°

OPHELIA: 'Tis brief, my lord.

HAMLET: As woman's love.   130

(Enter two PLAYERS *as* KING *and* QUEEN.)

PLAYER KING: Full thirty times hath Phoebus' cart° gone round
    Neptune's salt wash° and Tellus'° orbed ground,
    And thirty dozen moons with borrowed° sheen
    About the world have times twelve thirties been,
    Since love our hearts and Hymen° did our hands   135
    Unite commutual° in most sacred bands.

PLAYER QUEEN: So many journeys may the sun and moon
    Make us again count o'er ere love be done!
    But, woe is me, you are so sick of late,
    So far from cheer and from your former state.   140
    That I distrust you. Yet, though I distrust,°
    Discomfort you, my lord, it nothing° must.
    For women's fear and love hold quantity;°
    In neither aught, or in extremity.
    Now, what my love is, proof° hath made you know,   145
    And as my love is siz'd, my fear is so.
    Where love is great, the littlest doubts are fear;
    Where little fears grow great, great love grows there.

PLAYER KING: Faith, I must leave thee, love, and shortly too;
    My operant° powers their functions leave to do.°   150
    And thou shalt live in this fair world behind,
    Honor'd, belov'd; and haply one as kind
    For husband shalt thou—

PLAYER QUEEN: O, confound the rest!

---

122 *Be not you:* If you are not. 124 *naught:* Indecent. 126 *stooping:* Bowing. 128 *posy . . . ring:*
Brief motto in verse inscribed in a ring. 131 *Phoebus' cart:* The sun god's chariot. 132 *salt wash:*
The sea; *Tellus':* Goddess of the earth, of the *orbed ground.* 133 *borrowed:* Reflected. 135 *Hymen:*
God of matrimony. 136 *commutual:* Mutually. 141 *distrust:* Am anxious about. 142 *nothing:* Not
at all. 143 *hold quantity:* Keep proportion with one another. 145 *proof:* Experience. 150 *operant:*
Active; *leave to do:* Cease to perform.

        Such love must needs be treason in my breast.
155   In second husband let me be accurst!
        None wed the second but who kill'd the first.
HAMLET: Wormwood, wormwood.
PLAYER QUEEN: The instances° that second marriage move°
        Are base respects of thrift,° but none of love.
160   A second time I kill my husband dead,
        When second husband kisses me in bed.
PLAYER KING: I do believe you think what now you speak,
        But what we do determine oft we break.
        Purpose is but the slave to memory,°
165   Of violent birth, but poor validity,°
        Which now, like fruit unripe, sticks on the tree,
        But fall unshaken when they mellow be.
        Most necessary 'tis that we forget
        To pay ourselves what to ourselves is debt.°
170   What to ourselves in passion we propose,
        The passion ending, doth the purpose lose.
        The violence of either grief or joy
        Their own enactures° with themselves destroy.
        Where joy most revels, grief doth most lament;
175   Grief joys, joy grieves, on slender accident.
        This world is not for aye,° nor 'tis not strange
        That even our loves should with our fortunes change;
        For 'tis a question left us yet to prove,
        Whether love lead fortune, or else fortune love.
180   The great man down, you mark his favorite flies;
        The poor advanc'd makes friends of enemies.
        And hitherto doth love on fortune tend;
        For who not needs° shall never lack a friend,
        And who in want° a hollow friend doth try,°
185   Directly seasons him° his enemy.
        But, orderly to end where I begun,
        Our wills and fates do so contrary run
        That our devices still° are overthrown;

---

158 *instances:* Motives; *move:* Motivate. 159 *base . . . thrift:* Ignoble considerations of material prosperity. 164 *Purpose . . . memory:* Our good intentions are subject to forgetfulness. 165 *validity:* Strength, durability. 168–69 *Most . . . debt:* It's inevitable that in time we forget the obligations we have imposed on ourselves. 173 *enactures:* Fulfillments. 176 *aye:* Ever. 183 *who not needs:* He who is not in need (of wealth). 184 *who in want:* He who is in need; *try:* Test (his generosity). 185 *seasons him:* Ripens him into. 188 *devices still:* Intentions continually.

Our thoughts are ours, their ends° none of our own.

So think thou wilt no second husband wed,   190

But die thy thoughts when thy first lord is dead.

PLAYER QUEEN: Nor earth to me give food, nor heaven light,

Sport and repose lock from me day and night,

To desperation turn my trust and hope,

An anchor's cheer° in prison be my scope!°   195

Each opposite° that blanks° the face of joy

Meet what I would have well and it destroy!

Both here and hence° pursue me lasting strife,

If, once a widow, ever I be wife!

HAMLET: If she should break it now!   200

PLAYER KING: 'Tis deeply sworn. Sweet, leave me here awhile;

My spirits grow dull, and fain I would beguile

The tedious day with sleep.   *(Sleeps.)*

PLAYER QUEEN: Sleep rock thy brain,

And never come mischance between us twain!   *(Exit.)*

HAMLET: Madam, how like you this play?   205

QUEEN: The lady doth protest too much, methinks.

HAMLET: O, but she'll keep her word.

KING: Have you heard the argument?° Is there no offense in 't?

HAMLET: No, no, they do but jest, poison in jest; no offense i' th' world.

KING: What do you call the play?   210

HAMLET: "The Mousetrap." Marry, how? Tropically.° This play is the image
of a murder done in Vienna. Gonzago is the Duke's name; his wife, Bap-
tista. You shall see anon. 'Tis a knavish piece of work, but what of that?
Your Majesty, and we that have free° souls, it touches us not. Let the
gall'd jade° winch,° our withers° are unwrung.°   215

(Enter LUCIANUS.*)*

This is one Lucianus, nephew to the King.

OPHELIA: You are as good as a chorus,° my lord.

HAMLET: I could interpret between you and your love, if I could see the pup-
pets dallying.°

---

189 *ends:* Results. 195 *anchor's cheer:* Anchorite's or hermit's fare; *my scope:* The extent of my
happiness. 196 *opposite:* Adverse thing; *blanks:* Causes to blanch or grow pale. 198 *hence:* In the
life hereafter. 208 *argument:* Plot. 211 *Tropically:* Figuratively. 214 *free:* Guiltless. 215 *gall'd jade:*
Horse whose hide is rubbed by saddle or harness; *winch:* Wince; *withers:* The part between the
horse's shoulder blades; *unwrung:* Not rubbed sore. 217 *chorus:* In many Elizabethan plays the
forthcoming action was explained by an actor known as the "chorus"; at a puppet show the actor
who spoke the dialogue was known as an "interpreter," as indicated by the lines following. 219
dallying: With sexual suggestion, continued in *keen,* i.e., sexually aroused, *groaning,* i.e., moaning
in pregnancy, and *edge,* i.e., sexual desire or impetuosity.

220   OPHELIA: You are keen, my lord, you are keen.

HAMLET: It would cost you a groaning to take off mine edge.

OPHELIA: Still better, and worse.°

HAMLET: So° you mistake° your husbands. Begin, murderer; leave thy damnable faces, and begin. Come, the croaking raven doth bellow for

225   revenge.

LUCIANUS: Thoughts black, hands apt, drugs fit, and time agreeing,

Confederate season,° else no creature seeing,

Thou mixture rank, of midnight weeds collected,

With Hecate's ban° thrice blasted, thrice infected,

230   Thy natural magic and dire property

On wholesome life usurp immediately.

(Pours the poison into the sleeper's ears.)

HAMLET: 'A poisons him i' th' garden for his estate. His name's Gonzago. The story is extant, and written in very choice Italian. You shall see anon how the murderer gets the love of Gonzago's wife.

(CLAUDIUS rises.)

235   OPHELIA: The King rises.

HAMLET: What, frighted with false fire?°

QUEEN: How fares my lord?

POLONIUS: Give o'er the play.

KING: Give me some light. Away!

240   POLONIUS: Lights, lights, lights!

(Exeunt all but HAMLET and HORATIO.)

HAMLET: "Why, let the strucken deer go weep,

The hart ungalled° play.

For some must watch,° while some must sleep;

Thus runs the world away."°

245   Would not this,° sir, and a forest of feathers°—if the rest of my fortunes turn Turk with° me—with two Provincial roses° on my raz'd° shoes, get me a fellowship in a cry of players?°

HORATIO: Half a share.

HAMLET: A whole one, I.

---

222 *Still . . . worse:* More keen-witted and less decorous. 223 *So:* Even thus (in marriage); *mistake:* Mis-take, take erringly, falseheartedly. 227 *Confederate season:* The time and occasion conspiring (to assist the murderer). 229 *Hecate's ban:* The curse of Hecate, the goddess of witchcraft. 236 *false fire:* The blank discharge of a gun loaded with powder but not shot. 242 *ungalled:* Unafflicted. 243 *watch:* Remain awake. 243–44 *while . . . away:* Probably from an old ballad, with allusion to the popular belief that a wounded deer retires to weep and die. 245 *this:* The play; *feathers:* Allusion to the plumes which Elizabethan actors were fond of wearing. 246 *turn Turk with:* Turn renegade against, go back on; *Provincial roses:* Rosettes of ribbon like the roses of Provence, an area in France; *raz'd:* With ornamental slashing. 247 *fellowship . . . players:* Partnership in a theatrical company.

"For thou dost know, O Damon dear,   *250*
      This realm dismantled° was
    Of Jove himself, and now reigns here
        A very, very—pajock."°
HORATIO: You might have rhym'd.
HAMLET: O good Horatio, I'll take the ghost's word for a thousand pound.   *255*
    Didst perceive?
HORATIO: Very well, my lord.
HAMLET: Upon the talk of pois'ning?
HORATIO: I did very well note him.
HAMLET: Ah, ha! Come, some music! Come, the recorders!°   *260*
    "For if the King like not the comedy,
    Why then, belike, he likes it not, perdy."°
    Come, some music!

    (Enter ROSENCRANTZ *and* GUILDENSTERN.*)*

GUILDENSTERN: Good my lord, vouchsafe me a word with you.
HAMLET: Sir, a whole history.   *265*
GUILDENSTERN: The King, sir—
HAMLET: Ay, sir, what of him?
GUILDENSTERN: Is in his retirement marvelous distemp'red.
HAMLET: With drink, sir?
GUILDENSTERN: No, my lord, with choler.°   *270*
HAMLET: Your wisdom should show itself more richer to signify this to the
    doctor, for, for me to put him to his purgation would perhaps plunge
    him into more choler.
GUILDENSTERN: Good my lord, put your discourse into some frame° and
    start not so wildly from my affair.   *275*
HAMLET: I am tame, sir. Pronounce.
GUILDENSTERN: The Queen, your mother, in most great affliction of spirit,
    hath sent me to you.
HAMLET: You are welcome.
GUILDENSTERN: Nay, good my lord, this courtesy is not of the right breed.   *280*
    If it shall please you to make me a wholesome answer, I will do your
    mother's commandment; if not, your pardon° and my return shall be the
    end of my business.
HAMLET: Sir, I cannot.

---

251 *dismantled:* Stripped, divested. 253 *pajock:* Peacock, a bird with a bad reputation (here substituted for the obvious rhyme-word *ass*). 260 *recorders:* Wind instruments like the flute. 262 *perdy:*
A corruption of the French "par dieu," by God. 270 *choler:* Anger. (But Hamlet takes the word
in its more basic humors sense of "bilious disorder.") 274 *frame:* Order. 282 *pardon:* Permission
to depart.

285   ROSENCRANTZ: What, my lord?

HAMLET: Make you a wholesome answer; my wit's diseas'd. But, sir, such answer as I can make, you shall command, or rather, as you say, my mother. Therefore no more, but to the matter. My mother, you say—

ROSENCRANTZ: Then thus she says: your behavior hath struck her into

290   amazement and admiration.°

HAMLET: O wonderful son, that can so stonish a mother! But is there no sequel at the heels of this mother's admiration? Impart.

ROSENCRANTZ: She desires to speak with you in her closet,° ere you go to bed.

295   HAMLET: We shall obey, were she ten times our mother. Have you any further trade with us?

ROSENCRANTZ: My lord, you once did love me.

HAMLET: And do still, by these pickers and stealers.°

ROSENCRANTZ: Good my lord, what is your cause of distemper? You do

300   surely bar the door upon your own liberty, if you deny your griefs to your friend.

HAMLET: Sir, I lack advancement.

ROSENCRANTZ: How can that be, when you have the voice of the King himself for your succession in Denmark?

305   HAMLET: Ay, sir, but "While the grass grows"°—the proverb is something° musty.

(Enter the PLAYERS *with recorders.)*

O, the recorders! Let me see one. *(He takes a recorder.)* To withdraw° with you: why do you go about to recover the wind° of me, as if you would drive me into a toil?°

310   GUILDENSTERN: O, my lord, if my duty be too bold, my love is too unmannerly.°

HAMLET: I do not well understand that. Will you play upon this pipe?

GUILDENSTERN: My lord, I cannot.

HAMLET: I pray you.

315   GUILDENSTERN: Believe me, I cannot.

HAMLET: I do beseech you.

GUILDENSTERN: I know no touch of it, my lord.

---

290 *admiration:* Wonder. 293 *closet:* Private chamber. 298 *pickers and stealers:* Hands (so called from the catechism, "to keep my hands from picking and stealing"). 305 *While . . . grows:* The rest of the proverb is "the silly horse starves"; Hamlet may not live long enough to succeed to the kingdom; *something:* Somewhat. 307 *withdraw:* Speak privately. 308 *recover the wind:* Get on the windward side. 309 *toil:* Snare. 310–11 *if . . . unmannerly:* If I am using an unmannerly boldness, it is my love which occasions it.

HAMLET: It is as easy as lying. Govern these ventages° with your fingers and thumb, give it breath with your mouth, and it will discourse most eloquent music. Look you, these are the stops.   320
GUILDENSTERN: But these cannot I command to any utt'rance of harmony; I have not the skill.
HAMLET: Why, look you now, how unworthy a thing you make of me! You would play upon me, you would seem to know my stops, you would pluck out the heart of my mystery, you would sound me from my lowest   325
note to the top of my compass,° and there is much music, excellent voice, in this little organ,° yet cannot you make it speak. 'Sblood, do you think I am easier to be play'd on than a pipe? Call me what instrument you will, though you can fret° me, you cannot play upon me.

(Enter POLONIUS.*)*

God bless you, sir!   330
POLONIUS: My lord, the Queen would speak with you, and presently.°
HAMLET: Do you see yonder cloud that's almost in shape of a camel?
POLONIUS: By th' mass, and 'tis like a camel, indeed.
HAMLET: Methinks it is like a weasel.
POLONIUS: It is back'd like a weasel.   335
HAMLET: Or like a whale?
POLONIUS: Very like a whale.
HAMLET: Then I will come to my mother by and by.° *(Aside.)* They fool me° to the top of my bent.°—I will come by and by.
POLONIUS: I will say so.   *(Exit.)*   340
HAMLET: "By and by" is easily said. Leave me, friends.
                                          (Exeunt all but HAMLET.*)*
'Tis now the very witching time° of night,
When churchyards yawn and hell itself breathes out
Contagion to this world. Now could I drink hot blood,
And do such bitter business as the day   345
Would quake to look on. Soft, now to my mother.
O heart, lose not thy nature! Let not ever
The soul of Nero° enter this firm bosom.
Let me be cruel, not unnatural;

318 *ventages:* Stops of the recorder. 326 *compass:* Range (of voice). 327 *organ:* Musical instrument. 329 *fret:* Irritate (with a quibble on *fret* meaning the piece of wood, gut, or metal that regulates the fingering on an instrument). 331 *presently:* At once. 338 *by and by:* Immediately; *fool me:* Make me play the fool. 339 *top of my bent:* Limit of my ability or endurance (literally, the extent to which a bow may be bent). 342 *witching time:* Time when spells are cast and evil is abroad. 348 *Nero:* Murderer of his mother, Agrippina.

350   I will speak daggers to her, but use none.
      My tongue and soul in this be hypocrites:
      How in my words somever° she be shent,°
      To give them seals° never, my soul, consent!   (Exit.)

SCENE III°

(Enter KING, ROSENCRANTZ, *and* GUILDENSTERN.*)*

KING: I like him not, nor stands it safe with us
      To let his madness range. Therefore prepare you.
      I your commission will forthwith dispatch,°
      And he to England shall along with you.
5   The terms° of our estate° may not endure
      Hazard so near 's as doth hourly grow
      Out of his brows.°
GUILDENSTERN: We will ourselves provide.
      Most holy and religious fear it is
      To keep those many many bodies safe
10   That live and feed upon your Majesty.
ROSENCRANTZ: The single and peculiar° life is bound
      With all the strength and armor of the mind
      To keep itself from noyance,° but much more
      That spirit upon whose weal depends and rests
15   The lives of many. The cess° of majesty
      Dies not alone, but like a gulf° doth draw
      What's near it with it; or it is a massy wheel
      Fix'd on the summit of the highest mount,
      To whose huge spokes ten thousand lesser things
20   Are mortis'd and adjoin'd, which, when it falls,
      Each small annexment, petty consequence,
      Attends° the boist'rous ruin. Never alone
      Did the King sigh, but with a general groan.
KING: Arm° you, I pray you, to this speedy voyage,
25   For we will fetters put about this fear,
      Which now goes too free-footed.
ROSENCRANTZ: We will haste us.

(Exeunt GENTLEMEN *[*ROSENCRANTZ *and* GUILDENSTERN*].)*

---

352 *How . . . somever:* However much by my words; *shent:* Rebuked. 353 *give them seals:* Confirm
them with deeds. ACT III, SCENE III. *Location:* The castle. 3 *dispatch:* Prepare, cause to be drawn
up. 5 *terms:* Condition, circumstances; *our estate:* My royal position. 7 *brows:* Effronteries, threatening frowns (?), brain (?). 11 *single and peculiar:* Individual and private. 13 *noyance:* Harm. 15
cess: Decease. 16 *gulf:* Whirlpool. 22 *Attends:* Participates in. 24 *Arm:* Prepare.

(Enter POLONIUS.*)*

POLONIUS: My lord, he's going to his mother's closet.
 Behind the arras° I'll convey myself
 To hear the process.° I'll warrant she'll tax him home,°
 And, as you said, and wisely was it said,   30
 'Tis meet that some more audience than a mother,
 Since nature makes them partial, should o'erhear
 The speech, of vantage.° Fare you well, my liege.
 I'll call upon you ere you go to bed,
 And tell you what I know.
KING: Thanks, dear my lord. *(Exit* POLONIUS.*)* 35
 O, my offense is rank, it smells to heaven;
 It hath the primal eldest curse° upon 't,
 A brother's murder. Pray can I not,
 Though inclination be as sharp as will.°
 My stronger guilt defeats my strong intent,   40
 And, like a man to double business bound,
 I stand in pause where I shall first begin,
 And both neglect. What if this cursed hand
 Were thicker than itself with brother's blood,
 Is there not rain enough in the sweet heavens   45
 To wash it white as snow? Whereto serves mercy
 But to confront the visage of offense?°
 And what's in prayer but this twofold force,
 To be forestalled° ere we come to fall,
 Or pardon'd being down? Then I'll look up;   50
 My fault is past. But, O, what form of prayer
 Can serve my turn? "Forgive me my foul murder"?
 That cannot be, since I am still possess'd
 Of those effects for which I did the murder,
 My crown, mine own ambition, and my queen.   55
 May one be pardon'd and retain th' offense?
 In the corrupted currents° of this world
 Offense's gilded hand° may shove by justice,
 And oft 'tis seen the wicked prize° itself

---

28 *arras:* Screen of tapestry placed around the walls of household apartments. (On the Elizabethan stage, the arras was presumably over a door or discovery space in the tiring-house facade.) 29 *process:* Proceedings; *tax him home:* Reprove him severely. 33 *of vantage:* From an advantageous place. 37 *primal eldest curse:* The curse of Cain, the first murderer; he killed his brother, Abel. 39 *Though . . . will:* Though my desire is as strong as my determination. 46–47 *Whereto . . . offense:* For what function does mercy serve other than to undo the effects of sin? 49 *forestalled:* Prevented (from sinning). 57 *currents:* Courses. 58 *gilded hand:* Hand offering gold as a bribe. 59 *wicked prize:* Prize won by wickedness.

60   Buys out the law. But 'tis not so above.
     There is no shuffling,° there the action lies°
     In his° true nature, and we ourselves compell'd,
     Even to the teeth and forehead° of our faults,
     To give in evidence. What then? What rests?°
65   Try what repentance can. What can it not?
     Yet what can it, when one cannot repent?
     O wretched state! O bosom black as death!
     O limed° soul, that, struggling to be free,
     Art more engag'd!° Help, angels! Make assay.°
70   Bow, stubborn knees, and heart with strings of steel,
     Be soft as sinews of the new-born babe!
     All may be well.   *(He kneels.)*

(Enter HAMLET *with sword drawn.)*

HAMLET: Now might I do it pat,° now 'a is a-praying;
     And now I'll do 't. And so 'a goes to heaven;
75   And so am I reveng'd. That would be scann'd:°
     A villain kills my father, and for that,
     I, his sole son, do this same villain send
     To heaven.
     Why, this is hire and salary, not revenge.
80   'A took my father grossly,° full of bread,°
     With all his crimes broad blown,° as flush° as May;
     And how his audit° stands who knows save heaven?
     But in our circumstance and course° of thought,
     'Tis heavy with him. And am I then reveng'd,
85   To take him in the purging of his soul,
     When he is fit and season'd for his passage?
     No!
     Up, sword, and know thou a more horrid hent.°   *(Puts up his sword.)*
     When he is drunk asleep, or in his rage,
90   Or in th' incestuous pleasure of his bed,
     At game a-swearing, or about some act
     That has no relish of salvation in 't—

61 *shuffling:* Escape by trickery; *the action lies:* The accusation is made manifest, comes up for consideration (a legal metaphor). 62 *his:* Its. 63 *teeth and forehead:* Face to face, concealing nothing.
64 *rests:* Remains. 68 *limed:* Caught as with birdlime, a sticky substance used to ensnare birds.
69 *engag'd:* Embedded; *assay:* Trial. 73 *pat:* Opportunely. 75 *would be scann'd:* Needs to be looked
into. 80 *grossly:* Not spiritually prepared; *full of bread:* Enjoying his worldly pleasures. (See Ezek.
16:49.) 81 *crimes broad blown:* Sins in full bloom; *flush:* Lusty. 82 *audit:* Account. 83 *in . . . course:*
As we see it in our mortal situation. 88 *know . . . hent:* Await to be grasped by me on a more
horrid occasion.

Then trip him, that his heels may kick at heaven,
And that his soul may be as damn'd and black
As hell, whereto it goes. My mother stays.   95
This physic° but prolongs thy sickly days.   *(Exit.)*
KING: My words fly up, my thoughts remain below.
Words without thoughts never to heaven go.   *(Exit.)*

SCENE IV°

(Enter QUEEN GERTRUDE *and* POLONIUS.*)*

POLONIUS: 'A will come straight. Look you lay° home to him.
Tell him his pranks have been too broad° to bear with,
And that your Grace hath screen'd and stood between
Much heat° and him. I'll sconce° me even here.
Pray you, be round° with him.   5
HAMLET *(within)*: Mother, mother, mother!
QUEEN: I'll warrant you, fear me not.
Withdraw, I hear him coming.   (POLONIUS *hides behind the arras.)*

(Enter HAMLET.*)*

HAMLET: Now, mother, what's the matter?
QUEEN: Hamlet, thou hast thy father° much offended.   10
HAMLET: Mother, you have my father much offended.
QUEEN: Come, come, you answer with an idle° tongue.
HAMLET: Go, go, you question with a wicked tongue.
QUEEN: Why, how now, Hamlet?
HAMLET: What's the matter now?
QUEEN: Have you forgot me?
HAMLET: No, by the rood,° not so: 15
You are the Queen, your husband's brother's wife,
And—would it were not so!—you are my mother.
QUEEN: Nay, then, I'll set those to you that can speak.
HAMLET: Come, come, and sit you down; you shall not budge.
You go not till I set you up a glass   20
Where you may see the inmost part of you.
QUEEN: What wilt thou do? Thou wilt not murder me?
Help, ho!
POLONIUS *(behind)*: What, ho! Help!

96 *physic:* Purging (by prayer). ACT III, SCENE IV. *Location:* The Queen's private chamber.
1 *lay:* Thrust (i.e., reprove him soundly). 2 *broad:* Unrestrained. 4 *Much heat:* The King's anger;
sconce: Ensconce, hide. 5 *round:* Blunt. 10 *thy father:* Your stepfather, Claudius. 12 *idle:* Foolish.
15 *rood:* Cross.

25 HAMLET *(drawing)*: How now? A rat? Dead, for a ducat, dead!

                                   (Makes a pass through the arras.)

POLONIUS *(behind)*: O, I am slain!   *(Falls and dies.)*

QUEEN: O me, what hast thou done?

HAMLET: Nay, I know not. Is it the King?

QUEEN: O, what a rash and bloody deed is this!

HAMLET: A bloody deed—almost as bad, good mother,

30   As kill a king, and marry with his brother.

QUEEN: As kill a king!

HAMLET: Ay, lady, it was my word.

                     (Parts the arras and discovers POLONIUS.*)*

    Thou wretched, rash, intruding fool, farewell!

    I took thee for thy better. Take thy fortune.

    Thou find'st to be too busy is some danger.—

35   Leave wringing of your hands. Peace, sit you down,

    And let me wring your heart, for so I shall,

    If it be made of penetrable stuff,

    If damned custom° have not braz'd° it so

    That it be proof° and bulwark against sense.°

40 QUEEN: What have I done, that thou dar'st wag thy tongue

    In noise so rude against me?

HAMLET: Such an act

    That blurs the grace and blush of modesty,

    Calls virtue hypocrite, takes off the rose

    From the fair forehead of an innocent love

45   And sets a blister° there, makes marriage-vows

    As false as dicers' oaths. O, such a deed

    As from the body of contraction° plucks

    The very soul, and sweet religion° makes

    A rhapsody° of words. Heaven's face does glow

50   O'er this solidity and compound mass

    With heated visage, as against the doom,

    Is thought-sick at the act.°

QUEEN: Ay me, what act,

    That roars so loud and thunders in the index?°

HAMLET: Look here, upon this picture, and on this,

---

38 *damned custom:* Habitual wickedness; *braz'd:* Brazened, hardened. 39 *proof:* Armor; *sense:* Feeling. 45 *sets a blister:* Brands as a harlot. 47 *contraction:* The marriage contract. 48 *religion:* Religious vows. 49 *rhapsody:* Senseless string. 49–52 *Heaven's . . . act:* Heaven's face flushes with anger to look down upon this solid world, this compound mass, with hot face as though the day of doom were near, and is thought-sick at the deed (i.e., Gertrude's marriage). 53 *index:* Table of contents, prelude, or preface.

The counterfeit presentment° of two brothers.   *55*

(Shows her two likenesses.)

See, what a grace was seated on this brow:
Hyperion's° curls, the front° of Jove himself,
An eye like Mars, to threaten and command,
A station° like the herald Mercury
New-lighted on a heaven-kissing hill—   *60*
A combination and a form indeed,
Where every god did seem to set his seal,
To give the world assurance of a man.
This was your husband. Look you now, what follows:
Here is your husband, like a mildew'd ear,°   *65*
Blasting his wholesome brother. Have you eyes?
Could you on this fair mountain leave to feed,
And batten° on this moor?° Ha, have you eyes?
You cannot call it love, for at your age
The heyday° in the blood is tame, it's humble,   *70*
And waits upon the judgment, and what judgment
Would step from this to this? Sense,° sure, you have,
Else could you not have motion, but sure that sense
Is apoplex'd,° for madness would not err,
Nor sense to ecstasy was ne'er so thrall'd   *75*
But it reserv'd some quantity of choice
To serve in such a difference. What devil was 't
That thus hath cozen'd° you at hoodman-blind?°
Eyes without feeling, feeling without sight,
Ears without hands or eyes, smelling sans° all,   *80*
Or but a sickly part of one true sense
Could not so mope.°
O shame, where is thy blush? Rebellious hell,
If thou canst mutine° in a matron's bones,
To flaming youth let virtue be as wax,   *85*
And melt in her own fire. Proclaim no shame
When the compulsive ardor gives the charge,
Since frost itself as actively doth burn,

---

55 *counterfeit presentment:* Portrayed representation. 57 *Hyperion:* The sun god; *front:* Brow. 59 *station:* Manner of standing. 65 *ear:* I.e., of grain. 68 *batten:* Gorge; *moor:* Barren upland. 70 *heyday:* State of excitement. 72 *Sense:* Perception through the five senses (the functions of the middle or sensible soul). 74 *apoplex'd:* Paralyzed. (Hamlet goes on to explain that without such a paralysis of will, mere madness would not so err, nor would the five senses so enthrall themselves to *ecstasy* or lunacy; even such deranged states of mind would be able to make the obvious choice between Hamlet Senior and Claudius.) 78 *cozen'd:* Cheated; *hoodman-blind:* Blindman's buff. 80 *sans:* Without. 82 *mope:* Be dazed, act aimlessly. 84 *mutine:* Mutiny.

And reason panders will.°
QUEEN: O Hamlet, speak no more!
90   Thou turn'st mine eyes into my very soul,
And there I see such black and grained° spots
As will not leave their tinct.°
HAMLET: Nay, but to live
In the rank sweat of an enseamed° bed,
Stew'd in corruption, honeying and making love
Over the nasty sty—
95   QUEEN: O, speak to me no more.
These words, like daggers, enter in my ears.
No more, sweet Hamlet!
HAMLET: A murderer and a villain,
A slave that is not twentieth part the tithe°
Of your precedent° lord, a vice° of kings,
100   A cutpurse of the empire and the rule,
That from a shelf the precious diadem stole,
And put it in his pocket!
QUEEN: No more!

(Enter GHOST in his nightgown.)

HAMLET: A king of shreds and patches°—
105   Save me, and hover o'er me with your wings,
You heavenly guards! What would your gracious figure?
QUEEN: Alas, he's mad!
HAMLET: Do you not come your tardy son to chide,
That, laps'd in time and passion,° lets go by
110   Th' important° acting of your dread command?
O, say!
GHOST: Do not forget. This visitation
Is but to whet thy almost blunted purpose.
But, look, amazement° on thy mother sits.
115   O, step between her and her fighting soul!
Conceit° in weakest bodies strongest works.
Speak to her, Hamlet.
HAMLET: How is it with you, lady?

86–89 *Proclaim . . . will:* Call it no shameful business when the compelling ardor of youth delivers the attack, i.e., commits lechery, since the frost of advanced age burns with as active a fire of lust and reason perverts itself by fomenting lust rather than restraining it. 91 *grained:* Dyed in grain, indelible. 92 *tint:* Color. 93 *enseamed:* Laden with grease. 98 *tithe:* Tenth part. 99 *precedent:* Former (i.e., the elder Hamlet); *vice:* Buffoon (a reference to the vice of the morality plays). 104 *shreds and patches:* Motley, the traditional costume of the clown or fool. 109 *laps'd . . . passion:* Having allowed time to lapse and passion to cool. 110 *important:* Importunate, urgent. 114 *amazement:* Distraction. 116 *Conceit:* Imagination.

QUEEN: Alas, how is 't with you,
    That you do bend your eye on vacancy,
    And with th' incorporal° air do hold discourse?   120
    Forth at your eyes your spirits wildly peep,
    And, as the sleeping soldiers in th' alarm,
    Your bedded° hair, like life in excrements,°
    Start up and stand an° end. O gentle son,
    Upon the heat and flame of thy distemper   125
    Sprinkle cool patience. Whereon do you look?
HAMLET: On him, on him! Look you how pale he glares!
    His form and cause conjoin'd,° preaching to stones,
    Would make them capable.°—Do not look upon me,
    Lest with this piteous action you convert   130
    My stern effects.° Then what I have to do
    Will want true color°—tears perchance for blood.
QUEEN: To whom do you speak this?
HAMLET: Do you see nothing there?
QUEEN: Nothing at all; yet all that is I see.   135
HAMLET: Nor did you nothing hear?
QUEEN: No, nothing but ourselves.
HAMLET: Why, look you there, look how it steals away!
    My father, in his habit° as he lived!
    Look, where he goes, even now, out at the portal!   *(Exit* GHOST.)   140
QUEEN: This is the very coinage of your brain.
    This bodiless creation ecstasy°
    Is very cunning in.
HAMLET: Ecstasy?
    My pulse, as yours, doth temperately keep time,
    And makes as healthful music. It is not madness   145
    That I have utter'd. Bring me to the test,
    And I the matter will reword, which madness
    Would gambol° from. Mother, for love of grace,
    Lay not that flattering unction° to your soul
    That not your trespass but my madness speaks.   150
    It will but skin and film the ulcerous place,
    Whiles rank corruption, mining° all within,
    Infects unseen. Confess yourself to heaven,

---

120 *incorporal:* Immaterial. 123 *bedded:* Laid in smooth layers; *excrements:* Outgrowths. 124 *an:* On. 128 *His . . . conjoin'd:* His appearance joined to his cause for speaking. 129 *capable:* Receptive. 130–31 *convert . . . effects:* Divert me from my stern duty. 132 *want true color:* Lack plausibility so that (with a play on the normal sense of "color") I shall shed tears instead of blood. 139 *habit:* Dress. 142 *ecstasy:* Madness. 148 *gambol:* Skip away. 149 *unction:* Ointment. 152 *mining:* Working under the surface.

Repent what's past, avoid what is to come,
155 And do not spread the compost° on the weeds
To make them ranker. Forgive me this my virtue;°
For in the fatness° of these pursy° times
Virtue itself of vice must pardon beg,
Yea, curb° and woo for leave° to do him good.
160 QUEEN: O Hamlet, thou hast cleft my heart in twain.
HAMLET: O, throw away the worser part of it,
And live the purer with the other half.
Good night. But go not to my uncle's bed;
Assume a virtue, if you have it not.
165 That monster, custom, who all sense doth eat,°
Of habits devil,° is angel yet in this,
That to the use of actions fair and good
He likewise gives a frock or livery°
That aptly is put on. Refrain tonight,
170 And that shall lend a kind of easiness
To the next abstinence; the next more easy;
For use° almost can change the stamp of nature,
And either° . . . the devil, or throw him out
With wondrous potency. Once more, good night;
175 And when you are desirous to be bless'd,°
I'll blessing beg of you. For this same lord,   *(Pointing to* POLONIUS.*)*
I do repent; but heaven hath pleas'd it so
To punish me with this, and this with me,
That I must be their scourge and minister.°
180 I will bestow° him, and will answer well
The death I gave him. So, again, good night.
I must be cruel only to be kind.
Thus bad begins and worse remains behind.°
One word more, good lady.
QUEEN: What shall I do?
185 HAMLET: Not this, by no means, that I bid you do:
Let the bloat° king tempt you again to bed,

---

155 *compost:* Manure. 156 *this my virtue:* My virtuous talk in reproving you. 157 *fatness:* Grossness; *pursy:* Short-winded, corpulent. 159 *curb:* Bow, bend the knee; *leave:* Permission. 165 *who . . . eat:* Who consumes all proper or natural feeling. 166 *Of habits devil:* Devil-like in prompting evil habits. 168 *livery:* An outer appearance, a customary garb (and hence a predisposition easily assumed in time of stress). 172 *use:* Habit. 173 *And either:* A defective line usually emended by inserting the word "master" after "either." 175 *be bless'd:* Become blessed, i.e., repentant. 179 *their scourge and minister:* Agent of heavenly retribution. (By *scourge,* Hamlet also suggests that he himself will eventually suffer punishment in the process of fulfilling heaven's will.) 180 *bestow:* Stow, dispose of. 183 *behind:* To come. 186 *bloat:* Bloated.

Pinch wanton on your cheek, call you his mouse,
And let him, for a pair of reechy° kisses,
Or paddling in your neck with his damn'd fingers,
Make you to ravel all this matter out,   *190*
That I essentially am not in madness,
But mad in craft. 'Twere good° you let him know,
For who that's but a queen, fair, sober, wise,
Would from a paddock,° from a bat, a gib,°
Such dear concernings° hide? Who would do so?   *195*
No, in despite of sense and secrecy,
Unpeg the basket° on the house's top,
Let the birds fly, and, like the famous ape,°
To try conclusions,° in the basket creep
And break your own neck down.   *200*
QUEEN: Be thou assur'd, if words be made of breath,
And breath of life, I have no life to breathe
What thou hast said to me.
HAMLET: I must to England; you know that?
QUEEN: Alack,
I had forgot. 'Tis so concluded on.   *205*
HAMLET: There's letters seal'd, and my two schoolfellows,
Whom I will trust as I will adders fang'd,
They bear the mandate; they must sweep my way,°
And marshal me to knavery. Let it work.
For 'tis the sport to have the enginer°   *210*
Hoist with° his own petar,° and 't shall go hard
But I will delve one yard below their mines,°
And blow them at the moon. O, 'tis most sweet,
When in one line two crafts° directly meet.
This man shall set me packing.°   *215*
I'll lug the guts into the neighbor room.
Mother, good night indeed. This counselor
Is now most still, most secret, and most grave,

188 *reechy:* Dirty, filthy. 192 *good:* Said ironically; also the following eight lines. 194 *paddock:* Toad; *gib:* Tomcat. 195 *dear concernings:* Important affairs. 197 *Unpeg the basket:* Open the cage, i.e., let out the secret. 198 *famous ape:* In a story now lost. 199 *conclusions:* Experiments (in which the ape apparently enters a cage from which birds have been released and then tries to fly out of the cage as they have done, falling to his death). 208 *sweep my way:* Go before me. 210 *enginer:* Constructor of military contrivances. 211 *Hoist with:* Blown up by; *petar:* Petard, an explosive used to blow in a door or make a breach. 212 *mines:* Tunnels used in warfare to undermine the enemy's emplacements; Hamlet will countermine by going under their mines. 214 *crafts:* Acts of guile, plots. 215 *set me packing:* Set me to making schemes, and set me to lugging (him) and, also, send me off in a hurry.

Who was in life a foolish prating knave.
220   Come, sir, to draw toward an end° with you.
Good night, mother.

(Exeunt severally, HAMLET *dragging in* POLONIUS.*)*

ACT IV
SCENE I°

(Enter KING *and* QUEEN, *with* ROSENCRANTZ *and* GUILDENSTERN.*)*

KING: There's matter in these sighs, these profound heaves
You must translate; 'tis fit we understand them.
Where is your son?
QUEEN: Bestow this place on us a little while.

(Exeunt ROSENCRANTZ *and* GUILDENSTERN.*)*

5   Ah, mine own lord, what have I seen tonight!
KING: What, Gertrude? How does Hamlet?
QUEEN: Mad as the sea and wind when both contend
Which is the mightier. In his lawless fit,
Behind the arras hearing something stir,
10   Whips out his rapier, cries, "A rat, a rat!"
And, in this brainish apprehension,° kills
The unseen good old man.
KING: O heavy deed!
It had been so with us, had we been there.
His liberty is full of threats to all—
15   To you yourself, to us, to everyone.
Alas, how shall this bloody deed be answer'd?
It will be laid to us, whose providence°
Should have kept short,° restrain'd, and out of haunt°
This mad young man. But so much was our love
20   We would not understand what was most fit,
But, like the owner of a foul disease,
To keep it from divulging,° let it feed
Even on the pith of life. Where is he gone?
QUEEN: To draw apart the body he hath kill'd,
25   O'er whom his very madness, like some ore°
Among a mineral° of metals base,
Shows itself pure: 'a weeps for what is done.

---

220 *draw . . . end:* Finish up (with a pun on "draw," pull). ACT IV, SCENE I. *Location:* The castle.
11 *brainish apprehension:* Headstrong conception. 17 *providence:* Foresight. 18 *short:* On a short
tether; *out of haunt:* Secluded. 22 *divulging:* Becoming evident. 25 *ore:* Vein of gold. 26 *mineral:*
Mine.

KING: O Gertrude, come away!
  The sun no sooner shall the mountains touch
  But we will ship him hence; and this vile deed   *30*
  We must, with all our majesty and skill,
  Both countenance and excuse. Ho, Guildenstern!

(Enter ROSENCRANTZ *and* GUILDENSTERN.*)*

  Friends both, go join you with some further aid.
  Hamlet in madness hath Polonius slain,
  And from his mother's closet hath he dragg'd him.   *35*
  Go seek him out; speak fair, and bring the body
  Into the chapel. I pray you, haste in this.
                 (Exeunt ROSENCRANTZ *and* GUILDENSTERN.*)*
  Come, Gertrude, we'll call up our wisest friends
  And let them know both what we mean to do
  And what's untimely done° *40*
  Whose whisper o'er the world's diameter,°
  As level° as the cannon to his blank,°
  Transports his pois'ned shot, may miss our name,
  And hit the woundless° air. O, come away!
  My soul is full of discord and dismay.   *(Exeunt.)* *45*

SCENE II°

(Enter HAMLET.*)*

HAMLET: Safely stow'd.
ROSENCRANTZ, GUILDENSTERN *(within)*: Hamlet! Lord Hamlet!
HAMLET: But soft, what noise? Who calls on Hamlet? O, here they come.

(Enter ROSENCRANTZ *and* GUILDENSTERN.*)*

ROSENCRANTZ: What have you done, my lord, with the dead body?
HAMLET: Compounded it with dust, whereto 'tis kin.   *5*
ROSENCRANTZ: Tell us where 'tis, that we may take it thence
    And bear it to the chapel.
HAMLET: Do not believe it.
ROSENCRANTZ: Believe what?
HAMLET: That I can keep your counsel and not mine own. Besides, to be   *10*
   demanded of° a sponge, what replication° should be made by the son
   of a king?

---

40 *And . . . done:* A defective line. 41 *diameter:* Extent from side to side. 42 *As level:* With
as direct aim; *blank:* White spot in the center of a target. 44 *woundless:* Invulnerable. ACT IV,
SCENE II. *Location:* The castle. 11 *demanded of:* Questioned by; *replication:* Reply.

ROSENCRANTZ: Take you me for a sponge, my lord?

HAMLET: Ay, sir, that soaks up the King's countenance,° his rewards, his au-
15 thorities. But such officers do the King best service in the end. He keeps
them, like an ape an apple, in the corner of his jaw, first mouth'd, to be
last swallow'd. When he needs what you have glean'd, it is but squeezing
you, and, sponge, you shall be dry again.

ROSENCRANTZ: I understand you not, my lord.

20 HAMLET: I am glad of it. A knavish speech sleeps in° a foolish ear.

ROSENCRANTZ: My lord, you must tell us where the body is, and go with us
to the King.

HAMLET: The body is with the King, but the King is not with the body.° The
King is a thing—

25 GUILDENSTERN: A thing, my lord?

HAMLET: Of nothing.° Bring me to him. Hide fox, and all after.°   *(Exeunt.)*

SCENE III°

(Enter KING, and two or three.)

KING: I have sent to seek him, and to find the body.
How dangerous is it that this man goes loose!
Yet must not we put the strong law on him.
He's lov'd of the distracted° multitude,
5 Who like not in their judgment, but their eyes,
And where 'tis so, th' offender's scourge° is weigh'd,°
But never the offense. To bear° all smooth and even,
This sudden sending him away must seem
Deliberate pause.° Diseases desperate grown
10 By desperate appliance are reliev'd,
Or not at all.

(Enter ROSENCRANTZ, GUILDENSTERN, and all the rest.)

How now? What hath befall'n?

ROSENCRANTZ: Where the dead body is bestow'd, my lord,
We cannot get from him.

KING: But where is he?

ROSENCRANTZ: Without, my lord; guarded, to know your pleasure.

---

14 *countenance:* Favor. 20 *sleeps in:* Has no meaning to. 23 *The . . . body:* Perhaps alludes to the legal commonplace of "the king's two bodies," which drew a distinction between the sacred office of kingship and the particular mortal who possessed it at any given time. 26 *Of nothing:* Of no account; *Hide . . . after:* An old signal cry in the game of hide-and-seek, suggesting that Hamlet now runs away from them. ACT IV, SCENE III. *Location:* The castle. 4 *distracted:* Fickle, unstable. 6 *scourge:* Punishment; *weigh'd:* Taken into consideration. 7 *bear:* Manage. 9 *Deliberate pause:* Carefully considered action.

KING: Bring him before us.

ROSENCRANTZ: Ho! Bring in the lord.   15

(They enter with HAMLET.*)*

KING: Now, Hamlet, where's Polonius?

HAMLET: At supper.

KING: At supper? Where?

HAMLET: Not where he eats, but where 'a is eaten. A certain convocation of
politic worms° are e'en at him. Your worm is your only emperor for   20
diet.° We fat all creatures else to fat us, and we fat ourselves for maggots.
Your fat king and your lean beggar is but variable service,° two dishes,
but to one table—that's the end.

KING: Alas, alas!

HAMLET: A man may fish with the worm that hath eat° of a king, and eat of   25
the fish that hath fed of that worm.

KING: What dost thou mean by this?

HAMLET: Nothing but to show you how a king may go a progress° through
the guts of a beggar.

KING: Where is Polonius?   30

HAMLET: In heaven. Send thither to see. If your messenger find him not there,
seek him i' th' other place yourself. But if indeed you find him not within
this month, you shall nose him as you go up the stairs into the lobby.

KING *(to some* ATTENDANTS*)*: Go seek him there.

HAMLET: 'A will stay till you come.   *(Exit* ATTENDANTS.*)*   35

KING: Hamlet, this deed, for thine especial safety,—
Which we do tender,° as we dearly° grieve
For that which thou hast done—must send thee hence
With fiery quickness. Therefore prepare thyself.
The bark° is ready, and the wind at help,   40
Th' associates tend,° and everything is bent°
For England.

HAMLET: For England!

KING: Ay, Hamlet.

HAMLET: Good.

KING: So is it, if thou knew'st our purposes.

HAMLET: I see a cherub° that sees them. But, come, for England! Farewell,
dear mother.   45

---

20 *politic worms:* Crafty worms (suited to a master spy like Polonius).   21 *diet:* Food, eating (with
perhaps a punning reference to the Diet of Worms, a famous convocation held in 1521).   22 *vari-*
able service: Different courses of a single meal.   25 *eat* (pronounced "et"): Eaten.   28 *progress:* Royal
journey of state.   37 *tender:* Regard, hold dear; *dearly:* Intensely.   40 *bark:* Sailing vessel.   41 *tend:*
Wait; *bent:* In readiness.   44 *cherub:* Cherubim are angels of knowledge.

KING: Thy loving father, Hamlet.

HAMLET: My mother. Father and mother is man and wife, man and wife is
    one flesh, and so, my mother. Come, for England!   *(Exit.)*

KING: Follow him at foot;° tempt him with speed aboard.
50   Delay it not; I'll have him hence tonight.
    Away! For everything is seal'd and done
    That else leans on° th' affair. Pray you, make haste.
                 (Exeunt all but the KING.)
    And, England,° if my love thou hold'st at aught—
    As my great power thereof may give thee sense,
55   Since yet thy cicatrice° looks raw and red
    After the Danish sword, and thy free awe°
    Pays homage to us—thou mayst not coldly set°
    Our sovereign process,° which imports at full,
    By letters congruing° to that effect,
60   The present° death of Hamlet. Do it, England,
    For like the hectic° in my blood he rages,
    And thou must cure me. Till I know 'tis done,
    Howe'er my haps,° my joys were ne'er begun.   *(Exit.)*

SCENE IV°

    (Enter FORTINBRAS *with his* ARMY *over the stage.)*

FORTINBRAS: Go, captain, from me greet the Danish king.
    Tell him that, by his license,° Fortinbras
    Craves the conveyance° of a promis'd march
    Over his kingdom. You know the rendezvous.
5   If that his Majesty would aught with us,
    We shall express our duty in his eye;°
    And let him know so.
CAPTAIN: I will do 't, my lord.
FORTINBRAS: Go softly° on.   *(Exeunt all but the* CAPTAIN.)

    (Enter HAMLET, ROSENCRANTZ, GUILDENSTERN, *etc.)*

HAMLET: Good sir, whose powers° are these?
10 CAPTAIN: They are of Norway, sir.
HAMLET: How purposed, sir, I pray you?
CAPTAIN: Against some part of Poland.

---

49 *at foot:* Close behind, at heel. 52 *leans on:* Bears upon, is related to. 53 *England:* King of England. 55 *cicatrice:* Scar. 56 *free awe:* Voluntary show of respect. 57 *set:* Esteem. 58 *process:* Command. 59 *congruing:* Agreeing. 60 *present:* Immediate. 61 *hectic:* Persistent fever. 63 *haps:* Fortunes. ACT IV, SCENE IV. *Location:* The coast of Denmark. 2 *license:* Permission. 3 *conveyance:* Escort, convoy. 6 *eye:* Presence. 8 *softly:* Slowly. 9 *powers:* Forces.

HAMLET: Who commands them, sir?

CAPTAIN: The nephew to old Norway, Fortinbras.

HAMLET: Goes it against the main° of Poland, sir,   *15*
  Or for some frontier?

CAPTAIN: Truly to speak, and with no addition,°
  We go to gain a little patch of ground
  That hath in it no profit but the name.
  To pay° five ducats, five, I would not farm it;°   *20*
  Nor will it yield to Norway or the Pole
  A ranker° rate, should it be sold in fee.°

HAMLET: Why, then the Polack never will defend it.

CAPTAIN: Yes, it is already garrison'd.

HAMLET: Two thousand souls and twenty thousand ducats   *25*
  Will not debate the question of this straw.°
  This is th' imposthume° of much wealth and peace,
  That inward breaks, and shows no cause without
  Why the man dies. I humbly thank you, sir.

CAPTAIN: God buy you, sir.   *(Exit.)*

ROSENCRANTZ: Will 't please you go, my lord?   *30*

HAMLET: I'll be with you straight. Go a little before.

                              (Exit all except HAMLET.*)*

  How all occasions do inform against° me,
  And spur my dull revenge! What is a man,
  If his chief good and market of° his time
  Be but to sleep and feed? A beast, no more.   *35*
  Sure he that made us with such large discourse,°
  Looking before and after, gave us not
  That capability and god-like reason
  To fust° in us unus'd. Now, whether it be
  Bestial oblivion,° or some craven scruple   *40*
  Of thinking too precisely on th' event°—
  A thought which, quarter'd, hath but one part wisdom
  And ever three parts coward—I do not know
  Why yet I live to say "This thing's to do,"
  Sith° I have cause and will and strength and means   *45*
  To do 't. Examples gross° as earth exhort me:
  Witness this army of such mass and charge°

---

15 *main:* Main part. 17 *addition:* Exaggeration. 20 *To pay:* I.e., for a yearly rental of; *farm it:* Take a lease of it. 22 *ranker:* Higher; *in fee:* Fee simple, outright. 26 *debate . . . straw:* Settle this trifling matter. 27 *imposthume:* Abscess. 32 *inform against:* Denounce, betray; take shape against. 34 *market of:* Profit of, compensation for. 36 *discourse:* Power of reasoning. 39 *fust:* Grow moldy. 40 *oblivion:* Forgetfulness. 41 *event:* Outcome. 45 *Sith:* Since. 46 *gross:* Obvious. 47 *charge:* Expense.

Led by a delicate and tender prince,
Whose spirit, with divine ambition puff'd
50   Makes mouths° at the invisible event,
Exposing what is mortal and unsure
To all that fortune, death, and danger dare,
Even for an egg-shell. Rightly to be great
Is not to stir without great argument,
55   But greatly to find quarrel in a straw
When honor's at the stake. How stand I then,
That have a father kill'd, a mother stain'd,
Excitements of° my reason and my blood,
And let all sleep, while, to my shame, I see
60   The imminent death of twenty thousand men,
That, for a fantasy° and trick° of fame,
Go to their graves like beds, fight for a plot°
Whereon the numbers cannot try the cause,°
Which is not tomb enough and continent°
65   To hide the slain? O, from this time forth,
My thoughts be bloody, or be nothing worth!   *(Exit.)*

SCENE V°

(Enter HORATIO, QUEEN GERTRUDE, *and a* GENTLEMAN.)

QUEEN: I will not speak with her.
GENTLEMAN: She is importunate, indeed distract.
Her mood will needs be pitied.
QUEEN: What would she have?
GENTLEMAN: She speaks much of her father, says she hears
5   There's tricks° i' th' world, and hems, and beats her heart,°
Spurns enviously at straws,° speaks things in doubt°
That carry but half sense. Her speech is nothing,
Yet the unshaped use° of it doth move
The hearers to collection;° they yawn° at it,
10   And botch° the words up fit to their own thoughts,
Which, as her winks and nods and gestures yield° them,
Indeed would make one think there might be thought,°

---

50 *Makes mouths:* Makes scornful faces. 58 *Excitements of:* Promptings by. 61 *fantasy:* Fanciful
caprice; *trick:* Trifle. 62 *plot:* I.e., of ground. 63 *Whereon . . . cause:* On which there is insufficient
room for the soldiers needed to engage in a military contest. 66 *continent:* Receptacle, container.
ACT IV, SCENE V. *Location:* The castle. 5 *tricks:* Deceptions; *heart:* Breast. 6 *Spurns . . . straws:*
Kicks spitefully, takes offense at trifles; *in doubt:* Obscurely. 8 *unshaped use:* Distracted manner.
9 *collection:* Inference, a guess at some sort of meaning; *yawn:* Wonder, gasp. 10 *botch:* Patch. 11
yield: Delivery, bring forth (her words). 12 *thought:* Conjectured.

Though nothing sure, yet much unhappily.
HORATIO: 'Twere good she were spoken with, for she may strew
    Dangerous conjectures in ill-breeding° minds.   15
QUEEN: Let her come in.   *(Exit* GENTLEMEN.*)*
    (Aside.) To my sick soul, as sin's true nature is,
    Each toy° seems prologue to some great amiss.°
    So full of artless jealousy is guilt,
    It spills itself in fearing to be spilt.°   20

(Enter OPHELIA *distracted.)*

OPHELIA: Where is the beauteous majesty of Denmark?
QUEEN: How now, Ophelia?
OPHELIA *(she sings)*: "How should I your true love know
      From another one?
    By his cockle hat° and staff,   25
      And his sandal shoon."°
QUEEN: Alas, sweet lady, what imports this song?
OPHELIA: Say you? Nay, pray you, mark.
    "He is dead and gone, lady,   *(Song.)*
      He is dead and gone;   30
    At his head a grass-green turf,
      At his heels a stone."
    O, ho!
QUEEN: Nay, but Ophelia—
OPHELIA: Pray you mark.   35
    (Sings.) "What his shroud as the mountain snow"—

(Enter KING.*)*

QUEEN: Alas, look here, my lord.
OPHELIA: "Larded° all with flowers   *(Song.)*
    Which bewept to the ground did not go
      With true-love showers."   40
KING: How do you, pretty lady?
OPHELIA: Well, God 'ild° you! They say the owl° was a baker's daughter. Lord,
    we know what we are, but know not what we may be. God be at your
    table!

---

15 *ill-breeding:* Prone to suspect the worst. 18 *toy:* Trifle; *amiss:* Calamity. 19–20 *So . . . spilt:*
Guilt is so full of suspicion that it unskillfully betrays itself in fearing betrayal. 25 *cockle hat:* Hat
with cockleshell stuck in it as a sign that the wearer had been a pilgrim to the shrine of St. James
of Compostella in Spain. 26 *shoon:* Shoes. 38 *Larded:* Decorated. 42 *God 'ild:* God yield or reward; *owl:* Refers to a legend about a baker's daughter who was turned into an owl for refusing
Jesus bread.

45   KING: Conceit° upon her father.
       OPHELIA: Pray let's have no words of this; but when they ask you what it
              means, say you this:
              "Tomorrow is Saint Valentine's° day.   (*Song.*)
                   All in the morning betime,
50   And I a maid at your window,
                   To be your Valentine.
              Then up he rose, and donn'd his clo'es,
                   And dupp'd° the chamber-door,
              Let in the maid, that out a maid
55   Never departed more."
       KING: Pretty Ophelia!
       OPHELIA: Indeed, la, without an oath, I'll make an end on 't:
              (Sings.) "By Gis° and by Saint Charity,
                   Alack, and fie for shame!
60   Young men will do 't, if they come to 't;
                   By Cock,° they are to blame.
              Quoth she, 'Before you tumbled me,
                   You promised me to wed.' "
              He answers:
65   " 'So would I ha' done, by yonder sun,
                   And thou hadst not come to my bed.' "
       KING: How long hath she been thus?
       OPHELIA: I hope all will be well. We must be patient, but I cannot choose but
              weep, to think they would lay him i' th' cold ground. My brother shall know
70   of it; and so I thank you for your good counsel. Come, my coach! Good
              night, ladies; good night, sweet ladies; good night, good night.   *(Exit.)*
       KING: Follow her close; give her good watch, I pray you.   *(Exit* HORATIO.*)*
              O, this is the poison of deep grief; it springs
              All from her father's death—and now behold!
75   O Gertrude, Gertrude,
              When sorrows come, they come not single spies,°
              But in battalions. First, her father slain;
              Next, your son gone, and he most violent author
              Of his own just remove; the people muddied,°
80   Thick and unwholesome in their thoughts and whispers,
              For good Polonius' death; and we have done but greenly,°

---

45 *Conceit:* Brooding. 48 *Valentine's:* This song alludes to the belief that the first girl seen by a
man on the morning of this day was his valentine or true love. 53 *dupp'd:* Opened. 58 *Gis:*
Jesus. 61 *Cock:* A perversion of "God" in oaths. 76 *spies:* Scouts sent in advance of the main
force. 79 *muddied:* Stirred up, confused. 81 *greenly:* Imprudently, foolishly.

In hugger-mugger° to inter him; poor Ophelia
Divided from herself and her fair judgment,
Without the which we are pictures, or mere beasts;
Last, and as much containing as all these,   *85*
Her brother is in secret come from France,
Feeds on his wonder, keeps himself in clouds,°
And wants° not buzzers° to infect his ear
With pestilent speeches of his father's death,
Wherein necessity, of matter beggar'd,°   *90*
Will nothing stick our person to arraign
In ear and ear.° O my dear Gertrude, this,
Like to a murd'ring-piece,° in many places
Gives me superfluous death.   *(A noise within.)*
QUEEN: Alack, what noise is this?   *95*
KING: Attend!
    Where are my Switzers?° Let them guard the door.

(Enter a MESSENGER.*)*

    What is the matter?
MESSENGER: Save yourself, my lord!
    The ocean, overpeering of his list,°
    Eats not the flats° with more impiteous° haste   *100*
    Than young Laertes, in a riotous head,°
    O'erbears your officers. The rabble call him lord,
    And, as° the world were now but to begin,
    Antiquity forgot, custom not known,
    The ratifiers and props° of every word,°   *105*
    They cry, "Choose we! Laertes shall be king!"
    Caps, hands, and tongues applaud it to the clouds,
    "Laertes shall be king, Laertes king!"   *(A noise within.)*
QUEEN: How cheerfully on the false trail they cry!
    O, this is counter,° you false Danish dogs!   *110*

(Enter LAERTES *with others.)*

82 *hugger-mugger:* Secret haste. 87 *in clouds:* I.e., of suspicion and rumor. 88 *wants:* Lacks; *buzzers:* Gossipers, informers. 90 *of matter beggar'd:* Unprovided with facts. 91–92 *Will . . . and ear:* Will not hesitate to accuse my (royal) person in everybody's ears. 93 *murd'ring-piece:* Cannon loaded so as to scatter its shot. 97 *Switzers:* Swiss guards, mercenaries. 99 *overpeering of his list:* Overflowing its shore. 100 *flats:* Flatlands near shore; *impiteous:* Pitiless. 101 *head:* Armed force. 103 *as:* As if. 105 *ratifiers and props:* Refer to *antiquity* and *custom; word:* Promise. 110 *counter:* A hunting term meaning to follow the trail in a direction opposite to that which the game has taken.

KING: The doors are broke.

LAERTES: Where is this King? Sirs, stand you all without.

ALL: No, let's come in.

LAERTES: I pray you, give me leave.

ALL: We will, we will.   *(They retire without the door.)*

115 LAERTES: I thank you. Keep the door. O thou vile king,
          Give me my father!

QUEEN: Calmly, good Laertes.   *(She tries to hold him back.)*

LAERTES: That drop of blood that's calm proclaims me bastard,
          Cries cuckold to my father, brands the harlot
          Even here, between the chaste unsmirched brow
          Of my true mother.

120 KING: What is the cause, Laertes,
          That thy rebellion looks so giant-like?
          Let him go, Gertrude. Do not fear our° person.
          There's such divinity doth hedge a king
          That treason can but peep to what it would,°

125   Acts little of his will.° Tell me, Laertes,
          Why thou art thus incens'd. Let him go, Gertrude.
          Speak, man.

LAERTES: Where is my father?

KING: Dead.

QUEEN: But not by him.

KING: Let him demand his fill.

130 LAERTES: How came he dead? I'll not be juggled with.
          To hell, allegiance! Vows, to the blackest devil!
          Conscience and grace, to the profoundest pit!
          I dare damnation. To this point I stand,
          That both the worlds I give to negligence,°

135   Let come what comes, only I'll be reveng'd
          Most throughly° for my father.

KING: Who shall stay you?

LAERTES: My will, not all the world's.°
          And for my means, I'll husband them so well,
          They shall go far with little.

KING: Good Laertes,

140   If you desire to know the certainty

---

122 *fear our:* Fear for my.   124 *can . . . would:* Can only glance; as from far off or through a barrier, at what it would intend.   125 *Acts . . . will:* (But) performs little of what it intends.   134 *both . . . negligence:* Both this world and the next are of no consequence to me.   136 *throughly:* Thoroughly. 137 *My will . . . world's:* I'll stop *(stay)* when my will is accomplished, not for anyone else's.

Of your dear father, is 't writ in your revenge
That, swoopstake,° you will draw both friend and foe,
Winner and loser?
LAERTES: None but his enemies.
KING: Will you know them then?
LAERTES: To his good friends thus wide I'll ope my arms,   145
And, like the kind life-rend'ring pelican,°
Repast° them with my blood.
KING: Why, now you speak
Like a good child and a true gentleman.
That I am guiltless of your father's death,
And am most sensibly° in grief for it,   150
It shall as level° to your judgment 'pear
As day does to your eye.
                    (A noise within:) "Let her come in."
LAERTES: How now? What noise is that?

(Enter OPHELIA.)

O heat, dry up my brains! Tears seven times salt
Burn out the sense and virtue° of mine eye!   155
By heaven, thy madness shall be paid with weight°
Till our scale turn the beam.° O rose of May!
Dear maid, kind sister, sweet Ophelia!
O heavens, is 't possible a young maid's wits
Should be as mortal as an old man's life?   160
Nature is fine in° love, and where 'tis fine,
It sends some precious instance° of itself
After the thing it loves.°
OPHELIA: "They bore him barefac'd on the bier;   (Song.)
Hey non nonny, nonny, hey nonny,   165
And in his grave rain'd many a tear"—
Fare you well, my dove!
LAERTES: Hadst thou thy wits, and didst persuade° revenge,
It could not move thus.
OPHELIA: You must sing "A-down a-down,   170

142 *swoopstake:* Literally, taking all stakes on the gambling table at once, i.e., indiscriminately; "draw" is also a gambling term. 146 *pelican:* Refers to the belief that the female pelican fed its young with its own blood. 147 *Repast:* Feed. 150 *sensibly:* Feelingly. 151 *level:* Plain. 155 *virtue:* Faculty, power. 156 *paid with weight:* Repaid, avenged equally or more. 157 *beam:* Crossbar of a balance. 161 *fine in:* Refined by. 162 *instance:* Token. 163 *After . . . loves:* Into the grave, along with Polonius. 168 *persuade:* Argue cogently for.

And you call him a-down-a."
    O, how the wheel° becomes it! It is the false steward° that stole his mas-
    ter's daughter.
LAERTES: This nothing's more than matter.°
175 OPHELIA: There's rosemary,° that's for remembrance; pray you, love, remem-
    ber. And there is pansies,° that's for thoughts.
LAERTES: A document° in madness, thoughts and remembrance fitted.
OPHELIA: There's fennel° for you, and columbines.° There's rue° for you, and
    here's some for me; we may call it herb of grace o' Sundays. You may
180 wear your rue with a difference.° There's a daisy.° I would give you some
    violets,° but they wither'd all when my father died. They say 'a made a
    good end—
    (Sings.) "For bonny sweet Robin is all my joy."
LAERTES: Thought° and affliction, passion, hell itself,
185 She turns to favor° and to prettiness.
OPHELIA: "And will 'a not come again?   (Song.)
    And will 'a not come again?
        No, no, he is dead,
        Go to thy death-bed,
190 He never will come again.

    "His beard was as white as snow,
    All flaxen was his poll.°
        He is gone, he is gone,
        And we cast away moan.
195 God 'a' mercy on his soul!"
    And of all Christians' souls, I pray God. God buy you.   (Exit.)
LAERTES: Do you see this, O God?
KING: Laertes, I must commune with your grief,
    Or you deny me right. Go but apart,
200 Make choice of whom your wisest friends you will,
    And they shall hear and judge 'twixt you and me.
    If by direct or by collateral° hand

---

172 *wheel:* Spinning wheel as accompaniment to the song, or refrain; *false steward:* The story is
unknown. 174 *This . . . matter:* This seeming nonsense is more meaningful than sane utterance.
175 *rosemary:* Used as a symbol of remembrance both at weddings and at funerals. 176 *pansies:*
Emblems of love and courtship; perhaps from French "pensées," thoughts. 177 *document:* Instruction, lesson. 178 *fennel:* Emblem of flattery; *columbines:* Emblems of unchastity (?) or ingratitude
(?); *rue:* Emblem of repentance; when mingled with holy water, it was known as "herb of grace."
180 *with a difference:* Suggests that Ophelia and the Queen have different causes of sorrow and repentance; perhaps with a play on "rue" in the sense of ruth, pity; *daisy:* Emblem of dissembling,
faithlessness. 181 *violets:* Emblems of faithfulness. 184 *Thought:* Melancholy. 185 *favor:* Grace.
192 *poll:* Head. 202 *collateral:* Indirect.

They find us touch'd,° we will our kingdom give,
Our crown, our life, and all that we call ours,
To you in satisfaction; but if not,   205
Be you content to lend your patience to us,
And we shall jointly labor with your soul
To give it due content.
LAERTES: Let this be so.
His means of death, his obscure funeral—
No trophy,° sword, nor hatchment° o'er his bones,   210
No noble rite nor formal ostentation°—
Cry to be heard, as 'twere from heaven to earth,
That I must call 't in question.
KING: So you shall;
And where th' offense is, let the great ax fall.
I pray you go with me.   *(Exeunt.)*   215

SCENE VI°

(Enter HORATIO *and others.)*

HORATIO: What are they that would speak with me?
GENTLEMAN: Seafaring men, sir. They say they have letters for you.
HORATIO: Let them come in.   *(Exit* GENTLEMAN.*)*
I do not know from what part of the world
I should be greeted, if not from lord Hamlet.   5

(Enter SAILORS.*)*

FIRST SAILOR: God bless you sir.
HORATIO: Let him bless thee too.
FIRST SAILOR: 'A shall, sir, an 't please him. There's a letter for you, sir— it
    came from th' ambassador that was bound for England—if your name be
    Horatio, as I am let to know it is.   *(Gives letter.)*   10
HORATIO *(reads)*: "Horatio, when thou shalt have overlook'd this, give these
    fellows some means° to the King; they have letters for him. Ere we were
    two days old at sea, a pirate of very warlike appointment° gave us chase.
    Finding ourselves too slow of sail, we put on a compell'd valor, and in
    the grapple I boarded them. On the instant they got clear of our ship, so   15
    I alone became their prisoner. They have dealt with me like thieves of
    mercy,° but they knew what they did: I am to do a good turn for them.

---

203 *us touch'd:* Me implicated. 210 *trophy:* Memorial; *hatchment:* Tablet displaying the armorial
bearings of a deceased person. 211 *ostentation:* Ceremony. ACT IV, SCENE VI. *Location:* The
castle. 12 *means:* Means of access. 13 *appointment:* Equipage. 16–17 *thieves of mercy:* Merciful
thieves.

Let the King have the letters I have sent, and repair thou to me with as
much speed as thou wouldest fly death. I have words to speak in thine
20   ear will make thee dumb; yet are they much too light for the bore° of
the matter. These good fellows will bring thee where I am. Rosencrantz
and Guildenstern hold their course for England. Of them I have much
to tell thee. Farewell.

                                        He that thou knowest thine, Hamlet."

25   Come, I will give you way for these your letters,
And do 't the speedier that you may direct me
To him from whom you brought them.   *(Exeunt.)*

SCENE VII°

(Enter KING *and* LAERTES.*)*

KING: Now must your conscience my acquittance seal,°
        And you must put me in your heart for friend,
        Sith you have heard, and with a knowing ear,
        That he which hath your noble father slain
        Pursued my life.
5   LAERTES: It well appears. But tell me
        Why you proceeded not against these feats°
        So criminal and so capital° in nature,
        As by your safety, greatness, wisdom, all things else,
        You mainly° were stirr'd up.
    KING: O, for two special reasons,
10   Which may to you, perhaps, seem much unsinew'd,°
        But yet to me th' are strong. The Queen his mother
        Lives almost by his looks, and for myself—
        My virtue or my plague, be it either which—
        She's so conjunctive° to my life and soul
15   That, as the star moves not but in his sphere,°
        I could not but by her. The other motive,
        Why to a public count° I might not go,
        Is the great love the general gender° bear him,
        Who, dipping all his faults in their affection,
20   Would, like the spring° that turneth wood to stone,

---

20 *bore:* Caliber, i.e., importance. ACT IV, SCENE VII. *Location:* The castle. 1 *my acquittance seal:*
Confirm or acknowledge my innocence. 6 *feats:* Acts. 7 *capital:* Punishable by death. 9 *mainly:*
Greatly. 10 *unsinew'd:* Weak. 14 *conjunctive:* Closely united. 15 *sphere:* The hollow sphere in
which, according to Ptolemaic astronomy, the planets moved. 17 *count:* Account, reckoning. 18
general gender: Common people. 20 *spring:* A spring with such a concentration of lime that it
coats a piece of wood with limestone, in effect gilding it.

Convert his gyves° to graces, so that my arrows,
Too slightly timber'd° for so loud° a wind,
Would have reverted to my bow again
And not where I had aim'd them.

LAERTES: And so have I a noble father lost,   *25*
A sister driven into desp'rate terms,°
Whose worth, if praises may go back° again,
Stood challenger on mount° of all the age
For her perfections. But my revenge will come.

KING: Break not your sleeps for that. You must not think   *30*
That we are made of stuff so flat and dull
That we can let our beard be shook with danger
And think it pastime. You shortly shall hear more.
I lov'd your father, and we love ourself;
And that, I hope, will teach you to imagine—   *35*

(Enter a MESSENGER *with letters.)*

How now? What news?
MESSENGER: Letters, my lord, from Hamlet:
These to your Majesty, this to the Queen.   *(Gives letters.)*
KING: From Hamlet? Who brought them?
MESSENGER: Sailors, my lord, they say; I saw them not.
They were given me by Claudio. He receiv'd them   *40*
Of him that brought them.
KING: Laertes, you shall hear them.
Leave us.   *(Exit* MESSENGER.*)*
(Reads.) "High and mighty, you shall know I am set naked° on your king-
dom. Tomorrow shall I beg leave to see your kingly eyes, when I shall,
first asking your pardon° thereunto, recount the occasion of my sudden   *45*
and more strange return.   Hamlet." What should this mean? Are all the
rest come back? Or is it some abuse,° and no such thing?
LAERTES: Know you the hand?
KING: 'Tis Hamlet's character.° "Naked!"
And in a postscript here, he says "alone."
Can you devise° me?   *50*
LAERTES: I am lost in it, my lord. But let me come.
It warms the very sickness in my heart
That I shall live and tell him to his teeth,

21 *gyves:* Fetters (which, gilded by the people's praise, would look like badges of honor). 22
slightly timber'd: Light; *loud:* Strong. 26 *terms:* State, condition. 27 *go back:* Recall Ophelia's former virtues. 28 *on mount:* On high. 42 *naked:* Destitute, unarmed, without following. 45 *pardon:* Permission. 47 *abuse:* Deceit. 48 *character:* Handwriting. 50 *devise:* Explain to.

   "Thus didst thou."
 KING: If it be so, Laertes—
55   As how should it be so? How otherwise?°—
   Will you be ruled by me?
 LAERTES: Ay, my lord,
   So° you will not o'errule me to a peace.
 KING: To thine own peace. If he be now returned,
   As checking at° his voyage, and that he means
60   No more to undertake it, I will work him
   To an exploit, now ripe in my device,
   Under the which he shall not choose but fall;
   And for his death no wind of blame shall breathe,
   But even his mother shall uncharge the practice°
   And call it accident.
65 LAERTES: My lord, I will be rul'd,
   The rather if you could devise it so
   That I might be the organ.°
 KING: It falls right.
   You have been talk'd of since your travel much,
   And that in Hamlet's hearing, for a quality
70   Wherein, they say, you shine. Your sum of parts°
   Did not together pluck such envy from him
   As did that one, and that, in my regard,
   Of the unworthiest siege.°
 LAERTES: What part is that, my lord?
 KING: A very riband in the cap of youth,
75   Yet needful too, for youth no less becomes
   The light and careless livery that it wears
   Than settled age his sables° and his weeds,°
   Importing health° and graveness. Two months since
   Here was a gentleman of Normandy.
80   I have seen myself, and serv'd against, the French,
   And they can well° on horseback, but this gallant
   Had witchcraft in 't; he grew unto his seat,
   And to such wondrous doing brought his horse

---

55 *As . . . otherwise:* How can this (Hamlet's return) be true? Yet how otherwise than true (since we have the evidence of his letter). 57 *So:* Provided that. 59 *checking at:* Turning aside from (like a falcon leaving the quarry to fly at a chance bird). 64 *uncharge the practice:* Acquit the stratagem of being a plot. 67 *organ:* Agent, instrument. 70 *Your . . . parts:* All your other virtues. 73 *unworthiest siege:* Least important rank. 77 *sables:* Rich robes furred with sable; *weeds:* Garments. 78 *Importing health:* Indicating prosperity. 81 *can well:* Are skilled.

As had he been incorps'd and demi-natured°
With the brave beast. So far he topp'd° my thought   *85*
That I, in forgery° of shapes and tricks,
Come short of what he did.

LAERTES: A Norman was 't?

KING: A Norman.

LAERTES: Upon my life, Lamord.

KING: The very same.

LAERTES: I know him well. He is the brooch° indeed   *90*
And gem of all the nation.

KING: He made confession° of you,
And gave you such a masterly report
For art and exercise in your defense,
And for your rapier most especial,   *95*
That he cried out, 'twould be a sight indeed,
If one could match you. The scrimers° of their nation,
He swore, had neither motion, guard, nor eye,
If you oppos'd them. Sir, this report of his
Did Hamlet so envenom with his envy   *100*
That he could nothing do but wish and beg
Your sudden coming o'er to play° with you.
Now, out of this—

LAERTES: What out of this, my lord?

KING: Laertes, was your father dear to you?
Or are you like the painting of a sorrow,   *105*
A face without a heart?

LAERTES: Why ask you this?

KING: Not that I think you did not love your father,
But that I know love is begun by time,°
And that I see, in passages of proof,°
Time qualifies° the spark and fire of it.   *110*
There lives within the very flame of love
A kind of wick or snuff° that will abate it,
And nothing is at a like goodness still,°
For goodness, growing to a plurisy,°
Dies in his own too much.° That° we would do,   *115*

84 *incorps'd and demi-natured:* Of one body and nearly of one nature (like the centaur). 85 *topp'd:* Surpassed. 86 *forgery:* Invention. 90 *brooch:* Ornament. 92 *confession:* Admission of superiority. 97 *scrimers:* Fences. 102 *play:* Fence. 108 *begun by time:* Subject to change. 109 *passages of proof:* Actual instances. 110 *qualifies:* Weakens. 112 *snuff:* The charred part of a candlewick. 113 *nothing . . . still:* Nothing remains at a constant level of perfection. 114 *plurisy:* Excess, plethora. 115 *in . . . much:* Of its own excess; *That:* That which.

We should do when we would; for this "would" changes
And hath abatements° and delays as many
As there are tongues, are hands, are accidents,°
And then this "should" is like a spendthrift's sigh,°
120   That hurts by easing.° But, to the quick o' th' ulcer;
Hamlet comes back. What would you undertake
To show yourself your father's son in deed
More than in words?

LAERTES: To cut his throat i' th' church!

KING: No place, indeed, should murder sanctuarize;°
125   Revenge should have no bounds. But, good Laertes,
Will you do this,° keep close within your chamber.
Hamlet return'd shall know you are come home.
We'll put on those° shall praise your excellence
And set a double varnish on the fame
130   The Frenchman gave you, bring you in fine° together,
And wager on your heads. He, being remiss,°
Most generous,° and free from all contriving,
Will not peruse the foils, so that, with ease,
Or with a little shuffling, you may choose
135   A sword unbated,° and in a pass of practice°
Requite him for your father.

LAERTES: I will do 't.
And for that purpose I'll anoint my sword.
I bought an unction° of a mountebank°
So mortal that, but dip a knife in it,
140   Where it draws blood no cataplasm° so rare,
Collected from all simples° that have virtue
Under the moon, can save the thing from death
That is but scratch'd withal. I'll touch my point
With this contagion, that, if I gall° him slightly,
It may be death.

145 KING: Let's further think of this,
Weigh what convenience both of time and means

---

117 *abatements:* Diminutions. 118 *accidents:* Occurrences, incidents. 119 *spendthrift's sigh:* An allusion to the belief that each sigh costs the heart a drop of blood. 120 *hurts by easing:* Costs the heart blood even while it affords emotional relief. 124 *sanctuarize:* Protect from punishment (alludes to the right of sanctuary with which certain religious places were invested). 126 *Will you do this:* If you wish to do this. 128 *put on those:* Instigate those who. 130 *in fine:* Finally. 131 *remiss:* Negligently unsuspicious. 132 *generous:* Noble-minded. 135 *unbated:* Not blunted, having no button; *pass of practice:* Treacherous thrust. 138 *unction:* Ointment; *mountebank:* Quack doctor. 140 *cataplasm:* Plaster or poultice. 141 *simples:* Herbs. 144 *gall:* Graze, wound.

May fit us to our shape.° If this should fail,
And that our drift look through our bad performance,°
'Twere better not assay'd. Therefore this project
Should have a back or second, that might hold   150
If this did blast in proof.° Soft, let me see.
We'll make a solemn wager on your cunnings—
I ha 't!
When in your motion you are hot and dry—
As° make your bouts more violent to that end—   155
And that he calls for drink, I'll have prepar'd him
A chalice for the nonce,° whereon but sipping,
If he by chance escape your venom'd stuck,°
Our purpose may hold there. *(A cry within.)* But stay, what noise?

(Enter QUEEN.*)*

QUEEN: One woe doth tread upon another's heel,   160
        So fast they follow. Your sister's drowned, Laertes.
LAERTES: Drown'd! O, where?
QUEEN: There is a willow grows askant° the brook,
        That shows his hoar° leaves in the glassy stream;
        Therewith fantastic garlands did she make   165
        Of crow-flowers, nettles, daisies, and long purples°
        That liberal° shepherds give a grosser name,
        But our cold° maids do dead men's fingers call them.
        There on the pendent boughs her crownet° weeds
        Clamb'ring to hang, an envious sliver° broke,   170
        When down her weedy° trophies and herself
        Fell in the weeping brook. Her clothes spread wide,
        And mermaid-like awhile they bore her up,
        Which time she chanted snatches of old lauds,°
        As one incapable° of her own distress,   175
        Or like a creature native and indued°
        Unto that element. But long it could not be
        Till that her garments, heavy with their drink,

147 *shape:* Part that we propose to act. 148 *drift . . . performance:* I.e., intention be disclosed by
our bungling. 151 *blast in proof:* Burst in the test (like a cannon). 155 *As:* And you should. 157
nonce: Occasion. 158 *stuck:* Thrust (from "stoccado," a fencing term). 163 *askant:* Aslant. 164
hoar: White or gray. 166 *long purples:* Early purple orchids. 167 *liberal:* Free-spoken. 168 *cold:*
Chaste. 169 *crownet:* Made into a chaplet or coronet. 170 *envious sliver:* Malicious branch. 171
weedy: I.e., of plants. 174 *lauds:* Hymns. 175 *incapable:* Lacking capacity to apprehend. 176 *in-
dued:* Adapted by nature.

Pull'd the poor wretch from her melodious lay
To muddy death.

180   LAERTES: Alas, then she is drown'd?

QUEEN: Drown'd, drown'd.

LAERTES: Too much of water hast thou, poor Ophelia,
And therefore I forbid my tears. But yet
It is our trick;° nature her custom holds,

185   Let shame say what it will. *(He weeps.)* When these are gone,
The woman will be out.° Adieu, my lord.
I have a speech of fire, that fain would blaze,
But that this folly drowns it.   *(Exit.)*

KING: Let's follow, Gertrude.
How much I had to do to calm his rage!

190   Now fear I this will give it start again;
Therefore let's follow.   *(Exeunt.)*

ACT V
SCENE I°

(Enter two CLOWNS° *with spades, etc.)*

FIRST CLOWN: Is she to be buried in Christian burial when she willfully
seeks her own salvation?

SECOND CLOWN: I tell thee she is; therefore make her grave straight.° The
crowner° hath sat on her, and finds it Christian burial.

5   FIRST CLOWN: How can that be, unless she drown'd herself in her own
defense?

SECOND CLOWN: Why, 'tis found so.

FIRST CLOWN: It must be "se offendendo";° it cannot be else. For here lies
the point: if I drown myself wittingly, it argues an act, and an act hath

10   three branches—it is to act, to do, and to perform. Argal,° she drown'd
herself wittingly.

SECOND CLOWN: Nay, but hear you, goodman delver—

FIRST CLOWN: Give me leave. Here lies the water; good. Here stands the
man; good. If the man go to this water, and drown himself, it is, will he,

15   nill he°, he goes, mark you that. But if the water come to him and drown
him, he drowns not himself. Argal, he that is not guilty of his own death
shortens not his own life.

---

184 *It is our trick:* Weeping is our natural way (when sad). 185–86 *When . . . out:* When my tears
are all shed, the woman in me will be expended, satisfied. ACT V, SCENE I. *Location:* A churchyard. s.d. *Clowns:* Rustics. 3 *straight:* Straightway, immediately. 4 *crowner:* Coroner. 8 *se offendendo:* A comic mistake for "*se defendendo,*" term used in verdicts of justifiable homicide. 10
Argal: Corruption of "ergo," therefore. 14–15 *will . . . he:* Like it or not.

SECOND CLOWN: But is this law?

FIRST CLOWN: Ay, marry, is 't—crowner's quest° law.

SECOND CLOWN: Will you ha' the truth on 't? If this had not been a gentle-   *20*
woman, she should have been buried out o' Christian burial.

FIRST CLOWN: Why, there thou say'st.° And the more pity that great folk
should have count'nance° in this world to drown or hang themselves,
more than their even-Christen.° Come, my spade. There is no ancient
gentlemen but gard'ners, ditchers, and grave-makers. They hold up   *25*
Adam's profession.

SECOND CLOWN: Was he a gentleman?

FIRST CLOWN: 'A was the first that ever bore arms.

SECOND CLOWN: Why, he had none.

FIRST CLOWN: What, art a heathen? How dost thou understand the Scrip-   *30*
ture? The Scripture says "Adam digg'd." Could he dig without arms? I'll
put another question to thee. If thou answerest me not to the purpose,
confess thyself°—

SECOND CLOWN: Go to.

FIRST CLOWN: What is he that builds stronger than either the mason, the   *35*
shipwright, or the carpenter?

SECOND CLOWN: The gallows-maker, for that frame outlives a thousand
tenants.

FIRST CLOWN: I like thy wit well, in good faith. The gallows does well; but
how does it well? It does well to those that do ill. Now thou dost ill to   *40*
say the gallows is built stronger than the church. Argal, the gallows may
do well to thee. To 't again, come.

SECOND CLOWN: "Who builds stronger than a mason, a shipwright, or a
carpenter?"

FIRST CLOWN: Ay, tell me that, and unyoke.°   *45*

SECOND CLOWN: Marry, now I can tell.

FIRST CLOWN: To 't.

SECOND CLOWN: Mass,° I cannot tell.

(Enter HAMLET and HORATIO at a distance.)

FIRST CLOWN: Cudgel thy brains no more about it, for your dull ass will not
mend his pace with beating; and, when you are ask'd this question next,   *50*
say "a grave-maker." The houses he makes lasts till doomsday. Go, get
thee in, and fetch me a stoup° of liquor.

(Exit SECOND CLOWN. FIRST CLOWN digs.)

---

19 *quest:* Inquest. 22 *there thou say'st:* That's right. 23 *count'nance:* Privilege. 24 *even-Christen:*
Fellow Christian. 33 *confess thyself:* The saying continues, "and be hanged." 45 *unyoke:* After this
great effort you may unharness the team of your wits. 48 *Mass:* By the Mass. 52 *stoup:* Two-
quart measure.

        "In youth, when I did love, did love,°   *(Song.)*
        Methought it was very sweet,
55   To contract—O—the time for—a—my behove,°
        O, methought there—a—was nothing—a—meet."°

HAMLET: Has this fellow no feeling of his business, that 'a sings at grave-making?

HORATIO: Custom hath made it in him a property of easiness.°

HAMLET: 'Tis e'en so. The hand of little employment hath the daintier sense.°

60 FIRST CLOWN: "But age, with his stealing steps,   *(Song.)*
        Hath claw'd me in his clutch,
        And hath shipped me into the land,°
        As if I had never been such."   *(Throws up a skull.)*

HAMLET: That skull had a tongue in it, and could sing once. How the knave
65   jowls° it to the ground, as if 'twere Cain's jaw-bone, that did the first
      murder! This might be the pate of a politician,° which this ass now o'er-
      reaches,° one that would circumvent God, might it not?

HORATIO: It might, my lord.

HAMLET: Or of a courtier, which could say "Good morrow, sweet lord! How
70   dost thou, sweet lord?" This might be my Lord Such-a-one, that prais'd
      my Lord Such-a-one's horse when 'a meant to beg it, might it not?

HORATIO: Ay, my lord.

HAMLET: Why, e'en so, and now my Lady Worm's, chapless,° and knock'd
      about the mazzard° with a sexton's spade. Here's fine revolution,° an°
75   we had the trick to see 't. Did these bones cost no more the breeding,°
      but to play at loggats° with them? Mine ache to think on 't.

FIRST CLOWN: "A pick-axe, and a spade, a spade,   *(Song.)*
        For and° a shrouding sheet;
        O, a pit of clay for to be made
80   For such a guest is meet."   *(Throws up another skull.)*

HAMLET: There's another. Why may not that be the skull of a lawyer? Where
      be his quiddities° now, his quillities,° his cases, his tenures,° and his
      tricks? Why does he suffer this mad knave now to knock him about the

---

53 *In . . . love:* This and the two following stanzas, with nonsensical variations, are from a poem attributed to Lord Vaux and printed in *Tottel's Miscellany* (1557). The O and *a* (for "ah") seemingly are the grunts of the digger. 55 *To contract . . . behove:* To make a betrothal agreement for my benefit (?). 56 *meet:* Suitable, i.e., more suitable. 58 *property of easiness:* Something he can do easily and without thinking. 59 *daintier sense:* More delicate sense of feeling. 62 *into the land:* Toward my grave (?) (but note the lack of rhyme in *steps, land*). 65 *jowls:* Dashes. 66 *politician:* Schemer, plotter. 66–67 *o'erreaches:* Circumvents, gets the better of (with a quibble on the literal sense). 73 *chapless:* Having no lower jaw. 74 *mazzard:* Head (literally, a drinking vessel); *revolution:* Change; *an:* If. 75 *the breeding:* In the breeding, raising. 76 *loggats:* A game in which pieces of hardwood are thrown to lie as near as possible to a stake. 78 *For and:* And moreover. 82 *quiddities:* Subtleties, quibbles (from Latin "quid," a thing); *quillities:* Verbal niceties, subtle distinctions (variation of "quiddities"); *tenures:* The holding of a piece of property or office, or the conditions or period of such holding.

sconce° with a dirty shovel, and will not tell him of his action of battery? Hum! This fellow might be in 's time a great buyer of land, with   *85*
his statutes, his recognizances,° his fines, his double° vouchers,° his recoveries.° Is this the fine of his fines, and the recovery of his recoveries,
to have his fine pate full of fine dirt?° Will his vouchers vouch him no
more of his purchases, and double ones too, than the length and breadth
of a pair of indentures?° The very conveyances° of his lands will scarcely   *90*
lie in this box,° and must th' inheritor° himself have no more, ha?

HORATIO: Not a jot more, my lord.

HAMLET: Is not parchment made of sheep-skins?

HORATIO: Ay, my lord, and of calf-skins too.

HAMLET: They are sheep and calves which seek out assurance in that.° I will   *95*
speak to this fellow.— Whose grave's this, sirrah?°

FIRST CLOWN: Mine, sir.
(Sings.) "O, a pit of clay for to be made
For such a guest is meet."

HAMLET: I think it be thine, indeed, for thou liest in 't.   *100*

FIRST CLOWN: You lie out on 't, sir, and therefore 'tis not yours. For my part,
I do not lie in 't, yet it is mine.

HAMLET: Thou dost lie in 't, to be in 't and say it is thine. 'Tis for the dead,
not for the quick;° therefore thou liest.

FIRST CLOWN: 'Tis a quick lie, sir; 'twill away again from me to you.   *105*

HAMLET: What man dost thou dig it for?

FIRST CLOWN: For no man, sir.

HAMLET: What woman, then?

FIRST CLOWN: For none, neither.

HAMLET: Who is to be buried in 't?   *110*

FIRST CLOWN: One that was a woman, sir, but, rest her soul, she's dead.

HAMLET: How absolute° the knave is! We must speak by the card°, or equiv-
ocation° will undo us. By the Lord, Horatio, this three years I have taken
note of it: the age is grown so pick'd° that the toe of the peasant comes

---

83 *sconce:* Head. 85–86 *statutes, recognizances:* Legal documents guaranteeing a debt by attaching
land and property. 86–87 *fines, recoveries:* Ways of converting entailed estates into "fee simple" or
freehold. 86 *double:* Signed by two signatories; *vouchers:* Guarantees of the legality of a title to
real estate. 87–88 *fine of his fines . . . fine pate . . . fine dirt:* End of his legal maneuvers . . . elegant
head . . . minutely sifted dirt. 89–90 *pair of indentures:* Legal document drawn up in duplicate on
a single sheet and then cut apart on a zigzag line so that each pair was uniquely matched. (Hamlet may refer to two rows of teeth, or dentures.) 90 *conveyances:* Deeds. 90–91 *this box:* The skull.
91 *inheritor:* Possessor, owner. 95 *assurance in that:* Safety in legal parchments. 96 *sirrah:* Term of
address to inferiors. 104 *quick:* Living. 112 *absolute:* Positive, decided; *by the card:* By the mariner's
card on which the points of the compass were marked, i.e., with precision. 112–13 *equivocation:*
Ambiguity in the use of terms 114 *pick'd:* Refined, fastidious

115   so near the heel of the courtier, he galls his kibe.° How long hast thou
     been a grave-maker?

FIRST CLOWN: Of all the days i' th' year, I came to 't that day that our last
     king Hamlet overcame Fortinbras.

HAMLET: How long is that since?

120 FIRST CLOWN: Cannot you tell that? Every fool can tell that. It was that very
     day that young Hamlet was born—he that is mad, and sent into England.

HAMLET: Ay, marry, why was he sent into England?

FIRST CLOWN: Why, because 'a was mad. 'A shall recover his wits there, or, if
     'a do not, 'tis no great matter there.

125 HAMLET: Why?

FIRST CLOWN: 'Twill not be seen in him there. There the men are as mad as he.

HAMLET: How came he mad?

FIRST CLOWN: Very strangely, they say.

HAMLET: How strangely?

130 FIRST CLOWN: Faith, e'en with losing his wits.

HAMLET: Upon what ground?

FIRST CLOWN: Why, here in Denmark. I have been sexton here, man and
     boy, thirty years.

HAMLET: How long will a man lie i' th' earth ere he rot?

135 FIRST CLOWN: Faith, if 'a be not rotten before 'a die—as we have many
     pocky° corses now-a-days, that will scarce hold the laying in—'a will
     last you some eight year or nine year. A tanner will last you nine year.

HAMLET: Why he more than another?

FIRST CLOWN: Why, sir, his hide is so tann'd with his trade that 'a will keep
140   out water a great while, and your water is a sore decayer of your whore-
     son dead body. *(Picks up a skull.)* Here's a skull now hath lain you° i' th'
     earth three and twenty years.

HAMLET: Whose was it?

FIRST CLOWN: A whoreson mad fellow's it was. Whose do you think it was?

145 HAMLET: Nay, I know not.

FIRST CLOWN: A pestilence on him for a mad rogue! 'A pour'd a flagon of
     Rhenish° on my head once. This same skull, sir, was Yorick's skull, the
     King's jester.

HAMLET: This?

150 FIRST CLOWN: E'en that.

HAMLET: Let me see. *(Takes the skull.)* Alas, poor Yorick! I knew him, Horatio,
     a fellow of infinite jest, of most excellent fancy. He hath borne me on
     his back a thousand times; and now, how abhorr'd in my imagination it
     is! My gorge rises at it. Here hung those lips that I have kiss'd I know

---

115 *galls his kibe:* Chafes the courtier's chilblain (a swelling or sore caused by cold). 136 *pocky:*
Rotten, diseased (literally, with the pox, or syphilis). 141 *lain you:* Lain. 147 *Rhenish:* Rhine
wine.

not how oft. Where be your gibes now? Your gambols, your songs, your   155
flashes of merriment that were wont to set the table on a roar? Not one
now, to mock your own grinning? Quite chap-fall'n?° Now get you to
my lady's chamber, and tell her, let her paint an inch thick, to this favor°
she must come; make her laugh at that. Prithee, Horatio, tell me one
thing.   160

HORATIO: What's that, my lord?

HAMLET: Dost thou think Alexander look'd o' this fashion i' th' earth?

HORATIO: E'en so.

HAMLET: And smelt so? Pah! *(Puts down the skull.)*

HORATIO: E'en so, my lord.   165

HAMLET: To what base uses we may return, Horatio! Why may not imagina-
    tion trace the noble dust of Alexander, till a' find it stopping a bunghole!

HORATIO: 'Twere to consider too curiously,° to consider so.

HAMLET: No, faith, not a jot, but to follow him thither with modesty°
    enough, and likelihood to lead it. As thus: Alexander died, Alexander was   170
    buried, Alexander returneth to dust; the dust is earth; of earth we make
    loam;° and why of that loam, whereto he was converted, might they not
    stop a beer-barrel?
    Imperious° Caesar, dead and turn'd to clay,
    Might stop a hole to keep the wind away.   175
    O, that that earth which kept the world in awe
    Should patch a wall t' expel the winter's flaw!°
    But soft, but soft awhile! Here comes the King.

(Enter KING, QUEEN, LAERTES, *and the Corse of* OPHELIA, *in procession,*
with PRIEST, LORDS *etc.)*

    The Queen, the courtiers. Who is this they follow?
    And with such maimed rites? This doth betoken   180
    The corse they follow did with desp'rate hand
    Fordo it° own life. 'Twas of some estate.°
    Couch° we awhile, and mark.

                                        (He and HORATIO *conceal themselves.*
                                    OPHELIA'*s body is taken to the grave.)*

LAERTES: What ceremony else?

HAMLET *(to* HORATIO*)*: That is Laertes, a very noble youth. Mark.   185

LAERTES: What ceremony else?

PRIEST: Her obsequies have been as far enlarg'd
    As we have warranty. Her death was doubtful,

---

157 *chap-fall'n:* (1) Lacking the lower jaw, (2) dejected. 158 *favor:* Aspect, appearance. 168 *curi-*
ously: Minutely. 169 *modesty:* Moderation. 172 *loam:* Clay mixture for brickmaking or other
clay use. 174 *Imperious:* Imperial. 177 *flaw:* Gust of wind. 182 *Fordo it:* Destroy its; *estate:* Rank.
183 *Couch:* Hide, lurk.

And, but that great command o'ersways the order,
190 She should in ground unsanctified been lodg'd
Till the last trumpet. For° charitable prayers,
Shards,° flints, and pebbles should be thrown on her.
Yet here she is allow'd her virgin crants,°
Her maiden strewments,° and the bringing home
195 Of bell and burial.°

LAERTES: Must there no more be done?

PRIEST: No more be done.
We should profane the service of the dead
To sing a requiem and such rest to her
As to peace-parted souls.

LAERTES: Lay her i' th' earth,
200 And from her fair and unpolluted flesh
May violets° spring! I tell thee, churlish priest,
A minist'ring angel should my sister be
When thou liest howling!

HAMLET *(to* HORATIO*)*:   What, the fair Ophelia!

QUEEN *(scattering flowers)*: Sweets to the sweet! Farewell.
205 I hoped thou shouldst have been my Hamlet's wife.
I thought thy bride-bed to have deck'd, sweet maid,
And not have strew'd thy grave.

LAERTES: O, treble woe
Fall ten times treble on that cursed head
Whose wicked deed thy most ingenious sense°
210 Depriv'd thee of! Hold off the earth awhile,
Till I have caught her once more in mine arms.

                    (Leaps into the grave and embraces OPHELIA.*)*
Now pile your dust upon the quick and dead,
Till of this flat a mountain you have made
T'o'ertop old Pelion,° or the skyish head
Of blue Olympus.°

215 HAMLET *(coming forward)*:   What is he whose grief
Bears such an emphasis, whose phrase of sorrow
Conjures the wand'ring stars,° and makes them stand
Like wonder-wounded hearers? This is I,
Hamlet the Dane.°

---

191 *For:* In place of. 192 *Shards:* Broken bits of pottery. 193 *crants:* Garland. 194 *strewments:* Traditional strewing of flowers. 194–95 *bringing . . . burial:* Laying to rest of the body in conse- crated ground, to the sound of the bell. 201 *violets:* see IV.v.181 and note. 209 *ingenious sense:* Mind endowed with finest qualities. 214–15 *Pelion, Olympus:* Mountains in the north of Thes- saly; see also *Ossa* at line 244. 217 *wand'ring stars:* Planets. 219 *the Dane:* This title normally sig- nifies the King; see I.I.15 and note.

LAERTES: The devil take thy soul!   *(Grappling with him.)*
HAMLET: Thou pray'st not well.   220
    I prithee, take thy fingers from my throat;
    For, though I am not splenitive° and rash,
    Yet have I in me something dangerous,
    Which let thy wisdom fear. Hold off thy hand.
KING: Pluck them asunder.
QUEEN: Hamlet, Hamlet!
ALL: Gentlemen!   225
HORATIO: Good my lord, be quiet.   (HAMLET *and* HORATIO *are parted.*)
HAMLET: Why, I will fight with him upon this theme
    Until my eyelids will no longer wag.
QUEEN: O my son, what theme?
HAMLET: I lov'd Ophelia. Forty thousand brothers   230
    Could not with all their quantity of love
    Make up my sum. What wilt thou do for her?
KING: O, he is mad, Laertes.
QUEEN: For love of God, forbear him.
HAMLET: 'Swounds,° show me what thou't do.   235
    Woo 't° weep? Woo 't fight? Woo 't fast? Woo 't tear thyself?
    Woo 't drink up eisel?° Eat a crocodile?
    I'll do 't. Dost thou come here to whine?
    To outface me with leaping in her grave?
    Be buried quick° with her, and so will I.   240
    And, if thou prate of mountains, let them throw
    Millions of acres on us, till our ground,
    Singeing his pate° against the burning zone,°
    Make Ossa° like a wart! Nay, an thou 'lt mouth,°
    I'll rant as well as thou.
QUEEN: This is mere° madness,   245
    And thus a while the fit will work on him;
    Anon, as patient as the female dove
    When that her golden couplets° are disclos'd,°
    His silence will sit drooping.
HAMLET: Hear you, sir.
    What is the reason that you use me thus?   250
    I lov'd you ever. But it is no matter.
    Let Hercules himself do what he may,

---

222 *splenitive:* Quick-tempered. 235 *'Swounds:* By His (Christ's) wounds. 236 *Woo 't:* Wilt thou.
237 *eisel:* Vinegar. 240 *quick:* Alive. 243 *his pate:* Its head, i.e., top; *burning zone:* Sun's orbit. 244
Ossa: Another mountain in Thessaly. (In their war against the Olympian gods, the giants attempted to heap Ossa, Pelion, and Olympus on one another to scale heaven.); *mouth:* Rant. 245
mere: Utter. 248 *golden couplets:* Two baby pigeons, covered with yellow down; *disclos'd:* Hatched.

The cat will mew, and dog will have his day.°
KING: I pray thee, good Horatio, wait upon him.

(*Exit* HAMLET *and* HORATIO.)

255   (To LAERTES.) Strengthen your patience in° our last night's speech;
We'll put the matter to the present push.°—
Good Gertrude, set some watch over your son.—
This grave shall have a living° monument.
An hour of quiet shortly shall we see;
260   Till then, in patience our proceeding be.   (*Exeunt.*)

SCENE II°

(*Enter* HAMLET *and* HORATIO.)

HAMLET: So much for this, sir; now shall you see the other.°
You do remember all the circumstance?
HORATIO: Remember it, my lord!
HAMLET: Sir, in my heart there was a kind of fighting
5   That would not let me sleep. Methought I lay
Worse than the mutines° in the bilboes.° Rashly,°
And prais'd be rashness for it—let us know,°
Our indiscretion sometime serves us well
When our deep plots do pall,° and that should learn° us
10   There's a divinity that shapes our ends,
Rough-hew° them how we will—
HORATIO: That is most certain.
HAMLET: Up from my cabin,
My sea-grown scarf'd about me, in the dark
Grop'd I to find out them, had my desire,
15   Finger'd° their packet, and in fine° withdrew
To mine own room again, making so bold,
My fears forgetting manners, to unseal
Their grand commission; where I found, Horatio—
Ah, royal knavery!—an exact command,
20   Larded° with many several sorts of reasons
Importing° Denmark's health and England's too,
With, ho, such bugs° and goblins in my life,°

252–53 *Let . . . day:* Despite any blustering attempts at interference, every person will sooner or later do what he must do. 255 *in:* By recalling. 256 *present push:* Immediate test. 258 *living:* Lasting; also refers (for Laertes' benefit) to the plot against Hamlet. ACT V, SCENE II. *Location:* The castle. 1 *see the other:* Hear the other news. 6 *mutines:* Mutineers; *bilboes:* Shackles; *Rashly:* On impulse (this adverb goes with line 12ff.). 7 *know:* Acknowledge. 9 *pall:* Fail; *learn:* Teach. 11 *Rough-hew:* Shape roughly. 15 *Finger'd:* Pilfered, pinched; *in fine:* Finally, in conclusion. 20 *Larded:* Enriched. 21 *Importing:* Relating to. 22 *bugs:* Bugbears, hobgoblins; *in my life:* To be feared if I were allowed to live.

That, on the supervise,° no leisure bated,°
No, not to stay the grinding of the axe,
My head should be struck off.

HORATIO: Is 't possible?   *25*

HAMLET: Here's the commission; read it at more leisure.   *(Gives document.)*
But wilt thou hear now how I did proceed?

HORATIO: I beseech you.

HAMLET: Being thus benetted round with villainies,
Or I could make a prologue to my brains,   *30*
They had begun the play.° I sat me down,
Devis'd a new commission, wrote it fair.°
I once did hold it, as our statists° do,
A baseness° to write fair, and labor'd much
How to forget that learning, but, sir, now   *35*
It did me yeoman's° service. Wilt thou know
Th' effect° of what I wrote?

HORATIO: Ay, good my lord.

HAMLET: An earnest conjuration from the King,
As England was his faithful tributary,
As love between them like the palm might flourish,   *40*
As peace should still her wheaten garland° wear
And stand a comma° 'tween their amities,
And many such-like as's° of great charge,°
That, on the view and knowing of these contents,
Without debatement further, more or less,   *45*
He should those bearers put to sudden death,
Not shriving time° allow'd.

HORATIO: How was this seal'd?

HAMLET: Why, even in that was heaven ordinant.°
I had my father's signet° in my purse,
Which was the model of that Danish seal;   *50*
Folded the writ up in the form of th' other,
Subscrib'd° it, gave 't th' impression,° plac'd it safely,
The changeling° never known. Now, the next day
Was our sea-fight, and what to this was sequent
Thou knowest already.   *55*

23 *supervise:* Reading; *leisure bated:* Delay allowed. 30–31 *Or . . . play:* Before I could consciously turn my brain to the matter, it had started working on a plan. (*Or* means ere.) 32 *fair:* In a clear hand. 33 *statists:* Statesmen. 34 *baseness:* Lower-class trait. 36 *yeoman's:* Substantial, workman-like. 37 *effect:* Purport. 41 *wheaten garland:* Symbolic of fruitful agriculture, of peace. 42 *comma:* Indicating continuity, link. 43 *as's:* (1) The "whereases" of formal document, (2) asses; *charge:* (1) Import, (2) burden. 47 *shriving time:* Time for confession and absolution. 48 *ordinant:* Directing. 49 *signet:* Small seal. 52 *Subscrib'd:* Signed; *impression:* With a wax seal. 53 *changeling:* The substituted letter (literally, a fairy child substituted for a human one).

HORATIO: So Guildenstern and Rosencrantz go to 't.

HAMLET: Why, man, they did make love to this employment.
They are not near my conscience. Their defeat
Does by their own insinuation° grow.

60   'Tis dangerous when the baser nature comes
Between the pass° and fell° incensed points
Of mighty opposites.

HORATIO: Why, what a king is this!

HAMLET: Does it not, think thee, stand° me now upon—
He that hath killed my king and whor'd my mother,

65   Popp'd in between th' election° and my hopes,
Thrown out his angle° for my proper° life,
And with such coz'nage°—is 't not perfect conscience
To quit° him with this arm? And is 't not to be damn'd
To let this canker° of our nature come

70   In further evil?

HORATIO: It must be shortly known to him from England
What is the issue of the business there.

HAMLET: It will be short. The interim is mine,
And a man's life 's no more than to say "One."°

75   But I am very sorry, good Horatio,
That to Laertes I forgot myself,
For by the image of my cause I see
The portraiture of his. I'll court his favors.
But, sure, the bravery° of his grief did put me
Into a tow'ring passion.

80 HORATIO: Peace, who comes here?

(Enter a COURTIER *[*OSRIC*].)*

OSRIC: Your lordship is right welcome back to Denmark.

HAMLET: I humbly thank you, sir. *(To* HORATIO.*)* Dost know this water-fly?

HORATIO: No, my good lord.

HAMLET: Thy state is the more gracious, for 'tis a vice to know him. He hath

85   much land, and fertile. Let a beast be lord of beasts, and his crib shall
stand at the King's mess.° 'Tis a chough,° but, as I say, spacious in the
possession of dirt.

---

59 *insinuation:* Interference. 61 *pass:* Thrust; *fell:* Fierce. 63 *stand:* Become incumbent. 65 *election:* The Danish monarch was "elected" by a small number of high-ranking electors. 66 *angle:* Fishing line; *proper:* Very. 67 *coz'nage:* Trickery. 68 *quit:* Repay. 69 *canker:* Ulcer. 74 *a man's . . . "One":* To take a man's life requires no more than to count to one as one duels. 79 *bravery:* Bravado. 85-86 *Let . . . mess:* If a man, no matter how beastlike, is as rich in possessions as Osric, he may eat at the King's table. 86 *chough:* Chattering jackdaw.

OSRIC: Sweet lord, if your lordship were at leisure, I should impart a thing to
  you from his Majesty.

HAMLET: I will receive it, sir, with all diligence of spirit. Put your bonnet to   *90*
  his right use; 'tis for the head.

OSRIC: I thank your lordship, it is very hot.

HAMLET: No, believe me, 'tis very cold; the wind is northerly.

OSRIC: It is indifferent° cold, my lord, indeed.

HAMLET: But yet methinks it is very sultry and hot for my complexion.°   *95*

OSRIC: Exceedingly, my lord; it is very sultry, as 'twere—I cannot tell how.
  My lord, his Majesty bade me signify to you that 'a has laid a great wager
  on your head. Sir, this is the matter—

HAMLET: I beseech you, remember—

  (HAMLET moves him to put on his hat.)

OSRIC: Nay, good my lord; for my ease,° in good faith. Sir, here is newly come   *100*
  to court Laertes—believe me, an absolute gentleman, full of most excellent differences,° of very soft society° and great showing.° Indeed, to
  speak feelingly° of him, he is the card° or calendar° of gentry,° for you
  shall find in him the continent of what part° a gentleman would see.

HAMLET: Sir, his definement° suffers no perdition° in you, though, I know, to   *105*
  divide him inventorially° would dozy° th' arithmetic of memory, and yet
  but yaw° neither° in respect of° his quick sail. But, in the verity of extolment,° I take him to be a soul of great article,° and his infusion° of such
  dearth and rareness,° as, to make true diction° of him, his semblable° is
  his mirror, and who else would trace° him, his umbrage,° nothing more.   *110*

OSRIC: Your lordship speaks most infallibly of him.

HAMLET: The concernancy,° sir? Why do we wrap the gentleman in our
  more rawer breath?°

OSRIC: Sir?

HORATIO: Is 't not possible to understand in another tongue?° You will do   *115*
  't,° sir, really.

---

94 *indifferent:* Somewhat. 95 *complexion:* Temperament. 100 *for my ease:* A conventional reply declining the invitation to put his hat back on. 102 *differences:* Special qualities; *soft society:* Agreeable manners; *great showing:* Distinguished appearance. 103 *feelingly:* With just perception; *card:*
Chart, map; *calendar:* Guide; *gentry:* Good breeding. 104 *the continent . . . part:* One who contains
in him all the qualities (a *continent* is that which contains). 105 *definement:* Definition. (Hamlet
proceeds to mock Osric by using his lofty diction back at him.); *perdition:* Loss, diminution. 106
divide him inventorially: Enumerate his graces; *dozy:* Dizzy. 107 *yaw:* To move unsteadily (said of a
ship); *neither:* For all that; *in respect of:* In comparison with. 107–108 *in . . . extolment:* In true
praise (of him). 108 *article:* Moment or importance; *infusion:* Essence, character imparted by nature. 109 *dearth and rareness:* Rarity; *make true diction:* Speak truly; *semblable:* Only true likeness.
110 *who . . . trace:* Any other person who would wish to follow; *umbrage:* Shadow. 112 *concernancy:* Import, relevance. 113 *breath:* Speech. 115 *to understand . . . tongue:* For Osric to understand when someone else speaks in his manner. (Horatio twits Osric for not being able to
understand the kind of flowery speech he himself uses when Hamlet speaks in such a vein.)
115–16 *You will do 't:* You can if you try.

HAMLET: What imports the nomination° of this gentleman?

OSRIC: Of Laertes?

HORATIO *(to* HAMLET*)*: His purse is empty already; all 's golden words are
120   spent.

HAMLET: Of him, sir.

OSRIC: I know you are not ignorant—

HAMLET: I would you did, sir; yet, in faith, if you did, it would not much ap-
         prove° me. Well, sir?

125   OSRIC: You are not ignorant of what excellence Laertes is—

HAMLET: I dare not confess that, lest I should compare° with him in excel-
         lence; but to know a man well were to know himself.°

OSRIC: I mean, sir, for his weapon; but in the imputation laid on him by
        them,° in his meed° he's unfellow'd.°

130   HAMLET: What's his weapon?

OSRIC: Rapier and dagger.

HAMLET: That's two of his weapons—but well.

OSRIC: The King, sir, hath wager'd with him six Barbary horses, against the
        which he has impawn'd,° as I take it, six French rapiers and poniards,
135   with their assigns,° as girdle, hangers,° and so. Three of the carriages,° in
        faith, are very dear to fancy,° very responsive° to the hilts, most delicate°
        carriages, and of very liberal conceit.°

HAMLET: What call you the carriages?

HORATIO *(to* HAMLET*)*: I knew you must be edified by the margent° ere
140   you had done.

OSRIC: The carriages, sir, are the hangers.

HAMLET: The phrase would be more germane to the matter if we could carry
         a cannon by our sides; I would it might be hangers till then. But, on: six
         Barb'ry horses against six French swords, their assigns, and three liberal-
145   conceited carriages; that's the French bet against the Danish. Why is this
         impawn'd, as you call it?

OSRIC: The King, sir, hath laid,° sir, that in a dozen passes° between yourself
        and him, he shall not exceed you three hits. He hath laid on twelve for
        nine, and it would come to immediate trial, if your lordship would
150   vouchsafe the answer.

---

117 *nomination:* Naming. 124 *approve:* Commend. 126 *compare:* Seem to compete. 127 *but . . .
himself:* For, to recognize excellence in another man, one must know oneself. 128–129 *imputation . . . them:* Reputation given him by others. 129 *meed:* Merit; *unfellow'd:* Unmatched. 134 *im-
pawn'd:* Staked, wagered. 135 *assigns:* Appurtenances; *hangers:* Straps on the sword belt (*girdle*)
from which the sword hung; *carriages:* An affected way of saying *hangers;* literally, gun-carriages.
136 *dear to fancy:* Fancifully designed, tasteful; *responsive:* Corresponding closely, matching; *delicate:*
I.e., in workmanship. 137 *liberal conceit:* Elaborate design. 139 *margent:* Margin of a book, place
for explanatory notes. 147 *laid:* Wagered; *passes:* Bouts. (The odds of the betting are hard to explain. Possibly the King bets that Hamlet will win at least five out of twelve, at which point
Laertes raises the odds against himself by betting he will win nine.)

HAMLET: How if I answer no?

OSRIC: I mean, my lord, the opposition of your person in trial.

HAMLET: Sir, I will walk here in the hall. If it please his Majesty, it is the
breathing time° of day with me. Let the foils be brought, the gentleman
willing, and the King hold his purpose, I will win for him an I can; if   *155*
not, I will gain nothing but my shame and the odd hits.

OSRIC: Shall I deliver you so?

HAMLET: To this effect, sir—after what flourish your nature will.

OSRIC: I commend my duty to your lordship.

HAMLET: Yours, yours. *(Exit* OSRIC.*)* He does well to commend it himself;   *160*
there are no tongues else for 's turn.

HORATIO: This lapwing° runs away with the shell on his head.

HAMLET: 'A did comply, sir, with his dug,° before 'a suck'd it. Thus has he—
and many more of the same breed that I know the drossy° age dotes
on—only got the tune° of the time and, out of an habit of encounter,° a   *165*
kind of yesty° collection,° which carries them through and through the
most fann'd and winnow'd° opinions; and do but blow them to their
trial, the bubbles are out.°

(Enter a LORD.*)*

LORD: My lord, his Majesty commended him to you by young Osric, who
brings back to him that you attend him in the hall. He sends to know if   *170*
your pleasure hold to play with Laertes, or that you will take longer time.

HAMLET: I am constant to my purposes; they follow the King's pleasure. If his
fitness speaks,° mine is ready; now or whensoever, provided I be so able
as now.

LORD: The King and Queen and all are coming down.   *175*

HAMLET: In happy time.°

LORD: The Queen desires you to use some gentle entertainment° to Laertes
before you fall to play.

HAMLET: She well instructs me.   *(Exit* LORD.*)*

HORATIO: You will lose, my lord.   *180*

HAMLET: I do not think so. Since he went into France, I have been in continual practice; I shall win at the odds. But thou wouldst not think how ill
all's here about my heart; but it is no matter.

HORATIO: Nay, good my lord—

---

154 *breathing time:* Exercise period. 162 *lapwing:* A bird that draws intruders away from its nest
and was thought to run about when newly hatched with its head in the shell; a seeming reference to Osric's hat. 163 *comply . . . dug:* Observe ceremonious formality toward his mother's teat.
164 *drossy:* Frivolous. 165 *tune:* Temper, mood, manner of speech; *habit of encounter:* Demeanor
of social intercourse. 166 *yesty:* Yeasty, frothy; *collection:* I.e., of current phrases. 167 *fann'd and
winnow'd:* Select and refined. 167–68 *blow . . . out:* Put them to the test, and their ignorance is
exposed. 172–73 *If . . . speaks:* If his readiness answers to the time. 176 *In happy time:* A phrase
of courtesy indicating acceptance. 177 *entertainment:* Greeting.

185 HAMLET: It is but foolery, but it is such a kind of gain-giving,° as would perhaps trouble a woman.

HORATIO: If your mind dislike anything, obey it. I will forestall their repair
hither, and say you are not fit.

HAMLET: Not a whit, we defy augury. There is special providence in the fall
190 of a sparrow. If it be now, 'tis not to come; if it be not to come, it will be
now; if it be not now; yet it will come. The readiness is all. Since no man
of aught he leaves knows what is 't to leave betimes,° let be.

(A table prepar'd. Enter trumpets, drums, and OFFICERS with cushions; KING,
QUEEN, OSRIC, and all the State; foils, daggers, and wine borne in; and
LAERTES.)

KING: Come, Hamlet, come, and take this hand from me.
(The KING puts LAERTES' hand into HAMLET's.)

HAMLET: Give me your pardon, sir. I have done you wrong,
195 But pardon 't, as you are a gentleman.
This presence° knows,
And you must needs have heard, how I am punish'd
With a sore distraction. What I have done
That might your nature, honor, and exception°
200 Roughly awake, I here proclaim was madness.
Was 't Hamlet wrong'd Laertes? Never Hamlet.
If Hamlet from himself be ta'en away,
And when he's not himself does wrong Laertes,
Then Hamlet does it not, Hamlet denies it.
205 Who does it, then? His madness. If 't be so,
Hamlet is of the faction that is wrong'd;
His madness is poor Hamlet's enemy.
Sir, in this audience,
Let my disclaiming from a purpos'd evil
210 Free me so far in your most generous thoughts
That I have shot my arrow o'er the house
And hurt my brother.

LAERTES: I am satisfied in nature,°
Whose motive in this case should stir me most
To my revenge. But in my terms of honor
215 I stand aloof, and will no reconcilement
Till by some elder masters of known honor
I have a voice° and precedent of peace
To keep my name ungor'd. But till that time,

185 gain-giving: Misgiving. 192 what . . . betimes: What is the best time to leave it. 196 presence:
Royal assembly. 199 exception: Disapproval. 212 in nature: As to my personal feelings. 217 voice:
Authoritative pronouncement.

I do receive your offer'd love like love,
And will not wrong it.

HAMLET: I embrace it freely,   220
And will this brothers' wager frankly play.
Give us the foils. Come on.

LAERTES: Come, one for me.

HAMLET: I'll be your foil,° Laertes. In mine ignorance
Your skill shall, like a star i' th' darkest night,
Stick fiery off° indeed.

LAERTES: You mock me, sir.   225

HAMLET: No, by this hand.

KING: Give them the foils, young Osric. Cousin Hamlet,
You know the wager?

HAMLET: Very well, my lord.
Your Grace has laid the odds o' th' weaker side.

KING: I do not fear it; I have seen you both.   230
But since he is better'd,° we have therefore odds.

LAERTES: This is too heavy, let me see another.

                         (Exchanges his foil for another.)

HAMLET: This likes me well. These foils have all a length?

                         (They prepare to play.)

OSRIC: Ay, my good lord.

KING: Set me the stoups of wine upon that table.   235
If Hamlet give the first or second hit,
Or quit° in answer of the third exchange,
Let all the battlements their ordnance fire.
The King shall drink to Hamlet's better breath,
And in the cup an union° shall he throw,   240
Richer than that which four successive kings
In Denmark's crown have worn. Give me the cups,
And let the kettle° to the trumpet speak,
The trumpet to the cannoneer without,
The cannons to the heavens, the heaven to earth,   245
"Now the King drinks to Hamlet." Come, begin.   *(Trumpets the while.)*
And you, the judges, bear a wary eye.

HAMLET: Come on sir.

LAERTES: Come, my lord.   *(They play.* HAMLET *scores a hit.)*

HAMLET: One.

LAERTES: No.

---

223 *foil:* Thin metal background which sets a jewel off (with pun on the blunted rapier for fencing). 225 *Stick fiery off:* Stand out brilliantly. 231 *is better'd:* Has improved; is the odds-on favorite. 237 *quit:* Repay (with a hit). 240 *union:* Pearl (so called, according to Pliny's *Natural History,* IX, because pearls are *unique,* never identical). 243 *kettle:* Kettledrum.

HAMLET: Judgment.
OSRIC: A hit, a very palpable hit.
                         (Drum, trumpets, and shot. Flourish. A piece goes off.)
250 LAERTES: Well, again.
KING: Stay, give me drink. Hamlet, this pearl is thine.
                     (He throws a pearl in HAMLET's *cup and drinks.)*
    Here's to thy health. Give him the cup.
HAMLET: I'll play this bout first; set it by awhile.
    Come. *(They play.)* Another hit; what say you?
255 LAERTES: A touch, a touch, I do confess 't.
KING: Our son shall win.
QUEEN: He's fat,° and scant of breath.
    Here, Hamlet, take my napkin,° rub thy brows.
    The Queen carouses° to thy fortune, Hamlet.
HAMLET: Good madam!
260 KING: Gertrude, do not drink.
QUEEN: I will, my lord; I pray you pardon me.   *(Drinks.)*
KING *(aside)*: It is the pois'ned cup. It is too late.
HAMLET: I dare not drink yet, madam; by and by.
QUEEN: Come, let me wipe thy face.
LAERTES *(to* KING*)*: My lord, I'll hit him now.
265 KING: I do not think 't.
LAERTES *(aside)*: And yet it is almost against my conscience.
HAMLET: Come, for the third, Laertes. You do but dally.
    I pray you, pass with your best violence;
    I am afeard you make a wanton of me.°
270 LAERTES: Say you so? Come on.   *(They play.)*
OSRIC: Nothing, neither way.
LAERTES: Have at you now!
                    *(*LAERTES *wounds* HAMLET; *then, in scuffling,*
             they change rapiers,° and HAMLET *wounds* LAERTES.*)*
KING: Part them! They are incens'd.
HAMLET: Nay, come, again.   *(The* QUEEN *falls.)*
OSRIC: Look to the Queen there, ho!
HORATIO: They bleed on both sides. How is it, my lord?
275 OSRIC: How is 't, Laertes?
LAERTES: Why, as a woodcock° to mine own springe,° Osric;
    I am justly kill'd with mine own treachery.

---

256 *fat:* Not physically fit, out of training. 257 *napkin:* Handkerchief. 258 *carouses:* Drinks a
toast. 269 *make . . . me:* Treat me like a spoiled child, holding back to give me an advantage. 272
s.d. *in scuffling, they change rapiers:* According to a widespread stage tradition, Hamlet receives a
scratch, realizes that Laertes' sword is unbated, and accordingly forces an exchange. 276 *woodcock:*
A bird, a type of stupidity or as a decoy; *springe:* Trap, snare.

HAMLET: How does the Queen?

KING: She swoons to see them bleed.

QUEEN: No, no, the drink, the drink—O my dear Hamlet—
    The drink, the drink! I am pois'ned.   *(Dies.)*   *280*

HAMLET: O villainy! Ho, let the door be lock'd!
    Treachery! Seek it out.   *(LAERTES falls.)*

LAERTES: It is here, Hamlet. Hamlet, thou art slain.
    No med'cine in the world can do thee good;
    In thee there is not half an hour's life.   *285*
    The treacherous instrument is in thy hand,
    Unbated° and envenom'd. The foul practice
    Hath turn'd itself on me. Lo, here I lie,
    Never to rise again. Thy mother's pois'ned.
    I can no more. The King, the King's to blame.   *290*

HAMLET: The point envenom'd too? Then, venom, to thy work.

                                                (Stabs the KING.)

ALL: Treason! Treason!

KING: O, yet defend me, friends; I am but hurt.

HAMLET: Here, thou incestuous, murd'rous, damned Dane,
                    (He forces the KING to drink the poisoned cup.)
    Drink off this potion. Is thy union° here?   *295*
    Follow my mother.   *(KING dies.)*

LAERTES: He is justly serv'd.
    It is a poison temper'd° by himself.
    Exchange forgiveness with me, noble Hamlet.
    Mine and my father's death come not upon thee,
    Nor thine on me!   *(Dies.)*   *300*

HAMLET: Heaven make thee free of it! I follow thee.
    I am dead, Horatio. Wretched Queen, adieu!
    You that look pale and tremble at this chance,
    That are but mutes° or audience to this act,
    Had I but time—as this fell° sergeant,° Death,   *305*
    Is strict in his arrest—O, I could tell you—
    But let it be. Horatio, I am dead;
    Thou livest. Report me and my cause aright
    To the unsatisfied.

HORATIO: Never believe it.
    I am more an antique Roman° than a Dane.   *310*
    Here's yet some liquor left.

---

287 *Unbated:* Not blunted with a button. 295 *union:* Pearl (see line 240; with grim puns on the word's other meanings: marriage, shared death [?]). 297 *temper'd:* Mixed. 304 *mutes:* Silent observers. 305 *fell:* Cruel; *sergeant:* Sheriff's officer. 310 *Roman:* It was the Roman custom to follow masters in death.

(He attempts to drink from the poisoned cup. HAMLET *prevents him.)*

HAMLET: As th' art a man,
Give me the cup! Let go! By heaven, I'll ha 't.
O God, Horatio, what a wounded name,
Things standing thus unknown, shall I leave behind me!
315   If thou didst ever hold me in thy heart,
Absent thee from felicity awhile,
And in this harsh world draw thy breath in pain
To tell my story.   *(A march afar off and a volley within.)*
What warlike noise is this?
OSRIC: Young Fortinbras, with conquest come from Poland,
320   To the ambassadors of England gives
This warlike volley.
HAMLET: O, I die, Horatio!
The potent poison quite o'ercrows° my spirit.
I cannot live to hear the news from England,
But I do prophesy th' election lights
325   On Fortinbras. He has my dying voice.°
So tell him, with th' occurrents° more and less
Which have solicited°—the rest is silence.   *(Dies.)*
HORATIO: Now cracks a noble heart. Good night, sweet prince;
And flights of angels sing thee to thy rest!   *(March within.)*
330   Why does the drum come hither?

(Enter FORTINBRAS, *with the English* AMBASSADORS *with drum, colors, and* attendants.*)*

FORTINBRAS: Where is this sight?
HORATIO: What is it you would see?
If aught of woe or wonder, cease your search.
FORTINBRAS: This quarry° cries on havoc.° O proud Death,
What feast is toward° in thine eternal cell,
335   That thou so many princes at a shot
So bloodily hast struck?
FIRST AMBASSADOR: The sight is dismal;
And our affairs from England come too late.
The ears are senseless that should give us hearing,
To tell him his commandment is fulfill'd,
340   That Rosencrantz and Guildenstern are dead.

---

322 *o'ercrows:* Triumphs over.   325 *voice:* Vote.   326 *occurrents:* Events, incidents.   327 *solicited:*
Moved, urged.   333 *quarry:* Heap of dead; *cries on havoc:* Proclaims a general slaughter.   334 *to-*
ward: In preparation.

Where should we have our thanks?

HORATIO: Not from his° mouth,
Had it th' ability of life to thank you.
He never gave commandment for their death.
But since, so jump° upon this bloody question,°
You from the Polack wars, and you from England,   345
Are here arriv'd, give order that these bodies
High on a stage° be placed to the view,
And let me speak to th' yet unknowing world
How these things came about. So shall you hear
Of carnal, bloody, and unnatural acts,   350
Of accidental judgments,° casual° slaughters,
Of deaths put on° by cunning and forc'd cause,
And, in this upshot, purposes mistook
Fall'n on th' inventors' heads. All this can I
Truly deliver.

FORTINBRAS: Let us haste to hear it,   355
And call the noblest to the audience.
For me, with sorrow I embrace my fortune.
I have some rights of memory° in this kingdom,
Which now to claim my vantage° doth invite me.

HORATIO: Of that I shall have also cause to speak,   360
And from his mouth whose voice will draw on more.°
But let this same be presently° perform'd,
Even while men's minds are wild, lest more mischance
On° plots and errors happen.

FORTINBRAS: Let four captains
Bear Hamlet, like a soldier, to the stage,   365
For he was likely, had he been put on,°
To have prov'd most royal; and, for his passage,°
The soldiers' music and the rite of war
Speak loudly for him.
Take up the bodies. Such a sight as this   370
Becomes the field,° but here shows much amiss.
Go, bid the soldiers shoot.

(Exeunt marching, bearing off the dead bodies; a peal of ordnance is shot off.)

c. 1600

341 *his:* Claudius's. 344 *jump:* Precisely; *question:* Dispute. 347 *stage:* Platform. 351 *judgments:* Retributions; *casual:* Occurring by chance. 352 *put on:* Instigated. 358 *of memory:* Traditional, remembered. 359 *vantage:* Presence at this opportune moment. 361 *voice . . . more:* Vote will influence still others. 362 *presently:* Immediately. 364 *On:* On the basis of. 366 *put on:* Invested in royal office and so put to the test. 367 *passage:* Death. 371 *field:* I.e., of battle.

CONSIDERATIONS

1. Reread the "dram of eale (evil)" passage (I.iv.13ff.). In this speech, Hamlet suggests three possible ways of looking at the problem of evil. Explain each of these responses and then discuss how any (or all) of them might apply to the actions (or failure to act) of any of the play's characters.
2. Identify passages that show the change in Hamlet's character after his father's death. Consider not only what Hamlet himself says but also what other characters say and how they react to or interact with Hamlet.
3. Choose any one of Hamlet's soliloquies. Based on what he says, evaluate his ability to make reliable assessments of himself and of other characters' motivations and behaviors.
4. What do you think of Gertrude? Is she an innocent victim of Claudius's villainy? Or does she seem to have some complicity in her husband's death? Can you identify evidence suggesting that she did or did not know how King Hamlet met his death?
5. Evaluate Hamlet's relationship with Ophelia. Consider especially his behavior toward her after the "To be or not to be" soliloquy. To what extent would you hold Hamlet responsible for Ophelia's suicide?
6. How important is the Ghost's role in the play? Why does Hamlet first accept the "honesty" of the Ghost and then express deep doubts about the truth of the Ghost's message? How does Hamlet's reaction to and interaction with the Ghost suggest one of the play's major conflicts?
7. Consider any one of the play's minor characters: Laertes, Rosencrantz and Guildenstern, Horatio, or Polonius. What roles do these characters play? How do they contribute to the conflict or to the development of the major characters?
8. What motivates Hamlet to refrain from killing Claudius in Act III? Do you find his hesitation valid or simply a form of procrastination and rationalization? Explain.
9. Analyze the actions and reactions of the major characters during the "Mousetrap" (play within a play) scene. How does this scene contribute to developing the conflicts, themes, and characterizations of *Hamlet?*
10. What would be lost (or gained) if the gravedigger scene (V.i.1ff.) were omitted? As you respond to this question, consider whether the scene simply provides a moment of comic relief or does more.

More resources on
William Shakespeare

 In *ARIEL*
- Brief biography of Shakespeare
- Text of a scene from *Othello*, with hyperlinked comments
- Video clip of a scene from *Othello*
- Video discussion of Shakespeare's writing
- Bibliography of scholarly works on Shakespeare

 In the Online Learning Center for *Responding to Literature*
- Brief biography of Shakespeare
- List of major works by Shakespeare
- Web links to more resources on Shakespeare
- Additional questions for experiencing and interpreting Shakespeare's writing

Commentary

CAROLYN HEILBRUN (1926–2003)

The Character of Hamlet's Mother

The character of Hamlet's mother has not received the specific critical attention it deserves. Moreover, the traditional account of her personality as rendered by the critics will not stand up under close scrutiny of Shakespeare's play.

None of the critics of course has failed to see Gertrude as vital to the action of the play; not only is she the mother of the hero, the widow of the Ghost, and the wife of the current King of Denmark, but the fact of her hasty and, to the Elizabethans, incestuous marriage, the whole question of her "falling off," occupies a position of barely secondary importance in the mind of her son, and of the Ghost. Indeed, Freud and Jones see her, the object of Hamlet's Oedipus complex, as central to the motivation of the play.[1] But the critics, with no exception that I have been able to find, have accepted Hamlet's word "fraility" as applying to her whole personality, and have seen in her not one weakness, or passion in the Elizabethan sense, but a character of which weakness and lack of depth and vigorous intelligence are the entire explanation. Of her can it truly be said that carrying the "stamp of one defect," she did "in the general censure take corruption from that particular fault" (I.iv.35–36).

The critics are agreed that Gertrude was not a party to the late King's murder and indeed knew nothing of it, a point which, on the clear evidence of the play, is indisputable. They have also discussed whether or not Gertrude, guilty of more than an "o'er-hasty marriage," had committed adultery with Claudius before her husband's death. I will return to this point later on. Beyond discussing these two points, those critics who have dealt specifically with the Queen have traditionally seen her as well-meaning but shallow and feminine, in the pejorative sense of the word: incapable of any sustained rational process, superficial and flighty. It is this tradition which a closer reading of the play will show to be erroneous.

Professor Bradley describes the traditional Gertrude thus:

> The Queen was not a bad-hearted woman, not at all the woman to think little of murder. But she had a soft animal nature and was very dull and very shallow. She loved to be happy, like a sheep in the sun, and to do her justice, it pleased her to see others happy, like more sheep in the sun.... It was pleasant to sit upon her throne and see smiling faces around her, and foolish and unkind in Hamlet to persist in grieving for his father instead of marrying Ophelia and making everything comfortable.... The belief at the bottom of her heart was that the world is a place constructed simply that people may be happy in it in a good-humored sensual fashion.[2]

Later on, Bradley says of her that when affliction comes to her "the good in her nature struggles to the surface through the heavy mass of sloth."

Granville-Barker is not quite so extreme. Shakespeare, he says,   5

> gives us in Gertrude the woman who does not mature, who clings to her youth and all that belongs to it, whose charm will not change but at last fade and wither, a pretty creature, as we see her, desperately refusing to grow old. . . . She is drawn for us with unemphatic strokes, and she has but a passive part in the play's action. She moves throughout in Claudius' shadow; he holds her as he won her, by the witchcraft of his wit.[3]

Elsewhere Granville-Barker says "Gertrude who will certainly never see forty-five again, might better be 'old.' [That is, portrayed by an older, mature actress.] But that would make her relations with Claudius—and *their* likelihood is vital to the play—quite incredible" (p. 226). Granville-Barker is saying here that a woman about forty-five years of age cannot feel any sexual passion nor arouse it. This is one of the mistakes which lie at the heart of the misunderstanding about Gertrude.

Professor Dover Wilson sees Gertrude as more forceful than either of these two critics will admit, but even he finds the Ghost's unwillingness to shock her with knowledge of his murder to be one of the basic motivations of the play, and he says of her "Gertrude is always hoping for the best."[4]

Now whether Claudius won Gertrude before or after her husband's death, it was certainly not, as Granville-Barker implies, with "the witchcraft of his wit" alone. Granville-Barker would have us believe that Claudius won her simply by the force of his persuasive tongue. "It is plain," he writes, that the Queen "does little except echo his [Claudius'] wishes; sometimes—as in the welcome to Rosencrantz and Guildenstern—she repeats his very words" (p. 227), though Wilson must admit later that Gertrude does not tell Claudius everything. Without dwelling here on the psychology of the Ghost, or the greater burden borne by the Elizabethan words "witchcraft" and "wit," we can plainly see, for the Ghost tells us, how Claudius won the Queen: the Ghost considers his brother to be garbage, and "lust," the Ghost says, "will sate itself in a celestial bed and prey on garbage" [I.v.56–57]. "Lust"—in a woman of forty-five or more—is the key word here. Bradley, Granville-Barker, and to a lesser extent Professor Dover Wilson, misunderstand Gertrude largely because they are unable to see lust, the desire for sexual relations, as the passion, in the Elizabethan sense of the word, the flaw, the weakness which drives Gertrude to an incestuous marriage, appalls her son, and keeps him from the throne. Unable to explain her marriage to Claudius as the act of any but a weak-minded vacillating woman, they fail to see Gertrude for the strong-minded, intelligent, succinct, and, apart from this passion, sensible woman that she is.

To understand Gertrude properly, it is only necessary to examine the lines Shakespeare has chosen for her to say. She is, except for her description of Ophelia's death, concise and pithy in speech, with a talent for seeing the essence of every situation presented before her eyes. If she is not profound, she is certainly never silly. We first hear her asking Hamlet to stop wearing black, to stop walking about with his eyes downcast, and to realize that death is an inevitable part of life. She is, in short, asking him not to give way to the passion of grief, a passion of whose force and dangers the Elizabethans are aware, as Miss Campbell has shown.[5] Claudius echoes her with a well-reasoned argument against grief which was, in its philosophy if not in its language, a piece of commonplace Elizabethan lore. After Claudius' speech, Gertrude asks Hamlet to remain in Denmark, where he is rightly loved. Her speeches have been short, however warm and loving, and conciseness of statement is not the mark of a dull and shallow woman.

We next hear her, as Queen and gracious hostess, welcoming Rosencrantz and Guildenstern to the court, hoping, with the King, that they may cheer Hamlet and discover what is depressing him. Claudius then tells Gertrude, when they are alone, that Polonius believes he knows what is upsetting Hamlet. The Queen answers:

> I doubt it is no other than the main,
> His father's death and our o'er-hasty marriage. (II.ii.56–57)

This statement is concise, remarkably to the point, and not a little courageous. It is not the statement of a dull, slothful woman who can only echo her husband's words. Next, Polonius enters with his most unbrief apotheosis to brevity. The Queen interrupts him with five words: "More matter with less art" (II.ii.95). It would be difficult to find a phrase more applicable to Polonius. When this gentleman, in no way deterred from his loquacity, after purveying the startling news that he has a daughter, begins to read a letter, the Queen asks pointedly "Came this from Hamlet to her?" (II.ii.114).

10

We see Gertrude next in Act III, asking Rosencrantz and Guildenstern, with her usual directness, if Hamlet received them well, and if they were able to tempt him to any pastime. But before leaving the room, she stops for a word of kindness to Ophelia. It is a humane gesture, for she is unwilling to leave Ophelia, the unhappy tool of the King and Polonius, without some kindly and intelligent appreciation of her help:

> And for your part, Ophelia, I do wish
> That your good beauties be the happy cause
> Of Hamlet's wildness. So shall I hope your virtues
> Will bring him to his wonted way again,
> To both your honors. (III.i.38–42)

It is difficult to see in this speech, as Bradley apparently does, the gushing shallow wish of a sentimental woman that class distinctions shall not stand in the way of true love.

At the play, the Queen asks Hamlet to sit near her. She is clearly trying to make him feel he has a place in the court of Denmark. She does not speak again until Hamlet asks her how she likes the play. "The lady doth protest too much, methinks" [III.ii.206) is her immortal comment on the player queen. The scene gives her four more words: when Claudius leaps to his feet, she asks "How fares my Lord?" [III.ii.237].

I will for the moment pass over the scene in the Queen's closet, to follow her quickly through the remainder of the play. After the closet scene, the Queen comes to speak to Claudius. She tells him, as Hamlet has asked her to, that he, Hamlet, is mad, and has killed Polonius. She adds, however, that he now weeps for what he has done. She does not wish Claudius to know what she now knows, how wild and fearsome Hamlet has become. Later, she does not wish to see Ophelia, but hearing how distracted she is, consents. When Laertes bursts in ready to attack Claudius, she immediately steps between Claudius and Laertes to protect the King, and tells Laertes it is not Claudius who has killed his father. Laertes will of course soon learn this, but it is Gertrude who manages to tell him before he can do any meaningless damage. She leaves Laertes and the King together, and then returns to tell Laertes that his sister is drowned. She gives her news directly, realizing that suspense will increase the pain of it, but this is the one time in the play when her usual pointed conciseness would be the mark neither of intelligence nor kindness, and so, gently, and at some length, she tells Laertes of his sister's death, giving him time to recover from the shock of grief, and to absorb the meaning of her words. At Ophelia's funeral the Queen scatters flowers over the grave:

> Sweets to the sweet; farewell!
> I hop'd thou shouldst have been my Hamlet's wife.
> I thought thy bride-bed to have deck'd, sweet maid,
> And not t' have strew'd thy grave. [V.i.204–7]

She is the only one present decently mourning the death of someone young, and not heated in the fire of some personal passion.

At the match between Hamlet and Laertes, the Queen believes that Hamlet is out of training, but glad to see him at some sport, she gives him her handkerchief to wipe his brow, and drinks to his success. The drink is poisoned and she dies. But before she dies she does not waste time on vituperation; she warns Hamlet that the drink is poisoned to prevent his drinking it. They are her last words. Those critics who have thought her stupid admire her death; they call it uncharacteristic.

In Act III, when Hamlet goes to his mother in her closet his nerves are pitched at the very height of tension; he is on the edge of hysteria. The possibility of murdering his mother has in fact entered his mind, and he has just met and refused an opportunity to kill Claudius. His mother, meanwhile, waiting for him, has told Polonius not to fear for her, but she knows when she sees

Hamlet that he may be violently mad. Hamlet quips with her, insults her, tells her he wishes she were not his mother, and when she, still retaining dignity, attempts to end the interview, Hamlet seizes her and she cries for help. The important thing to note is that the Queen's cry "Thou wilt not murder me" [III.iv.22] is not foolish. She has seen from Hamlet's demeanor that he is capable of murder, as indeed in the next instant he proves himself to be.

15   We next learn from the Queen's startled "As kill a king" (III.iv.30) that she has no knowledge of the murder, though of course this is only confirmation here of what we already know. Then the Queen asks Hamlet why he is so hysterical:

> What have I done, that thou dar'st wag thy tongue
> In noise so rude against me? [III.iv.40–41]

Hamlet tells her: it is her lust, the need of sexual passion, which has driven her from the arms and memory of her husband to the incomparably cruder charms of his brother. He cries out that she has not even the excuse of youth for her lust:

> O Shame! where is thy blush? Rebellious hell,
> If thou canst mutine in a matron's bones,
> To flaming youth let virtue be as wax
> And melt in her own fire. Proclaim no shame
> When the compulsive ardor gives the charge,
> Since frost itself as actively doth burn,
> And reason panders will. (III.iv.83–89)

This is not only a lust, but a lust which throws out of joint all the structure of human morality and relationships. And the Queen admits it. If there is one quality that has characterized, and will characterize, every speech of Gertrude's in the play, it is the ability to see reality clearly, and to express it. This talent is not lost when turned upon herself:

> O Hamlet, speak no more!
> Thou turn'st mine eyes into my very soul,
> And there I see such black and grained spots
> As will not leave their tinct. [III.iv.89–92]

She knows that lust has driven her, that this is her sin, and she admits it. Not that she wishes to linger in the contemplation of her sin. No more, she cries, no more. And then the Ghost appears to Hamlet. The Queen thinks him mad again—as well she might—but she promises Hamlet that she will not betray him—and she does not.

Where, in all that we have seen of Gertrude, is there the picture of "a soft animal nature, very dull and very shallow"? She may indeed be "animal" in the sense of "lustful." But it does not follow that because she wishes to continue a life of sexual experience, her brain is soft or her wit unperceptive.

Some critics, having accepted Gertrude as a weak and vacillating woman, see no reason to suppose that she did not fall victim to Claudius' charms before the death of her husband and commit adultery with him. These critics, Professor Bradley among them (p. 166), claim that the elder Hamlet clearly tells his son that Gertrude has committed adultery with Claudius in the speech beginning "Ay that incestuous, that adulterate beast" [I.v.42ff.]. Professor Dover Wilson presents the argument:

> Is the Ghost speaking here of the o'er-hasty marriage of Claudius and Gertrude? Assuredly not. His "certain term" is drawing rapidly to an end, and he is already beginning to "scent the morning air." Hamlet knew of the marriage, and his whole soul was filled with nausea at the thought of the speedy hasting to "incestuous sheets." Why then should the Ghost waste precious moments in telling Hamlet what he was fully cognisant of before? . . . Moreover, though the word "incestuous" was applicable to the marriage, the rest of the passage is entirely inapplicable to it. Expressions like "witchcraft", "traitorous gifts", "seduce", "shameful lust", and "seeming virtuous" may be noted in passing. But the rest of the quotation leaves no doubt upon the matter. (p. 293)

Professor Dover Wilson and other critics have accepted the Ghost's word "adulterate" in its modern meaning. The Elizabethan word "adultery," however, was not restricted to its modern meaning, but was used to define any sexual relationship which could be called unchaste, including of course an incestuous one.[6] Certainly the elder Hamlet considered the marriage of Claudius and Gertrude to be unchaste and unseemly, and while his use of the word "adulterate" indicates his very strong feelings about the marriage, it would not to an Elizabethan audience necessarily mean that he believed Gertrude to have been false to him before his death. It is important to notice, too, that the Ghost does not apply the term "adulterate" to Gertrude, and he may well have considered the term a just description of Claudius' entire sexual life.

But even if the Ghost used the word "adulterate" in full awareness of its modern restricted meaning, it is not necessary to assume on the basis of this single speech (and it is the only shadow of evidence we have for such a conclusion) that Gertrude was unfaithful to him while he lived. It is quite probable that the elder Hamlet still considered himself married to Gertrude, and he is moreover revolted that her lust for him ("why she would hang on him as if increase of appetite had grown by what it fed on") should have so easily transferred itself to another. This is why he uses the expressions "seduce," "shameful lust," and others. Professor Dover Wilson has himself said "Hamlet knew of the marriage, and his whole soul was filled with nausea at the thought of the

speedy hasting to incestuous sheets"; the soul of the elder Hamlet was undoubtedly filled with nausea too, and this could well explain his using such
strong language, as well as his taking the time to mention the matter at all. It is
not necessary to consider Gertrude an adulteress to account for the speech of
the Ghost.

20   Gertrude's lust was, of course, more important to the plot than we may
at first perceive. Charlton Lewis, among others, has shown how Shakespeare
kept many of the facts of the plots from which he borrowed without maintaining the structures which explained them. In the original Belleforest story,
Gertrude (substituting Shakespeare's more familiar names) was daughter of the
king; to become king, it was necessary to marry her. The elder Hamlet, in marrying Gertrude, ousted Claudius from the throne.[7] Shakespeare retained the
shell of this in his play. When she no longer has a husband, the form of election would be followed to declare the next king, in this case undoubtedly her
son Hamlet. By marrying Gertrude, Claudius "popp'd in between th' election
and my hopes" (V.ii.65), that is, kept young Hamlet from the throne. Gertrude's
flaw of lust made Claudius' ambition possible, for without taking advantage of
the Queen's desire still to be married, he could not have been king.

But Gertrude, if she is lustful, is also intelligent, penetrating, and gifted
with a remarkable talent for concise and pithy speech. In all the play, the person whose language hers most closely resembles is Horatio. "Sweets to the
sweet," she has said at Ophelia's grave. "Good night sweet prince," Horatio says
at the end. They are neither of them dull, or shallow, or slothful, though one of
them is passion's slave.   *1990*

ENDNOTES

1. William Shakespeare, *Hamlet,* with a psycholoanalytical study by
Ernest Jones, M.D. (London: Vision Press, 1947), pp. 7–42.

2. A. C. Bradley, *Shakespearean Tragedy* (New York: Macmillan, 1949),
p. 167.

3. Harley Granville-Barker, *Prefaces to Shakespeare* (Princeton: Princeton
University Press, 1946), 1:227.

4. J. Dover Wilson, *What Happens in Hamlet* (Cambridge: Cambridge
University Press, 1951), p. 125.

5. Lily B. Campbell, *Shakespeare's Tragic Heroes* (New York: Barnes &
Noble, 1952), pp. 112–113.

6. See Bertram Joseph, *Conscience and the King* (London: Chatto and
Windus, 1953), pp. 16–19.

7. Charlton M. Lewis, *The Genesis of Hamlet* (New York: Henry Holt,
1907), p. 36.

<u>Commentary</u>

LAURA BOHANNAN (1922–   )
Shakespeare in the Bush

Scholar and anthropologist Laura Bohannon had always understood Shakespeare's Hamlet *through the lens of her British education. However, when she described the plot and characters of this play to the elders in a small, remote African village, she found that they interpreted this classic of English literature in a very different way from her former professors and classmates.*

Just before I left Oxford for the Tiv in West Africa, conversation turned to the season at Stratford. "You Americans," said a friend, "often have difficulty with Shakespeare. He was, after all, a very English poet, and one can easily misinterpret the universal by misunderstanding the particular."

I protested that human nature is pretty much the same the whole world over; at least the general plot and motivation of the greater tragedies would always be clear—everywhere—although some details of custom might have to be explained and difficulties of translation might produce other slight changes. To end an argument we could not conclude, my friend gave me a copy of *Hamlet* to study in the African bush: It would, he hoped, lift my mind above its primitive surroundings, and possibly I might, by prolonged meditation, achieve the grace of correct interpretation.

It was my second field trip to the African tribe, and I thought myself ready to live in one of its remote sections—an area difficult to cross even on foot. I eventually settled on the hillock of a very knowledgeable old man, the head of a homestead of some hundred and forty people, all of whom were either his close relatives or their wives and children. Like the other elders of the vicinity, the old man spent most of his time performing ceremonies seldom seen these days in the more accessible parts of the tribe. I was delighted. Soon there would be three months of enforced isolation and leisure, between the harvest that takes place just before the rising of the swamps and the clearing of new farms when the water goes down. Then, I thought, they would have even more time to perform ceremonies and explain them to me.

I was quite mistaken. Most of the ceremonies demanded the presence of elders from several homesteads. As the swamps rose, the old men found it too difficult to walk from one homestead to the next, and the ceremonies gradually ceased. As the swamps rose even higher, all activities but one came to an end. The women brewed beer from maize and millet. Men, women, and children sat on their hillocks and drank it.

People began to drink at dawn. By midmorning the whole homestead was singing, dancing, and drumming. When it rained, people had to sit inside   5 their huts: There they drank and sang or they drank and told stories. In any case, by noon or before, I either had to join the party or retire to my own hut and my books. "One does not discuss serious matters when there is beer. Come, drink with us." Since I lacked their capacity for the thick native beer, I spent more and more time with *Hamlet*. Before the end of the second month, grace descended on me. I was quite sure that *Hamlet* had only one possible interpretation, and that one universally obvious.

Early every morning, in the hope of having some serious talk before the beer party, I used to call on the old man at his reception hut—a circle of posts supporting a thatched roof above a low mud wall to keep out wind and rain. One day I crawled through the low doorway and found most of the men of the homestead sitting huddled in their ragged cloths on stools, low plank beds, and reclining chairs, warming themselves against the chill of the rain around a smoky fire. In the center were three pots of beer. The party had started.

The old man greeted me cordially. "Sit down and drink." I accepted a large calabash full of beer, poured some into a small drinking gourd, and tossed it down. Then I poured some more into the same gourd for the man second in seniority to my host before I handed my calabash over to a young man for further distribution. Important people shouldn't ladle beer themselves.

"It is better like this," the old man said, looking at me approvingly and plucking at the thatch that had caught in my hair. "You should sit and drink with us more often. Your servants tell me that when you are not with us, you sit inside your hut looking at a paper."

The old man was acquainted with four kinds of "papers": tax receipts, bride price receipts, court fee receipts, and letters. The messenger who brought him letters from the chief used them mainly as a badge of office, for he always knew what was in them and told the old man. Personal letters for the few who had relatives in the government or mission stations were kept until someone went to a large market where there was a letter writer and reader. Since my arrival, letters were brought to me to be read. A few men also brought me bride price receipts, privately, with requests to change the figures to a higher sum. I found moral arguments were of no avail, since in-laws are fair game, and the technical hazards of forgery difficult to explain to an illiterate people. I did not wish them to think me silly enough to look at any such papers for days on end, and I hastily explained that my "paper" was one of the "things of long ago" of my country.

10   "Ah," said the old man. "Tell us."

I protested that I was not a storyteller. Storytelling is a skilled art among them; their standards are high, and the audiences critical—and vocal in their criticism. I protested in vain. This morning they wanted to hear a story while they drank. They threatened to tell me no more stories until I told them one of mine. Finally, the old man promised that no one would criticize my style "for we know you are struggling with our language." "But," put in one of the elders, "you must explain what we do not understand, as we do when we tell you our stories." Realizing that here was my chance to prove *Hamlet* universally intelligible, I agreed.

The old man handed me some more beer to help me on with my storytelling. Men filled their long wooden pipes and knocked coals from the fire to place in the pipe bowls; then, puffing contentedly, they sat back to listen. I began in the proper style, "Not yesterday, not yesterday, but long ago, a thing occurred. One night three men were keeping watch outside the homestead of the great chief, when suddenly they saw the former chief approach them."

"Why was he no longer their chief?"

"He was dead," I explained. "That is why they were troubled and afraid when they saw him."

"Impossible," began one of the elders, handing his pipe on to his neighbor, who interrupted, "Of course it wasn't the dead chief. It was an omen sent by a witch. Go on."   15

Slightly shaken, I continued. "One of these three was a man who knew things"—the closest translation of scholar, but unfortunately it also meant witch. The second elder looked triumphantly at the first. "So he spoke to the dead chief saying, 'Tell us what we must do so you may rest in your grave,' but the dead chief did not answer. He vanished, and they could see him no more. Then the man who knew things—his name was Horatio—said this event was the affair of the dead chief's son, Hamlet."

There was a general shaking of heads round the circle. "Had the dead chief no living brothers? Or was this son the chief?"

"No," I replied. "That is, he had one living brother who became the chief when the elder brother died."

The old men muttered: Such omens were matters for chiefs and elders, not for youngsters; no good could come of going behind a chief's back; clearly Horatio was not a man who knew things.

"Yes, he was," I insisted, shooing a chicken away from my beer. "In our   20
country the son is next to the father. The dead chief's younger brother had become the great chief. He had also married his elder brother's widow only about a month after the funeral."

"He did well," the old man beamed and announced to the others, "I told you that if we knew more about Europeans, we would find they really were very like us. In our country also," he added to me, "the younger brother marries the elder brother's widow and becomes the father of his children. Now, if your uncle, who married your widowed mother, is your father's full brother, then he will be a real father to you. Did Hamlet's father and uncle have one mother?"

His question barely penetrated my mind; I was too upset and thrown too far off balance by having one of the most important elements of *Hamlet* knocked straight out of the picture. Rather uncertainly I said that I thought they had the same mother, but I wasn't sure—the story didn't say. The old man told me severely that these genealogical details made all the difference and that when I got home I must ask the elders about it. He shouted out the door to one of his younger wives to bring his goatskin bag.

Determined to save what I could of the mother motif, I took a deep breath and began again. "The son Hamlet was very sad because his mother had married again so quickly. There was no need for her to do so, and it is our custom for a widow not to go to her next husband until she has mourned for two years."

"Two years is too long," objected the wife, who had appeared with the old man's battered goatskin bag. "Who will hoe your farms for you while you have no husband?"

25 "Hamlet," I retorted without thinking, "was old enough to hoe his mother's farms himself. There was no need for her to remarry." No one looked convinced. I gave up. "His mother and the great chief told Hamlet not to be sad, for the great chief himself would be a father to Hamlet. Furthermore, Hamlet would be the next chief: Therefore he must stay to learn the things of a chief. Hamlet agreed to remain, and all the rest went off to drink beer."

While I paused, perplexed at how to render Hamlet's disgusted soliloquy to an audience convinced that Claudius and Gertrude had behaved in the best possible manner, one of the younger men asked me who had married the other wives of the dead chief.

"He had no other wives," I told him.

"But a chief must have many wives! How else can he brew beer and pre-pare food for all his guests?"

I said firmly that in our country even chiefs had only one wife, that they had servants to do their work, and that they paid them from tax money.

30 It was better, they returned, for a chief to have many wives and sons who would help him hoe his farms and feed his people; then everyone loved the chief who gave much and took nothing—taxes were a bad thing.

I agreed with the last comment, but for the rest fell back on their fa-vorite way of fobbing off my questions: "That is the way it is done, so that is how we do it."

I decided to skip the soliloquy. Even if Claudius was here thought quite right to marry his brother's widow, there remained the poison motif, and I knew they would disapprove of fratricide. More hopefully I resumed, "That night Hamlet kept watch with the three who had seen his dead father. The dead chief again appeared, and although the others were afraid, Hamlet fol-lowed his dead father off to one side. When they were alone, Hamlet's dead fa-ther spoke."

"Omens can't talk!" The old man was emphatic.

"Hamlet's dead father wasn't an omen. Seeing him might have been an omen, but he was not." My audience looked as confused as I sounded. "It was Hamlet's dead father. It was a thing we call a 'ghost.'" I had to use the English word, for unlike many of the neighboring tribes, these people didn't believe in the survival after death of any individuating part of the personality.

"What is a 'ghost?' An omen?"   *35*

"No, a 'ghost' is someone who is dead but who walks around and can talk, and people can hear him and see him but not touch him."

They objected. "One can touch zombis."

"No, no! It was not a dead body the witches had animated to sacrifice and eat. No one else made Hamlet's dead father walk. He did it himself."

"Dead men can't walk," protested my audience as one man.

I was quite willing to compromise. "A 'ghost' is the dead man's shadow."   *40*

But again they objected. "Dead men cast no shadows."

"They do in my country," I snapped.

The old man quelled the babble of disbelief that arose immediately and told me with that insincere, but courteous, agreement one extends to the fancies of the young, ignorant, and superstitious, "No doubt in your country the dead can also walk without being zombis." From the depths of his bag he produced a withered fragment of kola nut, bit off one end to show it wasn't poisoned, and handed me the rest as a peace offering.

"Anyhow," I resumed, "Hamlet's dead father said that his own brother, the one who became chief, had poisoned him. He wanted Hamlet to avenge him. Hamlet believed this in his heart, for he did not like his father's brother." I took another swallow of beer. "In the country of the great chief, living in the same homestead, for it was a very large one, was an important elder who was often with the chief to advise and help him. His name was Polonius. Hamlet was courting his daughter, but her father and her brother . . . [I cast hastily about for some tribal analogy] warned her not to let Hamlet visit her when she was alone on her farm, for he would be a great chief and so could not marry her."

"Why not?" asked the wife, who had settled down on the edge of the   *45*
old man's chair. He frowned at her for asking stupid questions and growled, "They lived in the same homestead."

"That was not the reason," I informed them. "Polonius was a stranger who lived in the homestead because he helped the chief, not because he was a relative."

"Then why couldn't Hamlet marry her?"

"He could have," I explained, "but Polonius didn't think he would. After all, Hamlet was a man of great importance who ought to marry a chief's daughter, for in his country a man could have only one wife. Polonius was afraid that if Hamlet made love to his daughter, then no one else would give a high price for her."

"That might be true," remarked one of the shrewder elders, "but a chief's son would give his mistress's father enough presents and patronage to more than make up the difference. Polonius sounds like a fool to me."

"Many people think he was," I agreed. "Meanwhile Polonius sent his son   *50*
Laertes off to Paris to learn the things of that country, for it was the homestead of a very great chief indeed. Because he was afraid that Laertes might waste a

lot of money on beer and women and gambling, or get into trouble by fighting, he sent one of his servants to Paris secretly, to spy out what Laertes was doing. One day Hamlet came upon Polonius's daughter Ophelia. He behaved so oddly he frightened her. Indeed"—I was fumbling for words to express the dubious quality of Hamlet's madness—"the chief and many others had also noticed that when Hamlet talked one could understand the words but not what they meant. Many people thought that he had become mad." My audience suddenly became much more attentive. "The great chief wanted to know what was wrong with Hamlet, so he sent for two of Hamlet's age mates [school friends would have taken long explanation] to talk to Hamlet and find out what troubled his heart. Hamlet, seeing that they had been bribed by the chief to betray him, told them nothing. Polonius, however, insisted that Hamlet was mad because he had been forbidden to see Ophelia, whom he loved."

"Why," inquired a bewildered voice, "should anyone bewitch Hamlet on that account?"

"Bewitch him?"

"Yes, only witchcraft can make anyone mad, unless, of course, one sees the beings that lurk in the forest."

I stopped being a storyteller, took out my notebook and demanded to be told more about these two causes of madness. Even while they spoke and I jotted notes, I tried to calculate the effect of this new factor on the plot. Hamlet had not been exposed to the beings that lurk in the forests. Only his relatives in the male line could bewitch him. Barring relatives not mentioned by Shakespeare, it had to be Claudius who was attempting to harm him. And, of course, it was.

55   For the moment I staved off questions by saying that the great chief also refused to believe that Hamlet was mad for the love of Ophelia and nothing else. "He was sure that something much more important was troubling Hamlet's heart."

"Now Hamlet's age mates," I continued, "had brought with them a famous storyteller. Hamlet decided to have this man tell the chief and all his homestead a story about a man who had poisoned his brother because he desired his brother's wife and wished to be chief himself. Hamlet was sure the great chief could not hear the story without making a sign if he was indeed guilty, and then he would discover whether his dead father had told him the truth."

The old man interrupted, with deep cunning, "Why should a father lie to his son?" he asked.

I hedged: "Hamlet wasn't sure that it really was his dead father." It was impossible to say anything, in that language, about devil-inspired visions.

"You mean," he said, "it actually was an omen, and he knew witches sometimes send false ones. Hamlet was a fool not to go to one skilled in reading omens and divining the truth in the first place. A man-who-sees-the-truth could have told him how his father died, if he really had been poisoned, and if there was witchcraft in it; then Hamlet could have called the elders to settle the matter."

The shrewd elder ventured to disagree. "Because his father's brother was a great chief, one who sees the truth might therefore have been afraid to tell it. I think it was for that reason that a friend of Hamlet's father—a witch and an elder—sent an omen so his friend's son would know. Was the omen true?"

"Yes," I said, abandoning ghosts and the devil; a witch-sent omen it would have to be. "It was true, for when the storyteller was telling his tale before all the homestead, the great chief rose in fear. Afraid that Hamlet knew his secret he planned to have him killed."

The stage set of the next bit presented some difficulties of translation. I began cautiously. "The great chief told Hamlet's mother to find out from her son what he knew. But because a woman's children are always first in her heart, he had the important elder Polonius hide behind a cloth that hung against the wall of Hamlet's mother's sleeping hut. Hamlet started to scold his mother for what she had done."

There was a shocked murmur from everyone. A man should never scold his mother.

"She called out in fear, and Polonius moved behind the cloth. Shouting, 'A rat!' Hamlet took his machete and slashed through the cloth." I paused for dramatic effect. "He had killed Polonius!"

The old men looked at each other in supreme disgust. "That Polonius truly was a fool and a man who knew nothing! What child would not know enough to shout, 'It's me!' "With a pang, I remembered that these people are ardent hunters, always armed with bow, arrow, and machete; at the first rustle in the grass an arrow is aimed and ready, and the hunter shouts "Game!" If no human voice answers immediately, the arrow speeds on its way. Like a good hunter Hamlet had shouted, "A rat!"

I rushed in to save Polonius's reputation. "Polonius did speak. Hamlet heard him. But he thought it was the chief and wished to kill him to avenge his father. He had meant to kill him earlier that evening. . . ." I broke down, unable to describe to these pagans, who had no belief in individual afterlife, the difference between dying at one's prayers and dying "unhousell'd, disappointed, unaneled."

This time I had shocked my audience seriously. "For a man to raise his hand against his father's brother and the one who has become his father—that is a terrible thing. The elders ought to let such a man be bewitched."

I nibbled at my kola nut in some perplexity, then pointed out that after all the man had killed Hamlet's father.

"No," pronounced the old man, speaking less to me than to the young men sitting behind the elders. "If your father's brother has killed your father, you must appeal to your father's age mates; *they* may avenge him. No man may use violence against his senior relatives." Another thought struck him. "But if his father's brother had indeed been wicked enough to bewitch Hamlet and make him mad that would be a good story indeed, for it would be his fault that Hamlet, being mad, no longer had any sense and thus was ready to kill his father's brother."

70   There was a murmur of applause. *Hamlet* was again a good story to them, but it no longer seemed quite the same story to me. As I thought over the coming complications of plot and motive, I lost courage and decided to skim over dangerous ground quickly.

"The great chief," I went on, "was not sorry that Hamlet had killed Polonius. It gave him a reason to send Hamlet away, with his two treacherous age mates, with letters to a chief of a far country, saying that Hamlet should be killed. But Hamlet changed the writing on their papers, so that the chief killed his age mates instead." I encountered a reproachful glare from one of the men whom I had told undetectable forgery was not merely immoral but beyond human skill. I looked the other way.

"Before Hamlet could return, Laertes came back for his father's funeral. The great chief told him Hamlet had killed Polonius. Laertes swore to kill Hamlet because of this, and because his sister Ophelia, hearing her father had been killed by the man she loved, went mad and drowned in the river."

"Have you already forgotten what we told you?" The old man was reproachful. "One cannot take vengeance on a madman; Hamlet killed Polonius in his madness. As for the girl, she not only went mad, she was drowned. Only witches can make people drown. Water itself can't hurt anything. It is merely something one drinks and bathes in."

I began to get cross. "If you don't like the story, I'll stop."

75   The old man made soothing noises and himself poured me some more beer. "You tell the story well, and we are listening. But it is clear that the elders of your country have never told you what the story really means. No, don't interrupt! We believe you when you say your marriage customs are different, or your clothes and weapons. But people are the same everywhere; therefore, there are always witches and it is we, the elders, who know how witches work. We told you it was the great chief who wished to kill Hamlet, and now your own words have proved us right. Who were Ophelia's male relatives?"

"There were only her father and her brother." Hamlet was clearly out of my hands.

"There must have been many more; this also you must ask of your elders when you get back to your country. From what you tell us, since Polonius was dead, it must have been Laertes who killed Ophelia, although I do not see the reason for it."

We had emptied one pot of beer, and the old men argued the point with slightly tipsy interest. Finally one of them demanded of me, "What did the servant of Polonius say on his return?"

With difficulty I recollected Reynaldo and his mission. "I don't think he did return before Polonius was killed."

"Listen," said the elder, "and I will tell you how it was and how your   *80*
story will go, then you may tell me if I am right. Polonius knew his son would
get into trouble, and so he did. He had many fines to pay for fighting, and
debts from gambling. But he had only two ways of getting money quickly.
One was to marry off his sister at once, but it is difficult to find a man who
will marry a woman desired by the son of a chief. For if the chief's heir commits adultery with your wife, what can you do? Only a fool calls a case against
a man who will someday be his judge. Therefore Laertes had to take the second way: He killed his sister by witchcraft, drowning her so he could secretly
sell her body to the witches."

I raised an objection. "They found her body and buried it. Indeed Laertes
jumped into the grave to see his sister once more—so, you see, the body was
truly there. Hamlet, who had just come back, jumped in after him."

"What did I tell you?" The elder appealed to the others. "Laertes was up
to no good with his sister's body. Hamlet prevented him, because the chief's
heir, like a chief, does not wish any other man to grow rich and powerful.
Laertes would be angry, because he would have killed his sister without benefit to himself. In our country he would try to kill Hamlet for that reason. Is
this not what happened?"

"More or less," I admitted. "When the great chief found Hamlet was still
alive, he encouraged Laertes to try to kill Hamlet and arranged a fight with
machetes between them. In the fight both the young men were wounded to
death. Hamlet's mother drank the poisoned beer that the chief meant for Hamlet in case he won the fight. When he saw his mother die of poison, Hamlet,
dying, managed to kill his father's brother with his machete."

"You see, I was right!" exclaimed the elder.

"That was a very good story," added the old man, "and you told it with   *85*
very few mistakes. There was just one more error, at the very end. The poison
Hamlet's mother drank was obviously meant for the survivor of the fight,
whichever it was. If Laertes had won, the great chief would have poisoned
him, for no one would know that he arranged Hamlet's death. Then, too, he
need not fear Laertes' witchcraft; it takes a strong heart to kill one's only sister
by witchcraft.

"Sometime," concluded the old man, gathering his ragged toga about
him, "you must tell us some more stories of your country. We, who are elders,
will instruct you in their true meaning, so that when you return to your own
land your elders will see that you have not been sitting in the bush, but among
those who know things and who have taught you wisdom."   *1966*

Photo Essay

THEN AND NOW

Images of Hamlet

The following sketches and photographs suggest the rich possibilities for the staging of William Shakespeare's *Hamlet*. While information on visual aspects of Elizabethan staging is extremely hard to come by, scholar C. Walter Hodges (b. 1909) has devoted much of his career to studying the plays of Shakespeare and in discovering rare primary source materials on the production of these plays. Based on his research, he has created a series of drawings suggesting how theaters and actors may have appeared in Shakespeare's lifetime. The drawing, included here (below), shows Hamlet in several scenes with his father's ghost. These images indicate the demeanor Hodges envisions for Hamlet, for his courtiers, and for the ghost. In addition, the sketches suggest probable ways that Elizabethan staging permitted the entrance, exit, and off-stage dialogue of the ghost.

This drawing by C. Walter Hodges shows the possibilities for the ghost scenes in *Hamlet* as presented on the Elizabethan stage.

Booth's Theatre Production, c. 1870, sketch by Thomas B. Glessing. Hamlet played by Edwin Booth. Courtesy the Walter Hampden–Edwin Booth Theatre Collection and Library, New York.

The second sketch (above), made by Thomas B. Glessing around 1870, shows another version of the act 1 ghost scene, this one from a production in which Edwin Booth (1833–1893), a renowned nineteenth-century Shakespearean actor, portrays Hamlet. Booth, who played this role hundreds of times both in the United States and in Britain, is said to have brought a quiet, understated, brooding quality to the role. In the minds of nineteenth-century theatergoers, he was so closely associated with the role that his interpretation of Hamlet overshadowed all others for many years. The photo of Booth (right) suggests the costuming and affect typical for his stage appearances as Hamlet.

Edwin Booth as Hamlet.

In the twentieth century, *Hamlet* has been staged in many ways, including some productions with contemporary, rather than Elizabethean, settings and costumes. For instance, in the photo below, a 1991 American Repertory Theatre production, the characters wear costumes reminiscent of the 1940's. This scene shows Hamlet and Laertes in modern fencing garb, and the court members wear contemporary clothing. The overall design of the set suggests a large, spacious modern room (with a dizzily tilted window) rather than an ancient castle. Another contemporary setting, present day New York City, creates yet another interpretation of Hamlet (page 379, top). In this 2000 Miramax film, Ethan Hawke, in the title role, wears a modern knit winter hat with the ties dangling as he walks beside Gertrude with Claudius in the background. (See page 380 for further discussion of this film.) Finally, Jamaican-born actor Adrian Lester (page 379, bottom) portrays Hamlet in the final act. This photograph is from the 2001 production co-produced by Peter Brook's International Center of Theatre Research and the Vienna *Festwochen*. This production, with an international cast, toured many theaters, bringing intriguing new possibilities to Shakespeare's Elizabethan play.

American Repertory Theatre production, 1991, directed by Ron Daniels. Hamlet (Mark Rylance) fences with Laertes (Derek Smith) as court members watch. Seated just in back of the crossed swords are Gertrude (Christine Estabrook) and Claudius (Mark Metcalf).

Miramax film production, 2000. Left to right: Hamlet (Ethan Hawke), Gertrude (Diane Venora), and Claudius (Kyle MacLachlan).

International Center of Theatre Research and the Vienna *Festwochen,* 2001 International Tour. Directed by Peter Brook. Hamlet played by Adrian Lester is seen here in the final act.

Considerations

1. Choose any two images of Hamlet and discuss their similarities and differences. In addition, consider the differences and similarities between these images and your own interpretation of the character of Hamlet as you were reading the play.

2. The first two visuals show Hamlet with his fathers' ghost. How do you think that the ghost might be presented in the other three productions represented? In what ways do you think modern views of the supernatural might affect the way directors would decide to present the ghost?

3. Consider the sixth image, showing Jamaican actor Adrian Lester portraying Hamlet. How might the Jamaican setting of this production of the play affect the way various audiences would respond? How might the interpretation of the play's conflicts be affected by this setting?

4. Look carefully at all the images of Hamlet. What does each image suggest about the relationship of the title character to the other characters? Consider details such as costume, posture, gestures, and the position of Hamlet in the scene in relation to the other characters.

5. If you were to direct the ghost scene for an audience of your fellow students, what choices would you make regarding staging, costumes, and, particularly, the appearance of the ghost? Explain your choices.

■■■ Film Connection: *Hamlet*

While film and other genres of literature share certain elements, such as word choice and plot development, there are some elements unique to film. Of course, it is obvious that a film, unlike a written work, offers visual images that can be seen with the eye, rather than imagined in the mind. These visual aspects contribute to the viewers' response, to their pleasure, and to their ability to analyze and evaluate the film. Consider, as an example, the Miramax production of *Hamlet* (2000), with Ethan Hawke playing the title role. (For a still shot from this film, see page 379.)

Color and Light   In the Miramax *Hamlet,* almost immediately the color blue becomes a motif. The initial shot of Hamlet shows him through a blue lens, suggesting his melancholy as well as the somber themes of the film. Throughout the film, blue suggests pensive or impulsive moves into the dangerous hidden world of the depressed or distraught mind. For instance, while Polonius, Claudius, and Gertrude plan how to use Ophelia as a pawn in their scheme to trap Hamlet, she stands on the edge of the swimming pool. The camera focuses on her, brightly dressed, then immediately cuts to a shot of her plunging into the water, submersed in blue tones and eerie light. The use of blue here suggests not only her distress at what is happening, but also foreshadows her tragic drowning.

> *Exercise* Identify and discuss another color that provides visual support to the themes, characterizations, and conflicts in the film. For example, consider the color red or the bright flashes of light that appear throughout this work.

Camera Angles and Movement Extreme close up images create powerful representations of the characters' emotions and conflicts. Consider, for instance, the stunning shot of Hamlet's bloodied eye near the end of the film. The blood, along with the widening look in the eye, suggests the theme of the death of innocence and brings home the violence and loss that are an integral part of this work.

> *Exercises*
> 1. Note other extreme close up shots, and choose one or two to discuss. How do the shots you chose contribute to the development of character, conflict, or theme?
> 2. Consider other camera angles and movement. For instance, identify scenes where the camera moves backward while the character or characters appear to walk directly at the viewer. Or note scenes where the camera seems to circle the character or characters. Then consider what these camera angles and movements contribute to the development of character, conflict, or theme.

Visual Symbols of Setting One of the most prominent symbolic elements of setting in this film is the window. Windows appear in almost every scene, often dominating the background. In many cases, the images of characters are reflected in the light that seems to hover beyond the windows. Viewers then have an uncanny sense of characters and actions, who are shadowed by fainter, often distorted reflections of themselves. These window scenes underscore one of the film's key themes: the challenge in distinguishing between appearance and reality, between what is false and what is true. Contributing further to this theme, the windows, in some cases, seem to form barriers between the interior and exterior settings, perhaps suggesting the way the characters are trapped within the confines of the world they have created, unable to reach or define their true selves.

Exercise   Consider some of the other symbolic elements of setting. For example, the video equipment that is both watched and watching or the photographs that function as props in several significant scenes. Watch for patterns in the use of these symbols. What do these patterns of symbols suggest about the development of characters, themes, and conflicts?

Essays

LANGSTON HUGHES (1902–1967)
Salvation

Born in Joplin, Missouri, Langston Hughes graduated from Lincoln University in 1929 and gained an outstanding literary reputation as one of the key figures of the Harlem Renaissance of the 1920s, a period that saw a rich proliferation of art, music, and literature that celebrated African-American heritage and experience in the United States. In addition to writing poetry, Hughes worked as a reporter for the Baltimore Afro-American *and for the Chicago* Defender. *He wrote more than twenty-five plays and, in addition, created jazz scores to accompany many of his poems and dramas. "Salvation," an autobiographical essay, first appeared in his collection* The Big Sea *(1940).*

I was saved from sin when I was going on thirteen. But not really saved. It happened like this. There was a big revival at my Auntie Reed's church. Every night for weeks there had been much preaching, singing, praying, and shouting, and some very hardened sinners had been brought to Christ, and the membership of the church had grown by leaps and bounds. Then just before the revival ended, they held a special meeting for children, "to bring the young lambs to the fold." My aunt spoke of it for days ahead. That night I was escorted to the front row and placed on the mourners' bench with all the other young sinners, who had not yet been brought to Jesus.

My aunt told me that when you were saved you saw a light, and something happened to you inside! And Jesus came into your life! And God was with you from then on! She said you could see and hear and feel Jesus in your soul. I believed her. I had heard a great many old people say the same thing and it seemed to me they ought to know. So I sat there calmly in the hot, crowded church, waiting for Jesus to come to me.

The preacher preached a wonderful rhythmical sermon, all moans and shouts and lonely cries and dire pictures of hell, and then he sang a song about the ninety and nine safe in the fold, but one little lamb was left out in the cold. Then he said: "Won't you come? Won't you come to Jesus? Young lambs, won't you come?" And he held out his arms to all us young sinners there on the mourners' bench. And the little girls cried. And some of them jumped up and went to Jesus right away. But most of us just sat there.

A great many old people came and knelt around us and prayed, old women with jet-black faces and braided hair, old men with work-gnarled hands. And the church sang a song about the lower lights are burning, some poor sinners to be saved. And the whole building rocked with prayer and song.

Still I kept waiting to *see* Jesus.   5

Finally all the young people had gone to the altar and were saved, but one boy and me. He was a rounder's son named Westley. Westley and I were surrounded by sisters and deacons praying. It was very hot in the church, and getting late now. Finally Westley said to me in a whisper: "God damn! I'm tired o' sitting here. Let's get up and be saved." So he got up and was saved.

Then I was left all alone on the mourners' bench. My aunt came and knelt at my knees and cried, while prayers and song swirled all around me in the little church. The whole congregation prayed for me alone, in a mighty wail of moans and voices. And I kept waiting serenely for Jesus, waiting, waiting—but he didn't come. I wanted to see him, but nothing happened to me. Nothing! I wanted something to happen to me, but nothing happened.

I heard the songs and the minister saying: "Why don't you come? My dear child, why don't you come to Jesus? Jesus is waiting for you. He wants you. Why don't you come? Sister Reed, what is this child's name?"

"Langston," my aunt sobbed.

"Langston, why don't you come? Why don't you come and be saved?   10 Oh, Lamb of God! Why don't you come?"

Now it was really getting late. I began to be ashamed of myself, holding everything up so long. I began to wonder what God thought about Westley, who certainly hadn't seen Jesus either, but who was now sitting proudly on the platform, swinging his knickerbockered legs and grinning down at me, surrounded by deacons and old women on their knees praying. God had not struck Westley dead for taking his name in vain or for lying in the temple. So I decided that maybe to save further trouble, I'd better lie, too, and say that Jesus had come, and get up and be saved.

So I got up.

Suddenly the whole room broke into a sea of shouting, as they saw me rise. Waves of rejoicing swept the place. Women leaped in the air. My aunt threw her arms around me. The minister took me by the hand and led me to the platform.

More Resources on
Langston Hughes

In *ARIEL*
- Brief biography of Hughes
- Complete texts of additional Hughes poems such as "I, Too" and "Dream Deferred"
- Analysis of figurative writing in Hughes's poetry
- Bibliography of scholarly works on Hughes

In the Online Learning Center for *Responding to Literature*
- Brief biography of Hughes
- List of major works by Hughes
- Web links to more resources on Hughes
- Additional questions for experiencing and interpreting Hughes's writing

When things quieted down, in a hushed silence, punctuated by a few ecstatic "Amens," all the new young lambs were blessed in the name of God. Then joyous singing filled the room.

15   That night, for the last time in my life but one—for I was a big boy twelve years old—I cried. I cried, in bed alone, and couldn't stop. I buried my head under the quilts, but my aunt heard me. She woke up and told my uncle I was crying because the Holy Ghost had come into my life, and because I had seen Jesus. But I was really crying because I couldn't bear to tell her that I had lied, that I had deceived everybody in the church, that I hadn't seen Jesus, and that now I didn't believe there was a Jesus any more, since he didn't come to help me.   *1940*

CONSIDERATIONS

1. Compare the narrator to Westley. Keep in mind the narrator's hopes, fears, and expectations and, using evidence provided by the words and actions of the two boys, speculate on how they might contrast with Westley's.
2. What is your definition of "salvation"? How many possible meanings of "salvation" are stated or implied in Hughes's memoir?

3. Evaluate Auntie Reed's motives and expectations. What does she want for the narrator? What does she want for herself?

4. Why does the narrator cry? Consider the reasons he states and speculate on other reasons (and on the implications of those reasons).

5. This essay describes a moment when a young man comes to doubt a strongly held belief. Notice that he recalls in detail the sights, sounds, and feelings of that moment. Think about a strongly held belief that you have come to question and describe an incident that led you to doubt that belief. Use Hughes's essay as an example; recreate for your readers the sights, sounds, and feelings of the moment you describe.

MAYA ANGELOU (1928–   )

Graduation in Stamps

Originally named Marguerite Johnson, Maya Angelou was born in St. Louis in 1928. From age three to age eight, Angelou and her brother grew up in Stamps, Arkansas, under the watchful, loving eye of their grandmother, whom they called "Momma." Unfortunately, her grandmother's boundless energy and affection could not protect Angelou from the pain of poverty, segregated schools, and violence at the hands of both whites and blacks. At age eight, she went to stay with her mother. At her mother's home, she was raped by her mother's lover; subsequently, Angelou refused to talk for more than a year. Shortly after the rape, she returned to her grandmother's home, where she began to read voraciously, memorizing extensive passages from writers varying from Shakespeare to the poets of the Harlem Renaissance. The cadences and rhythms of her early love affair with poetry weave throughout her works. In 1972 her book of poems Just Give Me a Cool Drink of Water 'fore I Die *was nominated for a Pulitzer Prize. In 1993, as Poet Laureate of the United States, she wrote and read a poem for the inauguration of President Clinton.*

A champion of the narrative as complex, serious art, Angelou sees her work as "stemming from the slave narrative and developing into a new American literary form." This selection, a chapter from Angelou's highly praised autobiography, I Know Why the Caged Bird Sings *(1969), demonstrates her strong and hopeful vision of the African-American experience.*

The children in Stamps trembled visibly with anticipation. Some adults were excited too, but to be certain the whole young population had come down with graduation epidemic. Large classes were graduating from both the grammar school and the high school. Even those who were years removed from their own day of glorious release were anxious to help with preparations as a kind of dry run. The junior students who were moving into the vacating classes' chairs were tradition-bound to show their talents for leadership and management. They strutted through the school and around the campus exerting pressure on the lower grades. Their authority was so new that occasionally if they pressed a little too hard it had to be overlooked. After all, next term was coming, and it never hurt a sixth grader to have a play sister in the eighth grade, or a tenth-year student to be able to call a twelfth grader Bubba. So all was endured in a spirit of shared understanding. But the graduating classes themselves were the nobility. Like travelers with exotic destinations on their minds, the graduates were remarkably forgetful. They came to school without their books, or tablets or even pencils. Volunteers fell over themselves to secure replacements for the missing equipment. When accepted, the willing workers might or might not be thanked, and it was of no importance to the pre-graduation rites. Even teachers were respectful of the now quiet and aging seniors, and tended to speak to them, if not as equals, as beings only slightly lower than themselves. After tests were returned and grades given, the student body, which acted like an extended family, knew who did well, who excelled, and what piteous ones had failed.

Unlike the white high school, Lafayette County Training School distinguished itself by having neither lawn, nor hedges, nor tennis court, nor climbing ivy. Its two buildings (main classrooms, the grade school and home economics) were set on a dirt hill with no fence to limit either its boundaries or those of bordering farms. There was a large expanse to the left of the school which was used alternately as a baseball diamond or a basketball court. Rusty hoops on the swaying poles represented the permanent recreational equipment, although bats and balls could be borrowed from the P.E. teacher if the borrower was qualified and if the diamond wasn't occupied.

Over this rocky area relieved by a few shady tall persimmon trees the graduating class walked. The girls often held hands and no longer bothered to speak to the lower students. There was a sadness about them, as if this old world was not their home and they were bound for higher ground. The boys, on the other hand, had become more friendly, more outgoing. A decided change from the closed attitude they projected while studying for finals. Now they seemed not ready to give up the old school, the familiar paths and classrooms. Only a small percentage would be continuing on to college—one of the South's A & M (agricultural and mechanical) schools, which trained Negro youths to be carpenters, farmers, handymen, masons, maids, cooks and baby nurses. Their future rode heavily on their shoulders, and blinded them to the collective joy that had pervaded the lives of the boys and girls in the grammar school graduating class.

Parents who could afford it had ordered new shoes and ready-made clothes for themselves from Sears and Roebuck or Montgomery Ward. They also engaged the best seamstresses to make the floating graduating dresses and to cut down secondhand pants which would be pressed to a military slickness for the important event.

Oh, it was important, all right. Whitefolks would attend the ceremony,   5 and two or three would speak of God and home, and the Southern way of life, and Mrs. Parsons, the principal's wife, would play the graduation march while the lower-grade graduates paraded down the aisles and took their seats below the platform. The high school seniors would wait in empty classrooms to make their dramatic entrance.

In the Store I was the person of the moment. The birthday girl. The center. Bailey had graduated the year before, although to do so he had had to forfeit all pleasures to make up for his time lost in Baton Rouge.

My class was wearing butter-yellow piqué dresses, and Momma launched out on mine. She smocked the yoke into tiny crisscrossing puckers, then shirred the rest of the bodice. Her dark fingers ducked in and out of the lemony cloth as she embroidered raised daisies around the hem. Before she considered herself finished she had added a crocheted cuff on the puff sleeves, and a pointy crocheted collar.

I was going to be lovely. A walking model of all the various styles of fine hand sewing and it didn't worry me that I was only twelve years old and merely graduating from the eighth grade. Besides, many teachers in Arkansas Negro schools had only that diploma and were licensed to impart wisdom.

The days had become longer and more noticeable. The faded beige of former times had been replaced with strong and sure colors. I began to see my classmates' clothes, their skin tones, and the dust that waved off pussy willows. Clouds that lazed across the sky were objects of great concern to me. Their shiftier shapes might have held a message that in my new happiness and with a little bit of time I'd soon decipher. During that period I looked at the arch of heaven so religiously my neck kept a steady ache. I had taken to smiling more often, and my jaws hurt from the unaccustomed activity. Between the two physical sore spots, I suppose I could have been uncomfortable, but that was not the case. As a member of the winning team (the graduating class of 1940) I had outdistanced unpleasant sensations by miles. I was headed for the freedom of open fields.

Youth and social approval allied themselves with me and we trammeled   10 memories of slights and insults. The wind of our swift passage remodeled my features. Lost tears were pounded to mud and then to dust. Years of withdrawal were brushed aside and left behind, as hanging ropes of parasitic moss.

My work alone had awarded me a top place and I was going to be one of the first called in the graduating ceremonies. On the classroom blackboard, as well as on the bulletin board in the auditorium, there were blue stars and white stars and red stars. No absences, no tardinesses, and my academic work was among the best of the year. I could say the preamble to the Constitution even faster than Bailey. We timed ourselves often: "WethepeopleoftheUnited-Statesinordertoformamoreperfectunion . . ." I had memorized the Presidents of the United States from Washington to Roosevelt in chronological as well as alphabetical order.

My hair pleased me too. Gradually the black mass had lengthened and thickened, so that it kept at last to its braided pattern, and I didn't have to yank my scalp off when I tried to comb it.

Louise and I had rehearsed the exercises until we tired out ourselves. Henry Reed was class valedictorian. He was a small, very black boy with hooded eyes, a long, broad nose and an oddly shaped head. I had admired him for years because each term he and I vied for the best grades in our class. Most often he bested me, but instead of being disappointed, I was pleased that we shared top places between us. Like many Southern black children, he lived with his grandmother, who was as strict as Momma and as kind as she knew how to be. He was courteous, respectful and soft-spoken to elders, but on the playground he chose to play the roughest games. I admired him. Anyone, I reckoned, sufficiently afraid or sufficiently dull could be polite. But to be able to operate at a top level with both adults and children was admirable.

His valedictory speech was entitled "To Be or Not to Be." The rigid tenth-grade teacher had helped him write it. He'd been working on the dramatic stresses for months.

15   The weeks until graduation were filled with heady activities. A group of small children were to be presented in a play about buttercups and daisies and bunny rabbits. They could be heard throughout the building practicing their hops and their little songs that sounded like silver bells. The older girls (non-graduates, of course) were assigned the task of making refreshments for the night's festivities. A tangy scent of ginger, cinnamon, nutmeg and chocolate wafted around the home economics building as the budding cooks made samples for themselves and their teachers.

In every corner of the workshop, axes and saws split fresh timber as the woodshop boys made sets and stage scenery. Only the graduates were left out of the general bustle. We were free to sit in the library at the back of the building or look in quite detachedly, naturally, on the measures being taken for our event.

Even the minister preached on graduation the Sunday before. His subject was, "Let your light so shine that men will see your good works and praise your Father, Who is in Heaven." Although the sermon was purported to be addressed to us, he used the occasion to speak to backsliders, gamblers and general ne'er-do-wells. But since he had called our names at the beginning of the service we were mollified.

Among Negroes the tradition was to give presents to children going only from one grade to another. How much more important this was when the person was graduating at the top of the class. Uncle Willie and Momma had sent away for a Mickey Mouse watch like Bailey's. Louise gave me four embroidered handkerchiefs. (I gave her three crocheted doilies.) Mrs. Sneed, the minister's wife, made me an underskirt to wear for graduation, and nearly every customer gave me a nickel or maybe even a dime with the instruction "Keep on moving to higher ground," or some such encouragement.

Amazingly the great day finally dawned and I was out of bed before I knew it. I threw open the back door to see it more clearly, but Momma said, "Sister, come away from that door and put your robe on."

I hoped the memory of that morning would never leave me. Sunlight   20
was itself still young, and the day had none of the insistence maturity would bring it in a few hours. In my robe and barefoot in the backyard, under cover of going to see about my new beans, I gave myself up to the gentle warmth and thanked God that no matter what evil I had done in my life He had allowed me to live to see this day. Somewhere in my fatalism I had expected to die, accidentally, and never have the chance to walk up the stairs in the auditorium and gracefully receive my hard-earned diploma. Out of God's merciful bosom I had won reprieve.

Bailey came out in his robe and gave me a box wrapped in Christmas paper. He said he had saved his money for months to pay for it. It felt like a box of chocolates, but I knew Bailey wouldn't save money to buy candy when we had all we could want under our noses.

He was as proud of the gift as I. It was a soft-leather-bound copy of a collection of poems by Edgar Allan Poe,° or, as Bailey and I called him, "Eap." I turned to "Annabel Lee" and we walked up and down the garden rows, the cool dirt between our toes, reciting the beautifully sad lines.

Momma made a Sunday breakfast although it was only Friday. After we finished the blessing, I opened my eyes to find the watch on my plate. It was a dream of a day. Everything went smoothly and to my credit. I didn't have to be reminded or scolded for anything. Near evening I was too jittery to attend to chores, so Bailey volunteered to do all before his bath.

Days before, we had made a sign for the Store, and as we turned out the lights Momma hung the cardboard over the doorknob. It read clearly: CLOSED: GRADUATION.

My dress fitted perfectly and everyone said that I looked like a sunbeam in   25
it. On the hill, going toward the school, Bailey walked behind with Uncle Willie, who muttered, "Go on, Ju." He wanted him to walk ahead with us because it

Edgar Allan Poe (1809–1849): American editor, critic, poet, and short-story writer. A brilliant, haunted man, Poe created poems and stories that combined the beautiful with the grotesque, the real with the fantastic.

embarrassed him to have to walk so slowly. Bailey said he'd let the ladies walk together, and the men would bring up the rear. We all laughed, nicely.

Little children dashed by out of the dark like fireflies. Their crepe paper dresses and butterfly wings were not made for running and we heard more than one rip, dryly, and the regretful "uh uh" that followed.

The school blazed without gaiety. The windows seemed cold and unfriendly from the lower hill. A sense of ill-fated timing crept over me, and if Momma hadn't reached for my hand I would have drifted back to Bailey and Uncle Willie, and possibly beyond. She made a few slow jokes about my feet getting cold, and tugged me along to the now-strange building.

Around the front steps, assurance came back. There were my fellow "greats," the graduating class. Hair brushed back, legs oiled, new dresses and pressed pleats, fresh pocket handkerchiefs and little handbags, all home-sewn. Oh, we were up to snuff, all right. I joined my comrades and didn't even see my family go in to find seats in the crowded auditorium.

The school band struck up a march and all classes filed in as had been rehearsed. We stood in front of our seats, as assigned, and on a signal from the choir director, we sat. No sooner had this been accomplished than the band started to play the national anthem. We rose again and sang the song, after which we recited the pledge of allegiance. We remained standing for a brief minute before the choir director and the principal signaled to us, rather desperately I thought, to take our seats. The command was so unusual that our carefully rehearsed and smooth-running machine was thrown off. For a full minute we fumbled for our chairs and bumped into each other awkwardly. Habits change or solidify under pressure, so in our state of nervous tension we had been ready to follow our usual assembly pattern: the American national anthem, then the pledge of allegiance, then the song every Black person I knew called the Negro National Anthem. All done in the same key, with the same passion and most often standing on the same foot.

30   Finding my seat at last, I was overcome with a presentiment of worse things to come. Something unrehearsed, unplanned, was going to happen, and we were going to be made to look bad. I distinctly remember being explicit in the choice of pronoun. It was "we," the graduating class, the unit, that concerned me then.

The principal welcomed "parents and friends" and asked the Baptist minister to lead us in prayer. His invocation was brief and punchy, and for a second I thought we were getting back on the high road to right action. When the principal came back to the dais, however, his voice had changed. Sounds always affected me profoundly and the principal's voice was one of my favorites. During assembly it melted and lowed weakly into the audience. It had not been in my plan to listen to him, but my curiosity was piqued and I straightened up to give him my attention.

He was talking about Booker T. Washington,° our "late great leader," who said we can be as close as the fingers on the hand, etc. . . . Then he said a few vague things about friendship and the friendship of kindly people to those less fortunate than themselves. With that his voice nearly faded, thin, away. Like a river diminishing to a stream and then to a trickle. But he cleared his throat and said, "Our speaker tonight, who is also our friend, came from Texarkana to deliver the commencement address, but due to the irregularity of the train schedule, he's going to, as they say, 'speak and run.'" He said that we understood and wanted the man to know that we were most grateful for the time he was able to give us and then something about how we were willing always to adjust to another's program; and without more ado—"I give you Mr. Edward Donleavy."

Not one but two white men came through the door offstage. The shorter one walked to the speaker's platform, and the tall one moved over to the center seat and sat down. But that was our principal's seat, and already occupied. The dislodged gentleman bounced around for a long breath or two before the Baptist minister gave him his chair, then with more dignity than the situation deserved, the minister walked off the stage.

Donleavy looked at the audience once (on reflection, I'm sure that he wanted only to reassure himself that we were really there), adjusted his glasses and began to read from a sheaf of papers.

He was glad "to be here and to see the work going on just as it was in   35 the other schools."

At the first "Amen" from the audience I willed the offender to immediate death by choking on the word. But Amens and Yes, sir's began to fall around the room like rain through a ragged umbrella.

He told us of the wonderful changes we children in Stamps had in store. The Central School (naturally, the white school was Central) had already been granted improvements that would be in use in the fall. A well-known artist was coming from Little Rock to teach art to them. They were going to have the newest microscopes and chemistry equipment for their laboratory. Mr. Donleavy didn't leave us long in the dark over who made these improvements available to Central High. Nor were we to be ignored in the general betterment scheme he had in mind.

He said that he had pointed out to people at a very high level that one of the first-line football tacklers at Arkansas Agricultural and Mechanical College

---

Booker T. Washington (1856–1915): African-American educator who founded Tuskegee Institute, a post–high school institution of learning for black students who were not, at that time, permitted to most colleges and universities. He was criticized by many African-American leaders because he argued that social equality could not be attained—and should not be a goal for African Americans—until they had, on their own, attained economic independence.

had graduated from good old Lafayette County Training School. Here fewer Amen's were heard. Those few that did break through lay dully in the air with the heaviness of habit.

He went on to praise us. He went on to say how he had bragged that "one of the best basketball players at Fisk sank his first ball right here at Lafayette County Training School."

40   The white kids were going to have a chance to become Galileos° and Madame Curies° and Edisons° and Gauguins,° and our boys (the girls weren't even in on it) would try to be Jesse Owenses° and Joe Louises.°

Owens and the Brown Bomber were great heroes in our world, but what school official in the white-goddom of Little Rock had the right to decide that those two men must be our only heroes? Who decided that for Henry Reed to become a scientist he had to work like George Washington Carver,° as a bootblack, to buy a lousy microscope? Bailey was obviously always going to be too small to be an athlete, so which concrete angel glued to what county seat had decided that if my brother wanted to become a lawyer he had to first pay penance for his skin by picking cotton and hoeing corn and studying correspondence books at night for twenty years?

The man's dead words fell like bricks around the auditorium and too many settled in my belly. Constrained by hard-learned manners I couldn't look behind me, but to my left and right the proud graduating class of 1940 had dropped their heads. Every girl in my row had found something new to do with her handkerchief. Some folded the tiny squares into love knots, some into triangles, but most were wadding them, then pressing them flat on their yellow laps.

On the dais, the ancient tragedy was being replayed. Professor Parsons sat, a sculptor's reject, rigid. His large, heavy body seemed devoid of will or willingness, and his eyes said he was no longer with us. The other teachers ex-

Galileo (1564–1642): Italian astronomer and physicist. He discovered many physical laws, constructed the first telescope, and confirmed the theory that the earth moves around the sun. *Madame Curie* (1867–1934): Polish-born French physicist. She won the Nobel Prize in 1911 for the discovery of metallic radium. *Thomas Alva Edison* (1847–1931): One of the most productive American inventors. Among his significant inventions were the record player, the motion picture, the incandescent lamp, and a system for the distribution of electricity. *Paul Gauguin* (1848–1903): French painter, associated with the Impressionists, noted especially for rejecting traditional naturalism and, instead, using nature as an inspiration for abstract symbols and figures. *Jesse Owens* (1913–1981): African-American track star who won four gold medals at the 1936 Olympics, which were held in Berlin. Owens made a mockery of Hitler's contention that "Aryan" athletes were superior to all others. *Joe Louis* (1914–1981): African-American boxer. Holder of the heavyweight title, Louis was known as the Brown Bomber. *George Washington Carver* (1864–1943): African-American agriculture chemist. Born a slave, he later taught at Tuskegee Institute, where he carried out research that led to crop diversification in the South. He is particularly credited with discovering new uses for crops such as peanuts and soybeans.

amined the flag (which was draped stage right) or their notes, or the windows which opened on our now-famous playing diamond.

Graduation, the hush-hush magic time of frills and gifts and congratulations and diplomas, was finished for me before my name was called. The accomplishment was nothing. The meticulous maps, drawn in three colors of ink, learning and spelling decasyllabic words, memorizing the whole of *The Rape of Lucrece*°—it was for nothing. Donleavy had exposed us.

We were maids and farmers, handymen and washerwomen, and anything   45
higher that we aspired to was farcical and presumptuous.

Then I wished that Gabriel Prosser° and Nat Turner° had killed all whitefolks in their beds and that Abraham Lincoln had been assassinated before the signing of the Emancipation Proclamation, and that Harriet Tubman° had been killed by that blow on her head and Christopher Columbus had drowned in the *Santa Maria*.

It was awful to be Negro and have no control over my life. It was brutal to be young and already trained to sit quietly and listen to charges brought against my color with no chance of defense. We should all be dead. I thought I should like to see us all dead, one on top of the other. A pyramid of flesh with the whitefolks on the bottom, as the broad base, then the Indians with their silly tomahawks and tepees and wigwams and treaties, the Negroes with their mops and recipes and cotton sacks and spirituals sticking out of their mouths. The Dutch children should all stumble in their wooden shoes and break their necks. The French should choke to death on the Louisiana Purchase (1803) while silkworms ate all the Chinese with their stupid pigtails. As a species, we were an abomination. All of us.

Donleavy was running for election, and assured our parents that if he won we could count on having the only colored paved playing field in that part of Arkansas. Also—he never looked up to acknowledge the grunts of acceptance—also, we were bound to get some new equipment for the home economics building and the workshop.

He finished, and since there was no need to give any more than the most perfunctory thank-you's, he nodded to the men on the stage, and the tall white man who was never introduced joined him at the door. They left with the attitude that now they were off to something really important. (The graduation ceremonies at Lafayette County Training School had been a mere preliminary.)

The Rape of Lucrece: A narrative poem, 1855 lines long, written by William Shakespeare. *Gabriel Prosser, Nat Turner:* Leaders of slave rebellions. In 1800, Prosser recruited several hundred slaves to attack Richmond. Before they could attack, they were betrayed, and the leaders of the rebellion were captured and executed. In 1831, Turner led a group of slaves who eventually killed 57 white men, women, and children as a protest against slavery. *Harriet Tubman* (1820–1913): An African-American abolitionist who escaped from slavery in 1849 and worked with the Underground Railroad, leading more than 300 slaves north to freedom.

50   The ugliness they left was palpable. An uninvited guest who wouldn't leave. The choir was summoned and sang a modern arrangement of "Onward, Christian Soldiers," with new words pertaining to graduates seeking their place in the world. But it didn't work. Elouise, the daughter of the Baptist minister, recited "Invictus," and I could have cried at the impertinence of "I am the master of my fate, I am the captain of my soul."

My name had lost its ring of familiarity and I had to be nudged to go and receive my diploma. All my preparations had fled. I neither marched up to the stage like a conquering Amazon, nor did I look in the audience for Bailey's nod of approval. Marguerite Johnson, I heard the name again, my honors were read, there were noises in the audience of appreciation, and I took my place on the stage as rehearsed.

I thought about colors I hated: ecru, puce, lavender, beige and black.

There was shuffling and rustling around me, then Henry Reed was giving his valedictory address, "To Be or Not to Be." Hadn't he heard the whitefolks? We couldn't *be,* so the question was a waste of time. Henry's voice came clear and strong. I feared to look at him. Hadn't he got the message? There was no "nobler in the mind" for Negroes because the world didn't think we had minds, and they let us know it. "Outrageous fortune"? Now, that was a joke. When the ceremony was over I had to tell Henry Reed some things. That is, if I still cared. Not "rub," Henry, "erase." "Ah, there's the erase." Us.

Henry had been a good student in elocution. His voice rose on tides of promise and fell on waves of warnings. The English teacher had helped him to create a sermon winging through Hamlet's soliloquy. To be a man, a doer, a builder, a leader, or to be a tool, an unfunny joke, a crusher of funky toadstools. I marveled that Henry could go through the speech as if we had a choice.

55   I had been listening and silently rebutting each sentence with my eyes closed; then there was a hush, which in an audience warns that something unplanned is happening. I looked up and saw Henry Reed, the conservative, the proper, the A student, turn his back to the audience and turn to us (the proud graduating class of 1940) and sing, nearly speaking,

> Lift ev'ry voice and sing
> Till earth and heaven ring
> Ring with the harmonies of Liberty . . .★

It was the poem written by James Weldon Johnson. It was the music composed by J. Rosamond Johnson. It was the Negro national anthem. Out of habit we were singing it.

★"Lift Ev'ry Voice and Sing"—words by James Weldon Johnson and music by J. Rosamond Johnson. Copyright by Edward B. Marks Music Corporation. Used by permission.

Our mothers and fathers stood in the dark hall and joined the hymn of encouragement. A kindergarten teacher led the small children onto the stage and the buttercups and daisies and bunny rabbits marked time and tried to follow:

> Stony the road we trod
> Bitter the chastening rod
> Felt in the days when hope, unborn, had died.
> Yet with a steady beat
> Have not our weary feet
> Come to the place for which our fathers sighed?

Every child I knew had learned that song with his ABC's and along with "Jesus Loves Me This I Know." But I personally had never heard it before. Never heard the words, despite the thousands of times I had sung them. Never thought they had anything to do with me.

On the other hand, the words of Patrick Henry° had made such an impression on me that I had been able to stretch myself tall and trembling and say, "I know not what course others may take, but as for me, give me liberty or give me death."

And now I heard, really for the first time:

> We have come over a way that with tears has been watered,
> We have come, treading our path through the blood of the slaughtered.

While echoes of the song shivered in the air, Henry Reed bowed his   60
head, said "Thank you," and returned to his place in the line. The tears that slipped down many faces were not wiped away in shame.

We were on top again. As always, again. We survived. The depths had been icy and dark, but now a bright sun spoke to our souls. I was no longer simply a member of the proud graduating class of 1940; I was a proud member of the wonderful beautiful Negro race.   *1969*

CONSIDERATIONS

1. Although the word "graduation" appears in the title, the first half of the work focuses on preparation for the event. What effect does Maya Angelou (pen name of Marguerite Johnson) create by describing in such detail the

---

Patrick Henry (1726–1799): A leader of the American Revolution who was admired for his skills as a public speaker. The rallying cry "Give me liberty or give me death" is attributed to him.

community's involvement in and anticipation of the ceremony? What—if anything—would be lost if the first half of the essay were abbreviated or omitted?

2. Describe the attitude of the white officials who attend the graduation. Provide details from the essay to explain your analysis of their actions, words, and responses.

3. Henry Reed's speech is titled "To Be or Not to Be." Using a dictionary of quotations, identify the allusion made by the title as well as by Angelou's comments on the title. Speculate on the irony suggested by the title and by Reed's speech as contrasted to Mr. Donleavy's speech.

4. Describe Marguerite Johnson's response when she is called to receive her diploma. How does the reality compare with the way she had imagined the moment? How can you explain this change and its implications?

5. Maya Angelou describes an incident related to her formal education that taught her lessons different from those she learned from books. Think of your own school experiences, and describe an incident—apart from regular subject-matter study—that taught you something you consider valuable. As you write your essay, consider the strategies Angelou uses. For instance, notice her description of setting, her arrangement of events in chronological order, and her direct quotation of conversations and speeches.

CONNECTIONS: INNOCENCE AND EXPERIENCE

1. In the works "Araby," "The Bass, the River, and Sheila Mant," "When I was one-and-twenty," and "Oranges," young love is depicted in many ways. Compare and comment on the various ways that innocence moves to experience in love in any of these works. What is the impact on the character or speaker?

2. Choose one of the stories or essays, and trace the journey that a character experiences from childhood to adulthood. Explain the effects on the person moving from innocence to experience.

3. Parents or other adults play an important role in the passage from innocence to experience. Choose one of the following works to show the positive and negative effects on the development of the main character or speaker: "And the Soul Shall Dance," "Oranges," *Hamlet,* "Graduation in Stamps," "Salvation," "Ex-Basketball Player," or "Araby."

4. Cultural influences (socioeconomic, professional, gender, ethnic, religious) affect the passage from innocence to experience. Choose one of the works from this section that compares or contrasts to your own perspective on the role of one of these influences. For example, you might want to compare/contrast your growing up in a particular place to that of Maya Angelou in "Graduation in Stamps."

5. Differences are often seen between the ways that males and females deal with maturing and moving from innocence to experience in life. Choose one work relating to males and one relating to females, and compare/contrast some of these ways. For example, you might choose to compare "Araby" and "And the Soul Shall Dance" or "Spring and Fall" with "Mid-Term Break" to point out the similarities or differences between males and females in the actions and reactions of the characters.

SUGGESTIONS FOR EXTENDED CONNECTIONS AMONG CHAPTERS

1. Consider the connection between family relationships and the journey from innocence to experience. How do parents or other adults in these readings affect the childhood of the other central characters?

"Sonny's Blues"	412
"Who's Irish?"	724
"The Man Who Was Almost a Man"	402
"I Stand Here Ironing"	692
"A Rose for Emily"	1170
"How Far She Went"	717
Soul Gone Home	792
Wit	1085

2. In the following works, an extraordinary or unusual circumstance forces the central characters to learn something profound about themselves and the world around them—regardless of their age. In other words, the awareness that comes from the external experience changes them internally. Discuss this concept in any of the following works:

"Sonny's Blues"	412
Soul Gone Home	792
"The Management of Grief"	948
"The Shawl"	929
"How Far She Went"	717
"The Open Boat"	820
"The Deer at Providencia"	890
"The Death of a Moth"	895
Wit	1085

3. Consider how an encounter with death or the realization that one is vulnerable changes the people in the following pieces. Consider, too, what you learned about yourself through these literary encounters:

"Cathedral"	437
Soul Gone Home	792

Riders to the Sea	874
"The Management of Grief"	948
Wit	1085
"How to Watch Your Brother Die"	1199
"The Lost Boy"	1198
"A Crime of Compassion"	1230

4. Consider the forces of prejudice and/or stereotypical roles in the following pieces, and analyze the root of these forces and how they affect people:

"Who's Irish"	724
"The Man Who Was Almost a Man"	402
"Learning to Read and Write"	520
On Tidy Endings	1203
"To Any Would–Be Terrorists"	1018
"Master Harold" . . . and the Boys	474
Soul Gone Home	792

WEB CONNECTIONS

1. As many of the selections in this chapter have shown, the problems besetting children and adolescents often connect to the social factors and issues of the times in which they live. The issues may range from prejudice to violence to war—serious concerns that directly affect children's view of themselves and their purpose in a world that is ever-changing and full of fear. From the Web site *The Literature and Culture of the American 1950s* (http://www.writing.upenn.edu/~afilreis/50s/home.html), students can link to articles on a range of cultural issues that significantly impacted the lives of Americans in the 1950s. The site provides access to discussions of feminism, beat culture, folk music, McCarthyism, modern–day witch hunts, prejudice and discrimination, movies of teenage rebellion, and popular television programs.

2. Loss and human reaction to loss is a common literary theme. Loss is also usually a part of the adolescent experience, as young men and women make the transition from childhood to adulthood. What is lost during this transition? What is gained by those who move from a world of (relative) innocence to a world of experience? Psychologists have been grappling with these essential questions since life stage theories were first developed. To understand the major causes and effects of the adolescent conflicts that are central themes in many of this chapter's selections, consider consulting the authorities, such as Piaget, Erikson, Kohlberg, and Gilligan, on the moral, cognitive, and emotional development of children. Useful links to explana-

tions and critiques of the theories of these major psychologists can be found in Chapter 2 ("The Science of Adolescent Development") of the online edition of John W. Santrock's *Adolescence* (10th edition, McGraw-Hill) at: http://www.mhhe.com/santrocka10. Upon entering the site, click on "Student Edition" under "Online Learning Center." Choose "Chapter 2" from the drop-down menu, and click on "Web Links."

Consider the words these children are reciting. How might these word relate to their roots, identity, and culture?

7

Roots, Identity, and Culture

The selections in this chapter all look at some aspect of the various cultures that make up our world, both past and present. Culture may be defined as the ideas, customs, values, skills, and arts of a specific group of people. Most of us belong not solely to one cultural group but to several. For instance, our age places us in a culture such as childhood, youth, or middle age. We may be assigned to "Generation X" or labeled "baby boomers," and these phrases may be associated with certain images or values for those who hear or read them. In addition, we are all either male or female, and the ways various societies treat gender differences traditionally have created cultural distinctions between men and women. Another group we belong to relates to the country of our birth or to the country where our ancestors were born.

As you prepare to read the selections in this chapter, consider the following possibilities:

1. List as many cultural groups as possible of which you see yourself as a member. These groups may relate to age, ethnic background, religious affiliation, political beliefs, or current work status.
2. After completing your list, choose one or two cultural groups and describe the ideas, customs, values, skills, and/or arts you believe to be typical of that group.
3. Describe an example of something you read or heard in another class that gave you a view of a cultural perspective other than your own. What new ideas or possibilities were suggested by this perspective?
4. Describe an incident from a television program or a film you have seen that showed you a cultural perspective different from your own. What new ideas or possibilities were suggested by this perspective?
5. Describe an event from your work that showed you a cultural perspective different from your own. What new ideas or possibilities were suggested by this perspective?

Fiction

RICHARD WRIGHT (1908–1960)
The Man Who Was Almost a Man

The son of a sharecropper, Richard Wright was born on a farm outside Natchez, Mississippi. When Wright was six, his father abandoned the family. When he was eight, his mother became too ill to support him and his brother, and they were put in an orphanage for a while. After some relatives took them in, Wright was able to return to school and graduate as valedictorian of his high school. Soon he moved to Chicago, where he joined the Communist Party and began writing with the encouragement of some of its members. In 1937 he moved to New York, and a year later his first collection, Uncle Tom's Children, *was published. His first novel and his best-known work,* Native Son, *was published in 1940. It is the story of Bigger Thomas, a poor and angry young African American who is hired to work for a wealthy white family and accidentally kills their daughter. In 1945 he published* Black Boy, *an autobiography of his younger years. Disillusioned with racism and anti-Communist sentiments in the United States, he moved to France in 1946, one of a number of black intellectuals and artists to do so during that era. In Europe, he wrote several more books, both fiction and nonfiction, but none was as successful as the books he had written in the United States. His fiction usually employed a straightforward, realistic style, but he sometimes experimented with literary techniques, such as the dialect in "The Man Who Was Almost a Man."*

Dave struck out across the fields looking homeward through paling light. Whut's the use talking wid em niggers in the field? Anyhow, his mother was putting supper on the table. Them niggers can't understan nothing. One of these days he was going to get a gun and practice shooting, then they couldn't talk to him as though he were a little boy. He slowed, looking at the ground. Shucks, Ah ain scareda them even ef they are biggern me! Aw, Ah know whut Ahma do. Ahm going by ol Joe's sto n git that Sears Roebuck catlog n look at them guns. Mebbe Ma will lemme buy one when she gits mah pay from ol man Hawkins. Ahma beg her t gimme some money. Ahm ol ernough to hava gun. Ahm seventeen. Almost a man. He strode, feeling his long loose-jointed limbs. Shucks, a man oughta hava little gun aftah he done worked hard all day.

He came in sight of Joe's store. A yellow lantern glowed on the front porch. He mounted steps and went through the screen door, hearing it bang behind him. There was a strong smell of coal oil and mackerel fish. He felt very confident until he saw fat Joe walk in through the rear door, then his courage began to ooze.

"Howdy, Dave! Wutcha want?"

"How yuh, Mistah Joe? Aw, Ah don wanna buy nothing. Ah jus wanted t see ef yuhd lemme look at tha catlog erwhile."

"Sure! You wanna see it here?"   5

"Nawsuh. Ah wans t take it home wid me. Ah'll bring it back termorrow when Ah come in from the fiels."

"You plannin on buying something?"

"Yessuh."

"Your ma lettin you have your own money now?"

"Shucks. Mistah Joe, Ahm gittin t be a man like anybody else!"   10

Joe laughed and wiped his greasy white face with a red bandanna.

"Whut you plannin on buyin?"

Dave looked at the floor, scratched his head, scratched his thigh, and smiled. Then he looked up shyly.

"Ah'll tell yuh, Mistah Joe, ef yuh promise yuh won't tell."

"I promise."   15

"Waal, Ahma buy a gun."

"A gun? Whut you want with a gun?"

"Ah wanna keep it."

"You ain't nothing but a boy. You don't need a gun."

"Aw, lemme have the catlog, Mistah Joe. Ah'll bring it back."   20

Joe walked through the rear door. Dave was elated. He looked around at barrels of sugar and flour. He heard Joe coming back. He craned his neck to see if he were bringing the book. Yeah, he's got it. Gawddog, he's got it!

"Here, but be sure you bring it back. It's the only one I got."

"Sho, Mistah Joe."

"Say, if you wanna buy a gun, why don't you buy one from me? I gotta gun to sell."

"Will it shoot?"   25

"Sure it'll shoot."

"Whut kind is it?"

"Oh, it's kinda old . . . a left-handed Wheeler. A pistol. A big one."

"Is it got bullets in it?"

"It's loaded."   30

"Kin Ah see it?"

"Where's your money?"

"What yuh wan fer it?"

"I'll let you have it for two dollars."

"Just two dollahs! Shucks, Ah could buy tha when Ah git mah pay."   35

"I'll have it here when you want it."

"Awright, suh. Ah be in fer it."

He went through the door, hearing it slam again behind him. Ahma git some money from Ma n buy me a gun! Only two dollahs! He tucked the thick catalogue under his arm and hurried.

"Where yuh been, boy?" His mother held a steaming dish of black-eyed peas.

40   "Aw, Ma, Ah just stopped down the road t talk wid the boys."

"Yuh know bettah t keep suppah waitin."

He sat down, resting the catalogue on the edge of the table.

"Yuh git up from there and git to the well n wash yoself! Ah ain feedin no hogs in mah house!"

She grabbed his shoulder and pushed him. He stumbled out of the room, then came back to get the catalogue.

45   "Whut this?"

"Aw, Ma, it's jusa catlog."

"Who yuh git it from?"

"From Joe, down at the sto."

"Waal, thas good. We kin use it in the outhouse."

50   "Naw, Ma." He grabbed for it. "Gimme ma catlog, Ma."

She held onto it and glared at him.

"Quit hollerin at me! Whut's wrong wid yuh? Yuh crazy?"

"But, Ma, please. It ain mine! It's Joe's! He tol me t bring it back tim termorrow."

She gave up the book. He stumbled down the back steps, hugging the thick book under his arm. When he had splashed water on his face and hands, he groped back to the kitchen and fumbled in a corner for the towel. He bumped into a chair; it clattered to the floor. The catalogue sprawled at his feet. When he had dried his eyes he snatched up the book and held it again under his arm. His mother stood watching him.

55   "Now, ef yuh gonna act a fool over that ol book, Ah'll take it n burn it up."

"Naw, Ma, please."

"Waal, set down n be still!"

He sat down and drew the oil lamp close. He thumbed page after page, unaware of the food his mother set on the table. His father came in. Then his small brother.

"Whutcha got there, Dave?" his father asked.

60   "Jusa catlog," he answered, not looking up.

"Yeah, here they is!" His eyes glowed at blue-and-black revolvers. He glanced up, feeling sudden guilt. His father was watching him. He eased the book under the table and rested it on his knees. After the blessing was asked, he ate. He scooped up peas and swallowed fat meat without chewing. Butter-milk helped to wash it down. He did not want to mention money before his father. He would do much better by cornering his mother when she was alone! He looked at his father uneasily out of the edge of his eye.

"Boy, how come yuh don quit foolin wid tha book n eat yo suppah?"

"Yessuh."

"How you n ol man Hawkins gitten erlong?"

"Suh?"   ₆₅

"Can't yuh hear! Why don yuh lissen? Ah ast yu how wuz yuh n ol man Hawkins gittin erlong?"

"Oh, swell, Pa. Ah plows mo lan than anybody over there."

"Waal, yuh oughta keep yo mind on whut yuh doin."

"Yessuh."

He poured his plate full of molasses and sopped it up slowly with a chunk   ₇₀ of cornbread. When his father and brother had left the kitchen, he still sat and looked again at the guns in the catalogue, longing to muster courage enough to present his case to his mother. Lawd, ef Ah only had tha pretty one! He could almost feel the slickness of the weapon with his fingers. If he had a gun like that he would polish it and keep it shining so it would never rust. N Ah'd keep it loaded, by Gawd!

"Ma?" His voice was hesitant.

"Hunh?"

"Ol man Hawkins give yuh mah money yit?"

"Yeah, but ain no usa yuh thinking bout throwin nona it erway. Ahm keepin tha money sos yuh kin have cloes t go to school this winter."

He rose and went to her side with the open catalogue in his palms. She   ₇₅ was washing dishes, her head bent low over a pan. Shyly he raised the book. When he spoke, his voice was husky, faint.

"Ma, Gawd knows Ah wans one of these."

"One of whut?" she asked, not raising her eyes.

"One of these," he said again, not daring even to point. She glanced up at the page, then at him with wide eyes.

"Nigger, is yuh gone plumb crazy?"

"Aw, Ma—"   ₈₀

"Git outta here! Don yuh talk t me bout no gun! Yuh a fool!"

"Ma, Ah kin buy one fer two dollahs."

"Not ef Ah knows it, yuh ain!"

"But yuh promised me one—"

"Ah don care whut Ah promised! Yuh ain nothing but a boy yit!"   ₈₅

"Ma, if yuh lemme buy one ah'll *never* ast yuh fer nothing no mo."

"Ah tol yuh t git outta here! Yuh ain gonna toucha penny of tha money fer no gun! Thas how come Ah has Mistah Hawkins t pay yo wages to me, cause Ah knows yuh ain got no sense."

"But, Ma, we needa gun. Pa ain got no gun. We needa gun in the house. Yuh kin never tell whut might happen."

"Now don yuh try to maka fool outta me, boy! Ef we did hava gun, yuh wouldn't have it!"

He laid the catalogue down and slipped his arm around her waist.   ₉₀

"Aw, Ma, Ah done worked hard alla summer n ain ast yuh fer nothing, is Ah, now?"

"Thas whut yuh spose t do!"

"But Ma, Ah wans a gun. Yuh kin lemme have two dollahs outta mah money. Please, Ma. I kin give it to Pa . . . Please, Ma! Ah loves yuh, Ma."

When she spoke her voice came soft and low.

95 "Whut yu wan wida gun, Dave? Yuh don need no gun. Yuh'll git in trouble. N ef yo pa just thought Ah let yuh have money t buy a gun he'd hava fit."

"Ah'll hide it, Ma. It ain but two dollahs."

"Lawd, chil, whut's wrong wid yuh?"

"Ain nothin wrong, Ma. Ahm almos a man now. Ah wans a gun."

"Who gonna sell yuh a gun?"

100 "Ol Joe at the sto."

"N it don cos but two dollahs?"

"Thas all, Ma. Jus two dollahs. Please, Ma."

She was stacking the plates away; her hands moved slowly, reflectively. Dave kept an anxious silence. Finally, she turned to him.

"Ah'll let yuh git tha gun ef yuh promise me one thing."

105 "Whut's tha, Ma?"

"Yuh bring it straight back t me, yuh hear? It be fer Pa."

"Yessum! Lemme go now, Ma."

She stooped, turned slightly to one side, raised the hem of her dress, rolled down the top of her stocking, and came up with a slender wad of bills.

"Here," she said. "Lawd knows yuh don need no gun. But yer pa does. Yuh bring it right back t me, yuh hear? Ahma put it up. Now ef yuh don, Ahma have yuh pa lick yuh so hard yuh won fergit it."

110 "Yessum."

He took the money, ran down the steps, and across the yard.

"Dave! Yuuuuuh Daaaaave!"

He heard, but he was not going to stop now. "Naw, Lawd!"

The first movement he made the following morning was to reach under his pillow for the gun. In the gray light of dawn he held it loosely, feeling a sense of power. Could kill a man with a gun like this. Kill anybody, black or white. And if he were holding his gun in his hand, nobody could run over him; they would have to respect him. It was a big gun, with a long barrel and a heavy handle. He raised and lowered it in his hand, marveling at its weight.

115 He had not come straight home with it as his mother had asked; instead he had stayed out in the fields, holding the weapon in his hand, aiming it now and then at some imaginary foe. But he had not fired it; he had been afraid that his father might hear. Also he was not sure he knew how to fire it.

To avoid surrendering the pistol he had not come into the house until he knew that they were all asleep. When his mother had tiptoed to his bedside late that night and demanded the gun, he had first played possum; then he had told her that the gun was hidden outdoors, that he would bring it to her in the morning. Now he lay turning it slowly in his hands. He broke it, took out the cartridges, felt them, and then put them back.

He slid out of bed, got a long strip of old flannel from a trunk, wrapped the gun in it, and tied it to his naked thigh while it was still loaded. He did not go in to breakfast. Even though it was not yet daylight, he started for Jim Hawkins' plantation. Just as the sun was rising he reached the barns where the mules and plows were kept.

"Hey! That you, Dave?"

He turned. Jim Hawkins stood eying him suspiciously.

"What're yuh doing here so early?"   *120*

"Ah didn't know Ah wuz gittin up so early, Mistah Hawkins. Ah wuz fixin t hitch up ol Jenny n take her t the fiels."

"Good. Since you're so early, how about plowing that stretch down by the woods?"

"Suits me, Mistah Hawkins."

"O.K. Go to it!"

He hitched Jenny to a plow and started across the fields. Hot dog! This   *125* was just what he wanted. If he could get down by the woods, he could shoot his gun and nobody would hear. He walked behind the plow, hearing the traces creaking, feeling the gun tied tight to his thigh.

When he reached the woods, he plowed two whole rows before he decided to take out the gun. Finally, he stopped, looked in all directions, then untied the gun and held it in his hand. He turned to the mule and smiled.

"Know whut this is, Jenny? Naw, yuh wouldn know! Yuhs jusa ol mule! Anyhow, this is a gun, n it kin shoot, by Gawd!"

He held the gun at arm's length. Whut t hell, Ahma shoot this thing! He looked at Jenny again.

"Lissen here, Jenny! When Ah pull this ol trigger, Ah don wan yuh t run n acka fool now!"

Jenny stood with head down, her short ears pricked straight. Dave walked   *130* off about twenty feet, held the gun far out from him at arm's length, and turned his head. Hell, he told himself, Ah ain afraid. The gun felt loose in his fingers; he waved it wildly for a moment. Then he shut his eyes and tightened his forefinger. Bloom! A report half deafened him and he thought his right hand was torn from his arm. He heard Jenny whinnying and galloping over the field, and he found himself on his knees, squeezing his fingers hard between his legs. His hand was numb; he jammed it into his mouth, trying to warm it, trying to stop the pain. The gun lay at his feet. He did not quite know what had happened. He stood up and stared at the gun as though it were a living thing. He gritted his teeth and kicked the gun. Yuh almos broke mah arm! He turned to look for Jenny; she was far over the fields, tossing her head and kicking wildly.

"Hol on there, ol mule!"

When he caught up with her she stood trembling, walling her big white eyes at him. The plow was far away; the traces had broken. Then Dave stopped short, looking, not believing. Jenny was bleeding. Her left side was red and wet with blood. He went closer. Lawd, have mercy! Wondah did Ah shoot this mule? He grabbed for Jenny's mane. She flinched, snorted, whirled, tossing her head.

"Hol on now! Hol on."

Then he saw the hole in Jenny's side, right between the ribs. It was round, wet, red. A crimson stream streaked down the front leg, flowing fast. Good Gawd! Ah wuzn't shootin at tha mule. He felt panic. He knew he had to stop that blood, or Jenny would bleed to death. He had never seen so much blood in all his life. He chased the mule for a half a mile, trying to catch her. Finally she stopped, breathing hard, stumpy tail half arched. He caught her mane and led her back to where the plough and gun lay. Then he stooped and grabbed handfuls of damp black earth and tried to plug the bullet hole, Jenny shuddered, whinnied, and broke from him.

135   "Hol on! Hol on now!"

He tried to plug it again, but blood came anyhow. His fingers were hot and sticky. He rubbed dirt into his palms, trying to dry them. Then again he attempted to plug the bullet hole, but Jenny shied away, kicking her heels high. He stood helpless. He had to do something. He ran at Jenny; she dodged him. He watched a red stream of blood flow down Jenny's leg and form a bright pool at her feet.

"Jenny . . . Jenny," he called weakly.

His lips trembled. She's bleeding t death! He looked in the direction of home, wanting to go back, wanting to get help. But he saw the pistol lying in the damp black clay. He had a queer feeling that if he only did something, this would not be; Jenny would not be there bleeding to death.

When he went to her this time, she did not move. She stood with sleepy, dreamy eyes; and when he touched her she gave a low-pitched whinny and knelt to the ground, her front knees slopping in blood.

140   "Jenny . . . Jenny . . ." he whispered.

For a long time she held her neck erect; then her head sank, slowly. Her ribs swelled with a mighty heave and she went over.

Dave's stomach felt empty, very empty. He picked up the gun and held it gingerly between his thumb and forefinger. He buried it at the foot of a tree. He took a stick and tried to cover the pool of blood with dirt—but what was the use? There was Jenny lying with her mouth open and her eyes walled and glassy. He could not tell Jim Hawkins he had shot his mule. But he had to tell something. Yeah, Ah'll tell em Jenny started gittin wil n fell on the joint of the plow. . . . But that would hardly happen to a mule. He walked across the field slowly, head down.

It was sunset. Two of Jim Hawkins' men were over near the edge of the woods digging a hole in which to bury Jenny. Dave was surrounded by a knot of people, all of whom were looking down at the dead mule.

"I don't see how in the world it happened," said Jim Hawkins for the tenth time.

The crowd parted and Dave's mother, father, and small brother pushed into the center.   *145*

"Where Dave?" his mother called.

"There he is," said Jim Hawkins.

His mother grabbed him.

"Whut happened, Dave? Whut yuh done?"

"Nothin."   *150*

"C mon, boy, talk," his father said.

Dave took a deep breath and told the story he knew nobody believed.

"Waal," he drawled. "Ah brung ol Jenny down here sos Ah could do mah plowin. Ah plowed bout two rows, just like yuh see." He stopped and pointed at the long rows of upturned earth. "Then somethin musta been wrong wid ol Jenny. She wouldn ack right a-tall. She started snortin n kickin her heels. Ah tried t hol her, but she pulled erway, rearin n goin in. Then when the point of the plow was stickin up in the air, she swung erroun n twisted herself back on it . . . She stuck herself n started t bleed. N fo Ah could do anything, she wuz dead."

"Did you ever hear of anything like that in all your life?" asked Jim Hawkins.

There were white and black standing in the crowd. They murmured.   *155* Dave's mother came close to him and looked hard into his face. "Tell the truth, Dave," she said.

"Looks like a bullet hole to me," said one man.

"Dave, whut yuh do wid the gun?" his mother asked.

The crowd surged in, looking at him. He jammed his hands into his pockets, shook his head slowly from left to right, and backed away. His eyes were wide and painful.

"Did he hava gun?" asked Jim Hawkins.

"By Gawd, Ah tol yuh tha wuz a gun wound," said a man, slapping his   *160* thigh. His father caught his shoulders and shook him till his teeth rattled.

"Tell whut happened, yuh rascal! Tell whut . . ."

Dave looked at Jenny's stiff legs and began to cry.

"Whut yuh do wid tha gun?" his mother asked.

"Whut wuz he doin wida gun?" his father asked.

"Come on and tell the truth," said Hawkins. "Ain't nobody going to   *165* hurt you . . ."

His mother crowded close to him.

"Did yuh shoot tha mule, Dave?"

Dave cried, seeing blurred white and black faces.

"Ahh ddinn gggo tt sshooot hher . . . Ah ssswear ffo Gawd Ah ddin. . . . Ah wuz a-tryin t sssee ef the old gggun would sshoot—"

170   "Where yuh git the gun from?" his father asked.

"Ah got it from Joe, at the sto."

"Where yuh git the money?"

"Ma give it t me."

"He kept worryin me, Bob. Ah had t. Ah tol im t bring the gun right back t me . . . It was fer yuh, the gun."

175   "But how yuh happen to shoot that mule?" asked Jim Hawkins.

"Ah wuzn shootin at the mule, Mistah Hawkins. The gun jumped when Ah pulled the trigger . . . N fo Ah knowed anythin Jenny was there a-bleedin."

Somebody in the crowd laughed. Jim Hawkins walked close to Dave and looked into his face.

"Well, looks like you have bought you a mule, Dave."

"Ah sear fo Gawd, Ah didn go t kill the mule, Mistah Hawkins!"

180   "But you killed her!"

All the crowd was laughing now. They stood on tiptoe and poked heads over one another's shoulders.

"Well, boy, looks like yuh done bought a dead mule! Hahaha!"

"Ain tha ershame."

"Hohohohoho."

185   Dave stood, head down, twisting his feet in the dirt.

"Well, you needn't worry about it, Bob," said Jim Hawkins to Dave's father. "Just let the boy keep on working and pay me two dollars a month."

"Whut yuh wan fer yo mule, Mistah Hawkins?"

Jim Hawkins screwed up his eyes.

"Fifty dollars."

190   "Whut yuh do wid tha gun?" Dave's father demanded.

Dave said nothing.

"Yuh wan me t take a tree n beat yuh till yuh talk!"

"Nawsuh!"

"Whut yuh do wid it?"

195   "Ah throwed it erway."

"Where?"

"Ah . . . Ah throwed it in the creek."

"Waal, c mon home. N firs thing in the mawnin git to tha creek n fin tha gun."

"Yessuh."

200   "Whut yuh pay fer it?"

"Two dollahs."

"Take tha gun n git yo money back n carry it t Mistah Hawkins, yuh hear? N don fergit Ahma lam you black bottom good fer this! Now march yosef on home, suh!"

Dave turned and walked slowly. He heard people laughing. Dave glared, his eyes welling with tears. Hot anger bubbled in him. Then he swallowed and stumbled on.

That night Dave did not sleep. He was glad that he had gotten out of killing the mule so easily, but he was hurt. Something hot seemed to turn over inside him each time he remembered how they had laughed. He tossed on his bed, feeling his hard pillow. N Pa says he's gonna beat me . . . He remembered other beatings, and his back quivered. Naw, naw, Ah sho don wan im t beat me tha way no mo. Dam em all! Nobody ever gave him anything. All he did was work. They treat me like a mule, n then they beat me. He gritted his teeth. N Ma had t toll on me.

Well, if he had to, he would take old man Hawkins that two dollars. But   *205* that meant selling the gun. And he wanted to keep that gun. Fifty dollars for a dead mule.

He turned over, thinking how he fired the gun. He had an itch to fire it again. Ef other men kin shoota gun, by Gawd, Ah kin! He was still, listening. Mebbe they all sleepin now. The house was still. He heard the soft breathing of his brother. Yes, now! He would go down and get that gun and see if he could fire it! He eased out of bed and slipped into overalls.

The moon was bright. He ran almost all the way to the edge of the woods. He stumbled over the ground, looking for the spot where he had buried the gun. Yeah, here it is. Like a hungry dog scratching for a bone, he pawed it up. He puffed his black cheeks and blew dirt from the trigger and barrel. He broke it and found four cartridges unshot. He looked around; the fields were filled with silence and moonlight. He clutched the gun stiff and hard in his fingers. But, as soon as he wanted to pull the trigger, he shut his eyes and turned his head. Naw, Ah can't shoot wid mah eyes closed n mah head turned. With effort he held his eyes open; then he squeezed. *Blooooom!* He was stiff, not breathing. The gun was still in his hands. Dammit, he'd done it! He fired again. *Blooooom!* He smiled. *Blooooom! Blooooom! Click, click.* There! It was empty. If anybody could shoot a gun, he could. He put the gun into his hip pocket and started across the fields.

When he reached the top of a ridge he stood straight and proud in the moonlight, looking at Jim Hawkins' big white house, feeling the gun sagging in his pocket. Lawd, ef Ah had just one mo bullet Ah'd taka shot at tha house. Ah'd like t scare ol man Hawkins jusa little . . . Jusa enough t let im know Dave Saunders is a man.

To his left the road curved, running to the tracks of the Illinois Central. He jerked his head, listening. From far off came a faint *hoooof-hoooof; hoooof-hoooof; hoooof-hoooof.* . . . He stood rigid. Two dollahs a mont. Les see now . . . Tha means it'll take bout two years. Shucks! Ah'll be dam!

He started down the road, toward the tracks. Yeah, here she comes! He   *210* stood beside the track and held himself stiffly. Here she comes, erroun the ben . . . C mon, yuh slow poke! C mon! He had his hand on his gun; something quivered in his stomach. Then the train thundered past, the gray and brown box cars rumbling and clinking. He gripped the gun tightly; then he jerked his hand out of his pocket. Ah betcha Bill wouldn't do it! Ah betcha . . . The cars

slid past, steel grinding upon steel. Ahm ridin yuh ternight, so hep me Gawd!
He was hot all over. He hesitated just a moment; then he grabbed, pulled atop
of a car, and lay flat. He felt his pocket; the gun was still there. Ahead the long
rails were glinting in the moonlight, stretching away, away to somewhere,
somewhere where he could be a man . . .   *1940*

CONSIDERATIONS

1. If you could pick one word to describe the pervasive feeling within the
   culture in which Dave and his family live, what would it be? Explain.
2. Reread this story and find all of the references to darkness and light, black
   and white. In what ways do these opposing forces help explain Dave's actions?
3. Within Dave's own family, violence is an acceptable, perhaps even common
   way, of dealing with one's feelings. Examine the words and actions of Dave,
   his mother, and his father that reflect violence.
4. Wright writes that Dave's hurt was not of any physical nature nor was it related to guilt he might have had over killing the mule. Rather, he was hurt
   "each time he remembered how they had laughed" at him. Within this culture, who or what is most responsible for the humiliation that fosters Dave's
   feelings of anger and violence?
5. In the end, Dave is on the train with an empty gun, running away to some-
   place where "he could be a man." How might his definition of being a man,
   and thus his own identity, now differ from the opening paragraph when he
   says he is "almost a man"? What caused this change?

JAMES BALDWIN (1924–1987)

Sonny's Blues

> *Born to Emma Berdis, a single mother, James Baldwin became part of a large
> and complex family when his mother later married David Baldwin, with whom
> she subsequently had eight more children. James Baldwin often acted as a father
> figure to the younger children, and his fiction shows sensitivity to the complex
> relationships between parents and their sons and daughters. "Sonny's Blues,"
> published as part of his collection* Going to Meet the Man *(1965), demon-
> strates his concern with the theme of families, roots, and identity.*

I read about it in the paper, in the subway, on my way to work. I read it,
and I couldn't believe it, and I read it again. Then perhaps I just stared at it, at

the newsprint spelling out his name, spelling out the story. I stared at it in the swinging lights of the subway car, and in the faces and bodies of the people, and in my own face, trapped in the darkness which roared outside.

It was not to be believed and I kept telling myself that, as I walked from the subway station to the high school. And at the same time I couldn't doubt it. I was scared, scared for Sonny. He became real to me again. A great block of ice got settled in my belly and kept melting there slowly all day long, while I taught my classes algebra. It was a special kind of ice. It kept melting, sending trickles of ice water all up and down my veins, but it never got less. Sometimes it hardened and seemed to expand until I felt my guts were going to come spilling out or that I was going to choke or scream. This would always be at a moment when I was remembering some specific thing Sonny had once said or done.

When he was about as old as the boys in my class his face had been bright and open, there was a lot of copper in it; and he'd had wonderfully direct brown eyes, and great gentleness and privacy. I wondered what he looked like now. He had been picked up, the evening before, in a raid on an apartment downtown, for peddling and using heroin.

I couldn't believe it: but what I mean by that is that I couldn't find any room for it anywhere inside me. I had kept it outside me for a long time. I hadn't wanted to know. I had had suspicions, but I didn't name them, I kept putting them away. I told myself that Sonny was wild, but he wasn't crazy. And he'd always been a good boy, he hadn't ever turned hard or evil or disrespectful, the way kids can, so quick, so quick, especially in Harlem. I didn't want to believe that I'd ever see my brother going down, coming to nothing, all that light in his face gone out, in the condition I'd already seen so many others. Yet it had happened and here I was, talking about algebra to a lot of boys who might, every one of them for all I knew, be popping off needles every time they went to the head. Maybe it did more for them than algebra could.

I was sure that the first time Sonny had ever had horse, he couldn't have   5
been much older than these boys were now. These boys, now, were living as we'd been living then, they were growing up with a rush and their heads bumped abruptly against the low ceiling of their actual possibilities. They were filled with rage. All they really knew were two darknesses, the darkness of their lives, which was now closing in on them, and the darkness of the movies, which had blinded them to that other darkness, and in which they now, vindictively, dreamed, at once more together than they were at any other time, and more alone.

When the last bell rang, the last class ended, I let out my breath. It seemed I'd been holding it for all that time. My clothes were wet—I may have looked as though I'd been sitting in a steam bath, all dressed up, all afternoon. I sat alone in the classroom a long time. I listened to the boys outside, downstairs, shouting and cursing and laughing. Their laughter struck me for perhaps the first time. It was not the joyous laughter which—God knows why—one associates with children. It was mocking and insular, its intent was to denigrate. It was disenchanted, and in this, also, lay the authority of their curses. Perhaps I was listening to them because I was thinking about my brother and in them I heard my brother. And myself.

One boy was whistling a tune, at once very complicated and very simple, it seemed to be pouring out of him as though he were a bird, and it sounded very cool and moving through all that harsh, bright air, only just holding its own through all those other sounds.

I stood up and walked over to the window and looked down into the courtyard. It was the beginning of the spring and the sap was rising in the boys. A teacher passed through them every now and again, quickly, as though he or she couldn't wait to get out of that courtyard, to get those boys out of their sight and off their minds. I started collecting my stuff. I thought I'd better get home and talk to Isabel.

The courtyard was almost deserted by the time I got downstairs. I saw this boy standing in the shadow of a doorway, looking just like Sonny. I almost called his name. Then I saw that it wasn't Sonny, but somebody we used to know, a boy from around our block. He'd been Sonny's friend. He'd never been mine, having been too young for me, and, anyway, I'd never liked him. And now, even though he was a grown-up man, he still hung around that block, still spent hours on the street corners, was always high and raggy. I used to run into him from time to time and he'd often work around to asking me for a quarter or fifty cents. He always had some real good excuse, too, and I always gave it to him, I don't know why.

10   But now, abruptly, I hated him. I couldn't stand the way he looked at me, partly like a dog, partly like a cunning child. I wanted to ask him what the hell he was doing in the school courtyard.

He sort of shuffled over to me, and he said, "I see you got the papers. So you already know about it."

"You mean about Sonny? Yes, I already know about it. How come they didn't get you?"

He grinned. It made him repulsive and it also brought to mind what he'd looked like as a kid. "I wasn't there. I stay away from them people."

"Good for you." I offered him a cigarette and I watched him through the smoke. "You come all the way down here just to tell me about Sonny?"

15   "That's right." He was sort of shaking his head and his eyes looked strange, as though they were about to cross. The bright sun deadened his damp dark brown skin and it made his eyes look yellow and showed up the dirt in his kinked hair. He smelled funky. I moved a little away from him and I said, "Well, thanks. But I already know about it and I got to get home."

"I'll walk you a little ways," he said. We started walking. There were a couple of kids still loitering in the courtyard and one of them said goodnight to me and looked strangely at the boy beside me.

"What're you going to do?" he asked me. "I mean, about Sonny?"

"Look. I haven't seen Sonny for over a year, I'm not sure I'm going to do anything. Anyway, what the hell *can* I do?"

"That's right," he said quickly, "ain't nothing you can do. Can't much help old Sonny no more, I guess."

It was what I was thinking and so it seemed to me he had no right to say it.   *20*

"I'm surprised at Sonny, though," he went on—he had a funny way of talking, he looked straight ahead as though he were talking to himself—"I thought Sonny was a smart boy, I thought he was too smart to get hung."

"I guess he thought so too," I said sharply, "and that's how he got hung. And how about you? You're pretty goddamn smart, I bet."

Then he looked directly at me, just for a minute. "I ain't smart," he said. "If I was smart, I'd have reached for a pistol a long time ago."

"Look. Don't tell *me* your sad story, if it was up to me, I'd give you one." Then I felt guilty—guilty, probably, for never having supposed that the poor bastard *had* a story of his own, much less a sad one, and I asked, quickly, "What's going to happen to him now?"

He didn't answer this. He was off by himself some place. "Funny thing,"   *25* he said, and from his tone we might have been discussing the quickest way to get to Brooklyn, "when I saw the papers this morning, the first thing I asked myself was if I had anything to do with it. I felt sort of responsible."

I began to listen more carefully. The subway station was on the corner, just before us, and I stopped. He stopped, too. We were in front of a bar and he ducked slightly, peering in, but whoever he was looking for didn't seem to be there. The juke box was blasting away with something black and bouncy and I half watched the barmaid as she danced her way from the juke box to her place behind the bar. And I watched her face as she laughingly responded to something someone said to her, still keeping time to the music. When she smiled one saw the little girl, one sensed the doomed, still-struggling woman beneath the battered face of the semi-whore.

"I never *give* Sonny nothing," the boy said finally, "but a long time ago I come to school high and Sonny asked me how it felt." He paused, I couldn't bear to watch him, I watched the barmaid, and I listened to the music which seemed to be causing the pavement to shake. "I told him it felt great." The music stopped, the barmaid paused and watched the juke box until the music began again. "It did."

All this was carrying me some place I didn't want to go. I certainly didn't want to know how it felt. It filled everything, the people, the houses, the music, the dark, quicksilver barmaid, with menace; and this menace was their reality.

"What's going to happen to him now?" I asked again.

"They'll send him away some place and they'll try to cure him." He   *30* shook his head. "Maybe he'll even think he's kicked the habit. Then they'll let him loose"—he gestured, throwing his cigarette into the gutter. "That's all."

"What do you mean, that's *all?*"

But I knew what he meant.

"I *mean,* that's *all.*" He turned his head and looked at me, pulling down the corners of his mouth. "Don't you know what I mean?" he asked, softly.

"How the hell *would* I know what you mean?" I almost whispered it, I don't know why.

35 "That's right," he said to the air, "how would *he* know what I mean?" He turned toward me again, patient and calm, and yet I somehow felt him shaking, shaking as though he were going to fall apart. I felt that ice in my guts again, the dread I'd felt all afternoon; and again I watched the barmaid, moving about the bar, washing glasses, and singing. "Listen. They'll let him out and then it'll just start all over again. That's what I mean."

"You mean—they'll let him out. And then he'll just start working his way back in again. You mean he'll never kick the habit. Is that what you mean?"

"That's right," he said, cheerfully. "*You* see what I mean."

"Tell me," I said at last, "why does he want to die? He must want to die, he's killing himself, why does he want to die?"

He looked at me in surprise. He licked his lips. "He don't want to die. He wants to live. Don't nobody want to die, ever."

40 Then I wanted to ask him—too many things. He could not have answered, or if he had, I could not have borne the answers. I started walking. "Well, I guess it's none of my business."

"It's going to be rough on old Sonny," he said. We reached the subway station. "This is your station?" he asked. I nodded. I took one step down. "Damn!" he said, suddenly. I looked up at him. He grinned again. "Damn it if I didn't leave all my money home. You ain't got a dollar on you, have you? Just for a couple of days, is all."

All at once something inside gave and threatened to come pouring out of me. I didn't hate him any more. I felt that in another moment I'd start crying like a child.

"Sure," I said. "Don't swear." I looked in my wallet and didn't have a dollar, I only had a five. "Here," I said. "That hold you?"

He didn't look at it—he didn't want to look at it. A terrible, closed look came over his face, as though he were keeping the number on the bill a secret from him and me. "Thanks," he said, and now he was dying to see me go. "Don't worry about Sonny. Maybe I'll write him or something."

45 "Sure," I said. "You do that. So long."

"Be seeing you," he said. I went down the steps.

And I didn't write Sonny or send him anything for a long time. When I finally did, it was just after my little girl died, he wrote me back a letter which made me feel like a bastard.

Here's what he said:

Dear Brother,

You don't know how much I needed to hear from you. I wanted to write you many a time but I dug how much I must have hurt you and so I didn't write. But now I feel like a man who's been trying to climb up out of some deep, real deep and funky hole and just saw the sun up there, outside. I got to get outside.

I can't tell you much about how I got here. I mean I don't know how to tell you. I guess I was afraid of something or I was trying to escape from something and you know I have never been very strong in the head (smile). I'm glad Mama and Daddy are dead and can't see what's happened to their son and I swear if I'd known what I was doing I would never have hurt you so, you and a lot of other fine people who were nice to me and who believed in me.

I don't want you to think it had anything to do with me being a musician. It's more than that. Or maybe less than that. I can't get anything straight in my head down here and I try not to think about what's going to happen to me when I get outside again. Sometime I think I'm going to flip and *never* get outside and sometime I think I'll come straight back. I tell you one thing, though, I'd rather blow my brains out than go through this again. But that's what they all say, so they tell me. If I tell you when I'm coming to New York and if you could meet me, I sure would appreciate it. Give my love to Isabel and the kids and I was sure sorry to hear about little Gracie. I wish I could be like Mama and say the Lord's will be done, but I don't know it seems to me that trouble is the one thing that never does get stopped and I don't know what good it does to blame it on the Lord. But maybe it does some good if you believe it.

Your brother,
Sonny

Then I kept in constant touch with him and I sent him whatever I could and I went to meet him when he came back to New York. When I saw him many things I thought I had forgotten came flooding back to me. This was because I had begun, finally, to wonder about Sonny, about the life that Sonny lived inside. This life, whatever it was, had made him older and thinner and it had deepened the distant stillness in which he had always moved. He looked very unlike my baby brother. Yet, when he smiled, when we shook hands, the baby brother I'd never known looked out from the depths of his private life, like an animal waiting to be coaxed into the light.

"How you been keeping?" he asked me.

"All right. And you?"

"Just fine." He was smiling all over his face. "It's good to see you again."

50

"It's good to see you."

The seven years' difference in our ages lay between us like a chasm: I wondered if these years would ever operate between us as a bridge. I was remembering, and it made it hard to catch my breath, that I had been there when he was born; and I had heard the first words he had ever spoken. When he started to walk, he walked from our mother straight to me. I caught him just before he fell when he took the first steps he ever took in this world.

55   "How's Isabel?"

"Just fine. She's dying to see you."

"And the boys?"

"They're fine, too. They're anxious to see their uncle."

"Oh, come on. You know they don't remember me."

60   "Are you kidding? Of course they remember you."

He grinned again. We got into a taxi. We had a lot to say to each other, far too much to know how to begin.

As the taxi began to move, I asked, "You still want to go to India?"

He laughed. "You still remember that? Hell, no. This place is Indian enough for me."

"It used to belong to them," I said.

65   And he laughed again. "They damn sure knew what they were doing when they got rid of it."

Years ago, when he was around fourteen, he'd been all hipped on the idea of going to India. He read books about people sitting on rocks, naked, in all kinds of weather, but mostly bad, naturally, and walking barefoot through hot coals and arriving at wisdom. I used to say that it sounded to me as though they were getting away from wisdom as fast as they could. I think he sort of looked down on me for that.

"Do you mind," he asked, "if we have the driver drive alongside the park? On the west side—I haven't seen the city in so long."

"Of course not," I said. I was afraid that I might sound as though I were humoring him, but I hoped he wouldn't take it that way.

So we drove along, between the green of the park and the stony, lifeless elegance of hotels and apartment buildings, toward the vivid, killing streets of our childhood. These streets hadn't changed, though housing projects jutted up out of them now like rocks in the middle of a boiling sea. Most of the houses in which we had grown up had vanished, as had the stores from which we had stolen, the basements in which we had first tried sex, the rooftops from which we had hurled tin cans and bricks. But houses exactly like the houses of our past yet dominated the landscape, boys exactly like the boys we once had been found themselves smothering in these houses, came down into the streets for light and air and found themselves encircled by disaster. Some escaped the trap, most didn't. Those who got out always left something of themselves behind, as some animals amputate a leg and leave it in the trap. It might be said, perhaps, that I had escaped, after all, I was a school teacher; or that Sonny had, he hadn't lived in Harlem for years. Yet, as the cab moved uptown through streets which seemed, with a rush, to darken with dark people, and as I covertly studied Sonny's face, it came to me that what we were both seeking through our separate cab windows was that part of ourselves which had been left behind. It's always at the hour of trouble and confrontation that the missing member aches.

We hit 110th Street and started rolling up Lenox Avenue. And I'd known this avenue all my life, but it seemed to me again, as it had seemed on the day I'd first heard about Sonny's trouble, filled with a hidden menace which was its very breath of life.   70

"We almost there," said Sonny.

"Almost." We were both too nervous to say anything more.

We lived in a housing project. It hasn't been up long. A few days after it was up it seemed uninhabitably new, now, of course, it's already rundown. It looks like a parody of the good, clean, faceless life—God knows the people who live in it do their best to make it a parody. The beat-looking grass lying around isn't enough to make their lives green, the hedges will never hold out the streets, and they know it. The big windows fool no one, they aren't big enough to make space out of no space. They don't bother with the windows, they watch the TV screen instead. The playground is most popular with the children who don't play at jacks, or skip rope, or roller skate, or swing, and they can be found in it after dark. We moved in partly because it's not too far from where I teach, and partly for the kids; but it's really just like the houses in which Sonny and I grew up. The same things happen, they'll have the same things to remember. The moment Sonny and I started into the house I had the feeling that I was simply bringing him back into the danger he had almost died trying to escape.

Sonny has never been talkative. So I don't know why I was sure he'd be dying to talk to me when supper was over the first night. Everything went fine, the oldest boy remembered him, and the youngest boy liked him, and Sonny had remembered to bring something for each of them; and Isabel, who is really much nicer than I am, more open and giving, had gone to a lot of trouble about dinner and was genuinely glad to see him. And she's always been able to tease Sonny in a way that I haven't. It was nice to see her face so vivid again and to hear her laugh and watch her make Sonny laugh. She wasn't, or, anyway, she didn't seem to be, at all uneasy or embarrassed. She chatted as though there were no subject which had to be avoided and she got Sonny past his first, faint stiffness. And thank God she was there, for I was filled with that icy dread again. Everything I did seemed awkward to me, and everything I said sounded freighted with hidden meaning. I was trying to remember everything I'd heard about dope addiction and I couldn't help watching Sonny for signs. I wasn't doing it out of malice. I was trying to find out something about my brother. I was dying to hear him tell me he was safe.

75   "Safe!" my father grunted, whenever Mama suggested trying to move to a neighborhood which might be safer for children. "Safe, hell! Ain't no place safe for kids, nor nobody."

He always went on like this, but he wasn't, ever, really as bad as he sounded, not even on weekends, when he got drunk. As a matter of fact, he was always on the lookout for "something a little better," but he died before he found it. He died suddenly, during a drunken weekend in the middle of the war, when Sonny was fifteen. He and Sonny hadn't ever got on too well. And this was partly because Sonny was the apple of his father's eye. It was because he loved Sonny so much and was frightened for him, that he was always fighting with him. It doesn't do any good to fight with Sonny. Sonny just moves back, inside himself, where he can't be reached. But the principal reason that they never hit it off is that they were so much alike. Daddy was big and rough and loud-talking, just the opposite of Sonny, but they both had—that same privacy.

Mama tried to tell me something about this, just after Daddy died. I was home on leave from the army.

This was the last time I ever saw my mother alive. Just the same, this picture gets all mixed up in my mind with pictures I had of her when she was younger. The way I always see her is the way she used to be on a Sunday afternoon, say, when the old folks were talking after the big Sunday dinner. I always see her wearing pale blue. She'd be sitting on the sofa. And my father would be sitting in the easy chair, not far from her. And the living room would be full of church folks and relatives. There they sit, in chairs all around the living room, and the night is creeping up outside, but nobody knows it yet. You can see the darkness growing against the windowpanes and you hear the street noises every now and again, or maybe the jangling beat of a tambourine from one of the churches close by, but it's real quiet in the room. For a moment nobody's talking, but every face looks darkening, like the sky outside. And my mother rocks a little from the waist, and my father's eyes are closed. Everyone is looking at something a child can't see. For a minute they've forgotten the children. Maybe a kid is lying on the rug, half asleep. Maybe somebody's got a kid in his lap and is absent-mindedly stroking the kid's head. Maybe there's a kid, quiet and big-eyed, curled up in a big chair in the corner. The silence, the darkness coming, and the darkness in the faces frightens the child obscurely. He hopes that the hand which strokes his forehead will never stop—will never die. He hopes that there will never come a time when the old folks won't be sitting around the living room, talking about where they've come from, and what they've seen, and what's happening to them and their kinfolk.

But something deep and watchful in the child knows that this is bound to end, is already ending. In a moment someone will get up and turn on the light. Then the old folks will remember the children and they won't talk any more that day. And when light fills the room, the child is filled with darkness. He knows that every time this happens he's moved just a little closer to that darkness outside. The darkness outside is what the old folks have been talking about. It's what they've come from. It's what they endure. The child knows that they won't talk any more because if he knows too much about what's happened to *them,* he'll know too much too soon, about what's going to happen to *him.*

The last time I talked to my mother, I remember I was restless. I wanted   80
to get out and see Isabel. We weren't married then and we had a lot to
straighten out between us.

There Mama sat, in black, by the window. She was humming an old
church song, *Lord, you brought me from a long ways off.* Sonny was out somewhere. Mama kept watching the streets.

"I don't know," she said, "if I'll ever see you again, after you go off from
here. But I hope you'll remember the things I tried to teach you."

"Don't talk like that," I said, and smiled. "You'll be here a long time yet."

She smiled, too, but she said nothing. She was quiet for a long time. And
I said, "Mama, don't you worry about nothing. I'll be writing all the time, and
you be getting the checks. . . ."

"I want to talk to you about your brother," she said, suddenly. "If any-   85
thing happens to me he ain't going to have nobody to look out for him."

"Mama," I said, "ain't nothing going to happen to you *or* Sonny. Sonny's
all right. He's a good boy and he's got good sense."

"It ain't a question of his being a good boy," Mama said, "nor of his having good sense. It ain't only the bad ones, nor yet the dumb ones that gets
sucked under." She stopped, looking at me. "Your Daddy once had a brother,"
she said, and she smiled in a way that made me feel she was in pain. "You didn't
never know that, did you?"

"No," I said, "I never knew that," and I watched her face.

"Oh, yes," she said, "your Daddy had a brother." She looked out of the
window again. "I know you never saw your Daddy cry. But I did—many a
time, through all these years."

I asked her, "What happened to his brother? How come nobody's ever   90
talked about him?"

This was the first time I ever saw my mother look old.

"His brother got killed," she said, "when he was just a little younger than
you are now. I knew him. He was a fine boy. He was maybe a little full of the
devil, but he didn't mean nobody no harm."

Then she stopped and the room was silent, exactly as it had sometimes
been on those Sunday afternoons. Mama kept looking out into the streets.

"He used to have a job in the mill," she said, "and, like all young folks, he
just liked to perform on Saturday nights. Saturday nights, him and your father
would drift around to different places, go to dances and things like that, or just
sit around with people they knew, and your father's brother would sing, he had
a fine voice, and play along with himself on his guitar. Well, this particular Saturday night, him and your father was coming home from some place, and they

were both a little drunk and there was a moon that night, it was bright like day. Your father's brother was feeling kind of good, and he was whistling to himself, and he had his guitar slung over his shoulder. They was coming down a hill and beneath them was a road that turned off from the highway. Well, your father's brother, being always kind of frisky, decided to run down this hill, and he did, with that guitar banging and clanging behind him, and he ran across the road, and he was making water behind a tree. And your father was sort of amused at him and he was still coming down the hill, kind of slow. Then he heard a car motor and that same minute his brother stepped from behind the tree, into the road, in the moonlight. And he started to cross the road. And your father started to run down the hill, he says he don't know why. This car was full of white men. They was all drunk, and when they seen your father's brother they let out a great whoop and holler and they aimed the car straight at him. They was having fun, they just wanted to scare him, the way they do sometimes, you know. But they was drunk. And I guess the boy, being drunk, too, and scared, kind of lost his head. By the time he jumped it was too late. Your father says he heard his brother scream when the car rolled over him, and he heard the wood of that guitar when it give, and he heard them strings go flying, and he heard them white men shouting, and the car kept on a-going and it ain't stopped till this day. And, time your father got down the hill, his brother weren't nothing but blood and pulp."

95   Tears were gleaming on my mother's face. There wasn't anything I could say.

"He never mentioned it," she said, "because I never let him mention it before you children. Your Daddy was like a crazy man that night and for many a night thereafter. He says he never in his life seen anything as dark as that road after the lights of that car had gone away. Weren't nothing; weren't nobody on that road, just your Daddy and his brother and that busted guitar. Oh, yes. Your Daddy never did really get right again. Till the day he died he wasn't sure but that every white man he saw was the man that killed his brother."

She stopped and took out a handkerchief and dried her eyes and looked at me.

"I ain't telling you all this," she said, "to make you scared or bitter or to make you hate nobody. I'm telling you this because you got a brother. And the world ain't changed."

I guess I didn't want to believe this. I guess she saw this in my face. She turned away from me, toward the window again, searching those streets.

100   "But I praise my Redeemer," she said at last, "that He called your Daddy home before me. I ain't saying it to throw no flowers at myself, but, I declare, it keeps me from feeling too cast down to know I helped your father get safely through this world. Your father always acted like he was the roughest, strongest man on earth. And everybody took him to be like that. But if he hadn't had *me* there—to see his tears!"

She was crying again. Still, I couldn't move. I said, "Lord, Lord, Mama, I didn't know it was like that."

"Oh, honey," she said, "there's a lot that you don't know. But you are going to find out." She stood up from the window and came over to me. "You got to hold on to your brother," she said, "and don't let him fall, no matter what it looks like is happening to him and no matter how evil you gets with him. You going to be evil with him many a time. But don't you forget what I told you, you hear?"

"I won't forget," I said. "Don't you worry, I won't forget. I won't let nothing happen to Sonny."

My mother smiled as though she were amused at something she saw in my face. Then, "You may not be able to stop nothing from happening. But you got to let him know you's *there*."

Two days later I was married, and then I was gone. And I had a lot of things on my mind and I pretty well forgot my promise to Mama until I got shipped home on a special furlough for her funeral.   *105*

And, after the funeral, with just Sonny and me alone in the empty kitchen, I tried to find out something about him.

"What do you want to do?" I asked him.

"I'm going to be a musician," he said.

For he had graduated, in the time I had been away, from dancing to the juke box to finding out who was playing what, and what they were doing with it, and he had bought himself a set of drums.

"You mean, you want to be a drummer?" I somehow had the feeling   *110*
that being a drummer might be all right for other people but not for my brother Sonny.

"I don't think," he said, looking at me very gravely, "that I'll ever be a good drummer. But I think I can play a piano."

I frowned. I'd never played the role of the older brother quite so seriously before, had scarcely ever, in fact, *asked* Sonny a damn thing. I sensed myself in the presence of something I didn't really know how to handle, didn't understand. So I made my frown a little deeper as I asked: "What kind of musician do you want to be?"

He grinned. "How many kinds do you think there are?"

"Be *serious*," I said.

He laughed, throwing his head back, and looked at me. "I *am* serious."   *115*

"Well, then, for Christ's sake, stop kidding around and answer a serious question. I mean, do you want to be a concert pianist, you want to play classical music and all that, or—or what?" Long before I finished he was laughing again. "For Christ's *sake*, Sonny!"

He sobered, but with difficulty. "I'm sorry. But you sound so—*scared!*" and he was off again.

"Well, you may think it's funny now, baby, but it's not going to be so funny when you have to make your living at it, let me tell you *that*." I was furious because I knew he was laughing at me and I didn't know why.

"No," he said, very sober now, and afraid, perhaps, that he'd hurt me, "I don't want to be a classical pianist. That isn't what interests me. I mean"—he paused, looking hard at me, as though his eyes would help me to understand, and then gestured helplessly, as though perhaps his hand would help—"I mean, I'll have a lot of studying to do, and I'll have to study *everything,* but, I mean, I want to play *with*—jazz musicians." He stopped. "I want to play jazz," he said.

120 Well, the word had never before sounded as heavy, as real, as it sounded that afternoon in Sonny's mouth. I just looked at him and I was probably frowning a real frown by this time. I simply couldn't see why on earth he'd want to spend his time hanging around nightclubs, clowning around on bandstands, while people pushed each other around a dance floor. It seemed— beneath him, somehow. I had never thought about it before, had never been forced to, but I suppose I had always put jazz musicians in a class with what Daddy called "goodtime people."

"Are you *serious?*"

"Hell, *yes,* I'm serious."

He looked more helpless than ever, and annoyed, and deeply hurt.

I suggested, helpfully: "You mean—like Louis Armstrong?"

125 His face closed as though I'd struck him. "No. I'm not talking about none of that old-time, down home crap."

"Well, look, Sonny, I'm sorry, don't get mad. I just don't altogether get it, that's all. Name somebody—you know, a jazz musician you admire."

"Bird."

"Who?"

"Bird! Charlie Parker! Don't they teach you nothing in the goddamn army?"

130 I lit a cigarette. I was surprised and then a little amused to discover that I was trembling. "I've been out of touch," I said. "You'll have to be patient with me. Now. Who's this Parker character?"

"He's just one of the greatest jazz musicians alive," said Sonny, sullenly, his hands in his pockets, his back to me. "Maybe *the* greatest," he added, bitterly, "that's probably why *you* never heard of him."

"All right," I said, "I'm ignorant. I'm sorry. I'll go out and buy all the cat's records right away, all right?"

"It don't," said Sonny, with dignity, "make any difference to me. I don't care what you listen to. Don't do me no favors."

I was beginning to realize that I'd never seen him so upset before. With another part of my mind I was thinking that this would probably turn out to be one of those things kids go through and that I shouldn't make it seem important by pushing it too hard. Still, I didn't think it would do any harm to ask: "Doesn't all this take a lot of time? Can you make a living at it?"

He turned back to me and half leaned, half sat, on the kitchen table.   *135*
"Everything takes time," he said, "and—well, yes, sure, I can make a living at it.
But what I don't seem to be able to make you understand is that it's the only
thing I want to do."

"Well, Sonny," I said, gently, "you know people can't always do exactly
what they *want* to do—"

"*No,* I don't know that," said Sonny, surprising me. "I think people *ought*
to do what they want to do, what else are they alive for?"

"You getting to be a big boy," I said desperately, "it's time you started
thinking about your future."

"I'm thinking about my future," said Sonny, grimly. "I think about it all
the time."

I gave up. I decided, if he didn't change his mind, that we could always   *140*
talk about it later. "In the meantime," I said, "you got to finish school." We had
already decided that he'd have to move in with Isabel and her folks. I knew
this wasn't the ideal arrangement because Isabel's folks are inclined to be dicty
and they hadn't especially wanted Isabel to marry me. But I didn't know what
else to do. "And we have to get you fixed up at Isabel's."

There was a long silence. He moved from the kitchen table to the window. "That's a terrible idea. You know it yourself."

"Do you have a *better* idea?"

He just walked up and down the kitchen for a minute. He was as tall as
I was. He had started to shave. I suddenly had the feeling that I didn't know
him at all.

He stopped at the kitchen table and picked up my cigarettes. Looking at
me with a kind of mocking, amused defiance, he put one between his lips.
"You mind?"

"You smoking already?"   *145*

He lit the cigarette and nodded, watching me through the smoke. "I just
wanted to see if I'd have the courage to smoke in front of you." He grinned
and blew a great cloud of smoke to the ceiling. "It was easy." He looked at my
face. "Come on, now. I bet you was smoking at my age, tell the truth."

I didn't say anything but the truth was on my face, and he laughed. But
now there was something very strained in his laugh. "Sure. And I bet that ain't
all you was doing."

He was frightening me a little. "Cut the crap," I said. "We already decided that you was going to go and live at Isabel's. Now what's got into you all
of a sudden?"

"*You* decided it," he pointed out. "*I* didn't decide nothing." He stopped
in front of me, leaning against the stove, arms loosely folded. "Look, brother. I
don't want to stay in Harlem no more, I really don't." He was very earnest. He
looked at me, then over toward the kitchen window. There was something in
his eyes I'd never seen before, some thoughtfulness, some worry all his own.
He rubbed the muscle of one arm. "It's time I was getting out of here."

150   "Where do you want to go, Sonny?"

"I want to join the army. Or the navy, I don't care. If I say I'm old enough, they'll believe me."

Then I got mad. It was because I was so scared. "You must be crazy. You god-damn fool, what the hell do you want to go and join the *army* for?"

"I just told you. To get out of Harlem."

"Sonny, you haven't even finished *school*. And if you really want to be a musician, how do you expect to study if you're in the *army?*"

155   He looked at me, trapped, and in anguish. "There's ways. I might be able to work out some kind of deal. Anyway, I'll have the G.I. Bill when I come out."

"*If* you come out." We stared at each other. "Sonny, please. Be reasonable. I know the setup is far from perfect. But we got to do the best we can."

"I ain't learning nothing in school," he said. "Even when I go." He turned away from me and opened the window and threw his cigarette out into the narrow alley. I watched his back. "At least, I ain't learning nothing you'd want me to learn." He slammed the window so hard I thought the glass would fly out, and turned back to me. "And I'm sick of the stink of these garbage cans!"

"Sonny," I said, "I know how you feel. But if you don't finish school now, you're going to be sorry later that you didn't." I grabbed him by the shoulders. "And you only got another year. It ain't so bad. And I'll come back and I swear I'll help you do *whatever* you want to do. Just try to put up with it till I come back. Will you please do that? For me?"

He didn't answer and he wouldn't look at me.

160   "Sonny. You hear me?"

He pulled away. "I hear you. But you never hear anything I say."

I didn't know what to say to that. He looked out of the window and then back at me. "OK," he said, and sighed. "I'll try."

Then I said, trying to cheer him up a little, "They got a piano at Isabel's. You can practice on it."

And as a matter of fact, it did cheer him up for a minute. "That's right," he said to himself. "I forgot that." His face relaxed a little. But the worry, the thoughtfulness, played on it still, the way shadows play on a face which is staring into the fire.

165   But I thought I'd never hear the end of that piano. At first, Isabel would write me, saying how nice it was that Sonny was so serious about his music and how, as soon as he came in from school, or wherever he had been when he was supposed to be at school, he went straight to that piano and stayed there until suppertime. And, after supper, he went back to that piano and stayed there until everybody went to bed. He was at the piano all day Saturday and all day Sunday. Then he bought a record player and started playing records. He'd play one record over and over again, all day long sometimes, and he'd improvise along with it on the piano. Or he'd play one section of the record, one chord, one change, one progression, then he'd do it on the piano. Then back to the record. Then back to the piano.

Well, I really don't know how they stood it. Isabel finally confessed that it wasn't like living with a person at all, it was like living with sound. And the sound didn't make any sense to her, didn't make any sense to any of them—naturally. They began, in a way, to be afflicted by this presence that was living in their home. It was as though Sonny were some sort of god, or monster. He moved in an atmosphere which wasn't like theirs at all. They fed him and he ate, he washed himself, he walked in and out of their door; he certainly wasn't nasty or unpleasant or rude, Sonny isn't any of those things; but it was as though he were all wrapped up in some cloud, some fire, some vision all his own; and there wasn't any way to reach him.

At the same time, he wasn't really a man yet, he was still a child, and they had to watch out for him in all kinds of ways. They certainly couldn't throw him out. Neither did they dare to make a great scene about that piano because even they dimly sensed, as I sensed, from so many thousands of miles away, that Sonny was at that piano playing for his life.

But he hadn't been going to school. One day a letter came from the school board and Isabel's mother got it—there had, apparently, been other letters but Sonny had torn them up. This day, when Sonny came in, Isabel's mother showed him the letter and asked where he'd been spending his time. And she finally got it out of him that he'd been down in Greenwich Village, with musicians and other characters, in a white girl's apartment. And this scared her and she started to scream at him and what came up, once she began—though she denies it to this day—was what sacrifices they were making to give Sonny a decent home and how little he appreciated it.

Sonny didn't play the piano that day. By evening, Isabel's mother had calmed down but then there was the old man to deal with, and Isabel herself. Isabel says she did her best to be calm but she broke down and started crying. She says she just watched Sonny's face. She could tell, by watching him, what was happening with him. And what was happening was that they penetrated his cloud, they had reached him. Even if their fingers had been a thousand times more gentle than human fingers ever are, he could hardly help feeling that they had stripped him naked and were spitting on that nakedness. For he also had to see that his presence, that music, which was life or death to him, had been torture for them and that they had endured it, not at all for his sake, but only for mine. And Sonny couldn't take that. He can take it a little better today than he could then but he's still not very good at it and, frankly, I don't know anybody who is.

The silence of the next few days must have been louder than the sound   *170*
of all the music ever played since time began. One morning, before she went to work, Isabel was in his room for something and she suddenly realized that all of his records were gone. And she knew for certain that he was gone. And he was. He went as far as the navy would carry him. He finally sent me a postcard from some place in Greece and that was the first I knew that Sonny was still alive. I didn't see him any more until we were both back in New York and the war had long been over.

He was a man by then, of course, but I wasn't willing to see it. He came by the house from time to time, but we fought almost every time we met. I didn't like the way he carried himself, loose and dreamlike all the time, and I didn't like his friends, and his music seemed to be merely an excuse for the life he led. It sounded just that weird and disordered.

Then we had a fight, a pretty awful fight, and I didn't see him for months. By and by I looked him up, where he was living, in a furnished room in the Village, and I tried to make it up. But there were lots of other people in the room and Sonny just lay on his bed, and he wouldn't come downstairs with me, and he treated these other people as though they were his family and I weren't. So I got mad and then he got mad, and then I told him that he might just as well be dead as live the way he was living. Then he stood up and he told me not to worry about him any more in life, that he *was* dead as far as I was concerned. Then he pushed me to the door and the other people looked on as though nothing were happening, and he slammed the door behind me. I stood in the hallway, staring at the door. I heard somebody laugh in the room and then the tears came to my eyes. I started down the steps, whistling to keep from crying, I kept whistling to myself, *You going to need me, baby, one of these cold, rainy days.*

I read about Sonny's trouble in the spring. Little Grace died in the fall. She was a beautiful little girl. But she only lived a little over two years. She died of polio and she suffered. She had a slight fever for a couple of days, but it didn't seem like anything and we just kept her in bed. And we would certainly have called the doctor, but the fever dropped, she seemed to be all right. So we thought it had just been a cold. Then, one day, she was up, playing, Isabel was in the kitchen fixing lunch for the two boys when they'd come in from school, and she heard Grace fall down in the living room. When you have a lot of children you don't always start running when one of them falls, unless they start screaming or something. And, this time, Grace was quiet. Yet, Isabel says that when she heard that *thump* and then that silence, something happened in her to make her afraid. And she ran to the living room and there was little Grace on the floor, all twisted up, and the reason she hadn't screamed was that she couldn't get her breath. And when she did scream, it was the worst sound, Isabel says, that she'd ever heard in all her life, and she still hears it sometimes in her dreams. Isabel will sometimes wake me up with a low, moaning, strangled sound and I have to be quick to awaken her and hold her to me and where Isabel is weeping against me seems a mortal wound.

I think I may have written Sonny the very day that little Grace was buried. I was sitting in the living room in the dark, by myself, and I suddenly thought of Sonny. My trouble made his real.

175   One Saturday afternoon, when Sonny had been living with us, or, anyway, been in our house, for nearly two weeks, I found myself wandering aim-

lessly about the living room, drinking from a can of beer, and trying to work up the courage to search Sonny's room. He was out, he was usually out whenever I was home, and Isabel had taken the children to see their grandparents. Suddenly I was standing still in front of the living room window, watching Seventh Avenue. The idea of searching Sonny's room made me still. I scarcely dared to admit to myself what I'd be searching for. I didn't know what I'd do if I found it. Or if I didn't.

On the sidewalk across from me, near the entrance to a barbecue joint, some people were holding an old-fashioned revival meeting. The barbecue cook, wearing a dirty white apron, his conked° hair reddish and metallic in the pale sun, and a cigarette between his lips, stood in the doorway, watching them. Kids and older people paused in their errands and stood there, along with some older men and a couple of very tough-looking women who watched everything that happened on the avenue, as though they owned it, or were maybe owned by it. Well, they were watching this, too. The revival was being carried on by three sisters in black, and a brother. All they had were their voices and their Bibles and a tambourine. The brother was testifying and while he testified two of the sisters stood together, seeming to say, amen, and the third sister walked around with the tambourine outstretched and a couple of people dropped coins into it. Then the brother's testimony ended and the sister who had been taking up the collection dumped the coins into her palm and transferred them to the pocket of her long black robe. Then she raised both hands, striking the tambourine against the air, and then against one hand, and she started to sing. And the two other sisters and the brother joined in.

It was strange, suddenly, to watch, though I had been seeing these street meetings all my life. So, of course, had everybody else down there. Yet, they paused and watched and listened and I stood still at the window. *"Tis the old ship of Zion,"* they sang, and the sister with the tambourine kept a steady, jangling beat, *"it has rescued many a thousand!"* Not a soul under the sound of their voices was hearing this song for the first time, not one of them had been rescued. Nor had they seen much in the way of rescue work being done around them. Neither did they especially believe in the holiness of the three sisters and the brother, they knew too much about them, knew where they lived, and how. The woman with the tambourine, whose voice dominated the air, whose face was bright with joy, was divided by very little from the woman who stood watching her, a cigarette between her heavy, chapped lips, her hair a cuckoo's nest, her face scarred and swollen from many beatings, and her black eyes glittering like coal. Perhaps they both knew this, which was why, when, as rarely, they addressed each other, they addressed each other as Sister. As the singing filled the air the watching, listening faces underwent a change, the eyes focusing

---

conked: Straightened.

on something within; the music seemed to soothe a poison out of them; and time seemed, nearly, to fall away from the sullen, belligerent, battered faces, as though they were fleeing back to their first condition, while dreaming of their last. The barbecue cook half shook his head and smiled, and dropped his cigarette and disappeared into his joint. A man fumbled in his pockets for change and stood holding it in his hand impatiently, as though he had just remembered a pressing appointment further up the avenue. He looked furious. Then I saw Sonny, standing on the edge of the crowd. He was carrying a wide, flat notebook with a green cover, and it made him look, from where I was standing, almost like a schoolboy. The coppery sun brought out the copper in his skin, he was very faintly smiling, standing very still. Then the singing stopped, the tambourine turned into a collection plate again. The furious man dropped in his coins and vanished, so did a couple of the women, and Sonny dropped some change in the plate, looking directly at the woman with a little smile. He started across the avenue, toward the house. He has a slow, loping walk, something like the way Harlem hipsters walk, only he's imposed on this his own half-beat. I had never really noticed it before.

I stayed at the window, both relieved and apprehensive. As Sonny disappeared from my sight, they began singing again. And they were still singing when his key turned in the lock.

"Hey," he said.

180 "Hey, yourself. You want some beer?"

"No. Well, maybe." But he came up to the window and stood beside me, looking out. "What a warm voice," he said.

They were singing *If I could only hear my mother pray again!*

"Yes," I said, "and she can sure beat that tambourine."

"But what a terrible song," he said, and laughed. He dropped his notebook on the sofa and disappeared into the kitchen. "Where's Isabel and the kids?"

185 "I think they went to see their grandparents. You hungry?"

"No." He came back into the living room with his can of beer. "You want to come some place with me tonight?"

I sensed, I don't know how, that I couldn't possibly say no. "Sure. Where?"

He sat down on the sofa and picked up his notebook and started leafing through it. "I'm going to sit in with some fellows in a joint in the Village."

"You mean, you're going to play, tonight?"

190 "That's right." He took a swallow of his beer and moved back to the window. He gave me a sidelong look. "If you can stand it."

"I'll try," I said.

He smiled to himself and we both watched as the meeting across the way broke up. The three sisters and the brother, heads bowed, were singing *God be with you till we meet again.* The faces around them were very quiet. Then the song ended. The small crowd dispersed. We watched the three women and the lone man walk slowly up the avenue.

"When she was singing before," said Sonny, abruptly, "her voice reminded me for a minute of what heroin feels like sometimes—when it's in
your veins. It makes you feel sort of warm and cool at the same time. And distant. And—and sure." He sipped his beer, very deliberately not looking at me. I
watched his face. "It makes you feel—in control. Sometimes you've got to
have that feeling."

"Do you?" I sat down slowly in the easy chair.

"Sometimes." He went to the sofa and picked up his notebook again.   195
"Some people do."

"In order," I asked, "to play?" And my voice was very ugly, full of contempt and anger.

"Well"—he looked at me with great, troubled eyes, as though, in fact, he
hoped his eyes would tell me things he could never otherwise say—"they *think*
so. And *if* they think so—!"

"And what do *you* think?" I asked.

He sat on the sofa and put his can of beer on the floor. "I don't know,"
he said, and I couldn't be sure if he were answering my question or pursuing
his thoughts. His face didn't tell me. "It's not so much to *play*. It's to *stand* it, to
be able to make it at all. On any level." He frowned and smiled: "In order to
keep from shaking to pieces."

"But these friends of yours," I said, "they seem to shake themselves to   200
pieces pretty goddamn fast."

"Maybe." He played with his notebook. And something told me that I
should curb my tongue, that Sonny was doing his best to talk, that I should listen. "But of course you only know the ones that've gone to pieces. Some
don't—or at least they haven't *yet* and that's just about all *any* of us can say." He
paused. "And then there are some who just live, really, in hell, and they know
it and they see what's happening and they go right on. I don't know." He
sighed, dropped the notebook, folded his arms. "Some guys, you can tell from
the way they play, they on something *all* the time. And you can see that, well, it
makes something real for them. But of course," he picked up his beer from the
floor and sipped it and put the can down again, "they *want* to, too, you've got
to see that. Even some of them that say they don't—*some,* not all."

"And what about you?" I asked—I couldn't help it. "What about you?
Do *you* want to?"

He stood up and walked to the window and remained silent for a long
time. Then he sighed. "Me," he said. Then: "While I was downstairs before, on
my way here, listening to that woman sing, it struck me all of a sudden how
much suffering she must have had to go through—to sing like that. It's *repulsive* to think that you have to suffer that much."

I said: "But there's no way not to suffer—is there, Sonny?"

"I believe not," he said and smiled, "but that's never stopped anyone from   205
trying." He looked at me. "Has it?" I realized, with this mocking look, that
there stood between us, forever, beyond the power of time or forgiveness, the

fact that I had held silence—so long!—when he had needed human speech to help him. He turned back to the window. "No, there's no way not to suffer. But you try all kinds of ways to keep from drowning in it, to keep on top of it, and to make it seem—well, like *you*. Like you did something, all right, and now you're suffering for it. You know?" I said nothing. "Well you know," he said, impatiently, "why *do* people suffer? Maybe it's better to do something to give it a reason, *any* reason."

"But we just agreed," I said, "that there's no way not to suffer. Isn't it better, then, just to—take it?"

"But nobody just takes it," Sonny cried, "that's what I'm telling you! *Everybody* tries not to. You're just hung up on the *way* some people try—it's not *your* way!"

The hair on my face began to itch, my face felt wet. "That's not true," I said, "that's not true. I don't give a damn what other people do, I don't even care how they suffer. I just care how *you* suffer." And he looked at me. "Please believe me," I said, "I don't want to see you—die—trying not to suffer."

"I won't," he said, flatly, "die trying not to suffer. At least, not any faster than anybody else."

210   "But there's no need," I said, trying to laugh, "is there? in killing yourself."

I wanted to say more, but I couldn't. I wanted to talk about will power and how life could be—well, beautiful. I wanted to say that it was all within; but was it? or, rather, wasn't that exactly the trouble? And I wanted to promise that I would never fail him again. But it would all have sounded—empty words and lies.

So I made the promise to myself and prayed that I would keep it.

"It's terrible sometimes, inside," he said, "that's what's the trouble. You walk these streets, black and funky and cold, and there's not really a living ass to talk to, and there's nothing shaking, and there's no way of getting it out—that storm inside. You can't talk it and you can't make love with it, and when you finally try to get with it and play it, you realize *nobody's* listening. So *you've* got to listen. You got to find a way to listen."

And then he walked away from the window and sat on the sofa again, as though all the wind had suddenly been knocked out of him. "Sometimes you'll do *anything* to play, even cut your mother's throat." He laughed and looked at me. "Or your brother's." Then he sobered. "Or your own." Then: "Don't worry. I'm all right now and I think I'll *be* all right. But I can't forget—where I've been. I don't mean just the physical place I've been, I mean where I've *been*. And *what* I've been."

215   "What have you been, Sonny?" I asked.

He smiled—but sat sideways on the sofa, his elbow resting on the back, his fingers playing with his mouth and chin, not looking at me. "I've been something I didn't recognize, didn't know I could be. Didn't know anybody could be." He stopped, looking inward, looking helplessly young, looking old.

"I'm not talking about it now because I feel *guilty* or anything like that—maybe it would be better if I did, I don't know. Anyway, I can't really talk about it. Not to you, not to anybody," and now he turned and faced me. "Sometimes, you know, and it was actually when I was most *out* of the world, I felt that I was in it, that I was *with* it, really, and I could play or I didn't really have to *play*, it just came out of me, it was there. And I don't know how I played, thinking about it now, but I know I did awful things, those times, sometimes, to people. Or it wasn't that I *did* anything to them—it was that they weren't real." He picked up the beer can; it was empty; he rolled it between his palms: "And other times—well, I needed a fix, I needed to find a place to lean, I needed to clear a space to *listen*—and I couldn't find it, and I—went crazy, I did terrible things to *me*, I was terrible *for* me." He began pressing the beer can between his hands, I watched the metal begin to give. It glittered, as he played with it, like a knife, and I was afraid he would cut himself, but I said nothing. "Oh well. I can never tell you. I was all by myself at the bottom of something, stinking and sweating and crying and shaking, and I smelled it, you know? my stink, and I thought I'd die if I couldn't get away from it and yet, all the same, I knew that everything I was doing was just locking me in with it. And I didn't know," he paused, still flattening the beer can, "I didn't know, I still *don't* know, something kept telling me that maybe it was good to smell your own stink, but I didn't think that *that* was what I'd been trying to do—and—who can stand it?" and he abruptly dropped the ruined beer can, looking at me with a small, still smile, and then rose, walking to the window as though it were the lodestone rock. I watched his face, he watched the avenue. "I couldn't tell you when Mama died—but the reason I wanted to leave Harlem so bad was to get away from drugs. And then, when I ran away, that's what I was running from—really. When I came back, nothing had changed, I hadn't changed, I was just—older." And he stopped, drumming with his fingers on the windowpane. The sun had vanished, soon darkness would fall. I watched his face. "It can come again," he said, almost as though speaking to himself. Then he turned to me. "It can come again," he repeated. "I just want you to know that."

"All right," I said, at last. "So it can come again. All right."

He smiled, but the smile was sorrowful. "I had to try to tell you," he said.

"Yes," I said. "I understand that."

"You're my brother," he said, looking straight at me, and not smiling at all.   220

"Yes," I repeated, "yes. I understand that."

He turned back to the window, looking out. "All that hatred down there," he said, "all that hatred and misery and love. It's a wonder it doesn't blow the avenue apart."

We went to the only nightclub on a short, dark street, downtown. We squeezed through the narrow, chattering, jam-packed bar to the entrance of the big room, where the bandstand was. And we stood there for a moment, for the lights were very dim in this room and we couldn't see. Then, "Hello, boy," said a voice and an enormous black man, much older than Sonny or myself, erupted out of all that atmospheric lighting and put an arm around Sonny's shoulder. "I been sitting right here," he said, "waiting for you."

He had a big voice, too, and heads in the darkness turned toward us.

225 Sonny grinned and pulled a little away, and said, "Creole, this is my brother. I told you about him."

Creole shook my hand. "I'm glad to meet you, son," he said, and it was clear that he was glad to meet me *there* for Sonny's sake. And he smiled, "You got a real musician in *your* family," and he took his arm from Sonny's shoulder and slapped him, lightly, affectionately, with the back of his hand.

"Well. Now I've heard it all," said a voice behind us. This was another musician, and a friend of Sonny's, a coal-black, cheerful-looking man, built close to the ground. He immediately began confiding to me, at the top of his lungs, the most terrible things about Sonny, his teeth gleaming like a lighthouse and his laugh coming up out of him like the beginning of an earthquake. And it turned out that everyone at the bar knew Sonny, or almost everyone; some were musicians, working there, or nearby, or not working, some were simply hangers-on, and some were there to hear Sonny play. I was introduced to all of them and they were all very polite to me. Yet, it was clear that, for them, I was only Sonny's brother. Here, I was in Sonny's world. Or, rather: his kingdom. Here, it was not even a question that his veins bore royal blood.

They were going to play soon and Creole installed me, by myself, at a table in a dark corner. Then I watched them, Creole, and the little black man, and Sonny, and the others, while they horsed around, standing just below the bandstand. The light from the bandstand spilled just a little short of them and, watching them laughing and gesturing and moving about, I had the feeling that they, nevertheless, were being most careful not to step into that circle of light too suddenly: that if they moved into the light too suddenly, without thinking, they would perish in flame. Then, while I watched, one of them, the small, black man, moved into the light and crossed the bandstand and started fooling around with his drums. Then—being funny and being, also, extremely ceremonious—Creole took Sonny by the arm and led him to the piano. A woman's voice called Sonny's name and a few hands started clapping. And Sonny, also being funny and being ceremonious, and so touched, I think, that he could have cried, but neither hiding it nor showing it, riding it like a man, grinned, and put both hands to his heart and bowed from the waist.

Creole then went to the bass fiddle and a lean, very bright-skinned brown man jumped up on the bandstand and picked up his horn. So there they were, and the atmosphere on the bandstand and in the room began to change and tighten. Someone stepped up to the microphone and announced them. Then there were all kinds of murmurs. Some people at the bar shushed others. The waitress ran around, frantically getting in the last orders, guys and chicks got closer to each other, and the lights on the bandstand, on the quartet, turned to a kind of indigo. Then they all looked different there. Creole looked about him for the last time, as though he were making certain that all his chickens were in the coop, and then he—jumped and struck the fiddle. And there they were.

All I know about music is that not many people ever really hear it. And even then, on the rare occasions when something opens within, and the music enters, what we mainly hear, or hear corroborated, are personal, private, vanishing evocations. But the man who creates the music is hearing something else, is dealing with the roar rising from the void and imposing order on it as it hits the air. What is evoked in him, then, is of another order, more terrible because it has no words, and triumphant, too, for that same reason. And his triumph, when he triumphs, is ours. I just watched Sonny's face. His face was troubled, he was working hard, but he wasn't with it. And I had the feeling that, in a way, everyone on the bandstand was waiting for him, both waiting for him and pushing him along. But as I began to watch Creole, I realized that it was Creole who held them all back. He had them on a short rein. Up there, keeping the beat with his whole body, wailing on the fiddle, with his eyes half closed, he was listening to everything, but he was listening to Sonny. He was having a dialogue with Sonny. He wanted Sonny to leave the shoreline and strike out for the deep water. He was Sonny's witness that deep water and drowning were not the same thing—he had been there, and he knew. And he wanted Sonny to know. He was waiting for Sonny to do the things on the keys which would let Creole know that Sonny was in the water.

And, while Creole listened, Sonny moved, deep within, exactly like someone in torment. I had never before thought of how awful the relationship must be between the musician and his instrument. He has to fill it, this instrument, with the breath of life, his own. He has to make it do what he wants it to do. And a piano is just a piano. It's made out of so much wood and wires and little hammers and big ones, and ivory. While there's only so much you can do with it, the only way to find this out is to try; to try and make it do everything.

And Sonny hadn't been near a piano for over a year. And he wasn't on much better terms with his life, not the life that stretched before him now. He and the piano stammered, started one way, got scared, stopped; started another way, panicked, marked time, started again; then seemed to have found a direction, panicked again, got stuck. And the face I saw on Sonny I'd never seen before. Everything had been burned out of it, and, at the same time, things usually hidden were being burned in, by the fire and fury of the battle which was occurring in him up there.

Yet, watching Creole's face as they neared the end of the first set, I had the feeling that something had happened, something I hadn't heard. Then they finished, there was scattered applause, and then, without an instant's warning,

Creole started into something else, it was almost sardonic, it was *Am I Blue*. And, as though he commanded, Sonny began to play. Something began to happen. And Creole let out the reins. The dry, low, black man said something awful on the drums, Creole answered, and the drums talked back. Then the horn insisted, sweet and high, slightly detached perhaps, and Creole listened, commenting now and then, dry, and driving, beautiful and calm and old. Then they all came together again, and Sonny was part of the family again. I could tell this from his face. He seemed to have found, right there beneath his fingers, a damn brand-new piano. It seemed that he couldn't get over it. Then, for awhile, just being happy with Sonny, they seemed to be agreeing with him that brand-new pianos certainly were a gas.

Then Creole stepped forward to remind them that what they were playing was the blues. He hit something in all of them, he hit something in me, myself, and the music tightened and deepened, apprehension began to beat the air. Creole began to tell us what the blues were all about. They were not about anything very new. He and his boys up there were keeping it new, at the risk of ruin, destruction, madness, and death, in order to find new ways to make us listen. For, while the tale of how we suffer, and how we are delighted, and how we may triumph is never new, it always must be heard. There isn't any other tale to tell, it's the only light we've got in all this darkness.

235 And this tale, according to that face, that body, those strong hands on those strings, has another aspect in every country, and a new depth in every generation. Listen, Creole seemed to be saying, listen. Now these are Sonny's blues. He made the little black man on the drums know it, and the bright, brown man on the horn. Creole wasn't trying any longer to get Sonny in the water. He was wishing him Godspeed. Then he stepped back, very slowly, filling the air with the immense suggestion that Sonny speak for himself.

Then they all gathered around Sonny and Sonny played. Every now and again one of them seemed to say, amen. Sonny's fingers filled the air with life, his life. But that life contained so many others. And Sonny went all the way back, he really began with the spare, flat statement of the opening phrase of the song. Then he began to make it his. It was very beautiful because it wasn't hurried and it was no longer a lament. I seemed to hear with what burning he had made it his, with what burning we had yet to make it ours, how we could cease lamenting. Freedom lurked around us and I understood, at last, that he could help us to be free if we would listen, that he would never be free until we did. Yet, there was no battle in his face now. I heard what he had gone through, and would continue to go through until he came to rest in earth. He had made it his: that long line, of which we knew only Mama and Daddy. And he was giving it back, as everything must be given back, so that, passing through death, it can live forever. I saw my mother's face again, and felt, for the first time, how the stones of the road she had walked on must have bruised her feet. I saw the moonlit road where my father's brother died. And it brought something else back to me, and carried me past it, I saw my little girl again and felt Isabel's tears again, and I felt my own tears begin to rise. And I was yet aware that this was only a moment, that the world waited outside, as hungry as a tiger, and that trouble stretched above us, longer than the sky.

Then it was over. Creole and Sonny let out their breath, both soaking wet, and grinning. There was a lot of applause and some of it was real. In the dark, the girl came by and I asked her to take drinks to the bandstand. There was a long pause, while they talked up there in the indigo light and after awhile I saw the girl put a Scotch and milk on top of the piano for Sonny. He didn't seem to notice it, but just before they started playing again, he sipped from it and looked toward me, and nodded. Then he put it back on top of the piano. For me, then, as they began to play again, it glowed and shook above my brother's head like the very cup of trembling.   *1957*

CONSIDERATIONS

1. How does the story's chronology affect your response? Consider, for example, how the story would change for you if the events were recounted as they occurred rather than retrospectively.
2. Describe the relationship between Sonny and his brother. Explain the changes they go through in the course of the story, and speculate on the reason for those changes.
3. How do the song lyrics that appear throughout the story relate to the conflict, action, and character?
4. How do the following forces relate to Sonny's search for identity: his parents, his neighborhood, his brother, and his music?
5. Compare and contrast the brothers in "Sonny's Blues" with those in "The Red Convertible" (page 218).

RAYMOND CARVER (1939–1988)

Cathedral

> *Born in Clatskanie, a logging town in Oregon, Raymond Carver graduated from California State University at Humboldt. After a year in the Writer's Workshop at the University of Iowa, he taught writing at the University of California, the University of Texas, and Syracuse University. When he was not teaching, he held various jobs, including truck driver, custodian, and deliveryman, to support himself while he wrote poetry and fiction. "Cathedral" appears in the collection* Cathedral *(1983).*

This blind man, an old friend of my wife's, he was on his way to spend the night. His wife had died. So he was visiting the dead wife's relatives in Connecticut. He called my wife from his in-laws'. Arrangements were made. He would come by train, a five-hour trip, and my wife would meet him at the station. She hadn't seen him since she worked for him one summer in Seattle ten years ago. But she and the blind man had kept in touch. They made tapes and mailed them back and forth. I wasn't enthusiastic about his visit. He was no one I knew. And his being blind bothered me. My idea of blindness came from the movies. In the movies, the blind moved slowly and never laughed. Sometimes they were led by seeing-eye dogs. A blind man in my house was not something I looked forward to.

That summer in Seattle she had needed a job. She didn't have any money. The man she was going to marry at the end of the summer was in officers' training school. He didn't have any money, either. But she was in love with the guy, and he was in love with her, etc. She'd seen something in the paper: HELP WANTED—*Reading to Blind Man,* and a telephone number. She phoned and went over, was hired on the spot. She'd worked with this blind man all summer. She read stuff to him, case studies, reports, that sort of thing. She helped him organize his little office in the county social-service department. They'd become good friends, my wife and the blind man. How do I know these things? She told me. And she told me something else. On her last day in the office, the blind man asked if he could touch her face. She agreed to this. She told me he touched his fingers to every part of her face, her nose—even her neck! She never forgot it. She even tried to write a poem about it. She was always trying to write a poem. She wrote a poem or two every year, usually after something really important had happened to her.

When we first started going out together, she showed me the poem. In the poem, she recalled his fingers and the way they had moved around over her face. In the poem, she talked about what she had felt at the time, about what went through her mind when the blind man touched her nose and lips. I can remember I didn't think much of the poem. Of course, I didn't tell her that. Maybe I just don't understand poetry. I admit it's not the first thing I reach for when I pick up something to read.

Anyway, this man who'd first enjoyed her favors, the officer-to-be, he'd been her childhood sweetheart. So okay. I'm saying that at the end of the summer she let the blind man run his hands over her face, said goodbye to him, married her childhood etc., who was now a commissioned officer, and she moved away from Seattle. But they'd kept in touch, she and the blind man. She made the first contact after a year or so. She called him up one night from an Air Force base in Alabama. She wanted to talk. They talked. He asked her to send him a tape and tell him about her life. She did this. She sent the tape. On the tape, she told the blind man about her husband and about their life together in the military. She told the blind man she loved her husband but she didn't like it where they lived and she didn't like it that he was part of the military-industrial thing. She told the blind man she'd written a poem and he was in it. She told him that she was writing a poem about what it was like to be an Air Force officer's wife. The poem wasn't finished yet. She was still writing it. The blind man made a tape. He sent her the tape. She made a tape. This went on for years. My wife's officer was posted to one base and then another. She sent tapes from Moody AFB, McGuire, McConnell, and finally Travis, near Sacramento, where one night she got to feeling lonely and cut off from people she kept losing in that moving-around life. She got to feeling she couldn't go it another step. She went in and swallowed all the pills and capsules in the medicine chest and washed them down with a bottle of gin. Then she got into a hot bath and passed out.

But instead of dying, she got sick. She threw up. Her officer—why   5
should he have a name? he was the childhood sweetheart, and what more does he want?—came home from somewhere, found her, and called the ambulance. In time, she put it all on a tape and sent the tape to the blind man. Over the years, she put all kinds of stuff on tapes and sent the tapes off lickety-split. Next to writing a poem every year, I think it was her chief means of recreation. On one tape, she told the blind man she'd decided to live away from her officer for a time. On another tape, she told him about her divorce. She and I began going out, and of course she told her blind man about it. She told him everything, or so it seemed to me. Once she asked me if I'd like to hear the latest tape from the blind man. This was a year ago. I was on the tape, she said. So I said okay, I'd listen to it. I got us drinks and we settled down in the living room. We made ready to listen. First she inserted the tape into the player and adjusted a couple of dials. Then she pushed a lever. The tape squeaked and someone began to talk in this loud voice. She lowered the volume. After a few minutes of harmless chitchat, I heard my own name in the mouth of this stranger, this blind man I didn't even know! And then this: "From all you've said about him, I can only conclude—" But we were interrupted, a knock at the door, something, and we didn't ever get back to the tape. Maybe it was just as well. I'd heard all I wanted to.

Now this same blind man was coming to sleep in my house.

"Maybe I could take him bowling," I said to my wife. She was at the draining board doing scalloped potatoes. She put down the knife she was using and turned around.

"If you love me," she said, "you can do this for me. If you don't love me, okay. But if you had a friend, any friend, and the friend came to visit, I'd make him feel comfortable." She wiped her hands with the dish towel.

"I don't have any blind friends," I said.

"You don't have *any* friends," she said. "Period. Besides," she said, "god-   10
damn it, his wife's just died! Don't you understand that? The man's lost his wife!"

I didn't answer. She'd told me a little about the blind man's wife. Her name was Beulah. Beulah! That's a name for a colored woman.

"Was his wife a Negro?" I asked.

"Are you crazy?" my wife said. "Have you just flipped or something?" She picked up a potato. I saw it hit the floor, then roll under the stove. "What's wrong with you?" she said. "Are you drunk?"

"I'm just asking," I said.

15   Right then my wife filled me in with more detail than I cared to know. I made a drink and sat at the kitchen table to listen. Pieces of the story began to fall into place.

Beulah had gone to work for the blind man the summer after my wife had stopped working for him. Pretty soon Beulah and the blind man had themselves a church wedding. It was a little wedding—who'd want to go to such a wedding in the first place?—just the two of them, plus the minister and the minister's wife. But it was a church wedding just the same. It was what Beulah had wanted, he'd said. But even then Beulah must have been carrying the cancer in her glands. After they had been inseparable for eight years—my wife's word, *inseparable*—Beulah's health went into rapid decline. She died in a Seattle hospital room, the blind man sitting beside the bed and holding on to her hand. They'd married, lived and worked together, slept together—had sex, sure—and then the blind man had to bury her. All this without his having ever seen what the goddamned woman looked like. It was beyond my understanding. Hearing this, I felt sorry for the blind man for a little bit. And then I found myself thinking what a pitiful life this woman must have led. Imagine a woman who could never see herself as she was seen in the eyes of her loved one. A woman who could go on day after day and never receive the smallest compliment from her beloved. A woman whose husband could never read the expression on her face, be it misery or something better. Someone who could wear makeup or not—what difference to him? She could, if she wanted, wear green eye-shadow around one eye, a straight pin in her nostril, yellow slacks and purple shoes, no matter. And then to slip off into death, the blind man's hand on her hand, his blind eyes streaming tears—I'm imagining now—her last thought maybe this: that he never even knew what she looked like, and she on an express to the grave. Robert was left with a small insurance policy and half of a twenty-peso Mexican coin. The other half of the coin went into the box with her. Pathetic.

So when the time rolled around, my wife went to the depot to pick him up. With nothing to do but wait—sure, I blamed him for that—I was having a drink and watching the TV when I heard the car pull into the drive. I got up from the sofa with my drink and went to the window to have a look.

I saw my wife laughing as she parked the car. I saw her get out of the car and shut the door. She was still wearing a smile. Just amazing. She went around to the other side of the car to where the blind man was already starting to get out. This blind man, feature this, he was wearing a full beard! A beard on a blind man! Too much, I say. The blind man reached into the back seat and dragged out a suitcase. My wife took his arm, shut the car door, and, talking all the way, moved him down the drive and then up the steps to the front porch. I turned off the TV. I finished my drink, rinsed the glass, dried my hands. Then I went to the door.

My wife said, "I want you to meet Robert. Robert, this is my husband. I've told you all about him." She was beaming. She had this blind man by his coat sleeve.

The blind man let go of his suitcase and up came his hand.   *20*

I took it. He squeezed hard, held my hand, and then he let it go.

"I feel like we've already met," he boomed.

"Likewise," I said. I didn't know what else to say. Then I said, "Welcome. I've heard a lot about you." We began to move then, a little group, from the porch into the living room, my wife guiding him by the arm. The blind man was carrying his suitcase in his other hand. My wife said things like, "To your left here, Robert. That's right. Now watch it, there's a chair. That's it. Sit down right here. This is the sofa. We just bought this sofa two weeks ago."

I started to say something about the old sofa. I'd liked that old sofa. But I didn't say anything. Then I wanted to say something else, small-talk, about the scenic ride along the Hudson. How going *to* New York, you should sit on the right-hand side of the train, and coming *from* New York, the left-hand side.

"Did you have a good train ride?" I said. "Which side of the train did   *25* you sit on, by the way?"

"What a question, which side!" my wife said. "What's it matter which side?" she said.

"I just asked," I said.

"Right side," the blind man said. "I hadn't been on a train in nearly forty years. Not since I was a kid. With my folks. That's been a long time. I'd nearly forgotten the sensation. I have winter in my beard now," he said. "So I've been told, anyway. Do I look distinguished, my dear?" the blind man said to my wife.

"You look distinguished, Robert," she said. "Robert," she said. "Robert, it's just so good to see you."

My wife finally took her eyes off the blind man and looked at me. I had   *30* the feeling she didn't like what she saw. I shrugged.

I've never met, or personally known, anyone who was blind. This blind man was late forties, a heavy-set, balding man with stooped shoulders, as if he carried a great weight there. He wore brown slacks, brown shoes, a light-brown shirt, a tie, a sports coat. Spiffy. He also had this full beard. But he didn't use a cane and he didn't wear dark glasses. I'd always thought dark glasses were a must for the blind. Fact was, I wished he had a pair. At first glance, his eyes looked like anyone else's eyes. But if you looked close, there was something different about them. Too much white in the iris, for one thing, and the pupils seemed to move around in the sockets without his knowing it or being able to stop it.

Creepy. As I stared at his face, I saw the left pupil turn in toward his nose while the other made an effort to keep in one place. But it was only an effort, for that eye was on the roam without his knowing it or wanting it to be.

I said, "Let me get you a drink. What's your pleasure? We have a little of everything. It's one of our pastimes."

"Bub, I'm a Scotch man myself," he said fast enough in this big voice.

"Right," I said. Bub! "Sure you are. I knew it."

35   He let his fingers touch his suitcase, which was sitting alongside the sofa. He was taking his bearings. I didn't blame him for that.

"I'll move that up to your room," my wife said.

"No, that's fine," the blind man said loudly. "It can go up when I go up."

"A little water with the Scotch?" I said.

"Very little," he said.

40   "I knew it," I said.

He said, "Just a tad. The Irish actor, Barry Fitzgerald? I'm like that fellow. When I drink water, Fitzgerald said, I drink water. When I drink whiskey, I drink whiskey." My wife laughed. The blind man brought his hand up under his beard. He lifted his beard slowly and let it drop.

I did the drinks, three big glasses of Scotch with a splash of water in each. Then we made ourselves comfortable and talked about Robert's travels. First the long flight from the West Coast to Connecticut, we covered that. Then from Connecticut up here by train. We had another drink concerning that leg of the trip.

I remembered having read somewhere that the blind didn't smoke because, as speculation had it, they couldn't see the smoke they exhaled. I thought I knew that much and that much only about blind people. But this blind man smoked his cigarette down to the nubbin and then lit another one. This blind man filled his ashtray and my wife emptied it.

When we sat down at the table for dinner, we had another drink. My wife heaped Robert's plate with cube steak, scalloped potatoes, green beans. I buttered him up two slices of bread. I said, "Here's bread and butter for you." I swallowed some of my drink. "Now let us pray," I said, and the blind man lowered his head. My wife looked at me, her mouth agape. "Pray the phone won't ring and the food doesn't get cold," I said.

45   We dug in. We ate everything there was to eat on the table. We ate like there was no tomorrow. We didn't talk. We ate. We scarfed. We grazed that table. We were into serious eating. The blind man had right away located his foods, he knew just where everything was on his plate. I watched with admiration as he used his knife and fork on the meat. He'd cut two pieces of meat, fork the meat into his mouth, and then go all out for the scalloped potatoes, the beans next, and then he'd tear off a hunk of buttered bread and eat that. He'd follow this up with a big drink of milk. It didn't seem to bother him to use his fingers once in a while, either.

We finished everything, including half a strawberry pie. For a few moments, we sat as if stunned. Sweat beaded on our faces. Finally, we got up from the table and left the dirty plates. We didn't look back. We took ourselves into the living room and sank into our places again. Robert and my wife sat on the sofa. I took the big chair. We had us two or three more drinks while they talked about the major things that had come to pass for them in the past ten years. For the most part, I just listened. Now and then I joined in. I didn't want him to think I'd left the room, and I didn't want her to think I was feeling left out. They talked of things that had happened to them—to them—these past ten years. I waited in vain to hear my name on my wife's sweet lips: "And then my dear husband came into my life"—something like that. But I heard nothing of the sort. More talk of Robert. Robert had done a little of everything, it seemed, a regular blind jack-of-all-trades. But most recently he and his wife had had an Amway distributorship, from which, I gathered, they'd earned their living, such as it was. The blind man was also a ham radio operator. He talked in his loud voice about conversations he'd had with fellow operators in Guam, in the Philippines, in Alaska, and even in Tahiti. He said he'd have a lot of friends there if he ever wanted to go visit those places. From time to time, he'd turn his blind face toward me, put his hand under his beard, ask me something. How long had I been in my present position? (Three years.) Did I like my work? (I didn't.) Was I going to stay with it? (What were the options?) Finally, when I thought he was beginning to run down, I got up and turned on the TV.

My wife looked at me with irritation. She was heading toward a boil. Then she looked at the blind man and said, "Robert, do you have a TV?"

The blind man said, "My dear, I have two TVs. I have a color set and a black-and-white thing, an old relic. It's funny, but if I turn the TV on, and I'm always turning it on, I turn on the color set. It's funny, don't you think?"

I didn't know what to say to that. I had absolutely nothing to say to that. No opinion. So I watched the news program and tried to listen to what the announcer was saying.

"This is a color TV," the blind man said. "Don't ask me how, but I can tell."   *50*

"We traded up a while ago," I said.

The blind man had another taste of his drink. He lifted his beard, sniffed it, and let it fall. He leaned forward on the sofa. He positioned his ashtray on the coffee table, then put the lighter to his cigarette. He leaned back on the sofa and crossed his legs at the ankles.

My wife covered her mouth, and then she yawned. She stretched. She said, "I think I'll go upstairs and put on my robe. I think I'll change into something else. Robert, you make yourself comfortable," she said.

"I'm comfortable," the blind man said.

"I want you to feel comfortable in this house," she said.   *55*

"I am comfortable," the blind man said.

After she'd left the room, he and I listened to the weather report and then to the sports roundup. By that time, she'd been gone so long I didn't know if she was going to come back. I thought she might have gone to bed. I wished she'd come back downstairs. I didn't want to be left alone with a blind man. I asked him if he wanted another drink, and he said sure. Then I asked if he wanted to smoke some dope with me. I said I'd just rolled a number. I hadn't, but I planned to do so in about two shakes. "I'll try some with you," he said.

"Damn right," I said. "That's the stuff."

I got our drinks and sat down on the sofa with him. Then I roll us two fat numbers. I lit one and passed it. I brought it to his fingers. He took it and inhaled.

60   "Hold it as long as you can," I said. I could tell he didn't know the first thing.

My wife came back downstairs wearing her pink robe and her pink slippers.

"What do I smell?" she said.

"We thought we'd have us some cannabis," I said.

My wife gave me a savage look. Then she looked at the blind man and said, "Robert, I didn't know you smoked."

65   He said, "I do now, my dear. There's a first time for everything. But I don't feel anything yet."

"This stuff is pretty mellow," I said. "This stuff is mild. It's dope you can reason with," I said. "It doesn't mess you up."

"Not much it doesn't, bub," he said, and laughed.

My wife sat on the sofa between the blind man and me. I passed her the number. She took it and toked and then passed it back to me. "Which way is this going?" she said. Then she said, "I shouldn't be smoking this. I can hardly keep my eyes open as it is. That dinner did me in. I shouldn't have eaten so much."

"It was the strawberry pie," the blind man said. "That's what did it," he said, and he laughed his big laugh. Then he shook his head.

70   "There's more strawberry pie," I said.

"Do you want some more, Robert?" my wife said.

"Maybe in a little while," he said.

We gave our attention to the TV. My wife yawned again. She said, "Your bed is made up when you feel like going to bed, Robert. I know you must have had a long day. When you're ready to go to bed, say so." She pulled his arm. "Robert?"

He came to and said, "I've had a real nice time. This beats tapes, doesn't it?"

75   I said, "Coming at you," and I put the number between his fingers. He inhaled, held the smoke, and then let it go. It was like he'd been doing it since he was nine years old.

"Thanks, bub," he said. "But I think this is all for me. I think I'm beginning to feel it," he said. He held the burning roach out for my wife.

"Same here," she said. "Ditto. Me, too." She took the roach and passed it to me. "I may just sit here for a while between you two guys with my eyes closed. But don't let me bother you, okay? Either one of you. If it bothers you, say so. Otherwise, I may just sit here with my eyes closed until you're ready to go to bed," she said. "Your bed's made up, Robert, when you're ready. It's right next to our room at the top of the stairs. We'll show you up when you're ready. You wake me up now, you guys, if I fall asleep." She said that and then she closed her eyes and went to sleep.

The news program ended. I got up and changed the channel. I sat back down on the sofa. I wished my wife hadn't pooped out. Her head lay across the back of the sofa, her mouth open. She'd turned so that her robe had slipped away from her legs, exposing a juicy thigh. I reached to draw her robe back over her, and it was then that I glanced at the blind man. What the hell! I flipped the robe open again.

"You say when you want some strawberry pie," I said.

"I will," he said.   80

I said, "Are you tired? Do you want me to take you up to your bed? Are you ready to hit the hay?"

"Not yet," he said. "No, I'll stay up with you, bub. If that's all right. I'll stay up until you're ready to turn in. We haven't had a chance to talk. Know what I mean? I feel like me and her monopolized the evening." He lifted his beard and he let it fall. He picked up his cigarettes and his lighter.

"That's all right," I said. Then I said, "I'm glad for the company."

And I guess I was. Every night I smoked dope and stayed up as long as I could before I fell asleep. My wife and I hardly ever went to bed at the same time. When I did go to sleep, I had these dreams. Sometimes I'd wake up from one of them, my heart going crazy.

Something about the church and the Middle Ages was on the TV. Not   85
your run-of-the-mill TV fare. I wanted to watch something else. I turned to the other channels. But there was nothing on them, either. So I turned back to the first channel and apologized.

"Bub, it's all right," the blind man said. "It's fine with me. Whatever you want to watch is okay. I'm always learning something. Learning never ends. It won't hurt me to learn something tonight. I got ears," he said.

We didn't say anything for a time. He was leaning forward with his head turned at me, his right ear aimed in the direction of the set. Very disconcerting. Now and then his eyelids drooped and then they snapped open again. Now and then he put his fingers into his beard and tugged, like he was thinking about something he was hearing on the television.

On the screen, a group of men wearing cowls was being set upon and tormented by men dressed in skeleton costumes and men dressed as devils. The men dressed as devils wore devil masks, horns, and long tails. This pageant was part of a procession. The Englishman who was narrating the thing said it took place in Spain once a year. I tried to explain to the blind man what was happening.

"Skeletons," he said. "I know about skeletons," he said, and he nodded.

90   The TV showed this one cathedral. Then there was a long, slow look at another one. Finally, the picture switched to the famous one in Paris, with its flying buttresses and its spires reaching up to the clouds. The camera pulled away to show the whole of the cathedral rising above the skyline.

There were times when the Englishman who was telling the thing would shut up, would simply let the camera move around over the cathedrals. Or else the camera would tour the countryside, men in fields walking behind oxen. I waited as long as I could. Then I felt I had to say something. I said, "They're showing the outside of this cathedral now. Gargoyles. Little statues carved to look like monsters. Now I guess they're in Italy. Yeah, they're in Italy. There's paintings on the walls of this one church."

"Are those fresco paintings, bub?" he asked, and he sipped from his drink.

I reached for my glass. But it was empty. I tried to remember what I could remember. "You're asking me are those frescoes?" I said. "That's a good question. I don't know."

The camera moved to a cathedral outside Lisbon. The differences in the Portuguese cathedral compared with the French and Italian were not that great. But they were there. Mostly the interior stuff. Then something occurred to me, and I said, "Something has occurred to me. Do you have any idea what a cathedral is? What they look like, that is? Do you follow me? If somebody says cathedral to you, do you have any notion what they're talking about? Do you know the difference between that and a Baptist church, say?"

95   He let the smoke dribble from his mouth. "I know they took hundreds of workers fifty or a thousand years to build," he said. "I just heard the man say that, of course. I know generations of the same families worked on a cathedral. I heard him say that, too. The men who began their life's work on them, they never lived to see the completion of their work. In that wise, bub, they're no different from the rest of us, right?" He laughed. Then his eyelids drooped again. His head nodded. He seemed to be snoozing. Maybe he was imagining himself in Portugal. The TV was showing another cathedral now. This one was in Germany. The Englishman's voice droned on. "Cathedrals," the blind man said. He sat up and rolled his head back and forth. "If you want the truth, bub, that's about all I know. What I just said. What I heard him say. But maybe you could describe one to me? I wish you'd do it. I'd like that. If you want to know, I really don't have a good idea."

I stared hard at the shot of the cathedral on the TV. How could I even begin to describe it? But say my life depended on it. Say my life was being threatened by an insane guy who said I had to do it or else.

I stared some more at the cathedral before the picture flipped off into the countryside. There was no use. I turned to the blind man and said, "To begin with, they're very tall." I was looking around the room for clues. "They reach way up. Up and up. Toward the sky. They're so big, some of them, they have to have these supports. To help hold them up, so to speak. These supports are called buttresses. They remind me of viaducts, for some reason. But maybe you don't know viaducts, either? Sometimes the cathedrals have devils and such carved into the front. Sometimes lords and ladies. Don't ask me why this is," I said.

He was nodding. The whole upper part of his body seemed to be moving back and forth.

"I'm not doing so good, am I?" I said.

He stopped nodding and leaned forward on the edge of the sofa. As he listened to me, he was running his fingers through his beard. I wasn't getting through to him, I could see that. But he waited for me to go on just the same. He nodded, like he was trying to encourage me. I tried to think what else to say. "They're really big," I said. "They're massive. They're built of stone. Marble, too, sometimes. In those olden days, when they built cathedrals, men wanted to be close to God. In those olden days, God was an important part of everyone's life. You could tell this from their cathedral-building. I'm sorry," I said, "but it looks like that's the best I can do for you. I'm just no good at it."

"That's all right, bub," the blind man said. "Hey, listen. I hope you don't mind my asking you. Can I ask you something? Let me ask you a simple question, yes or no. I'm just curious and there's no offense. You're my host. But let me ask if you are in any way religious? You don't mind my asking?"

I shook my head. He couldn't see that, though. A wink is the same as a nod to a blind man. "I guess I don't believe in it. In anything. Sometimes it's hard. You know what I'm saying?"

"Sure, I do," he said.

"Right," I said.

The Englishman was still holding forth. My wife sighed in her sleep. She drew a long breath and went on with her sleeping.

"You'll have to forgive me," I said. "But I can't tell you what a cathedral looks like. It just isn't in me to do it. I can't do any more than I've done."

The blind man sat very still, his head down, as he listened to me.

I said, "The truth is, cathedrals don't mean anything special to me. Nothing. Cathedrals. They're something to look at on late-night TV. That's all they are."

It was then that the blind man cleared his throat. He brought something up. He took a handkerchief from his back pocket. Then he said, "I get it, bub. It's okay. It happens. Don't worry about it," he said. "Hey, listen to me. Will you do me a favor? I got an idea. Why don't you find us some heavy paper? And a pen. We'll do something. We'll draw one together. Get us a pen and some heavy paper. Go on, bub, get the stuff," he said.

So I went upstairs. My legs felt like they didn't have any strength in them. They felt like they did after I'd done some running. In my wife's room, I

100

105

110

looked around. I found some ballpoints in a little basket on her table. And then I tried to think where to look for the kind of paper he was talking about.

Downstairs, in the kitchen, I found a shopping bag with onion skins in the bottom of the bag. I emptied the bag and shook it. I brought it into the living room and sat down with it near his legs. I moved some things, smoothed the wrinkles from the bag, spread it out on the coffee table.

The blind man got down from the sofa and sat next to me on the carpet.

He ran his fingers over the paper. He went up and down the sides of the paper. The edges, even the edges. He fingered the corners.

"All right," he said. "All right, let's do her."

115   He found my hand, the hand with the pen. He closed his hand over my hand. "Go ahead, bub, draw," he said. "Draw. You'll see. I'll follow along with you. It'll be okay. Just begin now like I'm telling you. You'll see. Draw," the blind man said.

So I began. First I drew a box that looked like a house. It could have been the house I lived in. Then I put a roof on it. At either end of the roof, I drew spires. Crazy.

"Swell," he said. "Terrific. You're doing fine," he said. "Never thought anything like this could happen in your lifetime, did you, bub? Well, it's a strange life, we all know that. Go on now. Keep it up."

I put in windows with arches. I drew flying buttresses. I hung great doors. I couldn't stop. The TV station went off the air. I put down the pen and closed and opened my fingers. The blind man felt around over the paper. He moved the tips of his fingers over the paper, all over what I had drawn, and he nodded.

"Doing fine," the blind man said.

120   I took up the pen again, and he found my hand. I kept at it. I'm no artist. But I kept drawing just the same.

My wife opened her eyes and gazed at us. She sat up on the sofa, her robe hanging open. She said, "What are you doing? Tell me, I want to know."

I didn't answer her.

The blind man said, "We're drawing a cathedral. Me and him are working on it. Press hard," he said to me. "That's right. That's good," he said. "Sure, you got it, bub. I can tell. You didn't think you could. But you can, can't you? You're cooking with gas now. You know what I'm saying? We're going to really have us something here in a minute. How's the old arm?" he said. "Put some people in there now. What's a cathedral without people?"

My wife said, "What's going on? Robert, what are you doing? What's going on?"

125   "It's all right," he said to her. "Close your eyes now," the blind man said to me.

I did it. I closed them just like he said.

"Are they closed?" he said. "Don't fudge."

"They're closed," I said.

"Keep them that way," he said. "Don't stop now. Draw."

So we kept on with it. His fingers rode my fingers as my hand went over   *130*
the paper. It was like nothing else in my life up to now.

Then he said, "I think that's it. I think you got it," he said. "Take a look.
What do you think?"

But I had my eyes closed. I thought I'd keep them that way for a little
longer. I thought it was something I ought to do.

"Well?" he said. "Are you looking?"

My eyes were still closed. I was in my house. I knew that. But I didn't
feel like I was inside anything.

"It's really something," I said.   *1983*   *135*

CONSIDERATIONS

1. Read the first part of the story (through paragraph 16, when Robert arrives at the narrator's house), and then write a brief description of the narrator and your response to him.
2. In an article in *Studies in Short Fiction* (Summer 1986), Mark A. R. Facknitz suggests that what motivates one to continue reading this story, in spite of its unattractive narrator, is "a fear of the harm he may do to his wife and her blind friend." Do you agree with this observation? Explain.
3. In what ways do the narrator and Robert belong to different cultures? How are their identities related to these cultures?
4. What happens in the final scene? Why does Carver choose to have Robert and the narrator watch a television program about cathedrals rather than, for example, old schoolhouses or national monuments?
5. How does Robert contribute to the narrator's wife's search for identity? How does she contribute to Robert's sense of who he is?

JOSÉ ARMAS (1944–   )

El Tonto° del Barrio°

> *José Armas is a publisher, writer, and community activist who in 1974 won a fellowship associated with the Urban Planning Department at MIT. Armas has taught at the University of New Mexico and at the University of Albuquerque. In addition, he writes a column for* The Albuquerque Journal *on issues of*

El Tonto: Stupid one; *del Barrio:* Of the Spanish-speaking community.

particular importance to the Hispanic community. In 1980, the National En-
dowment for the Arts granted him a writing fellowship. "El Tonto del Barrio"
was first published in 1982.

Romero Estrada was called "El Cotoro"° because he was always whistling
and singing. He made nice music even though his songs were spontaneous
compositions made up of words with sounds that he liked but which seldom
made any sense. But that didn't seem to bother either Romero or anyone else
in the Golden Heights Centro where he lived. Not even the kids made fun of
him. It just was not permitted.

Romero had a ritual that he followed almost every day. After breakfast
he would get his broom and go up and down the main street of the Golden
Heights Centro whistling and singing and sweeping the sidewalks for all the
businesses. He would sweep in front of the Tortillería America, the XXX
Liquor Store, the Tres Milpas Bar run by Tino Gabaldon, Barelas' Barber Shop,
the used furniture store owned by Goldstein, El Centro Market of the Avila
family, the Model Cities Office, and Lourdes Printing Store. Then, in the afternoons, he would come back and sit in Barelas' Barber Shop and spend the day
looking at magazines and watching and waving to the passing people as he
sang and composed his songs without a care in the world.

When business was slow, Barelas would let him sit in the barber's chair.
Romero loved it. It was a routine that Romero kept every day except Sundays
and Mondays when Barelas' Barber Shop was closed. After a period of years,
people in the barrio got used to seeing Romero do his little task of sweeping
the sidewalks and sitting in Barelas' Barber Shop. If he didn't show up one day
someone assumed the responsibility to go to his house to see if he was ill. People would stop to say hello to Romero on the street and although he never
initiated a conversation while he was sober, he always smiled and responded
cheerfully to everyone. People passing the barber shop in the afternoons made
it a point to wave even though they couldn't see him; they knew he was in
there and was expecting some salutation.

When he was feeling real good, Romero would sweep in front of the
houses on both sides of the block also. He took his job seriously and took
great care to sweep cleanly, between the cracks and even between the sides of
the buildings. The dirt and small scraps went into the gutter. The bottles and
bigger pieces of litter were put carefully in cardboard boxes, ready for the
garbage man.

5   If he did it the way he wanted, the work took him the whole morning.
And always cheerful—always with some song.

Only once did someone call attention to his work. Frank Avila told him
in jest that Romero had forgotten to pick up an empty bottle of wine from

---

El Cotoro: The parrot or magpie; chatterbox (slang).

his door. Romero was so offended and made such a commotion that it got around very quickly that no one should criticize his work. There was, in fact, no reason to.

Although it had been long acknowledged that Romero was a little "touched," he fit very well into the community. He was a respected citizen.

He could be found at the Tres Milpas Bar drinking his occasional beer in the evenings. Romero had a rivalry going with the Ranchera° songs on the jukebox. He would try to outsing the songs using the same melody but inserting his own selection of random words. Sometimes, like all people, he would "bust out" and get drunk.

One could always tell when Romero was getting drunk because he would begin telling everyone that he loved them.

"I looov youuu," he would sing to someone and offer to compose them   10
a song.

"Ta bueno, Romero. Ta bueno, ya bete,"° they would tell him.

Sometimes when he got too drunk he would crap in his pants and then Tino would make him go home.

Romero received some money from Social Security but it wasn't much. None of the merchants gave him any credit because he would always forget to pay his bills. He didn't do it on purpose, he just forgot and spent his money on something else. So instead, the businessmen preferred to do little things for him occasionally. Barelas would trim his hair when things were slow. The Tortillería America would give him menudo° and fresh-made tortillas at noon when he was finished with his sweeping. El Centro Market would give him the overripe fruit and broken boxes of food that no one else would buy. Although it was unspoken and unwritten, there was an agreement that existed between Romero and the Golden Heights Centro. Romero kept the sidewalks clean and the barrio looked after him. It was a contract that worked well for a long time.

Then, when Seferino, Barelas' oldest son, graduated from high school he went to work in the barber shop for the summer. Seferino was a conscientious and sensitive young man and it wasn't long before he took notice of Romero and came to feel sorry for him.

One day when Romero was in the shop Seferino decided to act.   15

"Mira, Romero. Yo te doy 50 centavos por cada dia que me barres la banqueta.° Fifty cents for every day you sweep the sidewalk for us. Qué te parece?"°

Romero thought about it carefully.

"Hecho! Done!" he exclaimed. He started for home right away to get his broom.

"Why did you do that for, m'ijo?"° asked Barelas.

Ranchera: Spanish-language songs originating with those who worked on ranches. *Ta bueno, ya bete:* It's all right; go away now. *menudo:* Dish made with internal organs. *Mira, Romero. . . . la banqueta:* Look here, Romero. I'll give you 50 cents for every day you sweep the sidewalk for me. *Qué te parece?:* How does that seem to you? *m'ijo:* My son.

20   "It don't seem right, Dad. The man works and no one pays him for his
work. Everyone should get paid for what they do."
        "He don't need no pay. Romero has everything he needs."
        "It's not the same, Dad. How would you like to do what he does and be
treated the same way? It's degrading the way he has to go around getting scraps
and handouts."
        "I'm not Romero. Besides you don't know about these things, m'ijo.
Romero would be unhappy if his schedule was upset. Right now everyone
likes him and takes care of him. He sweeps the sidewalks because he wants
something to do, not because he wants money."
        "I'll pay him out of my money, don't worry about it then."
25   "The money is not the point. The point is that money will not help
Romero. Don't you understand that?"
        "Look, Dad. Just put yourself in his place. Would you do it? Would you
cut hair for nothing?"
        Barelas just knew his son was putting something over on him but he
didn't know how to answer. It seemed to make sense the way Seferino explained it. But it still went against his "instinct." On the other hand, Seferino
had gone and finished high school. He must know something. There were few
kids who had finished high school in the barrio, and fewer who had gone to
college. Barelas knew them all. He noted (with some pride) that Seferino was
going to be enrolled at Harvard University this year. That must count for something, he thought. Barelas himself had never gone to school. So maybe his son
had something there. On the other hand . . . it upset Barelas that he wasn't able
to get Seferino to see the issue. How can we be so far apart on something so
simple, he thought. But he decided not to say anything else about it.
        Romero came back right away and swept the front of Barelas' shop again
and put what little dirt he found into the curb. He swept up the gutter, put the
trash in a shoe box and threw it in a garbage can.
        Seferino watched with pride as Romero went about his job and when
he was finished he went outside and shook Romero's hand. Seferino told him
he had done a good job. Romero beamed.
30   Manolo was coming into the shop to get his hair cut as Seferino was
giving Romero his wages. He noticed Romero with his broom.
        "What's going on?" he asked. Barelas shrugged his shoulders. "Qué tiene
Romero?° Is he sick or something?"
        "No, he's not sick," explained Seferino, who had now come inside. He
told Manolo the story.
        "We're going to make Romero a businessman," said Seferino. "Do you
realize how much money Romero would make if everyone paid him just fifty

Qué tiene Romero?: What's wrong with Romero?

cents a day. Like my dad says, 'Everyone should be able to keep his dignity, no matter how poor.' And he does a job, you know."

"Well, it makes sense," said Manolo.

"Hey. Maybe I'll ask people to do that," said Seferino. "That way the   35
poor old man could make a decent wage. Do you want to help, Manolo? You can go with me to ask people to pay him."

"Well," said Manolo as he glanced at Barelas, "I'm not too good at asking people for money."

This did not discourage Seferino. He went out and contacted all the businesses on his own, but no one else wanted to contribute. This didn't discourage Seferino either. He went on giving Romero fifty cents a day.

After a while, Seferino heard that Romero had asked for credit at the grocery store. "See, Dad. What did I tell you? Things are getting better for him already. He's becoming his own man. And look. It's only been a couple of weeks." Barelas did not reply.

But then the next week Romero did not show up to sweep any sidewalks. He was around but he didn't do any work for anybody the entire week. He walked around Golden Heights Centro in his best gray work pants and his slouch hat, looking important and making it a point to walk right past the barber shop every little while.

Of course, the people in the Golden Heights Centro noticed the change   40
immediately, and since they saw Romero in the street, they knew he wasn't ill. But the change was clearly disturbing the community. They discussed him in the Tortillería America where people got together for coffee, and at the Tres Milpas Bar. Everywhere the topic of conversation was the great change that had come over Romero. Only Barelas did not talk about it.

The following week Romero came into the barber shop and asked to talk with Seferino in private. Barelas knew immediately something was wrong. Romero never initiated a conversation unless he was drunk.

They went into the back room where Barelas could not hear and then Romero informed Seferino, "I want a raise."

"What? What do you mean, a raise? You haven't been around for a week. You only worked a few weeks and now you want a raise?" Seferino was clearly angry but Romero was calm and insistent.

Romero correctly pointed out that he had been sweeping the sidewalks for a long time. Even before Seferino finished high school.

"I deserve a raise," he repeated after an eloquent presentation.   45

Seferino looked coldly at Romero. It was clearly a stand-off.

Then Seferino said, "Look, maybe we should forget the whole thing. I was just trying to help you out and look at what you do."

Romero held his ground. "I helped you out too. No one told me to do it and I did it anyway. I helped you many years."

"Well, let's forget about the whole thing then," said Seferino.

454 ROOTS, IDENTITY, AND CULTURE

50   "I quit then," said Romero.
            "Quit?" exclaimed Seferino as he laughed at Romero.
            "Quit! I quit!" said Romero as he walked out the front of the shop past
Barelas who was cutting a customer's hair.
            Seferino came out shaking his head and laughing.
            "Can you imagine that old guy?"
55   Barelas did not seem too amused. He felt he could have predicted that
something bad like this would happen.
            Romero began sweeping the sidewalks again the next day with the ex-
ception that when he came to the barber shop he would go around it and
continue sweeping the rest of the sidewalks. He did this for the rest of the
week. And the following Tuesday he began sweeping the sidewalk all the way
up to the shop and then pushing the trash to the sidewalk in front of the barber shop. Romero then stopped coming to the barber shop in the afternoon.
            The barrio buzzed with fact and rumor about Romero. Tino com-
mented that Romero was not singing anymore. Even if someone offered to
buy him a beer he wouldn't sing. Frank Avila said the neighbors were complaining because he was leaving his TV on loud the whole day and night. He
still greeted people but seldom smiled. He had run up a big bill at the liquor
store and when the manager stopped his credit, he caught Romero stealing
bottles of whiskey. He was also getting careless about his dress. He didn't shave
and clean like he used to. Women complained that he walked around in soiled
pants, that he smelled bad. Even one of the little kids complained that Romero
had kicked his puppy, but that seemed hard to believe.
            Barelas felt terrible. He felt responsible. But he couldn't convince Se-
ferino that what he had done was wrong. Barelas himself stopped going to the
Tres Milpas Bar after work to avoid hearing about Romero. Once he came
across Romero on the street and Barelas said hello but with a sense of guilt.
Romero responded, avoiding Barelas' eyes and moving past him awkwardly
and quickly. Romero's behavior continued to get erratic and some people
started talking about having Romero committed.
            "You can't do that," said Barelas when he was presented with a petition.
60   "He's flipped," said Tino, who made up part of the delegation circulating
the petition. "No one likes Romero more than I do, you know that Barelas."
            "But he's really crazy," said Frank Avila.
            "He was crazy before. No one noticed," pleaded Barelas.
            "But it was a crazy we could depend on. Now he just wants to sit on the
curb and pull up the women's skirts. It's terrible. The women are going crazy.
He's also running into the street stopping traffic. You see how he is. What
choice do we have?"
            "It's for his own good," put in one of the workers from the Model Cities
Office. Barelas dismissed them as outsiders. Seferino was there and wanted to
say something but a look from Barelas stopped him.

"We just can't do that," insisted Barelas. "Let's wait. Maybe he's just going   65
through a cycle. Look. We've had a full moon recently, qué no?° That must be
it. You know how the moon affects people in his condition."

"I don't know," said Tino. "What if he hurts . . ."

"He's not going to hurt anyone," cut in Barelas.

"No, Barelas. I was going to say, what if he hurts himself. He has no one
at home. I'd say, let him come home with me for a while but you know how
stubborn he is. You can't even talk to him any more."

"He gives everyone the finger when they try to pull him out of the traffic," said Frank Avila. "The cops have missed him, but it won't be long before
they see him doing some of his antics and arrest him. Then what? Then the
poor guy is in real trouble."

"Well, look," said Barelas. "How many names you got on the list?"   70

Tino responded slowly, "Well, we sort of wanted you to start off the list."

"Let's wait a while longer," said Barelas. "I just know that Romero will
come around. Let's wait just a while, okay?"

No one had the heart to fight the issue and so they postponed the petition.

There was no dramatic change in Romero even though the full moon
had completed its cycle. Still, no one initiated the petition again and then in
the middle of August Seferino left for Cambridge to look for housing and to
register early for school. Suddenly everything began to change again. One day
Romero began sweeping the entire sidewalk again. His spirits began to pick
up and his strange antics began to disappear.

At the Tortillería America the original committee met for coffee and the   75
talk turned to Romero.

"He's going to be all right now," said a jubilant Barelas. "I guarantee it."

"Well, don't hold your breath yet," said Tino. "The full moon is coming
up again."

"Yeah," said Frank Avila dejectedly.

When the next full moon was in force the group was together again
drinking coffee and Tino asked, "Well, how's Romero doing?"

Barelas smiled and said, "Well. Singing songs like crazy." *1982*   80

CONSIDERATIONS

1. Is Romero Estrada "El Tonto del Barrio" (the stupid one of the neighborhood)? Is there another person or are there other persons in the story to
   whom the title could be awarded? Explain.

qué no?: Haven't we?

2. Make a list of the qualities and characteristics you see in Barelas. Why do the other barrio dwellers cast him in the role of leader? Do you agree with their view of Barelas? Explain.

3. Barelas and his son Seferino argue about paying Romero for his work. Seferino thinks paying Romero will give him dignity. Do you agree that being paid for work generally grants the worker dignity that is not granted to unpaid labor? Explain.

4. Why do you think Romero reacts to the pay as he does? Write a monologue describing the thoughts that explain the changes he goes through after he is offered 50 cents a day to sweep the sidewalk.

5. What do you think of the story's ending? Are there any clear winners or losers? Explain.

TONI CADE BAMBARA (1939–1995)

The Lesson

Toni Cade Bambara grew up in Harlem and Bedford-Stuyvesant, New York. After earning a bachelor of arts from Queens College and a master of arts from the City College of New York and studying in Italy and Paris, she took a position as a social worker with the New York State Department of Welfare. In addition, she worked as a youth counselor, a community organizer, and a freelance writer. Many of her stories focus on the lives of African-American women and their varied experiences in relationship to their families, their professional lives, and their communities. "The Lesson" appeared in her collection of short fiction Gorilla, My Love *(1972).*

Back in the days when everyone was old and stupid or young and foolish and me and Sugar were the only ones just right, this lady moved on our block with nappy hair and proper speech and no makeup. And quite naturally we laughed at her, laughed the way we did at the junk man who went about his business like he was some big-time president and his sorry-ass horse his secretary. And we kinda hated her too, hated the way we did the winos who cluttered up our parks and pissed on our handball walls and stank up our hallways and stairs so you couldn't halfway play hide-and-seek without a goddamn gas mask. Miss Moore was her name. The only woman on the block with no first name. And she was black as hell, cept for her feet, which were fish-white and spooky. And she was always planning these boring-ass things for us to do, us being my cousin, mostly, who lived on the block cause we all moved North the same time and to the same apartment then spread out gradual to breathe. And our parents would yank our heads into some kinda shape and crisp up our clothes so we'd be presentable for travel with Miss Moore, who always looked like she was going to church, though she never did. Which is just one of the things the grownups talked about when they talked behind her back like a dog. But when she came calling with some sachet she'd sewed up or some gingerbread she'd made or some book, why then they'd all be too embarrassed to turn her down and we'd get handed over all spruced up. She'd been to college and said it was only right that she should take responsibility for the young ones' education, and she not even related by marriage or blood. So they'd go for it. Specially Aunt Gretchen. She was the main gofer in the family. You got some ole dumb shit foolishness you want somebody to go for, you send for Aunt Gretchen. She been screwed into the go-along for so long, it's a blood-deep natural thing with her. Which is how she got saddled with me and Sugar and Junior in the first place while our mothers were in a la-de-da apartment up the block having a good ole time.

So this one day Miss Moore rounds us all up at the mailbox and it's puredee hot and she's knockin herself out about arithmetic. And school suppose to let up in summer I heard, but she don't never let up. And the starch in my pinafore scratching the shit outta me and I'm really hating this nappy-head bitch and her goddamn college degree. I'd much rather go to the pool or to the show where it's cool. So me and Sugar leaning on the mailbox being surly, which is a Miss Moore word. And Flyboy checking out what everybody brought for lunch. And Fat Butt already wasting his peanut-butter-and-jelly sandwich like the pig he is. And Junebug punchin on Q.T.'s arm for potato chips. And Rosie Giraffe shifting from one hip to the other waiting for somebody to step on her foot or ask her if she from Georgia so she can kick ass, preferably Mercedes'. And Miss Moore asking us do we know what money is, like we a bunch of retards. I mean real money, she say, like it's only poker chips or monopoly papers we lay on the grocer. So right away I'm tired of this and say so. And would much rather snatch Sugar and go to the Sunset and terrorize the West Indian kids and take their hair ribbons and their money too. And Miss Moore files that remark away for next week's lesson on brotherhood, I can tell. And finally I say we oughta get to the subway cause it's cooler and besides we might meet some cute boys. Sugar done swiped her mama's lipstick, so we ready.

So we heading down the street and she's boring us silly about what things cost and what our parents make and how much goes for rent and how money ain't divided up right in this country. And then she gets to the part about we all poor and live in the slums, which I don't feature. And I'm ready to speak on that, but she steps out in the street and hails two cabs just like that. Then she hustles half the crew in with her and hands me a five-dollar bill and tells me to calculate 10 percent tip for the driver. And we're off. Me and Sugar and

Junebug and Flyboy hangin out the window and hollering to everybody, putting lipstick on each other cause Flyboy a faggot anyway, and making farts with our sweaty armpits. But I'm mostly trying to figure how to spend this money. But they all fascinated with the meter ticking and Junebug starts laying bets as to how much it'll read when Flyboy can't hold his breath no more. Then Sugar lays bets as to how much it'll be when we get there. So I'm stuck. Don't nobody want to go for my plan, which is to jump out at the next light and run off to the first bar-b-que we can find. Then the driver tells us to get the hell out cause we there already. And the meter reads eighty-five cents. And I'm stalling to figure out the tip and Sugar say give him a dime. And I decide he don't need it bad as I do, so later for him. But then he tries to take off with Junebug foot still in the door so we talk about his mama something ferocious. Then we check out that we on Fifth Avenue and everybody dressed up in stockings. One lady in a fur coat, hot as it is. White folks crazy.

"This is the place," Miss Moore say, presenting it to us in the voice she uses at the museum. "Let's look in the windows before we go in."

5 "Can we steal?" Sugar asks very serious like she's getting the ground rules squared away before she plays. "I beg your pardon," say Miss Moore, and we fall out. So she leads us around the windows of the toy store and me and Sugar screamin, "This is mine, that's mine, I gotta have that, that was made for me, I was born for that," till Big Butt drowns us out.

"Hey, I'm going to buy that there."

"That there? You don't even know what it is, stupid."

"I do so," he say punchin on Rosie Giraffe. "It's a microscope."

"Whatcha gonna do with a microscope, fool?"

10 "Look at things."

"Like what, Ronald?" ask Miss Moore. And Big Butt ain't got the first notion. So here go Miss Moore gabbing about the thousands of bacteria in a drop of water and the somethinorother in a speck of blood and the million and one living things in the air around us is invisible to the naked eye. And what she say that for? Junebug go to town on that "naked" and we rolling. Then Miss Moore ask what it cost. So we all jam into the window smudgin it up and the price tag say $300. So then she ask how long'd take for Big Butt and Junebug to save up their allowances. "Too long" I say. "Yeh," adds Sugar, "outgrown it by that time." And Miss Moore say no, you never outgrow learning instruments. "Why, even medical students and interns and," blah, blah, blah. And we ready to choke Big Butt for bringing it up in the first damn place.

"This here costs four hundred eighty dollars," say Rosie Giraffe. So we pile up all over her to see what she pointin out. My eyes tells me it's a chunk of glass cracked with something heavy, and different-color inks dripped into the splits, then the whole thing put into a oven or something. But for $480 it don't make sense.

"That's a paperweight made of semi-precious stones fused together under tremendous pressure," she explains slowly, with her hands doing the mining and all the factory work.

"So what's a paperweight?" asks Rosie Giraffe.

"To weigh paper with, dumbbell," say Flyboy, the wise man from the East.   *15*

"Not exactly," say Miss Moore, which is what she say when you warm or way off too. "It's to weigh paper down so it won't scatter and make your desk untidy." So right away me and Sugar curtsy to each other and then to Mercedes who is more the tidy type.

"We don't keep paper on top of the desk in my class," say Junebug, figuring Miss Moore crazy or lyin one.

"At home, then," she say. "Don't you have a calendar and a pencil case and a blotter and a letter-opener on your desk at home where you do your homework?" And she know damn well what our homes look like cause she nosys around in them every chance she gets.

"I don't even have a desk," say Junebug. "Do we?"

"No. And I don't get no homework neither," says Big Butt.   *20*

"And I don't even have a home," say Flyboy like he do at school to keep the white folks off his back and sorry for him. Send this poor kid to camp posters, is his specialty.

"I do," says Mercedes. "I have a box of stationery on my desk and a picture of my cat. My godmother bought the stationery and the desk. There's a big rose on each sheet and the envelopes smell like roses."

"Who wants to know about your smelly-ass stationery," say Rosie Giraffe fore I can get my two cents in.

"It's important to have a work area all your own so that . . ."

"Will you look at this sailboat, please," say Flyboy, cuttin her off and   *25* pointin to the thing like it was his. So once again we tumble all over each other to gaze at this magnificent thing in the toy store which is just big enough to maybe sail two kittens across the pond if you strap them to the posts tight. We all start reciting the price tag like we in assembly. "Hand-crafted sailboat of fiberglass at one thousand one hundred ninety-five dollars."

"Unbelievable," I hear myself say and am really stunned. I read it again for myself just in case the group recitation put me in a trance. Same thing. For some reason this pisses me off. We look at Miss Moore and she lookin at us, waiting for I dunno what.

"Who'd pay all that when you can buy a sailboat set for a quarter at Pop's, a tube of glue for a dime, and a ball of string for eight cents? It must have a motor and a whole lot else besides," I say. "My sailboat cost me about fifty cents."

"But will it take water?" say Mercedes with her smart ass.

"Took mine to Alley Pond Park once," say Flyboy. "String broke. Lost it. Pity."

30   "Sailed mine in Central Park and it keeled over and sank. Had to ask my father for another dollar."

"And you got the strap," laugh Big Butt. "The jerk didn't even have a string on it. My old man wailed on his behind."

Little Q.T. was staring hard at the sailboat and you could see he wanted it bad. But he too little and somebody'd just take it from him. So what the hell. "This boat for kids, Miss Moore?"

"Parents silly to buy something like that just to get all broke up," say Rosie Giraffe.

"That much money it should last forever," I figure.

35   "My father'd buy it for me if I wanted it."

"Your father, my ass," say Rosie Giraffe getting a chance to finally push Mercedes.

"Must be rich people shop here," say Q.T.

"You are a very bright boy," say Flyboy. "What was your first clue?" And he rap him on the head with the back of his knuckles, since Q.T. the only one he could get away with. Though Q.T. liable to come up behind you years later and get his licks in when you half expect it.

"What I want to know is," I says to Miss Moore though I never talk to her, I wouldn't give the bitch that satisfaction, "is how much a real boat costs? I figure a thousand'd get you a yacht any day."

40   "Why don't you check that out," she says, "and report back to the group?" Which really pains my ass. If you gonna mess up a perfectly good swim day least you could do is have some answers. "Let's go in," she say like she got something up her sleeve. Only she don't lead the way. So me and Sugar turn the corner to where the entrance is, but when we get there I kinda hang back. Not that I'm scared, what's there to be afraid of, just a toy store. But I feel funny, shame. But what I got to be shamed about? Got as much right to go in as anybody. But somehow I can't seem to get hold of the door, so I step away for Sugar to lead. But she hangs back too. And I look at her and she looks at me and this is ridiculous. I mean, damn, I have never ever been shy about doing nothing or going nowhere. But then Mercedes steps up and then Rosie Giraffe and Big Butt crowd in behind and shove, and next thing we all stuffed into the doorway with only Mercedes squeezing past us, smoothing out her jumper and walking right down the aisle. Then the rest of us tumble in like a glued-together jigsaw done all wrong. And people lookin at us. And it's like the time me and Sugar crashed into the Catholic church on a dare. But once we got in there and everything so hushed and holy and the candles and the bowin and the handkerchiefs on all the drooping heads, I just couldn't go through with the plan. Which was for me to run up to the altar and do a tap dance while Sugar played the nose flute and messed around in the holy water. And Sugar kept givin me the elbow. Then later teased me so bad I tied her up

in the shower and turned it on and locked her in. And she'd be there till this day if Aunt Gretchen hadn't finally figured I was lyin about the boarder takin a shower.

Same thing in the store. We all walkin on tiptoe and hardly touchin the games and puzzles and things. And I watched Miss Moore who is steady watchin us like she waitin for a sign. Like Mama Drewery watches the sky and sniffs the air and takes note of just how much slant is in the bird formation. Then me and Sugar bump smack into each other, so busy gazing at the toys, 'specially the sailboat. But we don't laugh and go into our fat-lady bump-stomach routine. We just stare at that price tag. Then Sugar run a finger over the whole boat. And I'm jealous and want to hit her. Maybe not her, but I sure want to punch somebody in the mouth.

"Watcha bring us here for, Miss Moore?"

"You sound angry, Sylvia. Are you mad about something?" Givin me one of them grins like she tellin a grown-up joke that never turns out to be funny. And she's lookin very closely at me like maybe she plannin to do my portrait from memory. I'm mad, but I won't give her that satisfaction. So I slouch around the store bein very bored and say, "Let's go."

Me and Sugar at the back of the train watchin the tracks whizzin by large then small then gettin gobbled up in the dark. I'm thinkin about this tricky toy I saw in the store. A clown that somersaults on a bar then does chin-ups just cause you yank lightly at his leg. Cost $35. I could see me askin my mother for a $35 birthday clown. "You wanna who that costs what?" she'd say, cocking her head to the side to get a better view of the hole in my head. Thirty-five dollars could buy new bunk beds for Junior and Gretchen's boy. Thirty-five dollars and the whole household could go visit Granddaddy Nelson in the country. Thirty-five dollars would pay for the rent and the piano bill too. Who are these people that spend that much for performing clowns and $1000 for toy sailboats? What kinda work they do and how they live and how come we ain't in on it? Where we are is who we are, Miss Moore always pointin out. But it don't necessarily have to be that way, she always adds then waits for somebody to say that poor people have to wake up and demand their share of the pie and don't none of us know what kind of pie she talking about in the first damn place. But she ain't so smart cause I still got her four dollars from the taxi and she sure ain't gettin it. Messin up my day with this shit. Sugar nudges me in my pocket and winks.

Miss Moore lines us up in front of the mailbox where we started from,   45
seem like years ago, and I got a headache for thinkin so hard. And we lean all over each other so we can hold up under the draggy-ass lecture she always finishes us off with at the end before we thank her for borin us to tears. But she just looks at us like she readin tea leaves. Finally she say, "Well, what did you think of F.A.O. Schwartz?"

Rosie Giraffe mumbles, "White folks crazy."

"I'd like to go there again when I get my birthday money," says Mercedes, and we shove her out the pack so she has to lean on the mailbox by herself.

"I'd like a shower. Tiring day," say Flyboy.

Then Sugar surprises me by sayin, "You know, Miss Moore, I don't think all of us here put together eat in a year what that sailboat costs." And Miss Moore lights up like somebody goosed her. "And?" she say, urging Sugar on. Only I'm standin on her foot so she don't continue.

50   "Imagine for a minute what kind of society it is in which some people can spend on a toy what it would cost to feed a family of six or seven. What do you think?"

"I think," say Sugar pushing me off her feet like she never done before, cause I whip her ass in a minute, "that this is not much of a democracy if you ask me. Equal chance to pursue happiness means an equal crack at the dough, don't it?" Miss Moore is beside herself and I am disgusted with Sugar's treachery. So I stand on her foot one more time to see if she'll shove me. She shuts up, and Miss Moore looks at me, sorrowfully I'm thinkin. And somethin weird is goin on, I can feel it in my chest.

"Anybody else learn anything today?" lookin dead at me. I walk away and Sugar has to run to catch up and don't even seem to notice when I shrug her arm off my shoulder.

"Well, we got four dollars anyway," she says.

"Uh hunh."

55   "We could go to Hascombs and get half a chocolate layer and then go to the Sunset and still have plenty money for potato chips and ice cream sodas."

"Uh hunh."

"Race you to Hascombs," she say.

We start down the block and she gets ahead which is O.K. by me cause I'm going to the West End and then over to the Drive to think this day through. She can run if she want to and even run faster. But ain't nobody gonna beat me at nuthin.   *1972*

CONSIDERATIONS

1. Although Miss Moore does not teach Sugar, Sylvia, and their friends in a traditional classroom, in what ways does she fit the stereotype of an elementary schoolteacher? In what ways does she challenge or escape the stereotype?

2. Explain Miss Moore's attitude toward the children she teaches and toward their parents. How is her attitude reflected by her teaching methods?

3. What do you see as Miss Moore's purpose for bringing Sugar, Sylvia, and their friends to F.A.O. Schwartz? What speculations do the children make about the trip and its purpose?
4. Identify and discuss some of the comic elements in the story. Do you find these elements distracting, or do they in some way contribute to the theme(s) you see?
5. Sugar and Sylvia react differently to the trip to F.A.O. Schwartz. What do you think each learns? Based on their different reactions to Miss Moore's lesson, what future can you predict for each girl?

Poetry

PAUL LAURENCE DUNBAR (1872–1906)
We wear the mask

> *Paul Laurence Dunbar was born in Dayton, Ohio, to parents who were former slaves. His first collection of poetry,* Oak and Ivy, *was published in 1893. Dunbar's poems often address the themes of culture and race, and his works include traditional rhythms and forms as well as experimental rhythms that incorporate black dialect.*

We wear the mask that grins and lies,
It hides our cheeks and shades our eyes—
This debt we pay to human guile;
With torn and bleeding hearts we smile,
And mouth with myriad subtleties.   5

Why should the world be over-wise,
In counting all our tears and sighs?
Nay, let them only see us, while
    We wear the mask.

We smile, but, O great Christ, our cries   10
To thee from tortured souls arise.
We sing, but oh the clay is vile
Beneath our feet, and long the mile;
But let the world dream otherwise,
    We wear the mask!   *1913*   15

CONSIDERATIONS

1. The speaker suggests that we all wear masks and that these masks serve a purpose. Do you see this purpose as positive? Explain.
2. Do you agree that nearly everyone wears masks? If so, do you believe that you and other people wear the same mask throughout life or change them? Explain.
3. Do you think that the concept of wearing masks is related to one's cultural identity? Explain, using examples from the poem as well as from your own observations and experiences.

LUCILLE CLIFTON (1936–   )
Quilting

> *Lucille Clifton was born in Depew, New York, and attended Howard University and Fredonia State Teachers College. Before publishing her first book of poetry at the age of thirty-three (*Good Times, *1969), she worked as a claims clerk in a New York State Division of Employment office and as a literature assistant in the Office of Education in Washington, D.C. Since then she has written eight more books of poetry celebrating the events of everyday life, two of which were nominated for Pulitzer Prizes. "Quilting" comes from* Quilting: Poems 1987– 1990 *(1991). The mother of six children, Clifton has also written* Generations: A Memoir, *a free-verse chronicle of five generations of her family, and more than fifteen children's books. Clifton has summed up her approach to poetry by saying, "I am a black woman poet, and I sound like one."*

somewhere in the unknown world
a yellow eyed woman
sits with her daughter
quilting.
5 some other where
alchemists mumble over pots.
their chemistry stirs
into science. their science
freezes into stone.

10 in the unknown world
the woman
threading together her need
and her needle

nods toward the smiling girl
remember   *15*
this will keep us warm.

how does this poem end?
    do the daughters' daughters quilt?
    do the alchemists practice their tables?
    do the worlds continue spinning   *20*
    away from each other forever?   *1991*

CONSIDERATIONS

1. What two different groups do quilters and alchemists represent in this poem? Do they have anything in common? Explain.
2. Compare/contrast the use of the image of "their science / freezes into stone" with the warning to "remember / this will keep us warm." What is the significance of these two opposing images?
3. Explain the image of the woman "threading together her need / and her needle." What is the meaning and how does it relate to the whole poem?
4. Why does the last stanza contain only questions? How would you answer each question?

---

in the inner city

in the inner city
or
like we call it
home
we think a lot about uptown   *5*
and the silent nights
and the houses straight as
dead men
and the pastel lights
and we hang on to our no place   *10*
happy to be alive
and in the inner city
or
like we call it
home   *1969*   *15*

CONSIDERATIONS

1. Who is the "we" in this poem, and what do the two opposing terms "inner city" and "home" reflect about the "them" that is never named?
2. Based on the images that describe "uptown," what impression does the narrator have of the people who live there, and what is the irony of this impression? What does this poem suggest about different cultures within one city?

WOLE SOYINKA (1934–   )

Telephone Conversation

> Born in Nigeria and educated at Leeds College in England, Wole Soyinka integrates his tribal and European cultures in his works. A diverse writer, Soyinka is an acclaimed poet, novelist, playwright, translator, and essayist.

The price seemed reasonable, location
Indifferent. The landlady swore she lived
Off premises. Nothing remained
But self-confession. 'Madam,' I warned,
5   'I hate a wasted journey—I am African.'
Silence. Silenced transmission of
Pressurized good-breeding. Voice, when it came,
Lipstick coated, long gold-rolled
Cigarette-holder pipped. Caught I was, foully.
10   'HOW DARK?' . . . I had not misheard. . . . 'ARE YOU LIGHT
OR VERY DARK?' Button B. Button A. Stench
Of rancid breath of public hide-and-speak.
Red booth. Red pillar-box. Red double-tiered
Omnibus squelching tar. It *was* real! Shamed
15   By ill-mannered silence, surrender
Pushed dumbfoundment to beg simplification.
Considerate she was, varying the emphasis—
'ARE YOU DARK? OR VERY LIGHT?' Revelation came.
'You mean—like plain or milk chocolate?'
20   Her assent was clinical, crushing in its light
Impersonality. Rapidly, wave-length adjusted.
I chose. 'West African sepia'—and as afterthought,
'Down in my passport.' Silence for spectroscopic
Flight of fancy, till truthfulness clanged her accent
25   Hard on the mouthpiece. 'WHAT'S THAT?' conceding

'DON'T KNOW WHAT THAT IS.' 'Like brunette.'
'THAT'S DARK, ISN'T IT?' 'Not altogether.
Facially, I am brunette, but madam, you should see
The rest of me. Palm of my hand, soles of my feet
Are a peroxide blonde. Friction, caused—   30
Foolishly madam—by sitting down, has turned
My bottom raven black—One moment madam!'—sensing
Her receiver rearing on the thunderclap
About my ears—'Madam,' I pleaded, 'wouldn't you rather
See for yourself?'   *1960*   35

CONSIDERATIONS

1. What cultural expectations, both on the part of the speaker and on the part
   of the prospective landlady, does this telephone conversation suggest?
2. Write a dialogue (or monologue) in which the landlady describes this telephone encounter to a friend. What are her fears? What are her concerns?
   How does she explain and justify her responses?
3. How might this encounter have differed if the speaker had applied for the
   room in person? Write a dialogue describing this encounter, perhaps in poetic form, similar to Soyinka's original poem.

MARTÍN ESPADA (1957–   )

Coca-Cola and Coco Frío

> *Martín Espada was born in Brooklyn. He earned a bachelor's degree at the Uni-
> versity of Wisconsin and a law degree at Northeastern University. Before practic-
> ing law in Boston, Espada had a variety of jobs ranging from bouncer to radio
> journalist in Nicaragua. He is currently teaching at the University of Massachu-
> setts at Amherst. His books of poetry include* The Immigrant Iceboy's Bolero
> *(1982);* Trumpets from the Islands of Their Eviction *(1987);* City of
> Coughing and Dead Radiators *(1994), where "Coca-Cola and Coco Frío"
> appears; and* Imagine the Angels of Bread *(1996). He has also edited two
> bilingual collections of poetry,* Poetry like Bread: Poets of the Political Imag-
> ination from Curbstone Press *(1994) and* El Coro: A Chorus of Latino
> and Latina Poetry *(1997).*

On his first visit to Puerto Rico,
island of family folklore,

the fat boy wandered
from table to table
5   with his mouth open.
At every table, some great-aunt
would steer him with cool spotted hands
to a glass of Coca-Cola.
One even sang to him, in all the English
10   she could remember, a Coca-Cola jingle
from the forties. He drank obediently, though
he was bored with this potion, familiar
from soda fountains in Brooklyn.
Then, at a roadside stand off the beach, the fat boy
15   opened his mouth to coco frío, a coconut
chilled, then scalped by a machete
so that a straw could inhale the clear milk.
The boy tilted the green shell overhead
and drooled coconut milk down his chin;
20   suddenly, Puerto Rico was not Coca-Cola
or Brooklyn, and neither was he.

For years afterward, the boy marveled at an island
where the people drank Coca-Cola
and sang jingles from World War II
25   in a language they did not speak,
while so many coconuts in the trees
sagged heavy with milk, swollen
and unsuckled.   *1993*

CONSIDERATIONS

1. Why does everyone serve the boy Coca-Cola? Why is he bored with this? Explain.
2. What do you make of this statement: "suddenly, Puerto Rico was not Coca-Cola / or Brooklyn, and neither was he." Why did the boy react in this way?
3. Explain the last stanza and show why the boy "marveled at an island / where the people drank Coca-Cola . . . while so many coconuts in the trees / sagged heavy with milk, swollen / and unsuckled." Why is the final image so powerful?
4. How does this poem point out the cultural differences between countries and different time periods? Relate this to some of your own experiences if you have visited another country or part of the United States.

CATHY SONG (1955–   )

The Youngest Daughter

> *Cathy Song was born in Honolulu, Hawaii, to a Chinese mother and Korean father. As "The Youngest Daughter," from* Picture Bride *(1983), demonstrates, many of her poems balance themes of commitment to family and tradition with the theme of commitment to oneself.*

The sky has been dark
for many years.
My skin has become as damp
and pale as rice paper
and feels the way   5
mother's used to before the drying sun
parched it out there in the fields.

Lately, when I touch my eyelids,
my hands react as if
I had just touched something   10
hot enough to burn.
My skin, aspirin colored,
tingles with migraine. Mother
has been massaging the left side of my face
especially in the evenings   15
when the pain flares up.

This morning
her breathing was graveled,
her voice gruff with affection
when I wheeled her into the bath.   20
She was in a good humor,
making jokes about her great breasts,
floating in the milky water
like two walruses,
flaccid and whiskered around the nipples.   25
I scrubbed them with a sour taste
in my mouth, thinking:
six children and an old man
have sucked from these brown nipples.

I was almost tender   30
when I came to the blue bruises
that freckle her body,

places where she has been injecting insulin
for thirty years. I soaped her slowly,
35   she sighed deeply, her eyes closed.
It seems it has always
been like this: the two of us
in this sunless room,
the splashing of the bathwater.

40   In the afternoons
when she has rested,
she prepares our ritual of tea and rice,
garnished with a shred of gingered fish,
a slice of pickled turnip,
45   a token for my white body.
We eat in the familiar silence.
She knows I am not to be trusted,
even now planning my escape.
As I toast to her health
50   with the tea she has poured,
a thousand cranes curtain the window,
fly up in a sudden breeze.   *1983*

CONSIDERATIONS

1. Often, important truths in a poem are found in the spaces between the
    lines. While this poem gives a vivid description of a typical day in the life of
    the youngest daughter, what would her life be like if she were not the one
    who had to care for her aging mother? Why doesn't Song include this in-
    formation in the poem? Why doesn't she include any names for the mother
    or the daughter? How do these choices relate to tradition and culture?
2. List all of the objects and rituals that seem related to the narrator's culture.
    In what ways do these traditions connect the mother and daughter? In what
    ways do they drive a wedge between them?

JUDITH ORTIZ COFER (1952–   )
Latin Women Pray

*Born in Puerto Rico, Judith Ortiz Cofer spent her early years moving from place
to place in Puerto Rico and the mainland United States in accordance with the*

orders received by her father, a career officer in the United States Navy. Because
of these moves, she attended school in many different cultural environments, even-
tually earning a master's degree in English from the University of Florida and
pursuing further graduate work at Oxford University in England. "Latin
Women Pray" is from Reaching for the Mainland and Selected New
Poems *(1995).*

Latin women pray
In incense sweet churches
They pray in Spanish to an Anglo God
With a Jewish heritage.
And this Great White Father   5
Imperturbable on his marble pedestal
Looks down upon his brown daughters
Votive candles shining like lust
In his all seeing eyes
Unmoved by their persistent prayers.   10

Yet year after year
Before his image they kneel
Margarita Josefina Maria and Isabel
All fervently hoping
That if not omnipotent   15
At least he be bilingual.   *1987*

CONSIDERATIONS

1. In what ways does the physical arrangement of the women kneeling before
   God reflect the power—and powerlessness—of traditional beliefs?
2. Examine all the possible cultural, social, and moral implications of the relationship between "Great White Father" and "his brown daughters." Cofer
   includes the women's names in the last stanza. What is the effect of that
   choice?

N. SCOTT MOMADAY (1934–   )
New World

Born in Oklahoma, Navarre Scott Momaday spent the first year of his life on
the Kiowa Indian Reservation where his grandparents lived. His father, an artist,

and his mother, who is of Anglo and Cherokee descent, encouraged Momaday to
understand and appreciate the diverse Native American cultures, including those
of the Kiowa, Apache, Navajo, and Pueblo Indians. In 1969, his first novel,
House Made of Dawn, *was awarded the Pulitzer Prize. In addition to pub-*
lishing several volumes of poetry and memoirs, Momaday has taught at a number
of universities, including the University of California at Berkeley.

1.
First Man,
behold:
the earth
5   glitters
with leaves;
the sky
glistens
with rain.   2.
10 Pollen   At dawn
is borne   eagles
on winds   hie and
that low   hover
and lean   above   3.
15 upon   the plain At noon
mountains. where light turtles
Cedars   gathers   enter
blacken   in pools. slowly
the slopes— Grasses   into   4.
20 and pines. shimmer the warm At dusk
and shine. dark loam. the gray
Shadows Bees hold foxes
withdraw the swarm. stiffen
and lie   Meadows in cold;
25   away   recede   blackbirds
like smoke. through planes are fixed
of heat   in the
and pure branches.
distance. Rivers
30   follow
the moon,
the long
white track
of the
35   full moon. *1975*

CONSIDERATIONS

1. Trace the evolution of the natural world from the first stanza to the last, paying special attention to the change in colors as well as light and darkness. Why might these changes be important, and what, based on the patterns the poet has laid out, is to come?
2. Discuss the effect of Momaday's ordering of the images in the poem. In addition, consider why he begins with the three words "First Man/behold." What are we humans to make of our roots?

SHERMAN J. ALEXIE, JR. (1966–   )
Evolution

> *Born in Spokane, Washington, Sherman J. Alexie, Jr. grew up on the Spokane/
> Coeur d'Alene Indian Reservation. Although he suffered from severe health
> problems in his early years, he learned to read by the time he was three years old
> and excelled in both academic pursuits and athletics throughout his school years.
> In addition to publishing poetry, Alexie has also written short stories and film
> scripts, including the highly acclaimed* Smoke Signals, *which received the
> Christopher Award (an award for works that "affirm the highest values of the
> human spirit") in 1999.*

Buffalo Bill opens a pawn shop on the reservation
right across the border from the liquor store
and he stays open 24 hours a day, 7 days a week

and the Indians come running in with jewelry
television sets, a VCR, a full-length beaded buckskin outfit   5
it took Inez Muse 12 years to finish. Buffalo Bill

takes everything the Indians have to offer, keeps it
all catalogued and filed in a storage room. The Indians
pawn their hands, saving the thumbs for last, they pawn

their skeletons, falling endlessly from the skin   10
and when the last Indian has pawned everything
but his heart, Buffalo Bill takes that for twenty bucks

closes up the pawn shop, paints a new sign over the old
calls his venture THE MUSEUM OF NATIVE AMERICAN CULTURES
charges the Indians five bucks a head to enter.   *1992*   15

CONSIDERATIONS

1. Discuss all the levels of irony (there are at least three) in the two words that open his poem. What do these levels say about mainstream American culture and the Native Americans?
2. Look back to the title of this poem and the way that the poem is arranged. Trace the evolution of the American Indian and explain the evolution of Buffalo Bill. Who is responsible for how the history between these two cultures has evolved?

Drama

ATHOL FUGARD (1932–   )
"Master Harold"... and the Boys

South African playwright, director, and actor Athol Fugard was born in Port Elizabeth, South Africa; his mother was an Afrikaner but his father was of English descent, thus representing South Africa's two different white communities. Fugard established a theater group in Port Elizabeth that includes people from all racial groups; his play Blood Knot *(1961) was the first play ever performed in South Africa with a mixed-race cast. The play, which was also performed in London and New York City, is about two brothers who fall on opposite sides of the color line. How apartheid restricted the lives and spirits of individuals is the common theme of all Fugard's plays, including* Sizwe Banzi Is Dead *(1966),* Boesman and Lena *(1969),* The Island *(1972), and* A Lesson from Aloes *(1981).* "Master Harold"... and the Boys *is based on an autobiographical incident that Fugard recounts in his memoirs,* Notebooks 1960–1977 *(1983) and* Cousins: A Memoir *(1997).*

(The St. George's Park Tea Room on a wet and windy Port Elizabeth afternoon.)
    (Tables and chairs have been cleared and are stacked on one side except for one which stands apart with a single chair. On this table a knife, fork, spoon and side plate in anticipation of a simple meal, together with a pile of comic books.)
        (Other elements: a serving counter with a few stale cakes under glass and a not very impressive display of sweets, cigarettes and cool drinks, etc.; a few cardboard advertising handouts—Cadbury's Chocolate, Coca-Cola—and a blackboard on which an untrained hand has chalked up the prices of Tea, Coffee, Scones, Milkshakes—all flavors—and Cool Drinks; a few sad ferns in pots; a telephone; an old-style jukebox.)

(There is an entrance on one side and an exit into a kitchen on the other.)
(Leaning on the solitary table, his head cupped in one hand as he pages through one of the comic books, is SAM. *A black man in his mid-forties. He wears the white coat of a waiter. Behind him on his knees, mopping down the floor with a bucket of water and a rag, is* WILLIE. *Also black and about the same age as* SAM. *He has his sleeves and trousers rolled up.)*
(The year: 1950.)

WILLIE *(singing as he works)*: "She was scandalizin' my name,
   She took my money
   She called me honey
   But she was scandalizin' my name.
   Called it love but was playin' a game. . . ."

(He gets up and moves the bucket. Stands thinking for a moment, then, raising his arms to hold an imaginary partner, he launches into an intricate ballroom dance step. Although a mildly comic figure, he reveals a reasonable degree of accomplishment.)

Hey, Sam.

*(*SAM, *absorbed in the comic book, does not respond.)*

Hey, Boet° Sam!

*(*SAM *looks up.)*

I'm getting it. The quickstep. Look now and tell me. *(He repeats the step.)* Well?
SAM *(encouragingly)*: Show me again.
WILLIE: Okay, count for me.
SAM: Ready?
WILLIE: Ready.   5
SAM: Five, six, seven, eight. . . . *(*WILLIE *starts to dance.)* A-n-d one two three four . . . and one two three four. . . . *(Ad libbing as* WILLIE *dances.)* Your shoulders, Willie . . . your shoulders! Don't look down! Look happy, Willie! Relax, Willie!
WILLIE *(desperate but still dancing)*: I am relax.
SAM: No, you're not.
WILLIE *(he falters)*: Ag no man, Sam! Mustn't talk. You make me make mistakes.
SAM: But you're stiff.   10
WILLIE: Yesterday I'm not straight . . . today I'm too stiff!
SAM: Well, you are. You asked me and I'm telling you.
WILLIE: Where?

Boet: Brother.

SAM: Everywhere. Try to glide through it.

15 WILLIE: Glide?

SAM: Ja, make it smooth. And give it more style. It must look like you're enjoying yourself.

WILLIE *(emphatically)*: I wasn't.

SAM: Exactly.

WILLIE: How can I enjoy myself? Not straight, too stiff and now it's also glide,
give it more style, make it smooth. . . . Haai! Is hard to remember all those
things, Boet Sam.

20 SAM: That's your trouble. You're trying too hard.

WILLIE: I try hard because it *is* hard.

SAM: But don't let me see it. The secret is to make it look easy. Ballroom must
look happy, Willie, not like hard work. It must. . . . Ja! . . . it must look like
romance.

WILLIE: Now another one! What's romance?

SAM: Love story with happy ending. A handsome man in tails, and in his arms,
smiling at him, a beautiful lady in evening dress!

25 WILLIE: Fred Astaire, Ginger Rogers.

SAM: You got it. Tapdance or ballroom, it's the same. Romance. In two weeks'
time when the judges look at you and Hilda, they must see a man and a
woman who are dancing their way to a happy ending. What I saw was
you holding her like you were frightened she was going to run away.

WILLIE: Ja! Because that is what she wants to do! I got no romance left for
Hilda anymore, Boet Sam.

SAM: Then pretend. When you put your arms around Hilda, imagine she is
Ginger Rogers.

WILLIE: With no teeth? You try.

30 SAM: Well, just remember, there's only two weeks left.

WILLIE: I know, I know! *(To the jukebox.)* I do it better with music. You got
sixpence for Sarah Vaughan°?

SAM: That's a slow foxtrot. You're practicing the quickstep.

WILLIE: I'll practice slow foxtrot.

SAM *(shaking his head)*: It's your turn to put money in the jukebox.

35 WILLIE: I only got bus fare to go home. *(He returns disconsolately to his work.)*
Love story and happy ending! She's doing it all right, Boet Sam, but is
not me she's giving happy endings. Fuckin' whore! Three nights now she
doesn't come practice. I wind up gramophone, I get record ready and I
sit and wait. What happens? Nothing. Ten o'clock I start dancing with
my pillow. You try and practice romance by yourself, Boet Sam. Struesgod, she doesn't come tonight I take back my dress and ballroom shoes
and I find me new partner. Size twenty-six. Shoe size seven. And now

Sarah Vaughan (1924–1990): Legendary jazz singer.

she's also making trouble for me with the baby again. Reports me to Child Wellfed, that I'm not giving her money. She lies! Every week I am giving her money for milk. And how do I know is my baby? Only his hair looks like me. She's fucking around all the time I turn my back. Hilda Samuels is a bitch! *(Pause.)* Hey, Sam!

SAM: Ja.

WILLIE: You listening?

SAM: Ja.

WILLIE: So what you say?

SAM: About Hilda?   *40*

WILLIE: Ja.

SAM: When did you last give her a hiding?

WILLIE *(reluctantly)*: Sunday night.

SAM: And today is Thursday.

WILLIE *(he knows what's coming)*: Okay.   *45*

SAM: Hiding on Sunday night, then Monday, Tuesday, and Wednesday she doesn't come to practice . . . and you are asking me why?

WILLIE: I said okay, Boet Sam!

SAM: You hit her too much. One day she's going to leave you for good.

WILLIE: So? She makes me the hell-in too much.

SAM *(emphasizing his point)*: *Too* much and *too* hard. You had the same trouble   *50*
with Eunice.

WILLIE: Because she also make the hell-in, Boet Sam. She never got the steps right. Even the waltz.

SAM: Beating her up every time she makes a mistake in the waltz? *(Shaking his head.)* No, Willie! That takes the pleasure out of ballroom dancing.

WILLIE: Hilda is not too bad with the waltz, Boet Sam. Is the quickstep where the trouble starts.

SAM *(teasing him gently)*: How's your pillow with the quickstep?

WILLIE *(ignoring the tease)*: Good! And why? Because it got no legs. That's her   *55*
trouble. She can't move them quick enough, Boet Sam. I start the record and before halfway Count Basie° is already winning. Only time we catch up with him is when gramophone runs down. *(Sam laughs.)* Haaikona, Boet Sam, is not funny.

SAM *(snapping his fingers)*: I got it! Give her a handicap.

WILLIE: What's that?

SAM: Give her a ten-second start and then let Count Basie go. Then I put my money on her. Hot favorite in the Ballroom Stakes: Hilda Samuels ridden by Willie Malopo.

WILLIE *(turning away)*: I'm not talking to you no more.

SAM *(relenting)*: Sorry, Willie. . . .   *60*

Count Basie (1904–1984): Jazz composer and bandleader.

WILLIE: It's finish between us.

SAM: Okay, okay . . . I'll stop.

WILLIE: You can also fuck off.

SAM: Willie, listen! I want to help you!

65   WILLIE: No more jokes?

SAM: I promise.

WILLIE: Okay. Help me.

SAM (*his turn to hold an imaginary partner*): Look and learn. Feet together. Back straight. Body relaxed. Right hand placed gently in the small of her back and wait for the music. Don't start worrying about making mistakes or the judges or the other competitors. It's just you, Hilda and the music, and you're going to have a good time. What Count Basie do you play?

WILLIE: "You the cream in my coffee, you the salt in my stew."

70   SAM: Right. Give it to me in strict tempo.

WILLIE: Ready?

SAM: Ready.

WILLIE: A–n–d . . . (*Singing.*)
"You the cream in my coffee.
You the salt in my stew.
You will always be my necessity.
I'd be lost without you. . . . (*etc.*)

(SAM *launches into the quickstep. He is obviously a much more accomplished dancer than* WILLIE. HALLY *enters. A seventeen-year-old white boy. Wet raincoat and school case. He stops and watches* SAM. *The demonstration comes to an end with a flourish. Applause from* HALLY *and* WILLIE.)

HALLY: Bravo! No question about it. First place goes to Mr. Sam Semela.

75   WILLIE (*in total agreement*): You was gliding with style, Boet Sam.

HALLY (*cheerfully*): How's it, chaps?

SAM: Okay, Hally.

WILLIE (*springing to attention like a soldier and saluting*): At your service, Master Harold!

HALLY: Not long to the big event, hey!

80   SAM: Two weeks.

HALLY: You nervous?

SAM: No.

HALLY: Think you stand a chance?

SAM: Let's just say I'm ready to go out there and dance.

85   HALLY: It looked like it. What about you, Willie?

(WILLIE *groans.*)

What's the matter?

SAM: He's got leg trouble.

HALLY (*innocently*): Oh, sorry to hear that, Willie.

WILLIE: Boet Sam! You promised. *(WILLIE returns to his work.)*

(HALLY deposits his school case and takes off his raincoat. His clothes are a little neglected and untidy: black blazer with school badge, gray flannel trousers in need of an ironing, khaki shirt and tie, black shoes. SAM has fetched a towel for HALLY to dry his hair.)

HALLY: God, what a lousy bloody day. It's coming down cats and dogs out there. Bad for business, chaps. . . . *(Conspiratorial whisper.)* . . . but it also means we're in for a nice quiet afternoon.

SAM: You can speak loud. Your Mom's not here.   *90*

HALLY: Out shopping?

SAM: No. The hospital.

HALLY: But it's Thursday. There's no visiting on Thursday afternoons. Is my Dad okay?

SAM: Sounds like it. In fact, I think he's going home.

HALLY *(stopped short by SAM's remark)*: What do you mean?   *95*

SAM: The hospital phoned.

HALLY: To say what?

SAM: I don't know. I just heard your Mom talking.

HALLY: So what makes you say he's going home?

SAM: It sounded as if they were telling her to come and fetch him.   *100*

(HALLY thinks about what SAM has said for a few seconds.)

HALLY: When did she leave?

SAM: About an hour ago. She said she would phone you. Want to eat?

(HALLY doesn't respond.)

Hally, want your lunch?

HALLY: I suppose so. *(His mood has changed.)* What's on the menu? . . . as if I don't know.

SAM: Soup, followed by meat pie and gravy.

HALLY: Today's?   *105*

SAM: No.

HALLY: And the soup?

SAM: Nourishing pea soup.

HALLY: Just the soup. *(The pile of comic books on the table.)* And these?

SAM: For your Dad. Mr. Kempston brought them.   *110*

HALLY: You haven't been reading them, have you?

SAM: Just looking.

HALLY *(examining the comics)*: Jungle Jim . . . Batman and Robin . . . Tarzan . . . God, what rubbish! Mental pollution. Take them away.

(SAM exits waltzing into the kitchen. HALLY turns to WILLIE.)

HALLY: Did you hear my Mom talking on the telephone, Willie?

115   WILLIE: No, Master Hally. I was at the back.

HALLY: And she didn't say anything to you before she left?

WILLIE: She said I must clean the floors.

HALLY: I mean about my Dad.

WILLIE: She didn't say nothing to me about him, Master Hally.

120   HALLY *(with conviction)*: No! It can't be. They said he needed at least another three weeks of treatment. Sam's definitely made a mistake. *(Rummages through his school case, finds a book and settles down at the table to read.)* So, Willie!

WILLIE: Yes, Master Hally! Schooling okay today?

HALLY: Yes, okay. . . . *(He thinks about it.)* . . . No, not really. Ag, what's the difference? I don't care. And Sam says you've got problems.

WILLIE: Big problems.

HALLY: Which leg is sore?

(WILLIE *groans.*)

Both legs.

125   WILLIE: There is nothing wrong with my legs. Sam is just making jokes.

HALLY: So then you *will* be in the competition.

WILLIE: Only if I can find a partner.

HALLY: But what about Hilda?

SAM *(returning with a bowl of soup)*: She's the one who's got trouble with her legs.

130   HALLY: What sort of trouble, Willie?

SAM: From the way he describes it, I think the lady has gone a bit lame.

HALLY: Good God! Have you taken her to see a doctor?

SAM: I think a vet would be better.

HALLY: What do you mean?

135   SAM: What do you call it again when a racehorse goes very fast?

HALLY: Gallop?

SAM: That's it!

WILLIE: Boet Sam!

HALLY: "A gallop down the homestretch to the winning post." But what's that got to do with Hilda?

140   SAM: Count Basie always gets there first.

(WILLIE *lets fly with his slop rag. It misses* SAM *and hits* HALLY.)

HALLY *(furious)*: For Christ's sake, Willie! What the hell do you think you're doing?

WILLIE: Sorry, Master Hally, but it's him. . . .

HALLY: Act your bloody age! *(Hurls the rag back at* WILLIE.)* Cut out the nonsense now and get on with your work. And you too, Sam. Stop fooling around.

(SAM *moves away.*)

No. Hang on. I haven't finished! Tell me exactly what my Mom said.

SAM: I have. "When Hally comes, tell him I've gone to the hospital and I'll phone him."

HALLY: She didn't say anything about taking my Dad home?   145

SAM: No. It's just that when she was talking on the phone. . . .

HALLY *(interrupting him)*: No, Sam. They can't be discharging him. She would have said so if they were. In any case, we saw him last night and he wasn't in good shape at all. Staff nurse even said there was talk about taking more X-rays. And now suddenly today he's better? If anything, it sounds more like a bad turn to me . . . which I sincerely hope it isn't. Hang on . . . how long ago did you say she left?

SAM: Just before two . . . *(His wrist watch.)* . . . hour and a half.

HALLY: I know how to settle it. *(Behind the counter to the telephone. Talking as he dials.)* Let's give her ten minutes to get to the hospital, ten minutes to load him up, another ten, at the most, to get home, and another ten to get him inside. Forty minutes. They should have been home for at least half an hour already. *(Pause—he waits with the receiver to his ear.)* No reply, chaps. And you know why? Because she's at his bedside in hospital helping him pull through a bad turn. You definitely heard wrong.

SAM: Okay.   150

(As far as HALLY is concerned, the matter is settled. He returns to his table, sits down, and divides his attention between the book and his soup. SAM is at his school case and picks up a textbook.)

Modern Graded Mathematics for Standards Nine and Ten. (Opens it at random and laughs at something he sees.) Who is this supposed to be?

HALLY: Old fart-face Prentice.

SAM: Teacher?

HALLY: Thinks he is. And believe me, that is not a bad likeness.

SAM: Has he seen it?

HALLY: Yes.   155

SAM: What did he say?

HALLY: Tried to be clever, as usual. Said I was no Leonardo da Vinci and that bad art had to be punished. So, six of the best, and his are bloody good.

SAM: On your bum?

HALLY: Where else? The days when I got them on my hands are gone forever, Sam.

SAM: With your trousers down!   160

HALLY: No. He's not quite that barbaric.

SAM: That's the way they do it in jail.

HALLY *(flicker of morbid interest)*: Really?

SAM: Ja. When the magistrate sentences you to "strokes with a light cane."

165 HALLY: Go on.

SAM: They make you lie down on a bench. One policeman pulls down your trousers and holds your ankles, another one pulls your shirt over your head and holds your arms. . . .

HALLY: Thank you! That's enough.

SAM: . . . and the one that gives you the strokes talks to you gently and for a long time between each one. *(He laughs.)*

HALLY: I've heard enough, Sam! It's a bloody awful world when you come to think of it. People can be real bastards.

170 SAM: That's the way it is, Hally.

HALLY: It doesn't *have* to be that way. There is something called progress, you know. We don't exactly burn people at the stake anymore.

SAM: Like Joan of Arc.

HALLY: Correct. If she was captured today, she'd be given a fair trial.

SAM: And then the death sentence.

175 HALLY *(a world-weary sigh)*: I know, I know! I oscillate between hope and despair for this world as well, Sam. But things will change, you wait and see. One day somebody is going to get up and give history a kick up the backside and get it going again.

SAM: Like who?

HALLY *(after thought)*: They're called social reformers. Every age, Sam, has got its social reformer. My history book is full of them.

SAM: So where's ours?

HALLY: Good question. And I hate to say it, but the answer is: I don't know. Maybe he hasn't even been born yet. Or is still only a babe in arms at his mother's breast. God, what a thought.

180 SAM: So we just go on waiting.

HALLY: Ja, looks like it. *(Back to his soup and the book.)*

SAM *(reading from the textbook)*: "Introduction: In some mathematical problems only the magnitude. . . . *(He mispronounces the word "magnitude.")*

HALLY *(correcting him without looking up)*: Magnitude.

SAM: What's it mean?

185 HALLY: How big it is. The size of the thing.

SAM *(reading)*: ". . . magnitude of the quantities is of importance. In other problems we need to know whether these quantities are negative or positive. For example, whether there is a debit or credit bank balance . . ."

HALLY: Whether you're broke or not.

SAM: ". . . whether the temperature is above or below Zero. . . ."

HALLY: Naught degrees. Cheerful state of affairs! No cash and you're freezing to death. Mathematics won't get you out of that one.

190 SAM: "All these quantities are called . . ." *(spelling the word)* . . . s-c-a-l. . . .

HALLY: Scalars.

SAM: Scalars! *(Shaking his head with a laugh.)* You understand all that?

HALLY *(turning a page)*: No. And I don't intend to try.

SAM: So what happens when the exams come?

HALLY: Failing a maths exam isn't the end of the world, Sam. How many times   *195*
have I told you that examination results don't measure intelligence?

SAM: I would say about as many times as you've failed one of them.

HALLY *(mirthlessly)*: Ha, ha, ha.

SAM *(simultaneously)*: Ha, ha, ha.

HALLY: Just remember Winston Churchill° didn't do particularly well at
school.

SAM: You've also told me that one many times.   *200*

HALLY: Well, it just so happens to be the truth.

SAM *(enjoying the word)*: Magnitude! Magnitude! Show me how to use it.

HALLY *(after thought)*: An intrepid social reformer will not be daunted by the
magnitude of the task he has undertaken.

SAM *(impressed)*: Couple of jaw-breakers in there!

HALLY: I gave you three for the price of one. Intrepid, daunted, and magni-   *205*
tude. I did that once in an exam. Put five of the words I had to explain
in one sentence. It was half a page long.

SAM: Well, I'll put my money on you in the English exam.

HALLY: Piece of cake. Eighty percent without even trying.

SAM *(another textbook from* HALLY's *case)*: And history?

HALLY: So-so. I'll scrape through. In the fifties if I'm lucky.

SAM: You didn't do too badly last year.   *210*

HALLY: Because we had World War One. That at least has some action. You try
to find that in the South African Parliamentary system.

SAM *(reading from the history textbook)*: "Napoleon and the principle of equality." Hey! This sounds interesting. "After concluding peace with Britain
in 1802, Napoleon used a brief period of calm to in-sti-tute . . ."

HALLY: Introduce.

SAM: ". . . many reforms. Napoleon regarded all people as equal before the law
and wanted them to have equal opportunities for advancement. All ves-
ti-ges of the feu-dal sys-tem with its oppression of the poor were abolished." Vestiges, feudal system, and abolished. I'm all right on oppression.

HALLY: I'm thinking. He swept away . . . abolished . . . the last remains . . .   *215*
vestiges . . . of the bad old days . . . feudal system.

SAM: Ha! There's the social reformer we're waiting for. He sounds like a man
of some magnitude.

HALLY: I'm not so sure about that. It's a damn good title for a book, though.
A man of magnitude!

Winston Churchill (1874–1965): British statesman who served as prime minister.

SAM: He sounds pretty big to me, Hally.

HALLY: Don't confuse historical significance with greatness. But maybe I'm being a bit prejudiced. Have a look in there and you'll see he's two chapters long. And hell! . . . has he only got dates, Sam, all of which you've got to remember! This campaign and that campaign, and then, because of all the fighting, the next thing is we get Peace Treaties all over the place. And what's the end of the story? Battle of Waterloo, which he loses. Wasn't worth it. No, I don't know about him as a man of magnitude.

220   SAM: Then who would you say was?

HALLY: To answer that, we need a definition of greatness, and I suppose that would be somebody who . . . somebody who benefited all mankind.

SAM: Right. But like who?

HALLY *(he speaks with total conviction)*: Charles Darwin. Remember him? That big book from the library. *The Origin of the Species.*

SAM: Him?

225   HALLY: Yes. For his Theory of Evolution.

SAM: You didn't finish it.

HALLY: I ran out of time. I didn't finish it because my two weeks was up. But I'm going to take it out again after I've digested what I read. It's safe. I've hidden it away in the Theology section. Nobody ever goes in there. And anyway who are you to talk? You hardly even looked at it.

SAM: I tried. I looked at the chapters in the beginning and I saw one called "The Struggle for an Existence." Ah ha, I thought. At last! But what did I get? Something called the mistletoe which needs the apple tree and there's too many seeds and all are going to die except one . . . ! No, Hally.

HALLY *(intellectually outraged)*: What do you mean, No! The poor man had to start somewhere. For God's sake, Sam, he revolutionized science. Now we know.

230   SAM: What?

HALLY: Where we come from and what it all means.

SAM: And that's a benefit to mankind? Anyway, I still don't believe it.

HALLY: God, you're impossible. I showed it to you in black and white.

SAM: Doesn't mean I got to believe it.

235   HALLY: It's the likes of you that kept the Inquisition in business. It's called bigotry. Anyway, that's my man of magnitude. Charles Darwin! Who's yours?

SAM *(without hesitation)*: Abraham Lincoln.

HALLY: I might have guessed as much. Don't get sentimental, Sam. You've never been a slave, you know. And anyway we freed your ancestors here in South Africa long before the Americans. But if you want to thank somebody on their behalf, do it to Mr. William Wilberforce.° Come on. Try again! I want a real genius.

Mr. William Wilberforce (1759–1833): British political leader who worked to outlaw slavery in the British Empire.

(Now enjoying himself, and so is SAM. HALLY *goes behind the counter and helps himself to a chocolate.)*

SAM: William Shakespeare.

HALLY *(no enthusiasm)*: Oh. So you're also one of them, are you? You're basing that opinion on only one play, you know. You've only read my *Julius Caesar* and even I don't understand half of what they're talking about. They should do what they did with the old Bible: bring the language up to date.

SAM: That's all you've got. It's also the only one *you've* read.   240

HALLY: I know. I admit it. That's why I suggest we reserve our judgment until we've checked up on a few others. I've got a feeling, though, that by the end of this year one is going to be enough for me, and I can give you the names of twenty-nine other chaps in the Standard Nine class of the Port Elizabeth Technical College who feel the same. But if you want him, you can have him. My turn now. *(Pacing.)* This is a damned good exercise, you know! It started off looking like a simple question and here it's got us really probing into the intellectual heritage of our civilization.

SAM: So who is it going to be?

HALLY: My next man . . . and he gets the title on two scores: social reform and literary genius . . . is Leo Nikolaevich Tolstoy.°

SAM: That Russian.

HALLY: Correct. Remember the picture of him I showed you?   245

SAM: With the long beard.

HALLY *(trying to look like Tolstoy)*: And those burning, visionary eyes. My God, the face of a social prophet if ever I saw one! And remember my words when I showed it to you? Here's a *man,* Sam!

SAM: Those were words, Hally!

HALLY: Not many intellectuals are prepared to shovel manure with the peasants and then go home and write a "little book" called *War and Peace.* Incidentally, Sam, he was somebody else who, to quote, ". . . did not distinguish himself scholastically."

SAM: Meaning?   250

HALLY: He was also no good at school.

SAM: Like you and Winston Churchill.

HALLY *(mirthlessly)*: Ha, ha, ha.

SAM *(simultaneously)*: Ha, ha, ha.

HALLY: Don't get clever, Sam. That man freed his serfs of his own free will.   255

SAM: No argument. He was a somebody, all right. I accept him.

HALLY: I'm sure Count Tolstoy will be very pleased to hear that. Your turn. Shoot. *(Another chocolate from behind the counter.)* I'm waiting, Sam.

SAM: I've got him.

HALLY: Good. Submit your candidate for examination.

Tolstoy (1828–1910): Russian novelist and intellectual.

260   SAM: Jesus.

      HALLY *(stopped dead in his tracks)*: Who?

      SAM: Jesus Christ.

      HALLY: Oh, come on, Sam!

      SAM: The Messiah.

265   HALLY: Ja, but still . . . No, Sam. Don't let's get started on religion. We'll just
            spend the whole afternoon arguing again. Suppose I turn around and say
            Mohammed?

      SAM: All right.

      HALLY: You can't have them both on the same list!

      SAM: Why not? You like Mohammed, I like Jesus.

      HALLY: I *don't* like Mohammed. I never have. I was merely being hypotheti-
            cal. As far as I'm concerned, the Koran is as bad as the Bible. No. Reli-
            gion is out! I'm not going to waste my time again arguing with you
            about the existence of God. You know perfectly well I'm an atheist . . .
            and I've got homework to do.

270   SAM: Okay, I take him back.

      HALLY: You've got time for one more name.

      SAM *(after thought)*: I've got one I know we'll agree on. A simple straightfor-
            ward great Man of Magnitude . . . and no arguments. And *he* really *did*
            benefit all mankind.

      HALLY: I wonder. After your last contribution I'm beginning to doubt
            whether anything in the way of an intellectual agreement is possible be-
            tween the two of us. Who is he?

      SAM: Guess.

275   HALLY: Socrates? Alexandre Dumas? Karl Marx, Dostoevsky? Nietzsche?

      (SAM shakes his head after each name.)

      Give me a clue.

      SAM: The letter *P* is important. . . .

      HALLY: Plato!

      SAM: . . . and his name begins with an *F.*

      HALLY: I've got it. Freud and Psychology.

280   SAM: No. I didn't understand him.

      HALLY: That makes two of us.

      SAM: Think of moldy apricot jam.

      HALLY *(after a delighted laugh)*: Penicillin and Sir Alexander Fleming! And the
            title of the book: *The Microbe Hunters. (Delighted.)* Splendid, Sam! Splen-
            did. For once we are in total agreement. The major breakthrough in
            medical science in the Twentieth Century. If it wasn't for him, we might
            have lost the Second World War. It's deeply gratifying, Sam, to know that
            I haven't been wasting my time in talking to you. *(Strutting around
            proudly.)* Tolstoy may have educated his peasants, but I've educated you.

SAM: Standard Four to Standard Nine.

HALLY: Have we been at it as long as that?   285

SAM: Yep. And my first lesson was geography.

HALLY (*intrigued*): Really? I don't remember.

SAM: My room there at the back of the old Jubilee Boarding House. I had
just started working for your Mom. Little boy in short trousers walks in
one afternoon and asks me seriously: "Sam, do you want to see South
Africa?" Hey man! Sure I wanted to see South Africa!

HALLY: Was that me?

SAM: . . . So the next thing I'm looking at a map you had just done for home-   290
work. It was your first one and you were very proud of yourself.

HALLY: Go on.

SAM: Then came my first lesson. "Repeat after me, Sam: Gold in the Trans-
vaal, mealies in the Free State, sugar in Natal, and grapes in the Cape." I
still know it!

HALLY: Well, I'll be buggered. So that's how it all started.

SAM: And your next map was one with all the rivers and the mountains they
came from. The Orange, the Vaal, the Limpopo, the Zambezi. . . .

HALLY: You've got a phenomenal memory!   295

SAM: You should be grateful. That is why you started passing your exams. You
tried to be better than me.

(They laugh together. WILLIE is attracted by the laughter and joins them.)

HALLY: The old Jubilee Boarding House. Sixteen rooms with board and lodging, rent in advance and one week's notice. I haven't thought about it for
donkey's years . . . and I don't think that's an accident. God, was I glad
when we sold it and moved out. Those years are not remembered as the
happiest ones of an unhappy childhood.

WILLIE (*knocking on the table and trying to imitate a woman's voice*): "Hally, are
you there?"

HALLY: Who's that supposed to be?

WILLIE: "What you doing in there, Hally? Come out at once!"   300

HALLY (*to SAM*): What's he talking about?

SAM: Don't you remember?

WILLIE: "Sam, Willie . . . is he in there with you boys?"

SAM: Hiding away in our room when your mother was looking for you.

HALLY (*another good laugh*): Of course! I used to crawl and hide under your   305
bed! But finish the story, Willie. Then what used to happen? You chaps
would give the game away by telling her I was in there with you. So
much for friendship.

SAM: We couldn't lie to her. She knew.

HALLY: Which meant I got another rowing for hanging around the "servants'
quarters." I think I spent more time in there with you chaps than any-

where else in that dump. And do you blame me? Nothing but bloody misery wherever you went. Somebody was always complaining about the food, or my mother was having a fight with Micky Nash because she'd caught her with a petty officer in her room. Maud Meiring was another one. Remember those two? They were prostitutes, you know. Soldiers and sailors from the troopships. Bottom fell out of the business when the war ended. God, the flotsam and jetsam that life washed up on our shores! No joking, if it wasn't for your room, I would have been the first certified ten-year-old in medical history. Ja, the memories are coming back now. Walking home from school and thinking: "What can I do this afternoon?" Try out a few ideas, but sooner or later I'd end up in there with you fellows. I bet you I could still find my way to your room with my eyes closed. *(He does exactly that.)* Down the corridor . . . telephone on the right, which my Mom keeps locked because somebody is using it on the sly and not paying . . . past the kitchen and unappetizing cooking smells . . . around the corner into the backyard, hold my breath again because there are more smells coming when I pass your lavatory, then into that little passageway, first door on the right and into your room. How's that?

SAM: Good. But, as usual, you forgot to knock.

HALLY: Like that time I barged in and caught you and Cynthia . . . at it. Remember? God, was I embarrassed! I didn't know what was going on at first.

310   SAM: Ja, that taught you a lesson.

HALLY: And about a lot more than knocking on doors, I'll have you know, and I don't mean geography either. Hell, Sam, couldn't you have waited until it was dark?

SAM: No.

HALLY: Was it that urgent?

SAM: Yes, and if you don't believe me, wait until your time comes.

315   HALLY: No, thank you. I am not interested in girls. *(Back to his memories . . . Using a few chairs he re-creates the room as he lists the items.)* A gray little room with a cold cement floor. Your bed against that wall . . . and I now know why the mattress sags so much! . . . Willie's bed . . . it's propped up on bricks because one leg is broken . . . that wobbly little table with the washbasin and jug of water . . . Yes! . . . stuck to the wall above it are some pin-up pictures from magazines. Joe Louis. . . .

WILLIE: Brown Bomber. World Title. *(Boxing pose.)* Three rounds and knockout.

HALLY: Against who?

SAM: Max Schmeling.

HALLY: Correct. I can also remember Fred Astaire and Ginger Rogers, and Rita Hayworth in a bathing costume which always made me hot and bothered when I looked at it. Under Willie's bed is an old suitcase with all his clothes in a mess, which is why I never hide there. Your things are

neat and tidy in a trunk next to your bed, and on it there is a picture of
you and Cynthia in your ballroom clothes, your first silver cup for third
place in a competition and an old radio which doesn't work anymore.
Have I left out anything?

SAM: No.   *320*

HALLY: Right, so much for the stage directions. Now the characters. *(SAM and
WILLIE move to their appropriate positions in the bedroom.)* Willie is in bed,
under his blankets with his clothes on, complaining nonstop about something, but we can't make out a word of what he's saying because he's got
his head under the blankets as well. You're on your bed trimming your
toenails with a knife—not a very edifying sight—and as for me. . . . What
am I doing?

SAM: You're sitting on the floor giving Willie a lecture about being a good
loser while you get the checkerboard and pieces ready for a game. Then
you go to Willie's bed, pull off the blankets and make him play with you
first because you know you're going to win, and that gives you the second game with me.

HALLY: And you certainly were a bad loser, Willie!

WILLIE: Haai!

HALLY: Wasn't he, Sam? And so slow! A game with you almost took the whole   *325*
afternoon. Thank God I gave up trying to teach you how to play chess.

WILLIE: You and Sam cheated.

HALLY: I never saw Sam cheat, and mine were mostly the mistakes of youth.

WILLIE: Then how is it you two was always winning?

HALLY: Have you ever considered the possibility, Willie, that it was because
we were better than you?

WILLIE: Every time better?   *330*

HALLY: Not every time. There were occasions when we deliberately let you
win a game so that you would stop sulking and go on playing with us.
Sam used to wink at me when you weren't looking to show me it was
time to let you win.

WILLIE: So then you two didn't play fair.

HALLY: It was for your benefit, Mr. Malopo, which is more than being fair. It
was an act of self-sacrifice. *(To Sam.)* But you know what my best memory is, don't you?

SAM: No.

HALLY: Come on, guess. If your memory is so good, you must remember it as   *335*
well.

SAM: We got up to a lot of tricks in there, Hally.

HALLY: This one was special, Sam.

SAM: I'm listening.

HALLY: It started off looking like another of those useless nothing-to-do afternoons. I'd already been down to Main Street looking for adventure,

but nothing had happened. I didn't feel like climbing trees in the Donkin Park or pretending I was a private eye and following a stranger . . . so as usual: See what's cooking in Sam's room. This time it was you on the floor. You had two thin pieces of wood and you were smoothing them down with a knife. It didn't look particularly interesting, but when I asked you what you were doing, you just said, "Wait and see, Hally. Wait . . . and see" . . . in that secret sort of way of yours, so I knew there was a surprise coming. You teased me, you bugger, by being deliberately slow and not answering my questions!

(SAM *laughs.*)

And whistling while you worked away! God, it was infuriating! I could have brained you! It was only when you tied them together in a cross and put that down on the brown paper that I realized what you were doing. "Sam is making a kite?" And when I asked you and you said "Yes" . . . ! *(Shaking his head with disbelief.)* The sheer audacity of it took my breath away. I mean, seriously, what the hell does a black man know about flying a kite? I'll be honest with you, Sam, I had no hopes for it. If you think I was excited and happy, you got another guess coming. In fact, I was shit-scared that we were going to make fools of ourselves. When we left the boarding house to go up onto the hill, I was praying quietly that there wouldn't be any other kids around to laugh at us.

340   SAM   *(enjoying the memory as much as* HALLY*)*: Ja, I could see that.

HALLY: I made it obvious, did I?

SAM: Ja. You refused to carry it.

HALLY: Do you blame me? Can you remember what the poor thing looked like? Tomato-box wood and brown paper! Flour and water for glue! Two of my mother's old stockings for a tail, and then all those bits and pieces of string you made me tie together so that we could fly it! Hell, no, that was now only asking for a miracle to happen.

SAM: Then the big argument when I told you to hold the string and run with it when I let go.

345   HALLY: I was prepared to run, all right, but straight back to the boarding house.

SAM   *(knowing what's coming)*: So what happened?

HALLY: Come on, Sam, you remember as well as I do.

SAM: I want to hear it from you.

(HALLY *pauses. He wants to be as accurate as possible.*)

HALLY: You went a little distance from me down the hill, you held it up ready to let it go. . . . "This is it," I thought. "Like everything else in my life, here comes another fiasco." Then you shouted, "Go, Hally!" and I started to run. *(Another pause.)* I don't know how to describe it, Sam. Ja! The miracle happened! I was running, waiting for it to crash to the ground, but instead suddenly there was something alive behind me at the end of the string, tugging at it as if it wanted to be free. I looked back . . . *(Shakes his head.)* . . . I still can't believe my eyes. It was flying! Looping around and trying to climb even higher into the sky. You shouted to me to let it have more string. I did, until there was none left and I was just holding that piece of wood we had tied it to. You came up and joined me. You were laughing.

SAM: So were you. And shouting, "It works, Sam! We've done it!"   *350*

HALLY: And we had! I was so proud of us! It was the most splendid thing I had ever seen. I wished there were hundreds of kids around to watch us. The part that scared me, though, was when you showed me how to make it dive down to the ground and then just when it was on the point of crashing, swoop up again!

SAM: You didn't want to try yourself.

HALLY: Of course not! I would have been suicidal if anything had happened to it. Watching you do it made me nervous enough. I was quite happy just to see it up there with its tail fluttering behind it. You left me after that, didn't you? You explained how to get it down, we tied it to the bench so that I could sit and watch it, and you went away. I wanted you to stay, you know. I was a little scared of having to look after it by myself.

SAM *(quietly)*: I had work to do, Hally.

HALLY: It was sort of sad bringing it down, Sam. And it looked sad again when   *355*
it was lying there on the ground. Like something that had lost its soul. Just tomato-box wood, brown paper and two of my mother's old stockings! But, hell, I'll never forget that first moment when I saw it up there. I had a stiff neck the next day from looking up so much.

(SAM laughs. HALLY turns to him with a question he never thought of asking before.)

Why did you make that kite, Sam?

SAM *(evenly)*: I can't remember.

HALLY: Truly?

SAM: Too long ago, Hally.

HALLY: Ja, I suppose it was. It's time for another one, you know.

SAM: Why do you say that?   *360*

HALLY: Because it feels like that. Wouldn't be a good day to fly it, though.

SAM: No. You can't fly kites on rainy days.

HALLY *(He studies SAM. Their memories have made him conscious of the man's presence in his life.)*: How old are you, Sam?

SAM: Two score and five.

HALLY: Strange, isn't it?   *365*

SAM: What?

HALLY: Me and you.

SAM: What's strange about it?

HALLY: Little white boy in short trousers and a black man old enough to be his father flying a kite. It's not every day you see that.

370   SAM: But why strange? Because the one is white and the other black?

HALLY: I don't know. Would have been just as strange, I suppose, if it had been me and my Dad . . . cripple man and a little boy! Nope! There's no chance of me flying a kite without it being strange. *(Simple statement of fact—no self-pity.)* There's a nice little short story there. "The Kite-Flyers." But we'd have to find a twist in the ending.

SAM: Twist?

HALLY: Yes. Something unexpected. The way it ended with us was too straightforward . . . me on the bench and you going back to work. There's no drama in that.

WILLIE: And me?

375   HALLY: You?

WILLIE: Yes me.

HALLY: You want to get into the story as well, do you? I got it! Change the title: "Afternoons in Sam's Room" . . . expand it and tell all the stories. It's on its way to being a novel. Our days in the old Jubilee. Sad in a way that they're over. I almost wish we were still in that little room.

SAM: We're still together.

HALLY: That's true. It's just that life felt the right size in there . . . not too big and not too small. Wasn't so hard to work up a bit of courage. It's got so bloody complicated since then.

(The telephone rings. SAM answers it.)

380   SAM: St. George's Park Tea Room . . . Hello, Madam . . . Yes, Madam, he's here. . . . Hally, it's your mother.

HALLY: Where is she phoning from?

SAM: Sounds like the hospital. It's a public telephone.

HALLY *(relieved)*: You see! I told you. *(The telephone.)* Hello, Mom . . . Yes . . . Yes no fine. Everything's under control here. How's things with poor old Dad? . . . Has he had a bad turn? . . . What? . . . Oh, God! . . . Yes, Sam told me, but I was sure he'd made a mistake. But what's this all about, Mom? He didn't look at all good last night. How can he get better so quickly? . . . Then very obviously you must say no. Be firm with him. You're the boss. . . . You know what it's going to be like if he comes home. . . . Well then, don't blame me when I fail my exams at the end of the year. . . . Yes! How am I expected to be fresh for school when I spend half the night massaging his gammy leg? . . . So am I! . . . So tell him a white lie. Say Dr. Colley wants more X-rays of his stump. Or bribe him. We'll sneak in double tots of brandy in future....What? ... Order him to get back into bed at once! If he's going to behave like a child, treat him like one....All right, Mom! I was just trying to ... I'm sorry.... I said I'm sorry.... Quick, give me your number. I'll phone you back. *(He hangs up and waits a few seconds.)* Here we go again! *(He dials.)* I'm sorry, Mom.... Okay.... But now listen to me carefully. All it needs is for you to put your foot down. Don't take no for an answer.... Did you hear me? And whatever you do, don't discuss it with him.... Because I'm frightened you'll give in to him.... Yes, Sam gave me lunch.... I ate all of it! ... No, Mom not a soul. It's still raining here.... Right, I'll tell them. I'll just do some homework and then lock up.... But remember now, Mom. Don't listen to anything he says. And phone me back and let me know what happens.... Okay. Bye, Mom. *(He hangs up. The men are staring at him.)* My Mom says that when you're finished with the floors you must do the windows. *(Pause.)* Don't misunderstand me, chaps. All I want is for him to get better. And if he was, I'd be the first person to say: "Bring him home." But he's not, and we can't give him the medical care and attention he needs at home. That's what hospitals are there for. *(Brusquely.)* So don't just stand there! Get on with it!

(SAM clears HALLY's table.)

You heard right. My Dad wants to go home.

SAM: Is he better?

HALLY *(sharply)*: No! How the hell can he be better when last night he was groaning with pain? This is not an age of miracles!   *385*

SAM: Then he should stay in hospital.

HALLY *(seething with irritation and frustration)*: Tell me something I don't know, Sam. What the hell do you think I was saying to my Mom? All I can say is fuck-it-all.

SAM: I'm sure he'll listen to your Mom.

HALLY: You don't know what she's up against. He's already packed his shaving kit and pajamas and is sitting on his bed with his crutches, dressed and ready to go. I know him when he gets in that mood. If she tries to reason with him, we've had it. She's no match for him when it comes to a battle of words. He'll tie her up in knots. *(Trying to hide his true feelings.)*

SAM: I suppose it gets lonely for him in there.   *390*

HALLY: With all the patients and nurses around? Regular visits from the Salvation Army? Balls! It's ten times worse for him at home. I'm at school and my mother is here in the business all day.

SAM: He's at least got you at night.

HALLY *(before he can stop himself)*: And we've got him! Please! I don't want to talk about it anymore. *(Unpacks his school case, slamming down books on the table.)* Life is just a plain bloody mess, that's all. And people are fools.

SAM: Come on, Hally.

395 HALLY: Yes, they are! They bloody well deserve what they get.

SAM: Then don't complain.

HALLY: Don't try to be clever, Sam. It doesn't suit you. Anybody who thinks there's nothing wrong with this world needs to have his head examined. Just when things are going along all right, without fail someone or something will come along and spoil everything. Somebody should write that down as a fundamental law of the Universe. The principle of perpetual disappointment. If there is a God who created this world, he should scrap it and try again.

SAM: All right, Hally, all right. What you got for homework?

HALLY: Bullshit, as usual. *(Opens an exercise book and reads.)* "Write five hundred words describing an annual event of cultural or historical significance."

400 SAM: That should be easy enough for you.

HALLY: And also plain bloody boring. You know what he wants, don't you? One of their useless old ceremonies. The commemoration of the landing of the 1820 Settlers, or if it's going to be culture, Carols by Candlelight every Christmas.

SAM: It's an impressive sight. Make a good description, Hally. All those candles glowing in the dark and the people singing hymns.

HALLY: And it's called religious hysteria. *(Intense irritation.)* Please, Sam! Just leave me alone and let me get on with it. I'm not in the mood for games this afternoon. And remember my Mom's orders . . . you're to help Willie with the windows. Come on now, I don't want any more nonsense in here.

SAM: Okay, Hally, okay.

(HALLY settles down to his homework; determined preparations . . . pen, ruler, exercise book, dictionary, another cake . . . all of which will lead to nothing.)

(SAM waltzes over to WILLIE and starts to replace tables and chairs. He practices a ballroom step while doing so. WILLIE watches. When SAM is finished, WILLIE tries.)

Good! But just a little bit quicker on the turn and only move in to her after she's crossed over. What about this one?

(Another step. When SAM is finished, WILLIE again has a go.)

Much better. See what happens when you just relax and enjoy yourself? Remember that in two weeks' time and you'll be all right.

405 WILLIE: But I haven't got partner, Boet Sam.

SAM: Maybe Hilda will turn up tonight.

WILLIE: No, Boet Sam. *(Reluctantly.)* I gave her a good hiding.

SAM: You mean a bad one.

WILLIE: Good bad one.

SAM: Then you mustn't complain either. Now you pay the price for losing   410
    your temper.
WILLIE: I also pay two pounds ten shilling entrance fee.
SAM: They'll refund you if you withdraw now.
WILLIE *(appalled)*: You mean, don't dance?
SAM: Yes.
WILLIE: No! I wait too long and I practice too hard. If I find me new partner,   415
    you think I can be ready in two weeks? I ask madam for my leave now
    and we practice every day.
SAM: Quickstep nonstop for two weeks. World record, Willie, but you'll be
    mad at the end.
WILLIE: No jokes, Boet Sam.
SAM: I'm not joking.
WILLIE: So then what?
SAM: Find Hilda. Say you're sorry and promise you won't beat her again.   420
WILLIE: No.
SAM: Then withdraw. Try again next year.
WILLIE: No.
SAM: Then I give up.
WILLIE: Haaikona, Boet Sam, you can't.   425
SAM: What do you mean, I can't? I'm telling you: I give up.
WILLIE *(adamant)*: No! *(Accusingly.)* It was you who start me ballroom dancing.
SAM: So?
WILLIE: Before that I use to be happy. And is you and Miriam who bring me
    to Hilda and say here's partner for you.
SAM: What are you saying, Willie?   430
WILLIE: You!
SAM: But me what? To blame?
WILLIE: Yes.
SAM: Willie . . . ? *(Bursts into laughter.)*
WILLIE: And now all you do is make jokes at me. You wait. When Miriam   435
    leaves you is my turn to laugh. Ha! Ha! Ha!
SAM *(he can't take* WILLIE *seriously any longer)*: She can leave me tonight! I
    know what to do. *(Bowing before an imaginary partner.)* May I have the
    pleasure? *(He dances and sings.)*
    "Just a fellow with his pillow . . .
    Dancin' like a willow . . .
    In an autumn breeze. . . ."
WILLIE: There you go again!

(SAM goes on dancing and singing.)

    Boet Sam!

SAM: There's the answer to your problem! Judges' announcement in two weeks' time: "Ladies and gentlemen, the winner in the open section . . . Mr. Willie Malopo and his pillow!"

(This is too much for a now really angry WILLIE. *He goes for* SAM, *but the latter is too quick for him and puts* HALLY's *table between the two of them.)*

HALLY *(exploding)*: For Christ's sake, you two!

440   WILLIE *(still trying to get at* SAM*)*: I donner you, Sam! Struesgod!

SAM *(still laughing)*: Sorry, Willie . . . Sorry. . . .

HALLY: Sam! Willie! *(Grabs his ruler and gives* WILLIE *a vicious whack on the bum.)* How the hell am I supposed to concentrate with the two of you behaving like bloody children!

WILLIE: Hit him too!

HALLY: Shut up, Willie.

445   WILLIE: He started jokes again.

HALLY: Get back to your work. You too, Sam. *(His ruler.)* Do you want another one, Willie?

*(*SAM *and* WILLIE *return to their work.* HALLY *uses the opportunity to escape from his unsuccessful attempt at homework. He struts around like a little despot, ruler in hand, giving vent to his anger and frustration.)*

Suppose a customer had walked in then? Or the Park Superintendent. And seen the two of you behaving like a pair of hooligans. That would have been the end of my mother's license, you know. And your jobs? Well, this is the end of it. From now on there will be no more of your ballroom nonsense in here. This is a business establishment, not a bloody New Brighton dancing school. I've been far too lenient with the two of you. *(Behind the counter for a green cool drink and a dollop of ice cream. He keeps up his tirade as he prepares it.)* But what really makes me bitter is that I allow you chaps a little freedom in here when business is bad and what do you do with it? The foxtrot! Specially you, Sam. There's more to life than trotting around a dance floor and I thought at least you knew it.

SAM: It's a harmless pleasure, Hally. It doesn't hurt anybody.

HALLY: It's also a rather simple one, you know.

SAM: You reckon so? Have you ever tried?

450   HALLY: Of course not.

SAM: Why don't you? Now.

HALLY: What do you mean? Me dance?

SAM: Yes. I'll show you a simple step—the waltz—then you try it.

HALLY: What will that prove?

455   SAM: That it might not be as easy as you think.

HALLY: I didn't say it was easy. I said it was simple—like in simple-minded, meaning mentally retarded. You can't exactly say it challenges the intellect.

SAM: It does other things.

HALLY: Such as?

SAM: Make people happy.

HALLY *(the glass in his hand)*: So do American cream sodas with ice cream.   460
For God's sake, Sam, you're not asking me to take ballroom dancing serious, are you?

SAM: Yes.

HALLY *(sigh of defeat)*: Oh, well, so much for trying to give you a decent education. I've obviously achieved nothing.

SAM: You still haven't told me what's wrong with admiring something that's
beautiful and then trying to do it yourself.

HALLY: Nothing. But we happen to be talking about a foxtrot, not a thing of
beauty.

SAM: But that is just what I'm saying. If you were to see two champions doing,   465
two masters of the art . . . !

HALLY: Oh God, I give up. So now it's also art!

SAM: Ja.

HALLY: There's a limit, Sam. Don't confuse art and entertainment.

SAM: So then what is art?

HALLY: You want a definition?   470

SAM: Ja.

HALLY *(He realizes he has got to be careful. He gives the matter a lot of thought before
answering.)*: Philosophers have been trying to do that for centuries. What
is Art? What is Life? But basically I suppose it's . . . the giving of meaning
to matter.

SAM: Nothing to do with beautiful?

HALLY: It goes beyond that. It's the giving of form to the formless.

SAM: Ja, well, maybe it's not art, then. But I still say it's beautiful.   475

HALLY: I'm sure the word you mean to use is entertaining.

SAM *(adamant)*: No. Beautiful. And if you want proof come along to the Centenary Hall in New Brighton in two weeks' time.

(The mention of the Centenary Hall draws WILLIE *over to them.)*

HALLY: What for? I've seen the two of you prancing around in here often
enough.

SAM *(he laughs)*: This isn't the real thing, Hally. We're just playing around in here.

HALLY: So? I can use my imagination.   480

SAM: And what do you get?

HALLY: A lot of people dancing around and having a so-called good time.

SAM: That's all?

HALLY: Well, basically it is that, surely.

SAM: No, it isn't. Your imagination hasn't helped you at all. There's a lot more   485
to it than that. We're getting ready for the championships, Hally, not just

another dance. There's going to be a lot of people, all right, and they're going to have a good time, but they'll only be spectators, sitting around and watching. It's just the competitors out there on the dance floor. Party decorations and fancy lights all around the walls! The ladies in beautiful evening dresses!

HALLY: My mother's got one of those, Sam, and, quite frankly, it's an embarrassment every time she wears it.

SAM *(undeterred)*: Your imagination left out the excitement.

(HALLY scoffs.)

Oh, yes. The finalists are not going to be out there just to have a good time. One of those couples will be the 1950 Eastern Province Champions. And your imagination left out the music.

WILLIE: Mr. Elijah Gladman Guzana and his Orchestral Jazzonions.

SAM: The sound of the big band, Hally. Trombone, trumpet, tenor and alto sax. And then, finally, your imagination also left out the climax of the evening when the dancing is finished, the judges have stopped whispering among themselves and the Master of Ceremonies collects their scorecards and goes up onto the stage to announce the winners.

490 HALLY: All right. So you make it sound like a bit of a do. It's an occasion. Satisfied?

SAM *(victory)*: So you admit that!

HALLY: Emotionally yes, intellectually no.

SAM: Well, I don't know what you mean by that, all I'm telling you is that it is going to be *the* event of the year in New Brighton. It's been sold out for two weeks already. There's only standing room left. We've got competitors coming from Kingwilliamstown, East London, Port Alfred.

(HALLY starts pacing thoughtfully.)

HALLY: Tell me a bit more.

495 SAM: I thought you weren't interested . . . intellectually.

HALLY *(mysteriously)*: I've got my reasons.

SAM: What do you want to know?

HALLY: It takes place every year?

SAM: Yes. But only every third year in New Brighton. It's East London's turn to have the championships next year.

500 HALLY: Which, I suppose, makes it an even more significant event.

SAM: Ah ha! We're getting somewhere. Our "occasion" is now a "significant event."

HALLY: I wonder.

SAM: What?

HALLY: I wonder if I would get away with it.

505 SAM: But what?

HALLY *(to the table and his exercise book)*: "Write five hundred words describing an annual event of cultural or historical significance." Would I be stretching poetic license a little too far if I called your ballroom championships a cultural event?

SAM: You mean . . . ?

HALLY: You think we could get five hundred words out of it, Sam?

SAM: Victor Sylvester has written a whole book on ballroom dancing.

WILLIE: You going to write about it, Master Hally?   510

HALLY: Yes, gentlemen, that is precisely what I am considering doing. Old Doc Bromely—he's my English teacher—is going to argue with me, of course. He doesn't like natives. But I'll point out to him that in strict anthropological terms the culture of a primitive black society includes its dancing and singing. To put my thesis in a nutshell: The war-dance has been replaced by the waltz. But it still amounts to the same thing: the release of primitive emotions through movement. Shall we give it a go?

SAM: I'm ready.

WILLIE: Me also.

HALLY: Ha! This will teach the old bugger a lesson. *(Decision taken.)* Right. Let's get ourselves organized. *(This means another cake on the table. He sits.)* I think you've given me enough general atmosphere, Sam, but to build the tension and suspense I need facts. *(Pencil poised.)*

WILLIE: Give him facts, Boet Sam.   515

HALLY: What you called the climax . . . how many finalists?

SAM: Six couples.

HALLY *(making notes)*: Go on. Give me the picture.

SAM: Spectators seated right around the hall. (WILLIE *becomes a spectator.*)

HALLY: . . . and it's a full house.   520

SAM: At one end, on the stage, Gladman and his Orchestral Jazzonions. At the other end is a long table with the three judges. The six finalists go onto the dance floor and take up their positions. When they are ready and the spectators have settled down, the Master of Ceremonies goes to the microphone. To start with, he makes some jokes to get people laughing. . . .

HALLY: Good touch. *(As he writes.)* ". . . creating a relaxed atmosphere which will change to one of tension and drama as the climax is approached."

SAM *(onto a chair to act out the M.C.)*: "Ladies and gentlemen, we come now to the great moment you have all been waiting for this evening. . . . The finals of the 1950 Eastern Province Open Ballroom Dancing Championships. But first let me introduce the finalists! Mr. and Mrs. Welcome Tchabalala from Kingwilliamstown . . ."

WILLIE *(he applauds after every name)*: Is when the people clap their hands and whistle and make a lot of noise, Master Hally.

SAM: "Mr. Mulligan Njikelane and Miss Nomhle Nkonyeni of Grahamstown;   525
Mr. and Mrs. Norman Nchinga from Port Alfred; Mr. Fats Bokolane and

Miss Dina Plaatjies from East London; Mr. Sipho Dugu and Mrs. Mable Magada from Peddie; and from New Brighton our very own Mr. Willie Malopo and Miss Hilda Samuels."

(WILLIE *can't believe his ears. He abandons his role as spectator and scrambles into position as a finalist.*)

WILLIE: Relaxed and ready to romance!

SAM: The applause dies down. When everybody is silent, Gladman lifts up his sax, nods at the Orchestral Jazzonions. . . .

WILLIE: Play the jukebox please, Boet Sam!

SAM: I also only got bus fare, Willie.

530   HALLY: Hold it, everybody. (*Heads for the cash register behind the counter.*) How much is in the till, Sam?

SAM: Three shillings, Hally . . . Your Mom counted it before she left.

(HALLY *hesitates.*)

HALLY: Sorry, Willie, You know how she carried on the last time I did it. We'll just have to pool our combined imaginations and hope for the best. (*Returns to the table.*) Back to work. How are the points scored, Sam?

SAM: Maximum of ten points each for individual style, deportment, rhythm, and general appearance.

WILLIE: Must I start?

535   HALLY: Hold it for a second, Willie. And penalties?

SAM: For what?

HALLY: For doing something wrong. Say you stumble or bump into somebody . . . do they take off any points?

SAM (*aghast*): Hally . . . !

HALLY: When you're dancing. If you and your partner collide into another couple.

(HALLY *can get no further.* SAM *has collapsed with laughter. He explains to* WILLIE.)

540   SAM: If me and Miriam bump into you and Hilda. . . .

(WILLIE *joins him in another good laugh.*)

Hally, Hally . . . !

HALLY (*perplexed*): Why? What did I say?

SAM: There's no collisions out there, Hally. Nobody trips or stumbles or bumps into anybody else. That's what that moment is all about. To be one of those finalists on that dance floor is like . . . like being in a dream about a world in which accidents don't happen.

HALLY (*genuinely moved by* SAM's *image*): Jesus, Sam! That's beautiful!

WILLIE (*can endure waiting no longer*): I'm starting!

*(*WILLIE *dances while* SAM *talks.)*

SAM: Of course it is. That's what I've been trying to say to you all afternoon.   545
And it's beautiful because that is what we want life to be like. But instead, like you said, Hally, we're bumping into each other all the time.
Look at the three of us this afternoon: I've bumped into Willie, the two
of us have bumped into you, you've bumped into your mother, she
bumping into your Dad. . . . None of us knows the steps and there's no
music playing. And it doesn't stop with us. The whole world is doing it
all the time. Open a newspaper and what do you read? America has
bumped into Russia, England is bumping into India, rich man bumps
into poor man. Those are big collisions, Hally. They make for a lot of
bruises. People get hurt in all that bumping, and we're sick and tired of it
now. It's been going on for too long. Are we never going to get it right?
. . . Learn to dance life like champions instead of always being just a
bunch of beginners at it?

HALLY *(deep and sincere admiration of the man)*: You've got a vision, Sam!

SAM: Not just me. What I'm saying to you is that everybody's got it. That's
why there's only standing room left for the Centenary Hall in two weeks'
time. For as long as the music lasts, we are going to see six couples get it
right, the way we want life to be.

HALLY: But is that the best we can do, Sam . . . watch six finalists dreaming
about the way it should be?

SAM: I don't know. But it starts with that. Without the dream we won't know
what we're going for. And anyway I reckon there are a few people who
have got past just dreaming about it and are trying for something real.
Remember that thing we read once in the paper about the Mahatma
Gandhi? Going without food to stop those riots in India?

HALLY: You're right. He certainly was trying to teach people to get the steps   550
right.

SAM: And the Pope.

HALLY: Yes, he's another one. Our old General Smuts° as well, you know. He's
also out there dancing. You know, Sam, when you come to think of it,
that's what the United Nations boils down to . . . a dancing school for
politicians!

SAM: And let's hope they learn.

HALLY *(a little surge of hope)*: You're right. We mustn't despair. Maybe there's
some hope for mankind after all. Keep it up, Willie. *(Back to his table with
determination.)* This is a lot bigger than I thought. So what have we got?
Yes, our title: "A World without Collisions."

General Smuts: Jan Christiaan Smuts (1870–1950), a South-African political leader who helped to
form both the Union of South Africa in 1910 and later the United Nations.

555   SAM: That sounds good! "A World without Collisions."
      HALLY: Subtitle: "Global Politics on the Dance Floor." No. A bit too heavy,
      hey? What about "Ballroom Dancing as a Political Vision"?

(The telephone rings. SAM answers it.)

SAM: St. George's Park Tea Room . . . Yes, Madam . . . Hally, it's your Mom.
HALLY *(back to reality)*:   O, God, yes! I'd forgotten all about that. Shit! Re-
      member my words, Sam? Just when you're enjoying yourself, someone
      or something will come along and wreck everything.
SAM: You haven't heard what she's got to say yet.
560   HALLY: Public telephone?
SAM: No.
HALLY: Does she sound happy or unhappy?
SAM: I couldn't tell. *(Pause.)* She's waiting, Hally.
HALLY *(to the telephone)*:   Hello, Mom . . . No, everything is okay here. Just
      doing my homework. . . . ? What's your news? . . . You've what? . . . *(Pause.*
      He takes the receiver away from his ear for a few seconds. In the course of HALLY's
      telephone conversation, SAM *and* WILLIE *discreetly position the stacked tables*
      and chairs. HALLY *places the receiver back to his ear.)* Yes, I'm still here. Oh,
      well, I give up now. Why did you do it, Mom? . . . Well, I just hope you
      know what you've let us in for. . . . *(Loudly.)* I said I hope you know what
      you've let us in for! It's the end of the peace and quiet we've been hav-
      ing. *(Softly.)* Where is he? *(Normal voice.)* He can't hear us from in there.
      But for God's sake, Mom, what happened? I told you to be firm with
      him. . . . Then you and the nurses should have held him down, taken his
      crutches away. . . . I know only too well he's my father! . . . I'm not being
      disrespectful, but I'm sick and tired of emptying stinking chamber pots
      full of phlegm and piss. . . . Yes, I do! When you're not there, he asks *me*
      to do it. . . . If you really want to know the truth, that's why I've got no
      appetite for my food. . . . Yes! There's a lot of things you don't know
      about. For your information, I still haven't got that science textbook I
      need. And you know why? He borrowed the money you gave me for it.
      . . . Because I didn't want to start another fight between you two. . . . He
      says that every time. . . . All right, Mom! *(Viciously.)* Then just remember
      to start hiding your bag away again, because he'll be at your purse before
      long for money for booze. And when he's well enough to come down
      here, you better keep an eye on the till as well, because that is also going
      to develop a leak. . . . Then don't complain to me when he starts his old
      tricks. . . . Yes, you do, I get it from you on one side and from him on the
      other, and it makes life hell for me. I'm not going to be the peacemaker
      anymore. I'm warning you now: when the two of you start fighting
      again, I'm leaving home. . . . Mom, if you start crying, I'm going to put
      down the receiver. . . . Okay. . . . *(Lowering his voice to a vicious whisper.)*

Okay, Mom. I heard you. *(Desperate.)* No. . . . Because I don't want to. I'll see him when I get home! Mom! . . . *(Pause. When he speaks again, his tone changes completely. It is not simply pretense. We sense a genuine emotional conflict.)* Welcome home, chum! . . . What's that . . . Don't be silly, Dad. You being home is just about the best news in the world. . . . I bet you are. Bloody depressing there with everybody going on about their ailments, hey! . . . How you feeling? . . . Good. . . . Here as well, pal. Coming down cats and dogs. . . . That's right. Just the day for a kip and a toss in your old Uncle Ned. . . . Everything's just hunky-dory on my side, Dad. . . . Well, to start with, there's a nice pile of comics for you on the counter. . . . Yes, old Kemple brought them in. *Batman and Robin, Submariner* . . . just your cup of tea. . . . I will. . . . Yes, we'll spin a few yarns tonight. . . . Okay, chum, see you in a little while. . . . No, I promise. I'll come straight home. . . . *(Pause—his mother comes back on the phone.)* Mom? Okay. I'll lock up now. . . . What? . . . Oh, the brandy . . . Yes, I'll remember! . . . I'll put it in my suitcase now, for God's sake. I know well enough what will happen if he doesn't get it. . . . *(Places a bottle of brandy on the counter.)* I *was* kind to him, Mom. I didn't say anything nasty! . . . All right. Bye. *(End of telephone conversation. A desolate HALLY doesn't move. A strained silence.)*

SAM *(quietly):* That sounded like a bad bump, Hally.   565

HALLY *(Having a hard time controlling his emotions. He speaks carefully.):* Mind your own business, Sam.

SAM: Sorry. I wasn't trying to interfere. Shall we carry on? Hally? *(He indicates the exercise book. No response from HALLY.)*

WILLIE *(also trying):* Tell him about when they give out the cups, Boet Sam.

SAM: Ja! That's another big moment. The presentation of the cups after the winners have been announced. You've got to put that in.

(Still no response from HALLY.)

WILLIE: A big silver one, Master Hally, called floating trophy for the champions.   570

SAM: We always invite some big-shot personality to hand them over. Guest of honor this year is going to be His Holiness Bishop Jabulani of the All African Free Zionist Church.

(HALLY gets up abruptly, goes to his table, and tears up the page he was writing on.)

HALLY: So much for a bloody world without collisions.

SAM: Too bad. It was on its way to being a good composition.

HALLY: Let's stop bullshitting ourselves, Sam.

SAM: Have we been doing that?   575

HALLY: Yes! That's what all our talk about a decent world has been . . . just so much bullshit.

SAM: We did say it was still only a dream.

HALLY: And a bloody useless one at that. Life's a fuckup and it's never going to change.

SAM: Ja, maybe that's true.

580   HALLY: There's no maybe about it. It's a blunt and brutal fact. All we've done this afternoon is waste our time.

SAM: Not if we'd got your homework done.

HALLY: I don't give a shit about my homework, so, for Christ's sake, just shut up about it. *(Slamming books viciously into his school case.)* Hurry up now and finish your work. I want to lock up and get out of here. *(Pause.)* And then go where? Home-sweet-fucking-home. Jesus, I hate that word.

(HALLY goes to the counter to put the brandy bottle and comics in his school case. After a moment's hesitation, he smashes the bottle of brandy. He abandons all further attempts to hide his feelings. SAM and WILLIE work away as unobtrusively as possible.)

Do you want to know what is really wrong with your lovely little dream, Sam? It's not just that we are all bad dancers. That does happen to be perfectly true, but there's more to it than just that. You left out the cripples.

SAM: Hally!

HALLY *(now totally reckless)*: Ja! Can't leave them out, Sam. That's why we always end up on our backsides on the dance floor. They're also out there dancing . . . like a bunch of broken spiders trying to do the quickstep! *(An ugly attempt at laughter.)* When you come to think of it, it's a bloody comical sight. I mean, it's bad enough on two legs . . . but one and a pair of crutches! Hell, no, Sam. That's guaranteed to turn that dance floor into a shambles. Why you shaking your head? Picture it, man. For once this afternoon let's use our imaginations sensibly.

585   SAM: Be careful, Hally.

HALLY: Of what? The truth? I seem to be the only one around here who is prepared to face it. We've had the pretty dream, it's time now to wake up and have a good long look at the way things really are. Nobody knows the steps, there's no music, the cripples are also out there tripping up everybody and trying to get into the act, and it's all called the All-Comers-How-to-Make-a-Fuckup-of-Life Championships. *(Another ugly laugh.)* Hang on, Sam! The best bit is still coming. Do you know what the winner's trophy is? A beautiful big chamber pot with roses on the side, and it's full to the brim with piss. And guess who I think is going to be this year's winner.

SAM *(almost shouting)*: Stop now!

HALLY *(suddenly appalled by how far he has gone)*: Why?

SAM: Hally? It's your father you're talking about.

590   HALLY: So?

SAM: Do you know what you've been saying?

(HALLY can't answer. He is rigid with shame. SAM speaks to him sternly.)

No, Hally, you mustn't do it. Take back those words and ask for forgiveness! It's a terrible sin for a son to mock his father with jokes like that. You'll be punished if you carry on. Your father is your father, even if he is a . . . cripple man.

WILLIE: Yes, Master Hally. Is true what Sam say.

SAM: I understand how you are feeling, Hally, but even so. . . .

HALLY: No, you don't!

SAM: I think I do.   595

HALLY: And I'm telling you you don't. Nobody does. *(Speaking carefully as his shame turns to rage at SAM.)* It's your turn to be careful, Sam. Very careful! You're treading on dangerous ground. Leave me and my father alone.

SAM: I'm not the one who's been saying things about him.

HALLY: What goes on between me and my Dad is none of your business!

SAM: Then don't tell me about it. If that's all you've got to say about him, I don't want to hear.

(For a moment HALLY is at a loss for a response.)

HALLY: Just get on with your bloody work and shut up.   600

SAM: Swearing at me won't help you.

HALLY: Yes, it does! Mind your own fucking business and shut up!

SAM: Okay. If that's the way you want it, I'll stop trying.

(He turns away. This infuriates HALLY even more.)

HALLY: Good. Because what you've been trying to do is meddle in something you know nothing about. All that concerns you in here, Sam, is to try and do what you get paid for—keep the place clean and serve the customers. In plain words, just get on with your job. My mother is right. She's always warning me about allowing you to get too familiar. Well, this time you've gone too far. It's going to stop right now.

(No response from SAM.)

You're only a servant in here, and don't forget it.

(Still no response. HALLY is trying hard to get one.)

And as far as my father is concerned, all you need to remember is that he is your boss.

SAM *(needled at last)*: No, he isn't. I get paid by your mother.   605

HALLY: Don't argue with me, Sam!

SAM: Then don't say he's my boss.

HALLY: He's a white man and that's good enough for you.

SAM: I'll try to forget you said that.

610   HALLY: Don't! Because you won't be doing me a favor if you do. I'm telling you to remember it.

(A pause. SAM *pulls himself together and makes one last effort.)*

SAM: Hally, Hally . . . ! Come on now. Let's stop before it's too late. You're right. We *are* on dangerous ground. If we're not careful, somebody is going to get hurt.

HALLY: It won't be me.

SAM: Don't be so sure.

HALLY: I don't know what you're talking about, Sam.

615   SAM: Yes, you do.

HALLY *(furious)*: Jesus, I wish you would stop trying to tell me what I do and what I don't know.

*(*SAM *gives up. He turns to* WILLIE.*)*

SAM: Let's finish up.

HALLY: Don't turn your back on me! I haven't finished talking.

(He grabs SAM *by the arm and tries to make him turn around.* SAM *reacts with a flash of anger.)*

SAM: Don't do that, Hally! *(Facing the boy.)* All right, I'm listening. Well? What do you want to say to me?

620   HALLY *(pause as* HALLY *looks for something to say)*: To begin with, why don't you also start calling me Master Harold, like Willie.

SAM: Do you mean that?

HALLY: Why the hell do you think I said it?

SAM: And if I don't?

HALLY: You might just lose your job.

625   SAM *(quietly and very carefully)*: If you make me say it once, I'll never call you anything else again.

HALLY: So? *(The boy confronts the man.)* Is that meant to be a threat?

SAM: Just telling you what will happen if you make me do that. You must decide what it means to you.

HALLY: Well, I have. It's good news. Because that is exactly what Master Harold wants from now on. Think of it as a little lesson in respect, Sam, that's long overdue, and I hope you remember it as well as you do your geography. I can tell you now that somebody who will be glad to hear I've finally given it to you will be my Dad. Yes! He agrees with my Mom. He's always going on about it as well. "You must teach the boys to show you more respect, my son."

SAM: So now you can stop complaining about going home. Everybody is going to be happy tonight.

HALLY: That's perfectly correct. You see, you mustn't get the wrong idea about   *630*
me and my Dad, Sam. We also have our good times together. Some
bloody good laughs. He's got a marvelous sense of humor. Want to know
what our favorite joke is? He gives out a big groan, you see, and says:
"It's not fair, is it, Hally?" Then I have to ask: "What, chum?" And then
he says: "A nigger's arse" . . . and we both have a good laugh.

(The men stare at him with disbelief.)

What's the matter, Willie? Don't you catch the joke? You always were a
bit slow on the uptake. It's what is called a pun. You see, fair means both
light in color and to be just and decent. *(He turns to* SAM.*)* I thought *you*
would catch it, Sam.
SAM: Oh ja, I catch it all right.
HALLY: But it doesn't appeal to your sense of humor.
SAM: Do you really laugh?
HALLY: Of course.
SAM: To please him? Make him feel good?   *635*
HALLY: No, for heaven's sake! I laugh because I think it's a bloody good joke.
SAM: You're really trying hard to be ugly, aren't you? And why drag poor old
Willie into it? He's done nothing to you except show you the respect
you want so badly. That's also not being fair, you know . . . and *I* mean
just or decent.
WILLIE: It's all right, Sam. Leave it now.
SAM: It's me you're after. You should just have said "Sam's arse" . . . because
that's the one you're trying to kick. Anyway, how do you know it's not
fair? You've never seen it. Do you want to? *(He drops his trousers and un-
derpants and presents his backside for* HALLY*'s inspection.)* Have a good look.
A real Basuto arse . . . which is about as nigger as they can come. Satisfied? *(Trousers up.)* Now you can make your Dad even happier when you
go home tonight. Tell him I showed you my arse and he is quite right.
It's not fair. And if it will give him an even better laugh next time, I'll
also let *him* have a look. Come, Willie, let's finish up and go.

*(*SAM *and* WILLIE *start to tidy up the tea room.* HALLY *doesn't move. He waits
for a moment when* SAM *passes him.)*

HALLY *(quietly)*: Sam . . .   *640*

*(*SAM *stops and looks expectantly at the boy.* HALLY *spits in his face. A long
and heartfelt groan from* WILLIE. *For a few seconds* SAM *doesn't move.)*

SAM *(taking out a handkerchief and wiping his face)*: It's all right, Willie.

(To HALLY.*)*

Ja, well, you've done it . . . Master Harold. Yes, I'll start calling you that from now on. It won't be difficult anymore. You've hurt yourself, Master Harold. I saw it coming. I warned you, but you wouldn't listen. You've just hurt yourself *bad*. And you're a coward, Master Harold. The face you should be spitting in is your father's . . . but you used mine, because you think you're safe inside your fair skin . . . and this time I don't mean just or decent. *(Pause, then moving violently toward* HALLY.*)* Should I hit him, Willie?

WILLIE *(stopping* SAM*)*: No, Boet Sam.

SAM *(violently)*: Why not?

WILLIE: It won't help, Boet Sam.

645 SAM: I don't want to help! I want to hurt him.

WILLIE: You also hurt yourself.

SAM: And if he had done it to you, Willie?

WILLIE: Me? Spit at me like I was a dog? *(A thought that had not occurred to him before. He looks at* HALLY.*)* Ja. Then I want to hit him. I want to hit him hard!

(A dangerous few seconds as the men stand staring at the boy. WILLIE *turns away, shaking his head.)*

But maybe all I do is go cry at the back. He's little boy, Boet Sam. Little *white* boy. Long trousers now, but he's still little boy.

SAM *(his violence ebbing away into defeat as quickly as it flooded)*: You're right. So go on, then: groan again, Willie. You do it better than me. *(To* HALLY.*)* You don't know all of what you've just done . . . Master Harold. It's not just that you've made me feel dirtier than I've ever been in my life . . . I mean, how do I wash off yours and your father's filth? . . . I've also failed. A long time ago I promised myself I was going to try and do something, but you've just shown me . . . Master Harold . . . that I've failed. *(Pause.)* I've also got a memory of a little white boy when he was still wearing short trousers and a black man, but they're not flying a kite. It was the old Jubilee days, after dinner one night. I was in my room. You came in and just stood against the wall, looking down at the ground, and only after I'd asked you what you wanted, what was wrong, I don't know how many times, did you speak and even then so softly I almost didn't hear you. "Sam, please help me to go and fetch my Dad." Remember? He was dead drunk on the floor of the Central Hotel Bar. They'd phoned for your Mom, but you were the only one at home. And do you remember how we did it? You went in first by yourself to ask permission for me to go into the bar. Then I loaded him onto my back like a baby and carried him back to the boarding house with you following behind carrying his crutches. *(Shaking his head as he remembers.)* A crowded Main Street with all the people watching a little white boy following his drunk father on a nigger's back! I felt for that little boy . . . Master Harold. I felt for him. After that we still had to clean him up, remember? He'd messed in his trousers, so we had to clean him up and get him into bed.

HALLY (*great pain*): I love him, Sam.   650

SAM: I know you do. That's why I tried to stop you from saying these things about him. It would have been so simple if you could have just despised him for being a weak man. But he's your father. You love him and you're ashamed of him. You're ashamed of so much! . . . And now that's going to include yourself. That was the promise I made to myself: to try and stop that happening. (*Pause.*) After we got him to bed you came back with me to my room and sat in a corner and carried on just looking down at the ground. And for days after that! You hadn't done anything wrong, but you went around as if you owed the world an apology for being alive. I didn't like seeing that! That's not the way a boy grows up to be a man! . . . But the one person who should have been teaching you what that means was the cause of your shame. If you really want to know, that's why I made you that kite. I wanted you to look up, be proud of something, of yourself . . . (*bitter smile at the memory*) . . . and you certainly were that when I left you with it up there on the hill. Oh, ja . . . something else! . . . If you ever do write it as a short story, there *was* a twist in our ending. I couldn't sit down there and stay with you. It was a "Whites Only" bench. You were too young, too excited to notice then. But not anymore. If you're not careful . . . Master Harold . . . you're going to be sitting up there by your-self for a long time to come, and there won't be a kite in the sky. (*SAM has got nothing more to say. He exits into the kitchen, taking off his waiter's jacket.*)

WILLIE: Is bad. Is all bad in here now.

HALLY (*books into his school case, raincoat on*): Willie . . . (*It is difficult to speak.*) Will you lock up for me and look after the keys?

WILLIE: Okay.

(*SAM returns.* HALLY *goes behind the counter and collects the few coins in the cash register. As he starts to leave. . . .*)

SAM: Don't forget the comic books.   655

(*HALLY returns to the counter and puts them in his case. He starts to leave again.*)

SAM (*to the retreating back of the boy*): Stop . . . Hally. . . .

(*HALLY stops, but doesn't turn to face him.*)

Hally . . . I've got no right to tell you what being a man means if I don't behave like one myself, and I'm not doing so well at that this afternoon. Should we try again, Hally?

HALLY: Try what?

SAM: Fly another kite, I suppose. It worked once, and this time I need it as much as you do.

HALLY: It's still raining, Sam. You can't fly kites on rainy days, remember.

660   SAM: So what do we do? Hope for better weather tomorrow?

HALLY *(helpless gesture)*: I don't know. I don't know anything anymore.

SAM: You sure of that, Hally? Because it would be pretty hopeless if that was true. It would mean nothing has been learnt in here this afternoon, and there was a hell of a lot of teaching going on . . . one way or the other. But anyway, I don't believe you. I reckon there's one thing you know. You don't *have* to sit up there by yourself. You know what that bench means now, and you can leave it any time you choose. All you've got to do is stand up and walk away from it.

(HALLY leaves. WILLIE goes up quietly to SAM.)

WILLIE: Is okay, Boet Sam. You see. Is . . . *(he can't find any better words)* . . . is going to be okay tomorrow. *(Changing his tone.)* Hey, Boet Sam! *(He is trying hard.)* You right. I think about it and you right. Tonight I find Hilda and say sorry. And make promise I won't beat her no more. You hear me, Boet Sam?

SAM: I hear you, Willie.

665   WILLIE: And when we practice I relax and romance with her from beginning to end. Nonstop! You watch! Two weeks' time: "First prize for promising newcomers: Mr. Willie Malopo and Miss Hilda Samuels." *(Sudden impulse.)* To hell with it! I walk home. *(He goes to the jukebox, puts in a coin and selects a record. The machine comes to life in the gray twilight, blushing its way through a spectrum of soft, romantic colors.)* How did you say it, Boet Sam? Let's dream. *(WILLIE sways with the music and gestures for SAM to dance.)*

(Sarah Vaughan sings.)

"Little man you're crying,
I know why you're blue,
Someone took your kiddy car away;
Better go to sleep now,
Little man you've had a busy day." *(etc., etc.)*
You lead. I follow.

(The men dance together.)

"Johnny won your marbles,
Tell you what we'll do;
Dad will get you new ones right away;
Better go to sleep now,
Little man you've had a busy day."   *1982*

CONSIDERATIONS

1. The play's three characters, two of them black and one white, identify themselves differently. Explain how and why they do so.
2. Who seems to be the most intelligent character? Explain and justify your choice.
3. What is your response to Willie's attitude toward Hilda? Does his change of mind later in the play seem plausible? Why? Why not?
4. The play's action takes place in a tea room, which is a place that could be seen as inoffensive, innocuous. Why do you suppose the playwright chose to use a tea room for the setting? Can you think of other settings that the playwright might have used? Brainstorm a list with some description of other possible locations.
5. Describe Hally's treatment of Sam and Willie in the first part of the play. Compare that to what happens later in the play.
6. Respond to Sam's description of a ballroom:

   > There's no collisions out there, Hally. Nobody trips or stumbles or bumps into anybody else. That's what that moment is all about. To be one of those finalists on that dance floor is like . . . like being in a dream about a world in which accidents don't happen.

   Does it seem idyllic, romantic, or just downright irrational to think that people and life should or could be like a dance?
7. Explain the significance of the closing of the play with Sarah Vaughan's singing. What is its purpose? Why does it make an effective conclusion to the play? Explain your reasons.

More Resources on
Athol Fugard

 In the Online Learning Center for *Responding to Literature*
- Brief biography of Fugard
- List of major works by Fugard
- Web links to more resources on Fugard
- Additional questions for experiencing and interpreting Fugard's writing

Commentary

ERVIN BECK
Fugard's **Master Harold and the Boys**

In *Master Harold and the Boys,* Athol Fugard uses intertextual references to the literary canon as well as to texts from popular culture to clarify the characters and issues in the play. The play concludes with Harold appropriating a borrowed, morally problematic text and with Sam encouraging Harold to write a new liberating text of his own.

Harold's father and Willie, who are the least complex characters, embrace the least complex sets of texts. For instance, all of the texts associated with Harold's father are comic books: Jungle Jim, Batman and Robin, Tarzan, Submariner. In psychoanalytic terms, the macho, superhuman heroes of these comics are compensatory projections for his own personal and social insecurity and immaturity. As Harold says, his father "behave[s] like a child" in his hospital room (26). Just as Harold initially condemns his father, so he also initially condemns his father's favorite reading: "God what rubbish. Mental pollution" (9). Isofar as the heroes of Tarzan and Jungle Jim are white supermen lording it over a stereotypical jungle culture, these comic books also embody the racist ideas of Harold's father, as revealed in his favorite joke, which Harold tells Sam at the climax of the play.

Because Willie is illiterate, his texts come from popular, mass media culture. They include the Hollywood films of Ginger Rogers and Fred Astaire, a pinup of Rita Hayworth in a bathing suit, a photograph of Joe Louis, and popular music by Count Basie and, especially, Sarah Vaughn. All of these come from American and European mainstream culture and communicate that culture's stereotypes of gender and race. To Willie's credit, in Count Basie, Joe Louis, and Sarah Vaughn, he does adopt some attractive black entertainers as his models. However, in his own life he mimics the macho behavior of the Brown Bomber in his abusive, destructive relationship with his dance partner Hilda, a fellow African. And in Ginger Rogers and Fred Astaire he sees only the surface glamour of ballroom dancing, not Sam's vision of a "world without collisions." A victim of alien and alienating cultural norms, Willie's unenlightened, even slavelike, condition is symbolized onstage as he continues to scrub the floor "on his knees" (3), smiling.

The schoolbooks that Harold shares with Sam make Sam into the Christian humanist hero that he is seen to be at the end of the play. Sam knows but does not choose as his "man of magnitude" either Socrates, Dumas, Marx, Dostoevsky, or Nietzsche. Since those names appear in a simple list (18), the negative meanings that those people hold for Sam remain ambiguous. However, in light of Sam's subsequent self-revelation, they may represent for him such alternatives as utopianism (Socrates), escapism (Dumas), communism (Marx), existentialism (Dostoevsky), and "God is dead" and the will to power (Nietzsche). Instead of any of these, Sam understandably chooses Abraham Lincoln as his first man of magnitude because of Lincoln's dramatic liberation of black people in the United States. Sam also chooses Jesus Christ and then even takes on the role of a Christ-figure by enduring Harold's insults (which include spitting in Sam's face) and by preserving his accepting, forgiving attitude toward Harold at the end of the play.

Sam's enthusiasm for Shakespeare, whom he knows only through Julius   5
Caesar, is more subtle. That play is relevant to Sam's own situation under apartheid, because it is a politically charged revenge tragedy with many complex, ambiguous ramifications. Cassius and Brutus rise up against Julius Caesar and assassinate him, but with ensuing social chaos and eventually a new tyranny under Mark Anthony. Perhaps the play has influenced Sam's own temptation to, but ultimate rejection of, violence in reforming an evil social order.

That Harold and Sam share a common belief in human progress is suggested by their mutual endorsement of Sir Alexander Fleming, whose contribution to human physical survival and well-being is documented in *Microbe Hunters,* which both have enjoyed reading. But Harold's choice of two other texts in his man of magnitude game betrays his confused thinking on political and moral issues. Harold chooses Charles Darwin, author of *The Origin of the Species* (Harold's version of Darwin's title), as his main man of magnitude. It is appropriate that Harold has put the book in the "Theology" section of his bookshelves, since he is a self-named "atheist" (18) foil to Sam, the Christian theist. At that point in the play Harold has not yet articulated his embrace of his father's racism, which might also be grounded in his admiration of Darwin. Although Sam is disappointed in Darwin's chapter "The Struggle for an Existence" (15), Harold may be positively impressed by Darwin's notion of the survival of the fittest, which in the South African context implies the white race and white supremacy.

As an atheist, Harold does not perceive the self-contradiction found in his choice of Leo Tolstoy, author of *War and Peace,* as a model social reformer. Tolstoy was a Christian, and both *War and Peace* and his liberation of serfs sprang from his profoundly held Christian pacifism. In choosing Tolstoy, Harold chooses what Sam is and what Sam thinks Harold should become at the end of the play. But in choosing Darwin, Harold chooses what his father is and what Harold apparently becomes at the end of the play through his racist joke and other abuse of Sam. In so subtle a manner, and so early in the play, does the association of books and authors with the key characters, especially the initially unformed character of Harold, foreshadow the outcome of the play.

As a politically liberal Christian humanist who believes in education instead of violence and in freedom instead of determinism, Sam persists throughout the play in helping Harold write himself into a text that will be more liberating and humanizing than the one Harold has committed himself to at the end of the play, which is his father's racist joke about "a Kaffir's arse" (44). Harold's assignment for school is to write an essay for his English class. Admirably, he first rejects the topic "Landing of the 1820 settlers" (which would be white chauvinism) and also "Carols by Candlelight" (28) (which would be mindlessly sentimental, given South Africa's cultural crisis). To his credit, he is then attracted to an anthropological report on native Africans' "ballroom championship" events, which is politically subversive and risky for him because his teacher "doesn't like natives" (34). He is even drawn to Sam's politically symbolic interpretation of ballroom dancing and subsequently titles his paper, "Ballroom Dancing as a Political Vision" (38).

A telephone call from his mother and father immediately follows that noble decision and eventually leads to Harold's abandoning the essay and, instead, internalizing as his own text the Tarzan-like, racist joke that he shares with his father. Although momentarily crushed and discouraged, Sam recovers and by the end of the play encourages Harold to change his mind and write something new—about the time in his childhood when Harold and Sam flew a kite, the play's chief symbol of racial harmony and spiritual liberation. "If you ever do write it as a short story, there was a twist in our ending" (47), Sam reminds Harold. He has in mind, of course, that the hero—Harold or any other South African—need not sit forever, crying, on a bench labeled "Whites Only." They can get off that bench. They can change the system.

Work Cited

Fugard, Athol. *Master Harold and the Boys. Selected Plays.* Oxford: Oxford UP, 1987.

BRIAN SUTTON
Fugard's "Master Harold" . . . and the Boys

(A Response to Ervin Beck)[19]

In a recent article in *The Explicator,* Ervin Beck states that in Athol Fugard's play *"Master Harold" . . . and the Boys,* Sam is a "Christian humanist hero" who "even takes on the role of a Christ-figure by enduring Harold's insults (which include spitting in Sam's face) and by preserving his accepting, forgiving attitude toward Harold at the end of the play" (110). Beck is correct in calling Sam a Christ-figure, but the central point of his article lies elsewhere. Thus, he says nothing more about this idea in his essay, never suggesting that

---

19. Editor's subtitle.

Sam is a symbol of Christ in other ways beyond those demonstrated at the end of the play. Nor has any other article about *"Master Harold"* mentioned the concept of Sam as Christ-symbol. But in fact, Fugard develops Sam as a symbol of Christ throughout, in part by portraying him as a servant literally suffering, who must bear the cross of racism in the play's apartheid South Africa.

Fugard begins establishing this concept early, when Sam describes to Willie, his fellow servant, and to Hally (Harold), a young white man, his experience of being whipped on the backside after being arrested (apparently for little more than being black) and sentenced. By giving Sam an experience so similar to Christ's—being arrested, almost certainly unjustly, and whipped by henchmen working for corrupt authorities—Fugard begins to associate the concept of the suffering servant with apartheid policies. Although Sam describes the experience with no trace of bitterness, Hally is moved to say to Sam, "Jesus! It's a bloody awful world when you come to think of it" (15), a wording that further encourages the audience to view Sam as a Christ-symbol.

Even when the play treats happier memories, images underscoring Sam's Christlike suffering remain prominent. A prime example is Hally's discussion of his favorite memory from childhood, the time Sam made a kite for him. Hally states that when he first observed Sam smoothing down two pieces of wood with a knife, he couldn't tell what Sam was making. He adds, "It was only when you tied them together in a cross . . . that I realized what you were doing" (28). Hally describes himself as having been initially so pessimistic about the kite that he refused to carry it, convinced that expecting it to fly was like "asking for a miracle to happen" (29). So Sam was left to carry his cross, hidden within a kite, up a hill where, as Hally recalls, "The miracle happened!" (30)

Although the relationship between the cross that Sam bears and the apartheid system is not made manifest until later in the play, it is already implicit in the kite-flying episode. First, Sam makes the kite while in the servants' quarters of the Jubilee Boarding House. The name of the boarding house, like many other elements in *"Master Harold,"* is unchanged from the autobiographical events on which Fugard based the play (Fugard, *Notebooks* 25–26); "jubilee" in the Bible refers to a holy time occurring every fifty years (and the play is set in 1950), when slaves were freed and land was returned to its original owners (Leviticus 25.8–12). Thus, the name of the boarding house emphasizes the dispossessed natives' suffering within a biblical context. Second, Hally describes Sam's holding the kite and telling Hally to run with the string and then describes himself running and feeling "something alive behind me at the end of the string, tugging at it as if it wanted to be free" (30). The tugging, of course comes from the airborne kite, but Fugard's handling of the dialogue encourages us to think that Hally might be referring to Sam and his desire for freedom. Finally, Hally describes the sadness he felt when Sam left him to bring the kite down alone and adds that the kite, after being brought down, looked "like something that had lost its soul" (30). We don't learn about it until later in the play, but there is a simple reason why Sam had to leave: Though too young to notice it at the time, Hally was sitting on a whites-only bench (58). Although the symbolism of the kite isn't entirely consistent—at times it appears to be a cross Sam must bear, whereas at other times it appears to symbolize Sam himself—the incident is steeped in overtones involving religion, oppression, and apartheid.

5   Later in the play Fugard uses another incident, one carefully correlated with the kite-flying scene, to underscore the relationship between apartheid racism and Sam's role as suffering servant. Sam introduces the incident, from what he calls "the old Jubilee days," by saying, "I've also got a memory of a little white boy when he was still wearing short trousers and a black man, but they're not flying a kite" (57). He then describes the time when Hally's father, a disabled alcoholic, passed out in a bar and had to be carried home by Sam, with little Hally forced to come along to enable Sam to enter the whites-only bar. Fugard's handling of the imagery of this scene encourages the audience to associate the incident with the kite-flying scene. For example, Hally says that when they left the boarding house with Sam carrying the kite, "I was praying quietly that there wouldn't be other kids around to laugh at us" (29). Similarly, Sam describes carrying Hally's father down "a crowded Main street with all the people watching a little white boy following his drunk father on a nigger's back!" (58). In both scenes, Sam carries the physical burden while Hally carries the burden of knowing that others are seeing him in a humiliating situation. The two scenes are further correlated when Sam adds that the reason he made the kite for Hally in the first place was to help the boy overcome his shame after the incident with his father (58).

Clearly we are expected to associate Sam's carrying Hally's father with his carrying the kite—and thus, with Jesus' burden of the cross. But Hally's father, besides being an alcoholic, is also the play's embodiment of apartheid racism, a man whose favorite joke has the punch line "A nigger's arse" (55). Thus, the nature of the cross that Sam must carry finally becomes symbolically explicit.

What the scene of Sam carrying Hally's father establishes symbolically, Hally establishes literally within the plot, through the insults mentioned by Beck (110). For by the time Sam describes the scene, Hally has already used his society's racial standards as a pretext for attacking Sam, although Sam is blameless and the real roots of Hally's anger lie in his being ashamed of his father and himself. Early in his tirade, in a line that underscores Sam's role as Christ-symbol, Hally tells Sam, "You're only a servant here and don't forget it" (53). Eventually, in the play's most famous image, Hally spits in Sam's face. Sam says to Hally, "You don't know all of what you've just done" (57). And moments later, in a passage criticized by some (Asahina 445; Seidenspinner 211) but clearly consistent with Fugard's own philosophy of nonviolence and forgiveness (Fugard, "Problems" 389-90; Gussow 93; Kalem 86), Sam reaches out to Hally in an attempt to reestablish their friendship. The echo of Christ's words and actions is unmistakable: Sam forgives Hally after telling him that he knows not what he does.

Just before this, as his anger builds toward its shameful culmination, Hally insists that Sam start calling him "Master Harold" rather than "Hally," adding that his father has told him, "You must teach the boys to show you more respect" (54–55). It is from this sequence, presumably, that Fugard derived the play's title. Other writers have mentioned the irony of the title, noting that it is Hally, not Sam or Willie, who is the boy (Post 101; Simon 76; Wertheim 146). A further irony is that it is Sam, not Hally, who is the Master.

Works Cited

Asahina, Robert. "Theatre Chronicle." *Hudson Review* 35 (1982):439–46.

Beck, Ervin. "Fugard's '*Master Harold' and the Boys*." *Explicator* 58 (2000): 109–12.

Fugard, Athol. *"Master Harold" . . . and the Boys.* New York: Knopf, 1982.

————. *Notebooks: 1960–1977.* New York: Theatre Communications Group, 1983.

————. "Some Problems of a Playwright from South Africa." *Twentieth Century Literature* 39 (1983): 381–93.

Gussow, Mel. "Witness." *New Yorker* 20 December 1982: 47–94.

Kalem, T. E. "Dance Marathon." *Time* 17 May 1982: 86.

Post, Robert. "Racism in Athol Fugard's '*Master Harold' . . . and the Boys.*" *World Literature Written in English* 30.1 (1990): 97–102.

Seidenspinner, Margaret. *Exploring the Labyrinth: Athol Fugard's Approach to South African Drama.* Essen: Blaue Eule, 1986.

Simon, John. "Two Harolds and No Medea." *New Yorker* 17 May 1982. 76+.

Wertheim, Albert. "Ballroom Dancing, Kites and Politics: Athol Fugard's '*Master Harold' . . . and the Boys. Journal of the South Pacific Association for Commonwealth Literature* 30 (April 1990): 141–55.

Essays

CHIEF SEATTLE (c. 1786–1866)

My People

Chief of the Suquamish and leader of other tribes in what is now Washington state, Chief Seattle was born around 1786. In 1853, the governor of Washington Territories, Isaac Stevens, proposed to buy two million acres of land from the tribes Seattle led. This speech is Seattle's reply to the offer. His words offer a chilling prediction of the massacres and relocations that decimated Native American tribes beginning in the 1860s.

Yonder sky that has wept tears upon my people for centuries untold, and which to us appears changeless and eternal, may change. Today is fair. Tomorrow may be overcast with clouds. My words are like the stars that never change. Whatever Seattle says the great chief at Washington can rely upon with as much certainty as he can upon the return of the sun or the seasons. The White Chief says that Big Chief at Washington sends us greetings of friendship and goodwill. That is kind of him for we know he has little need of our friendship in return. His people are many. They are like the grass that covers vast prairies. My people are few. They resemble the scattering trees of a storm-swept plain. The great, and—I presume—good, White Chief sends us word that he wishes to buy our lands but is willing to allow us enough to live comfortably. This indeed appears just, even generous, for the Red Man no longer has rights that he need respect, and the offer may be wise also, as we are no longer in need of an extensive country. . . . I will not dwell on, nor mourn over, our untimely decay, nor reproach our paleface brothers with hastening it, as we too may have been somewhat to blame.

Youth is impulsive. When our young men grow angry at some real or imaginary wrong, and disfigure their faces with black paint, it denotes that their hearts are black, and then they are often cruel and relentless, and our old men and old women are unable to restrain them. Thus it has ever been. Thus it was when the white men first began to push our forefathers further westward. But let us hope that the hostilities between us may never return. We would have everything to lose and nothing to gain. Revenge by young men is considered gain, even at the cost of their own lives, but old men who stay at home in times of war, and mothers who have sons to lose, know better.

Our good father at Washington—for I presume he is now our father as well as yours, since King George has moved his boundaries further north— our great good father, I say, sends us word that if we do as he desires he will protect us. His brave warriors will be to us a bristling wall of strength, and his wonderful ships of war will fill our harbors so that our ancient enemies far to the northward—the Hydas and Tsimpsians—will cease to frighten our women, children, and old men. Then in reality will he be our father and we his children. But can that ever be? Your God is not our God! Your God loves your people and hates mine. He folds his strong and protecting arms lovingly about the paleface and leads him by the hand as a father leads his infant son—but He has forsaken His red children—if they really are his. Our God, the Great Spirit, seems also to have forsaken us. Your God makes your people wax strong every day. Soon they will fill the land. Our people are ebbing away like a rapidly receding tide that will never return. The white man's God cannot love our people or He would protect them. They seem to be orphans who can look nowhere for help. How then can we be brothers? How can your God become our God and renew our prosperity and awaken in us dreams of returning greatness? If we have a common heavenly father He must be partial—for He came to his paleface children. We never saw Him. He gave you laws but

He had no word for His red children whose teeming multitudes once filled this vast continent as stars fill the firmament. No; we are two distinct races with separate origins and separate destinies. There is little in common between us.

To us the ashes of our ancestors are sacred and their resting place is hallowed ground. You wander far from the graves of your ancestors and seemingly without regret. Your religion was written upon tables of stone by the iron finger of your God so that you could not forget. The Red Man could never comprehend nor remember it. Our religion is the traditions of our ancestors—the dreams of our old men, given them in solemn hours of night by the Great Spirit; and the visions of our sachems°; and it is written in the hearts of our people.

Your dead cease to love you and the land of their nativity as soon as they   5 pass the portals of the tomb and wander way beyond the stars. They are soon forgotten and never return. Our dead never forget the beautiful world that gave them being.

Day and night cannot dwell together. The Red Man has ever fled the approach of the White Man, as the morning mist flees before the morning sun. However, your proposition seems fair and I think that my people will accept it and will retire to the reservation you offer them. Then we will dwell apart in peace, for the words of the Great White Chief seem to be the words of nature speaking to my people out of dense darkness.

It matters little where we pass the remnant of our days. They will not be many. A few more moons; a few more winters—and not one of the descendants of the mighty hosts that once moved over this broad land or lived in happy homes, protected by the Great Spirit, will remain to mourn over the graves of a people once more powerful and hopeful than yours. But why should I mourn at the untimely fate of my people? Tribe follows tribe, and nation follows nation, like the waves of the sea. It is the order of nature, and regret is useless. Your time of decay may be distant, but it will surely come, for even the White Man whose God walked and talked with him as friend with friend, cannot be exempt from the common destiny. We may be brothers after all. We will see.

We will ponder your proposition, and when we decide we will let you know. But should we accept it, I here and now make this condition that we will not be denied the privilege without molestation of visiting at any time the tombs of our ancestors, friends and children. Every part of this soil is sacred in the estimation of my people. Every hillside, every valley, every plain and grove, has been hallowed by some sad or happy event in days long vanished. . . . The very dust upon which you now stand responds more lovingly to their footsteps than to yours, because it is rich with the blood of our ancestors

sachems: Tribal chiefs.

and our bare feet are conscious of the sympathetic touch. . . . Even the little children who lived here and rejoiced here for a brief season will love these somber solitudes and at eventide they greet shadowy returning spirits. And when the last Red Man shall have perished, and the memory of my tribe shall have become a myth among the White Men, these shores will swarm with the invisible dead of my tribe, and when your children's children think themselves alone in the field, the store, the shop, upon the highway, or in the silence of the pathless woods, they will not be alone. . . . At night when the streets of your cities and villages are silent and you think them deserted, they will throng with the returning hosts that once filled and still love this beautiful land. The White Man will never be alone.

Let him be just and deal kindly with my people, for the dead are not powerless. Dead, did I say? There is not death, only a change of worlds.   *1853*

CONSIDERATIONS

1. Note the images and comparisons Chief Seattle chooses to express his ideas. What does his language suggest about his view of the world?
2. The tone of Seattle's message is complex. Identify and discuss specific passages that suggest his view of white people and of their offer to buy the lands where his tribe has lived.
3. This message was composed in 1853. To what extent has Seattle's prophecy been proved true? Consider particularly the vision he projects in the last part of paragraph 8.
4. Briefly describe the audience to whom Chief Seattle delivers his message. What tone does he take? Cite specific examples to argue either for or against the following proposition: Chief Seattle's speech is a masterpiece of diplomacy.
5. In paragraph 2, Chief Seattle describes the young men of his tribe in this way: "Youth is impulsive. When our young men grow angry at some real or imaginary wrong . . . then they are often cruel and relentless." What is his attitude toward this cruelty and relentlessness? Comment on the application of Seattle's observations to any of your own present-day actions or observations.

FREDERICK DOUGLASS (1817?–1895)
Learning to Read and Write

> *Born a slave in Talbot County, Maryland, Frederick Douglass grew up on a plantation and was later sent to Baltimore to live with and work for the Auld family. During this period of his life, Douglass became aware of the essential rela-*

tionship between literacy and independence. Although the Auld family thwarted him whenever they could, he discovered innovative ways of learning to read and write. He describes this phase of his education in the following excerpt from his autobiography, The Narrative of the Life of Frederick Douglass, *an American Slave, Written by Himself (1845).*

I lived in Master Hugh's family about seven years. During this time, I succeeded in learning to read and write. In accomplishing this, I was compelled to resort to various stratagems. I had no regular teacher. My mistress, who had kindly commenced to instruct me, had, in compliance with the advice and direction of her husband, not only ceased to instruct, but had set her face against my being instructed by any one else. It is due, however, to my mistress to say of her, that she did not adopt this course of treatment immediately. She at first lacked the depravity indispensable to shutting me up in mental darkness. It was at least necessary for her to have some training in the exercise of irresponsible power, to make her equal to the task of treating me as though I were a brute.

My mistress was, as I have said, a kind and tender-hearted woman; and in the simplicity of her soul she commenced, when I first went to live with her, to treat me as she supposed one human being ought to treat another. In entering upon the duties of a slaveholder, she did not seem to perceive that I sustained to her the relation of a mere chattel, and that for her to treat me as a human being was not only wrong, but dangerously so. Slavery proved as injurious to her as it did to me. When I went there, she was a pious, warm, and tender-hearted woman. There was no sorrow or suffering for which she had not a tear. She had bread for the hungry, clothes for the naked, and comfort for every mourner that came within her reach. Slavery soon proved its ability to divest her of these heavenly qualities. Under its influence, the tender heart became stone, and the lamblike disposition gave way to one of tiger-like fierceness. The first step in her downward course was in her ceasing to instruct me. She now commenced to practise her husband's precepts. She finally became even more violent in her opposition than her husband himself. She was not satisfied with simply doing as well as he had commanded; she seemed anxious to do better. Nothing seemed to make her more angry than to see me with a newspaper. She seemed to think that here lay the danger. I have had her rush at me with a face made all up of fury, and snatch from me a newspaper, in a manner that fully revealed her apprehension. She was an apt woman; and a little experience soon demonstrated, to her satisfaction, that education and slavery were incompatible with each other.

From this time I was most narrowly watched. If I was in a separate room any considerable length of time, I was sure to be suspected of having a book, and was at once called to give an account of myself. All this, however, was too late. The first step had been taken. Mistress, in teaching me the alphabet, had given me the *inch,* and no precaution could prevent me from taking the *ell.*

The plan which I adopted, and the one by which I was most successful, was that of making friends of all the little white boys whom I met in the street. As many of these as I could, I converted into teachers. With their kindly aid, obtained at different times and in different places, I finally succeeded in learning to read. When I was sent on errands, I always took my book with me, and by doing one part of my errand quickly, I found time to get a lesson before my return. I used also to carry bread with me, enough of which was always in the house, and to which I was always welcome; for I was much better off in this regard than many of the poor white children in our neighborhood. This bread I used to bestow upon the hungry little urchins, who, in return, would give me that more valuable bread of knowledge. I am strongly tempted to give the names of two or three of those little boys, as a testimonial of the gratitude and affection I bear them; but prudence forbids;—not that it would injure me, but it might embarrass them; for it is almost an unpardonable offence to teach slaves to read in this Christian country. It is enough to say of the dear little fellows, that they lived on Philpot Street, very near Durgin and Bailey's shipyard. I used to talk this matter of slavery over with them. I would sometimes say to them, I wished I could be as free as they would be when they got to be men. "You will be free as soon as you are twenty-one, *but I am a slave for life!* Have not I as good a right to be free as you have?" These words used to trouble them; they would express for me the liveliest sympathy, and console me with the hope that something would occur by which I might be free.

5   I was now about twelve years old, and the thought of being *a slave for life* began to bear heavily upon my heart. Just about this time, I got hold of a book entitled "The Columbian Orator." Every opportunity I got, I used to read this book. Among much of other interesting matter, I found in it a dialogue between a master and his slave. The slave was represented as having run away from his master three times. The dialogue represented the conversation which took place between them, when the slave was retaken the third time. In this dialogue, the whole argument in behalf of slavery was brought forward by the master, all of which was disposed of by the slave. The slave was made to say some very smart as well as impressive things in reply to his master—things which had the desired though unexpected effect; for the conversation resulted in the voluntary emancipation of the slave on the part of the master.

In the same book, I met with one of Sheridan's° mighty speeches on and in behalf of Catholic emancipation. These were choice documents to me. I read them over and over again with unabated interest. They gave tongue to interesting thoughts of my own soul, which had frequently flashed through my mind, and died away for want of utterance. The moral which I gained from the dialogue was the power of truth over the conscience of even a slaveholder. What I got from Sheridan was a bold denunciation of slavery, and a powerful

---

Sheridan's: Richard Brinsley Sheridan (1751–1861), English playwright and politician who wrote and spoke about the need for Catholic emancipation in England.

vindication of human rights. The reading of these documents enabled me to utter my thoughts, and to meet the arguments brought forward to sustain slavery; but while they relieved me of one difficulty, they brought on another even more painful than the one of which I was relieved. The more I read, the more I was led to abhor and detest my enslavers. I could regard them in no other light than a band of successful robbers, who had left their homes, and gone to Africa, and stolen us from our homes, and in a strange land reduced us to slavery. I loathed them as being the meanest as well as the most wicked of men. As I read and contemplated the subject, behold! that very discontentment which Master Hugh had predicted would follow my learning to read had already come, to torment and sting my soul to unutterable anguish. As I writhed under it, I would at times feel that learning to read had been a curse rather than a blessing. It had given me a view of my wretched condition, without the remedy. It opened my eyes to the horrible pit, but to no ladder upon which to get out. In moments of agony, I envied my fellow-slaves for their stupidity. I have often wished myself a beast. I preferred the condition of the meanest reptile to my own. Any thing, no matter what, to get rid of thinking! It was this everlasting thinking of my condition that tormented me. There was no getting rid of it. It was pressed upon me by every object within sight or hearing, animate or inanimate. The silver trump° of freedom had roused my soul to eternal wakefulness. Freedom now appeared, to disappear no more forever. It was heard in every sound, and seen in every thing. It was ever present to torment me with a sense of my wretched condition. I saw nothing without seeing it, I heard nothing without hearing it, and felt nothing without feeling it. It looked from every star, it smiled in every calm, breathed in every wind, and moved in every storm.

I often found myself regretting my own existence, and wishing myself dead; and but for the hope of being free, I have no doubt but that I should have killed myself, or done something for which I should have been killed. While in this state of mind, I was eager to hear any one speak of slavery. I was a ready listener. Every little while, I could hear something about the abolitionists. It was some time before I found what the word meant. It was always used in such connections as to make it an interesting word to me. If a slave ran away and succeeded in getting clear, or if a slave killed his master, set fire to a barn, or did any thing very wrong in the mind of a slaveholder, it was spoken of as the fruit of *abolition*. Hearing the word in this connection very often, I set about learning what it meant. The dictionary afforded me little or no help. I found it was "the act of abolishing"; but then I did not know what was to be abolished. Here I was perplexed. I did not dare to ask any one about its meaning, for I was satisfied that it was something they wanted me to know very little about. After a patient waiting, I got one of our city papers, containing an account of the number of petitions from the north, praying for the abolition

trump: Trumpet.

of slavery in the District of Columbia, and of the slave trade between the States. From this time I understood the words *abolition* and *abolitionist,* and always drew near when that word was spoken, expecting to hear something of importance to myself and fellow-slaves. The light broke in upon me by degrees. I went one day down on the wharf of Mr. Waters; and seeing two Irishmen unloading a scow of stone, I went, unasked, and helped them. When we had finished, one of them came to me and asked me if I were a slave. I told him I was. He asked, "Are ye a slave for life?" I told him that I was. The good Irishman seemed to be deeply affected by the statement. He said to the other that it was a pity so fine a little fellow as myself should be a slave for life. He said it was a shame to hold me. They both advised me to run away to the north; that I should find friends there, and that I should be free. I pretended not to be interested in what they said, and treated them as if I did not understand them; for I feared they might be treacherous. White men have been known to encourage slaves to escape, and then, to get the reward, catch them and return them to their masters. I was afraid that these seemingly good men might use me so; but I nevertheless remembered their advice, and from that time I resolved to run away. I looked forward to a time at which it would be safe for me to escape. I was too young to think of doing so immediately; besides, I wished to learn how to write, as I might have occasion to write my own pass. I consoled myself with the hope that I should one day find a good chance. Meanwhile, I would learn to write.

The idea as to how I might learn to write was suggested to me by being in Durgin and Bailey's ship-yard, and frequently seeing the ship carpenters, after hewing, and getting a piece of timber ready to use, write on the timber the name of that part of the ship for which it was intended. When a piece of timber was intended for the larboard side, it would be marked thus—"L." When a piece was for the starboard side, it would be marked thus—"S." A piece for the larboard side forward, would be marked thus—"L. F." When a piece was for starboard side forward, it would be marked thus—"S. F." For larboard aft, it would be marked thus—"L. A." For starboard aft, it would be marked thus—"S. A." I soon learned the names of these letters, and for what they were intended when placed upon a piece of timber in the ship-yard. I immediately commenced copying them, and in a short time was able to make the four letters named. After that, when I met with any boy who I knew could write, I would tell him I could write as well as he. The next word would be, "I don't believe you. Let me see you try it." I would then make the letters which I had been so fortunate as to learn, and ask him to beat that. In this way I got a good many lessons in writing, which it is quite possible I should never have gotten in any other way. During this time, my copy-book was the board fence, brick wall, and pavement; my pen and ink was a lump of chalk. With these, I learned mainly how to write. I then commenced and continued copying the Italics in Webster's Spelling Book, until I could make them all without looking on the book. By this time, my little Master Thomas had gone to school, and learned how to write, and had written over a number of copy-books. These had been brought home, and shown to some of our near neighbors, and then laid aside. My mistress used to go to class meeting at the Wilk Street meeting-house every Monday afternoon, and leave me to take care of the house. When left thus, I used to spend the time in writing in the spaces left in Master Thomas's copy-book, copying what he had written. I continued to do this until I could write a hand very similar to that of Master Thomas. Thus, after a long, tedious effort for years, I finally succeeded in learning how to write.   *1845*

CONSIDERATIONS

1. Douglass chooses to report certain incidents in his process of learning to read and write and to show other incidents by dramatizing them. Summarize one of these dramatized incidents and discuss why you think this episode might have been particularly significant to Douglass.
2. Although this selection, a chapter from Douglass's book *The Narrative of the Life of Frederick Douglass: An American Slave* (1845), is told primarily in story form, it also makes a profound argument against slavery. Explain how Douglass develops this argument, and evaluate the evidence he uses to support his contentions.
3. Douglass compares the circumstances of slaves to the circumstances of Irish Catholics. Locate and list every mention of the Irish or of Catholicism in this selection and explain how Douglass uses this comparison to argue his case persuasively.

More Resources on
Frederick Douglass and "Learning to Read and Write"

 In *ARIEL*

- Brief biography of Douglass
- Complete text of Chapters 1 to 3 of *Narrative of the Life of Frederick Douglass*
- Video clip of dramatic production of a speech by Douglass
- Analysis of narrative in Douglass's writing
- Bibliography of scholarly works on Douglass

4. Discuss the role of Master Hugh's wife. What might her motives be as she first sets out to educate Douglass and then becomes almost fanatic in her attempts to keep him away from books?

5. Put yourself in the place of one of the people who chooses to help Douglass. Describe the circumstances of your decision from that person's point of view. Keep in mind that it was against the law to educate slaves.

CONNECTIONS: ROOTS, IDENTITY, AND CULTURE

1. How do people recognize their identities? Explain and illustrate your response using examples from any of the following works: "Sonny's Blues," "Quilting," "Coca-Cola and Coco Frío," *"Master Harold"... and the Boys,* "My People," and "The Man Who Was Almost a Man."

2. Do you relate to or empathize with any one particular character, group, or situation depicted in the works in this chapter? If so, describe how and why.

3. Contrast your culture with the culture depicted in one of the following works that is very different from your own: "El Tonto del Barrio," "Telephone Conversation," "The Youngest Daughter," "Latin Women Pray," or "in the inner city."

4. In many of the works in this chapter, differences cause conflict, which makes for a better story. Describe how the world in which you live or society in general would be better served without these sorts of differences. Can or should differences between people and groups ever be resolved? Explain your answer.

5. "Sonny's Blues," "The Lesson," "We wear the mask," "Telephone Conversation," *"Master Harold"... and the Boys,* and "Learning to Read and Write" all look at the experiences of African or African-American men and women living in a predominantly white culture. From reading these works, what observations can you make about the similarities and differences in these experiences?

6. Examine ways in which people's life choices are or are not controlled by their roots and culture. Consider some of the following works: "Sonny's Blues," "The Youngest Daughter," "Latin Women Pray," *"Master Harold"... and the Boys,* "Learning to Read and Write," and "The Man Who Was Almost a Man."

SUGGESTIONS FOR EXTENDED CONNECTIONS AMONG CHAPTERS

1. How do the cultural expectations and backgrounds of parents and other adults affect the way these individuals influence a central character's view of her- or himself? Consider the following as you explore this topic:

"Graduation in Stamps"	385
"Roman Fever"	547
"I Stand Here Ironing"	692
"Everyday Use"	709
A Doll's House	608
"My Flamboyant Grandson"	1067
"To Any Would-Be Terrorists"	1018
"My Father's Life"	797

2. How do external circumstances and social expectations shape gender roles and development of identity? Consider the following as you explore this issue:

"Young Goodman Brown"	194
"Araby"	206
"The Bass, the River, and Sheila Mant"	227
"The Yellow Wallpaper"	532
"Second-Hand Man"	585
Trifles	666
A Doll's House	608
"The Man Who Was Almost a Man"	402
"The Birthmark"	1034
"The Things They Carried"	934

3. Often, characters cannot express their true selves or their true feelings because of the restraints their cultures place on them. As you think about this conflict between an individual's social self and an individual's interior self, consider the following selections:

"Araby"	206
"The Red Convertible"	218
Trifles	666
"The Things They Carried"	934
"The Yellow Wallpaper"	532
"Who's Irish?"	724
"How to Watch Your Brother Die"	1199
Wit	1085
"A Chinese Banquet"	606
"My Flamboyant Grandson"	1067

4. Choose any of the following selections and compare and contrast the experience of the central characters with your own experiences within the culture in which you grew up.

"Learning to Read and Write"	520
"Who's Irish?"	724
"A Jury of Her Peers"	558
"A Partial Remembrance of a Puerto Rican Childhood"	804
"The Management of Grief"	948

SUGGESTIONS FOR COLLABORATIVE LEARNING

1. Working in groups of two or three, choose one of the short stories in this section, and carefully record the most vivid images and descriptions contained in these stories. Once you've collected the most powerful words and phrases, use these words to construct a poem that will reflect the conflict, central theme, or main character in this piece. You may also convert this poem into a song if you so choose. You may also want to compare your new piece of writing with the original story, noting the different responses your piece evokes.

2. Working in groups of three or four, choose one of the poems in this section with the intent of having two or three people outside your class read and respond to it. Write up the responses of those who read this poem outside of class, and share these new responses with your group members. Individually, write up an analysis of how this poem affected those who read it, as well as any new insights you gained from others' responses.

WEB CONNECTIONS

1. What forces go into shaping our identity? In this chapter, all of the selections deal with how much our environment, especially our ethnic background, shapes our perspective on our relationships with ourselves and others. Sociologists and anthropologists study the effects of culture on the individual and the community. To gain insight into some of their theories, check out the following two Web sites, which provide many links to cultural theorists and other resources related to the study of cultures. The first is Athabasca University's *Centre for Psychology Resources*; the second is Georgetown University's *New American Studies Web,* where you can scroll down to "19. Race, Ethnicity, and Identity" for links to resources.

     http://psych.athabascau.ca/html/aupr/social.shtml
     http://cfdev.Georgetown.edu/cndls/asw/

2. Diversity and race are two vital aspects of every culture, most especially in America, which is sometimes described as the melting pot of the world's cultures. In actuality, though, how well do people from different backgrounds blend together? What are some of the current struggles and issues

that still divide people who have different backgrounds? The following Web site provides an extensive list of links to sites that contain information about diversity and acceptance, and include information and readings on affirmative action, white privilege, multiracial individuals, gays and lesbians of color, race and media, and art, literature, and music.

http://racerelations.about.com/mlibrary.htm

Imagine two dialogues between these people, one that reflects love and one that reflects hate.

8

Love and Hate

Selections in this chapter look at many aspects of love and hate, inviting readers to consider the complex circumstances, beliefs, hopes, fears, and desires that evoke these human emotions. From romantic love to the love of a long-married couple to the love of a neighbor or street person, these works explore the ways people connect and the reasons for those connections. Looking at hate, the emotion that so often intimately relates to love, these stories, poems and plays also show how misunderstanding, prejudice, abuse of power, and jealousy tear people apart and destroy lives.

As you read the selections in the section, keep in mind the following questions:

1. How does romantic love differ from the love of a long-married couple? In what ways might hate also intertwine with love in these relationships?
2. How do the use and misuse of power relate to love relationships and to the hate that sometimes infects these relationships?
3. How do the ethics, customs, and laws of various cultures relate to the way people living in these cultures love and hate?
4. How do gender issues and stereotypes relate to the themes of love and hate as portrayed in these works?
5. How would you define love? How would you define hate? Do you consider these emotions to be opposites?

Fiction

CHARLOTTE PERKINS GILMAN (1860–1935)
The Yellow Wallpaper

Charlotte Perkins Gilman was born in Hartford, Connecticut. Her father left the family shortly after her birth, and she and her brother were raised by her mother. As a young adult, Gilman attended the Rhode Island School of Design, which provided the training she needed to work as an art teacher. In 1884, she married her first husband, Charles Walter Stetson. Following the birth of their first child, a daughter, Gilman suffered a severe breakdown. After she recovered, she moved with her mother and daughter to California, obtained a divorce, and finally sent her daughter back to Connecticut to live with her former husband and his new wife. Gilman remained in California, supporting herself by lecturing, editing, writing, and teaching. In 1900, she married George Houghton Gilman, and the two were happily married for many years, during which Charlotte became a prominent lecturer and writer on feminism and the labor movement. "The Yellow Wallpaper" was first published in 1892 in the New England Magazine.

It is very seldom that mere ordinary people like John and myself secure ancestral halls for the summer.

A colonial mansion, a hereditary estate, I would say a haunted house and reach the height of romantic felicity—but that would be asking too much of fate!

Still I will proudly declare that there is something queer about it.

Else, why should it be let so cheaply? And why have stood so long untenanted?

5   John laughs at me, of course, but one expects that.

John is practical in the extreme. He has no patience with faith, an intense horror of superstition, and he scoffs openly at any talk of things not to be felt and seen and put down in figures.

John is a physician, and *perhaps*—(I would not say it to a living soul, of course, but this is dead paper and a great relief to my mind)—*perhaps* that is one reason I do not get well faster.

You see, he does not believe I am sick! And what can one do?

If a physician of high standing, and one's own husband, assures friends and relatives that there is really nothing the matter with one but temporary nervous depression—a slight hysterical tendency—what is one to do?

10   My brother is also a physician, and also of high standing, and he says the same thing.

So I take phosphates or phosphites—whichever it is—and tonics, and air and exercise, and journeys, and am absolutely forbidden to "work" until I am well again.

Personally, I disagree with their ideas.

Personally, I believe that congenial work, with excitement and change, would do me good.

But what is one to do?

I did write for a while in spite of them; but it *does* exhaust me a good   *15*
deal—having to be so sly about it, or else meet with heavy opposition.

I sometimes fancy that in my condition, if I had less opposition and more society and stimulus—but John says the very worst thing I can do is to think about my condition, and I confess it always makes me feel bad.

So I will let it alone and talk about the house.

The most beautiful place! It is quite alone, standing well back from the road, quite three miles from the village. It makes me think of English places that you read about, for there are hedges and walls and gates that lock, and lots of separate little houses for the gardeners and people.

There is a *delicious* garden! I never saw such a garden—large and shady, full of box-bordered paths, and lined with long grape-covered arbors with seats under them.

There were greenhouses, but they are all broken now.   *20*

There was some legal trouble, I believe, something about the heirs and co-heirs; anyhow, the place has been empty for years.

That spoils my ghostliness, I am afraid, but I don't care—there is something strange about the house—I can feel it.

I even said so to John one moonlight evening, but he said what I felt was a draught, and shut the window.

I get unreasonably angry with John sometimes. I'm sure I never used to be so sensitive. I think it is due to this nervous condition.

But John says if I feel so I shall neglect proper self-control; so I take pains   *25*
to control myself—before him, at least, and that makes me very tired.

I don't like our room a bit. I wanted one downstairs that opened onto the piazza and had roses all over the window, and such pretty old-fashioned chintz hangings! But John would not hear of it.

He said there was only one window and not room for two beds, and no near room for him if he took another.

He is very careful and loving, and hardly lets me stir without special direction.

I have a schedule prescription for each hour in the day; he takes all care from me, and so I feel basely ungrateful not to value it more.

He said he came here solely on my account, that I was to have perfect   *30*
rest and all the air I could get. "Your exercise depends on your strength, my

dear," said he, "and your food somewhat on your appetite; but air you can absorb all the time." So we took the nursery at the top of the house.

It is a big, airy room, the whole floor nearly, with windows that look all
ways, and air and sunshine galore. It was a nursery first, and then playroom and
gymnasium, I should judge, for the windows are barred for little children, and
there are rings and things in the walls.

The paint and paper look as if a boys' school had used it. It is stripped
off—the paper—in great patches all around the head of my bed, about as far as
I can reach, and in a great place on the other side of the room low down. I
never saw a worse paper in my life. One of those sprawling, flamboyant patterns committing every artistic sin.

It is dull enough to confuse the eye in following, pronounced enough
constantly to irritate and provoke study, and when you follow the lame uncertain curves for a little distance they suddenly commit suicide—plunge off at
outrageous angles, destroy themselves in unheard-of contradictions.

The color is repellent, almost revolting: a smouldering unclean yellow,
strangely faded by the slow-turning sunlight. It is a dull yet lurid orange in
some places, a sickly sulphur tint in others.

35   No wonder the children hated it! I should hate it myself if I had to live
in this room long.

There comes John, and I must put this away—he hates to have me write
a word.

We have been here two weeks, and I haven't felt like writing before,
since that first day.

I am sitting by the window now, up in this atrocious nursery, and there is
nothing to hinder my writing as much as I please, save lack of strength.

John is away all day, and even some nights when his cases are serious.

40   I'm glad my case is not serious!

But these nervous troubles are dreadfully depressing.

John does not know how much I really suffer. He knows there is no reason to suffer, and that satisfies him.

Of course it is only nervousness. It does weigh on me so not to do my
duty in any way!

I meant to be such a help to John, such a real rest and comfort, and here
I am a comparative burden already!

45   Nobody would believe what an effort it is to do what little I am able—
to dress and entertain, and order things.

It is fortunate Mary is so good with the baby. Such a dear baby!

And yet I *cannot* be with him, it makes me so nervous.

I suppose John never was nervous in his life. He laughs at me so about
this wallpaper!

At first he meant to repaper the room, but afterward he said that I was letting it get the better of me, and that nothing was worse for a nervous patient than to give way to such fancies.

He said that after the wallpaper was changed it would be the heavy bedstead, and then the barred windows, and then that gate at the head of the stairs, and so on.

"You know the place is doing you good," he said, "and really, dear, I don't care to renovate the house just for a three months' rental."

"Then do let us go downstairs," I said. "There are such pretty rooms there."

Then he took me in his arms and called me a blessed little goose, and said he would go down to the cellar, if I wished, and have it whitewashed into the bargain.

But he is right enough about the beds and windows and things.

It is as airy and comfortable a room as anyone need wish, and, of course, I would not be so silly as to make him uncomfortable just for a whim.

I'm really getting quite fond of the big room, all but that horrid paper.

Out of one window I can see the garden—those mysterious deep-shaded arbors, the riotous old-fashioned flowers, and bushes and gnarly trees.

Out of another I get a lovely view of the bay and a little private wharf belonging to the estate. There is a beautiful shaded lane that runs down there from the house. I always fancy I see people walking in these numerous paths and arbors, but John has cautioned me not to give way to fancy in the least. He says that with my imaginative power and habit of story-making, a nervous weakness like mine is sure to lead to all manner of excited fancies, and that I ought to use my will and good sense to check the tendency. So I try.

I think sometimes that if I were only well enough to write a little it would relieve the press of ideas and rest me.

But I find I get pretty tired when I try.

It is so discouraging not to have any advice and companionship about my work. When I get really well, John says we will ask Cousin Henry and Julia down for a long visit; but he says he would as soon put fireworks in my pillowcase as to let me have those stimulating people about now.

I wish I could get well faster.

But I must not think about that. This paper looks to me as if it *knew* what a vicious influence it had!

There is a recurrent spot where the pattern lolls like a broken neck and two bulbous eyes stare at you upside down.

I get positively angry with the impertinence of it and the everlastingness. Up and down and sideways they crawl, and those absurd unblinking eyes are everywhere. There is one place where two breadths didn't match, and the eyes go all up and down the line, one a little higher than the other.

I never saw so much expression in an inanimate thing before, and we all know how much expression they have! I used to lie awake as a child and get

more entertainment and terror out of blank walls and plain furniture than
most children could find in a toy-store.

I remember what a kindly wink the knobs of our big old bureau used to
have, and there was one chair that always seemed like a strong friend.

I used to feel that if any of the other things looked too fierce I could always hop into that chair and be safe.

The furniture in this room is no worse than inharmonious, however, for
we had to bring it all from downstairs. I suppose when this was used as a playroom they had to take the nursery things out, and no wonder! I never saw
such ravages as the children have made here.

70   The wallpaper, as I said before, is torn off in spots, and it sticketh closer
than a brother—they must have had perseverance as well as hatred.

Then the floor is scratched and gouged and splintered, the plaster itself is
dug out here and there, and this great heavy bed, which is all we found in the
room, looks as if it had been through the wars.

But I don't mind it a bit—only the paper.

There comes John's sister. Such a dear girl as she is, and so careful of me!
I must not let her find me writing.

She is a perfect and enthusiastic housekeeper, and hopes for no better
profession. I verily believe she thinks it is the writing which made me sick!

75   But I can write when she is out, and see her a long way off from these
windows.

There is one that commands the road, a lovely shaded winding road, and
one that just looks off over the country. A lovely country, too, full of great elms
and velvet meadows.

This wallpaper has a kind of sub-pattern in a different shade, a particularly irritating one, for you can only see it in certain lights, and not clearly
then.

But in the places where it isn't faded and where the sun is just so—I can
see a strange, provoking, formless sort of figure that seems to skulk about behind that silly and conspicuous front design.

There's sister on the stairs!

80   Well, the Fourth of July is over! The people are all gone, and I am tired
out. John thought it might do me good to see a little company, so we just had
Mother and Nellie and the children down for a week.

Of course I didn't do a thing. Jennie sees to everything now.

But it tired me all the same.

John says if I don't pick up faster he shall send me to Weir Mitchell in
the fall.

But I don't want to go there at all. I had a friend who was in his hands
once, and she says he is just like John and my brother, only more so!

Besides, it is such an undertaking to go so far.   *85*

I don't feel as if it was worthwhile to turn my hand over for anything, and I'm getting dreadfully fretful and querulous.

I cry at nothing, and cry most of the time.

Of course I don't when John is here, or anybody else, but when I am alone.

And I am alone a good deal just now. John is kept in town very often by serious cases, and Jennie is good and lets me alone when I want her to.

So I walk a little in the garden or down that lovely lane, sit on the porch   *90* under the roses, and lie down up here a good deal.

I'm getting really fond of the room in spite of the wallpaper. Perhaps *because* of the wallpaper.

It dwells in my mind so!

I lie here on this great immovable bed—it is nailed down, I believe— and follow that pattern about by the hour. It is as good as gymnastics, I assure you. I start, we'll say, at the bottom, down in the corner over there where it has not been touched, and I determine for the thousandth time that I *will* follow that pointless pattern to some sort of a conclusion.

I know a little of the principle of design, and I know this thing was not arranged on any laws of radiation, or alternation, or repetition, or symmetry, or anything else that I ever heard of.

It is repeated, of course, by the breadths, but not otherwise.   *95*

Looked at in one way, each breadth stands alone; the bloated curves and flourishes—a kind of "debased Romanesque" with delirium tremens—go waddling up and down in isolated columns of fatuity.

But, on the other hand, they connect diagonally, and the sprawling outlines run off in great slanting waves of optic horror, like a lot of wallowing sea-weeds in full chase.

The whole thing goes horizontally, too, at least it seems so, and I exhaust myself trying to distinguish the order of its going in that direction.

They have used a horizontal breadth for a frieze, and that adds wonderfully to the confusion.

There is one end of the room where it is almost intact, and there, when   *100* the crosslights fade and the low sun shines directly upon it, I can almost fancy radiation after all—the interminable grotesque seems to form around a common center and rush off in headlong plunges of equal distraction.

It makes me tired to follow it. I will take a nap, I guess.

I don't know why I should write this.

I don't want to.

I don't feel able.

And I know John would think it absurd. But I *must* say what I feel and   *105* think in some way—it is such a relief!

But the effort is getting to be greater than the relief.

Half the time now I am awfully lazy, and lie down ever so much. John says I musn't lose my strength, and has me take cod liver oil and lots of tonics and things, to say nothing of ale and wine and rare meat.

Dear John! He loves me very dearly, and hates to have me sick. I tried to have a real earnest reasonable talk with him the other day, and tell him how I wish he would let me go and make a visit to Cousin Henry and Julia.

But he said I wasn't able to go, nor able to stand it after I got there; and I did not make out a very good case for myself, for I was crying before I had finished.

110   It is getting to be a great effort for me to think straight. Just this nervous weakness, I suppose.

And dear John gathered me up in his arms, and just carried me upstairs and laid me on the bed, and sat by me and read to me till it tired my head.

He said I was his darling and his comfort and all he had, and that I must take care of myself for his sake, and keep well.

He says no one but myself can help me out of it, that I must use my will and self-control and not let any silly fancies run away with me.

There's one comfort—the baby is well and happy, and does not have to occupy this nursery with the horrid wallpaper.

115   If we had not used it, that blessed child would have! What a fortunate escape! Why, I wouldn't have a child of mine, an impressionable little thing, live in such a room for worlds.

I never thought of it before, but it is lucky that John kept me here after all; I can stand it so much easier than a baby, you see.

Of course I never mention it to them any more—I am too wise—but I keep watch for it all the same.

There are things in that wallpaper that nobody knows about but me, or ever will.

Behind that outside pattern the dim shapes get clearer every day.

120   It is always the same shape, only very numerous.

And it is like a woman stooping down and creeping about behind that pattern. I don't like it a bit. I wonder—I begin to think—I wish John would take me away from here!

It is so hard to talk with John about my case, because he is so wise, and because he loves me so.

But I tried it last night.

It was moonlight. The moon shines in all around just as the sun does.

125   I hate to see it sometimes, it creeps so slowly, and always comes in by one window or another.

John was asleep and I hated to waken him, so I kept still and watched the moonlight on that undulating wallpaper till I felt creepy.

The faint figure behind seemed to shake the pattern, just as if she wanted to get out.

I got up softly and went to feel and see if the paper *did* move, and when I came back John was awake.

"What is it, little girl?" he said. "Don't go walking about like that—you'll get cold."

I thought it was a good time to talk, so I told him that I really was not   *130* gaining here, and that I wished he would take me away.

"Why, darling!" said he. "Our lease will be up in three weeks, and I can't see how to leave before.

"The repairs are not done at home, and I cannot possibly leave town just now. Of course, if you were in any danger, I could and would, but you really are better, dear, whether you can see it or not. I am a doctor, dear, and I know. You are gaining flesh and color, your appetite is better, I feel really much easier about you."

"I don't weigh a bit more," said I, "nor as much; and my appetite may be better in the evening when you are here but it is worse in the morning when you are away!"

"Bless her little heart!" said he with a big hug. "She shall be as sick as she pleases! But now let's improve the shining hours by going to sleep, and talk about it in the morning!"

"And you won't go away?" I asked gloomily.   *135*

"Why, how can I, dear? It is only three weeks more and then we will take a nice little trip of a few days while Jennie is getting the house ready. Really, dear, you are better!"

"Better in body perhaps—" I began, and stopped short, for he sat up straight and looked at me with such a stern, reproachful look that I could not say another word.

"My darling," said he, "I beg of you, for my sake and for our child's sake, as well as for your own, that you will never for one instant let that idea enter your mind! There is nothing so dangerous, so fascinating, to a temperament like yours. It is a false and foolish fancy. Can you not trust me as a physician when I tell you so?"

So of course I said no more on that score, and we went to sleep before long. He thought I was asleep first, but I wasn't, and lay there for hours trying to decide whether that front pattern and the back pattern really did move together or separately.

On a pattern like this, by daylight, there is a lack of sequence, a defiance   *140* of law, that is a constant irritant to a normal mind.

The color is hideous enough, and unreliable enough, and infuriating enough, but the pattern is torturing.

You think you have mastered it, but just as you get well under way in following, it turns a back-somersault and there you are. It slaps you in the face, knocks you down, and tramples upon you. It is like a bad dream.

The outside pattern is a florid arabesque, reminding one of a fungus. If you can imagine a toadstool in joints, an interminable string of toadstools, budding and sprouting in endless convolutions—why, that is something like it.

That is, sometimes!

145   There is one marked peculiarity about this paper, a thing nobody seems to notice but myself, and that is that it changes as the light changes.

When the sun shoots in through the east window—I always watch for that first long, straight ray—it changes so quickly that I never can quite believe it.

That is why I watch it always.

By moonlight—the moon shines in all night when there is a moon—I wouldn't know it was the same paper.

At night in any kind of light, in twilight, candlelight, lamplight, and worst of all by moonlight, it becomes bars! The outside pattern, I mean, and the woman behind it is as plain as can be.

150   I didn't realize for a long time what the thing was that showed behind, that dim sub-pattern, but now I am quite sure it is a woman.

By daylight she is subdued, quiet. I fancy it is the pattern that keeps her so still. It is so puzzling. It keeps me quiet by the hour.

I lie down ever so much now. John says it is good for me, and to sleep all I can.

Indeed he started the habit by making me lie down for an hour after each meal.

It is a very bad habit, I am convinced, for you see, I don't sleep.

155   And that cultivates deceit, for I don't tell them I'm awake—oh, no!

The fact is I am getting a little afraid of John.

He seems very queer sometimes, and even Jennie has an inexplicable look.

It strikes me occasionally, just as a scientific hypothesis, that perhaps it is the paper!

I have watched John when he did not know I was looking, and come into the room suddenly on the most innocent excuses, and I've caught him several times *looking at the paper!* And Jennie too. I caught Jennie with her hand on it once.

160   She didn't know I was in the room, and when I asked her in a quiet, a very quiet voice, with the most restrained manner possible, what she was doing with the paper, she turned around as if she had been caught stealing, and looked quite angry—asked me why I should frighten her so!

Then she said that the paper stained everything it touched, that she had found yellow smooches on all my clothes and John's and she wished we would be more careful!

Did not that sound innocent? But I know she was studying that pattern, and I am determined that nobody shall find it out but myself!

Life is very much more exciting now than it used to be. You see, I have something more to expect, to look forward to, to watch. I really do eat better, and am more quiet than I was.

John is so pleased to see me improve! He laughed a little the other day, and said I seemed to be flourishing in spite of my wallpaper.

I turned it off with a laugh. I had no intention of telling him it was *because* of the wallpaper—he would make fun of me. He might even want to take me away.   165

I don't want to leave now until I have found it out. There is a week more, and I think that will be enough.

I'm feeling so much better!

I don't sleep much at night, for it is so interesting to watch developments; but I sleep a good deal during the daytime.

In the daytime it is tiresome and perplexing.

There are always new shoots on the fungus, and new shades of yellow all   170
over it. I cannot keep count of them, though I have tried conscientiously.

It is the strangest yellow, that wallpaper! It makes me think of all the yellow things I ever saw—not beautiful like buttercups, but old, foul, bad yellow things.

But there is something else about that paper—the smell! I noticed it the moment we came into the room, but with so much air and sun it was not bad. Now we have had a week of fog and rain, and whether the windows are open or not, the smell is here.

It creeps all over the house.

I find it hovering in the dining-room, skulking in the parlor, hiding in the hall, lying in wait for me on the stairs.

It gets into my hair.   175

Even when I go to ride, if I turn my head suddenly and surprise it—there is that smell!

Such a peculiar odor, too! I have spent hours in trying to analyze it, to find what it smelled like.

It is not bad—at first—and very gentle, but quite the subtlest, most enduring odor I ever met.

In this damp weather it is awful. I wake up in the night and find it hanging over me.

It used to disturb me at first. I thought seriously of burning the house—   180
to reach the smell.

But now I am used to it. The only thing I can think of that it is like is the *color* of the paper! A yellow smell.

There is a very funny mark on this wall, low down, near the mopboard. A streak that runs round the room. It goes behind every piece of furniture, except the bed, a long, straight, even *smooch,* as if it had been rubbed over and over.

I wonder how it was done and who did it, and what they did it for. Round and round and round—round and round and round—it makes me dizzy!

I really have discovered something at last.

185   Through watching so much at night, when it changes so, I have finally found out.

The front pattern *does* move—and no wonder! The woman behind shakes it!

Sometimes I think there are a great many women behind, and sometimes only one, and she crawls around fast, and her crawling shakes it all over.

Then in the very bright spots she keeps still, and in the very shady spots she just takes hold of the bars and shakes them hard.

And she is all the time trying to climb through. But nobody could climb through that pattern—it strangles so; I think that is why it has so many heads.

190   They get through, and then the pattern strangles them off and turns them upside down and makes their eyes white!

If those heads were covered or taken off it would not be half so bad.

I think that woman gets out in the daytime!

And I'll tell you why—privately—I've seen her!

I can see her out of every one of my windows!

195   It is the same woman, I know, for she is always creeping, and most women do not creep by daylight.

I see her in that long shaded lane, creeping up and down. I see her in those dark grape arbors, creeping all around the garden.

I see her on that long road under the trees, creeping along, and when a carriage comes she hides under the blackberry vines.

I don't blame her a bit. It must be very humiliating to be caught creeping by daylight!

I always lock the door when I creep by daylight. I can't do it at night, for I know John would suspect something at once.

200   And John is so queer now that I don't want to irritate him. I wish he would take another room! Besides, I don't want anybody to get that woman out at night but myself.

I often wonder if I could see her out of all the windows at once.

But, turn as fast as I can, I can only see out of one at one time.

And though I always see her, she *may* be able to creep faster than I can turn! I have watched her sometimes away off in the open country, creeping as fast as a cloud shadow in a high wind.

If only that top pattern could be gotten off from the under one! I mean to try it, little by little.

I have found out another funny thing, but I shan't tell it this time! It does   *205*
not do to trust people too much.

There are only two more days to get this paper off, and I believe John is
beginning to notice. I don't like the look in his eyes.

And I hear him ask Jennie a lot of professional questions about me. She
had a very good report to give.

She said I slept a good deal in the daytime.

John knows I don't sleep very well at night, for all I'm so quiet!

He asked me all sorts of questions, too, and pretended to be very loving   *210*
and kind.

As if I couldn't see through him!

Still, I don't wonder he acts so, sleeping under this paper for three months.

It only interests me, but I feel sure John and Jennie are affected by it.

Hurrah! This is the last day, but it is enough. John is to stay in town over
night, and won't be out until this evening.

Jennie wanted to sleep with me—the sly thing; but I told her I should   *215*
undoubtedly rest better for a night all alone.

That was clever, for really I wasn't alone a bit! As soon as it was moonlight and that poor thing began to crawl and shake the pattern, I got up and
ran to help her.

I pulled and she shook. I shook and she pulled, and before morning we
had peeled off yards of that paper.

A strip about as high as my head and half around the room.

And then when the sun came and that awful pattern began to laugh at
me, I declared I would finish it today!

We go away tomorrow, and they are moving all my furniture down again   *220*
to leave things as they were before.

Jennie looked at the wall in amazement, but I told her merrily that I did
it out of pure spite at the vicious thing.

She laughed and said she wouldn't mind doing it herself, but I must not
get tired.

How she betrayed herself that time!

But I am here, and no person touches this paper but Me—not *alive!*

She tried to get me out of the room—it was too patent! But I said it was   *225*
so quiet and empty and clean now that I believed I would lie down again and
sleep all I could, and not to wake me even for dinner—I would call when I woke.

So now she is gone, and the servants are gone, and the things are gone,
and there is nothing left but that great bedstead nailed down, with the canvas
mattress we found on it.

We shall sleep downstairs tonight, and take the boat home tomorrow.

I quite enjoy the room, now it is bare again.

How those children did tear about here!

230   This bedstead is fairly gnawed!

But I must get to work.

I have locked the door and thrown the key down into the front path.

I don't want to go out, and I don't want to have anybody come in, till John comes.

I want to astonish him.

235   I've got a rope up here that even Jennie did not find. If that woman does get out, and tries to get away, I can tie her!

But I forgot I could not reach far without anything to stand on!

This bed will *not* move!

I tried to lift and push it until I was lame, and then I got so angry I bit off a little piece at one corner—but it hurt my teeth.

Then I peeled off all the paper I could reach standing on the floor. It sticks horribly and the pattern just enjoys it! All those strangled heads and bulbous eyes and waddling fungus growths just shriek with derision!

240   I am getting angry enough to do something desperate. To jump out of the window would be admirable exercise, but the bars are too strong even to try.

Besides I wouldn't do it. Of course not. I know well enough that a step like that is improper and might be misconstrued.

I don't like to *look* out of the windows even—there are so many of those creeping women, and they creep so fast.

I wonder if they all come out of that wallpaper as I did?

But I am securely fastened now by my well-hidden rope—you don't get *me* out in the road there!

245   I suppose I shall have to get back behind the pattern when it comes night, and that is hard!

It is so pleasant to be out in this great room and creep around as I please!

I don't want to go outside. I won't, even if Jennie asks me to.

For outside you have to creep on the ground, and everything is green instead of yellow.

But here I can creep smoothly on the floor, and my shoulder just fits in that long smooch around the wall, so I cannot lose my way.

250   Why, there's John at the door!

It is no use, young man, you can't open it!

How he does call and pound!

Now he's crying to Jennie for an axe.

It would be a shame to break down that beautiful door!

255   "John, dear!" said I in the gentlest voice. "The key is down by the front steps, under a plantain leaf!"

That silenced him for a few moments.

Then he said, very quietly indeed, "Open the door, my darling!"

"I can't," said I. "The key is down by the front door under a plantain leaf!" And then I said it again, several times, very gently and slowly, and said it so often that he had to go and see, and he got it of course, and came in. He stopped short by the door.

"What is the matter?" he cried. "For God's sake, what are you doing!"

I kept on creeping just the same, but I looked at him over my shoulder.   260

"I've got out at last," said I, "in spite of you and Jane. And I've pulled off most of the paper, so you can't put me back!"

Now why should that man have fainted? But he did, and right across my path by the wall, so that I had to creep over him every time!   *1892*

CONSIDERATIONS

1. Describe the work of the narrator. How is her work significant to the conflicts and themes of the story?
2. Explain how John's profession relates to the development of the plot. How does the narrator regard John's work? How does John regard the narrator's work?
3. Make a list of details describing the room the narrator occupies. She interprets these details as indicators that the room was once a nursery. What other possibilities would fit the same details?
4. "The Yellow Wallpaper" has often been anthologized as a ghost story. Do you see the woman in the wallpaper as a supernatural element? What other possibilities can you suggest?
5. Read the following commentary on "The Yellow Wallpaper." Then write a response explaining how reading it has changed or confirmed your own views of the story.

More Resources on
Charlotte Perkins Gilman and "The Yellow Wallpaper"

In *ARIEL*
- Brief biography of Gilman
- Complete text of "The Yellow Wallpaper," with hyperlinked comments
- Video clip of a dramatic production of "The Yellow Wallpaper"
- Analysis of narrator reliability in "The Yellow Wallpaper"
- Bibliography of scholarly works on Gilman

Commentary

CHARLOTTE PERKINS GILMAN
Why I Wrote "The Yellow Wallpaper"

Many and many a reader has asked that. When the story first came out, in the *New England Magazine* about 1891, a Boston physician made protest in *The Transcript*. Such a story ought not to be written, he said; it was enough to drive anyone mad to read it.

Another physician, in Kansas I think, wrote to say that it was the best description of incipient insanity he had ever seen, and—begging my pardon—had I been there?

Now the story of the story is this:

For many years I suffered from a severe and continuous nervous breakdown tending to melancholia—and beyond. During about the third year of this trouble I went, in devout faith and some faint stir of hope, to a noted specialist in nervous diseases, the best known in the country.° This wise man put me to bed and applied the rest cure, to which a still-good physique responded so promptly that he concluded there was nothing much the matter with me, and sent me home with solemn advice to "live as domestic a life as far as possible," to "have but two hours' intellectual life a day," and "never to touch pen, brush, or pencil again" as long as I lived. This was in 1887.

5   I went home and obeyed those directions for some three months, and came so near the borderline of utter mental ruin that I could see over.

Then, using the remnants of intelligence that remained, and helped by a wise friend, I cast the noted specialist's advice to the winds and went to work again—work, the normal life of every human being; work, in which is joy and growth and service, without which one is a pauper and a parasite—ultimately recovering some measure of power.

Being naturally moved to rejoicing by this narrow escape, I wrote "The Yellow Wallpaper," with its embellishments and additions, to carry out the ideal (I never had hallucinations or objections to my mural decorations) and sent a copy to the physician who so nearly drove me mad. He never acknowledged it.

The little book is valued by alienists° and as a good specimen of one kind of literature. It has, to my knowledge, saved one woman from a similar fate—so terrifying her family that they let her out into normal activity and she recovered.

---

noted specialist . . . best known in the country: Dr. S. Weir Mitchell of Philadelphia, a famous "nerve specialist" of the time. Mitchell is mentioned by the narrator of "The Yellow Wallpaper." *alienist:* Nineteenth-century word for "psychiatrist."

But the best result is this. Many years later I was told that the great specialist had admitted to friends of his that he had altered his treatment of neurasthenia since reading "The Yellow Wallpaper."

It was not intended to drive people crazy, but to save people from being   10
driven crazy, and it worked.

EDITH WHARTON (1862–1937)
Roman Fever

Edith Wharton was born to a wealthy New York family and was taught how to behave as a well-bred young lady, although she would later rebel. When she was twenty-three, she married Teddy Wharton, who came from a similar social background but had little interest in artistic or intellectual pursuits. During the 1890s, she suffered from depression and revived her spirits with annual trips to France and Italy. In 1897, she published her first book, The Decoration of Houses, *in which she criticized the Victorian style of heavily curtained rooms full of overstuffed furniture and advocated a simpler style that reflected the owners' personalities rather than the fashions of the day. By 1905, she had moved to fiction, publishing the novel* The House of Mirth, *a critical look at New York's high society. In 1907, her marriage to Teddy crumbling, she began spending winters in Paris, where, a year later, she began an affair with journalist Morton Fullerton, a friend of novelist Henry James. Wharton published* Ethan Frome *in 1911, a novel about a man caught between his wife and his true love. She and Teddy were divorced in 1913, and she spent most of her time in Europe with a circle of French and American writers and artists. In 1920, she published* The Age of Innocence, *a novel about a man who cannot escape the conventions of elite New York society. For this book, Wharton won the Pulitzer Prize in 1921, and she returned to the United States for the last time to accept it. In 1927, she was nominated for the Nobel Prize in literature. Until the end of her life, she published a book almost every year. The following story, first printed in* Liberty Magazine *in 1934, was included in her collection* The World Over *(1936).*

I

From the table at which they had been lunching two American ladies of ripe but well-cared-for middle age moved across the lofty terrace of the Roman restaurant and, leaning on its parapet, looked first at each other, and then down on the outspread glories of the Palatine and the Forum, with the same expression of vague but benevolent approval.

As they leaned there a girlish voice echoed up gaily from the stairs leading to the court below. "Well, come along, then," it cried, not to them but to an invisible companion, "and let's leave the young things to their knitting"; and a voice as fresh laughed back: "Oh, look here, Babs, not actually *knitting*—" "Well, I mean figuratively," rejoined the first. "After all, we haven't left our poor parents much else to do. . . ." and at that point the turn of the stairs engulfed the dialogue.

The two ladies looked at each other again, this time with a tinge of smiling embarrassment, and the smaller and paler one shook her head and colored slightly.

"Barbara!" she murmured, sending an unheard rebuke after the mocking voice in the stairway.

5   The other lady, who was fuller, and higher in color, with a small determined nose supported by vigorous black eyebrows, gave a good-humored laugh. "That's what our daughters think of us!"

Her companion replied by a deprecating gesture. "Not of us individually. We must remember that. It's just the collective modern idea of Mothers. And you see—" Half-guiltily she drew from her handsomely mounted black handbag a twist of crimson silk run through by two fine knitting needles. "One never knows," she murmured. "The new system has certainly given us a good deal of time to kill; and sometimes I get tired just looking—even at this." Her gesture was now addressed to the stupendous scene at their feet.

The dark lady laughed again, and they both relapsed upon the view, contemplating it in silence, with a sort of diffused serenity which might have been borrowed from the spring effulgence of the Roman skies. The luncheon hour was long past, and the two had their end of the vast terrace to themselves. At its opposite extremity a few groups, detained by a lingering look at the outspread city, were gathering up guidebooks and fumbling for tips. The last of them scattered, and the two ladies were alone on the air-washed height.

"Well, I don't see why we shouldn't just stay here," said Mrs. Slade, the lady of the high color and energetic brows. Two derelict basket chairs stood near and she pushed them into the angle of the parapet, and settled herself in one, her gaze upon the Palatine. "After all, it's still the most beautiful view in the world."

"It always will be, to me," assented her friend Mrs. Ansley, with so slight a stress on the "me" that Mrs. Slade, though she noticed it, wondered if it were not merely accidental, like the random underlinings of old-fashioned letter writers.

10   "Grace Ansley was always old-fashioned," she thought; and added aloud, with a retrospective smile: "It's a view we've both been familiar with for a good many years. When we first met here we were younger than our girls are now. You remember?"

"Oh, yes, I remember," murmured Mrs. Ansley, with the same undefinable stress. "There's that headwaiter wondering," she interpolated. She was evidently far less sure than her companion of herself and of her rights in the world.

"I'll cure him of wondering," said Mrs. Slade, stretching her hand toward a bag as discreetly opulent-looking as Mrs. Ansley's. Signing to the headwaiter, she explained that she and her friend were old lovers of Rome, and would like to spend the end of the afternoon looking down on the view—that is, if it did not disturb the service? The headwaiter, bowing over her gratuity, assured her that the ladies were most welcome, and would be still more so if they would condescend to remain for dinner. A full-moon night, they would remember. . . .

Mrs. Slade's black brows drew together, as though references to the moon were out of place and even unwelcome. But she smiled away her frown as the headwaiter retreated. "Well, why not? We might do worse. There's no knowing, I suppose, when the girls will be back. Do you even know back from *where?* I don't!"

Mrs. Ansley again colored slightly. "I think those young Italian aviators we met at the Embassy invited them to fly to Tarquinia for tea. I suppose they'll want to wait and fly back by moonlight."

"Moonlight—moonlight! What a part it still plays. Do you suppose they're as sentimental as we were?"   *15*

"I've come to the conclusion that I don't in the least know what they are," said Mrs. Ansley. "And perhaps we didn't know much more about each other."

"No; perhaps we didn't."

Her friend gave her a shy glance. "I never should have supposed you were sentimental, Alida."

"Well, perhaps I wasn't." Mrs. Slade drew her lids together in retrospect; and for a few moments the two ladies, who had been intimate since childhood, reflected how little they knew each other. Each one, of course, had a label ready to attach to the other's name; Mrs. Delphin Slade, for instance, would have told herself, or anyone who asked her, that Mrs. Horace Ansley, twenty-five years ago, had been exquisitely lovely—no, you wouldn't believe it, would you? . . . though, of course, still charming, distinguished. . . . Well, as a girl she had been exquisite; far more beautiful than her daughter Barbara, though certainly Babs, according to the new standards at any rate, was more effective—had more *edge,* as they say. Funny where she got it, with those two nullities as parents. Yes; Horace Ansley was—well, just the duplicate of his wife. Museum specimens of old New York. Good-looking, irreproachable, exemplary. Mrs. Slade and Mrs. Ansley had lived opposite each other—actually as well as figuratively—for years. When the drawing-room curtains in No. 20 East 73rd Street were renewed, No. 23, across the way, was always aware of it. And of all the movings, buyings, travels, anniversaries, illnesses—the tame chronicle of an estimable pair. Little of it escaped Mrs. Slade. But she had grown bored with it by the time her husband made his big *coup* in Wall Street, and when they bought in upper Park Avenue had already begun to think: "I'd rather live opposite a speakeasy for a change; at least one might see it raided." The idea of seeing Grace raided was so amusing that (before the move) she launched it at a woman's lunch. It made a hit, and went the rounds—she sometimes wondered if it had crossed the street, and reached Mrs. Ansley. She hoped not, but didn't much mind. Those were the days when respectability was at a discount, and it did the irreproachable no harm to laugh at them a little.

20   A few years later, and not many months apart, both ladies lost their husbands. There was an appropriate exchange of wreaths and condolences, and a brief renewal of intimacy in the half-shadow of their mourning; and now, after another interval, they had run across each other in Rome, at the same hotel, each of them the modest appendage of a salient daughter. The similarity of their lot had again drawn them together, lending itself to mild jokes, and the mutual confession that, if in old days it must have been tiring to "keep up" with daughters, it was now, at times, a little dull not to.

No doubt, Mrs. Slade reflected, she felt her unemployment more than poor Grace ever would. It was a big drop from being the wife of Delphin Slade to being his widow. She had always regarded herself (with a certain conjugal pride) as his equal in social gifts, as contributing her full share to the making of the exceptional couple they were: but the difference after his death was irremediable. As the wife of the famous corporation lawyer, always with an international case or two on hand, every day brought its exciting and unexpected obligation: the impromptu entertaining of eminent colleagues from abroad, the hurried dashes on legal business to London, Paris or Rome, where the entertaining was so handsomely reciprocated; the amusement of hearing in her wake: "What, that handsome woman with the good clothes and the eyes is Mrs. Slade— *the* Slade's wife? Really? Generally the wives of celebrities are such frumps."

Yes; being *the* Slade's widow was a dullish business after that. In living up to such a husband all her faculties had been engaged; now she had only her daughter to live up to, for the son who seemed to have inherited his father's gifts had died suddenly in boyhood. She had fought through that agony because her husband was there, to be helped and to help; now, after the father's death, the thought of the boy had become unbearable. There was nothing left but to mother her daughter; and dear Jenny was such a perfect daughter that she needed no excessive mothering. "Now with Babs Ansley I don't know that I *should* be so quiet," Mrs. Slade sometimes half-enviously reflected; but Jenny, who was younger than her brilliant friend, was that rare accident, an extremely pretty girl who somehow made youth and prettiness seem as safe as their absence. It was all perplexing—and to Mrs. Slade a little boring. She wished that Jenny would fall in love—with the wrong man, even; that she might have to be watched, out-maneuvered, rescued. And instead, it was Jenny who watched her mother, kept her out of drafts, made sure that she had taken her tonic. . . .

Mrs. Ansley was much less articulate than her friend, and her mental portrait of Mrs. Slade was slighter, and drawn with fainter touches. "Alida Slade's awfully brilliant; but not as brilliant as she thinks," would have summed it up; though she would have added, for the enlightenment of strangers, that Mrs. Slade had been an extremely dashing girl; much more so than her daughter, who was pretty, of course, and clever in a way, but had none of her mother's—

well, "vividness," someone had once called it. Mrs. Ansley would take up current words like this, and cite them in quotation marks, as unheard-of audacities. No; Jenny was not like her mother. Sometimes Mrs. Ansley thought Alida Slade was disappointed; on the whole she had had a sad life. Full of failures and mistakes; Mrs. Ansley had always been rather sorry for her. . . .

So these two ladies visualized each other, each through the wrong end of her little telescope.

II

For a long time they continued to sit side by side without speaking. It seemed as though, to both, there was a relief in laying down their somewhat futile activities in the presence of the vast Memento Mori° which faced them. Mrs. Slade sat quite still, her eyes fixed on the golden slope of the Palace of the Caesars, and after a while Mrs. Ansley ceased to fidget with her bag, and she too sank into meditation. Like many intimate friends, the two ladies had never before had occasion to be silent together, and Mrs. Ansley was slightly embarrassed by what seemed, after so many years, a new stage in their intimacy, and one with which she did not yet know how to deal.

Suddenly the air was full of that deep clangor of bells which periodically covers Rome with a roof of silver. Mrs. Slade glanced at her wristwatch. "Five o'clock already," she said, as though surprised.

Mrs. Ansley suggested interrogatively: "There's bridge at the Embassy at five." For a long time Mrs. Slade did not answer. She appeared to be lost in contemplation, and Mrs. Ansley thought the remark had escaped her. But after a while she said, as if speaking out of a dream: "Bridge, did you say? Not unless you want to. . . . But I don't think I will, you know."

"Oh, no," Mrs. Ansley hastened to assure her. "I don't care to at all. It's so lovely here; and so full of old memories, as you say." She settled herself in her chair, and almost furtively drew forth her knitting. Mrs. Slade took sideway note of this activity, but her own beautifully cared-for hands remained motionless on her knee.

"I was just thinking," she said slowly, "what different things Rome stands for to each generation of travelers. To our grandmothers, Roman fever; to our mothers, sentimental dangers—how we used to be guarded!—to our daughters, no more dangers than the middle of Main Street. They don't know it—but how much they're missing!"

The long golden light was beginning to pale, and Mrs. Ansley lifted her knitting a little closer to her eyes. "Yes; how we were guarded!"

"I always used to think," Mrs. Slade continued, "that our mothers had a much more difficult job than our grandmothers. When Roman fever stalked the streets it must have been comparatively easy to gather in the girls at the

25

30

Memento Mori: Monument or memorial to the dead.

danger hour; but when you and I were young, with such beauty calling us, and the spice of disobedience thrown in, and no worse risk than catching cold during the cool hour after sunset, the mothers used to be put to it to keep us in—didn't they?"

She turned again toward Mrs. Ansley, but the latter had reached a delicate point in her knitting. "One, two, three—slip two; yes, they must have been," she assented, without looking up.

Mrs. Slade's eyes rested on her with a deepened attention. "She can knit—in the face of *this!* How like her. . . ."

Mrs. Slade leaned back, brooding, her eyes ranging from the ruins which faced her to the long green hollow of the Forum, the fading glow of the church fronts beyond it, and the outlying immensity of the Colosseum. Suddenly she thought: "It's all very well to say that our girls have done away with sentiment and moonlight. But if Babs Ansley isn't out to catch that young aviator—the one who's a Marchese—then I don't know anything. And Jenny has no chance beside her. I know that too. I wonder if that's why Grace Ansley likes the two girls to go everywhere together? My poor Jenny as a foil—!" Mrs. Slade gave a hardly audible laugh, and at the sound Mrs. Ansley dropped her knitting.

35   "Yes—?"

"I—oh, nothing. I was only thinking how your Babs carries everything before her. That Campolieri boy is one of the best matches in Rome. Don't look so innocent, my dear—you know he is. And I was wondering, ever so respectfully, you understand . . . wondering how two such exemplary characters as you and Horace had managed to produce anything quite so dynamic." Mrs. Slade laughed again, with a touch of asperity.

Mrs. Ansley's hands lay inert across her needles. She looked straight out at the great accumulated wreckage of passion and splendor at her feet. But her small profile was almost expressionless. At length she said: "I think you overrate Babs, my dear."

Mrs. Slade's tone grew easier. "No; I don't. I appreciate her. And perhaps envy you. Oh, my girl's perfect; if I were a chronic invalid I'd—well, I think I'd rather be in Jenny's hands. There must be times . . . but there! I always wanted a brilliant daughter . . . and never quite understood why I got an angel instead."

Mrs. Ansley echoed her laugh in a faint murmur. "Babs is an angel too."

40   "Of course—of course! But she's got rainbow wings. Well, they're wandering by the sea with their young men; and here we sit . . . and it all brings back the past a little too acutely."

Mrs. Ansley had resumed her knitting. One might almost have imagined (if one had known her less well, Mrs. Slade reflected) that, for her also, too many memories rose from the lengthening shadows of those august ruins. But no; she was simply absorbed in her work. What was there for her to worry about? She knew that Babs would almost certainly come back engaged to the extremely eligible Campolieri. "And she'll sell the New York house, and settle down near them in Rome, and never be in their way . . . she's much too tactful. But she'll have an excellent cook, and just the right people in for bridge and cocktails . . . and a perfectly peaceful old age among her grandchildren."

Mrs. Slade broke off this prophetic flight with a recoil of self-disgust. There was no one of whom she had less right to think unkindly than of Grace Ansley. Would she never cure herself of envying her? Perhaps she had begun too long ago.

She stood up and leaned against the parapet, filling her troubled eyes with the tranquilizing magic of the hour. But instead of tranquilizing her the sight seemed to increase her exasperation. Her gaze turned toward the Colosseum. Already its golden flank was drowned in purple shadow, and above it the sky curved crystal clear, without light or color. It was the moment when afternoon and evening hang balanced in mid-heaven.

Mrs. Slade turned back and laid her hand on her friend's arm. The gesture was so abrupt that Mrs. Ansley looked up, startled.

"The sun's set. You're not afraid, my dear?"   45

"Afraid—?"

"Of Roman fever or pneumonia? I remember how ill you were that winter. As a girl you had a very delicate throat, hadn't you?"

"Oh, we're all right up here. Down below, in the Forum, it does get deathly cold, all of a sudden . . . but not here."

"Ah, of course you know because you had to be so careful." Mrs. Slade turned back to the parapet. She thought: "I must make one more effort not to hate her." Aloud she said: "Whenever I look at the Forum from up here, I remember that story about a great-aunt of yours, wasn't she? A dreadfully wicked great-aunt?"

"Oh, yes; great-aunt Harriet. The one who was supposed to have sent   50
her young sister out to the Forum after sunset to gather a night-blooming flower for her album. All our great-aunts and grandmothers used to have albums of dried flowers."

Mrs. Slade nodded. "But she really sent her because they were in love with the same man—"

"Well, that was the family tradition. They said Aunt Harriet confessed it years afterward. At any rate, the poor little sister caught the fever and died. Mother used to frighten us with the story when we were children."

"And you frightened *me* with it, that winter when you and I were here as girls. The winter I was engaged to Delphin."

Mrs. Ansley gave a faint laugh. "Oh, did I? Really frightened you? I don't believe you're easily frightened."

"Not often; but I was then. I was easily frightened because I was too   55
happy. I wonder if you know what that means?"

"I—yes . . ." Mrs. Ansley faltered.

"Well, I suppose that was why the story of your wicked aunt made such an impression on me. And I thought: 'There's no more Roman fever, but the Forum is deathly cold after sunset—especially after a hot day. And the Colosseum's even colder and damper.'"

"The Colosseum—?"

"Yes. It wasn't easy to get in, after the gates were locked for the night. Far from easy. Still, in those days it could be managed; it *was* managed, often. Lovers met there who couldn't meet elsewhere. You knew that?"

60   "I—I dare say. I don't remember."

"You don't remember? You don't remember going to visit some ruins or other one evening, just after dark, and catching a bad chill? You were supposed to have gone to see the moon rise. People always said that expedition was what caused your illness."

There was a moment's silence; then Mrs. Ansley rejoined: "Did they? It was all so long ago."

"Yes. And you got well again—so it didn't matter. But I suppose it struck your friends—the reason given for your illness, I mean—because everybody knew you were so prudent on account of your throat, and your mother took such care of you. . . . You *had* been out late sight-seeing, hadn't you, that night?"

"Perhaps I had. The most prudent girls aren't always prudent. What made you think of it now?"

65   Mrs. Slade seemed to have no answer ready. But after a moment she broke out: "Because I simply can't bear it any longer—!"

Mrs. Ansley lifted her head quickly. Her eyes were wide and very pale. "Can't bear what?"

"Why—your not knowing that I've always known why you went."

"Why I went—?"

"Yes. You think I'm bluffing, don't you? Well, you went to meet the man I was engaged to—and I can repeat every word of the letter that took you there."

70   While Mrs. Slade spoke Mrs. Ansley had risen unsteadily to her feet. Her bag, her knitting and gloves, slid in a panic-stricken heap to the ground. She looked at Mrs. Slade as though she were looking at a ghost.

"No, no—don't," she faltered out.

"Why not? Listen, if you don't believe me. 'My one darling, things can't go on like this. I must see you alone. Come to the Colosseum immediately after dark tomorrow. There will be somebody to let you in. No one whom you need fear will suspect'—but perhaps you've forgotten what the letter said?"

Mrs. Ansley met the challenge with an unexpected composure. Steadying herself against the chair she looked at her friend, and replied: "No; I know it by heart too."

"And the signature? 'Only *your* D.S.' Was that it? I'm right, am I? That was the letter that took you out that evening after dark?"

75   Mrs. Ansley was still looking at her. It seemed to Mrs. Slade that a slow struggle was going on behind the voluntarily controlled mask of her small

quiet face. "I shouldn't have thought she had herself so well in hand," Mrs. Slade reflected, almost resentfully. But at this moment Mrs. Ansley spoke. "I don't know how you knew. I burnt that letter at once."

"Yes; you would, naturally—you're so prudent!" The sneer was open now. "And if you burnt the letter you're wondering how on earth I know what was in it. That's it, isn't it?"

Mrs. Slade waited, but Mrs. Ansley did not speak.

"Well, my dear, I know what was in that letter because I wrote it!"

"You wrote it?"

"Yes."   80

The two women stood for a minute staring at each other in the last golden light. Then Mrs. Ansley dropped back into her chair. "Oh," she murmured, and covered her face with her hands.

Mrs. Slade waited nervously for another word or movement. None came, and at length she broke out: "I horrify you."

Mrs. Ansley's hands dropped to her knee. The face they uncovered was streaked with tears. "I wasn't thinking of you. I was thinking—it was the only letter I ever had from him!"

"And I wrote it. Yes; I wrote it! But I was the girl he was engaged to. Did you happen to remember that?"

Mrs. Ansley's head drooped again. "I'm not trying to excuse myself . . . I   85
remembered. . . ."

"And still you went?"

"Still I went."

Mrs. Slade stood looking down on the small bowed figure at her side. The flame of her wrath had already sunk, and she wondered why she had ever thought there would be any satisfaction in inflicting so purposeless a wound on her friend. But she had to justify herself.

"You do understand? I found out—and I hated you, hated you. I knew you were in love with Delphin—and I was afraid; afraid of you, of your quiet ways, your sweetness . . . your . . . well, I wanted you out of the way, that's all. Just for a few weeks; just till I was sure of him. So in a blind fury I wrote that letter . . . I don't know why I'm telling you now."

"I suppose," said Mrs. Ansley slowly, "it's because you've always gone on   90
hating me."

"Perhaps. Or because I wanted to get the whole thing off my mind." She paused. "I'm glad you destroyed the letter. Of course I never thought you'd die."

Mrs. Ansley relapsed into silence, and Mrs. Slade, leaning above her, was conscious of a strange sense of isolation, of being cut off from the warm current of human communion. "You think me a monster!"

"I don't know. . . . It was the only letter I had, and you say he didn't write it?"

"Ah, how you care for him still!"

"I cared for that memory," said Mrs. Ansley.   95

Mrs. Slade continued to look down on her. She seemed physically reduced by the blow—as if, when she got up, the wind might scatter her like a
puff of dust. Mrs. Slade's jealousy suddenly leapt up again at the sight. All these
years the woman had been living on that letter. How she must have loved him,
to treasure the mere memory of its ashes! The letter of the man her friend was
engaged to. Wasn't it she who was the monster?

"You tried your best to get him away from me, didn't you? But you
failed; and I kept him. That's all."

"Yes. That's all."

"I wish now I hadn't told you. I'd no idea you'd feel about it as you do; I
thought you'd be amused. It all happened so long ago, as you say; and you must
do me the justice to remember that I had no reason to think you'd ever taken
it seriously. How could I, when you were married to Horace Ansley two
months afterward? As soon as you could get out of bed your mother rushed
you off to Florence and married you. People were rather surprised—they wondered at its being done so quickly; but I thought I knew. I had an idea you did
it out of *pique*—to be able to say you'd got ahead of Delphin and me. Girls
have such silly reasons for doing the most serious things. And your marrying
so soon convinced me that you'd never really cared."

100   "Yes. I suppose it would," Mrs. Ansley assented.

The clear heaven overhead was emptied of all its gold. Dusk spread over
it, abruptly darkening the Seven Hills. Here and there lights began to twinkle
through the foliage at their feet. Steps were coming and going on the deserted
terrace—waiters looking out of the doorway at the head of the stairs, then
reappearing with trays and napkins and flasks of wine. Tables were moved,
chairs straightened. A feeble string of electric lights flickered out. Some vases
of faded flowers were carried away, and brought back replenished. A stout lady
in a dust coat suddenly appeared, asking in broken Italian if anyone had seen
the elastic band which held together her tattered Baedeker. She poked with
her stick under the table at which she had lunched, the waiters assisting.

The corner where Mrs. Slade and Mrs. Ansley sat was still shadowy and
deserted. For a long time neither of them spoke. At length Mrs. Slade began
again: "I suppose I did it as a sort of joke—"

"A joke?"

"Well, girls are ferocious sometimes, you know. Girls in love especially. And
I remember laughing to myself all that evening at the idea that you were waiting
around there in the dark, dodging out of sight, listening for every sound, trying
to get in— Of course I was upset when I heard you were so ill afterward."

105   Mrs. Ansley had not moved for a long time. But now she turned slowly
toward her companion. "But I didn't wait. He'd arranged everything. He was
there. We were let in at once," she said.

Mrs. Slade sprang up from her leaning position. "Delphin there? They let
you in?—Ah, now you're lying!" she burst out with violence.

Mrs. Ansley's voice grew clearer, and full of surprise. "But of course he was there. Naturally he came—"

"Came? How did he know he'd find you there? You must be raving!"

Mrs. Ansley hesitated, as though reflecting. "But I answered the letter. I told him I'd be there. So he came."

Mrs. Slade flung her hands up to her face. "Oh, God—you answered! I   *110* never thought of your answering. . . ."

"It's odd you never thought of it, if you wrote the letter."

"Yes. I was blind with rage."

Mrs. Ansley rose, and drew her fur scarf about her. "It is cold here. We'd better go . . . I'm sorry for you," she said, as she clasped the fur about her throat.

The unexpected words sent a pang through Mrs. Slade. "Yes; we'd better go." She gathered up her bag and cloak. "I don't know why you should be sorry for me," she muttered.

Mrs. Ansley stood looking away from her toward the dusky secret mass   *115* of the Colosseum. "Well—because I didn't have to wait that night."

Mrs. Slade gave an unquiet laugh. "Yes; I was beaten there. But I oughtn't to begrudge it to you, I suppose. At the end of all these years. After all, I had everything; I had him for twenty-five years. And you had nothing but that one letter that he didn't write."

Mrs. Ansley was again silent. At length she turned toward the door of the terrace. She took a step, and turned back, facing her companion.

"I had Barbara," she said, and began to move ahead of Mrs. Slade toward the stairway.   *1934*

CONSIDERATIONS

1. In what ways do the setting and description of Rome in this story contribute to the revelation of the hidden secret and conflicts that lie between the two women?

2. What might be Wharton's purpose in not distinguishing the two women by name until the seventh paragraph? How do the descriptions, actions, and reflections of these two women differ? In what ways are they alike?

3. At the end of part I, Wharton writes that "these two ladies visualized each other, each through the wrong end of her little telescope." What does she mean by this statement, and what does it say about these two friends?

4. At what point in this story do the two women begin to disagree with one another, and who, exactly, spurs this conflict? Explain.

5. With which woman, if either, do your sympathies lie at the end of this story? Explain, with specific references to the facts provided in the story.

SUSAN GLASPELL (1882–1948)

A Jury of Her Peers

> *Born in Davenport, Iowa, Susan Glaspell was the daughter of an Irish immigrant mother; her father was a feed dealer. Following her graduation from Drake University, she worked as a reporter and began to publish short stories and novels. In 1911, she moved to New York City, where she met and married George Cram Cook, who also came from Davenport, Iowa. Collaborating with her husband, Glaspell wrote plays, and her husband directed them. During the summer, they resided on Cape Cod, where they helped to found the Playwrights' Theater and devoted their time to the Provincetown Players, a theatrical group that performed Glaspell's plays as well as those by other renowned playwrights such as Eugene O'Neill and Edna St. Vincent Millay. In 1930, Glaspell won the Pulitzer Prize for drama for* Alison's House, *a dramatization of the life of a poet, thought to be based on Emily Dickinson. "A Jury of Her Peers" was published in 1917, two years before women in the United States were granted the right to vote.*

When Martha Hale opened the storm-door and got a cut of the north wind, she ran back for her big woolen scarf. As she hurriedly wound that round her head her eye made a scandalized sweep of her kitchen. It was no ordinary thing that called her away—it was probably farther from ordinary than anything that had ever happened in Dickson County. But what her eye took in was that her kitchen was in no shape for leaving: her bread all ready for mixing, half the flour sifted and half unsifted.

She hated to see things half done; but she had been at that when the team from town stopped to get Mr. Hale, and then the sheriff came running in to say his wife wished Mrs. Hale would come too—adding, with a grin, that he guessed she was getting scarey and wanted another woman along. So she had dropped everything right where it was.

"Martha!" now came her husband's impatient voice. "Don't keep folks waiting out here in the cold."

She again opened the storm-door, and this time joined the three men and the one woman waiting for her in the big two-seated buggy.

5   After she had the robes tucked around her she took another look at the woman who sat beside her on the back seat. She had met Mrs. Peters the year before at the county fair, and the thing she remembered about her was that she didn't seem like a sheriff's wife. She was small and thin and didn't have a strong voice. Mrs. Gorman, sheriff's wife before Gorman went out and Peters came in, had a voice that somehow seemed to be backing up the law with every word. But if Mrs. Peters didn't look like a sheriff's wife, Peters made it up in looking like a sheriff. He was to a dot the kind of man who could get

himself elected sheriff—a heavy man with a big voice, who was particularly genial with the law-abiding, as if to make it plain that he knew the difference between criminals and non-criminals. And right there it came into Mrs. Hale's mind, with a stab, that this man who was so pleasant and lively with all of them was going to the Wrights' now as a sheriff.

"The country's not very pleasant this time of year," Mrs. Peters at last ventured, as if she felt they ought to be talking as well as the men.

Mrs. Hale scarcely finished her reply, for they had gone up a little hill and could see the Wright place now, and seeing it did not make her feel like talking. It looked very lonesome this cold March morning. It had always been a lonesome-looking place. It was down in a hollow, and the poplar trees around it were lonesome-looking trees. The men were looking at it and talking about what had happened. The county attorney was bending to one side of the buggy, and kept looking steadily at the place as they drew up to it.

"I'm glad you came with me," Mrs. Peters said nervously, as the two women were about to follow the men in through the kitchen door.

Even after she had her foot on the door-step, her hand on the knob, Martha Hale had a moment of feeling she could not cross that threshold. And the reason it seemed she couldn't cross it now was simply because she hadn't crossed it before. Time and time again it had been in her mind, "I ought to go over and see Minnie Foster"—she still thought of her as Minnie Foster, though for twenty years she had been Mrs. Wright. And then there was always something to do and Minnie Foster would go from her mind. But *now* she could come.

The men went over to the stove. The women stood close together by the door. Young Henderson, the county attorney, turned around and said, "Come up to the fire, ladies."   10

Mrs. Peters took a step forward, then stopped. "I'm not—cold," she said.

And so the two women stood by the door, at first not even so much as looking around the kitchen.

The men talked for a minute about what a good thing it was, the sheriff had sent his deputy out that morning to make a fire for them, and then Sheriff Peters stepped back from the stove, unbuttoned his outer coat, and leaned his hands on the kitchen table in a way that seemed to mark the beginning of official business. "Now, Mr. Hale," he said in a sort of semi-official voice, "before we move things about, you tell Mr. Henderson just what it was you saw when you came here yesterday morning."

The county attorney was looking around the kitchen.

"By the way," he said, "has anything been moved?" He turned to the   15
sheriff. "Are things just as you left them yesterday?"

Peters looked from cupboard to sink; from that to a small worn rocker a little to one side of the kitchen table.

"It's just the same."

"Somebody should have been left here yesterday," said the county attorney.

"Oh—yesterday," returned the sheriff, with a little gesture as of yesterday having been more than he could bear to think of. "When I had to send Frank to Morris Center for that man who went crazy—let me tell you. I had my hands full yesterday. I knew you could get back from Omaha by today, George, and as long as I went over everything here myself—"

20   "Well, Mr. Hale," said the county attorney, in a way of letting what was past and gone go, "tell just what happened when you came here yesterday morning."

Mrs. Hale, still leaning against the door, had that sinking feeling of the mother whose child is about to speak a piece. Lewis often wandered along and got things mixed up in a story. She hoped he would tell this straight and plain, and not say unnecessary things that would just make things harder for Minnie Foster. He didn't begin at once, and she noticed that he looked queer—as if standing in that kitchen and having to tell what he had seen there yesterday morning made him almost sick.

"Yes, Mr. Hale?" the county attorney reminded.

"Harry and I had started to town with a load of potatoes," Mrs. Hale's husband began.

Harry was Mrs. Hale's oldest boy. He wasn't with them now, for the very good reason that those potatoes never got to town yesterday and he was taking them this morning, so he hadn't been home when the sheriff stopped to say he wanted Mr. Hale to come over to the Wright place and tell the county attorney his story there, where he could point it all out. With all Mrs. Hale's other emotions came the fear now that maybe Harry wasn't dressed warm enough—they hadn't any of them realized how that north wind did bite.

25   "We come along this road," Hale was going on, with a motion of his hand to the road over which they had just come, "and as we got in sight of the house I says to Harry, 'I'm goin' to see if I can't get John Wright to take a telephone.' You see," he explained to Henderson, "unless I can get somebody to go in with me they won't come out this branch road except for a price *I* can't pay. I'd spoke to Wright about it once before; but he put me off, saying folks talked too much anyway, and all he asked was peace and quiet—guess you know about how much he talked himself. But I thought maybe if I went to the house and talked about it before his wife, and said all the women-folks liked the telephones, and that in this lonesome stretch of road it would be a good thing—well, I said to Harry that that was what I was going to say— though I said at the same time that I didn't know as what his wife wanted made much difference to John—"

Now there he was!—saying things he didn't need to say. Mrs. Hale tried to catch her husband's eye, but fortunately the county attorney interrupted with:

"Let's talk about that a little later, Mr. Hale. I do want to talk about that, but I'm anxious now to get along to just what happened when you got here."

When he began this time, it was very deliberately and carefully:

"I didn't see or hear anything. I knocked at the door. And still it was all quiet inside. I knew they must be up—it was past eight o'clock. So I knocked again, louder, and I thought I heard somebody say, 'Come in.' I wasn't sure—I'm not sure yet. But I opened the door—this door," jerking a hand toward the door by which the two women stood. "and there, in that rocker"—pointing to it—"sat Mrs. Wright."

Everyone in the kitchen looked at the rocker. It came into Mrs. Hale's   *30* mind that that rocker didn't look in the least like Minnie Foster—the Minnie Foster of twenty years before. It was a dingy red, with wooden rungs up the back, and the middle rung was gone, and the chair sagged to one side.

"How did she—look?" the county attorney was inquiring.

"Well," said Hale, "she looked—queer."

"How do you mean—queer?"

As he asked it he took out a note-book and pencil. Mrs. Hale did not like the sight of that pencil. She kept her eye fixed on her husband, as if to keep him from saying unnecessary things that would go into that note-book and make trouble.

Hale did speak guardedly, as if the pencil had affected him too.   *35*

"Well, as if she didn't know what she was going to do next. And kind of—done up."

"How did she seem to feel about your coming?"

"Why, I don't think she minded—one way or other. She didn't pay much attention. I said, 'Ho' do, Mrs. Wright? It's cold, ain't it?' And she said. 'Is it?'—and went on pleatin' at her apron.

"Well, I was surprised. She didn't ask me to come up to the stove, or to sit down, but just set there, not even lookin' at me. And so I said: 'I want to see John.'

"And then she—laughed. I guess you would call it a laugh.   *40*

"I thought of Harry and the team outside, so I said, a little sharp, 'Can I see John?' 'No,' says she—kind of dull like. 'Ain't he home?' says I. Then she looked at me. 'Yes,' says she, 'he's home.' 'Then why can't I see him?' I asked her, out of patience with her now. 'Cause he's dead' says she, just as quiet and dull—and fell to pleatin' her apron. 'Dead?' says, I, like you do when you can't take in what you've heard.

"She just nodded her head, not getting a bit excited, but rockin' back and forth.

"'Why—where is he?' says I, not knowing *what* to say.

"She just pointed upstairs—like this"—pointing to the room above.

"I got up, with the idea of going up there myself. By this time I—didn't   *45* know what to do. I walked from there to here; then I says: "Why, what did he die of?"

"'He died of a rope around his neck,' says she; and just went on pleatin' at her apron."

Hale stopped speaking, and stood staring at the rocker, as if he were still seeing the woman who had sat there the morning before. Nobody spoke; it was as if every one were seeing the woman who had sat there the morning before.

"And what did you do then?" the county attorney at last broke the silence.

"I went out and called Harry. I thought I might—need help. I got Harry in, and we went upstairs." His voice fell almost to a whisper. "There he was— lying over the—"

50   "I think I'd rather have you go into that upstairs," the county attorney interrupted, "where you can point it all out. Just go on now with the rest of the story."

"Well, my first thought was to get that rope off. It looked—"

He stopped, his face twitching.

"But Harry, he went up to him, and he said, 'No, he's dead all right, and we'd better not touch anything.' So we went downstairs.

"She was still sitting that same way. 'Has anybody been notified?' I asked. 'No,' says she, unconcerned.

55   "'Who did this, Mrs. Wright?' said Harry. He said it businesslike, and she stopped pleatin' at her apron. 'I don't know,' she says. 'You don't *know*?' says Harry. 'Weren't you sleepin' in the bed with him?' 'Yes,' says she, 'but I was on the inside.' 'Somebody slipped a rope round his neck and strangled him, and you didn't wake up?' says Harry. 'I didn't wake up,' she said after him.

"We may have looked as if we didn't see how that could be, for after a minute she said, 'I sleep sound.'

"Harry was going to ask her more questions, but I said maybe that weren't our business; maybe we ought to let her tell her story first to the coroner or the sheriff. So Harry went fast as he could over to High Road—the Rivers' place, where there's a telephone."

"And what did she do when she knew you had gone for the coroner?" The attorney got his pencil in his hand all ready for writing.

"She moved from that chair to this one over here"—Hale pointed to a small chair in the corner—"and just sat there with her hands held together and looking down. I got a feeling that I ought to make some conversation, so I said I had come in to see if John wanted to put in a telephone; and at that she started to laugh, and then she stopped and looked at me—scared."

60   At the sound of a moving pencil the man who was telling the story looked up.

"I dunno—maybe it wasn't scared," he hastened: "I wouldn't like to say it was. Soon Harry got back, and then Dr. Lloyd came, and you, Mr. Peters, and so I guess that's all I know that you don't."

He said that last with relief, and moved a little, as if relaxing. Everyone moved a little. The county attorney walked toward the stair door.

"I guess we'll go upstairs first—then out to the barn and around there."

He paused and looked around the kitchen.

"You're convinced there was nothing important here?" he asked the   65
sheriff. "Nothing that would—point to any motive?"

The sheriff too looked all around, as if to re-convince himself.

"Nothing here but kitchen things," he said, with a little laugh for the in-
significance of kitchen things.

The county attorney was looking at the cupboard—a peculiar, ungainly
structure, half closet and half cupboard, the upper part of it being built in the
wall, and the lower part just the old-fashioned kitchen cupboard. As if its
queerness attracted him, he got a chair and opened the upper part and looked
in. After a moment he drew his hand away sticky.

"Here's a nice mess," he said resentfully.

The two women had drawn nearer, and now the sheriff's wife spoke.   70

"Oh—her fruit," she said, looking to Mrs. Hale for sympathetic understanding. She turned back to the county attorney and explained: "She worried
about that when it turned so cold last night. She said the fire would go out
and her jars might burst."

Mrs. Peters' husband broke into a laugh.

"Well, can you beat the women! Held for murder, and worrying about
her preserves!"

The young attorney set his lips.

"I guess before we're through with her she may have something more   75
serious than preserves to worry about."

"Oh, well," said Mrs. Hale's husband, with good-natured superiority,
"women are used to worrying over trifles."

The two women moved a little closer together. Neither of them spoke.
The county attorney seemed suddenly to remember his manners—and think
of his future.

"And yet," said he, with the gallantry of a young politician, "for all their
worries, what would we do without the ladies?"

The women did not speak, did not unbend. He went to the sink and
began washing his hands. He turned to wipe them on the roller towel—
whirled it for a cleaner place.

"Dirty towels! Not much of a housekeeper, would you say, ladies?"   80

He kicked his foot against some dirty pans under the sink.

"There's a great deal of work to be done on a farm," said Mrs. Hale stiffly.

"To be sure. And yet"—with a little bow to her—"I know there are some
Dickson County farm-houses that do not have such roller towels." He gave it
a pull to expose its full length again.

"Those towels get dirty awful quick. Men's hands aren't always as clean
as they might be."

"Ah, loyal to your sex, I see," he laughed. He stopped and gave her a keen   85
look. "But you and Mrs. Wright were neighbors. I suppose you were friends, too."

Martha Hale shook her head.

"I've seen little enough of her of late years. I've not been in this house—it's more than a year."

"And why was that? You didn't like her?"

"I liked her well enough," she replied with spirit. "Farmers' wives have their hands full, Mr. Henderson. And then"—She looked around the kitchen.

90   "Yes?" he encouraged.

"It never seemed a very cheerful place," said she, more to herself than to him.

"No," he agreed; "I don't think anyone would call it cheerful. I shouldn't say she had the home-making instinct."

"Well, I don't know as Wright had, either," she muttered.

"You mean they didn't get on very well?" he was quick to ask.

95   "No; I don't mean anything," she answered, with decision. As she turned a little away from him, she added: "But I don't think a place would be any the cheerfuler for John Wright's bein' in it."

"I'd like to talk to you about that a little later, Mrs. Hale," he said. "I'm anxious to get the lay of things upstairs now."

He moved toward the stair door, followed by the two men.

"I suppose anything Mrs. Peters does'll be all right?" the sheriff inquired. "She was to take in some clothes for her, you know—and a few little things. We left in such a hurry yesterday."

The county attorney looked at the two women they were leaving alone there among the kitchen things.

100   "Yes—Mrs. Peters," he said, his glance resting on the woman who was not Mrs. Peters, the big farmer woman who stood behind the sheriff's wife. "Of course Mrs. Peters is one of us," he said, in a manner of entrusting responsibility. "And keep your eye out, Mrs. Peters, for anything that might be of use. No telling; you women might come upon a clue to the motive—and that's the thing we need."

Mr. Hale rubbed his face after the fashion of a show man getting ready for a pleasantry.

"But would the women know a clue if they did come upon it?" he said; and, having delivered himself of this, he followed the others through the stair door.

The women stood motionless and silent, listening to the footsteps, first upon the stairs, then in the room above them.

Then, as if releasing herself from something strange, Mrs. Hale began to arrange the dirty pans under the sink, which the county attorney's disdainful push of the foot had deranged.

105   "I'd hate to have men comin' into my kitchen," she said testily—"snoopin' round and criticizin'."

"Of course it's no more than their duty," said the sheriff's wife, in her manner of timid acquiescence.

"Duty's all right," replied Mrs. Hale bluffly; "but I guess that deputy sheriff that come out to make the fire might have got a little of this on." She gave the roller towel a pull. "Wish I'd thought of that sooner! Seems mean to talk about her for not having things slicked up, when she had to come away in such a hurry."

She looked around the kitchen. Certainly it was not "slicked up." Her eye was held by a bucket of sugar on a low shelf. The cover was off the wooden bucket, and beside it was a paper bag—half full.

Mrs. Hale moved toward it.

"She was putting this in there," she said to herself—slowly.   *110*

She thought of the flour in her kitchen at home—half sifted, half not sifted. She had been interrupted, and had left things half done. What had interrupted Minnie Foster? Why had that work been left half done? She made a move as if to finish it,—unfinished things always bothered her,—and then she glanced around and saw that Mrs. Peters was watching her—and she didn't want Mrs. Peters to get that feeling she had got of work begun and then—for some reason—not finished.

"It's a shame about her fruit," she said, and walked toward the cupboard that the county attorney had opened, and got on the chair, murmuring: "I wonder if it's all gone."

It was a sorry enough looking sight, but "Here's one that's all right," she said at last. She held it toward the light. "This is cherries, too." She looked again. "I declare I believe that's the only one."

With a sigh, she got down from the chair, went to the sink, and wiped off the bottle.

"She'll feel awful bad, after all her hard work in the hot weather. I re-   *115* member the afternoon I put up my cherries last summer."

She set the bottle on the table, and, with another sigh, started to sit down in the rocker. But she did not sit down. Something kept her from sitting down in that chair. She straightened—stepped back, and, half turned away, stood looking at it, seeing the woman who had sat there "pleatin' at her apron."

The thin voice of the sheriff's wife broke in upon her: "I must be getting those things from the front-room closet." She opened the door into the other room, started in, stepped back. "You coming with me, Mrs. Hale?" she asked nervously. "You—you could help me get them."

They were soon back—the stark coldness of that shut-up room was not a thing to linger in.

"My!" said Mrs. Peters, dropping the things on the table and hurrying to the stove.

Mrs. Hale stood examining the clothes the woman who was being de-   *120* tained in town had said she wanted.

"Wright was close!" she exclaimed, holding up a shabby black skirt that bore the marks of much making over. "I think maybe that's why she kept so much to herself. I s'pose she felt she couldn't do her part; and then, you don't enjoy things when you feel shabby. She used to wear pretty clothes and be lively—when she was Minnie Foster, one of the town girls, singing in the choir. But that—oh, that was twenty years ago."

With a carefulness in which there was something tender, she folded the shabby clothes and piled them at one corner of the table. She looked up at Mrs. Peters, and there was something in the other woman's look that irritated her.

"She don't care," she said to herself. "Much difference it makes to her whether Minnie Foster had pretty clothes when she was a girl."

Then she looked again, and she wasn't so sure; in fact, she hadn't at any time been perfectly sure about Mrs. Peters. She had that shrinking manner, and yet her eyes looked as if they could see a long way into things.

125 "This all you was to take in?" asked Mrs. Hale.

"No," said the sheriff's wife; "she said she wanted an apron. Funny thing to want," she ventured in her nervous little way, "for there's not much to get you dirty in jail, goodness knows. But I suppose just to make her feel more natural. If you're used to wearing an apron—. She said they were in the bottom drawer of this cupboard. Yes—here they are. And then her little shawl that always hung on the stair door."

She took the small gray shawl from behind the door leading upstairs, and stood a minute looking at it.

Suddenly Mrs. Hale took a quick step toward the other woman,

"Mrs. Peters!"

130 "Yes, Mrs. Hale?"

"Do you think she—did it?"

A frightened look blurred the other things in Mrs. Peters' eyes.

"Oh, I don't know," she said, in a voice that seemed to shink away from the subject.

"Well, I don't think she did," affirmed Mrs. Hale stoutly. "Asking for an apron, and her little shawl. Worryin' about her fruit."

135 "Mr. Peters says—" Footsteps were heard in the room above; she stopped, looked up, then went on in a lowered voice: "Mr. Peters says—it looks bad for her. Mr. Henderson is awful sarcastic in a speech, and he's going to make fun of her saying she didn't—wake up."

For a moment Mrs. Hale had no answer. Then, "Well, I guess John Wright didn't wake up—when they was slippin' that rope under his neck," she muttered.

"No, it's *strange*," breathed Mrs. Peters. "They think it was such a—funny way to kill a man."

She began to laugh; at sound of the laugh, abruptly stopped.

"That's just what Mr. Hale said," said Mrs. Hale, in a resolutely natural voice. "There was a gun in the house. He says that's what he can't understand."

140 "Mr. Henderson said, coming out, that what was needed for the case was a motive. Something to show anger—or sudden feeling."

"Well, I don't see any signs of anger around here," said Mrs. Hale, "I don't—"

She stopped. It was as if her mind tripped on something. Her eye was caught by a dish-towel in the middle of the kitchen table. Slowly she moved toward the table. One half of it was wiped clean, the other half messy. Her eyes made a slow, almost unwilling turn to the bucket of sugar and the half empty bag beside it. Things begun—and not finished.

After a moment she stepped back, and said, in that manner of releasing herself:

"Wonder how they're finding things upstairs? I hope she had it a little more red up up there. You know,"—she paused, and feeling gathered,—"it seems kind of *sneaking:* locking her up in town and coming out here to get her own house to turn against her!"

"But, Mrs. Hale," said the sheriff's wife, "the law is the law."   145

"I s'pose 'tis," answered Mrs. Hale shortly.

She turned to the stove, saying something about that fire not being much to brag of. She worked with it a minute, and when she straightened up she said aggressively:

"The law is the law—and a bad stove is a bad stove. How'd you like to cook on this?"—pointing with the poker to the broken lining. She opened the oven door and started to express her opinion of the oven; but she was swept into her own thoughts, thinking of what it would mean, year after year, to have that stove to wrestle with. The thought of Minnie Foster trying to bake in that oven—and the thought of her never going over to see Minnie Foster—.

She was startled by hearing Mrs. Peters say: "A person gets discouraged—and loses heart."

The sheriff's wife had looked from the stove to the sink—to the pail of   150
water which had been carried in from outside. The two women stood there silent, above them the footsteps of the men who were looking for evidence against the woman who had worked in that kitchen. That look of seeing into things, of seeing through a thing to something else, was in the eyes of the sheriff's wife now. When Mrs. Hale next spoke to her, it was gently:

"Better loosen up your things, Mrs. Peters. We'll not feel them when we go out."

Mrs. Peters went to the back of the room to hang up the fur tippet she was wearing. A moment later she exclaimed, "Why, she was piecing a quilt," and held up a large sewing basket piled high with quilt pieces.

Mrs. Hale spread some of the blocks on the table.

"It's log-cabin pattern," she said, putting several of them together, "Pretty, isn't it?"

They were so engaged with the quilt that they did not hear the footsteps   155
on the stairs. Just as the stair door opened Mrs. Hale was saying:

"Do you suppose she was going to quilt it or just knot it?"

The sheriff threw up his hands.

"They wonder whether she was going to quilt it or just knot it!"

There was a laugh for the ways of women, a warming of hands over the stove, and then the county attorney said briskly:

160   "Well, let's go right out to the barn and get that cleared up."

"I don't see as there's anything so strange," Mrs. Hale said resentfully, after the outside door had closed on the three men—"our taking up our time with little things while we're waiting for them to get the evidence. I don't see as it's anything to laugh about."

"Of course they've got awful important things on their minds," said the sheriff's wife apologetically.

They returned to an inspection of the blocks for the quilt. Mrs. Hale was looking at the fine, even sewing, and preoccupied with thoughts of the woman who had done that sewing, when she heard the sheriff's wife say, in a queer tone:

"Why, look at this one."

165   She turned to take the block held out to her.

"The sewing," said Mrs. Peters, in a troubled way, "All the rest of them have been so nice and even—but—this one. Why, it looks as if she didn't know what she was about!"

Their eyes met—something flashed to life, passed between them; then, as if with an effort, they seemed to pull away from each other. A moment Mrs. Hale sat there, her hands folded over that sewing which was so unlike all the rest of the sewing. Then she had pulled a knot and drawn the threads.

"Oh, what are you doing, Mrs. Hale?" asked the sheriff's wife, startled.

"Just pulling out a stitch or two that's not sewed very good," said Mrs. Hale mildly.

170   "I don't think we ought to touch things," Mrs. Peters said, a little helplessly.

"I'd just finish up this end," answered Mrs. Hale, still in that mild, matter-of-fact fashion.

She threaded a needle and started to replace bad sewing with good. For a little while she sewed in silence. Then, in that thin, timid voice, she heard:

"Mrs. Hale!"

"Yes, Mrs. Peters?"

175   "What do you suppose she was so—nervous about?"

"Oh, I don't know," said Mrs. Hale, as if dismissing a thing not important enough to spend much time on. "I don't know as she was—nervous. I sew awful queer sometimes when I'm just tired."

She cut a thread, and out of the corner of her eye looked up at Mrs. Peters. The small, lean face of the sheriff's wife seemed to have tightened up. Her eyes had that look of peering into something. But next moment she moved, and said in her thin, indecisive way:

"Well, I must get those clothes wrapped. They may be through sooner than we think. I wonder where I could find a piece of paper—and string."

"In that cupboard, maybe," suggested to Mrs. Hale, after a glance around.

One piece of the crazy sewing remained unripped. Mrs. Peter's back   *180*
turned, Martha Hale now scrutinized that piece, compared it with the dainty, accurate sewing of the other blocks. The difference was startling. Holding this block
made her feel queer, as if the distracted thoughts of the woman who had perhaps
turned to it to try and quiet herself were communicating themselves to her.

Mrs. Peters' voice roused her.

"Here's a bird-cage," she said. "Did she have a bird, Mrs. Hale?"

"Why, I don't know whether she did or not." She turned to look at the
cage Mrs. Peters was holding up. "I've not been here in so long." She sighed.
"There was a man round last year selling canaries cheap—but I don't know as
she took one. Maybe she did. She used to sing real pretty herself."

Mrs. Peters looked around the kitchen.

"Seems kind of funny to think of a bird here." She half laughed—an at-   *185*
tempt to put up a barrier. "But she must have had one—or why would she
have a cage? I wonder what happened to it."

"I suppose maybe the cat got it," suggested Mrs. Hale, resuming her sewing.

"No; she didn't have a cat. She's got that feeling some people have about
cats—being afraid of them. When they brought her to our house yesterday, my
cat got in the room, and she was real upset and asked me to take it out."

"My sister Bessie was like that," laughed Mrs. Hale.

The sheriff's wife did not reply. The silence made Mrs. Hale turn round.
Mrs. Peters was examining the bird-cage.

"Look at this door," she said slowly. "It's broke. One hinge has been   *190*
pulled apart."

Mrs. Hale came nearer.

"Looks as if someone must have been—rough with it."

Again their eyes met—startled, questioning, apprehensive. For a moment
neither spoke nor stirred. Then Mrs. Hale, turning away, said brusquely:

"If they're going to find any evidence, I wish they'd be about it. I don't
like this place."

"But I'm awful glad you came with me, Mrs. Hale." Mrs. Peters put the   *195*
bird-cage on the table and sat down. "It would be lonesome for me—sitting
here alone."

"Yes, it would, wouldn't it?" agreed Mrs. Hale, a certain determined nat-
uralness in her voice. She had picked up the sewing, but now it dropped in her
lap, and she murmured in a different voice: "But I tell you what I *do* wish, Mrs.
Peters. I wish I had come over sometimes when she was here. I wish—I had."

"But of course you were awful busy, Mrs. Hale. Your house—and your
children."

"I could've come," retorted Mrs. Hale shortly. "I stayed away because it
weren't cheerful—and that's why I ought to have come. I"—she looked
around—"I've never liked this place. Maybe because it's down in a hollow and
you don't see the road. I don't know what it is, but it's a lonesome place, and

always was. I wish I had come over to see Minnie Foster sometimes. I can see now—" She did not put it into words.

"Well, you mustn't reproach yourself," counseled Mrs. Peters. "Somehow, we just don't see how it is with other folks till—something comes up."

200   "Not having children makes less work," mused Mrs. Hale, after a silence, "but it makes a quiet house—and Wright out to work all day—and no company when he did come in. Did you know John Wright, Mrs. Peters?"

"Not to know him. I've seen him in town. They say he was a good man."

"Yes—good," conceded John Wright's neighbor grimly. "He didn't drink, and kept his word as well as most, I guess, and paid his debts. But he was a hard man, Mrs. Peters. Just to pass the time of day with him—." She stopped, shivered a little. "Like a raw wind that gets to the bone." Her eye fell upon the cage on the table before her, and she added, almost bitterly: "I should think she would've wanted a bird!"

Suddenly she leaned forward, looking intently at the cage. "But what do you s'pose went wrong with it?"

"I don't know," returned Mrs. Peters; "unless it got sick and died."

205   But after she said it she reached over and swung the broken door. Both women watched it as if somehow held by it.

"You didn't know—her?" Mrs. Hale asked, a gentler note in her voice.

"Not till they brought her yesterday," said the sheriff's wife.

"She—come to think of it, she was kind of like a bird herself. Real sweet and pretty, but kind of timid and—fluttery. How—she—did—change."

That held her for a long time. Finally, as if struck with a happy thought and relieved to get back to everyday things, she exclaimed:

210   "Tell you what, Mrs. Peters, why don't you take the quilt in with you? It might take up her mind."

"Why, I think that's a real nice idea, Mrs. Hale," agreed the sheriff's wife, as if she too were glad to come into the atmosphere of a simple kindness. "There couldn't possibly be any objection to that, could there? Now, just what will I take? I wonder if her patches are in here—and her things?"

They turned to the sewing basket.

"Here's some red," said Mrs. Hale, bringing out a roll of cloth. Underneath that was a box. "Here, maybe her scissors are in here—and her things." She held it up. "What a pretty box! I'll warrant that was something she had a long time ago—when she was a girl."

She held it in her hand a moment; then, with a little sigh, opened it.

215   Instantly her hand went to her nose.

"Why—!"

Mrs. Peters drew nearer—then turned away.

"There's something wrapped up in this piece of silk," faltered Mrs. Hale.

"This isn't her scissors," said Mrs. Peters, in a shrinking voice.

220   Her hand not steady, Mrs. Hale raised the piece of silk. "Oh, Mrs. Peters!" she cried. "It's—"

Mrs. Peters bent closer.

"It's the bird," she whispered.

"But, Mrs. Peters!" cried Mrs. Hale. "*Look* at it! Its *neck*—look at its neck! It's all—other side *to*."

She held the box away from her.

The sheriff's wife again bent closer.   *225*

"Somebody wrung its neck," said she, in a voice that was slow and deep.

And then again the eyes of the two women met—this time clung together in a look of dawning comprehension, of growing horror. Mrs. Peters looked from the dead bird to the broken door of the cage. Again their eyes met. And just then there was a sound at the outside door.

Mrs. Hale slipped the box under the quilt pieces in the basket, and sank into the chair before it. Mrs. Peters stood holding to the table. The county attorney and the sheriff came in from outside.

"Well, ladies," said the county attorney, as one turning from serious things to little pleasantries, "have you decided whether she was going to quilt it or knot it?"

"We think," began the sheriff's wife in a flurried voice, "that she was   *230* going to—knot it."

He was too preoccupied to notice the change that came in her voice on that last.

"Well, that's very interesting, I'm sure," he said tolerantly. He caught sight of the bird-cage. "Has the bird flown?"

"We think the cat got it," said Mrs. Hale in a voice curiously even.

He was walking up and down, as if thinking something out.

"Is there a cat?" he asked absently.   *235*

Mrs. Hale shot a look up at the sheriff's wife.

"Well, not *now*," said Mrs. Peters. "They're superstitious, you know; they leave."

She sank into her chair.

The county attorney did not heed her. "No sign at all of anyone having come in from the outside," he said to Peters, in the manner of continuing an interrupted conversation. "Their own rope. Now let's go upstairs again and go over it, piece by piece. It would have to have been someone who knew just the—"

The stair door closed behind them and their voices were lost.   *240*

The two women sat motionless, not looking at each other, but as if peering into something and at the same time holding back. When they spoke now it was as if they were afraid of what they were saying, but as if they could not help saying it.

"She liked the bird," said Martha Hale, low and slowly. "She was going to bury it in that pretty box."

"When I was a girl," said Mrs. Peters, under her breath, "my kitten—there was a boy took a hatchet, and before my eyes—before I could get there—" She covered her face an instant. "If they hadn't held me back I would have"—

she caught herself, looked upstairs where footsteps were heard, and finished weakly—"hurt him."

Then they sat without speaking or moving.

245   "I wonder how it would seem," Mrs. Hale at last began, as if feeling her way over strange ground—"never to have had any children around?" Her eyes made a slow sweep of the kitchen, as if seeing what that kitchen had meant through all the years. "No, Wright wouldn't like the bird," she said after that— "a thing that sang. She used to sing. He killed that too." Her voice tightened.

Mrs. Peters moved uneasily.

"Of course we don't know who killed the bird."

"I knew John Wright," was Mrs. Hale's answer.

"It was an awful thing was done in this house that night, Mrs. Hale," said the sheriff's wife. "Killing a man while he slept—slipping a thing round his neck that choked the life out of him."

250   Mrs. Hale's hand went out to the bird-cage.

"His neck. Choked the life out of him."

"We don't *know* who killed him," whispered Mrs. Peters wildly. "We don't *know.*"

Mrs. Hale had not moved. "If there had been years and years of—nothing, then a bird to sing to you, it would be awful—still—after the bird was still."

It was as if something within her not herself had spoken, and it found in Mrs. Peters something she did not know as herself.

255   "I know what stillness is," she said, in a queer, monotonous voice. "When we homesteaded in Dakota, and my first baby died—after he was two years old—and me with no other then—"

Mrs. Hale stirred.

"How soon do you suppose they'll be through looking for the evidence?"

"I know what stillness is," repeated Mrs. Peters, in just that same way. Then she too pulled back. "The law has got to punish crime, Mrs. Hale," she said in her tight little way.

"I wish you'd seen Minnie Foster," was the answer, "when she wore a white dress with blue ribbons, and stood up there in the choir and sang."

260   The picture of that girl, the fact that she had lived neighbor to that girl for twenty years, and had let her die for lack of life, was suddenly more than she could bear.

"Oh, I *wish* I'd come over here once in a while!" she cried. "That was a crime! That was a crime. Who's going to punish that?"

"We mustn't take on," said Mrs. Peters, with a frightened look toward the stairs.

"I might 'a' *known* she needed help! I tell you, it's *queer,* Mrs. Peters. We live close together, and we live far apart. We all go through the same things— it's all just a different kind of the same thing! If it weren't—why do you and I *understand?* Why do we *know*—what we know this minute?"

She dashed her hand across her eyes. Then, seeing the jar of fruit on the table she reached for it and choked out:

"If I was you I wouldn't *tell* her her fruit was gone! Tell her it *ain't*. Tell   265
her it's all right—all of it. Here—take this in to prove it to her! She—she may never know whether it was broke or not."

She turned away.

Mrs. Peters reached out for the bottle of fruit as if she were glad to take it—as if touching a familiar thing, having something to do, could keep her from something else. She got up, looked about for something to wrap the fruit in, took a petticoat from the pile of clothes she had brought from the front room, and nervously started winding that round the bottle.

"My!" she began, in a high, false voice, "it's a good thing the men couldn't hear us! Getting all stirred up over a little thing like a—dead canary." She hurried over that. "As if that could have anything to do with—with—My, wouldn't they *laugh*?"

Footsteps were heard on the stairs.

"Maybe they would," muttered Mrs. Hale—"maybe they wouldn't."   270

"No, Peters," said the county attorney incisively; "it's all perfectly clear, except the reason for doing it. But you know juries when it comes to women. If there was some definite thing—something to show. Something to make a story about. A thing that would connect up with this clumsy way of doing it."

In a covert way Mrs. Hale looked at Mrs. Peters. Mrs. Peters was looking at her. Quickly they looked away from each other. The outer door opened and Mr. Hale came in.

"I've got the team round now," he said. "Pretty cold out there."

"I'm going to stay here awhile by myself," the county attorney suddenly announced. "You can send Frank out for me, can't you?" he asked the sheriff. "I want to go over everything. I'm not satisfied we can't do better."

Again, for one brief moment, the two women's eyes found one another.   275

The sheriff came up to the table.

"Did you want to see what Mrs. Peters was going to take in?"

The county attorney picked up the apron. He laughed.

"Oh, I guess they're not very dangerous things the ladies have picked out."

Mrs. Hale's hand was on the sewing basket in which the box was con-   280
cealed. She felt that she ought to take her hand off the basket. She did not seem able to. He picked up one of the quilt blocks which she had piled on to cover the box. Her eyes felt like fire. She had a feeling that if he took up the basket she would snatch it from him.

But he did not take it up. With another little laugh, he turned away, saying:

"No; Mrs. Peters doesn't need supervising. For that matter, a sheriff's wife is married to the law. Ever think of it that way, Mrs. Peters?"

Mrs. Peters was standing beside the table. Mrs. Hale shot a look up at her; but she could not see her face. Mrs. Peters had turned away. When she spoke, her voice was muffled.

285   "Not—just that way," she said.

"Married to the law!" chuckled Mrs. Peters' husband. He moved toward the door into the front room, and said to the county attorney:

"I just want you to come in here a minute, George. We ought to take a look at these windows."

"Oh—windows," said the county attorney scoffingly.

"We'll be right out, Mr. Hale," said the sheriff to the farmer, who was still waiting by the door.

Hale went to look after the horses. The sheriff followed the county attorney into the other room. Again—for one final moment—the two women were alone in that kitchen.

290   Martha Hale sprang up, her hands tight together, looking at that other woman, with whom it rested. At first she could not see her eyes, for the sheriff's wife had not turned back, since she turned away at that suggestion of being married to the law. But now Mrs. Hale made her turn back. Her eyes made her turn back. Slowly, unwillingly, Mrs. Peters turned her head until her eyes met the eyes of the other woman. There was a moment when they held each other in a steady, burning look in which there was no evasion or flinching. Then Martha Hale's eyes pointed the way to the basket in which was hidden the thing that would make certain the conviction of the other woman—that woman who was not there and yet who had been there with them all through the hour.

For a moment Mrs. Peters did not move. And then she did it. With a rush forward, she threw back the quilt pieces, got the box, tried to put it in her handbag. It was too big. Desperately she opened it, started to take the bird out. But there she broke—she could not touch the bird. She stood there helpless, foolish.

There was the sound of a knob turning in the inner door. Martha Hale snatched the box from the sheriff's wife, and got it in the pocket of her big coat just as the sheriff and the county attorney came back into the kitchen.

"Well, Henry," said the county attorney facetiously, "at least we found out that she was not going to quilt it. She was going to—what is it you call it, ladies?"

Mrs. Hale's hand was against the pocket of her coat.

295   "We call it—knot it, Mr. Henderson."   *1917*

CONSIDERATIONS

1. What does the opening scene reveal about the concerns that women have compared to the concerns that men have? From the opening alone, what is your impression of the marriages these women have? Explain.
2. Trace the presence of the element of cold in this story. What role does it play, and how does its meaning change, depending on the scene?
3. Many images connected with Mrs. Wright connote warmth and love, such as the homemade preserves, the stove, the quilt, the singing bird, the red rocking chair. What images are associated with John Wright, and in what

ways do these contrasting images suggest the relationship between Mr. and Mrs. Wright?

4. Mrs. Wright has been married for twenty years, sleeps in the same bed with her husband, and yet she has no children. What reasons can you offer for the absence of children in her life?

5. In the end, why do the two women hide the evidence that most surely would convict Mrs. Wright? Would you argue that despite the illegality of this act, it is compassionate and loving and therefore justified? Or do you think that their action cannot be defended, no matter what the motive?

More Resources on
Susan Glaspell and "A Jury of Her Peers" and *Trifles*

In *ARIEL*

- Brief biography of Glaspell
- An excerpt from "A Jury of Her Peers" and an excerpt from *Trifles* with hyperlinked comments
- Video discussion of Glaspell
- Analysis of dramatic irony in *Trifles*
- Bibliography of scholarly works on Glaspell

In the Online Learning Center for *Responding to Literature*

- Brief biography of Glaspell
- List of major works by Glaspell
- Complete text of *Trifles*
- Web links to more resources on Glaspell
- Additional questions for experiencing and interpreting Glaspell's writing

NADINE GORDIMER (1923–   )

Town and Country Lovers

Nadine Gordimer was born in South Africa, the daughter of parents who had immigrated from Europe. The theme of all Gordimer's writing since her first novel, A World of Strangers (1958), has been the relationship between the races in South Africa. Apartheid became the official government policy in 1948. The population was officially classified according to racial category—Bantu (black), white, Colored (of mixed race), or Asian (Indian or Pakistani)—and the

different groups had different rights in terms of where they could live and work,
what property they could own, where they could travel, whether they could vote
and be represented in the government, and whom they could marry. Gordimer's
opposition to apartheid grew stronger over the years, and some of her later work
was banned in her own country, for example, Burger's Daughter, *a novel writ-*
ten in 1979 about a woman whose parents were imprisoned for their anti-
apartheid beliefs. In 1991 Gordimer won the Nobel Prize for literature, a
recognition of her success in showing readers around the world how apartheid
affected every aspect of South Africans' lives. In 1994 the South African govern-
ment, after decades of opposition by the black majority in South Africa and by
the people around the world, began dismantling the policies of apartheid.
Gordimer's latest novel, The House Gun *(1998), explores apartheid's legacy:*
the violence that still permeates South African society.

Dr. Franz-Josef von Leinsdorf is a geologist absorbed in his work;
wrapped up in it, as the saying goes—year after year the experience of this
work enfolds him, swaddling him away from the landscapes, the cities and the
people, wherever he lives: Peru, New Zealand, the United States. He's always
been like that, his mother could confirm from their native Austria. There, even
as a handsome small boy he presented only his profile to her: turned away to
his bits of rock and stone. His few relaxations have not changed much since
then. An occasional skiing trip, listening to music, reading poetry—Rainer
Maria Rilke° once stayed in his grandmother's hunting lodge in the forests of
Styria and the boy was introduced to Rilke's poems while very young.

Layer upon layer, country after country, wherever his work takes him—
and now he has been almost seven years in Africa. First the Côte d'Ivoire, and
for the past five years, South Africa. The shortage of skilled manpower brought
about his recruitment here. He has no interest in the politics of the countries
he works in. His private preoccupation-within-the-preoccupation of his work
has been research into underground water-courses, but the mining company
that employs him in a senior though not executive capacity is interested only
in mineral discovery. So he is much out in the field—which is the veld,°
here—seeking new gold, copper, platinum and uranium deposits. When he is
at home—on this particular job, in this particular country, this city—he lives
in a two-roomed flat in a suburban block with a landscaped garden, and does
his shopping at a supermarket conveniently across the street. He is not married—yet. That is how his colleagues, and the typists and secretaries at the mining company's head office, would define his situation. Both men and women
would describe him as a good-looking man, in a foreign way, with the lower
half of the face dark and middle-aged (his mouth is thin and curving, and no
matter how close-shaven his beard shows like fine shot embedded in the skin

---

Rainer Maria Rilke: Influential German poet (1875–1926).   *veld:* Grasslands.

round mouth and chin) and the upper half contradictorily young, with deep-set eyes (some would say grey, some black), thick eyelashes and brows. A tangled gaze: through which concentration and gleaming thoughtfulness perhaps appear as fire and languor. It is this that the women in the office mean when they remark he's not unattractive. Although the gaze seems to promise, he has never invited any one of them to go out with him. There is the general assumption he probably has a girl who's been picked for him, he's bespoken by one of his own kind, back home in Europe where he comes from. Many of these well-educated Europeans have no intention of becoming permanent immigrants; neither the remnant of white colonial life nor idealistic involvement with Black Africa appeals to them.

One advantage, at least, of living in underdeveloped or half-developed countries is that flats are serviced. All Dr. von Leinsdorf has to do for himself is buy his own supplies and cook an evening meal if he doesn't want to go to a restaurant. It is simply a matter of dropping in to the supermarket on his way from his car to his flat after work in the afternoon. He wheels a trolley up and down the shelves, and his simple needs are presented to him in the form of tins, packages, plastic-wrapped meat, cheeses, fruit and vegetables, tubes, bottles. . . . At the cashiers' counters where customers must converge and queue there are racks of small items uncategorized, for last-minute purchase. Here, as the coloured girl cashier punches the adding machine, he picks up cigarettes and perhaps a packet of salted nuts or a bar of nougat. Or razor-blades, when he remembers he's running short. One evening in winter he saw that the cardboard display was empty of the brand of blades he preferred, and he drew the cashier's attention to this. These young coloured girls are usually pretty unhelpful, taking money and punching their machines in a manner that asserts with the time-serving obstinacy of the half-literate the limit of any responsibility towards customers, but this one ran an alert glance over the selection of razor-blades, apologized that she was not allowed to leave her post, and said she would see that the stock was replenished "next time." A day or two later she recognized him, gravely, as he took his turn before her counter—"I ahssed them, but it's out of stock. You can't get it. I did ahss about it." He said this didn't matter. "When it comes in, I can keep a few packets for you." He thanked her.

He was away with the prospectors the whole of the next week. He arrived back in town just before nightfall on Friday, and was on his way from car to flat with his arms full of briefcase, suitcase and canvas bags when someone stopped him by standing timidly in his path. He was about to dodge round unseeingly on the crowded pavement but she spoke. "We got the blades in now. I didn't see you in the shop this week, but I kept some for when you come. So . . ."

He recognized her. He had never seen her standing before, and she was   5
wearing a coat. She was rather small and finely-made, for one of them. The coat was skimpy but no big backside jutted. The cold brought an apricot-

graining of warm color to her cheekbones, beneath which a very small face was quite delicately hollowed, and the skin was smooth, the subdued satiny color of certain yellow wood. That crêpey hair, but worn drawn back flat and in a little knot pushed into one of the cheap wool chignons that (he recognized also) hung in the miscellany of small goods along with the razor-blades, at the supermarket. He said thanks, he was in a hurry, he'd only just got back from a trip—shifting the burdens he carried, to demonstrate. "Oh shame." She acknowledged his load. "But if you want I can run in and get it for you quickly. If you want."

He saw at once it was perfectly clear that all the girl meant was that she would go back to the supermarket, buy the blades and bring the packet to him there where he stood, on the pavement. And it seemed that it was this certainty that made him say, in the kindly tone of assumption used for an obliging underling, "I live just across there—*Atlantis*—that flat building. Could you drop them by, for me—number seven-hundred-and-eighteen, seventh floor—"

She had not before been inside one of these big flat buildings near where she worked. She lived a bus- and train-ride away to the West of the city, but this side of the black townships, in a township for people her tint. There was a pool with ferns, not plastic, and even a little waterfall pumped electrically over rocks, in the entrance of the building *Atlantis;* she didn't wait for the lift marked goods but took the one meant for whites and a white woman with one of those sausage-dogs on a lead got in with her but did not pay her any attention. The corridors leading to the flats were nicely glassed-in, not draughty.

He wondered if he should give her a twenty-cent piece for her trouble—ten cents would be right for a black; but she said, "Oh no—please, here—" standing outside his open door and awkwardly pushing back at his hand the change from the money he'd given her for the razor-blades. She was smiling, for the first time, in the dignity of refusing a tip. It was difficult to know how to treat these people, in this country; to know what they expected. In spite of her embarrassing refusal of the coin, she stood there, completely unassuming, fists thrust down the pockets of her cheap coat against the cold she'd come in from, rather pretty thin legs neatly aligned, knee to knee, ankle to ankle.

"Would you like a cup of coffee or something?"

10   He couldn't very well take her into his study-cum-living room and offer her a drink. She followed him to his kitchen, but at the sight of her pulling out the single chair to drink her cup of coffee at the kitchen table, he said, "No—bring it in here—" and led the way into the big room where, among his books and his papers, his files of scientific correspondence (and the cigar boxes of stamps from the envelopes), his racks of records, his specimens of minerals and rocks, he lived alone.

It was no trouble to her; she saved him the trips to the supermarket and brought him his groceries two or three times a week. All he had to do was to leave a list and the key under the doormat, and she would come up in her lunch-hour to collect them, returning to put his supplies in the flat after work.

Sometimes he was home and sometimes not. He bought a box of chocolates and left it, with a note, for her to find; and that was acceptable, apparently, as a gratuity.

Her eyes went over everything in the flat although her body tried to conceal its sense of being out of place by remaining as still as possible, holding its contours in the chair offered her as a stranger's coat is set aside and remains exactly as left until the owner takes it up to go. "You collect?"

"Well, these are specimens—connected with my work."

"My brother used to collect. Miniatures. With brandy and whisky and that, in them. From all over. Different countries."

The second time she watched him grinding coffee for the cup he had   15
offered her she said, "You always do that? Always when you make coffee?"

"But of course. Is it no good, for you? Do I make it too strong?"

"Oh it's just I'm not used to it. We buy it ready—you know, it's in a bottle, you just add a bit to the milk or water."

He laughed, instructive: "That's not coffee, that's a synthetic flavoring. In my country we drink only real coffee, fresh, from the beans—you smell how good it is as it's being ground?"

She was stopped by the caretaker and asked what she wanted in the building. Heavy with the *bona fides*° of groceries clutched to her body, she said she was working at number 718, on the seventh floor. The caretaker did not tell her not to use the whites' lift; after all, she was not black; her family was very light-skinned.

There was the item "gray button for trousers" on one of his shopping   20
lists. She said as she unpacked the supermarket carrier, "Give me the pants, so long, then," and sat on his sofa that was always gritty with fragments of pipe tobacco, sewing in and out through the four holes of the button with firm, fluent movements of the right hand, gestures supplying the articulacy missing from her talk. She had a little yokel's, peasant's (he thought of it) gap between her two front teeth when she smiled that he didn't much like, but, face ellipsed to three-quarter angle, eyes cast down in concentration with soft lips almost closed, this didn't matter. He said, watching her sew, "You're a good girl"; and touched her.

She remade the bed every late afternoon when they left it and she dressed again before she went home. After a week there was a day when late afternoon became evening, and they were still in the bed.

"Can't you stay the night?"

"My mother," she said.

"Phone her. Make an excuse." He was a foreigner. He had been in the country five years, but he didn't understand that people don't usually have telephones in their houses, where she lived. She got up to dress. He didn't want

bona fides: Latin for "good faith"; here, evidence of her legitimate reason for being in the building.

that tender body to go out in the night cold and kept hindering her with the interruption of his hands; saying nothing. Before she put on her coat, when the body had already disappeared, he spoke. "But you must make some arrangement."

25   "Oh my mother!" Her face opened to fear and vacancy he could not read.

He was not entirely convinced the woman would think of her daughter as some pure and unsullied virgin. . . . "Why?"

The girl said, "S'e'll be scared. S'e'll be scared we get caught."

"Don't tell her anything. Say I'm employing you." In this country he was working in now there were generally rooms on the roofs of flat buildings for tenants' servants.

She said: "That's what I told the caretaker."

30   She ground fresh coffee beans every time he wanted a cup while he was working at night. She never attempted to cook anything until she had watched in silence while he did it the way he liked, and she learned to reproduce exactly the simple dishes he preferred. She handled his pieces of rock and stone, at first admiring the colors—"It'd make a beautiful ring or a necklace, ay." Then he showed her the striations, the formation of each piece, and explained what each was, and how, in the long life of the earth, it had been formed. He named the mineral it yielded, and what that was used for. He worked at his papers, writing, writing, every night, so it did not matter that they could not go out together to public places. On Sundays she got into his car in the basement garage and they drove to the country and picnicked away up in the Magaliesberg, where there was no one. He read or poked about among the rocks; they climbed together, to the mountain pools. He taught her to swim. She had never seen the sea. She squealed and shrieked in the water, showing the gap between her teeth, as—it crossed his mind—she must do when among her own people. Occasionally he had to go out to dinner at the houses of colleagues from the mining company; she sewed and listened to the radio in the flat and he found her in the bed, warm and already asleep, by the time he came in. He made his way into her body without speaking; she made him welcome without a word. Once he put on evening dress for a dinner at his country's consulate; watching him brush one or two fallen hairs from the shoulders of the dark jacket that sat so well on him, she saw a huge room, all chandeliers and people dancing some dance from a costume film—stately, hand-to-hand. She supposed he was going to fetch, in her place in the car, a partner for the evening. They never kissed when either left the flat; he said, suddenly, kindly, pausing as he picked up cigarettes and keys, "Don't be lonely." And added, "Wouldn't you like to visit your family sometimes, when I have to go out?"

He had told her he was going home to his mother in the forests and mountains of his country near the Italian border (he showed her on the map) after Christmas. She had not told him how her mother, not knowing there was any other variety, assumed he was a medical doctor, so she had talked to her about the doctor's children and the doctor's wife who was a very kind lady, glad to have someone who could help out in the surgery as well as the flat.

She remarked wonderingly on his ability to work until midnight or later, after a day at work. She was so tired when she came home from her cash register at the supermarket that once dinner was eaten she could scarcely keep awake. He explained in a way she could understand that while the work she did was repetitive, undemanding of any real response from her intelligence, requiring little mental or physical effort and therefore unrewarding, his work was his greatest interest, it taxed his mental capacities to their limit, exercised all his concentration, and rewarded him constantly as much with the excitement of a problem presented as with the satisfaction of a problem solved. He said later, putting away his papers, speaking out of a silence: "Have you done other kinds of work?" She said, "I was in a clothing factory before. Sportbeau shirts; you know? But the pay's better in the shop."

Of course. Being a conscientious newspaper-reader in every country he lived in, he was aware that it was only recently that the retail consumer trade in this one had been allowed to employ coloreds as shop assistants; even punching a cash register represented advancement. With the continuing shortage of semi-skilled whites a girl like this might be able to edge a little farther into the white-collar category. He began to teach her to type. He was aware that her English was poor, even though, as a foreigner, in his ears her pronunciation did not offend, nor categorize her as it would in those of someone of his education whose mother tongue was English. He corrected her grammatical mistakes but missed the less obvious ones because of his own sometimes exotic English usage—she continued to use the singular pronoun "it" when what was required was the plural "they." Because he was a foreigner (although so clever, as she saw) she was less inhibited than she might have been by the words she knew she misspelled in her typing. While she sat at the typewriter she thought how one day she would type notes for him, as well as making coffee the way he liked it, and taking him inside her body without saying anything, and sitting (even if only through the empty streets of quiet Sundays) beside him in his car, like a wife.

On a summer night near Christmas—he had already bought and hidden a slightly showy but nevertheless good watch he thought she would like—there was a knocking at the door that brought her out of the bathroom and him to his feet, at his work-table. No one ever came to the flat at night; he had no friends intimate enough to drop in without warning. The summons was an imperious banging that did not pause and clearly would not stop until the door was opened.

She stood in the open bathroom doorway gazing at him across the passage into the living-room; her bare feet and shoulders were free of a big bath-towel. She said nothing, did not even whisper. The flat seemed to shake with the strong unhurried blows.

35

He made as if to go to the door, at last, but now she ran and clutched him by both arms. She shook her head wildly; her lips drew back but her teeth were clenched, she didn't speak. She pulled him into the bedroom, snatched some clothes from the clean laundry laid out on the bed and got into the wall-cupboard, thrusting the key at his hand. Although his arms and calves felt weakly cold he was horrified, distastefully embarrassed at the sight of her pressed back crouching there under his suits and coat; it was horrible and ridiculous. *Come out!* he whispered. *No! Come out!* She hissed: *Where? Where can I go?*

Never mind! Get out of there!

He put out his hand to grasp her. At bay, she said with all the force of her terrible whisper, baring the gap in her teeth: *I'll throw myself out the window.*

She forced the key into his hand like the handle of a knife. He closed the door on her face and drove the key home in the lock, then dropped it among coins in his trouser pocket.

40   He unslotted the chain that was looped across the flat door. He turned the serrated knob of the Yale lock. The three policemen, two in plain clothes, stood there without impatience although they had been banging on the door for several minutes. The big dark one with an elaborate moustache held out in a hand wearing a plaited gilt ring some sort of identity card.

Dr. von Leinsdorf said quietly, the blood coming strangely back to legs and arms, "What is it?"

The sergeant told him they knew there was a colored girl in the flat. They had had information; "I been watching this flat three months, I know."

"I am alone here." Dr. von Leinsdorf did not raise his voice.

"I know, I know who is here. Come—" And the sergeant and his two assistants went into the living-room, the kitchen, the bathroom (the sergeant picked up a bottle of after-shave cologne, seemed to study the French label) and the bedroom. The assistants removed the clean laundry that was laid upon the bed and then turned back the bedding, carrying the sheets over to be examined by the sergeant under the lamp. They talked to one another in Afrikaans, which the Doctor did not understand. The sergeant himself looked under the bed, and lifted the long curtains at the window. The wall cupboard was of the kind that has no knobs; he saw that it was locked and began to ask in Afrikaans, then politely changed to English, "Give us the key."

45   Dr. von Leinsdorf said, "I'm sorry, I left it at my office—I always lock and take my keys with me in the mornings."

"It's no good, man, you better give me the key."

He smiled a little, reasonably. "It's on my office desk."

The assistants produced a screwdriver and he watched while they inserted it where the cupboard doors met, gave it quick, firm but not forceful leverage. He heard the lock give.

She had been naked, it was true, when they knocked. But now she was wearing a long-sleeved T-shirt with an appliquéd butterfly motif on one breast, and a pair of jeans. Her feet were still bare; she had managed, by feel, in the dark, to get into some of the clothing she had snatched from the bed, but she had no shoes. She had perhaps been weeping behind the cupboard door (her cheeks looked stained) but now her face was sullen and she was breathing heavily, her diaphragm contracting and expanding exaggeratedly and her breasts pushing against the cloth. It made her appear angry; it might simply have been that she was half-suffocated in the cupboard and needed oxygen. She did not look at Dr. von Leinsdorf. She would not reply to the sergeant's questions.

They were taken to the police station where they were at once separated and in turn led for examination by the district surgeon. The man's underwear was taken away and examined, as the sheets had been, for signs of his seed. When the girl was undressed, it was discovered that beneath her jeans she was wearing a pair of men's briefs with his name on the neatly-sewn laundry tag; in her haste, she had taken the wrong garment to her hiding-place.

Now she cried, standing there before the district surgeon in a man's underwear.

He courteously pretended not to notice it. He handed briefs, jeans and T-shirt round the door, and motioned her to lie on a white-sheeted high table where he placed her legs apart, resting in stirrups, and put into her where the other had made his way so warmly a cold hard instrument that expanded wider and wider. Her thighs and knees trembled uncontrollably while the doctor looked into her and touched her deep inside with more hard instruments, carrying wafers of gauze.

When she came out of the examining room back to the charge office, Dr. von Leinsdorf was not there; they must have taken him somewhere else. She spent what was left of the night in a cell, as he must be doing; but early in the morning she was released and taken home to her mother's house in the colored township by a white man who explained he was the clerk of the lawyer who had been engaged for her by Dr. von Leinsdorf. Dr. von Leinsdorf, the clerk said, had also been bailed out that morning. He did not say when, or if, she would see him again.

A statement made by the girl to the police was handed in to Court when she and the man appeared to meet charges of contravening the Immorality Act in a Johannesburg flat on the night of — December, 19— *I lived with the white man in his flat. He had intercourse with me sometimes. He gave me tablets to take to prevent me becoming pregnant.*

Interviewed by the Sunday papers, the girl said, "I'm sorry for the sadness brought to my mother." She said she was one of nine children of a female laundry worker. She had left school in Standard Three° because there was no money at home for gym clothes or a school blazer. She had worked as a

50

55

Standard Three: Eighth grade in the South African school system.

machinist in a factory and a cashier in a supermarket. Dr. von Leinsdorf taught her to type his notes.

Dr. Franz-Josef von Leinsdorf, described as the grandson of a baroness, a cultured man engaged in international mineralogical research, said he accepted social distinctions between people but didn't think they should be legally imposed. "Even in my own country it's difficult for a person from a higher class to marry one from a lower class."

The two accused gave no evidence. They did not greet or speak to each other in Court. The Defense argued that the sergeant's evidence that they had been living together as man and wife was hearsay. (The woman with the dachshund, the caretaker?) The magistrate acquitted them because the State failed to prove carnal intercourse had taken place on the night of — December, 19—.

The girl's mother was quoted, with photograph, in the Sunday papers: "I won't let my daughter work as a servant for a white man again."   *1980*

CONSIDERATIONS

1. If you erased the occupations and backgrounds of Franz and the unnamed young woman, how would you expect this story to end, given the journey their relationship was taking? Who was more loving in this relationship? Explain.
2. In what way is the relationship between Franz and the young woman typical of any two people who are courting? In what way do they change each other? Explain.
3. The woman in this story is never named while Franz is always addressed by his professional name. How does the way the two characters are presented relate to a central conflict in this story?
4. Comment on Gordimer's style. Find two or three places where she omits transitions of time, and assess the effect of this strategy on you as a reader. In what ways does this absence of clearly stated time transitions reflect the true relationship between the two lovers?
5. What are the beliefs and attitudes of the South African government and culture (at the time the story takes place) that cause the lovers' actions to be viewed as a crime? How will the lovers' futures be affected without one another's company? Who, do you think, will suffer the most?

RITA DOVE (1952–   )

Second-Hand Man

Poet laureate of the United States from 1993 to 1995, Rita Dove was born in 1952 in Akron, Ohio. Her father was the first African-American chemist to break the racial barrier in the tire and rubber industry. After graduating from Miami University in Ohio, Dove attended the University of Tübingen in Germany and then the University of Iowa Writers' Workshop, where she met her future husband, German-born writer Fred Viebahn. She published two chapbooks of poems before her official literary debut with the poetry collection Yellow House on the Corner *in 1980. Since then she has published eight other books of poetry, including* Thomas and Beulah *(1986), for which she won the Pulitzer Prize for poetry in 1987. Although primarily a poet, she has also published a novel (*Through the Ivory Gate, *1992), a play (*The Darker Face of the Earth, *1994), and a volume of short stories (*Fifth Sunday, *1985), the source of the selection here. Most of Dove's writings have an autobiographical base, ranging from her travels in Europe (*Museum, *1983) to scenes from middle-class black life (*Grace Notes, *1989) to the story of her maternal grandparents (*Thomas and Beulah*), who both grew up in the South in the early years of the twentieth century. Currently, Dove teaches English at the University of Virginia in Charlottesville.*

Virginia couldn't stand it when someone tried to shorten her name—like *Ginny,* for example. But James Evans didn't. He set his twelve-string guitar down real slow.

"Miss Virginia," he said, "you're a fine piece of woman."

Seemed he'd been asking around. Knew everything about her. Knew she was bold and proud and didn't cotton to no silly niggers. Vir-gin-ee-a he said, nice and slow. Almost Russian, the way he said it. Right then and there she knew this man was for her.

He courted her just inside a year, came by nearly every day. First she wouldn't see him for more than half an hour at a time. She'd send him away; he knew better than to try to force her. Another fellow did that once—kept coming by when she said she had other things to do. She told him he do it once more, she'd be waiting at the door with a pot of scalding water to teach him some manners. Did, too. Fool didn't believe her—she had the pot waiting on the stove and when he came up those stairs, she was standing in the door. He took one look at her face and turned and ran. He was lucky those steps were so steep. She only got a little piece of his pant leg.

No, James knew his stuff. He'd come on time and stay till she told him   5
he needed to go.

She'd met him out at Summit Beach one day. In the Twenties, that was the place to go on hot summer days! Clean yellow sand all around the lake, and an amusement park that ran from morning to midnight. She went there with a couple of girl friends. They were younger than her and a little silly. But they were sweet. Virginia was nineteen then. "High time," everyone used to say to her, but she'd just lift her head and go on about her business. She weren't going to marry just any old Negro. He had to be perfect.

There was a man who was chasing her around about that time, too. Tall dark Negro—Sterling Williams was his name. Pretty as a panther. Married, he was. Least that's what everyone said. Left a wife in Washington, D.C. A little crazy, the wife—poor Sterling was trying to get a divorce.

Well, Sterling was at Summit Beach that day, too. He followed Virginia around, trying to buy her root beer. Everybody loved root beer that summer. Root beer and vanilla ice cream—the Boston Cooler. But she wouldn't pay him no mind. People said she was crazy—Sterling was the best catch in Akron, they said.

"Not for me," Virginia said. "I don't want no second-hand man."

10   But Sterling wouldn't give up. He kept buying root beers and having to drink them himself.

Then she saw James. He'd just come up from Tennessee, working his way up on the riverboats. Folks said his best friend had been lynched down there and he turned his back on the town and said he was never coming back. Well, when she saw this cute little man in a straw hat and a twelve-string guitar under his arm, she got a little flustered. Her girlfriends whispered around to find out who he was, but she acted like she didn't even see him.

He was the hit of Summit Beach. Played that twelve-string guitar like a devil. They'd take off their shoes and sit on the beach toward evening. All the girls loved James. "Oh, Jimmy," they'd squeal, "play us a *loooove* song!" He'd laugh and pick out a tune:

> I'll give you a dollar if you'll come out tonight
> If you'll come out tonight,
> If you'll come out tonight.
> I'll give you a dollar if you'll come out tonight
> And dance by the light of the moon.

Then the girls would giggle. "Jimmy," they screamed, "you outta be 'shamed of yourself!" He'd sing the second verse then:

> I danced with a girl with a hole in her stockin',
> And her heel kep 'a-rockin',
> And her heel kep 'a-rockin';
> I danced with a girl with a hole in her stockin',
> And we danced by the light of the moon.

Then they'd all priss and preen their feathers and wonder which would be best—to be in fancy clothes and go on being courted by these dull factory fellows, or to have a hole in their stockings and dance with James.

Virginia never danced. She sat a bit off to one side and watched them   *15*
make fools of themselves.

Then one night near season's end, they were all sitting down by the
water, and everyone had on sweaters and was in a foul mood because the cold
weather was coming and there wouldn't be no more parties. Someone said
something about hating having the good times end, and James struck up a nice
and easy tune, looking across the fire straight at Virginia:

> As I was lumb'ring down de street,
> Down de street, down de street,
> A han some gal I chanced to meet,
> Oh, she was fair to view!
>
> I'd like to make dat gal my wife,
> Gal my wife, gal my wife.
> I'd be happy all my life
> If I had her by me.

She knew he was the man. She'd known it a long while, but she was just
biding her time. He called on her the next day. She said she was busy canning
peaches. He came back the day after. They sat on the porch and watched the
people go by. He didn't talk much, except to say her name like that:

"Vir–gin–ee–a," he said, "you're a mighty fine woman."

She sent him home a little after that. He showed up again a week later.
She was angry at him and told him she didn't have time for playing around.
But he'd brought his twelve-string guitar, and he said he'd been practicing all
week just to play a couple of songs for her. She let him in then and made him
sit on the stool while she sat on the porch swing. He sang the first song. It was
a floor thumper.

> There is a gal in our town,
> She wears a yellow striped gown,
> And when she walks the streets aroun',
> The hollow of her foot makes a hole in the ground.
>
> Ol' folks, young folks, cl'ar the kitchen,
> Ol' folks, young folks, cl'ar the kitchen,
> Ol' Virginny never tire.

She got a little mad then, but she knew he was baiting her. Seeing how   *20*
much she would take. She knew he wasn't singing about her, and she'd already
heard how he said her name. It was time to let the dog in out of the rain, even
if he shook his wet all over the floor. So she leaned back and put her hands on
her hips, real slow.

"I just *know* you ain't singing about me."

"Virginia," he replied, with a grin would've put Rudolph Valentino to
shame, "I'd *never* sing about you that way."

He pulled a yellow scarf out of his trouser pocket. Like melted butter it was, with fringes.

"I saw it yesterday and thought how nice it would look against your skin," he said.

25   That was the first present she ever accepted from a man. Then he sang his other song:

> I'm coming, I'm coming!
> Virginia, I'm coming to stay.
> Don't hold it agin' me
> For running away.
>
> And if I can win ya,
> I'll never more roam,
> I'm coming Virginia,
> My dixie land home.

She was gone for him. Not like those girls on the beach: she had enough sense left to crack a joke or two. "You saying I look like the state of Virginia?" she asked, and he laughed. But she was gone.

She didn't let him know it, though, not for a long while. Even when he asked her to marry him, eight months later, he was trembling and thought she just might refuse out of some woman's whim. No, he courted her proper. Every day for a little while. They'd sit on the porch until it got too cold and then they'd sit in the parlor with two or three bright lamps on. Her mother and father were glad Virginia'd found a beau, but they weren't taking any chances. Everything had to be proper.

He got down, all trembly, on one knee and asked her to be his wife. She said yes. There's a point when all this dignity and stuff get in the way of Destiny. He kept on trembling; he didn't believe her.

"What?" he said.

30   "I said yes," Virginia answered. She was starting to get angry. Then he saw that she meant it, and he went into the other room to ask her father for her hand in marriage.

But people are too curious for their own good, and there's some things they never need to know, but they're going to find them out one way or the other. James had come all the way up from Tennessee and that should have been far enough, but he couldn't hide that snake any more. It just crawled out from under the rock when it was good and ready.

The snake was Jeremiah Morgan. Some fellows from Akron had gone off for work on the riverboats, and some of these fellows had heard about James. That twelve-string guitar and straw hat of his had made him pretty popular. So, story got to town that James had a baby somewhere. And joined up to this baby—but long dead and buried—was a wife.

Virginia had been married six months when she found out from sweettalking, side-stepping Jeremiah Morgan who never liked her no-how after she'd laid his soul to rest one night when he'd taken her home from a dance. (She always carried a brick in her purse—no man could get the best of her!)

Jeremiah must have been the happiest man in Akron the day he found out. He found it out later than most people—things like that have a way of circulating first among those who know how to keep it from spreading to the wrong folks—then when the gossip's gotten to everyone else, it's handed over to the one who knows what to do with it.

"Ask that husband of your'n what else he left in Tennessee besides his   *35* best friend," was all Jeremiah said at first.

No no-good Negro like Jeremiah Morgan could make Virginia beg for information. She wouldn't bite.

"I ain't got no need for asking my husband nothing," she said, and walked away. She was going to choir practice.

He stood where he was, yelled after her like any old common person. "Mrs. Evans always talking about being Number 1! It looks like she's Number 2 after all."

Her ears burned from the shame of it. She went on to choir practice and sang her prettiest; and straight when she was back home she asked:

"What's all this number two business?"   *40*

James broke down and told her the whole story—how he'd been married before, when he was seventeen, and his wife dying in childbirth and the child not quite right because of being blue when it was born. And how when his friend was strung up he saw no reason for staying. And how when he met Virginia, he found out pretty quick what she'd done to Sterling Williams and that she'd never have no second-hand man, and he had to have her, so he never said a word about his past.

She took off her coat and hung it in the front closet. She unpinned her hat and set it in its box on the shelf. She reached in the back of the closet and brought out his hunting rifle and the box of bullets. She didn't see no way out but to shoot him.

"Put that down!" he shouted. "I love you!"

"You were right not to tell me," she said, "because I sure as sin wouldn't have married you. I don't want you now."

"Virginia!" he said. He was real scared. "How can you shoot me down   *45* like this?"

No, she couldn't shoot him when he stood there looking at her with those sweet brown eyes, telling her how much he loved her.

"You have to sleep sometime," she said, and sat down to wait.

He didn't sleep for three nights. He knew she meant business. She sat up in their best chair with the rifle across her lap, but he wouldn't sleep. He sat at the table and told her over and over that he loved her and he hadn't known what else to do at the time.

"When I get through killing you," she told him. "I'm going to write to Tennessee and have them send that baby up here. It won't do, farming a child out to any relative with an extra plate."

50   She held onto that rifle. Not that he would have taken it from her—not that that would've saved him. No, the only thing would've saved him was running away. But he wouldn't run either.

Sitting there, Virginia had lots of time to think. He was afraid of what she might do, but he wouldn't leave her, either. Some of what he was saying began to sink in. He had lied, but that was the only way to get her—she could see the reasoning behind that. And except for that, he was perfect. It was hardly like having a wife before at all. And the baby—anyone could see the marriage wasn't meant to be anyway.

On the third day about midnight, she laid down the rifle.

"You will join the choir and settle down instead of plucking on that guitar anytime anyone drop a hat," she said. "And we will write to your aunt in Tennessee and have that child sent up here." Then she put the rifle back in the closet.

The child never made it up to Ohio—it had died a month before Jeremiah ever opened his mouth. That hit James hard. He thought it was his fault and all, but Virginia made him see the child was sick and was probably better off with its Maker than it would be living out half a life.

55   James made a good tenor in the choir. The next spring, Virginia had her first baby and they decided to name her Belle. That's French for beautiful. And she was, too.   *1985*

CONSIDERATIONS

1. Comment on Dove's style and tone in this piece. How effective do you find it? Why might Dove have chosen to write it in this way? Explain.
2. How do you think Virginia came to be so independent, so different from other girls her age? What might have contributed to her steadfastness against "a second-hand man"?
3. What role does the color yellow play in this story? What does it reveal about Virginia? About James? About love, perhaps?
4. Although "running away" would have saved James from Virginia's rifle, why doesn't he leave? Why does Virginia decide to spare his life in the end? Explain.
5. What might be the author's purpose in writing this piece? In other words, what do you think her own thoughts are on men, marriage, and love? Does your philosophy on these same topics match hers? Explain.

More Resources on
Rita Dove

In *ARIEL*
- Brief biography of Dove
- Complete texts of several of Dove's poems, including "Dusting" and "Testimonial," both with hyperlinked comments
- Video clip of Dove reading her poem "Canary"
- Analysis of understatement in Dove's writing
- Bibliography of scholarly works on Dove

In the Online Learning Center for *Responding to Literature*
- Brief biography of Dove
- List of major works by Dove
- Web links to more resources on Dove.

Poetry

SAPPHO (c. 610 B.C.–c. 580 B.C.)
To me he seems like a god

TRANSLATED BY WILLIS BARNSTONE

Although little is known of her life, Sappho is acknowledged as the finest woman poet of the ancient world. Born to an aristocratic Greek family, she wrote poetry that was extremely innovative for its time because of her use of common language rather than the formal diction used by conventional poets.

To me he seems like a god
as he sits facing you and
hears you near as you speak
softly and laugh
in a sweet echo that jolts   5
the heart in my ribs. For now
as I look at you my voice
is empty and

can say nothing as my tongue
10   cracks and slender fire is quick
under my skin. My eyes are dead
to light, my ears
pound, and sweat pours over me.
I convulse, paler than grass,
15   and feel my mind slip as I
go close to death

[but must suffer all, being poor.]   *c. 6th century* B.C.

CONSIDERATIONS

1. From clues in the poem, what can you surmise about the speaker, her life, and her work?
2. Would you characterize the effects the man has on the speaker as the result of a great love or something else? Explain.

WILLIAM SHAKESPEARE (1564–1616)

Let me not to the marriage of true minds

For biographical information about William Shakespeare, see page 244.

Let me not to the marriage of true minds
Admit impediments. Love is not love
Which alters when it alteration finds,
Or bends with the remover to remove:
5   Oh, no! it is an ever-fixéd mark,
That looks on tempests and is never shaken;
It is the star to every wandering bark,
Whose worth's unknown, although his height be taken.
Love's not Time's fool, though rosy lips and cheeks
10   Within his bending sickle's compass come;
Love alters not with his brief hours and weeks,
But bears it out even to the edge of doom.
     If this be error and upon me proved,
     I never writ, nor no man ever loved.   *1609*

CONSIDERATIONS

1. On what basic belief about love does this sonnet rely? How realistic do you think this belief about love is for most couples? Explain.
2. What purpose do the final two lines serve in relation to the rest of the sonnet?

More Resources on
William Shakespeare and
"Let me not to the marriage of true minds"

 In *ARIEL*

- Brief biography of Shakespeare
- Text of several additional sonnets
- Audio clip of reading of "Let me not to the marriage of true minds" and of "Shall I compare thee to a summer's day?"
- Analysis of the sonnet form
- Bibliography of scholarly works on Shakespeare

 In the Online Learning Center for *Responding to Literature*

- Brief biography of Shakespeare
- List of major works by Shakespeare
- Web links to more resources on Shakespeare
- Additional questions for experiencing and interpreting Shakespeare's writing

 ## JOHN DONNE (1572–1631)
The Sun Rising

For biographical information about John Donne, see page 1186.

> Busy old fool, unruly sun,
> Why dost thou thus,
> Through windows, and through curtains call on us?
> Must to thy motions lovers' seasons run?
> Saucy pedantic wretch, go chide   5
> Late schoolboys, and sour prentices,

Go tell court-huntsmen that the King will ride,
    Call country ants to harvest offices;
Love, all alike, no season knows, nor clime,
10   Nor hours, days, months, which are the rags of time.

        Thy beams, so reverend and strong
            Why shouldst thou think?
I could eclipse and cloud them with a wink,
But that I would not lose her sight so long;
15   If her eyes have not blinded thine,
            Look, and tomorrow late, tell me
Whether both the Indias of spice and mine
Be where thou left'st them, or lie here with me.
Ask for those kings whom thou saw'st yesterday,
20   And thou shalt hear, All here in one bed lay.

        She's all states, and all princes, I,
            Nothing else is.
Princes do but play us; compared to this,
All's honor's mimic, all wealth alchemy.
25   Thou, sun, art half as happy as we,
            In that the world's contracted thus;
Thine age asks ease, and since thy duties be
To warm the world, that's done in warming us.
Shine here to us, and thou art everywhere;
30   This bed thy center is, these walls, thy sphere.   *1633*

CONSIDERATIONS

1. Go through this poem and note all the exaggerations that Donne uses. What effect do such exaggerations achieve?
2. Consider the order, or syntax, of the words in this poem. What effect does the author achieve by regularly withholding verbs until the end of his lines? What might be his purpose in arranging the words in this manner?
3. How would you describe the narrator's tone in this piece? In what ways does his tone relate to the theme of men and women—and love?
4. While many poets use the moon as a symbol of love, Donne chooses to use the sun as his focal point. What are the implications of the sun, and how do these implications change from one stanza to the next? Explain.

More Resources on
John Donne and "The Sun Rising"

In *ARIEL*

- Brief biography of Donne
- Text of "The Sun Rising," with hyperlinked comments, in addition to several other hyperlinked Donne poems
- Audio clip of dramatic reading of "The Sun Rising" and of "Death, be not proud"
- Video clip of documentary on the metaphysical poets
- Analysis of figurative language in Donne's writing
- Bibliography of scholarly works on Donne

ANDREW MARVELL (1621–1678)
To His Coy Mistress

> *Born in Yorkshire, England, Andrew Marvell was educated at Cambridge and then traveled on the European continent for four years. Following his return to England, he supported the Puritans during the civil war, although he was not himself a member of the Puritan party. Just before the restoration of the monarchy in 1660, Marvell was elected to Parliament, where he continued to serve for the rest of his life. In addition to his love poems, for which he is best known today, Marvell also wrote and published many political satires.*

Had we but world enough, and time,
This coyness, lady, were no crime.
We would sit down, and think which way
To walk, and pass our long love's day.
Thou by the Indian Ganges'° side   5
Shoudst rubies find; I by the tide
Of Humber° would complain. I would
Love you ten years before the flood,
And you should, if you please, refuse
Till the conversion of the Jews.   10

---

5 *Ganges:* River in northern India. 7 *Humber:* Estuary in northern England formed by the Ouse and Trent rivers.

My vegetable love should grow
Vaster than empires and more slow;
An hundred years should go to praise
Thine eyes, and on thy forehead gaze;
15   Two hundred to adore each breast,
But thirty thousand to the rest;
An age at least to every part,
And the last age should show your heart.
For, lady, you deserve this state,
20   Nor would I love at lower rate.
      But at my back I always hear
Time's wingèd chariot hurrying near;
And yonder all before us lie
Deserts of vast eternity.
25   Thy beauty shall no more be found;
Nor, in thy marble vault, shall sound
My echoing song; then worms shall try
That long-preserved virginity,
And your quaint honor turn to dust,
30   And into ashes all my lust:
The grave's a fine and private place,
But none, I think, do there embrace.
      Now therefore, while the youthful hue
Sits on thy skin like morning dew
35   And while thy willing soul transpires
At every pore with instant fires,
Now let us sport us while we may,
And now, like amorous birds of prey,
Rather at once our time devour
40   Than languish in his slow-chapped power.
Let us roll all our strength and all
Our sweetness up into one ball,
And tear our pleasures with rough strife
Thorough the iron gates of life:
45   Thus, though we cannot make our sun
Stand still, yet we will make him run.   *1681*

CONSIDERATIONS

1. What subject—love or time—is the main theme of this poem? How do the
   images of the poem connect and relate the two?

2. Write a prose version of this argument, listing each new point separately. How convincing do you find the argument? Explain your reasons.
3. Imagine that you are the woman to whom this poem is addressed. Write a letter giving the speaker your answer. Consider each point of his argument in your response.

APHRA BEHN (1640–1689)

The Willing Mistress

> *In* A Room of One's Own, *Virginia Woolf said, "All women together ought to let flowers fall upon the tomb of Aphra Behn, for it was she who earned them the right to speak their minds." Woolf's tribute refers to Behn's unprecedented literary career. Widowed in 1666, she desperately needed a way to support herself. She turned first to working as a spy for King Charles II in Antwerp and then, in 1670, published her first play,* The Forced Marriage. *In doing so, she became the first woman in the history of England to earn her living by writing. In addition to her plays, for which she is best known, Behn also wrote poems such as "The Willing Mistress," first published in 1673.*

Amyntas led me to a grove,
   Where all the trees did shade us;
The sun itself, though it had strove,
   It could not have betrayed us.
The place secured from human eyes   5
   No other fear allows
But when the winds that gently rise
   Do kiss the yielding boughs.

Down there we sat upon the moss,
   And did begin to play   10
A thousand amorous tricks, to pass
   The heat of all the day.
A many kisses did he give
   And I returned the same,
Which made me willing to receive   15
   That which I dare not name.

His charming eyes no aid required
   To tell their softening tale;
On her that was already fired
   'Twas easy to prevail.   20

598   LOVE AND HATE

He did but kiss and clasp me round,
   Whilst those his thoughts expressed:
And laid me gently on the ground;
   Ah who can guess the rest?   *1673*

CONSIDERATIONS

1. What does the language of the poem suggest about the speaker's attitude toward sexual love? Cite specific images to support your view.
2. Compare the view of women suggested by this poem to the view of women suggested by "To His Coy Mistress."
3. This poem is part of a play, in which it is sung by a maidservant to her mistress. Create the scene that leads up to the maid's decision to reveal this love affair to the woman who employs her.

CHRISTOPHER MARLOWE (1564–1593)

The Passionate Shepherd to His Love

> *Born in Canterbury, Christopher Marlowe attended Cambridge University, intending to become a priest. His career as a writer led him to set aside this plan. In 1593, he was arrested for being an atheist, but he was murdered before he was brought to trial. Best known for his plays, Marlowe also wrote and published many poems.*

Come live with me and be my love,
And we will all the pleasures prove
That valleys, groves, hills, and fields,
Woods, or steepy mountain yields.

5   And we will sit upon the rocks,
Seeing the shepherds feed their flocks,
By shallow rivers to whose falls
Melodious birds sing madrigals.

And I will make thee beds of roses
10 And a thousand fragrant posies,
A cap of flowers, and a kirtle
Embroidered all with leaves of myrtle;

A gown made of the finest wool
Which from our pretty lambs we pull;

Fair lined slippers for the cold,   *15*
With buckles of the purest gold;

A belt of straw and ivy buds,
With coral clasps and amber studs:
And if these pleasures may thee move
Come live with me, and be my love.   *20*

The shepherds' swains shall dance and sing
For thy delight each May morning:
If these delights thy mind may move,
Then live with me and be my love.   *1600*

CONSIDERATIONS

1. What does the speaker wish for? What specific persuasive arguments does
    he use in order to have his wish fulfilled? How effective do you find his
    persuasions to be?
2. What "proof" does the speaker offer to his love that he will be true to his
    promises?
3. What are the connections between the images of nature and the theme of
    this poem?

SIR WALTER RALEIGH (c. 1552–1618)

The Nymph's Reply to the Shepherd

> *Best known as a key adviser who fell in and out of favor with Queen Eliza-*
> *beth I and was later executed during the reign of James I, Sir Walter Raleigh*
> *loved adventure and exploration. In addition to his poetry, he is also the author*
> *of* A History of the World *(1614), written while he was imprisoned in the*
> *Tower of London.*

If all the world and love were young,
And truth in every shepherd's tongue,
These pretty pleasures might me move
To live with thee and be thy love.

Time drives the flocks from field to fold   *5*
When rivers rage and rocks grow cold,
And Philomel becometh dumb;
The rest complains of cares to come.

The flowers do fade, and wanton fields
10   To wayward winter reckoning yields;
A honey tongue, a heart of gall,
Is fancy's spring, but sorrow's fall.

Thy gowns, thy shoes, thy beds of roses,
Thy cap, thy kirtle, and thy posies
15   Soon break, soon wither, soon forgotten—
In folly ripe, in reason rotten.

Thy belt of straw and ivy buds,
Thy coral clasps and amber studs,
All these in me no means can move
20   To come to thee and be thy love.

But could youth last and love still breed,
Had joys no date nor age no need,
Then these delights my mind might move
To live with thee and be thy love.   *1600*

CONSIDERATIONS

1. In this poem, Raleigh creates the voice of a woman to answer Christopher Marlowe's shepherd (pages 598–99). In what lines does the speaker begin dismantling the shepherd's argument? Why might the author have placed the opposing point of view here?
2. What images does this poem employ that are not found in Marlowe's poem? What do these images reveal about the speaker in this poem?
3. What is the one major difference between the shepherd and the nymph? If this argument were to continue, who do you think would win? Explain.

W. S. MERWIN (1927–   )

Separation

> *Born in New York City, W. S. Merwin spent his early years in New Jersey and Pennsylvania. He graduated from Princeton University and soon thereafter, in 1952, his first book of poems won the prestigious Yale Series of Younger Poets Award. While many of Merwin's early poems drew heavily on the classical tradition, his later work shows innovative experimentation with verse and metrical forms.*

Your absence has gone through me
Like thread through a needle.
Everything I do is stitched with its color.   *1963*

CONSIDERATIONS

Explore all the implications of the central metaphor of this tiny poem, which
compares separation to a needle and thread.

KRISTINE BATEY (1951–   )
Lot's Wife

> *Kristine Batey, who decided at age six to be a writer, lives in a suburb of
> Chicago. She describes herself as "a writer, cartoonist, wife, mother, grandmother,
> university administrator, and cat owner." "Lot's Wife," which was first published
> in 1978, won a Pushcart Prize as one of the best poems appearing in a small-
> press publication for that year. Batey describes the poem as follows: "'Lot's
> Wife'" is a poem about being a woman and, therefore, a human being."*

While Lot, the conscience of a nation,
struggles with the Lord,
she struggles with the housework.
The City of Sin is where
she raises the children.   5
Ba'al or Adonai°—
Whoever is God—
the bread must still be made
and the doorsill swept.
The Lord may kill the children tomorrow,   10
but today they must be bathed and fed.
Well and good to condemn your neighbors' religion,
but weren't they there
when the baby was born,
and when the well collapsed?   15
While her husband communes with God,
she tucks the children into bed.

Ba'al: Old Testament name for the chief god of the Canaanites, whose cult practices prostitution
and child sacrifice. This cult was denounced by Jewish prophets. *Adonai:* Hebrew term for God.

In the morning, when he tells her of the judgment,°
she puts down the lamp she is cleaning
20   and calmly begins to pack.
In between bundling up the children
and deciding what will go,
she runs for a moment
to say goodbye to the herd,
25   gently patting each soft head
with tears in her eyes for the animals that will not understand.
She smiles blindly to the woman
who held her hand at childbed.
It is easy for eyes that have always turned to heaven
30   not to look back;
those who have been—by necessity—drawn to earth
cannot forget that life is lived from day to day.
Good, to a God, and good in human terms
are two different things.
35   On the breast of the hill, she chooses to be human,
and turns, in farewell—
and never regrets
the sacrifice.   *1978*

CONSIDERATIONS

1. Read the biblical story of Lot and his wife (Genesis 19:1–26), and compare that story with the account in the poem.
2. What values are suggested by the details that describe Lot? By the details that describe his wife? In the poem, it is suggested that these values conflict. Do you think such values still conflict today? Explain.
3. In what ways are the concepts of love and hate suggested in this poem?

DONALD HALL (1928–   )

The Wedding Couple

Poet Donald Hall was born in New Haven, Connecticut, in 1928 but left New England in 1957 to become a professor of English at the University of Michigan,

---

the judgment: God's decision to destroy the city.

Ann Arbor, where he taught for almost twenty years. In 1975, he and his wife,
the poet Jane Kenyon, decided to move to the farm that had belonged to his
grandparents in New Hampshire to devote themselves to writing full-time. Since
his first work was published at the age of sixteen, he has published over a dozen
volumes of poetry; numerous volumes of prose on a variety of topics, including his
own life, the sculpture of Henry Moore, poetry, and baseball; and eleven children's
books. The One Day *(1988), a book of poetry in which Hall speaks in several*
narrative voices about mid-life crisis, won the National Book Critics Circle
Award for poetry and was nominated for a Pulitzer Prize. In 1995, at the age
of forty-seven, Kenyon died of leukemia; Hall had been her caregiver for the pre-
ceding fifteen months. The poem here first appeared in the Atlantic Monthly *in*
1996. His latest collection, Without *(1998), contains poems written during his*
wife's illness and "letters" written to her after her death.

Fifteen years ago his heart
infarcted and he stopped smoking.
　At eighty he trembled
like a birch but remained vigorous
　　and acute.　　　　　　　　　　5
　　　　　When they married,
fifty years ago, I was twelve.
　I observed the white lace
veil, the mumbling preacher, and the flowers
　of parlor silence　　　　　　　10
and ordinary absurdity; but
　I thought I stood outside
the parlor.
　　　　　For two years she dwindled
　by small strokes　　　　　　　15
into a mannequin—speechless almost, almost
　unmoving, eyes open
and blinking, fitful in perception
　but a mannequin that suffered
shame when it stained the bed sheet.　　20
　Slowly, shaking with purpose,
he carried her to the bathroom,
　undressed and washed her,
dressed her in clean clothes, and carried her back
　to CNN and bed. "All　　　　25
you need is love," sang John and Paul:
　He touched her shoulder; her eyes
caressed him like a bride's bold eyes.　*1996*

CONSIDERATIONS

1. What reasons might Hall have for beginning this poem 35 years after the couple has married and when the husband has had a heart attack?
2. What do the details of the wedding reveal about the young couple?
3. According to this poem, what is love? How does the speaker tie the love he now feels for his wife with the idea of a young bride and groom? Consider lines 6–10 and the final lines of the poem.

TESS GALLAGHER (1943–   )

The Hug

> *Tess Gallagher was born in Washington State, the daughter of loggers. She has degrees from the University of Washington and the University of Iowa and has taught creative writing at several schools. Her first book of poetry,* Instructions to the Double *(1976), won the Elliston Award in 1977 for the best book of poetry published by a small press. Since then, she has written two collections of short stories, a collection of essays about poetry, and several more poetry collections exploring the complexities of family relationships and everyday life. She was married to the writer Raymond Carver, who died in 1988. (One of Carver's short stories, "Cathedral," appears on pages 437–49.) In 1992, she published a collection of poems,* Moon Crossing Bridge, *that traces the course of her grieving after his death.*

A woman is reading a poem on the street
and another woman stops to listen. We stop too,
with our arms around each other. The poem
is being read and listened to out here
5   in the open. Behind us
no one is entering or leaving the houses.

Suddenly a hug comes over me and I'm
giving it to you, like a variable star shooting light
off to make itself comfortable, then
10   subsiding. I finish but keep on holding
you. A man walks up to us and we know he hasn't
come out of nowhere, but if he could, he
would have. He looks homeless because of how
he needs. "Can I have one of those?" he asks you,
15   and I feel you nod. I'm surprised,
surprised you don't tell him how
it is—that I'm yours, only

yours, etc., exclusive as a nose to
its face. Love—that's what we're talking about, love
that nabs you with "for me   *20*
only" and holds on.

So I walk over to him and put my
arms around him and try to
hug him like I mean it. He's got an overcoat on
so thick I can't feel   *25*
him past it. I'm starting the hug
and thinking, "How big a hug is this supposed to be?
How long shall I hold this hug?" Already
we could be eternal, his arms falling over my
shoulders, my hands not   *30*
meeting behind his back, he is so big!
I put my head into his chest and snuggle
in. I lean into him. I lean my blood and my wishes
into him. He stands for it. This is his
and he's starting to give it back so well I know he's   *35*
getting it. This hug. So truly, so tenderly

we stop having arms and I don't know if
my lover has walked away or what, or
if the woman is still reading the poem, or the houses—
what about them?—the houses.   *40*

Clearly, a little permission is a dangerous thing.
But when you hug someone you want it
to be a masterpiece of connection, the way the button
on his coat will leave the imprint of
a planet in my cheek   *45*
when I walk away. When I try to find some place
to go back to.   *1987*

CONSIDERATIONS

1. Based on the first two stanzas, how would you describe the relationship between the speaker and her lover? How well do you think they know each
   other? Explain.
2. What are the differences between the hug with the lover and the hug with
   the homeless stranger? What does this say, perhaps, about the woman herself?
3. What does the speaker mean by finding "some place / to go back to" at the
   end of this poem?

KITTY TSUI (1953–)

a chinese banquet

Born in Hong Kong, Kitty Tsui moved with her family to England. In 1969, she moved the United States where, in addition to writing poetry, she has become an actor, a bodybuilder, and an artist. She is particularly noted for her contributions to the body of work by Asian-American lesbian writers.

for the one who was not invited

it was not a very formal affair but
all the women over twelve
wore long gowns and a corsage,
5 except for me.

it was not a very formal affair, just
the family getting together,
poa poa, kuw fu without *kuw mow*°
(her excuse this year is a headache).

10 aunts and uncles and cousins,
the grandson who is a dentist,
the one who drives a mercedes benz,
sitting down for shark's fin soup.

they talk about buying a house and
15 taking a two week vacation in beijing.
i suck on shrimp and squab,
dreaming of the cloudscape in your eyes.

my mother, her voice beaded with sarcasm;
you're twenty six and not getting younger.
20 it's about time you got a decent job.
she no longer asks when i'm getting married.

you're twenty six and not getting younger.
what are you doing with your life?
you've got to make a living.
25 why don't you study computer programming?

she no longer asks when i'm getting married.
one day, wanting desperately to
bridge the boundaries that separate us,
wanting desperately to touch her,

---

poa poa: Maternal grandmother. *kuw fu:* Uncle. *kuw mow:* Aunt.

tell her: mother i'm gay,   *30*
mother i'm gay and so happy with her.
but she will not listen,
she shakes her head.

she sits across from me,
emotions invading her face.   *35*
her eyes are wet but
she will not let tears fall.

mother, i say,
you love a man.
i love a woman.   *40*
it is not what she wants to hear.

aunts and uncles and cousins,
very much a family affair.
but you are not invited,
being neither my husband nor my wife.   *45*

aunts and uncles and cousins
eating longevity noodles
fragrant with ham inquire:
sold that old car of yours yet?

i want to tell them: my back is healing,   *50*
i dream of dragons and water.
my home is in her arms,
our bedroom ceiling the wide open sky.   *1983*

CONSIDERATIONS

1. What is it that the speaker's relatives seem to value most in a relationship?
   How do the speaker's values differ from these? How are they the same?
2. How would you characterize the relationship between the mother and her
   daughter? Would you describe it as loving? Explain.
3. What is your reaction to the final stanza? How would you describe the relationship between the speaker and her lover?

Drama

HENRIK IBSEN (1828–1906)
A Doll's House

TRANSLATED BY ROLF FJELDE

> *Henrik Ibsen was the son of a wealthy merchant in Norway. In 1836, however, the elder Ibsen filed for bankruptcy. The family was forced to move to a small house, and Henrik had to leave his beloved private school to attend a public school, which he always believed left him with an inferior education. He left home as soon as he was old enough to become a druggist's apprentice. As a young man, Ibsen was both a social and political rebel, founding a radical club that worked to promote issues of personal and national freedom. He drank and gambled heavily, and at the age of 18 he became an unwed father. In 1850 he wrote his first play, and in 1857 he became the director of the Norwegian Theater in the city that is now Oslo. Following the bankruptcy of the Norwegian Theater, he and his family moved abroad. They lived primarily in Italy until 1891, and Ibsen wrote his major plays during this time:* Peer Gynt *(1867),* A Doll's House *(1879),* Ghosts *(1881), and* An Enemy of the People *(1882). Ibsen and his family returned to Norway in 1891, and in 1900 he suffered a stroke that left him an invalid until his death in 1906. Of this major pioneer in modern realistic theater, the playwright Luigi Pirandello said, "After Shakespeare, I put Ibsen first."*

Characters
TORVALD HELMER, *a lawyer*
NORA, *his wife*
DR. RANK
MRS. LINDE
NILS KROGSTAD, *a bank clerk*
THE HELMERS' THREE SMALL CHILDREN
ANNE-MARIE, *their nurse*
HELENE, *a maid*
A DELIVERY BOY

Scene   *The action takes place in* HELMER*'s residence.*

ACT I

Scene   *A comfortable room, tastefully but not expensively furnished. A door to the right in the back wall leads to the entryway, another to the left leads to* HELMER*'s* *study. Between these doors, a piano. Midway in the left-hand wall a door, and further back a window. Near the window a round table with an armchair and a small sofa. In the right-hand wall, toward the rear a door, and nearer the foreground a porcelain stove with two armchairs and a rocking chair beside it. Between the stove and the side door, a small table. Engravings on the walls. An étagère with china figures and other small art objects; a small bookcase with richly bound books; the floor carpeted; a fire burning in the stove. It is a winter day.*

A bell rings in the entryway; shortly after, we hear the door being unlocked. NORA *comes into the room, humming happily to herself; she is wearing street clothes and carries an armload of packages, which she puts down on the table to the right. She has left the hall door open; and through it a* DELIVERY BOY *is seen, holding a Christmas tree and a basket which he gives to the* MAID *who let them in.*

NORA: Hide the tree well, Helene. The children mustn't get a glimpse of it till this evening, after it's trimmed. *(To the* DELIVERY BOY, *taking out her purse.)* How much?

DELIVERY BOY: Fifty, ma'am.

NORA: There's a crown. No, keep the change. *(The* BOY *thanks her and leaves.* NORA *shuts the door. She laughs softly to herself while taking off her street things. Drawing a bag of macaroons from her pocket, she eats a couple, then steals over and listens at her husband's study door.)* Yes, he's home. *(Hums again as she moves to the table, right.)*

HELMER *(from the study)*: Is that my little lark twittering out there?

NORA *(busy opening some packages)*: Yes, it is.   5

HELMER: Is that my squirrel rummaging around?

NORA: Yes!

HELMER: When did my squirrel get in?

NORA: Just now. *(Putting the macaroon bag in her pocket and wiping her mouth.)* Do come in, Torvald, and see what I've bought.

HELMER: Can't be disturbed. *(After a moment he opens the door and peers in, pen*   10 *in hand.)* Bought, you say? All that there? Has the little spendthrift been out throwing money around again?

NORA: Oh, but Torvald, this year we really should let ourselves go a bit. It's the first Christmas we haven't had to economize.

HELMER: But you know we can't go squandering.

NORA: Oh yes, Torvald, we can squander a little now. Can't we? Just a tiny, wee bit. Now that you've got a big salary and are going to make piles and piles of money.

HELMER: Yes—starting New Year's. But then it's a full three months till the raise comes through.

NORA: Pooh! We can borrow that long.   15

HELMER: Nora! *(Goes over and playfully takes her by the ear.)* Are your scatter-brains off again? What if today I borrowed a thousand crowns, and you

squandered them over Christmas week, and then on New Year's Eve a
roof tile fell on my head, and I lay there—

NORA *(putting her hand on his mouth)*: Oh! Don't say such things!

HELMER: Yes, but what if it happened—then what?

NORA: If anything so awful happened, then it just wouldn't matter if I had
debts or not.

20   HELMER: Well, but the people I'd borrowed from?

NORA: Them? Who cares about them! They're strangers.

HELMER: Nora, Nora, how like a woman! No, but seriously, Nora, you know
what I think about that. No debts! Never borrow! Something of freedom's lost—and something of beauty, too—from a home that's founded
on borrowing and debt. We've made a brave stand up to now, the two of
us; and we'll go right on like that the little while we have to.

NORA *(going toward the stove)*: Yes, whatever you say, Torvald.

HELMER *(following her)*: Now, now, the little lark's wings mustn't droop. Come
on, don't be a sulky squirrel. *(Taking out his wallet.)* Nora, guess what I
have here.

25   NORA *(turning quickly)*: Money!

HELMER: There, see. *(Hands her some notes.)* Good grief, I know how costs go
up in a house at Christmastime.

NORA: Ten—twenty—thirty—forty. Oh, thank you, Torvald; I can manage
no end on this.

HELMER: You really will have to.

NORA: Oh yes, I promise I will! But come here so I can show you everything
I bought. And so cheap! Look, new clothes for Ivar here—and a sword.
Here a horse and a trumpet for Bob. And a doll and a doll's bed here for
Emmy; they're nothing much, but she'll tear them to bits in no time any-
way. And here I have dress material and handkerchiefs for the maids. Old
Anne-Marie really deserves something more.

30   HELMER: And what's in that package there?

NORA *(with a cry)*: Torvald, no! You can't see that till tonight!

HELMER: I see. But tell me now, you little prodigal, what have you thought of
for yourself?

NORA: For myself? Oh, I don't want anything at all.

HELMER: Of course you do. Tell me just what—within reason—you'd most
like to have.

35   NORA: I honestly don't know. Oh, listen, Torvald—

HELMER: Well?

NORA *(fumbling at his coat buttons, without looking at him)*: If you want to give
me something, then maybe you could—you could—

HELMER: Come on, out with it.

NORA *(hurriedly)*: You could give me money, Torvald. No more than you
think you can spare, then one of these days I'll buy something with it.

HELMER: But Nora—   40

NORA: Oh, please, Torvald darling, do that! I beg you, please. Then I could hang
the bills in pretty gilt paper on the Christmas tree. Wouldn't that be fun?

HELMER: What are those little birds called that always fly through their
fortunes?

NORA: Oh yes, spendthrifts. I know all that. But let's do as I say, Torvald; then
I'll have time to decide what I really need most. That's very sensible, isn't it?

HELMER *(smiling)*: Yes, very—that is, if you actually hung onto the money I
give you, and you actually used it to buy yourself something. But it goes
for the house and for all sorts of foolish things, and then I only have to
lay out some more.

NORA: Oh, but Torvald—   45

HELMER: Don't deny it, my dear little Nora. *(Putting his arm around her waist.)*
Spendthrifts are sweet, but they use up a frightful amount of money. It's
incredible what it costs a man to feed such birds.

NORA: Oh, how can you say that! Really, I save everything I can.

HELMER *(laughing)*: Yes, that's the truth. Everything you can. But that's nothing at all.

NORA *(humming, with a smile of quiet satisfaction)*: Hm, if you only knew what
expenses we larks and squirrels have, Torvald.

HELMER: You're an odd little one. Exactly the way your father was. You're   50
never at a loss for scaring up money; but the moment you have it, it runs
right out through your fingers; you never know what you've done with
it. Well, one takes you as you are. It's deep in your blood. Yes, these things
are hereditary, Nora.

NORA: Ah, I could wish I'd inherited many of Papa's qualities.

HELMER: And I couldn't wish you anything but just what you are, my sweet
little lark. But wait; it seems to me you have a very—what should I call
it?—a very suspicious look today—

NORA: I do?

HELMER: You certainly do. Look me straight in the eye.

NORA *(looking at him)*: Well?   55

HELMER *(shaking an admonitory finger)*: Surely my sweet tooth hasn't been
running riot in town today, has she?

NORA: No. Why do you imagine that?

HELMER: My sweet tooth really didn't make a little detour through the
confectioner's?

NORA: No, I assure you, Torvald—

HELMER: Hasn't nibbled some pastry?   60

NORA: No, not at all.

HELMER: Nor even munched a macaroon or two?

NORA: No, Torvald, I assure you, really—

HELMER: There, there now. Of course I'm only joking.

65   NORA *(going to the table, right)*: You know I could never think of going against
you.

HELMER: No, I understand that; and you *have* given me your word. *(Going
over to her.)* Well, you keep your little Christmas secrets to yourself, Nora
darling. I expect they'll come to light this evening, when the tree is lit.

NORA: Did you remember to ask Dr. Rank?

HELMER: No. But there's no need for that; it's assumed he'll be dining with
us. All the same, I'll ask him when he stops by here this morning. I've
ordered some fine wine. Nora, you can't imagine how I'm looking forward to this evening.

NORA: So am I. And what fun for the children, Torvald!

70   HELMER: Ah, it's so gratifying to know that one's gotten a safe, secure job,
and with a comfortable salary. It's a great satisfaction, isn't it?

NORA: Oh, it's wonderful!

HELMER: Remember last Christmas? Three whole weeks before, you shut
yourself in every evening till long after midnight, making flowers for the
Christmas tree, and all the other decorations to surprise us. Ugh, that
was the dullest time I've ever lived through.

NORA: It wasn't at all dull for me.

HELMER *(smiling)*: But the outcome *was* pretty sorry, Nora.

75   NORA: Oh, don't tease me with that again. How could I help it that the cat
came in and tore everything to shreds.

HELMER: No, poor thing, you certainly couldn't. You wanted so much to
please us all, and that's what counts. But it's just as well that the hard
times are past.

NORA: Yes, it's really wonderful.

HELMER: Now I don't have to sit here alone, boring myself, and you don't
have to tire your precious eyes and your fair little delicate hands—

NORA *(clapping her hands)*: No, is it really true, Torvald, I don't have to? Oh,
how wonderfully lovely to hear! *(Taking his arm.)* Now I'll tell you just
how I've thought we should plan things. Right after Christmas—*(The
doorbell rings.)* Oh, the bell. *(Straightening the room up a bit.)* Somebody
would have to come. What a bore!

80   HELMER: I'm not at home to visitors, don't forget.

MAID *(from the hall doorway)*: Ma'am, a lady to see you—

NORA: All right, let her come in.

MAID *(to* HELMER*)*: And the doctor's just come too.

HELMER: Did he go right to my study?

85   MAID: Yes, he did.

*(*HELMER *goes into his room. The* MAID *shows in* MRS. LINDE, *dressed in
traveling clothes, and shuts the door after her.)*

MRS. LINDE *(in a dispirited and somewhat hesitant voice)*: Hello, Nora.

NORA *(uncertain)*: Hello—

MRS. LINDE: You don't recognize me.

NORA: No, I don't know—but wait, I think—*(Exclaiming.)* What! Kristine! Is it really you?

MRS. LINDE: Yes, it's me.   90

NORA: Kristine! To think I didn't recognize you. But then, how could I? *(More quietly.)* How you've changed, Kristine!

MRS. LINDE: Yes, no doubt I have. In nine—ten long years.

NORA: Is it so long since we met! Yes, it's all of that. Oh, these last eight years have been a happy time, believe me. And so now you've come in to town, too. Made the long trip in the winter. That took courage.

MRS. LINDE: I just got here by ship this morning.

NORA: To enjoy yourself over Christmas, of course. Oh, how lovely! Yes, enjoy   95
ourselves, we'll do that. But take your coat off. You're not still cold? *(Helping her.)* There now, let's get cozy here by the stove. No, the easy chair there! I'll take the rocker here. *(Seizing her hands.)* Yes, now you have your old look again; it was only in that first moment. You're a bit more pale, Kristine—and maybe a bit thinner.

MRS. LINDE: And much, much older, Nora.

NORA: Yes, perhaps, a bit older; a tiny, tiny bit; not much at all. *(Stopping short; suddenly serious.)* Oh, but thoughtless me, to sit here, chattering away. Sweet, good Kristine, can you forgive me?

MRS. LINDE: What do you mean, Nora?

NORA *(softly)*: Poor Kristine, you've become a widow.

MRS. LINDE: Yes, three years ago.   100

NORA: Oh, I knew it, of course; I read it in the papers. Oh Kristine, you must believe me; I often thought of writing you then, but I kept postponing it, and something always interfered.

MRS. LINDE: Nora dear, I understand completely.

NORA: No, it was awful of me, Kristine. You poor thing, how much you must have gone through. And he left you nothing?

MRS. LINDE: No.

NORA: And no children?   105

MRS. LINDE: No.

NORA: Nothing at all, then?

MRS. LINDE: Not even a sense of loss to feed on.

NORA *(looking incredulously at her)*: But Kristine, how could that be?

MRS. LINDE *(smiling wearily and smoothing her hair)*: Oh, sometimes it happens,   110
Nora.

NORA: So completely alone. How terribly hard that must be for you. I have three lovely children. You can't see them now; they're out with the maid. But now you must tell me everything—

MRS. LINDE: No, no, no, tell me about yourself.

NORA: No, you begin. Today I don't want to be selfish. I want to think only of you today. But there *is* something I must tell you. Did you hear of the wonderful luck we had recently?

MRS. LINDE: No, what's that?

115 NORA: My husband's been made manager in the bank, just think!

MRS. LINDE: Your husband? How marvelous!

NORA: Isn't it? Being a lawyer is such an uncertain living, you know, especially if one won't touch any cases that aren't clean and decent. And of course Torvald would never do that, and I'm with him completely there. Oh, we're simply delighted, believe me! He'll join the bank right after New Year's and start getting a huge salary and lots of commissions. From now on we can live quite differently—just as we want. Oh, Kristine, I feel so light and happy! Won't it be lovely to have stacks of money and not a care in the world?

MRS. LINDE: Well, anyway, it would be lovely to have enough for necessities.

NORA: No, not just for necessities, but stacks and stacks of money!

120 MRS. LINDE *(smiling)*: Nora, Nora, aren't you sensible yet? Back in school you were such a free spender.

NORA *(with a quiet laugh)*: Yes, that's what Torvald still says. *(Shaking her finger.)* But "Nora, Nora" isn't as silly as you all think. Really, we've been in no position for me to go squandering. We've had to work, both of us.

MRS. LINDE: You too?

NORA: Yes, at odd jobs—needlework, crocheting, embroidery, and such— *(casually)* and other things too. You remember that Torvald left the department when we were married? There was no chance of promotion in his office, and of course he needed to earn more money. But that first year he drove himself terribly. He took on all kinds of extra work that kept him going morning and night. It wore him down, and then he fell deathly ill. The doctors said it was essential for him to travel south.

MRS. LINDE: Yes, didn't you spend a whole year in Italy?

125 NORA: That's right. It wasn't easy to get away, you know. Ivar had just been born. But of course we had to go. Oh, that was a beautiful trip, and it saved Torvald's life. But it cost a frightful sum, Kristine.

MRS. LINDE: I can well imagine.

NORA: Four thousand, eight hundred crowns it cost. That's really a lot of money.

MRS. LINDE: But it's lucky you had it when you needed it.

NORA: Well, as it was, we got it from Papa.

130 MRS. LINDE: I see. It was just about the time your father died.

NORA: Yes, just about then. And, you know, I couldn't make the trip out to nurse him. I had to stay here, expecting Ivar any moment, and with my poor sick Torvald to care for. Dearest Papa, I never saw him again, Kristine. Oh, that was the worst time I've known in all my marriage.

MRS. LINDE: I know how you loved him. And then you went off to Italy?

NORA: Yes. We had the means now, and the doctors urged us. So we left a month after.

MRS. LINDE: And your husband came back completely cured?

NORA: Sound as a drum! 135

MRS. LINDE: But—the doctor?

NORA: Who?

MRS. LINDE: I thought the maid said he was a doctor, the man who came in with me.

NORA: Yes, that was Dr. Rank—but he's not making a sick call. He's our clos-est friend, and he stops by at least once a day. No, Torvald hasn't had a sick moment since, and the children are fit and strong, and I am, too. *(Jumping up and clapping her hands.)* Oh, dear God, Kristine, what a lovely thing to live and be happy! But how disgusting of me—I'm talking of nothing but my own affairs. *(Sits on a stool close by* KRISTINE, *arms resting across her knees.)* Oh, don't be angry with me! Tell me, is it really true that you weren't in love with your husband? Why did you marry him, then?

MRS. LINDE: My mother was still alive, but bedridden and helpless—and I 140 had two younger brothers to look after. In all conscience, I didn't think I could turn him down.

NORA: No, you were right there. But was he rich at the time?

MRS. LINDE: He was very well off, I'd say. But the business was shaky, Nora. When he died, it all fell apart, and nothing was left.

NORA: And then—?

MRS. LINDE: Yes, so I had to scrape up a living with a little shop and a little teaching and whatever else I could find. The last three years have been like one endless workday without a rest for me. Now it's over, Nora. My poor mother doesn't need me, for she's passed on. Nor the boys, either; they're working now and can take care of themselves.

NORA: How free you must feel— 145

MRS. LINDE: No—only unspeakably empty. Nothing to live for now. *(Stand-ing up anxiously.)* That's why I couldn't take it any longer out in that des-olate hole. Maybe here it'll be easier to find something to do and keep my mind occupied. If I could only be lucky enough to get a steady job, some office work—

NORA: Oh, but Kristine, that's so dreadfully tiring, and you already look so tired. It would be much better for you if you could go off to a bathing resort.

MRS. LINDE *(going toward the window)*: I have no father to give me travel money, Nora.

NORA *(rising)*: Oh, don't be angry with me.

MRS. LINDE *(going to her)*: Nora dear, don't you be angry with me. The worst 150 of my kind of situation is all the bitterness that's stored away. No one to work for, and yet you're always having to snap up your opportunities.

You have to live; and so you grow selfish. When you told me the happy change in your lot, do you know I was delighted less for your sake than for mine?

NORA: How so? Oh, I see. You think maybe Torvald could do something for you.

MRS. LINDE: Yes, that's what I thought.

NORA: And he will, Kristine! Just leave it to me; I'll bring it up so delicately— find something attractive to humor him with. Oh, I'm so eager to help you.

MRS. LINDE: How very kind of you, Nora, to be so concerned over me— doubly kind, considering you really know so little of life's burdens yourself.

155 NORA: I—? I know so little—?

MRS. LINDE *(smiling)*: Well, my heavens—a little needlework and such— Nora, you're just a child.

NORA *(tossing her head and pacing the floor)*: You don't have to act so superior.

MRS. LINDE: Oh?

NORA: You're just like the others. You all think I'm incapable of anything serious—

160 MRS. LINDE: Come now—

NORA: That I've never had to face the raw world.

MRS. LINDE: Nora dear, you've just been telling me all your troubles.

NORA: Hm! Trivia! *(Quietly.)* I haven't told you the big thing.

MRS. LINDE: Big thing? What do you mean?

165 NORA: You look down on me so, Kristine, but you shouldn't. You're proud that you worked so long and hard for your mother.

MRS. LINDE: I don't look down on a soul. But it is true; I'm proud—and happy, too—to think it was given to me to make my mother's last days almost free of care.

NORA: And you're also proud thinking of what you've done for your brothers.

MRS. LINDE: I feel I've a right to be.

NORA: I agree. But listen to this, Kristine—I've also got something to be proud and happy for.

170 MRS. LINDE: I don't doubt it. But whatever do you mean?

NORA: Not so loud. What if Torvald heard! He mustn't, not for anything in the world. Nobody must know, Kristine. No one but you.

MRS. LINDE: But what is it, then?

NORA: Come here. *(Drawing her down beside her on the sofa.)* It's true—I've also got something to be proud and happy for. I'm the one who saved Torvald's life.

MRS. LINDE: Saved—? Saved how?

175 NORA: I told you about the trip to Italy. Torvald never would have lived if he hadn't gone south—

MRS. LINDE: Of course, your father gave you the means—

NORA *(smiling)*: That's what Torvald and all the rest think, but—

MRS. LINDE: But—?

NORA: Papa didn't give us a pin. I was the one who raised the money.

MRS. LINDE: You? The whole amount?   *180*

NORA: Four thousand, eight hundred crowns. What do you say to that?

MRS. LINDE: But Nora, how was it possible? Did you win the lottery?

NORA *(disdainfully)*: The lottery? Pooh! No art to that.

MRS. LINDE: But where did you get it from then?

NORA *(humming, with a mysterious smile)*: Hmm, tra-la-la-la.   *185*

MRS. LINDE: Because you couldn't have borrowed it.

NORA: No? Why not?

MRS. LINDE: A wife can't borrow without her husband's consent.

NORA *(tossing her head)*: Oh, but a wife with a little business sense, a wife
    who knows how to manage—

MRS. LINDE: Nora, I simply don't understand—   *190*

NORA: You don't have to. Whoever said I *borrowed* the money? I could have
    gotten it other ways. *(Throwing herself back on the sofa.)* I could have gotten
    it from some admirer or other. After all, a girl with my ravishing appeal—

MRS. LINDE: You lunatic.

NORA: I'll bet you're eaten up with curiosity, Kristine.

MRS. LINDE: Now listen here, Nora—you haven't done something indiscreet?

NORA *(sitting up again)*: Is it indiscreet to save your husband's life?   *195*

MRS. LINDE: I think it's indiscreet that without his knowledge you—

NORA: But that's the point: he mustn't know! My Lord, can't you under-
    stand? He mustn't ever know the close call he had. It was to *me* the doc-
    tors came to say his life was in danger—that nothing could save him but
    a stay in the south. Didn't I try strategy then! I began talking about how
    lovely it would be for me to travel abroad like other young wives; I
    begged and I cried; I told him please to remember my condition, to be
    kind and indulge me; and then I dropped a hint that he could easily take
    out a loan. But at that, Kristine, he nearly exploded. He said I was frivo-
    lous, and it was his duty as man of the house not to indulge me in whims
    and fancies—as I think he called them. Aha, I thought, now you'll just
    have to be saved—and that's when I saw my chance.

MRS. LINDE: And your father never told Torvald the money wasn't from him?

NORA: No, never. Papa died right about then. I'd considered bringing him
    into my secret and begging him never to tell. But he was too sick at the
    time—and then, sadly, it didn't matter.

MRS. LINDE: And you've never confided in your husband since?   *200*

NORA: For heaven's sake, no! Are you serious? He's so strict on that subject.
    Besides—Torvald, with all his masculine pride—how painfully humiliat-
    ing for him if he ever found out he was in debt to me. That would just
    ruin our relationship. Our beautiful happy home would never be the
    same.

MRS. LINDE: Won't you ever tell him?

NORA *(thoughtfully, half smiling)*: Yes—maybe sometime, years from now, when I'm no longer so attractive. Don't laugh! I only mean when Torvald loves me less than now, when he stops enjoying my dancing and dressing up and reciting for him. Then it might be wise to have something in reserve—*(Breaking off.)* How ridiculous! That'll never happen— Well, Kristine, what do you think of my big secret? I'm capable of something too, hm? You can imagine, of course, how this thing hangs over me. It really hasn't been easy meeting the payments on time. In the business world there's what they call quarterly interest and what they call amortization, and these are always so terribly hard to manage. I've had to skimp a little here and there, wherever I could, you know. I could hardly spare anything from my house allowance, because Torvald has to live well. I couldn't let the children go poorly dressed; whatever I got for them, I felt I had to use up completely—the darlings!

MRS. LINDE: Poor Nora, so it had to come out of your own budget, then?

205 NORA: Yes, of course. But I was the one most responsible, too. Every time Torvald gave me money for new clothes and such, I never used more than half; always bought the simplest, cheapest outfits. It was a godsend that everything looks so well on me that Torvald never noticed. But it did weigh me down at times, Kristine. It *is* such a joy to wear fine things. You understand.

MRS. LINDE: Oh, of course.

NORA: And then I found other ways of making money. Last winter I was lucky enough to get a lot of copying to do. I locked myself in and sat writing every evening till late in the night. Ah, I was tired so often, dead tired. But still it was wonderful fun, sitting and working like that, earning money. It was almost like being a man.

MRS. LINDE: But how much have you paid off this way so far?

NORA: That's hard to say, exactly. These accounts, you know, aren't easy to figure. I only know that I've paid out all I could scrape together. Time and again I haven't known where to turn. *(Smiling.)* Then I'd sit here dreaming of a rich old gentleman who had fallen in love with me—

210 MRS. LINDE: What! Who is he?

NORA: Oh, really! And that he'd died, and when his will was opened, there in big letters it said, "All my fortune shall be paid over in cash, immediately, to that enchanting Mrs. Nora Helmer."

MRS. LINDE: But Nora dear—who *was* this gentleman?

NORA: Good grief, can't you understand? The old man never existed; that was only something I'd dream up time and again whenever I was at my wits' end for money. But it makes no difference now; the old fossil can go where he pleases for all I care; I don't need him or his will—because now I'm free. *(Jumping up.)* Oh, how lovely to think of that, Kristine! Carefree! To know you're carefree, utterly carefree, to be able to romp

and play with the children, and to keep up a beautiful, charming home—
everything just the way Torvald likes it! And think, spring is coming,
with big blue skies. Maybe we can travel a little then. Maybe I'll see the
ocean again. Oh yes, it *is* so marvelous to live and be happy!

(The front doorbell rings.)

MRS. LINDE *(rising)*: There's the bell. It's probably best that I go.

NORA: No, stay. No one's expected. It must be for Torvald.   *215*

MAID *(from the hall doorway)*: Excuse me, ma'am—there's a gentleman here to
see Mr. Helmer, but I didn't know—since the doctor's with him—

NORA: Who is the gentleman?

KROGSTAD *(from the doorway)*: It's me, Mrs. Helmer.

(MRS. LINDE starts and turns away toward the window.)

NORA *(stepping toward him, tense, her voice a whisper)*: You? What is it? Why do
you want to speak to my husband?

KROGSTAD: Bank business—after a fashion. I have a small job in the invest-   *220*
ment bank, and I hear now your husband is going to be our chief—

NORA: In other words, it's—

KROGSTAD: Just dry business, Mrs. Helmer. Nothing but that.

NORA: Yes, then please be good enough to step into the study.

*(She nods indifferently, as she sees him out by the hall door, then returns and
begins stirring up the stove.)*

MRS. LINDE: Nora—who was that man?

NORA: That was a Mr. Krogstad—a lawyer.   *225*

MRS. LINDE: Then it really was him.

NORA: Do you know that person?

MRS. LINDE: I did once—many years ago. For a time he was a law clerk in
our town.

NORA: Yes, he's been that.

MRS. LINDE: How he's changed.   *230*

NORA: I understand he had a very unhappy marriage.

MRS. LINDE: He's a widower now.

NORA: With a number of children. There now, it's burning. *(She closes the stove
door and moves the rocker a bit to one side.)*

MRS. LINDE: They say he has a hand in all kinds of business.

NORA: Oh? That may be true; I wouldn't know. But let's not think about   *235*
business. It's so dull.

(DR. RANK enters from HELMER's study.)

RANK *(still in the doorway)*: No, no, really—I don't want to intrude, I'd just as
soon talk a little while with your wife. *(Shuts the door, then notices MRS.
LINDE.)* Oh, beg pardon, I'm intruding here too.

NORA: No, not at all. *(Introducing him.)* Dr. Rank, Mrs. Linde.

RANK: Well now, that's a name much heard in this house. I believe I passed the lady on the stairs as I came.

MRS. LINDE: Yes, I take the stairs very slowly. They're rather hard on me.

240 RANK: Uh-hm, some touch of internal weakness?

MRS. LINDE: More overexertion, I'd say.

RANK: Nothing else? Then you're probably here in town to rest up in a round of parties?

MRS. LINDE: I'm here to look for work.

RANK: Is that the best cure for overexertion?

245 MRS. LINDE: One has to live, Doctor.

RANK: Yes, there's a common prejudice to that effect.

NORA: Oh, come on, Dr. Rank—you really do want to live yourself.

RANK: Yes, I really do. Wretched as I am, I'll gladly prolong my torment indefinitely. All my patients feel like that. And it's quite the same, too, with the morally sick. Right at this moment there's one of those moral invalids in there with Helmer—

MRS. LINDE *(softly)*: Ah!

250 NORA: Who do you mean?

RANK: Oh, it's a lawyer, Krogstad, a type you wouldn't know. His character is rotten to the root—but even he began chattering all-importantly about how he had to *live.*

NORA: Oh? What did he want to talk to Torvald about?

RANK: I really don't know. I only heard something about the bank.

NORA: I didn't know that Krog—that this man Krogstad had anything to do with the bank.

255 RANK: Yes, he's gotten some kind of berth down there. *(To* MRS. LINDE.*)* I don't know if you also have, in your neck of the woods, a type of person who scuttles about breathlessly, sniffing out hints of moral corruption, and then maneuvers his victim into some sort of key position where he can keep an eye on him. It's the healthy these days that are out in the cold.

MRS. LINDE: All the same, it's the sick who most need to be taken in.

RANK *(with a shrug)*: Yes, there we have it. That's the concept that's turning society into a sanatorium.

*(*NORA, *lost in her thoughts, breaks out into quiet laughter and claps her hands.)*

RANK: Why do you laugh at that? Do you have any real idea of what society is?

NORA: What do I care about dreary old society? I was laughing at something quite different—something terribly funny. Tell me, Doctor—is everyone who works in the bank dependent now on Torvald?

260 RANK: Is that what you find so terribly funny?

NORA *(smiling and humming)*: Never mind, never mind! *(Pacing the floor.)* Yes, that's really immensely amusing: that we—that Torvald has so much power now over all those people. *(Taking the bag out of her pocket.)* Dr. Rank, a little macaroon on that?

RANK: See here, macaroons! I thought they were contraband here.

NORA: Yes, but these are some that Kristine gave me.

MRS. LINDE: What? I—?

NORA: Now, now, don't be afraid. You couldn't possibly know that Torvald   265
had forbidden them. You see, he's worried they'll ruin my teeth. But
hmp! Just this once! Isn't that so, Dr. Rank? Help yourself! *(Puts a macaroon in his mouth.)* And you too, Kristine. And I'll also have one, only a
little one—or two, at the most. *(Walking about again.)* Now I'm really
tremendously happy. Now there's just one last thing in the world that I
have an enormous desire to do.

RANK: Well! And what's that?

NORA: It's something I have such a consuming desire to say so Torvald could
hear.

RANK: And why can't you say it?

NORA: I don't dare. It's quite shocking.

MRS. LINDE: Shocking?   270

RANK: Well, then it isn't advisable. But in front of us you certainly can. What
do you have such a desire to say so Torvald could hear?

NORA: I have such a huge desire to say—to hell and be damned!

RANK: Are you crazy?

MRS. LINDE: My goodness, Nora!

RANK: Go on, say it. Here he is.   275

NORA *(hiding the macaroon bag)*: Shh, shh, shh!

*(*HELMER *comes in from his study, hat in hand, overcoat over his arm.)*

NORA *(going toward him)*: Well, Torvald dear, are you through with him?

HELMER: Yes, he just left.

NORA: Let me introduce you—this is Kristine, who's arrived here in town.

HELMER: Kristine—? I'm sorry, but I don't know—   280

NORA: Mrs. Linde, Torvald dear. Mrs. Kristine Linde.

HELMER: Of course. A childhood friend of my wife's, no doubt?

MRS. LINDE: Yes, we knew each other in those days.

NORA: And just think, she made the long trip down here in order to talk
with you.

HELMER: What's this?   285

MRS. LINDE: Well, not exactly—

NORA: You see, Kristine is remarkably clever in office work, and so she's terribly eager to come under a capable man's supervision and add more to
what she already knows—

HELMER: Very wise, Mrs. Linde.

NORA: And then when she heard that you'd become a bank manager—the
story was wired out to the papers—then she came in as fast as she could

and—Really, Torvald, for my sake you can do a little something for Kristine, can't you?

290 HELMER: Yes, it's not at all impossible. Mrs. Linde, I suppose you're a widow?

MRS. LINDE: Yes.

HELMER: Any experience in office work?

MRS. LINDE: Yes, a good deal.

HELMER: Well, it's quite likely that I can make an opening for you—

295 NORA *(clapping her hands)*: You see, you see!

HELMER: You've come at a lucky moment, Mrs. Linde.

MRS. LINDE: Oh, how can I thank you?

HELMER: Not necessary. *(Putting his overcoat on.)* But today you'll have to excuse me—

RANK: Wait, I'll go with you. *(He fetches his coat from the hall and warms it at the stove.)*

300 NORA: Don't stay out long, dear.

HELMER: An hour; no more.

NORA: Are you going too, Kristine?

MRS. LINDE *(putting on her winter garments)*: Yes, I have to see about a room now.

HELMER: Then perhaps we can all walk together.

305 NORA *(helping her)*: What a shame we're so cramped here, but it's quite impossible for us to—

MRS. LINDE: Oh, don't even think of it! Good-bye, Nora dear, and thanks for everything.

NORA: Good-bye for now. Of course you'll be back again this evening. And you too, Dr. Rank. What? If you're well enough? Oh, you've got to be! Wrap up tight now.

(In a ripple of small talk the company moves out into the hall; CHILDREN's *voices are heard outside on the steps.)*

NORA: There they are! There they are! *(She runs to open the door. The* CHILDREN *come in with their nurse,* ANNE-MARIE.*)* Come in, come in! *(Bends down and kisses them.)* Oh, you darlings—! Look at them, Kristine. Aren't they lovely!

RANK: No loitering in the draft here.

310 HELMER: Come, Mrs. Linde—this place is unbearable now for anyone but mothers.

(DR. RANK, HELMER, and MRS. LINDE *go down the stairs.* ANNE-MARIE *goes into the living room with the* CHILDREN. NORA *follows, after closing the hall door.)*

NORA: How fresh and strong you look. Oh, such red cheeks you have! Like apples and roses. *(The children interrupt her throughout the following.)* And it was so much fun? That's wonderful. Really? You pulled both Emmy and Bob on the sled? Imagine, all together! Yes, you're a clever boy, Ivar. Oh, let me hold her a bit, Anne-Marie. My sweet little doll baby! *(Takes the smallest from the nurse and dances with her.)* Yes, yes, Mama will dance with Bob as well. What? Did you throw snowballs? Oh, if I'd only been there! No, don't bother, Anne-Marie—I'll undress them myself. Oh yes, let me. It's such fun. Go in and rest; you look half frozen. There's hot coffee waiting for you on the stove. *(The* NURSE *goes into the room to the left.* NORA *takes the children's winter things off, throwing them about, while the* children *talk to her all at once.)* Is that so? A big dog chased you? But it didn't bite? No, dogs never bite little, lovely doll babies. Don't peek in the packages, Ivar! What is it? Yes, wouldn't you like to know. No, no, it's an ugly something. Well? Shall we play? What shall we play? Hide-and-seek? Yes, let's play hide-and-seek. Bob must hide first. I must? Yes, let me hide first.

(Laughing and shouting, she and the CHILDREN *play in and out of the living room and the adjoining room to the right. At last* NORA *hides under the table. The* CHILDREN *come storming in, search, but cannot find her, then hear her muffled laughter, dash over to the table, lift the cloth and find her. Wild shouting. She creeps forward as if to scare them. More shouts. Meanwhile, a knock at the hall door; no one has noticed it. Now the door half opens, and* KROGSTAD *appears. He waits a moment; the game goes on.)*

KROGSTAD: Beg pardon, Mrs. Helmer—

NORA *(with a strangled cry, turning and scrambling to her knees)*: Oh! what do you want?

KROGSTAD: Excuse me. The outer door was ajar; it must be someone forgot to shut it—

NORA *(rising)*: My husband isn't home, Mr. Krogstad.   *315*

KROGSTAD: I know that.

NORA: Yes—then what do you want here?

KROGSTAD: A word with you.

NORA: With—? *(To the* CHILDREN, *quietly.)* Go in to Anne-Marie. What? No, the strange man won't hurt Mama. When he's gone, we'll play some more. *(She leads the* CHILDREN *into the room to the left and shuts the door after them. Then, tense and nervous.)* You want to speak to me?

KROGSTAD: Yes, I want to.   *320*

NORA: Today? But it's not yet the first of the month—

KROGSTAD: No, it's Christmas Eve. It's going to be up to you how merry a Christmas you have.

NORA: What is it you want? Today I absolutely can't—

KROGSTAD: We won't talk about that till later. This is something else. You do have a moment to spare, I suppose?

NORA: Oh yes, of course—I do, except—   *325*

KROGSTAD: Good. I was sitting over at Olsen's Restaurant when I saw your husband go down the street—

NORA: Yes?

KROGSTAD: With a lady.

NORA: Yes. So?

330   KROGSTAD: If you'll pardon my asking: wasn't that lady a Mrs. Linde?

NORA: Yes.

KROGSTAD: Just now come into town?

NORA: Yes, today.

KROGSTAD: She's a good friend of yours?

335   NORA: Yes, she is. But I don't see—

KROGSTAD: I also knew her once.

NORA: I'm aware of that.

KROGSTAD: Oh? You know all about it. I thought so. Well, then let me ask
you short and sweet: is Mrs. Linde getting a job at the bank?

NORA: What makes you think you can cross-examine me, Mr. Krogstad—
you, one of my husband's employees? But since you ask, you might as
well know—yes, Mrs. Linde's going to be taken on at the bank. And I'm
the one who spoke for her, Mr. Krogstad. Now you know.

340   KROGSTAD: So I guessed right.

NORA (pacing up and down): Oh, one does have a tiny bit of influence, I should
hope. Just because I am a woman, don't think it means that—When one
has a subordinate position, Mr. Krogstad, one really ought to be careful
about pushing somebody who—hm—

KROGSTAD: Who has influence?

NORA: That's right.

KROGSTAD (in a different tone): Mrs. Helmer, would you be good enough to
use your influence on my behalf?

345   NORA: What? What do you mean?

KROGSTAD: Would you please make sure that I keep my subordinate position
in the bank?

NORA: What does that mean? Who's thinking of taking away your position?

KROGSTAD: Oh, don't play the innocent with me. I'm quite aware that your
friend would hardly relish the chance of running into me again; and I'm
also aware now whom I can thank for being turned out.

NORA: But I promise you—

350   KROGSTAD: Yes, yes, yes, to the point: there's still time, and I'm advising you
to use your influence to prevent it.

NORA: But Mr. Krogstad, I have absolutely no influence.

KROGSTAD: You haven't? I thought you were just saying—

NORA: You shouldn't take me so literally. I! How can you believe that I have
any such influence over my husband?

KROGSTAD: Oh, I've known your husband from our student days. I don't think
the great bank manager's more steadfast than any other married man.

355   NORA: You speak insolently about my husband, and I'll show you the door.

KROGSTAD: The lady has spirit.

NORA: I'm not afraid of you any longer. After New Year's, I'll soon be done with the whole business.

KROGSTAD *(restraining himself)*: Now listen to me, Mrs. Helmer. If necessary, I'll fight for my little job in the bank as if it were life itself.

NORA: Yes, so it seems.

KROGSTAD: It's not just a matter of income; that's the least of it. It's some-   *360*
thing else—All right, out with it! Look, this is the thing. You know, just like all the others, of course, that once, a good many years ago, I did something rather rash.

NORA: I've heard rumors to that effect.

KROGSTAD: The case never got into court; but all the same, every door was closed in my face from then on. So I took up those various activities you know about. I had to grab hold somewhere; and I dare say I haven't been among the worst. But now I want to drop all that. My boys are growing up. For their sakes, I'll have to win back as much respect as possible here in town. That job in the bank was like the first rung in my ladder. And now your husband wants to kick me right back down in the mud again.

NORA: But for heaven's sake, Mr. Krogstad, it's simply not in my power to help you.

KROGSTAD: That's because you haven't the will to—but I have the means to make you.

NORA: You certainly won't tell my husband that I owe you money?   *365*

KROGSTAD: Hm—what if I told him that?

NORA: That would be shameful of you. *(Nearly in tears.)* This secret—my joy and my pride—that he should learn it in such a crude and disgusting way—learn it from you. You'd expose me to the most horrible unpleasantness—

KROGSTAD: Only unpleasantness?

NORA *(vehemently)*: But go on and try. It'll turn out the worst for you, because then my husband will really see what a crook you are, and then you'll *never* be able to hold your job.

KROGSTAD: I asked if it was just domestic unpleasantness you were afraid of?   *370*

NORA: If my husband finds out, then of course he'll pay what I owe at once, and then we'd be through with you for good.

KROGSTAD *(a step closer)*: Listen, Mrs. Helmer—you've either got a very bad memory, or else no head at all for business. I'd better put you a little more in touch with the facts.

NORA: What do you mean?

KROGSTAD: When your husband was sick, you came to me for a loan of four thousand, eight hundred crowns.

NORA: Where else could I go?   *375*

KROGSTAD: I promised to get you that sum—

NORA: And you got it.

KROGSTAD: I promised to get you that sum, on certain conditions. You were so involved in your husband's illness, and so eager to finance your trip, that I guess you didn't think out all the details. It might just be a good idea to remind you. I promised you the money on the strength of a note I drew up.

NORA: Yes, and that I signed.

380 KROGSTAD: Right. But at the bottom I added some lines for your father to guarantee the loan. He was supposed to sign down there.

NORA: Supposed to? He did sign.

KROGSTAD: I left the date blank. In other words, your father would have dated his signature himself. Do you remember that?

NORA: Yes, I think—

KROGSTAD: Then I gave you the note for you to mail to your father. Isn't that so?

385 NORA: Yes.

KROGSTAD: And naturally you sent it at once—because only some five, six days later you brought me the note, properly signed. And with that, the money was yours.

NORA: Well, then; I've made my payments regularly, haven't I?

KROGSTAD: More or less. But—getting back to the point—those were hard times for you then, Mrs. Helmer.

NORA: Yes, they were.

390 KROGSTAD: Your father was very ill, I believe.

NORA: He was near the end.

KROGSTAD: He died soon after?

NORA: Yes.

KROGSTAD: Tell me, Mrs. Helmer, do you happen to recall the date of your father's death? The day of the month, I mean.

395 NORA: Papa died the twenty-ninth of September.

KROGSTAD: That's quite correct; I've already looked into that. And now we come to a curious thing—*(taking out a paper)* which I simply cannot comprehend.

NORA: Curious thing? I don't know—

KROGSTAD: This is the curious thing: that your father co-signed the note for your loan three days after his death.

NORA: How—? I don't understand.

400 KROGSTAD: Your father died the twenty-ninth of September. But look. Here your father dated his signature October second. Isn't that curious, Mrs. Helmer? *(NORA is silent.)* Can you explain it to me? *(NORA remains silent.)* It's also remarkable that the words "October second" and the year aren't written in your father's hand, but rather in one that I think I know. Well, it's easy to understand. Your father forgot perhaps to date his signature, and then someone or other added it, a bit sloppily, before anyone

knew of his death. There's nothing wrong in that. It all comes down to the signature. And there's no question about *that,* Mrs. Helmer. It really *was* your father who signed his own name here, wasn't it?

NORA *(after a short silence, throwing her head back and looking squarely at him)*: No, it wasn't. I signed Papa's name.

KROGSTAD: Wait, now—are you fully aware that this is a dangerous confession?

NORA: Why? You'll soon get your money.

KROGSTAD: Let me ask you a question—why didn't you send the paper to your father?

NORA: That was impossible. Papa was so sick. If I'd asked him for his signa-   405
ture, I also would have had to tell him what the money was for. But I couldn't tell him, sick as he was, that my husband's life was in danger. That was just impossible.

KROGSTAD: Then it would have been better if you'd given up the trip abroad.

NORA: I couldn't possibly. The trip was to save my husband's life. I couldn't give that up.

KROGSTAD: But didn't you ever consider that this was a fraud against me?

NORA: I couldn't let myself be bothered by that. You weren't any concern of mine. I couldn't stand you, with all those cold complications you made, even though you knew how badly off my husband was.

KROGSTAD: Mrs. Helmer, obviously you haven't the vaguest idea of what   410
you've involved yourself in. But I can tell you this: it was nothing more and nothing worse than I once did—and it wrecked my whole reputation.

NORA: You? Do you expect me to believe that you ever acted bravely to save your wife's life?

KROGSTAD: Laws don't inquire into motives.

NORA: Then they must be very poor laws.

KROGSTAD: Poor or not—if I introduce this paper in court, you'll be judged according to law.

NORA: This I refuse to believe. A daughter hasn't a right to protect her dying   415
father from anxiety and care? A wife hasn't a right to save her husband's life? I don't know much about laws, but I'm sure that somewhere in the books these things are allowed. And you don't know anything about it— you who practice the law? You must be an awful lawyer, Mr. Krogstad.

KROGSTAD: Could be. But business—the kind of business we two are mixed up in—don't you think I know about that? All right. Do what you want now. But I'm telling you *this:* if I get shoved down a second time, you're going to keep me company.

(He bows and goes out through the hall.)

NORA *(pensive for a moment, then tossing her head)*: Oh, really! Trying to frighten me! I'm not so silly as all that. *(Begins gathering up the children's clothes, but soon stops.)* But—? No, but that's impossible! I did it out of love.

THE CHILDREN *(in the doorway, left)*: Mama, that strange man's gone out
the door.

NORA: Yes, yes, I know it. But don't tell anyone about the strange man. Do
you hear. Not even Papa!

420   THE CHILDREN: No, Mama. But now will you play again?

NORA: No, not now.

THE CHILDREN: Oh, but Mama, you promised.

NORA: Yes, but I can't now. Go inside; I have too much to do. Go in, go in,
my sweet darlings. *(She herds them gently back in the room and shuts the door
after them. Settling on the sofa, she takes up a piece of embroidery and makes
some stitches, but soon stops abruptly.)* No! *(Throws the work aside, rises, goes to
the hall door and calls out.)* Helene! Let me have the tree in here. *(Goes to
the table, left, opens the table drawer, and stops again.)* No, but that's utterly
impossible!

MAID *(with the Christmas tree)*: Where should I put it, Ma'am?

425   NORA: There. The middle of the floor.

MAID: Should I bring anything else?

NORA: No, thanks. I have what I need.

(The MAID, who has set the tree down, goes out.)

NORA *(absorbed in trimming the tree)*: Candles here—and flowers here. That
terrible creature! Talk, talk, talk! There's nothing to it at all. The tree's
going to be lovely. I'll do anything to please you, Torvald. I'll sing for
you, dance for you—

(HELMER comes in from the hall, with a sheaf of papers under his arm.)

NORA: Oh! You're back so soon?

430   HELMER: Yes. Has anyone been here?

NORA: Here? No.

HELMER: That's odd. I saw Krogstad leaving the front door.

NORA: So? Oh yes, that's true. Krogstad was here a moment.

HELMER: Nora, I can see by your face that he's been here, begging you to
put in a good word for him.

435   NORA: Yes.

HELMER: And it was supposed to seem like your own idea? You were to hide
it from me that he'd been here. He asked you that, too, didn't he?

NORA: Yes, Torvald, but—

HELMER: Nora, Nora, and you could fall for that? Talk with that sort of person
and promise him anything? And then in the bargain, tell me an untruth.

NORA: An untruth—?

440   HELMER: Didn't you say that no one had been here? *(Wagging his finger.)* My
little songbird must never do that again. A songbird needs a clean beak

to warble with. No false notes. *(Putting his arm about her waist.)* That's the way it should be, isn't it? Yes, I'm sure of it. *(Releasing her.)* And so, enough of that. *(Sitting by the stove.)* Ah, how snug and cozy it is here. *(Leafing among his papers.)*

NORA *(busy with the tree, after a short pause)*: Torvald!

HELMER: Yes.

NORA: I'm so much looking forward to the Stenborgs' costume party, day after tomorrow.

HELMER: And I can't wait to see what you'll surprise me with.

NORA: Oh, that stupid business.   445

HELMER: What?

NORA: I can't find anything that's right. Everything seems so ridiculous, so inane.

HELMER: So my little Nora's come to *that* recognition?

NORA *(going behind his chair, her arms resting on its back)*: Are you very busy, Torvald?

HELMER: Oh—   450

NORA: What papers are those?

HELMER: Bank matters.

NORA: Already?

HELMER: I've gotten full authority from the retiring management to make all necessary changes in personnel and procedure. I'll need Christmas week for that. I want to have everything in order by New Year's.

NORA: So that was the reason this poor Krogstad—   455

HELMER: Hm.

NORA *(still leaning on the chair and slowly stroking the nape of his neck)*: If you weren't so very busy, I would have asked you an enormous favor, Torvald.

HELMER: Let's hear. What is it?

NORA: You know, there isn't anyone who has your good taste—and I want so much to look well at the costume party. Torvald, couldn't you take over and decide what I should be and plan my costume?

HELMER: Ah, is my stubborn little creature calling for a lifeguard?   460

NORA: Yes, Torvald, I can't get anywhere without your help.

HELMER: All right—I'll think it over. We'll hit on something.

NORA: Oh, how sweet of you. *(Goes to the tree again. Pause.)* Aren't the red flowers pretty—? But tell me, was it really such a crime that this Krogstad committed?

HELMER: Forgery. Do you have any idea what that means?

NORA: Couldn't he have done it out of need?   465

HELMER: Yes, or thoughtlessness, like so many others. I'm not so heartless that I'd condemn a man categorically for just one mistake.

NORA: No, of course not, Torvald!

HELMER: Plenty of men have redeemed themselves by openly confessing their crimes and taking their punishments.

NORA: Punishment—?

470   HELMER: But now Krogstad didn't go that way. He got himself out by sharp practices, and that's the real cause of his moral breakdown.

NORA: Do you really think that would—?

HELMER: Just imagine how a man with that sort of guilt in him has to lie and cheat and deceive on all sides, has to wear a mask even with the nearest and dearest he has, even with his own wife and children. And with the children, Nora—that's where it's most horrible.

NORA: Why?

HELMER: Because that kind of atmosphere of lies infects the whole life of a home. Every breath the children take in is filled with the terms of something degenerate.

475   NORA *(coming closer behind him)*: Are you sure of that?

HELMER: Oh, I've seen it often enough as a lawyer. Almost everyone who goes bad early in life has a mother who's a chronic liar.

NORA: Why just—the mother?

HELMER: It's usually the mother's influence that's dominant, but the father's works in the same way, of course. Every lawyer is quite familiar with it. And still this Krogstad's been going home year in, year out, poisoning his own children with lies and pretense; that's why I call him morally lost. *(Reaching his hands out toward her.)* So my sweet little Nora must promise me never to plead his cause. Your hand on it. Come, come, what's this? Give me your hand. There, now. All settled. I can tell you it'd be impossible for me to work alongside of him. I literally feel physically revolted when I'm anywhere near such a person.

NORA *(withdraws her hand and goes to the other side of the Christmas tree)*: How hot it is here! And I've got so much to do.

480   HELMER *(getting up and gathering his papers)*: Yes, and I have to think about getting some of these read through before dinner. I'll think about your costume, too. And something to hang on the tree in gilt paper, I may even see about that. *(Putting his hand on her head.)* Oh you, my darling little songbird.

(He goes into his study and closes the door after him.)

NORA *(softly, after a silence)*: Oh, really! It isn't so. It's impossible. It must be impossible.

ANNE-MARIE *(in the doorway, left)*: The children are begging so hard to come in to Mama.

NORA: No, no, no, don't let them in to me! You stay with them, Anne-Marie.

ANNE-MARIE: Of course, Ma'am. *(Closes the door.)*

NORA *(pale with terror)*: Hurt my children—! Poison my home? *(A moment's*   485
    pause; then she tosses her head.) That's not true. Never. Never in all the world.

ACT II

Scene *Same room. Beside the piano the Christmas tree now stands stripped of ornament, burned-down candle stubs on its ragged branches.* NORA's *street clothes lie on the sofa.* NORA, *alone in the room, moves restlessly about; at last she stops at the sofa and picks up her coat.*

NORA *(dropping the coat again)*: Someone's coming! *(Goes toward the door, lis-tens.)* No—there's no one. Of course—nobody's coming today, Christ-mas Day—or tomorrow, either. But maybe—*(Opens the door and looks out.)* No, nothing in the mailbox. Quite empty. *(Coming forward.)* What nonsense! He won't do anything serious. Nothing terrible could hap-pen. It's impossible. Why, I have three small children.

    *(*ANNE-MARIE, *with a large carton, comes in from the room to the left.)*

ANNE-MARIE: Well, at last I found the box with the masquerade clothes.
NORA: Thanks. Put it on the table.
ANNE-MARIE *(does so)*: But they're all pretty much of a mess.
NORA: Ahh! I'd love to rip them in a million pieces!   5
ANNE-MARIE: Oh, mercy, they can be fixed right up. Just a little patience.
NORA: Yes, I'll go get Mrs. Linde to help me.
ANNE-MARIE: Out again now? In this nasty weather? Miss Nora will catch
    cold—get sick.
NORA: Oh, worse things could happen—How are the children?
ANNE-MARIE: The poor mites are playing with their Christmas presents, but—   10
NORA: Do they ask for me much?
ANNE-MARIE: They're so used to having Mama around, you know.
NORA: Yes, but Anne-Marie, I *can't* be together with them as much as I was.
ANNE-MARIE: Well, small children get used to anything.
NORA: You think so? Do you think they'd forget their mother if she was   15
    gone for good?
ANNE-MARIE: Oh, mercy—gone for good!
NORA: Wait, tell me, Anne-Marie—I've wondered so often—how could you
    ever have the heart to give your child over to strangers?
ANNE-MARIE: But I had to, you know, to become little Nora's nurse.
NORA: Yes, but how could you *do* it?
ANNE-MARIE: When I could get such a good place? A girl who's poor and   20
    who's gotten in trouble is glad enough for that. Because that slippery
    fish, he didn't do a thing for me, you know.
NORA: But your daughter's surely forgotten you.

ANNE-MARIE: Oh, she certainly has not. She's written to me, both when she was confirmed and when she was married.

NORA *(clasping her about the neck)*: You old Anne-Marie, you were a good mother for me when I was little.

ANNE-MARIE: Poor little Nora, with no other mother but me.

25 NORA: And if the babies didn't have one, then I know that you'd—What silly talk! *(Opening the carton.)* Go in to them. Now I'll have to—Tomorrow you can see how lovely I'll look.

ANNE-MARIE: Oh, there won't be anyone at the party as lovely as Miss Nora.

(She goes off into the room, left.)

NORA *(begins unpacking the box, but soon throws it aside)*: Oh, if I dared to go out. If only nobody would come. If only nothing would happen here while I'm out. What craziness—nobody's coming. Just don't think. This muff—needs a brushing. Beautiful gloves, beautiful gloves. Let it go. Let it go! One, two, three, four, five, six—*(With a cry.)* Oh, there they are! *(Poises to move toward the door, but remains irresolutely standing.* MRS. LINDE *enters from the hall, where she has removed her street clothes.)*

NORA: Oh, it's you, Kristine. There's no one else out there? How good that you've come.

MRS. LINDE: I hear you were up asking for me.

30 NORA: Yes, I just stopped by. There's something you really can help me with. Let's get settled on the sofa. Look, there's going to be a costume party tomorrow evening at the Stenborgs' right above us, and now Torvald wants me to go as a Neapolitan peasant girl and dance the tarantella that I learned in Capri.

MRS. LINDE: Really, you are giving a whole performance?

NORA: Torvald says yes, I should. See, here's the dress. Torvald had it made for me down there; but now it's all so tattered that I just don't know—

MRS. LINDE: Oh, we'll fix that up in no time. It's nothing more than the trimmings—they're a bit loose here and there. Needle and thread? Good, now we have what we need.

NORA: Oh, how sweet of you!

35 MRS. LINDE *(sewing)*: So you'll be in disguise tomorrow, Nora. You know what? I'll stop by then for a moment and have a look at you all dressed up. But listen, I've absolutely forgotten to thank you for that pleasant evening yesterday.

NORA *(getting up and walking about)*: I don't think it was as pleasant as usual yesterday. You should have come to town a bit sooner, Kristine—Yes, Torvald really knows how to give a home elegance and charm.

MRS. LINDE: And you do, too, if you ask me. You're not your father's daughter for nothing. But tell me, is Dr. Rank always so down in the mouth as yesterday?

NORA: No, that was quite an exception. But he goes around critically ill all the time—tuberculosis of the spine, poor man. You know, his father was a disgusting thing who kept mistresses and so on—and that's why the son's been sickly from birth.

MRS. LINDE *(lets her sewing fall to her lap)*: But my dearest Nora, how do you know about such things?

NORA *(walking more jauntily)*: Hmp! When you've had three children, then you've had a few visits from—women who know something of medicine, and they tell you this and that.

MRS. LINDE *(resumes sewing; a short pause)*: Does Dr. Rank come here every day?

NORA: Every blessed day. He's Torvald's best friend from childhood, and *my* good friend, too. Dr. Rank almost belongs to this house.

MRS. LINDE: But tell me—is he quite sincere? I mean, doesn't he rather enjoy flattering people?

NORA: Just the opposite. Why do you think that?

MRS. LINDE: When you introduced us yesterday, he was proclaiming that he'd often heard my name in this house; but later I noticed that your husband hadn't the slightest idea who I really was. So how could Dr. Rank—?

NORA: But it's all true, Kristine. You see, Torvald loves me beyond words, and, as he puts it, he'd like to keep me all to himself. For a long time he'd almost be jealous if I even mentioned any of my old friends back home. So of course I dropped that. But with Dr. Rank I talk a lot about such things, because he likes hearing about them.

MRS. LINDE: Now listen, Nora; in many ways you're still like a child. I'm a good deal older than you, with a little more experience. I'll tell you something; you ought to put an end to all this with Dr. Rank.

NORA: What should I put an end to?

MRS. LINDE: Both parts of it, I think. Yesterday you said something about a rich admirer who'd provide you with money—

NORA: Yes, one who doesn't exist—worse luck. So?

MRS. LINDE: Is Dr. Rank well off?

NORA: Yes, he is.

MRS. LINDE: With no dependents?

NORA: No, no one. But—

MRS. LINDE: And he's over here every day?

NORA: Yes, I told you that.

MRS. LINDE: How can a man of such refinement be so grasping?

NORA: I don't follow you at all.

MRS. LINDE: Now don't try to hide it, Nora. You think I can't guess who loaned you the forty-eight hundred crowns?

NORA: Are you out of your mind? How could you think of such a thing! A friend of ours, who comes here every single day. What an intolerable situation that would have been!

MRS. LINDE: Then it really wasn't him.

NORA: No, absolutely not. It never even crossed my mind for a moment—
  And he had nothing to lend in those days; his inheritance came later.

MRS. LINDE: Well, I think that was a stroke of luck for you, Nora dear.

NORA: No, it never would have occurred to me to ask Dr. Rank—Still, I'm
  quite sure that if I had asked him—

65 MRS. LINDE: Which you won't, of course.

NORA: No, of course not. I can't see that I'd ever need to. But I'm quite positive that if I talked to Dr. Rank—

MRS. LINDE: Behind your husband's back?

NORA: I've got to clear up this other thing: *that's* also behind his back. I've *got*
  to clear it all up.

MRS. LINDE: Yes, I was saying that yesterday, but—

70 NORA *(pacing up and down)*: A man handles these problems so much better
  than a woman—

MRS. LINDE: One's husband does, yes.

NORA: Nonsense. *(Stopping.)* When you pay everything you owe, then you
  get your note back, right?

MRS. LINDE: Yes, naturally.

NORA: And can rip it into a million pieces and burn it up—that filthy scrap
  of paper!

75 MRS. LINDE *(looking hard at her, laying her sewing aside, and rising slowly)*: Nora,
  you're hiding something from me.

NORA: You can see it in my face?

MRS. LINDE: Something's happened to you since yesterday morning. Nora,
  what is it?

NORA *(hurrying toward her)*: Kristine! *(Listening.)* Shh! Torvald's home. Look,
  go in with the children a while. Torvald can't bear all this snipping and
  stitching. Let Anne-Marie help you.

MRS. LINDE *(gathering up some of the things)*: All right, but I'm not leaving
  here until we've talked this out. *(She disappears into the room, left, as* TOR-
  VALD *enters from the hall.)*

80 NORA: Oh, how I've been waiting for you, Torvald dear.

HELMER: Was that the dressmaker?

NORA: No, that was Kristine. She's helping me fix up my costume. You know,
  it's going to be quite attractive.

HELMER: Yes, wasn't that a bright idea I had?

NORA: Brilliant! But then wasn't I good as well to give in to you?

85 HELMER: Good—because you give in to your husband's judgment? All right,
  you little goose, I know you didn't mean it like that. But I won't disturb
  you. You'll want to have a fitting, I suppose.

NORA: And you'll be working?

HELMER: Yes. *(Indicating a bundle of papers.)* See. I've been down to the bank.
  (Starts toward his study.)

NORA: Torvald.

HELMER *(stops)*: Yes.

NORA: If your little squirrel begged you, with all her heart and soul, for   *90*
something—?

HELMER: What's that?

NORA: Then would you do it?

HELMER: First, naturally, I'd have to know what it was.

NORA: Your squirrel would scamper about and do tricks, if you'd only be
sweet and give in.

HELMER: Out with it.   *95*

NORA: Your lark would be singing high and low in every room—

HELMER: Come on, she does that anyway.

NORA: I'd be a wood nymph and dance for you in the moonlight.

HELMER: Nora—don't tell me it's that same business from this morning?

NORA *(coming closer)*: Yes, Torvald, I beg you, please!   *100*

HELMER: And you actually have the nerve to drag that up again?

NORA: Yes, yes, you've got to give in to me; you have to let Krogstad keep his
job in the bank.

HELMER: My dear Nora, I've slated his job for Mrs. Linde.

NORA: That's awfully kind of you. But you could just fire another clerk instead of Krogstad.

HELMER: This is the most incredible stubbornness! Because you go and give   *105*
an impulsive promise to speak up for him, I'm expected to—

NORA: That's not the reason, Torvald. It's for your own sake. That man does
writing for the worst papers; you said it yourself. He could do you any
amount of harm. I'm scared to death of him—

HELMER: Ah, I understand. It's the old memories haunting you.

NORA: What do you mean by that?

HELMER: Of course, you're thinking about your father.

NORA: Yes, all right. Just remember how those nasty gossips wrote in the pa-   *110*
pers about Papa and slandered him so cruelly. I think they'd have had
him dismissed if the department hadn't sent you up to investigate, and if
you hadn't been so kind and open-minded toward him.

HELMER: My dear Nora, there's a notable difference between your father and
me. Your father's official career was hardly above reproach. But mine is;
and I hope it'll stay that way as long as I hold my position.

NORA: Oh, who can ever tell what vicious minds can invent? We could be so
snug and happy now in our quiet, carefree home—you and I and the
children, Torvald! That's why I'm pleading with you so—

HELMER: And just by pleading for him you make it impossible for me to
keep him on. It's already known at the bank that I'm firing Krogstad.
What if it's rumored around now that the new bank manager was ve-
toed by his wife—

NORA: Yes, what then—?

115   HELMER: Oh yes—as long as your little bundle of stubbornness gets her way—I should go and make myself ridiculous in front of the whole office—give people the idea I can be swayed by all kinds of outside pressure. Oh, you can bet I'd feel the effects of that soon enough! Besides—there's something that rules Krogstad right out at the bank as long as I'm the manager.

NORA: What's that?

HELMER: His moral failings I could maybe overlook if I had to—

NORA: Yes, Torvald, why not?

HELMER: And I hear he's quite efficient on the job. But he was a crony of mine back in my teens—one of those rash friendships that crop up again and again to embarrass you later in life. Well, I might as well say it straight out: we're on a first-name basis. And that tactless fool makes no effort at all to hide it in front of others. Quite the contrary—he thinks that entitles him to take a familiar air around me, and so every other second he comes booming out with his "Yes, Torvald!" and "Sure thing, Torvald!" I tell you, it's been excruciating for me. He's out to make my place in the bank unbearable.

120   NORA: Torvald, you can't be serious about all this.

HELMER: Oh no? Why not?

NORA: Because these are such petty considerations.

HELMER: What are you saying? Petty? You think I'm petty!

NORA: No, just the opposite, Torvald dear. That's exactly why—

125   HELMER: Never mind. You call my motives petty; then I might as well be just that. Petty! All right! We'll put a stop to this for good. (Goes to the hall door and calls.) Helene!

NORA: What do you want?

HELMER (searching among his papers): A decision. (The MAID comes in.) Look here; take this letter, go out with it at once. Get hold of a messenger and have him deliver it. Quick now. It's already addressed. Wait, here's some money.

MAID: Yes, sir. (She leaves with the letter.)

HELMER (straightening his papers): There, now, little Miss Willful.

130   NORA (breathlessly): Torvald, what was that letter?

HELMER: Krogstad's notice.

NORA: Call it back, Torvald! There's still time. Oh Torvald, call it back! Do it for my sake—for your sake, for the children's sake! Do you hear, Torvald; do it! You don't know how this can harm us.

HELMER: Too late.

NORA: Yes, too late.

135   HELMER: Nora dear, I can forgive you this panic, even though basically you're insulting me. Yes, you are! Or isn't it an insult to think that I should be afraid of a courtroom hack's revenge? But I forgive you anyway, because

this shows so beautifully how much you love me. *(Takes her in his arms.)* This is the way it should be, my darling Nora. Whatever comes, you'll see: when it really counts, I have strength and courage enough as a man to take on the whole weight myself.

NORA *(terrified)*: What do you mean by that?

HELMER: The whole weight, I said.

NORA *(resolutely)*: No, never in all the world.

HELMER: Good. So we'll share it, Nora, as man and wife. That's as it should be. *(Fondling her.)* Are you happy now? There, there, there—not these frightened dove's eyes. It's nothing at all but empty fantasies—Now you should run through your tarantella and practice your tambourine. I'll go to the inner office and shut both doors, so I won't hear a thing; you can make all the noise you like. *(Turning in the doorway.)* And when Rank comes, just tell him where he can find me. *(He nods to her and goes with his papers into the study, closing the door.)*

NORA *(standing as though rooted, dazed with fright, in a whisper)*: He really could   *140* do it. He will do it. He'll do it in spite of everything. No, not that, never, never! Anything but that! Escape! A way out—*(The doorbell rings.)* Dr. Rank! Anything but that! Anything, whatever it is! *(Her hands pass over her face, smoothing it; she pulls herself together, goes over and opens the hall door. DR. RANK stands outside, hanging his fur coat up. During the following scene, it begins getting dark.)*

NORA: Hello, Dr. Rank. I recognized your ring. But you mustn't go in to Torvald yet; I believe he's working.

RANK: And you?

NORA: For you, I always have an hour to spare—you know that.

(He has entered, and she shuts the door after him.)

RANK: Many thanks. I'll make use of these hours while I can.

NORA: What do you mean by that? While you can?   *145*

RANK: Does that disturb you?

NORA: Well, it's such an odd phrase. Is anything going to happen?

RANK: What's going to happen is what I've been expecting so long—but I honestly didn't think it would come so soon.

NORA *(gripping his arm)*: What is it you've found out? Dr. Rank, you have to tell me!

RANK *(sitting by the stove)*: It's all over with me. There's nothing to be done   *150* about it.

NORA *(breathing easier)*: Is it you—then—?

RANK: Who else? There's no point in lying to one's self. I'm the most miserable of all my patients, Mrs. Helmer. These past few days I've been auditing my internal accounts. Bankrupt! Within a month I'll probably be laid out and rotting in the churchyard.

NORA: Oh, what a horrible thing to say.

RANK: The thing itself is horrible. But the worst of it is all the other horror before it's over. There's only one final examination left; when I'm finished with that, I'll know about when my disintegration will begin. There's something I want to say. Helmer with his sensitivity has such a sharp distaste for anything ugly. I don't want him near my sickroom.

155 NORA: Oh, but Dr. Rank—

RANK: I won't have him in there. Under no condition. I'll lock my door to him—As soon as I'm completely sure of the worst, I'll send you my calling card marked with a black cross, and you'll know then the wreck has started to come apart.

NORA: No, today you're completely unreasonable. And I wanted you so much to be in a really good humor.

RANK: With death up my sleeve? And then to suffer this way for somebody else's sins. Is there any justice in that? And in every single family, in some way or another, this inevitable retribution of nature goes on—

NORA *(her hands pressed over her ears)*: Oh, stuff! Cheer up! Please—be gay!

160 RANK: Yes, I'd just as soon laugh at it all. My poor, innocent spine, serving time for my father's gay army days.

NORA *(by the table, left)*: He was so infatuated with asparagus tips and *pâté de foie gras,* wasn't that it?

RANK: Yes—and with truffles.

NORA: Truffles, yes. And then with oysters, I suppose?

RANK: Yes, tons of oysters, naturally.

165 NORA: And then the port and champagne to go with it. It's so sad that all these delectable things have to strike at our bones.

RANK: Especially when they strike at the unhappy bones that never shared in the fun.

NORA: Ah, that's the saddest of all.

RANK *(looks searchingly at her)*: Hm.

NORA *(after a moment)*: Why did you smile?

170 RANK: No, it was you who laughed.

NORA: No, it was you who smiled, Dr. Rank!

RANK *(getting up)*: You're even a bigger tease than I'd thought.

NORA: I'm full of wild ideas today.

RANK: That's obvious.

175 NORA *(putting both hands on his shoulders)*: Dear, dear Dr. Rank, you'll never die for Torvald and me.

RANK: Oh, that loss you'll easily get over. Those who go away are soon forgotten.

NORA *(looks fearfully at him)*: You believe that?

RANK: One makes new connections, and then—

NORA: Who makes new connections?

RANK: Both you and Torvald will when I'm gone. I'd say you're well under   *180*
    way already. What was that Mrs. Linde doing here last evening?

NORA: Oh, come—you can't be jealous of poor Kristine?

RANK: Oh yes, I am. She'll be my successor here in the house. When I'm
    down under, that woman will probably—

NORA: Shh! Not so loud. She's right in there.

RANK: Today as well. So you see.

NORA: Only to sew on my dress. Good gracious, how unreasonable you are.   *185*
    (Sitting on the sofa.) Be nice now, Dr. Rank. Tomorrow you'll see how
    beautifully I'll dance, and you can imagine then that I'm dancing only
    for you—yes, and of course for Torvald, too—that's understood. *(Takes
    various items out of the carton.)* Dr. Rank, sit over here and I'll show you
    something.

RANK *(sitting)*: What's that?

NORA: Look here. Look.

RANK: Silk stockings.

NORA: Flesh-colored. Aren't they lovely? Now it's so dark here, but tomor-
    row—No, no, no, just look at the feet. Oh well, you might as well look
    at the rest.

RANK: Hm—   *190*

NORA: Why do you look so critical? Don't you believe they'll fit?

RANK: I've never had any chance to form an opinion on that.

NORA *(glancing at him a moment)*: Shame on you. *(Hits him lightly on the ear
    with the stockings.)* That's for you. *(Puts them away again.)*

RANK: And what other splendors am I going to see now?

NORA: Not the least bit more, because you've been naughty. *(She hums a little   *195*
    and rummages among her things.)*

RANK *(after a short silence)*: When I sit here together with you like this, com-
    pletely easy and open, then I don't know—I simply can't imagine—
    whatever would have become of me if I'd never come into this house.

NORA *(smiling)*: Yes, I really think you feel completely at ease with us.

RANK *(more quietly, staring straight ahead)*: And then to have to go away from
    it all—

NORA: Nonsense, you're not going away.

RANK *(his voice unchanged)*: —and not even be able to leave some poor show   *200*
    of gratitude behind, scarcely a fleeting regret—no more than a vacant
    place that anyone can fill.

NORA: And if I asked you now for—? No—

RANK: For what?

NORA: For a great proof of your friendship—

RANK: Yes, yes?

NORA: No, I mean—for an exceptionally big favor—   *205*

RANK: Would you really, for once, make me so happy?

NORA: Oh, you haven't the vaguest idea what it is.

RANK: All right, then tell me.

NORA: No, but I can't, Dr. Rank—it's all out of reason. It's advice and help, too—and a favor—

210 RANK: So much the better. I can't fathom what you're hinting at. Just speak out. Don't you trust me?

NORA: Of course. More than anyone else. You're my best and truest friend, I'm sure. That's why I want to talk to you. All right, then, Dr. Rank: there's something you can help me prevent. You know how deeply, how inexpressibly dearly Torvald loves me; he'd never hesitate a second to give up his life for me.

RANK *(leaning close to her)*: Nora—do you think he's the only one—

NORA *(with a slight start)*: Who—?

RANK: Who'd gladly give up his life for you.

215 NORA *(heavily)*: I see.

RANK: I swore to myself you should know this before I'm gone. I'll never find a better chance. Yes, Nora, now you know. And also you know now that you can trust me beyond anyone else.

NORA *(rising, natural and calm)*: Let me by.

RANK *(making room for her, but still sitting)*: Nora—

NORA *(in the hall doorway)*: Helene, bring the lamp in. *(Goes over to the stove.)* Ah, dear Dr. Rank, that was really mean of you.

220 RANK *(getting up)*: That I've loved you just as deeply as somebody else? Was *that* mean?

NORA: No, but that you came out and told me. That was quite unnecessary—

RANK: What do you mean? Have you known—?

(The MAID comes in with the lamp, sets it on the table, and goes out again.)

RANK: Nora—Mrs. Helmer—I'm asking you: have you known about it?

NORA: Oh, how can I tell what I know or don't know? Really, I don't know what to say—Why did you have to be so clumsy, Dr. Rank! Everything was so good.

225 RANK: Well, in any case, you now have the knowledge that my body and soul are at your command. So won't you speak out?

NORA *(looking at him)*: After that?

RANK: Please, just let me know what it is.

NORA: You can't know anything now.

RANK: I have to. You mustn't punish me like this. Give me the chance to do whatever is humanly possible for you.

230 NORA: Now there's nothing you can do for me. Besides, actually, I don't need any help. You'll see—it's only my fantasies. That's what it is. Of course! *(Sits in the rocker, looks at him, and smiles.)* What a nice one you are, Dr. Rank. Aren't you a little bit ashamed, now that the lamp is here?

RANK: No, not exactly. But perhaps I'd better go—for good?

NORA: No, you certainly can't do that. You must come here just as you always have. You know Torvald can't do without you.

RANK: Yes, but *you?*

NORA: You know how much I enjoy it when you're here.

RANK: That's precisely what threw me off. You're a mystery to me. So many   235
times I've felt you'd almost rather be with me than with Helmer.

NORA: Yes—you see, there are some people that one loves most and other people that one would almost prefer being with.

RANK: Yes, there's something to that.

NORA: When I was back home, of course I loved Papa most. But I always thought it was so much fun when I could sneak down to the maids' quarters, because they never tried to improve me, and it was always so amusing, the way they talked to each other.

RANK: Aha, so it's *their* place that I've filled.

NORA *(jumping up and going to him)*: Oh, dear sweet Dr. Rank, that's not what   240
I meant at all. But you can understand that with Torvald it's just the same as with Papa—

(The MAID enters from the hall.)

MAID: Ma'am—please! *(She whispers to NORA and hands her a calling card.)*

NORA *(glancing at the card)*: Ah! *(Slips it into her pocket.)*

RANK: Anything wrong?

NORA: No, no, not at all. It's only some—it's my new dress—

RANK: Really? But—there's your dress.   245

NORA: Oh, that. But this is another one—I ordered it—Torvald mustn't know—

RANK: Ah, now we have the big secret.

NORA: That's right. Just go in with him—he's back in the inner study. Keep him there as long as—

RANK: Don't worry. He won't get away.   *(Goes into the study.)*

NORA *(to the MAID)*: And he's standing waiting in the kitchen.   250

MAID: Yes, he came up by the back stairs.

NORA: But didn't you tell him somebody was here?

MAID: Yes, but that didn't do any good.

NORA: He won't leave?

MAID: No, he won't go till he's talked with you, ma'am.   255

NORA: Let him come in, then—but quietly. Helene, don't breathe a word about this. It's a surprise for my husband.

MAID: Yes, yes, I understand—   *(Goes out.)*

NORA: This horror—it's going to happen. No, no, no, it can't happen, it mustn't. *(She goes and bolts HELMER's door. The MAID opens the hall door for KROGSTAD and shuts it behind him. He is dressed for travel in a fur coat, boots and a fur cap.)*

NORA *(going toward him)*: Talk softly. My husband's home.

260 KROGSTAD: Well, good for him.

NORA: What do you want?

KROGSTAD: Some information.

NORA: Hurry up, then. What is it?

KROGSTAD: You know, of course, that I got my notice.

265 NORA: I couldn't prevent it, Mr. Krogstad. I fought for you to the bitter end, but nothing worked.

KROGSTAD: Does your husband's love for you run so thin? He knows everything I can expose you to, and all the same he dares to—

NORA: How can you imagine he knows anything about this?

KROGSTAD: Ah, no—I can't imagine it either, now. It's not at all like my fine Torvald Helmer to have so much guts—

NORA: Mr. Krogstad, I demand respect for my husband!

270 KROGSTAD: Why, of course—all due respect. But since the lady's keeping it so carefully hidden, may I presume to ask if you're also a bit better informed than yesterday about what you've actually done?

NORA: More than you ever could teach me.

KROGSTAD: Yes, I *am* such an awful lawyer.

NORA: What is it you want from me?

KROGSTAD: Just a glimpse of how you are, Mrs. Helmer. I've been thinking about you all day long. A cashier, a night-court scribbler, a—well, a type like me also has a little of what they call a heart, you know.

275 NORA: Then show it. Think of my children.

KROGSTAD: Did you or your husband ever think of mine? But never mind. I simply wanted to tell you that you don't need to take this thing too seriously. For the present, I'm not proceeding with any action.

NORA: Oh no, really! Well—I knew that.

KROGSTAD: Everything can be settled in a friendly spirit. It doesn't have to get around town at all; it can stay just among us three.

NORA: My husband may never know anything of this.

280 KROGSTAD: How can you manage that? Perhaps you can pay me the balance?

NORA: No, not right now.

KROGSTAD: Or you know some way of raising the money in a day or two?

NORA: No way that I'm willing to use.

KROGSTAD: Well, it wouldn't have done you any good, anyway. If you stood in front of me with a fistful of bills, you still couldn't buy your signature back.

285 NORA: Then tell me what you're going to do with it.

KROGSTAD: I'll just hold onto it—keep it on file. There's no outsider who'll even get wind of it. So if you've been thinking of taking some desperate step—

NORA: I have!
KROGSTAD: Been thinking of running away from home—
NORA: I have!
KROGSTAD: Or even of something worse   *290*
NORA: How could you guess that?
KROGSTAD: You can drop those thoughts.
NORA: How could you guess I was thinking of *that?*
KROGSTAD: Most of us think about *that* at first. I thought about it too, but I
    discovered I hadn't the courage—
NORA *(lifelessly)*: I don't either.   *295*
KROGSTAD *(relieved)*: That's true, you haven't the courage? You too?
NORA: I don't have it—I don't have it.
KROGSTAD: It would be terribly stupid, anyway. After that first storm at home
    blows out, why, then—I have here in my pocket a letter for your hus-
    band—
NORA: Telling everything?
KROGSTAD: As charitably as possible.   *300*
NORA *(quickly)*: He mustn't ever get that letter. Tear it up. I'll find some way
    to get money.
KROGSTAD: Beg pardon, Mrs. Helmer, but I think I just told you—
NORA: Oh, I don't mean the money I owe you. Let me know how much you
    want from my husband, and I'll manage it.
KROGSTAD: I don't want any money from your husband.
NORA: What do you want, then?   *305*
KROGSTAD: I'll tell you what. I want to recoup, Mrs. Helmer; I want to get
    on in the world—and there's where your husband can help me. For a
    year and a half I've kept myself clean of anything disreputable—all that
    time struggling with the worst conditions; but I was satisfied, working
    my way up step by step. Now I've been written right off, and I'm just
    not in the mood to come crawling back. I tell you, I want to move on. I
    want to get back in the bank—in a better position. Your husband can set
    up a job for me—
NORA: He'll never do that!
KROGSTAD: He'll do it. I know him. He won't dare breathe a word of protest.
    And once I'm in there together with him, you just wait and see! Inside
    of a year, I'll be the manager's right-hand man. It'll be Nils Krogstad, not
    Torvald Helmer, who runs the bank.
NORA: You'll never see the day!
KROGSTAD: Maybe you think you can—   *310*
NORA: I have the courage now—for *that.*
KROGSTAD: Oh, you don't scare me. A smart, spoiled lady like you—
NORA: You'll see; you'll see!

KROGSTAD: Under the ice, maybe? Down in the freezing, coal-black water? There, till you float up in the spring, ugly, unrecognizable, with your hair falling out—

315   NORA: You don't frighten me.

KROGSTAD: Nor do you frighten me. One doesn't do these things, Mrs. Helmer. Besides, what good would it be? I'd still have him safe in my pocket.

NORA: Afterwards? When I'm no longer—?

KROGSTAD: Are you forgetting that *I'll* be in control then over your final reputation? *(NORA stands speechless, staring at him.)* Good; now I've warned you. Don't do anything stupid. When Helmer's read my letter, I'll be waiting for his reply. And bear in mind that it's your husband himself who's forced me back to my old ways. I'll never forgive him for that. Good-bye, Mrs. Helmer.

(He goes out through the hall.)

NORA *(goes to the hall door, opens it a crack, and listens)*: He's gone. Didn't leave the letter. Oh no, no, that's impossible too! *(Opening the door more and more.)* What's that? He's standing outside—not going downstairs. He's thinking it over? Maybe he'll—? *(A letter falls in the mailbox; then* KROGSTAD's *footsteps are heard, dying away down a flight of stairs.* NORA *gives a muffled cry and runs over toward the sofa table. A short pause.)* In the mailbox. *(Slips warily over to the hall door.)* It's lying there. Torvald, Torvald—now we're lost!

320   MRS. LINDE *(entering with the costume from the room, left)*: There now, I can't see anything else to mend. Perhaps you'd like to try—

NORA *(in a hoarse whisper)*: Kristine, come here.

MRS. LINDE *(tossing the dress on the sofa)*: What's wrong? You look upset.

NORA: Come here. See that letter? *There!* Look—through the glass in the mailbox.

MRS. LINDE: Yes, yes, I see it.

325   NORA: That letter's from Krogstad—

MRS. LINDE: Nora—it's Krogstad who loaned you the money!

NORA: Yes, and now Torvald will find out everything.

MRS. LINDE: Believe me, Nora, it's best for both of you.

NORA: There's more you don't know. I forged a name.

330   MRS. LINDE: But for heaven's sake—?

NORA: I only want to tell you that, Kristine, so that you can be my witness.

MRS. LINDE: Witness? Why should I—?

NORA: If I should go out of my mind—it could easily happen—

MRS. LINDE: Nora!

335   NORA: Or anything else occurred—so I couldn't be present here—

MRS. LINDE: Nora, Nora, you aren't yourself at all!

NORA: And someone should try to take on the whole weight, all of the guilt, you follow me—

MRS. LINDE: Yes, of course, but why do you think—?

NORA: Then you're the witness that it isn't true, Kristine. I'm very much myself; my mind right now is perfectly clear; and I'm telling you: nobody else has known about this; I alone did everything. Remember that.

MRS. LINDE: I will. But I don't understand all this.   340

NORA: Oh, how could you ever understand it? It's the miracle now that's going to take place.

MRS. LINDE: The miracle?

NORA: Yes, the miracle. But it's so awful, Kristine. It mustn't take place, not for anything in the world.

MRS. LINDE: I'm going right over and talk with Krogstad.

NORA: Don't go near him; he'll do you some terrible harm!   345

MRS. LINDE: There was a time once when he'd gladly have done anything for me.

NORA: He?

MRS. LINDE: Where does he live?

NORA: Oh, how do I know? Yes. *(Searches in her pocket.)* Here's his card. But the letter, the letter—!

HELMER *(from the study, knocking on the door)*: Nora!   350

NORA *(with a cry of fear)*: Oh! What is it? What do you want?

HELMER: Now, now, don't be so frightened. We're not coming in. You locked the door—are you trying on the dress?

NORA: Yes, I'm trying it. I'll look just beautiful, Torvald.

MRS. LINDE *(who has read the card)*: He's living right around the corner.

NORA: Yes, but what's the use? We're lost. The letter's in the box.   355

MRS. LINDE: And your husband has the key?

NORA: Yes, always.

MRS. LINDE: Krogstad can ask for his letter back unread; he can find some excuse—

NORA: But it's just this time that Torvald usually—

MRS. LINDE: Stall him. Keep him in there. I'll be back as quick as I can. *(She   360 hurries out through the hall entrance.)*

NORA *(goes to* HELMER'*s door, opens it, and peers in)*: Torvald!

HELMER *(from the inner study)*: Well—does one dare set foot in one's own living room at last? Come on, Rank, now we'll get a look—*(In the doorway.)* But what's this?

NORA: What, Torvald dear?

HELMER: Rank had me expecting some grand masquerade.

RANK *(in the doorway)*: That was my impression, but I must have been wrong.   365

NORA: No one can admire me in my splendor—not until tomorrow.

HELMER: But Nora dear, you look so exhausted. Have you practiced too hard?

NORA: No, I haven't practiced at all yet.

HELMER: You know, it's necessary—

370 NORA: Oh, it's absolutely necessary, Torvald. But I can't get anywhere without your help. I've forgotten the whole thing completely.

HELMER: Ah, we'll soon take care of that.

NORA: Yes, take care of me, Torvald, please! Promise me that? Oh, I'm so nervous. That big party—You must give up everything this evening for me.
No business—don't even touch your pen. Yes? Dear Torvald, promise?

HELMER: It's a promise. Tonight I'm totally at your service—you little helpless thing. Hm—but first there's one thing I want to—*(Goes toward the
hall door.)*

NORA: What are you looking for?

375 HELMER: Just to see if there's any mail.

NORA: No, no, don't do that, Torvald!

HELMER: Now what?

NORA: Torvald, please. There isn't any.

HELMER: Let me look, though. *(Starts out. NORA, at the piano, strikes the first
notes of the tarantella. HELMER, at the door, stops.)* Aha!

380 NORA: I can't dance tomorrow if I don't practice with you.

HELMER *(going over to her)*: Nora dear, are you really so frightened?

NORA: Yes, so terribly frightened. Let me practice right now; there's still time
before dinner. Oh, sit down and play for me, Torvald. Direct me. Teach
me, the way you always have.

HELMER: Gladly, if it's what you want. *(Sits at the piano.)*

NORA *(snatches the tambourine up from the box, then a long, varicolored shawl, which
she throws around herself, whereupon she springs forward and cries out)*: Play
for me now! Now I'll dance!

*(HELMER plays and NORA dances. RANK stands behind HELMER at the
piano and looks on.)*

385 HELMER *(as he plays)*: Slower. Slow down.

NORA: Can't change it.

HELMER: Not so violent, Nora!

NORA: Has to be just like this.

HELMER *(stopping)*: No, no, that won't do at all.

390 NORA *(laughing and swinging her tambourine)*: Isn't that what I told you?

RANK: Let me play for her.

HELMER *(getting up)*: Yes, go on, I can teach her more easily then.

*(RANK sits at the piano and plays; NORA dances more and more wildly.
HELMER has stationed himself by the stove and repeatedly gives her directions;*

she seems not to hear them; her hair loosens and falls over her shoulders; she does not notice, but goes on dancing. MRS. LINDE *enters.)*

MRS. LINDE *(standing dumbfounded at the door)*: Ah—!

NORA *(still dancing)*: See what fun, Kristine!

HELMER: But Nora darling, you dance as if your life were at stake.   *395*

NORA: And it is.

HELMER: Rank, stop! This is pure madness. Stop it, I say!

(RANK breaks off playing, and NORA *halts abruptly.)*

(going over to her): I never would have believed it. You've forgotten everything I taught you.

NORA *(throwing away the tambourine)*: You see for yourself.

HELMER: Well, there's certainly room for instruction here.   *400*

NORA: Yes, you see how important it is. You've got to teach me to the very last minute. Promise me that, Torvald?

HELMER: You can bet on it.

NORA: You mustn't, either today or tomorrow, think about anything else but me; you mustn't open any letters—or the mailbox—

HELMER: Ah, it's still the fear of that man—

NORA: Oh yes, yes, that too.   *405*

HELMER: Nora, it's written all over you—there's already a letter from him out there.

NORA: I don't know. I guess so. But you mustn't read such things now; there mustn't be anything ugly between us before it's all over.

RANK *(quietly to* HELMER*)*: You shouldn't deny her.

HELMER *(putting his arm around her)*: The child can have her way. But tomorrow night, after you've danced—

NORA: Then you'll be free.   *410*

MAID *(in the doorway, right)*: Ma'am, dinner is served.

NORA: We'll be wanting champagne, Helene.

MAID: Very good, ma'am.   *(Goes out.)*

HELMER: So—a regular banquet, hm?

NORA: Yes, a banquet—champagne till daybreak! *(Calling out.)* And some   *415* macaroons, Helene. Heaps of them—just this once.

HELMER *(taking her hands)*: Now, now, now—no hysterics. Be my own little lark again.

NORA: Oh, I will soon enough. But go on in—and you, Dr. Rank. Kristine, help me put up my hair.

RANK *(whispering, as they go)*: There's nothing wrong—really wrong, is there?

HELMER: Oh, of course not. It's nothing more than this childish anxiety I was telling you about.   *(They go out, right.)*

420   NORA: Well?

MRS. LINDE: Left town.

NORA: I could see by your face.

MRS. LINDE: He'll be home tomorrow evening. I wrote him a note.

NORA: You shouldn't have. Don't try to stop anything now. After all, it's a wonderful joy, this waiting here for the miracle.

425   MRS. LINDE: What is it you're waiting for?

NORA: Oh, you can't understand that. Go in to them, I'll be along in a moment.

(MRS. LINDE *goes into the dining room.* NORA *stands a short while as if composing herself; then she looks at her watch.*)

NORA: Five. Seven hours to midnight. Twenty-four hours to the midnight after, and then the tarantella's done. Seven and twenty-four? Thirty-one hours to live.

HELMER *(in the doorway, right)*: What's become of the little lark?

NORA *(going toward him with open arms)*: Here's your lark!

ACT III

Scene *Same scene. The table, with chairs around it, has been moved to the center of the room. A lamp on the table is lit. The hall door stands open. Dance music drifts down from the floor above.* MRS. LINDE *sits at the table, absently paging through a book, trying to read, but apparently unable to focus her thoughts. Once or twice she pauses, tensely listening for a sound at the outer entrance.*

MRS. LINDE *(glancing at her watch)*: Not yet—and there's hardly any time left. If only he's not—*(Listening again.)* Ah, there he is. *(She goes out in the hall and cautiously opens the outer door. Quiet footsteps are heard on the stairs. She whispers.)* Come in. Nobody's here.

KROGSTAD *(in the doorway)*: I found a note from you at home. What's back of all this?

MRS. LINDE: I just *had* to talk to you.

KROGSTAD: Oh? And it just *had* to be here in this house?

5   MRS. LINDE: At my place it was impossible; my room hasn't a private entrance. Come in; we're all alone. The maid's asleep, and the Helmers are at the dance upstairs.

KROGSTAD *(entering the room)*: Well, well, the Helmers are dancing tonight? Really?

MRS. LINDE: Yes, why not?

KROGSTAD: How true—why not?

MRS. LINDE: All right, Krogstad, let's talk.

10   KROGSTAD: Do we two have anything more to talk about?

MRS. LINDE: We have a great deal to talk about.

KROGSTAD: I wouldn't have thought so.

MRS. LINDE: No, because you've never understood me, really.

KROGSTAD: Was there anything more to understand—except what's all too common in life? A calculating woman throws over a man the moment a better catch comes by.

MRS. LINDE: You think I'm so thoroughly calculating? You think I broke it   15
off lightly?

KROGSTAD: Didn't you?

MRS. LINDE: Nils—is that what you really thought?

KROGSTAD: If you cared, then why did you write me the way you did?

MRS. LINDE: What else could I do? If I had to break off with you, then it was my job as well to root out everything you felt for me.

KROGSTAD *(wringing his hands)*: So that was it. And this—all this, simply for   20
money!

MRS. LINDE: Don't forget I had a helpless mother and two small brothers. We couldn't wait for you, Nils; you had such a long road ahead of you then.

KROGSTAD: That may be; but you still hadn't the right to abandon me for somebody else's sake.

MRS. LINDE: Yes—I don't know. So many, many times I've asked myself if I did have that right.

KROGSTAD *(more softly)*: When I lost you, it was as if all the solid ground dissolved from under my feet. Look at me; I'm a half-drowned man now, hanging onto a wreck.

MRS. LINDE: Help may be near.   25

KROGSTAD: It was near—but then you came and blocked it off.

MRS. LINDE: Without my knowing it, Nils. Today for the first time I learned that it's you I'm replacing at the bank.

KROGSTAD: All right—I believe you. But now that you know, will you step aside?

MRS. LINDE: No, because that wouldn't benefit you in the slightest.

KROGSTAD: Not "benefit" me, hm! I'd step aside anyway.   30

MRS. LINDE: I've learned to be realistic. Life and hard, bitter necessity have taught me that.

KROGSTAD: And life's taught me never to trust fine phrases.

MRS. LINDE: Then life's taught you a very sound thing. But you do have to trust in actions, don't you?

KROGSTAD: What does that mean?

MRS. LINDE: You said you were hanging on like a half-drowned man to a wreck.   35

KROGSTAD: I've good reason to say that.

MRS. LINDE: I'm also like a half-drowned woman on a wreck. No one to suffer with; no one to care for.

KROGSTAD: You made your choice.

MRS. LINDE: There wasn't any choice then.

KROGSTAD: So—what of it?   40

MRS. LINDE: Nils, if only we two shipwrecked people could reach across to each other.

KROGSTAD: What are you saying?

MRS. LINDE: Two on one wreck are at least better off than each on his own.

KROGSTAD: Kristine!

45 MRS. LINDE: Why do you think I came into town?

KROGSTAD: Did you really have some thought of me?

MRS. LINDE: I have to work to go on living. All my born days, as long as I can remember, I've worked, and it's been my best and my only joy. But now I'm completely alone in the world; it frightens me to be so empty and lost. To work for yourself—there's no joy in that. Nils, give me something—someone to work for.

KROGSTAD: I don't believe all this. It's just some hysterical feminine urge to go out and make a noble sacrifice.

MRS. LINDE: Have you ever found me to be hysterical?

50 KROGSTAD: Can you honestly mean this? Tell me—do you know everything about my past?

MRS. LINDE: Yes.

KROGSTAD: And you know what they think I'm worth around here.

MRS. LINDE: From what you were saying before, it would seem that with me you could have been another person.

KROGSTAD: I'm positive of that.

55 MRS. LINDE: Couldn't it happen still?

KROGSTAD: Kristine—you're saying this in all seriousness? Yes, you are! I can see it in you. And do you really have the courage, then—?

MRS. LINDE: I need to have someone to care for; and your children need a mother. We both need each other. Nils, I have faith that you're good at heart—I'll risk everything together with you.

KROGSTAD (gripping her hands): Kristine, thank you, thank you—Now I know I can win back a place in their eyes. Yes—but I forgot—

MRS. LINDE (listening): Shh! The tarantella. Go now! Go on!

60 KROGSTAD: Why? What is it?

MRS. LINDE: Hear the dance up there? When that's over, they'll be coming down.

KROGSTAD: Oh, then I'll go. But—it's all pointless. Of course, you don't know the move I made against the Helmers.

MRS. LINDE: Yes, Nils, I know.

KROGSTAD: And all the same, you have the courage to—?

65 MRS. LINDE: I know how far despair can drive a man like you.

KROGSTAD: Oh, if I only could take it all back.

MRS. LINDE: You easily could—your letter's still lying in the mailbox.

KROGSTAD: Are you sure of that?

MRS. LINDE: Positive. But—

KROGSTAD *(looks at her searchingly)*: Is that the meaning of it, then? You'll   *70*
    have your friend at any price. Tell me straight out. Is that it?

MRS. LINDE: Nils—anyone who's sold herself for somebody else once isn't
    going to do it again.

KROGSTAD: I'll demand my letter back.

MRS. LINDE: No, no.

KROGSTAD: Yes, of course. I'll stay here till Helmer comes down; I'll tell him
    to give me my letter again—that it only involves my dismissal—that he
    shouldn't read it—

MRS. LINDE: No, Nils, don't call the letter back.   *75*

KROGSTAD: But wasn't that exactly why you wrote me to come here?

MRS. LINDE: Yes, in that first panic. But it's been a whole day and night since
    then, and in that time I've seen such incredible things in this house.
    Helmer's got to learn everything; this dreadful secret has to be aired;
    those two have to come to a full understanding; all these lies and eva-
    sions can't go on.

KROGSTAD: Well, then, if you want to chance it. But at least there's one thing
    I can do, and do right away—

MRS. LINDE *(listening)*: Go now, go quick! The dance is over. We're not safe
    another second.

KROGSTAD: I'll wait for you downstairs.   *80*

MRS. LINDE: Yes, please do; take me home.

KROGSTAD: I can't believe it; I've never been so happy. *(He leaves by way of the
    outer door; the door between the room and the hall stays open.)*

MRS. LINDE *(straightening up a bit and getting together her street clothes)*: How
    different now! How different! Someone to work for, to live for—a home
    to build. Well, it is worth the try! Oh, if they'd only come! *(Listening.)*
    Ah, there they are. Bundle up. *(She picks up her hat and coat.* NORA's *and*
    HELMER's *voices can be heard outside; a key turns in the lock, and* HELMER
    brings NORA *into the hall almost by force. She is wearing the Italian costume
    with a large black shawl about her; he has on evening dress, with a black domino°
    open over it.)*

NORA *(struggling in the doorway)*: No, no, no, not inside! I'm going up again. I
    don't want to leave so soon.

HELMER: But Nora dear—   *85*

NORA: Oh, I beg you, please, Torvald. From the bottom of my heart, *please*—
    only an hour more!

HELMER: Not a single minute, Nora darling. You know our agreement. Come
    on, in we go; you'll catch cold out here. *(In spite of her resistance, he gently
    draws her into the room.)*

---

domino: Long, hooded cloak.

MRS. LINDE: Good evening.

NORA: Kristine!

90 HELMER: Why, Mrs. Linde—are you here so late?

MRS. LINDE: Yes, I'm sorry, but I did want to see Nora in costume.

NORA: Have you been sitting here, waiting for me?

MRS. LINDE: Yes. I didn't come early enough; you were all upstairs; and then I thought I really couldn't leave without seeing you.

HELMER *(removing* NORA's *shawl)*: Yes, take a good look. She's worth looking at, I can tell you that, Mrs. Linde. Isn't she lovely?

95 MRS. LINDE: Yes, I should say—

HELMER: A dream of loveliness, isn't she? That's what everyone thought at the party, too. But she's horribly stubborn—this sweet little thing. What's to be done with her? Can you imagine, I almost had to use force to pry her away.

NORA: Oh, Torvald, you're going to regret you didn't indulge me, even for just a half hour more.

HELMER: There, you see. She danced her tarantella and got a tumultuous hand—which was well earned, although the performance may have been a bit too naturalistic—I mean it rather overstepped the proprieties of art. But never mind—what's important is, she made a success, an overwhelming success. You think I could let her stay on after that and spoil the effect? Oh no; I took my lovely little Capri girl—my capricious little Capri girl, I should say—took her under my arm; one quick tour of the ballroom, a curtsy to every side, and then—as they say in novels—the beautiful vision disappeared. An exit should always be effective, Mrs. Linde, but that's what I can't get Nora to grasp. Phew, it's hot in here. *(Flings the domino on a chair and opens the door to his room.)* Why's it dark in here? Oh yes, of course. Excuse me. *(He goes in and lights a couple of candles.)*

NORA *(in a sharp, breathless whisper)*: So?

100 MRS. LINDE *(quietly)*: I talked with him.

NORA: And—?

MRS. LINDE: Nora—you must tell your husband everything.

NORA *(dully)*: I knew it.

MRS. LINDE: You've got nothing to fear from Krogstad, but you have to speak out.

105 NORA: I won't tell.

MRS. LINDE: Then the letter will.

NORA: Thanks, Kristine. I know now what's to be done. Shh!

HELMER *(reentering)*: Well, then, Mrs. Linde—have you admired her?

MRS. LINDE: Yes, and now I'll say good night.

110 HELMER: Oh, come, so soon? Is this yours, this knitting?

MRS. LINDE: Yes, thanks. I nearly forgot it.

HELMER: Do you knit, then?

MRS. LINDE: Oh yes.

HELMER: You know what? You should embroider instead.

MRS. LINDE: Really? Why?   115

HELMER: Yes, because it's a lot prettier. See here, one holds the embroidery
    so, in the left hand, and then one guides the needle with the right—so—
    in an easy, sweeping curve—right?

MRS. LINDE: Yes, I guess that's—

HELMER: But, on the other hand, knitting—it can never be anything but ugly.
    Look, see here, the arms tucked in, the knitting needles going up and
    down—there's something Chinese about it. Ah, that was really a glorious
    champagne they served.

MRS. LINDE: Yes, good night, Nora, and don't be stubborn anymore.

HELMER: Well put, Mrs. Linde!   120

MRS. LINDE: Good night, Mr. Helmer.

HELMER (accompanying her to the door): Good night, good night. I hope you
    get home all right. I'd be very happy to—but you don't have far to go.
    Good night, good night. (She leaves. He shuts the door after her and returns.)
    There, now, at last we got her out the door. She's a deadly bore, that
    creature.

NORA: Aren't you pretty tired, Torvald?

HELMER: No, not a bit.

NORA: You're not sleepy?   125

HELMER: Not at all. On the contrary, I'm feeling quite exhilarated. But you?
    Yes, you really look tired and sleepy.

NORA: Yes, I'm very tired. Soon now I'll sleep.

HELMER: See! You see! I was right all along that we shouldn't stay longer.

NORA: Whatever you do is always right.

HELMER (kissing her brow): Now my little lark talks sense. Say, did you notice   130
    what a time Rank was having tonight?

NORA: Oh, was he? I didn't get to speak with him.

HELMER: I scarcely did either, but it's a long time since I've seen him in such
    high spirits. (Gazes at her a moment, then comes nearer her.) Hm—it's mar-
    velous, though, to be back home again—to be completely alone with
    you. Oh, you bewitchingly lovely young woman!

NORA: Torvald, don't look at me like that!

HELMER: Can't I look at my richest treasure? At all that beauty that's mine,
    mine alone—completely and utterly.

NORA (moving around to the other side of the table): You mustn't talk to me that   135
    way tonight.

HELMER (following her): The tarantella is still in your blood, I can see—and it
    makes you even more enticing. Listen. The guests are beginning to go.
    (Dropping his voice.) Nora—it'll soon be quiet through this whole house.

NORA: Yes, I hope so.

HELMER: You do, don't you, my love? Do you realize—when I'm out at a party like this with you—do you know why I talk to you so little, and keep such a distance away; just send you a stolen look now and then— you know why I do it? It's because I'm imagining then that you're my secret darling, my secret young bride-to-be, and that no one suspects there's anything between us.

NORA: Yes, yes; oh, yes, I know you're always thinking of me.

140   HELMER: And then when we leave and I place the shawl over those fine young rounded shoulders—over that wonderful curving neck—then I pretend that you're my young bride, that we're just coming from the wedding, that for the first time I'm bringing you into my house—that for the first time I'm alone with you—completely alone with you, your trembling young beauty! All this evening I've longed for nothing but you. When I saw you turn and sway in the tarantella—my blood was pounding till I couldn't stand it—that's why I brought you down here so early—

NORA: Go away, Torvald! Leave me alone. I don't want all this.

HELMER: What do you mean? Nora, you're teasing me. You will, won't you? Aren't I your husband—?

(A knock at the outside door.)

NORA *(startled)*: What's that?

HELMER *(going toward the hall)*: Who is it?

145   RANK *(outside)*: It's me. May I come in a moment?

HELMER *(with quiet irritation)*: Oh, what does he want now? *(Aloud.)* Hold on. *(Goes and opens the door.)* Oh, how nice that you didn't just pass us by!

RANK: I thought I heard your voice, and then I wanted so badly to have a look in. *(Lightly glancing about.)* Ah, me, these old familiar haunts. You have it snug and cozy in here, you two.

HELMER: You seemed to be having it pretty cozy upstairs, too.

RANK: Absolutely. Why shouldn't I? Why not take in everything in life? As much as you can, anyway, and as long as you can. The wine was superb—

150   HELMER: The champagne especially.

RANK: You noticed that too? It's amazing how much I could guzzle down.

NORA: Torvald also drank a lot of champagne this evening.

RANK: Oh?

NORA: Yes, and that always makes him so entertaining.

155   RANK: Well, why shouldn't one have a pleasant evening after a well-spent day?

HELMER: Well spent? I'm afraid I can't claim that.

RANK *(slapping him on the back)*: But I can, you see!

NORA: Dr. Rank, you must have done some scientific research today.

RANK: Quite so.

160   HELMER: Come now—little Nora talking about scientific research!

NORA: And can I congratulate you on the results?

RANK: Indeed you may.

NORA: Then they were good?

RANK: The best possible for both doctor and patient—certainty.

NORA (quickly and searchingly): Certainty?   165

RANK: Complete certainty. So don't I owe myself a gay evening afterwards?

NORA: Yes, you're right, Dr. Rank.

HELMER: I'm with you—just so long as you don't have to suffer for it in the morning.

RANK: Well, one never gets something for nothing in life.

NORA: Dr. Rank—are you very fond of masquerade parties?   170

RANK: Yes, if there's a good array of odd disguises—

NORA: Tell me, what should we two go as at the next masquerade?

HELMER: You little feather head—already thinking of the next!

RANK: We two? I'll tell you what: you must go as Charmed Life—

HELMER: Yes, but find a costume for *that!*   175

RANK: Your wife can appear just as she looks every day.

HELMER: That was nicely put. But don't you know what you're going to be?

RANK: Yes, Helmer, I've made up my mind.

HELMER: Well?

RANK: At the next masquerade I'm going to be invisible.   180

HELMER: That's a funny idea.

RANK: They say there's a hat—black, huge—have you never heard of the hat that makes you invisible? You put it on, and then no one on earth can see you.

HELMER (suppressing a smile): Ah, of course.

RANK: But I'm quite forgetting what I came for. Helmer, give me a cigar, one of the dark Havanas.

HELMER: With the greatest pleasure. (Holds out his case.)   185

RANK: Thanks. (Takes one and cuts off the tip.)

NORA (striking a match): Let me give you a light.

RANK: Thank you. (She holds the match for him; he lights the cigar.) And now good-bye.

HELMER: Good-bye, good-bye, old friend.

NORA: Sleep well, Doctor.   190

RANK: Thanks for that wish.

NORA: Wish me the same.

RANK: You? All right, if you like—Sleep well. And thanks for the light.

(He nods to them both and leaves.)

HELMER (his voice subdued): He's been drinking heavily.

NORA (absently): Could be. (HELMER takes his keys from his pocket and goes out   195
in the hall.) Torvald—what are you after?

HELMER: Got to empty the mailbox; it's nearly full. There won't be room for the morning papers.

NORA: Are you working tonight?

HELMER: You know I'm not. Why—what's this? Someone's been at the lock.

NORA: At the lock—?

200   HELMER: Yes, I'm positive. What do you suppose—? I can't imagine one of
the maids—? Here's a broken hairpin. Nora, it's yours—

NORA *(quickly)*: Then it must be the children.

HELMER: You'd better break them of that. Hm, hm—well, opened it after all.
(Takes the contents out and calls into the kitchen.) Helene! Helene, would
you put out the lamp in the hall. *(He returns to the room, shutting the hall
door, then displays the handful of mail.)* Look how it's piled up. *(Sorting
through them.)* Now what's this?

NORA *(at the window)*: The letter! Oh, Torvald, no!

HELMER: Two calling cards—from Rank.

205   NORA: From Dr. Rank?

HELMER *(examining them)*: "Dr. Rank, Consulting Physician." They were on
top. He must have dropped them as he left.

NORA: Is there anything on them?

HELMER: There's a black cross over the name. See? That's a gruesome notion.
He could almost be announcing his own death.

NORA: That's just what he's doing.

210   HELMER: What! You've heard something? Something he's told you?

NORA: Yes. That when those cards came, he'd be taking his leave of us. He'll
shut himself in now and die.

HELMER: Ah, my poor friend! Of course I knew he wouldn't be here much
longer. But so soon—And then to hide himself away like a wounded
animal.

NORA: If it has to happen, then it's best it happens in silence—don't you think
so, Torvald?

HELMER *(pacing up and down)*: He's grown right into our lives. I simply can't
imagine him gone. He with his suffering and loneliness—like a dark
cloud setting off our sunlit happiness. Well, maybe it's best this way. For
him, at least. *(Standing still.)* And maybe for us too, Nora. Now we're
thrown back on each other completely. *(Embracing her.)* Oh you, my darling wife, how can I hold you close enough? You know what, Nora—
time and again I've wished you were in some terrible danger, just so I
could stake my life and soul and everything, for your sake.

215   NORA *(tearing herself away, her voice firm and decisive)*: Now you must read your
mail, Torvald.

HELMER: No, no, not tonight. I want to stay with you, dearest.

NORA: With a dying friend on your mind?

HELMER: You're right. We've both had a shock. There's ugliness between us—
these thoughts of death and corruption. We'll have to get free of them
first. Until then—we'll stay apart.

NORA *(clinging about his neck)*: Torvald—good night! Good night!

HELMER *(kissing her on the cheek)*: Good night, little songbird. Sleep well,   *220*
    Nora. I'll be reading my mail now.

(He takes the letters into his room and shuts the door after him.)

NORA *(with bewildered glances, groping about, seizing* HELMER*'s domino, throwing
    it around her, and speaking in short, hoarse, broken whispers)*: Never see him
    again. Never, never. (Putting her shawl over her head.) Never see the chil-
    dren either—them, too. Never, never. Oh, the freezing black water! The
    depths—down—Oh, I wish it were over—He has it now; he's reading
    it—now. Oh no, no, not yet. Torvald, good-bye, you and the children—
    (She starts for the hall; as she does, HELMER *throws open his door and stands
    with an open letter in his hand.)*
HELMER: Nora!
NORA *(screams)*: Oh—!
HELMER: What is this? You know what's in this letter?
NORA: Yes, I know. Let me go! Let me out!   *225*
HELMER *(holding her back)*: Where are you going?
NORA *(struggling to break loose)*: You can't save me, Torvald!
HELMER *(slumping back)*: True! Then it's true what he writes? How horrible!
    No, no, it's impossible—it can't be true.
NORA: It *is* true. I've loved you more than all this world.
HELMER: Ah, none of your slippery tricks.   *230*
NORA *(taking one step toward him)*: Torvald—!
HELMER: What *is* this you've blundered into!
NORA: Just let me loose. You're not going to suffer for my sake. You're not
    going to take on my guilt.
HELMER: No more playacting. *(Locks the hall door.)* You stay right here and
    give me a reckoning. You understand what you've done? Answer! You
    understand?
NORA *(looking squarely at him, her face hardening)*: Yes. I'm beginning to un-   *235*
    derstand everything now.
HELMER *(striding about)*: Oh, what an awful awakening! In all these eight
    years—she who was my pride and joy—a hypocrite, a liar—worse,
    worse—a criminal! How infinitely disgusting it all is! The shame! *(NORA
    says nothing and goes on looking straight at him. He stops in front of her.)* I
    should have suspected something of the kind. I should have known. All
    your father's flimsy values—Be still! All your father's flimsy values have
    come out in you. No religion, no morals, no sense of duty—Oh, how
    I'm punished for letting him off! I did it for your sake, and you repay me
    like this.
NORA: Yes, like this.
HELMER: Now you've wrecked all my happiness—ruined my whole future.
    Oh, it's awful to think of. I'm in a cheap little grafter's hands; he can do

anything he wants with me, ask for anything, play with me like a puppet—and I can't breathe a word. I'll be swept down miserably into the depths on account of a featherbrained woman.

NORA: When I'm gone from this world, you'll be free.

240 HELMER: Oh, quit posing. Your father had a mess of those speeches too. What good would that ever do me if you were gone from this world, as you say? Not the slightest. He can still make the whole thing known; and if he does, I could be falsely suspected as your accomplice. They might even think that I was behind it—that I put you up to it. And all that I can thank you for—you that I've coddled the whole of our marriage. Can you see now what you've done to me?

NORA *(icily calm)*: Yes.

HELMER: It's so incredible, I just can't grasp it. But we'll have to patch up whatever we can. Take off the shawl. I said, take it off! I've got to appease him somehow or other. The thing has to be hushed up at any cost. And as for you and me, it's got to seem like everything between us is just as it was—to the outside world, that is. You'll go right on living in this house, of course. But you can't be allowed to bring up the children; I don't dare trust you with them—Oh, to have to say this to someone I've loved so much! Well, that's done with. From now on happiness doesn't matter; all that matters is saving the bits and pieces, the appearance—*(The doorbell rings.* HELMER *starts.)* What's that? And so late. Maybe the worst—? You think he'd—? Hide, Nora! Say you're sick. *(*NORA *remains standing motionless.* HELMER *goes and opens the door.)*

MAID *(half dressed, in the hall)*: A letter for Mrs. Helmer.

HELMER: I'll take it. *(Snatches the letter and shuts the door.)* Yes, it's from him. You don't get it; I'm reading it myself.

245 NORA: Then read it.

HELMER *(by the lamp)*: I hardly dare. We may be ruined, you and I. But—I've got to know. *(Rips open the letter, skims through a few lines, glances at an enclosure, then cries out joyfully.)* Nora! *(*NORA *looks inquiringly at him.)* Nora! Wait—better check it again—Yes, yes, it's true. I'm saved. Nora, I'm saved!

NORA: And I?

HELMER: You too, of course. We're both saved, both of us. Look. He's sent back your note. He says he's sorry and ashamed—that a happy development in his life—oh, who cares what he says! Nora, we're saved! No one can hurt you. Oh, Nora, Nora—but first, this ugliness all has to go. Let me see—*(Takes a look at the note.)* No, I don't want to see it; I want the whole thing to fade like a dream. *(Tears the note and both letters to pieces, throws them into the stove and watches them burn.)* There—now there's nothing left—He wrote that since Christmas Eve you—Oh, they must have been three terrible days for you, Nora.

NORA: I fought a hard fight.

HELMER: And suffered pain and saw no escape but—No, we're not going to   *250*
dwell on anything unpleasant. We'll just be grateful and keep on repeat-
ing, it's over now, it's over! You hear me, Nora? You don't seem to realize—it's over. What's it mean—that frozen look? Oh, poor little Nora, I
understand. You can't believe I've forgiven you. But I have, Nora; I swear
I have. I know that what you did, you did out of love for me.

NORA: That's true.

HELMER: You love me the way a wife ought to love her husband. It's simply
the means that you couldn't judge. But you think I love you any the less
for not knowing how to handle your affairs? No, no—just lean on me:
I'll guide you and teach you. I wouldn't be a man if this feminine helplessness didn't make you twice as attractive to me. You mustn't mind those
sharp words I said—that was all in the first confusion of thinking my
world had collapsed. I've forgiven you, Nora; I swear I've forgiven you.

NORA: My thanks for your forgiveness. *(She goes out through the door, right.)*

HELMER: No, wait—*(Peers in.)* What are you doing in there?

NORA *(inside)*: Getting out of my costume.   *255*

HELMER *(by the open door)*: Yes, do that. Try to calm yourself and collect your
thoughts again, my frightened little songbird. You can rest easy now; I've
got wide wings to shelter you with. *(Walking about close by the door.)* How
snug and nice our home is, Nora. You're safe here; I'll keep you like a
hunted dove I've rescued out of a hawk's claws. I'll bring peace to your
poor, shuddering heart. Gradually it'll happen, Nora; you'll see. Tomorrow all this will look different to you; then everything will be as it was. I
won't have to go on repeating I forgive you; you'll feel it for yourself.
How can you imagine I'd ever conceivably want to disown you—or even
blame you in any way? Ah, you don't know a man's heart, Nora. For a
man there's something indescribably sweet and satisfying in knowing
he's forgiven his wife—and forgiven her out of a full and open heart. It's
as if she belongs to him in two ways now: in a sense he's given her fresh
into the world again, and she's become his wife and his child as well.
From now on that's what you'll be to me—you little bewildered, helpless thing. Don't be afraid of anything, Nora; just open your heart to me,
and I'll be conscience and will to you both—*(NORA enters in her regular
clothes.)* What's this? Not in bed? You've changed your dress?

NORA: Yes, Torvald, I've changed my dress.

HELMER: But why now, so late?

NORA: Tonight I'm not sleeping.

HELMER: But Nora dear—   *260*

NORA *(looking at her watch)*: It's still not so very late. Sit down, Torvald; we
have a lot to talk over. *(She sits at one side of the table.)*

HELMER: Nora—what is this? That hard expression—

NORA: Sit down. This'll take some time. I have a lot to say.

HELMER *(sitting at the table directly opposite her)*: You worry me, Nora. And I don't understand you.

265   NORA: No, that's exactly it. You don't understand me. And I've never understood you either—until tonight. No, don't interrupt. You can just listen to what I say. We're closing out accounts, Torvald.

HELMER: How do you mean that?

NORA *(after a short pause)*: Doesn't anything strike you about our sitting here like this?

HELMER: What's that?

NORA: We've been married now eight years. Doesn't it occur to you that this is the first time we two, you and I, man and wife, have ever talked seriously together?

270   HELMER: What do you mean—seriously?

NORA: In eight whole years—longer even—right from our first acquaintance, we've never exchanged a serious word on any serious thing.

HELMER: You mean I should constantly go and involve you in problems you couldn't possibly help me with?

NORA: I'm not talking of problems, I'm saying that we've never sat down seriously together and tried to get to the bottom of anything.

HELMER: But dearest, what good would that ever do you?

275   NORA: That's the point right there: you've never understood me. I've been wronged greatly, Torvald—first by Papa, and then by you.

HELMER: What! By us—the two people who've loved you more than anyone else?

NORA *(shaking her head)*: You never loved me. You've thought it fun to be in love with me, that's all.

HELMER: Nora, what a thing to say!

NORA: Yes, it's true now, Torvald. When I lived at home with Papa, he told me all his opinions, so I had the same ones too; or if they were different I hid them, since he wouldn't have cared for that. He used to call me his doll-child, and he played with me the way I played with my dolls. Then I came into your house—

280   HELMER: How can you speak of our marriage like that?

NORA *(unperturbed)*: I mean, then I went from Papa's hands into yours. You arranged everything to your own taste, and so I got the same taste as you—or I pretended to; I can't remember. I guess a little of both, first one, then the other. Now when I look back, it seems as if I'd lived here like a beggar—just from hand to mouth. I've lived by doing tricks for you, Torvald. But that's the way you wanted it. It's a great sin what you and Papa did to me. You're to blame that nothing's become of me.

HELMER: Nora, how unfair and ungrateful you are! Haven't you been happy here?

NORA: No, never. I thought so—but I never have.

HELMER: Not—not happy!

NORA: No, only lighthearted. And you've always been so kind to me. But our   *285*
home's been nothing but a playpen. I've been your doll-wife here, just as
at home I was Papa's doll-child. And in turn the children have been my
dolls. I thought it was fun when you played with me, just as they thought
it fun when I played with them. That's been our marriage, Torvald.

HELMER: There's some truth in what you're saying—under all the raving exaggeration. But it'll all be different after this. Playtime's over; now for the
schooling.

NORA: Whose schooling—mine or the children's?

HELMER: Both yours and the children's, dearest.

NORA: Oh, Torvald, you're not the man to teach me to be a good wife to you.

HELMER: And you can say that?   *290*

NORA: And I—how am I equipped to bring up children?

HELMER: Nora!

NORA: Didn't you say a moment ago that that was no job to trust me with?

HELMER: In a flare of temper! Why fasten on that?

NORA: Yes, but you were so very right. I'm not up to the job. There's another   *295*
job I have to do first. I have to try to educate myself. You can't help me
with that. I've got to do it alone. And that's why I'm leaving you now.

HELMER *(jumping up)*: What's that?

NORA: I have to stand completely alone, if I'm ever going to discover myself
and the world out there. So I can't go on living with you.

HELMER: Nora, Nora!

NORA: I want to leave right away. Kristine should put me up for the night—

HELMER: You're insane! You've no right! I forbid you!   *300*

NORA: From here on, there's no use forbidding me anything. I'll take with
me whatever is mine. I don't want a thing from you, either now or later.

HELMER: What kind of madness is this!

NORA: Tomorrow I'm going home—I mean, home where I came from. It'll
be easier up there to find something to do.

HELMER: Oh, you blind, incompetent child!

NORA: I must learn to be competent, Torvald.   *305*

HELMER: Abandon your home, your husband, your children! And you're not
even thinking what people will say.

NORA: I can't be concerned about that. I only know how essential this is.

HELMER: Oh, it's outrageous. So you'll run out like this on your most sacred
vows.

NORA: What do you think are my most sacred vows?

HELMER: And I have to tell you that! Aren't they your duties to your hus-   *310*
band and children?

NORA: I have other duties equally sacred.

HELMER: That isn't true. What duties are they?

NORA: Duties to myself.

HELMER: Before all else, you're a wife and a mother.

315 NORA: I don't believe in that anymore. I believe that, before all else, I'm a human being, no less than you—or anyway, I ought to try to become one. I know the majority thinks you're right, Torvald, and plenty of books agree with you, too. But I can't go on believing what the majority says, or what's written in books. I have to think over these things myself and try to understand them.

HELMER: Why can't you understand your place in your own home? On a point like that, isn't there one everlasting guide you can turn to? Where's your religion?

NORA: Oh, Torvald, I'm really not sure what religion is.

HELMER: What—?

NORA: I only know what the minister said when I was confirmed. He told me religion was this thing and that. When I get clear and away by myself, I'll go into that problem too. I'll see if what the minister said was right, or, in any case, if it's right for me.

320 HELMER: A young woman your age shouldn't talk like that. If religion can't move you, I can try to rouse your conscience. You do have some moral feeling? Or, tell me—has that gone too?

NORA: It's not easy to answer that, Torvald. I simply don't know. I'm all confused about these things. I just know I see them so differently from you. I find out, for one thing, that the law's not at all what I'd thought—but I can't get it through my head that the law is fair. A woman hasn't a right to protect her dying father or save her husband's life! I can't believe that.

HELMER: You talk like a child. You don't know anything of the world you live in.

NORA: No, I don't. But now I'll begin to learn for myself. I'll try to discover who's right, the world or I.

HELMER: Nora, you're sick; you've got a fever. I almost think you're out of your head.

325 NORA: I've never felt more clearheaded and sure in my life.

HELMER: And—clearheaded and sure—you're leaving your husband and children?

NORA: Yes.

HELMER: Then there's only one possible reason.

NORA: What?

330 HELMER: You no longer love me.

NORA: No. That's exactly it.

HELMER: Nora! You can't be serious!

NORA: Oh, this is so hard, Torvald—you've been so kind to me always. But I can't help it. I don't love you anymore.

HELMER (*struggling for composure*): Are you also clearheaded and sure about that?

NORA: Yes, completely. That's why I can't go on staying here.   *335*

HELMER: Can you tell me what I did to lose your love?

NORA: Yes, I can tell you. It was this evening when the miraculous thing didn't come—then I knew you weren't the man I'd imagined

HELMER: Be more explicit; I don't follow you.

NORA: I've waited now so patiently eight long years—for, my Lord, I know miracles don't come every day. Then this crisis broke over me, and such a certainty filled me: *now* the miraculous event would occur. While Krogstad's letter was lying out there, I never for an instant dreamed that you could give in to his terms. I was so utterly sure you'd say to him: go on, tell your tale to the whole wide world. And when he'd done that—

HELMER: Yes, what then? When I'd delivered my own wife into shame and   *340* disgrace—!

NORA: When he'd done that, I was so utterly sure that you'd step forward, take the blame on yourself and say: I am the guilty one.

HELMER: Nora—!

NORA: You're thinking I'd never accept such a sacrifice from you? No, of course not. But what good would my protests be against you? That was the miracle I was waiting for, in terror and hope. And to stave that off, I would have taken my life.

HELMER: I'd gladly work for you day and night, Nora—and take on pain and deprivation. But there's no one who gives up honor for love.

NORA: Millions of women have done just that.   *345*

HELMER: Oh, you think and talk like a silly child.

NORA: Perhaps. But you neither think nor talk like the man I could join myself to. When your big fright was over—and it wasn't from any threat against me, only for what might damage you—when all the danger was past, for you it was just as if nothing had happened. I was exactly the same, your little lark, your doll, that you'd have to handle with double care now that I'd turned out so brittle and frail. *(Gets up.)* Torvald—in that instant it dawned on me that for eight years I've been living here with a stranger, and that I'd even conceived three children—oh, I can't stand the thought of it! I could tear myself to bits.

HELMER *(heavily)*: I see. There's a gulf that's opened between us—that's clear. Oh, but Nora, can't we bridge it somehow?

NORA: The way I am now, I'm no wife for you.

HELMER: I have the strength to make myself over.   *350*

NORA: Maybe—if your doll gets taken away.

HELMER: But to part! To part from you! No, Nora, no—I can't imagine it.

NORA *(going out, right)*: All the more reason why it has to be. *(She reenters with her coat and a small overnight bag, which she puts on a chair by the table.)*

HELMER: Nora, Nora, not now! Wait till tomorrow.

NORA: I can't spend the night in a strange man's room.   *355*

HELMER: But couldn't we live here like brother and sister—

NORA: You know very well how long that would last. *(Throws her shawl about her.)* Good-bye, Torvald. I won't look in on the children. I know they're in better hands than mine. The way I am now, I'm no use to them.

HELMER: But someday, Nora—someday—?

NORA: How can I tell? I haven't the least idea what'll become of me.

360   HELMER: But you're my wife, now and wherever you go.

NORA: Listen, Torvald—I've heard that when a wife deserts her husband's house just as I'm doing, then the law frees him from all responsibility. In any case, I'm freeing you from being responsible. Don't feel yourself bound, any more than I will. There has to be absolute freedom for us both. Here, take your ring back. Give me mine.

HELMER: That too?

NORA: That too.

HELMER: There it is.

365   NORA: Good. Well, now it's all over. I'm putting the keys here. The maids know all about keeping up the house—better than I do. Tomorrow, after I've left town, Kristine will stop by to pack up everything that's mine from home. I'd like those things shipped to me.

HELMER: Over! All over! Nora, won't you ever think about me?

NORA: I'm sure I'll think of you often, and about the children and the house here.

HELMER: May I write you?

NORA: No—never. You're not to do that.

370   HELMER: Oh, but let me send you—

NORA: Nothing. Nothing.

HELMER: Or help if you need it.

NORA: No. I accept nothing from strangers.

HELMER: Nora—can I never be more than a stranger to you?

375   NORA *(picking up the overnight bag)*: Ah, Torvald—it would take the greatest miracle of all—

HELMER: Tell me the greatest miracle!

NORA: You and I both would have to transform ourselves to the point that— Oh, Torvald, I've stopped believing in miracles.

HELMER: But I'll believe. Tell me! Transform ourselves to the point that—?

NORA: That our living together could be a true marriage.

(She goes out down the hall.)

380   HELMER *(sinks down on a chair by the door, face buried in his hands)*: Nora! Nora! *(Looking about and rising.)* Empty. She's gone. *(A sudden hope leaps in him.)* The greatest miracle—?

(From below, the sound of a door slamming shut.)   1879

CONSIDERATIONS

1. How does Nora change from the beginning of the play to the end? Do you find her changes convincing? Explain.
2. Describe the relationships Nora has with each of the male characters. Do you believe she relates to any of these men as an equal? Does she relate to any of them as an inferior? As someone who is superior?
3. Comment on Torvald's values. What does he consider to be most important in life? Does he remain consistent throughout the play, or do you see him as having changed by the play's end?
4. Describe the setting, noting both time and place. How do the details of setting change throughout the play? Do these changes reflect the development of plot, conflict, and character?
5. Describe the values of each of the female characters in the play. Do you admire Nora's values more than those of Kristine? Explain.

More Resources on
Henrik Ibsen and *A Doll's House*

In *ARIEL*
- Brief biography of Ibsen
- Act I, scene 1 of *A Doll's House,* with hyperlinked comments
- Analysis of setting in *A Doll's House*
- Bibliography of scholarly works on Ibsen

In the Online Learning Center for *Responding to Literature*
- Brief biography of Ibsen
- List of major works by Ibsen
- Web links to more resources on Ibsen
- Additional questions for experiencing and interpreting Ibsen's writing

SUSAN GLASPELL (1882–1948)

Trifles

For a biography of Susan Glaspell, see page 558.

Characters

GEORGE HENDERSON, *county attorney*
HENRY PETERS, *sheriff*
LEWIS HALE, *a neighboring farmer*
MRS. PETERS
MRS. HALE

Scene *The kitchen in the now abandoned farmhouse of John Wright, a gloomy kitchen, and left without having been put in order—unwashed pans under the sink, a loaf of bread outside the breadbox, a dish towel on the table—other signs of incompleted work. At the rear the outer door opens and the* SHERIFF *comes in followed by the* COUNTY ATTORNEY *and* HALE. *The* SHERIFF *and* HALE *are men in middle life, the* COUNTY ATTORNEY *is a young man; all are much bundled up and go at once to the stove. They are followed by two women—the* SHERIFF'S WIFE *first; she is a slight wiry woman, a thin nervous face.* MRS. HALE *is larger and would ordinarily be called more comfortable looking, but she is disturbed now and looks fearfully about as she enters. The women have come in slowly, and stand close together near the door.*

COUNTY ATTORNEY *(rubbing his hands)*: This feels good. Come up to the fire, ladies.

MRS. PETERS *(after taking a step forward)*: I'm not—cold.

SHERIFF *(unbuttoning his overcoat and stepping away from the stove as if to mark the beginning of official business)*: Now, Mr. Hale, before we move things about, you explain to Mr. Henderson just what you saw when you came here yesterday morning.

COUNTY ATTORNEY: By the way, has anything been moved? Are things just as you left them yesterday?

5 SHERIFF *(looking about)*: It's just the same. When it dropped below zero last night I thought I'd better send Frank out this morning to make a fire for us—no use getting pneumonia with a big case on, but I told him not to touch anything except the stove—and you know Frank.

COUNTY ATTORNEY: Somebody should have been left here yesterday.

SHERIFF: Oh—yesterday. When I had to send Frank to Morris Center for that man who went crazy—I want you to know I had my hands full yesterday, I knew you could get back from Omaha by today and as long as I went over everything here myself—

COUNTY ATTORNEY: Well, Mr. Hale, tell just what happened when you came here yesterday morning.

HALE: Harry and I had started to town with a load of potatoes. We came along the road from my place and as I got here I said, "I'm going to see if I can't get John Wright to go in with me on a party telephone." I spoke to Wright about it once before and he put me off, saying folks talked too much anyway, and all he asked was peace and quiet—I guess you know about how much he talked himself; but I thought maybe if I went to the house and talked about it before his wife, though I said to Harry that I didn't know as what his wife wanted made such difference to John—

COUNTY ATTORNEY: Let's talk about that later, Mr. Hale. I do want to talk   10
about that, but tell now just what happened when you got to the house.

HALE: I didn't hear or see anything; I knocked at the door, and still it was all quiet inside. I knew they must be up, it was past eight o'clock. So I knocked again, and I thought I heard somebody say, "Come in." I wasn't sure, I'm not sure yet, but I opened the door—this door *(indicating the door by which the two women are still standing)* and there in that rocker— *(pointing to it)* sat Mrs. Wright.

(They all look at the rocker.)

COUNTY ATTORNEY: What—was she doing?

HALE: She was rockin' back and forth. She had her apron in her hand and was kind of—pleating it.

COUNTY ATTORNEY: And how did she—look?

HALE: Well, she looked queer.   15

COUNTY ATTORNEY: How do you mean—queer?

HALE: Well, as if she didn't know what she was going to do next. And kind of done up.

COUNTY ATTORNEY: How did she seem to feel about your coming?

HALE: Why, I don't think she minded—one way or other. She didn't pay much attention. I said, "How do, Mrs. Wright, it's cold, ain't it?" And she said, "Is it?"—and went on kind of pleating at her apron. Well, I was surprised; she didn't ask me to come up to the stove, or to set down, but just sat there, not even looking at me, so I said, "I want to see John." And then she—laughed. I guess you would call it a laugh. I thought of Harry and the team outside, so I said a little sharp: "Can't I see John?" "No," she says, kind o' dull like. "Ain't he home?" says I. "Yes," says she, "he's home." "Then why can't I see him?" I asked her, out of patience. "'Cause he's dead," says she. "Dead?" says I. She just nodded her head, not getting a bit excited, but rockin' back and forth. "Why—where is he?" says I, not knowing what to say. She just pointed upstairs—like that *(himself pointing to the room above)*. I got up, with the idea of going up there. I walked from there to here—then I says, "Why, what did he die of?" "He died of a rope around his neck," says she, and just went on pleatin' at her apron. Well, I went out and called Harry. I thought I might—need help. We went upstairs and there he was lyin'—

20   COUNTY ATTORNEY: I think I'd rather have you go into that upstairs, where you can point it all out. Just go on now with the rest of the story.

HALE: Well, my first thought was to get that rope off. It looked . . . *(stops, his face twitches)* . . . but Harry, he went up to him, and he said, "No, he's dead all right, and we'd better not touch anything." So we went back down stairs. She was still sitting that same way. "Has anybody been notified?" I asked. "No," says she, unconcerned. "Who did this, Mrs. Wright?" said Harry. He said it businesslike—and she stopped pleatin' of her apron. "I don't know," she says. "You don't *know?*" says Harry. "No," says she. "Weren't you sleepin' in the bed with him?" says Harry. "Yes," says she, "but I was on the inside." "Somebody slipped a rope around his neck and strangled him and you didn't wake up?" says Harry. "I didn't wake up," she said after him. We must 'a looked as if we didn't see how that could be, for after a minute she said, "I sleep sound." Harry was going to ask her more questions but I said maybe we ought to let her tell her story first to the coroner, or the sheriff, so Harry went fast as he could to Rivers' place, where there's a telephone.

COUNTY ATTORNEY: And what did Mrs. Wright do when she knew that you had gone for the coroner?

HALE: She moved from that chair to this one over here *(pointing to a small chair in the corner)* and just sat there with her hands held together and looking down. I got a feeling that I ought to make some conversation, so I said I had come in to see if John wanted to put in a telephone, and at that she started to laugh, and then she stopped and looked at me—scared. *(The* COUNTY ATTORNEY, *who has had his notebook out, makes a note.)* I dunno, maybe it wasn't scared. I wouldn't like to say it was. Soon Harry got back, and then Dr. Lloyd came, and you, Mr. Peters, and so I guess that's all I know that you don't.

COUNTY ATTORNEY *(looking around)*: I guess we'll go upstairs first—and then out to the barn and around there. *(To the* SHERIFF.*)* You're convinced that there was nothing important here—nothing that would point to any motive.

25   SHERIFF: Nothing here but kitchen things.

(The COUNTY ATTORNEY, *after again looking around the kitchen, opens the door of a cupboard closet. He gets up on a chair and looks on a shelf. Pulls his hand away, sticky.)*

COUNTY ATTORNEY: Here's a nice mess.

(The women draw nearer.)

MRS. PETERS *(to the other woman)*: Oh, her fruit; it did freeze. *(To the* COUNTY ATTORNEY.*)* She worried about that when it turned so cold. She said the fire'd go out and her jars would break.

SHERIFF: Well, can you beat the women! Held for murder and worryin' about her preserves.

COUNTY ATTORNEY: I guess before we're through she may have something more serious than preserves to worry about.

HALE: Well, women are used to worrying over trifles.   30

(The two women move a little closer together.)

COUNTY ATTORNEY *(with the gallantry of a young politician)*: And yet, for all their worries, what would we do without the ladies? *(The women do not unbend. He goes to the sink, takes a dipperful of water from the pail and pouring it into a basin, washes his hands. Starts to wipe them on the roller towel, turns it for a cleaner place.)* Dirty towels! *(Kicks his foot against the pans under the sink.)* Not much of a housekeeper, would you say ladies?

MRS. HALE *(stiffly)*: There's a great deal of work to be done on a farm.

COUNTY ATTORNEY: To be sure. And yet *(with a little bow to her)* I know there are some Dickson county farmhouses which do not have such roller towels.

(He gives it a pull to expose its full length again.)

MRS. HALE: Those towels get dirty awful quick. Men's hands aren't always as clean as they might be.

COUNTY ATTORNEY: Ah, loyal to your sex, I see. But you and Mrs. Wright   35
were neighbors. I suppose you were friends, too.

MRS. HALE *(shaking her head)*: I've not seen much of her of late years. I've not been in this house—it's more than a year.

COUNTY ATTORNEY: And why was that? You didn't like her?

MRS. HALE: I liked her all well enough. Farmers' wives have their hands full, Mr. Henderson. And then—

COUNTY ATTORNEY: Yes—?

MRS. HALE *(looking about)*: It never seemed a very cheerful place.   40

COUNTY ATTORNEY: No—it's not cheerful. I shouldn't say she had the homemaking instinct.

MRS. HALE: Well, I don't know as Wright had, either.

COUNTY ATTORNEY: You mean that they didn't get on very well?

MRS. HALE: No, I don't mean anything. But I don't think a place'd be any cheerfuller for John Wright's being in it.

COUNTY ATTORNEY: I'd like to talk more of that a little later. I want to get   45
the lay of things upstairs now.

(He goes to the left, where three steps lead to a stair door.)

SHERIFF: I suppose anything Mrs. Peters does'll be all right. She was to take in some clothes for her, you know, and a few little things. We left in such a hurry yesterday.

COUNTY ATTORNEY: Yes, but I would like to see what you take, Mrs. Peters, and keep an eye out for anything that might be of use to us.

MRS. PETERS: Yes, Mr. Henderson.

(The women listen to the men's steps on the stairs, then look about the kitchen.)

MRS. HALE: I'd hate to have men coming into my kitchen, snooping around and criticizing.

(She arranges the pans under sink which the COUNTY ATTORNEY *had shoved out of place.)*

50 MRS. PETERS: Of course it's no more than their duty.

MRS. HALE: Duty's all right, but I guess that deputy sheriff that came out to make the fire might have got a little of this on. *(Gives the roller towel a pull.)* Wish I'd thought of that sooner. Seems mean to talk about her for not having things slicked up when she had to come away in such a hurry.

MRS. PETERS *(who has gone to a small table in the left rear corner of the room, and lifted one end of a towel that covers a pan)*: She had bread set.

(Stands still.)

MRS. HALE *(Eyes fixed on a loaf of bread beside the breadbox, which is on a low shelf at the other side of the room. Moves slowly toward it.)*: She was going to put this in there. *(Picks up loaf, then abruptly drops it. In a manner of returning to familiar things.)* It's a shame about her fruit. I wonder if it's all gone. *(Gets up on the chair and looks.)* I think there's some here that's all right, Mrs. Peters. Yes—here; *(holding it toward the window)* this is cherries, too. *(Looking again.)* I declare I believe that's the only one. *(Gets down, bottle in her hand. Goes to the sink and wipes it off on the outside.)* She'll feel awful bad after all her hard work in the hot weather. I remember the afternoon I put up my cherries last summer.

(She puts the bottle on the big kitchen table, center of the room. With a sigh, is about to sit down in the rocking-chair. Before she is seated realizes what chair it is; with a slow look at it, steps back. The chair which she has touched rocks back and forth.)

MRS. PETERS: Well, I must get those things from the front room closet. *(She goes to the door at the right, but after looking into the other room, steps back.)* You coming with me, Mrs. Hale? You could help me carry them.

(They go in the other room; reappear, MRS. PETERS *carrying a dress and skirt,* MRS. HALE *following with a pair of shoes.)*

MRS. PETERS: My, it's cold in there.   *55*

(She puts the clothes on the big table, and hurries to the stove.)

MRS. HALE *(examining her skirt)*: Wright was close. I think maybe that's why she kept so much to herself. She didn't even belong to the Ladies Aid. I suppose she felt she couldn't do her part, and then you don't enjoy things when you feel shabby. She used to wear pretty clothes and be lively, when she was Minnie Foster, one of the town girls singing in the choir. But that—oh, that was thirty years ago. This all you was to take in?

MRS. PETERS: She said she wanted an apron. Funny thing to want, for there isn't much to get you dirty in jail, goodness knows. But I suppose just to make her feel more natural. She said they was in the top drawer in this cupboard. Yes, here. And then her little shawl that always hung behind the door. *(Opens stair door and looks.)* Yes, here it is.

(Quickly shuts door leading upstairs.)

MRS. HALE *(abruptly moving toward her)*: Mrs. Peters?

MRS. PETERS: Yes, Mrs. Hale?

MRS. HALE: Do you think she did it?   *60*

MRS. PETERS *(in a frightened voice)*: Oh, I don't know.

MRS. HALE: Well, I don't think she did. Asking for an apron and her little shawl. Worrying about her fruit.

MRS. PETERS *(Starts to speak, glances up, where footsteps are heard in the room above. In a low voice.)*: Mr. Peters says it looks bad for her. Mr. Henderson is awful sarcastic in a speech and he'll make fun of her sayin' she didn't wake up.

MRS. HALE: Well, I guess John Wright didn't wake when they was slipping that rope under his neck.

MRS. PETERS: No, it's strange. It must have been done awful crafty and still.   *65*
They say it was such a—funny way to kill a man, rigging it all up like that.

MRS. HALE: That's just what Mr. Hale said. There was a gun in the house. He says that's what he can't understand.

MRS. PETERS: Mr. Henderson said coming out that what was needed for the case was a motive; something to show anger, or—sudden feeling.

MRS. HALE *(who is standing by the table)*: Well, I don't see any signs of anger around here. *(She puts her hand on the dish towel which lies on the table, stands looking down at table, one half of which is clean, the other half messy.)* It's wiped to here. *(Makes a move as if to finish work, then turns and looks at loaf of bread outside the breadbox. Drops towel. In that voice of coming back to familiar things.)* Wonder how they are finding things upstairs. I hope she had it a little more red-up up there. You know, it seems kind of *sneaking*. Locking her up in town and then coming out here and trying to get her own house to turn against her!

MRS. PETERS: But Mrs. Hale, the law is the law.

70   MRS. HALE: I s'pose 'tis. *(Unbuttoning her coat.)* Better loosen up your things, Mrs. Peters. You won't feel them when you go out.

(MRS. PETERS takes off her fur tippet, goes to hang it on hook at back of room, stands looking at the under part of the small corner table.)

MRS. PETERS: She was piecing a quilt.

(She brings the large sewing basket and they look at the bright pieces.)

MRS. HALE: It's log cabin pattern. Pretty, isn't it? I wonder if she was goin' to quilt it or just knot it?

(Footsteps have been heard coming down the stairs. The sheriff enters followed by HALE and the COUNTY ATTORNEY.)

SHERIFF: They wonder if she was going to quilt it or just knot it!

(The men laugh; the women look abashed.)

COUNTY ATTORNEY *(rubbing his hands over the stove)*: Frank's fire didn't do much up there, did it? Well, let's go out to the barn and get that cleared up.

(The men go outside.)

75   MRS. HALE *(resentfully)*: I don't know as there's anything so strange, our takin' up our time with little things while we're waiting for them to get the evidence. *(She sits down at the big table smoothing out a block with decision.)* I don't see as it's anything to laugh about.

MRS. PETERS *(apologetically)*: Of course they've got awful important things on their minds.

(Pulls up a chair and joins MRS. HALE at the table.)

MRS. HALE *(examining another block)*: Mrs. Peters, look at this one. Here, this is the one she was working on, and look at the sewing! All the rest of it has been so nice and even. And look at this! It's all over the place! Why, it looks as if she didn't know what she was about!

(After she has said this they look at each other, then start to glance back at the door. After an instant MRS. HALE has pulled at a knot and ripped the sewing.)

MRS. PETERS: Oh, what are you doing, Mrs. Hale?

MRS. HALE *(mildly)*: Just pulling out a stitch or two that's not sewed very good. *(Threading a needle.)* Bad sewing always made me fidgety.

80   MRS. PETERS *(nervously)*: I don't think we ought to touch things.

MRS. HALE: I'll just finish up this end. *(Suddenly stopping and leaning forward.)* Mrs. Peters?

MRS. PETERS: Yes, Mrs. Hale?

MRS. HALE: What do you suppose she was so nervous about?

MRS. PETERS: Oh—I don't know. I don't know as she was nervous. I sometimes sew awful queer when I'm just tired. *(*MRS. HALE *starts to say something, looks at* MRS. PETERS, *then goes on sewing.)* Well, I must get these
things wrapped up. They may be through sooner than we think. *(Putting
apron and other things together.)* I wonder where I can find a piece of paper,
and string.

MRS. HALE: In that cupboard, maybe.   85

MRS. PETERS *(looking in cupboard)*: Why, here's a birdcage. *(Holds it up.)* Did
she have a bird, Mrs. Hale?

MRS. HALE: Why, I don't know whether she did or not—I've not been here for
so long. There was a man around last year selling canaries cheap, but I don't
know as she took one; maybe she did. She used to sing real pretty herself.

MRS. PETERS *(glancing around)*: Seems funny to think of a bird here. But she
must have had one, or why would she have a cage? I wonder what happened to it.

MRS. HALE: I s'pose maybe the cat got it.

MRS. PETERS: No, she didn't have a cat. She's got that feeling some people   90
have about cats—being afraid of them. My cat got in her room and she
was real upset and asked me to take it out.

MRS. HALE: My sister Bessie was like that. Queer, ain't it?

MRS. PETERS *(examining the cage)*: Why, look at this door. It's broke. One
hinge is pulled apart.

MRS. HALE *(looking too)*: Looks as if someone must have been rough with it.

MRS. PETERS: Why, yes.

(She brings the cage forward and puts it on the table.)

MRS. HALE: I wish if they're going to find any evidence they'd be about it. I   95
don't like this place.

MRS. PETERS: But I'm awful glad you came with me, Mrs. Hale. It would be
lonesome for me sitting here alone.

MRS. HALE: It would, wouldn't it? *(Dropping her sewing.)* But I tell you what I
do wish, Mrs. Peters. I wish I had come over sometimes when *she* was
here. I—*(looking around the room)*—wish I had.

MRS. PETERS: But of course you were awful busy, Mrs. Hale—your house
and your children.

MRS. HALE: I could've come. I stayed away because it weren't cheerful—and
that's why I ought to have come. I—I've never liked this place. Maybe
because it's down in a hollow and you don't see the road. I dunno what
it is but it's a lonesome place and always was. I wish I had come over to
see Minnie Foster sometimes. I can see now—

(Shakes her head.)

100   MRS. PETERS: Well, you mustn't reproach yourself, Mrs. Hale. Somehow we
just don't see how it is with other folks until—something comes up.

MRS. HALE: Not having children makes less work—but it makes a quiet
house, and Wright out to work all day, and no company when he did
come in. Did you know John Wright, Mrs. Peters?

MRS. PETERS: Not to know him; I've seen him in town. They say he was a
good man.

MRS. HALE: Yes—good; he didn't drink, and kept his word as well as most, I
guess, and paid his debts. But he was a hard man, Mrs. Peters. Just to pass
the time of day with him—*(Shivers.)* Like a raw wind that gets to the
bone. *(Pauses, her eye falling on the cage.)* I should think she would 'a wanted
a bird. But what do you suppose went with it?

MRS. PETERS: I don't know, unless it got sick and died.

*(She reaches over and swings the broken door, swings it again. Both women
watch it.)*

105   MRS. HALE: You weren't raised round here, were you? (MRS. PETERS *shakes
her head.)* You didn't know—her?

MRS. PETERS: Not till they brought her yesterday.

MRS. HALE: She—come to think of it, she was kind of like a bird herself—
real sweet and pretty, but kind of timid and—fluttery. How—she—did—
change. *(Silence; then as if struck by a happy thought and relieved to get back to
everyday things.)* Tell you what, Mrs. Peters, why don't you take the quilt
in with you? It might take up her mind.

MRS. PETERS: Why, I think that's a real nice idea, Mrs. Hale. There couldn't
possibly be any objection to it, could there? Now, just what would I take?
I wonder if her patches are in here—and her things.

(They look in the sewing basket.)

MRS. HALE: Here's some red. I expect this has got sewing things in it. *(Brings
out a fancy box.)* What a pretty box. Looks like something somebody
would give you. Maybe her scissors are in here. *(Opens box. Suddenly puts
her hand to her nose.)* Why—(MRS. PETERS *bends nearer, then turns her face
away.)* There's something wrapped up in this piece of silk.

110   MRS. PETERS: Why, this isn't her scissors.

MRS. HALE *(lifting the silk)*: Oh, Mrs. Peters—it's—

*(MRS. PETERS *bends closer.)*

MRS. PETERS: It's the bird.

MRS. HALE *(jumping up)*: But, Mrs. Peters—look at it! Its neck! Look at its
neck! It's all—other side *to.*

MRS. PETERS: Somebody—wrung—its—neck.

(Their eyes meet. A look of growing comprehension, of horror. Steps are heard outside. MRS. HALE *slips box under quilt pieces, and sinks into her chair. Enter* SHERIFF *and* COUNTY ATTORNEY. MRS. PETERS *rises.)*

COUNTY ATTORNEY *(as one turning from serious things to little pleasantries)*: Well, ladies, have you decided whether she was going to quilt it or knot it?   115

MRS. PETERS: We think she was going to—knot it.

COUNTY ATTORNEY: Well, that's interesting, I'm sure. *(Seeing the birdcage.)* Has the bird flown?

MRS. HALE *(putting more quilt pieces over the box)*: We think the—cat got it.

COUNTY ATTORNEY *(preoccupied)*: Is there a cat?

*(*MRS. HALE *glances in a quick covert way at* MRS. PETERS.*)*

MRS. PETERS: Well, not *now*. They're superstitious, you know. They leave.   120

COUNTY ATTORNEY *(to* SHERIFF PETERS, *continuing an interrupted conversation)*: No sign at all of anyone having come from the outside. Their own rope. Now let's go up again and go over it piece by piece. *(They start upstairs.)* It would have to have been someone who knew just the—

*(*MRS. PETERS *sits down. The two women sit there not looking at one another, but as if peering into something and at the same time holding back. When they talk now it is in the manner of feeling their way over strange ground, as if afraid of what they are saying, but as if they can not help saying it.)*

MRS. HALE: She liked the bird. She was going to bury it in that pretty box.

MRS. PETERS *(in a whisper)*: When I was a girl—my kitten—there was a boy took a hatchet, and before my eyes—and before I could get there—*(Covers her face an instant.)* If they hadn't held me back I would have—*(catches herself, looks upstairs where steps are heard, falters weakly)*—hurt him.

MRS. HALE *(with a slow look around her)*: I wonder how it would seem never to have had any children around. *(Pause.)* No, Wright wouldn't like the bird—a thing that sang. She used to sing. He killed that, too.

MRS. PETERS *(moving uneasily)*: We don't know who killed the bird.   125

MRS. HALE: I knew John Wright.

MRS. PETERS: It was an awful thing was done in this house that night, Mrs. Hale. Killing a man while he slept, slipping a rope around his neck that choked the life out of him.

MRS. HALE: His neck. Choked the life out of him.

(Her hand goes out and rests on the birdcage.)

MRS. PETERS *(with rising voice)*: We don't know who killed him. We don't know.

MRS. HALE *(her own feeling not interrupted)*: If there'd been years and years of nothing, then a bird to sing to you, it would be awful—still, after the bird was still.   130

MRS. PETERS *(something within her speaking)*: I know what stillness is. When we homesteaded in Dakota, and my first baby died—after he was two years old, and me with no other then—

MRS. HALE *(moving)*: How soon do you suppose they'll be through, looking for the evidence?

MRS. PETERS: I know what stillness is. *(Pulling herself back.)* The law has got to punish crime, Mrs. Hale.

MRS. HALE *(not as if answering that)*: I wish you'd seen Minnie Foster when she wore a white dress with blue ribbons and stood up there in the choir and sang. *(A look around the room.)* Oh, I *wish* I'd come over here once in a while! That was a crime! That was a crime! Who's going to punish that?

135   MRS. PETERS *(looking upstairs)*: We mustn't—take on.

MRS. HALE: I might have known she needed help! I know how things can be—for women. I tell you, it's queer, Mrs. Peters. We live close together and we live far apart. We all go through the same things—it's all just a different kind of the same thing. *(Brushes her eyes; noticing the bottle of fruit, reaches out for it.)* If I was you I wouldn't tell her her fruit was gone. Tell her it *ain't.* Tell her it's all right. Take this in to prove it to her. She—she may never know whether it was broke or not.

MRS. PETERS *(Takes the bottle, looks about for something to wrap it in; takes petticoat from the clothes brought from the other room, very nervously begins winding this around the bottle. In a false voice.)*: My, it's a good thing the men couldn't hear us. Wouldn't they just laugh! Getting all stirred up over a little thing like a—dead canary. As if that could have anything to do with—with—wouldn't they *laugh!*

(The men are heard coming down stairs.)

MRS. HALE *(under her breath)*: Maybe they would—maybe they wouldn't.

COUNTY ATTORNEY: No, Peters, it's all perfectly clear except a reason for doing it. But you know juries when it comes to women. If there was some definite thing. Something to show—something to make a story about—a thing that would connect up with this strange way of doing it—

(The women's eyes meet for an instant. Enter HALE from outer door.)

140   HALE: Well, I've got the team around. Pretty cold out there.

COUNTY ATTORNEY: I'm going to stay here a while by myself. *(To the SHERIFF.)* You can send Frank out for me, can't you? I want to go over everything. I'm not satisfied that we can't do better.

SHERIFF: Do you want to see what Mrs. Peters is going to take in?

(The COUNTY ATTORNEY goes to the table, picks up the apron, laughs.)

COUNTY ATTORNEY: Oh, I guess they're not very dangerous things the ladies have picked out. *(Moves a few things about, disturbing the quilt pieces which cover the box. Steps back.)* No, Mrs. Peters doesn't need supervising. For that matter, a sheriff's wife is married to the law. Ever think of it that way, Mrs. Peters?

MRS. PETERS: Not—just that way.

SHERIFF *(chuckling)*: Married to the law. *(Moves toward the other room.)* I just   145
want you to come in here a minute, George. We ought to take a look at these windows.

COUNTY ATTORNEY *(scoffingly)*: Oh, windows!

SHERIFF: We'll be right out, Mr. Hale.

(HALE goes outside. The SHERIFF *follows the* COUNTY ATTORNEY *into the other room. Then* MRS. HALE *rises, hands tight together, looking intensely at* MRS. PETERS, *whose eyes make a slow turn, finally meeting* MRS. HALE's. *A moment* MRS. HALE *holds her, then her own eyes point the way to where the box is concealed. Suddenly* MRS. PETERS *throws back quilt pieces and tries to put the box in the bag she is wearing. It is too big. She opens box, starts to take bird out, cannot touch it, goes to pieces, stands there helpless. Sound of a knob turning in the other room.* MRS. HALE *snatches the box and puts it in the pocket of her big coat. Enter* COUNTY ATTORNEY *and* SHERIFF.)

COUNTY ATTORNEY *(facetiously)*: Well, Henry, at least we found out that she was not going to quilt it. She was going to—what is it you call it, ladies?

MRS. HALE *(her hand against her pocket)*: We call it—knot it, Mr. Henderson.
1916

CONSIDERATIONS

1. If this play began with Mr. and Mrs. Wright sitting at night in their living room, what would this scene look like? What would they be doing or saying? Why might Glaspell have decided not to show either John Wright or his wife when she wrote this play?

2. Go through the list of characters in this play and rate them on a scale from one to five, with one being cold and hateful and five being warm and loving. What conclusions can you draw about the men and women in this play based on your scale?

3. Who in this play would you characterize as being more concerned about justice and who would be more concerned with mercy?

4. Compare the short story "A Jury of Her Peers" with this play, *Trifles*. List the differences you discover. How do those differences affect your understanding of the characters and your response to their actions?

5. Comment on the final line of the play and how it connects to both love and hate.

More Resources on
Susan Glaspell and "A Jury of Her Peers" and *Trifles*

In *ARIEL*
- Brief biography of Glaspell
- An excerpt from "A Jury of Her Peers" and an excerpt from *Trifles* with hyperlinked comments
- Video discussion of Glaspell
- Analysis of dramatic irony in *Trifles*
- Bibliography of scholarly works on Glaspell

In the Online Center for *Responding to Literature*
- Brief biography of Glaspell
- List of major works by Glaspell
- Complete text of *Trifles*
- Web links to more resources on Glaspell
- Additional questions for experiencing and interpreting Glaspell's writing

Essays

C. S. LEWIS (1898–1963)
We Have No "Right to Happiness"

C. S. Lewis, author of the children's books known as The Chronicles of Narnia *as well as several books of science fiction, was also a respected literary scholar and critic. For forty years, he taught medieval and Renaissance English literature, first at Oxford and then at Cambridge. In addition, he wrote several books about Christianity from the point of view of a believer. One of the most popular,* Mere Christianity *(1952), was a collection of radio talks he delivered in England during World War II. Lewis was known for not only his intellect but also his strongly held opinions, which can be seen in this selection, collected in* God in the Dock: Essays on Theology and Ethics *(1970). In 1994 the film* Shadowlands, *starring Anthony Hopkins and Debra Winger, portrayed Lewis's falling in love with American poet Joy Gresham; they married when he was fifty-eight (his first marriage), and she died of cancer four years later.*

"After all," said Clare, "they had a right to happiness."

We were discussing something that once happened in our own neighborhood. Mr. A. had deserted Mrs. A. and got his divorce in order to marry Mrs. B., who had likewise got her divorce in order to marry Mr. A. And there was certainly no doubt that Mr. A. and Mrs. B. were very much in love with one another. If they continued to be in love, and if nothing went wrong with their health or their income, they might reasonably expect to be very happy.

It was equally clear that they were not happy with their old partners. Mrs. B. had adored her husband at the outset. But then he got smashed up in the war. It was thought he had lost his virility, and it was known that he had lost his job. Life with him was no longer what Mrs. B. had bargained for. Poor Mrs. A., too. She had lost her looks—and all her liveliness. It might be true, as some said, that she consumed herself by bearing his children and nursing him through the long illness that overshadowed their earlier married life.

You mustn't, by the way, imagine that A. was the sort of man who nonchalantly threw a wife away like the peel of an orange he'd sucked dry. Her suicide was a terrible shock to him. We all knew this, for he told us so himself. "But what could I do?" he said. "A man has a right to happiness. I had to take my one chance when it came."

I went away thinking about the concept of a "right to happiness."   5

At first this sounds to me as odd as a right to good luck. For I believe—whatever one school of moralists may say—that we depend for a very great deal of our happiness or misery on circumstances outside all human control. A right to happiness doesn't, for me, make much more sense than a right to be six feet tall, or to have a millionaire for your father, or to get good weather whenever you want to have a picnic.

I can understand a right as a freedom guaranteed me by the laws of the society I live in. Thus, I have a right to travel along the public roads because society gives me that freedom; that's what we mean by calling the roads "public." I can also understand a right as a claim guaranteed me by the laws, and correlative to an obligation on someone else's part. If I have a right to receive £100 from you, this is another way of saying that you have a duty to pay me £100. If the laws allow Mr. A. to desert his wife and seduce his neighbor's wife, then, by definition, Mr. A. has a legal right to do so, and we need bring in no talk about "happiness."

But of course that was not what Clare meant. She meant that he had not only a legal but a moral right to act as he did. In other words, Clare is—or would be if she thought it out—a classical moralist after the style of Thomas Aquinas, Grotius, Hooker and Locke. She believes that behind the laws of the state there is a Natural Law.

I agree with her. I hold this conception to be basic to all civilization. Without it, the actual laws of the state become an absolute, as in Hegel. They cannot be criticized because there is no norm against which they should be judged.

10   The ancestry of Clare's maxim, "They have a right to happiness," is august. In words that are cherished by all civilized men, but especially by Americans, it has been laid down that one of the rights of man is a right to "the pursuit of happiness." And now we get to the real point.

What did the writers of that august declaration mean?

It is quite certain what they did not mean. They did not mean that man was entitled to pursue happiness by any and every means—including, say, murder, rape, robbery, treason and fraud. No society could be built on such a basis.

They meant "to pursue happiness by all lawful means"; that is, by all means which the Law of Nature eternally sanctions and which the laws of the nation shall sanction.

Admittedly this seems at first to reduce their maxim to the tautology that men (in pursuit of happiness) have a right to do whatever they have a right to do. But tautologies, seen against their proper historical context, are not always barren tautologies. The declaration is primarily a denial of the political principles which long governed Europe: a challenge flung down to the Austrian and Russian empires, to England before the Reform Bills, to Bourbon France. It demands that whatever means of pursuing happiness are lawful for any should be lawful for all; that "man," not men of some particular caste, class, status or religion, should be free to use them. In a century when this is being unsaid by nation after nation and party after party, let us not call it a barren tautology.

15   But the question as to what means are "lawful"—what methods of pursuing happiness are either morally permissible by the Law of Nature or should be declared legally permissible by the legislature of a particular nation—remains exactly where it did. And on that question I disagree with Clare. I don't think it is obvious that people have the unlimited "right to happiness" which she suggests.

For one thing, I believe that Clare, when she says "happiness," means simply and solely "sexual happiness." Partly because women like Clare never use the word "happiness" in any other sense. But also because I never heard Clare talk about the "right" to any other kind. She was rather leftist in her politics, and would have been scandalized if anyone had defended the actions of a ruthless man-eating tycoon on the ground that his happiness consisted in making money and he was pursuing his happiness. She was also a rabid teetotaler; I never heard her excuse an alcoholic because he was happy when he was drunk.

A good many of Clare's friends, and especially her female friends, often felt—I've heard them say so—that their own happiness would be perceptibly increased by boxing her ears. I very much doubt if this would have brought her theory of a right to happiness into play.

Clare, in fact, is doing what the whole Western world seems to me to have been doing for the last forty-odd years. When I was a youngster, all the progressive people were saying, "Why all this prudery? Let us treat sex just as we treat all our other impulses." I was simple-minded enough to believe they meant what they said. I have since discovered that they meant exactly the opposite. They meant that sex was to be treated as no other impulse in our nature has ever been treated by civilized people. All the others, we admit, have to be bridled. Absolute obedience to your instinct for self-preservation is what we call cowardice; to your acquisitive impulse, avarice. Even sleep must be resisted if you're a sentry. But every unkindness and breach of faith seems to be condoned provided that the object aimed at is "four bare legs in a bed."

It is like having a morality in which stealing fruit is considered wrong—unless you steal nectarines.

And if you protest against this view you are usually met with chatter   *20* about the legitimacy and beauty and sanctity of "sex" and accused of harboring some Puritan prejudice against it as something disreputable or shameful. I deny the charge. Foam-born Venus . . . golden Aphrodite . . . Our Lady of Cyprus . . . I never breathed a word against you. If I object to boys who steal my nectarines, must I be supposed to disapprove of nectarines in general? Or even of boys in general? It might, you know, be stealing that I disapproved of.

The real situation is skillfully concealed by saying that the question of Mr. A.'s "right" to desert his wife is one of "sexual morality." Robbing an orchard is not an offense against some special morality called "fruit morality." It is an offense against honesty. Mr. A.'s action is an offense against good faith (to solemn promises), against gratitude (toward one to whom he was deeply indebted) and against common humanity.

Our sexual impulses are thus being put in a position of preposterous privilege. The sexual motive is taken to condone all sorts of behavior which, if it had any other end in view, would be condemned as merciless, treacherous and unjust.

Now though I see no good reason for giving sex this privilege, I think I see a strong cause. It is this.

It is part of the nature of a strong erotic passion—as distinct from a transient fit of appetite—that it makes more towering promises than any other emotion. No doubt all our desires make promises, but not so impressively. To be in love involves the almost irresistible conviction that one will go on being in love until one dies, and that possession of the beloved will confer, not merely frequent ecstasies, but settled, fruitful, deep-rooted, lifelong happiness. Hence *all* seems to be at stake. If we miss this chance we shall have lived in vain. At the very thought of such a doom we sink into fathomless depths of self-pity.

Unfortunately these promises are found often to be quite untrue. Every   *25* experienced adult knows this to be so as regards all erotic passions (except the one he himself is feeling at the moment). We discount the world-without-end pretensions of our friends' amours easily enough. We know that such things sometimes last—and sometimes don't. And when they do last, this is not because they promised at the outset to do so. When two people achieve lasting happiness, this is not solely because they are great lovers but because they are also—I must put it crudely—good people; controlled, loyal, fairminded, mutually adaptable people.

If we establish a "right to (sexual) happiness" which supersedes all the ordinary rules of behavior, we do so not because of what our passion shows itself to be in experience but because of what it professes to be while we are in the grip of it. Hence, while the bad behavior is real and works miseries and degradations, the happiness which was the object of the behavior turns out again and again to be illusory. Everyone (except Mr. A. and Mrs. B.) knows that Mr. A. in a year or so may have the same reason for deserting his new wife as for deserting his old. He will feel again that all is at stake. He will see himself again as the great lover, and his pity for himself will exclude all pity for the woman.

Two further points remain.

One is this. A society in which conjugal infidelity is tolerated must always be in the long run a society adverse to women. Women, whatever a few male songs and satires may say to the contrary, are more naturally monogamous than men; it is a biological necessity. Where promiscuity prevails, they will therefore always be more often the victims than the culprits. Also, domestic happiness is more necessary to them than to us. And the quality by which they most easily hold a man, their beauty, decreases every year after they have come to maturity, but this does not happen to those qualities of personality— women don't really care twopence about our *looks*—by which we hold women. Thus in the ruthless war of promiscuity women are at a double disadvantage. They play for higher stakes and are also more likely to lose. I have no sympathy with moralists who frown at the increasing crudity of female provocativeness. These signs of desperate competition fill me with pity.

Secondly, though the "right to happiness" is chiefly claimed for the sexual impulse, it seems to me impossible that the matter should stay there. The fatal principle, once allowed in that department, must sooner or later seep through our whole lives. We thus advance toward a state of society in which not only each man but every impulse in each man claims *carte blanche*. And then, though our technological skill may help us survive a little longer, our civilization will have died at heart, and will—one dare not even add "unfortunately"—be swept away.   *1963*

CONSIDERATIONS

1. State in your own words Lewis's underlying argument or premise in this piece. Do you agree or disagree with this basic premise? Please explain.
2. According to Lewis, what does "the pursuit of happiness" imply? How strong is his argument here?

3. On what specific points does Lewis agree with Clare? On what points do the two differ? Considering these differences, what would you say is Clare's underlying premise, and how does that conflict with Lewis's?
4. How would you describe Lewis's tone? Is he self-righteous, pompous, understanding, conciliatory, or something else? Please support your stance with specific instances from the text.
5. What are the factors that contribute to true happiness, according to the author? What are the illusions to which many people cling, according to Lewis? What are their reasons for clinging to such illusions? On this matter of realistic happiness and the illusions of love, what points make the most sense to you? What points have you yet to embrace? Explain.

JOAN DIDION (1934–   )

Marrying Absurd

> *Born and raised primarily in California, Joan Didion was educated at the University of California at Berkeley. While at Berkeley, she entered and won an essay contest run by* Vogue Magazine, *which led to her first job as an editor at* Vogue. *While she is best known for her sharp-witted, precisely detailed essays, she has also published several novels and has written several screenplays. Her best known collections of essays include* Slouching Towards Bethlehem *(1968) and* The White Album *(1979).*

To be married in Las Vegas, Clark County, Nevada, a bride must swear that she is eighteen or has parental permission and a bridegroom that he is twenty-one or has parental permission. Someone must put up five dollars for the license. (On Sundays and holidays, fifteen dollars. The Clark County Courthouse issues marriage licenses at any time of the day or night except between noon and one in the afternoon, between eight and nine in the evening, and between four and five in the morning). Nothing else is required. The State of Nevada, alone among these United States, demands neither a premarital blood test nor a waiting period before or after the issuance of a marriage license. Driving in across the Mojave from Los Angeles, one sees the signs way out on the desert, looming up from that moonscape of rattlesnakes and mesquite, even before the Las Vegas lights appear like a mirage on the horizon: "GETTING MARRIED? Free License Information First Strip Exit." Perhaps the Las Vegas wedding industry achieved its peak operational efficiency between 9:00 p.m. and midnight of August 26, 1965, an otherwise unremarkable Thursday which happened to be, by Presidential order, the last day on which anyone could improve his draft status merely by getting married. One hundred and seventy-one couples were pronounced man and wife in the name of Clark County and the State of Nevada that night, sixty-seven of them by a single justice of the peace, Mr. James A. Brennan. Mr. Brennan did one wedding at the Dunes and the other sixty-six in his office, and charged each couple eight dollars. One bride lent her veil to six others. "I got it down from five to three minutes," Mr. Brennan said later of his feat. "I could've married them *en masse,* but they're people, not cattle. People expect more when they get married."

What people who get married in Las Vegas actually do expect—what, in the largest sense, their "expectations" are—strikes one as a curious and self-contradictory business. Las Vegas is the most extreme and allegorical of American settlements, bizarre and beautiful in its venality and in its devotion to immediate gratification, a place the tone of which is set by mobsters and call girls and ladies' room attendants with amyl nitrite poppers in their uniform pockets. Almost everyone notes that there is no "time" in Las Vegas, no night and no day and no past and no future (no Las Vegas casino, however, has taken the obliteration of the ordinary time sense quite so far as Harold's Club in Reno, which for a while issued, at odd intervals in the day and night, mimeographed "bulletins" carrying news from the world outside); neither is there any logical sense of where one is. One is standing on a highway in the middle of a vast hostile desert looking at an eighty-foot sign which blinks "Stardust" or "Caesar's Palace." Yes, but what does that explain? This geographical implausibility reinforces the sense that what happens there has no connection with "real" life; Nevada cities like Reno and Carson are ranch towns, Western towns, places behind which there is some historical imperative. But Las Vegas seems to exist only in the eye of the beholder. All of which makes it an extraordinarily stimulating and interesting place, but an odd one in which to want to wear a candlelight satin Priscilla of Boston wedding dress with Chantilly lace insets, tapered sleeves and a detachable modified train.

And yet the Las Vegas wedding business seems to appeal to precisely that impulse. "Sincere and Dignified Since 1954," one wedding chapel advertises. There are nineteen such wedding chapels in Las Vegas, intensely competitive, each offering better, faster, and, by implication, more sincere services than the next: Our Photos Best Anywhere, Your Wedding on A Phonograph Record, Candlelight with Your Ceremony, Honeymoon Accommodations, Free Transportation from Your Motel to Courthouse to Chapel and Return to Motel, Religious or Civil Ceremonies, Dressing Rooms, Flowers, Rings, Announcements, Witnesses Available, and Ample Parking. All of these services, like most others in Las Vegas (sauna baths, payroll-check cashing, chinchilla coats for sale or rent) are offered twenty-four hours a day, seven days a week, presumably on the premise that marriage, like craps, is a game to be played when the table seems hot.

But what strikes one most about the Strip chapels, with their wishing wells and stained-glass paper windows and their artificial bouvardia, is that so much of their business is by no means a matter of simple convenience, of late-night liaisons between show girls and baby Crosbys.★ Of course there is some of that. (One night about eleven o'clock in Las Vegas I watched a bride in an orange minidress and masses of flame-colored hair stumble from a Strip chapel on the arm of her bridegroom, who looked the part of the expendable nephew in movies like *Miami Syndicate.* "I gotta get the kids," the bride whimpered. "I gotta pick up the sitter, I gotta get to the midnight show." "What you gotta get," the bridegroom said, opening the door of a Cadillac Coupe de Ville and watching her crumple on the seat, "is sober.") But Las Vegas seems to offer something other than "convenience"; it is merchandising "niceness," the facsimile of proper ritual, to children who do not know how else to find it, how to make the arrangements, how to do it "right." All day and evening long on the Strip, one sees actual wedding parties, waiting under the harsh lights at a crosswalk, standing uneasily in the parking lot of the Frontier while the photographer hired by The Little Church of the West ("Wedding Place of the Stars") certifies the occasion, takes the picture: the bride in a veil and white satin pumps, the bridegroom usually in a white dinner jacket, and even an attendant or two, a sister or best friend in hot-pink *peau de soier*, a flirtation veil, a carnation nosegay. "When I Fall in Love It Will Be Forever," the organist plays, and then a few bars of Lohengrin. The mother cries; the stepfather, awkward in his role, invites the chapel hostess to join them for a drink at the Sands. The hostess declines with a professional smile; she has already transferred her interest to the group waiting outside. One bride out, another in, and again the sign goes up on the chapel door: "One moment please—Wedding."

I sat next to one such wedding party in a Strip restaurant the last time I   5
was in Las Vegas. The marriage had just taken place; the bride still wore her dress, the mother her corsage. A bored waiter poured out a few swallows of pink champagne ("on the house") for everyone but the bride, who was too young to be served. "You'll need something with more kick than that," the bride's father said with heavy jocularity to his new son-in-law; the ritual jokes about the wedding night had a certain Panglossian character, since the bride was clearly several months pregnant. Another round of pink champagne, this time not on the house, and the bride began to cry. "It was just as nice," she sobbed, "as I hoped and dreamed it would be."   *1968*

CONSIDERATIONS

1. Read the opening paragraph closely. What American values are suggested in Didion's description of the marriage laws and rituals in Las Vegas?

★People who aspire to singing careers like that of Bing Crosby (1903–1977), a popular singer of the 1930s to 1960s.

2. Discuss the symbolism of the following words Didion uses to describe the setting as one enters Las Vegas from the West: "moonscape," "mirage," "desert," and "rattlesnakes." In your discussion, consider both the denotation and connotation of the words and how they relate to the topic of marriage.

3. If, as Didion writes, what happens in Las Vegas seems to have no connection with "real" life, then what connections does she see between Las Vegas and what Americans value and how they view marriage?

4. What do the chapels on the Strip offer the couples who use their services? Is Didion implying that those who go to Vegas are a different breed of Americans—or something else?

5. What does Didion gain by presenting the anecdote at the end of this essay instead of at the beginning? How does it reflect the values suggested throughout the essay?

6. What is Didion saying about love in this piece?

7. Didion wrote this essay in the late 1960s. What (if anything) do you think she might change if she rewrote "Marrying Absurd" today? Explain your response.

CONNECTIONS: LOVE AND HATE

1. Compare the views of male and female sexuality as suggested by these works: "Roman Fever," "The Hug," "To His Coy Mistress," and "The Willing Mistress."

2. Consider the theme of fidelity (and infidelity) in marriage in "Roman Fever," "The Hug," "The Wedding Couple," and "We Have No Right to Happiness."

3. "The Yellow Wallpaper" and *A Doll's House* both depict relationships that are failing for one reason or another. Compare the roles played by the men and women and the way those roles relate to the failure of the relationships.

4. Consider the various ways of defining the roles of men and women as evident in "The Yellow Wallpaper," "Second-Hand Man," and "To me he seems like a god." Choose two of these to compare and contrast. What conclusion do you draw based on your comparison/contrast?

5. Consider the depiction of relationships—real and ideal—that are found in "The Yellow Wallpaper," "Roman Fever," "A Chinese Banquet," and "Let me not to the marriage of true minds." Explain the effect on any future relationships that the characters may have with someone other than those depicted in the stories or poems.

6. Consider how traditional male and female roles have changed and how these changes can be traced through some of the works in this chapter. Write an essay that examines these changes and expresses your attitude toward them.

SUGGESTIONS FOR EXTENDED CONNECTIONS AMONG CHAPTERS

1. How would you define a good love relationship or a bad love relationship? Consider the relationships depicted in the following works as you develop your definition:

"Astronomer's Wife"	1047
"The Wedding Couple"	602
"Town and Country Lovers"	575
On Tidy Endings	1203
"Old Man and Old Woman"	1152
"Hills Like White Elephants"	839
"A Partial Remembrance of a Puerto Rican Childhood"	804
"The Jilting of Granny Weatherall"	1162

2. Suppose you were a sociologist trying to explain the definition of love as depicted by standards set within a certain time period in a certain society. Use the following selections to determine standards that seem to transcend time and culture.

"Araby"	206
Hamlet	244
"Cathedral"	437
"How Far She Went"	717
"A Worn Path"	844
"The Shawl"	929
On Tidy Endings	1203

3. Consider the different ways in which people communicate and to what extent they reveal their deepest emotions. Come to some conclusions as to what circumstances or characteristics promote honesty and openness in communicating one's true feelings:

Hamlet	244
"Sonny's Blues"	412
"Cathedral"	437
"Master Harold" . . . and the Boys	474
"Roman Fever"	547
Trifles	666
"I Stand Here Ironing"	692
"A Partial Rememberance of a Puerto Rican Childhood"	804
"The Things They Carried"	934
Wit	1085

4. Consider the differences and similarities in how males and females express their deepest emotions, such as love, hate, fear, joy, sorrow, regret:

"The Red Convertible"	218
"Araby"	206

SUGGESTION FOR COLLABORATIVE LEARNING

Working in groups of three or four, choose four selections from the various genres in this chapter. As a group, choose three or four good, open-ended questions that address the topics of love, marriage, men, and women. After the questions and selections have been agreed on, each member of the group then chooses one selection to analyze in terms of how the character or narrator in the piece would answer the given questions. Collectively, the group then synthesizes their responses and creates a screenplay or script of sorts in which four different characters/speakers answer the question and respond to one another. If you like, you can set this up as a popular talk show panel and perform it for the class when you are ready.

WEB CONNECTIONS

1. In many of the selections in this chapter, human emotions play an integral part in the major conflicts within and among the characters. How does an individual control an emotion, and how is that emotion born in the first place? What happens when emotions end up controlling people instead of the other way around? Are there distinct differences between men and women when it comes to emotions? If so, are these differences based on genetic predisposition or on social expectations? To consider the complexity of emotions and the role they play in our lives, visit the *Great Ideas in Personality* Web site at http://personalityresearch.org. This site links to student and professional essays on emotions, as well as modern gender roles. Under "Personality Research Programs," click on "Basic Emotions" for links. The link for the "Emotions Home Page" leads to more links to scholarly publications.
2. In what ways are our expectations and views on emotions shaped by the early literature we read as well as the fictional characters we celebrate both in the United States and around the world? In order to gain a better understanding of gender roles and stereotyping in children's literature, go to *Children's*

Literature: Gender Roles and Sex Stereotyping at www.indiana.edu/~reading/ ieo/bibs/childgen.html, where you will find research links on this subject. Another helpful site, *The Fictional 100* at http://www.fictional100.com/ index.html, lists the top 100 fictional characters in literature and provides analysis and links for each one of these characters. Consider analyzing any one of these characters in terms of how their emotions direct them in their journeys.

Who might the people in this photograph be? What might be their relationship to each other? How do these possible relationships suggest the structure of today's families?

9

Families

The frustrations, rewards, pains, and pleasures of family life both absorb and renew enormous amounts of energy in almost everyone's life. The works in this section examine family relationships from many different vantage points.

As you read the selections in this chapter, keep in mind the following questions:

1. What do you believe are the five most significant conflicts that arise within families?
2. What are the five most important things children can learn from their parents?
3. What are the five most important things parents can learn from their children?
4. Do you believe that parent–child relationships have changed significantly since the time when your parents and grandparents were growing up? Explain.
5. How would you define the ideal mother, father, daughter, or son?

Fiction

TILLIE OLSEN (1913–)

I Stand Here Ironing

Born in Nebraska, Tillie Olsen left high school after her junior year, educating herself through wide reading in public libraries. In the 1930s, she published many poems and prose writings. Her next published work was Tell Me a Riddle, *a 1961 short story collection that includes "I Stand Here Ironing." The years from the late 1930s until the late 1950s were filled with the work of raising a family. Her 1978 book* Silences *examines the forces that often keep women writers from their work, referring frequently to Olsen's own twenty-year hiatus. She has received the O. Henry Award and has taught at Amherst College, Stanford University, and MIT.*

I stand here ironing, and what you asked me moves tormented back and forth with the iron.

"I wish you would manage the time to come in and talk with me about your daughter. I'm sure you can help me understand her. She's a youngster who needs help and whom I'm deeply interested in helping."

"Who needs help." . . . Even if I came, what good would it do? You think because I am her mother I have a key, or that in some way you could use me as a key? She has lived for nineteen years. There is all that life that has happened outside of me, beyond me.

And when is there time to remember, to sift, to weigh, to estimate, to total? I will start and there will be an interruption and I will have to gather it all together again. Or I will become engulfed with all I did or did not do, with what should have been and what cannot be helped.

5   She was a beautiful baby. The first and only one of our five that was beautiful at birth. You do not guess how new and uneasy her tenancy in her now-loveliness. You did not know her all those years she was thought homely, or see her poring over her baby pictures, making me tell her over and over how beautiful she had been—and would be, I would tell her—and was now, to the seeing eye. But the seeing eyes were few or nonexistent. Including mine.

I nursed her. They feel that's important nowadays. I nursed all the children, but with her, with all the fierce rigidity of first motherhood, I did like the books then said. Though her cries battered me to trembling and my breasts ached with swollenness, I waited till the clock decreed.

Why do I put that first? I do not even know if it matters, or if it explains anything.

She was a beautiful baby. She blew shining bubbles of sound. She loved motion, loved light, loved color and music and textures. She would lie on the floor in her blue overalls patting the surface so hard in ecstasy her hands and feet would blur. She was a miracle to me, but when she was eight months old I had to leave her daytimes with the woman downstairs to whom she was no miracle at all, for I worked or looked for work and for Emily's father, who "could no longer endure" (he wrote in his good-bye note) "sharing want with us."

I was nineteen. It was the pre-relief, pre-WPA world of the depression. I would start running as soon as I got off the streetcar, running up the stairs, the place smelling sour, and awake or asleep to startle awake, when she saw me she would break into a clogged weeping that could not be comforted, a weeping I can hear yet.

After a while I found a job hashing at night so I could be with her days, and it was better. But it came to where I had to bring her to his family and leave her.

It took a long time to raise the money for her fare back. Then she got chicken pox and I had to wait longer. When she finally came, I hardly knew her, walking quick and nervous like her father, looking like her father, thin, and dressed in a shoddy red that yellowed her skin and glared at the pockmarks. All the baby loveliness gone.

She was two. Old enough for nursery school they said, and I did not know then what I know now—the fatigue of the long day, and the lacerations of group life in the kinds of nurseries that are only parking places for children.

Except that it would have made no difference if I had known. It was the only place there was. It was the only way we could be together, the only way I could hold a job.

And even without knowing, I knew. I knew the teacher that was evil because all these years it has curdled into my memory, the little boy hunched in the corner, her rasp, "why aren't you outside, because Alvin hits you? that's no reason, go out, scaredy." I knew Emily hated it even if she did not clutch and implore "don't go Mommy" like the other children, mornings.

She always had a reason why we should stay home. Momma, you look sick. Momma, I feel sick. Momma, the teachers aren't there today, they're sick. Momma, we can't go, there was a fire there last night. Momma, it's a holiday today, no school, they told me.

But never a direct protest, never rebellion. I think of our others in their three-, four-year-oldness—the explosions, the tempers, the denunciations, the demands—and I feel suddenly ill. I put the iron down. What in me demanded that goodness in her? And what was the cost, the cost to her of such goodness?

The old man living in the back once said in his gentle way: "You should smile at Emily more when you look at her." What *was* in my face when I looked at her? I loved her. There were all the acts of love.

It was only with the others I remembered what he said, and it was the face of joy, and not of care or tightness or worry I turned to them—too late for Emily. She does not smile easily, let alone almost always as her brothers and sisters do. Her face is closed and sombre, but when she wants, how fluid. You must have seen it in her pantomimes, you spoke of her rare gift for comedy on the stage that rouses a laughter out of the audience so dear they applaud and applaud and do not want to let her go.

Where does it come from, that comedy? There was none of it in her when she came back to me that second time, after I had had to send her away again. She had a new daddy now to learn to love, and I think perhaps it was a better time.

20   Except when we left her alone nights, telling ourselves she was old enough.

"Can't you go some other time, Mommy, like tomorrow?" she would ask. "Will it be just a little while you'll be gone? Do you promise?"

The time we came back, the front door open, the clock on the floor in the hall. She rigid awake. "It wasn't just a little while. I didn't cry. Three times I called you, just three times, and then I ran downstairs to open the door so you could come faster. The clock talked loud. I threw it away, it scared me what it talked."

She said the clock talked loud again that night I went to the hospital to have Susan. She was delirious with the fever that comes before red measles, but she was fully conscious all the week I was gone and the week after we were home when she could not come near the new baby or me.

She did not get well. She stayed skeleton thin, not wanting to eat, and night after night she had nightmares. She would call for me, and I would rouse from exhaustion to sleepily call back: "You're all right, darling, go to sleep, it's just a dream," and if she still called, in a sterner voice, "now go to sleep, Emily, there's nothing to hurt you." Twice, only twice, when I had to get up for Susan anyhow, I went in to sit with her.

25   Now when it is too late (as if she would let me hold and comfort her like I do the others) I get up and go to her at once at her moan or restless stirring. "Are you awake, Emily? Can I get you something?" And the answer is always the same: "No, I'm all right, go back to sleep, Mother."

They persuaded me at the clinic to send her away to a convalescent home in the country where "she can have the kind of food and care you can't manage for her, and you'll be free to concentrate on the new baby." They still send children to that place. I see pictures on the society page of sleek young women planning affairs to raise money for it, or dancing at the affairs, or decorating Easter eggs or filling Christmas stockings for the children.

They never have a picture of the children so I do not know if the girls still wear those gigantic red bows and the ravaged looks on the every other Sunday when the parents can come to visit "unless otherwise notified"—as we were notified the first six weeks.

Oh it is a handsome place, green lawns and tall trees and fluted flower beds. High up on the balconies of each cottage the children stand, the girls in their red bows and white dresses, the boys in white suits and giant red ties. The parents stand below shrieking up to be heard and the children shriek down to be heard, and between them the invisible wall "Not To Be Contaminated by Parental Germs or Physical Affection."

There was a tiny girl who always stood hand in hand with Emily. Her parents never came. One visit she was gone. "They moved her to Rose Cottage" Emily shouted in explanation. "They don't like you to love anybody here."

She wrote once a week, the labored writing of a seven-year-old. "I am   *30* fine. How is the baby. If I write my leter nicely I will have a star. Love." There never was a star. We wrote every other day, letters she could never hold or keep but only hear read—once. "We simply do not have room for children to keep any personal possessions," they patiently explained when we pieced one Sunday's shrieking together to plead how much it would mean to Emily, who loved so to keep things, to be allowed to keep her letters and cards.

Each visit she looked frailer. "She isn't eating," they told us.

(They had runny eggs for breakfast or mush with lumps, Emily said later, I'd hold it in my mouth and not swallow. Nothing ever tasted good, just when they had chicken.)

It took us eight months to get her released home, and only the fact that she gained back so little of her seven lost pounds convinced the social worker.

I used to try to hold and love her after she came back, but her body would stay stiff, and after a while she'd push away. She ate little. Food sickened her, and I think much of life too. Oh she had physical lightness and brightness, twinkling by on skates, bouncing like a ball up and down up and down over the jump rope, skimming over the hill; but these were momentary.

She fretted about her appearance, thin and dark and foreign-looking at a   *35* time when every little girl was supposed to look or thought she should look a chubby blonde replica of Shirley Temple. The doorbell sometimes rang for her, but no one seemed to come and play in the house or be a best friend. Maybe because we moved so much.

There was a boy she loved painfully through two school semesters. Months later she told me how she had taken pennies from my purse to buy him candy. "Licorice was his favorite and I brought him some every day, but he still liked Jennifer better'n me. Why, Mommy?" The kind of question for which there is no answer.

School was a worry to her. She was not glib or quick in a world where glibness and quickness were easily confused with ability to learn. To her overworked and exasperated teachers she was an overconscientious "slow learner" who kept trying to catch up and was absent entirely too often.

I let her be absent, though sometimes the illness was imaginary. How different from my now-strictness about attendance with the others. I wasn't working. We had a new baby, I was home anyhow. Sometimes, after Susan grew old enough, I would keep her home from school, too, to have them all together.

Mostly Emily had asthma, and her breathing, harsh and labored, would fill the house with a curiously tranquil sound. I would bring the two old dresser mirrors and her boxes of collections to her bed. She would select beads and single earrings, bottle tops and shells, dried flowers and pebbles, old post-cards and scraps, all sorts of oddments; then she and Susan would play King-dom, setting up landscapes and furniture, peopling them with action.

40   Those were the only times of peaceful companionship between her and Susan. I have edged away from it, that poisonous feeling between them, that terrible balancing of hurts and needs I had to do between the two, and did so badly, those earlier years.

Oh there are conflicts between the others too, each one human, need-ing, demanding, hurting, taking—but only between Emily and Susan, no, Emily toward Susan that corroding resentment. It seems so obvious on the surface, yet it is not obvious. Susan, the second child, Susan, golden- and curly-haired and chubby, quick and articulate and assured, everything in appearance and manner Emily was not; Susan, not able to resist Emily's precious things, losing or sometimes clumsily breaking them; Susan telling jokes and riddles to company for applause while Emily sat silent (to say to me later; that was *my* riddle, Mother, I told it to Susan); Susan, who for all the five years' difference in age was just a year behind Emily in developing physically.

I am glad for that slow physical development that widened the differ-ence between her and her contemporaries, though she suffered over it. She was too vulnerable for that terrible world of youthful competition, of preen-ing and parading, of constant measuring of yourself against every other, of envy, "If I had that copper hair," "If I had that skin. . . ." She tormented herself enough about not looking like the others, there was enough of the unsure-ness, the having to be conscious of words before you speak, the constant car-ing—what are they thinking of me? without having it all magnified by the merciless physical drives.

Ronnie is calling. He is wet and I change him. It is rare there is such a cry now. That time of motherhood is almost behind me when the ear is not one's own but must always be racked and listening for the child cry, the child call. We sit for a while and I hold him, looking out over the city spread in char-coal with its soft aisles of light. "*Shoogily*," he breathes and curls closer. I carry him back to bed, asleep. *Shoogily*. A funny word, a family word, inherited from Emily, invented by her to say: *comfort*.

In this and other ways she leaves her seal, I say aloud. And startle at my saying it. What do I mean? What did I start to gather together, to try and make coherent? I was at the terrible, growing years. War years. I do not remember them well. I was working, there were four smaller ones now, there was not time for her. She had to help be a mother, and housekeeper, and shopper. She had to set her seal. Mornings of crisis and near hysteria trying to get lunches packed, hair combed, coats and shoes found, everyone to school or Child Care on time, the baby ready for transportation. And always the paper scribbled on by a smaller one, the book looked at by Susan then mislaid, the homework not done. Running out to that huge school where she was one, she was lost, she was a drop; suffering over the unpreparedness, stammering and unsure in her classes.

There was so little time left at night after the kids were bedded down.   45
She would struggle over books, always eating (it was in those years she developed her enormous appetite that is legendary in our family) and I would be ironing, or preparing food for the next day, or writing V-mail to Bill, or tending the baby. Sometimes, to make me laugh, or out of her despair, she would imitate happenings or types at school.

I think I said once: "Why don't you do something like this in the school amateur show?" One morning she phoned me at work, hardly understandable through the weeping: "Mother, I did it. I won, I won; they gave me first prize; they clapped and clapped and wouldn't let me go."

Now suddenly she was Somebody, and as imprisoned in her difference as she had been in anonymity.

She began to be asked to perform at other high schools, even in colleges, then at city and statewide affairs. The first one we went to, I only recognized her that first moment when thin, shy, she almost drowned herself into the curtains. Then: Was this Emily? The control, the command, the convulsing and deadly clowning, the spell, then the roaring, stamping audience, unwilling to let this rare and precious laughter out of their lives.

Afterwards: You ought to do something about her with a gift like that—but without money or knowing how, what does one do? We have left it all to her, and the gift has as often eddied inside, clogged and clotted, as been used and growing.

She is coming. She runs up the stairs two at a time with her light grace-   50
ful step, and I know she is happy tonight. Whatever it was that occasioned your call did not happen today.

"Aren't you ever going to finish the ironing, Mother? Whistler painted his mother in a rocker. I'd have to paint mine standing over an ironing board." This is one of her communicative nights and she tells me everything and nothing as she fixes herself a plate of food out of the icebox.

She is so lovely. Why did you want me to come in at all? Why were you concerned? She will find her way.

She starts up the stairs to bed. "Don't get me up with the rest in the morning." "But I thought you were having midterms." "Oh, those," she comes back in, kisses me, and says quite lightly, "in a couple of years when we'll all be atom-dead they won't matter a bit."

She has said it before. She *believes* it. But because I have been dredging the past, and all that compounds a human being is so heavy and meaningful in me, I cannot endure it tonight.

55   I will never total it all. I will never come in to say: She was a child seldom smiled at. Her father left me before she was a year old. I had to work her first six years when there was work, or I sent her home and to his relatives. There were years she had care she hated. She was dark and thin and foreign-looking in a world where the prestige went to blondeness and curly hair and dimples, she was slow where glibness was prized. She was a child of anxious, not proud, love. We were poor and could not afford for her the soil of easy growth. I was a young mother, I was a distracted mother. There were the other children pushing up, demanding. Her younger sister seemed all that she was not. There were years she did not want me to touch her. She kept too much in herself, her life was such she had to keep too much in herself. My wisdom came too late. She has much to her and probably little will come of it. She is a child of her age, of depression, of war, of fear.

Let her be. So all that is in her will not bloom—but in how many does it? There is still enough left to live by. Only help her to know—help make it so there is cause for her to know—that she is more than this dress on the ironing board, helpless before the iron.   *1961*

CONSIDERATIONS

1. What incident prompts the mother's long meditation as she stands at the ironing board? How does this incident suggest the relationship between the mother, her daughter, and the authority figures who have, to one degree or another, controlled the lives of both mother and daughter?
2. Make a list of the circumstances the mother sees as having prevented her from taking care of her children as she would have liked. To what extent do you find her explanations valid? To what extent do you find her explanations to be rationalizations?
3. The act of ironing is mentioned in the title, in the opening section, and in the conclusion. How does ironing serve as a metaphor for the mother's life? How does the mother use ironing as a metaphor to suggest the hopes she holds for her daughter's life?
4. How has Emily been affected by the circumstances of her life? Have the effects of these circumstances been entirely negative? Entirely positive?
5. Imagine that you are Emily and you have come across "I Stand Here Ironing" written as a meditation in the diary your mother has left open on the dining room table. Write a response to the feelings and ideas she has expressed.

JOYCE CAROL OATES (1938–   )
Shopping

Joyce Carol Oates grew up in rural upstate New York and began writing as a child. When she was an undergraduate at Syracuse University, she won Mademoiselle *magazine's fiction contest. She earned a master's degree in English at the University of Wisconsin and later taught English at the University of Detroit, at the University of Windsor, and in Princeton's creative writing program. By the time she was thirty-five, Oates had published 18 books, including the National Book Award winner* them *(1969). In the 1980s she departed from the psychological realism of her earlier work and began writing a series of gothic novels, including* Bellefleur *(1980) and* The Bloodsmoor Romance *(1982). After these experiments, Oates returned to more realistic fiction in the form of family chronicles, such as* You Must Remember This *(1987), and novels of female experience, such as* Marya: A Life *(1986). At the same time, she was also publishing a series of suspense thrillers under the pseudonym "Rosamond Smith." In addition to writing over 60 novels, Oates has written short stories, poetry, plays, and essays.*

An old ritual, Saturday morning shopping. Mother and daughter. Mrs. Dietrich and Nola. Shops in the village, stores and boutiques at the splendid Livingstone Mall on Route 12. Bloomingdale's, Saks, Lord & Taylor, Bonwit's, Neiman-Marcus: and the rest. Mrs. Dietrich would know her way around the stores blindfolded but there is always the surprise of lavish seasonal displays, extraordinary holiday sales, the openings of new stores at the Mall like Laura Ashley, Paraphernalia. On one of their Mall days Mrs. Dietrich and Nola would try to get there at midmorning, have lunch around 1 P.M. at one or another of their favorite restaurants, shop for perhaps an hour after lunch, then come home. Sometimes the shopping trips were more successful than at other times but you have to have faith, Mrs. Dietrich tells herself. Her interior voice is calm, neutral, free of irony. Ever since her divorce her interior voice has been free of irony. You have to have faith.

Tomorrow morning Nola returns to school in Maine; today will be a day at the Mall. Mrs. Dietrich has planned it for days. At the Mall, in such crowds of shoppers, moments of intimacy are possible as they rarely are at home. (Seventeen-year-old Nola, home on spring break for a brief eight days, seems always to be *busy*, always out with her *friends*—the trip to the Mall has been postponed twice.) But Saturday, 10:30 A.M., they are in the car at last headed south on Route 12, a bleak March morning following a night of freezing rain, there's a metallic cast to the air and no sun anywhere in the sky but the light hurts Mrs. Dietrich's eyes just the same. "Does it seem as if spring will ever come?—it must be twenty degrees colder up in Maine," she says. Driving in heavy traffic always makes Mrs. Dietrich nervous and she is overly sensitive to her daughter's silence, which seems deliberate, perverse, when they have so little time remaining together—not even a full day.

Nola asks politely if Mrs. Dietrich would like her to drive and Mrs. Dietrich says no, of course not, she's fine, it's only a few more miles and maybe traffic will lighten. Nola seems about to say something more, then thinks better of it. So much between them that is precarious, chancy—but they've been kind to each other these past seven days. Mrs. Dietrich loves Nola with a fierce unreasoned passion stronger than any she felt for the man who had been her husband for thirteen years, certainly far stronger than any she ever felt for her own mother. Sometimes in weak despondent moods, alone, lonely, self-pitying, when she has had too much to drink, Mrs. Dietrich thinks she is in love with her daughter—but this is a thought she can't contemplate for long. And how Nola would snort in amused contempt, incredulous, mocking—"Oh *Mother!*"—if she were told.

Mrs. Dietrich tries to engage her daughter in conversation of a harmless sort but Nola answers in monosyllables, Nola is rather tired from so many nights of partying with her friends, some of whom attend the local high school, some of whom are home for spring break from prep schools—Exeter, Lawrenceville, Concord, Andover, Portland. Late nights, but Mrs. Dietrich doesn't consciously lie awake waiting for Nola to come home: they've been through all that before. Now Nola sits beside her mother looking wan, subdued, rather melancholy. Thinking her private thoughts. She is wearing a bulky quilted jacket Mrs. Dietrich has never liked, the usual blue jeans, black calfskin boots zippered tightly to mid-calf. Mrs. Dietrich must resist the temptation to ask, "Why are you so quiet, Nola? What are you thinking?" They've been through all that before.

5   Route 12 has become a jumble of small industrial parks, high-rise office and apartment buildings, torn-up landscapes—mountains of raw earth, uprooted trees, ruts and ditches filled with muddy water. There is no natural sequence to what you see—buildings, construction work, leveled woods, the lavish grounds owned by Squibb. Though she has driven this route countless times, Mrs. Dietrich is never quite certain where the Mall is and must be prepared for a sudden exit. She remembers getting lost the first several times, remembers the excitement she and her friends felt about the grand opening of the Mall, stores worthy of serious shopping at last. Today is much the same. No, today is worse. Like Christmas when she was a small child, Mrs. Dietrich thinks. She'd hoped so badly to be happy she'd felt actual pain, a constriction in her throat like crying.

"*Are* you all right, Nola?—you've been so quiet all morning," Mrs. Dietrich asks, half-scolding. Nola stirs from her reverie, says she's fine, a just perceptible edge to her reply, and for the remainder of the drive there's some stiffness between them. Mrs. Dietrich chooses to ignore it. In any case she is fully absorbed in driving—negotiating a tricky exit across two lanes of traffic, then the hairpin curve of the ramp, the numerous looping drives of the Mall. Then the enormous parking lot, daunting to the inexperienced, but Mrs. Dietrich always heads for the area behind Lord & Taylor on the far side of the Mall, Lot D; her luck holds and she finds a space close in. "Well—we made it," she says, smiling happily at Nola. Nola laughs in reply—what does a seventeen-year-old's laughter *mean?*—but she remembers, getting out, to lock both doors on her side of the car. The smile Nola gives Mrs. Dietrich across the car's roof is careless and beautiful and takes Mrs. Dietrich's breath away.

The March morning tastes of grit with an undercurrent of something acrid, chemical; inside the Mall, beneath the first of the elegant brass-buttressed glass domes, the air is fresh and tonic, circulating from invisible vents. The Mall is crowded, rather noisy—it *is* Saturday morning—but a feast for the eyes after that long trip on Route 12. Tall slender trees grow out of the mosaic-tiled pavement, there are beds of Easter lilies, daffodils, jonquils, tulips of all colors. Mrs. Dietrich smiles with relief. She senses that Nola too is relieved, cheered. It's like coming home.

The shopping excursions began when Nola was a small child but did not acquire their special significance until she was twelve or thirteen years old and capable of serious, sustained shopping with her mother. This was about the time when Mr. Dietrich moved out of the house and back into their old apartment in the city—a separation, he'd called it initially, to give them perspective—though Mrs. Dietrich had no illusions about what "perspective" would turn out to entail—so the shopping trips were all the more significant. Not that Mrs. Dietrich and Nola spent very much money—they really didn't, *really* they didn't, when compared to friends and neighbors.

At seventeen Nola is shrewd and discerning as a shopper, not easy to please, knowledgeable as a mature woman about certain aspects of fashion, quality merchandise, good stores. Her closets, like Mrs. Dietrich's, are crammed, but she rarely buys anything that Mrs. Dietrich thinks shoddy or merely faddish. Up in Portland, at the Academy, she hasn't as much time to shop but when she is home in Livingstone it isn't unusual for her and her girlfriends to shop nearly every day. Like all her friends she has charge accounts at the better stores, her own credit cards, a reasonable allowance. At the time of their settlement Mr. Dietrich said guiltily that it was the least he could do for them—if Mrs. Dietrich wanted to work part-time, she could (she was trained, more or less, in public relations of a small-scale sort); if not, not. Mrs. Dietrich thought, It's the most you can do for us too.

Near Bloomingdale's entrance mother and daughter see a disheveled   10
woman sitting by herself on one of the benches. Without seeming to look at her, shoppers are making a discreet berth around her, a stream following a natural

course. Nola, taken by surprise, stares. Mrs. Dietrich has seen the woman from time to time at the Mall, always alone, smirking and talking to herself, frizzed gray hair in a tangle, puckered mouth. Always wearing the same black wool coat, a garment of fairly good quality but shapeless, rumpled, stained, as if she sleeps in it. She might be anywhere from forty to sixty years of age. Once Mrs. Dietrich saw her make menacing gestures at children who were teasing her, another time she'd seen the woman staring belligerently at *her*. A white paste had gathered in the corners of her mouth. . . . "My God, that poor woman," Nola says. "I didn't think there were people like her here—I mean, I didn't think they would allow it."

"She doesn't seem to cause any disturbance," Mrs. Dietrich says. "She just sits—Don't stare, Nola, she'll see you."

"You've seen her here before? Here?"

"A few times this winter."

"Is she always like that?"

15 "I'm sure she's harmless, Nola. She just *sits*."

Nola is incensed, her pale blue eyes like washed glass. "I'm sure *she's* harmless, Mother. It's the harm the poor woman has to endure that is the tragedy."

Mrs. Dietrich is surprised and a little offended by her daughter's passionate tone but she knows enough not to argue. They enter Bloomingdale's, taking their habitual route. So many shoppers!—so much merchandise! Nola speaks of the tragedy of women like that woman—the tragedy of the homeless, the mentally disturbed—bag ladies out on the street—outcasts of an affluent society—but she's soon distracted by the busyness on all sides, the attractive items for sale. They take the escalator up to the third floor, to the Juniors department where Nola often buys things. From there they will move on to Young Collector, then to New Impressions, then to Petites, then one or another boutique and designer—Liz Claiborne, Christian Dior, Calvin Klein, Carlos Falchi, and the rest. And after Bloomingdale's the other stores await, to be visited each in turn. Mrs. Dietrich checks her watch and sees with satisfaction that there's just enough time before lunch but not *too* much time. She gets ravenously hungry, shopping at the Mall.

Nola is efficient and matter-of-fact about shopping, though she acts solely upon instinct. Mrs. Dietrich likes to watch her at a short distance—holding items of clothing up to herself in the three-way mirrors, modeling things she thinks especially promising. A twill blazer with rounded shoulders and blouson jacket, a funky zippered jumpsuit in white sailcloth, a pair of straight-leg Evan-Picone pants, a green leather vest: Mrs. Dietrich watches her covertly. At such times Nola is perfectly content, fully absorbed in the task at hand; Mrs. Dietrich knows she isn't thinking about anything that would distress her. (Like Mr. Dietrich's betrayal. Like Nola's difficulties with her friends. Like her difficulties at school—as much as Mrs. Dietrich knows of them.)

Once, at the Mall, perhaps in this very store in this very department, Nola saw Mrs. Dietrich watching her and walked away angrily and when Mrs. Dietrich caught up with her she said, "I can't stand it, Mother." Her voice was choked and harsh, a vein prominent in her forehead. "Let me go. For Christ's sake will you let me go." Mrs. Dietrich didn't dare touch her though she could see Nola was trembling. For a long terrible moment mother and daughter stood side by side near a display of bright brash Catalina beachwear while Nola whispered, "Let me go. *Let me go.*"

Difficult to believe that girl standing so poised and self-assured in front of the three-way mirror was once a plain, rather chunky, unhappy child. She'd been unpopular at school. Overly serious. Anxious. Quick to tears. Aged eleven she hid herself away in her room for hours at a time, reading, drawing pictures, writing little stories she could sometimes be prevailed upon to read aloud to her mother, sometimes even to her father, though she dreaded his judgment. She went through a "scientific" phase a while later—Mrs. Dietrich remembers an ambitious bas-relief map of North America, meticulous illustrations for "photosynthesis," a pastel drawing of an eerie ball of fire labeled "Red Giant" (a dying star?) which won a prize in a state competition for junior high students. Then for a season it was stray facts Nola confronted them with, often at the dinner table. Interrupting her parents' conversation to say brightly: "Did you know that Nero's favorite color was green?—he carried a giant emerald and held it up to his eye to watch Christians being devoured by lions." And once at a large family gathering: "Did you know that last week downtown a little baby's nose was chewed off by rats in his crib?—a little *black* baby?" Nola meant only to call attention to herself but you couldn't blame her listeners for being offended. They stared at her, not knowing what to say. What a strange child! What queer glassy-pale eyes! Mr. Dietrich told her curtly to leave the table—he'd had enough of the game she was playing and so had everyone else.

Nola stared at him, her eyes filling with tears. Game? 20

When they were alone Mr. Dietrich said angrily to Mrs. Dietrich: "Can't you control her in front of other people, at least?" Mrs. Dietrich was angry too, and frightened. She said "I *try.*"

They sent her off aged fourteen to the Portland Academy up in Maine and without their help she matured into a girl of considerable beauty. A heart-shaped face, delicate features, glossy red-brown hair scissor-cut to her shoulders. Five feet seven inches tall, weighing less than one hundred pounds—the result of constant savage dieting. (Mrs. Dietrich, who has weight problems herself, doesn't dare to inquire as to details. They've been through that already.) Thirty days after they'd left her at the Portland Academy Nola telephoned home at 11:00 P.M. one Sunday giggly and high telling Mrs. Dietrich she adored the school she adored her suite mates she adored most of her teachers particularly her riding instructor Terri, Terri the Terrier they called the woman because she was so fierce, such a character, eyes that bore right through your skull, wore belts with the most amazing silver buckles! Nola loved Terri but she wasn't *in* love—there's a difference!

Mrs. Dietrich broke down weeping, *that* time.

Now of course Nola has boyfriends. Mrs. Dietrich has long since given up trying to keep track of their names. There is even one "boy"—or young man—who seems to be married: who seems to be, in fact, one of the junior instructors at the school. (Mrs. Dietrich does not eavesdrop on her daughter's telephone conversations but there are things she cannot help overhearing.) Is your daughter on the Pill? the women in Mrs. Dietrich's circle asked one another for a while, guiltily, surreptitiously. Now they no longer ask.

25   But Nola has announced recently that she loathes boys—she's fed up.

She's never going to get married. She'll study languages in college, French, Italian, something exotic like Arabic, go to work for the American foreign service. Unless she drops out of school altogether to become a model.

"Do you think I'm fat, Mother?" she asks frequently, worriedly, standing in front of the mirror twisted at the waist to reveal her small round belly which, it seems, can't help being round: she bloats herself on diet Cokes all day long. "Do you think it *shows?*"

When Mrs. Dietrich was pregnant with Nola she'd been twenty-nine years old and she and Mr. Dietrich had tried to have a baby for nearly five years. She'd lost hope, begun to despise herself, then suddenly it happened: like grace. Like happiness swelling so powerfully it can barely be contained. I can hear its heartbeat! Her husband exclaimed. He'd been her lover then, young, vigorous, dreamy. Caressing the rock-hard belly, splendid white tight-stretched skin. Mr. Dietrich gave Mrs. Dietrich a reproduction on stiff glossy paper of Dante Gabriel Rossetti's *Beata Beatrix,* embarrassed, apologetic, knowing it was sentimental and perhaps a little silly but that was how he thought of her—so beautiful, rapturous, pregnant with their child. She told no one but she knew the baby was to be a girl. It would be herself again, reborn and this time perfect.

"Oh, Mother—isn't it *beautiful?*" Nola exclaims.

30   It is past noon. Past twelve-thirty. Mrs. Dietrich and Nola have made the rounds of a half-dozen stores, traveled countless escalators, one clothing department has blended into the next and the chic smiling saleswomen have become indistinguishable and Mrs. Dietrich is beginning to feel the urgent need for a glass of white wine. Just a glass. "Isn't it beautiful?—it's *perfect,*" Nola says. Her eyes glow with pleasure, her smooth skin is radiant. As Nola models in the three-way mirror a queer little yellow-and-black striped sweater with a ribbed waist, punk style, mock-cheap, Mrs. Dietrich feels the motherly obligation to register a mild protest, knowing that Nola will not hear. She must have it and

will have it. She'll wear it a few times, then retire it to the bottom of a drawer with so many other novelty sweaters, accumulated since sixth grade. (She's like her mother in that regard—can't bear to throw anything away.)

"*Isn't* it beautiful?" Nola demands, studying her reflection in the mirror.

Mrs. Dietrich pays for the sweater on her charge account.

Next, they buy Nola a good pair of shoes. And a handbag to go with them. In Paraphernalia, where rock music blasts overhead and Mrs. Dietrich stands to one side, rather miserable, Nola chats companionably with two girls—tall, pretty, cutely made up—she'd gone to public school in Livingstone with, says afterward with an upward rolling of her eyes, "God, I was afraid they'd latch on to us!" Mrs. Dietrich has seen women friends and acquaintances of her own in the Mall this morning but has shrunk from being noticed, not wanting to share her daughter with anyone. She has a sense of time passing ever more swiftly, cruelly.

She watches Nola preening in a mirror, watches other shoppers watching her. My daughter. Mine. But of course there is no connection between them—they don't even resemble each other. A seventeen-year-old, a forty-seven-year-old. When Nola is away she seems to forget her mother entirely—doesn't telephone, certainly doesn't write. It's the way all their daughters are, Mrs. Dietrich's friends tell her. It doesn't *mean* anything. Mrs. Dietrich thinks how when she was carrying Nola, those nine long months, they'd been completely happy—not an instant's doubt or hesitation. The singular weight of the body. A trancelike state you are tempted to mistake for happiness because the body is incapable of thinking, therefore incapable of anticipating change. Hot rhythmic blood, organs, packed tight and moist, the baby upside down in her sac in her mother's belly, always present tense, always *now.* It was a shock when the end came so abruptly but everyone told Mrs. Dietrich she was a natural mother, praised and pampered her. For a while. Then of course she'd had her baby, her Nola. Even now Mrs. Dietrich can't really comprehend the experience. *Giving birth. Had a baby. Was born.* Mere words, absurdly inadequate. She knows no more of how love ends than she knew as a child, she knows only of how love begins—in the belly, in the womb, where it is always present tense.

The morning's shopping has been quite successful but lunch at La Crêperie doesn't go well for some reason. La Crêperie is Nola's favorite Mall restaurant—always amiably crowded, bustling, a simulated sidewalk café with red-striped umbrellas, wrought-iron tables and chairs, menus in French, music piped in overhead. Mrs. Dietrich's nerves are chafed by the pretense of gaiety, the noise, the openness onto one of the Mall's busy promenades where at any minute a familiar face might emerge, but she is grateful for her glass of chilled white wine. She orders a small tossed salad and a creamed-chicken crepe and devours it hungrily—she *is* hungry. While Nola picks at her seafood crepe with a disdainful look. A familiar scene: mother watching while daughter

35

pushes food around on her plate. Suddenly Nola is tense, moody, corners of her mouth downturned. Mrs. Dietrich wants to ask, What's wrong? She wants to ask, Why are you unhappy? She wants to smooth Nola's hair back from her forehead, check to see if her forehead is overly warm, wants to hug her close, hard. Why, why? What did I do wrong? Why do you hate me?

Calling the Portland Academy a few weeks ago Mrs. Dietrich suddenly lost control, began crying. She hadn't been drinking and she hadn't known she was upset. A girl unknown to her, one of Nola's suite mates, was saying, "Please, Mrs. Dietrich, it's all right, I'm sure Nola will call you back later tonight, or tomorrow, Mrs. Dietrich?—I'll tell her you called, all right?—Mrs. Dietrich?" as embarrassed as if Mrs. Dietrich had been her own mother.

How love begins. How love ends.

Mrs. Dietrich orders a third glass of wine. This is a celebration of sorts isn't it?—their last shopping trip for a long time. But Nola resists, Nola isn't sentimental. In casual defiance of Mrs. Dietrich she lights up a cigarette—yes, Mother, Nola has said ironically, since *you* stopped smoking *everybody* is supposed to stop—and sits with her arms crossed, watching streams of shoppers pass. Mrs. Dietrich speaks lightly of practical matters, tomorrow morning's drive to the airport, and will Nola telephone when she gets to Portland to let Mrs. Dietrich know she has arrived safely?

Then with no warning—though of course she'd been planning this all along—Nola brings up the subject of a semester in France, in Paris and Rouen, the fall semester of her senior year it would be; she has put in her application, she says, and is waiting to hear if she's been accepted. She smokes her cigarette calmly, expelling smoke from her nostrils in a way Mrs. Dietrich thinks particularly coarse. Mrs. Dietrich, who believed that particular topic was finished, takes care to speak without emotion. "I just don't think it's a very practical idea right now, Nola," she says. "We've been through it haven't we? I—"

40   "I'm going," Nola says.

"The extra expense, for one thing. Your father—"

"If I get accepted, I'm going."

"Your father—"

"The hell with him too."

45   Mrs. Dietrich would like to slap her daughter's face. Bring tears to those steely eyes. But she sits stiff, turning her wine glass between her fingers, patient, calm, she's heard all this before; she says, "Surely this isn't the best time to discuss it, Nola."

Mrs. Dietrich is afraid her daughter will leave the restaurant, simply walk away, that has happened before and if it happens today she doesn't know what she will do. But Nola sits unmoving; her face closed, impassive. Mrs. Dietrich feels her quickened heartbeat. Once after one of their quarrels Mrs. Dietrich told a friend of hers, the mother too of a teenage daughter, "I just don't know her any longer, how can you keep living with someone you don't know?" and the woman said, "Eventually you can't."

Nola says, not looking at Mrs. Dietrich: "Why don't we talk about it, Mother?"

"Talk about what?" Mrs. Dietrich asks.

"You know."

"The semester in France? Again?" 50

"No."

"What, then?"

"You *know.*"

"I don't know, really. Really!" Mrs. Dietrich smiles, baffled. She feels the corners of her eyes pucker white with strain.

Nola says, sighing, "How exhausting it is." 55

"How *what?*"

"How exhausting it is."

"What is?"

"You and me—"

"What?" 60

"Being together—"

"Being together how—?"

"The two of us, like this—"

"But we're hardly ever together, Nola," Mrs. Dietrich says.

Her expression is calm but her voice is shaking. Nola turns away, cover- 65 ing her face with a hand, for a moment she looks years older than her age—in fact exhausted. Mrs. Dietrich sees with pity that her daughter's skin is fair and thin and dry—unlike her own, which tends to be oily—it will wear out before she's forty. Mrs. Dietrich reaches over to squeeze her hand. The fingers are limp, ungiving. "You're going back to school tomorrow, Nola," she says. "You won't come home again until June 12. And you probably will go to France—if your father consents."

Nola gets to her feet, drops her cigarette to the flagstone terrace and grinds it beneath her boot. A dirty thing to do, Mrs. Dietrich thinks, consider- ing there's an ashtray right on the table, but she says nothing. She dislikes La Crêperie anyway.

Nola laughs, showing her lovely white teeth. "Oh, the hell with him," she says. "Fuck Daddy, right?"

They separate for an hour, Mrs. Dietrich to Neiman-Marcus to buy a birthday gift for her elderly aunt, Nola to the trendy new boutique Pour Vous. By the time Mrs. Dietrich rejoins her daughter she's quite angry, blood beating hot and hard and measured in resentment, she has had time to relive old quarrels between them, old exchanges, stray humiliating memories of her marriage as well, these last-hour disagreements are the cruelest and they are Nola's specialty. She locates Nola in the rear of the boutique amid blaring rock music, flashing neon lights, chrome-edged mirrors, her face still hard, closed, prim, pale. She stands beside another teenage girl looking in a desultory way through a rack of blouses, shoving the hangers roughly along, taking no care when a blouse falls to the floor. As Nola glances up, startled, not prepared to see her mother in front of her, their eyes lock for an instant and Mrs. Dietrich stares at her with hatred. Cold calm clear unmistakable hatred. She is thinking, Who are *you?* What have I to do with *you?* I don't know *you,* I don't love *you,* why should I?

Has Nola seen, heard?—she turns aside as if wincing, gives the blouses a final dismissive shove. Her eyes look tired, the corners of her mouth downturned. Anxious, immediately repentant, Mrs. Dietrich asks if she has found anything worth trying on. Nola says with a shrug, "Not a thing, Mother."

70   On their way out of the Mall Mrs. Dietrich and Nola see the disheveled woman in the black coat again, this time sitting prominently on a concrete ledge in front of Lord & Taylor's busy main entrance. Shopping bag at her feet, shabby purse on the ledge beside her. She is shaking her head in a series of annoyed twitches as if arguing with someone but her hands are loose, palms up, in her lap. Her posture is unfortunate—she sits with her knees parted, inner thighs revealed, fatty, dead white, the tops of cotton stockings rolled tight cutting into the flesh. Again, streams of shoppers are making a careful berth around her. Alone among them Nola hesitates, seems about to approach the woman—Please don't, Nola! please! Mrs. Dietrich thinks—then changes her mind and keeps on walking. Mrs. Dietrich murmurs isn't it a pity, poor thing, don't you wonder where she lives, who her family is, but Nola doesn't reply. Her pace through the first door of Lord & Taylor is so rapid that Mrs. Dietrich can barely keep up.

But Nola's upset. Strangely upset. As soon as they are in the car, packages and bags in the backseat, she begins crying.

It's childish helpless crying, as though her heart is broken. But Mrs. Dietrich knows it isn't broken, she has heard these very sobs before. Many times before. Still she comforts her daughter, embraces her, hugs her hard, hard. A sudden fierce passion. Vehemence. "Nola honey. Nola dear, what's wrong, dear, everything will be all right, dear," she says, close to weeping herself. She would embrace Nola even more tightly except for the girl's quilted jacket, that bulky L. L. Bean thing she has never liked, and Nola's stubborn lowered head. Nola has always been ashamed, crying, frantic to hide her face. Strangers are passing close by the car, curious, staring. Mrs. Dietrich wishes she had a cloak to draw over her daughter and herself, so that no one else would see.   *1991*

CONSIDERATIONS

1. Why is Mrs. Dietrich overly sensitive to Nola's silence? Is her silence meant to be "deliberate, perverse," or is her mother imagining it this way? What would be your reaction under these circumstances—having "so little time remaining together"? Is there something more profound about that last statement? Explain.

2. Describe the relationship between Nola and her mother. Is it "typical" for a seventeen-year-old girl? Why or why not?

3. Why does Mrs. Dietrich choose to ignore Nola's stiffness and quietness?

4. Explain the symbolism of "the Mall" in this story. Does the Mall represent anything larger outside this story? Explain.

5. When Mrs. Dietrich and Nola are eating lunch, Mrs. Dietrich wants to ask several questions and do several things. Why doesn't she ask these questions or perform these actions? What would you do in this sort of situation if you were Mrs. Dietrich? If you were Nola?

6. Compare Nola's earlier reaction to the homeless woman with her later one. Why does she hesitate and then keep on walking away?

7. What do you make of Nola's crying? Why does she cry? Why does Mrs. Dietrich wish no one else could see her comforting and embracing Nola?

8. Predict what may or may not happen in Mrs. Dietrich and Nola's relationship. Explain your prediction.

ALICE WALKER (1944–   )

Everyday Use
For Your Grandmama

> As the youngest of eight children born in Eatonton, Georgia, to sharecroppers Minnie and Willie Lee Walker, Alice Walker was exposed to a number of contradictory forces that shaped her early life. On the one hand, she suffered from economic deprivation and the hardships imposed by segregation. On the other hand, she derived strength from her closely knit family and the extended black church congregation and community. She credits her mother with passing on the creativity she expressed through the flower gardens she nurtured and the stories she told. Walker describes the pivotal role her mother played in her life in the moving essay "In Search of Our Mothers' Gardens," which traces the roots of current black women writers to the artistry of their mothers and grandmothers. This artistry often came to light through handwork such as quilting (as reflected in "Everyday Use") or, as in her own mother's case, through growing flowers to provide beauty and sustenance for the spirits of their families.
>
> Walker has been widely acclaimed for her novel The Color Purple, which was awarded both the Pulitzer Prize and the American Book Award in 1983 and was later made into a highly praised film. Since then, she has published two more novels, The Temple of My Familiar (1989) and Possessing the Secret of Joy (1992). "Everyday Use" comes from the collection In Love and In Trouble (1973).

I will wait for her in the yard that Maggie and I made so clean and wavy yesterday afternoon. A yard like this is more comfortable than most people know. It is not just a yard. It is like an extended living room. When the hard clay is swept clean as a floor and the fine sand around the edges lined with tiny, irregular grooves anyone can come and sit and look up into the elm tree and wait for the breezes that never come inside the house.

Maggie will be nervous until after her sister goes: she will stand hopelessly in corners homely and ashamed of the burn scars down her arms and legs, eyeing her sister with a mixture of envy and awe. She thinks her sister has held life always in the palm of one hand, that "no" is a word the world never learned to say to her.

You've no doubt seen those TV shows where the child who has "made it" is confronted, as a surprise, by her own mother and father, tottering in weakly from backstage. (A pleasant surprise, of course: What would they do if parent and child came on the show only to curse out and insult each other?) On TV mother and child embrace and smile into each other's faces. Sometimes the mother and father weep, the child wraps them in her arms and leans across the table to tell how she would not have made it without their help. I have seen these programs.

Sometimes I dream a dream in which Dee and I are suddenly brought together on a TV program of this sort. Out of a dark and soft-seated limousine I am ushered into a bright room filled with many people. There I meet a smiling, gray, sporty man like Johnny Carson who shakes my hand and tells me what a fine girl I have. Then we are on the stage and Dee is embracing me with tears in her eyes. She pins on my dress a large orchid, even though she has told me once that she thinks orchids are tacky flowers.

5   In real life I am a large, big-boned woman with rough, man-working hands. In the winter I wear flannel nightgowns to bed and overalls during the day. I can kill and clean a hog as mercilessly as a man. My fat keeps me hot in zero weather. I can work outside all day, breaking ice to get water for washing; I can eat pork liver cooked over the open fire minutes after it comes steaming from the hog. One winter I knocked a bull calf straight in the brain between the eyes with a sledge hammer and had the meat hung up to chill before nightfall. But of course all this does not show on television. I am the way my daughter would want me to be: a hundred pounds lighter, my skin like an uncooked barley pancake. My hair glistens in the hot bright lights. Johnny Carson has much to do to keep up with my quick and witty tongue.

But that is a mistake. I know even before I wake up. Who ever knew a Johnson with a quick tongue? Who can even imagine me looking a strange white man in the eye? It seems to me I have talked to them always with one foot raised in flight, with my head turned in whichever way is farthest from them. Dee, though. She would always look anyone in the eye. Hesitation was no part of her nature.

"How do I look, Mama?" Maggie says, showing just enough of her thin body enveloped in pink skirt and red blouse for me to know she's there, almost hidden by the door.

"Come out into the yard," I say.

Have you ever seen a lame animal, perhaps a dog run over by some careless person rich enough to own a car, sidle up to someone who is ignorant enough to be kind to him? That is the way my Maggie walks. She has been like this, chin on chest, eyes on ground, feet in shuffle, ever since the fire that burned the other house to the ground.

Dee is lighter than Maggie, with nicer hair and a fuller figure. She's a   *10* woman now, though sometimes I forget. How long ago was it that the other house burned? Ten, twelve years? Sometimes I can still hear the flames and feel Maggie's arms sticking to me, her hair smoking and her dress falling off her in little black papery flakes. Her eyes seemed stretched open, blazed open by the flames reflected in them. And Dee. I see her standing off under the sweet gum tree she used to dig gum out of; a look of concentration on her face as she watched the last dingy gray board of the house fall in toward the red-hot brick chimney. Why don't you do a dance around the ashes? I'd wanted to ask her. She had hated the house that much.

I used to think she hated Maggie, too. But that was before we raised the money, the church and me, to send her to Augusta to school. She used to read to us without pity; forcing words, lies, other folks' habits, whole lives upon us two, sitting trapped and ignorant underneath her voice. She washed us in a river of make-believe, burned us with a lot of knowledge we didn't necessarily need to know. Pressed us to her with the serious way she read, to shove us away at just the moment, like dimwits, we seemed about to understand.

Dee wanted nice things. A yellow organdy dress to wear to her graduation from high school; black pumps to match a green suit she'd made from an old suit somebody gave me. She was determined to stare down any disaster in her efforts. Her eyelids would not flicker for minutes at a time. Often I fought off the temptation to shake her. At sixteen she had a style of her own: and knew what style was.

I never had an education myself. After second grade the school was closed down. Don't ask me why: in 1927 colored asked fewer questions than they do now. Sometimes Maggie reads to me. She stumbles along good-naturedly but can't see well. She knows she is not bright. Like good looks and money, quickness passed her by. She will marry John Thomas (who has mossy teeth in an earnest face) and then I'll be free to sit here and I guess just sing church songs to myself. Although I never was a good singer. Never could carry a tune. I was always better at a man's job. I used to love to milk till I was hooked in the side in '49. Cows are soothing and slow and don't bother you, unless you try to milk them the wrong way.

I have deliberately turned my back on the house. It is three rooms, just like the one that burned, except the roof is tin; they don't make shingle roofs any more. There are no real windows, just some holes cut in the sides, like the portholes in a ship, but not round and not square, with rawhide holding the shutters up on the outside. This house is in a pasture, too, like the other one. No doubt when Dee sees it she will want to tear it down. She wrote me once that no matter where we "choose" to live, she will manage to come see us. But she will never bring her friends. Maggie and I thought about this and Maggie asked me, "Mama, when did Dee ever *have* any friends?"

15   She had a few. Furtive boys in pink shirts hanging about on washday after school. Nervous girls who never laughed. Impressed with her they worshiped the well-turned phrase, the cute shape, the scalding humor that erupted like bubbles in lye. She read to them.

When she was courting Jimmy T she didn't have much time to pay to us, but turned all her faultfinding power on him. He *flew* to marry a cheap gal from a family of ignorant flashy people. She hardly had time to recompose herself.

When she comes I will meet—but there they are!

Maggie attempts to make a dash for the house, in her shuffling way, but I stay her with my hand. "Come back here," I say. And she stops and tries to dig a well in the sand with her toe.

It is hard to see them clearly through the strong sun. But even the first glimpse of leg out of the car tells me it is Dee. Her feet were always neat-looking, as if God himself had shaped them with a certain style. From the other side of the car comes a short, stocky man. Hair is all over his head a foot long and hanging from his chin like a kinky mule tail. I hear Maggie suck in her breath. "Uhnnnh," is what it sounds like. Like when you see the wriggling end of a snake just in front of your foot on the road. "Uhnnnh."

20   Dee next. A dress down to the ground, in this hot weather. A dress so loud it hurts my eyes. There are yellows and oranges enough to throw back the light of the sun. I feel my whole face warming from the heat waves it throws out. Earrings gold, too, and hanging down to her shoulders. Bracelets dangling and making noises when she moves her arm up to shake the folds of the dress out of her armpits. The dress is loose and flows, and as she walks closer, I like it. I hear Maggie go "Uhnnnh" again. It is her sister's hair. It stands straight up like the wool on a sheep. It is black as night and around the edges are two long pigtails that rope about like small lizards disappearing behind her ears.

"Wa-su-zo-Tean-o!" she says, coming on in that gliding way the dress makes her move. The short stocky fellow with the hair to his navel is all grinning and he follows up with "Asalamalakim, my mother and sister!" He moves to hug Maggie but she falls back, right up against the back of my chair. I feel her trembling there and when I look up I see the perspiration falling off her chin.

"Don't get up," says Dee. Since I am stout it takes something of a push. You can see me trying to move a second or two before I make it. She turns, showing white heels through her sandals, and goes back to the car. Out she peeks next with a Polaroid. She stoops down quickly and lines up picture after picture of me sitting there in front of the house with Maggie cowering behind me. She never takes a shot without making sure the house is included. When a cow comes nibbling around the edge of the yard she snaps it and me and Maggie *and* the house. Then she puts the Polaroid in the back seat of the car, and comes up and kisses me on the forehead.

Meanwhile Asalamalakim is going through the motions with Maggie's hand. Maggie's hand is as limp as a fish, and probably as cold, despite the sweat, and she keeps trying to pull it back. It looks like Asalamalakim wants to shake hands but wants to do it fancy. Or maybe he don't know how people shake hands. Anyhow, he soon gives up on Maggie.

"Well," I say. "Dee."

"No, Mama," she says. "Not 'Dee,' Wangero Leewanika Kemanjo!"   25

"What happened to 'Dee'?" I wanted to know.

"She's dead," Wangero said. "I couldn't bear it any longer being named after the people who oppress me."

"You know as well as me you was named after your aunt Dicie," I said. Dicie is my sister. She named Dee. We called her "Big Dee" after Dee was born.

"But who was *she* named after?" asked Wangero.

"I guess after Grandma Dee," I said.   30

"And who was she named after?" asked Wangero.

"Her mother," I said, and saw Wangero was getting tired. "That's about as far back as I can trace it," I said. Though, in fact, I probably could have carried it back beyond the Civil War through the branches.

"Well," said Asalamalakim, "there you are."

"Uhnnnh," I heard Maggie say.

"There I was not," I said, "before 'Dicie' cropped up in our family, so   35 why should I try to trace it that far back?"

He just stood there grinning, looking down on me like somebody inspecting a Model A car. Every once in a while he and Wangero sent eye signals over my head.

"How do you pronounce this name?" I asked.

"You don't have to call me by it if you don't want to," said Wangero.

"Why shouldn't I?" I asked. "If that's what you want us to call you, we'll call you."

"I know it might sound awkward at first," said Wangero.   40

"I'll get used to it," I said. "Ream it out again."

Well, soon we got the name out of the way. Asalamalakim had a name twice as long and three times as hard. After I tripped over it two or three times he told me to just call him Hakim-a-barber. I wanted to ask him was he a barber, but I didn't really think he was, so I didn't ask.

"You must belong to those beef-cattle peoples down the road," I said. They said "Asalamalakim" when they met you, too, but they didn't shake hands. Always too busy: feeding the cattle, fixing the fences, putting up salt-lick shelters, throwing down hay. When the white folks poisoned some of the herd the men stayed up all night with rifles in their hands. I walked a mile and a half just to see the sight.

Hakim-a-barber said, "I accept some of their doctrines, but farming and raising cattle is not my style." (They didn't tell me, and I didn't ask, whether Wangero [Dee] had really gone and married him.)

45   We sat down to eat and right away he said he didn't eat collards and pork was unclean. Wangero, though, went on through the chitlins and corn bread, the greens and everything else. She talked a blue streak over the sweet pota-toes. Everything delighted her. Even the fact that we still used the benches her daddy made for the table when we couldn't afford to buy chairs.

"Oh, Mama!" she cried. Then turned to Hakim-a-barber. "I never knew how lovely these benches are. You can feel the rump prints," she said, running her hands underneath her and along the bench. Then she gave a sigh and her hand closed over Grandma Dee's butter dish. "That's it!" she said. "I knew there was something I wanted to ask you if I could have." She jumped up from the table and went over in the corner where the churn stood, the milk in it clab-ber by now. She looked at the churn and looked at it.

"This churn top is what I need," she said. "Didn't Uncle Buddy whittle it out of a tree you all used to have?"

"Yes," I said.

"Uh huh," she said happily. "And I want the dasher, too."

50   "Uncle Buddy whittle that, too?" asked the barber.

Dee (Wangero) looked up at me.

"Aunt Dee's first husband whittled the dash," said Maggie so low you al-most couldn't hear her. "His name was Henry, but they called him Stash."

"Maggie's brain is like an elephant's," Wangero said, laughing. "I can use the churn top as a centerpiece for the alcove table," she said, sliding a plate over the churn, "and I'll think of something artistic to do with the dasher."

When she finished wrapping the dasher the handle stuck out. I took it for a moment in my hands. You didn't even have to look close to see where hands pushing the dasher up and down to make butter had left a kind of sink in the wood. In fact, there were a lot of small sinks; you could see where thumbs and fingers had sunk into the wood. It was beautiful light yellow wood, from a tree that grew in the yard where Big Dee and Stash had lived.

55   After dinner Dee (Wangero) went to the trunk at the foot of my bed and started rifling through it. Maggie hung back in the kitchen over the dishpan. Out came Wangero with two quilts. They had been pieced by Grandma Dee and then Big Dee and me had hung them on the quilt frames on the front porch and quilted them. One was in the Lone Star pattern. The other was Walk Around the Mountain. In both of them were scraps of dresses Grandma Dee had worn fifty and more years ago. Bits and pieces of Grandpa Jarrell's paisley

shirts. And one teeny faded blue piece, about the size of a penny matchbox, that was from Great Grandpa Ezra's uniform that he wore in the Civil War.

"Mama," Wangero said sweet as a bird. "Can I have these old quilts?"

I heard something fall in the kitchen, and a minute later the kitchen door slammed.

"Why don't you take one or two of the others?" I asked. "These old things was just done by me and Big Dee from some tops your grandma pieced before she died."

"No," said Wangero. "I don't want those. They are stitched around the borders by machine."

"That'll make them last better," I said.   60

"That's not the point," said Wangero. "These are all pieces of dresses Grandma used to wear. She did all this stitching by hand. Imagine!" She held the quilts securely in her arms, stroking them.

"Some of the pieces, like those lavender ones, come from old clothes her mother handed down to her," I said, moving up to touch the quilts. Dee (Wangero) moved back just enough so that I couldn't reach the quilts. They already belonged to her.

"Imagine!" she breathed again, clutching them closely to her bosom.

"The truth is," I said, "I promised to give them quilts to Maggie, for when she marries John Thomas."

She gasped like a bee had stung her.   65

"Maggie can't appreciate these quilts!" she said. "She'd probably be backward enough to put them to everyday use."

"I reckon she would," I said. "God knows I been saving 'em for long enough with nobody using 'em. I hope she will!" I didn't want to bring up how I had offered Dee (Wangero) a quilt when she went away to college. Then she had told me they were old-fashioned, out of style.

"But they're *priceless!*" she was saying now, furiously; for she has a temper. "Maggie would put them on the bed and in five years they'd be in rags. Less than that!"

"She can always make some more," I said. "Maggie knows how to quilt."

Dee (Wangero) looked at me with hatred. "You just will not understand.   70
The point is these quilts, *these* quilts!"

"Well," I said, stumped. "What would *you* do with them?"

"Hang them," she said. As if that was the only thing you *could* do with quilts.

Maggie by now was standing in the door. I could almost hear the sound her feet made as they scraped over each other.

"She can have them, Mama," she said, like somebody used to never winning anything, or having anything reserved for her. "I can 'member Grandma Dee without the quilts."

I looked at her hard. She had filled her bottom lip with checkerberry   75
snuff and it gave her face a kind of dopey, hangdog look. It was Grandma Dee

and Big Dee who taught her how to quilt herself. She stood there with her scarred hands hidden in the folds of her skirt. She looked at her sister with something like fear but she wasn't mad at her. This was Maggie's portion. This was the way she knew God to work.

When I looked at her like that something hit me in the top of my head and ran down to the soles of my feet. Just like when I'm in church and the spirit of God touches me and I get happy and shout. I did something I never had done before: hugged Maggie to me, then dragged her on into the room, snatched the quilts out of Miss Wangero's hands and dumped them into Maggie's lap. Maggie just sat there on my bed with her mouth open.

"Take one or two of the others," I said to Dee.

But she turned without a word and went out to Hakim-a-barber.

"You just don't understand," she said, as Maggie and I came out to the car.

80   "What don't I understand?" I wanted to know.

"Your heritage," she said. And then she turned to Maggie, kissed her, and said, "You ought to try to make something of yourself, too, Maggie. It's really a new day for us. But from the way you and Mama still live you'd never know it."

She put on some sunglasses that hid everything above the tip of her nose and her chin.

Maggie smiled; maybe at the sunglasses. But a real smile, not scared. After we watched the car dust settle I asked Maggie to bring me a dip of snuff. And then the two of us sat there just enjoying, until it was time to go in the house and go to bed.   *1973*

CONSIDERATIONS

1. Why does Walker subtitle her story "For Your Grandmama"? Whose grandmama is she talking about?

2. Speculate on Dee's motives for coming home with her friend even though she had told her mother that she would never bring friends to the family's house. What is it that she now values about her past? Why, for example, does she want the churn top and the quilts? What is it that Maggie and her mother value about their past and the objects that reflect their past?

3. Analyze the implications of the story's title. For example, consider Dee's statement that if Maggie got the quilts, "she'd probably be backward enough to put them to everyday use." If you were to arbitrate this disagreement, whose side would you be on? Should the quilts be put to everyday use? Why or why not?

4. How would you describe the relationship between Dee and Maggie? Between the mother and her two daughters? What creates a close relationship here? A distant one?

5. Discuss the significance of Dee's name change. How does her adoption of this new name explain, in part, the relationship she has with Maggie and her mother?

MARY HOOD (1946–   )

How Far She Went

Mary Hood was born in 1946 in Brunswick, Georgia, and has spent most of her life near Atlanta. She began writing in 1967 after graduating from college. But it took almost twenty years before she found a publisher for her collection of short stories about the people and places of backwoods Georgia, How Far She Went, *in 1984. During those years, she worked at a variety of jobs—substitute teacher, library assistant, and department store clerk—and she had a small business painting portraits of deceased pets. And she read voraciously.* How Far She Went *(the source of the selection here) won the Flannery O'Connor award for short fiction in 1984. Because of that acclaim, it was easier to find a publisher for her second collection of short stories,* And Venus Is Blue, *in 1986. For the next nine years, before her novel* Familiar Heat *in 1995, she published short stories and essays in periodicals. She has held teaching positions at the University of Georgia, the University of Mississippi at Oxford, Berry College, and Reinhardt College.*

They had quarreled all morning, squalled all summer about the incidentals: how tight the girl's cut-off jeans were, the "Every Inch a Woman" T-shirt, her choice of music and how loud she played it, her practiced inattention, her sullen look. Her granny wrung out the last boiled dishcloth, pinched it to the line, giving the basin a sling and a slap, the water flying out in a scalding arc onto the Queen Anne's lace by the path, never mind if it bloomed, that didn't make it worth anything except to chiggers, but the girl would cut it by the everlasting armload and cherish it in the old churn, going to that much trouble for a weed but not bending once—unbegged—to pick the nearest bean; she was sulking now. Bored. Displaced.

"And what do you think happens to a chigger if nobody ever walks by his weed?" her granny asked, heading for the house with that sidelong uneager unanswered glance, hoping for what? The surprise gift of a smile? Nothing. The woman shook her head and said it. "Nothing." The door slammed behind her. Let it.

"I hate it here!" the girl yelled then. She picked up a stick and broke it and threw the pieces—one from each hand—at the laundry drying in the noon. Missed. Missed.

Then she turned on her bare, haughty heel and set off high-shouldered into the heat, quick but not far, not far enough—no road was *that* long—only as far as she dared. At the gate, a rusty chain swinging between two lichened posts, she stopped, then backed up the raw drive to make a run at the barrier, lofting, clearing it clean, her long hair wild in the sun. Triumphant, she looked back at the house where she caught at the dark window her granny's face in its perpetual eclipse of disappointment, old at fifty. She stepped back, but the girl saw her.

5 "You don't know me!" the girl shouted, chin high, and ran till her ribs ached.

As she rested in the rattling shade of the willows, the little dog found her. He could be counted on. He barked all the way, and squealed when she pulled the burr from his ear. They started back to the house for lunch. By then the mailman had long come and gone in the old ruts, leaving the one letter folded now to fit the woman's apron pocket.

If bad news darkened her granny's face, the girl ignored it. Didn't talk at all, another of her distancings, her defiances. So it was as they ate that the woman summarized, "Your daddy wants you to cash in the plane ticket and buy you something. School clothes. For here."

Pale, the girl stared, defenseless only an instant before blurting out, "You're lying."

The woman had to stretch across the table to leave her handprint on that blank cheek. She said, not caring if it stung or not, "He's been planning it since he sent you here."

10 "I could turn this whole house over, dump it! Leave you slobbering over that stinking jealous dog in the dust!" The girl trembled with the vision, with the strength it gave her. It made her laugh. "Scatter the Holy Bible like confetti and ravel the crochet into miles of stupid string! I could! I will! I won't stay here!" But she didn't move, not until her tears rose to meet her color, and then to escape the shame of minding so much she fled. Just headed away, blind. It didn't matter, this time, how far she went.

The woman set her thoughts against fretting over their bickering, just went on unalarmed with chores, clearing off after the uneaten meal, bringing in the laundry, scattering corn for the chickens, ladling manure tea onto the porch flowers. She listened though. She always had been a listener. It gave her a cocked look. She forgot why she had gone into the girl's empty room, that ungirlish, tenuous lodging place with its bleak order, its ready suitcases never unpacked, the narrow bed, the contested radio on the windowsill. The woman drew the cracked shade down between the radio and the August sun. There wasn't anything else to do.

It was after six when she tied on her rough oxfords and walked down the drive and dropped the gate chain and headed back to the creosoted shed where she kept her tools. She took a hoe for snakes, a rake, shears to trim the grass where it grew, and seed in her pocket to scatter where it never had grown at all. She put the tools and her gloves and the bucket in the trunk of the old Chevy, its prime and rust like an Appaloosa's spots through the chalky white finish. She left the trunk open and the tool handles sticking out. She wasn't going far.

The heat of the day had broken, but the air was thick, sultry, weighted with honeysuckle in second bloom and the Nu-Grape scent of kudzu. The maple and poplar leaves turned over, quaking, silver. There wouldn't be any rain. She told the dog to stay, but he knew a trick. He stowed away when she turned her back, leaped right into the trunk with the tools, then gave himself away with exultant barks. Hearing him, her court jester, she stopped the car and welcomed him into the front seat beside her. Then they went on. Not a mile from her gate she turned onto the blue gravel of the cemetery lane, hauled the gearshift into reverse to whoa them, and got out to take the idle walk down to her buried hopes, bending all along to rout out a handful of weeds from between the markers of old acquaintance. She stood there and read, slow. The dog whined at her hem; she picked him up and rested her chin on his head, then he wriggled and whined to run free, contrary and restless as a child.

The crows called strong and bold MOM! MOM! A trick of the ear to hear it like that. She knew it was the crows, but still she looked around. No one called her that now. She was done with that. And what was it worth anyway? It all came to this: solitary weeding. The sinful fumble of flesh, the fear, the listening for a return that never came, the shamed waiting, the unanswered prayers, the perjury on the certificate—hadn't she lain there weary of the whole lie and it only beginning? and a voice telling her, "Here's your baby, here's your girl," and the swaddled package meaning no more to her than an extra anything, something store-bought, something she could take back for a refund.

"Tie her to the fence and give her a bale of hay," she had murmured,   *15* drugged, and they teased her, excused her for such a welcoming, blaming the anesthesia, but it went deeper than that; *she* knew, and the *baby* knew: there was no love in the begetting. That was the secret, unforgivable, that not another good thing could ever make up for, where all the bad had come from, like a visitation, a punishment. She knew that was why Sylvie had been wild, had gone to earth so early, and before dying had made this child in sudden wedlock, a child who would be just like her, would carry the hurting on into another generation. A matter of time. No use raising her hand. But she *had* raised her hand. Still wore on its palm the memory of the sting of the collision with the girl's cheek; had she broken her jaw? Her heart? Of course not. She said it aloud: "Takes more than that."

She went to work then, doing what she could with her old tools. She pecked the clay on Sylvie's grave, new-looking, unhealed after years. She tried again, scattering seeds from her pocket, every last possible one of them. Off in the west she could hear the pulpwood cutters sawing through another acre across the lake. Nearer, there was the racket of motorcycles laboring cross-country, insect-like, distracting.

She took her bucket to the well and hung it on the pump. She had half filled it when the bikers roared up, right down the blue gravel, straight at her. She let the bucket overflow, staring. On the back of one of the machines was the girl. Sylvie's girl! Her bare arms wrapped around the shirtless man riding between her thighs. They were first. The second biker rode alone. She studied their strangers' faces as they circled her. They were the enemy, all of them. Laughing. The girl was laughing too, laughing like her mama did. Out in the middle of nowhere the girl had found these two men, some moth-musk about her drawing them (too soon!) to what? She shouted it: "What in God's—" They roared off without answering her, and the bucket of water tipped over, spilling its stain blood-dark on the red dust.

The dog went wild barking, leaping after them, snapping at the tires, and there was no calling him down. The bikers made a wide circuit of the churchyard, then roared straight across the graves, leaping the ditch and landing upright on the road again, heading off toward the reservoir.

Furious, she ran to her car, past the barking dog, this time leaving him behind, driving after them, horn blowing nonstop, to get back what was not theirs. She drove after them knowing what they did not know, that all the roads beyond that point dead-ended. She surprised them, swinging the Impala across their path, cutting them off; let them hit it! They stopped. She got out, breathing hard, and said, when she could, "She's underage." Just that. And put out her claiming hand with an authority that made the girl's arms drop from the man's insolent waist and her legs tremble.

20   "I was just riding," the girl said, not looking up.

Behind them the sun was heading on toward down. The long shadows of the pines drifted back and forth in the same breeze that puffed the distant sails on the lake. Dead limbs creaked and clashed overhead like the antlers of locked and furious beasts.

"Sheeeut," the lone rider said. "I told you." He braced with his muddy boot and leaned out from his machine to spit. The man the girl had been riding with had the invading sort of eyes the woman had spent her lifetime bolting doors against. She met him now, face to face.

"Right there, missy," her granny said, pointing behind her to the car.

The girl slid off the motorcycle and stood halfway between her choices. She started slightly at the poosh! as he popped another top and chugged the beer in one uptilting of his head. His eyes never left the woman's. When he was through, he tossed the can high, flipping it end over end. Before it hit the ground he had his pistol out and, firing once, winged it into the lake.

25   "Freaking lucky shot," the other one grudged.

"I don't need luck," he said. He sighted down the barrel of the gun at the woman's head. "POW!" he yelled, and when she recoiled, he laughed. He swung around to the girl; he kept aiming the gun, here, there, high, low, all around. "Y'all settle it," he said, with a shrug.

The girl had to understand him then, had to know him, had to know better. But still she hesitated. He kept looking at her, then away.

"She's fifteen," her granny said. "You can go to jail."

"You can go to hell," he said.

"Probably will," her granny told him. "I'll save you a seat by the fire."   *30*
She took the girl by the arm and drew her to the car; she backed up, swung around, and headed out the road toward the churchyard for her tools and dog. The whole way the girl said nothing, just hunched against the far door, staring hard-eyed out at the pines going past.

The woman finished watering the seed in, and collected her tools. As she worked, she muttered, "It's your own kin buried here, you might have the decency to glance this way one time . . ." The girl was finger-tweezing her eyebrows in the side mirror. She didn't look around as the dog and the woman got in. Her granny shifted hard, sending the tools clattering in the trunk.

When they came to the main road, there were the men. Watching for them. Waiting for them. They kicked their machines into life and followed, close, bumping them, slapping the old fenders, yelling. The girl gave a wild glance around at the one by her door and said, "Gran'ma?" and as he drew his pistol, "Gran'ma!" just as the gun nosed into the open window. She frantically cranked the glass up between her and the weapon, and her granny, seeing, spat, "Fool!" She never had been one to pray for peace or rain. She stamped the accelerator right to the floor.

The motorcycles caught up. Now she braked, hard, and swerved off the road into an alley between the pines, not even wide enough for the school bus, just a fire scrape that came out a quarter mile from her own house, if she could get that far. She slewed on the pine straw, then righted, tearing along the dark tunnel through the woods. She had for the time being bested them; they were left behind. She was winning. Then she hit the wallow where the tadpoles were already five weeks old. The Chevy plowed in and stalled. When she got it cranked again, they were stuck. The tires spattered mud three feet up the near trunks as she tried to spin them out, to rock them out. Useless. "Get out and run!" she cried, but the trees were too close on the passenger side. The girl couldn't open her door. She wasted precious time having to crawl out under the steering wheel. The woman waited but the dog ran on.

They struggled through the dusky woods, their pace slowed by the thick straw and vines. Overhead, in the last light, the martins were reeling free and sure after their prey.

"Why? Why?" the girl gasped, as they lunged down the old deer trail.   *35*
Behind them they could hear shots, and glass breaking as the men came to the bogged car. The woman kept on running, swatting their way clear through the shoulder-high weeds. They could see the Greer cottage, and made for it. But it

was ivied-over, padlocked, the woodpile dry-rotting under its tarp, the electric meterbox empty on the pole. No help there.

The dog, excited, trotted on, yelping, his lips white-flecked. He scented the lake and headed that way, urging them on with thirsty yips. On the clay shore, treeless, deserted, at the utter limit of land, they stood defenseless, listening to the men coming on, between them and home. The woman pressed her hands to her mouth, stifling her cough. She was exhausted. She couldn't think.

"We can get under!" the girl cried suddenly, and pointed toward the Greers' dock, gap-planked, its walkway grounded on the mud. They splashed out to it, wading in, the woman grabbing up the telltale, tattletale dog in her arms. They waded out to the far end and ducked under. There was room between the foam floats for them to crouch neck-deep.

The dog wouldn't hush, even then; never had yet, and there wasn't time to teach him. When the woman realized that, she did what she had to do. She grabbed him whimpering; held him; held him under till the struggle ceased and the bubbles rose silver from his fur. They crouched there then, the two of them, submerged to the shoulders, feet unsteady on the slimed lake bed. They listened. The sky went from rose to ocher to violet in the cracks over their heads. The motorcycles had stopped now. In the silence there was the glissando of locusts, the dry crunch of boots on the flinty beach, their low man-talk drifting as they prowled back and forth. One of them struck a match.

"—they in these woods we could burn 'em out."

40   The wind carried their voices away into the pines. Some few words eddied back.

"—lippy old smartass do a little work on her knees besides praying—"

Laughter. It echoed off the deserted house. They were getting closer.

One of them strode directly out to the dock, walked on the planks over their heads. They could look up and see his boot soles. He was the one with the gun. He slapped a mosquito on his bare back and cursed. The carp, roused by the troubling of the waters, came nosing around the dock, guzzling and snorting. The girl and her granny held still, so still. The man fired his pistol into the shadows, and a wounded fish thrashed, dying. The man knelt and reached for it, chuffing out his beery breath. He belched. He pawed the lake for the dead fish, cursing as it floated out of reach. He shot it again, firing at it till it sank and the gun was empty. Cursed that too. He stood then and unzipped and relieved himself of some of the beer. They had to listen to that. To know that about him. To endure that, unprotesting.

Back and forth on shore the other one ranged, restless. He lit another cigarette. He coughed. He called, "Hey! They got away, man, that's all. Don't get your shorts in a wad. Let's go."

45   "Yeah." He finished. He zipped. He stumped back across the planks and leaped to shore, leaving the dock tilting amid widening ripples. Underneath, they waited.

The bike cranked. The other ratcheted, ratcheted, then coughed, caught, roared. They circled, cut deep ruts, slung gravel, and went. Their roaring died away and away. Crickets resumed and a near frog bic-bic-bicked.

Under the dock, they waited a little longer to be sure. Then they ducked below the water, scraped out from under the pontoon, and came up into free air, slogging toward shore. It had seemed warm enough in the water. Now they shivered. It was almost night. One streak of light still stood reflected on the darkening lake, drew itself thinner, narrowing into a final cancellation of day. A plane winked its way west.

The girl was trembling. She ran her hands down her arms and legs, shedding water like a garment. She sighed, almost a sob. The woman held the dog in her arms; she dropped to her knees upon the random stones and murmured, private, haggard, "Oh, honey," three times, maybe all three times for the dog, maybe once for each of them. The girl waited, watching. Her granny rocked the dog like a baby, like a dead child, rocked slower and slower and was still.

"I'm sorry," the girl said then, avoiding the dog's inert, empty eye.

"It was him or you," her granny said, finally, looking up. Looking her *50*
over. "Did they mess with you? With your britches? Did they?"

"No!" Then, quieter, "No, ma'am."

When the woman tried to stand up she staggered, lightheaded, clumsy with the freight of the dog. "No, ma'am," she echoed, fending off the girl's "Let me." And she said again, "It was him or you. I know that. I'm not going to rub your face in it." They saw each other as well as they could in that failing light, in any light.

The woman started toward home, saying, "Around here, we bear our own burdens." She led the way along the weedy shortcuts. The twilight bleached the dead limbs of the pines to bone. Insects sang in the thickets, silencing at their oncoming.

"We'll see about the car in the morning," the woman said. She bore her armful toward her own moth-ridden dusk-to-dawn security light with that country grace she had always had when the earth was reliably progressing underfoot. The girl walked close behind her, exactly where *she* walked, matching her pace, matching her stride, close enough to put her hand forth (if the need arose) and touch her granny's back where the faded voile was clinging damp, the merest gauze between their wounds.   *1984*

CONSIDERATIONS

1. Discuss the implications of the title and how these implications develop character, plot, conflict, and the theme of this piece.
2. Review the details associated with the grandmother as well as the girl in this story. What do these details reveal about them? What do their actions

say about them? With these details in mind, in what ways are the two characters alike? In what ways are they different? Explain.

3. What purpose does the natural landscape—the plants, the birds, the animals, weather—serve in this piece? In what ways does this setting reflect the theme as well as the conflict?

4. What background can you piece together from the scene at the cemetery? What difference does this make to the story?

5. In the end, the narrator writes that the grandmother and the girl "saw each other as well as they could in that failing light, in any light." What do you think they saw in each other? Explain.

GISH JEN (1956–   )
Who's Irish?

An American with Chinese roots, Gish Jen grew up in Scarsdale, New York, and was educated at Harvard, Stanford, and the Iowa Writers' Workshop. She has received grants from the National Endowment for the Arts, the James Michener/ Copernicus Society, The Bunting Institute, and the Massachusetts Artists' Foundation. Her work has appeared in many magazines and collections, including the New Yorker *and the* Atlantic Monthly. *She is the author of several novels, including the widely acclaimed* Typical Americans *(1991), which depicts the life of contemporary Chinese immigrants. The following selection, which appeared in* The Best American Short Stories of the Century *comes from her book of short fiction,* Who's Irish *(1998).*

In China, people say mixed children are supposed to be smart, and definitely my granddaughter Sophie is smart. But Sophie is wild, Sophie is not like my daughter Natalie, or like me. I am work hard my whole life, and fierce besides. My husband always used to say he is afraid of me, and in our restaurant, busboys and cooks all afraid of me too. Even the gang members come for protection money, they try to talk to my husband. When I am there, they stay away. If they come by mistake, they pretend they are come to eat. They hide behind the menu, they order a lot of food. They talk about their mothers. Oh, my mother have some arthritis, need to take herbal medicine, they say. Oh, my mother getting old, her hair all white now.

I say, Your mother's hair used to be white, but since she dye it, it become black again. Why don't you go home once in a while and take a look? I tell them, Confucious say a filial son knows what color his mother's hair is.

My daughter is fierce too, she is vice president in the bank now. Her new house is big enough for everybody to have their own room, including me. But Sophie take after Natalie's husband's family, their name is Shea. Irish. I always thought Irish people are like Chinese people, work so hard on the railroad, but now I know why the Chinese beat the Irish. Of course, not all Irish are like the Shea family, of course not. My daughter tell me I should not say Irish this, Irish that.

How do you like it when people say the Chinese this, the Chinese that, she say.

You know the British call the Irish heathen, just like they call the Chinese, she say.   5

You think the Opium War was bad, how would you like to live right next door to the British, she say.

And that is that. My daughter have a funny habit when she win an argument, she take a sip of something and look away, so the other person is not embarrassed. So I am not embarrassed. I do not call anybody anything either. I just happen to mention about the Shea family, an interesting fact: four brothers in the family, and not one of them work. The mother, Bess, have a job before she got sick, she was executive secretary in a big company. She is handle everything for a big shot, you would be surprised how complicated her job is, not just type this, type that. Now she is a nice woman with a clean house. But her boys, every one of them is on welfare, or so-called severance pay, or so-called disability pay. Something. They say they cannot find work, this is not the economy of the fifties, but I say, Even the black people doing better these days, some of them live so fancy, you'd be surprised. Why the Shea family have so much trouble? They are white people, they speak English. When I come to this country, I have no money and do not speak English. But my husband and I own our restaurant before he die. Free and clear, no mortgage. Of course, I understand I am just lucky, come from a country where the food is popular all over the world. I understand it is not the Shea family's fault they come from a country where everything is boiled. Still, I say.

She's right, we should broaden our horizons, say one brother, Jim, at Thanksgiving. Forget about the car business. Think about egg rolls.

Pad thai, say another brother, Mike. I'm going to make my fortune in pad thai. It's going to be the new pizza.

I say, You people too picky about what you sell. Selling egg rolls not   10
good enough for you, but at least my husband and I can say, We made it. What can you say? Tell me. What can you say?

Everybody chew their tough turkey.

I especially cannot understand my daughter's husband John, who has no job but cannot take care of Sophie either. Because he is a man, he say, and that's the end of the sentence.

Plain boiled food, plain boiled thinking. Even his names is plain boiled: John. Maybe because I grew up with black bean sauce and hoisin sauce and garlic sauce, I always feel something is missing when my son-in-law talk.

But, okay: so my son-in-law can be man, I am baby-sitter. Six hours a day, same as the old sitter, crazy Amy, who quit. This is not so easy, now that I am sixty-eight, Chinese age almost seventy. Still, I try. In China, daughter take care of mother. Here it is the other way around. Mother help daughter, mother ask, Anything else I can do? Otherwise daughter complain mother is not supportive. I tell daughter, We do not have this word in Chinese, *supportive*. But my daughter too busy to listen, she has to go to meeting, she has to write memo while her husband go to the gym to be a man. My daughter say otherwise he will be depressed. Seems like all his life he has this trouble, depression.

15   No one wants to hire someone who is depressed, she say. It is important for him to keep his spirits up.

       Beautiful wife, beautiful daughter, beautiful house, oven can clean itself automatically. No money left over, because only one income, but lucky enough, got the baby-sitter for free. If John lived in China, he would be very happy. But he is not happy. Even at the gym things go wrong. One day, he pull a muscle. Another day, weight room too crowded. Always something.

       Until finally, hooray, he has a job. Then he feel pressure.

       I need to concentrate, he say. I need to focus.

       He is going to work for insurance company. Salesman job. A paycheck, he say, and at least he will wear clothes instead of gym shorts. My daughter buy him some special candy bars from the health-food store. They say THINK! on them, and are supposed to help John think.

20   John is a good-looking boy, you have to say that, especially now that he shave so you can see his face.

       I am an old man in a young man's game, say John.

       I will need a new suit, say John.

       This time I am not going to shoot myself in the foot, say John.

       Good, I say.

25   She means to be supportive, my daughter say. Don't start the send her back to China thing, because we can't.

Sophie is three years old American age, but already I see her nice Chinese side swallowed up by her wild Shea side. She looks like mostly Chinese. Beautiful black hair, beautiful black eyes. Nose perfect size, not so flat looks like something fell down, not so large looks like some big deal got stuck in wrong face. Everything just right, only her skin is a brown surprise to John's family. So brown, they say. Even John say it. She never goes in the sun, still she is that color, he say. Brown. They say, Nothing the matter with brown. They are just surprised. So brown, Nattie is not that brown, they say. They say, It seems like Sophie should be a color in between Nattie and John. Seems funny, a girl names Sophie Shea be brown. But she is brown, maybe her name should be Sophie Brown. She never go in the sun, still she is that color, they say. Nothing the matter with brown. They are just surprised.

       The Shea family talk is like this sometimes, going around and around like a Christmas-tree train.

       Maybe John is not her father, I say one day, to stop the train. And sure enough, train wreck. None of the brothers ever say the word *brown* to me again.

Instead, John's mother, Bess, say, I hope you are not offended.

She say, I did my best on those boys. But raising four boys with no father   *30*
is no picnic.

You have a beautiful family, I say.

I'm getting old, she say.

You deserve a rest, I say. Too many boys make you old.

I never had a daughter, she say. You have a daughter.

I have a daughter, I say. Chinese people don't think a daughter is so great,   *35*
but you're right. I have a daughter.

I was never against the marriage, you know, she say. I never thought John
was marrying down. I always thought Nattie was just as good as white.

I was never against the marriage either, I say. I just wonder if they look at
the whole problem.

Of course you pointed out the problem, you are a mother, she say. And
now we both have a granddaughter. A little brown granddaughter, she is so
precious to me.

I laugh. A little brown granddaughter, I say. To tell you the truth, I don't
know how she came out so brown.

We laugh some more. These days Bess need a walker to walk. She take   *40*
so many pills, she need two glasses of water to get them all down. Her favorite
TV show is about bloopers, and she love her bird feeder. All day long, she can
watch that bird feeder, like a cat.

I can't wait for her to grow up, Bess say. I could use some female company.

Too many boys, I say.

Boys are fine, she say. But they do surround you after a while.

You should take a break, come live with us, I say. Lots of girls at our house.

Be careful what you offer, say Bess with a wink. Where I come from,   *45*
people mean for you to move in when they say a thing like that.

Nothing the matter with Sophie's outside, that's the truth. It is inside that she
is like not any Chinese girl I ever see. We go to the park, and this is what she
does. She stand up in the stroller. She take off all her clothes and throw them in
the fountain.

Sophie! I say. Stop!

But she just laugh like a crazy person. Before I take over as baby-sitter,
Sophie has that crazy-person sitter, Amy the guitar player. My daughter
thought this Amy very creative—another word we do not talk about in China.
In China, we talk about whether we have difficulty or no difficulty. We talk
about whether life is bitter or not bitter. In America, all day long people talk
about creative. Never mind that I cannot even look at this Amy, with her shirt
so short that her belly button showing. This Amy think Sophie should love
her body. So when Sophie take off her diaper, Amy laugh. When Sophie run
around naked, Amy say she wouldn't want to wear a diaper either. When Sophie go *shu-shu* in her lap, Amy laugh and say there are no germs in pee. When

Sophie take off her shoes, Amy say bare feet is best, even the pediatrician say so. That is why Sophie now walks around with no shoes like a beggar child. Also why Sophie love to take off her clothes.

Turn around! say the boys in the park. Let's see that ass!

50 Of course, Sophie does not understand. Sophie clap her hands, I am the only one to say, No! This is not a game.

It has nothing to do with John's family, my daughter say. Amy was too permissive, that's all.

But I think if Sophie was not wild inside, she would not take off her shoes and clothes to begin with.

You never take off your clothes when you were little, I say. All my Chinese friends had babies, I never saw one of them act wild like that.

Look, my daughter say. I have a big presentation tomorrow.

55 John and my daughter agree Sophie is a problem, but they don't know what to do.

You spank her, she'll stop, I say another day.

But they say, Oh no.

In America, parents not supposed to spank the child.

It gives them low self-esteem, my daughter say. And that leads to problems later, as I happen to know.

60 My daughter never have big presentation the next day when the subject of spanking come up.

I don't want you to touch Sophie, she say. No spanking, period.

Don't tell me what to do, I say.

I'm not telling you what to do, say my daughter. I'm telling you how I feel.

I am not your servant I say. Don't you dare talk to me like that.

65 My daughter have another funny habit when she lose an argument. She spread out all her fingers and look at them, as if she like to make sure they are still there.

My daughter is fierce like me. But she and John think it is better to explain to Sophie that clothes are a good idea. This is not so hard in the cold weather. In the warm weather, it is very hard.

Use your words, my daughter say. That's what we tell Sophie. How about if you set a good example.

As if good example mean anything to Sophie. I am so fierce, the gang members who used to come to the restaurant all afraid of me, but Sophie is not afraid.

I say, Sophie, if you take off your clothes, no snack.

70 I say, Sophie, if you take off your clothes, no lunch.

I say, Sophie, if you take off your clothes, no park.

Pretty soon we are stay home all day, and by the end of six hours she still did not have one thing to eat. You never saw a child stubborn like that.

I'm hungry! she cry when my daughter come home.

What's the matter, doesn't your grandmother feed you? My daughter laugh.

No! Sophie say. She doesn't feed me anything! 75

My daughter laugh again. Here you go, she say.

She say to John, Sophie must be growing.

Growing like a weed, I say.

Still Sophie take off her clothes until one day I spank her. Not too hard, but she cry and cry, and when I tell her if she doesn't put her clothes back on I'll spank her again, she put her clothes back on. Then I tell her she is good girl, and give her some food to eat. The next day we go to the park and, like a nice Chinese girl, she does not take off her clothes.

She stop taking off her clothes, I report. Finally! 80

How did you do it? my daughter ask.

After twenty-eight years experience with you, I guess I learn something, I say.

It must have been a phase, John say, and his voice is suddenly like an expert.

His voice is like an expert about everything these days, now that he carry a leather briefcase, and wear shiny shoes, and can go shopping for a new car. On the company, he say. The company will pay for it, but he will be able to drive it whenever he want.

A free car, he say. How do you like that. 85

It's good to see you in the saddle again, my daughter say. Some of your family patterns are scary.

At least I don't drink, he say. He say, And I'm not the only one with scary family patterns.

That's for sure, say my daughter.

Everyone is happy. Even I am happy, because there is more trouble with Sophie, but now I think I can help her Chinese side fight against her wild side. I teach her to eat food with fork or spoon or chopsticks, she cannot just grab into the middle of a bowl of noodles. I teach her not to play with garbage cans. Sometimes I spank her, but not too often, and not too hard.

Still, there are problems. Sophie like to climb everything. If there is a rail- 90 ing, she is never next to it. Always she is on top of it. Also, Sophie like to hit the mommies of her friends. She learn this from her playground best friend, Sinbad, who is four. Sinbad wear army clothes every day and like to ambush his mommy. He is the one who dug a big hole under the play structure, a foxhole he call it, all by himself. Very hardworking. Now he wait in the foxhole with a shovel full of wet sand. When his mommy come, he throw it right at her.

Oh, it's all right, his mommy say. You can't get rid of war games, it's part of their imaginative play. All the boys go through it.

Also, he like to kick his mommy, and one day he tell Sophie to kick his mommy too.

I wish this story is not true.

Kick her, kick her! Sinbad say.

95   Sophie kick her. A little kick, as if she just so happened was swinging her little leg and didn't realize that big mommy leg was in the way. Still I spank Sophie and make Sophie say sorry, and what does the mommy say?

Really, it's all right, she say. It didn't hurt.

After that, Sophie learn she can attack mommies in the playground, and some will say, Stop, but others will say, Oh, she didn't mean it, especially if they realize Sophie will be punished.

This is how, one day, bigger trouble come. The bigger trouble start when Sophie hide in the foxhole with that shovel full of sand. She wait, and when I come look for her, she throw it at me. All over my nice clean clothes.

Did you ever see a Chinese girl act this way?

100   Sophie! I say. Come out of there, say you're sorry.

But she does not come out. Instead, she laugh. Naaah, naah-na, naaa-naaa, she say.

I am not exaggerate: millions of children in China, not one act like this.

Sophie! I say. Now! Come out now!

But she know she is in big trouble. She know if she come out, what will happen next. So she does not come out. I am sixty-eight, Chinese age almost seventy, how can I crawl under there to catch her? Impossible. So I yell, yell, yell, and what happen? Nothing. A Chinese mother would help, but American mothers, they look at you, they shake their head, they go home. And, of course, a Chinese child would give up, but not Sophie.

105   I hate you! she yell. I hate you, Meanie!

Meanie is my new name these days.

Long time this goes on, long long time. The foxhole is deep, you cannot see too much, you don't know where is the bottom. You cannot hear too much either. If she does not yell, you cannot even know she is still there or not. After a while, getting cold out, getting dark out. No one left in the playground, only us.

Sophie, I say. How did you become stubborn like this? I am go home without you now.

I try to use a stick, chase her out of there, and once or twice I hit her, but still she does not come out. So finally I leave. I go outside the gate.

110   Bye-bye! I say. I'm go home now.

But still she does not come out and does not come out. Now it is dinnertime, the sky is black. I think I should maybe go get help, but how can I leave a little girl by herself in the playground? A bad man could come. A rat could come. I go back in to see what is happen to Sophie. What if she have a shovel and is making a tunnel to escape?

Sophie! I say.

No answer.

Sophie!

115   I don't know if she is alive. I don't know if she is fall asleep down there. If she is crying, I cannot hear her.

So I take the stick and poke.

Sophie! I say. I promise I no hit you. If you come out, I give you a lollipop.

No answer. By now I worried. What to do, what to do, what to do? I poke some more, even harder, so that I am poking and poking when my daughter and John suddenly appear.

What are you doing? What is going on? say my daughter.

Put down that stick! say my daughter. *120*

You are crazy! say my daughter.

John wiggle under the structure, into the foxhole, to rescue Sophie.

She fell asleep, say John the expert. She's okay. That is one big hole.

Now Sophie is crying and crying.

Sophia, my daughter say, hugging her. Are you okay, peanut? Are you okay? *125*

She's just scared, say John.

Are you okay? I say too. I don't know what happen, I say.

She's okay, say John. He is not like my daughter, full of questions. He is full of answers until we get home and can see by the lamplight.

Will you look at her? he yell then. What the hell happened?

Bruises all over her brown skin, and a swollen-up eye. *130*

You are crazy! say my daughter. Look at what you did! You are crazy!

I try very hard, I say.

How could you use a stick? I told you to use your words!

She is hard to handle, I say.

She's three years old! You cannot use a stick! say my daughter. *135*

She is not like any Chinese girl I ever saw, I say.

I brush some sand off my clothes. Sophie's clothes are dirty too, but at least she has her clothes on.

Has she done this before? ask my daughter. Has she hit you before?

She hits me all the time, Sophie say, eating ice cream.

Your family, say John. *140*

Believe me, say my daughter.

A daughter I have, a beautiful daughter. I took care of her when she could not hold her head up. I took care of her before she could argue with me, when she was a little girl with two pigtails, one of them always crooked. I took care of her when we have to escape from China, I take care of her when suddenly we live in a country with cars everywhere, if you are not careful your little girl get run over. When my husband die, I promise him I will keep the family together, even though it was just two of us, hardly a family at all.

But now my daughter take me around to look at apartments. After all, I can cook, I can clean, there's no reason I cannot live by myself, all I need is a telephone. Of course, she is sorry. Sometimes she cry, I am the one to say everything will be okay. She say she have no choice, she doesn't want to end up divorced. I say divorce is terrible, I don't know who invented this terrible idea. Instead of live with a telephone, though, surprise, I come to live with

Bess. Imagine that. Bess make an offer and, sure enough, where she come from, people mean for you to move in when they say things like that. A crazy idea, go to live with someone else's family, but she like to have some female company, not like my daughter, who does not believe in company. These days when my daughter visit, she does not bring Sophie. Bess say we should give Nattie time, we will see Sophie again soon. But seems like my daughter have more presentation than ever before, every time she come she have to leave.

I have a family to support, she say, and her voice is heavy, as if soaking wet. I have a young daughter and a depressed husband and no one to turn to.

145   When she say no one to turn to, she mean me.

These days my beautiful daughter is so tired she can just sit there in a chair and fall asleep. John lost his job again, already, but still they rather hire a baby-sitter than ask me to help, even they can't afford it. Of course, the new baby-sitter is much younger, can run around. I don't know if Sophie these days is wild or not wild. She call me Meanie, but she like to kiss me too, sometimes. I remember that every time I see a child on TV. Sophie like to grab my hair, a fistful in each hand, and then kiss me smack on the nose. I never see any other child kiss that way.

The satellite TV has so many channels, more channels than I can count, including a Chinese channel from the Mainland and a Chinese channel from Taiwan, but most of the time I watch bloopers with Bess. Also, I watch the bird feeder—so many, many kinds of birds come. The Shea sons hang around all the time, asking when will I go home, but Bess tell them, Get lost.

She's a permanent resident, say Bess. She isn't going anywhere.

Then she wink at me, and switch the channel with the remote control.

150   Of course, I shouldn't say Irish this, Irish that, especially now I am become honorary Irish myself, according to Bess. Me! Who's Irish? I say, and she laugh. All the same, if I could mention one thing about some of the Irish, not all of them of course, I like to mention this: Their talk just stick. I don't know how Bess Shea learn to use her words, but sometimes I hear what she say a long time later. *Permanent resident. Not going anywhere.* Over and over I hear it, the voice of Bess.   *1998*

CONSIDERATIONS

1. Using specific traits, describe the narrator as a mother, a woman, a grandmother, a person. Which traits overlap all of these roles? Which ones are exclusive to a specific role? What conclusions can you draw about her as a "whole" character?

2. Out of the four people in the narrator's family—herself, Natalie, John, and Sophie—which one lives with the most stress and conflict? Explore the reasons for this conflict.

3. Explore the differences between the narrator and Bess, and explain the deeper connections between them.

4. What are the primary influences on Sophie' personality: nature or nurture? To what extent do you think the grandmother's spanking really affects Sophie?

5. Who is in charge in John, Natalie, and Sophie's family? What are the major differences in parenting philosophies between Natalie and her mother? Who do you think exhibits the most wisdom as far as parenting goes? Explain.

6. What does the last paragraph say about Bess? About the narrator? In what way does this ending define what a family really is?

Poetry

THEODORE ROETHKE (1903–1963)
My Papa's Waltz

Born in Saginaw, Michigan, Theodore Roethke was the son of a greenhouse owner. After completing graduate study at Harvard, Roethke taught at several universities and was known as both a great teacher and a great poet. His collection The Waking: Poems 1933–1953 *won the Pulitzer Prize in 1954.*

The whiskey on your breath
Could make a small boy dizzy;
But I hung on like death
Such waltzing was not easy.

We romped until the pans   5
Slid from the kitchen shelf;
My mother's countenance
Could not unfrown itself.

The hand that held my wrist
Was battered on one knuckle;   10
At every step you missed
My right ear scraped a buckle.

You beat time on my head
With a palm caked hard by dirt,
Then waltzed me off to bed   15
Still clinging to your shirt.   *1942*

CONSIDERATIONS

1. List the images describing the father and his bedtime dance with his son. Do these words suggest the experience was positive? Negative? A mix? Explain.
2. Why is the mother frowning? Speculate on her reasons for refusing to join in the kitchen romp.
3. Rewrite this poem as a prose description of the same scene. Evaluate the changes that you make, and comment on the way these changes alter the view of the experience described in the poem.

 GWENDOLYN BROOKS (1917–2000)

The Mother

    For biographical information about Gwendolyn Brooks, see page 236.

Abortions will not let you forget.
You remember the children you got that you did not get,
The damp small pulps with a little or with no hair,
The singers and workers that never handled the air.
5 You will never neglect or beat
Them, or silence or buy with a sweet.
You will never wind up the sucking-thumb
Or scuttle off ghosts that come.
You will never leave them, controlling your luscious sigh,
10 Return for a snack of them, with gobbling mother-eye.

I have heard in the voices of the wind the voices of my dim killed children.
I have contracted. I have eased
My dim dears at the breasts they could never suck.
I have said, Sweets, if I sinned, if I seized
15 Your luck
And your lives from your unfinished reach,
If I stole your births and your names,
Your straight baby tears and your games,
Your stilted or lovely loves, your tumults, your marriages, aches, and your
     deaths,
20 If I poisoned the beginnings of your breaths,
Believe that even in my deliberateness I was not deliberate.
Though why should I whine,
Whine that the crime was other than mine?—
Since anyhow you are dead.

Or rather, or instead,   *25*
You were never made.
But that too, I am afraid,
Is faulty: oh, what shall I say, how is the truth to be said?
You were born, you had body, you died.
It is just that you never giggled or planned or cried.   *30*

Believe me, I loved you all.
Believe me, I knew you, though faintly, and I loved,
       I loved you all.   *1945*

CONSIDERATIONS

1. What images convey the conflicting emotions of the speaker? How do
   those images suggest the theme of this poem?
2. To whom does the speaker address her thoughts? How might this choice
   suggest the tone of the poet toward the speaker and toward the subject of
   the poem?

More Resources on
Gwendolyn Brooks

  In *ARIEL*
   • Brief biography of Brooks
   • Complete text of three Brooks poems, all with hyperlinked
     comments
   • Video discussion of Brooks's writing
   • Analysis of imagery in Brooks's poetry
   • Bibliography of scholarly works on Brooks

  In the Online Learning Center for *Responding to Literature*
   • Brief biography of Brooks
   • List of major works by Brooks
   • Web links to more resources on Brooks
   • Additional questions for experiencing and interpreting Brooks's
     writing

SHARON OLDS (1942–   )

The Possessive

> *Born in San Francisco, Sharon Olds did her undergraduate work at Stanford*
> *University and then earned her doctorate at Columbia University. Currently, she*
> *is on the faculty of the Graduate Creative Writing Program at New York Univer-*
> *sity. She published her first book of poetry,* Satan Says, *in 1980. In 1983 her*
> *second book of poetry,* The Dead and the Living, *won the National Book*
> *Critics Circle Award. In 1984 she founded a poetry workshop at New York's*
> *Goldwater Hospital, a hospital for the severely disabled. Other collections include*
> The Gold Cell *(1987),* The Father *(1992), and* The Wellspring *(1996).*
> *Like "The Possessive," many of Olds's poems are uncomfortable observations*
> *sparked by simple events of family life, often relating to her own son and daughter.*

My daughter—as if I
owned her—that girl with the
hair wispy as a frayed bellpull

has been to the barber, that knife grinder,
5   and had the edge of her hair sharpened.

Each strand now cuts
both ways. The blade of new bangs
hangs over her red-brown eyes
like carbon steel.

10   All the little
spliced ropes are sliced. the curtain of
dark paper-cuts veils the face that
started from next to nothing in my body—

My body. My daughter. I'll have to find
15   another word. In her bright helmet
she looks at me as if across a
great distance. Distant fires can be
glimpsed in the resin light of her eyes:
the watch fires of an enemy, a while before
20   the war starts.   *1980*

CONSIDERATIONS

1. Explain the significance and meaning of the title of the poem, "The Possessive."
2. What has happened between the mother and daughter? What is the effect
   on their relationship because of it?

3. Why does the mother say she will "have to find another word"—what word?
4. Identify the images of war used throughout the poem. Why would the mother refer to her daughter as "an enemy"? How would it be different if the daughter were "the" enemy?

SYLVIA PLATH (1932–1963)

Metaphors

> *Born in Boston, Sylvia Plath graduated summa cum laude from Smith College in 1955. She then became a Fulbright scholar and studied in England, where she met and married poet Ted Hughes in 1956. An extremely prolific poet, Plath also wrote* The Bell Jar, *an autobiographical novel that describes her battle with depression. This novel was published in 1963, the year Plath committed suicide.*

I'm a riddle in nine syllables,
An elephant, a ponderous house,
A melon strolling on two tendrils.
O red fruit, ivory, fine timbers!
This loaf's big with its yeasty rising.   5
Money's new-minted in this fat purse.
I'm a means, a stage, a cow in calf.
I've eaten a bag of green apples,
Boarded the train there's no getting off.   *1960*

More Resources on
Sylvia Plath

In *ARIEL*
- Brief biography of Plath
- Texts of additional poems by Plath such as "Lady Lazarus" and "Mirror"
- Video of a reading of "Mirror"
- Analysis of allusions in "Lady Lazarus"
- Bibliography of scholarly works on Plath

CONSIDERATIONS

1. List possible associations with the word "nine" in the first line. How might any of these associations relate to solving the riddle?
2. What do you make of the image "red fruit, ivory, fine timbers"? Once you have solved the riddle, how does this image fit with your solution?
3. What does the final line in the poem suggest about the speaker's response to the situation described in the poem?

DONALD HALL (1928–   )

My son, my executioner

> *Donald Hall was born and grew up in New Haven, Connecticut. He now lives in New Hampshire on a farm that was once owned by his grandparents. Hall is widely respected as a teacher, poet, and essayist, and his book* The One Day: A Poem in Three Parts *(1988) won the National Book Critics Circle Award.*

My son, my executioner,
   I take you in my arms,
Quiet and small and just astir,
   And whom my body warms.

5   Sweet death, small son, our instrument
    Of immortality,
Your cries and hungers document
   Our bodily decay.

We twenty-five and twenty-two,
10   Who seemed to live forever,
Observe enduring life in you
   And start to die together.   *1955*

CONSIDERATIONS

1. What was your initial response to the poem's title? Did your response change after you had read the poem? Explain.
2. Do you see birth and death as complete opposites or as somehow intimately connected? Explain.

NEAL BOWERS (1948–   )

Driving Lessons

*Neal Bowers was born in Tennessee. He received a doctorate in English at the University of Florida and started teaching at Iowa State University in 1977. He has published two books of poetry (*The Golf Ball Diver, *1983, and* Night Vision, *1992) as well as books about the poets James Dickey and Theodore Roethke. In 1997 he published* Words for the Taking: The Hunt for a Plagiarist. *This book began in 1992, when Bowers learned that someone had plagiarized one of his poems and published it under another name in a poetry magazine. Bowers discovered that the same person had plagiarized other poems by him and by other poets as well.* Words for the Taking *is about his search for the plagiarist and about the worth of poetry.*

I learned to drive in a parking lot
on Sundays, when the stores were closed—
slow maneuvers out beyond the light-poles,
no destination, just the ritual of clutch and gas,
my father clenching with the grinding gears,   5
finally giving up and leaving my mother
to buck and plunge with me and say,
repeatedly, "Once more. Try just once more."

She walked out on him once
when I was six or seven, my father   10
driving beside her, slow as a beginner,
pleading, my baby brother and I
crying out the windows, "Mama, don't go!"
It was a scene to break your heart
or make you laugh—those wailing kids,   15
a woman walking briskly with a suitcase,
the slow car following like a faithful dog.

I don't know why she finally got in
and let us take her back
to whatever she had made up her mind to leave;   20
but the old world swallowed her up
as soon as she opened that door,
and the other life she might have lived
lay down forever in its dark infancy.

Sometimes, when I'm home, driving   25
through the old neighborhoods, stopping
in front of each little house we rented,

my stillborn other life gets in,
the boy I would have been if
30   my mother had kept on walking.

He wants to be just like her,
far away and gone forever, wants
me to press down on the gas;
but however fast I squeal away,
35   the shaggy past keeps loping behind,
sniffing every turn.

When I stop in the weedy parking lot,
the failed stores of the old mall
make a dark wall straight ahead;
40   and I'm alone again, until my parents get in,
unchanged after all these years,
my father, impatient, my mother
trying hard to smile, waiting for me
to steer my way across this emptiness.   *1992*

CONSIDERATIONS

1. Identify the lessons that the speaker learned from the parents. Which parent taught him the most? The least? Explain.
2. Explain the metaphoric use of the cars, driving, and parking lots in the poem. Why are these images effective?
3. Why does the speaker claim that the time his mother "walked out on" his father "was a scene to break your heart / or make you laugh"?
4. What is revealed about being a "teacher" when you compare the father's and mother's teaching the son to drive?

ROBERT HAYDEN (1913–1980)

Those Winter Sundays

Robert Hayden grew up in a poor neighborhood in Detroit, where he was shuttled between the home of his parents and that of a foster family next door. In 1932 he graduated from high school and, with the help of a scholarship, attended Detroit City College (which became Wayne State University). In 1936, he joined the Federal Writers Project, researching black folklore and the history of the Underground Railroad in Michigan. Hayden published his first book of poems, Heart-Shape in the Dust, *in 1940. He enrolled in a graduate English literature program at the University of Michigan, where he studied with W. H. Auden, who became an influential guide in the development of his writing. In 1946, he published his two most famous poems about African-American history, "Middle Passage" and "Frederick Douglass." His poetry gained international recognition in 1966 when he was awarded a grand prize for poetry at the First World Festival of Negro Arts in Dakar, Senegal, for his book* Ballad of Remembrance. *In 1976, he became the first African American to be appointed Consultant in Poetry to the Library of Congress. His last book was* American Journal *(1980).*

Sundays too my father got up early
and put his clothes on in the blueblack cold,
then with cracked hands that ached
from labor in the weekday weather made
banked fires blaze. No one ever thanked him.   5

I'd wake and hear the cold splintering, breaking.
When the rooms were warm, he'd call,
and slowly I would rise and dress,
fearing the chronic angers of that house,

Speaking indifferently to him,   10
who had driven out the cold
and polished my good shoes as well.
What did I know, what did I know
of love's austere and lonely offices?°   1966

CONSIDERATIONS

1. Isolate one powerful phrase or image from each stanza. Based on your three selections, what conclusions can you draw about the father and how his presence affected the speaker as a young boy?
2. At what point in his life is the speaker reflecting on his childhood? Explain.
3. The word "cold" appears in each stanza. Explore the many different connotations of this word and how they relate to the theme of family.

---

14 *offices:* Tasks, works; here, with the implication of "offerings."

Commentary

DAVID HUDDLE
The "Banked Fire" of Robert Hayden's "Those Winter Sundays"

For twenty years I've been teaching Robert Hayden's most frequently anthologized poem to undergraduate poetry-writing students. By "teach," I mean that from our textbook I read the poem aloud in the classroom, I ask one of the students to read it aloud, I make some observations about it, I invite the students to make some observations about it, then we talk about it a while longer. Usually to wrap up the discussion, I'll read the poem through once more. Occasions for such teaching come up about half a dozen times a year, and so let's say that during my life I've been privileged to read this poem aloud approximately 240 times. "Those Winter Sundays" has withstood my assault upon it. It remains a poem I look forward to reading and discussing in my classroom. The poem remains alive to me, so that for hours and sometimes days after it visits my classroom, I'm hearing its lines in my mind's ear.

Though a fourteen-liner, "Those Winter Sundays" is only loosely a sonnet. Its stanzas are five, four, and five lines long. There are rhymes and near-rhymes, but no rhyme scheme. The poem's lines probably average about eight syllables. There are only three strictly iambic lines: the fourth, the eighth, and (significantly) the fourteenth. It's a poem that's powerfully informed by the sonnet form; it's a poem that "feels like" a sonnet—it has the density and gravity of a sonnet—which is to say that in its appearance on the page, in its diction and syntax, in its tone, cadence, and argumentative strategy, "Those Winter Sundays" presents the credentials of a work of literary art in the tradition of English letters. But it's also a poem that has gone its own way, a definite departure from that most conventional of all the poetic forms of English and American verse.

The abstract issue of this poem's sonnethood is of less value to my beginning poets than the tangible matter of the sounds the poem makes, especially those *k*-sounding words of the first eleven lines that one comes to associate with discomfort: "clothes . . . blueblack cold . . . cracked . . . ached . . . weekday . . . banked . . . thanked . . . wake . . . cold . . . breaking . . . call . . . chronic . . . cold." What's missing from the final three lines? The *k* sounds have been driven from the poem, as the father has "driven out the cold" from the house. The sounds that have replaced those *k* sounds are the *o* sounds of "good . . . shoes . . . know . . . know . . . love . . . lonely offices." The poem lets us associate the *o* sounds with love and loneliness. Sonically the poem tells the same story the poem narrates for us. The noise of this poem moves us through its emotional journey from discomfort to lonely love. If ever there was a poem that could teach a beginning poet the viability of the element of sound-crafting, it is "Those Winter Sundays."

Quote its first two words, and a great many poets and English teachers will be able to finish the first line (if not the whole poem) from memory. Somewhat remarkably, the poem's thesis—that the office of love can be relentless, thankless, and more than a little mysterious—resides in that initially odd-sounding two-word beginning, "Sundays too." The rest of the line—the rest of the independent clause—is ordinary. Nowhere else in Anglo-American literature does the word *too* carry the weight it carries in "Those Winter Sundays."

Not as immediately apparent as its opening words but very nearly as im-   5
portant to the poem's overall strategy is the two-sentence engineering of the first stanza. Because they will appreciate it more if they discover it for themselves, I often maneuver Socratically to have my students describe the poem's first two sentences: long and complex, followed by short and simple. It almost always seems to me worthwhile to ask, "Why didn't Hayden begin his poem this way: 'No one ever thanked my father for getting up early on Sundays, too'? Wouldn't that be a more direct and hospitable way to bring the reader into the poem?" After I've taken my students that far, they are quick to see how that ordinary five-word unit, "No one ever thanked him," gains meaning and emotion, weight, and force, from the elaborate preparation given it by the thirty-two-word "Sundays too" first sentence.

So much depends on "No one ever thanked him" that it requires the narrative enhancement of the first four and a half lines. It is the crux of the poem. What is this poem about? It is about a son's remorse over never thanking his father not only for what he did for him but also for how (he now realizes) he felt about him. And what is the poem if not an elegantly fashioned, permanent expression of gratitude?

"Those Winter Sundays" tells a story, or it describes a circumstance, of father-son conflict, and it even makes some excuses for the son's "speaking indifferently" to the father: there was a good deal of anger between them; "chronic angers of that house" suggests that the circumstances were complicated somewhat beyond the usual and ordinary conflict between fathers and sons. Of the father, we know that he labored outdoors with his hands. Of the son, we know that he was, in the classic manner of youth, heedless of the ways in which his father served him.

Though the evidence of his "labor" is visible in every stanza of this poem, the father himself is somewhere else. We don't see him. He is in some other room of the house than the one where our speaker is. That absence suggests the emotional distance between the father and the son as well as the current absence, through death, of the father on the occasion of this utterance. It's easy enough to imagine this poem as a graveside meditation, an elegy, and a rather impassioned one at that, "What did I know, what did I know?"

The grinding of past against present gives the poem its urgency. The story is being told with such clarity, thoughtfulness, and apparent calm that we are surprised by the outburst of the repeated question of the thirteenth line.

The fourteenth line returns to a tone of tranquillity. Its diction is formal, even arch, and its phrasing suggests an extremely considered conclusion; the fourteenth line is the answer to a drastic rephrasing of the original question: *What is the precise name of what as a youth I was incapable of perceiving but that as a life-examining adult, I now suddenly understand?*

10   I tell my students that they may someday need this poem, they may someday be walking along downtown and find themselves asking aloud, "What did I know, what did I know?" But what I mean to suggest to them is that Hayden has made them the gift of this final phrase like a package that in ten years' time they may open and find immensely valuable: "love's austere and lonely offices." Like "the banked fires" his father made, Hayden has made a poem that will be of value to readers often years after they've first read it.   *1996*

URSULA K. LEGUIN (1929–   )

The Old Falling Down

> *Born in Berkeley, California, Ursula LeGuin spent her early years in an academic family. Both her parents were accomplished anthropologists. She was educated at Radcliffe College and Columbia University and is best known for her highly acclaimed works of science fiction, particularly the Earthsea tetralogy, published in the 1960s.*

In the old falling-down
house of my childhood
I go down-
stairs to sleep out-
5   side on the porch
under stars and dream
of trying to go up-
stairs but there are no
stairs so I climb
10   hand over hand clambering
scared and when I get there
to my high room, find
no bed, no chair, bare floor.   *1988*

CONSIDERATIONS

1. Think about what is implied in the word "old" in both the title and the first line of this poem. Read it out loud with the stress on the word "old,"

and the implications will become more apparent. What does this one word
have to do with the narrator's family experience?
2. What do the levels in the house reflect about the family relationships? What
feeling are you left with after reading (and rereading) this poem? Explain.

LOUISE GLÜCK (1943–   )

Terminal Resemblance

*Born in New York City, Louise Glück attended Sarah Lawrence College and
Columbia University. She has taught at many colleges and universities. She has
been the recipient of both Rockefeller and Guggenheim fellowships and has won
the Pulitzer Prize for poetry. In 2003, she was named poet laureate of the United
States. Isolation, alienation, and rejected love are common themes in her work.*

When I saw my father for the last time, we both did the same thing.
He was standing in the doorway to the living room,
waiting for me to get off the telephone.
That he wasn't also pointing to his watch
was a signal he wanted to talk.   5

Talk for us always meant the same thing.
He'd say a few words. I'd say a few back.
That was about it.

It was the end of August, very hot, very humid.
Next door, workmen dumped new gravel on the driveway.   10

My father and I avoided being alone;
we didn't know how to connect, to make small talk—
there didn't seem to be
any other possibilities.
So this was special: when a man's dying,   15
he has a subject.

It must have been early morning. Up and down the street
sprinklers started coming on. The gardener's truck
appeared at the end of the block,
then stopped, parking.   20
My father wanted to tell me what it was like to be dying.
He told me he wasn't suffering.
He said he kept expecting pain, waiting for it, but it never came.
All he felt was a kind of weakness.
I said I was glad for him, that I thought he was lucky.   25

Some of the husbands were getting in their cars, going to work.
Not people we knew anymore. New families,
families with young children.
The wives stood on the steps, gesturing or calling.

30 We said goodbye in the usual way,
no embrace, nothing dramatic.
When the taxi came, my parents watched from the front door,
arm in arm, my mother blowing kisses as she always does,
because it frightens her when a hand isn't being used.
35 But for a change, my father didn't just stand there.
This time, he waved.

That's what I did, at the door to the taxi.
Like him, waved to disguise my hand's trembling.   *1990*

CONSIDERATIONS

1. Discuss the significance of the title in terms of each stanza. What patterns/habits have been passed down from father to daughter?
2. What is your response when the speaker says to her dying father that she thought he was lucky? What else could she have said here? What is her father's response? What does this interaction reveal about their relationship?
3. Is the speaker revealing a truth about how men and women communicate differently, or is this situation unique to her and her father? Upon what evidence in the poem do you base your answer?

GAIL MAZUR
Family Plot, October

Gail Mazur is the author of four books of poetry and her poems have been published in such anthologies as Best American Poetry of the 1990s, The Pushcart Anthology, *and* The Ploughshares Poetry Reader. *She was the founder and first director of the Blacksmith House Poetry Center in Cambridge, Massachusetts, and has taught at many colleges and universities, including Harvard, the University of Massachusetts, and Wellesley.*

I'm digging at my father's grave,
my mother holding the rusty mums
she's carried here to make a little garden

before the first frost. Three years today,
and the grass is a damp brown rectangle   5
over his cryptic body that's guarded

by earth from my more morbid speculations.
Perpetual care's contracted out here,
so no one's responsible for the dried-out

tap, the graveyard's shameless posture   10
of neglect, certainly not this pair
of purposeful mourners with trowels

and sturdy annuals we've chosen
for their profusions of unopened buds.
I'm not good at this, thudding my shovel   15

at stones, setting pots in the ground
off-center. Alone, I'd plant a little dogwood,
a Japanese drift of flowing branch

above his name, but my mother sees this
as her future home and wants, as usual,   20
something else, whatever's harder to nurture.

I'll never lie here. I don't want anyone
to stand, icy-handed, imagining
my ruined body. My father liked so much

to laugh—would he enjoy his clumsy girl,   25
hacking away at clumps of sod, or his wife's
sensible blue shoes sinking in mud?

It doesn't matter. I can't even say
if he or I believed in God,
or in any kind of hereafter. . . .   30

A drizzle mists the raw new hole,
mists the one white rose from my table,
and the pebble I place on his headstone

like a good Orthodox daughter
leaving a memorial relic   35
as if it were a talisman of devotion

that nothing—no eternities of neglect
by myself or others, no drought or blight
or storm or holocaust—could erode.   *1995*

CONSIDERATIONS

1. What emotions are apparent within the speaker? What one overwhelming emotion would you say permeates this piece? Explain.
2. From the evidence given in the poem, how close were the speaker and her father? How close are the speaker and her mother?
3. Explore the contrasting images between the graveyard scene and how the speaker would have decorated this plot had it been up to her. What does her contribution in the third-to-last stanza reveal about her?

Drama

SOPHOCLES (c. 496?–406 B.C.)
Oedipus Rex

TRANSLATED BY DUDLEY FITTS AND ROBERT FITZGERALD

Born at Colonus, a village near Athens, Sophocles grew to be a handsome young man who was often chosen to lead the chorus at major festivals because of his handsome appearance and graceful dramatic performance. (See page 72 for more on these festivals.) In the traditional Athenian spring drama competition in 468 B.C., Sophocles, not yet thirty, submitted a tragedy that triumphed over the play submitted by Aeschylus, an older playwright favored to win. Sophocles' victory was attributed in part to his willingness to take risks and to break old conventions; until the 468 B.C. competition, tragedies were written so that no more than two actors appeared on stage at the same time. Sophocles, however, added a third. During his lifetime, Sophocles—who lived for nearly a century—saw the Greeks rise to power over the Persian Empire. Toward the end of his life, however, Athenian power declined. Sophocles, unlike his native country, maintained his power until the end of his life. He wrote more than 120 plays, including seven that remain today, Ajax, Antigone, Oedipus Rex, Electra, Philoctetes, The Trachinian Women, *and his final play,* Oedipus at Colonus, *which was written when he was nearly ninety.*

Characters

OEDIPUS, *King of Thebes, supposed son of Polybos and Merope, King and Queen of Corinth*
IOKASTE, *wife of Oedipus and widow of the late King Laios*
KREON, *brother of Iokaste, a prince of Thebes*
TEIRESIAS, *a blind seer who serves Apollo*

PRIEST
MESSENGER, *from Corinth*
SHEPHERD, *former servant of Laios*
SECOND MESSENGER, *from the palace*
CHORUS OF THEBAN ELDERS
CHORAGOS, *leader of the Chorus*
ANTIGONE *and* ISMENE, *young daughters of Oedipus and Iokaste. They appear in the Exodos but do not speak.*
SUPPLIANTS, GUARDS, SERVANTS

Scene *Before the palace of Oedipus, King of Thebes. A central door and two lateral doors open onto a platform which runs the length of the facade. On the platform, right and left, are altars; and three steps lead down into the orchestra, or chorus-ground. At the beginning of the action these steps are crowded by suppliants who have brought branches and chaplets of olive leaves and who sit in various attitudes of despair. Oedipus enters.*

PROLOGUE

OEDIPUS: My children, generations of the living
    In the line of Kadmos,° nursed at his ancient hearth:
    Why have you strewn yourselves before these altars
    In supplication, with your boughs and garlands?
    The breath of incense rises from the city   5
    With a sound of prayer and lamentation.
                                Children,
    I would not have you speak through messengers,
    And therefore I have come myself to hear you—
    I, Oedipus, who bear the famous name.
    (To a PRIEST.*)* You, there, since you are eldest in the company,   10
    Speak for them all, tell me what preys upon you,
    Whether you come in dread, or crave some blessing:
    Tell me, and never doubt that I will help you
    In every way I can; I should be heartless
    Were I not moved to find you suppliant here.   15
PRIEST: Great Oedipus, O powerful king of Thebes!
    You see how all the ages of our people
    Cling to your altar steps: here are boys
    Who can barely stand alone, and here are priests
    By weight of age, as I am a priest of God,   20
    And young men chosen from those yet unmarried;
    As for the others, all that multitude,

2 *Kadmos:* Founder of Thebes, according to legend.

They wait with olive chaplets in the squares,
At the two shrines of Pallas,° and where Apollo°
Speaks in the glowing embers.

25   Your own eyes
Must tell you: Thebes is tossed on a murdering sea
And can not lift her head from the death surge.
A rust consumes the buds and fruits of the earth;
The herds are sick; children die unborn,

30 And labor is vain. The god of plague and pyre
Raids like detestable lightning through the city,
And all the house of Kadmos is laid waste,
All emptied, and all darkened: Death alone
Battens upon the misery of Thebes.

35 You are not one of the immortal gods, we know;
Yet we have come to you to make our prayer
As to the man surest in mortal ways
And wisest in the ways of God. You saved us
From the Sphinx,° that flinty singer, and the tribute

40 We paid to her so long; yet you were never
Better informed than we, nor could we teach you:
A god's touch, it seems, enabled you to help us.

Therefore, O mighty power, we turn to you:
Find us our safety, find us a remedy,

45 Whether by counsel of the gods or of men.
A king of wisdom tested in the past
Can act in a time of troubles, and act well.
Noblest of men, restore
Life to your city! Think how all men call you

50 Liberator for your boldness long ago;
Ah, when your years of kingship are remembered,
Let them not say *We rose, but later fell*—
Keep the State from going down in the storm!
Once, years ago, with happy augury,

55 You brought us fortune; be the same again!
No man questions your power to rule the land:
But rule over men, not over a dead city!
Ships are only hulls, high walls are nothing,

---

24 *Pallas:* Pallas Athena, Zeus's daughter; goddess of wisdom; *Apollo:* Zeus's son, god of the sun, truth, and poetry. 39 *Sphinx:* A monster with the body of a lion, the wings of a bird, and the face of a woman. The Sphinx had challenged Thebes with a riddle, killing those who failed to solve it. When Oedipus answered correctly, the Sphinx killed herself.

When no life moves in the empty passageways.
OEDIPUS: Poor children! You may be sure I know   *60*
    All that you longed for in your coming here.
    I know that you are deathly sick; and yet,
    Sick as you are, not one is as sick as I.
    Each of you suffers in himself alone
    His anguish, not another's; but my spirit   *65*
    Groans for the city, for myself, for you.

    I was not sleeping, you are not waking me.
    No, I have been in tears for a long while
    And in my restless thought walked many ways.
    In all my search I found one remedy,   *70*
    And I have adopted it: I have sent Kreon,
    Son of Menoikeus, brother of the queen,
    To Delphi,° Apollo's place of revelation,
    To learn there, if he can,
    What act or pledge of mine may save the city.   *75*
    I have counted the days, and now, this very day,
    I am troubled, for he has overstayed his time.
    What is he doing? He has been gone too long.
    Yet whenever he comes back, I should do ill
    Not to take any action the god orders.   *80*
PRIEST: It is a timely promise. At this instant
    They tell me Kreon is here.
OEDIPUS: O Lord Apollo!
    May his news be fair as his face is radiant!
PRIEST: Good news, I gather! he is crowned with bay,
    The chaplet is thick with berries.
OEDIPUS: We shall soon know;   *85*
    He is near enough to hear us now. *(Enter* KREON.*)* O prince:
    Brother: son of Menoikeus:
    What answer do you bring us from the god?
KREON: A strong one. I can tell you, great afflictions
    Will turn out well, if they are taken well.   *90*
OEDIPUS: What was the oracle? These vague words
    Leave me still hanging between hope and fear.
KREON: Is it your pleasure to hear me with all these
    Gathered around us? I am prepared to speak,
    But should we not go in?

73 *Delphi:* Location of the prophetic oracle, regarded as the keeper of religious truth.

95   OEDIPUS: Speak to them all,
     It is for them I suffer, more than for myself.
   KREON: Then I will tell you what I heard at Delphi.
     In plain words
     The god commands us to expel from the land of Thebes
100   An old defilement we are sheltering.
     It is a deathly thing, beyond cure;
     We must not let it feed upon us longer.
   OEDIPUS: What defilement? How shall we rid ourselves of it?
   KREON: By exile or death, blood for blood. It was
105   Murder that brought the plague-wind on the city.
   OEDIPUS: Murder of whom? Surely the god has named him?
   KREON: My Lord: Laios once ruled this land,
     Before you came to govern us.
   OEDIPUS: I know;
     I learned of him from others; I never saw him.
110 KREON: He was murdered; and Apollo commands us now
     To take revenge upon whoever killed him.
   OEDIPUS: Upon whom? Where are they? Where shall we find a clue
     To solve that crime, after so many years?
   KREON: Here in this land, he said. Search reveals
115   Things that escape an inattentive man.
   OEDIPUS: Tell me: Was Laios murdered in his house,
     Or in the fields, or in some foreign country?
   KREON: He said he planned to make a pilgrimage.
     He did not come home again.
   OEDIPUS: And was there no one,
120   No witness, no companion, to tell what happened?
   KREON: They were all killed but one, and he got away
     So frightened that he could remember one thing only.
   OEDIPUS: What was that one thing? One may be the key
     To everything, if we resolve to use it.
125 KREON: He said that a band of highwaymen attacked them,
     Outnumbered them, and overwhelmed the king.
   OEDIPUS: Strange, that a highwayman should be so daring—
     Unless some faction here bribed him to do it.
   KREON: We thought of that. But after Laios' death
130   New troubles arose and we had no avenger.
   OEDIPUS: What troubles could prevent your hunting down the killers?
   KREON: The riddling Sphinx's song
     Made us deaf to all mysteries but her own.
   OEDIPUS: Then once more I must bring what is dark to light.
135   It is most fitting that Apollo shows,
     As you do, this compunction for the dead.

You shall see how I stand by you, as I should,
Avenging this country and the god as well,
And not as though it were for some distant friend,
But for my own sake, to be rid of evil.   *140*
Whoever killed King Laios might—who knows?—
Lay violent hands even on me—and soon.
I act for the murdered king in my own interest.

Come, then, my children: leave the altar steps,
Lift up your olive boughs!
                      One of you go   *145*
And summon the people of Kadmos to gather here.
I will do all that I can; you may tell them that   *(Exit a* PAGE.*)*
So, with the help of God,
We shall be saved—or else indeed we are lost.
PRIEST: Let us rise, children. It was for this we came,   *150*
And now the king has promised it.
Phoibos° has sent us an oracle; may he descend
Himself to save us and drive out the plague.

    *(Exeunt° * OEDIPUS *and* KREON *into the palace by the central door. The*
    PRIEST *and the* SUPPLIANTS *disperse right and left. After a short pause*
                     the CHORUS *enters the orchestra.)*

PARODOS

Strophe 1
CHORUS: What is God singing in his profound
    Delphi of gold and shadow?
    What oracle for Thebes, the Sunwhipped city?
    Fear unjoints me, the roots of my heart tremble.
    Now I remember, O Healer, your power, and wonder: *5*
    Will you send doom like a sudden cloud, or weave it
    Like nightfall of the past?
    Speak to me, tell me, O
    Child of golden Hope, immortal Voice.

Antistrophe 1
    Let me pray to Athene, the immortal daughter of Zeus,   *10*
    And to Artemis° her sister
    Who keeps her famous throne in the market ring,

---

152 *Phoibos:* Apollo. s.d. *Exeunt:* Latin term meaning "they exit." 11 *Artemis:* Goddess of
the hunt.

And to Apollo, archer from distant heaven—
O gods, descend! Like three streams leap against
The fires of our grief, the fires of darkness;
Be swift to bring us rest!
As in the old time from the brilliant house
Of air you stepped to save us, come again!

15

Strophe 2

Now our afflictions have no end,
Now all our stricken host lies down
And no man fights off death with his mind;
The noble plowland bears no grain,
And groaning mothers can not bear—
See, how our lives like birds take wing,
Like sparks that fly when a fire soars,
To the shore of the god of evening.

20

25

Antistrophe 2

The plague burns on, it is pitiless,
Though pallid children laden with death
Lie unwept in the stony ways,
And old gray women by every path
Flock to the strand about the altars
There to strike their breasts and cry
Worship of Phoibos in wailing prayers:
Be kind, God's golden child!

30

Strophe 3

There are no swords in this attack by fire,
No shields, but we are ringed with cries.
Send the besieger plunging from our homes
Into the vast sea-room of the Atlantic
Or into the waves that foam eastward of Thrace—
For the day ravages what the night spares—
Destroy our enemy, lord of the thunder!
Let him be riven by lightning from heaven!

35

40

Antistrophe 3

Phoibos Apollo, stretch the sun's bowstring,
That golden cord, until it sing for us,
Flashing arrows in heaven!
                    Artemis, Huntress,

45

Race with flaring lights upon our mountains!
O scarlet god,° O golden-banded brow,
O Theban Bacchos in a storm of Maenads,°

(Enter OEDIPUS, *center.)*

Whirl upon Death, that all the Undying hate!
Come with blinding torches, come in joy!   *50*

SCENE 1

OEDIPUS: Is this your prayer? It may be answered. Come,
    Listen to me, act as the crisis demands,
    And you shall have relief from all these evils.

    Until now I was a stranger to this tale,
    As I had been a stranger to the crime.   *5*
    Could I track down the murderer without a clue?
    But now, friends,
    As one who became a citizen after the murder,
    I make this proclamation to all Thebans:
    If any man knows by whose hand Laios, son of Labdakos,   *10*
    Met his death, I direct that man to tell me everything,
    No matter what he fears for having so long withheld it.
    Let it stand as promised that no further trouble
    Will come to him, but he may leave the land in safety.
    Moreover: If anyone knows the murderer to be foreign,   *15*
    Let him not keep silent: he shall have his reward from me.
    However, if he does conceal it; if any man
    Fearing for his friend or for himself disobeys this edict,
    Hear what I propose to do:

    I solemnly forbid the people of this country,   *20*
    Where power and throne are mine, ever to receive that man
    Or speak to him, no matter who he is, or let him
    Join in sacrifice, lustration, or in prayer.
    I decree that he be driven from every house,
    Being, as he is, corruption itself to us: the Delphic   *25*
    Voice of Apollo has pronounced this revelation.
    Thus I associate myself with the oracle
    And take the side of the murdered king.

    As for the criminal, I pray to God—

47 *scarlet god:* Bacchos, god of wine and revelry. 48 *Maenads:* Female attendants of Bacchos.

30   Whether it be a lurking thief, or one of a number—
        I pray that that man's life be consumed in evil and wretchedness.
        And as for me, this curse applies no less
        If it should turn out that the culprit is my guest here,
        Sharing my hearth.
                              You have heard the penalty.
35   I lay it on you now to attend to this
        For my sake, for Apollo's, for the sick
        Sterile city that heaven has abandoned.
        Suppose the oracle had given you no command:
        Should this defilement go uncleansed for ever?
40   You should have found the murderer: your king,
        A noble king, had been destroyed!
                              Now I,
        Having the power that he held before me,
        Having his bed, begetting children there
        Upon his wife, as he would have, had he lived—
45   Their son would have been my children's brother,
        If Laios had had luck in fatherhood!
        (And now his bad fortune has struck him down)—
        I say I take the son's part, just as though
        I were his son, to press the fight for him
50   And see it won! I'll find the hand that brought
        Death to Labdakos' and Polydoros' child,
        Heir of Kadmos' and Agenor's line.°
        And as for those who fail me,
        May the gods deny them the fruit of the earth,
55   Fruit of the womb, and may they rot utterly!
        Let them be wretched as we are wretched, and worse!

        For you, for loyal Thebans, and for all
        Who find my actions right, I pray the favor
        Of justice, and of all the immortal gods.
60 CHORAGOS: Since I am under oath, my lord, I swear
        I did not do the murder, I can not name
        The murderer. Phoibos ordained the search;
        Why did he not say who the culprit was?
    OEDIPUS: An honest question. But no man in the world
65   Can make the gods do more than the gods will.
    CHORAGOS: There is an alternative, I think—
    OEDIPUS: Tell me.

51–52 *Labdakos, Polydoros, Kadmos,* and *Agenor:* Ancestors of Laios.

Any or all, you must not fail to tell me.
CHORAGOS: A lord clairvoyant to the lord Apollo,
      As we all know, is the skilled Teiresias.
      One might learn much about this from him, Oedipus.   70
OEDIPUS: I am not wasting time:
      Kreon spoke of this, and I have sent for him—
      Twice, in fact; it is strange that he is not here.
CHORAGOS: The other matter—that old report—seems useless.
OEDIPUS: What was that? I am interested in all reports.   75
CHORAGOS: The king was said to have been killed by highwaymen.
OEDIPUS: I know. But we have no witnesses to that.
CHORAGOS: If the killer can feel a particle of dread,
      Your curse will bring him out of hiding!
OEDIPUS: No.
      The man who dared that act will fear no curse.   80

(Enter the blind seer TEIRESIAS, *led by a* PAGE.*)*

CHORAGOS: But there is one man who may detect the criminal.
      This is Teiresias, this is the holy prophet
      In whom, alone of all men, truth was born.
OEDIPUS: Teiresias: seer: student of mysteries,
      Of all that's taught and all that no man tells,   85
      Secrets of Heaven and secrets of the earth:
      Blind though you are, you know the city lies
      Sick with plague; and from this plague, my lord,
      We find that you alone can guard or save us.

      Possibly you did not hear the messengers?   90
      Apollo, when we sent to him,
      Sent us back word that this great pestilence
      Would lift, but only if we established clearly
      The identity of those who murdered Laios.
      They must be killed or exiled.
                                       Can you use   95
      Birdflight° or any art of divination
      To purify yourself, and Thebes, and me
      From this contagion? We are in your hands.
      There is no fairer duty
      Than that of helping others in distress.   100
TEIRESIAS: How dreadful knowledge of the truth can be
      When there's no help in truth! I knew this well,

96 *Birdflight:* The flight of birds was one sign used to predict the future.

But did not act on it; else I should not have come.

OEDIPUS: What is troubling you? Why are your eyes so cold?

105　TEIRESIAS: Let me go home. Bear your own fate, and I'll
　　　　Bear mine. It is better so: trust what I say.

OEDIPUS: What you say is ungracious and unhelpful
　　　　To your native country. Do not refuse to speak.

TEIRESIAS: When it comes to speech, your own is neither temperate

110　　　　Nor opportune. I wish to be more prudent.

OEDIPUS: In God's name, we all beg you—

TEIRESIAS:　　　　　　　　　　　　　You are all ignorant.
　　　　No; I will never tell you what I know.
　　　　Now it is my misery; then, it would be yours.

OEDIPUS: What! You do know something, and will not tell us?

115　　　　You would betray us all and wreck the State?

TEIRESIAS: I do not intend to torture myself, or you.
　　　　Why persist in asking? You will not persuade me.

OEDIPUS: What a wicked old man you are! You'd try a stone's
　　　　Patience! Out with it! Have you no feeling at all?

120　TEIRESIAS: You call me unfeeling. If you could only see
　　　　The nature of your own feelings . . .

OEDIPUS:　　　　　　　　　　　　　　　Why,
　　　　Who would not feel as I do? Who could endure
　　　　Your arrogance toward the city?

TEIRESIAS:　　　　　　　　　　　　　　What does it matter?
　　　　Whether I speak or not, it is bound to come.

125　OEDIPUS: Then, if "it" is bound to come, you are bound to tell me.

TEIRESIAS: No, I will not go on. Rage as you please.

OEDIPUS: Rage? Why not!
　　　　　　　　　　　　　And I'll tell you what I think:
　　　　You planned it, you had it done, you all but
　　　　Killed him with your own hands: if you had eyes,

130　　　　I'd say the crime was yours, and yours alone.

TEIRESIAS: So? I charge you, then,
　　　　Abide by the proclamation you have made:
　　　　From this day forth
　　　　Never speak again to these men or to me;

135　　　　You yourself are the pollution of this country.

OEDIPUS: You dare say that! Can you possibly think you have
　　　　Some way of going free, after such insolence?

TEIRESIAS: I have gone free. It is the truth sustains me.

OEDIPUS: Who taught you shamelessness? It was not your craft.

140　TEIRESIAS: You did. You made me speak. I did not want to.

OEDIPUS: Speak what? Let me hear it again more clearly.

TEIRESIAS: Was it not clear before? Are you tempting me?

OEDIPUS: I did not understand it. Say it again.

TEIRESIAS: I say that you are the murderer whom you seek.

OEDIPUS: Now twice you have spat out infamy. You'll pay for it!   *145*

TEIRESIAS: Would you care for more? Do you wish to be really angry?

OEDIPUS: Say what you will. Whatever you say is worthless.

TEIRESIAS: I say you live in hideous shame with those
        Most dear to you. You can not see the evil.

OEDIPUS: Can you go on babbling like this for ever?   *150*

TEIRESIAS: I can, if there is power in truth.

OEDIPUS: There is:
        But not for you, not for you,
        You sightless, witless, senseless, mad old man!

TEIRESIAS: You are the madman. There is no one here
        Who will not curse you soon, as you curse me.   *155*

OEDIPUS: You child of total night! I would not touch you;
        Neither would any man who sees the sun.

TEIRESIAS: True: it is not from you my fate will come.
        That lies within Apollo's competence,
        As it is his concern.

OEDIPUS: Tell me, who made   *160*
        These fine discoveries? Kreon? or someone else?

TEIRESIAS: Kreon is no threat. You weave your own doom.

OEDIPUS: Wealth, power, craft of statemanship!
        Kingly position, everywhere admired!
        What savage envy is stored up against these,   *165*
        If Kreon, whom I trusted, Kreon my friend,
        For this great office which the city once
        Put in my hands unsought—if for this power
        Kreon desires in secret to destroy me!

        He has bought this decrepit fortune-teller, this   *170*
        Collector of dirty pennies, this prophet fraud—
        Why, he is no more clairvoyant than I am!
                                        Tell us:
        Has your mystic mummery ever approached the truth?
        When that hellcat the Sphinx was performing here,
        What help were you to these people?   *175*
        Her magic was not for the first man who came along:
        It demanded a real exorcist. Your birds—
        What good were they? or the gods, for the matter of that?
        But I came by,
        Oedipus, the simple man, who knows nothing—   *180*
        I thought it out for myself, no birds helped me!
        And this is the man you think you can destroy,

That you may be close to Kreon when he's king!
Well, you and your friend Kreon, it seems to me,
185   Will suffer most. If you were not an old man,
You would have paid already for your plot.
CHORAGOS: We can not see that his words or yours
Have been spoken except in anger, Oedipus,
And of anger we have no need. How to accomplish
190   The god's will best: that is what most concerns us.
TEIRESIAS: You are a king. But where argument's concerned
I am your man, as much a king as you.
I am not your servant, but Apollo's.
I have no need of Kreon or Kreon's name.

195   Listen to me. You mock my blindness, do you?
But I say that you, with both your eyes, are blind:
You can not see the wretchedness of your life,
Nor in whose house you live, no, nor with whom.
Who are your father and mother? Can you tell me?
200   You do not even know the blind wrongs
That you have done them, on earth and in the world below.
But the double lash of your parents' curse will whip you
Out of this land some day, with only night
Upon your precious eyes.
205   Your cries then—where will they not be heard?
What fastness of Kithairon° will not echo them?
And that bridal-descant of yours—you'll know it then,
The song they sang when you came here to Thebes
And found your misguided berthing.
210   All this, and more, that you can not guess at now,
Will bring you to yourself among your children.

Be angry, then. Curse Kreon. Curse my words.
I tell you, no man that walks upon the earth
Shall be rooted out more horribly than you.
215   OEDIPUS: Am I to bear this from him?—Damnation
Take you! Out of this place! Out of my sight!
TEIRESIAS: I would not have come at all if you had not asked me.
OEDIPUS: Could I have told that you'd talk nonsense, that
You'd come here to make a fool of yourself, and of me?
220   TEIRESIAS: A fool? Your parents thought me sane enough.
OEDIPUS: My parents again!—Wait: who were my parents?

206 *Kithairon:* Mountain where the infant Oedipus was left for dead.

TEIRESIAS: This day will give you a father, and break your heart.
OEDIPUS: Your infantile riddles! Your damned abracadabra!
TEIRESIAS: You were a great man once at solving riddles.
OEDIPUS: Mock me with that if you like; you will find it true.   225
TEIRESIAS: It was true enough. It brought about your ruin.
OEDIPUS: But if it saved this town?
TEIRESIAS: *(to the* PAGE*)*:   Boy, give me your hand.
OEDIPUS: Yes, boy; lead him away.
                         —While you are here
        We can do nothing. Go; leave us in peace.
TEIRESIAS: I will go when I have said what I have to say.   230
        How can you hurt me? And I tell you again:
        The man you have been looking for all this time,
        The damned man, the murderer of Laios,
        That man is in Thebes. To your mind he is foreign-born,
        But it will soon be shown that he is a Theban,   235
        A revelation that will fail to please.
                         A blind man,
        Who has his eyes now; a penniless man, who is rich now;
        And he will go tapping the strange earth with his staff.
        To the children with whom he lives now he will be
        Brother and father—the very same; to her   240
        Who bore him, son and husband—the very same
        Who came to his father's bed, wet with his father's blood.
        Enough. Go think that over.
        If later you find error in what I have said,
        You may say that I have no skill in prophecy.   245

            (Exit TEIRESIAS, *led by his* PAGE. OEDIPUS *goes into the palace.)*

ODE 1

Strophe 1
CHORUS: The Delphic stone of prophecies
        Remembers ancient regicide
        And a still bloody hand.
        That killer's hour of flight has come.
        He must be stronger than riderless   5
        Coursers of untiring wind,
        For the son of Zeus° armed with his father's thunder
        Leaps in lightning after him;
        And the Furies° hold his track, the sad Furies.

---

7 *son of Zeus:* Apollo. 9 *Furies:* Female spirits who avenged evil deeds.

Antistrophe 1

10   Holy Parnassos'° peak of snow
        Flashes and blinds that secret man,
        That all shall hunt him down:
        Though he may roam the forest shade
        Like a bull gone wild from pasture
15   To rage through glooms of stone.
        Doom comes down on him; flight will not avail him;
        For the world's heart calls him desolate,
        And the immortal voices follow, for ever follow.

Strophe 2

        But now a wilder thing is heard
20   From the old man skilled at hearing Fate in the wing-beat of a bird.
        Bewildered as a blown bird, my soul hovers and can not find
        Foothold in this debate, or any reason or rest of mind.
        But no man ever brought—none can bring
        Proof of strife between Thebes' royal house,
25   Labdakos' line, and the son of Polybos;°
        And never until now has any man brought word
        Of Laios' dark death staining Oedipus the King.

Antistrophe 2

        Divine Zeus and Apollo hold
        Perfect intelligence alone of all tales ever told;
30   And well though this diviner works, he works in his own night;
        No man can judge that rough unknown or trust in second sight,
        For wisdom changes hands among the wise.
        Shall I believe my great lord criminal
        At a raging word that a blind old man let fall?
35   I saw him, when the carrion woman° faced him of old,
        Prove his heroic mind. These evil words are lies.

SCENE 2

KREON: Men of Thebes:
        I am told that heavy accusations
        Have been brought against me by King Oedipus.

        I am not the kind of man to bear this tamely.

---

10 *Parnassos:* Holy mountain, dwelling place of Zeus, king of the gods. 25 *Polybos:* Oedipus's
adoptive father, king of Corinth. 35 *woman:* The Sphinx.

If in these present difficulties   5
He holds me accountable for any harm to him
Through anything I have said or done—why, then,
I do not value life in this dishonor.
It is not as though this rumor touched upon
Some private indiscretion. The matter is grave.   10
The fact is that I am being called disloyal
To the State, to my fellow citizens, to my friends.
CHORAGOS: He may have spoken in anger, not from his mind.
KREON: But did you not hear him say I was the one
    Who seduced the old prophet into lying?   15
CHORAGOS: The thing was said; I do not know how seriously.
KREON: But you were watching him! Were his eyes steady?
    Did he look like a man in his right mind?
CHORAGOS: I do not know.
    I can not judge the behavior of great men.
    But here is the king himself.

    (Enter OEDIPUS.*)*

OEDIPUS: So you dared come back.   20
    Why? How brazen of you to come to my house,
    You murderer!
            Do you think I do not know
    That you plotted to kill me, plotted to steal my throne?
    Tell me, in God's name: am I coward, a fool,
    That you should dream you could accomplish this?   25
    A fool who could not see your slippery game?
    A coward, not to fight back when I saw it?
    You are the fool, Kreon, are you not? hoping
    Without support or friends to get a throne?
    Thrones may be won or bought: you could do neither.   30
KREON: Now listen to me. You have talked; let me talk, too.
    You can not judge unless you know the facts.
OEDIPUS: You speak well: there is one fact; but I find it hard
    To learn from the deadliest enemy I have.
KREON: That above all I must dispute with you.   35
OEDIPUS: That above all I will not hear you deny.
KREON: If you think there is anything good in being stubborn
    Against all reason, then I say you are wrong.
OEDIPUS: If you think a man can sin against his own kind
    And not be punished for it, I say you are mad.   40
KREON: I agree. But tell me: what have I done to you?
OEDIPUS: You advised me to send for that wizard, did you not?

KREON: I did. I should do it again.

OEDIPUS:　　　　　　　　　　Very well. Now tell me:
　　How long has it been since Laios—

KREON:　　　　　　　　　　　　What of Laios?

45　OEDIPUS: Since he vanished in that onset by the road?

KREON: It was long ago, a long time.

OEDIPUS:　　　　　　　　　And this prophet,
　　Was he practicing here then?

KREON:　　　　　　　　　　He was; and with honor, as now.

OEDIPUS: Did he speak of me at that time?

KREON:　　　　　　　　　　He never did,
　　At least, not when I was present.

OEDIPUS:　　　　　　　　　But . . . the enquiry?
　　I suppose you held one?

50　KREON:　　　　　　　　We did, but we learned nothing.

OEDIPUS: Why did the prophet not speak against me then?

KREON: I do not know; and I am the kind of man
　　Who holds his tongue when he has no facts to go on.

OEDIPUS: There's one fact that you know, and you could tell it.

55　KREON: What fact is that? If I know it, you shall have it.

OEDIPUS: If he were not involved with you, he could not say
　　That it was I who murdered Laios.

KREON: If he says that, you are the one that knows it!—
　　But now it is my turn to question you.

60　OEDIPUS: Put your questions. I am no murderer.

KREON: First, then: You married my sister?

OEDIPUS:　　　　　　　　　　　I married your sister.

KREON: And you rule the kingdom equally with her?

OEDIPUS: Everything that she wants she has from me.

KREON: And I am the third, equal to both of you?

65　OEDIPUS: That is why I call you a bad friend.

KREON: No. Reason it out, as I have done.
　　Think of this first: would any sane man prefer
　　Power, with all a king's anxieties,
　　To that same power and the grace of sleep?
70　　Certainly not I.
　　I have never longed for the king's power—only his rights.
　　Would any wise man differ from me in this?
　　As matters stand, I have my way in everything
　　With your consent, and no responsibilities.
75　　If I were king, I should be a slave to policy.
　　How could I desire a scepter more
　　Than what is now mine—untroubled influence?

No, I have not gone mad; I need no honors,
Except those with the perquisites I have now.
I am welcome everywhere; every man salutes me,   *80*
And those who want your favor seek my ear,
Since I know how to manage what they ask.
Should I exchange this ease for that anxiety?
Besides, no sober mind is treasonable.
I hate anarchy   *85*
And never would deal with any man who likes it.
Test what I have said. Go to the priestess
At Delphi, ask if I quoted her correctly.
And as for this other thing: if I am found
Guilty of treason with Teiresias,   *90*
Then sentence me to death. You have my word
It is a sentence I should cast my vote for—
But not without evidence!
                            You do wrong
When you take good men for bad, bad men for good.
A true friend thrown aside—why, life itself   *95*
Is not more precious!
                            In time you will know this well:
For time, and time alone, will show the just man,
Though scoundrels are discovered in a day.
CHORAGOS: This is well said, and a prudent man would ponder it.
    Judgments too quickly formed are dangerous.   *100*
OEDIPUS: But is he not quick in his duplicity?
    And shall I not be quick to parry him?
    Would you have me stand still, hold my peace, and let
    This man win everything, through my inaction?
KREON: And you want—what is it, then? To banish me?   *105*
OEDIPUS: No, not exile. It is your death I want,
    So that all the world may see what treason means.
KREON: You will persist, then? You will not believe me?
OEDIPUS: How can I believe you?
KREON: Then you are a fool.
OEDIPUS: To save myself?
KREON: In justice, think of me.   *110*
OEDIPUS: You are evil incarnate.
KREON: But suppose that you are wrong?
OEDIPUS: Still I must rule.
KREON: But not if you rule badly.
OEDIPUS: O city, city!
KREON: It is my city, too!

CHORAGOS: Now, my lords, be still. I see the queen,
115   Iokaste, coming from her palace chambers;
      And it is time she came, for the sake of you both.
      This dreadful quarrel can be resolved through her.

      (Enter IOKASTE.*)*

IOKASTE: Poor foolish men, what wicked din is this?
      With Thebes sick to death, is it not shameful
120   That you should rake some private quarrel up?
      (To OEDIPUS.*)* Come into the house.
                            —And you, Kreon, go now:
      Let us have no more of this tumult over nothing.
KREON: Nothing? No, sister: what your husband plans for me
      Is one of two great evils: exile or death.
OEDIPUS: He is right.
125   Why, woman I have caught him squarely
      Plotting against my life.
KREON: No! Let me die
      Accurst if ever I have wished you harm!
IOKASTE: Ah, believe it, Oedipus!
      In the name of the gods, respect this oath of his
130   For my sake, for the sake of these people here!

Strophe 1

CHORAGOS: Open your mind to her, my lord. Be ruled by her, I beg you!
OEDIPUS: What would you have me do?
CHORAGOS: Respect Kreon's word. He has never spoken like a fool,
      And now he has sworn an oath.
OEDIPUS: You know what you ask?
CHORAGOS: I do.
OEDIPUS: Speak on, then.
135 CHORAGOS: A friend so sworn should not be baited so,
      In blind malice, and without final proof.
OEDIPUS: You are aware, I hope, that what you say
      Means death for me, or exile at the least.

Strophe 2

CHORAGOS: No, I swear by Helios, first in heaven!
140   May I die friendless and accurst,
      The worst of deaths, if ever I meant that!
      It is the withering fields
        That hurt my sick heart:

Must we bear all these ills,
And now your bad blood as well?   *145*
OEDIPUS: Then let him go. And let me die, if I must,
Or be driven by him in shame from the land of Thebes.
It is your unhappiness, and not his talk,
That touches me.
                        As for him—
Wherever he goes, hatred will follow him.   *150*
KREON: Ugly in yielding, as you were ugly in rage!
Natures like yours chiefly torment themselves.
OEDIPUS: Can you not go? Can you not leave me?
KREON: I can.
You do not know me; but the city knows me,
And in its eyes I am just, if not in yours.   *(Exit* KREON.*)*   *155*

Antistrophe 1
CHORAGOS: Lady Iokaste, did you not ask the King to go to his chambers?
IOKASTE: First tell me what has happened.
CHORAGOS: There was suspicion without evidence; yet it rankled
As even false charges will.
IOKASTE: On both sides?
CHORAGOS: On both.
IOKASTE: But what was said?   *160*
CHORAGOS: Oh let it rest, let it be done with!
Have we not suffered enough?
OEDIPUS: You see to what your decency has brought you:
You have made difficulties where my heart saw none.

Antistrophe 2
CHORAGOS: Oedipus, it is not once only I have told you—   *165*
You must know I should count myself unwise
To the point of madness, should I now forsake you—
        You, under whose hand,
            In the storm of another time,
            Our dear land sailed out free.   *170*
        But now stand fast at the helm!
IOKASTE: In God's name, Oedipus, inform your wife as well:
Why are you so set in this hard anger?
OEDIPUS: I will tell you, for none of these men deserves
My confidence as you do. It is Kreon's work,   *175*
His treachery, his plotting against me.
IOKASTE: Go on, if you can make this clear to me.
OEDIPUS: He charges me with the murder of Laios.

IOKASTE: Has he some knowledge? Or does he speak from hearsay?

180   OEDIPUS: He would not commit himself to such a charge,
But he has brought in that damnable soothsayer
To tell his story.

IOKASTE: Set your mind at rest.
If it is a question of soothsayers, I tell you
That you will find no man whose craft gives knowledge
Of the unknowable.

185   Here is my proof:
An oracle was reported to Laios once
(I will not say from Phoibos himself, but from
His appointed ministers, at any rate)
That his doom would be death at the hands of his own son—

190   His son, born of his flesh and of mine!

Now, you remember the story: Laios was killed
By marauding strangers where three highways meet;
But his child had not been three days in this world
Before the king had pierced the baby's ankles

195   And left him to die on a lonely mountainside.
Thus, Apollo never caused that child
To kill his father, and it was not Laios' fate
To die at the hands of his son, as he had feared.
This is what prophets and prophecies are worth!
Have no dread of them.

200   It is God himself
Who can show us what he wills, in his own way.

OEDIPUS: How strange a shadowy memory crossed my mind,
Just now while you were speaking; it chilled my heart.

IOKASTE: What do you mean? What memory do you speak of?

205   OEDIPUS: If I understand you, Laios was killed
At a place where three roads meet.

IOKASTE: So it was said;
We have no later story.

OEDIPUS: Where did it happen?

IOKASTE: Phokis, it is called: at a place where the Theban Way
Divides into the roads toward Delphi and Daulia.

OEDIPUS: When?

210   IOKASTE: We had the news not long before you came
And proved the right to your succession here.

OEDIPUS: Ah, what net has God been weaving for me?

IOKASTE: Oedipus! Why does this trouble you?

OEDIPUS: Do not ask me yet.
First, tell me how Laios looked, and tell me

How old he was.

IOKASTE: He was tall, his hair just touched   215
　　　With white; his form was not unlike your own.

OEDIPUS: I think that I myself may be accurst
　　　By my own ignorant edict.

IOKASTE: You speak strangely.
　　　It makes me tremble to look at you, my king.

OEDIPUS: I am not sure that the blind man can not see.   220
　　　But I should know better if you were to tell me—

IOKASTE: Anything—though I dread to hear you ask it.

OEDIPUS: Was the king lightly escorted, or did he ride
　　　With a large company, as a ruler should?

IOKASTE: There were five men with him in all: one was a herald;   225
　　　And a single chariot, which he was driving.

OEDIPUS: Alas, that makes it plain enough!
　　　　　　　　　　　　　　　　But who—
　　　Who told you how it happened?

IOKASTE: A household servant,
　　　The only one to escape.

OEDIPUS: And is he still
　　　A servant of ours?

IOKASTE: No; for when he came back at last   230
　　　And found you enthroned in the place of the dead king,
　　　He came to me, touched my hand with his, and begged
　　　That I would send him away to the frontier district
　　　Where only the shepherds go—
　　　As far away from the city as I could send him.   235
　　　I granted his prayer; for although the man was a slave,
　　　He had earned more than this favor at my hands.

OEDIPUS: Can he be called back quickly?

IOKASTE: Easily.
　　　But why?

OEDIPUS: I have taken too much upon myself
　　　Without enquiry; therefore I wish to consult him.   240

IOKASTE: Then he shall come.
　　　　　　　　　　　　But am I not one also
　　　To whom you might confide these fears of yours?

OEDIPUS: That is your right; it will not be denied you,
　　　Now least of all; for I have reached a pitch
　　　Of wild foreboding. Is there anyone   245
　　　To whom I should sooner speak?

　　　Polybos of Corinth is my father.
　　　My mother is a Dorian: Merope.

I grew up chief among the men of Corinth
250   Until a strange thing happened—
Not worth my passion, it may be, but strange.
At a feast, a drunken man maundering in his cups
Cries out that I am not my father's son!
I contained myself that night, though I felt anger
255   And a sinking heart. The next day I visited
My father and mother, and questioned them. They stormed,
Calling it all the slanderous rant of a fool;
And this relieved me. Yet the suspicion
Remained always aching in my mind;
260   I knew there was talk; I could not rest;
And finally, saying nothing to my parents,
I went to the shrine at Delphi.

The god dismissed my question without reply;
He spoke of other things.
                              Some were clear,
265   Full of wretchedness, dreadful, unbearable:
As, that I should lie with my own mother, breed
Children from whom all men would turn their eyes;
And that I should be my father's murderer.

I heard all this, and fled. And from that day
270   Corinth to me was only in the stars
Descending in that quarter of the sky,
As I wandered farther and farther on my way
To a land where I should never see the evil
Sung by the oracle. And I came to this country
275   Where, so you say, King Laios was killed.

I will tell you all that happened there, my lady.
There were three highways
Coming together at a place I passed;
And there a herald came towards me, and a chariot
280   Drawn by horses, with a man such as you describe
Seated in it. The groom leading the horses
Forced me off the road at his lord's command;
But as this charioteer lurched over towards me
I struck him in my rage. The old man saw me
285   And brought his double goad down upon my head
As I came abreast.
                              He was paid back, and more!

Swinging my club in this right hand I knocked him
Out of his car, and he rolled on the ground.
                                       I killed him.

I killed them all.
Now if that stranger and Laios were—kin,   *290*
Where is a man more miserable than I?
More hated by the gods? Citizen and alien alike
Must never shelter me or speak to me—
I must be shunned by all.
                       And I myself
Pronounced this malediction upon myself!   *295*

Think of it: I have touched you with these hands,
These hands that killed your husband. What defilement!

Am I all evil, then? It must be so,
Since I must flee from Thebes, yet never again
See my own countrymen, my own country,   *300*
For fear of joining my mother in marriage
And killing Polybos, my father.
                        Ah,
If I was created so, born to this fate,
Who could deny the savagery of God?

O holy majesty of heavenly powers!   *305*
May I never see that day! Never!
Rather let me vanish from the race of men
Than know the abomination destined me!
CHORAGOS: We too, my lord, have felt dismay at this.
    But there is hope: you have yet to hear the shepherd.   *310*
OEDIPUS: Indeed, I fear no other hope is left me.
IOKASTE: What do you hope from him when he comes?
OEDIPUS: This much:
    If his account of the murder tallies with yours,
    Then I am cleared.
IOKASTE: What was it that I said
    Of such importance?
OEDIPUS: Why, "marauders," you said,   *315*
    Killed the king, according to this man's story.
    If he maintains that still, if there were several,
    Clearly the guilt is not mine: I was alone.
    But if he says one man, singlehanded, did it,

320   Then the evidence all points to me.
      IOKASTE: You may be sure that he said there were several;
              And can he call back that story now? He can not.
              The whole city heard it as plainly as I.
              But suppose he alters some detail of it:
325   He can not ever show that Laios' death
              Fulfilled the oracle: for Apollo said
              My child was doomed to kill him; and my child—
              Poor baby!—it was my child that died first.

              No. From now on, where oracles are concerned,
330   I would not waste a second thought on any.
      OEDIPUS: You may be right.
      OEDIPUS: But come: let someone go
              For the shepherd at once. This matter must be settled.
      IOKASTE: I will send for him.
              I would not wish to cross you in anything,
335   And surely not in this.—Let us go in.   *(Exeunt into the palace.)*

ODE 2

Strophe 1

CHORUS: Let me be reverent in the ways of right,
        Lowly the paths I journey on;
        Let all my words and actions keep
        The laws of the pure universe
5   From highest Heaven handed down.
        For Heaven is their bright nurse,
        Those generations of the realms of light;
        Ah, never of mortal kind were they begot,
        Nor are they slaves of memory, lost in sleep:
10   Their Father is greater than Time, and ages not.

Antistrophe 1

        The tyrant is a child of Pride
        Who drinks from his great sickening cup
        Recklessness and vanity,
        Until from his high crest headlong
15   He plummets to the dust of hope.
        That strong man is not strong.
        But let no fair ambition be denied;
        May God protect the wrestler for the State

In government, in comely policy,
Who will fear God, and on his ordinance wait.   *20*

Strophe 2

Haughtiness and the high hand of disdain
Tempt and outrage God's holy law;
And any mortal who dares hold
No immortal Power in awe
Will be caught up in a net of pain: *25*
The price for which his levity is sold.
Let each man take due earnings, then,
And keep his hands from holy things,
And from blasphemy stand apart—
Else the crackling blast of heaven   *30*
Blows on his head, and on his desperate heart.
Though fools will honor impious men,
In their cities no tragic poet sings.

Antistrophe 2

Shall we lose faith in Delphi's obscurities,
We who have heard the world's core   *35*
Discredited, and the sacred wood
Of Zeus at Elis praised no more?
The deeds and the strange prophecies
Must make a pattern yet to be understood.
Zeus, if indeed you are lord of all,   *40*
Throned in light over night and day,
Mirror this in your endless mind:
Our masters call the oracle
Words on the wind, and the Delphic vision blind!
Their hearts no longer know Apollo,   *45*
And reverence for the gods has died away.

SCENE 3

(Enter IOKASTE.*)*

IOKASTE: Princes of Thebes, it has occurred to me
To visit the altars of the gods, bearing
These branches as a suppliant, and this incense.
Our king is not himself: his noble soul
Is overwrought with fantasies of dread,   *5*

Else he would consider
The new prophecies in the light of the old.
He will listen to any voice that speaks disaster,
And my advice goes for nothing. *(She approaches the altar, right.)*
                                   To you, then, Apollo,
10   Lycean lord, since you are nearest, I turn in prayer
Receive these offerings, and grant us deliverance
From defilement. Our hearts are heavy with fear
When we see our leader distracted, as helpless sailors
Are terrified by the confusion of their helmsman.

(Enter MESSENGER.*)*

15   MESSENGER: Friends, no doubt you can direct me:
    Where shall I find the house of Oedipus,
    Or, better still, where is the king himself?
  CHORAGOS: It is this very place, stranger; he is inside.
    This is his wife and mother of his children.
20   MESSENGER: I wish her happiness in a happy house,
    Blest in all the fulfillment of her marriage.
  IOKASTE: I wish as much for you: your courtesy
    Deserves a like good fortune. But now, tell me:
    Why have you come? What have you to say to us?
25   MESSENGER: Good news, my lady, for your house and your husband.
  IOKASTE: What news? Who sent you here?
  MESSENGER: I am from Corinth.
    The news I bring ought to mean joy for you,
    Though it may be you will find some grief in it.
  IOKASTE: What is it? How can it touch us in both ways?
30   MESSENGER: The word is that the people of the Isthmus
                 Intend to call Oedipus to be their king.
  IOKASTE: But old King Polybos—is he not reigning still?
  MESSENGER: No. Death holds him in his sepulchre.
  IOKASTE: What are you saying? Polybos is dead?
35   MESSENGER: If I am not telling the truth, may I die myself.
  IOKASTE *(to a* MAIDSERVANT*)*: Go in, go quickly; tell this to your master.
    O riddlers of God's will, where are you now!
    This was the man whom Oedipus, long ago,
    Feared so, fled so, in dread of destroying him—
40   But it was another fate by which he died.

(Enter OEDIPUS, *center.)*

OEDIPUS: Dearest Iokaste, why have you sent for me?
IOKASTE: Listen to what this man says, and then tell me

What has become of the solemn prophecies.
OEDIPUS: Who is this man? What is his news for me?
IOKASTE: He has come from Corinth to announce your father's death!   45
OEDIPUS: Is it true, stranger? Tell me in your own words.
MESSENGER: I can not say it more clearly: the king is dead.
OEDIPUS: Was it by treason? Or by an attack of illness?
MESSENGER: A little thing brings old men to their rest.
OEDIPUS: It was sickness, then?
MESSENGER: Yes, and his many years.   50
OEDIPUS: Ah!
    Why should a man respect the Pythian hearth,° or
    Give heed to the birds that jangle above his head?
    They prophesied that I should kill Polybos,
    Kill my own father; but he is dead and buried,   55
    And I am here—I never touched him, never,
    Unless he died of grief for my departure,
    And thus, in a sense, through me. No. Polybos
    Has packed the oracles off with him underground.
    They are empty words.
IOKASTE: Had I not told you so?   60
OEDIPUS: You had; it was my faint heart that betrayed me.
IOKASTE: From now on never think of those things again.
OEDIPUS: And yet—must I not fear my mother's bed?
IOKASTE: Why should anyone in this world be afraid,
    Since Fate rules us and nothing can be foreseen?   65
    A man should live only for the present day.

    Have no more fear of sleeping with your mother:
    How many men, in dreams, have lain with their mothers!
    No reasonable man is troubled by such things.
OEDIPUS: That is true; only—   70
    If only my mother were not still alive!
    But she is alive. I can not help my dread.
IOKASTE: Yet this news of your father's death is wonderful.
OEDIPUS: Wonderful. But I fear the living woman.
MESSENGER: Tell me, who is this woman that you fear?   75
OEDIPUS: It is Merope, man; the wife of King Polybos.
MESSENGER: Merope? Why should you be afraid of her?
OEDIPUS: An oracle of the gods, a dreadful saying.
MESSENGER: Can you tell me about it or are you sworn to silence?

52 *Pythian hearth:* Delphi; the alternative name came from the dragon Python, which once
guarded Delphi until Apollo vanquished it.

80   OEDIPUS: I can tell you, and I will.
      Apollo said through his prophet that I was the man
      Who should marry his own mother, shed his father's blood
      With his own hands. And so, for all these years
      I have kept clear of Corinth, and no harm has come—
85   Though it would have been sweet to see my parents again.
  MESSENGER: And is this the fear that drove you out of Corinth?
  OEDIPUS: Would you have me kill my father?
  MESSENGER: As for that
      You must be reassured by the news I gave you.
  OEDIPUS: If you could reassure me, I would reward you.
90   MESSENGER: I had that in mind, I will confess: I thought
      I could count on you when you returned to Corinth.
  OEDIPUS: No: I will never go near my parents again.
  MESSENGER: Ah, son, you still do not know what you are doing—
  OEDIPUS: What do you mean? In the name of God tell me!
95   MESSENGER: —If these are your reasons for not going home.
  OEDIPUS: I tell you, I fear the oracle may come true.
  MESSENGER: And guilt may come upon you through your parents?
  OEDIPUS: That is the dread that is always in my heart.
  MESSENGER: Can you not see that all your fears are groundless?
100   OEDIPUS: Groundless? Am I not my parents' son?
  MESSENGER: Polybos was not your father.
  OEDIPUS: Not my father?
  MESSENGER: No more your father than the man speaking to you.
  OEDIPUS: But you are nothing to me!
  MESSENGER: Neither was he.
  OEDIPUS: Then why did he call me son?
  MESSENGER: I will tell you:
105   Long ago he had you from my hands, as a gift.
  OEDIPUS: Then how could he love me so, if I was not his?
  MESSENGER: He had no children, and his heart turned to you.
  OEDIPUS: What of you? Did you buy me? Did you find me by chance?
  MESSENGER: I came upon you in the woody vales of Kithairon.
  OEDIPUS: And what were you doing there?
110   MESSENGER: Tending my flocks.
  OEDIPUS: A wandering shepherd?
  MESSENGER: But your savior, son, that day.
  OEDIPUS: From what did you save me?
  MESSENGER: Your ankles should tell you that.
  OEDIPUS: Ah, stranger, why do you speak of that childhood pain?
  MESSENGER: I pulled the skewer that pinned your feet together.
115   OEDIPUS: I have had the mark as long as I can remember.

MESSENGER: That was why you were given the name you bear.°
OEDIPUS: God! Was it my father or my mother who did it?
    Tell me!
MESSENGER: I do not know. The man who gave you to me
    Can tell you better than I.
OEDIPUS: It was not you that found me, but another?   *120*
MESSENGER: It was another shepherd gave you to me.
OEDIPUS: Who was he? Can you tell me who he was?
MESSENGER: I think he was said to be one of Laios' people.
OEDIPUS: You mean the Laios who was king here years ago?
MESSENGER: Yes; King Laios; and the man was one of his herdsmen.   *125*
OEDIPUS: Is he still alive? Can I see him?
MESSENGER: These men here
    Know best about such things.
OEDIPUS: Does anyone here
    Know this shepherd that he is talking about?
    Have you seen him in the fields, or in the town?
    If you have, tell me. It is time things were made plain.   *130*
CHORAGOS: I think the man he means is that same shepherd
    You have already asked to see. Iokaste perhaps
    Could tell you something.
OEDIPUS: Do you know anything
    About him, Lady? Is he the man we have summoned?
    Is that the man this shepherd means?
IOKASTE: Why think of him?   *135*
    Forget this herdsman. Forget it all.
    This talk is a waste of time.
OEDIPUS: How can you say that,
    When the clues to my true birth are in my hands?
IOKASTE: For God's love, let us have no more questioning!
    Is your life nothing to you?   *140*
    My own is pain enough for me to bear.
OEDIPUS: You need not worry. Suppose my mother a slave,
    And born of slaves: no baseness can touch you.
IOKASTE: Listen to me, I beg you: do not do this thing!
OEDIPUS: I will not listen; the truth must be made known.   *145*
IOKASTE: Everything that I say is for your own good!
OEDIPUS: My own good
    Snaps my patience, then; I want none of it.
IOKASTE: You are fatally wrong! May you never learn who you are!

---

116 *the name you bear:* "Oedipus" translates as "the one with a swollen foot."

OEDIPUS: Go, one of you, and bring the shepherd here.
150   Let us leave this woman to brag of her royal name.
IOKASTE: Ah, miserable!
    That is the only word I have for you now.
    That is the only word I can ever have.   *(Exit into the palace.)*
CHORAGOS: Why has she left us, Oedipus? Why has she gone
155   In such a passion of sorrow? I fear this silence:
    Something dreadful may come of it.
OEDIPUS: Let it come!
    However base my birth, I must know about it.
    The Queen, like a woman, is perhaps ashamed
    To think of my low origin. But I
160   Am a child of Luck; I can not be dishonored.
    Luck is my mother; the passing months, my brothers,
    Have seen me rich and poor.
                    If this is so,
    How could I wish that I were someone else?
    How could I not be glad to know my birth?

ODE 3

Strophe
CHORUS: If ever the coming time were known
    To my heart's pondering,
    Kithairon, now by Heaven I see the torches
    At the festival of the next full moon,
5   And see the dance, and hear the choir sing
    A grace to your gentle shade:
    Mountain where Oedipus was found,
    O mountain guard of a noble race!
    May the god° who heals us lend his aid,
10   And let that glory come to pass
    For our king's cradling-ground.

Antistrophe
    Of the nymphs that flower beyond the years,
    Who bore you,° royal child,
    To Pan° of the hills or the timberline Apollo,
15   Cold in delight where the upland clears,

9 *god:* Apollo. 13 *Who bore you:* The Chorus wonders whether Oedipus might be the son of a nymph and a god: Pan, Apollo, Hermes, or Dionysus. 14 *Pan:* God of nature; from the waist up, he is human, from the waist down, a goat.

Or Hermes° for whom Kyllene's° heights are piled?
Or flushed as evening cloud,
Great Dionysos,° roamer of mountains,
He—was it he who found you there,
And caught you up in his own proud   20
Arms from the sweet god-ravisher
Who laughed by the Muses'° fountains?

SCENE 4

OEDIPUS: Sirs: though I do not know the man,
    I think I see him coming, this shepherd we want:
    He is old, like our friend here, and the men
    Bringing him seem to be servants of my house.
    But you can tell, if you have ever seen him.   5

(Enter SHEPHERD escorted by SERVANTS.)

CHORAGOS: I know him, he was Laios' man. You can trust him.
OEDIPUS: Tell me first, you from Corinth: is this the shepherd
    We were discussing?
MESSENGER: This is the very man.
OEDIPUS *(to SHEPHERD)*: Come here. No, look at me. You must answer
    Everything I ask.—You belonged to Laios?   10
SHEPHERD: Yes: born his slave, brought up in his house.
OEDIPUS: Tell me: what kind of work did you do for him?
SHEPHERD: I was a shepherd of his, most of my life.
OEDIPUS: Where mainly did you go for pasturage?
SHEPHERD: Sometimes Kithairon, sometimes the hills near-by.   15
OEDIPUS: Do you remember ever seeing this man out there?
SHEPHERD: What would he be doing there? This man?
OEDIPUS: This man standing here. Have you ever seen him before?
SHEPHERD: No. At least, not to my recollection.
MESSENGER: And that is not strange, my lord. But I'll refresh   20
    His memory: he must remember when we two
    Spent three whole seasons together, March to September,
    On Kithairon or thereabouts. He had two flocks;
    I had one. Each autumn I'd drive mine home
    And he would go back with his to Laios' sheepfold.—   25
    Is this not true, just as I have described it?

16 *Hermes:* Zeus's son, messenger of the gods; *Kyllene:* Sacred mountain, the birthplace of Hermes. 18 *Dionysos:* (Dionysus) God of wine, sometimes called Bacchos. 22 *Muses:* Nine goddesses, sisters, who are the patronesses of poetry, music, art, and the sciences.

SHEPHERD: True, yes; but it was all so long ago.
MESSENGER: Well, then: do you remember, back in those days,
　　　That you gave me a baby boy to bring up as my own?
30 SHEPHERD: What if I did? What are you trying to say?
MESSENGER: King Oedipus was once that little child.
SHEPHERD: Damn you, hold your tongue!
OEDIPUS:　　　　　　　　　　　No more of that!
　　　It is your tongue needs watching, not this man's.
SHEPHERD: My king, my master, what is it I have done wrong?
35 OEDIPUS: You have not answered his question about the boy.
SHEPHERD: He does not know . . . He is only making trouble . . .
OEDIPUS: Come, speak plainly, or it will go hard with you.
SHEPHERD: In God's name, do not torture an old man!
OEDIPUS: Come here, one of you; bind his arms behind him.
40 SHEPHERD: Unhappy king! What more do you wish to learn?
OEDIPUS: Did you give this man the child he speaks of?
SHEPHERD:　　　　　　　　　　　　　　　I did.
　　　And I would to God I had died that very day.
OEDIPUS: You will die now unless you speak the truth.
SHEPHERD: Yet if I speak the truth, I am worse than dead.
45 OEDIPUS (to ATTENDANT): He intends to draw it out, apparently—
SHEPHERD: No! I have told you already that I gave him the boy.
OEDIPUS: Where did you get him? From your house? From somewhere else?
SHEPHERD: Not from mine, no. A man gave him to me.
OEDIPUS: Is that man here? Whose house did he belong to?
50 SHEPHERD: For God's love, my king, do not ask me any more!
OEDIPUS: You are a dead man if I have to ask you again.
SHEPHERD: Then . . . Then the child was from the palace of Laios.
OEDIPUS: A slave child? or a child of his own line?
SHEPHERD: Ah, I am on the brink of dreadful speech!
55 OEDIPUS: And I of dreadful hearing. Yet I must hear.
SHEPHERD: If you must be told, then . . .
　　　　　　　　　　　　　　They said it was Laios' child;
　　　But it is your wife who can tell you about that.
OEDIPUS: My wife—Did she give it to you?
SHEPHERD:　　　　　　　　　　　My lord, she did.
OEDIPUS: Do you know why?
SHEPHERD:　　　　　　　　I was told to get rid of it.
OEDIPUS: Oh heartless mother!
60 SHEPHERD:　　　　　　　　But in dread of prophecies . . .
OEDIPUS: Tell me.
SHEPHERD:　　　　It was said that the boy would kill his own father.
OEDIPUS: Then why did you give him over to this old man?
SHEPHERD: I pitied the baby, my king,

And I thought that this man would take him far away
To his own country.
                        He saved him—but for what a fate!   65
For if you are what this man says you are,
No man living is more wretched than Oedipus.
OEDIPUS: Ah God!
    It was true!
            All the prophecies!
                        —Now,
O Light, may I look on you for the last time!   70
I, Oedipus,
Oedipus, damned in his birth, in his marriage damned,
Damned in the blood he shed with his own hand!
(He rushes into the palace.)

ODE 4

Strophe 1
CHORUS: Alas for the seed of men.
    What measure shall I give these generations
    That breathe on the void and are void
    And exist and do not exist?
    Who bears more weight of joy   5
    Than mass of sunlight shifting in images,
    Or who shall make his thought stay on
    That down time drifts away?
    Your splendor is all fallen.
    O naked brow of wrath and tears,   10
    O change of Oedipus!
    I who saw your days call no man blest—
    Your great days like ghosts gone.

Antistrophe 1
    That mind was a strong bow.
    Deep, how deep you drew it then, hard archer,   15
    At a dim fearful range,
    And brought dear glory down!
    You overcame the stranger°—
    The virgin with her hooking lion claws—
    And though death sang, stood like a tower   20
    To make pale Thebes take heart.
    Fortress against our sorrow!

18 *stranger:* The Sphinx.

True king, giver of laws,
Majestic Oedipus!
25   No prince in Thebes had ever such renown,
No prince won such grace of power.

Strophe 2

And now of all men ever known
Most pitiful is this man's story:
His fortunes are most changed; his state
30   Fallen to a low slave's
Ground under bitter fate.
O Oedipus, most royal one!
The great door° that expelled you to the light
Gave at night—ah, gave night to your glory:
35   As to the father, to the fathering son.
All understood too late.
How could that queen whom Laios won,
The garden that he harrowed at his height,
Be silent when that act was done?

Antistrophe 2

40   But all eyes fail before time's eye,
All actions come to justice there.
Though never willed, though far down the deep past,
Your bed, your dread sirings,
Are brought to book at last.
45   Child by Laios doomed to die,
Then doomed to lose that fortunate little death,
Would God you never took breath in this air
That with my wailing lips I take to cry:
For I weep the world's outcast.
50   I was blind, and now I can tell why:
Asleep, for you had given ease of breath
To Thebes, while the false years went by.

EXODOS°

(Enter, from the palace, SECOND MESSENGER.)

SECOND MESSENGER: Elders of Thebes, most honored in this land,
What horrors are yours to see and hear, what weight
Of sorrow to be endured, if, true to your birth,

---

33 *door:* Refers to the birth process. *Exodos:* Final scene.

You venerate the line of Labdakos!
I think neither Istros nor Phasis, those great rivers,   5
Could purify this place of all the evil
It shelters now, or soon must bring to light—
Evil not done unconsciously, but willed.

The greatest griefs are those we cause ourselves.
CHORAGOS: Surely, friend, we have grief enough already;   10
    What new sorrow do you mean?
SECOND MESSENGER: The queen is dead.
CHORAGOS: O miserable queen! But at whose hand?
SECOND MESSENGER: Her own.
    The full horror of what happened you can not know,
    For you did not see it; but I, who did, will tell you
    As clearly as I can how she met her death.   15

When she had left us,
In passionate silence, passing through the court,
She ran to her apartment in the house,
Her hair clutched by the fingers of both hands.
She closed the doors behind her; then, by that bed   20
Where long ago the fatal son was conceived—
That son who should bring about his father's death—
We heard her call upon Laios, dead so many years,
And heard her wail for the double fruit of her marriage,
A husband by her husband, children by her child.   25
Exactly how she died I do not know:
For Oedipus burst in moaning and would not let us
Keep vigil to the end: it was by him
As he stormed about the room that our eyes were caught.
From one to another of us he went, begging a sword,   30
Hunting the wife who was not his wife, the mother
Whose womb had carried his own children and himself.
I do not know: it was none of us aided him,
But surely one of the gods was in control!
For with a dreadful cry   35
He hurled his weight, as though wrenched out of himself,
At the twin doors: the bolts gave, and he rushed in.
And there we saw her hanging, her body swaying
From the cruel cord she had noosed about her neck.
A great sob broke from him, heartbreaking to hear,   40
As he loosed the rope and lowered her to the ground.

I would blot out from my mind what happened next!

For the king ripped from her gown the golden brooches
That were her ornament, and raised them, and plunged them down
45   Straight into his own eyeballs, crying, "No more,
No more shall you look on the misery about me,
The horrors of my own doing! Too long you have known
The faces of those whom I should never have seen,
Too long been blind to those for whom I was searching!
50   From this hour, go in darkness!" And as he spoke,
He struck at his eyes—not once, but many times;
And the blood spattered his beard,
Bursting from his ruined sockets like red hail.

So from the unhappiness of two this evil has sprung,
55   A curse on the man and woman alike. The old
Happiness of the house of Labdakos
Was happiness enough: where is it today?
It is all wailing and ruin, disgrace, death—all
The misery of mankind that has a name—
60   And it is wholly and for ever theirs.
CHORAGOS: Is he in agony still? Is there no rest for him?
SECOND MESSENGER: He is calling for someone to open the doors wide
So that all the children of Kadmos may look upon
His father's murderer, his mother's—no,
I can not say it!
65   And then he will leave Thebes,
Self-exiled, in order that the curse
Which he himself pronounced may depart from the house.
He is weak, and there is none to lead him,
So terrible is his suffering.
But you will see:
70   Look, the doors are opening; in a moment
You will see a thing that would crush a heart of stone.

(The central door is opened; OEDIPUS, *blinded, is led in.)*

CHORAGOS: Dreadful indeed for men to see.
Never have my own eyes
Looked on a sight so full of fear.

75   Oedipus!
What madness came upon you, what demon
Leaped on your life with heavier
Punishment than a mortal man can bear?
No: I can not even
80   Look at you, poor ruined one.

And I would speak, question, ponder,
If I were able. No.
You make me shudder.
OEDIPUS: God. God.
    Is there a sorrow greater?   85
    Where shall I find harbor in this world?
    My voice is hurled far on a dark wind.
    What has God done to me?
CHORAGOS: Too terrible to think of, or to see.

Strophe 1
OEDIPUS: O cloud of night,   90
    Never to be turned away: night coming on,
    I can not tell how: night like a shroud!
    My fair winds brought me here.
                        O God. Again
    The pain of the spikes where I had sight,
    The flooding pain   95
    Of memory, never to be gouged out.
CHORAGOS: This is not strange.
    You suffer it all twice over, remorse in pain,
    Pain in remorse.

Antistrophe 1
OEDIPUS: Ah dear friend   100
    Are you faithful even yet, you alone?
    Are you still standing near me, will you stay here,
    Patient, to care for the blind?
                        The blind man!
    Yet even blind I know who it is attends me,
    By the voice's tone—   105
    Though my new darkness hide the comforter.
CHORAGOS: Oh fearful act!
    What god was it drove you to rake black
    Night across your eyes?

Strophe 2
OEDIPUS: Apollo. Apollo. Dear   110
    Children, the god was Apollo.
    He brought my sick, sick fate upon me.
    But the blinding hand was my own!
    How could I bear to see

115   When all my sight was horror everywhere?

CHORAGOS: Everywhere; that is true.

OEDIPUS: And now what is left?

        Images? Love? A greeting even,

        Sweet to the senses? Is there anything?

120   Ah, no, friends: lead me away.

        Lead me away from Thebes.

                        Lead the great wreck

        And hell of Oedipus, whom the gods hate.

CHORAGOS: Your misery, you are not blind to that.

        Would God you had never found it out!

Antistrophe 2

125 OEDIPUS: Death take the man who unbound

        My feet on that hillside

        And delivered me from death to life! What life?

        If only I had died,

        This weight of monstrous doom

130   Could not have dragged me and my darlings down.

CHORAGOS: I would have wished the same.

OEDIPUS: Oh never to have come here

        With my father's blood upon me! Never

        To have been the man they call his mother's husband!

135   Oh accurst! Oh child of evil,

        To have entered that wretched bed—

                        the selfsame one!

        More primal than sin itself, this fell to me.

CHORAGOS: I do not know what words to offer you.

        You were better dead than alive and blind.

140 OEDIPUS: Do not counsel me any more. This punishment

        That I have laid upon myself is just.

        If I had eyes,

        I do not know how I could bear the sight

        Of my father, when I came to the house of Death,

145   Or my mother: for I have sinned against them both

        So vilely that I could not make my peace

        By strangling my own life.

                        Or do you think my children,

        Born as they were born, would be sweet to my eyes?

        Ah never, never! Nor this town with its high walls,

        Nor the holy images of the gods.

150   For I,

        Thrice miserable!—Oedipus, noblest of all the line

Of Kadmos, have condemned myself to enjoy
These things no more, by my own malediction
Expelling that man whom the gods declared
To be a defilement in the house of Laios.   *155*
After exposing the rankness of my own guilt,
How could I look men frankly in the eyes?
No, I swear it,
If I could have stifled my hearing at its source,
I would have done it and made all this body   *160*
A tight cell of misery, blank to light and sound:
So I should have been safe in my dark mind
Beyond external evil.
                    Ah Kithairon!
Why did you shelter me? When I was cast upon you,
Why did I not die? Then I should never   *165*
Have shown the world my execrable birth.

Ah Polybos! Corinth, city that I believed
The ancient seat of my ancestors: how fair
I seemed, your child! And all the while this evil
Was cancerous within me!
                    For I am sick   *170*
In my own being, sick in my origin.
O three roads, dark ravine, woodland and way
Where three roads met; you, drinking my father's blood,
My own blood, spilled by my own hand: can you remember
The unspeakable things I did there, and the things   *175*
I went on from there to do?
                    O marriage, marriage!
The act that engendered me, and again the act
Performed by the son in the same bed—
                                        Ah, the net
Of incest, mingling fathers, brothers, sons,
With brides, wives, mothers: the last evil   *180*
That can be known by men: no tongue can say
How evil!
            No. For the love of God, conceal me
Somewhere far from Thebes; or kill me; or hurl me
Into the sea, away from men's eyes for ever.

Come, lead me. You need not fear to touch me.   *185*
Of all men, I alone can bear this guilt.

(Enter KREON.*)*

CHORAGOS: Kreon is here now. As to what you ask,
  He may decide the course to take. He only
  Is left to protect the city in your place.

190 OEDIPUS: Alas, how can I speak to him? What right have I
  To beg his courtesy whom I have deeply wronged?

KREON: I have not come to mock you, Oedipus,
  Or to reproach you, either.

(To ATTENDANTS.*)*   —You, standing there:
  If you have lost all respect for man's dignity,
195 At least respect the flame of Lord Helios:
  Do not allow this pollution to show itself
  Openly here, an affront to the earth
  And Heaven's rain and the light of day. No, take him
  Into the house as quickly as you can.
200 For it is proper
  That only the close kindred see his grief.

OEDIPUS: I pray you in God's name, since your courtesy
  Ignores my dark expectation, visiting
  With mercy this man of all men most execrable:
205 Give me what I ask—for your good, not for mine.

KREON: And what is it that you turn to me begging for?

OEDIPUS: Drive me out of this country as quickly as may be
  To a place where no human voice can ever greet me.

KREON: I should have done that before now—only,
210 God's will had not been wholly revealed to me.

OEDIPUS: But his command is plain: the parricide
  Must be destroyed. I am that evil man.

KREON: That is the sense of it, yes; but as things are,
  We had best discover clearly what is to be done.

215 OEDIPUS: You would learn more about a man like me?

KREON: You are ready now to listen to the god.

OEDIPUS: I will listen. But it is to you
  That I must turn for help. I beg you, hear me.

  The woman is there—
220 Give her whatever funeral you think proper:
  She is your sister.
     —But let me go, Kreon!
  Let me purge my father's Thebes of the pollution
  Of my living here, and go out to the wild hills,
  To Kithairon, that has won such fame with me,
225 The tomb my mother and father appointed for me,
  And let me die there, as they willed I should.
  And yet I know

Death will not ever come to me through sickness
Or in any natural way: I have been preserved
For some unthinkable fate. But let that be.   *230*

As for my sons, you need not care for them.
They are men, they will find some way to live.
But my poor daughters, who have shared my table,
Who never before have been parted from their father—
Take care of them, Kreon; do this for me.   *235*

And will you let me touch them with my hands
A last time, and let us weep together?
Be kind, my lord,
Great prince, be kind!
                      Could I but touch them,
They would be mine again, as when I had my eyes.   *240*

(Enter ANTIGONE *and* ISMENE, *attended.)*

Ah, God!
Is it my dearest children I hear weeping?
Has Kreon pitied me and sent my daughters?
KREON: Yes, Oedipus: I knew that they were dear to you
    In the old days, and know you must love them still.   *245*
OEDIPUS: May God bless you for this—and be a friendlier
    Guardian to you than he has been to me!

Children, where are you?
Come quickly to my hands: they are your brother's—
Hands that have brought your father's once clear eyes   *250*
To this way of seeing—
                      Ah dearest ones,
I had neither sight nor knowledge then, your father
By the woman who was the source of his own life!
And I weep for you—having no strength to see you—,
I weep for you when I think of the bitterness   *255*
That men will visit upon you all your lives.
What homes, what festivals can you attend
Without being forced to depart again in tears?
And when you come to marriageable age,
Where is the man, my daughters, who would dare   *260*
Risk the bane that lies on all my children?
Is there any evil wanting? Your father killed
His father; sowed the womb of her who bore him;
Engendered you at the fount of his own existence!

That is what they will say of you.

265   Then, whom
Can you ever marry? There are no bridegrooms for you,
And your lives must wither away in sterile dreaming.

O Kreon, son of Menoikeus!
You are the only father my daughters have,
270   Since we, their parents, are both of us gone for ever.
They are your own blood: you will not let them
Fall into beggary and loneliness;
You will keep them from the miseries that are mine!
Take pity on them; see, they are only children,
275   Friendless except for you. Promise me this,
Great prince, and give me your hand in token of it.

(KREON *clasps his right hand.*)

Children:
I could say much, if you could understand me,
But as it is, I have only this prayer for you:
280   Live where you can, be as happy as you can—
Happier, please God, than God has made your father.
KREON: Enough. You have wept enough. Now go within.
OEDIPUS: I must; but it is hard.
KREON: Time eases all things.
OEDIPUS: You know my mind, then?
KREON: Say what you desire.
OEDIPUS: Send me from Thebes!
285   KREON: God grant that I may!
OEDIPUS: But since God hates me . . .
KREON: No, he will grant your wish.
OEDIPUS: You promise?
KREON: I can not speak beyond my knowledge.
OEDIPUS: Then lead me in.
KREON: Come now, and leave your children.
OEDIPUS: No! Do not take them from me!
KREON: Think no longer
290   That you are in command here, but rather think
How, when you were, you served your own destruction.

(*Exeunt into the house all but the* CHORUS; *the* CHORAGOS *chants directly to the audience.*)

CHORAGOS: Men of Thebes: look upon Oedipus.

This is the king who solved the famous riddle
And towered up, most powerful of men.
No mortal eyes but looked on him with envy,   *295*
Yet in the end ruin swept over him.

Let every man in mankind's frailty
Consider his last day; and let none
Presume on his good fortune until he find
Life, at his death, a memory without pain.   *c. 430 B.C.*   *300*

CONSIDERATIONS

1. How do the references to light and darkness and seeing (vision) and blindness suggest the theme of the play? Consider especially the conflicts Oedipus faces and the way he resolves (or fails to resolve) these conflicts.
2. What are your responses to the gods as you finish reading the play? Consider, for example, the havoc they have brought to the lives of the people of Thebes. Do you see these actions as justified or as random and cruel? In your response, consider also the attitudes of the play's characters toward the gods. Do these characters seem reverent or merely fearful as they talk about and act in reaction to the will of the gods?
3. How would you evaluate the character of Iokaste? To what extent, if any, does she contribute to Oedipus's tragic downfall? How would you defend Iokaste's actions and decisions to people who might view her as an unsympathetic character?
4. Reread the Prologue, Scene 1, and Ode 1. Then list details that suggest the qualities of Oedipus's character as a leader, a son, and a husband. Write a description of Oedipus, incorporating these details where they are appropriate to support your observations about his strengths and weaknesses. What conclusions can you draw about the qualities necessary to be a father of a country? About the qualities necessary to be a good person? What, if any, conflict do you find between the public and personal roles Oedipus plays?
5. According to Freud, what exactly is an "Oedipus complex"? (You might do a search on the Internet for a definition of this concept.) How valid do you find this theory to be in terms of real life? At the heart of it, what is Freud saying about the mother–son relationship and human nature? What is the real need that all children have of their mothers? Explain.

More Resources on
Sophocles and *Oedipus Rex*

In *ARIEL*
- Brief biography of Sophocles
- Excerpt from *Oedipus Rex,* with hyperlinked comments
- Video clip of a performance from *Oedipus Rex*
- Video clip on theater in ancient Greece
- Analysis of Greek tragedy
- Bibliography of scholarly works on Sophocles

In the Online Learning Center for *Responding to Literature*
- Brief biography of Sophocles
- List of major works by Sophocles
- Scene III from *Oedipus Rex*
- Web links to more resources on Sophocles
- Additional questions for experiencing and interpreting Sophocles's writing

LANGSTON HUGHES (1902–1967)
Soul Gone Home

For biographical information about Langston Hughes see page 382.

Characters
THE MOTHER
THE SON
TWO MEN

Night.
  A tenement room, bare, ugly, dirty. An unshaded electric-light bulb. In the middle of the room a cot on which the body of a Negro youth is lying. His hands are folded across his chest. There are pennies on his eyes. He is a soul gone home.
  As the curtain rises, his mother, a large, middle-aged woman in a red sweater, kneels weeping beside the cot, loudly simulating grief.

MOTHER: Oh, Gawd! Oh Lawd! Why did you take my son from me? Oh, Gawd, why did you do it? He was all I had! Oh, Lawd, what am I gonna do? [*Looking at the dead boy and stroking his head.*] Oh, son! Oh, Ronnie!

Oh, my boy, speak to me! Ronnie, say something to me! Son, why don't
you talk to your mother? Can't you see she's bowed down in sorrow?   5
Son, speak to me, just a word! Come back from the spirit-world and speak
to me! Ronnie, come back from the dead and speak to your mother!

SON: [*lying there dead as a doornail, speaking loudly*]: I wish I wasn't dead, so I
could speak to you. You been a hell of a mama!

MOTHER: [*falling back from the cot in astonishment, but still on her knees*]: Ron-   10
nie! Ronnie! What's that you say? What you sayin' to your mother?
[*Wild-eyed.*] Is you done opened your mouth and spoke to me?

SON: I said you a hell of a mama!

MOTHER: [*rising suddenly and backing away, screaming loudly*]: Awo-oo-o! Ronnie, that ain't you talkin'!   15

SON: Yes, it is me talkin', too! I say you been a no-good mama.

MOTHER: What for you talkin' to me like that, Ronnie! You ain't never said
nothin' like that to me before.

SON: I know it, but I'm dead now—and I can say what I want to say. [*Stirring.*] You done called on me to talk, ain't you? Lemme take these pennies   20
off my eyes so I can see. [*He takes the coins off his eyes, throws them across the
room and sits up in bed. He is a very dark boy in a torn white shirt. He looks
hard at his mother.*] Mama, you know you ain't done me right.

MOTHER: What you mean, I ain't done you right? [*She is rooted in horror.*]
What you mean, huh?   25

SON: You know what I mean.

MOTHER: No, I don't neither. [*Trembling violently.*] What you mean comin'
back to haunt your poor old mother? Ronnie, what does you mean?

SON: [*leaning forward*]: I'll tell you just what I mean! You been a bad mother
to me.   30

MOTHER: Shame! Shame! Shame, talkin' to your mama that away. Damn it!
Shame! I'll slap your face. [*She starts toward him, but he rolls his big white
eyes at her, and she backs away.*] Me, what borned you! Me, what suffered
the pains o'death to bring you into this world! Me, what raised you up,
what washed your dirty didies. [*Sorrowfully.*] And now I'm left here   35
mighty nigh prostrate 'cause you gone from me! Ronnie, what you mean
talkin' to *me* like that—what brought you into this world?

SON: You never did feed me good, that's what I mean! Who wants to come
into the world hongry, and go out the same way?

MOTHER: What you mean hongry? When I had money, ain't I fed you?   40

SON: [*sullenly*]: Most of the time you ain't had no money.

MOTHER: Twarn't my fault then.

SON: Twarn't *my* fault neither.

MOTHER: [*defensively*]: You always was so weak and sickly, you couldn't earn
nothin' sellin' papers.   45

SON: I know it.

MOTHER: You never was no use to me.

SON: So you just lemme grow up in the street, and I ain't had no manners nor morals, neither.

50 MOTHER: Manners and morals? Ronnie, where'd you learn all them big words?

SON: I learnt 'em just now in the spirit-world.

MOTHER: [*coming nearer*]: But you ain't been dead no more'n an hour.

SON: That's long enough to learn a lot.

MOTHER: Well, what else did you find out?

55 SON: I found out you was a hell of a mama puttin' me out in the cold to sell papers soon as I could even walk.

MOTHER: What? You little liar!

SON: If I'm lyin', I'm dyin'! And lettin' me grow up all bowlegged and stunted from undernourishment.

60 MOTHER: Under-nurse-mint?

SON: Undernourishment. You heard what the doctor said last week?

MOTHER: Naw, what'd he say?

SON: He said I was dyin' o' undernourishment, that's what he said. He said I had TB 'cause I didn't have enough to eat never when I were a child.

65 And he said I couldn't get well, nohow eating nothin' but beans ever since I been sick. Said I needed milk and eggs. And you said you ain't got no money for milk and eggs, which I know you ain't. [*Gently*] We never had no money, mama, not even since you took up hustlin' on the streets

MOTHER: Son, money ain't everything.

70 SON: Naw, but when you got TB you have to have milk and eggs.

MOTHER: [*advancing sentimentally*]: Anyhow, I love you, Ronnie!

SON: [*rudely*]: Sure you love me—but here I am dead.

MOTHER: [*angrily*]: Well, damn your hide, you ain't even decent dead. If you was, you wouldn't be sittin' there jawin' at your mother when she's shed-

75 din' every tear she's got for you tonight.

SON: First time you ever did cry for me, far as I know.

MOTHER: Tain't! You's a liar! I cried when I borned you—you was such a big child—ten pounds.

SON: Then *I* did the cryin' after that, I reckon.

80 MOTHER: [*proudly*]: Sure, I could of let you die, but I didn't. Naw, I kept you with me—off and on. And I lost the chance to marry many a good man, too—if it weren't for you. No man wants to take care o' nobody else's child [*Self-pityingly.*] You been a burden to me, Randolph.

SON: [*angrily*]: What did you have me for then, in the first place?

85 MOTHER: How could I help havin' you, you little bastard? Your father ruint me—and you's the result. And I been worried with you for sixteen years. [*Disgustedly.*] Now, just when you get big enough to work and do me some good, you have to go and die.

SON: I sure am dead!

90 MOTHER: But you ain't decent dead! Here you come back to haunt your poor old mama and spoil her cryin' spell, and spoil the mournin'. [*There*

is the noise of an ambulance going outside. The mother goes to the window and looks down into the street. Turns to son.] Ronnie, lay down quick! Here comes the city's ambulance to take you to the undertaker's. Don't let them white men see you dead, sitting up here quarrelin' with your 95 mother. Lay down and fold your hands back like I had 'em.

SON: [*passing his hand across his head*]: All right, but gimme that comb yonder and my stocking cap. I don't want to go out of here with my hair standin' straight up in front, even if I is dead. [*The mother hands him a comb and his stocking cap. The son combs his hair and puts the cap on. Noise of men coming* 100 *up the stairs.*]

MOTHER: Hurry up, Ronnie, they'll be here in no time.

SON: Aw, they got another flight to come yet. Don't rush me, ma!

MOTHER: Yes, but I got to put these pennies back on your eyes, boy! [*She searches in a corner for the coins as her son lies down and folds his hands, stiff in* 105 *death. She finds the coins and puts them nervously on his eyes, watching the door meanwhile. A knock.*] Come in.

[*Enter two men in the white coats of city health employees.*]

MAN: Somebody sent for us to get the body of Ronnie Bailey? Third floor, apartment five.

MOTHER: Yes, sir, here he is! [*Weeping loudly.*] He's my boy! Oh, Lawd, 110 he's done left me! Oh, Lawdy, he's done gone home! His soul's gone home! Oh, what am I gonna do? Mister! Mister! Mister, the Lawd's done took him home! [*As the men unfold the stretchers, she continues to weep hysterically. They place the boy's thin body on the stretchers and cover it with a rubber cloth. Each man takes his end of the stretchers. Silently, they walk out the door* 115 *as the mother wails.*] Oh, my son! Oh, my boy! Come back, come back, come back! Ronnie, come back! [*One loud scream as the door closes.*] Awo-ooo-o!

[*As the footsteps of the men die down on the stairs, the mother becomes suddenly quiet. She goes to a broken mirror and begins to rouge and powder her face. In the street the ambulance gong sounds fainter and fainter in the distance. The mother takes down an old fur coat from a nail and puts it on. Before she leaves, she smoothes back the quilts on the cot from which the dead boy has been removed. She looks into the mirror again, and once more whitens her face with powder. She dons a red hat. From a handbag she takes a cigarette, lights it, and walks slowly out the door. At the door she switches off the light. The hallway is dimly illuminated. She turns before closing the door, looks back into the room and speaks.*]

MOTHER: Tomorrow, Ronnie, I'll buy you some flowers—if I can pick up a dollar tonight. You was a hell of a no-good son, I swear! 120

Curtain.

CONSIDERATIONS

1. In what ways do the details of the opening scene foreshadow the conflicts within this family as well as within their community? What relationship can you see between this isolated room and the African-American experience in the United States?

2. Who appears to be more resentful and angry in this play—the mother or the son? Explain your answer with specifics from the play.

3. Discuss the significance of the "ghost" in this play—the soul of the son that does all the speaking. What might Hughes be saying about the experience of African-American men in America? To what extent is this experience the same today?

4. React to the mother's character in this piece. To what extent is she to blame for the condition of her son and their life of poverty? Explain.

5. Trace the references to "white" in this play and discuss their symbolic value.

More Resources on
Langston Hughes

 In ARIEL
- Brief biography of Hughes
- Complete texts Hughes poems, such as "I, Too" and "Dream Deferred"
- Audio clip of reading of "Theme for English B"
- Analysis of figurative writing in Hughes's poetry
- Bibliography of scholarly works on Hughes

 In the Online Learning Center for *Responding to Literature*
- Brief biography of Hughes
- List of major works by Hughes
- Web links to more resources on Hughes
- Additional questions for experiencing and interpreting Hughes's writing

Essays

RAYMOND CARVER (1939–1988)
My Father's Life

For Biographical information on Raymond Carver, see page 437.

My dad's name was Clevie Raymond Carver. His family called him Raymond and friends called him C.R. I was named Raymond Clevie Carver Jr. I hated the "Junior" part. When I was little my dad called me Frog, which was okay. But later, like everybody else in the family, he began calling me Junior. He went on calling me this until I was thirteen or fourteen and announced that I wouldn't answer to that name any longer. So he began calling me Doc. From then until his death, on June 17, 1967, he called me Doc, or else Son.

When he died, my mother telephoned my wife with the news. I was away from my family at the time, between lives, trying to enroll in the School of Library Science at the University of Iowa. When my wife answered the phone, my mother blurted out, "Raymond's dead!" For a moment, my wife thought my mother was telling her that I was dead. Then my mother made it clear *which* Raymond she was talking about and my wife said, "Thank God, I thought you meant *my* Raymond."

My dad walked, hitched rides, and rode in empty boxcars when he went from Arkansas to Washington State in 1934, looking for work. I don't know whether he was pursuing a dream when he went out to Washington. I doubt it. I don't think he dreamed much. I believe he was simply looking for steady work at decent pay. Steady work was meaningful work. He picked apples for a time and then landed a construction laborer's job on the Grand Coulee Dam. After he'd put aside a little money, he bought a car and drove back to Arkansas to help his folks, my grandparents, pack up for the move west. He said later that they were about to starve down there, and this wasn't meant as a figure of speech. It was during that short while in Arkansas, in a town called Leola, that my mother met my dad on the sidewalk as he came out of a tavern.

"He was drunk," she said. "I don't know why I let him talk to me. His eyes were glittery. I wish I'd had a crystal ball." They'd met once, a year or so before, at a dance. He'd had girlfriends before her, my mother told me. "Your dad always had a girlfriend, even after we married. He was my first and last. I never had another man. But I didn't miss anything."

They were married by a justice of the peace on the day they left for Washington, this big, tall country girl and a farmhand-turned-construction worker. My mother spent her wedding night with my dad and his folks, all of them camped beside the road in Arkansas. 5

In Omak, Washington, my dad and mother lived in a little place not much bigger than a cabin. My grandparents lived next door. My dad was still working on the dam, and later, with the huge turbines producing electricity and the water backed up for a hundred miles into Canada, he stood in the crowd and heard Franklin D. Roosevelt when he spoke at the construction site. "He never mentioned those guys who died building that dam," my dad said. Some of his friends had died there, men from Arkansas, Oklahoma, and Missouri.

He then took a job in a sawmill in Clatskanie, Oregon, a little town alongside the Columbia River. I was born there, and my mother has a picture of my dad standing in front of the gate to the mill, proudly holding me up to face the camera. My bonnet is on crooked and about to come untied. His hat is pushed back on his forehead, and he's wearing a big grin. Was he going in to work or just finishing his shift? It doesn't matter. In either case, he had a job and a family. These were his salad days.

In 1941 we moved to Yakima, Washington, where my dad went to work as a saw filer, a skilled trade he'd learned in Clatskanie. When war broke out, he was given a deferment because his work was considered necessary to the war effort. Finished lumber was in demand by the armed services, and he kept his saws so sharp they could shave the hair off your arm.

After my dad had moved us to Yakima, he moved his folks into the same neighborhood. By the mid-1940s the rest of my dad's family—his brother, his sister, and her husband, as well as uncles, cousins, nephews, and most of their extended family and friends—had come out from Arkansas. All because my dad came out first. The men went to work at Boise Cascade, where my dad worked, and the women packed apples in the canneries. And in just a little while, it seemed—according to my mother—everybody was better off than my dad. "Your dad couldn't keep money," my mother said. "Money burned a hole in his pocket. He was always doing for others."

10   The first house I clearly remember living in, at 1515 South Fifteenth Street, in Yakima, had an outdoor toilet. On Halloween night, or just any night, for the hell of it, neighbor kids, kids in their early teens, would carry our toilet away and leave it next to the road. My dad would have to get somebody to help him bring it home. Or these kids would take the toilet and stand it in somebody else's backyard. Once they actually set it on fire. But ours wasn't the only house that had an outdoor toilet. When I was old enough to know what I was doing, I threw rocks at the other toilets when I'd see someone go inside. This was called bombing the toilets. After a while, though, everyone went to indoor plumbing until, suddenly, our toilet was the last outdoor one in the neighborhood. I remember the shame I felt when my third-grade teacher, Mr. Wise, drove me home from school one day. I asked him to stop at the house just before ours, claiming I lived there.

I can recall what happened one night when my dad came home late to find that my mother had locked all the doors on him from the inside. He was drunk, and we could feel the house shudder as he rattled the door. When he'd managed to force open a window, she hit him between the eyes with a colander and knocked him out. We could see him down there on the grass. For years afterward, I used to pick up this colander—it was as heavy as a rolling pin—and imagine what it would feel like to be hit in the head with something like that.

It was during this period that I remember my dad taking me into the bedroom, sitting me down on the bed, and telling me that I might have to go live with my Aunt LaVon for a while. I couldn't understand what I'd done that meant I'd have to go away from home to live. But this, too—whatever prompted it—must have blown over, more or less, anyway, because we stayed together, and I didn't have to go live with her or anyone else.

I remember my mother pouring his whiskey down the sink. Sometimes she'd pour it all out and sometimes, if she was afraid of getting caught, she'd only pour half of it out and then add water to the rest. I tasted some of his whiskey once myself. It was terrible stuff, and I don't see how anybody could drink it.

After a long time without one, we finally got a car, in 1949 or 1950, a 1938 Ford. But it threw a rod the first week we had it, and my dad had to have the motor rebuilt.

"We drove the oldest car in town," my mother said. "We could have had   15
a Cadillac for all he spent on car repairs." One time she found someone else's tube of lipstick on the floorboard, along with a lacy handkerchief. "See this?" she said to me. "Some floozy left this in the car."

Once I saw her take a pan of warm water into the bedroom where my dad was sleeping. She took his hand from under the covers and held it in the water. I stood in the doorway and watched. I wanted to know what was going on. This would make him talk in his sleep, she told me. There were things she needed to know, things she was sure he was keeping from her.

Every year or so, when I was little, we would take the North Coast Limited across the Cascade Range from Yakima to Seattle and stay in the Vance Hotel and eat, I remember, at a place called the Dinner Bell Cafe. Once we went to Ivar's Acres of Clams and drank glasses of warm clam broth.

In 1956, the year I was to graduate from high school, my dad quit his job at the mill in Yakima and took a job in Chester, a little sawmill town in northern California. The reasons given at the time for his taking the job had to do with a higher hourly wage and the vague promise that he might, in a few year's time, succeed to the job of head filer in this new mill. But I think, in the main, that my dad had grown restless and simply wanted to try his luck elsewhere. Things had gotten a little too predictable for him in Yakima. Also, the year before, there had been the deaths, within six months of each other, of both his parents.

But just a few days after graduation, when my mother and I were packed to move to Chester, my dad penciled a letter to say he'd been sick for a while. He didn't want us to worry, he said, but he'd cut himself on a saw. Maybe he'd got a tiny sliver of steel in his blood. Anyway, something had happened and he'd had to miss work, he said. In the same mail was an unsigned postcard from somebody down there telling my mother that my dad was about to die and that he was drinking "raw whiskey."

20   When we arrived in Chester, my dad was living in a trailer that belonged to the company. I didn't recognize him immediately. I guess for a moment I didn't want to recognize him. He was skinny and pale and looked bewildered. His pants wouldn't stay up. He didn't look like my dad. My mother began to cry. My dad put his arm around her and patted her shoulder vaguely, like he didn't know what this was all about, either. The three of us took up life together in the trailer, and we looked after him as best we could But my dad was sick, and he couldn't get any better. I worked with him in the mill that summer and part of the fall. We'd get up in the mornings and eat eggs and toast while we listened to the radio, and then go out the door with our lunch pails. We'd pass through the gate together at eight in the morning, and I wouldn't see him again until quitting time. In November I went back to Yakima to be closer to my girlfriend, the girl I'd made up my mind I was going to marry.

He worked at the mill in Chester until the following February, when he collapsed on the job and was taken to the hospital. My mother asked if I would come down there and help. I caught a bus from Yakima to Chester, intending to drive them back to Yakima. But now, in addition to being physically sick, my dad was in the midst of a nervous breakdown, though none of us knew to call it that at the time. During the entire trip back to Yakima, he didn't speak, not even when asked a direct question. ("How do you feel, Raymond?" "You okay, Dad?") He'd communicate, if he communicated at all, by moving his head or by turning his palms up as if to say he didn't know or care. The only time he said anything on the trip, and for nearly a month afterward, was when I was speeding down a gravel road in Oregon and the car muffler came loose. "You were going too fast," he said.

Back in Yakima a doctor saw to it that my dad went to a psychiatrist. My mother and dad had to go on relief, as it was called, and the county paid for the psychiatrist. The psychiatrist asked my dad, "Who is the President?" He'd had a question put to him that he could answer. "Ike," my dad said. Nevertheless, they put him on the fifth floor of Valley Memorial Hospital and began giving him electroshock treatments. I was married by then and about to start my own family. My dad was still locked up when my wife went into this same hospital, just one floor down, to have our first baby. After she had delivered, I went upstairs to give my dad the news. They let me in through a steel door and showed me where I could find him. He was sitting on a couch with a blanket over his lap. *Hey*, I thought. *What in hell is happening to my dad?* I sat down next to him and told him he was a grandfather. He waited a minute and then he said, "I feel like a grandfather." That's all he said. He didn't smile or move. He was in a big room with a lot of other people. Then I hugged him, and he began to cry.

Somehow he got out of there. But now came the years when he couldn't work and just sat around the house trying to figure what next and what he'd done wrong in his life that he'd wound up like this. My mother went from job to crummy job. Much later she referred to that time he was in the hospital, and those years just afterward, as "when Raymond was sick." The word *sick* was never the same for me again.

In 1964, through the help of a friend, he was lucky enough to be hired on at a mill in Klamath, California. He moved down there by himself to see if he could hack it. He lived not far from the mill, in a one-room cabin not much different from the place he and my mother had started out living in when they went west. He scrawled letters to my mother, and if I called she'd read them aloud to me over the phone. In the letters, he said it was touch and go. Every day that he went to work, he felt like it was the most important day of his life. But every day, he told her, made the next day that much easier. He said for her to tell me he said hello. If he couldn't sleep at night, he said, he thought about me and the good times we used to have. Finally, after a couple of months, he regained some of his confidence. He could do the work and didn't think he had to worry that he'd let anybody down ever again. When he was sure, he sent for my mother.

He'd been off from work for six years and had lost everything in that time—home, car, furniture, and appliances, including the big freezer that had been my mother's pride and joy. He'd lost his good name too—Raymond Carver was someone who couldn't pay his bills—and his self-respect was gone. He'd even lost his virility. My mother told my wife, "All during that time Raymond was sick we slept together in the same bed, but we didn't have relations. He wanted to a few times, but nothing happened. I didn't miss it, but I think he wanted to, you know." 25

During those years I was trying to raise my own family and earn a living. But, one thing and another, we found ourselves having to move a lot. I couldn't keep track of what was going down in my dad's life. But I did have a chance one Christmas to tell him I wanted to be a writer. I might as well have told him I wanted to become a plastic surgeon. "What are you going to write about?" he wanted to know. Then, as if to help me out, he said "Write about stuff you know about. Write about some of those fishing trips we took." I said I would, but I knew I wouldn't. "Send me what you write," he said. I said I'd do that, but then I didn't. I wasn't writing anything about fishing, and I didn't think he'd particularly care about, or even necessarily understand, what I was writing in those days. Besides, he wasn't a reader. Not the sort, anyway, I imagined I was writing for.

Then he died. I was a long way off, in Iowa City, with things still to say to him. I didn't have the chance to tell him goodbye, or that I thought he was doing great at his new job. That I was proud of him for making a comeback.

My mother said he came in from work that night and ate a big supper. Then he sat at the table by himself and finished what was left of a bottle of whiskey, a bottle she found hidden in the bottom of the garbage under some coffee grounds a day or so later. Then he got up and went to bed, where my mother joined him a little later. But in the night she had to get up and make a bed for herself on the couch. "He was snoring so loud I couldn't sleep," she said. The next morning when she looked in on him, he was on his back with his mouth open, his cheeks caved in. *Graylooking* she said. She knew he was dead—she didn't need a doctor to tell her that. But she called one anyway, and then she called my wife.

Among the pictures my mother kept of my dad and herself during those early days in Washington was a photograph of him standing in front of a car, holding a beer and a stringer of fish. In the photograph he is wearing his hat back on his forehead and has this awkward grin on his face. I asked her for it and she gave it to me, along with some others. I put it up on my wall, and each time we moved, I took the picture along and put it up on another wall. I looked at it carefully from time to time, trying to figure out some things about my dad, and maybe myself in the process. But I couldn't. My dad just kept moving further and further away from me and back into time. Finally, in the course of another move, I lost the photograph. It was then that I tried to recall it, and at the same time make an attempt to say something about my dad, and how I thought that in some important ways we might be alike. I wrote the poem when I was living in an apartment house in an urban area south of San Francisco, at a time when I found myself, like my dad, having trouble with alcohol. The poem was a way of trying to connect up with him.

PHOTOGRAPH OF MY FATHER IN HIS TWENTY-SECOND YEAR

> *October.* Here in this dank, unfamiliar kitchen
> I study my father's embarrassed young man's face.
> Sheepish grin, he holds in one hand a string
> of spiny yellow perch, in the other
> a bottle of Carlsberg beer.
>
> In jeans and flannel shirt, he leans
> against the front fender of a 1934 Ford.
> He would like to pose brave and hearty for his posterity,
> wear his old hat cocked over his ear.
> All his life my father wanted to be bold.
>
> But the eyes give him away, and the hands
> that limply offer the string of dead perch
> and the bottle of beer. Father, I love you,
> yet how can I say thank you, I who can't hold my liquor either
> and don't even know the places to fish.

30   The poem is true in its particulars, except that my dad died in June and not October, as the first word of the poem says. I wanted a word with more

than one syllable to it to make it linger a little. But more than that, I wanted a month appropriate to what I felt at the time I wrote the poem—a month of short days and failing light, smoke in the air, things perishing. June was summer nights and days, graduations, my wedding anniversary, the birthday of one of my children. June wasn't a month your father died in.

After the service at the funeral home, after we had moved outside, a woman I didn't know came over to me and said, "He's happier where he is now." I stared at this woman until she moved away. I still remember the little knob of a hat she was wearing. Then one of my dad's cousins—I didn't know the man's name—reached out and took my hand. "We all miss him," he said, and I knew he wasn't saying it just to be polite.

I began to weep for the first time since receiving the news. I hadn't been able to before. I hadn't had the time, for one thing. Now, suddenly, I couldn't stop. I held my wife and wept while she said and did what she could do to comfort me there in the middle of that summer afternoon.

I listened to people saying consoling things to my mother, and I was glad that my dad's family had turned up, had come to where he was. I thought I'd remember everything that was said and done that day and maybe find a way to tell it sometime. But I didn't. I forgot it all, or nearly. What I do remember is that I heard our name used a lot that afternoon, my dad's name and mine. But I knew they were talking about my dad. *Raymond*, these people kept saying in their beautiful voices out of my childhood. *Raymond*.

CONSIDERATIONS

1. From the opening paragraph alone, what conclusions can you draw about Carver, his father, and their relationship?
2. What are some possible reasons Carver's mother stayed on with her husband despite all of his shortcomings? In what way does time and place shape a family's identity?
3. What forces, including social, historical, and personal, contribute to the downfall of Carver's father? Which one do you think is most powerful in determining the course this family takes? Explain.
4. In his poem, Carver shows a picture of his father with a string of fish in one hand and a beer in the other. Analyze the opposing forces that these objects symbolize.
5. As writers know, the more specific details they provide to support their ideas, the more universal the message becomes. What then are the universal messages that this essay might be delivering regarding fathers and sons? Husbands and wives? Mothers and sons? Family dynamics in general?

JUDITH ORTIZ COFER (1952–   )

A Partial Remembrance of a Puerto Rican Childhood

Born in Puerto Rico, Judith Ortiz Cofer spent her early years moving from place to place within Puerto Rico and the mainland United States in accordance with the orders received by her father, a career officer in the navy. Because of these moves, she attended school in many different cultural environments, earning an M.A. in English from the University of Florida and pursuing further graduate work at Oxford University in England. In "Casa," Ortiz Cofer focuses on the importance of the afternoons she spent visiting at her grandmother's house, where she came to know well the wit and wisdom of the female members of her extended family.

At three or four o'clock in the afternoon, the hour of *café con leche*, the women of my family gathered in Mamá's living room to speak of important things and retell familiar stories meant to be overheard by us young girls, their daughters. In Mamá's house (everyone called my grandmother Mamá) was a large parlor built by my grandfather to his wife's exact specifications so that it was always cool, facing away from the sun. The doorway was on the side of the house so no one could walk directly into her living room. First they had to take a little stroll through and around her beautiful garden where prize-winning orchids grew in the trunk of an ancient tree she had hollowed out for that purpose. This room was furnished with several mahogany rocking chairs, acquired at the births of her children, and one intricately carved rocker that had passed down to Mamá at the death of her own mother.

It was on these rockers that my mother, her sisters, and my grandmother sat on these afternoons of my childhood to tell their stories, teaching each other, and my cousin and me, what it was like to be a woman, more specifically, a Puerto Rican woman. They talked about life on the island, and life in *Los Nueva Yores*, their way of referring to the United States from New York City to California: the other place, not home, all the same. They told real-life stories though, as I later learned, always embellishing them with a little or a lot of dramatic detail. And they told *cuentos*, the morality and cautionary tales told by the women in our family for generations: stories that became a part of my subconscious as I grew up in two worlds, the tropical island and the cold city, and that would later surface in my dreams and in my poetry.

One of these tales was about the woman who was left at the altar. Mamá liked to tell that one with histrionic intensity. I remember the rise and fall of her voice, the sighs, and her constantly gesturing hands, like two birds swooping through her words. This particular story usually would come up in a conversation as a result of someone mentioning a forthcoming engagement or wedding. The first time I remember hearing it, I was sitting on the floor at Mamá's feet, pretending to read a comic book. I may have been eleven or twelve years old, at that difficult age when a girl was no longer a child who could be ordered to leave the room if the women wanted freedom to take their talk into forbidden zones, nor really old enough to be considered a part of their conclave. I could only sit quietly, pretending to be in another world, while absorbing it all in a sort of unspoken agreement of my status as silent auditor. On this day, Mamá had taken my long, tangled mane of hair into her ever-busy hands. Without looking down at me and with no interruption of her flow of words, she began braiding my hair, working at it with the quickness and determination that characterized all her actions. My mother was watching us impassively from her rocker across the room. On her lips played a little ironic smile. I would never sit still for *her* ministrations, but even then, I instinctively knew that she did not possess Mamá's matriarchal power to command and keep everyone's attention. This was never more evident than in the spell she cast when telling a story.

"It is not like it used to be when I was a girl," Mamá announced. "Then, a man could leave a girl standing at the church altar with a bouquet of fresh flowers in her hands and disappear off the face of the earth. No way to track him down if he was from another town. He could be a married man, with maybe even two or three families all over the island. There was no way to know. And there were men who did this. Hombres with the devil in their flesh who would come to a pueblo, like this one, take a job at one of the haciendas, never meaning to stay, only to have a good time and to seduce the women."

The whole time she was speaking, Mamá would be weaving my hair   5 into a flat plait that required pulling apart the two sections of hair with little jerks that made my eyes water; but knowing how grandmother detested whining and *boba* (sissy) tears, as she called them, I just sat up as straight and stiff as I did at La Escuela San José, where the nuns enforced good posture with a flexible plastic ruler they bounced off of slumped shoulders and heads. As Mamá's story progressed, I noticed how my young Aunt Laura lowered her eyes, refusing to meet Mamá's meaningful gaze. Laura was seventeen, in her last year of high school, and already engaged to a boy from another town who had staked his claim with a tiny diamond ring, then left for Los Nueva Yores to make his fortune. They were planning to get married in a year. Mamá had expressed serious doubts that the wedding would ever take place. In Mamá's eyes, a man set free without a legal contract was a man lost. She believed that marriage was not something men desired, but simply the price they had to pay for the privilege of children and, of course, for what no decent (synonymous with "smart") woman would give away for free.

"María La Loca was only seventeen when *it* happened to her." I listened closely at the mention of this name. María was a town character, a fat middle-aged woman who lived with her old mother on the outskirts of town. She was to be seen around the pueblo delivering the meat pies the two women made for a living. The most peculiar thing about María, in my eyes, was that she walked and moved like a little girl though she had the thick body and wrinkled face of an old woman. She would swing her hips in an exaggerated, clownish way, and sometimes even hop and skip up to someone's house. She spoke to no one. Even if you asked her a question, she would just look at you and smile, showing her yellow teeth. But I had heard that if you got close enough, you could hear her humming a tune without words. The kids yelled out nasty things to her, calling her *La Loca*, and the men who hung out at the bodega playing dominoes sometimes whistled mockingly as she passed by with her funny, out-landish walk. But María seemed impervious to it all, carrying her basket of *pasteles* like a grotesque Little Red Riding Hood through the forest.

María La Loca interested me, as did all the eccentrics and crazies of our pueblo. Their weirdness was a measuring stick I used in my serious quest for a definition of normal. As a Navy brat shuttling between New Jersey and the pueblo, I was constantly made to feel like an oddball by my peers, who made fun of my two-way accent: a Spanish accent when I spoke English, and when I spoke Spanish I was told that I sounded like a *Gringa*. Being the outsider had already turned my brother and me into cultural chameleons. We developed early on the ability to blend into a crowd, to sit and read quietly in a fifth story apartment building for days and days when it was too bitterly cold to play out-side, or, set free, to run wild in Mamá's realm, where she took charge of our lives, releasing Mother for a while from the intense fear for our safety that our father's absences instilled in her. In order to keep us from harm when Father was away, Mother kept us under strict surveillance. She even walked us to and from Public School No. 11, which we attended during the months we lived in Paterson, New Jersey, our home base in the states. Mamá freed all three of us like pigeons from a cage. I saw her as my liberator and my model. Her stories were like parables from which to glean the *Truth*.

"María La Loca was once a beautiful girl. Everyone thought she would marry the Méndez boy." As everyone knew, Rogelio Méndez was the richest man in town. "But," Mamá continued, knitting my hair with the same inten-sity she was putting into her story, "this *macho* made a fool out of her and ru-ined her life." She paused for the effect of her use of the word *macho*, which at that time had not yet become a popular epithet for an unliberated man. This word had for us the crude and comical connotation of "male of the species," stud; a *macho* was what you put in a pen to increase your stock.

I peeked over my comic book at my mother. She too was under Mamá's spell, smiling conspiratorially at this little swipe at men. She was safe from Mamá's contempt in this area. Married at an early age, an unspotted lamb, she had been accepted by a good family of strict Spaniards whose name was old and respected, though their fortune had been lost long before my birth. In a rocker Papá had painted sky blue sat Mamá's oldest child, Aunt Nena. Mother of three children, step-mother of two more, she was a quiet woman who liked books but had married an ignorant and abusive widower whose main interest in life was accumulating wealth. He too was in the mainland working on his dream of returning home rich and triumphant to buy the *finca* of his dreams. She was waiting for him to send for her. She would leave her children with Mamá for several years while the two of them slaved away in factories. He would one day be a rich man, and she a sadder woman. Even now her life-light was dimming. She spoke little, an aberration in Mamá's house, and she read avidly, as if storing up spiritual food for the long winters that awaited her in Los Nueva Yores without her family. But even Aunt Nena came alive to Mamá's words, rocking gently, her hands over a thick book in her lap.

Her daughter, my cousin Sara, played jacks by herself on the tile porch   *10* outside the room where we sat. She was a year older than I. We shared a bed and all our family's secrets. Collaborators in search of answers, Sara and I discussed everything we heard the women say, trying to fit it all together like a puzzle that, once assembled, would reveal life's mysteries to us. Though she and I still enjoyed taking part in boys' games—chase, vollyball and even *vaqueros*, the island version of cowboys and Indian involving capgun battles and violent shoot-outs under the mango tree in Mamá's backyard—we loved best the quiet hours in the afternoon when the men were still at work and the boys had gone to play serious baseball at the park. Then Mamá's house belonged only to us women. The aroma of coffee perking in the kitchen, the mesmerizing creaks and groans of the rockers, and the women telling their lives in *cuentos* are forever woven into the fabric of my imagination, braided like my hair that day I felt my grandmother's hands teaching me about strength, her voice convincing me of the power of storytelling.

That day Mamá told how the beautiful María had fallen prey to a man whose name was never the same in subsequent versions of the story; it was Juan one time, José, Rafael, Diego, another. We understood that neither the name nor any of the *facts* were important, only that a woman had allowed love to defeat her. Mamá put each of us in María's place by describing her wedding dress in loving detail: how she looked like a princess in her lace as she waited at the altar. Then, as Mamá approached the tragic denouement of her story, I was distracted by the sound of my Aunt Laura's violent rocking. She seemed on the verge of tears. She knew the fable was intended for her. That week she was going to have her wedding gown fitted, though no firm date had been set for the marriage. Mamá ignored Laura's obvious discomfort, digging out a ribbon from the sewing basket she kept by her rocker while describing María's long illness, "a fever that would not break for days." She spoke of a mother's despair: "that woman climbed the church steps on her knees every morning, wore only black as a *promesa* to the Holy Virgin in exchange for her daughter's health." By the time María returned from her honeymoon with death, she was ravished, no longer young or sane. "As you can see, she is almost as old as her mother already," Mamá lamented while tying the ribbon to the ends of my hair, pulling it back with such force that I just knew I would never be able to close my eyes completely again.

"That María is getting crazier every day." Mamá's voice would take a lighter tone now, expressing satisfaction, either for the perfection of my braid, or for a story well told—it was hard to tell. "You know that tune María is always humming?" Carried away by her enthusiasm, I tried to nod, but Mamá still had me pinned between her knees.

"Well, that's the wedding march." Surprising us all, Mama sang out, "Da, da, dara . . . da, da, dara." Then lifting me off the floor by my skinny shoulders, she would lead me around the room in an impromptu waltz—another session ending with the laughter of women, all of us caught up in the infectious joke of our lives.

CONSIDERATIONS

1. What do all three generations of women in this piece have in common? In what ways are they different?
2. What is Mamá's purpose in retelling the story of María La Loca, and what effect does it have on the women in her audience? What effect did it have on you?
3. Respond to Mamá's belief that "marriage was not something men desired, but simply the price they had to pay for the privilege of children and, of course, for what no decent (synonymous with 'smart') woman would give away for free."
4. Although not stated, what might Mamá say about the reasons that women get married? What is the moral of the María La Loca story and women's reasons for marrying?
5. Compare and contrast the relationships that females in this essay have with males depending on their ages. In what ways are these relationships unique to the culture described in this essay? In what ways are they universal.

Photo Essay

THEN AND NOW
Images of Families

The images in this photo essay all depict some aspect of family life, and provide snapshots of the family at various points in history, from the early Greek civilization and to the present day. Some of the images suggest the peace, strength, joy, and comfort that family members gain from living together. Some suggest the problems, pain, and challenges that sometimes result from conflicts within families.

PHOTO 1   The first image, a detail from the marble relief on a sarcophagus, was created in the third century, C.E., in Greece and depicts the infant prince, Oedipus, being abandoned on a remote mountainside. The shepherd who leaves him there has been directed to take him from the palace in response to the oracle's prediction that he will someday kill his father. The complicated relationships and tragedies that result from the abandonment and subsequent rescue of Oedipus might stand as the prototype of what today is termed the "dysfunctional family."

PHOTO 1

PHOTO 2

PHOTO 2   Jacob Lawrence's depiction of an African-American family, rejoicing at the birth of their child, comes from the series on Harriet Tubman's life called *Harriet and the Promised Land*. As an adult, Tubman, who was born a slave in 1819 or 1820 in Maryland, led approximately 300 slaves to freedom in the North as a conductor on the Underground Railroad. One of the most tragic aspects of slavery was the way this institution tore families apart. Among the first people Tubman led to freedom, guided according to legend by the North Star, were members of her own family. The joy and possibility suggested in this painting come from the eager, engaged posture of both parents, from the suggestions of smiles on their faces, and, of course, from the star in the sky, which serves as an allusion to the birth of Christ.

PHOTO 3   The third photograph shows an extended
family from the early decades
of the twentieth century
standing on a porch. Each
person holds a banjo, ready to
play. The house, which is in
need of paint, the weeds that
grow near the porch, and the
clothing of the family members all indicate that these are
not wealthy people. Yet, the
banjos suggest that these family members experience at
least some moments of harmony and creativity in their
lives. In addition, this family
group reminds us that playing
instruments, singing, reading,
and other such activities were
often important activities for
nineteenth and early twentieth-
century families.

PHOTO 3

PHOTO 4

PHOTO 4   With the advent
and spread of television in the
1950s and 1960s, family life
began to be portrayed in dramas and situation comedies.
The still from the 1954–1963
family situation comedy
Father Knows Best captures a
moment when the children,
played by Billy Gray, Elinor
Donahue, and Lauren Chapin,
all gather around Father,
played by Robert Young. As
the children gaze adoringly at
their father, their mother,
played by Jane Wyatt, stands
off to the side and seems to

puzzle over a problem. While the television programs of the 1950s and early 1960s often portrayed family life as idyllic, with the characters experiencing only temporary and humorous problems, this photo (probably inadvertently) suggests that not all family members were endlessly overjoyed with the traditional structure.

PHOTOS 5 AND 6   The last two photos, along with the photo at the beginning of this chapter, offer images of the changes in family life that are part of the late twentieth and early twenty-first centuries. The photograph by Sally Mann, "The New Mothers," shows two young girls with their dolls. Yet their clothes, hairstyles, and especially their posture suggest that constant exposure to influences, perhaps from within their families and perhaps from beyond their families (including from the media), have made them sophisticated beyond their years. The photo of a lesbian couple with their daughter suggests a nontraditional family structure. Another nontraditional family structure blends children from previous marriages into the lives of new partners. The photograph at the beginning of the chapter on page 690 shows a firefighter and massage therapist who met in the aftermath of the terrorist attack on

PHOTO 5

Photo 6

September 11, 2001, and subsequently married and formed a blended family
that includes his daughter and her son from previous marriages.

CONSIDERATIONS

1. Consider the relationships between mothers and daughters as suggested in
   the photographs of Jacob Lawrence's *Harriet and the Promised Land*, the still
   from *Father Knows Best*, and the lesbian couple with their daughter. Compare these images with the depiction of the relationship between mothers
   and daughters in any of the following selections: "I Stand Here Ironing,"
   "Shopping," "Everyday Use," and "A Partial Remembrance of a Puerto
   Rican Childhood."
2. Consider the relationships between fathers and their children as suggested
   in the photographs of the sculpture of Oedipus being abandoned, the still
   from *Father Knows Best*, and the wedding of the New York firefighter.
   Compare these images with the depictions of the relationship between fathers and their children in any of the following selections: "My Papa's
   Waltz," "Those Winter Sundays," *Oedipus Rex*, and "My Father's Life."

3. Jacob Lawrence's *Harriet and the Promised Land* suggests one aspect of the African-American experience in the United States. Compare and contrast the details in this painting with the details in "Everyday Use" and "Soul Gone Home."

4. After looking at these images, write a definition of what you would consider to be a strong, happy family. Use details from the photographs to illustrate and develop your definition. Consider the definition you have written in relationship to the story "Who's Irish?" the poem "Those Winter Sundays," and the essay "A Partial Remembrance of a Puerto Rican Childhood." According to your definition, would you consider the families depicted in these selections to be strong and happy? Explain.

5. Choose any of the images and any of the selections in this chapter as possible examples for discussing the ways in which family structure and family life seem to have changed or remained the same from the time of the Greek civilization to the present.

CONNECTIONS: FAMILIES

1. In this chapter, many of the works deal in some way with children who are separated from (or are becoming separate from) their parents. Consider issues relating to separation as part of the parent-child relationship. In what ways do you see separation as harmful? As necessary? Important for growth?

2. Several selections in this unit reveal parents and children experiencing varying degrees of conflict. Why does conflict seem to occur between parents and children? Consider all of the works you have read and write an essay that illustrates the different levels of the reasons for, and the results of, conflict.

3. In some of the selections, respect and love for a parent or caretaker is obvious. Using two or more of these works, define what it means to have respect and love for a parent, and discuss how these two terms are not the same. In some of these pieces, you could also explore how love and respect change as a child matures and grows to adulthood. Possibilities for consideration include "How Far She Went," "Who's Irish?" "My Father's Life," "Family Plot, October," and "Terminal Resemblance."

4. The works in this chapter offer many different portraits of family life and the relationships between parents and children. Analyze these relationships in terms of specific pairings: Mother/son relationships: "My Father's Life," "Driving Lessons'" *Oedipus Rex*, and *Soul Gone Home*. Mother/daughter relationships: "I Stand Here Ironing," "Everyday Use," "Who's Irish?" "The Possessive," and "How Far She Went." Father/children relationships: "My Papa's Waltz," "My Son, My Executioner," "Those Winter Sundays," "Terminal Resemblance," and "My Father's Life."

5. Consider the impact of economic circumstances on relationships within the family as suggested in "I Stand Here Ironing," "Shopping," *Soul Gone Home*, and "My Father's Life."

SUGGESTIONS FOR EXTENDED CONNECTIONS AMONG CHAPTERS

1. Consider the family patterns that add to the conflict in the following selections. In addition to destructive patterns, note patterns that help heal and promote individual wellness and family unity. What are the forces that hinder family relationships and what are the ones that foster successful relationships?

"The Red Convertible"	218
"Sonny's Blues"	412
Oedipus Rex	748
"The Management of Grief"	948
"Videotape"	1063
"The Man Who Was Almost a Man"	402
Trifles	666
"My Flamboyant Grandson"	1067

2. Investigate how traditions and cultures affect family members in different ways in the following pieces. In addition, consider synthesizing observations and experiences from within your own family as you think about the following selections.

"The Red Convertible"	218
"Salvation"	382
"Graduation in Stamps"	385
"The Lesson"	456
A Doll's House	608
"The Things They Carried"	934
"The Management of Grief"	948
Riders to the Sea	874

3. Often, forces outside of the family, natural as well as social, cause conflicts within the family. Use the following selections to examine how outside forces affect a family and to what extent family members are able to control or change these forces or to alter their own responses to them.

"The Red Convertible"	218
"The Management of Grief"	948
"Sonny's Blues"	412
Oedipus Rex	748
"Goodbye, Saigon, Finally"	1011
"The Shawl"	929
Trifles	666

4. In what ways do mothers and fathers affect their children's growth and development? What similarities do they have? What are their differences? What is it that children need most in order to become stable adults? Consider the following selections as you explore these questions:

SUGGESTIONS FOR COLLABORATIVE LEARNING

1. Often, the secret of understanding poetry is in listening to the unspoken words, the spaces in between. Working in groups of two or three, select any one poem from this section and transform it into a short story, focusing on probable dialogue, description, and actions that are beneath the surface of the poem. Once the story has been written, compare it to the original poem. What has been lost? What has been gained?

2. The version of the truth in any story, essay, or poem often depends on the narrator's slant or perspective. Is the narrator a detached observer or an active participant who is coming to terms with a problem? Working in groups of two or three, discuss one piece from this chapter where another narrator could change the reader's perception of truth. For example, "Everyday Use" could be told from Dee's, Maggie's, or a distant narrator's viewpoint. Likewise, "I Stand Here Ironing" could be told by Emily or the psychologist. "My Papa's Waltz" could be seen through the father's eyes as well as the mother's. After discussing your choice, rewrite the selection you chose with each member of the group assuming a different perspective. Once the individual writing is finished, share it with the group, and come to some conclusion as to the difference perspective makes in terms of the work's theme.

WEB CONNECTIONS

1. Many selections in this section show families that are struggling with living in poverty. How does poverty affect the family, and how does it affect the roles that people have in families, as children, mothers, or fathers? To re-

search issues related to families living in poverty—including single mothers, government statistics, effects of poverty on children, myths surrounding poverty, recent articles in newspapers and journals, current projects, reforms and educational aids—consult the Web site of the Joint Commission on Poverty Research at http://jcpr.org/sitemap.html.

2. Many of the selections in this chapter show families in conflict, in which families are facing extremely difficult and challenging situations. To consider a different side of family life, visit the following Web site—http://aspe.hhs.gov/daltcp/reports/idsucfam.htm—that offers links to a thoughtful article titled "Identifying Successful Families" from the U.S. Department of Heath and Human Services on the factors that contribute to a healthy family environment. While this site does not provide links to other sites, it does contain a wealth of citations from experts in the fields of psychology and sociology, thus providing a list of resources for further research into the sources of the article.

Is nature a friend, a foe, or a challenger to the human figure in this photograph?

10

Nature

The connections between humans and the natural environment invoke endless conflicts, challenges, joys, and sorrows. Often people find new strengths, previously undiscovered gifts, or surprising weaknesses through their interactions with and observations of nature.

As you read the selections in this chapter, keep in mind the following questions:

1. If you had to define "nature" for someone unfamiliar with the concept, what would you say?
2. What changes might be anticipated in humans as they encounter or observe various aspects of nature?
3. What comparisons can you make between the experiences of the characters in these works and your own experiences with nature?
4. Do you think of nature as primarily beautiful and benign or as primarily a system of forces, ready at any moment to be hostile? Consider which selections might support or challenge your view.
5. What obligations do humans have to the natural environment?

Fiction

STEPHEN CRANE (1871–1900)

The Open Boat

A Tale Intended to Be after the Fact: Being the Experience of Four Men from the Sunk Steamer Commodore

> *Born in Newark, New Jersey, Stephen Crane grew up in a small town in New York as the youngest of fourteen children. He started to write stories at about age nine, close to the time when his father, a Methodist minister, died. While he was not considered academically talented and in fact dropped out of Syracuse University after one semester, he was determined to become a professional writer and moved to New York City in pursuit of his goal. There he became a journalist and in 1893 published his first book,* Maggie, A Girl of the Streets. *He is best known, however, for his second novel,* The Red Badge of Courage *(1895), the moving story of a young Civil War soldier. The following selection is a work of fiction based on Crane's experiences and observations when the steamship* Commodore, *on which he was a passenger, sunk off the coast of Florida in 1897. Although most people on board were drowned, Crane and a few others survived, living for days in an open lifeboat. "The Open Boat" serves as a testimony to their ordeal.*

I

None of them knew the color of the sky. Their eyes glanced level, and were fastened upon the waves that swept toward them. These waves were of the hue of slate, save for the tops, which were of foaming white, and all of the men knew the colors of the sea. The horizon narrowed and widened, and dipped and rose, and at all times its edge was jagged with waves that seemed thrust up in points like rocks.

Many a man ought to have a bathtub larger than the boat which here rode upon the sea. These waves were most wrongfully and barbarously abrupt and tall, and each froth-top was a problem in small-boat navigation.

The cook squatted in the bottom, and looked with both eyes at the six inches of gunwale which separated him from the ocean. His sleeves were rolled over his fat forearms, and the two flaps of his unbuttoned vest dangled as he bent to bail out the boat. Often he said, "Gawd! that was a narrow clip." As he remarked it he invariably gazed eastward over the broken sea.

The oiler, steering with one of the two oars in the boat, sometimes raised himself suddenly to keep clear of water that swirled in over the stern. It was a thin little oar, and it seemed often ready to snap.

The correspondent, pulling at the other oar, watched the waves and won-   *5*
dered why he was there.

The injured captain, lying in the bow, was at this time buried in that profound dejection and indifference which comes, temporarily at least, to even
the bravest and most enduring when, willy-nilly, the firm fails, the army loses,
the ship goes down. The mind of the master of a vessel is rooted deep in the
timbers of her, though he command for a day or a decade; and this captain had
on him the stern impression of a scene in the grays of dawn of seven turned
faces, and later a stump of a top-mast with a white ball on it that slashed to
and fro at the waves, went low and lower, and down. Thereafter there was
something strange in his voice. Although steady, it was deep with mourning,
and of a quality beyond oration or tears.

"Keep'er a little more south, Billie," said he.

"A little more south, sir," said the oiler in the stern.

A seat in this boat was not unlike a seat upon a bucking broncho, and, by
the same token a broncho is not much smaller. The craft pranced and reared
and plunged like an animal. As each wave came, and she rose for it, she seemed
like a horse making at a fence outrageously high. The manner of her scramble
over these walls of water is a mystic thing, and, moreover, at the top of them
were ordinarily these problems in white water, the foam racing down from the
summit of each wave requiring a new leap, and a leap from the air. Then, after
scornfully bumping a crest, she would slide and race and splash down a long
incline, and arrive bobbing and nodding in front of the next menace.

A singular disadvantage of the sea lies in the fact that after successfully   *10*
surmounting one wave you discover that there is another behind it just as important and just as nervously anxious to do something effective in the way of
swamping boats. In a ten-foot dinghy one can get an idea of the resources of
the sea in the line of waves that is not probable to the average experience,
which is never at sea in a dinghy. As each slaty wall of water approached, it
shut all else from the view of the men in the boat, and it was not difficult to
imagine that this particular wave was the final outburst of the ocean, the last
effort of the grim water. There was a terrible grace in the move of the waves,
and they came in silence, save for the snarling of the crests.

In the wan light the faces of the men must have been gray. Their eyes
must have glinted in strange ways as they gazed steadily astern. Viewed from a
balcony, the whole thing would doubtlessly have been weirdly picturesque.
But the men in the boat had no time to see it, and if they had had leisure,
there were other things to occupy their minds. The sun swung steadily up the
sky, and they knew it was broad day because the color of the sea changed from
slate to emerald-green streaked with amber lights, and the foam was like tumbling snow. The process of the breaking day was unknown to them. They were
aware only of this effect upon the color of the waves that rolled toward them.

In disjointed sentences the cook and the correspondent argued as to the difference between a lifesaving station and a house of refuge. The cook had said: "There's a house of refuge just north of the Mosquito Inlet Light, and as soon as they see us they'll come off in their boat and pick us up."

"As soon as who see us?" said the correspondent.

"The crew," said the cook.

15   "Houses of refuge don't have crews," said the correspondent. "As I understand them, they are only places where clothes and grub are stored for the benefit of shipwrecked people. They don't carry crews."

"Oh, yes, they do," said the cook.

"No, they don't," said the correspondent.

"Well, we're not there yet, anyhow," said the oiler, in the stern.

"Well," said the cook, "perhaps it's not a house of refuge that I'm thinking of as being near Mosquito Inlet Light; perhaps it's a lifesaving station."

20   "We're not there yet," said the oiler, in the stern.

II

As the boat bounced from the top of each wave the wind tore through the hair of the hatless men, and as the craft plopped her stern down again the spray slashed past them. The crest of each of these waves was a hill, from the top of which the men surveyed for a moment a broad tumultuous expanse, shining and wind-riven. It was probably splendid. It was probably glorious, this play of the free sea, wild with lights of emerald and white and amber.

"Bully good thing it's an onshore wind," said the cook. "If not, where would we be? Wouldn't have a show."

"That's right," said the correspondent.

The busy oiler nodded his assent.

25   Then the captain, in the bow, chuckled in a way that expressed humor, contempt, tragedy, all in one. "Do you think we've got much of a show now, boys?" said he.

Whereupon the three were silent, save for a trifle of hemming and hawing. To express any particular optimism at this time they felt to be childish and stupid, but they all doubtless possessed this sense of the situation in their minds. A young man thinks doggedly at such times. On the other hand, the ethics of their condition was decidedly against any open suggestion of hopelessness. So they were silent.

"Oh, well," said the captain, soothing his children, "we'll get ashore all right."

But there was that in his tone which made them think; so the oiler quoth, "Yes! if this wind holds."

The cook was bailing. "Yes! if we don't catch hell in the surf."

30   Canton-flannel gulls flew near and far. Sometimes they sat down on the sea, near patches of brown seaweed that rolled over the waves with a move-

ment like carpets on a line in a gale. The birds sat comfortably in groups, and they were envied by some in the dinghy, for the wrath of the sea was no more to them than it was to a covey of prairie chickens a thousand miles inland. Often they came very close and stared at the men with black bead-like eyes. At these times they were uncanny and sinister in their unblinking scrutiny, and the men hooted angrily at them, telling them to be gone. One came, and evidently decided to alight on the top of the captain's head. The bird flew parallel to the boat and did not circle, but made short sidelong jumps in the air in chicken fashion. His black eyes were wistfully fixed upon the captain's head. "Ugly brute," said the oiler to the bird. "You look as if you were made with a jackknife." The cook and the correspondent swore darkly at the creature. The captain naturally wished to knock it away with the end of the heavy painter, but he did not dare do it, because anything resembling an emphatic gesture would have capsized this freighted boat; and so, with his open hand, the captain gently and carefully waved the gull away. After it had been discouraged from the pursuit the captain breathed easier on account of his hair, and others breathed easier because the bird struck their minds at this time as being somehow gruesome and ominous.

In the meantime the oiler and the correspondent rowed. And also they rowed. They sat together in the same seat, and each rowed an oar. Then the oiler took both oars; then the correspondent took both oars; then the oiler; then the correspondent. They rowed and they rowed. The very ticklish part of the business was when the time came for the reclining one in the stern to take his turn at the oars. By the very last star of truth, it is easier to steal eggs from under a hen than it was to change seats in the dinghy. First the man in the stern slid his hand along the thwart and moved with care, as if he were of Sèvres.[1] Then the man in the rowing-seat slid his hand along the other thwart. It was all done with the most extraordinary care. As the two sidled past each other, the whole party kept watchful eyes on the coming wave, and the captain cried: "Look out, now! Steady, there!"

The brown mats of seaweed that appeared from time to time were like islands, bits of earth. They were traveling, apparently, neither one way nor the other. They were, to all intents, stationary. They informed the men in the boat that it was making progress slowly toward the land.

The captain, rearing cautiously in the bow after the dinghy soared on a great swell, said that he had seen the lighthouse at Mosquito Inlet. Presently the cook remarked that he had seen it. The correspondent was at the oars then, and for some reason he too wished to look at the lighthouse; but his back was toward the far shore and the waves were important, and for some time he could not seize an opportunity to turn his head. But at last there came a wave more

[1] A fine chinaware.

gentle than the others, and when at the crest of it he swiftly scoured the western horizon.

"See it?" said the captain.

35 "No," said the correspondent, slowly. "I didn't see anything."

"Look again," said the captain. He pointed. "It's exactly in that direction."

At the top of another wave the correspondent did as he was bid, and this time his eyes chanced on a small, still thing on the edge of the swaying horizon. It was precisely like the point of a pin. It took an anxious eye to find a lighthouse so tiny.

"Think we'll make it, Captain?"

"If this wind holds and the boat don't swamp, we can't do much else," said the captain.

40 The little boat, lifted by each towering sea and splashed viciously by the crests, made progress that in the absence of seaweed was not apparent to those in her. She seemed just a wee thing wallowing, miraculously top up, at the mercy of five oceans. Occasionally, a great spread of water, like white flames, swarmed into her.

"Bail her, cook," said the captain, serenely.

"All right, Captain," said the cheerful cook.

III

It would be difficult to describe the subtle brotherhood of men that was here established on the seas. No one said that it was so. No one mentioned it. But it dwelt in the boat, and each man felt it warm him. They were a captain, an oiler, a cook, and correspondent, and they were friends—friends in a more curiously ironbound degree than may be common. The hurt captain, lying against the water jar in the bow, spoke always in a low voice and calmly; but he could never command a more ready and swiftly obedient crew than the motley three of the dinghy. It was more than a mere recognition of what was best for the common safety. There was surely in it a quality that was personal and heartfelt. And after this devotion to the commander of the boat, there was this comradeship, that the correspondent, for instance, who had been taught to be cynical of men, knew even at the time was the best experience of his life. But no one said that it was so. No one mentioned it.

"I wish we had a sail," remarked the captain. "We might try my overcoat on the end of an oar, and give you two boys a chance to rest." So the cook and the correspondent held the mast and spread wide the overcoat; the oiler steered, and the little boat made good way with her new rig. Sometimes the oiler had to scull sharply to keep a sea from breaking into the boat, but otherwise sailing was a success.

45 Meanwhile the lighthouse had been growing slowly larger. It had now almost assumed color, and appeared like a little gray shadow on the sky. The

man at the oars could not be prevented from turning his head rather often to try for a glimpse of this little gray shadow.

At last, from the top of each wave, the men in the tossing boat could see land. Even as the lighthouse was an upright shadow on the sky, this land seemed but a long black shadow on the sea. It certainly was thinner than paper. "We must be about opposite New Smyrna," said the cook, who had coasted this shore often in schooners. "Captain, by the way, I believe they abandoned that lifesaving station there about a year ago."

"Did they?" said the captain.

The wind slowly died away. The cook and the correspondent were not now obliged to slave in order to hold high the oar. But the waves continued their old impetuous swooping at the dinghy, and the little craft, no longer under way, struggled woundily over them. The oiler or the correspondent took the oars again.

Shipwrecks are *apropos* of nothing. If men could only train for them and have them occur when the men had reached pink condition, there would be less drowning at sea. Of the four in the dinghy none had slept any time worth mentioning for two days and two nights previous to embarking in the dinghy, and in the excitement of clambering about the deck of a foundering ship they had also forgotten to eat heartily.

For these reasons, and for others, neither the oiler nor the correspondent   *50*
was fond of rowing at this time. The correspondent wondered ingenuously how in the name of all that was sane could there be people who thought it amusing to row a boat. It was not an amusement; it was a diabolical punishment, and even a genius of mental aberrations could never conclude that it was anything but a horror to the muscles and a crime against the back. He mentioned to the boat in general how the amusement of rowing struck him, and the weary-faced oiler smiled in full sympathy. Previously to the foundering, by the way, the oiler had worked a double-watch in the engine room of the ship.

"Take her easy now, boys," said the captain. "Don't spend yourselves. If we have to run a surf you'll need all your strength, because we'll sure have to swim for it. Take your time."

Slowly the land arose from the sea. From a black line it became a line of black and a line of white—trees and sand. Finally the captain said that he could make out a house on the shore. "That's the house of refuge, sure," said the cook. "They'll see us before long, and come out after us."

The distant lighthouse reared high. "The keeper ought to be able to make us out now, if he's looking through a glass," said the captain. "He'll notify the lifesaving people."

"None of those other boats could have got ashore to give word of this wreck," said the oiler, in a low voice. "Else the lifeboat would be out hunting us."

55   Slowly and beautifully the land loomed out of the sea. The wind came again. It had veered from the northeast to the southeast. Finally, a new sound struck the ears of the men in the boat. It was the low thunder of the surf on the shore. "We'll never be able to make the lighthouse now," said the captain. "Swing her head a little more north, Billie," said the captain.

"A little more north, sir," said the oiler.

Whereupon the little boat turned her nose once more down the wind, and all but the oarsman watched the shore grow. Under the influence of this expansion doubt and direful apprehension were leaving the minds of the men. The management of the boat was still most absorbing, but it could not prevent a quiet cheerfulness. In an hour, perhaps, they would be ashore.

Their backbones had become thoroughly used to balancing in the boat, and they now rode this wild colt of a dinghy like circus men. The correspondent thought that he had been drenched to the skin, but happening to feel in the top pocket of his coat, he found therein eight cigars. Four of them were soaked with sea-water; four were perfectly scatheless. After a search, somebody produced three dry matches, and thereupon the four waifs rode impudently in their little boat and, with an assurance of an impending rescue shining in their eyes, puffed at the big cigars, and judged well and ill of all men. Everybody took a drink of water.

IV

"Cook," remarked the captain, "there don't seem to be any signs of life about your house of refuge."

60   "No," replied the cook. "Funny they don't see us!"

A broad stretch of lowly coast lay before the eyes of the men. It was of low dunes topped with dark vegetation. The roar of the surf was plain, and sometimes they could see the white lip of a wave as it spun up the beach. A tiny house was blocked out black upon the sky. Southward, the slim lighthouse lifted its little gray length.

Tide, wind, and waves were swinging the dinghy northward. "Funny they don't see us," said the men.

The surf's roar was here dulled, but its tone was nevertheless thunderous and mighty. As the boat swam over the great rollers the men sat listening to this roar. "We'll swamp sure," said everybody.

It is fair to say here that there was not a lifesaving station within twenty miles in either direction; but the men did not know this fact, and in consequence they made dark and opprobrious remarks concerning the eyesight of the nation's lifesavers. Four scowling men sat in the dinghy and surpassed records in the invention of epithets.

65   "Funny they don't see us."

The light-heartedness of a former time had completely faded. To their sharpened minds it was easy to conjure pictures of all kinds of incompetency and blindness and, indeed, cowardice. There was the shore of the populous land, and it was bitter and bitter to them that from it came no sign.

"Well," said the captain, ultimately, "I suppose we'll have to make a try for ourselves. If we stay out here too long, we'll none of us have strength left to swim after the boat swamps."

And so the oiler, who was at the oars, turned the boat straight for the shore. There was a sudden tightening of muscles. There was some thinking.

"If we don't all get ashore," said the captain—"if we don't all get ashore, I suppose you fellows know where to send news of my finish?"

They then briefly exchanged some addresses and admonitions. As for the reflections of the men, there was a great deal of rage in them. Perchance they might be formulated thus: "If I am going to be drowned—if I am going to be drowned—if I am going to be drowned, why, in the name of the seven mad gods who rule the sea, was I allowed to come thus far and contemplate sand and trees? Was I brought here merely to have my nose dragged away as I was about to nibble the sacred cheese of life? It is preposterous. If this old ninny-woman, Fate, cannot do better than this, she should be deprived of the man-agement of men's fortunes. She is an old hen who knows not her intention. If she has decided to drown me, why did she not do it in the beginning and save me all this trouble? The whole affair is absurd. . . . But, no, she cannot mean to drown me. She dare not drown me. She cannot drown me. Not after all this work." Afterward the man might have had an impulse to shake his fist at the clouds: "Just you drown me, now, and then hear what I call you!"

The billows that came at this time were more formidable. They seemed always just about to break and roll over the little boat in a turmoil of foam. There was a preparatory and long growl in the speech of them. No mind un-used to the sea would have concluded that the dinghy could ascend these sheer heights in time. The shore was still afar. The oiler was a wily surfman. "Boys," he said swiftly, "she won't live three minutes more and we're too far out to swim. Shall I take her to sea again, Captain?"

"Yes; go ahead!" said the captain.

This oiler, by a series of quick miracles and fast and steady oarsmanship, turned the boat in the middle of the surf and took her safely to sea again.

There was a considerable silence as the boat bumped over the furrowed sea to deeper water. Then somebody in gloom spoke: "Well, anyhow, they must have seen us from the shore by now."

The gulls went in slanting flight up the wind toward the gray desolate east. A squall, marked by dingy clouds and clouds brick-red, like smoke from a burning building, appeared from the southeast.

"What do you think of those lifesaving people? Ain't they peaches?"

"Funny they haven't seen us."

"Maybe they think we're out here for sport! Maybe they think we're fishin'. Maybe they think we're damned fools."

It was a long afternoon. A changed tide tried to force them southward, but wind and wave said northward. Far ahead, where coastline, sea, and sky formed their mighty angle, there were little dots which seemed to indicate a city on the shore.

80 "St. Augustine?"

The captain shook his head. "Too near Mosquito Inlet."

And the oiler rowed, and then the correspondent rowed; then the oiler rowed. It was a weary business. The human back can become the seat of more aches and pains than are registered in books for the composite anatomy of a regiment. It is a limited area, but it can become the theater of innumerable muscular conflicts, tangles, wrenches, knots, and other comforts.

"Did you ever like to row, Billie?" asked the correspondent.

"No," said the oiler; "hang it."

85 When one exchanged the rowing-seat for a place in the bottom of the boat, he suffered a bodily depression that caused him to be careless of everything save an obligation to wiggle one finger. There was cold seawater swashing to and fro in the boat, and he lay in it. His head, pillowed on a thwart, was within an inch of the swirl of a wave-crest, and sometimes a particularly obstreperous sea came inboard and drenched him once more. But these matters did not annoy him. It is almost certain that if the boat had capsized he would have tumbled comfortably out upon the ocean as if he felt sure that it was a great soft mattress.

"Look! There's a man on the shore?"

"Where?"

"There! See 'im? See 'im?"

"Yes, sure! He's walking along."

90 "Now he's stopped. Look! He's facing us!"

"He's waving at us!"

"So he is! By thunder!"

"Ah, now, we're all right! Now we're all right! There'll be a boat out here for us in half an hour."

"He's going on. He's running. He's going up to that house there."

95 The remote beach seemed lower than the sea, and it required a searching glance to discern the little black figure. The captain saw a floating stick and they rowed to it. A bath towel was by some weird chance in the boat, and, tying this on the stick, the captain waved it. The oarsman did not dare turn his head, so he was obliged to ask questions.

"What's he doing now?"

"He's standing still again. He's looking, I think.... There he goes again— toward the house.... Now he's stopped again."

"Is he waving at us?"

"No, not now; he was, though."

100 "Look! There comes another man!"

"He's running."

"Look at him go, would you!"

"Why, he's on a bicycle. Now he's met the other man. They're both waving at us. Look!"

"There comes something up the beach."

"What the devil is that thing?"   105

"Why, it looks like a boat."

"Why, certainly, it's a boat."

"No; it's on wheels."

"Yes, so it is. Well, that must be the lifeboat. They drag them along shore on a wagon."

"That's the lifeboat, sure."   110

"No, by God, it's—it's an omnibus."

"I tell you it's a lifeboat."

"It is not! It's an omnibus. I can see it plain. See? One of these big hotel omnibuses."

"By thunder, you're right. It's an omnibus, sure as fate. What do you suppose they are doing with an omnibus? Maybe they are going around collecting the life-crew, hey?"

"That's it, likely. Look! There's a fellow waving a little black flag. He's   115
standing on the steps of the omnibus. There come those other two fellows. Now they're all talking together. Look at the fellow with the flag. Maybe he ain't waving it!"

"That ain't a flag, is it? That's his coat. Why, certainly, that's his coat."

"So it is; it's his coat. He's taken it off and is waving it around his head. But would you look at him swing it!"

"Oh, say, there isn't any lifesaving station there. That's just a winter resort hotel omnibus that has brought over some of the boarders to see us drown."

"What's that idiot with the coat mean? What's he signaling, anyhow?"

"It looks as if he were trying to tell us to go north. There must be a life-   120
saving station up there."

"No; he thinks we're fishing. Just giving us a merry hand. See? Ah, there, Willie."

"Well, I wish I could make something out of those signals. What do you suppose he means?"

"He don't mean anything; he's just playing."

"Well, if he'd just signal us to try the surf again, or to go to sea and wait, or go north, or go south, or go to hell, there would be some reason in it. But look at him. He just stands there and keeps his coat revolving like a wheel. The ass!"

"There come more people."   125

"Now there's quite a mob. Look! Isn't that a boat?"

"Where? Oh, I see where you mean. No, that's no boat."

"That fellow is still waving his coat."

"He must think we like to see him do that. Why don't he quit it? It don't mean anything."

130   "I don't know. I think he is trying to make us go north. It must be that there's a lifesaving station there somewhere."

"Say, he ain't tired yet. Look at 'im wave!"

"Wonder how long he can keep that up. He's been revolving his coat ever since he caught sight of us. He's an idiot. Why aren't they getting men to bring a boat out? A fishing boat—one of those big yawls—could come out here all right. Why don't he do something?"

"Oh, it's all right, now."

"They'll have a boat out here for us in less than no time, now that they've seen us."

135   A faint yellow tone came into the sky over the low land. The shadows on the sea slowly deepened. The wind bore coldness with it, and the men began to shiver.

"Holy smoke!" said one, allowing his voice to express his impious mood, "if we keep on monkeying out here! If we've got to flounder out here all night!"

"Oh, we'll never have to stay here all night! Don't you worry. They've seen us now, and it won't be long before they'll come chasing out after us."

The shore grew dusky. The man waving a coat blended gradually into this gloom, and it swallowed in the same manner the omnibus and the group of people. The spray, when it dashed uproariously over the sides, made the voyagers shrink and swear like men who were being branded.

"I'd like to catch the chump who waved the coat. I feel like socking him one, just for luck."

140   "Why? What did he do?"

"Oh, nothing, but then he seemed so damned cheerful."

In the meantime the oiler rowed, and then the correspondent rowed, and then the oiler rowed. Gray-faced and bowed forward, they mechanically, turn by turn, plied the leaden oars. The form of the lighthouse had vanished from the southern horizon, but finally a pale star appeared, just lifting from the sea. The streaked saffron in the west passed before the all-merging darkness, and the sea to the east was black. The land had vanished, and was expressed only by the low and drear thunder of the surf.

"If I am going to be drowned—if I am going to be drowned—if I am going to be drowned, why, in the name of the seven mad gods who rule the sea, was I allowed to come thus far and contemplate sand and trees? Was I brought here merely to have my nose dragged away as I was about to nibble the sacred cheese of life?"

The patient captain, drooped over the water jar, was sometimes obliged to speak to the oarsman.

145   "Keep her head up! Keep her head up!"

"Keep her head up, sir." The voices were weary and low.

This was surely a quiet evening. All save the oarsman lay heavily and list-lessly in the boat's bottom. As for him, his eyes were just capable of noting the tall black waves that swept forward in a most sinister silence, save for an occasional subdued growl of a crest.

The cook's head was on a thwart, and he looked without interest at the water under his nose. He was deep in other scenes. Finally he spoke. "Billie," he murmured, dreamfully, "what kind of pie do you like best?"

V

"Pie!" said the oiler and the correspondent, agitatedly. "Don't talk about those things, blast you!"

"Well," said the cook, "I was just thinking about ham sandwiches, and—"   150

A night on the sea in an open boat is a long night. As darkness settled finally, the shine of the light, lifting from the sea in the south, changed to full gold. On the northern horizon a new light appeared, a small bluish gleam on the edge of the waters. These two lights were the furniture of the world. Otherwise there was nothing but waves.

Two men huddled in the stern, and distances were so magnificent in the dinghy that the rower was enabled to keep his feet partly warm by thrusting them under his companions. Their legs indeed extended far under the rowing-seat until they touched the feet of the captain forward. Sometimes, despite the efforts of the tired oarsman, a wave came piling into the boat, an icy wave of the night, and the chilling water soaked them anew. They would twist their bodies for a moment and groan, and sleep the dead sleep once more, while the water in the boat gurgled about them as the craft rocked.

The plan of the oiler and the correspondent was for one to row until he lost the ability, and then arouse the other from his sea-water couch in the bottom of the boat.

The oiler plied the oars until his head drooped forward and the over-powering sleep blinded him; and he rowed yet afterward. Then he touched a man in the bottom of the boat, and called his name. "Will you spell me for a little while?" he said meekly.

"Sure, Billie," said the correspondent, awaking and dragging himself to a   155
sitting position. They exchanged places carefully, and the oiler, cuddling down in the seawater at the cook's side, seemed to go to sleep instantly.

The particular violence of the sea had ceased. The waves came without snarling. The obligation of the man at the oars was to keep the boat headed so that the tilt of the rollers would not capsize her, and to preserve her from filling when the crests rushed past. The black waves were silent and hard to be seen in the darkness. Often one was almost upon the boat before the oarsman was aware.

In a low voice the correspondent addressed the captain. He was not sure that the captain was awake, although this iron man seemed to be always awake. "Captain, shall I keep her making for that light north, sir?"

The same steady voice answered him. "Yes. Keep it about two points off the port bow."

The cook had tied a lifebelt around himself in order to get even the warmth which this clumsy cork contrivance could donate, and he seemed almost stovelike when a rower, whose teeth invariably chattered wildly as soon as he ceased his labor, dropped down to sleep.

160   The correspondent, as he rowed, looked down at the two men sleeping underfoot. The cook's arm was around the oiler's shoulders, and, with their fragmentary clothing and haggard faces, they were the babes of the sea—a grotesque rendering of the old babes in the wood.

Later he must have grown stupid at his work, for suddenly there was a growling of water, and a crest came with a roar and a swash into the boat, and it was a wonder that it did not set the cook afloat in his lifebelt. The cook continued to sleep, but the oiler sat up, blinking his eyes and shaking with the new cold.

"Oh, I'm awful sorry, Billie," said the correspondent, contritely.

"That's all right, old boy," said the oiler, and lay down again and was asleep.

Presently it seemed that even the captain dozed, and the correspondent thought that he was the one man afloat on all the oceans. The wind had a voice as it came over the waves, and it was sadder than the end.

165   There was a long, loud swishing astern of the boat, and a gleaming trail of phosphorescence, like blue flame, was furrowed on the black waters. It might have been made by a monstrous knife.

Then there came a stillness, while the correspondent breathed with open mouth and looked at the sea.

Suddenly there was another swish and another long flash of bluish light, and this time it was alongside the boat, and might almost have been reached with an oar. The correspondent saw an enormous fin speed like a shadow through the water, hurling the crystalline spray and leaving the long glowing trail.

The correspondent looked over his shoulder at the captain. His face was hidden, and he seemed to be asleep. He looked at the babes of the sea. They certainly were asleep. So, being bereft of sympathy, he leaned a little way to one side and swore softly into the sea.

But the thing did not then leave the vicinity of the boat. Ahead or astern, on one side or the other, at intervals long or short, fled the long sparkling streak, and there was to be heard the *whirroo* of the dark fin. The speed and power of the thing was greatly to be admired. It cut the water like a gigantic and keen projectile.

170   The presence of this biding thing did not affect the man with the same horror that it would if he had been a picnicker. He simply looked at the sea dully and swore in an undertone.

Nevertheless, it is true that he did not wish to be alone with the thing. He wished one of his companions to awake by chance and keep him company with it. But the captain hung motionless over the water jar, and the oiler and the cook in the bottom of the boat were plunged in slumber.

VI

"If I am going to be drowned—if I am going to be drowned—if I am going to be drowned, why, in the name of the seven mad gods who rule the sea, was I allowed to come thus far and contemplate sand and trees?"

During this dismal night, it may be remarked that a man would conclude that it was really the intention of the seven mad gods to drown him, despite the abominable injustice of it. For it was certainly an abominable injustice to drown a man who had worked so hard, so hard. The man felt it would be a crime most unnatural. Other people had drowned at sea since galleys swarmed with painted sails, but still—

When it occurs to a man that nature does not regard him as important, and that she feels she would not maim the universe by disposing of him, he at first wishes to throw bricks at the temple, and he hates deeply the fact that there are no bricks and no temples. Any visible expression of nature would surely be pelted with his jeers.

Then, if there be no tangible thing to hoot, he feels, perhaps, the desire   175
to confront a personification and indulge in pleas, bowed to one knee, and with hands supplicant, saying, "Yes, but I love myself."

A high cold star on a winter's night is the word he feels that she says to him. Thereafter he knows the pathos of his situation.

The men in the dinghy had not discussed these matters, but each had, no doubt, reflected upon them in silence and according to his mind. There was seldom any expression upon their faces save the general one of complete weariness. Speech was devoted to the business of the boat.

To chime the notes of his emotion, a verse mysteriously entered the correspondent's head. He had even forgotten that he had forgotten this verse, but it suddenly was in his mind.

A soldier of the Legion lay dying in Algiers;
There was lack of woman's nursing, there was dearth of woman's tears;
But a comrade stood beside him, and he took that comrade's hand,
And he said, "I never more shall see my own, my native land."

In his childhood, the correspondent had been made acquainted with the fact that a soldier of the Legion lay dying in Algiers, but he had never regarded the fact as important. Myriads of his schoolfellows had informed him of the soldier's plight, but the dinning had naturally ended by making him perfectly indifferent. He had never considered it his affair that a soldier of the Legion lay dying in Algiers, nor had it appeared to him as a matter for sorrow. It was less to him than breaking of a pencil's point.

Now, however, it quaintly came to him as a human, living thing. It was   180
no longer merely a picture of a few throes in the breast of a poet, meanwhile

drinking tea and warming his feet at the grate; it was an actuality—stern, mournful, and fine.

The correspondent plainly saw the soldier. He lay on the sand with his feet out straight and still. While his pale left hand was upon his chest in an attempt to thwart the going of his life, the blood came between his fingers. In the far Algerian distance, a city of low square forms was set against a sky that was faint with the last sunset hues. The correspondent, plying the oars and dreaming of the slow and slower movements of the lips of the soldier, was moved by a profound and perfectly impersonal comprehension. He was sorry for the soldier of the Legion who lay dying in Algiers.

The thing which had followed the boat and waited had evidently grown bored at the delay. There was no longer to be heard the slash of the cut-water, and there was no longer the flame of the long trail. The light in the north still glimmered, but it was apparently no nearer to the boat. Sometimes the boom of the surf rang in the correspondent's ears, and he turned the craft seaward then and rowed harder. Southward, some one had evidently built a watch fire on the beach. It was too low and too far to be seen, but it made a shimmering, roseate reflection upon the bluff in back of it, and this could be discerned from the boat. The wind came stronger, and sometimes a wave suddenly raged out like a mountain cat, and there was to be seen the sheen and sparkle of a broken crest.

The captain, in the bow, moved on his water jar and sat erect. "Pretty long night," he observed to the correspondent. He looked at the shore. "Those lifesaving people take their time."

"Did you see that shark playing around?"

185   "Yes, I saw him. He was a big fellow, all right."

"Wish I had known you were awake."

Later the correspondent spoke into the bottom of the boat. "Billie!" There was a slow and gradual disentanglement. "Billie, will you spell me?"

"Sure," said the oiler.

As soon as the correspondent touched the cold, comfortable seawater in the bottom of the boat and had huddled close to the cook's lifebelt he was deep in sleep, despite the fact that his teeth played all the popular airs. This sleep was so good to him that it was but a moment before he heard a voice call his name in a tone that demonstrated the last stages of exhaustion. "Will you spell me?"

190   "Sure, Billie."

The light in the north had mysteriously vanished, but the correspondent took his course from the wide-awake captain.

Later in the night they took the boat farther out to sea, and the captain directed the cook to take one oar at the stern and keep the boat facing the seas. He was to call out if he should hear the thunder of the surf. This plan enabled the oiler and the correspondent to get respite together. "We'll give those boys a chance to get into shape again," said the captain. They curled down and, after a few preliminary chatterings and trembles, slept once more the dead sleep. Neither knew they had bequeathed to the cook the company of another shark, or perhaps the same shark.

As the boat caroused on the waves, spray occasionally bumped over the side and gave them a fresh soaking, but this had no power to break their repose. The ominous slash of the wind and the water affected them as it would have affected mummies.

"Boys," said the cook, with the notes of every reluctance in his voice, "she's drifted in pretty close. I guess one of you had better take her to sea again." The correspondent, aroused, heard the crash of the toppled crests.

As he was rowing, the captain gave him some whiskey-and-water, and   *195* this steadied the chills out of him. "If I ever get ashore and anybody shows me even a photograph of an oar—"

At last there was a short conversation.

"Billie.... Billie, will you spell me?"

"Sure," said the oiler.

VII

When the correspondent again opened his eyes, the sea and the sky were each of the gray hue of the dawning. Later, carmine and gold was painted upon the waters. The morning appeared finally, in its splendor, with a sky of pure blue, and the sunlight flamed on the tips of the waves.

On the distant dunes were set many little black cottages, and a tall white   *200* windmill reared above them. No man, nor dog, nor bicycle appeared on the beach. The cottages might have formed a deserted village.

The voyagers scanned the shore. A conference was held in the boat. "Well," said the captain, "if no help is coming, we might better try a run through the surf right away. If we stay out here much longer we will be too weak to do anything for ourselves at all." The others silently acquiesced in this reasoning. The boat was headed for the beach. The correspondent wondered if none ever ascended the tall windtower, and if then they never looked seaward. This tower was a giant, standing with its back to the plight of the ants. It represented in a degree, to the correspondent, the serenity of nature amid the struggles of the individual—nature in the wind, and nature in the vision of men. She did not seem cruel to him then, nor beneficent, nor treacherous, nor wise. But she was indifferent, flatly indifferent. It is, perhaps, plausible that a man in this situation, impressed with the unconcern of the universe, should see the innumerable flaws of his life, and have them taste wickedly in his mind, and wish for another chance. A distinction between right and wrong seems absurdly clear to him, then, in this new ignorance of the grave-edge, and he understands that if he were given another opportunity he would mend his conduct and his words, and be better and brighter during an introduction or at a tea.

"Now, boys," said the captain, "she is going to swamp sure. All we can do is to work her in as far as possible, and then when she swamps, pile out and scramble for the beach. Keep cool now, and don't jump until she swamps sure."

The oiler took the oars. Over his shoulders he scanned the surf. "Captain," he said, "I think I'd better bring her about, and keep her head-on to the seas and back her in."

"All right, Billie," said the captain. "Back her in." The oiler swung the boat then, and, seated in the stern, the cook and the correspondent were obliged to look over their shoulders to contemplate the lonely and indifferent shore.

205   The monstrous inshore rollers heaved the boat high until the men were again enabled to see the white sheets of water scudding up the slanted beach. "We won't get in very close," said the captain. Each time a man could wrest his attention from the rollers, he turned his glance toward the shore, and in the expression of the eyes during this contemplation there was a singular quality. The correspondent, observing the others, knew that they were not afraid, but the full meaning of their glances was shrouded.

As for himself, he was too tired to grapple fundamentally with the fact. He tried to coerce his mind into thinking of it, but the mind was dominated at this time by the muscles, and the muscles said they did not care. It merely occurred to him that if he should drown it would be a shame.

There were no hurried words, no pallor, no plain agitation. The men simply looked at the shore. "Now, remember to get well clear of the boat when you jump," said the captain.

Seaward the crest of a roller suddenly fell with a thunderous crash, and the long white comber came roaring down upon the boat.

"Steady now," said the captain. The men were silent. They turned their eyes from the shore to the comber and waited. The boat slid up the incline, leaped at the furious top, bounced over it, and swung down the long back of the waves. Some water had been shipped, and the cook bailed it out.

210   But the next crest crashed also. The tumbling, boiling flood of white water caught the boat and whirled it almost perpendicular. Water swarmed in from all sides. The correspondent had his hands on the gunwale at this time, and when the water entered at that place he swiftly withdrew his fingers, as if he objected to wetting them.

The little boat, drunken with this weight of water, reeled and snuggled deeper into the sea.

"Bail her out, cook! Bail her out," said the captain.

"All right, Captain," said the cook.

"Now, boys, the next one will do for us sure," said the oiler. "Mind to jump clear of the boat."

215   The third wave moved forward, huge, furious, implacable. It fairly swallowed the dinghy, and almost simultaneously the men tumbled into the sea. A piece of lifebelt had lain in the bottom of the boat, and as the correspondent went overboard he held this to his chest with his left hand.

The January water was icy, and he reflected immediately that it was colder than he had expected to find it off the coast of Florida. This appeared to his dazed mind as a fact important enough to be noted at the time. The coldness of the water was sad; it was tragic. This fact was somehow mixed and confused with his opinion of his own situation, so that it seemed almost a proper reason for tears. The water was cold.

When he came to the surface he was conscious of little but the noisy water. Afterward he saw his companions in the sea. The oiler was ahead in the race. He was swimming strongly and rapidly. Off to the correspondent's left, the cook's great white and corked back bulged out of the water, and in the rear the captain was hanging with his one good hand to the keel of the overturned dinghy.

There is a certain immovable quality to a shore, and the correspondent wondered at it amid the confusion of the sea.

It seemed also very attractive; but the correspondent knew that it was a long journey, and he paddled leisurely. The piece of life preserver lay under him, and sometimes he whirled down the incline of a wave as if he were on a hand-sled.

But finally he arrived at a place in the sea where travel was beset with   220
difficulty. He did not pause swimming to inquire what manner of current had caught him, but there his progress ceased. The shore was set before him like a bit of scenery on a stage, and he looked at it and understood with his eyes each detail of it.

As the cook passed, much farther to the left, the captain was calling to him, "Turn over on your back, cook! Turn over on your back and use the oar."

"All right, sir." The cook turned on his back, and, paddling with an oar, went ahead as if he were a canoe.

Presently the boat also passed to the left of the correspondent with the captain clinging with one hand to the keel. He would have appeared like a man raising himself to look over a board fence if it were not for the extraordinary gymnastics of the boat. The correspondent marveled that the captain could still hold to it.

They passed on nearer to shore—the oiler, the cook, the captain—and following them went the water jar, bouncing gaily over the seas.

The correspondent remained in the grip of this strange new enemy—a   225
current. The shore, with its white slope of sand and its green bluff topped with little silent cottages, was spread like a picture before him. It was very near to him then, but he was impressed as one who in a gallery looks at a scene from Brittany or Algiers.

He thought: "I am going to drown? Can it be possible? Can it be possible? Can it be possible?" Perhaps an individual must consider his own death to be the final phenomenon of nature.

But later a wave perhaps whirled him out of this small deadly current, for he found suddenly that he could again make progress toward the shore.

Later still he was aware that the captain, clinging with one hand to the keel of the dinghy, had his face turned away from the shore and toward him, and was calling his name. "Come to the boat! Come to the boat!"

In his struggle to reach the captain and the boat, he reflected that when one gets properly wearied, drowning must really be a comfortable arrangement—a cessation of hostilities accompanied by a large degree of relief; and he was glad of it, for the main thing in his mind for some moments had been horror of the temporary agony. He did not wish to be hurt.

Presently he saw a man running along the shore. He was undressing with most remarkable speed. Coat, trousers, shirt, everything flew magically off him.

230   "Come to the boat," called the captain.

"All right, Captain." As the correspondent paddled, he saw the captain let himself down to bottom and leave the boat. Then the correspondent performed his one little marvel of the voyage. A large wave caught him and flung him with ease and supreme speed completely over the boat and far beyond it. It struck him even then as an event in gymnastics and a true miracle of the sea. An overturned boat in the surf is not a plaything to a swimming man.

The correspondent arrived in water that reached only to his waist, but his condition did not enable him to stand for more than a moment. Each wave knocked him into a heap, and the undertow pulled at him.

Then he saw the man who had been running and undressing, and undressing and running, come bounding into the water. He dragged ashore the cook, and then waded toward the captain; but the captain waved him away, and sent him to the correspondent. He was naked, naked as a tree in winter; but a halo was about his head, and he shone like a saint. He gave a strong pull, and a long drag, and a bully heave at the correspondent's hand. The correspondent, schooled in the minor formulae, said, "Thanks, old man." But suddenly the man cried, "What's that?" He pointed a swift finger. The correspondent said, "Go."

In the shallows, face downward, lay the oiler. His forehead touched sand that was periodically, between each wave, clear of the sea.

235   The correspondent did not know all that transpired afterward. When he achieved safe ground he fell, striking the sand with each particular part of his body. It was as if he had dropped from a roof, but the thud was grateful to him.

It seems that instantly the beach was populated with men with blankets, clothes, and flasks, and women with coffeepots and all the remedies sacred to their minds. The welcome of the land to the men from the sea was warm and generous; but a still and dripping shape was carried slowly up the beach, and the land's welcome for it could only be the different and sinister hospitality of the grave.

When it came night, the white waves paced to and fro in the moonlight, and the wind brought the sound of the great sea's voice to the men on the shore, and they felt that they could then be interpreters. *1898*

CONSIDERATIONS

1. In what ways do the first nine words of this piece set up and forecast the major conflict?
2. Read the paragraph (10) that begins "A singular disadvantage of the sea lies in," paying close attention to the contrasts within the sentences of that paragraph. Focus on one sentence that includes opposing forces, and analyze the effects of describing such forces within one sentence.
3. In what ways does the battle against nature in part 3 improve human relationships? Looking further to part 4, how does nature divide men against each other?
4. In addition to the ocean, what other forces in nature appear as "characters" in this story, and what purpose do they serve?
5. Discuss the epiphany (insight) that occurs within the narrator when the verse relating to the "soldier of the legion" mysteriously enters his mind (part 6). What does this insight reveal about not only the narrator but also the human condition in general?
6. In *Being Peace,* Zen master, poet, and peace activist Thich Nhat Hanh compares the planet Earth to a small boat in the sea. For the human race to survive, he writes, all must work together or our world and everyone in it will be destroyed. In what ways does this thinking connect to "The Open Boat"? In what ways does it not?

ERNEST HEMINGWAY (1899–1961)
Hills like White Elephants

After he graduated from high school in 1917, Ernest Hemingway went to work as a reporter for the Kansas City Star. *Although he stayed only seven months, he was introduced to what he called "the best rules I ever learned for the business of writing." These rules included "Use short sentences. Use short first paragraphs. Use vigorous English, not forgetting to strive for smoothness."*

In the spring of 1918, Hemingway left the Star *to become an ambulance driver for the Red Cross in Italy during World War I. Shortly after he arrived, he was wounded and spent months convalescing. His experiences in Italy, however, inspired his novel* A Farewell to Arms *(1929). After returning to Michigan, he accepted a job as the European correspondent for the Toronto* Star. *In December of 1921, he and his new bride moved to Paris, where he became friends with a number of prominent writers, including Ezra Pound, James Joyce, and Gertrude Stein. During the next two years, he reported on news events, wrote lifestyle pieces about topics such as fishing, bullfighting, and social life in Europe, and started to become known as a fiction writer. In 1923, the couple moved to*

Toronto for the birth of their son. The next year the family moved back to Paris.
During the next five years, Hemingway produced some of his most important
works, including the short story collections In Our Time *(1925) and* Men
without Women *(1927) and the novels* The Sun Also Rises *(1926) and*
A Farewell to Arms *(1929). The story here was first published in* Men without Women.

The hills across the valley of the Ebro were long and white. On this side
there was no shade and no trees and the station was between two lines of rails
in the sun. Close against the side of the station there was the warm shadow of
the building and a curtain, made of strings of bamboo beads, hung across the
open door into the bar, to keep out flies. The American and the girl with him
sat at a table in the shade, outside the building. It was very hot and the express
from Barcelona would come in forty minutes. It stopped at this junction for
two minutes and went on to Madrid.

"What should we drink?" the girl asked. She had taken off her hat and
put it on the table.

"It's pretty hot," the man said.

"Let's drink beer."

5   "*Dos cervezas,*" the man said into the curtain.

"Big ones?" a woman asked from the doorway.

"Yes. Two big ones."

The woman brought two glasses of beer and two felt pads. She put the
felt pads and the beer glasses on the table and looked at the man and the girl.
The girl was looking off at the line of hills. They were white in the sun and
the country was brown and dry.

"They look like white elephants," she said.

10   "I've never seen one," the man drank his beer.

"No, you wouldn't have."

"I might have," the man said. "Just because you say I wouldn't have doesn't
prove anything."

The girl looked at the bead curtain. "They've painted something on it,"
she said. "What does it say?"

"Anis del Toro. It's a drink."

15   "Could we try it?"

The man called "Listen" through the curtain. The woman came out from
the bar.

"Four *reales.*"

"We want two Anis del Toro."

"With water?"

20   "Do you want it with water?"

"I don't know," the girl said. "Is it good with water?"

"It's all right."

"You want them with water?" asked the woman.

"Yes, with water."

"It tastes like licorice," the girl said and put the glass down.   *25*

"That's the way with everything."

"Yes," said the girl. "Everything tastes of licorice. Especially all the things you've waited so long for, like absinthe."

"Oh, cut it out."

"You started it," the girl said. "I was being amused. I was having a fine time."

"Well, let's try and have a fine time."   *30*

"All right. I was trying. I said the mountains looked like white elephants. Wasn't that bright?"

"That was bright."

"I wanted to try this new drink. That's all we do, isn't it—look at things and try new drinks?"

"I guess so."

The girl looked across at the hills.   *35*

"They're lovely hills," she said. "They don't really look like white elephants. I just meant the coloring of their skin through the trees."

"Should we have another drink?"

"All right."

The warm wind blew the bead curtain against the table.

"The beer's nice and cool," the man said.   *40*

"It's lovely," the girl said.

"It's really an awfully simple operation, Jig," the man said. "It's not really an operation at all."

The girl looked at the ground the table legs rested on.

"I know you wouldn't mind it, Jig. It's really not anything. It's just to let the air in."

The girl did not say anything.   *45*

"I'll go with you and I'll stay with you all the time. They just let the air in and then it's all perfectly natural."

"Then what will we do afterward?"

"We'll be fine afterward. Just like we were before."

"What makes you think so?"

"That's the only thing that bothers us. It's the only thing that's made us   *50*
unhappy."

The girl looked at the bead curtain, put her hand out, and took hold of two of the strings of beads.

"And you think then we'll be all right and be happy."

"I know we will. You don't have to be afraid. I've known lots of people that have done it."

"So have I," said the girl. "And afterward they were all so happy."

"Well," the man said, "if you don't want to you don't have to. I wouldn't   *55*
have you do it if you didn't want to. But I know it's perfectly simple."

"And you really want to?"

"I think it's the best thing to do. But I don't want you to do it if you don't really want to."

"And if I do it you'll be happy and things will be like they were and you'll love me?"

"I love you now. You know I love you."

60   "I know. But if I do it, then it will be nice again if I say things are like white elephants, and you'll like it?"

"I'll love it. I love it now but I just can't think about it. You know how I get when I worry."

"If I do it you won't ever worry?"

"I won't worry about that because it's perfectly simple."

"Then I'll do it. Because I don't care about me."

65   "What do you mean?"

"I don't care about me."

"Well, I care about you."

"Oh, yes. But I don't care about me. And I'll do it and then everything will be fine."

"I don't want you to do it if you feel that way."

70   The girl stood up and walked to the end of the station. Across, on the other side, were fields of grain and trees along the banks of the Ebro. Far away, beyond the river, were mountains. The shadow of a cloud moved across the field of grain and she saw the river through the trees.

"And we could have all this," she said. "And we could have everything and every day we make it more impossible."

"What did you say?"

"I said we could have everything."

"We can have everything."

75   "No, we can't."

"We can have the whole world."

"No, we can't."

"We can go everywhere."

"No, we can't. It isn't ours any more."

80   "It's ours."

"No, it isn't. And once they take it away, you never get it back."

"But they haven't taken it away."

"We'll wait and see."

"Come on back in the shade," he said. "You mustn't feel that way."

85   "I don't feel any way," the girl said. "I just know things."

"I don't want you to do anything that you don't want to do—"

"Nor that isn't good for me," she said. "I know. Could we have another beer?"

"All right. But you've got to realize—"

"I realize," the girl said. "Can't we maybe stop talking?"

They sat down at the table and the girl looked across at the hills on the   *90*
dry side of the valley and the man looked at her and at the table.

"You've got to realize," he said, "that I don't want you to do it if you
don't want to. I'm perfectly willing to go through with it if it means anything
to you."

"Doesn't it mean anything to you? We could get along."

"Of course it does. But I don't want anybody but you. I don't want any
one else. And I know it's perfectly simple."

"Yes, you know it's perfectly simple."

"It's all right for you to say that, but I do know it."   *95*

"Would you do something for me now?"

"I'd do anything for you."

"Would you please please please please please please please stop talking?"

He did not say anything but looked at the bags against the wall of the station. There were labels on them from all the hotels where they had spent nights.

"But I don't want you to," he said, "I don't care anything about it."   *100*

"I'll scream," the girl said.

The woman came out through the curtains with two glasses of beer
and put them down on the damp felt pads. "The train comes in five minutes,"
she said.

"What did she say?" asked the girl.

"That the train is coming in five minutes."

The girl smiled brightly at the woman, to thank her.   *105*

"I'd better take the bags over to the other side of the station," the man
said. She smiled at him.

"All right. Then come back and we'll finish the beer."

He picked up the two heavy bags and carried them around the station
to the other tracks. He looked up the tracks but could not see the train. Coming back, he walked through the barroom, where people waiting for the train
were drinking. He drank an Anis at the bar and looked at the people. They
were all waiting reasonably for the train. He went out through the bead curtain. She was sitting at the table and smiled at him.

"Do you feel better?" he asked.

"I feel fine," she said. "There's nothing wrong with me. I feel fine."   *1927*   *110*

CONSIDERATIONS

1. Reflect on the elements of nature that Hemingway uses in this setting.
   Which character seems to notice the outdoor surroundings most often?
   Why might this be important to the story's conflict itself?

2. Consider the contrast between the outdoor setting and the indoor scene. If you were staging this story as a play, what props would be central to the café setting? Which ones would be central beyond the café? What do these contrasts reveal, perhaps, about the couple themselves and the situation in which they find themselves?

3. Analyze the dialogue between these two people. Who most often asks the questions? Who seems most confident? In general, how would you describe the man's personality? The woman's? Explain.

4. What is the dilemma that the couple is talking about? Find the pronouns that they use to name this dilemma. What effect does Hemingway achieve with the short, quick dialogue pattern here?

5. Throughout this story, one simple line can hold several meanings. For example, what might Hemingway mean by "It isn't ours any more"? Find several other places where the meaning can be interpreted several ways in order to deepen the conflict.

EUDORA WELTY (1909–2001)

A Worn Path

Eudora Welty was born in Jackson, Mississippi, and spent nearly her whole life in the South. In her mid-twenties, she began to publish stories in the Southern Review *and the* Atlantic Monthly, *and during World War II she was a staff member of the* New York Times Book Review. *She wrote many collections of short fiction, and her novel* The Optimist's Daughter *won the Pulitzer Prize in 1972. In the preface to her collected stories, published in 1980, Welty said, "I have been told, both in approval and in accusation, that I seem to love all my characters. What I do in writing of any character is to try to enter into the mind, heart, and skin of a human being who is not myself. Whether this happens to be a man or a woman, old or young, with skin black or white, the primary challenge lies in making the jump itself. It is the act of a writer's imagination that I set most high."*

It was December—a bright frozen day in the early morning. Far out in the country there was an old Negro woman with her head tied in a red rag, coming along a path through the pinewoods. Her name was Phoenix Jackson. She was very old and small and she walked slowly in the dark pine shadows, moving a little from side to side in her steps, with the balanced heaviness and lightness of a pendulum in a grandfather clock. She carried a thin, small cane made from an umbrella, and with this she kept tapping the frozen earth in front of her. This made a grave and persistent noise in the still air, that seemed meditative like the chirping of a solitary little bird.

She wore a dark striped dress reaching down to her shoetops, and an equally long apron of bleached sugar sacks, with a full pocket; all neat and tidy, but every time she took a step she might have fallen over her shoelaces, which dragged from her unlaced shoes. She looked straight ahead. Her eyes were blue with age. Her skin had a pattern all its own of numberless branching wrinkles and as though a whole little tree stood in the middle of her forehead, but a golden color ran underneath, and the two knobs of her cheeks were illuminated by a yellow burning under the dark. Under the red rag her hair came down on her neck in the frailest of ringlets, still black, and with an odor like copper.

Now and then there was a quivering in the thicket. Old Phoenix said, "Out of my way, all you foxes, owls, beetles, jack rabbits, coons, and wild animals! . . . Keep out from under these feet, little bobwhites. . . . Keep the big wild hogs out of my path. Don't let none of those come running my direction. I got a long way." Under her small black-freckled hand her cane, limber as a buggy whip, would switch at the brush as if to rouse up any hiding things.

On she went. The woods were deep and still. The sun made the pine needles almost too bright to look at, up where the wind rocked. The cones dropped as light as feathers. Down in the hollow was the mourning dove—it was not too late for him.

The path ran up a hill. "Seems like there is chains about my feet, time I get this far," she said, in the voice of argument old people keep to use with themselves. "Something always take a hold on this hill—pleads I should stay." 5

After she got to the top she turned and gave a full, severe look behind her where she had come. "Up through pines," she said at length. "Now down through oaks."

Her eyes opened their widest and she started down gently. But before she got to the bottom of the hill a bush caught her dress.

Her fingers were busy and intent, but her skirts were full and long, so that before she could pull them free in one place they were caught in another. It was not possible to allow the dress to tear. "I in the thorny bush," she said. "Thorns, you doing your appointed work. Never want to let folks pass—no sir. Old eyes thought you was a pretty little green bush."

Finally, trembling all over, she stood free, and after a moment dared to stoop for her cane.

"Sun so high!" she cried, leaning back and looking, while the thick tears went over her eyes. "The time getting all gone here." 10

At the foot of this hill was a place where a log was laid across the creek.

"Now comes the trial," said Phoenix.

Putting her right foot out, she mounted the log and shut her eyes. Lifting her skirt, levelling her cane fiercely before her, like a festival figure in some parade, she began to march across. Then she opened her eyes and she was safe on the other side.

"I wasn't as old as I thought," she said.

15   But she sat down to rest. She spread her skirts on the bank around her and folded her hands over her knees. Up above her was a tree in a pearly cloud of mistletoe. She did not dare to close her eyes, and when a little boy brought her a little plate with a slice of marble-cake on it she spoke to him. "That would be acceptable," she said. But when she went to take it there was just her own hand in the air.

So she left that tree, and had to go through a barbed-wire fence. There she had to creep and crawl, spreading her knees and stretching her fingers like a baby trying to climb the steps. But she talked loudly to herself: she could not let her dress be torn now, so late in the day, and she could not pay for having her arm or her leg sawed off if she got caught fast where she was.

At last she was safe through the fence and risen up out in the clearing. Big dead trees, like black men with one arm, were standing in the purple stalks of the withered cotton field. There sat a buzzard.

"Who you watching?"

In the burrow she made her way along.

20   "Glad this not the season for bulls," she said, looking sideways, "and the good Lord made his snakes to curl up and sleep in the winter. A pleasure I don't see no two-headed snake coming around that tree, where it come once. It took a while to get by him, back in the summer."

She passed through the old cotton and went into a field of dead corn. It whispered and shook, and was taller than her head. "Through the maze now," she said, for there was no path.

Then there was something tall, black, and skinny there, moving before her.

At first she took it for a man. It could have been a man dancing in the field. But she stood still and listened, and it did not make a sound. It was as silent as a ghost.

"Ghost," she said sharply, "who be you the ghost of? For I have heard of nary death close by."

25   But there was no answer, only the ragged dancing in the wind.

She shut her eyes, reached out her hand, and touched a sleeve. She found a coat and inside that an emptiness, cold as ice.

"You scarecrow," she said. Her face lighted. "I ought to be shut up for good," she said with laughter. "My senses is gone. I too old. I the oldest people I ever know. Dance, old scarecrow," she said, "while I dancing with you."

She kicked her foot over the furrow, and with mouth drawn down shook her head once or twice in a little strutting way. Some husks blew down and whirled in streamers about her skirts.

Then she went on, parting her way from side to side with the cane, through the whispering field. At last she came to the end, to a wagon track, where the silver grass blew between the red ruts. The quail were walking around like pullets, seeming all dainty and unseen.

"Walk pretty," she said. "This the easy place. This the easy going."   30

She followed the track, swaying through the quiet bare fields, through the little strings of trees silver in their dead leaves, past cabins silver from weather, with the doors and windows boarded shut, all like old women under a spell sitting there. "I walking in their sleep," she said, nodding her head vigorously.

In a ravine she went where a spring was silently flowing through a hollow log. Old Phoenix bent and drank. "Sweetgum makes the water sweet," she said, and drank more. "Nobody knows who made this well, for it was here when I was born."

The track crossed a swampy part where the moss hung as white as lace from every limb. "Sleep on, alligators, and blow your bubbles." Then the track went into the road.

Deep, deep the road went down between the high green-colored banks. Overhead the live-oaks met, and it was as dark as a cave.

A black dog with a lolling tongue came up out of the weeds by the ditch.   35
She was meditating, and not ready, and when he came at her she only hit him a little with her cane. Over she went in the ditch, like a little puff of milk-weed.

Down there, her senses drifted away. A dream visited her, and she reached her hand up, but nothing reached down and gave her a pull. So she lay there and presently went to talking. "Old woman," she said to herself, "that black dog came up out of the weeds to stall you off, and now there he sitting on his fine tail, smiling at you."

A white man finally came along and found her—a hunter, a young man, with his dog on a chain.

"Well, Granny!" he laughed. "What are you doing there?"

"Lying on my back like a June-bug waiting to be turned over, mister," she said, reaching up her hand.

He lifted her up, gave her a swing in the air, and set her down, "Any-   40
thing broken, Granny?"

"No sir, them old dead weeds is springy enough," said Phoenix, when she had got her breath. "I thank you for your trouble."

"Where do you live, Granny?" he asked, while the two dogs were growling at each other.

"Away back yonder, sir, behind the ridge. You can't even see it from here."

"On your way home?"

"No, sir, I going to town."   45

"Why, that's too far! That's as far as I walk when I come out myself, and I get something for my trouble." He patted the stuffed bag he carried, and there hung down a little closed claw. It was one of the bobwhites, with its beak hooked bitterly to show it was dead. "Now you go on home, Granny!"

"I bound to go to town, mister," said Phoenix. "The time come around."

He gave another laugh, filling the whole landscape. "I know you colored people! Wouldn't miss going to town to see Santa Claus!"

But something held Old Phoenix very still. The deep lines in her face went into a fierce and different radiation. Without warning she had seen with her own eyes a flashing nickel fall out of the man's pocket on to the ground.

50   "How old are you, Granny?" he was saying.

"There is no telling, mister," she said, "no telling."

Then she gave a little cry and clapped her hands, and said, "Git on away from here, dog! Look at that dog!" She laughed as if in admiration. "He ain't scared of nobody. He a big black dog." She whispered, "Sick him!"

"Watch me get rid of that cur," said the man. "Sick him, Pete! Sick him!"

Phoenix heard the dogs fighting and heard the man running and throwing sticks. She even heard a gunshot. But she was slowly bending forward by that time, further and further forward, the lids stretched down over her eyes, as if she were doing this in her sleep. Her chin was lowered almost to her knees. The yellow palm of her hand came out from the fold of her apron. Her fingers slid down and along the ground under the piece of money with the grace and care they would have in lifting an egg from under a sitting hen. Then she slowly straightened up, she stood erect, and the nickel was in her apron pocket. A bird flew by. Her lips moved. "God watching me the whole time. I come to stealing."

55   The man came back, and his own dog panted about them. "Well, I scared him off that time," he said, and then he laughed and lifted his gun and pointed it at Phoenix.

She stood straight and faced him.

"Doesn't the gun scare you?" he said, still pointing it.

"No, sir, I seen plenty go off closer by, in my day, and for less than what I done," she said, holding utterly still.

He smiled, and shouldered the gun. "Well, Granny," he said, "you must be a hundred years old and scared of nothing. I'd give you a dime if I had any money with me. But you take my advice and stay home, and nothing will happen to you."

60   "I bound to go on my way, mister," said Phoenix. She inclined her head in the red rag. Then they went in different directions, but she could hear the gun shooting again and again over the hill.

She walked on. The shadows hung from the oak trees to the road like curtains. Then she smelled wood-smoke, and smelled the river, and she saw a steeple and the cabins on their steep steps. Dozens of little black children whirled around her. There ahead was Natchez shining. Bells were ringing. She walked on.

In the paved city it was Christmas time. There were red and green electric lights strung and crisscrossed everywhere, and all turned on in the daytime. Old Phoenix would have been lost if she had not distrusted her eyesight and depended on her feet to know where to take her.

She paused quietly on the sidewalk, where people were passing by. A lady came along in the crowd, carrying an armful of red-, green-, and silver-wrapped presents; she gave off perfume like the red roses in hot summer, and Phoenix stopped her.

"Please, missy, will you lace up my shoe?" She held up her foot.

"What do you want, Grandma?"

"See my shoe," said Phoenix. "Do all right for out in the country, but wouldn't look right to go in a big building."

"Stand still then, Grandma," said the lady. She put her packages down carefully on the sidewalk beside her and laced and tied both shoes tightly.

"Can't lace 'em with a cane," said Phoenix. "Thank you, missy. I doesn't mind asking a nice lady to tie up my shoe when I gets out on the street."

Moving slowly and from side to side, she went into the stone building and into a tower of steps, where she walked up and around and around until her feet knew to stop.

She entered a door, and there she saw nailed up on the wall the document that had been stamped with the gold seal and framed in the gold frame which matched the dream that was hung up in her head.

"Here I be," she said. There was a fixed and ceremonial stiffness over her body.

"A charity case, I suppose," said an attendant who sat at the desk before her.

But Phoenix only looked above her head. There was sweat on her face; the wrinkles shone like a bright net.

"Speak up, Grandma," the woman said. "What's your name? We must have your history, you know. Have you been here before? What seems to be the trouble with you?"

Old Phoenix only gave a twitch to her face as if a fly were bothering her.

"Are you deaf?" cried the attendant.

But then the nurse came in.

"Oh, that's just old Aunt Phoenix," she said. "She doesn't come for herself—she has a little grandson. She makes these trips just as regular as clockwork. She lives away back off the Old Natchez Trace." She bent down. "Well, Aunt Phoenix, why don't you just take a seat? We won't keep you standing after your long trip." She pointed.

The old woman sat down, bolt upright in the chair.

"Now, how is the boy?" asked the nurse.

Old Phoenix did not speak.

"I said, how is the boy?"

But Phoenix only waited and stared straight ahead, her face very solemn and withdrawn into rigidity.

"Is his throat any better?" asked the nurse. "Aunt Phoenix, don't you hear me? Is your grandson's throat any better since the last time you came for the medicine?"

85   With her hand on her knees, the old woman waited, silent, erect and motionless, just as if she were in armor.

"You mustn't take up our time this way, Aunt Phoenix," the nurse said. "Tell us quickly about your grandson, and get it over. He isn't dead, is he?"

At last there came a flicker and then a flame of comprehension across her face, and she spoke.

"My grandson. It was my memory had left me. There I sat and forgot why I made my long trip."

"Forgot?" The nurse frowned. "After you came so far?"

90   Then Phoenix was like an old woman begging a dignified forgiveness for waking up frightened in the night. "I never did go to school—I was too old at the Surrender," she said in a soft voice. "I'm an old woman without an education. It was my memory fail me. My little grandson, he is just the same, and I forgot it in the coming."

"Throat never heals, does it?" said the nurse, speaking in a loud, sure voice to Old Phoenix. By now she had a card with something written on it, a little list. "Yes. Swallowed lye. When was it—January—two—three years ago—"

Phoenix spoke unasked now. "No, missy, he not dead, he just the same. Every little while his throat begin to close up again, and he not able to swallow. He not get his breath. He not able to help himself. So the time come around, and I go on another trip for the soothing-medicine."

"All right. The doctor said as long as you came to get it you could have it," said the nurse. "But it's an obstinate case."

"My little grandson, he sit up there in the house all wrapped up, waiting by himself," Phoenix went on. "We is the only two left in the world. He suffer and it don't seem to put him back at all. He got a sweet look. He going to last. He wear a little patch quilt and peep out, holding his mouth open like a little bird. I remembers so plain now. I not going to forget him again, no, the whole enduring time. I could tell him from all the others in creation."

95   "All right." The nurse was trying to hush her now. She brought her a bottle of medicine. "Charity," she said, making a check mark in a book.

Old Phoenix held the bottle close to her eyes and then carefully put it into her pocket.

"I thank you," she said.

"It's Christmas time, Grandma," said the attendant. "Could I give you a few pennies out of my purse?"

"Five pennies is a nickel," said Phoenix stiffly.

100   "Here's a nickel," said the attendant.

Phoenix rose carefully and held out her hand. She received the nickel and then fished the other nickel out of her pocket and laid it beside the new one. She stared at her palm closely, with her head on one side.

Then she gave a tap with her cane on the floor.

"This is what come to me to do," she said. "I going to the store and buy my child a little windmill they sells, made out of paper. He going to find it hard to believe there such a thing in the world. I'll march myself back where he waiting, holding it straight up in this hand."

She lifted her free hand, gave a little nod, turned round, and walked out of the doctor's office. Then her slow step began on the stairs, going down.   *1941*

CONSIDERATIONS

1. Discuss the significance of the title. Why does Welty label the path "worn" when, in fact, it often seems overgrown and difficult to pass through?
2. What do the colors contribute to this story? In what way might they be related to Phoenix's name and personality? You might have to research the legend of the phoenix in order to make a good guess here.
3. Describe Phoenix from the point of view of the hunter and the nurse at the clinic. In what ways are their insights about Phoenix correct? What do they not see about her?
4. Comment on the story's ending. How is it related to the rest of the story? Consider especially any possible irony in the setting and the action.
5. Read the following commentary. How does it affect your initial reading of the story? Does it prompt you to go back and reread the story? Explain.

Commentary

EUDORA WELTY
Is Phoenix Jackson's Grandson Really Dead?

A story writer is more than happy to be read by students; the fact that these serious readers think and feel something in response to his work he finds life-giving. At the same time he may not always be able to reply to their specific questions in kind. I wondered if it might clarify something, for both the questioners and myself, if I set down a general reply to the question that comes to me most often in the mail, from both students and their teachers, after some classroom discussion. The unrivaled favorite is this: "Is Phoenix Jackson's grandson really *dead?*"

It refers to a short story I wrote years ago called "A Worn Path," which tells of a day's journey an old woman makes on foot from deep in the country into town and into a doctor's office on behalf of her little grandson; he is at home, periodically ill, and periodically she comes for his medicine; they give it to her as usual, she receives it and starts the journey back.

I had not meant to mystify readers by withholding any fact; it is not a writer's business to tease. The story is told through Phoenix's mind as she undertakes her errand. As the author at one with the character as I tell it, I must assume that the boy is alive. As the reader, you are free to think as you like, of course: The story invites you to believe that no matter what happens, Phoenix for as long as she is able to walk and can hold to her purpose will make her journey. The *possibility* that she would keep on even if he were dead is there in her devotion and its single-minded, single-track errand. Certainly the *artistic* truth, which should be good enough for the fact, lies in Phoenix's own answer to that question. When the nurse asks, "He isn't dead, is he?" she speaks for herself: "He still the same. He going to last."

The grandchild is the incentive. But it is the journey, the going of the errand, that is the story, and the question is not whether the grandchild is in reality alive or dead. It doesn't affect the outcome of the story or its meaning from start to finish. But it is not the question itself that has struck me as much as the idea, almost without exception implied in the asking, that for Phoenix's grandson to be dead would somehow make the story "better."

5 It's *all right,* I want to say to the students who write to me, for things to be what they appear to be, and for words to mean what they say. It's all right, too, for words and appearances to mean more than one thing—ambiguity is a fact of life. A fiction writer's responsibility covers not only what he presents as the facts of a given story but what he chooses to stir up as their implications; in the end, these implications, too, become facts, in the larger, fictional sense. But it is not all right, not in good faith, for things *not* to mean what they say.

The grandson's plight was real and it made the truth of the story, which is the story of an errand of love carried out. If the child no longer lived, the truth would persist in the "wornness" of the path. But his being dead can't increase the truth of the story, can't affect it one way or the other. I think I signal this, because the end of the story has been reached before Old Phoenix gets home again: she simply starts back. To the question "Is the grandson really dead?" I could reply that it doesn't make any difference. I could also say that I did not make him up in order to let him play a trick on Phoenix. But my best answer would be: "*Phoenix is alive.*"

The origin of a story is sometimes a trustworthy clue to the author—or can provide him with the clue—to its key image; maybe in this case it will do the same for the reader. One day I saw a solitary old woman like Phoenix. She was walking; I saw her, at middle distance, in a winter country landscape, and watched her slowly make her way across my line of vision. That sight of her made me write the story. I invented an errand for her, but that only seemed a living part of the figure she was herself: What errand other than for someone else could be making her go? And her going was the first thing, her persisting in her landscape was the real thing, and the first and the real were what I wanted and worked to keep. I brought her up close enough, by imagination, to describe her face, make her present to the eyes, but the full-length figure moving across the winter fields was the indelible one and the image to keep, and the perspective extending into the vanishing distance the true one to hold in mind.

I invented for my character, as I wrote, some passing adventures—some dreams and harassments and a small triumph or two, some jolts to her pride, some flights of fancy to console her, one or two encounters to scare her, a moment that gave her cause to feel ashamed, a moment to dance and preen— for it had to be a *journey,* and all these things belonged to that, parts of life's uncertainty.

A narrative line is in its deeper sense, of course, the tracing out of a meaning, and the real continuity of a story lies in this probing forward. The real dramatic force of a story depends on the strength of the emotion that has set it going. The emotional value is the measure of the reach of the story. What gives any such content to "A Worn Path" is not its circumstances but its *subject:* the deep-grained habit of love.

What I hoped would come clear was that in the whole surround of this   10 story, the world it threads through, the only certain thing at all is the worn path. The habit of love cuts through confusion and stumbles or contrives its way out of difficulty, it remembers the way even when it forgets, for a dumfounded moment, its reason for being. The path is the thing that matters.

Her victory—old Phoenix's—is when she sees the diploma in the doctor's office, when she finds "nailed up on the wall the document that had been stamped with the gold seal and framed in the gold frame, which matched the dream that was hung up in her head." The return with the medicine is just a matter of retracing her own footsteps. It is the part of the journey, and of the story, that can now go without saying.

In the matter of function, old Phoenix's way might even do as a sort of parallel to your way of work if you are a writer of stories. The way to get there is the all-important, all-absorbing problem, and this problem is your reason for undertaking the story. Your only guide, too, is your sureness about your subject, about what this subject is. Like Phoenix, you work all your life to find your way, through all the obstructions and the false appearances and the upsets you may have brought on yourself, to reach a meaning—using inventions of your imagination, perhaps helped out by your dreams and bits of good luck. And finally too, like Phoenix, you have to assume that what you are working in aid of is life, not death.

But you would make the trip anyway—wouldn't you?—just on hope.

LESLIE MARMON SILKO (1948–   )

The Man to Send Rain Clouds

> *Born in Albuquerque, New Mexico, Leslie Marmon Silko, grew up on the Laguna Pueblo Reservation. She has noted that her mixed ancestry—white, Mexican, and Native American—made her early years difficult, as she was not fully accepted by any culture. Nevertheless, her strongest identification is with the Laguna Pueblo. After graduating from the University of New Mexico and attending law school, she returned to the Laguna Pueblo where she currently lives and writes. She has published many short stories and poems, including a volume of poetry,* Laguna Woman: Poems *(1974), and a novel,* Ceremony *(1977). In interviews, Silko has stressed the importance of storytelling and, especially, the role of women in preserving the oral tradition. The short story that follows reflects this tradition.*

They found him under a big cottonwood tree. His Levi jacket and pants were faded light blue so that he had been easy to find. The big cottonwood tree stood apart from a small grove of winterbare cottonwoods which grew in the wide, sandy arroyo. He had been dead for a day or more, and the sheep had wandered and scattered up and down the arroyo. Leon and his brother-in-law, Ken, gathered the sheep and left them in the pen at the sheep camp before they returned to the cottonwood tree. Leon waited under the tree while Ken drove the truck through the deep sand to the edge of the arroyo. He squinted up at the sun and unzipped his jacket—it sure was hot for this time of year. But high and northwest the blue mountains were still in snow. Ken came sliding down the low, crumbling bank about fifty yards down, and he was bringing the red blanket.

Before they wrapped the old man, Leon took a piece of string out of his pocket and tied a small gray feather in the old man's long white hair. Ken gave him the paint. Across the brown wrinkled forehead he drew a streak of white and along the high cheekbones he drew a strip of blue paint. He paused and watched Ken throw pinches of corn meal and pollen into the wind that fluttered the small gray feather. Then Leon painted with yellow under the old man's broad nose, and finally, when he had painted green across the chin, he smiled.

"Send us rain clouds, Grandfather." They laid the bundle in the back of the pickup and covered it with a heavy tarp before they started back to the pueblo.

They turned off the highway onto the sandy pueblo road. Not long after they passed the store and post office they saw Father Paul's car coming toward them. When he recognized their faces he slowed his car and waved them to stop. The young priest rolled down the car window.

"Did you find old Teofilo?" he asked loudly.   5

Leon stopped the truck. "Good morning, Father. We were just out to the sheep camp. Everything is O.K. now."

"Thank God for that. Teofilo is a very old man. You really shouldn't allow him to stay at the sheep camp alone."

"No, he won't do that any more now."

"Well, I'm glad you understand. I hope I'll be seeing you at Mass this week—we missed you last Sunday. See if you can get old Teofilo to come with you." The priest smiled and waved at them as they drove away.

Louise and Teresa were waiting. The table was set for lunch, and the coffee   10
was boiling on the black iron stove. Leon looked at Louise and then at Teresa.

"We found him under a cottonwood tree in the big arroyo near sheep camp. I guess he sat down to rest in the shade and never got up again." Leon walked toward the old man's bed. The red plaid shawl had been shaken and spread carefully over the bed, and a new brown flannel shirt and pair of stiff new Levi's were arranged neatly beside the pillow. Louise held the screen door open while Leon and Ken carried in the red blanket. He looked small and shriveled, and after they dressed him in the new shirt and pants he seemed more shrunken.

It was noontime now because the church bells rang the Angelus. They ate the beans with hot bread, and nobody said anything until after Teresa poured the coffee.

Ken stood up and put on his jacket. "I'll see about the gravediggers. Only the top layer of soil is frozen. I think it can be ready before dark."

Leon nodded his head and finished his coffee. After Ken had been gone for a while, the neighbors and clanspeople came quietly to embrace Teofilo's family and to leave food on the table because the gravediggers would come to eat when they were finished.

———

15   The sky in the west was full of pale yellow light. Louise stood outside with her hands in the pockets of Leon's green army jacket that was too big for her. The funeral was over, and the old men had taken their candles and medicine bags and were gone. She waited until the body was laid into the pickup before she said anything to Leon. She touched his arm, and he noticed that her hands were still dusty from the corn meal that she had sprinkled around the old man. When she spoke, Leon could not hear her.

"What did you say? I didn't hear you."

"I said that I had been thinking about something."

"About what?"

"About the priest sprinkling holy water for Grandpa. So he won't be thirsty."

20   Leon stared at the new moccasins that Teofilo had made for the ceremonial dances in the summer. They were nearly hidden by the red blanket. It was getting colder, and the wind pushed gray dust down the narrow pueblo road. The sun was approaching the long mesa where it disappeared during the winter. Louise stood there shivering and watching his face. Then he zipped up his jacket and opened the truck door. "I'll see if he's there."

Ken stopped the pickup at the church, and Leon got out; and then Ken drove down the hill to the graveyard where people were waiting. Leon knocked at the old carved door with its symbols of the Lamb. While he waited he looked up at the twin bells from the king of Spain with the last sunlight pouring around them in their tower.

The priest opened the door and smiled when he saw who it was. "Come in! What brings you here this evening?"

The priest walked toward the kitchen, and Leon stood with his cap in his hand, playing with the earflaps and examining the living room—the brown sofa, the green armchair, and the brass lamp that hung down from the ceiling by links of chain. The priest dragged a chair out of the kitchen and offered it to Leon.

"No thank you, Father. I only came to ask you if you would bring your holy water to the graveyard."

25   The priest turned away from Leon and looked out the window at the patio full of shadows and the dining-room windows of the nuns' cloister across the patio. The curtains were heavy, and the light from within faintly penetrated; it was impossible to see the nuns inside eating supper. "Why didn't you tell me he was dead? I could have brought the Last Rites anyway."

Leon smiled. "It wasn't necessary, Father."

The priest stared down at his scuffed brown loafers and the worn hem of his cassock. "For a Christian burial it was necessary."

His voice was distant, and Leon thought that his blue eyes looked tired.

"It's O.K. Father, we just want him to have plenty of water."

The priest sank down into the green chair and picked up a glossy mis-   *30*
sionary magazine. He turned the colored pages full of lepers and pagans without looking at them.

"You know I can't do that, Leon. There should have been the Last Rites
and a funeral Mass at the very least."

Leon put on his green cap and pulled the flaps down over his ears. "It's
getting late, Father. I've got to go."

When Leon opened the door Father Paul stood up and said, "Wait." He
left the room and came back wearing a long brown overcoat. He followed
Leon out the door and across the dim churchyard to the adobe steps in front
of the church. They both stooped to fit through the low adobe entrance. And
when they started down the hill to the graveyard only half of the sun was visible above the mesa.

The priest approached the grave slowly, wondering how they had managed to dig into the frozen ground, and then he remembered that this was
New Mexico, and saw the pile of cold loose sand beside the hole. The people
stood close to each other with little clouds of steam puffing from their faces.
The priest looked at them and saw a pile of jackets, gloves, and scarves in the
yellow, dry tumbleweeds that grew in the graveyard. He looked at the red blanket, not sure that Teofilo was so small, wondering if it wasn't some perverse
Indian trick—something they did in March to ensure a good harvest—wondering if maybe old Teofilo was actually at sheep camp corraling the sheep for
the night. But there he was, facing into a cold dry wind and squinting at the
last sunlight, ready to bury a red wool blanket while the faces of his parish-
ioners were in shadow with the last warmth of the sun on their backs.

His fingers were stiff, and it took him a long time to twist the lid off the   *35*
holy water. Drops of water fell on the red blanket and soaked into dark icy spots.
He sprinkled the grave and the water disappeared almost before it touched the
dim, cold sand; it reminded him of something—he tried to remember what it
was, because he thought if he could remember he might understand this. He
sprinkled more water; he shook the container until it was empty, and the water
fell through the light from sundown like August rain that fell while the sun was
still shining, almost disappearing before it touched the wilted squash flowers.

The wind pulled at the priest's brown Franciscan robe and swirled away
the corn meal and pollen that had been sprinkled on the blanket. They lowered
the bundle into the ground, and they didn't bother to untie the stiff pieces of
new rope that were tied around the ends of the blanket. The sun was gone, and
over on the highway the eastbound lane was full of headlights. The priest walked
away slowly. Leon watched him climb the hill, and when he had disappeared
within the tall, thick walls, Leon turned to look up at the high blue mountains
in the deep snow that reflected a faint red light from the west. He felt good because it was finished, and he was happy about the sprinkling of the holy water;
now the old man could send them big thunderclouds for sure.   *1981*

CONSIDERATIONS

1. Reread this piece, noting the colors that Silko weaves through this story. How do these descriptions explain and connect the two different cultures? In what ways do they suggest divisions?
2. What are Father Paul's real reasons for not initially participating in the sprinkling of the holy water? Of whom or of what might he be afraid, and why does he change his mind?
3. Discuss the symbolism of the rain in terms of the Native American culture and of the Catholic Church as well. At a deep human level, where do these symbols converge?
4. Regarding the title, who is "the man" who will send the rain clouds, and what does this say about the relationship between nature and human beings?
5. In what ways does the weather reflect both the plight of the Native Americans *and* the plight of Father Paul's soul? Who is in greatest need or conflict in this piece? Explain.

Poetry

HAIKU

Haiku is a popular form of Japanese poetry that consists of seventeen syllables arranged in three lines containing five, seven, and five syllables. Traditionally, it must mention the season, the time of day, and the dominant features of the landscape. In the seventeenth century, the most famous haiku master, Basho, broadened the subject range, but it was still a form that expressed much and implied more in just a few words about daily affairs in everyday language.

Preceding Basho were haiku creators Arakida Moritake and Yamazaki Sokan, under whom haiku gained wide popularity. More modern practitioners of haiku include Meisetsu Naito and Kyoshi Takahama.

MORITAKE (1452–1540)

Fallen petals rise

TRANSLATED BY HAROLD G. HENDERSON

Fallen petals rise
back to the branch—I watch
oh . . . butterflies!

SÔKAN (1465–1553)

If only we could

TRANSLATED BY KENNETH YASUDA

If only we could
Add a handle to the moon
It would make a good fan.

MEISETSU (1847–1926)

City People

Townsfolk, it is plain—
    carrying red maple leaves
        in the homebound train.

KYOSHI (1874–1959)

The Snake

A snake! Though it passes,
    eyes that had glared at me
        stay in the grasses.

CONSIDERATIONS

1. Consider these four haiku. Which one(s) contain the most peaceful moods and tones? Which one(s) contain the most emotion? Which one(s) affect you most? Explain your answers to all of these questions.
2. List the most vivid images within these four pieces. Based on the images, what conclusions can you draw about haiku?
3. Either choose one piece and illustrate it, or choose one piece and write it in a paragraph in which you add more description. How does your creation compare to the original haiku? Explain.
4. Take a stand: Is haiku a simplistic form of poetry, or is it complex? Support your stance with three specific examples from these four pieces.

WILLIAM BLAKE (1757–1827)

The Tyger

For biographical information about William Blake, see page 233.

Tyger! Tyger! burning bright
In the forests of the night,
What immortal hand or eye
Could frame thy fearful symmetry?

5　In what distant deeps or skies
Burnt the fire of thine eyes?
On what wings dare he aspire?
What the hand, dare seize the fire?

And what shoulder, & what art,
10　Could twist the sinews of thy heart?
And when thy heart began to beat,
What dread hand? & what dread feet?

What the hammer? what the chain?
In what furnace was thy brain?
15　What the anvil? what dread grasp
Dare its deadly terrors clasp?

When the stars threw down their spears,
And water'd heaven with their tears,
Did he smile his work to see?
20　Did he who made the Lamb make thee?

Tyger! Tyger! burning bright
In the forests of the night,
What immortal hand or eye
Dare frame thy fearful symmetry?

CONSIDERATIONS

1. Note all the direct and indirect references to fire in this piece, and discuss
   the possible meanings behind this pattern of images.
2. Based on the descriptions in the fourth stanza, what role does Blake assign
   to the one who created the tyger? What does this imply about the creator
   and the created?

3. This poem was paired with a poem titled "The Lamb," which you can find on the Internet. On a concrete as well as a symbolic level, what is the relationship between the Lamb and the Tyger?
4. The first and last stanzas are exactly the same. What purpose might Blake have for this repetition, and how does it relate to the central conflict in this poem?

 WILLIAM WORDSWORTH (1770–1850)

The world is too much with us

> *William Wordsworth was born in the rural Lake District in the northwest of England and lived most of his life there. His poetry often celebrates the beauty and spiritual values of nature. In 1798, he and fellow poet Samuel Taylor Coleridge revolutionized English poetry with the publication of* Lyrical Ballads, *which used the language of ordinary people rather than the stylized idioms of the upper classes. This book launched the literary movement in England known as romanticism, which valued emotion over reason and the senses over intellect and held that the creative spirit of the artist was more important than following formal rules and conventions. At first, the critics harshly attacked this innovation, but in 1843, Wordsworth was named England's poet laureate. The sonnet here was probably written in 1803 and was first published in* Poems in Two Volumes *(1807).*

The world is too much with us; late and soon,
Getting and spending, we lay waste our powers:
Little we see in Nature that is ours;
We have given our hearts away, a sordid boon!
This Sea that bares her bosom to the moon;   5
The winds that will be howling at all hours,
And are up-gathered now like sleeping flowers;
For this, for everything, we are out of tune;
It moves us not.—Great God! I'd rather be
A Pagan suckled in a creed outworn;   10
So might I, standing on this pleasant lea,
Have glimpses that would make me less forlorn;
Have sight of Proteus rising from the sea;
Or hear old Triton blow his wreathèd horn.   *1803*

CONSIDERATIONS

1. The first sentence in this poem is often quoted with a sigh. What does the speaker mean: "The world is too much with us"? What does the author achieve by using such simple words to convey this message?
2. What does Wordsworth achieve by the use of the pronouns "we" and "us"? What might his shift to "I" imply?
3. The sonnet form is traditionally used to convey feelings of love and longing. What does the speaker here long for? What does he love most of all? Support your answer with details from the poem.
4. In what ways do the two mythical images in the last couplet connect with the theme and the conflict in this poem? Explain.

More Resources on
William Wordsworth and "The world is too much with us"

In *ARIEL*

- Brief biography of Wordsworth
- Complete texts of additional Wordsworth poems such as "Composed upon Westminster Bridge" and "I Wandered Lonely as a Cloud"

- Audio clip of reading of "The world is too much with us"
- Video clip of Wordsworth documentary
- Analysis of tone in Wordsworth's poetry
- Bibliography of scholarly works on Wordsworth

JOHN KEATS (1795–1821)
La Belle Dame Sans Merci[1]

Born the oldest of four children to working-class parents in Moorfields, England, John Keats was left an orphan at age fourteen. His maternal grandmother convinced two wealthy London merchants to become his guardians; they promptly took him out of school and apprenticed him to an apothecary (pharmacist). Although he had to hide his talent from his guardians, Keats knew that writing was his life's passion. When he turned twenty-one, and was thus an independent

[1]French: "The Beautiful Lady Without Pity."

adult, he left work as a pharmacist and devoted his life full-time to poetry. He
published several volumes of poetry, which were well received, but contracted tu-
berculosis, probably as a result of caring for his brother who had the disease. The
pall of darkness and death weighed heavily on Keats, which is often reflected in
the images of his poems. In 1821, he died from complications of the disease he
had been fighting for three years.

1

Ah, what can ail thee, knight at arms,
 Alone and palely loitering?
The sedge is withered from the lake,
 And no birds sing.

2

Ah, what can ail thee, knight at arms,   *5*
 So haggard and so woe-begone?
The squirrel's granary is full,
 And the harvest's done.

3

I see a lily on thy brow,
 With anguish moist and fever dew;   *10*
And on thy cheek a fading rose
 Fast withereth too.

4

"I met a lady in the meads,
 Full beautiful—a faery's child;
Her hair was long, her foot was light,   *15*
 And her eyes were wild.

5

"I set her on my pacing steed,
 And nothing else saw all day long,
For sideways would she lean, and sing
 A faery's song.   *20*

6

"I made a garland for her head,
 And bracelets too, and fragrant zone;
She looked at me as she did love,
 And made sweet moan.

7

25   "She found me roots of relish sweet,
        And honey wild, and manna dew;
      And sure in language strange she said—
        "I love thee true."

8

      "She took me to her elfin grot,
30   And there she gazed, and sighed deep,
      And there I shut her wild wild eyes
        So kissed to sleep.

9

      "And there we slumbered on the moss,
        And there I dreamed—Ah! woe betide!
35   The latest dream I ever dreamed.
        On the cold hill side.

10

      "I saw pale kings, and princes too,
        Pale warriors, death pale were they all;
      They cried—"La Belle Dame sans Merci
40   Hath thee in thrall!"

11

      "I saw their starved lips in the gloam,
        With horrid warning gaped wide,
      And I awoke, and found me here
        On the cold hill side.

12

45   "And this is why I sojourn here,
        Alone and palely loitering,
      Though the sedge is withered from the lake,
        And no birds sing."   *1819/1820*

CONSIDERATIONS

1. Imagine this poem as a three-act play. What is the central action in each
   act, and where does the central conflict reside? Explain.

2. What role do the seasons play in this poem, and how do they contribute to the central conflict?
3. What are the underlying causes of the knight's despondency, and what are the reasons that he remains alone in the end?

GERARD MANLEY HOPKINS (1844–1889)

God's Grandeur

Born in England into a High Church Anglican family, Gerard Manley Hopkins converted to Catholicism in 1866 while studying at Oxford. In 1877, he became a priest and worked in the slums of Manchester, Liverpool, and Glasgow. He had written some poetry as a student, but when he became a Jesuit, he decided that writing poetry was too self-indulgent for a priest who was supposed to sacrifice personal ambition. After a few years, however, he began writing again, exploring the struggle between his faith and his delight in the sensuous world in his poetry. He is considered the inventor of "sprung rhythm," which attempts to follow the rhythms of everyday speech rather than conventional patterns of stressed and unstressed syllables. This sonnet was written in 1877 but was not published until 1918, after his death, by his literary caretaker, poet laureate Robert Bridges.

The world is charged with the grandeur of God.
   It will flame out, like shining from shook foil;
   It gathers to a greatness, like the ooze of oil
Crushed. Why do men then now not reck his rod?°

Generations have trod, have trod, have trod;   5
   And all is seared with trade; bleared, smeared with toil;
   And wears man's smudge and shares man's smell: the soil
Is bare now, nor can foot feel, being shod.

And for all this, nature is never spent;
   There lives the dearest freshness deep down things;   10
And though the last lights off the black West went
   Oh, morning, at the brown brink eastward, springs—
Because the Holy Ghost over the bent
   World broods with warm breast and with ah! bright wings.   *1877*

°*reck his rod:* Heed his right to rule.

CONSIDERATIONS

1. In your own words, summarize the basic message within each stanza.
2. Make a list of the verbs Hopkins uses in this poem. How do they differ
   from stanza to stanza? What do the differences reflect about the relationship
   between man and God? Man and the world? The world and God?
3. Analyze the sounds in this poem, the alliteration as well as the assonance.
   What effect is achieved by the use of these devices? Explain.

JEAN TOOMER (1894–1967)

November Cotton Flower

> *Jean Toomer was born to an upper-class African-American family in Washington,
> D.C. Like many African Americans, Toomer's background was racially mixed. Both
> of his mother's grandfathers were white, and some sources say that Toomer's own
> father, who deserted the family shortly after Toomer's birth, was also white. Never-
> theless, his best known work* Cane *(1923), from which the following selection is
> taken, movingly describes the life of poor black people living in rural Georgia.*

Boll-weevil's coming, and the winter's cold,
Made cotton-stalks look rusty, seasons old,
And cotton, scarce as any southern snow,
Was vanishing; the branch, so pinched and slow,
5   Failed in its function as the autumn rake;
Drouth fighting soil had caused the soil to take
All water from the streams; dead birds were found
In wells a hundred feet below the ground—
Such was the season when the flower bloomed.
10   Old folks were startled, and it soon assumed
Significance. Superstition saw
Something it had never seen before:
Brown eyes that loved without a trace of fear,
Beauty so sudden for that time of year.   *1923*

CONSIDERATIONS

1. Explore the reasons why Toomer might have composed this poem in a strict
   sonnet form, and then discuss the relationship between the first eight lines
   and the last six lines.

2. In what ways could this poem be a metaphor for the African-American experience in the South? How do the elements of nature relate to this experience?

H. D. (HILDA DOOLITTLE) (1886–1961)

Sheltered Garden

> *Born in Bethlehem, Pennsylvania, Hilda Doolittle learned early to appreciate and recognize different cultures from her mother, who was Moravian, and to imagine the wonders of the universe from her father, who was an astronomer. She was educated at Bryn Mawr College, and during her years there developed friendships with noted poets such as Marianne Moore and Ezra Pound, who encouraged Doolittle to develop her own considerable talents. She became known as one of the leading poets of the Imagist movement, writing poems that treated their subject directly, sparely, and with attention to the musical sounds of the lines, rather than to the strict count of traditional metrics.*

I have had enough.
I gasp for breath.

Every way ends, every road,
every foot-path leads at last
to the hill-crest—   5
then you retrace your steps,
or find the same slope on the other side,
precipitate.

I have had enough—
border-pinks, clove-pinks, wax-lilies,   10
herbs, sweet-cress.

O for some sharp swish of a branch—
there is no scent of resin
in this place,
no taste of bark, of coarse weeds,   15
aromatic, astringent—
only border on border of scented pinks.

Have you seen fruit under cover
that wanted light—
pears wadded in cloth,   20
protected from the frost,
melons, almost ripe,
smothered in straw?

Why not let the pears cling
25   to the empty branch?
All your coaxing will only make
a bitter fruit—
let them cling, ripen of themselves,
test their own worth,
30   nipped, shriveled by the frost,
to fall at last but fair
with a russet coat.

Or the melon—
let it bleach yellow
35   in the winter light,
even tart to the taste—
it is better to taste of frost—
the exquisite frost—
than of wadding and of dead grass.

40   For this beauty,
beauty without strength,
chokes out life.
I want wind to break,
scatter these pink-stalks,
45   snap off their spiced heads,
fling them about with dead leaves—
spread the paths with twigs,
limbs broken off,
trail great pine branches,
50   hurled from some far wood
right across the melon patch,
break pear and quince—
leave half-trees, torn, twisted
but showing the fight was valiant.

55   O to blot out this garden
to forget, to find a new beauty
in some terrible
wind-tortured place.

CONSIDERATIONS

1. Respond to the language and tone in this piece. How would you characterize both—as feminine, masculine, neutral? Explain.

2. Explore the ways in which the narrator is like the pear on the "empty branch" and how this explains the conflict between social expectations and human nature.
3. What exactly has the narrator had "enough" of? To what degree can you relate to or sympathize with the narrator? Explain.

ELIZABETH BISHOP (1911–1979)

The Fish

After her father died and her mother was committed to a mental hospital, Eliza-beth Bishop spent her childhood shuttling between various relatives and boarding schools. She went to college at Vassar, where she and three fellow students founded a literary magazine. After college, she moved to Greenwich Village, where she lived with Louise Crane, a classmate from Vassar. During these years, Bishop met Marianne Moore, a poet with whom she would have a long friend-ship and literary correspondence. In 1938, Bishop and Crane bought a house in Key West, Florida. Bishop lived there for nine years, working on her poetry. A perfectionist, she would often revise a poem for years before judging it ready for publication. The poem here was first published in Partisan Review *in 1940 and later appeared in Bishop's first collection,* North and South *(1946). As she was working on "The Fish," Bishop wrote to Moore, "I'm afraid it is very bad and, if not like Robert Frost, perhaps like Ernest Hemingway! I left the last line on so it wouldn't be, but I don't know . . ." In 1951, Bishop moved to Brazil, where she lived with Lota de Macedo Soares. In 1953, she published* Poems: North and South—a Cold Spring, *which won the Pulitzer Prize for poetry in 1956. In 1965 she accepted a position as writer-in-residence at the Univer-sity of Washington, and her third book of poetry,* Questions of Travel, *won the National Book Award. After Lota's suicide in 1967, Bishop moved back to Brazil to live in Lota's house. In 1970, she returned to the United States to teach at Harvard. In 1976, she published* Geography III, *which won the National Book Critics Circle Award. At the time of her death, she had just begun the fall term as a visiting professor of poetry at the Massachusetts Institute of Technology.*

I caught a tremendous fish
and held him beside the boat
half out of water, with my hook
fast in a corner of his mouth.
He didn't fight.   5
He hadn't fought at all.
He hung a grunting weight,

battered and venerable
and homely. Here and there
10   his brown skin hung in strips
like ancient wallpaper,
and its pattern of darker brown
was like wallpaper:
shapes like full-blown roses
15   stained and lost through age.
He was speckled with barnacles,
fine rosettes of lime,
and infested
with tiny white sea-lice,
20   and underneath two or three
rags of green weed hung down.
While his gills were breathing in
the terrible oxygen
—the frightening gills,
25   fresh and crisp with blood,
that can cut so badly—
I thought of the coarse white flesh
packed in like feathers,
the big bones and the little bones,
30   the dramatic reds and blacks
of his shiny entrails,
and the pink swim-bladder
like a big peony.
I looked into his eyes
35   which were far larger than mine
but shallower, and yellowed,
the irises backed and packed
with tarnished tinfoil
seen through the lenses
40   of old scratched isinglass.°
They shifted a little, but not
to return my stare.
—It was more like the tipping
of an object toward the light.
45   I admired his sullen face,
the mechanism of his jaw,
and then I saw
that from his lower lip

40 *isinglass:* Very thin mica used for windshields in early automobiles.

—if you could call it a lip
grim, wet, and weaponlike,   *50*
hung five old pieces of fish-line,
or four and a wire leader
with the swivel still attached,
with all their five big hooks
grown firmly in his mouth.   *55*
A green line, frayed at the end
where he broke it, two heavier lines,
and a fine black thread
still crimped from the strain and snap
when it broke and he got away.   *60*
Like medals with their ribbons
frayed and wavering,
a five-haired beard of wisdom
trailing from his aching jaw.
I stared and stared   *65*
and victory filled up
the little rented boat,
from the pool of bilge
where oil had spread a rainbow
around the rusted engine   *70*
to the bailer rusted orange,
the sun-cracked thwarts,
the oarlocks on their strings,
the gunnels—until everything
was rainbow, rainbow, rainbow!   *75*
And I let the fish go.   *1940*

CONSIDERATIONS

1. How do the descriptions of the fish in the first 17 lines of the poem reflect the speaker's attitude toward the fish? Explain.
2. At what point do you think the speaker decides to free the fish? Explain.
3. What do the fish and the speaker have in common? What separates them? What is more important here, the differences or the common elements? Explain.
4. Comment on Bishop's use of color and description in this piece. What words or phrases affect you the most? Can you figure out why?

WILLIAM STAFFORD (1914–1993)
Traveling through the dark

> Born in Kansas, William Stafford lived and worked in that state, earning bachelor's and master's degrees at the University of Kansas and a doctorate at the University of Iowa. Beginning in 1948, he taught literature and writing at Lewis and Clark College in Portland, Oregon. "Traveling through the dark" appears in Stafford's collection Stories That Could Be True: New and Collected Poems (1960).

Traveling through the dark I found a deer
dead on the edge of the Wilson River road.
It is usually best to roll them into the canyon:
that road is narrow; to swerve might make more dead.

5   By glow of the tail-light I stumbled back of the car
and stood by the heap, a doe, a recent killing;
she had stiffened already, almost cold.
I dragged her off; she was large in the belly.

My fingers touching her side brought me the reason—
10   her side was warm; her fawn lay there waiting,
alive, still, never to be born.
Beside that mountain road I hesitated.

The car aimed ahead its lowered parking lights;
under the hood purred the steady engine.
15   I stood in the glare of the warm exhaust turning red;
around our group I could hear the wilderness listen.

I thought hard for us all—my only swerving—,
then pushed her over the edge into the river.   1960

CONSIDERATIONS

1. In what ways does the mountain setting contribute to the conflict in this piece?
2. Trace the images of light in this piece. How do they change from the beginning to the end?
3. What effect does the poet achieve by calling the doe "she" instead of "it"?
4. Stafford writes that "around our group I could hear the wilderness listen." What could it be listening to? What could it be listening for?
5. Would you have decided to do what the speaker in this poem did? Explain.

MARY OLIVER (1935–   )

A Certain Sharpness in the Morning Air

> *Mary Oliver was born in Maple Heights, Ohio. She attended Ohio State University and Vassar College, each for one year. Six years later, in 1963, she published her first book of poetry,* No Voyage and Other Poems. *In 1972, she chaired the writing department at the Fine Arts Work Center in Provincetown, Massachusetts, and published her second book of poetry,* The River Styx, Ohio, and Other Poems. *Between 1980 and 1995, she was visiting professor at Case Western Reserve University, Bucknell University, the University of Cincinnati, and Sweet Briar College. Since 1996, she has taught at Bennington College in Vermont. During that time, she has published thirteen more books of poetry, as well as* A Poetry Handbook *(1994) and* Rules for the Dance: A Handbook for Writing and Reading Metrical Verse *(1998). She won the Pulitzer Prize for poetry in 1984 for* American Primitive *(1983). Poet Maxine Kumin has called her "an indefatigable guide to the natural world." This poem first appeared in* New and Selected Poems *(1993).*

In the morning
it shuffles, unhurried,
across the wet fields
in its black slippers,
in its coal–colored coat   5
with the white stripe like a river
running down its spine—
a glossy animal with a quick temper
and two bulbs of such diatribe under its tail
that when I see it I pray   10
not to be noticed—
not to be struck
by the flat boards of its anger—
for the whole haul of its smell
is unendurable—   15
like tragedy
that can't be borne,
like death
that has to be buried, or burned—
but a little of it is another story—   20
for it's true, isn't it,
in our world,
that the petals pooled with nectar, and the polished thorns
are a single thing—

25   that even the purest light, lacking the robe of darkness,
       would be without expression—
       that love itself, without its pain, would be
       no more than a shruggable comfort.
       Lately, I have noticed, when the skunk's temper has tilted
30   in the distance,
       and the acids are floating everywhere,
       and I am touched, it is all, even in my nostrils and my throat,
         as the brushing of thorns;
       and I stand there
35   thinking of the old, wild life of the fields, when, as I remember it,
       I was shaggy, and beautiful,
       like the rose.   *1993*

CONSIDERATIONS

1. In what ways is the personification at the beginning of this poem connected to the ending? In this piece, is Oliver more intent on highlighting
   the similarities between humans and nature—or on discussing their differences? Explain.
2. In addition to the polarities between humans and the natural world, what
   are the other opposing realities at work in this poem?
3. What is it that the speaker may fear far more than being noticed by the
   skunk? Explain.

Drama

JOHN MILLINGTON SYNGE (1871–1909)

Riders to the Sea

*Born to wealthy parents, John Millington Synge (pronounced "Sing") lived dur-
ing his early years in the country outside of Dublin. Growing up as a Protestant
in a strongly Roman Catholic country, Synge often found himself isolated from
his peers. He left Ireland as a young man to travel through Europe, settling finally in Paris. It was there, in 1899, that Irish poet William Butler Yeats came
to read and admire his writing. Yeats convinced Synge to return to Ireland, where
he became profoundly moved by and concerned with the Irish political situation,
and, especially, with the dire circumstances of the Irish working class. During the*

final six years of his life, he wrote six plays, including the comedy Playboy of
the Western World *(1907), for which he is best known.* Riders to the Sea
*(1904) is a brief masterpiece that captures in one act the inexorable struggle of
Irish peasants with the sea on which they must depend for their living.*

Characters

MAURYA, *an old woman*
BARTLEY, *her son*
CATHLEEN, *her daughter*
NORA, *a younger daughter*
MEN AND WOMEN

Scene *An island off the West of Ireland*

> *Cottage kitchen, with nets, oilskins, spinning-wheel, some new boards standing
> by the wall, etc.* CATHLEEN, *a girl of about twenty, finishes kneading cake, and
> puts it down in the pot-oven by the fire; then wipes her hands, and begins to spin
> at the wheel.* NORA, *a young girl, puts her head in at the door.*

NORA *(in a low voice)*: Where is she?
CATHLEEN: She's lying down, God help her, and maybe sleeping, if she's able.

> NORA *comes in softly, and takes a bundle from under her shawl.*

CATHLEEN *(spinning the wheel rapidly)*: What is it you have?
NORA: The young priest is after bringing them. It's a shirt and a plain stocking were got off a drowned man in Donegal.   5

> CATHLEEN *stops her wheel with a sudden movement, and leans out to listen.*

NORA: We're to find out if it's Michael's they are, some time herself will be
down looking by the sea.
CATHLEEN: How would they be Michael's, Nora? How would he go the
length of that way to the far north?
NORA: The young priest says he's known the like of it. 'If it's Michael's they   10
are,' says he, 'you can tell herself he's got a clean burial, by the grace of
God; and if they're not his, let no one say a word about them, for she'll
be getting her death,' says he, 'with crying and lamenting.'

> *The door which* NORA *half closed is blown open by a gust of wind.*

CATHLEEN *(looking out anxiously)*: Did you ask him would he stop Bartley
going this day with the horses to the Galway fair?   15
NORA: 'I won't stop him,' says he; 'but let you not be afraid. Herself does be
saying prayers half through the night, and the Almighty God won't leave
her destitute,' says he, 'with no son living.'
CATHLEEN: Is the sea bad by the white rocks, Nora?

20 NORA: Middling bad, God help us. There's a great roaring in the west, and it's
      worse it'll be getting when the tide's turned to the wind. *(She goes over to
      the table with the bundle.)* Shall I open it now?

    CATHLEEN: Maybe she'd wake up on us, and come in before we'd done
      (coming to the table). It's a long time we'll be, and the two of us crying.

25 NORA *(goes to the inner door and listens)*: She's moving about on the bed. She'll
      be coming in a minute.

    CATHLEEN: Give me the ladder, and I'll put them up in the turf-loft, the way
      she won't know of them at all, and maybe when the tide turns she'll be
      going down to see would he be floating from the east.

    *They put the ladder against the gable of the chimney; CATHLEEN goes up a few
    steps and hides the bundle in the turf-loft. MAURYA comes from the inner room.*

30 MAURYA *(looking up at CATHLEEN and speaking querulously)*: Isn't it turf
      enough you have for this day and evening?

    CATHLEEN: There's a cake baking at the fire for a short space *(throwing down the
      turf)*, and Bartley will want it when the tide turns if he goes to Connemara.

    NORA picks up the turf and puts it round the pot-oven.

    MAURYA *(sitting down on a stool at the fire)*: He won't go this day with the
35   wind rising from the south and west. He won't go this day, for the young
      priest will stop him surely.

    NORA: He'll not stop him, mother; and I heard Eamon Simon and Stephen
      Pheety and Colum Shawn saying he would go.

    MAURYA: Where is he itself?

40 NORA: He went down to see would there be another boat sailing in the
      week, and I'm thinking it won't be long till he's here now, for the tides
      turning at the green head, and the hooker's tacking from the east.

    CATHLEEN: I hear some one passing the big stones.

    NORA *(looking out)*: He's coming now, and he in a hurry.

45 BARTLEY *(comes in and looks round the room. Speaking sadly and quietly)*: Where
      is the bit of new rope, Cathleen, was bought in Connemara?

    CATHLEEN *(coming down)*: Give it to him, Nora; it's on a nail by the white
      boards. I hung it up this morning, for the pig with the black feet was
      eating it.

50 NORA *(giving him a rope)*: Is that it, Bartley?

    MAURYA: You'd do right to leave that rope, Bartley, hanging by the boards
      (BARTLEY *takes the rope)*. It will be wanting in this place, I'm telling
      you, if Michael is washed up tomorrow morning or the next morning,
      or any morning in the week; for it's a deep grave we'll make him, by the
55   grace of God.

    BARTLEY *(beginning to work with the rope)*: I've no halter the way I can ride
      down on the mare, and I must go now quickly. This is the one boat going

for two weeks or beyond it, and the fair will be a good fair for horses, I
    heard them saying below.

MAURYA: It's a hard thing they'll be saying below if the body is washed up   *60*
    and there's no man in it to make the coffin, and I after giving a big price
    for the finest white boards you'd find in Connemara.

She looks round at the boards.

BARTLEY: How would it be washed up, and we after looking each day for nine
    days, and a strong wind blowing a while back from the west and south?

MAURYA: If it isn't found itself, that wind is raising the sea, and there was a   *65*
    star up against the moon, and it rising in the night. If it was a hundred
    horses, or a thousand horses, you had itself, what is the price of a thou-
    sand horses against a son where there is one son only?

BARTLEY *(working at the halter, to* CATHLEEN*)*: Let you go down each day,
    and see the sheep aren't jumping in on the rye, and if the jobber comes   *70*
    you can sell the pig with the black feet if there is a good price going.

MAURYA: How would the like of her get a good price for a pig?

BARTLEY *(to* CATHLEEN*)*: If the west wind holds with the last bit of the moon
    let you and Nora get up weed enough for another cock for the kelp. It's
    hard set we'll be from this day with no one in it but one man to work.   *75*

MAURYA: It's hard set we'll be surely the day you're drowned with the rest.
    What way will I live and the girls with me, and I an old woman looking
    for the grave?

    BARTLEY *lays down the halter, takes off his old coat, and puts on a newer one
    of the same flannel.*

BARTLEY *(to* NORA*)*: Is she coming to the pier?

NORA *(Looking out)*: She's passing the green head and letting fall her sails.   *80*

BARTLEY *(getting his purse and tobacco)*: I'll have half an hour to go down, and
    you'll see me coming again in two days, or in three days, or maybe in
    four days if the wind is bad.

MAURYA *(turning round to the fire, and putting her shawl over her head)*: Isn't it a
    hard and cruel man won't hear a word from an old woman, and she hold-   *85*
    ing him from the sea?

CATHLEEN: It's the life of a young man to be going on the sea, and who
    would listen to an old woman with one thing and she saying it over?

BARTLEY *(taking the halter)*: I must go now quickly. I'll ride down on the red
    mare, and the grey pony 'ill run behind me . . . The blessing of God on you.   *90*

    He goes out.

MAURYA *(crying out as he is in the door)*: He's gone now, God spare us, and
    we'll not see him again. He's gone now, and when the black night is
    falling I'll have no son left me in the world.

CATHLEEN: Why wouldn't you give him your blessing and he looking round
95 in the door? Isn't it sorrow enough is on every one in this house without you sending him out with an unlucky word behind him, and a hard
  word in his ear?

  MAURYA *takes up the tongs and begins raking the fire aimlessly without look-*
  ing round.

NORA *(turning towards her)*: You're taking away the turf from the cake.

CATHLEEN *(crying out)*: The Son of God forgive us, Nora, we're after forget-
100 ting his bit of bread. *(She comes over to the fire.)*

NORA: And it's destroyed he'll be going till dark night, and he after eating
  nothing since the sun went up.

CATHLEEN *(turning the cake out of the oven)*: It's destroyed he'll be, surely.
  There's no sense left on any person in a house where an old woman will
105 be talking for ever.

  MAURYA *sways herself on her stool*

CATHLEEN *(cutting off some of the bread and rolling it in a cloth; to* MAURYA*)*: Let
  you go down now to the spring well and give him this and he passing.
  You'll see him then and the dark word will be broken, and you can say
  'God speed you,' the way he'll be easy in his mind.

110 MAURYA *(taking the bread)*: Will I be in it as soon as himself?

CATHLEEN: If you go now quickly.

MAURYA *(standing up unsteadily)*: It's hard set I am to walk.

CATHLEEN *(looking at her anxiously)*: Give her the stick, Nora, or maybe she'll
  slip on the big stones.

115 NORA: What stick?

CATHLEEN: The stick Michael brought from Connemara.

MAURYA *(taking a stick* NORA *gives her)*: In the big world the old people do
  be leaving things after them for their sons and children, but in this place
  it is the young men do be leaving things behind for them that do be old.

  She goes out slowly. NORA *goes over to the ladder.*

120 CATHLEEN: Wait, Nora, maybe she'd turn back quickly. She's that sorry, God
  help her, you wouldn't know the thing she'd do.

NORA: Is she gone round by the bush?

CATHLEEN *(looking out)*: She's gone now. Throw it down quickly for the Lord
  knows when she'll be out of it again.

125 NORA *(getting the bundle from the loft)*: The young priest said he'd be passing
  tomorrow, and we might go down and speak to him below if it's
  Michael's they are surely.

CATHLEEN *(taking the bundle)*: Did he say what way they were found?

NORA *(coming down)*: 'There were two men,' says he, 'and they rowing round   *130*
with poteen before the cocks crowed, and the oar of one of them caught
the body, and they passing the black cliffs of the north.'

CATHEEN *(trying to open the bundle)*: Give me a knife, Nora; the string's perished with salt water, and there's a black knot on it you wouldn't loosen
in a week.

NORA *(giving her a knife)*: I've heard tell it was a long way to Donegal.   *135*

CATHLEEN *(cutting the string)*: It is surely. There was a man in here a while
ago—the man sold us that knife—and he said if you set off walking from
the rocks beyond, it would be in seven days you'd be in Donegal.

NORA: And what time would a man take, and he floating?

*CATHLEEN opens the bundle and takes out a bit of a shirt and a stocking. They
look at them eagerly.*

CATHLEEN *(in a low voice)*: The Lord spare us, Nora! Isn't it a queer hard   *140*
thing to say if it's his they are surely?

NORA: I'll get his shirt off the hook the way we can put the one flannel on
the other. *(She looks through some clothes hanging in the corner.)* It's not
with them, Cathleen, and where will it be?

CATHLEEN: I'm thinking Bartley put it on him in the morning, for his own   *145*
shirt was heavy with the salt in it. *(Pointing to the corner.)* There's a bit of
a sleeve was of the same stuff. Give me that and it will do.

NORA *brings it to her and they compare the flannel.*

CATHLEEN: It's the same stuff, Nora; but if it is itself, aren't there great rolls of
it in the shops of Galway, and isn't it many another man may have a shirt
of it as well as Michael himself?   *150*

NORA *(who has taken up the stocking and counted the stitches, crying out)*: It's
Michael, Cathleen, it's Michael; God spare his soul, and what will herself
say when she hears this story, and Bartley on the sea?

CATHLEEN *(taking the stocking)*: It's a plain stocking.

NORA: It's the second one of the third pair I knitted, and I put up three-score   *155*
stitches, and I dropped four of them.

CATHLEEN *(counts the stitches)*: It's that number is in it *(crying out)*. Ah, Nora,
isn't it a bitter thing to think of him floating that way to the far north, and
no one to keen him but the black hags that do be flying on the sea?

NORA *(swinging herself half round, and throwing out her arms on the clothes)*: And   *160*
isn't it a pitiful thing when there is nothing left of a man who was a great
rower and fisher but a bit of an old shirt and a plain stocking?

CATHLEEN *(after an instant)*: Tell me is herself coming, Nora? I hear a little
sound on the path.

NORA *(looking out)*: She is, Cathleen. She's coming up to the door.   *165*

CATHLEEN: Put these things away before she'll come in. Maybe it's easier she'll be after giving her blessing to Bartley, and we won't let on we've heard anything the time he's on the sea.

NORA *(helping* CATHLEEN *to close the bundle)*: We'll put them here in the corner.

They put them into a hole in the chimney corner. CATHLEEN *goes back to the spinning-wheel.*

170 NORA: Will she see it was crying I was?

CATHLEEN: Keep your back to the door the way the light'll not be on you.

NORA sits down at the chimney corner, with her back to the door. MAURYA comes in very slowly, without looking at the girls, and goes over to her stool at the other side of the fire. The cloth with the bread is still in her hand. The girls look at each other, and NORA points to the bundle of bread.

CATHLEEN *(after spinning for a moment)*: You didn't give him his bit of bread?

MAURYA *begins to keen softly, without turning round.*

CATHLEEN: Did you see him riding down?

MAURYA *goes on keening.*

CATHLEEN *(a little impatiently)*: God forgive you; isn't it a better thing to raise
175 your voice and tell what you seen, than to be making lamentation for a thing that's done? Did you see Bartley, I'm saying to you?

MAURYA *(with a weak voice)*: My heart's broken from this day.

CATHLEEN *(as before)*: Did you see Bartley?

MAURYA: I seen the fearfulest thing.

180 CATHLEEN *(leaves her wheel and looks out)*: God forgive you: he's riding the mare now over the green head, and the grey pony behind him.

MAURYA *(Starts, so that her shawl falls back from her head and shows her white tossed hair. With a frightened voice)*: The grey pony behind him. . . .

CATHLEEN *(coming to the fire)*: What is it ails you at all?

185 MAURYA *(speaking very slowly)*: I've seen the fearfulest thing any person has seen since the day Bride Dara seen the dead man with the child in his arms.

CATHLEEN *and* NORA: Uah.

They crouch down in front of the old woman at the fire.

NORA: Tell us what it is you seen.

MAURYA: I went down to the spring well, and I stood there saying a prayer to
190 myself. Then Bartley came along, and he riding on the red mare with the grey pony behind him *(she puts up her hands, as if to hide something from her eyes).* The Son of God spare us, Nora!

CATHLEEN: What is it you seen?

MAURYA: I seen Michael himself.

CATHLEEN *(speaking softly)*: You did not, mother. It wasn't Michael you seen, *195* for his body is after being found in the far north, and he's got a clean burial, by the grace of God.

MAURYA *(a little defiantly)*: I'm after seeing him this day, and he riding and galloping. Bartley came first on the red mare, and I tried to say 'God speed you,' but something choked the words in my throat. He went by *200* quickly; and 'the blessing of God on you,' says he, and I could say nothing. I looked up then, and I crying at the grey pony, and there was Michael upon it—with fine clothes on him, and new shoes on his feet.

CATHLEEN *(begins to keen)*: It's destroyed we are from this day. It's destroyed, surely.

NORA: Didn't the young priest say the Almighty God won't leave her desti- *205* tute with no son living?

MAURYA *(in a low voice, but clearly)*: It's little the like of him knows of the sea.... Bartley will be lost now, and let you call in Eamon and make me a good coffin out of the white boards, for I won't live after them. I've had a hus- band, and a husband's father, and six sons in this house—six fine men, *210* though it was a hard birth I had with every one of them and they com- ing to the world—and some of them were found and some of them were not found, but they're gone now the lot of them.... There were Stephan and Shawn were lost in the great wind, and found after in the Bay of Gregory of the Golden Mouth, and carried up the two of them on one *215* plank, and in by that door.

She pauses for a moment, the girls start as if they heard something through the door that is half open behind them.

NORA *(in a whisper)*: Did you hear that, Cathleen? Did you hear a noise in the north-east?

CATHLEEN *(in a whisper)*: There's someone after crying out by the seashore.

MAURYA *(continues without hearing anything)*: There was Sheamus and his fa- *220* ther, and his own father again, were lost in a dark night, and not a stick or sign was seen of them when the sun went up. There was Patch after was drowned out of a curagh that turned over. I was sitting here with Bartley, and he a baby lying on my two knees, and I seen two women, and three women, and four women coming in, and they crossing themselves and *225* not saying a word. I looked out then, and there were men coming after them, and they holding a thing in the half of a red sail, and water drip- ping out of it—it was a dry day, Nora—and leaving a track to the door.

She pauses again with her hand stretched out towards the door, It opens softly and old women begin to come in, crossing themselves on the threshold, and kneeling down in front of the stage with red petticoats over their heads.

MAURYA *(half in a dream, to* CATHLEEN*)*: Is it Patch, or Michael, or what is it at all? *230*

CATHLEEN: Michael is after being found in the far north, and when he is
found there how could he be here in this place?

MAURYA: There does be a power of young men floating round in the sea,
and what way would they know if it was Michael they had, or another
235   man like him, for when a man is nine days in the sea, and the wind blowing, it's hard set his own mother would be to say what man was in it.

CATHLEEN: It's Michael, God spare him, for they're after sending us a bit of
his clothes from the far north.

She reaches out and hands MAURYA *the clothes that belonged to Michael.*
MAURYA *stands up slowly, and takes them in her hands.* NORA *looks out.*

NORA: They're carrying a thing among them, and there's water dripping out
240   of it and leaving a track by the big stones.

CATHLEEN *(in a whisper to the women who have come in)*: Is it Bartley it is?

ONE OF THE WOMEN: It is, surely, God rest his soul.

*Two younger women come in and pull out the table. Then men carry in the body
of* BARTLEY, *laid on a plank, with a bit of a sail over it, and lay it on the table.*

CATHLEEN *(to the women as they are doing so)*: What way was he drowned?

ONE OF THE WOMEN: The grey pony knocked him over into the sea, and he
245   was washed out where there is a great surf on the white rocks.

MAURYA *has gone over and knelt down at the head of the table. The women
are keening softly and swaying themselves with a slow movement.* CATHLEEN
and NORA *kneel at the other end of the table. The men kneel near the door.*

MAURYA *(raising her head and speaking as if she did not see the people around her)*:
They're all gone now, and there isn't anything more the sea can do to
me. . . . I'll have no call now to be up crying and praying when the wind
breaks from the south, and you can hear the surf is in the east, and the
250   surf is in the west, making a great stir with the two noises, and they hitting one on the other. I'll have no call now to be going down and getting Holy Water in the dark nights after Samhain, and I won't care what
way the sea is when the other women will be keening. *(To* NORA.*)*
Give me the Holy Water, Nora; there's a small sup still on the dresser.

NORA *gives it to her.*

255   MAURYA *(drops Michael's clothes across* BARTLEY'S *feet, and sprinkles the Holy
Water over him)*: It isn't that I haven't prayed for you, Bartley, to the
Almighty God. It isn't that I haven't said prayers in the dark night till
you wouldn't know what I'd be saying; but it's a great rest I'll have now,
and it's time, surely. It's a great rest I'll have now, and great sleeping in the
260   long nights after Samhain, if it's only a bit of wet flour we do have to
eat, and maybe a fish that would be stinking.

She kneels down again, crossing herself, and saying prayers under her breath.

CATHLEEN *(to an old man)*: Maybe yourself and Eamon would make a coffin when the sun rises. We have fine white boards herself bought, God help her, thinking Michael would be found, and I have a new cake you can eat while you'll be working.   *265*

THE OLD MAN *(looking at the boards)*: Are there nails with them?

CATHLEEN: There are not, Colum; we didn't think of the nails.

ANOTHER MAN: It's a great wonder she wouldn't think of the nails, and all the coffins she's seen made already.

CATHLEEN: It's getting old she is, and broken.   *270*

MAURYA *stands up again very slowly and spreads out the pieces of Michael's clothes beside the body, sprinkling them with the last of the Holy Water.*

NORA *(in a whisper to CATHLEEN)*: She's quiet now and easy; but the day Michael was drowned you could hear her crying out from this to the spring well. It's fonder she was of Michael, and would anyone have thought that?

CATHLEEN *(slowly and clearly)*: An old woman will be soon tired with any-   *275* thing she will do, and isn't it nine days herself is after crying and keen-ing, and making great sorrow in the house?

MAURYA *(puts the empty cup mouth downwards on the table, and lays her hands to-gether on Bartley's feet)*: They're all together this time, and the end is come. May the Almighty God have mercy on Bartley's soul, and on Michael's   *280* soul, and on the souls of Sheamus and Patch, and Stephen and Shawn *(bending her head)*; and may He have mercy on my soul, Nora, and the soul of every one is left living in the world.

She pauses, and the keen rises a little more loudly from the women, then sinks away.

MAURYA *(continuing)*: Michael has a clean burial in the far north, by the grace of Almighty God. Bartley will have a fine coffin out of the white boards,   *285* and a deep grave surely. What more can we want than that? No man at all can be living for ever, and we must be satisfied.

She kneels down again and the curtain falls slowly.

CONSIDERATIONS

1. What is the significance of the title? In what ways does the sea become a character in the play? What images suggest the strength, power, and control the sea exerts in the lives of this family and their community?

2. List items that are described as part of the set, for example the oilskins and nets that hang on the wall. How are these objects significant to the conflicts and themes of this drama?
3. Compare and contrast the two daughters of the family, Cathleen and Nora. How do their similarities and differences suggest the roles they play in the family?
4. Scholar Thomas Kilroy has noted that Maurya "finds a freedom in isolation" and that she separates herself from the family and the community, showing "a contempt for the values that are left behind" *(Mosaic,* Spring 1971). Do you agree with this comment? What evidence can you offer to either support or refute Kilroy's view of Maurya?
5. Note examples of religious images and language in the play. How does the power of faith and religion relate to the power of nature as represented by the sea?

Essays

BARRY HOLSTUN LOPEZ (1945–   )

Landscape and Narrative

Although born in Port Chester, New York, Barry Lopez spent most of his first ten years in Southern California. His family moved back to New York, but after college at the University of Notre Dame, Lopez moved back to the West Coast to attend graduate school at the University of Oregon. His studies in folklore led him to write his first book, a retelling of Native American stories featuring the coyote as a trickster figure, which would later be published as Giving Birth to Thunder, Sleeping with His Daughter: Coyote Builds North America *(1978). In 1970, he decided to become a full-time writer and settled on the McKenzie River in western Oregon. A 1974 assignment for* Smithsonian *magazine led to his first major book,* Of Wolves and Men *(1978), which combines scientific information and wolf lore from aboriginal societies. During the next four years, Lopez traveled to the Arctic several times, and in 1986 he published an account of his travels,* Arctic Dreams: Imagination and Desire in a Northern Landscape, *which won the National Book Award. In this book, he explores man's relationship with "the landscape." "By landscape," he told an interviewer, "I mean the complete lay of the land—the animals that are there, the trees, the vegetation, the quality of soils, the drainage pattern of water, the annual cycles of temperature, and kinds of precipitation, the sounds common to the re-gion." Lopez also carries this theme into his short stories and fictional narratives, such as* River Notes: The Dance of Herons *(1979) and* Winter Count *(1981). In 1998, he published* About This Life: Journeys on the Threshold of Memory, *a collection of essays that span Lopez's career and observations. The following selection is from* Crossing Open Ground *(1988).*

One summer evening in a remote village in the Brooks Range of Alaska, I sat among a group of men listening to hunting stories about the trapping and pursuit of animals. I was particularly interested in several incidents involving wolverine, in part because a friend of mine was studying wolverine in Canada, among the Cree, but, too, because I find this animal such an intense creature. To hear about its life is to learn more about fierceness.

Wolverines are not intentionally secretive, hiding their lives from view, but they are seldom observed. The range of their known behavior is less than that of, say, bears or wolves. Still, that evening no gratuitous details were set out. This was somewhat odd, for wolverine easily excite the imagination; they can loom suddenly in the landscape with authority, with an aura larger than their compact physical dimensions, drawing one's immediate and complete attention. Wolverine also have a deserved reputation for resoluteness in the worst winters, for ferocious strength. But neither did these attributes induce the men to embellish.

I listened carefully to these stories, taking pleasure in the sharply observed detail surrounding the dramatic thread of events. The story I remember most vividly was about a man hunting a wolverine from a snow machine in the spring. He followed the animal's tracks for several miles over rolling tundra in a certain valley. Soon he caught sight ahead of a dark spot on the crest of a hill—the wolverine pausing to look back. The hunter was catching up, but each time he came over a rise the wolverine was looking back from the next rise, just out of range. The hunter topped one more rise and met the wolverine bounding toward him. Before he could pull his rifle from its scabbard, the wolverine flew across the engine cowl and the windshield, hitting him square in the chest. The hunter scrambled his arms wildly, trying to get the wolverine out of his lap, and fell over as he did so. The wolverine jumped clear as the snow machine rolled over, and fixed the man with a stare. He had not bitten, not even scratched the man. Then the wolverine walked away. The man thought of reaching for the gun, but no, he did not.

The other stories were like this, not so much making a point as evoking something about contact with wild animals that would never be completely understood.

When the stories were over, four or five of us walked out of the home of our host. The surrounding land, in the persistent light of a far northern   5 summer, was still visible for miles—the striated, pitched massifs° of the Brooks Range; the shy, willow-lined banks of the John River flowing south from Anaktuvuk Pass; and the flat tundra plain, opening with great affirmation to the north. The landscape seemed alive because of the stories. It was precisely these ocherous tones, this kind of willow, exactly this austerity that had informed the wolverine narratives. I felt exhilaration, and a deeper confirmation of the stories. The mundane tasks which awaited me I anticipated now with pleasure. The stories had renewed in me a sense of the purpose of my life.

This feeling, an inexplicable renewal of enthusiasm after storytelling, is familiar to many people. It does not seem to matter greatly what the subject is, as long as the context is intimate and the story is told for its own sake, not forced to serve merely as the vehicle for an idea. The tone of the story need not be solemn. The darker aspects of life need not be ignored. But I think intimacy is indispensable—a feeling that derives from the listener's trust and a storyteller's certain knowledge of his subject and regard for his audience. This intimacy deepens if the storyteller tempers his authority with humility, or when terms of idiomatic expression, or at least the physical setting for the story, are shared.

I think of two landscapes—one outside the self, the other within. The external landscape is the one we see—not only the line and color of the land and its shading at different times of the day, but also its plants and animals in season, its weather, its geology, the record of its climate and evolution. If you walk up, say, a dry arroyo in the Sonoran Desert you will feel a mounding and rolling of sand and silt beneath your foot that is distinctive. You will anticipate the crumbling of the sedimentary earth in the arroyo bank as your hand reaches out, and in that tangible evidence you will sense a history of water in the region. Perhaps a black-throated sparrow lands in a paloverde bush—the resiliency of the twig under the bird, that precise shade of yellowish-green against the milk-blue sky, the fluttering whir of the arriving sparrow, are what I mean by "the landscape." Draw on the smell of creosote bush, or clack stones together in the dry air. Feel how light is the desiccated dropping of the kangaroo rat. Study an animal track obscured by the wind. These are all elements of the land, and what makes the landscape comprehensible are the relationships between them. One learns a landscape finally not by knowing the name or identity of everything in it, but by perceiving the relationships in it—like that between the sparrow and the twig. The difference between the relationships and the elements is the same as that between written history and a catalog of events.

The second landscape I think of is an interior one, a kind of projection within a person of a part of the exterior landscape. Relationships in the exte-

---

massifs: Blocks of the earth's crust bounded by faults and displaced as a unit.

rior landscape include those that are named and discernible, such as the nitro-
gen cycle, or a vertical sequence of Ordovician° limestone, and others that are
uncodified or ineffable, such as winter light falling on a particular kind of
granite, or the effect of humidity on the frequency of a blackpoll warbler's
burst of song. That these relationships have purpose and order, however inscrutable they may seem to us, is a tenet of evolution. Similarly, the speculations, intuitions, and formal ideas we refer to as "mind" are a set of relationships
in the interior landscape with purpose and order; some of these are obvious,
many impenetrably subtle. The shape and character of these relationships in a
person's thinking, I believe, are deeply influenced by where on this earth one
goes, what one touches, the patterns one observes in nature—the intricate history of one's life in the land, even a life in the city, where wind, the chirp of
birds, the line of a falling leaf, are known. These thoughts are arranged, further,
according to the thread of one's moral, intellectual, and spiritual development.
The interior landscape responds to the character and subtlety of an exterior
landscape; the shape of the individual mind is affected by land as it is by genes.

   In stories like those I heard at Anaktuvuk Pass about wolverine, the relationship between separate elements in the land is set forth clearly. It is put in a
simple framework of sequential incidents and apposite detail. If the exterior
landscape is limned well, the listener often feels that he has heard something
pleasing and authentic—trustworthy. We derive this sense of confidence, I
think, not so much from verifiable truth as from an understanding that lying
has played no role in the narrative. The storyteller is obligated to engage the
reader with a precise vocabulary, to set forth a coherent and dramatic rendering of incidents—and to be ingenuous.

   When one hears a story one takes pleasure in it for different reasons—   10
for the euphony of its phrases, an aspect of the plot, or because one identifies
with one of the characters. With certain stories certain individuals may experience a deeper, more profound sense of well-being. This latter phenomenon, in
my understanding, rests at the heart of storytelling as an elevated experience
among aboriginal peoples. It results from bringing two landscapes together.
The exterior landscape is organized according to principles or laws or tenden-
cies beyond human control. It is understood to contain an integrity that is beyond human analysis and unimpeachable. Insofar as the storyteller depicts
various subtle and obvious relationships in the exterior landscape accurately in
his story, and insofar as he orders them along traditional lines of meaning to
create the narrative, the narrative will "ring true." The listener who "takes the
story to heart" will feel a pervasive sense of congruence within himself and
also with the world.

   Among the Navajo and, as far as I know, many other native peoples, the
land is thought to exhibit a sacred order. That order is the basis of ritual. The

---

Ordovician: Referring to the second period of the Paleozoic era.

rituals themselves reveal the power in that order. Art, architecture, vocabulary, and costume, as well as ritual, are derived from the perceived natural order of the universe—from observations and meditations on the exterior landscape. An indigenous philosophy—metaphysics, ethics, epistemology, aesthetics, and logic—may also be derived from a people's continuous attentiveness to both the obvious (scientific) and ineffable (artistic) orders of the local landscape. Each individual, further, undertakes to order his interior landscape according to the exterior landscape. To succeed in this means to achieve a balanced state of mental health.

I think of the Navajo for a specific reason. Among the various sung ceremonies of this people—Enemyway, Coyoteway, Red Antway, Uglyway—is one called Beautyway. In the Navajo view, the elements of one's interior life—one's psychological makeup and moral bearing—are subject to a persistent principle of disarray. Beautyway is, in part, a spiritual invocation of the order of the exterior universe, that irreducible, holy complexity that manifests itself as all things changing through time (a Navajo definition of beauty, hózhóó). The purpose of this invocation is to recreate in the individual who is the subject of the Beautyway ceremony that same order, to make the individual again a reflection of the myriad enduring relationships of the landscape.

I believe story functions in a similar way. A story draws on relationships in the exterior landscape and projects them onto the interior landscape. The purpose of storytelling is to achieve harmony between the two landscapes, to use all the elements of story—syntax, mood, figures of speech—in a harmonious way to reproduce the harmony of the land in the individual's interior. Inherent in story is the power to reorder a state of psychological confusion through contact with the pervasive truth of those relationships we call "the land."

These thoughts, of course, are susceptible to interpretation. I am convinced, however, that these observations can be applied to the kind of prose we call nonfiction as well as to traditional narrative forms such as the novel and the short story, and to some poems. Distinctions between fiction and nonfiction are sometimes obscured by arguments over what constitutes "the truth." In the aboriginal literature I am familiar with, the first distinction made among narratives is to separate the authentic from the inauthentic. Myth, which we tend to regard as fictitious or "merely metaphorical," is as authentic, as real, as the story of a wolverine in a man's lap. (A distinction is made, of course, about the elevated nature of myth—and frequently the circumstances of myth-telling are more rigorously prescribed than those for the telling of legends or vernacular stories—but all of these narratives are rooted in the local landscape. To violate *that* connection is to call the narrative itself into question.)

15   The power of narrative to nurture and heal, to repair a spirit in disarray, rests on two things: the skillful invocation of unimpeachable sources and a lis-

tener's knowledge that no hypocrisy or subterfuge is involved. This last simple fact is to me one of the most imposing aspects of the Holocene° history of man.

We are more accustomed now to thinking of "the truth" as something that can be explicitly stated, rather than as something that can be evoked in a metaphorical way outside science and Occidental° culture. Neither can truth be reduced to aphorism or formulas. It is something alive and unpronounceable. Story creates an atmosphere in which it becomes discernible as a pattern. For a storyteller to insist on relationships that do not exist is to lie. Lying is the opposite of story. (I do not mean to confuse ignorance with deception, or to imply that a storyteller can perceive all that is inherent in the land. Every storyteller falls short of a perfect limning of the landscape—perception and language both fail. Both to make up something that is not there, something which can never be corroborated in the land, to knowingly set forth a false relationship, is to be lying, no longer telling a story.)

Because of the intricate, complex nature of the land, it is not always possible for a storyteller to grasp what is contained in a story. The intent of the storyteller, then, must be to evoke, honestly, some single aspect of all that the land contains. The storyteller knows that because different individuals grasp the story at different levels, the focus of his regard for truth must be at the primary one— with who was there, what happened, when, where, and why things occurred. The story will then possess similar truth at other levels—the integrity inherent at the primary level of meaning will be conveyed everywhere else. As long as the storyteller carefully describes the order before him, and uses his storytelling skill to heighten and emphasize certain relationships, it is even possible for the story to be more successful than the storyteller himself is able to imagine.

I would like to make a final point about the wolverine stories I heard at Anaktuvuk Pass. I wrote down the details afterward, concentrating especially on aspects of the biology and ecology of the animals. I sent the information on to my friend living with the Cree. When, many months later, I saw him, I asked whether the Cree had enjoyed these insights of the Nunamiut into the nature of the wolverine. What had they said?

"You know," he told me, "how they are. They said, 'That could happen.'"

In these uncomplicated words the Cree declared their own knowledge   *20* of the wolverine. They acknowledged that although they themselves had never seen the things the Nunamiut spoke of, they accepted them as accurate observations, because they did not consider story a context for misrepresentation. They also preserved their own dignity by not overstating their confidence in the Nunamiut, a distant and unknown people.

Holocene: The past 11,000 years of Earth's history. *Occidental:* Western (including Europe and the Americas).

Whenever I think of this courtesy on the part of the Cree I think of the dignity that is ours when we cease to demand the truth and realize that the best we can have of those substantial truths that guide our lives is metaphorical—a story. And the most of it we are likely to discern comes only when we accord one another the respect the Cree showed the Nunamiut. Beyond this— that the interior landscape is a metaphorical representation of the exterior landscape, that the truth reveals itself most fully not in dogma but in the paradox, irony, and contradictions that distinguish compelling narratives—beyond this there are only failures of imagination: reductionism in science; fundamentalism in religion; fascism in politics.

Our national literatures should be important to us insofar as they sustain us with illumination and heal us. They can always do that so long as they are written with respect for both the source and the reader, and with an understanding of why the human heart and the land have been brought together so regularly in human history.   *1988*

CONSIDERATIONS

1. What is Lopez's main point about the power of stories as opposed to facts and knowledge? When the author writes that "the landscape seemed alive because of the stories," what does he mean?
2. What does Lopez believe stories must do in order to be considered worthy? In what ways can you apply his beliefs to the subject of writing in general?
3. What is the ultimate job of the storyteller, and what might she or he require in order to connect with her or his audience? Explain with quotes from the text.
4. What is the basic difference between interior and exterior landscapes, according to Lopez?
5. What is the relationship between the storyteller and the listener? What must each do in order for the spirit to be "healed"? Explain.

ANNIE DILLARD (1945–   )

The Deer at Providencia

The oldest of three daughters, Annie Dillard was born into an affluent Pittsburgh family. She and her sisters were raised to challenge authority and to think for themselves. Through the encouragement of her parents and teachers, Dillard became a passionate reader, as well as a lover of fine arts, such as music and dancing. She was educated at Hollins College, where she was particularly encouraged by Richard Dillard, her creative writing instructor, whom she married after her sophomore year. During those years, she also became deeply interested in the works of Ralph Waldo Emerson and of Henry David Thoreau and was particularly compelled by their writings on the natural world.

Following graduation, Dillard continued to live near Hollins College in a house in the Blue Ridge Mountains near Tinker Creek. Although still writing, she spent much of her time walking, lunching with friends, and enjoying the beauty of her surroundings. Then in 1971, she contracted a serious case of pneumonia, and during her difficult recovery period she began to keep a regular journal, eventually compiling thousands of pages of notations. The ultimate result of this extraordinary work was the book for which she is best known and for which she was awarded the Pulitzer Prize in 1974, Pilgrim at Tinker Creek. *Since then, she has published several more books and has won critical acclaim for her collections of essays such as* Pilgrim *and* Holy the Firm. *In addition, she has written a book of literary criticism and theory,* Living by Fiction; *an autobiography,* An American Childhood; *a highly regarded book of poetry,* Tickets for a Prayer Wheel; *and a novel,* The Living. *The following selection is from her collection of essays,* Teaching a Stone to Talk *(1983).*

There were four of us North Americans in the jungle, in the Ecuadorian jungle on the banks of the Napo River in the Amazon watershed. The other three North Americans were metropolitan men. We stayed in tents in one riverside village, and visited others. At the village called Providencia we saw a sight which moved us, and which shocked the men.

The first thing we saw when we climbed the riverbank to the village of Providencia was the deer. It was roped to a tree on the grass clearing near the thatch shelter where we would eat lunch.

The deer was small, about the size of a whitetail fawn, but apparently full-grown. It had a rope around its neck and three feet caught in the rope. Someone said that the dogs had caught it that morning and the villagers were going to cook and eat it that night.

This clearing lay at the edge of the little thatched-hut village. We could see the villagers going about their business, scattering feed corn for hens about their houses, and wandering down paths to the river to bathe. The village headman was our host; he stood beside us as we watched the deer struggle. Several village boys were interested in the deer; they formed part of the circle we made around it in the clearing. So also did four businessmen from Quito who were attempting to guide us around the jungle. Few of the very different people standing in this circle had a common language. We watched the deer, and no one said much.

The deer lay on its side at the rope's very end, so the rope lacked slack to   5
let it rest its head in the dust. It was "pretty," delicate of bone like all deer, and

thin-skinned for the tropics. Its skin looked virtually hairless, in fact, and almost translucent, like a membrane. Its neck was no thicker than my wrist; it was rubbed open on the rope, and gashed. Trying to paw itself free of the rope, the deer had scratched its own neck with its hooves. The raw underside of its neck showed red stripes and some bruises bleeding inside the muscles. Now three of its feet were hooked in the rope under its jaw. It could not stand, of course, on one leg, so it could not move to slacken the rope and ease the pull on its throat and enable it to rest its head.

Repeatedly the deer paused, motionless, its eyes veiled, with only its rib cage in motion, and its breaths the only sound. Then, after I would think, "It has given up; now it will die," it would heave. The rope twanged; the tree leaves clattered; the deer's free foot beat the ground. We stepped back and held our breaths. It thrashed, kicking, but only one leg moved; the other three legs tightened inside the rope's loop. Its hip jerked; its spine shook. Its eyes rolled; its tongue, thick with spittle, pushed in and out. Then it would rest again. We watched this for fifteen minutes.

Once three young native boys charged in, released its trapped legs, and jumped back to the circle of people. But instantly the deer scratched up its neck with its hooves and snared its forelegs in the rope again. It was easy to imagine a third and then a fourth leg soon stuck, like Brer Rabbit and the Tar Baby.

We watched the deer from the circle, and then we drifted on to lunch. Our palm-roofed shelter stood on a grassy promontory from which we could see the deer tied to the tree, pigs and hens walking under village houses, and black-and-white cattle standing in the river. There was even a breeze.

Lunch, which was the second and better lunch we had that day, was hot and fried. There was a big fish called *doncella,* a kind of catfish, dipped whole in corn flour and beaten egg, then deep fried. With our fingers we pulled soft fragments of it from its sides to our plates, and ate; it was delicate fish-flesh, fresh and mild. Someone found the roe, and I ate of that too—it was fat and stronger, like egg yolk, naturally enough, and warm.

10   There was also a stew of meat in shreds with rice and pale brown gravy. I had asked what kind of deer it was tied to the tree; Pepe had answered in Spanish, "*Gama.*" Now they told us this was *gama* too, stewed. I suspect the word means merely game or venison. At any rate, I heard that the village dogs had cornered another deer just yesterday, and it was this deer which we were now eating in full sight of the whole article. It was good. I was surprised at its tenderness. But it is a fact that high levels of lactic acid, which builds up in muscle tissues during exertion, tenderizes.

After the fish and meat we ate bananas fried in chunks and served on a tray; they were sweet and full of flavor. I felt terrific. My shirt was wet and cool from swimming; I had had a night's sleep, two decent walks, three meals, and a swim—everything tasted good. From time to time each one of us, separately, would look beyond our shaded roof to the sunny spot where the deer was still convulsing in the dust. Our meal completed, we walked around the deer and back to the boats.

That night I learned that while we were watching the deer, the others were watching me.

We four North Americans grew close in the jungle in a way that was not the usual artificial intimacy of travelers. We liked each other. We stayed up all that night talking, murmuring, as though we rocked on hammocks slung above time. The others were from big cities: New York, Washington, Boston. They all said that I had no expression on my face when I was watching the deer—or at any rate, not the expression they expected.

They had looked to see how I, the only woman, and the youngest, was taking the sight of the deer's struggles. I looked detached, apparently, or hard, or calm, or focused, still. I don't know. I was thinking. I remember feeling very old and energetic. I could say like Thoreau that I have traveled widely in Roanoke, Virginia. I have thought a great deal about carnivorousness; I eat meat. These things are not issues; they are mysteries.

Gentlemen of the city, what surprises you? That there is suffering here, or that I know it?   15

We lay in the tent and talked. "If it had been my wife," one man said with special vigor, amazed, "she wouldn't have cared *what* was going on; she would have dropped *everything* right at that moment and gone in the village from here to there to there, she would not have *stopped* until that animal was out of its suffering one way or another. She couldn't *bear* to see a creature in agony like that."

I nodded.

Now I am home. When I wake I comb my hair before the mirror above my dresser. Every morning for the past two years I have seen in that mirror, beside my sleep-softened face, the blackened face of a burnt man. It is a wire-service photograph clipped from a newspaper and taped to my mirror. The caption reads: "Alan McDonald in Miami hospital bed." All you can see in the photograph is a smudged triangle of face from his eyelids to his lower lip; the rest is bandages. You cannot see the expression in his eyes; the bandages shade them.

The story, headed MAN BURNED FOR SECOND TIME, begins:

"Why does God hate me?" Alan McDonald asked from his hospital bed.

"When the gunpowder went off, I couldn't believe it," he said. "I just couldn't believe it. I said, 'No, God couldn't do this to me again.'"

20 He was in a burn ward in Miami, in serious condition. I do not even know if he lived. I wrote him a letter at the time, cringing.

He had been burned before, thirteen years previously, by flaming gasoline. For years he had been having his body restored and his face remade in dozens of operations. He had been a boy, and then a burnt boy. He had already been stunned by what could happen, by how life could veer.

Once I read that people who survive bad burns tend to go crazy; they have a very high suicide rate. Medicine cannot ease their pain; drugs just leak away, soaking the sheets, because there is no skin to hold them in. The people just lie there and weep. Later they kill themselves. They had not known, before they were burned, that the world included such suffering, that life could permit them personally such pain.

This time a bowl of gunpowder had exploded on McDonald.

"I didn't realize what had happened at first," he recounted. "And then I heard that sound from 13 years ago. I was burning. I rolled to put the fire out and I thought, 'Oh God, not again.'

"If my friend hadn't been there, I would have jumped into a canal with a rock around my neck."

His wife concludes the piece, "Man, it just isn't fair."

25 I read the whole clipping again every morning. This is the Big Time here, every minute of it. Will someone please explain to Alan McDonald in his dignity, to the deer at Providencia in his dignity, what is going on? And mail me the carbon.

When we walked by the deer at Providencia for the last time, I said to Pepe, with a pitying glance at the deer, "*Pobrecito*"—"poor little thing." But I was trying out Spanish. I knew at the time it was a ridiculous thing to say.   *1983*

CONSIDERATIONS

1. What does the name of the place, Providencia, have to do with the events in this piece?
2. What is the narrator's overall attitude toward nature and suffering? Support your answer with details from the essay itself.
3. What does the writer gain by not mentioning her gender until later on in this piece? What is her purpose in doing this?

4. What commonalities do the deer and the burn victim share? What are the differences between these two situations?
5. Why does the narrator keep the newspaper clipping beside the mirror in her room? What does she mean by her final question, "What is going on?" How would you answer her?

VIRGINIA WOOLF (1882–1941)
The Death of the Moth

Born in England, Virginia Woolf was the daughter of Leslie Stephen, a well-known scholar. She was educated primarily at home and attributed her love of reading to the early and complete access she was given to her father's library. With her husband, Leonard Woolf, she founded the Hogarth Press and became known as a member of the Bloomsbury group of intellectuals, which included economist John Maynard Keynes, biographer Lytton Strachey, novelist E. M. Forster, and art historian Clive Bell. Although she was a central figure in London literary life, Woolf often saw herself as isolated from the mainstream because she was a woman. Her 1929 book A Room of One's Own *documents her desire for women to take their rightful place in literary history. Woolf is best known for her experimental, modernist novels, including* Mrs. Dalloway *(1925) and* To the Lighthouse *(1927). The following selection is taken from the collection* The Death of a Moth and Other Essays, *published in 1942, a year after her death.*

Moths that fly by day are not properly to be called moths; they do not excite that pleasant sense of dark autumn nights and ivy-blossom which the commonest yellow-underwing asleep in the shadow of the curtain never fails to rouse in us. They are hybrid creatures, neither gay like butterflies nor sombre like their own species. Nevertheless the present specimen, with his narrow hay-coloured wings, fringed with a tassel of the same colour, seemed to be content with life. It was a pleasant morning, mid-September, mild, benignant, yet with a keener breath than that of the summer months. The plough was already scoring the field opposite the window, and where the share had been, the earth was pressed flat and gleamed with moisture. Such vigour came rolling in from the fields and the down beyond that it was difficult to keep the eyes strictly turned upon the book. The rooks too were keeping one of their annual festivities; soaring round the tree tops until it looked as if a vast net with thousands of black knots in it had been cast up into the air; which, after a few moments sank slowly down upon the trees until every twig seemed to have a knot at the end of it. Then, suddenly, the net would be thrown into the air again in a wider circle this time, with the utmost clamour and vociferation, as though to be thrown into the air and settle slowly down upon the tree tops were a tremendously exciting experience.

The same energy which inspired the rooks, the ploughmen, the horses, and even, it seemed, the lean bare-backed downs, sent the moth fluttering from side to side of his square of the window-pane. One could not help watching him. One was, indeed, conscious of a queer feeling of pity for him. The possibilities of pleasure seemed that morning so enormous and so various that to have only a moth's part in life, and a day moth's at that, appeared a hard fate, and his zest in enjoying his meagre opportunities to the full, pathetic. He flew vigorously to one corner of his compartment, and, after waiting there a second, flew across to the other. What remained for him but to fly to a third corner and then to a fourth? That was all he could do, in spite of the size of the downs, the width of the sky, the far-off smoke of houses, and the romantic voice, now and then, of a steamer out at sea. What he could do he did. Watching him, it seemed as if a fibre, very thin but pure, of the enormous energy of the world had been thrust into his frail and diminutive body. As often as he crossed the pane, I could fancy that a thread of vital light became visible. He was little or nothing but life.

Yet, because he was so small, and so simple a form of the energy that was rolling in at the open window and driving its way through so many narrow and intricate corridors in my own brain and in those of other human beings, there was something marvellous as well as pathetic about him. It was as if someone had taken a tiny bead of pure life and decking it as lightly as possible with down and feathers, had set it dancing and zig zagging to show us the true nature of life. Thus displayed one could not get over the strangeness of it. One is apt to forget all about life, seeing it humped and bossed and garnished and cumbered so that it has to move with the greatest circumspection and dignity. Again, the thought of all that life might have been had he been born in any other shape caused one to view his simple activities with a kind of pity.

After a time, tired by his dancing apparently, he settled on the window ledge in the sun, and, the queer spectacle being at an end, I forgot about him. Then, looking up, my eye was caught by him. He was trying to resume his dancing, but seemed either so stiff or so awkward that he could only flutter to the bottom of the windowpane; and when he tried to fly across it he failed. Being intent on other matters I watched these futile attempts for a time without thinking, unconsciously waiting for him to resume his flight, as one waits for a machine, that has stopped momentarily, to start again without considering the reason of its failure. After perhaps a seventh attempt he slipped from the wooden ledge and fell, fluttering his wings, on to his back on the window sill. The helplessness of his attitude roused me. It flashed upon me that he was in difficulties; he could no longer raise himself; his legs struggled vainly. But, as I stretched out a pencil, meaning to help him to right himself, it came over me that the failure and awkwardness were the approach of death. I laid the pencil down again.

The legs agitated themselves once more. I looked as if for the enemy   5
against which he struggled. I looked out of doors. What had happened there? Presumably it was midday, and work in the fields had stopped. Stillness and quiet had replaced the previous animation. The birds had taken themselves off to feed in the brooks. The horses stood still. Yet the power was there all the same, massed outside, indifferent, impersonal, not attending to anything in particular. Somehow it was opposed to the little hay-coloured moth. It was useless to try to do anything. One could only watch the extraordinary efforts made by those tiny legs against an oncoming doom which could, had it chosen, have submerged an entire city, not merely a city, but masses of human beings; nothing, I knew, had any chance against death. Nevertheless after a pause of exhaustion the legs fluttered again. It was superb this last protest, and so frantic that he succeeded at last in righting himself. One's sympathies, of course, were all on the side of life. Also, when there was nobody to care or to know, this gigantic effort on the part of an insignificant little moth, against a power of such magnitude, to retain what no one else valued or desired to keep, moved one strangely. Again, somehow, one saw life, a pure bead. I lifted the pencil again, useless though I knew it to be. But even as I did so, the unmistakable tokens of death showed themselves. The body relaxed, and instantly grew stiff. The struggle was over. The insignificant little creature now knew death. As I looked at the dead moth, this minute wayside triumph of so great a force over so mean an antagonist filled me with wonder. Just as life had been strange a few minutes before, so death was now as strange. The moth having righted himself now lay most decently and uncomplainingly composed. O yes, he seemed to say, death is stronger than I am.   *1942*

CONSIDERATIONS

1. Why might the speaker be more engrossed with watching a moth than with what she has planned to do? What does this reflect about the speaker?
2. Woolf writes that the small moth was dancing around as if "to show the true nature of life." If that is the case, then what, according to Woolf's observations, is the true nature of life? If she means "life" to include human life, to what extent do you agree with her?
3. From the language, style, and tone of this piece, what is your impression of the speaker? To whom (or for whom) is she writing this piece, do you suppose?
4. What is the moth's apparent reaction to dying? To death? What insights does the speaker gain from watching the moth from the beginning to the end?

5. If you were to observe the human action of the speaker from the moth's point of view, how would this perspective affect your evaluation of the relationship between the two?

CONNECTIONS: NATURE

1. Compare and contrast the way the elements of nature reflect the conflicts of the characters who observe or experience these elements. Consider the following works in your analysis: "Hills like White Elephants," "The Open Boat," "The Man to Send Rain Clouds," "The Death of the Moth," "Sheltered Garden," "God's Grandeur," and "The Fish."
2. Discuss the contrasting images of living creatures and their relationships with humans in any of the following works: "The Fish," "The Deer at Providencia," "The Death of the Moth," "Traveling through the Dark," or "A Certain Sharpness in the Morning."
3. How do you see nature? As benign, hostile, indifferent, restorative, or wondrous? An inspiration or an obstacle? Compare your perspective with the perspectives offered in any of the following: "A Worn Path," "The Deer at Providencia," "The Open Boat," "God's Grandeur," "A Certain Sharpness in the Morning," "The Tyger," and "Riders to the Sea."
4. In a poem entitled "The Tables Turned," Wordsworth writes, "Come forth into the light of things / Let nature be your teacher." To what extent has nature been a teacher in your life? Include in your response your own experiences and a contrasting experience in any one of the pieces in this chapter.
5. Write an imaginative discourse or panel discussion about nature between or among characters in any of the following works: "A Worn Path," "The Open Boat," "The Death of the Moth," "God's Grandeur," "The Fish," "The Tyger," and "The Deer at Providencia."

SUGGESTIONS FOR EXTENDED CONNECTIONS AMONG CHAPTERS

1. The question of whether nature or nurture most profoundly influences the way humans grow and develop continues to foster spirited debates. Consider any of the following selections and discuss the way a central character is affected by these two forces.

2. The natural setting and landscape in a work of literature often reflect the conflict within the main character or between such contrasting forces as the individual and society, the individual and God, or the individual's relationship with another person. Examine how the setting contributes to the theme in any of the following:

3. Very often, images of heavenly objects—stars, sun, moon, the sky itself—symbolize the basic theme or conflict within a work of literature. Select any of the following and analyze the purpose and power of such objects:

4. In many cases, an internal conflict occurs because characters are not being true to their own real natures. Examine any of the following with the intent of understanding the conflict between a character's true nature and forces that work against the development of this nature. What forces causes someone to hide or fear an inner identity, and what is the outcome of not being true to one's self?

SUGGESTIONS FOR COLLABORATIVE LEARNING

1. Working in groups of three or four, choose any one of the authors within this section to research in terms of his or her relationship with nature and how he or she incorporates nature into other works. Assign separate sources for each member of the group to research. For example, one member may go to the library to search literary criticism texts, while others may look in electronic data bases or on the Internet. Once the sources have been found, the research is shared with the whole group, and then each member individually writes an analysis essay that explores the central question the group has raised.

2. Working in groups of two or three, choose one of the short stories and isolate the most powerful images and words in it. Once a long, complete list has been compiled by the group, use it to write individual poems that depend primarily on the words in this list. When the poems have been completed, share and compare the results with the whole group.

WEB CONNECTIONS

1. In American literature, the nineteenth-century transcendentalists explored as a major theme the contrast of nature with the growing industrialization of that era. The Web site American Transcendentalism Web (http://www.vcu .edu/engweb/transcendentalism/) offers writings by familiar nineteenth-century writers such as Henry David Thoreau and Ralph Waldo Emerson. This site also provides links to all of these two great writers' primary works, and includes links to the works of less well-known transcendentalists, such as Jones Very, who is called a "prophet, poet, and madman." Links to pri-

mary and secondary sources dealing with how transcendentalism affected all parts of American society, from education to politics, are also found on this site.

2. Haiku is a Japanese form of poetry, which, according to the traditional conventions, uses images related to one of the four seasons to convey a theme. Examples of haiku appear on pages 858–59. Explore both traditional and modern haiku through visiting links on the following web sites, and then consider the many ways in which nature is depicted by the poets that use this form.

   http://www.gardendigest.com/poetry/haiku1.htm

   http://www.toyomasu.com/haiku/

How does this photograph suggest the relationship between war and power?

War and Power

Since September 11, 2001, we have all lived with the memories, fears, and possibilities engendered by the terrorist attacks on the World Trade Center and the Pentagon. In addition, we live with the daily heartbreak of the wars in Iraq and Afghanistan. And in many other places throughout the world, other wars continue to rage. In addition, the repercussions of past wars—most particularly the Vietnam conflict—continue to reverberate, making this theme a timely and powerful part of our lives.

As you read the selections in this chapter, keep in mind the following questions:

1. How are civilians affected by war?
2. How do young people form their assumptions about war and power?
3. How do we define who is friend and who is foe in times of war?
4. What is the relationship between private and public duty in times of war?
5. Can a war ever be defined as "just" or "unjust"? Explain.

Fiction

AMBROSE BIERCE (1842–1914)
An Occurrence at Owl Creek Bridge

The tenth of thirteen children, Ambrose Bierce was born on his family's farm in Meigs County, Ohio. He enlisted in the Union army when the Civil War broke out and fought bravely in many battles, including Shiloh and Chickamauga, and accompanied Sherman on his March to the Sea. After the war, he traveled to San Francisco with a military expedition and then left the army to begin a career as a writer. From 1867 to 1872, he was writer, columnist, and managing editor of the San Francisco News Letter and California Advertiser, *forming friendships with the writers Mark Twain and Bret Harte. In 1872, Bierce and his wife moved to England for three years; his first three books of sketches were published during that time. The couple returned to San Francisco, and in 1887 Bierce began writing a regular column for William Randolph Hearst's* San Francisco Examiner. *His major fiction was collected in* Tales of Soldiers and Civilians *(1891), which is the source of the story here, and* Can Such Things Be? *(1893). Many of these stories are depictions of his experiences in the Civil War but are told from unusual, sometimes supernatural, perspectives. His most famous book,* The Devil's Dictionary, *was published in 1906 with the title* The Cynic's Word Book. *In 1914, Bierce told friends he was leaving for Mexico to join Pancho Villa's forces in that country's civil war; he was never heard from again. A 1989 movie (based on a novel by Carlos Fuentes),* Old Gringo, *presents a fictionalized version of how he might have died.*

I

A man stood upon a railroad bridge in northern Alabama, looking down into the swift water twenty feet below. The man's hands were behind his back, the wrists bound with a cord. A rope closely encircled his neck. It was attached to a stout cross-timber above his head and the slack fell to the level of his knees. Some loose boards laid upon the sleepers supporting the metals of the railway supplied a footing for him and his executioners—two private soldiers of the Federal army, directed by a sergeant who in civil life may have been a deputy sheriff. At a short remove upon the same temporary platform was an officer in the uniform of his rank, armed. He was a captain. A sentinel at each end of the bridge stood with his rifle in the position known as "support," that is to say, vertical in front of the left shoulder, the hammer resting on the forearm thrown straight across the chest—a formal and unnatural position, enforcing an erect carriage of the body. It did not appear to be the duty of these two men to know what was occurring at the center of the bridge; they merely blockaded the two ends of the foot planking that traversed it.

Beyond one of the sentinels nobody was in sight; the railroad ran straight away into a forest for a hundred yards, then, curving, was lost to view. Doubtless there was an outpost farther along. The other bank of the stream was open ground—a gentle acclivity topped with a stockade of vertical tree trunks, loopholed for rifles, with a single embrasure through which protruded the muzzle of a brass cannon commanding the bridge. Midway up the slope between bridge and fort were the spectators—a single company of infantry in line, at "parade rest," the butts of the rifles on the ground, the barrels inclining slightly backward against the right shoulder, the hands crossed upon the stock. A lieutenant stood at the right of the line, the point of his sword upon the ground, his left hand resting upon his right. Excepting the group of four at the center of the bridge, not a man moved. The company faced the bridge, staring stonily, motionless. The sentinels, facing the banks of the stream, might have been statues to adorn the bridge. The captain stood with folded arms, silent, observing the work of his subordinates, but making no sign. Death is a dignitary who when he comes announced is to be received with formal manifestations of respect, even by those most familiar with him. In the code of military etiquette silence and fixity are forms of deference.

The man who was engaged in being hanged was apparently about thirty-five years of age. He was a civilian, if one might judge from his habit, which was that of a planter. His features were good—a straight nose, firm mouth, broad forehead, from which his long, dark hair was combed straight back, falling behind his ears to the collar of his well-fitting frock-coat. He wore a mustache and pointed beard, but no whiskers; his eyes were large and dark gray, and had a kindly expression which one would hardly have expected in one whose neck was in the hemp. Evidently this was no vulgar assassin. The liberal military code makes provision for hanging many kinds of persons, and gentlemen are not excluded.

The preparations being complete, the two private soldiers stepped aside and each drew away the plank upon which he had been standing. The sergeant turned to the captain, saluted and placed himself immediately behind that officer, who in turn moved apart one pace. These movements left the condemned man and the sergeant standing on the two ends of the same plank, which spanned three of the cross-ties of the bridge. The end upon which the civilian stood almost, but not quite, reached a fourth. This plank had been held in place by the weight of the captain; it was now held by that of the sergeant. At a signal from the former the latter would step aside, the plank would tilt and the condemned man would go down between two ties. The arrangement commended itself to his judgment as simple and effective. His face had not been covered nor his eyes bandaged. He looked a moment at his "unsteadfast footing," then let his gaze wander to the swirling water of the stream racing madly beneath his feet. A piece of dancing driftwood caught his attention and his eyes followed it down the current. How slowly it appeared to move! What a sluggish stream!

5   He closed his eyes in order to fix his last thoughts upon his wife and children. The water, touched to gold by the early sun, the brooding mists under the banks at some distance down the stream, the fort, the soldiers, the piece of drift—all had distracted him. And now he became conscious of a new disturbance. Striking through the thought of his dear ones was a sound which he could neither ignore nor understand, a sharp, distinct, metallic percussion like the stroke of a blacksmith's hammer upon the anvil; it had the same ringing quality. He wondered what it was, and whether immeasurably distant or near by—it seemed both. Its recurrence was regular, but as slow as the tolling of a death knell. He awaited each stroke with impatience and—he knew not why—apprehension. The intervals of silence grew progressively longer; the delays became maddening. With their greater infrequency the sounds increased in strength and sharpness. They hurt his ear like the thrust of a knife; he feared he would shriek. What he heard was the ticking of his watch.

He unclosed his eyes and saw again the water below him. "If I could free my hands," he thought, "I might throw off the noose and spring into the stream. By diving I could evade the bullets and, swimming vigorously, reach the bank, take to the woods and get away home. My home, thank God, is as yet outside their lines; my wife and little ones are still beyond the invader's farthest advance."

As these thoughts, which have here to be set down in words, were flashed into the doomed man's brain rather than evolved from it the captain nodded to the sergeant. The sergeant stepped aside.

II

Peyton Farquhar was a well-to-do planter, of an old and highly respected Alabama family. Being a slave owner and like other slave owners a politician he was naturally an original secessionist and ardently devoted to the Southern cause. Circumstances of an imperious nature, which it is unnecessary to relate here, had prevented him from taking service with the gallant army that had fought the disastrous campaigns ending with the fall of Corinth, and he chafed under the inglorious restraint, longing for the release of his energies, the larger life of the soldier, the opportunity for distinction. That opportunity, he felt, would come, as it comes to all in war time. Meanwhile he did what he could. No service was too humble to him to perform in aid of the South, no adventure too perilous for him to undertake if consistent with the character of a civilian who was at heart a soldier, and who in good faith and without too much qualification assented to at least a part of the frankly villainous dictum that all is fair in love and war.

One evening while Farquhar and his wife were sitting on a rustic bench near the entrance to his grounds, a gray-clad soldier rode up to the gate and asked for a drink of water. Mrs. Farquhar was only too happy to serve him with her own white hands. While she was fetching the water her husband approached the dusty horseman and inquired eagerly for news from the front.

"The Yanks are repairing the railroads," said the man, "and are getting 10 ready for another advance. They have reached the Owl Creek bridge, put it in order and built a stockade on the north bank. The commandant has issued an order, which is posted everywhere, declaring that any civilian caught interfering with the railroad, its bridges, tunnels or trains will be summarily hanged. I saw the order."

"How far is it to the Owl Creek bridge?" Farquhar asked.

"About thirty miles."

"Is there no force on this side of the creek?"

"Only a picket post half a mile out, on the railroad, and a single sentinel at this end of the bridge."

"Suppose a man—a civilian and student of hanging—should elude the 15 picket post and perhaps get the better of the sentinel," said Farquhar, smiling, "what could he accomplish?"

The soldier reflected. "I was there a month ago," he replied. "I observed that the flood of last winter had lodged a great quantity of driftwood against the wooden pier at this end of the bridge. It is now dry and would burn like tow."

The lady had now brought the water, which the soldier drank. He thanked her ceremoniously, bowed to her husband and rode away. An hour later, after nightfall, he repassed the plantation, going northward in the direction from which he had come. He was a Federal scout.

III

As Peyton Farquhar fell straight downward through the bridge he lost consciousness and was as one already dead. From this state he was awakened— ages later, it seemed to him—by the pain of a sharp pressure upon his throat, followed by a sense of suffocation. Keen, poignant agonies seemed to shoot from his neck downward through every fiber of his body and limbs. These pains appeared to flash along well-defined lines of ramification and to beat with an inconceivably rapid periodicity. They seemed like streams of pulsating fire heating him to an intolerable temperature. As to his head, he was conscious of nothing but a feeling of fullness—of congestion. These sensations were unaccompanied by thought. The intellectual part of his nature was already effaced; he had power only to feel, and feeling was torment. He was conscious of motion. Encompassed in a luminous cloud, of which he was now merely the fiery heart, without material substance, he swung through unthinkable arcs of oscillation, like a vast pendulum. Then all at once, with terrible suddenness, the light about him shot upward with the noise of a loud plash; a frightful roaring was in his ears, and all was cold and dark. The power of thought was restored; he knew that the rope had broken and he had fallen into the stream. There was no additional strangulation; the noose about his neck was already suffocating him and kept the water from his lungs. To die of hanging at the bottom of a river!—the idea seemed to him ludicrous. He opened his eyes in the darkness and saw above him a gleam of light, but how distant, how inaccessible! He was still sinking, for the light became fainter and fainter until it was a mere glimmer. Then it began to grow and brighten, and he knew that he was rising toward the surface—knew it with reluctance, for he was now very comfortable. "To be hanged and drowned," he thought, "that is not so bad; but I do not wish to be shot. No; I will not be shot; that is not fair."

He was not conscious of an effort, but a sharp pain in his wrist apprised him that he was trying to free his hands. He gave the struggle his attention, as an idler might observe the feat of a juggler, without interest in the outcome. What splendid effort!—what magnificent, what superhuman strength! Ah, that was a fine endeavor! Bravo! The cord fell away; his arms parted and floated upward, the hands dimly seen on each side in the growing light. He watched them with a new interest as first one and then the other pounced upon the noose at his neck. They tore it away and thrust it fiercely aside, its undulations resembling those of a water-snake. "Put it back, put it back!" He thought he shouted these words to his hands, for the undoing of the noose had been succeeded by the direst pang that he had yet experienced. His neck ached horribly; his brain was on fire; his heart, which had been fluttering faintly, gave a great leap, trying to force itself out at his mouth. His whole body was racked and wrenched with an insupportable anguish! But his disobedient hands gave no heed to the command. They beat the water vigorously with quick, downward strokes, forcing him to the surface. He felt his head emerge; his eyes were blinded by the sunlight; his chest expanded convulsively, and with a supreme and crowning agony his lungs engulfed a great draught of air, which instantly he expelled in a shriek!

20   He was now in full possession of his physical senses. They were, indeed, preternaturally keen and alert. Something in the awful disturbance of his organic system had so exalted and refined them that they made record of things never before perceived. He felt the ripples upon his face and heard their separate sounds as they struck. He looked at the forest on the bank of the stream, saw the individual trees, the leaves and the veining of each leaf—saw the very insects upon them: the locusts, the brilliant-bodied flies, the gray spiders stretching their webs from twig to twig. He noted the prismatic colors in all the dewdrops upon a million blades of grass. The humming of the gnats that danced above the eddies of the stream, the beating of the dragon-flies' wings, the strokes of the water-spiders' legs, like oars which had lifted their boat—all these made audible music. A fish slid along beneath his eyes and he heard the rush of its body parting the water.

He had come to the surface facing down the stream; in a moment the visible world seemed to wheel slowly round, himself the pivotal point, and he saw the bridge, the fort, the soldiers upon the bridge, the captain, the sergeant, the two privates, his executioners. They were in silhouette against the blue sky. They shouted and gesticulated, pointing at him. The captain had drawn his pistol, but did not fire; the others were unarmed. Their movements were grotesque and horrible, their forms gigantic.

Suddenly he heard a sharp report and something struck the water smartly within a few inches of his head, spattering his face with spray. He heard a second report, and saw one of the sentinels with his rifle at his shoulder, a light cloud of blue smoke rising from the muzzle. The man in the water saw the eye of the man on the bridge gazing into his own through the sights of the rifle. He observed that it was a gray eye and remembered having read that gray eyes were keenest, and that all famous markmen had them. Nevertheless, this one had missed.

A counter-swirl had caught Farquhar and turned him half round; he was again looking into the forest on the bank opposite the fort. The sound of a clear, high voice in a monotonous singsong now rang out behind him and came across the water with a distinctness that pierced and subdued all other sounds, even the beating of the ripples in his ears. Although no soldier, he had frequented camps enough to know the dread significance of that deliberate, drawling, aspirated chant; the lieutenant on shore was taking a part in the morning's work. How coldly and pitilessly—with what an even, calm intonation, presaging, and enforcing tranquility in the men—with what accurately measured intervals fell those cruel words:

"Attention, company! . . . Shoulder arms! . . . Ready! . . . Aim! . . . Fire!"

Farquhar dived—dived as deeply as he could. The water roared in his ears like the voice of Niagara, yet he heard the dulled thunder of the volley and, rising again toward the surface, met shining bits of metal, singularly flattened, oscillating slowly downward. Some of them touched him on the face and hands, then fell away, continuing their descent. One lodged between his collar and neck; it was uncomfortably warm and he snatched it out.

As he rose to the surface, gasping for breath, he saw that he had been a long time under water; he was perceptibly farther down stream—nearer to safety. The soldiers had almost finished reloading; the metal ramrods flashed all at once in the sunshine as they were drawn from the barrels, turned in the air, and thrust into their sockets. The two sentinels fired again, independently and ineffectually.

The hunted man saw all this over his shoulder; he was now swimming vigorously with the current. His brain was as energetic as his arms and legs; he thought with the rapidity of lightning.

"The officer," he reasoned, "will not make that martinet's error a second time. It is as easy to dodge a volley as a single shot. He has probably already given the command to fire at will. God help me, I cannot dodge them all!"

25

An appalling plash within two yards of him was followed by a loud, rushing sound, *diminuendo*°, which seemed to travel back through the air to the fort and died in an explosion which stirred the very river to its deeps! A rising sheet of water curved over him, fell down upon him, blinded him, strangled him! The cannon had taken a hand in the game. As he shook his head free from the commotion of the smitten water he heard the deflected shot humming through the air ahead, and in an instant it was cracking and smashing the branches in the forest beyond.

30   "They will not do that again," he thought; "the next time they will use a charge of grape. I must keep my eye upon the gun; the smoke will apprise me—the report arrives too late; it lags behind the missile. That is a good gun."

Suddenly he felt himself whirled round and round—spinning like a top. The water, the banks, the forests, the now distant bridge, fort and men—all were commingled and blurred. Objects were represented by their colors only; circular horizontal streaks of color—that was all he saw. He had been caught in a vortex and was being whirled on with a velocity of advance and gyration that made him giddy and sick. In a few moments he was flung upon the gravel at the foot of the left bank of the stream—the southern bank—and behind a projecting point which concealed him from his enemies. The sudden arrest of his motion, the abrasion of one of his hands on the gravel, restored him, and he wept with delight. He dug his fingers into the sand, threw it over himself in handfuls and audibly blessed it. It looked like diamonds, rubies, emeralds; he could think of nothing beautiful which it did not resemble. The trees upon the bank were giant garden plants; he noted a definite order in their arrangement, inhaled the fragrance of their blooms. A strange, roseate light shone through the spaces among their trunks and the wind made in their branches the music of aeolian harps. He had no wish to perfect his escape—was content to remain in that enchanting spot until retaken.

A whiz and rattle of grapeshot among the branches high above his head roused him from his dream. The baffled cannoneer had fired him a random farewell. He sprang to his feet, rushed up the sloping bank, and plunged into the forest.

All that day he traveled, laying his course by the rounding sun. The forest seemed interminable; nowhere did he discover a break in it, not even a woodman's road. He had not known that he lived in so wild a region. There was something uncanny in the revelation.

By nightfall he was fatigued, footsore, famishing. The thought of his wife and children urged him on. At last he found a road which led him in what he knew to be the right direction. It was as wide and straight as a city street, yet it seemed untraveled. No fields bordered it, no dwelling anywhere. Not so much as the barking of a dog suggested human habitation. The black bodies of the

---

diminuendo: Gradually getting quieter.

trees formed a straight wall on both sides, terminating on the horizon in a point, like a diagram in a lesson in perspective. Overhead, as he looked up through this rift in the wood, shone great golden stars looking unfamiliar and grouped in strange constellations. He was sure they were arranged in some order which had a secret and malign significance. The wood on either side was full of singular noises, among which—once, twice, and again—he distinctly heard whispers in an unknown tongue.

His neck was in pain and lifting his hand to it he found it horribly   35
swollen. He knew that it had a circle of black where the rope had bruised it. His eyes felt congested; he could no longer close them. His tongue was swollen with thirst; he relieved its fever by thrusting it forward from between his teeth into the cold air. How softly the turf had carpeted the untraveled avenue—he could no longer feel the roadway beneath his feet!

Doubtless, despite his suffering, he had fallen asleep while walking, for now he sees another scene—perhaps he has merely recovered from a delirium. He stands at the gate of his own home. All is as he left it, and all bright and beautiful in the morning sunshine. He must have traveled the entire night. As he pushes open the gate and passes up the wide white walk, he sees a flutter of female garments; his wife, looking fresh and cool and sweet, steps down from the veranda to meet him. At the bottom of the steps she stands waiting, with a smile of ineffable joy, an attitude of matchless grace and dignity. Ah, how beautiful she is! He springs forward with extended arms. As he is about to clasp her he feels a stunning blow upon the back of the neck; a blinding white light blazes all about him with a sound like the shock of a cannon—then all is darkness and silence!

Peyton Farquhar was dead; his body, with a broken neck, swung gently from side to side beneath the timbers of the Owl Creek bridge.   *1891*

CONSIDERATIONS

1. The man on the bridge remains anonymous, and the descriptions focus primarily on the scene: the order of soldiers and their rank, the setting and its relationship to the forest. What do we learn, though, of the man in this first section, and why does Bierce withhold his name until section II?
2. From the description of the soldiers, especially the sentinels, what conclusions can you draw about men during times of war? Explain.
3. Analyze Bierce's choice of organization for this piece. How effective is it, and why might he have chosen to arrange the material as he did? Explain.
4. At what point did you find yourself rooting for Farquhar? What specifically does the author do to bring you, the reader, onto this character's side? At what point did you think Farquhar might or might not make it?
5. Discuss the significance of this quotation and its revelation about war: "and he saw the bridge, the fort, the soldiers upon the bridge, the captain, the

sergeant, the two privates, his executioners. They were in silhouette against the blue sky. . . . Their movements were grotesque and horrible, their forms gigantic."

6. Choose any other quotation from this story and discuss the effect it had on you, the reader.

FRANK O'CONNOR (1903–1966)

Guests of the Nation

Frank O'Connor is the pen name of Michael O'Donovan, who was born in County Cork, Ireland. Because of his family's poverty, he attended school only through the fourth grade, yet he developed a burning interest in reading and writing. Years later, after his brief service in the Irish Republican Army (IRA) during the Irish fight for independence from Great Britain, this interest in literature led him to work as a librarian. He later became director of the Abbey Theatre in Dublin. After moving to the United States in the 1950s, he enjoyed a brief stint as a Sunday morning television personality telling Irish stories. In addition, O'Connor taught creative writing at such renowned institutions as Harvard University and Northwestern University. Over the course of his life, O'Connor published many volumes of short stories and translations of traditional Gaelic poems and tales, as well as The Mirror in the Roadway *(1956), a critical study of the novel, and* The Lonely Voice *(1963), a critical study of the short story.*

"Guests of the Nation," which was O'Connor's first published short story, first appeared in the Atlantic Monthly *in 1931.*

I

At dusk the big Englishman, Belcher, would shift his long legs out of the ashes and say "Well, chums, what about it?" and Noble or me would say "All right, chum" (for we had picked up some of their curious expressions), and the little Englishman, Hawkins, would light the lamp and bring out the cards. Sometimes Jeremiah Donovan would come up and supervise the game and get excited over Hawkins's cards, which he always played badly, and shout at him as if he was one of our own "Ah, you divil, you, why didn't you play the trey?"

But ordinarily Jeremiah was a sober and contented poor devil like the big Englishman, Belcher, and was looked up to only because he was a fair hand at documents, though he was slow enough even with them. He wore a small cloth hat and big gaiters over his long pants, and you seldom saw him with his hands out of his pockets. He reddened when you talked to him, tilting from toe to heel and back, and looking down all the time at his big farmer's feet. Noble and me used to make fun of his broad accent, because we were from the town.

I couldn't at the time see the point of me and Noble guarding Belcher and Hawkins at all, for it was my belief that you could have planted that pair down anywhere from this to Claregalway and they'd have taken root there like a native weed. I never in my short experience seen two men to take to the country as they did.

They were handed on to us by the Second Battalion when the search for them became too hot, and Noble and myself, being young, took over with a natural feeling of responsibility, but Hawkins made us look like fools when he showed that he knew the country better than we did.

"You're the bloke they calls Bonaparte," he says to me. "Mary Brigid O'Connell told me to ask you what you done with the pair of her brother's socks you borrowed."   *5*

For it seemed, as they explained it, that the Second used to have little evenings, and some of the girls of the neighbourhood turned in, and, seeing they were such decent chaps, our fellows couldn't leave the two Englishmen out of them. Hawkins learned to dance "The Walls of Limerick," "The Siege of Ennis," and "The Waves of Tory" as well as any of them, though, naturally, he couldn't return the compliment, because our lads at that time did not dance foreign dances on principle.

So whatever privileges Belcher and Hawkins had with the Second they just naturally took with us, and after the first day or two we gave up all pretence of keeping a close eye on them. Not that they could have got far, for they had accents you could cut with a knife and wore khaki tunics and overcoats with civilian pants and boots. But it's my belief that they never had any idea of escaping and were quite content to be where they were.

It was a treat to see how Belcher got off with the old woman of the house where we were staying. She was a great warrant to scold, and cranky even with us, but before ever she had a chance of giving our guests, as I may call them, a lick of her tongue, Belcher had made her his friend for life. She was breaking sticks, and Belcher, who hadn't been more than ten minutes in the house, jumped up from his seat and went over to her.

"Allow me, madam," he says, smiling his queer little smile, "please allow me"; and he takes the bloody hatchet. She was struck too paralytic to speak, and after that, Belcher would be at her heels, carrying a bucket, a basket, or a load of turf, as the case might be. As Noble said, he got into looking before she leapt, and hot water, or any little thing she wanted, Belcher would have it ready for her. For such a huge man (and though I am five foot ten myself I had to look up at him) he had an uncommon shortness—or should I say lack?—of speech. It took us some time to get used to him, walking in and out, like a ghost, without a word. Especially because Hawkins talked enough for a platoon, it was strange to hear big Belcher with his toes in the ashes come out with a solitary "Excuse me, chum," or "That's right, chum." His one and only passion was cards, and I will say for him that he was a good card-player. He could have fleeced myself and Noble, but whatever we lost to him Hawkins lost to us, and Hawkins played with the money Belcher gave him.

10   Hawkins lost to us because he had too much old gab, and we probably lost to Belcher for the same reason. Hawkins and Noble would spit at one another about religion into the early hours of the morning, and Hawkins worried the soul out of Noble, whose brother was a priest, with a string of questions that would puzzle a cardinal. To make it worse even in treating of holy subjects, Hawkins had a deplorable tongue. I never in all my career met a man who could mix such a variety of cursing and bad language into an argument. He was a terrible man, and a fright to argue. He never did a stroke of work, and when he had no one else to talk to, he got stuck on the old woman.

He met his match in her, for one day when he tried to get her to complain profanely of the drought, she gave him a great come-down by blaming it entirely on Jupiter Pluvius (a deity neither Hawkins nor I had ever heard of, though Noble said that among the pagans it was believed that he had something to do with the rain). Another day he was swearing at the capitalists for starting the German war° when the old lady laid down her iron, puckered up her little crab's mouth, and said: "Mr. Hawkins, you can say what you like about the war, and think you'll deceive me because I'm only a simple poor countrywoman, but I know what started the war. It was the Italian Count that stole the heathen divinity out of the temple in Japan. Believe me, Mr. Hawkins, nothing but sorrow and want can follow the people that disturb the hidden powers."

A queer old girl, all right.

II

We had our tea one evening, and Hawkins lit the lamp and we all sat into cards. Jeremiah Donovan came in too, and sat down and watched us for a while, and it suddenly struck me that he had no great love for the two Englishmen. It came as a great surprise to me, because I hadn't noticed anything about him before.

Late in the evening a really terrible argument blew up between Hawkins and Noble, about capitalists and priests and love of your country.

15   "The capitalists," says Hawkins with an angry gulp, "pays the priests to tell you about the next world so as you won't notice what the bastards are up to in this."

"Nonsense, man!" says Noble, losing his temper. "Before ever a capitalist was thought of, people believed in the next world."

Hawkins stood up as though he was preaching a sermon.

"Oh, they did, did they?" he says with a sneer. "They believed all the things you believe, isn't that what you mean? And you believe that God created Adam,

German war: World War I.

and Adam created Shem, and Shem created Jehoshaphat. You believe all that silly old fairytale about Eve and Eden and the apple. Well, listen to me, chum. If you're entitled to hold a silly belief like that, I'm entitled to hold my silly belief—which is that the first thing your God created was a bleeding capitalist, with morality and Rolls-Royce complete. Am I right, chum?" he says to Belcher.

"You're right, chum," says Belcher with his amused smile, and got up from the table to stretch his long legs into the fire and stroke his moustache. So, seeing that Jeremiah Donovan was going, and that there was no knowing when the argument about religion would be over, I went out with him. We strolled down to the village together, and then he stopped and started blushing and mumbling and saying I ought to be behind, keeping guard on the prisoners. I didn't like the tone he took with me, and anyway I was bored with life in the cottage, so I replied by asking him what the hell we wanted guarding them at all for. I told him I'd talked it over with Noble, and that we'd both rather be out with a fighting column.

"What use are those fellows to us?" says I.   *20*

He looked at me in surprise and said: "I thought you knew we were keeping them as hostages."

"Hostages?" I said.

"The enemy have prisoners belonging to us," he says, "and now they're talking of shooting them. If they shoot our prisoners, we'll shoot theirs."

"Shoot them?" I said.

"What else did you think we were keeping them for?" he says.   *25*

"Wasn't it very unforeseen of you not to warn Noble and myself of that in the beginning?" I said.

"How was it?" says he. "You might have known it."

"We couldn't know it, Jeremiah Donovan," says I. "How could we when they were on our hands so long?"

"The enemy have our prisoners as long and longer," says he.

"That's not the same thing at all," says I.   *30*

"What difference is there?" says he.

I couldn't tell him, because I knew he wouldn't understand. If it was only an old dog that was going to the vet's, you'd try and not get too fond of him, but Jeremiah Donovan wasn't a man that would ever be in danger of that.

"And when is this thing going to be decided?" says I.

"We might hear tonight," he says. "Or tomorrow or the next day at latest. So if it's only hanging round here that's a trouble to you, you'll be free soon enough."

It wasn't the hanging round that was a trouble to me at all by this time. I   *35* had worse things to worry about. When I got back to the cottage the argument was still on. Hawkins was holding forth in his best style, maintaining that there was no next world, and Noble was maintaining that there was; but I could see that Hawkins had had the best of it.

"Do you know what, chum?" he was saying with a saucy smile. "I think you're just as big a bleeding unbeliever as I am. You say you believe in the next world, and you know just as much about the next world as I do, which is sweet damn-all. What's heaven? You don't know. Where's heaven? You don't know. You know sweet damn-all! I ask you again, do they wear wings?"

"Very well, then," says Noble, "they do. Is that enough for you? They do wear wings."

"Where do they get them, then? Who makes them? Have they a factory for wings? Have they a sort of store where you hands in your chit and takes your bleeding wings?"

"You're an impossible man to argue with," says Noble. "Now, listen to me—" And they were off again.

40   It was long after midnight when we locked up and went to bed. As I blew out the candle I told Noble what Jeremiah Donovan was after telling me. Noble took it very quietly. When we'd been in bed about an hour he asked me did I think we ought to tell the Englishmen. I didn't think we should, because it was more than likely that the English wouldn't shoot our men, and even if they did, the brigade officers, who were always up and down with the Second Battalion and knew the Englishmen well, wouldn't be likely to want them plugged. "I think so too," says Noble. "It would be great cruelty to put the wind up them now."

"It was very unforeseen of Jeremiah Donovan anyhow," says I.

It was next morning that we found it so hard to face Belcher and Hawkins. We went about the house all day scarcely saying a word. Belcher didn't seem to notice; he was stretched into the ashes as usual, with his usual look of waiting in quietness for something unforeseen to happen, but Hawkins noticed and put it down to Noble's being beaten in the argument of the night before.

"Why can't you take a discussion in the proper spirit?" he says severely. "You and your Adam and Eve! I'm a Communist, that's what I am. Communist or anarchist, it all comes to much the same thing." And for hours he went round the house, muttering when the fit took him. "Adam and Eve! Adam and Eve! Nothing better to do with their time than picking bleeding apples!"

III

I don't know how we got through that day, but I was very glad when it was over, the tea things were cleared away, and Belcher said in his peaceable way: "Well, chums, what about it?" We sat round the table and Hawkins took out the cards, and just then I heard Jeremiah Donovan's footstep on the path and a dark presentiment crossed my mind. I rose from the table and caught him before he reached the door.

45   "What do you want?" I asked.

"I want those two soldier friends of yours," he says, getting red.

"Is that the way, Jeremiah Donovan?" I asked.

"That's the way. There were four of our lads shot this morning, one of them a boy of sixteen."

"That's bad," I said.

At that moment Noble followed me out, and the three of us walked   *50*
down the path together, talking in whispers. Feeney, the local intelligence officer, was standing by the gate.

"What are you going to do about it?" I asked Jeremiah Donovan.

"I want you and Noble to get them out; tell them they're being shifted again; that'll be the quietest way."

"Leave me out of that," says Noble under his breath.

Jeremiah Donovan looks at him hard.

"All right," he says. "You and Feeney get a few tools from the shed and dig   *55*
a hole by the far end of the bog. Bonaparte and myself will be after you. Don't let anyone see you with the tools. I wouldn't like it to go beyond ourselves."

We saw Feeney and Noble go round to the shed and went in ourselves. I left Jeremiah Donovan to do the explanations. He told them that he had orders to send them back to the Second Battalion. Hawkins let out a mouthful of curses, and you could see that though Belcher didn't say anything, he was a bit upset too. The old woman was for having them stay in spite of us, and she didn't stop advising them until Jeremiah Donovan lost his temper and turned on her. He had a nasty temper, I noticed. It was pitch-dark in the cottage by this time, but no one thought of lighting the lamp, and in the darkness the two Englishmen fetched their topcoats and said good-bye to the old woman.

"Just as a man makes a home of a bleeding place, some bastard at headquarters thinks you're too cushy and shunts you off," says Hawkins, shaking her hand.

"A thousand thanks, madam," says Belcher. "A thousand thanks for everything"—as though he'd made it up.

We went round to the back of the house and down towards the bog. It was only then that Jeremiah Donovan told them. He was shaking with excitement.

"There were four of our fellows shot in Cork this morning and now   *60*
you're to be shot as a reprisal."

"What are you talking about?" snaps Hawkins. "It's bad enough being mucked about as we are without having to put up with your funny jokes."

"It isn't a joke," says Donovan. "I'm sorry, Hawkins, but it's true," and begins on the usual rigmarole about duty and how unpleasant it is.

I never noticed that people who talk a lot about duty find it much of a trouble to them.

"Oh, cut it out!" says Hawkins.

"Ask Bonaparte," says Donovan, seeing that Hawkins isn't taking him seriously. "Isn't it true, Bonaparte?"   *65*

"It is," I say, and Hawkins stops.

"Ah, for Christ's sake, chum!"

"I mean it, chum," I say.

"You don't sound as if you meant it."

70   "If he doesn't mean it, I do," says Donovan, working himself up.

"What have you against me, Jeremiah Donovan?"

"I never said I had anything against you. But why did your people take out four of our prisoners and shoot them in cold blood?"

He took Hawkins by the arm and dragged him on, but it was impossible to make him understand that we were in earnest. I had the Smith & Wesson in my pocket and I kept fingering it and wondering what I'd do if they put up a fight for it or ran, and wishing to God they'd do one or the other. I knew if they did run for it, that I'd never fire on them. Hawkins wanted to know was Noble in it, and when we said yes, he asked us why Noble wanted to plug him. Why did any of us want to plug him? What had he done to us? Weren't we all chums? Didn't we understand him and didn't he understand us? Did we imagine for an instant that he'd shoot us for all the so-and-so officers in the so-and-so British Army?

By this time we'd reached the bog, and I was so sick I couldn't even answer him. We walked along the edge of it in the darkness, and every now and then Hawkins would call a halt and begin all over again, as if he was wound up, about our being chums, and I knew that nothing but the sight of the grave would convince him that we had to do it. And all the time I was hoping that something would happen; that they'd run for it or that Noble would take over the responsibility from me. I had the feeling that it was worse on Noble than on me.

IV

75   At last we saw the lantern in the distance and made towards it. Noble was carrying it, and Feeney was standing somewhere in the darkness behind him, and the picture of them so still and silent in the bogland brought it home to me that we were in earnest, and banished the last bit of hope I had.

Belcher, on recognizing Noble, said: "Hallo, chum," in his quiet way, but Hawkins flew at him at once, and the argument began all over again, only this time Noble had nothing to say for himself and stood with his head down, holding the lantern between his legs.

It was Jeremiah Donovan who did the answering. For the twentieth time, as though it was haunting his mind, Hawkins asked if anybody thought he'd shoot Noble.

"Yes, you would," says Jeremiah Donovan.

"No, I wouldn't, damn you!"

80   "You would, because you'd know you'd be shot for not doing it."

"I wouldn't, not if I was to be shot twenty times over. I wouldn't shoot a pal. And Belcher wouldn't—isn't that right, Belcher?"

"That's right, chum," Belcher said, but more by way of answering the question than of joining in the argument. Belcher sounded as though whatever unforeseen thing he'd always been waiting for had come at last.

"Anyway, who says Noble would be shot if I wasn't? What do you think I'd do if I was in his place, out in the middle of a blasted bog?"

"What would you do?" asks Donovan.

"I'd go with him wherever he was going, of course. Share my last bob   85
with him and stick by him through thick and thin. No one can ever say of me that I let down a pal."

"We had enough of this," says Jeremiah Donovan, cocking his revolver. "Is there any message you want to send?"

"No, there isn't."

"Do you want to say your prayers?"

Hawkins came out with a cold-blooded remark that even shocked me and turned on Noble again.

"Listen to me, Noble," he says. "You and me are chums. You can't come   90
over to my side, so I'll come over to your side. That show you I mean what I say? Give me a rifle and I'll go along with you and the other lads."

Nobody answered him. We knew that was no way out.

"Hear what I'm saying?" he says. "I'm through with it. I'm a deserter or anything else you like. I don't believe in your stuff, but it's no worse than mine. That satisfy you?"

Noble raised his head, but Donovan began to speak and he lowered it again without replying.

"For the last time, have you any messages to send?" says Donovan in a cold, excited sort of voice.

"Shut up, Donovan! You don't understand me, but these lads do. They're   95
not the sort to make a pal and kill a pal. They're not the tools of any capitalist."

I alone of the crowd saw Donovan raise his Webley to the back of Hawkins's neck, and as he did so I shut my eyes and tried to pray. Hawkins had begun to say something else when Donovan fired, and as I opened my eyes at the bang, I saw Hawkins stagger at the knees and lie out flat at Noble's feet, slowly and as quiet as a kid falling asleep, with the lantern-light on his lean legs and bright farmer's boots. We all stood very still, watching him settle out in the last agony.

Then Belcher took out a handkerchief and began to tie it about his own eyes (in our excitement we'd forgotten to do the same for Hawkins), and, seeing it wasn't big enough, turned and asked for the loan of mine. I gave it to him and he knotted the two together and pointed with his foot at Hawkins.

"He's not quite dead," he says. "Better give him another."

Sure enough, Hawkins's left knee is beginning to rise. I bend down and put my gun to his head; then, recollecting myself, I get up again. Belcher understands what's in my mind.

100   "Give him his first," he says. "I don't mind. Poor bastard, we don't know what's happening to him now."

I knelt and fired. By this time I didn't seem to know what I was doing. Belcher, who was fumbling a bit awkwardly with the handkerchiefs, came out with a laugh as he heard the shot. It was the first time I heard him laugh and it sent a shudder down my back; it sounded so unnatural.

"Poor bugger!" he said quietly. "And last night he was so curious about it all. It's very queer, chums, I always think. Now he knows as much about it as they'll ever let him know, and last night he was all in the dark."

Donovan helped him to tie the handkerchiefs about his eyes. "Thanks, chum," he said. Donovan asked if there were any messages he wanted sent.

"No, chum," he says. "Not for me. If any of you would like to write to Hawkins's mother, you'll find a letter from her in his pocket. He and his mother were great chums. But my missus left me eight years ago. Went away with another fellow and took the kid with her. I like the feeling of a home, as you may have noticed, but I couldn't start again after that."

105   It was an extraordinary thing, but in those few minutes Belcher said more than in all the weeks before. It was just as if the sound of the shot had started a flood of talk in him and he could go on the whole night like that, quite happily, talking about himself. We stood round like fools now that he couldn't see us any longer. Donovan looked at Noble, and Noble shook his head. Then Donovan raised his Webley, and at that moment Belcher gives his queer laugh again. He may have thought we were talking about him, or perhaps he noticed the same thing I'd noticed and couldn't understand it.

"Excuse me, chums," he says. "I feel I'm talking the hell of a lot, and so silly, about my being so handy about a house and things like that. But this thing came on me suddenly. You'll forgive me, I'm sure."

"You don't want to say a prayer?" asks Donovan.

"No, chum," he says. "I don't think it would help. I'm ready, and you boys want to get it over."

"You understand that we're only doing our duty?" says Donovan.

110   Belcher's head was raised like a blind man's, so that you could only see his chin and the tip of his nose in the lantern-light.

"I never could make out what duty was myself," he said. "I think you're all good lads, if that's what you mean. I'm not complaining."

Noble, just as if he couldn't bear any more of it, raised his fist at Donovan, and in a flash Donovan raised his gun and fired. The big man went over like a sack of meal, and this time there was no need of a second shot.

I don't remember much about the burying, but that it was worse than all the rest because we had to carry them to the grave. It was all mad lonely with nothing but a patch of lantern-light between ourselves and the dark, and birds hooting and screeching all round, disturbed by the guns. Noble went through Hawkins's belongings to find the letter from his mother, and then joined his hands together. He did the same with Belcher. Then, when we'd filled in the grave, we separated from Jeremiah Donovan and Feeney and took our tools back to the shed. All the way we didn't speak a word. The kitchen was dark and cold as we'd left it, and the old woman was sitting over the hearth, saying her beads. We walked past her into the room, and Noble struck a match to light the lamp. She rose quietly and came to the doorway with all her cantankerousness gone.

"What did ye do with them?" she asked in a whisper, and Noble started so that the match went out in his hand.

"What's that?" he asked without turning round.   *115*

"I heard ye," she said.

"What did you hear?" asked Noble.

"I heard ye. Do ye think I didn't hear ye, putting the spade back in the houseen?"°

Noble struck another match and this time the lamp lit for him.

"Was that what ye did to them?" she asked.   *120*

Then, by God, in the very doorway, she fell on her knees and began praying, and after looking at her for a minute or two Noble did the same by the fireplace. I pushed my way out past her and left them at it. I stood at the door, watching the stars and listening to the shrieking of the birds dying out over the bogs. It is so strange what you feel at times like that you can't describe it. Noble says he saw everything ten times the size, as though there were nothing in the whole world but that little patch of bog with the two Englishmen stiffening into it, but with me it was as if the patch of bog where the Englishmen were was a million miles away, and even Noble and the old woman, mumbling behind me, and the birds and the bloody stars were all far away, and I was somehow very small and very lost and lonely like a child astray in the snow. And anything that happened to me afterwards, I never felt the same about again.   *1931*

CONSIDERATIONS

1. List the details that suggest the setting (both time and place) of this story. How important is this specific setting to the story's action and theme? Might a story like this take place in a different time and location? Explain.
2. The four major characters demonstrate striking similarities and differences. How do these suggest the story's theme(s)?
3. What roles do the minor characters—the old woman and Donovan— play? How would the story be different if these characters were absent (or different)?

---

houseen: Literally, "little house"; a small storage shed.

4. Throughout the story, several characters talk about "duty." What possible definitions of the word does the story suggest? How would you define the term? Consider, for example, different kinds of duty and evaluate whether one kind should take precedence over another.

5. Reread the details of the executions (section IV). What effect does O'Connor achieve—and what questions does he raise—by including the gory description of the prisoners' agonizing deaths as well as Belcher's and Hawkins's responses to the executions?

Commentary

STANLEY RENNER

The Theme of Hidden Powers: Fate vs. Human Responsibility in "Guests of the Nation"

In Frank O'Connor's "Guests of the Nation," the reader witnesses the cold-blooded execution of two English soldiers—a killing by the men who have been assigned to guard them and with whom they have become friends, done in reprisal for the soldiers' shooting four members of the Irish revolutionary movement. The story employs a first-person participant point of view to dramatize an irony much like Thomas Hardy's in "The Man He Killed":

> Yes; quaint and curious war is!
> You shoot a fellow down
> You'd treat if met where any bar is,
> Or help to half-a-crown.

Readers of the story, however, have not found the war-sanctioned shootings it dramatizes "quaint and curious." Commentators have been virtually unanimous in approving what they take to be O'Connor's condemnation of "the evil of murderous 'duty' which lies at the center of the story" (Briden 79).[1] O'Connor strongly invites this response by humanizing the two English soldiers, engaging the reader's sympathy for them in order to maximize the shock of their execution in the end. But he also heightens the story's disturbing effect through an extended figurative questioning of where responsibility for such evil lies—within the individuals involved or in forces beyond their control. At the heart of the story's design lies a preoccupation with certain mysterious "hidden powers" (19), the forces of chance or fate or other inexplicable supernatural machination that grips human lives in capricious, mostly unwelcome, ways. Analysis of the theme of "hidden powers" in "Guests of the Nation" clarifies its moral design, the role of its characters, the meaning of the ending—even the significance of the narrator's name, which has provoked surprisingly little critical curiosity.[2]

The concept of hidden powers is introduced at the outset of the story together with the fellow-feeling that develops between the English prisoners of war and their Irish guards. The opening paragraph establishes both that the men are becoming "chums" and that they spend a good deal of time playing cards, an activity that not only breaks down the military barriers between them but also introduces the notion of chance, a hidden force that plays a ubiquitous role in human events. Although one may exercise some control over how one's cards are played, chance governs what cards are dealt, both in card games and in life.

The card-playing in "Guests of the Nation" introduces the story's underlying preoccupation with the question of who or what is in charge of what happens on earth. Again reminiscent of Hardy, "Guests of the Nation" runs the gamut of possible answers to the question in much the same way as does Hardy's "Hap," in which the speaker, in the apparent absence of a benevolent Providence, prefers that "some vengeful god" were running things rather than nobody or nothing at all. The Christian view that the universe is controlled by a benevolent providence is represented in the story by Noble, who, in heated debates with Hawkins, argues for a supernatural being who promises an afterlife complete with angels who wear wings. The old woman who keeps the house in which the prisoners are being held introduces the notion of a vengeful deity who pays people off for violations of the divine order. She babbles nonsense as yet unexplained about how an "Italian Count that stole the heathen divinity out of the temple in Japan" brought on World War I because "nothing but sorrow and want can follow the people that disturb the hidden powers" (19). The card-playing in the story rounds out the possibilities: perhaps our lives, like games of chance, are governed by nothing but "Crass Casualty," as Hardy terms it in "Hap"—the random functioning of the universal machinery.

5   But there is another order of hidden powers in the design of "Guests of the Nation": human rather than cosmic. For not all the evil that happens to human beings is dealt out by forces beyond their control. Some of it they do to each other. These hidden human powers, visible only in their effect on human beings, appear in the story mainly in the obligations we impose on ourselves through our institutions of social organization and the human concerns that have created them and should make them work for the good of human beings. One of the institutional hidden powers in "Guests of the Nation" is that of capitalism, against which Hawkins, who calls himself a Communist, rails bitterly as an evil force working against an amelioration of the human condition. But the primary example in "Guests of the Nation" of the institutional power that human beings have imposed on themselves is the military organization which holds the intangible power of duty over the soldiers in the story. The other major human hidden power in the story is that of love in a broad sense—the power in the feelings that bind human beings together. Ironically, the institutional powers, such as the military, which have been created, ideally, to ensure the welfare and safety of human beings, may come to work to their harm: a human power meant for good may result in evil.

Some observers of the human lot have recognized two categories of evils and sorrows: those attributable to cosmic powers, whatever they may be, and those attributable to human powers. There are thus irremediable evils, those we can do nothing about, and remediable evils, those within our power to alleviate. Logically, then, we should cease wringing our hands about irremediable evils and concentrate on those we can do something about. Here again, the story is reminiscent of Hardy, who urges in "Apology"—the preface to his *Late Lyrics and Earlier*—that, to the extent permitted by "the mighty necessi-

tating forces—unconscious or otherwise," "pain to all upon [the globe],
tongued or dumb, shall be kept down to a minimum by loving-kindness, operating through scientific knowledge, and actuated by the modicum of free
will conjecturally possessed by organic life . . ." (527). A similar outlook is attributed to Clarissa Dalloway in Virginia Woolf's *Mrs. Dalloway:*

> As we are a doomed race, chained to a sinking ship . . . , as the whole
> thing is a bad joke, let us, at any rate, do our part; mitigate the sufferings
> of our fellow-prisoners . . . ; decorate the dungeon with flowers and air-
> cushions; be as decent as we possibly can. Those ruffians, the Gods, shan't
> have it all their own way (117).

—her notion being that the Gods, who never lost a chance of hurting, thwart-
ing and spoiling human lives were seriously put out if, all the same, you behaved like a lady.

These are precisely the issues against which the conflict between duty
and humanity in "Guests of the Nation" is posed, and it is the keenest irony of
the story that its protagonists, Bonaparte and Noble, commit a remediable brutality against fellow human beings as if compelled by a power beyond their
control. To be sure, chance has put them in their predicament. And it is easy to
judge them when one is safely detached from their situation, in which they
owe unquestioning obedience to a military organization not known for sweet
reasonableness. If they do not carry out the order to execute their prisoners,
they can be court-martialed and shot. Still, what they are ordered to do does
not fall within the province of the irremediable: they do have a choice, a "modicum," at least, "of free will." Bonaparte recognizes the patent inhumanity of
the order, although he seems less concerned about the brutality to the Englishmen than about the injury to his own feelings; and it is not promising
when he draws an analogy between how he would feel in shooting human
beings he has come to like and how he would feel in taking an old dog he is
fond of to the vet's to be put to sleep. But rather than taking action himself, he
merely drifts along as if helpless to defy the fates, "hoping that something
would happen," that the Englishmen would "run for it" or that "Noble would
take over the responsibility from me," but doing nothing himself (25).

The question that underlies the story, then, is whether one is driven
along by an irresistible destiny or can take a hand in the chances of life, remedy its remediable ills, and perhaps meliorate the pains and sorrows that cannot be prevented. This question informs not only the ending of "Guests of
the Nation" but also the design of its characters, and it is noteworthy that
O'Connor's Englishmen are more humane than his Irishmen. Presumably the
four Irish prisoners were executed by the English for something they had
done, whereas Belcher and Hawkins are to be shot in random cold-blooded
reprisal. Bonaparte and Noble, although they find the order shocking, nevertheless help carry it out, yielding with token resistance to what appears to be
their fate—Bonaparte by actually giving Hawkins the coup de grace, and

Noble by helping bury the Englishmen. Donovan and Feeney, who place devotion to the cause above humanity, personify a brutality unmediated by fellow-feeling. Donovan deliberately closes himself off from the human ties that should work against remediable evil, while Feeney has been linked to the Fenian brotherhood, the heart of the Irish nationalistic spirit, which brutally overrules the brotherhood of fellow-feeling that develops between the guards and prisoners in the story.[3]

The Englishmen are shown in a more positive light. Ironically, they fit in better with the local community than do the Irishmen, perhaps because their humanity is less numbed by divisive hatreds. Hawkins, the "quixotic Socialist-Atheist" (Briden 80), consistently takes the side of humanity against institutions of society he blames for evils that are or ought to be remediable—against "the capitalists" and their self-serving hypocrisy of "morality and Rolls-Royce complete" and "all the so-and-so officers" that enforce the prevailing social order (20, 24). But finally, it is the quiet Belcher who is most attuned to ameliorating the twists and toils of fate and necessity for his fellow human beings—this despite (or because of) the fact that he is himself a thoroughgoing fatalist, "with his usual look of waiting in quietness for something unforeseen to happen" (22). Belcher alone helps the old woman with her chores. He is a huge man, and to mitigate the inequalities of life, the strong should help the weak. Moved by the same spirit, he sees to it that things come out even in the card games with which the guards and prisoners pass the time. An object lesson for the capitalists railed at by Hawkins, he could have come out on top: "he was a good card player," Bonaparte admits, and "could have fleeced myself and Noble . . ." (19). Instead, he bankrolls Hawkins with the money he has won, knowing full well that Hawkins will lose it back to the Irishmen and there will be no winners and losers. True to the end, Belcher continues to put others' interests ahead of his own. As he is about to be shot, he asks that Hawkins, whom the initial bullet did not finish, be put out of his agony with a second shot. And he is almost unbelievably solicitous of his executioners' feelings in the affair, trying, apparently, to ease their shock and guilt in having to shoot him. Belcher's meliorating humanity, coupled with Hawkins's indignation against the remediable evils built into the established structures of society, seems to form the moral center of "Guests of the Nation" against which the actions of the Irishmen are judged. Thus the reader's shock at the execution of Hawkins and Belcher, guilty of nothing except being in the wrong uniform in the wrong place at the wrong time, is intensified by a sense that the power of fate which helped to contrive the situation need not have been allowed to dictate its brutal outcome.

10   The theme of hidden powers in "Guests of the Nation" may also help to answer a question left by the story—why is the narrator named Bonaparte?—that most commentators have ignored.[4] For among the hidden powers that control human life is destiny, and destiny was a life-long preoccupation of the original Bonaparte, Napoleon I—widely remembered, as he regarded himself,

as the Man of Destiny. Just as the story told by O'Connor's Bonaparte poses the question of the relationship between human responsibility and the workings of destiny, so Napoleon pondered his role as the instrument of oceanic forces working themselves out on the map of Europe. So important is the question of destiny in Napoleon's life that most of the numerous books about him address the subject. Especially pertinent to the present discussion is Emil Ludwig's *Napoleon,* published shortly before "Guests of the Nation" was written. A close similarity in the way both Ludwig's Napoleon and O'Connor's Bonaparte tend to shift the responsibility for their actions to destiny but suffer the consequences of such a view of life suggests the possibility that O'Connor might have drawn his character with Ludwig's Napoleon in mind.

Ludwig's book, whether or not O'Connor read it, throws light on several elements of the story's moral design, including the role of the ironically named Noble and the import of the final scene showing Bonaparte lost in a vacant cosmic immensity. In the spectrum of attitudes presented in the story, Noble is the Christian, who can resolve the problem of evil through faith in a hidden Providence and absolve his own sinful complicity in evil by seeking God's forgiveness. "How happy should we be here," Napoleon allows, "if I could confide my troubles to God, and could expect from him happiness and salvation!" (qtd. in Ludwig 601). Thus Noble, in the end, falls on his knees and begins praying to lighten his burden of sorrow and guilt, but neither Napoleon nor Bonaparte can accept this way of resolving the question of the scheme of things and his own place in it. The story also criticizes Noble's resort to the consolation of religion for his evasion of moral responsibility in this world through his fixation on the next.

O'Connor's Bonaparte, like Napoleon, tends to view himself as in the grip of an irresistible destiny. "In general," observes Ludwig, Napoleon "is resigned to fate." In "hundreds of sayings," he expressed the belief that "No one can escape his fate" and that "all things are linked together, and are subject to the unsearchable guidance of an unseen hand" (603). But both Napoleon and Bonaparte remain troubled by the terrible human consequences of the military actions their destinies commit them to—the former, in giving orders that cost human lives; the latter, in carrying out such orders. Napoleon, at the tomb of Rousseau, father of the Revolution, wondered "whether it would have been better for the peace of the world if neither Rousseau nor I had lived" (qtd. in Ludwig 605). O'Connor's Bonaparte suffers similarly from a troubling, if defective, sense that what fate seems to demand of him is wrong. Yet he does it anyway, as if governed by Napoleon's principle that "It is wise and politic to do what fate commands, and to march on the road along which we are led by the irresistible course of events" (qtd. in Ludwig 604). But neither Napoleon nor Bonaparte escapes the logical consequences—the spiritual desolation—of giving the world over to destiny. "What [Napoleon] never loses," Ludwig concludes, "is the sense of daimonic loneliness, which increases as his soaring flight leads him to chillier altitudes" (605). Similarly, Bonaparte in the end feels "very small and very lost and lonely like a child astray in the snow"—a feeling he will never lose, for, as he says, "anything that happened me [sic] afterwards, I never felt the same about again" (29). As a result of his world view, Ludwig's Napoleon faces "the desert, which to him is the image of the infinite . . . the sublime vacancy which expands before him when the myriad-faceted pictures of ordinary life sink from sight" (605). Similarly, O'Connor's Bonaparte stands in the end facing a vacant universe, nothing but the empty bogs and the distant stars, while the graves of Belcher and Hawkins, "even Noble and the old woman, mumbling behind me, and the birds and the bloody stars were all far away," "a million miles away."

Thus the moral judgment of "Guests of the Nation" comes down mainly on Bonaparte and Noble—not that the deliberate inhumanity of Donovan and Feeney is excused by O'Connor but that Bonaparte and Noble, who still entertain human feelings, allow themselves to contribute to the remediable brutality in the world in the mistaken impression that they have no choice. O'Connor wrings a further twist from his powerful ending by showing that the world views that allow Bonaparte and Noble to shift the responsibility for what they have done to the hidden powers that govern the cosmos are opposite forms of the same cop-out. In Noble's geocentric Christian world view, the human scene is predominant: "he saw everything ten times the size, as though there were nothing in the world but that little patch of bog with the two Englishmen stiffening into it . . ." (28). But he has failed to fulfill his Christian duty: to love, extend hospitality, and sacrifice oneself for others and especially for strangers and enemies. With Bonaparte, it is just the reverse. In his mechanistic sense of the universe, human doings seem insignificant, "as if the patch of bog where the Englishmen were was a million miles away" (29), in the vast empty universe of "Hap." And thus he has failed in the duty of human beings to band together, eliminate remediable evils, and mitigate the irremediable evils dealt out in a vacant, indifferent universe.

In the end, "Guests of the Nation" echoes the disillusionment that W. B. Yeats felt toward the Irish cause, which O'Connor implicitly in his story and Yeats explicitly in "Easter 1916" warn "Can make a stone of the heart." But the tone and gist of the story are surely best captured a decade later in E. M. Forster's memorable comment on where human duty lies: "I hate the idea of causes," he wrote in 1939, "and if I had to choose between betraying my country and betraying my friend, I hope I should have the guts to betray my country" (78).   *1990*

NOTES

1. To J. R. Crider, there is "virtual unanimity" in recognizing the story's theme of "the inhumanity of war" (407). Patricia Robinson notes O'Connor's disapproval of political fanaticism in the story (58). "'Duty,' as O'Connor projects it in the stories," writes Maurice Wohlgelertner, "becomes a shield for

monstrous acts of evil" (36). "Performing one's duty," Michael Liberman comments, can involve, as in the story, doing something "barbaric" (441).

2. Crider has noted the theme of hidden powers in the story, pointing out that Jupiter Pluvius, invoked by the old woman, is the god of human values such as hospitality—the protector of "strangers, guests, and supplicants." Thus by executing the Englishmen, the Irishmen do indeed "disturb the hidden powers" and "violate obligations and decencies that stem from the depths of human nature and immemorial custom" (410).

3. Earl F. Briden has linked Jeremiah Donovan in the story with Jeremiah O'Donovan, "a virtual legend of Irish revolutionary heroism," showing that O'Connor ironically attacks the movement for its admiration of violence in behalf of the cause. Briden also proposes that Feeney might be an allusion to the Fenian brotherhood (80), a suggestion later repeated by Robinson (58).

4. Only Briden, to my knowledge, has paused at the name Bonaparte, suggesting that the story's narrator "is a tragic parody of Napoleonic greatness" (79).

Works Cited

Briden, Earl F. "'Guests of the Nation': A Final Irony." *Studies in Short Fiction* 13 (1976): 79–81.

Crider, J. R. "Jupiter Pluvius in 'Guests of the Nation.'" *Studies in Short Fiction* 23 (1986): 407–11.

Forster, E. M. *Two Cheers for Democracy.* London: Edward Arnold, 1961.

Hardy, Thomas. "Apology." *The Collected Poems of Thomas Hardy.* London: Macmillan, 1962. 525–32.

Liberman, Michael. "Unforeseen Duty in Frank O'Connor's 'Guests of the Nation.'" *Studies II: Short Fiction* 24 (1987): 438–41.

Ludwig, Emil. *Napoleon.* New York: Liveright, 1954.

O'Connor, Frank. "Guests of the Nation." *More Stories by Frank O'Connor.* New York: Knopf, 1967. 17–29.

Robinson, Patricia. "O'Connor's 'Guests of the Nation.'" *Explicator 45* (1986): 58.

Wohlgelertner, Maurice. *Frank O'Connor: An Introduction.* New York: Columbia UP, 1977.

Woolf, Virginia. *Mrs. Dalloway.* New York: Harvest, 1925.

CYNTHIA OZICK (1928–   )

The Shawl

Cynthia Ozick was born in the Bronx, New York, where her parents owned a pharmacy, and her father was also a Hebrew scholar. Ozick graduated from New York University and earned a master's degree from Ohio State University. After a stint as an advertising copywriter and a year teaching at New York University, she devoted herself to writing. She published her first novel, Trust, *in 1966 and since then has written two more:* The Cannibal Galaxy *(1983) and* The Messiah of Stockholm *(1987). In addition to essays, poetry, and plays, she has also written four short story collections:* The Pagan Rabbi *(1971),* Bloodshed *(1976),* Levitation *(1982), and* The Shawl *(1989), which includes the following story as well as a companion piece, the novella "Rosa." "The Shawl" was first published in* The New Yorker *in 1980. She says the story grew from a line in William Shirer's history of Nazi Germany,* The Rise and Fall of the Third Reich: *it "spoke about babies being thrown against the electrified fences [surrounding the concentration camps], and I guess that image stayed with me."*

Stella, cold, cold, the coldness of hell. How they walked on the roads together, Rosa with Magda curled up between sore breasts, Magda wound up in the shawl. Sometimes Stella carried Magda. But she was jealous of Magda. A thin girl of fourteen, too small, with thin breasts of her own, Stella wanted to be wrapped in a shawl, hidden away, asleep, rocked by the march, a baby, a round infant in arms. Magda took Rosa's nipple, and Rosa never stopped walking, a walking cradle. There was not enough milk; sometimes Magda sucked air; then she screamed. Stella was ravenous. Her knees were tumors on sticks, her elbows chicken bones.

Rosa did not feel hunger; she felt light, not like someone walking but like someone in a faint, in trance, arrested in a fit, someone who is already a floating angel, alert and seeing everything, but in the air, not there, not touching the road. As if teetering on the tips of her fingernails. She looked into Magda's face through a gap in the shawl: a squirrel in a nest, safe, no one could reach her inside the little house of the shawl's windings. The face, very round, a pocket mirror of a face: but it was not Rosa's bleak complexion, dark like cholera, it was another kind of face altogether, eyes blue as air, smooth feathers of hair nearly as yellow as the Star sewn into Rosa's coat. You could think she was one of *their* babies.

Rosa, floating, dreamed of giving Magda away in one of the villages. She could leave the line for a minute and push Magda into the hands of any woman on the side of the road. But if she moved out of line they might shoot. And even if she fled the line for half a second and pushed the shawl-bundle at a stranger, would the woman take it? She might be surprised, or afraid; she might drop the shawl, and Magda would fall out and strike her head and die. The little round head. Such a good child, she gave up screaming, and sucked now only for the taste of the drying nipple itself. The neat grip of the tiny gums. One mite of a tooth tip sticking up in the bottom gum, how shining, an elfin tombstone of white marble, gleaming there. Without complaining, Magda relinquished Rosa's teats, first the left, then the right; both were cracked, not a sniff of milk. The duct crevice extinct, a dead volcano, blind eye, chill hole, so Magda took the corner of the shawl and milked it instead. She sucked and sucked, flooding the threads with wetness. The shawl's good flavor, milk of linen.

It was a magic shawl, it could nourish an infant for three days and three nights. Magda did not die, she stayed alive, although very quiet. A peculiar smell, of cinnamon and almonds, lifted out of her mouth. She held her eyes open every moment, forgetting how to blink or nap, and Rosa and sometimes Stella studied their blueness. On the road they raised one burden of a leg after another and studied Magda's face. "Aryan," Stella said, in a voice grown as thin as a string; and Rosa thought how Stella gazed at Magda like a young canni- bal. And the time that Stella said "Aryan," it sounded to Rosa as if Stella had really said, "Let us devour her."

But Magda lived to walk. She lived that long, but she did not walk very   5 well, partly because she was only fifteen months old, and partly because the spindles of her legs could not hold up her fat belly. It was fat with air, full and round. Rosa gave almost all her food to Magda. Stella gave nothing; Stella was ravenous, a growing child herself, but not growing much. Stella did not men- struate. Rosa did not menstruate. Rosa was ravenous, but also not; she learned from Magda how to drink the taste of a finger in one's mouth. They were in a place without pity, all pity was annihilated in Rosa, she looked at Stella's bones without pity. She was sure that Stella was waiting for Magda to die so she could put her teeth into the little thighs.

Rosa knew Magda was going to die very soon; she should have been dead already, but she had been buried away deep inside the magic shawl, mis- taken there for the shivering mound of Rosa's breasts; Rosa clung to the shawl as if it covered only herself. No one took it away from her. Magda was mute. She never cried. Rosa hid her in the barracks, under the shawl, but she knew that one day someone would inform; or one day someone, not even Stella, would steal Magda to eat her. When Magda began to walk Rosa knew that Magda was going to die very soon, something would happen. She was afraid to fall asleep; she slept with the weight of her thigh on Magda's body; she was afraid she would smother Magda under her thigh. The weight of Rosa was be- coming less and less, Rosa and Stella were slowly turning into air.

Magda was quiet, but her eyes were horribly alive, like blue tigers. She watched. Sometimes she laughed—it seemed a laugh, but how could it be? Magda had never seen anyone laugh. Still, Magda laughed at her shawl when the wind blew its corners, the bad wind with pieces of black in it, that made Stella's and Rosa's eyes tear. Magda's eyes were always clear and tearless. She watched like a tiger. She guarded her shawl. No one could touch it; only Rosa could touch it. Stella was not allowed. The shawl was Magda's own baby, her pet, her little sister. She tangled herself up in it and sucked on one of the cor- ners when she wanted to be very still.

Then Stella took the shawl away and made Magda die.

Afterward Stella said: "I was cold."

10   And afterward she was always cold, always. The cold went into her heart: Rosa saw that Stella's heart was cold. Magda flopped onward with her little pencil legs scribbling this way and that, in search of the shawl; the pencils faltered at the barracks opening, where the light began. Rosa saw and pursued. But already Magda was in the square outside the barracks, in the jolly light. It was the roll-call arena. Every morning Rosa had to conceal Magda under the shawl against a wall of the barracks and go out and stand in the arena with Stella and hundreds of others, sometimes for hours, and Magda, deserted, was quiet under the shawl, sucking on her corner. Every day Magda was silent, and so she did not die. Rosa saw that today Magda was going to die, and at the same time a fearful joy ran in Rosa's two palms, her fingers were on fire, she was astonished, febrile: Magda, in the sunlight, swaying on her pencil legs, was howling. Ever since the drying up of Rosa's nipples, ever since Magda's last scream on the road, Magda had been devoid of any syllable; Magda was a mute. Rosa believed that something had gone wrong with her vocal cords, with her windpipe, with the cave of her larynx; Magda was defective, without a voice; perhaps she was deaf; there might be something amiss with her intelligence; Magda was dumb. Even the laugh that came when the ash-stippled wind made a clown out of Magda's shawl was only the air-blown showing of her teeth. Even when the lice, head lice and body lice, crazed her so that she became as wild as one of the big rats that plundered the barracks at daybreak looking for carrion, she rubbed and scratched and kicked and bit and rolled without a whimper. But now Magda's mouth was spilling a long viscous rope of clamor.

"Maaaa—"

It was the first noise Magda had ever sent out from her throat since the drying up of Rosa's nipples.

"Maaaa . . . aaa!"

Again! Magda was wavering in the perilous sunlight of the arena, scribbling on such pitiful little bent shins. Rosa saw. She saw that Magda was grieving the loss of her shawl, she saw that Magda was going to die. A tide of commands hammered in Rosa's nipples: Fetch, get, bring! But she did not know which to go after first, Magda or the shawl. If she jumped out into the arena to snatch Magda up, the howling would not stop, because Magda would still not have the shawl; but if she ran back into the barracks to find the shawl, and if she found it, and if she came after Magda holding it and shaking it, then she would get Magda back, Magda would put the shawl in her mouth and turn dumb again.

15   Rosa entered the dark. It was easy to discover the shawl. Stella was heaped under it, asleep in her thin bones. Rosa tore the shawl free and flew— she could fly, she was only air—into the arena. The sunheat murmured of another life, of butterflies in summer. The light was placid, mellow. On the other side of the steel fence, far away, there were green meadows speckled with dandelions and deep-colored violets; beyond them, even farther, innocent tiger lilies, tall, lifting their orange bonnets. In the barracks they spoke of "flowers,"

of "rain": excrement, thick turd-braids, and the slow stinking maroon waterfall that slunk down from the upper bunks, the stink mixed with a bitter fatty floating smoke that greased Rosa's skin. She stood for an instant at the margin of the arena. Sometimes the electricity inside the fence would seem to hum; even Stella said it was only an imagining, but Rosa heard real sounds in the wire: grainy sad voices. The farther she was from the fence, the more clearly the voices crowded at her. The lamenting voices strummed so convincingly, so passionately, it was impossible to suspect them of being phantoms. The voices told her to hold up the shawl, high; the voices told her to shake it, to whip with it, to unfurl it like a flag. Rosa lifted, shook, whipped, unfurled. Far off, very far, Magda leaned across her air-fed belly, reaching out with the rods of her arms. She was high up, elevated, riding someone's shoulder. But the shoulder that carried Magda was not coming toward Rosa and the shawl, it was drifting away, the speck of Magda was moving more and more into the smoky distance. Above the shoulder a helmet glinted. A light tapped the helmet and sparkled it into a goblet. Below the helmet a black body like a domino and a pair of black boots hurled themselves in the direction of the electrified fence. The electric voices began to chatter wildly. "Maamaa, maaamaaa," they all hummed together. How far Magda was from Rosa now, across the whole square, past a dozen barracks, all the way on the other side! She was no bigger than a moth.

All at once Magda was swimming through the air. The whole of Magda traveled through loftiness. She looked like a butterfly touching a silver vine. And the moment Magda's feathered round head and her pencil legs and balloonish belly and zigzag arms splashed against the fence, the steel voices went mad in their growling, urging Rosa to run and run to the spot where Magda had fallen from her flight against the electrified fence; but of course Rosa did not obey them. She only stood, because if she ran they would shoot, and if she tried to pick up the sticks of Magda's body they would shoot, and if she let the wolf's screech ascending now through the ladder of her skeleton break out, they would shoot; so she took Magda's shawl and filled her own mouth with it, stuffed it in and stuffed it in, until she was swallowing up the wolf's screech and tasting the cinnamon and almond depth of Magda's saliva; and Rosa drank Magda's shawl until it dried.   *1980*

CONSIDERATIONS

1. Explain the use of the shawl to represent something beyond its normal or expected use.
2. Why is Stella jealous of the baby Magda even though Magda is the least likely to survive the march? What does she fear? Why?
3. What was your reaction to the guard's actions? What was your reaction to Rosa's inaction?

4. Explain the ending of the story. Why does Rosa stuff the shawl into her mouth?
5. This story seems to be in part about the inhumanity people suffer under conditions of war. Point out various examples of inhumanity in the story and comment on each.

TIM O'BRIEN (1947–   )
The Things They Carried

Tim O'Brien was born in Austin, Minnesota. He was drafted in 1968 at age twenty-one and subsequently served in the infantry in Vietnam. In response to his experiences as a reluctant soldier (he has stated that he had briefly considered dodging the draft), O'Brien has written a collection of short stories, The Things They Carried *(1990); a memoir,* If I Die in a Combat Zone *(1973); and three novels,* Northern Lights *(1975),* Going after Cacciato *(1979), which won the National Book Award, and* The Nuclear Age *(1994). O'Brien, who currently lives in Cambridge, Massachusetts, has received writing fellowships from the Guggenheim Foundation, the National Endowment for the Arts, and the Massachusetts Arts and Humanities Foundation.*

First Lieutenant Jimmy Cross carried letters from a girl named Martha, a junior at Mount Sebastian College in New Jersey. They were not love letters, but Lieutenant Cross was hoping, so he kept them folded in plastic at the bottom of his rucksack. In the late afternoon, after a day's march, he would dig his foxhole, wash his hands under a canteen, unwrap the letters, hold them with the tips of his fingers, and spend the last hour of light pretending. He would imagine romantic camping trips into the White Mountains in New Hampshire. He would sometimes taste the envelope flaps, knowing her tongue had been there. More than anything, he wanted Martha to love him as he loved her, but the letters were mostly chatty, elusive on the matter of love. She was a virgin, he was almost sure. She was an English major at Mount Sebastian, and she wrote beautifully about her professors and roommates and midterm exams, about her respect for Chaucer and her great affection for Virginia Woolf.° She often quoted lines of poetry; she never mentioned the war, except to say, Jimmy, take care of yourself. The letters weighed ten ounces. They were signed "Love, Martha," but Lieutenant Cross understood that "Love" was only a way of signing and did not mean what he sometimes pretended it meant. At dusk, he would carefully return the letters to his rucksack. Slowly, a bit distracted, he would get up and move among his men, checking the perimeter, then at full

---

Virginia Woolf (1882–1941): British writer.

dark he would return to his hole and watch the night and wonder if Martha was a virgin.

The things they carried were largely determined by necessity. Among the necessities or near necessities were P-38 can openers, pocket knives, heat tabs, wrist watches, dog tags, mosquito repellent, chewing gum, candy, cigarettes, salt tablets, packets of Kool-Aid, lighters, matches, sewing kits, Military Payment Certificates, C rations, and two or three canteens of water. Together, these items weighed between fifteen and twenty pounds, depending upon a man's habits or rate of metabolism. Henry Dobbins, who was a big man, carried extra rations; he was especially fond of canned peaches in heavy syrup over pound cake. Dave Jensen, who practiced field hygiene, carried a toothbrush, dental floss, and several hotel-size bars of soap he'd stolen on R&R° in Sydney, Australia. Ted Lavender, who was scared, carried tranquilizers until he was shot in the head outside the village of Than Khe in mid-April. By necessity, and because it was SOP,° they all carried steel helmets that weighed five pounds including the liner and camouflage cover. They carried the standard fatigue jackets and trousers. Very few carried underwear. On their feet they carried jungle boots—2.1 pounds—and Dave Jensen carried three pairs of socks and a can of Dr. Scholl's foot powder as a precaution against trench foot. Until he was shot, Ted Lavender carried six or seven ounces of premium dope, which for him was a necessity. Mitchell Sanders, the RTO, carried condoms. Norman Bowker carried a diary. Rat Kiley carried comic books. Kiowa, a devout Baptist, carried an illustrated New Testament that had been presented to him by his father, who taught Sunday school in Oklahoma City, Oklahoma. As a hedge against bad times, however, Kiowa also carried his grandmother's distrust of the white man, his grandfather's old hunting hatchet. Necessity dictated. Because the land was mined and booby-trapped, it was SOP for each man to carry a steel-centered, nylon-covered flak jacket, which weighed 6.7 pounds, but which on hot days seemed much heavier. Because you could die so quickly, each man carried at least one large compress bandage, usually in the helmet band for easy access. Because the nights were cold, and because the monsoons were wet, each carried a green plastic poncho that could be used as a raincoat or ground sheet or makeshift tent. With its quilted liner, the poncho weighed almost two pounds, but it was worth every ounce. In April, for instance, when Ted Lavender was shot, they used his poncho to wrap him up, then to carry him across the paddy, then to lift him into the chopper that took him away.

They were called legs or grunts.

To carry something was to "hump" it, as when Lieutenant Jimmy Cross humped his love for Martha up the hills and through the swamps. In its

---

R&R: Rest and recreation. *SOP:* Standard operating procedure.

intransitive form, "to hump" meant "to walk," or "to march," but it implied burdens far beyond the intransitive.

5   Almost everyone humped photographs. In his wallet, Lieutenant Cross carried two photographs of Martha. The first was a Kodachrome snapshot signed "Love," though he knew better. She stood against a brick wall. Her eyes were gray and neutral, her lips slightly open as she stared straight-on at the camera. At night, sometimes, Lieutenant Cross wondered who had taken the picture, because he knew she had boyfriends, because he loved her so much, and because he could see the shadow of the picture taker spreading out against the brick wall. The second photograph had been clipped from the 1968 Mount Sebastian yearbook. It was an action shot—women's volleyball—and Martha was bent horizontal to the floor, reaching, the palms of her hands in sharp focus, the tongue taut, the expression frank and competitive. There was no visible sweat. She wore white gym shorts. Her legs, he thought, were almost certainly the legs of a virgin, dry and without hair, the left knee cocked and carrying her entire weight, which was just over one hundred pounds. Lieutenant Cross remembered touching that left knee. A dark theater, he remembered, and the movie was *Bonnie and Clyde,* and Martha wore a tweed skirt, and during the final scene, when he touched her knee, she turned and looked at him in a sad, sober way that made him pull his hand back, but he would always remember the feel of the tweed skirt and the knee beneath it and the sound of the gunfire that killed Bonnie and Clyde, how embarrassing it was, how slow and oppressive. He remembered kissing her good night at the dorm door. Right then, he thought, he should've done something brave. He should've carried her up the stairs to her room and tied her to the bed and touched that left knee all night long. He should've risked it. Whenever he looked at the photographs, he thought of new things he should've done.

What they carried was partly a function of rank, partly of field specialty.

As a first lieutenant and platoon leader, Jimmy Cross carried a compass, maps, code books, binoculars, and a .45-caliber pistol that weighed 2.9 pounds fully loaded. He carried a strobe light and the responsibility for the lives of his men.

As an RTO, Mitchell Sanders carried the PRC-25 radio, a killer, twenty-six pounds with its battery.

As a medic, Rat Kiley carried a canvas satchel filled with morphine and plasma and malaria tablets and surgical tape and comic books and all the things a medic must carry, including M&M's for especially bad wounds, for a total weight of nearly twenty pounds.

10   As a big man, therefore a machine gunner, Henry Dobbins carried the M-60, which weighed twenty-three pounds unloaded, but which was almost always loaded. In addition, Dobbins carried between ten and fifteen pounds of ammunition draped in belts across his chest and shoulders.

As PFCs° or Spec 4s,° most of them were common grunts and carried the standard M-16 gas-operated assault rifle. The weapon weighed 7.5 pounds unloaded, 8.2 pounds with its full twenty-round magazine. Depending on numerous factors, such as topography and psychology, the riflemen carried anywhere from twelve to twenty magazines, usually in cloth bandoliers, adding on another 8.4 pounds at minimum, fourteen pounds at maximum. When it was available, they also carried M-16 maintenance gear—rods and steel brushes and swabs and tubes of LSA oil—all of which weighed about a pound. Among the grunts, some carried the M-79 grenade launcher, 5.9 pounds unloaded, a reasonably light weapon except for the ammunition, which was heavy. A single round weighed ten ounces. The typical load was twenty-five rounds. But Ted Lavender, who was scared, carried thirty-four rounds when he was shot and killed outside Than Khe, and he went down under an exceptional burden, more than twenty pounds of ammunition, plus the flak jacket and helmet and rations and water and toilet paper and tranquilizers and all the rest, plus the unweighed fear. He was dead weight. There was no twitching or flopping. Kiowa, who saw it happen, said it was like watching a rock fall, or a big sandbag or something—just boom, then down—not like the movies where the dead guy rolls around and does fancy spins and goes ass over teakettle—not like that, Kiowa said, the poor bastard just flat-fuck fell. Boom. Down. Nothing else. It was a bright morning in mid-April. Lieutenant Cross felt the pain. He blamed himself. They stripped off Lavender's canteens and ammo, all the heavy things, and Rat Kiley said the obvious, the guy's dead, and Mitchell Sanders used his radio to report one U.S. KIA° and to request a chopper. Then they wrapped Lavender in his poncho. They carried him out to a dry paddy, established security, and sat smoking the dead man's dope until the chopper came. Lieutenant Cross kept to himself. He pictured Martha's smooth young face, thinking he loved her more than anything, more than his men, and now Ted Lavender was dead because he loved her so much and could not stop thinking about her. When the dust-off arrived, they carried Lavender aboard. Afterward they burned Than Khe. They marched until dusk, then dug their holes, and that night Kiowa kept explaining how you had to be there, how fast it was, how the poor guy just dropped like so much concrete. Boom-down, he said. Like cement.

In addition to the three standard weapons—the M-60, M-16, and M-79— they carried whatever presented itself, or whatever seemed appropriate as a means of killing or staying alive. They carried catch-as-catch-can. At various times, in various situations, they carried M-14s and CAR-15s and Swedish Ks and grease guns and captured AK-47s and Chi-Coms and RPGs and Simonov

---

PFCs: Privates first class. *Spec 4s:* Fourth class, one rank higher than PFC. *KIA:* Killed in action.

carbines and black-market Uzis and .38-caliber Smith & Wesson handguns and 66 mm LAWs and shotguns and silencers and blackjacks and bayonets and C-4 plastic explosives. Lee Strunk carried a slingshot; a weapon of last resort, he called it. Mitchell Sanders carried brass knuckles. Kiowa carried his grandfather's feathered hatchet. Every third or fourth man carried a Claymore antipersonnel mine—3.5 pounds with its firing device. They all carried fragmentation grenades—fourteen ounces each. They all carried at least one M-18 colored smoke grenade—twenty-four ounces. Some carried CS or tear gas grenades. Some carried white-phosphorus grenades. They carried all they could bear, and then some, including a silent awe for the terrible power of the things they carried.

In the first week of April, before Lavender died, Lieutenant Jimmy Cross received a good-luck charm from Martha. It was a simple pebble, an ounce at most. Smooth to the touch, it was a milky-white color with flecks of orange and violet, oval-shaped, like a miniature egg. In the accompanying letter, Martha wrote that she had found the pebble on the Jersey shoreline, precisely where the land touched water at high tide, where things came together but also separated. It was this separate-but-together quality, she wrote, that had inspired her to pick up the pebble and to carry it in her breast pocket for several days, where it seemed weightless, and then to send it through the mail, by air, as a token of her truest feelings for him. Lieutenant Cross found this romantic. But he wondered what her truest feelings were, exactly, and what she meant by separate-but-together. He wondered how the tides and waves had come into play on that afternoon along the Jersey shoreline when Martha saw the pebble and bent down to rescue it from geology. He imagined bare feet. Martha was a poet, with the poet's sensibilities, and her feet would be brown and bare, the toenails unpainted, the eyes chilly and somber like the ocean in March, and though it was painful, he wondered who had been with her that afternoon. He imagined a pair of shadows moving along the strip of sand where things came together but also separated. It was phantom jealousy, he knew, but he couldn't help himself. He loved her so much. On the march, through the hot days of early April, he carried the pebble in his mouth, turning it with his tongue, tasting sea salts and moisture. His mind wandered. He had difficulty keeping his attention on the war. On occasion he would yell at his men to spread out the column, to keep their eyes open, but then he would slip away into daydreams, just pretending, walking barefoot along the Jersey shore, with Martha, carrying nothing. He would feel himself rising. Sun and waves and gentle winds, all love and lightness.

What they carried varied by mission.

15   When a mission took them to the mountains, they carried mosquito netting, machetes, canvas tarps, and extra bug juice.

If a mission seemed especially hazardous, or if it involved a place they knew to be bad, they carried everything they could. In certain heavily mined

AOs, where the land was dense with Toe Poppers and Bouncing Betties, they took turns humping a twenty-eight-pound mine detector. With its headphones and big sensing plate, the equipment was a stress on the lower back and shoulders, awkward to handle, often useless because of the shrapnel in the earth, but they carried it anyway, partly for safety, partly for the illusion of safety.

On ambush, or other night missions, they carried peculiar little odds and ends. Kiowa always took along his New Testament and a pair of moccasins for silence. Dave Jensen carried night-sight vitamins high in carotin. Lee Strunk carried his slingshot; ammo, he claimed, would never be a problem. Rat Kiley carried brandy and M&M's. Until he was shot, Ted Lavender carried the starlight scope, which weighed 6.3 pounds with its aluminum carrying case. Henry Dobbins carried his girlfriend's pantyhose wrapped around his neck as a comforter. They all carried ghosts. When dark came, they would move out single file across the meadows and paddies to their ambush coordinates, where they would quietly set up the Claymores and lie down and spend the night waiting.

Other missions were more complicated and required special equipment. In mid-April, it was their mission to search out and destroy the elaborate tunnel complexes in the Than Khe area south of Chu Lai. To blow the tunnels, they carried one-pound blocks of pentrite high explosives, four blocks to a man, sixty-eight pounds in all. They carried wiring, detonators, and battery-powered clackers. Dave Jensen carried earplugs. Most often, before blowing the tunnels, they were ordered by higher command to search them, which was considered bad news, but by and large they just shrugged and carried out orders. Because he was a big man, Henry Dobbins was excused from tunnel duty. The others would draw numbers. Before Lavender died there were seventeen men in the platoon, and whoever drew the number seventeen would strip off his gear and crawl in head first with a flashlight and Lieutenant Cross's .45-caliber pistol. The rest of them would fan out as security. They would sit down or kneel, not facing the hole, listening to the ground beneath them, imagining cobwebs and ghosts, whatever was down there—the tunnel walls squeezing in—how the flashlight seemed impossibly heavy in the hand and how it was tunnel vision in the very strictest sense, compression in all ways, even time, and how you had to wiggle in—ass and elbows—a swallowed-up feeling—and how you found yourself worrying about odd things—will your flashlight go dead? Do rats carry rabies? If you screamed, how far would the sound carry? Would your buddies hear it? Would they have the courage to drag you out? In some respects, though not many, the waiting was worse than the tunnel itself. Imagination was a killer.

On April 16, when Lee Strunk drew the number seventeen, he laughed and muttered something and went down quickly. The morning was hot and very still. Not good, Kiowa said. He looked at the tunnel opening, then out across a dry paddy toward the village of Than Khe. Nothing moved. No clouds or birds or people. As they waited, the men smoked and drank Kool-Aid, not talking much, feeling sympathy for Lee Strunk but also feeling the luck of the draw. You win some, you lose some, said Mitchell Sanders, and sometimes you settle for a rain check. It was a tired line and no one laughed.

20   Henry Dobbins ate a tropical chocolate bar. Ted Lavender popped a tranquilizer and went off to pee.

After five minutes, Lieutenant Jimmy Cross moved to the tunnel, leaned down, and examined the darkness. Trouble, he thought—a cave-in maybe. And then suddenly, without willing it, he was thinking about Martha. The stresses and fractures, the quick collapse, the two of them buried alive under all that weight. Dense, crushing love. Kneeling, watching the hole, he tried to concentrate on Lee Strunk and the war, all the dangers, but his love was too much for him, he felt paralyzed, he wanted to sleep inside her lungs and breathe her blood and be smothered. He wanted her to be a virgin and not a virgin, all at once. He wanted to know her. Intimate secrets—why poetry? Why so sad? Why that grayness in her eyes? Why so alone? Not lonely, just alone—riding her bike across campus or sitting off by herself in the cafeteria. Even dancing, she danced alone—and it was the aloneness that filled him with love. He remembered telling her that one evening. How she nodded and looked away. And how, later, when he kissed her, she received the kiss without returning it, her eyes wide open, not afraid, not a virgin's eyes, just flat and uninvolved.

Lieutenant Cross gazed at the tunnel. But he was not there. He was buried with Martha under the white sand at the Jersey shore. They were pressed together, and the pebble in his mouth was her tongue. He was smiling. Vaguely, he was aware of how quiet the day was, the sullen paddies, yet he could not bring himself to worry about matters of security. He was beyond that. He was just a kid at war, in love. He was twenty-two years old. He couldn't help it.

A few moments later Lee Strunk crawled out of the tunnel. He came up grinning, filthy but alive. Lieutenant Cross nodded and closed his eyes while the others clapped Strunk on the back and made jokes about rising from the dead.

Worms, Rat Kiley said. Right out of the grave. Fuckin' zombie.

25   The men laughed. They all felt great relief.

Spook City, said Mitchell Sanders.

Lee Strunk made a funny ghost sound, a kind of moaning, yet very happy, and right then, when Strunk made that high happy moaning sound, when he went *Ahhooooo,* right then Ted Lavender was shot in the head on his way back from peeing. He lay with his mouth open. The teeth were broken. There was a swollen black bruise under his left eye. The cheekbone was gone. Oh shit, Rat Kiley said, the guy's dead. The guy's dead, he kept saying, which seemed profound—the guy's dead. I mean really.

The things they carried were determined to some extent by superstition. Lieutenant Cross carried his good-luck pebble. Dave Jensen carried a rabbit's foot. Norman Bowker, otherwise a very gentle person, carried a thumb that had been presented to him as a gift by Mitchell Sanders. The thumb was dark brown, rubbery to the touch, and weighed four ounces at most. It had been cut from a VC° corpse, a boy of fifteen or sixteen. They'd found him at the bottom of an irrigation ditch, badly burned, flies in his mouth and eyes. The boy wore black shorts and sandals. At the time of his death he had been carrying a pouch of rice, a rifle, and three magazines of ammunition.

You want my opinion, Mitchell Sanders said, there's a definite moral here.

He put his hand on the dead boy's wrist. He was quiet for a time, as if   30
counting a pulse, then he patted the stomach, almost affectionately, and used Kiowa's hunting hatchet to remove the thumb.

Henry Dobbins asked what the moral was.

Moral?

You know. *Moral.*

Sanders wrapped the thumb in toilet paper and handed it across to Norman Bowker. There was no blood. Smiling, he kicked the boy's head, watched the flies scatter, and said, It's like with that old TV show—Paladin. Have gun, will travel.

Henry Dobbins thought about it.   35

Yeah, well, he finally said. I don't see no moral.

There it *is,* man.

Fuck off.

They carried USO stationery and pencils and pens. They carried Sterno, safety pins, trip flares, signal flares, spools of wire, razor blades, chewing tobacco, liberated joss sticks and statuettes of the smiling Buddha, candles, grease pencils, *The Stars and Stripes,*° fingernail clippers, Psy Ops leaflets, bush hats, bolos, and much more. Twice a week, when the resupply choppers came in, they carried hot chow in green Mermite cans and large canvas bags filled with iced beer and soda pop. They carried plastic water containers, each with a two-gallon capacity. Mitchell Sanders carried a set of starched tiger fatigues for special occasions. Henry Dobbins carried Black Flag insecticide. Dave Jensen carried empty sandbags that could be filled at night for added protection. Lee Strunk carried tanning lotion. Some things they carried in common. Taking turns, they carried the big PRC-77 scrambler radio, which weighed thirty pounds with its battery. They shared the weight of memory. They took up what others could no longer bear. Often, they carried each other, the wounded or weak. They carried infections. They carried chess sets, basketballs, Vietnamese-English dictionaries, insignia of rank, Bronze Stars and Purple Hearts, plastic cards imprinted with the Code of Conduct. They carried diseases, among them malaria and dysentery. They carried lice and ringworm and leeches and paddy algae and various rots and molds. They carried the land itself—Vietnam, the

---

VC: Viet Cong. The Stars and Stripes: The military's officially sanctioned overseas newspaper.

place, the soil—a powdery orange-red dust that covered their boots and fatigues and faces. They carried the sky. The whole atmosphere, they carried it, the humidity, the monsoons, the stink of fungus and decay, all of it, they carried gravity. They moved like mules. By daylight they took sniper fire, at night they were mortared, but it was not battle, it was just the endless march, village to village, without purpose, nothing won or lost. They marched for the sake of the march. They plodded along slowly, dumbly, leaning forward against the heat, unthinking, all blood and bone, simple grunts, soldiering with their legs, toiling up the hills and down into the paddies and across the rivers and up again and down, just humping, one step and then the next and then another, but no volition, no will, because it was automatic, it was anatomy, and the war was entirely a matter of posture and carriage, the hump was everything, a kind of inertia, a kind of emptiness, a dullness of desire and intellect and conscience and hope and human sensibility. Their principles were in their feet. Their calculations were biological. They had no sense of strategy or mission. They searched the villages without knowing what to look for, not caring, kicking over jars of rice, frisking children and old men, blowing tunnels, sometimes setting fires and sometimes not, then forming up and moving on to the next village, then other villages, where it would always be the same. They carried their own lives. The pressures were enormous. In the heat of early afternoon, they would remove their helmets and flak jackets, walking bare, which was dangerous but which helped ease the strain. They would often discard things along the route of march. Purely for comfort, they would throw away rations, blow their Claymores and grenades, no matter, because by nightfall the resupply choppers would arrive with more of the same, then a day or two later still more, fresh watermelons and crates of ammunition and sunglasses and woolen sweaters—the resources were stunning—sparklers for the Fourth of July, colored eggs for Easter. It was the great American war chest—the fruits of science, the smokestacks, the canneries, the arsenals at Hartford, the Minnesota forests, the machine shops, the vast fields of corn and wheat—they carried like freight trains; they carried it on their backs and shoulders—and for all the ambiguities of Vietnam, all the mysteries and unknowns, there was at least the single abiding certainty that they would never be at a loss for things to carry.

40   After the chopper took Lavender away, Lieutenant Jimmy Cross led his men into the village of Than Khe. They burned everything. They shot chickens and dogs, they trashed the village well, they called in artillery and watched the wreckage, then they marched for several hours through the hot afternoon, and then at dusk, while Kiowa explained how Lavender died, Lieutenant Cross found himself trembling.

He tried not to cry. With his entrenching tool, which weighed five pounds, he began digging a hole in the earth.

He felt shame. He hated himself. He had loved Martha more than his men, and as a consequence Lavender was now dead, and this was something he would have to carry like a stone in his stomach for the rest of the war.

All he could do was dig. He used his entrenching tool like an ax, slashing, feeling both love and hate, and then later, when it was full dark, he sat at the bottom of his foxhole and wept. It went on for a long while. In part, he was grieving for Ted Lavender, but mostly it was for Martha, and for himself, because she belonged to another world, which was not quite real, and because she was a junior at Mount Sebastian College in New Jersey, a poet and a virgin and uninvolved, and because he realized she did not love him and never would.

Like cement, Kiowa whispered in the dark. I swear to God—boom-down. Not a word.

I've heard this, said Norman Bowker.   45

A pisser, you know? Still zipping himself up. Zapped while zipping.

All right, fine. That's enough.

Yeah, but you had to see it, the guy just—

I *heard,* man. Cement. So why not shut the fuck *up?*

Kiowa shook his head sadly and glanced over at the hole where Lieutenant   50
Jimmy Cross sat watching the night. The air was thick and wet. A warm, dense fog had settled over the paddies and there was the stillness that precedes rain.

After a time Kiowa sighed.

One thing for sure, he said. The Lieutenant's in some deep hurt. I mean that crying jag—the way he was carrying on—it wasn't fake or anything, it was real heavy-duty hurt. The man cares.

Sure, Norman Bowker said.

Say what you want, the man does care.

We all got problems.   55

Not Lavender.

No, I guess not, Bowker said. Do me a favor, though.

Shut up?

That's a smart Indian. Shut up.

Shrugging, Kiowa pulled off his boots. He wanted to say more, just to   60
lighten up his sleep, but instead he opened his New Testament and arranged it beneath his head as a pillow. The fog made things seem hollow and unattached. He tried not to think about Ted Lavender, but then he was thinking how fast it was, no drama, down and dead, and how it was hard to feel anything except surprise. It seemed un-Christian. He wished he could find some great sadness, or even anger, but the emotion wasn't there and he couldn't make it happen. Mostly he felt pleased to be alive. He liked the smell of the New Testament under his cheek, the leather and ink and paper and glue, whatever the chemicals were. He liked hearing the sounds of night. Even his fatigue, it felt fine, the stiff muscles and the prickly awareness of his own body, a floating feeling.

He enjoyed not being dead. Lying there, Kiowa admired Lieutenant Jimmy Cross's capacity for grief. He wanted to share the man's pain, he wanted to care as Jimmy Cross cared. And yet when he closed his eyes, all he could think was boom-down, and all he could feel was the pleasure of having his boots off and the fog curling in around him and the damp soil and the Bible smells and the plush comfort of night.

After a moment Norman Bowker sat up in the dark.

What the hell, he said. You want to talk, *talk*. Tell it to me.

Forget it.

No, man, go on. One thing I hate, it's a silent Indian.

65   For the most part they carried themselves with poise, a kind of dignity. Now and then, however, there were times of panic, when they squealed or wanted to squeal but couldn't, when they twitched and made moaning sounds and covered their heads and said Dear Jesus and flopped around on the earth and fired their weapons blindly and cringed and sobbed and begged for the noise to stop and went wild and made stupid promises to themselves and to God and to their mothers and fathers, hoping not to die. In different ways, it happened to all of them. Afterward, when the firing ended, they would blink and peek up. They would touch their bodies, feeling shame, then quickly hiding it. They would force themselves to stand. As if in slow motion, frame by frame, the world would take on the old logic—absolute silence, then the wind, then sunlight, then voices. It was the burden of being alive. Awkwardly, the men would reassemble themselves, first in private, then in groups, becoming soldiers again. They would repair the leaks in their eyes. They would check for casualties, call in dust-offs, light cigarettes, try to smile, clear their throats and spit and begin cleaning their weapons. After a time someone would shake his head and say, No lie, I almost shit my pants, and someone else would laugh, which meant it was bad, yes, but the guy had obviously not shit his pants, it wasn't that bad, and in any case nobody would ever do such a thing and then go ahead and talk about it. They would squint into the dense, oppressive sunlight. For a few moments, perhaps, they would fall silent, lighting a joint and tracking its passage from man to man, inhaling, holding in the humiliation. Scary stuff, one of them might say. But then someone else would grin or flick his eyebrows and say, Roger-dodger, almost cut me a new asshole, *almost*.

There were numerous such poses. Some carried themselves with a sort of wistful resignation, others with pride or stiff soldierly discipline or good humor or macho zeal. They were afraid of dying but they were even more afraid to show it.

They found jokes to tell.

They used a hard vocabulary to contain the terrible softness. *Greased,* they'd say. *Offed, lit up, zapped while zipping.* It wasn't cruelty, just stage presence. They were actors and the war came at them in 3-D. When someone died, it wasn't quite dying, because in a curious way it seemed scripted, and because they had their lines mostly memorized, irony mixed with tragedy, and because they called it by other names, as if to encyst and destroy the reality of death itself. They kicked corpses. They cut off thumbs. They talked grunt lingo. They told stories about Ted Lavender's supply of tranquilizers, how the poor guy didn't feel a thing, how incredibly tranquil he was.

There's a moral here, said Mitchell Sanders.

They were waiting for Lavender's chopper, smoking the dead man's dope.   *70*

The moral's pretty obvious, Sanders said, and winked. Stay away from drugs. No joke, they'll ruin your day every time.

Cute, said Henry Dobbins.

Mind-blower, get it? Talk about wiggy—nothing left, just blood and brains.

They made themselves laugh.

There it is, they'd say, over and over, as if the repetition itself were an act   *75* of poise, a balance between crazy and almost crazy, knowing without going. There it is, which meant be cool, let it ride, because oh yeah, man, you can't change what can't be changed, there it is, there it absolutely and positively and fucking well *is*.

They were tough.

They carried all the emotional baggage of men who might die. Grief, terror, love, longing—these were intangibles, but the intangibles had their own mass and specific gravity, they had tangible weight. They carried shameful memories. They carried the common secret of cowardice barely restrained, the instinct to run or freeze or hide, and in many respects this was the heaviest burden of all, for it could never be put down, it required perfect balance and perfect posture. They carried their reputations. They carried the soldier's greatest fear, which was the fear of blushing. Men killed, and died, because they were embarrassed not to. It was what had brought them to the war in the first place, nothing positive, no dreams of glory or honor, just to avoid the blush of dishonor. They died so as not to die of embarrassment. They crawled into tunnels and walked point and advanced under fire. Each morning, despite the unknowns, they made their legs move. They endured. They kept humping. They did not submit to the obvious alternative, which was simply to close the eyes and fall. So easy, really. Go limp and tumble to the ground and let the muscles unwind and not speak and not budge until your buddies picked you up and lifted you into the chopper that would roar and dip its nose and carry you off to the world. A mere matter of falling, yet no one ever fell. It was not courage, exactly; the object was not valor. Rather, they were too frightened to be cowards.

By and large they carried these things inside, maintaining the masks of composure. They sneered at sick call. They spoke bitterly about guys who had found release by shooting off their own toes or fingers. Pussies, they'd say. Candyasses. It was fierce, mocking talk, with only a trace of envy or awe, but even so, the image played itself out behind their eyes.

They imagined the muzzle against flesh. They imagined the quick, sweet pain, then the evacuation to Japan, then a hospital with warm beds and cute geisha nurses.

80   They dreamed of freedom birds.

At night, on guard, staring into the dark, they were carried away by jumbo jets. They felt the rush of takeoff. *Gone!* they yelled. And then velocity, wings and engines, a smiling stewardess—but it was more than a plane, it was a real bird, a big sleek silver bird with feathers and talons and high screeching. They were flying. The weights fell off, there was nothing to bear. They laughed and held on tight, feeling the cold slap of wind and altitude, soaring, thinking *It's over, I'm gone!*—they were naked, they were light and free—it was all lightness, bright and fast and buoyant, light as light, a helium buzz in the brain, a giddy bubbling in the lungs as they were taken up over the clouds and the war, beyond duty, beyond gravity and mortification and global entanglements—*Sin loi!* they yelled, *I'm sorry, motherfuckers, but I'm out of it, I'm goofed, I'm on a space cruise, I'm gone!*—and it was a restful, disencumbered sensation, just riding the light waves, sailing that big silver freedom bird over the mountains and oceans, over America, over the farms and great sleeping cities and cemeteries and highways and the golden arches of McDonald's. It was flight, a kind of fleeing, a kind of falling, falling higher and higher, spinning off the edge of the earth and beyond the sun and through the vast, silent vacuum where there were no burdens and where everything weighed exactly nothing. *Gone!* they screamed, *I'm sorry but I'm gone!* And so at night, not quite dreaming, they gave themselves over to lightness, they were carried, they were purely borne.

On the morning after Ted Lavender died, First Lieutenant Jimmy Cross crouched at the bottom of his foxhole and burned Martha's letters. Then he burned the two photographs. There was a steady rain falling, which made it difficult, but he used heat tabs and Sterno to build a small fire, screening it with his body, holding the photographs over the tight blue flame with the tips of his fingers.

He realized it was only a gesture. Stupid, he thought. Sentimental, too, but mostly just stupid.

Lavender was dead. You couldn't burn the blame.

85   Besides, the letters were in his head. And even now, without photographs, Lieutenant Cross could see Martha playing volleyball in her white gym shorts and yellow T-shirt. He could see her moving in the rain.

When the fire died out, Lieutenant Cross pulled his poncho over his shoulders and ate breakfast from a can.

There was no great mystery, he decided.

In those burned letters Martha had never mentioned the war, except to say, Jimmy, take care of yourself. She wasn't involved. She signed the letters "Love," but it wasn't love, and all the fine lines and technicalities did not matter.

The morning came up wet and blurry. Everything seemed part of everything else, the fog and Martha and the deepening rain.

It was a war, after all.   *90*

Half smiling, Lieutenant Jimmy Cross took out his maps. He shook his head hard, as if to clear it, then bent forward and began planning the day's march. In ten minutes, or maybe twenty, he would rouse the men and they would pack up and head west, where the maps showed the country to be green and inviting. They would do what they had always done. The rain might add some weight, but otherwise it would be one more day layered upon all the other days.

He was realistic about it. There was that new hardness in his stomach.

No more fantasies, he told himself.

Henceforth, when he thought about Martha, it would be only to think that she belonged elsewhere. He would shut down the daydreams. This was not Mount Sebastian, it was another world, where there were no pretty poems or midterm exams, a place where men died because of carelessness and gross stupidity. Kiowa was right. Boom-down, and you were dead, never partly dead.

Briefly, in the rain, Lieutenant Cross saw Martha's gray eyes gazing back   *95* at him.

He understood.

It was very sad, he thought. The things men carried inside. The things men did or felt they had to do.

He almost nodded at her, but didn't.

Instead he went back to his maps. He was now determined to perform his duties firmly and without negligence. It wouldn't help Lavender, he knew that, but from this point on he would comport himself as a soldier. He would dispose of his good-luck pebble. Swallow it, maybe, or use Lee Strunk's slingshot, or just drop it along the trail. On the march he would impose strict field discipline. He would be careful to send out flank security, to prevent straggling or bunching up, to keep his troops moving at the proper pace and at the proper interval. He would insist on clean weapons. He would confiscate the remainder of Lavender's dope. Later in the day, perhaps, he would call the men together and speak to them plainly. He would accept the blame for what had happened to Ted Lavender. He would be a man about it. He would look them in the eyes, keeping his chin level, and he would issue the new SOPs in a calm, impersonal tone of voice, an officer's voice, leaving no room for argument or discussion. Commencing immediately, he'd tell them, they would no longer abandon equipment along the route of march. They would police up their acts. They would get their shit together, and keep it together, and maintain it neatly and in good working order.

100   He would not tolerate laxity. He would show strength, distancing himself.
    Among the men there would be grumbling, of course, and maybe worse, because their days would seem longer and their loads heavier, but Lieutenant Cross reminded himself that his obligation was not to be loved but to lead. He would dispense with love; it was not now a factor. And if anyone quarreled or complained, he would simply tighten his lips and arrange his shoulders in the correct command posture. He might give a curt little nod. Or he might not. He might just shrug and say Carry on, then they would saddle up and form into a column and move out toward the villages of Than Khe.   *1986*

CONSIDERATIONS

1. List the "things" carried by the men as they move through the Vietnamese countryside. Write a brief response to several of these "things," discussing what the men's choices suggest about their hopes, their fears, and their values.
2. To what extent is Lieutenant Cross responsible for Ted Lavender's death? Why does he think he is responsible? How does his response to Lavender's death change his attitude toward his command?
3. Evaluate the responses of the men to Lavender's death.
4. Mitchell Sanders says, "There's a moral here." Do you see any moral to the story of Lavender's death? To the story of the others' responses to his death?
5. How do Lieutenant Cross's fantasies about Martha change throughout the story? What significance do you see in these changes? Do you see them as negative? Positive? Or something else?

BHARATI MUKHERJEE (1940–   )
The Management of Grief

> *Bharati Mukherjee was born in Calcutta, India. After earning degrees at the universities of Calcutta and Baroda, she came to the United States to study writing at the University of Iowa. There she married a fellow student, Canadian writer Clark Blaise. They moved to Canada, where she taught at McGill University in Montreal. In 1980, Mukherjee and her family moved to the United States, and she became a naturalized citizen. Summing up her goals as a writer, Mukherjee has said, "My literary agenda begins by acknowledging that America has transformed me. It does not end until I show that I (along with hundreds of thousands of immigrants like me) am minute by minute transforming America." Her novels portray women living between the cultures of India and the West.*

They include The Tiger's Daughter *(1972),* Wife *(1975),* Jasmine *(1989),* The Holder of the World *(1993), and* Leave It to Me *(1997).*

A woman I don't know is boiling tea the Indian way in my kitchen. There are a lot of women I don't know in my kitchen, whispering and moving tactfully. They open doors, rummage through the pantry, and try not to ask me where things are kept. They remind me of when my sons were small, on Mother's Day or when Vikram and I were tired, and they would make big, sloppy omelets. I would lie in bed pretending I didn't hear them.

Dr. Sharma, the treasurer of the Indo-Canada Society, pulls me into the hallway. He wants to know if I am worried about money. His wife, who has just come up from the basement with a tray of empty cups and glasses, scolds him. "Don't bother Mrs. Bhave with mundane details." She looks so monstrously pregnant her baby must be days overdue. I tell her she shouldn't be carrying heavy things. "Shaila," she says, smiling, "this is the fifth." Then she grabs a teenager by his shirttails. He slips his Walkman off his head. He has to be one of her four children; they have the same domed and dented foreheads. "What's the official word now?" she demands. The boy slips the headphones back on. "They're acting evasive, Ma. They're saying it could be an accident or a terrorist bomb."

All morning, the boys have been muttering, Sikh bomb, Sikh bomb. The men, not using the word, bow their heads in agreement. Mrs. Sharma touches her forehead at such a word. At least they've stopped talking about space debris and Russian lasers.

Two radios are going in the dining room. They are tuned to different stations. Someone must have brought the radios down from my boys' bedrooms. I haven't gone into their rooms since Kusum came running across the front lawn in her bathrobe. She looked so funny, I was laughing when I opened the door.

The big TV in the den is being whizzed through American networks and cable channels.

"Damn!" some man swears bitterly. "How can these preachers carry on like nothing's happened?" I want to tell him we're not that important. You look at the audience, and at the preacher in his blue robe with his beautiful white hair, the potted palm trees under a blue sky, and you know they care about nothing.

The phone rings and rings. Dr. Sharma's taken charge. "We're with her," he keeps saying. "Yes, yes, the doctor has given calming pills. Yes, yes, pills are having necessary effect." I wonder if pills alone explain this calm. Not peace, just a deadening quiet. I was always controlled, but never repressed. Sound can reach me, but my body is tensed, ready to scream. I hear their voices all around me. I hear my boys and Vikram cry, "Mommy, Shaila!" and their screams insulate me, like headphones.

The woman boiling water tells her story again and again. "I got the news first. My cousin called from Halifax before six A.M., can you imagine? He'd gotten up for prayers and his son was studying for medical exams and heard on a rock channel that something had happened to a plane. They said first it had disappeared from the radar, like a giant eraser just reached out. His father called me, so I said to him, what do you mean, 'something bad'? You mean a hijacking? And he said, *Behn,* there is no confirmation of anything yet, but check with your neighbors because a lot of them must be on that plane. So I called poor Kusum straight-away. I knew Kusum's husband and daughter were booked to go yesterday."

Kusum lives across the street from me. She and Satish had moved in less than a month ago. They said they needed a bigger place. All these people, the Sharmas and friends from the Indo-Canada Society, had been there for the housewarming. Satish and Kusum made tandoori on their big gas grill and even the white neighbors piled their plates high with that luridly red, charred, juicy chicken. Their younger daughter had danced, and even our boys had broken away from the Stanley Cup telecast to put in a reluctant appearance. Everyone took pictures for their albums and for the community newspapers— another of our families had made it big in Toronto—and now I wonder how many of those happy faces are gone. "Why does God give us so much if all along He intends to take it away?" Kusum asks me.

10   I nod. We sit on carpeted stairs, holding hands like children. "I never once told him that I loved him," I say. I was too much the well-brought-up woman. I was so well brought up I never felt comfortable calling my husband by his first name.

"It's all right," Kusum says. "He knew. My husband knew. They felt it. Modern young girls have to say it because what they feel is fake."

Kusum's daughter Pam runs in with an overnight case. Pam's in her McDonald's uniform. "Mummy! You have to get dressed!" Panic makes her cranky. "A reporter's on his way here."

"Why?"

"You want to talk to him in your bathrobe?" She starts to brush her mother's long hair. She's the daughter who's always in trouble. She dates Canadian boys and hangs out in the mall, shopping for tight sweaters. The younger one, the goody-goody one according to Pam, the one with a voice so sweet that when she sang *bhajans* for Ethiopian relief even a frugal man like my husband wrote out a hundred-dollar check, *she* was on that plane. *She* was going to spend July and August with grandparents because Pam wouldn't go. Pam said she'd rather waitress at McDonald's. "If it's a choice between Bombay and Wonderland, I'm picking Wonderland," she'd said.

15   "Leave me alone," Kusum yells. "You know what I want to do? If I didn't have to look after you now, I'd hang myself."

Pam's young face goes blotchy with pain. "Thanks," she says, "don't let me stop you."

"Hush," pregnant Mrs. Sharma scolds Pam. "Leave your mother alone. Mr. Sharma will tackle the reporters and fill out the forms. He'll say what has to be said."

Pam stands her ground. "You think I don't know what Mummy's thinking? *Why her?* That's what. That's sick! Mummy wishes my little sister were alive and I were dead."

Kusum's hand in mine is trembly hot. We continue to sit on the stairs.

She calls before she arrives, wondering if there's anything I need. Her   20
name is Judith Templeton and she's an appointee of the provincial government. "Multiculturalism?" I ask, and she says "partially," but that her mandate is bigger. "I've been told you knew many of the people on the flight," she says. "Perhaps if you'd agree to help us reach the others . . . ?"

She gives me time at least to put on tea water and pick up the mess in the front room. I have a few *samosas* from Kusum's housewarming that I could fry up, but then I think, why prolong this visit?

Judith Templeton is much younger than she sounded. She wears a blue suit with a white blouse and a polka-dot tie. Her blond hair is cut short, her only jewelry is pearl-drop earrings. Her briefcase is new and expensive looking, a gleaming cordovan leather. She sits with it across her lap. When she looks out the front windows onto the street, her contact lenses seem to float in front of her light blue eyes.

"What sort of help do you want from me?" I ask. She has refused the tea, out of politeness, but I insist, along with some slightly stale biscuits.

"I have no experience," she admits. "That is, I have an M.S.W. and I've worked in liaison with accident victims, but I mean I have no experience with a tragedy of this scale—"

"Who could?" I ask.   25

"—and with the complications of culture, language, and customs. Someone mentioned that Mrs. Bhave is a pillar—because you've taken it more calmly."

At this, perhaps, I frown, for she reaches forward, almost to take my hand. "I hope you understand my meaning, Mrs. Bhave. There are hundreds of people in Metro directly affected, like you, and some of them speak no English. There are some widows who've never handled money or gone on a bus, and there are old parents who still haven't eaten or gone outside their bedrooms. Some houses and apartments have been looted. Some wives are still hysterical. Some husbands are in shock and profound depression. We want to help, but our hands are tied in so many ways. We have to distribute money to some people, and there are legal documents—these things can be done. We have interpreters, but we don't always have the human touch, or maybe the right human touch. We don't want to make mistakes, Mrs. Bhave, and that's why we'd like to ask you to help us."

"More mistakes, you mean," I say.

"Police matters are not in my hands," she answers.

30   "Nothing I can do will make any difference," I say. "We must all grieve in our own way."

"But you are coping very well. All the people said, Mrs. Bhave is the strongest person of all. Perhaps if the others could see you, talk with you, it would help them."

"By the standards of the people you call hysterical, I am behaving very oddly and very badly, Miss Templeton." I want to say to her, *I wish I could scream, starve, walk into Lake Ontario, jump from a bridge.* "They would not see me as a model. I do not see myself as a model."

I am a freak. No one who has ever known me would think of me reacting this way. This terrible calm will not go away.

She asks me if she may call again, after I get back from a long trip that we all must make. "Of course," I say. "Feel free to call, anytime."

35   Four days later, I find Kusum squatting on a rock overlooking a bay in Ireland. It isn't a big rock, but it juts sharply out over water. This is as close as we'll ever get to them. June breezes balloon out her sari and unpin her knee-length hair. She has the bewildered look of a sea creature whom the tides have stranded.

It's been one hundred hours since Kusum came stumbling and screaming across my lawn. Waiting around the hospital, we've heard many stories. The police, the diplomats, they tell us things thinking that we're strong, that knowledge is helpful to the grieving, and maybe it is. Some, I know, prefer ignorance, or their own versions. The plane broke into two, they say. Unconsciousness was instantaneous. No one suffered. My boys must have just finished their breakfasts. They loved eating on planes, they loved the smallness of plates, knives, and forks. Last year they saved the airline salt and pepper shakers. Half an hour more and they would have made it to Heathrow.

Kusum says that we can't escape our fate. She says that all those people— our husbands, my boys, her girl with the nightingale voice, all those Hindus, Christians, Sikhs, Muslims, Parsis, and atheists on that plane—were fated to die together off this beautiful bay. She learned this from a swami in Toronto.

I have my Valium.

Six of us "relatives"—two widows and four widowers—choose to spend the day today by the waters instead of sitting in a hospital room and scanning photographs of the dead. That's what they call us now: relatives. I've looked through twenty-seven photos in two days. They're very kind to us, the Irish are very understanding. Sometimes understanding means freeing a tourist bus for this trip to the bay, so we can pretend to spy our loved ones through the glassiness of waves or in sun-speckled cloud shapes.

40   I could die here, too, and be content.

"What is that, out there?" She's standing and flapping her hands, and for a moment I see a head shape bobbing in the waves. She's standing in the water, I, on the boulder. The tide is low, and a round, black, head-sized rock has just risen from the waves. She returns, her sari end dripping and ruined and her face is a twisted remnant of hope, the way mine was a hundred hours ago, still laughing but inwardly knowing that nothing but the ultimate tragedy could bring two women together at six o'clock on a Sunday morning. I watch her face sag into blankness.

"That water felt warm, Shaila," she says at length.

"You can't," I say. "We have to wait for our turn to come."

I haven't eaten in four days, haven't brushed my teeth.

"I know," she says. "I tell myself I have no right to grieve. They are in a   *45*
better place than we are. My swami says I should be thrilled for them. My swami says depression is a sign of our selfishness."

Maybe I'm selfish. Selfishly I break away from Kusum and run, sandals slapping against stones, to the water's edge. What if my boys aren't lying pinned under the debris? What if they aren't stuck a mile below that innocent blue chop? What if, given the strong currents. . . .

Now I've ruined my sari, one of my best. Kusum has joined me, knee-deep in water that feels to me like a swimming pool. I could settle in the water, and my husband would take my hand and the boys would slap water in my face just to see me scream.

"Do you remember what good swimmers my boys were, Kusum?"

"I saw the medals," she says.

One of the widowers, Dr. Ranganathan from Montreal, walks out to us,   *50*
carrying his shoes in one hand. He's an electrical engineer. Someone at the hotel mentioned his work is famous around the world, something about the place where physics and electricity come together. He has lost a huge family, something indescribable. "With some good luck," Dr. Ranganathan suggests to me, "a good swimmer could make it safely to some island. It is quite possible that there may be many, many microscopic islets scattered around."

"You're not just saying that?" I tell Dr. Ranganathan about Vinod, my elder son. Last year he took diving as well.

"It's a parent's duty to hope," he says. "It is foolish to rule out possibilities that have not been tested. I myself have not surrendered hope."

Kusum is sobbing once again. "Dear lady," he says, laying his free hand on her arm, and she calms down.

"Vinod is how old?" he asks me. He's very careful, as we all are. *Is,* not was.

"Fourteen. Yesterday he was fourteen. His father and uncle were going   *55*
to take him down to the Taj and give him a big birthday party. I couldn't go with them because I couldn't get two weeks off from my stupid job in June." I process bills for a travel agent. June is a big travel month.

Dr. Ranganathan whips the pockets of his suit jacket inside out. Squashed roses, in darkening shades of pink, float on the water. He tore the roses off creepers in somebody's garden. He didn't ask anyone if he could pluck the roses, but now there's been an article about it in the local papers. When you see an Indian person, it says, please give him or her flowers.

"A strong youth of fourteen," he says, "can very likely pull to safety a younger one."

My sons, though four years apart, were very close. Vinod wouldn't let Mithun drown. *Electrical engineering,* I think, foolishly perhaps: this man knows important secrets of the universe, things closed to me. Relief spins me light-headed. No wonder my boys' photographs haven't turned up in the gallery of photos of the recovered dead. "Such pretty roses," I say.

"My wife loved pink roses. Every Friday I had to bring a bunch home. I used to say, Why? After twenty-odd years of marriage you're still needing proof positive of my love?" He has identified his wife and three of his children. Then others from Montreal, the lucky ones, intact families with no survivors. He chuckles as he wades back to shore. Then he swings around to ask me a question. "Mrs. Bhave, you are wanting to throw in some roses for your loved ones? I have two big ones left."

60   But I have other things to float: Vinod's pocket calculator; a half-painted model B-52 for my Mithun. They'd want them on their island. And for my husband? For him I let fall into the calm, glassy waters a poem I wrote in the hospital yesterday. Finally he'll know my feelings for him.

"Don't tumble, the rocks are slippery," Dr. Ranganathan cautions. He holds out a hand for me to grab.

Then it's time to get back on the bus, time to rush back to our waiting posts on hospital benches.

Kusum is one of the lucky ones. The lucky ones flew here, identified in multiplicate their loved ones, then will fly to India with the bodies for proper ceremonies. Satish is one of the few males who surfaced. The photos of faces we saw on the walls in an office at Heathrow and here in the hospital are mostly of women. Women have more body fat, a nun said to me matter-of-factly. They float better.

Today I was stopped by a young sailor on the street. He had loaded bodies, he'd gone into the water when—he checks my face for signs of strength—when the sharks were first spotted. I don't blush, and he breaks down. "It's all right," I say. "Thank you." I heard about the sharks from Dr. Ranganathan. In his orderly mind, science brings understanding, it holds no terror. It is the shark's duty. For every deer there is a hunter, for every fish a fisherman.

65   The Irish are not shy; they rush to me and give me hugs and some are crying. I cannot imagine reactions like that on the streets of Toronto. Just strangers, and I am touched. Some carry flowers with them and give them to any Indian they see.

After lunch, a policeman I have gotten to know quite well catches hold of me. He says he thinks he has a match for Vinod. I explain what a good swimmer Vinod is.

"You want me with you when you look at photos?" Dr. Ranganathan walks ahead of me into the picture gallery. In these matters, he is a scientist, and I am grateful. It is a new perspective. "They have performed miracles," he says. "We are indebted to them."

The first day or two the policemen showed us relatives only one picture at a time; now they're in a hurry, they're eager to lay out the possibles, and even the probables.

The face on the photo is of a boy much like Vinod; the same intelligent eyes, the same thick brows dipping into a V. But this boy's features, even his cheeks, are puffier, wider, mushier.

"No." My gaze is pulled by other pictures. There are five other boys who   70
look like Vinod.

The nun assigned to console me rubs the first picture with a fingertip. "When they've been in the water for a while, love, they look a little heavier." The bones under the skin are broken, they said on the first day—try to adjust your memories. It's important.

"It's not him. I'm his mother. I'd know."

"I know this one!" Dr. Ranganathan cries out, and suddenly from the back of the gallery. "And this one!" I think he senses that I don't want to find my boys. "They are the Kutty brothers. They were also from Montreal." I don't mean to be crying. On the contrary, I am ecstatic. My suitcase in the hotel is packed heavy with dry clothes for my boys.

The policeman starts to cry. "I am so sorry, I am so sorry, ma'am. I really thought we had a match."

With the nun ahead of us and the policeman behind, we, the unlucky   75
ones without our children's bodies, file out of the makeshift gallery.

From Ireland most of us go on to India. Kusum and I take the same direct flight to Bombay, so I can help her clear customs quickly. But we have to argue with a man in uniform. He has large boils on his face. The boils swell and glow with sweat as we argue with him. He wants Kusum to wait in line and he refuses to take authority because his boss is on a tea break. But Kusum won't let her coffins out of sight, and I shan't desert her though I know that my parents, elderly and diabetic, must be waiting in a stuffy car in a scorching lot.

"You bastard!" I scream at the man with the popping boils. Other passengers press closer. "You think we're smuggling contraband in those coffins!"

Once upon a time we were well-brought-up women; we were dutiful wives who kept our heads veiled, our voices shy and sweet.

In India, I become, once again, an only child of rich, ailing parents. Old friends of the family come to pay their respects. Some are Sikh, and inwardly, involuntarily, I cringe. My parents are progressive people; they do not blame communities for a few individuals.

In Canada it is a different story now.   80

"Stay longer," my mother pleads. "Canada is a cold place. Why would you want to be all by yourself?" I stay.

Three months pass. Then another.

"Vikram wouldn't have wanted you to give up things!" they protest. They call my husband by the name he was born with. In Toronto he'd changed to Vik so the men he worked with at his office would find his name as easy as Rod or Chris. "You know, the dead aren't cut off from us!"

My grandmother, the spoiled daughter of a rich zamindar,[1] shaved her head with rusty razor blades when she was widowed at sixteen. My grandfather died of childhood diabetes when he was nineteen, and she saw herself as the harbinger of bad luck. My mother grew up without parents, raised indifferently by an uncle, while her true mother slept in a hut behind the main estate house and took her food with the servants. She grew up a rationalist. My parents abhor mindless mortification.

85   The zamindar's daughter kept stubborn faith in Vedic rituals; my parents rebelled. I am trapped between two modes of knowledge. At thirty-six, I am too old to start over and too young to give up. Like my husband's spirit, I flutter between worlds.

Courting aphasia, we travel. We travel with our phalanx of servants and poor relatives. To hill stations and to beach resorts. We play contract bridge in dusty gymkhana clubs. We ride stubby ponies up crumbly mountain trails. At tea dances, we let ourselves be twirled twice round the ballroom. We hit the holy spots we hadn't made time for before. In Varanasi, Kalighat, Rishikesh, Hardwar, astrologers and palmists seek me out and for a fee offer me cosmic consolations.

Already the widowers among us are being shown new bride candidates. They cannot resist the call of custom, the authority of their parents and older brothers. They must marry; it is the duty of a man to look after a wife. The new wives will be young widows with children, destitute but of good family. They will make loving wives, but the men will shun them. I've had calls from the men over crackling Indian telephone lines. "Save me," they say, these substantial, educated, successful men of forty. "My parents are arranging a marriage for me." In a month they will have buried one family and returned to Canada with a new bride and partial family.

I am comparatively lucky. No one here thinks of arranging a husband for an unlucky widow.

Then, on the third day of the sixth month into this odyssey, in an abandoned temple in a tiny Himalayan village, as I make my offering of flowers and sweetmeats to the god of a tribe of animists, my husband descends to me. He is squatting next to a scrawny sadhu[2] in moth-eaten robes. Vikram wears the vanilla suit he wore the last time I hugged him. The sadhu tosses petals on

---

[1]Landlord during the British regime in India. [2]Holy man.

a butter-fed flame, reciting Sanskrit mantras, and sweeps his face of flies. My husband takes my hands in his.

You're beautiful, he starts. Then, *What are you doing here?*   *90*

Shall I stay? I ask. He only smiles, but already the image is fading. *You must finish alone what we started together.* No seaweed wreathes his mouth. He speaks too fast, just as he used to when we were an envied family in our pink split-level. He is gone.

In the windowless altar room, smoky with joss sticks and clarified butter lamps, a sweaty hand gropes for my blouse. I do not shriek. The sadhu arranges his robe. The lamps hiss and sputter out.

When we come out of the temple, my mother says, "Did you feel something weird in there?"

My mother has no patience with ghosts, prophetic dreams, holy men, and cults.

"No," I lie. "Nothing."   *95*

But she knows that she's lost me. She knows that in days I shall be leaving.

Kusum's put up her house for sale. She wants to live in an ashram in Hardwar. Moving to Hardwar was her swami's idea. Her swami runs two ashrams, the one in Hardwar and another here in Toronto.

"Don't run away," I tell her.

"I'm not running away," she says. "I'm pursuing inner peace. You think you or that Ranganathan fellow are better off?"

Pam's left for California. She wants to do some modeling, she says. She   *100* says when she comes into her share of the insurance money she'll open a yoga-cum-aerobics studio in Hollywood. She sends me postcards so naughty I daren't leave them on the coffee table. Her mother has withdrawn from her and the world.

The rest of us don't lose touch, that's the point. Talk is all we have, says Dr. Ranganathan, who has also resisted his relatives and returned to Montreal and to his job, alone. He says, Whom better to talk with than other relatives? We've been melted down and recast as a new tribe.

He calls me twice a week from Montreal. Every Wednesday night and every Saturday afternoon. He is changing jobs, going to Ottawa. But Ottawa is over a hundred miles away, and he is forced to drive two hundred and twenty miles a day from his home in Montreal. He can't bring himself to sell his house. The house is a temple, he says; the king-sized bed in the master bedroom is a shrine. He sleeps on a folding cot. A devotee.

There are still some hysterical relatives. Judith Templeton's list of those needing help and those who've "accepted" is in nearly perfect balance. Acceptance means you speak of your family in the past tense and you make active plans for moving ahead with your life. There are courses at Seneca and Ryerson we could be taking. Her gleaming leather briefcase is full of college catalogues and lists of cultural societies that need our help. She has done impressive work, I tell her.

"In the textbooks on grief management," she replies—I am her confidante, I realize, one of the few whose grief has not sprung bizarre obsessions—"there are stages to pass through: rejection, depression, acceptance, reconstruction." She has compiled a chart and finds that six months after the tragedy, none of us still rejects reality, but only a handful are reconstructing. "Depressed acceptance" is the plateau we've reached. Remarriage is a major step in reconstruction (though she's a little surprised, even shocked, over *how* quickly some of the men have taken on new families). Selling one's house and changing jobs and cities is healthy.

105   How to tell Judith Templeton that my family surrounds me, and that like creatures in epics, they've changed shapes? She sees me as calm and accepting but worries that I have no job, no career. My closest friends are worse off than I. I cannot tell her my days, even my nights, are thrilling.

She asks me to help with families she can't reach at all. An elderly couple in Agincourt whose sons were killed just weeks after they had brought their parents over from a village in Punjab. From their names, I know they are Sikh. Judith Templeton and a translator have visited them twice with offers of money for airfare to Ireland, with bank forms, power-of-attorney forms, but they have refused to sign, or to leave their tiny apartment. Their sons' money is frozen in the bank. Their sons' investment apartments have been trashed by tenants, the furnishings sold off. The parents fear that anything they sign or any money they receive will end the company's or the country's obligations to them. They fear they are selling their sons for two airline tickets to a place they've never seen.

The high-rise apartment is a tower of Indians and West Indians, with a sprinkling of Orientals. The nearest bus-stop kiosk is lined with women in saris. Boys practice cricket in the parking lot. Inside the building, even I wince a bit from the ferocity of onion fumes, the distinctive and immediate Indian-ness of frying ghee, but Judith Templeton maintains a steady flow of information. These poor old people are in imminent danger of losing their place and all their services.

I say to her, "They are Sikh. They will not open up to a Hindu woman." And what I want to add is, as much as I try not to, I stiffen now at the sight of beards and turbans. I remember a time when we all trusted each other in this new country, it was only the new country we worried about.

The two rooms are dark and stuffy. The lights are off, and an oil lamp sputters on the coffee table. The bent old lady has let us in, and her husband is wrapping a white turban over his oiled, hip-length hair. She immediately goes to the kitchen, and I hear the most familiar sound of an Indian home, tap water hitting and filling a teapot.

They have not paid their utility bills, out of fear and inability to write a   *110*
check. The telephone is gone, electricity and gas and water are soon to follow.
They have told Judith their sons will provide. They are good boys, and they
have always earned and looked after their parents.

We converse a bit in Hindi. They do not ask about the crash and I wonder if I should bring it up. If they think I am here merely as a translator, then
they may feel insulted. There are thousands of Punjabi speakers, Sikhs, in
Toronto to do a better job. And so I say to the old lady, "I too have lost my
sons, and my husband, in the crash."

Her eyes immediately fill with tears. The man mutters a few words which
sound like a blessing. "God provides and God takes away," he says.

I want to say, But only men destroy and give back nothing. "My boys
and my husband are not coming back," I say. "We have to understand that."

Now the old woman responds. "But who is to say? Man alone does not
decide these things." To this her husband adds his agreement.

Judith asks about the bank papers, the release forms. With a stroke of the   *115*
pen, they will have a provincial trustee to pay their bills, invest their money,
send them a monthly pension.

"Do you know this woman?" I ask them.

The man raises his hand from the table, turns it over, and seems to regard
each finger separately before he answers. "This young lady is always coming
here, we make tea for her, and she leaves papers for us to sign." His eyes scan a
pile of papers in the corner of the room. "Soon we will be out of tea, then will
she go away?"

The old lady adds, "I have asked my neighbors and no one else gets *an-
grezi*[3] visitors. What have we done?"

"It's her job," I try to explain. "The government is worried. Soon you
will have no place to stay, no lights, no gas, no water."

"Government will get its money. Tell her not to worry, we are honorable   *120*
people."

I try to explain the government wishes to give money, not take. He raises
his hand. "Let them take," he says. "We are accustomed to that. That is no
problem."

"We are strong people," says the wife. "Tell her that."

"Who needs all this machinery?" demands the husband. "It is unhealthy,
the bright lights, the cold air on a hot day, the cold food, the four gas rings.
God will provide, not government."

"When our boys return," the mother says.

Her husband sucks his teeth. "Enough talk," he says.   *125*

Judith breaks in. "Have you convinced them?" The snaps on her cordovan briefcase go off like firecrackers in that quiet apartment. She lays the

[3] Anglo.

sheaf of legal papers on the coffee table. "If they can't write their names, an X will do—I've told them that."

Now the old lady has shuffled to the kitchen and soon emerges with a pot of tea and two cups. "I think my bladder will go first on a job like this," Judith says to me, smiling. "If only there was some way of reaching them. Please thank her for the tea. Tell her she's very kind."

I nod in Judith's direction and tell them in Hindi, "She thanks you for the tea. She thinks you are being very hospitable but she doesn't have the slightest idea what it means."

I want to say, Humor her. I want to say, My boys and my husband are with me too, more than ever. I look in the old man's eyes and I can read his stubborn, peasant's message: *I have protected this woman as best I can. She is the only person I have left. Give to me or take from me what you will, but I will not sign for it. I will not pretend that I accept.*

130   In the car, Judith says, "You see what I'm up against? I'm sure they're lovely people, but their stubbornness and ignorance are driving me crazy. They think signing a paper is signing their sons' death warrants, don't they?"

I am looking out the window. I want to say, *In our culture, it is a parent's duty to hope.*

"Now Shaila, this next woman is a real mess. She cries day and night, and she refuses all medical help. We may have to—"

"Let me out at the subway," I say.

"I beg your pardon?" I can feel those blue eyes staring at me.

135   It would not be like her to disobey. She merely disapproves, and slows at a corner to let me out. Her voice is plaintive. "Is there anything I said? Anything I did?"

I could answer her suddenly in a dozen ways, but I choose not to. "Shaila? Let's talk about it," I hear, then slam the door.

A wife and mother begins her life in a new country, and that life is cut short. Yet her husband tells her: Complete what we have started. We, who stayed out of politics and came half way around the world to avoid religious and political feuding, have been the first in the New World to die from it. I no longer know what we started, nor how to complete it. I write letters to the editors of local papers and to members of Parliament. Now at least they admit it was a bomb. One MP answers back, with sympathy, but with a challenge. You want to make a difference? Work on a campaign. Work on mine. Politicize the Indian voter.

My husband's old lawyer helps me set up a trust. Vikram was a saver and a careful investor. He had saved the boys' boarding school and college fees. I sell the pink house at four times what we paid for it and take a small apartment downtown. I am looking for a charity to support.

We are deep in the Toronto winter, gray skies, icy pavements. I stay indoors, watching television. I have tried to assess my situation, how best to live my life, to complete what we began so many years ago. Kusum has written me from Hardwar that her life is now serene. She has seen Satish and has heard her daughter sing again. Kusum was on a pilgrimage, passing through a village, when she heard a young girl's voice, singing one of her daughter's favorite *bhajans*. She followed the music through the squalor of a Himalayan village, to a hut where a young girl, an exact replica of her daughter, was fanning coals under the kitchen fire. When she appeared, the girl cried out, "Ma!" and ran away. What did I think of that?

I think I can only envy her.   140

Pam didn't make it to California, but writes me from Vancouver. She works in a department store, giving makeup hints to Indian and Oriental girls. Dr. Ranganathan has given up his commute, given up his house and job, and accepted an academic position in Texas, where no one knows his story and he has vowed not to tell it. He calls me now once a week.

I wait, I listen and I pray, but Vikram has not returned to me. The voices and the shapes and the nights filled with visions ended abruptly several weeks ago.

I take it as a sign.

One rare, beautiful, sunny day last week, returning from a small errand on Yonge Street, I was walking through the park from the subway to my apartment. I live equidistant from the Ontario Houses of Parliament and the University of Toronto. The day was not cold, but something in the bare trees caught my attention. I looked up from the gravel, into the branches and the clear blue sky beyond. I thought I heard the rustling of larger forms, and I waited a moment for voices. Nothing.

"What?" I asked.   145

Then as I stood in the path looking north to Queen's Park and west to the university, I heard the voices of my family one last time. *Your time has come,* they said. *Go, be brave.*

I do not know where this voyage I have begun will end. I do not know which direction I will take. I dropped the package on a park bench and started walking.   *1988*

CONSIDERATIONS

1. In December 1988, Pan Am Flight 103, on its way from London to New York City, exploded over Lockerbie, Scotland, as a result of an act of terrorism. How does Mukherjee's depiction of a similar act and its results suggest the many ramifications of such an event?
2. Categorize the qualities of the narrator that are typically North American and those that are typically Indian. Looking at these two categories, how would you characterize her—as predominantly one or the other?

3. Taking all the characters into account, what characteristics of their grieving are typically North American? Which reflect Eastern culture? Which characteristics cross over borders and touch on something that is universal within all peoples? Explain.

4. Explain the differences that the narrator notes between the Canadians and the Irish. On what does she base her opinions? How valid are these opinions? Explain.

5. Think about the religious differences between Eastern and Western thought and how death is viewed. How do those differences explain the old couple who keep waiting for their two sons to return? How do they explain the narrator's encounters with her husband and sons?

6. In addition to human life itself, what else do acts of terrorism and war destroy? According to this short story, to what extent do those left behind find closure?

Poetry

PERCY BYSSHE SHELLEY (1792–1822)
Ozymandias°

Born in Sussex, England to a wealthy, powerful family, Percy Bysshe Shelley attended Eton College and Oxford University, where he first began writing poetry. His poems and prose pamphlets, many of which expressed radical views, caused him to be expelled from Oxford. He then moved to the Lake District in the north of England, joining a community of writers, artists, and philosophers and continuing to write works, some of which expressed a socialist philosophy. Shelley traveled widely in Europe. Just before his thirtieth birthday, he drowned in a storm while he was sailing in the Bay of Spezia, near Lerici, Italy.

I met a traveler from an antique land,
Who said: Two vast and trunkless legs of stone
Stand in the desert . . . Near them, on the sand,
Half sunk, a shattered visage° lies, whose frown,
5   And wrinkled lip, and sneer of cold command,
Tell that its sculptor well those passions read
Which yet survive, stamped on these lifeless things,

Ozymandias: Greek name for the Egyptian ruler Ramses II, who ordered a huge statue of himself to be erected. *Visage:* Face.

The hand that mocked them, and the heart that fed:
And on the pedestal these words appear:
"My name is Ozymandias, king of kings: *10*
Look on my works, ye Mighty, and despair!"
Nothing beside remains. Round the decay
Of that colossal wreck, boundless and bare
The lone and level sands stretch far away.   *1818*

CONSIDERATIONS

1. This sonnet suggests the stories and voices of three different people. What role does each one play, and how do these roles relate to the theme of war and power?
2. What does the description of the sculpture in the desert suggest about the characteristics of warlords in general?
3. Discuss the irony of the message on the pedestal. What message might you inscribe instead?

WILLIAM BUTLER YEATS (1865–1939)

The Second Coming[1]

Born and raised in Ireland, William Butler Yeats wrote many poems and plays that reflect his connection with the history and culture of his native country. Yeats's achievement as a poet was recognized in 1923, when he won the Nobel Prize for literature. The following selection suggests Yeats' view of the Black and Tan War in Ireland, when British troops were sent in to subdue the Irish republicans. Yeats later noted that this poem has broader implications for what was happening in Europe both in 1919 and, later, in the years leading up to World War II.

Turning and turning in the widening gyre[2]
The falcon cannot hear the falconer;
Things fall apart; the centre cannot hold;
Mere anarchy is loosed upon the world,
The blood-dimmed tide is loosed, and everywhere   *5*
The ceremony of innocence is drowned;

---

[1] The title and the references to "the Second Coming" in the poem suggest the prediction of Christ's return to Earth (Matthew 24). [2] A gyre is the spiral shape a falcon makes as it rises from the hand of its trainer, the falconer.

The best lack all conviction, while the worst
Are full of passionate intensity.

Surely some revelation is at hand;
10   Surely the Second Coming is at hand.
The Second Coming! Hardly are those words out
When a vast image out of *Spiritus Mundi*[3]
Troubles my sight: somewhere in sands of the desert
A shape with lion body and the head of a man,[4]
15   A gaze blank and pitiless as the sun,
Is moving its slow thighs, while all about it
Reel shadows of the indignant desert birds.
The darkness drops again; but now I know
That twenty centuries of stony sleep
20   Were vexed to nightmare by a rocking cradle,
And what rough beast, its hour come round at last,
Slouches towards Bethlehem to be born?   *1919*

CONSIDERATIONS

1. Given that humankind is in the center of the widening gyre (spiral) in this poem, describe the world as depicted by the speaker in the first eight lines. What images are most disturbing? What do the Biblical allusions suggest?
2. What images are most powerful in the last stanza? Consider the symbolic and archetypal connotations of these images and come to some conclusion about what is coming this second time.
3. If the "turning and turning" in the first line is a reference to how history repeats itself, to what then, according to the line, is history turning? In what ways could the year when Yeats wrote the poem, 1919, have affected his vision of the world?

THOMAS HARDY (1840–1928)
The Man He Killed

> *Thomas Hardy was born and grew up in southeastern England, a region that he later fictionalized as "Wessex" in many of his novels. As a young man, he*

---

[3]*Spirtus Mundi* literally means the spirit of the world. Yeats refers here to his conviction that there exists a system of images and beliefs that all humans can access and share.   [4]The Sphinx in Egypt.

worked for several years as an apprentice to an ecclesiastical architect, but in
1861 he moved to London seeking an education. He practiced architecture while
attending King's College in the evenings. After completing his studies in 1867,
he devoted all his time to writing poetry and fiction. His best-known novels in-
clude Tess of the d'Urbervilles *(1891) and* Jude the Obscure *(1896).*

Had he and I but met
By some old ancient inn,
We should have sat us down to wet
Right many a nipperkin!

But ranged as infantry,   5
And staring face to face,
I shot at him as he at me,
And killed him in his place.

I shot him dead because—
Because he was my foe.   10
Just so: my foe of course he was;
That's clear enough; although

He thought he'd list,° perhaps,
Off-hand like—just as I—
Was out of work—had sold his traps—   15
No other reason why.

Yes; quaint and curious war is!
You shoot a fellow down
You'd treat, if met where any bar is,
Or help to half-a-crown.   *1902*   20

CONSIDERATIONS

1. Describe the speaker. What kind of man is he? What kind of work does he
   do? What does he enjoy in his free time? What are his values?
2. Reread lines 9 and 10. What is the effect of the repeated word "because"?
   How would the meaning change if one "because" were omitted?
3. What questions does the poem raise about war? Does it suggest any answers to those questions? Explain.

---

13 *list:* Enlist.

WILFRED OWEN (1893–1918)

Dulce et Decorum Est°

> After growing up in the peaceful countryside of his native Shropshire in England, Wilfred Owen attended London University. A few years later, after teaching in England and France, he enlisted in the British army. While serving in World War I, he wrote letters home, kept a journal, and composed poems describing and analyzing the horror he encountered every day. In 1917, he was wounded, but he returned to action only to be killed in 1918, a few days before the armistice was signed.

Bent double, like old beggars under sacks,
Knock-kneed, coughing like hags, we cursed through sludge,
Till on the haunting flares we turned our backs
And towards our distant rest began to trudge.
5   Men marched asleep. Many had lost their boots
But limped on, blood-shod. All went lame; all blind;
Drunk with fatigue; deaf even to the hoots
Of tired, outstripped Five-Nines° that dropped behind.

Gas! GAS! Quick, boys!—An ecstasy of fumbling,
10   Fitting the clumsy helmets just in time;
But someone still was yelling out and stumbling
And flound'ring like a man in fire or lime°. . .
Dim, through the misty panes and thick green light,
As under a green sea, I saw him drowning.

15   In all my dreams, before my helpless sight,
He plunges at me, guttering, choking, drowning.

If in some smothering dreams you too could pace
Behind the wagon that we flung him in,
And watch the white eyes writhing in his face,
20   His hanging face, like a devil's sick of sin;
If you could hear, at every jolt, the blood
Come gargling from the froth-corrupted lungs,
Obscene as cancer, bitter as the cud

Of vile, incurable sores on innocent tongues,—
25   My friend, you would not tell with such high zest

Dulce et Decorum Est: "It is sweet and fitting." The words come from Horace's Odes, II.ii.13. The full quotation, given in the poem's final line, means "It is sweet and fitting to die for one's country." 8 *Five-Nines:* Gas bombs used by Germans in World War I. 12 *lime:* Quick-lime, a chemical that dissolves flesh and bones.

To children ardent for some desperate glory,
The old Lie: *Dulce et decorum est*
Pro patria mori.   1918

CONSIDERATIONS

1. Who are the people described in the opening stanza? What do the images
   Owen chooses suggest about their response to the circumstances they must
   face?
2. What purpose is served by the graphic details of the gas attack and, particularly, of the death of the soldier?
3. The Latin sentence *Dulce et decorum est pro patria mori* means "It is sweet and
   fitting to die for one's country." Owen, along with other British schoolchildren, would have learned this motto in his Latin classes. Do children
   today receive similar messages in school? Explain.

RANDALL JARRELL (1914–1965)

Gunner

> *Randall Jarrell was born in Nashville, Tennessee, and served as a navigation
> tower operator in the United States Air Force during World War II. Following
> the war, he taught at Sarah Lawrence College, Kenyon College, and the
> Women's College of the University of North Carolina. He published a novel,*
> Pictures from an Institution *(1954), as well as several volumes of poetry, in-
> cluding* Little Friend, Little Friend *(1945),* Losses *(1948), and* The Lost
> World *(1965).*

Did they send me away from my cat and my wife
To a doctor who poked me and counted my teeth,
To a line on a plain, to a stove in a tent?
Did I nod in the flies of the schools?

And the fighters rolled into the tracer like rabbits,   5
The blood froze over my splints like a scab—
Did I snore, all still and grey in the turret,
Till the palms rose out of the sea with my death?

And the world ends here, in the sand of a grave,
All my wars over? . . . It was easy as that!   10
Has my wife a pension of so many mice?
Did the medals go home to my cat?   *1955*

CONSIDERATIONS

1. All of the sentences in this piece, with the exception of one, are questions. What purpose do these questions serve, and what is the purpose of the exception?
2. Isolate the references in this piece to the natural world of insects and other creatures. What is the connection between these images and the narrator's point about war?
3. What do you make of the last two questions in this poem? How do these last two lines suggest the writer's message about war?

DENISE LEVERTOV (1923–1997)

What Were They Like?

(Questions and Answers)

> *Born and raised in England, Denise Levertov was first exposed to war during World War II, when she worked as a nurse at a British hospital in Paris. She married Mitchell Goodman, an American writer, and emigrated to the United States in 1948. Her writing career led her to serve as poet-in-residence at several universities, including the Massachusetts Institute of Technology and Tufts University. A political activist, Levertov was deeply involved in antiwar protests and the antinuclear movement. Her works include* The Sorrow Dance *(1967),* Relearning the Alphabet *(1970),* Candles in Babylon *(1982), and* Sands of the Well *(1996).*

1) Did the people of Viet Nam
   use lanterns of stone?
2) Did they hold ceremonies
   to reverence the opening of buds?
5 3) Were they inclined to rippling laughter?
4) Did they use bone and ivory,
   jade and silver, for ornament?
5) Had they an epic poem?
6) Did they distinguish between speech and singing?

10 1) Sir, their light hearts turned to stone.
   It is not remembered whether in gardens
   stone lanterns illumined pleasant ways.
2) Perhaps they gathered once to delight in blossom,
   but after the children were killed
15   there were no more buds.
3) Sir, laughter is bitter to the burned mouth.

4) A dream ago, perhaps. Ornament is for joy.
   All the bones were charred.
5) It is not remembered. Remember,
   most were peasants; their life   *20*
   was in rice and bamboo
   When peaceful clouds were reflected in the paddies
   and the water-buffalo stepped surely along terraces,
   maybe fathers told their sons old tales.
   When bombs smashed the mirrors   *25*
   there was time only to scream.
6) There is an echo yet, it is said,
   of their speech which was like a song.
   It is reported their singing resembled
   the flight of moths in moonlight.   *30*
   Who can say? It is silent now.   *1966*

CONSIDERATIONS

1. Based on the content of the first six questions, who might be asking these questions, and why?
2. Discuss the organization of the poem and the effectiveness of the dual voices. Apart from the content of their questions and comments, in what ways are the voices different?
3. Analyze the images in the answer section of this poem. Based on this rich imagery, what would you say has been lost as a result of this war? Can what is lost ever be regained? Explain.

YUSEF KOMUNYAKAA (1947–   )

Facing It

Yusef Komunyakaa was born and raised in Bogalusa, Louisiana. After high school, he joined the army and served in Vietnam, where he was awarded the Bronze Star. When he returned to the United States, he entered college and earned degrees from the University of Colorado, Colorado State University, and the University of California at Irvine. Currently he is on the faculty of Princeton's creative writing program. He has written a number of books of poetry, including Copacetic *(1984),* Dien Cai Dau *(1988), and* Neon Vernacular: New and Selected Poems *(1993), which won the 1994 Pulitzer Prize for poetry. "Facing It," which comes from* Dien Cai Dau, *is about the Vietnam Veterans Memorial in Washington, a V-shaped black granite wall on which are engraved the names of the over 58,000 Americans who died in the Vietnam War.*

My black face fades,
hiding inside the black granite.
I said I wouldn't,
dammit: No tears.
5   I'm stone. I'm flesh.
My clouded reflection eyes me
like a bird of prey, the profile of night
slanted against morning. I turn
this way—the stone lets me go.
10 I turn that way—I'm inside
the Vietnam Veterans Memorial
again, depending on the light
to make a difference.
I go down the 58,022 names,
15 half-expecting to find
my own in letters like smoke.
I touch the name Andrew Johnson;
I see the booby trap's white flash.
Names shimmer on a woman's blouse
20 but when she walks away
the names stay on the wall.
Brushstrokes flash, a red bird's
wings cutting across my stare.
The sky. A plane in the sky.
25 A white vet's image floats
closer to me, then his pale eyes
look through mine. I'm a window.
He's lost his right arm
inside the stone. In the black mirror
30 a woman's trying to erase names:
No, she's brushing a boy's hair.   *1988*

CONSIDERATIONS

1. After reading this poem a few times, explore the possible meanings of the word "It" in the title.
2. Consider the organization in this poem and note how the perspective shifts. What effect does the poet achieve by shifting perspectives, and how does this shift relate to war?
3. Analyze the use of time in this piece—the present time, the flashbacks, and the future dreams. How are different times woven together in this poem, and how does the resulting tapestry of times relate to the soldier's experience?

CAROLYN FORCHÉ (1950–   )

The Colonel

Born in Detroit, Michigan, Carolyn Forché received a bachelor's degree from Michigan State University in 1972 and a master of fine arts from Bowling Green State University in 1975. That same year, she published her first book of poetry, Gathering the Tribes, *which won the Yale Series of Younger Poets Award. For a few years, she was a visiting lecturer at various schools, and then in 1978, she traveled to Central America as a journalist and human rights advocate. One result was her second book of poetry,* The Country between Us *(1981), which became a poetry bestseller. It is the source of the poem here, which is based on her meeting with a Salvadoran colonel who did indeed empty a bag of human ears in front of her. After two years in Central America, she returned to the United States and to teaching. After an assortment of posts, she started teaching at George Mason University in Fairfax, Virginia, in 1994. In 1993, she had published an anthology of poets speaking of human rights violations around the world,* Against Forgetting: Twentieth-Century Poetry of Witness. *The next year, she published another volume of her own poems,* The Angel of History, *which won the 1994* Los Angeles Times *Book Award for poetry. The five sections of the book deal with atrocities of war in France, Japan, Germany, Beirut, and El Salvador. According to* Contemporary Authors Online, *the* Angel of History, *"a figure imagined by German philosopher and critic Walter Benjamin—can record the miseries of humanity yet is unable either to prevent these miseries from happening or [to keep] from suffering from the pain associated with them."*

What you have heard is true. I was in his house. His wife carried a tray of coffee and sugar. His daughter filed her nails, his son went out for the night. There were daily papers, pet dogs, a pistol on the cushion beside him. The moon swung bare on its black cord over the house. On the television was a cop show. It was in English. Broken bottles were embedded in the walls round the house to scoop   5
the kneecaps from a man's legs or cut his hands to lace. On the windows there were gratings like those in liquor stores. We had dinner, rack of lamb, good wine, a gold bell was on the table for calling the maid. The maid brought green mangoes, salt, a type of bread. I was asked how I enjoyed the country. There was a brief commercial in Spanish. His wife took everything away. There was some   10
talk then of how difficult it had become to govern. The parrot said hello on the terrace. The colonel told it to shut up, and pushed himself from the table. My friend said to me with his eyes: say nothing. The colonel returned with a sack used to bring groceries home. He spilled many human ears on the table. They were like dried peach halves. There is no other way to say this. He took one of   15
them in his hands, shook it in our faces, dropped it into a water glass. It came alive there. I am tired of fooling around he said. As for the rights of anyone, tell

your people they can go fuck themselves. He swept the ears to the floor with his
arm and held the last of his wine in the air. Something for your poetry, no? he
20   said. Some of the ears on the floor caught this scrap of his voice. Some of the
ears on the floor were pressed to the ground.   *1981*

CONSIDERATIONS

1. Who is the speaker in this poem, and how does the paragraph form help
   suggest the speaker's situation? What are the reasons that the speaker is visiting the colonel?
2. Focus on the description of each family member and what she or he is
   doing. How do the details reflect a culture of war?
3. The narrator says that the human ears looked like "dried peach halves" and
   then says, "There is no other way to say this." Given that there could be
   countless ways to describe what the narrator saw, why does she say "there is
   no other way"?

STEPHEN DUNN (1939–   )

On Hearing the Airlines Will Use a Psychological Profile to Catch Potential Skyjackers

> *After college, Stephen Dunn served in the Army, played professional basketball,
> thought about becoming a sports reporter, and worked in advertising before en-
> rolling in Syracuse University to study writing. Since then, he has published fif-
> teen books of poetry and, since 1974, he has been a professor of creative writing
> at Stockton State College in New Jersey. This poem comes from* Looking for
> Holes in the Ceiling *(1974). The typical speaker in his poems, says Dunn, is
> "the normal man, gone public," whose "private little efforts / to fulfill himself /
> are not unlike yours, or anyone's." In 2001, Dunn was awarded the Pulitzer
> Prize for poetry for his collection* Different Hours *(2000).*

They will catch me
as sure as the check-out girls
in every Woolworths have caught me, the badge
of my imagined theft shining in their eyes.

5   I will be approaching the ticket counter
and knowing myself, myselves,
will effect the nonchalance of a baron.
That is what they'll be looking for.

I'll say "Certainly is nice that the
airlines are taking these precautions,"   *10*
and the man behind the counter
will press a secret button,

there'll be a hand on my shoulder
(this will have happened before in a dream),
and in a back room they'll ask me   *15*
"Why were you going to do it?"

I'll say "You wouldn't believe
I just wanted to get to Cleveland?"
"No," they'll say.
So I'll tell them everything,   *20*

the plot to get the Pulitzer Prize
in exchange for the airplane,
the bomb in my pencil,
heroin in the heel of my boot.

Inevitably, it'll be downtown for booking,   *25*
newsmen pumping me for deprivation
during childhood,
the essential cause.

"There is no one cause for any human act,"
I'll tell them, thinking *finally*,   *30*
a chance to let the public in
on the themes of great literature.

And on and on, celebrating myself, offering
no resistance, assuming what they assume,
knowing, in a sense, there is no such thing   *35*
as the wrong man.   *1974*

CONSIDERATIONS

1. How would you describe the tone of this piece? What reasons might Dunn
   have had for adopting this tone?
2. What point does the speaker make by using such details as "check-out girls"
   and "Woolworths" in the opening stanza? How is the point threaded
   throughout this poem?
3. What characteristics would be important in conducting a psychological profile of a hijacker, and what is the author's point about these characteristics
   and profiling in general? To what extent do you agree/disagree with him?

GALWAY KINNELL (1927–   )

When the Towers Fell

*Born in Providence, Rhode Island, Galway Kinnell was educated at Princeton
and the University of Rochester. After serving in the navy, he studied in Europe
as a Fulbright scholar. In addition, he has traveled widely in the Middle East.
While his early poems often reflect conventional Christian religious views, his
later poems are infused with a more expansive spirituality that praises and embraces a broader, more inclusive sense of the world.*

From our high window we saw the towers
with their bands and blocks of light
brighten against a fading sunset,
saw them at any hour glitter and live
5   as if the spirits inside them sat up all night
calculating profit and loss, saw them reach up
and steep their tops in the first yellow
of sunrise, grew so used to them
often we didn't see them, and now,
10   not seeing them, we see them.

The banker is talking to London.
Humberto is delivering breakfast sandwiches.
The trader is already working the phone.
The mail sorter has started sorting the mail.

15   . . . *povres et riches*
Sages et folz, prestres et laiz
Nobles, villains, larges et chiches
Petiz et grans et beaulx et laiz . . .[1]

The plane screamed low down lower Fifth Avenue,
20   lifted at the Arch, someone said, shaking the dog walkers
in Washington Square Park, drove for the north tower,
struck with a heavy thud, released a huge bright gush
of blackened fire, and vanished, leaving a hole
the size and shape a cartoon plane might make
25   if it had passed harmlessly through and were flying away now,
on the far side, back into the realm of the imaginary.

Some with torn clothing, some bloodied,
some limping at top speed like children in a three-legged race,
some half dragged,
30   some intact in neat suits and dresses,
they walk in silence up the avenues,

all dusted to a ghostly whiteness,
all but their eyes, which are rubbed red as the eyes of a Zahoris,
who can see the dead under the ground.

Some died while calling home to say they were O.K.   35
Some died after over an hour spent learning they would die.
Some died so abruptly they may have seen death from within it.
Some broke windows and leaned out and waited for rescue.
Some were asphyxiated.
Some burned, their very faces caught fire.   40
Some fell, letting gravity speed them through their long
        moment.
Some leapt hand in hand, the elasticity in their last bits of love
        time letting—I wish I could say—their vertical streaks down
        the sky happen more lightly.   45

At the high window, where I've often stood
to escape a nightmare, I meet
the single, unblinking eye
that lights the all-night lifting
and sifting for bodies, for pieces of bodies,   50
for anything that is not nothing,
in the search that always goes on
somewhere, now in New York and Kabul.

On a street corner she holds up a picture—
of a man who is smiling. In the gray air   55
of today few pass. Sorry sorry sorry.
She startles. Suppose, down the street, that headlong lope . . .
Or over there, that hair so black it's purple . . .
And yet, suppose some evening I forgot
The fare and transfer, yet got by that way   60
Without recall,—lost yet poised in traffic.
Then I might find your eyes . . .

It could happen. Sorry sorry good luck thank you.
On this side it is "amnesia"—forgetting the way home—;
on the other, "invisibleness"—never entirely returning.   65
Hard to see clearly in the metallic mist,
or through the sheet of supposed reality
cast over our world, bourne that no creature born
pokes its way back through, and no love can tear.

The towers burn and fall, burn and fall—   70
in a distant shot, like smokestacks spewing oily earth remnants.
Schwarze Milch der Frühe wir trinken sie abends

wir trinken sie mittage und morgens wir trinken sie nachts
wir trinken und trinken[2]
75   Here is not a comparison but a corollary,
not a likeness but a common lineage
in the twentieth-century history of violent death—
black men in the South castrated and hanged from trees,
soldiers advancing in mud at 90,000 dead per mile,
80   train upon train headed eastward of boxcars shoved full to the
            corners with Jews and Gypsies to be enslaved or gassed,
state murder of twenty, thirty, forty million of its own,
atomic blasts wiping cities off the earth, fire bombings the same,
death marches, starvations, assassinations, disappearances,
85   entire countries turned into rubble, minefields, mass graves.
Seeing the towers vomit these omens, that the last century
            dumped into this one, for us to dispose of, we know
they are our futures, that is our own black milk
            crossing the sky: *wir schaufeln ein Grab in den Lüften da*
90   *liegt man nicht eng*[3]

Burst jet fuel, incinerated aluminum, steel fume, volatized
            marble, exploded granite, pulverized wallboard, berserked
            plastic, mashed concrete, gasified mercury, scoria, vapor
of the vaporized—draped over our island up to streets regimented
95   into numbers and letters,
breathed across the great bridges to Brooklyn and the waiting
            sea:
astringent, sticky, miasmic, empyreumatic,
air too foul to take in, but we take it in,
100   too gruesome for seekers of lost beloveds
to breathe, but they breathe it and you breathe it.

A photograph of a woman hangs
from his neck. He doesn't look up.
He stares down at the sidewalk of flagstone slabs
105   laid down in Whitman's century, gutter edges
iron wheels rasped long ago to a melted roundedness:
conscious mind envying the stones.
Nie stają się, są,
Nic nad to, myślalem,
110   *zbrzydziwszy sobie*
wszystko co staje się.[4]

And I sat down by the waters of the Hudson,
by the North Cove Yacht Harbor, and thought
of what those on the high floors must have suffered: knowing

they would burn alive, and then, burning alive.   *115*
Could there be a mechanism of death
so mutilating to existence, that no one
gets over it ever, not even the dead?
And then I saw before me, in steel letters welded
to the steel railing posts, Walt Whitman's words   *120*
written when America plunged into war with itself:
City of the world! . . .
Proud and passionate city—mettlesome, mad, extravagant city!
Words of a time of illusions. And then I remembered
others of his words after the war was over and Lincoln dead: *125*
I saw the debris and debris of all the slain soldiers of the war,
But I saw they were not as was thought,
They themselves were fully at rest—they suffer'd not,
The living remain'd and suffer'd, the mother suffer'd,
And the wife and the child and the musing comrade suffer'd . . .   *130*

In our minds the glassy blocks
succumb over and over into themselves,
slam down floor by floor into themselves.

They blow up as if in reverse, explode
downward and outward, billowing   *135*
through the streets, engulfing the fleeing.

Each tower as it falls concentrates
into itself, as if transforming itself
infinitely slowly into a black hole

infinitesimally small: mass   *140*
without space, where each light,
each life, put out, lies down within us.⁵   *2002*

1. . . . poor and rich
Wise and foolish, priests and laymen
Noblemen, serfs, generous and mean
Short and tall and handsome and homely.

2. Black milk of daybreak, we drink it at nightfall
We drink it at midday and at morning we drink it at night
We drink it and drink it

3. We're digging a grave in the sky,
there'll be plenty of room to lie down there.

4. They do not become, they are
Nothing but that, I thought

Now loathing within myself
Everything that becomes.

5. Quotations (The sections that are printed in italics) are from the following: "The Testament," by François Villon; "For the Marriage of Faustus and Helen," by Hart Crane; "Death Fugue," by Paul Celan; "Songs of a Wanderer," by Aleksander Wat; "City of Ships" and "When Lilacs Last in the Door-yard Bloom'd," by Walt Whitman.

CONSIDERATIONS

1. Make a timeline, recording on it what is addressed in each stanza. What conclusions can you draw when you look at this timeline and the writer's message about the tragedy that struck America on 9/11?
2. What effect does Kinnell achieve by bringing in other historical references, such as the Holocaust and the Civil War? Explore the similarities and differences between these past wars and the events that took place on 9/11.
3. Examine the tone and shifting emotions in this piece. Where is the tone most detached? Where is it most emotional? Where does it moralize? Where does it intellectualize? As a reader, which do you find most effective? Explain.

Drama

SOPHOCLES (c. 496–406 B.C.)
Antigone

For biographical information on Sophocles, see page 748.

Characters

ANTIGONE ⎫ *daughters of Oedipus*
ISMENE   ⎭
EURYDICE, *wife of Kreon*
KREON, *King of Thebes*
HAIMON, *son of Kreon*
TEIRESIAS, *a blind seer*
A SENTRY
A MESSENGER
CHORUS

Scene *Before the palace of* KREON, *King of Thebes. A central double door, and two lateral doors. A platform extends the length of the façade, and from this platform three steps lead down into the orchestra, or chorus-ground.*

Time *Dawn of the day after the repulse of the Argive° army from the assault on Thebes.*

PROLOGUE° *(*ANTIGONE *and* ISMENE *enter from the central door of the palace.)*

ANTIGONE: Ismene, dear sister,
　　　You would think that we had already suffered enough
　　　For the curse on Oedipus.°
　　　I cannot imagine any grief
　　　That you and I have not gone through. And now—　　　　　　　　5
　　　Have they told you of the new decree of our King Kreon?
ISMENE: I have heard nothing: I know
　　　That two sisters lost two brothers, a double death
　　　In a single hour; and I know that the Argive army
　　　Fled in the night; but beyond this, nothing.　　　　　　　　10
ANTIGONE: I thought so. And that is why I wanted you
　　　To come out here with me. There is something we must do.
ISMENE: Why do you speak so strangely?
ANTIGONE: Listen, Ismene:
　　　Kreon buried our brother Eteocles　　　　　　　　15
　　　With military honors, gave him a soldier's funeral,
　　　And it was right that he should; but Polyneices,
　　　Who fought as bravely and died as miserably,—
　　　They say that Kreon has sworn
　　　No one shall bury him, no one mourn for him,　　　　　　　　20
　　　But his body must lie in the fields, a sweet treasure
　　　For carrion birds to find as they search for food.
　　　That is what they say, and our good Kreon is coming here

Argive: From Argos, a Greek city. *Prologue:* Section of the play that explains the background and current action. *3 curse on Oedipus:* Ismene's and Antigone's father, Oedipus, was formerly King of Thebes. As an infant, Oedipus was ordered to be killed when an oracle predicted that he would one day kill his father and marry his mother. Rescued by a shepherd and raised by the King and Queen of Corinth, Oedipus later returns to Thebes, where, unaware, he fulfills the prophecy by killing King Laios (his father) and marrying Iocaste (his mother). When Oedipus and Iokaste discover the truth, Iocaste kills herself and Oedipus blinds himself and leaves Thebes. His sons, Eteocles and Polyneices, later kill each other in battle. Kreon, Oedipus's uncle and now King of Thebes, orders Eteocles to be buried but commands that Polyneices, who has attacked Thebes, remain unburied.

To announce it publicly; and the penalty—
Stoning to death in the public square!

25   There it is,
And now you can prove what you are:
A true sister, or a traitor to your family.

ISMENE: Antigone, you are mad! What could I possibly do?

ANTIGONE: You must decide whether you will help me or not.

30   ISMENE: I do not understand you. Help you in what?

ANTIGONE: Ismene, I am going to bury him. Will you come?

ISMENE: Bury him! You have just said the new law forbids it.

ANTIGONE: He is my brother. And he is your brother, too.

ISMENE: But think of the danger! Think what Kreon will do!

35   ANTIGONE: Kreon is not strong enough to stand in my way.

ISMENE: Ah sister!
Oedipus died, everyone hating him
For what his own search brought to light, his eyes
Ripped out by his own hand; and Iocaste died,
40   His mother and wife at once: she twisted the cords
That strangled her life; and our two brothers died,
Each killed by the other's sword. And we are left:
But oh, Antigone,
Think how much more terrible than these
45   Our own death would be if we should go against Kreon
And do what he has forbidden! We are only women,
We cannot fight with men, Antigone!
The law is strong, we must give in to the law
In this thing, and in worse. I beg the Dead
50   To forgive me, but I am helpless: I must yield
To those in authority. And I think it is dangerous business
To be always meddling.

ANTIGONE: If that is what you think,
I should not want you, even if you asked to come.
You have made your choice, you can be what you want to be.
55   But I will bury him; and if I must die,
I say that this crime is holy: I shall lie down
With him in death, and I shall be as dear
To him as he is to me.
                            It is the dead,
Not the living, who make the longest demands:
We die for ever . . .
60   You may do as you like,
Since apparently the laws of the gods mean nothing to you.

ISMENE: They mean a great deal to me; but I have no strength

To break laws that were made for the public good.
ANTIGONE: That must be your excuse, I suppose. But as for me,
    I will bury the brother I love.
ISMENE: Antigone,   65
    I am so afraid for you!
ANTIGONE: You need not be:
    You have yourself to consider, after all.
ISMENE: But no one must hear of this, you must tell no one!
    I will keep it a secret, I promise!
ANTIGONE: O tell it! Tell everyone!
    Think how they'll hate you when it all comes out   70
    If they learn that you knew about it all the time!
ISMENE: So fiery! You should be cold with fear.
ANTIGONE: Perhaps. But I am doing only what I must.
ISMENE: But can you do it? I say that you cannot.
ANTIGONE: Very well: when my strength gives out,   75
    I shall do no more.
ISMENE: Impossible things should not be tried at all.
ANTIGONE: Go away, Ismene:
    I shall be hating you soon, and the dead will too,
    For your words are hateful. Leave me my foolish plan: 80
    I am not afraid of the danger; if it means death,
    It will not be the worst of deaths—death without honor.
ISMENE: Go then, if you feel that you must.
    You are unwise,
    But a loyal friend indeed to those who love you.   85

(Exit into the palace. ANTIGONE *goes off, left. Enter the* CHORUS.*)*

PARODOS°

Strophe° 1
CHORUS: Now the long blade of the sun, lying
    Level east to west, touches with glory
    Thebes of the Seven Gates. Open, unlidded
    Eye of golden day! O marching light
    Across the eddy and rush of Dirce's stream,°   5
    Striking the white shields of the enemy
    Thrown headlong backward from the blaze of morning!
CHORAGOS:° Polyneices their commander

Parodos: Chant sung by the Chorus as they enter; *Strophe:* Chant sung by the Chorus as they move from stage right to stage left. 5 *Dirce's stream:* River near Thebes. 8 *Choragos:* Leader of the Chorus.

Roused them with windy phrases,
10 He the wild eagle screaming
Insults above our land,
His wings their shields of snow,
His crest their marshalled helms.

Antistrophe° 1
CHORUS: Against our seven gates in a yawning ring
15   The famished spears came onward in the night;
But before his jaws were sated with our blood,
Or pinefire took the garland of our towers,
He was thrown back, and as he turned, great Thebes—
No tender victim for his noisy power—
20   Rose like a dragon behind him, shouting war.
CHORAGOS: For God hates utterly
The bray of bragging tongues;
And when he beheld their smiling,
Their swagger of golden helms,
25   The frown of his thunder blasted
Their first man from our walls.

Strophe 2
CHORUS: We heard his shout of triumph high in the air
Turn to a scream; far out in a flaming arc
He fell with his windy torch, and the earth struck him.
30   And others storming in fury no less than his
Found shock of death in the dusty joy of battle.
CHORAGOS: Seven captains at seven gates
Yielded their clanging arms to the god
That bends the battle-line and breaks it.
35   These two only, brothers in blood,
Face to face in matchless rage,
Mirroring each the other's death,
Clashed in long combat.

Antistrophe 2
CHORUS: But now in the beautiful morning of victory
40   Let Thebes of the many chariots sing for joy!
With hearts for dancing we'll take leave of war:

Antistrophe: Chant sung by the Chorus as they move from stage left to stage right.

Our temples shall be sweet with hymns of praise,
And the long nights shall echo with our chorus.

SCENE 1

CHORAGOS: But now at last our new King is coming:
  Kreon of Thebes, Menoikeus' son.
  In this auspicious dawn of his reign
  What are the new complexities
  That shifting Fate has woven for him?   5
  What is his counsel? Why has he summoned
  The old men to hear him?

(Enter KREON *from the palace, center. He addresses the* CHORUS *from the top step.)*

KREON: Gentlemen: I have the honor to inform you that our Ship of State, which recent storms have threatened to destroy, has come safely to harbor at last, guided by the merciful wisdom of Heaven. I have summoned   10
you here this morning because I know that I can depend upon you: your devotion to King Laios was absolute; you never hesitated in your duty to our late ruler Oedipus; and when Oedipus died, your loyalty was transferred to his children. Unfortunately, as you know, his two sons, the princes Eteocles and Polyneices, have killed each other in battle; and I, as   15
the next in blood, have succeeded to the full power of the throne.

    I am aware, of course, that no Ruler can expect complete loyalty from his subjects until he has been tested in office. Nevertheless, I say to you at the very outset that I have nothing but contempt for the kind of Governor who is afraid, for whatever reason, to follow the course that he   20
knows is best for the State; and as for the man who sets private friendship above the public welfare,—I have no use for him, either. I call God to witness that if I saw my country headed for ruin, I should not be afraid to speak out plainly; and I need hardly remind you that I would never have any dealings with an enemy of the people. No one values friend-   25
ship more highly than I; but we must remember that friends made at the risk of wrecking our Ship are not real friends at all.

    These are my principles, at any rate, and that is why I have made the following decision concerning the sons of Oedipus: Eteocles, who died as a man should die, fighting for his country, is to be buried with full   30
military honors, with all the ceremony that is usual when the greatest heroes die; but his brother Polyneices, who broke his exile to come back with fire and sword against his native city and the shrines of his fathers' gods, whose one idea was to spill the blood of his blood and sell his own people into slavery—Polyneices, I say, is to have no burial: no man is to   35

touch him or say the least prayer for him; he shall lie on the plain, unburied; and the birds and the scavenging dogs can do with him whatever
they like.

This is my command, and you can see the wisdom behind it. As long
40 as I am King, no traitor is going to be honored with the loyal man. But
whoever shows by word and deed that he is on the side of the State,—he
shall have my respect while he is living and my reverence when he is dead.

CHORAGOS: If that is your will, Kreon son of Menoikeus,
You have the right to enforce it: we are yours.

45 KREON: That is my will. Take care that you do your part.

CHORAGOS: We are old men: let the younger ones carry it out.

KREON: I do not mean that: the sentries have been appointed.

CHORAGOS: Then what is it that you would have us do?

KREON: You will give no support to whoever breaks this law.

50 CHORAGOS: Only a crazy man is in love with death!

KREON: And death it is; yet money talks, and the wisest
Have sometimes been known to count a few coins too many.

(Enter SENTRY *from left.)*

SENTRY: I'll not say that I'm out of breath from running, King, because every
time I stopped to think about what I have to tell you, I felt like going back.
55 And all the time a voice kept saying, "You fool, don't you know you're
walking straight into trouble?"; and then another voice: "Yes, but if you let
somebody else get the news to Kreon first, it will be even worse than that
for you!" But good sense won out, at least I hope it was good sense, and
here I am with a story that makes no sense at all; but I'll tell it anyhow, be-
60 cause, as they say, what's going to happen's going to happen and—

KREON: Come to the point. What have you to say?

SENTRY: I did not do it. I did not see who did it. You must not punish me for
what someone else has done.

KREON: A comprehensive defense! More effective, perhaps,
65 If I knew its purpose. Come: what is it?

SENTRY: A dreadful thing . . . I don't know how to put it—

KREON: Out with it!

SENTRY: Well, then;
The dead man—
            Polyneices—

(Pause. The SENTRY *is overcome, fumbles for words.* KREON *waits
impassively.)*

                    out there—
                                someone,—

New dust on the slimy flesh!

(Pause. No sign from KREON.*)*

Someone has given it burial that way, and   70
Gone . . .

(Long pause. KREON *finally speaks with deadly control.)*

KREON: And the man who dared do this?
SENTRY: I swear I
   Do not know! You must believe me!
                                        Listen:
The ground was dry, not a sign of digging, no,
Not a wheeltrack in the dust, no trace of anyone.   75
It was when they relieved us this morning: and one of them,
The corporal, pointed to it.
                                        There it was,
The strangest—
                Look:
The body, just mounded over with light dust: you see?
Not buried really, but as if they'd covered it   80
Just enough for the ghost's peace. And no sign
Of dogs or any wild animal that had been there.

And then what a scene there was! Every man of us
Accusing the other: we all proved the other man did it,
We all had proof that we could not have done it.   85
We were ready to take hot iron in our hands,
Walk through fire, swear by all the gods,
It was not I!
I do not know who it was, but it was not I!

*(*KREON's *rage has been mounting steadily, but the* SENTRY *is too intent upon
his story to notice it.)*

And then, when this came to nothing, someone said   90
A thing that silenced us and made us stare
Down at the ground: you had to be told the news,
And one of us had to do it! We threw the dice,
And the bad luck fell to me. So here I am,
No happier to be here than you are to have me: 95
Nobody likes the man who brings bad news.
CHORAGOS: I have been wondering, King: can it be that the gods have done
   this?

KREON (*furiously*): Stop!
100   Must you doddering wrecks
             Go out of your heads entirely? "The gods"!
             Intolerable!
             The gods favor this corpse? Why? How had he served them?
             Tried to loot their temples, burn their images,
105   Yes, and the whole State, and its laws with it!
             Is it your senile opinion that the gods love to honor bad men?
             A pious thought!—
                              No, from the very beginning
             There have been those who have whispered together,
             Stiff-necked anarchists, putting their heads together,
110   Scheming against me in alleys. These are the men,
             And they have bribed my own guard to do this thing.
             (*Sententiously.*) Money!
             There's nothing in the world so demoralizing as money.
             Down go your cities,
115   Homes gone, men gone, honest hearts corrupted,
             Crookedness of all kinds, and all for money!
             (*To* SENTRY.)   But you—
             I swear by God and by the throne of God,
             The man who has done this thing shall pay for it!
             Find that man, bring him here to me, or your death
120   Will be the least of your problems: I'll string you up
             Alive, and there will be certain ways to make you
             Discover your employer before you die;
             And the process may teach you a lesson you seem to have missed:
             The dearest profit is sometimes all too dear:
125   That depends on the source. Do you understand me?
             A fortune won is often misfortune.
SENTRY: King, may I speak?
KREON: Your very voice distresses me.
SENTRY: Are you sure that it is my voice, and not your conscience?
KREON: By God, he wants to analyze me now!
130 SENTRY: It is not what I say, but what has been done, that hurts you.
KREON: You talk too much.
SENTRY: Maybe; but I've done nothing.
KREON: Sold your soul for some silver: that's all you've done.
SENTRY: How dreadful it is when the right judge judges wrong!
KREON: Your figures of speech
135   May entertain you now; but unless you bring me the man,
             You will get little profit from them in the end.

(Exit KREON *into the palace.)*

SENTRY: "Bring me the man"—!
       I'd like nothing better than bringing him the man!
       But bring him or not, you have seen the last of me here.
       At any rate, I am safe!   *(Exit* SENTRY.*)*

ODE° 1

Strophe 1

CHORUS: Numberless are the world's wonders, but none
       More wonderful than man; the stormgray sea
       Yields to his prows, the huge crests bear him high;
       Earth, holy and inexhaustible, is graven
       With shining furrows where his plows have gone   5
       Year after year, the timeless labor of stallions.

Antistrophe 1

       The lightboned birds and beasts that cling to cover,
       The lithe fish lighting their reaches of dim water,
       All are taken, tamed in the net of his mind;
       The lion on the hill, the wild horse windy-maned,   10
       Resign to him; and his blunt yoke has broken
       The sultry shoulders of the mountain bull.

Strophe 2

       Words also, and thought as rapid as air,
       He fashions to his good use; statecraft is his,
       And his the skill that deflects the arrows of snow,   15
       The spears of winter rain: from every wind
       He has made himself secure—from all but one:
       In the late wind of death he cannot stand.

Antistrophe 2

       O clear intelligence, force beyond all measure!
       O fate of man, working both good and evil!   20
       When the laws are kept, how proudly his city stands!
       When the laws are broken, what of his city then?
       Never may the anarchic man find rest at my hearth,
       Never be it said that my thoughts are his thoughts.

Ode: Chant sung by the Chorus.

SCENE 2

(Reenter SENTRY *leading* ANTIGONE.*)*

CHORAGOS: What does this mean? Surely this captive woman
    Is the Princess, Antigone. Why should she be taken?
SENTRY: Here is the one who did it! We caught her
    In the very act of burying him.—Where is Kreon?
CHORAGOS: Just coming from the house.

(Enter KREON, *center.)*

5   KREON: What has happened?
    Why have you come back so soon?
SENTRY *(expansively)*:   O King,
    A man should never be too sure of anything:
    I would have sworn
    That you'd not see me here again: your anger
10   Frightened me so, and the things you threatened me with;
    But how could I tell then
    That I'd be able to solve the case so soon?
    No dice-throwing this time: I was only too glad to come!
    Here is this woman. She is the guilty one:
15   We found her trying to bury him.
    Take her, then; question her; judge her as you will.
    I am through with the whole thing now, and glad of it.
KREON: But this is Antigone! Why have you brought her here?
SENTRY: She was burying him, I tell you!
KREON *(severely)*:   Is this the truth?
20   SENTRY: I saw her with my own eyes. Can I say more?
KREON: The details: come, tell me quickly!
SENTRY: It was like this:
    After those terrible threats of yours, King,
    We went back and brushed the dust away from the body.
    The flesh was soft by now, and stinking,
25   So we sat on a hill to windward and kept guard.
    No napping this time! We kept each other awake.
    But nothing happened until the white round sun
    Whirled in the center of the round sky over us:
    Then, suddenly,
30   A storm of dust roared up from the earth, and the sky
    Went out, the plain vanished with all its trees
    In the stinging dark. We closed our eyes and endured it.
    The whirlwind lasted a long time, but it passed;
    And then we looked, and there was Antigone!

I have seen   *35*
A mother bird come back to a stripped nest, heard
Her crying bitterly a broken note or two
For the young ones stolen. Just so, when this girl
Found the bare corpse, and all her love's work wasted,
She wept, and cried on heaven to damn the hands   *40*
That had done this thing.
                          And then she brought more dust
And sprinkled wine three times for her brother's ghost.

We ran and took her at once. She was not afraid,
Not even when we charged her with what she had done.
She denied nothing.
                     And this was a comfort to me,   *45*
And some uneasiness: for it is a good thing
To escape from death, but it is no great pleasure
To bring death to a friend.
                            Yet I always say
There is nothing so comfortable as your own safe skin!
KREON *(slowly, dangerously)*: And you, Antigone,   *50*
    You with your head hanging,—do you confess this thing?
ANTIGONE: I do. I deny nothing.
KREON *(to* SENTRY*)*:   You may go.

                                                        (Exit SENTRY.*)*

(To ANTIGONE.*)* Tell me, tell me briefly:
    Had you heard my proclamation touching this matter?
ANTIGONE: It was public. Could I help hearing it?   *55*
KREON: And yet you dared defy the law.
ANTIGONE: I dared.
    It was not God's proclamation. That final Justice
    That rules the world below makes no such laws.

    Your edict, King, was strong,
    But all your strength is weakness itself against   *60*
    The immortal unrecorded laws of God.
    They are not merely now: they were, and shall be,
    Operative for ever, beyond man utterly.

    I knew I must die, even without your decree:
    I am only mortal. And if I must die   *65*
    Now, before it is my time to die,
    Surely this is no hardship: can anyone
    Living, as I live, with evil all about me,

Think Death less than a friend? This death of mine
70 Is of no importance; but if I had left my brother
Lying in death unburied, I should have suffered.
Now I do not.

                  You smile at me. Ah Kreon,
Think me a fool, if you like; but it may well be
That a fool convicts me of folly.

75 CHORAGOS: Like father, like daughter: both headstrong, deaf to reason!
She has never learned to yield:
KREON: She has much to learn.
The inflexible heart breaks first, the toughest iron
Cracks first, and the wildest horses bend their necks
At the pull of the smallest curb.

                          Pride? In a slave?
80 This girl is guilty of a double insolence,
Breaking the given laws and boasting of it.
Who is the man here,
She or I, if this crime goes unpunished?
Sister's child, or more than sister's child,
85 Or closer yet in blood—she and her sister
Win bitter death for this!
(To Servants.)   Go, some of you,
Arrest Ismene. I accuse her equally.
Bring her: you will find her sniffling in the house there.

Her mind's a traitor: crimes kept in the dark
90 Cry for light, and the guardian brain shudders;
But how much worse than this
Is brazen boasting of barefaced anarchy!
ANTIGONE: Kreon, what more do you want than my death?
KREON: Nothing.
That gives me everything.
ANTIGONE: Then I beg you: kill me.
95 This talking is a great weariness: your words
Are distasteful to me, and I am sure that mine
Seem so to you. And yet they should not seem so:
I should have praise and honor for what I have done.
All these men here would praise me
100 Were their lips not frozen shut with fear of you.
(Bitterly.) Ah the good fortune of kings,
Licensed to say and do whatever they please!
KREON: You are alone here in that opinion.
ANTIGONE: No, they are with me. But they keep their tongues in leash.

KREON: Maybe. But you are guilty, and they are not.   *105*
ANTIGONE: There is no guilt in reverence for the dead.
KREON: But Eteocles—was he not your brother too?
ANTIGONE: My brother too.
KREON: And you insult his memory?
ANTIGONE *(softly)*: The dead man would not say that I insult it.
KREON: He would: for you honor a traitor as much as him.   *110*
ANTIGONE: His own brother, traitor or not, and equal in blood.
KREON: He made war on his country. Eteocles defended it.
ANTIGONE: Nevertheless, there are honors due all the dead.
KREON: But not the same for the wicked as for the just.
ANTIGONE: Ah Kreon, Kreon,   *115*
     Which of us can say what the gods hold wicked?
KREON: An enemy is an enemy, even dead.
ANTIGONE: It is my nature to join in love, not hate.
KREON *(finally losing patience)*: Go join them then; if you must have
          your love,
     Find it in hell!   *120*
CHORAGOS: But see, Ismene comes:

     (Enter ISMENE, *guarded.)*

     Those tears are sisterly, the cloud
     That shadows her eyes rains down gentle sorrow.
KREON: You too, Ismene,
     Snake in my ordered house, sucking my blood   *125*
     Stealthily—and all the time I never knew
     That these two sisters were aiming at my throne!
                                             Ismene,
     Do you confess your share in this crime, or deny it?
     Answer me.
ISMENE: Yes, if she will let me say so. I am guilty.   *130*
ANTIGONE: *(coldly)*: No, Ismene. You have no right to say so.
     You would not help me, and I will not have you help me.
ISMENE: But now I know what you meant: and I am here
     To join you, to take my share of punishment.
ANTIGONE: The dead man and the gods who rule the dead   *135*
     Know whose act this was. Words are not friends.
ISMENE: Do you refuse me, Antigone? I want to die with you:
     I too have a duty that I must discharge to the dead.
ANTIGONE: You shall not lessen my death by sharing it.
ISMENE: What do I care for life when you are dead?   *140*
ANTIGONE: Ask Kreon. You're always hanging on his opinions.
ISMENE: You are laughing at me. Why, Antigone?

ANTIGONE: It's a joyless laughter, Ismene.

ISMENE: But can I do nothing?

ANTIGONE: Yes. Save yourself. I shall not envy you.

145   There are those who will praise you; I shall have honor, too.

ISMENE: But we are equally guilty!

ANTIGONE: No more, Ismene.
        You are alive, but I belong to Death.

KREON *(to the* CHORUS*)*: Gentlemen, I beg you to observe these girls:
        One has just now lost her mind; the other,

150   It seems, has never had a mind at all.

ISMENE: Grief teaches the steadiest minds to waver, King.

KREON: Yours certainly did, when you assumed guilt with the guilty!

ISMENE: But how could I go on living without her?

KREON: You are.
        She is already dead.

ISMENE: But your own son's bride!

155   KREON: There are places enough for him to push his plow.
        I want no wicked women for my sons!

ISMENE: O dearest Haimon, how your father wrongs you!

KREON: I've had enough of your childish talk of marriage!

CHORAGOS: Do you really intend to steal this girl from your son?

KREON: No; Death will do that for me.

160   CHORAGOS: Then she must die?

KREON *(ironically)*: You dazzle me.
                              —But enough of this talk!
        (To Guards.) You, there, take them away and guard them well:
        For they are but women, and even brave men run
        When they see Death coming.
                              (Exeunt° ISMENE, ANTIGONE, *and Guards.)*

ODE 2

Strophe 1

CHORUS: Fortunate is the man who has never tasted God's vengeance!
        Where once the anger of heaven has struck, that house is shaken
        For ever: damnation rises behind each child
        Like a wave cresting out of the black northeast,

5   When the long darkness under sea roars up
        And bursts drumming death upon the windwhipped sand.

Antistrophe 1

        I have seen this gathering sorrow from time long past

Exeunt: Latin for "they exit."

Loom upon Oedipus' children: generation from generation
Takes the compulsive rage of the enemy god.
So lately this last flower of Oedipus' line   *10*
Drank the sunlight! but now a passionate word
And a handful of dust have closed up all its beauty.

Strophe 2

What mortal arrogance
Transcends the wrath of Zeus?
Sleep cannot lull him nor the effortless long months   *15*
Of the timeless gods: but he is young for ever,
And his house is the shining day of high Olympos.
All that is and shall be,
And all the past, is his.
No pride on earth is free of the curse of heaven.   *20*

Antistrophe 2

The straying dreams of men
May bring them ghosts of joy:
But as they drowse, the waking embers burn them;
Or they walk with fixed eyes, as blind men walk.
But the ancient wisdom speaks for our own time: *25*
Fate works most for woe
With Folly's fairest show.
Man's little pleasure is the spring of sorrow.

SCENE 3

CHORAGOS: But here is Haimon, King, the last of all your sons.
    Is it grief for Antigone that brings him here,
    And bitterness at being robbed of his bride?

(Enter HAIMON.*)*

KREON: We shall soon see, and no need of diviners.
                                        —Son,
    You have heard my final judgment on that girl: *5*
    Have you come here hating me, or have you come
    With deference and with love, whatever I do?
HAIMON: I am your son, father. You are my guide.
    You make things clear for me, and I obey you.
    No marriage means more to me than your continuing wisdom.   *10*
KREON: Good. That is the way to behave: subordinate
    Everything else, my son, to your father's will.

This is what a man prays for, that he may get
Sons attentive and dutiful in his house,
15   Each one hating his father's enemies,
Honoring his father's friends. But if his sons
Fail him, if they turn out unprofitably,
What has he fathered but trouble for himself
And amusement for the malicious?
                                        So you are right
20   Not to lose your head over this woman.
Your pleasure with her would soon grow cold, Haimon,
And then you'd have a hellcat in bed and elsewhere.
Let her find her husband in Hell!
Of all the people in this city, only she
25   Has had contempt for my law and broken it.

Do you want me to show myself weak before the people?
Or to break my sworn word? No, and I will not.
The woman dies.
I suppose she'll plead "family ties." Well, let her.
30   If I permit my own family to rebel,
How shall I earn the world's obedience?
Show me the man who keeps his house in hand,
He's fit for public authority.
                                    I'll have no dealings
With lawbreakers, critics of the government:
35   Whoever is chosen to govern should be obeyed—
Must be obeyed, in all things, great and small,
Just and unjust! O Haimon,
The man who knows how to obey, and that man only,
Knows how to give commands when the time comes.
40   You can depend on him, no matter how fast
The spears come: he's a good soldier, he'll stick it out.
Anarchy, anarchy! Show me a greater evil!
This is why cities tumble and the great houses rain down,
This is what scatters armies!
45   No, no: good lives are made so by discipline.
We keep the laws then, and the lawmakers,
And no woman shall seduce us. If we must lose,
Let's lose to a man, at least! Is a woman stronger than we?
CHORAGOS: Unless time has rusted my wits,
50   What you say, King, is said with point and dignity.
HAIMON *(boyishly earnest)*: Father:
Reason is God's crowning gift to man, and you are right

To warn me against losing mine. I cannot say—
I hope that I shall never want to say!—that you
Have reasoned badly. Yet there are other men   *55*
Who can reason, too; and their opinions might be helpful.
You are not in a position to know everything
That people say or do, or what they feel:
Your temper terrifies—everyone
Will tell you only what you like to hear.   *60*
But I, at any rate, can listen; and I have heard them
Muttering and whispering in the dark about this girl.
They say no woman has ever, so unreasonably,
Died so shameful a death for a generous act:
"She covered her brother's body. Is this indecent?   *65*
She kept him from dogs and vultures. Is this a crime?
Death?—She should have all the honor that we can give her!"

This is the way they talk out there in the city.

You must believe me:
Nothing is closer to me than your happiness.   *70*
What could be closer? Must not any son
Value his father's fortune as his father does his?
I beg you, do not be unchangeable:
Do not believe that you alone can be right.
The man who thinks that,   *75*
The man who maintains that only he has the power
To reason correctly, the gift to speak, the soul—
A man like that, when you know him, turns out empty.
It is not reason never to yield to reason!

In flood time you can see how some trees bend,   *80*
And because they bend, even their twigs are safe,
While stubborn trees are torn up, roots and all.
And the same thing happens in sailing:
Make your sheet fast, never slacken,—and over you go,
Head over heels and under: and there's your voyage.   *85*
Forget you are angry! Let yourself be moved!
I know I am young; but please let me say this:
The ideal condition
Would be, I admit, that men should be right by instinct;
But since we are all too likely to go astray,   *90*
The reasonable thing is to learn from those who can teach.
CHORAGOS: You will do well to listen to him, King,

          If what he says is sensible. And you, Haimon,
          Must listen to your father.—Both speak well.

95   KREON: You consider it right for a man of my years and experience
          To go to school to a boy?
    HAIMON: It is not right
          If I am wrong. But if I am young, and right,
          What does my age matter?
    KREON: You think it is right to stand up for an anarchist?

100   HAIMON: Not at all. I pay no respect to criminals.
    KREON: Then she is not a criminal?
    HAIMON: The City would deny it, to a man.
    KREON: And the City proposes to teach me how to rule?
    HAIMON: Ah. Who is it that's talking like a boy now?

105   KREON: My voice is the one voice giving orders in this City!
    HAIMON: It is no City if it takes orders from one voice.
    KREON: The State is the King!
    HAIMON: Yes, if the State is a desert.

      (Pause.)

    KREON: This boy, it seems, has sold out to a woman.
    HAIMON: If you are a woman: my concern is only for you.

110   KREON: So? Your "concern"! In a public brawl with your father!
    HAIMON: How about you, in a public brawl with justice?
    KREON: With justice, when all that I do is within my rights?
    HAIMON: You have no right to trample on God's right.
    KREON *(completely out of control)*: Fool, adolescent fool! Taken in by a woman!

115   HAIMON: You'll never see me taken in by anything vile.
    KREON: Every word you say is for her!
    HAIMON *(quietly, darkly)*:   And for you.
          And for me. And for the gods under the earth.
    KREON: You'll never marry her while she lives.
    HAIMON: Then she must die.—But her death will cause another.

120   KREON: Another?
          Have you lost your senses? Is this an open threat?
    HAIMON: There is no threat in speaking to emptiness.
    KREON: I swear you'll regret this superior tone of yours!
          You are the empty one!
    HAIMON: If you were not my father,

125   I'd say you were perverse.
    KREON: You girl-struck fool, don't play at words with me!
    HAIMON: I am sorry. You prefer silence.
    KREON: Now, by God—
          I swear, by all the gods in heaven above us,

You'll watch it, I swear you shall!
    (To the Servants.)   Bring her out!
    Bring the woman out! Let her die before his eyes!   *130*
    Here, this instant, with her bridegroom beside her!
HAIMON: Not here, no; she will not die here, King.
    And you will never see my face again.
    Go on raving as long as you've a friend to endure you.

                                                (Exit HAIMON.*)*

CHORAGOS: Gone, gone.   *135*
    Kreon, a young man in a rage is dangerous!
KREON: Let him do, or dream to do, more than a man can.
    He shall not save these girls from death.
CHORAGOS: These girls?
    You have sentenced them both?
KREON: No, you are right.
    I will not kill the one whose hands are clean.   *140*
CHORAGOS: But Antigone?
KREON *(somberly)*:   I will carry her far away
    Out there in the wilderness, and lock her
    Living in a vault of stone. She shall have food,
    As the custom is, to absolve the State of her death.
    And there let her pray to the gods of hell: *145*
    They are her only gods:
    Perhaps they will show her an escape from death,
    Or she may learn,
                    though late,
    That piety shown the dead is pity in vain.

                                                (Exit KREON.*)*

ODE 3

Strophe
CHORUS: Love, unconquerable
    Waster of rich men, keeper
    Of warm lights and all-night vigil
    In the soft face of a girl:
    Sea-wanderer, forest-visitor!   *5*
    Even the pure Immortals cannot escape you,
    And mortal man, in his one day's dusk,
    Trembles before your glory.

Antistrophe
    Surely you swerve upon ruin

10   The just man's consenting heart,
     As here you have made bright anger
     Strike between father and son—
     And none has conquered but Love!
     A girl's glance working the will of heaven:
15   Pleasure to her alone who mocks us,
     Merciless Aphrodite.°

SCENE 4

CHORAGOS (as ANTIGONE enters guarded): But I can no longer stand in awe
          of this,
     Nor, seeing what I see, keep back my tears.
     Here is Antigone, passing to that chamber
     Where all find sleep at last.

Strophe 1

5   ANTIGONE: Look upon me, friends, and pity me
     Turning back at the night's edge to say
     Good-by to the sun that shines for me no longer;
     Now sleepy Death
     Summons me down to Acheron,° that cold shore:
10   There is no bridesong there, nor any music.
     CHORUS: Yet not unpraised, not without a kind of honor,
     You walk at last into the underworld;
     Untouched by sickness, broken by no sword.
     What woman has ever found your way to death?

Antistrophe 1

15   ANTIGONE: How often I have heard the story of Niobe,°
     Tantalos' wretched daughter, how the stone
     Clung fast about her, ivy-close: and they say
     The rain falls endlessly
     And sifting soft snow; her tears are never done.
20   I feel the loneliness of her death in mine.
     CHORUS: But she was born of heaven, and you
     Are woman, woman-born. If her death is yours,
     A mortal woman's, is this not for you

16 *Aphrodite:* Goddess of beauty and love. 9 *Acheron:* River in the underworld, the domain of the
dead. 15 *Niobe:* Mythological figure whose children were killed as punishment for her boastful-
ness. She was turned into a stone, and her tears became rushing streams that coursed down the
mountainside.

Glory in our world and in the world beyond?

Strophe 2

ANTIGONE: You laugh at me. Ah, friends, friends,   *25*
    Can you not wait until I am dead? O Thebes,
    O men many-charioted, in love with Fortune,
    Dear springs of Dirce, sacred Theban grove,
    Be witnesses for me, denied all pity,
    Unjustly judged! and think a word of love   *30*
    For her whose path turns
    Under dark earth, where there are no more tears.
CHORUS: You have passed beyond human daring and come at last
    Into a place of stone where Justice sits.
    I cannot tell   *35*
    What shape of your father's guilt appears in this.

Antistrophe 2

ANTIGONE: You have touched it at last: that bridal bed
    Unspeakable, horror of son and mother mingling:
    Their crime, infection of all our family!
    O Oedipus, father and brother!   *40*
    Your marriage strikes from the grave to murder mine.
    I have been a stranger here in my own land:
    All my life
    The blasphemy of my birth has followed me.
CHORUS: Reverence is a virtue, but strength   *45*
    Lives in established law: that must prevail.
    You have made your choice,
    Your death is the doing of your conscious hand.

Epode°

ANTIGONE: Then let me go, since all your words are bitter,
    And the very light of the sun is cold to me.   *50*
    Lead me to my vigil, where I must have
    Neither love nor lamentation; no song, but silence.

    (KREON interrupts impatiently.)

KREON: If dirges and planned lamentations could put off death,
    Men would be singing for ever.

Epode: Chant sung by the Chorus following the strophe and antistrophe.

(To the Servants.)   Take her, go!

55   You know your orders: take her to the vault
And leave her alone there. And if she lives or dies,
That's her affair, not ours: our hands are clean.

ANTIGONE: O tomb, vaulted bride-bed in eternal rock,
Soon I shall be with my own again

60   Where Persephone° welcomes the thin ghosts underground:
And I shall see my father again, and you, mother,
And dearest Polyneices—
                    dearest indeed
To me, since it was my hand
That washed him clean and poured the ritual wine:

65   And my reward is death before my time!

And yet, as men's hearts know, I have done no wrong,
I have not sinned before God. Or if I have,
I shall know the truth in death. But if the guilt
Lies upon Kreon who judged me, then, I pray,
May his punishment equal my own.

70   CHORAGOS: O passionate heart,
Unyielding, tormented still by the same winds!

KREON: Her guards shall have good cause to regret their delaying.

ANTIGONE: Ah! That voice is like the voice of death!

KREON: I can give you no reason to think you are mistaken.

75   ANTIGONE: Thebes, and you my fathers' gods,
And rulers of Thebes, you see me now, the last
Unhappy daughter of a line of kings,
Your kings, led away to death. You will remember
What things I suffer, and at what men's hands,

80   Because I would not transgress the laws of heaven.
(To the Guards, simply.) Come: let us wait no longer.
                    (Exit ANTIGONE, *left, guarded.)*

ODE 4

Strophe 1

CHORUS: All Danae's° beauty was locked away
In a brazen cell where the sunlight could not come:

---

60 *Persephone:* Kidnapped by Pluto, god of the underworld, to be his wife and queen. 1 *Danae:*
She was hidden away because of a prophecy that she would bear a son who would kill her father.
In spite of this precaution, she became pregnant when Zeus came to her in a shower of gold.
Her son later killed her father.

A small room still as any grave, enclosed her.
Yet she was a princess too,
And Zeus in a rain of gold poured love upon her.   *5*
O child, child,
No power in wealth or war
Or tough sea-blackened ships
Can prevail against untiring Destiny!

Antistrophe 1

And Dryas' son° also, that furious king,   *10*
Bore the god's prisoning anger for his pride:
Sealed up by Dionysos in deaf stone,
His madness died among echoes.
So at the last he learned what dreadful power
His tongue had mocked: *15*
For he had profaned the revels,
And fired the wrath of the nine
Implacable Sisters° that love the sound of the flute.

Strophe 2

And old men tell a half-remembered tale
Of horror where a dark ledge splits the sea   *20*
And a double surf beats on the gray shores:
How a king's new woman,° sick
With hatred for the queen he had imprisoned,
Ripped out his two sons' eyes with her bloody hands
While grinning Ares° watched the shuttle plunge   *25*
Four times: four blind wounds crying for revenge.

Antistrophe 2

Crying, tears and blood mingled.—Piteously born,
Those sons whose mother was of heavenly birth!
Her father was the god of the North Wind
And she was cradled by gales,   *30*
She raced with young colts on the glittering hills
And walked untrammeled in the open light:

---

10 *Dryas' son:* King Lycurgas of Thrace, who had been made insane by the god of wine and revelry, Dionysos.   18 *Implacable Sisters:* The muses.   22 *king's new woman:* Eidothea, the second wife of King Phineas, who blinded his sons after he had imprisoned their mother, Cleopatra, in a cave. 25 *Ares:* God of war.

But in her marriage deathless Fate found means
To build a tomb like yours for all her joy.

SCENE 5

(Enter blind TEIRESIAS, *led by a boy. The opening speeches of* TEIRESIAS *should be in singsong contrast to the realistic lines of* KREON.)

TEIRESIAS: This is the way the blind man comes, Princes, Princes,
    Lockstep, two heads lit by the eyes of one.
KREON: What new thing have you to tell us, old Teiresias?
TEIRESIAS: I have much to tell you: listen to the prophet, Kreon.
5   KREON: I am not aware that I have ever failed to listen.
TEIRESIAS: Then you have done wisely, King, and ruled well.
KREON: I admit my debt to you. But what have you to say?
TEIRESIAS: This, Kreon: you stand once more on the edge of fate.
KREON: What do you mean? Your words are a kind of dread.
10   TEIRESIAS: Listen, Kreon:
    I was sitting in my chair of augury, at the place
    Where the birds gather about me. They were all a-chatter,
    As is their habit, when suddenly I heard
    A strange note in their jangling, a scream, a
15   Whirring fury; I knew that they were fighting,
    Tearing each other, dying
    In a whirlwind of wings clashing. And I was afraid.
    I began the rites of burnt-offering at the altar,
    But Hephaistos° failed me: instead of bright flame,
20   There was only the sputtering slime of the fat thigh-flesh
    Melting: the entrails dissolved in gray smoke,
    The bare bone burst from the welter. And no blaze!
    This was a sign from heaven. My boy described it,
    Seeing for me as I see for others.
25   I tell you, Kreon, you yourself have brought
    This new calamity upon us. Our hearths and altars
    Are stained with the corruption of dogs and carrion birds
    That glut themselves on the corpse of Oedipus' son.
    The gods are deaf when we pray to them, their fire
30   Recoils from our offering, their birds of omen
    Have no cry of comfort, for they are gorged
    With the thick blood of the dead.
                      O my son,
    These are no trifles! Think: all men make mistakes,
    But a good man yields when he knows his course is wrong,

19 *Hephaistos:* God of fire.

And repairs the evil. The only crime is pride.   *35*

Give in to the dead man, then: do not fight with a corpse—
What glory is it to kill a man who is dead?
Think, I beg you:
It is for your own good that I speak as I do.
You should be able to yield for your own good.   *40*
KREON: It seems that prophets have made me their especial province.
     All my life long
     I have been a kind of butt for the dull arrows
     Of doddering fortune-tellers!
                              No, Teiresias:
     If your birds—if the great eagles of God himself   *45*
     Should carry him stinking bit by bit to heaven,
     I would not yield. I am not afraid of pollution:
     No man can defile the gods.
                              Do what you will,
     Go into business, make money, speculate
     In India gold or that synthetic gold from Sardis,   *50*
     Get rich otherwise than by my consent to bury him.
     Teiresias, it is a sorry thing when a wise man
     Sells his wisdom, lets out his words for hire!
TEIRESIAS: Ah Kreon! Is there no man left in the world—
KREON: To do what?—Come, let's have the aphorism!   *55*
TEIRESIAS: No man who knows that wisdom outweighs any wealth?
KREON: As surely as bribes are baser than any baseness.
TEIRESIAS: You are sick, Kreon! You are deathly sick!
KREON: As you say: it is not my place to challenge a prophet.
TEIRESIAS: Yet you have said my prophecy is for sale.   *60*
KREON: The generation of prophets has always loved gold.
TEIRESIAS: The generation of kings has always loved brass.
KREON: You forget yourself! You are speaking to your King.
TEIRESIAS: I know it. You are a king because of me.
KREON: You have a certain skill; but you have sold out.   *65*
TEIRESIAS: King, you will drive me to words that—
KREON: Say them, say them!
     Only remember: I will not pay you for them.
TEIRESIAS: No, you will find them too costly.
KREON: No doubt. Speak:
     Whatever you say, you will not change my will.
TEIRESIAS: Then take this, and take it to heart!   *70*
     The time is not far off when you shall pay back
     Corpse for corpse, flesh of your own flesh.
     You have thrust the child of this world into living night,

You have kept from the gods below the child that is theirs:
75   The one in a grave before her death, the other,
Dead, denied the grave. This is your crime:
And the Furies° and the dark gods of Hell
Are swift with terrible punishment for you.

Do you want to buy me now, Kreon?

                                    Not many days,
80   And your house will be full of men and women weeping,
And curses will be hurled at you from far
Cities grieving for sons unburied, left to rot
Before the walls of Thebes.

These are my arrows, Kreon: they are all for you.

85   (To Boy.) But come, child: lead me home.
Let him waste his fine anger upon younger men.
Maybe he will learn at last
To control a wiser tongue in a better head.
                                    (Exit TEIRESIAS.)
CHORAGOS: The old man has gone, King, but his words
90   Remain to plague us. I am old, too,
But I cannot remember that he was ever false.
KREON: That is true.... It troubles me.
Oh it is hard to give in! but it is worse
To risk everything for stubborn pride.
CHORAGOS: Kreon: take my advice.
95   KREON: What shall I do?
CHORAGOS: Go quickly: free Antigone from her vault
And build a tomb for the body of Polyneices.
KREON: You would have me do this!
CHORAGOS: Kreon, yes!
And it must be done at once: God moves
100   Swiftly to cancel the folly of stubborn men.
KREON: It is hard to deny the heart! But I
Will do it: I will not fight with destiny.
CHORAGOS: You must go yourself, you cannot leave it to others.
KREON: I will go.
            —Bring axes, servants:

---

77 *Furies:* Supernatural beings called upon to avenge crimes, especially those against relatives.

Come with me to the tomb. I buried her, I   *105*
Will set her free.
                    Oh, quickly!
My mind misgives—
The laws of the gods are mighty, and a man must serve them
To the last day of his life!   *(Exit* KREON.*)*

PAEAN°

Strophe 1
CHORAGOS: God of many names
CHORUS: O Iacchos°
                                                    son
    of Kadmeian Semele°
                        O born of the Thunder!
    Guardian of the West
                        Regent
    of Eleusis' plain
                    O Prince of maenad° Thebes
    and the Dragon Field by rippling Ismenos:°   *5*

Antistrophe 1
CHORAGOS: God of many names
CHORUS: the flame of torches
        flares on our hills
                        the nymphs of Iacchos
        dance at the spring of Castalia:°
        from the vine-close mountain
                                come ah come in ivy:
        Evohe evohe!° sings through the streets of Thebes.   *10*

Strophe 2
CHORAGOS: God of many names
CHORUS: Iacchos of Thebes
        heavenly Child
                    of Semele bride of the Thunderer!
        The shadow of plague is upon us:

Paean: A prayer, hymn, or song of praise. 1 *Iacchos:* Bacchos or Dionysos, god of wine. 2 *Semele:* Iacchos's mother; consort of Zeus. 4 *maenad:* Woman who worshipped Iacchos. 5 *Ismenos:* River near Thebes, where dragon's teeth were planted and the original residents of Thebes sprang forth. 8 *Castalia:* Spring on Mount Parnassus, used by priestesses of Dionysos in purification rites. 10 *Evohe evohe!:* "Come forth, come forth!" The maenads' call to Dionysos.

come

with clement feet

oh come from Parnasos

down the long slopes

15   across the lamenting water

Antistrophe 2

CHORAGOS: Io° Fire! Chorister of the throbbing stars!
    O purest among the voices of the night!
    Thou son of God, blaze for us!
CHORUS: Come with choric rapture of circling Maenads
    Who cry *Io Iacche!*
20   *God of many names!*

EXODOS°

(Enter MESSENGER *from left.)*

MESSENGER: Men of the line of Kadmos,° you who live
    Near Amphion's citadel,°
                    I cannot say
    Of any condition of human life "This is fixed,
    This is clearly good, or bad." Fate raises up,
5   And Fate casts down the happy and unhappy alike:
    No man can foretell his Fate.
                    Take the case of Kreon:
    Kreon was happy once, as I count happiness:
    Victorious in battle, sole governor of the land,
    Fortunate father of children nobly born.
10   And now it has all gone from him! Who can say
    That a man is still alive when his life's joy fails?
    He is a walking dead man. Grant him rich,
    Let him live like a king in his great house:
    If his pleasure is gone, I would not give
15   So much as the shadow of smoke for all he owns.
CHORAGOS: Your words hint at sorrow: what is your news for us?
MESSENGER: They are dead. The living are guilty of their death.
CHORAGOS: Who is guilty? Who is dead? Speak!
MESSENGER: Haimon.
    Haimon is dead; and the hand that killed him

---

16 *Io:* "Hail!" *Exodos:* Concluding scene. 1 *Kadmos:* Planted dragon's teeth from which grew
the founders of Thebes. 2 *Amphion's citadel:* Thebes.

Is his own hand.

CHORAGOS: His father's? or his own?   20

MESSENGER: His own, driven mad by the murder his father had done.

CHORAGOS: Teiresias, Teiresias, how clearly you saw it all!

MESSENGER: This is my news: you must draw what conclusions you can
    from it.

CHORAGOS: But look: Eurydice, our Queen:
    Has she overheard us?   25

(Enter EURYDICE *from the palace, center.)*

EURYDICE: I have heard something, friends:
    As I was unlocking the gate of Pallas'° shrine,
    For I needed her help today, I heard a voice
    Telling of some new sorrow. And I fainted
    There at the temple with all my maidens about me.   30
    But speak again: whatever it is, I can bear it:
    Grief and I are no strangers.

MESSENGER: Dearest Lady,
    I will tell you plainly all that I have seen.
    I shall not try to comfort you: what is the use,
    Since comfort could lie only in what is not true?   35
    The truth is always best.

                I went with Kreon
    To the outer plain where Polyneices was lying,
    No friend to pity him, his body shredded by dogs.
    We made our prayers in that place to Hecate
    And Pluto,° that they would be merciful. And we bathed   40
    The corpse with holy water, and we brought
    Fresh-broken branches to burn what was left of it,
    And upon the urn we heaped up a towering barrow
    Of the earth of his own land.
                When we were done, we ran
    To the vault where Antigone lay on her couch of stone.   45
    One of the servants had gone ahead,
    And while he was yet far off he heard a voice
    Grieving within the chamber, and he came back
    And told Kreon. And as the King went closer,
    The air was full of wailing, the words lost,   50
    And he begged us to make all haste. "Am I a prophet?"
    He said, weeping, "And must I walk this road,

---

27 *Pallas:* Pallas Athene, goddess of wisdom. 39–40 *Hecate and Pluto:* Goddess of witchcraft and
sorcery and King of Hades, the underworld, realm of the dead.

The saddest of all that I have gone before?
My son's voice calls me on. Oh quickly, quickly!
55   Look through the crevice there, and tell me
If it is Haimon, or some deception of the gods!"

We obeyed; and in the cavern's farthest corner
We saw her lying:
She had made a noose of her fine linen veil
60   And hanged herself. Haimon lay beside her,
His arms about her waist, lamenting her,
His love lost under ground, crying out
That his father had stolen her away from him.

When Kreon saw him the tears rushed to his eyes
65   And he called to him: "What have you done, child? speak to me.
What are you thinking that makes your eyes so strange?
O my son, my son, I come to you on my knees!"
But Haimon spat in his face. He said not a word,
Staring—
    And suddenly drew his sword
70   And lunged. Kreon shrank back, the blade missed; and the boy,
Desperate against himself, drove it half its length
Into his own side, and fell. And as he died
He gathered Antigone close in his arms again,
Choking, his blood bright red on her white cheek.
75   And now he lies dead with the dead, and she is his
At last, his bride in the house of the dead.
                                    (*Exit* EURYDICE *into the palace.*)
CHORAGOS: She has left us without a word. What can this mean?
MESSENGER: It troubles me, too; yet she knows what is best,
Her grief is too great for public lamentation,
80   And doubtless she has gone to her chamber to weep
For her dead son, leading her maidens in his dirge.

(*Pause*)

CHORAGOS: It may be so: but I fear this deep silence.
MESSENGER: I will see what she is doing. I will go in.
                                    (*Exit* MESSENGER *into the palace.*)

(*Enter* KREON *with attendants, bearing* HAIMON's *body.*)

CHORAGOS: But here is the king himself: oh look at him,
85   Bearing his own damnation in his arms.
KREON: Nothing you say can touch me any more.
My own blind heart has brought me

From darkness to final darkness. Here you see
The father murdering, the murdered son—
And all my civic wisdom!   *90*

Haimon my son, so young, so young to die,
I was the fool, not you; and you died for me.
CHORAGOS: That is the truth; but you were late in learning it.
KREON: This truth is hard to bear. Surely a god
     Has crushed me beneath the hugest weight of heaven,   *95*
     And driven me headlong a barbaric way
     To trample out the thing I held most dear.

The pains that men will take to come to pain!

(Enter MESSENGER *from the palace.)*

MESSENGER: The burden you carry in your hands is heavy,
     But it is not all: you will find more in your house.   *100*
KREON: What burden worse than this shall I find there?
MESSENGER: The Queen is dead.
KREON: O port of death, deaf world,
     Is there no pity for me? And you, Angel of evil,
     I was dead, and your words are death again.   *105*
     Is it true, boy? Can it be true?
     Is my wife dead? Has death bred death?
MESSENGER: You can see for yourself.

(The doors are opened and the body of EURYDICE *is disclosed within.)*

KREON: Oh pity!
     All true, all true, and more than I can bear!   *110*
     O my wife, my son!
MESSENGER: She stood before the altar, and her heart
     Welcomed the knife her own hand guided,
     And a great cry burst from her lips for Megareus° dead,
     And for Haimon dead, her sons; and her last breath   *115*
     Was a curse for their father, the murderer of her sons.
     And she fell, and the dark flowed in through her closing eyes.
KREON: O God, I am sick with fear.
     Are there no swords here? Has no one a blow for me?
MESSENGER: Her curse is upon you for the deaths of both.   *120*
KREON: It is right that it should be. I alone am guilty.
     I know it, and I say it. Lead me in,

114 *Megareus:* Haimon's brother, son of Kreon. He believed his death would save Thebes and so
sacrificed himself in the unsuccessful attack on the city.

Quickly, friends.
I have neither life nor substance. Lead me in.

125 CHORAGOS: You are right, if there can be right in so much wrong.
The briefest way is best in a world of sorrow.
KREON: Let it come,
Let death come quickly, and be kind to me.
I would not ever see the sun again.

130 CHORAGOS: All that will come when it will; but we, meanwhile,
Have much to do. Leave the future to itself.
KREON: All my heart was in that prayer!
CHORAGOS: Then do not pray any more: the sky is deaf.
KREON: Lead me away. I have been rash and foolish.

135 I have killed my son and my wife.
I look for comfort; my comfort lies here dead.
Whatever my hands have touched has come to nothing.
Fate has brought all my pride to a thought of dust.

(As KREON *is being led into the house, the* CHORAGOS *advances and speaks
directly to the audience.*)

CHORAGOS: There is no happiness where there is no wisdom;

140 No wisdom but in submission to the gods.
Big words are always punished,
And proud men in old age learn to be wise.   *441 B.C.*

CONSIDERATIONS

1. Summarize briefly the sections of the play, identifying significant action, conflict, and character development.
2. Explain the problem Antigone faces. How do her beliefs and values conflict with Kreon's? What arguments can you make for and against each character's position?
3. Sophocles entitled this play *Antigone,* and yet much of the action focuses on Kreon and his conflicts with his advisors and with his son Haimon. How do these conflicts relate to his struggle with Antigone?
4. From reading the opening dialogue between Ismene and Antigone, what inferences can you make about their relationship, about the character and value of each woman, and about the role of women in ancient Greece?
5. Choose a scene you find particularly significant, and describe the way you would stage it if you were directing the play. Consider the way the actors might move on the stage, where they will sit or stand, and what facial expressions and gestures you'll have them use. Feel free to use modern technology as you envision lighting, scenery, props, and costumes.

More Resources on
Sophocles

In *ARIEL*

- Brief biography of Sophocles
- Excerpt from *Oedipus Rex,* with hyperlinked comments
- Video clip on theater in ancient Greece
- Analysis of Greek tragedy
- Bibliography of scholarly works on Sophocles

In the Online Learning Center for *Responding to Literature*

- Brief biography of Sophocles
- List of major works by Sophocles
- Scene III from Sophocles's *Oedipus Rex*
- Web links to more resources on Sophocles
- Additional questions for experiencing and interpreting Sophocles's writing

Essays

ANDREW LAM   (1964–   )
Goodbye, Saigon, Finally

Andrew Lam was eleven when his family fled Saigon in 1975. His father had been a lieutenant general in the South Vietnamese Army. The family ended up in the San Francisco bay area, where Lam attended public schools and became fluent in English by reading everything he could get his hands on. Lam received a bachelor's degree in biochemistry from the University of California at Berkeley, but for his master's degree, he switched to creative writing at San Francisco State University. Currently, he is an associate editor at Pacific News Service, a multicultural media center in San Francisco. He is also a regular commentator on National Public Radio's All Things Considered *and is a regular contributor to the* San Jose Mercury-News *op-ed page and to Salon.com. His articles and essays have appeared in numerous newspapers and magazines, and his short stories have appeared in a number of literary reviews and fiction anthologies. The selection here first appeared as an op-ed piece in* The New York Times *in 1993. He is currently working on his first short story collection. Since 1991, Lam has returned to Vietnam frequently. He says, "While my father considers himself an exile living in America, I consider myself an American journalist who happens to make a yearly journey to Vietnam without much emotional fanfare. The irony is that he cannot return to the country to which he owes allegiance, so long as the current regime remains in power, while for me, my country of birth has become a point of departure, an occasional destination, but no longer home."*

Flipping through my United States passport as if it were a comic book, the customs man at the Noi Bai Airport, near Hanoi, appeared curious. "Brother, when did you leave Vietnam?"

"One day before National Defeat Day," I said without thinking. It was an exile's expression, not his.

"God! When did that happen?"

"The 30th of April, 1975."

5   "But, brother, don't you mean National Liberation Day?"

If this conversation had occurred a decade earlier, the difference would have created a dangerous gap between the Vietnamese and the returning Vietnamese-American. But this happened in 1992, when the walls were down, and as I studied the smiling young official, it occurred to me that there was something about this moment, an epiphany. "Yes, brother, I suppose I do mean liberation day."

Not everyone remembers the date with humor. It marked the Vietnamese diaspora, boat people, refugees.

On April 29, 1975, my family and I escaped from Saigon in a crowded C-130. We arrived in Guam the next day, to hear the BBC's tragic account of Saigon's demise: U.S. helicopters flying over the chaotic city, Vietcong tanks rolling in, Vietnamese climbing over the gate into the U.S. Embassy, boats fleeing down the Saigon River toward the South China Sea.

In time, April 30 became the birth date of an exile's culture built on defeatism and a sense of tragic ending. For a while, many Vietnamese in America talked of revenge, of blood debts, of the exile's anguish. Their songs had nostalgic titles: "The Day When I Return" and "Oh, Mother Vietnam, We Are Still Here."

10   April 30, 1976: A child of 12 with nationalistic fervor, I stood in front of San Francisco City Hall with other refugees. I waved the gold flag with three horizontal red stripes. I shouted (to no one in particular): "Give us back South Vietnam!"

April 30, 1979: An uncle told me there was an American plan to retake our homeland by force: "The way Douglas MacArthur did for the South Koreans in the 50's." My 17-year-old brother declared that he would join the anti-Communist guerrilla movement in Vietnam. My father sighed.

April 30, 1983: I stayed awake all night with Vietnamese classmates from Berkeley to listen to monotonous speeches by angry old men. "National defeat must be avenged by sweat and blood!" one vowed.

But through the years, April 30 has come to symbolize something entirely different to me. Although I sometimes mourn the loss of home and land, it's the American landscape and what it offers that solidify my hyphenated identity. This date of tragic ending, from an optimist's point of view, is also an American rebirth, something close to the Fourth of July.

I remember whispering to a young countryman during one of those monotonous April 30 rallies in the mid-1980's: "Even as the old man speaks of patriotic repatriation, we've already become Americans."

Assimilation, education, the English language, the American "I"—these have carried me and many others further from that beloved tropical country than the C-130 ever could. Each optimistic step the young Vietnamese takes toward America is tempered with a little betrayal of Little Saigon's parochialism, its sentimentalities and the old man's outdated passion.   *15*

When did this happen? Who knows? One night, America quietly seeps in and takes hold of one's mind and body, and the Vietnamese soul of sorrows slowly fades away. In the morning, the Vietnamese American speaks a new language of materialism: his vocabulary includes terms like career choices, down payment, escrow, overtime.

My brother never made it to the Indochinese jungle. The would-be guerrilla fighter became instead a civil engineer. My talk of endless possibilities is punctuated with favorite verbs—transcend, redefine, become. "I want to become a writer," I declared to my parents one morning. My mother gasped.

April 30, 1975: defeat or liberation?

"It was a day of joyous victory," said a retired Communist official in Hanoi. "We fought and realized Uncle Ho's dream of national independence." Then he asked for Marlboro cigarettes and a few precious dollars.

Nhon Nguyen, a real estate salesman in San Jose, a former South Vietnamese naval officer, said: "I could never forget the date. So many people died. So much blood. I could never tolerate Communism, you know."   *20*

Mai Huong, a young Vietnamese woman in Saigon, said that, of course, it was National Liberation Day. "But it's the South," she said with a wink, "that liberated the North." Indeed, conservative Uncle Ho has slowly admitted defeat to entrepreneurial and cosmopolitan Miss Saigon. She has taken her meaning from a different uncle, you know, Uncle Sam.

"April 30, 1975?" said Bobby To, my 22-year-old cousin in San Francisco. "I don't know that date. I don't remember Vietnam at all." April 29, 1992, is more meaningful to him, Bobby said. "It's when the race riots broke out all over our country. To me it's more realistic to worry about what's going on over here than there."

Sighing, the customs man, who offered me a ride into Hanoi, said: "In truth, there are no liberators. We are all defeated here." There is no job, no future, no direction, only a sense of collective malaise, something akin to the death of the national soul. He added: "You're lucky, brother. You left Vietnam and became an American."

April 30, 1993: My friends and I plan to watch *Gone with the Wind* for the umpteenth time and look for a scene of our unrequited romantic longings: Scarlett, teary-eyed with wind-blown hair, returning to forlorn Tara. We no longer can. Children of defeat, self-liberating adults, we promise to hug instead and recount to each other our own stories of flight.   *1993*

CONSIDERATIONS

1. What is the dual meaning of "National Liberation Day" in this piece? Explain the freedom that is implied in both meanings.
2. What is your impression of the author and his family? What do they value?
3. Explain how the process of Americanization parallels the subsequent celebrations between 1976 and 1983. In this short amount of time, what changes have taken place both within the country and within the narrator himself?
4. What does Lam mean when he says that April 30 is "an American rebirth" for him?
5. In the end, what do you think Lam has gained from being so closely aligned with the American culture? What, if anything, has he lost?

BARBARA KINGSOLVER (1955–   )

And Our Flag Was Still There

Born in Annapolis, Maryland, Barbara Kingsolver grew up in eastern Kentucky, where she was deeply affected by the contrast she saw between the wealthy owners of horse farms and the grinding poverty of families of coal miners. Her rural childhood was somewhat lonely, which may account for her early devotion to keeping prolific journals. After graduating from high school, Kingsolver attended DePauw University, initially majoring in music but later switching to biology. Following graduation, she traveled widely in Europe, working at such jobs as housecleaner, copy editor, biological researcher, and translator. She then returned to the United States to complete a graduate degree in biology and ecology at the University of Arizona. From 1985 to 1987, she worked as a freelance journalist and began writing fiction, publishing her first novel, The Bean Trees, *in 1988. In addition to five novels, she has published a collection of poetry,* Another America, *and a nonfiction book,* Holding the Line: Women in the Great Arizona Mine Strike of 1983. *She is best known for her fourth novel,* The*

Poisonwood Bible, *published in 1998, which was a finalist for the 1999
Book Critics Circle Award. Kingsolver has published numerous articles in publications such as The New York Times, The Nation, and Smithsonian and
has won many awards, including the American Library Association Best Book of
the Year, the Los Angeles Times Fiction Award, and the Edward Abbey Award
for Ecofiction. Currently, she lives in Tucson, Arizona, with her husband and two
daughters, where, in addition to pursing her writing career, she is an activist for
environmental and human rights issues.*

My daughter came home from kindergarten and announced, "Tomorrow we all have to wear red, white and blue."

"Why?" I asked, trying not to sound wary.

"For all the people that died when the airplanes hit the buildings."

I fear the sound of saber-rattling, dread that not just my taxes but even
my children are being dragged to the cause of death in the wake of death. I
asked quietly, "Why not wear black, then? Why the colors of the flag, what
does that mean?"

"It means we're a country. Just all people together."   5

So we sent her to school in red, white and blue, because it felt to her like
something she could do to help people who are hurting. And because my wise
husband put a hand on my arm and said, "You can't let hateful people steal the
flag from us."

He didn't mean terrorists, he meant Americans. Like the man in a city
near us who went on a rampage crying "I'm an American" as he shot at foreign-
born neighbors, killing a gentle Sikh man in a turban and terrifying every
brown-skinned person I know. Or the talk-radio hosts, who are viciously bully-
ing a handful of members of Congress for airing sensible skepticism at a time
when the White House was announcing preposterous things in apparent self-
interest, such as the "revelation" that terrorists had aimed to hunt down Air
Force One with a hijacked commercial plane. Rep. Barbara Lee cast the House's
only vote against handing over virtually unlimited war powers to one man that
a whole lot of us didn't vote for. As a consequence, so many red-blooded Americans have now threatened to kill her, she has to have additional bodyguards.

Patriotism seems to be falling to whoever claims it loudest, and we're left
struggling to find a definition in a clamor of reaction. This is what I'm hearing: Patriotism opposes the lone representative of democracy who was brave
enough to vote her conscience instead of following an angry mob. (Several
others have confessed they wanted to vote the same way, but chickened out.)
Patriotism threatens free speech with death. It is infuriated by thoughtful hesitation, constructive criticism of our leaders and pleas for peace. It despises people of foreign birth who've spent years learning our culture and contributing
their talents to our economy. It has specifically blamed homosexuals, feminists
and the American Civil Liberties Union. In other words, the American flag

stands for intimidation, censorship, violence, bigotry, sexism, homophobia, and shoving the Constitution through a paper shredder? Who are we calling terrorists here? Outsiders can destroy airplanes and buildings, but it is only we, the people, who have the power to demolish our own ideals.

It's a fact of our culture that the loudest mouths get the most airplay. And the loudmouths are saying now that in times of crisis it is treasonous to question our leaders. Nonsense. That kind of thinking let fascism grow out of the international depression of the 1930s. In critical times, our leaders need most to be influenced by the moderating force of dissent. That is the basis of democracy, in sickness and in health, and especially when national choices are difficult, and bear grave consequences.

10   It occurs to me that my patriotic duty is to recapture my flag from the men now waving it in the name of jingoism and censorship. This isn't easy for me.

The last time I looked at a flag with unambiguous pride, I was 13. Right after that, Vietnam began teaching me lessons in ambiguity, and the lessons have kept coming. I've learned of things my government has done to the world that made me direly ashamed. I've been further alienated from my flag by people who waved it at me declaring I should love it or leave it. I search my soul and find I cannot love killing for any reason. When I look at the flag, I see it illuminated by the rocket's red glare.

This is why the warmongers so easily gain the upper hand in the patriot game: Our nation was established with a fight for independence, so our iconography grew out of war. Our national anthem celebrates it; our language of patriotism is inseparable from a battle cry. Our every military campaign is still launched with phrases about men dying for the freedoms we hold dear, even when this is impossible to square with reality. In the Persian Gulf War we rushed to the aid of Kuwait, a monarchy in which women enjoyed approximately the same rights as a 19th century American slave. The values we fought for and won there are best understood, I think, by oil companies. Meanwhile, a country of civilians was devastated, and remains destroyed.

Stating these realities does not violate the principles of liberty, equality, and freedom of speech; it exercises them, and by exercise we grow stronger. I would like to stand up for my flag and wave it over a few things I believe in, including but not limited to the protection of dissenting points of view. After 225 years, I vote to retire the rocket's red glare and the bullet wound as obsolete symbols of Old Glory. We desperately need a new iconography of patriotism. I propose we rip stripes of cloth from the uniforms of public servants who rescued the injured and panic-stricken, remaining at their post until it fell down on them. The red glare of candles held in vigils everywhere as peace-loving people pray for the bereaved, and plead for compassion and restraint. The blood donated to the Red Cross. The stars of film and theater and music who are using their influence to raise money for recovery. The small hands of schoolchildren collecting pennies, toothpaste, teddy bears, anything they think might help the kids who've lost their moms and dads.

My town, Tucson, Ariz., has become famous for a simple gesture in which some 8,000 people wearing red, white or blue T-shirts assembled themselves in the shape of a flag on a baseball field and had their photograph taken from above. That picture has begun to turn up everywhere, but we saw it first on our newspaper's front page. Our family stood in silence for a minute looking at that photo of a human flag, trying to know what to make of it. Then my teenage daughter, who has a quick mind for numbers and a sensitive heart, did an interesting thing. She laid her hand over a quarter of the picture, leaving visible more or less 6,000 people, and said, "That many are dead." We stared at what that looked like—all those innocent souls, multi-colored and packed into a conjoined destiny—and shuddered at the one simple truth behind all the noise, which is that so many beloved people have suddenly gone from us. That is my flag, and that's what it means: We're all just people together.

CONSIDERATIONS

1. Although Kingsolver's essay does revolve around her reconciling two opposing views of patriotism, the theme is, on a deeper level, more than that. Discuss the less obvious truth that Kingsolver is writing about, and create a headline that reflects this topic and truth.
2. Discuss the tone in this piece, and make note of how many times it shifts and changes. In what ways might this shift in tone reflect the themes that are included here?
3. Within this essay, Kingsolver explores the evils and weaknesses that came to light in the aftermath of a tragedy that killed thousands of innocent people. What do you think: Are these evils primarily based in American culture, or are they inherent in human nature?
4. Kingsolver writes that "in critical times, our leaders need most to be influenced by the moderating force of dissent." What does she mean by these words, and do you agree or disagree with her? Explain.
5. Comment on Kingsolver's choices for her introduction and her conclusion. How might they reinforce an underlying theme that is woven throughout this piece? What effect might they have on her readers? Explain.

NAOMI SHIHAB NYE (1952–   )

To Any Would-Be Terrorists

For biographical information on Naomi Shihab Nye, see page 243.

I am sorry I have to call you that, but I don't know how else to get your attention. I hate that word. Do you know how hard some of us have worked to get rid of that word, to deny its instant connection to the Middle East? And now look. Look what extra work we have. Not only did your colleagues kill thousands of innocent, international people in those buildings and scar their families forever, they wounded a huge community of people in the Middle East, in the United States, and all over the world. If that's what they wanted to do, please know the mission was a terrible success, and you can stop now.

Because I feel a little closer to you than many Americans could possibly feel, or ever want to feel, I insist that you listen to me. Sit down and listen. I know what kinds of foods you like. I would feed them to you if you were right here, because it is very very important that you listen. I am humble in my country's pain and I am furious.

My Palestinian father became a refugee in 1948. He came to the United States as a college student. He is 74 years old now and still homesick. He has planted fig trees. He has invited all the Ethiopians in his neighborhood to fill their little paper sacks with his figs. He has written columns and stories saying the Arabs are not terrorists, he has worked all his life to defy that word. Arabs are businessmen and students and kind neighbors. There is no one like him and there are thousands like him—gentle Arab daddies who make everyone laugh around the dinner table, who have a hard time with headlines, who stand outside in the evenings with their hands in their pockets staring toward the far horizon.

I am sorry if you did not have a father like that. I wish everyone could have a father like that.

5   My hard-working American mother has spent 50 years trying to convince her fellow teachers and choir mates not to believe stereotypes about the Middle East. She always told them, there is a much larger story. If you knew the story, you would not jump to conclusions from what you see in the news. But now look at the news. What a mess has been made. Sometimes I wish everyone could have parents from different countries or ethnic groups so they would be forced to cross boundaries, to believe in mixtures, every day of their lives. Because this is what the world calls us to do. WAKE UP!

The Palestinian grocer in my Mexican-American neighborhood paints pictures of the Palestinian flag on his empty cartons. He paints trees and rivers. He gives his paintings away. He says, "Don't insult me" when I try to pay him for a lemonade. Arabs have always been famous for their generosity. Remember? My half-Arab brother with an Arabic name looks more like an Arab than many full-blooded Arabs do and he has to fly every week.

My Palestinian cousins in Texas have beautiful brown little boys. Many of them haven't gone to school yet. And now they have this heavy word to carry in their backpacks along with the weight of their papers and books. I repeat, the mission was a terrible success. But it was also a complete, total tragedy and I want you to think about a few things.

1. Many people, thousands of people, perhaps even millions of people, in the United States are very aware of the long unfairness of our country's policies regarding Israel and Palestine. We talk about this all the time. It exhausts us and we keep talking. We write letters to newspapers, to politicians, to each other. We speak out in public even when it is uncomfortable to do so, because that is our responsibility. Many of these people aren't even Arabs. Many happen to be Jews who are equally troubled by the inequity. I promise you this is true. Because I am Arab-American, people always express these views to me and I am amazed how many understand the intricate situation and have strong, caring feelings for Arabs and Palestinians even when they don't have to. Think of them, please: All those people who have been standing up for Arabs when they didn't have to. But as ordinary citizens we don't run the government and don't get to make all our government's policies, which makes us sad sometimes. We believe in the power of the word and we keep using it, even when it seems no one large enough is listening. That is one of the best things about this country: the free power of free words. Maybe we take it for granted too much. Many of the people killed in the World Trade Center probably believed in a free Palestine and were probably talking about it all the time.

But this tragedy could never help the Palestinians. Somehow, miraculously, if other people won't help them more, they are going to have to help themselves. And it will be peace, not violence, that fixes things. You could ask any one of the kids in the Seeds of Peace organization and they would tell you that. Do you ever talk to kids? Please, please, talk to more kids.

2. Have you noticed how many roads there are? Sure you have. You must   *10*
check out maps and highways and small alternate routes just like anyone else. There is no way everyone on earth could travel on the same road, or believe in exactly the same religion. It would be too crowded, it would be dumb. I don't believe you want us all to be Muslims. My Palestinian grandmother lived to be 106 years old, and did not read or write, but even she was much smarter than that. The only place she ever went beyond Palestine and Jordan was to Mecca, by bus, and she was very proud to be called a Hajji and to wear white clothes afterwards. She worked very hard to get stains out of everyone's dresses—scrubbing them with a stone. I think she would consider the recent tragedies a terrible stain on her religion and her whole part of the world. She would weep. She was scared of airplanes anyway. She wanted people to worship God in whatever ways they felt comfortable. Just worship. Just remember

God in every single day and doing. It didn't matter what they called it. When people asked her how she felt about the peace talks that were happening right before she died, she puffed up like a proud little bird and said, in Arabic, "I never lost my peace inside." To her, Islam was a welcoming religion. After her home in Jerusalem was stolen from her, she lived in a small village that contained a Christian shrine. She felt very tender toward the people who would visit it. A Jewish professor tracked me down a few years ago in Jerusalem to tell me she changed his life after he went to her village to do an oral history project on Arabs. "Don't think she only mattered to you!" he said. "She gave me a whole different reality to imagine—yet it was amazing how close we became. Arabs could never be just a 'project' after that."

Did you have a grandmother or two? Mine never wanted people to be pushed around. What did yours want? Reading about Islam since my grandmother died, I note the "tolerance" that was "typical of Islam" even in the old days. The Muslim leader Khalid ibn al-Walid signed a Jerusalem treaty which declared, "In the name of God, you have complete security for your churches which shall not be occupied by the Muslims or destroyed." It is the new millennium in which we should be even smarter than we used to be, right? But I think we have fallen behind.

3. Many Americans do not want to kill any more innocent people anywhere in the world. We are extremely worried about military actions killing innocent people. We didn't like this in Iraq, we never liked it anywhere. We would like no more violence, from us as well as from you. HEAR US! We would like to stop the terrifying wheel of violence, just stop it, right on the road, and find something more creative to do to fix these huge problems we have. Violence is not creative, it is stupid and scary and many of us hate all those terrible movies and TV shows made in our own country that try to pretend otherwise. Don't watch them. Everyone should stop watching them. An appetite for explosive sounds and toppling buildings is not a healthy thing for anyone in any country. The USA should apologize to the whole world for sending this trash out into the air and for paying people to make it.

But here's something good you may not know—one of the best-selling books of poetry in the United States in recent years is the Coleman Barks translation of Rumi, a mystical Sufi poet of the 13th century, and Sufism is Islam and doesn't that make you glad?

Everyone is talking about the suffering that ethnic Americans are going through. Many will no doubt go through more of it, but I would like to thank everyone who has sent me a consolation card. Americans are usually very kind people. Didn't your colleagues find that out during their time living here? It is hard to imagine they missed it. How could they do what they did, knowing that?

4. We will all die soon enough. Why not take the short time we have on this delicate planet and figure out some really interesting things we might do   *15*

together? I promise you, God would be happier. So many people are always trying to speak for God   I know it is a very dangerous thing to do. I tried my whole life not to do it. But this one time is an exception. Because there are so many people crying and scarred and confused and complicated and exhausted right now—it is as if we have all had a giant simultaneous breakdown. I beg you, as your distant Arab cousin, as your American neighbor, listen to me. Our hearts are broken, as yours may also feel broken in some ways we can't understand, unless you tell us in words. Killing people won't tell us. We can't read that message. Find another way to live. Don't expect others to be like you. Read Rumi. Read Arabic poetry. Poetry humanizes us in a way that news, or even religion, has a harder time doing. A great Arab scholar, Dr. Salma Jayyusi, said, "If we read one another, we won't kill one another." Read American poetry. Plant mint. Find a friend who is so different from you, you can't believe how much you have in common. Love them. Let them love you. Surprise people in gentle ways, as friends do. The rest of us will try harder too. Make our family proud.   *2001*

CONSIDERATIONS

1. Why does Nye address this piece to "would-be" terrorists instead of simply "terrorists"?
2. What stereotypes is the writer trying to dispel about Arab-Americans, and how effective do you find her attempts? What, specifically, impressed you the most? Explain.
3. This essay's title suggests that "Would-Be Terrorists" are its audience. How would you imagine the broader audience for whom the writer might intend her message?

Photo Essay

THEN AND NOW

Images of War

These images suggest the sorrow, heroism, cowardice, exhaustion, and confusion of war.

PHOTO 1

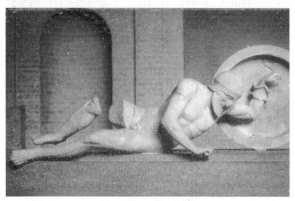

PHOTO 1 The first image shows a sculpted figure, *The Dying Warrior,* a detail from the Temple of Aphaia in Aegina, Greece. The warrior has fallen in battle, yet still clings to his shield and struggles to hold himself upright, suggesting his determination to hold on to life and, perhaps, his devotion to his cause. The fact that part of the warrior's leg has gone missing provides an un-intentional ironic emphasis on the physical loss war often brings to the young soldiers who are sent into battle.

PHOTO 2 Following an uprising against French occupiers in the Puerto del Sol section of Madrid in the early nineteenth century, French soldiers from Napoleon's army randomly executed Spanish citizens. Spanish artist Francisco de Goya's *The Third of May, 1808,* suggests the horror of these raids on civilians in many ways, including the light that illuminates the vic-tims, while Napoleon's troops, the executors, remain in dark shadow.

PHOTO 3 American GI's received strong acclaim during the libera-tion of Paris from Nazi occupation during World War II. This photo shows soldiers on an armored truck, riding into the city on August 25, 1944. The people of France extended an overwhelming welcome to the U.S. military during and immediately after this war, which was regarded by many to be a necessary and justified action against the aggression and atrocities of the Nazis and their allies.

PHOTO 2

PHOTO 3

PHOTO 4 Roughly twenty years after the end of World War II, the United States intervened in a conflict in the southeast Asian country of Vietnam. The name of every one of the over 58,000 American men and women who were killed in Vietnam is carved on the Vietnam Veterans Memorial in

PHOTO 4

Washington, D.C. The memorial, dedicated in 1982, reflects in its polished stone the images of visitors, some of whom may seek the names of relatives, friends, or comrades who died in Vietnam. When the memorial was first proposed in 1981, critics charged that it did not properly suggest the heroism of war. However, as suggested by the woman's hand reaching out to touch a name, most viewers came to see the Wall as starkly appropriate to the war it represents and as keenly evocative of the value of each life lost.

PHOTO 5 In 1990, Iraq invaded and occupied a neighboring country, Kuwait, triggering the first Persian Gulf War, which began with air strikes in January 1991 and ended with the expulsion of Iraqi forces from Kuwait by a

PHOTO 5

coalition of troops from the United States, Britain, France, and Arab countries in the following month. The invasion led to a rebellion against Saddam Hussein, the Iraqi dictator, by Shi'ite Muslims and Kurds in southern and northern Iraq, a rebellion that Hussein's forces put down while the U.S. forces stood by. In this still from the 1999 film *Three Kings,* actors Mark Wahlberg, George Clooney, and Ice Cube depict three American soldiers from this war. The desert stretches out behind them as dozens of Iraqi civilians follow, hoping to escape from Hussein's repressive regime. The film depicts the American soldiers both as renegades who leave their assigned posts to seek a reported cache of Kuwaiti gold and heroes who decide, after some time, to lead the Iraqis to freedom.

PHOTO 6 Both the final photo in this section and the image that appears on the opening page of this chapter show scenes from the second U.S. war against Iraq, which began in March 2003. The image on page 902 juxtaposes American soldiers who are trying to maintain security at an Iraqi passport office with Iraqi civilians, women in traditional Muslim dress, and a small boy who points at something just outside the photograph. This opening photo suggests at least the possibility of peace and order, while the photo of the flag-draped caskets marks the ending of all possibilities on this earth for the American troops who have been killed in Iraq. The life and energy of the young soldier who bends over to attend to one of the caskets contrasts poignantly with the stillness that surrounds him.

PHOTO 6

CONSIDERATIONS

1. Compare the images that portray or evoke death in war—for example, in *The Dying Warrior; The Third of May, 1808;* and the photo of the Vietnam Veterans Memorial—to the depictions of death in war that appear in any of the selections in this chapter. What similarities do you see? What differences do you observe?

2. The effects of war on civilians are suggested by the chapter's opening photograph of American soldiers at a passport office (page 902), by Goya's *The Third of May, 1808,* by the Parisian citizens greeting American soldiers at the end of World War II, by the individuals who touch and who are reflected by the Vietnam Memorial, and by the still from the film *Three Kings.* Compare these images to the way civilians during wartime are depicted in "Guests of the Nation," "The Shawl," and *Antigone.*

3. Consider the image of the Vietnam Veterans Memorial. In what ways do the details of this image relate to the following selections in this chapter that depict the Vietnam War: "The Things They Carried," "What Were They Like," "Facing It," and "Goodbye, Saigon, Finally"?

4. Choose any of the images and any of the selections in this chapter as possible examples for a discussion of the ways in which war and the effects of war seem to have changed or remained the same from the time of the Greek civilization until the present.

5. Create a dialogue between any of the individuals who are depicted in this photo section and a character or speaker from one of the literary sections in this chapter.

■■■   **Film Connection:** *Three Kings*

While film and other genres of literature share certain elements, such as word choice and plot development, there are some elements unique to film. Of course, it is obvious that a film, unlike a written work, offers visual and sound images that can be seen and heard rather than imagined in the mind. These aspects contribute to the viewers' response, to their pleasure, and to their ability to analyze and evaluate the film. Consider, as an example, the film *Three Kings* (1999, directed by David O. Russell).

This film, set just after the cease-fire at the declared end of the 1991 Gulf War, offers a thoughtful view of that war and provides images and sounds that suggest themes found in the poems, short stories, and play in this thematic chapter. Comparing various aspects of this film with the selections you have read will offer new perspectives and possibilities for writing and discussion related to the theme of war and power.

Color and Light   Throughout the film, the pale, bleached-out color casts an eerie light on the settings, on the characters, and on their actions. Although there are some comic moments, the strange and haunting color tones never allow the viewer to laugh at the jokes without also remembering the moral ambiguities that are part of the film's depiction of war and its aftermath. In addition, the many moments of cruelty and violence are made all the more powerful because they appear to be washed in the light of some cosmic examination.

> *Exercise*   Trace the use of another color that provides visual support to the theme, characterization, and conflicts in the film. For example, consider the blue and green light that often appears to halo characters and objects.

Camera Angles and Movement   Extreme long shots in this film create a sense of the vast stretches of desert and the startling cliffs, hills, and rises of land in the Iraq countryside. In several long shots, the screen shows just the landscape and holds this focus as people move into the scene. For example, in one long shot, we see a high ridge and then the silhouettes of the Iraqi people who are being accompanied by the American servicemen as the Iraqis try to escape over the border into Iran. The extreme difficulty and danger of this quest is suggested by the panoramic view the long shot provides to the viewer. We see how open, vulnerable, and unprotected the characters are as they move slowly toward their goal.

> *Exercises*
> 1. In some cases, the long shots are combined with quick camera movements and cuts. Identify some of these scenes and discuss

how the rapid changes, viewed from a distance, contribute to characterization or serve to create understanding of the actions they capture.

2. Consider other camera angles and movement. For instance, identify scenes where the camera shoots while moving backward or the character or characters appear to walk directly at the viewer. Or note scenes where the camera seems to circle the character or characters. Then consider what these camera angles and movements contribute to the development of character, conflict, or theme.

Visual Symbols and Sound Images   Many of the visual symbols and sound images suggest aspects of American culture. For instance, the Nerf footballs initially serve as sentimental reminders of the way the men cling to their memories of home. They seem to play at being soldiers, just as they play at tossing footballs. Yet later, the footballs take on a deeper and much darker significance, perhaps suggesting that if war is a game, it is deadly and terrible. The footballs have become bombs that can kill, yet paradoxically in the skilled hands of Sargent Chief Elgin, they also become a symbol of power and liberation.

The sound images, too, are often icons of American culture. For instance, as the three main characters set out on their mission, their vehicle carries a sign labeled "The Beach Boys," while the music and lyrics to "I Get Around" become louder, finally dominating the scene. The quintessentially American sound images suggest that the desert is being tacitly compared to a California beach.

> *Exercise*   Consider some of the other symbolic elements of setting. For example, the cache of cell phones, which provide Troy Barlow with an extraordinary means of addressing his dangerous situation. Or think about the treasure trove of American luxury cars. Watch for patterns in the use of these symbols. What do these patterns of symbols suggest about the development of characters, themes, and conflicts?

Connections: War and Power

1. Using several of the following works, consider the ways in which those who do not experience war directly or the survivors left behind to cope with their grief carry on with their lives. After exploring several pieces, what conclusions can you draw about the effects of war on those who are left behind? "The Management of Grief," "The Second Coming," "What

Were They Like?", "The Colonel," "When the Towers Fell," "Goodbye, Saigon, Finally," "To Any Would-Be Terrorists."

2. Many of these pieces suggest that defining the "enemy" is often not easy. Basing your analysis on several of the following pieces, what or who ends up defining "enemy" when it comes to war and acts of terrorism? "Guests of the Nation," "The Things They Carried," "The Management of Grief," "The Man He Killed," "Ozymandias," "When the Towers Fell," *Antigone,* "To Any Would-Be Terrorists."

3. Consider the concepts of loyalty and duty and to whom or what people pledge their loyalties in the following pieces: "Guests of the Nation," "The Things They Carried," "*Dulce et Decorum Est,*" *Antigone,* "And Our Flag Was Still There."

4. Choose any three works in this section, and compare or contrast your responses to the works with your responses to any war or act of terrorism you have experienced, either as a participant or an observer at home. How realistic and true do you find the works in this section compared to your own observations?

5. Analyze how a particular war is presented in this section when compared/contrasted with a film or television show about this same war. What similarities do you see? What differences emerge?

SUGGESTIONS FOR EXTENDED CONNECTIONS AMONG CHAPTERS

1. How do family members respond to their close relatives' war experiences? Consider the "wars" that are often waged on those who are innocent victims of crimes born out of ignorance, circumstances, power, passion, or terrorism:

"The Red Convertible"	218
Hamlet	244
"Sonny's Blues"	412
"The Yellow Wallpaper"	532
Trifles	666
"How Far She Went"	717
Antigone	978
Soul Gone Home	792
"The Birthmark"	1034
"The Black Cat"	1154

2. Create a dialogue or screenplay on the topic of duty, honor, and responsibility among any three to five characters from the following selections. While some of these selections are directly related to war, others are related to other kinds of power struggles that often cause the individual to question

where his or her loyalty lies. Is it to one's self, one's lover, one's family, one's community, or one's country?

3. What allows certain people to have power over others and control their lives? Examine this question in light of the following selections:

SUGGESTIONS FOR COLLABORATIVE LEARNING

1. The wars in this chapter range from ancient Greek times to the U.S. war in Iraq. Working in groups of three or four, choose one selection that refers to a relatively recent war or act of terror and find several primary sources that relate to that war or act. Consider, for example, interviews with victims, with protesters, or with members of the armed services. Share the findings with the whole group, and then individually write a paper that compares the primary sources with the reading you have chosen. In what ways does the reading support what you found? What differences exist between the primary documents and the piece you read?

2. As a group, choose two films that deal with war, one that was popular prior to 1960 and one that was produced more recently, such as *Three Kings, Sav-*

ing Private Ryan, Platoon, Glory, Schindler's List, The Pianist, or *Good Morning, Vietnam.* If possible, watch these two movies back to back as a group. Individually, write an essay in which you compare the two films, focusing primarily on the producer's intention and message concerning war.

WEB CONNECTIONS

1. The Web site "Virtual Seminars for Teaching Literature" (maintained by Oxford University Computing Services) at http://www.oucs.ox.ac.uk/ltg/projects/jtap/ links students to the poetry of World War I. In addition to Wilfred Owen, whose work is included in this chapter, there are links to trench poetry and songs and an intriguing link to a group whose voices are not usually heard—the women of WWI. While this is an introduction to WWI poetry, there are also links to historical sites and in-depth studies of individual authors. Upon entering the site, scroll down and click on "1. The Seminars." From there, scroll down and click on "Tutorial 1: An Introduction to WWI Poetry" for resources on the topic.

2. The Web site http://www.vietnamwomensmemorial.org, published by the Vietnam Women's Memorial Foundation, provides links to voices of women who either served in Vietnam or who suffered losses of loved ones in this war. There is a good link to poetry from Vietnam veterans as well as a link to the extensive online library sources regarding women's experiences in war. On the site introduction page, wait for the opening presentation to finish, then click on the "Library" link.

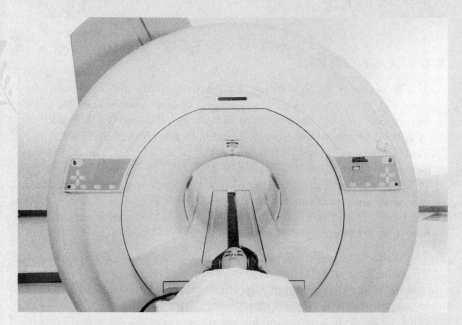

What ethical questions are raised by powerful and expensive medical technology such as the machine pictured above?

12

Technology and Ethics

The selections in this chapter all look at the ethical implications of technology. But what exactly is "technology"? One respected dictionary states that technology is "the totality of the means employed to provide objects necessary for human sustenance and comfort." The operative word in this definition may well be "necessary." For example, something that one generation or one group might consider a luxury, another generation or culture may consider a necessity. Another intriguing word in the definition is "comfort." What one person may deem essential to be comfortable, someone else might regard as an extravagance. Even those objects (or processes) that contribute to human sustenance—for example, increasingly complicated, expensive, and often painful medical procedures—raise ethical questions.

As you prepare to read the selections in this chapter, keep in mind the following questions:

1. What technological inventions have been made in your lifetime? In your parents' lifetime? In your grandparents' lifetime? How did these inventions change the lives of those living at the time they were invented?
2. What five technological inventions do you consider most important to your life? What are the reasons for your choices?
3. How have people benefitted from technological advances? How have technological advances caused problems?
4. What ethical issues are related to various advances in technology?
5. How have ethical and moral issues concerning technology affected you, your family, or your community?

Fiction

NATHANIEL HAWTHORNE (1804–1864)
The Birthmark

For biographical information on Nathaniel Hawthorne, see page 194.

In the latter part of the last century there lived a man of science, an eminent proficient in every branch of natural philosophy, who not long before our story opens had made experience of a spiritual affinity more attractive than any chemical one. He had left his laboratory to the care of an assistant, cleared his fine countenance from the furnace smoke, washed the stain of acids from his fingers, and persuaded a beautiful woman to become his wife. In those days when the comparatively recent discovery of electricity and other kindred mysteries of Nature seemed to open paths into the region of miracle, it was not unusual for the love of science to rival the love of woman in its depth and absorbing energy. The higher intellect, the imagination, the spirit, and even the heart might all find their congenial aliment in pursuits which, as some of their ardent votaries believed, would ascend from one step of powerful intelligence to another, until the philosopher should lay his hand on the secret of creative force and perhaps make new worlds for himself. We know not whether Aylmer possessed this degree of faith in man's ultimate control over Nature. He had devoted himself, however, too unreservedly to scientific studies ever to be weaned from them by any second passion. His love for his young wife might prove the stronger of the two; but it could only be by intertwining itself with his love of science, and uniting the strength of the latter to his own.

Such a union accordingly took place, and was attended with truly remarkable consequences and a deeply impressive moral. One day, very soon after their marriage, Aylmer sat gazing at his wife with a trouble in his countenance that grew stronger until he spoke.

"Georgiana," said he, "has it never occurred to you that the mark upon your cheek might be removed?"

"No, indeed," said she, smiling; but perceiving the seriousness of his manner, she blushed deeply. "To tell you the truth it has been so often called a charm that I was simple enough to imagine it might be so."

5   "Ah, upon another face perhaps it might," replied her husband; "but never on yours. No, dearest Georgiana, you came so nearly perfect from the hand of Nature that this slightest possible defect, which we hesitate whether to term a defect or a beauty, shocks me, as being the visible mark of earthly imperfection."

"Shocks you, my husband!" cried Georgiana, deeply hurt; at first reddening with momentary anger, but then bursting into tears. "Then why did you take me from my mother's side? You cannot love what shocks you!"

To explain this conversation it must be mentioned that in the centre of Georgiana's left cheek there was a singular mark, deeply interwoven, as it were, with the texture and substance of her face. In the usual state of her complexion—a healthy though delicate bloom—the mark wore a tint of deeper crimson, which imperfectly defined its shape amid the surrounding rosiness. When she blushed it gradually became more indistinct, and finally vanished amid the triumphant rush of blood that bathed the whole cheek with its brilliant glow. But if any shifting motion caused her to turn pale there was the mark again, a crimson stain upon the snow, in what Aylmer sometimes deemed an almost fearful distinctness. Its shape bore not a little similarity to the human hand, though of the smallest pygmy size. Georgiana's lovers were wont to say that some fairy at her birth hour had laid her tiny hand upon the infant's cheek, and left this impress there in token of the magic endowments that were to give her such sway over all hearts. Many a desperate swain would have risked life for the privilege of pressing his lips to the mysterious hand. It must not be concealed, however, that the impression wrought by this fairy sign manual varied exceedingly, according to the difference of temperament in the beholders. Some fastidious persons—but they were exclusively of her own sex—affirmed that the bloody hand, as they chose to call it, quite destroyed the effect of Georgiana's beauty, and rendered her countenance even hideous. But it would be as reasonable to say that one of those small blue stains which sometimes occur in the purest statuary marble would convert the Eve of Powers[1] to a monster. Masculine observers, if the birthmark did not heighten their admiration, contented themselves with wishing it away, that the world might possess one living specimen of ideal loveliness without the semblance of a flaw. After his marriage, — for he thought little or nothing of the matter before,—Aylmer discovered that this was the case with himself.

Had she been less beautiful, — if Envy's self could have found aught else to sneer at,— he might have felt his affection heightened by the prettiness of this mimic hand, now vaguely portrayed, now lost, now stealing forth again and glimmering to and fro with every pulse of emotion that throbbed within her heart; but seeing her otherwise so perfect, he found this one defect grow more and more intolerable with every moment of their united lives. It was the fatal flaw of humanity which Nature, in one shape or another, stamps ineffaceably on all her productions, either to imply that they are temporary and finite, or that their perfection must be wrought by toil and pain. The crimson hand expressed the ineludible gripe in which mortality clutches the highest and

---

[1]Eve of Powers: A beautiful and pure statue by American sculptor Hiram Powers (1805–1873).

purest of earthly mould, degrading them into kindred with the lowest, and even with the very brutes, like whom their visible frames return to dust. In this manner, selecting it as the symbol of his wife's liability to sin, sorrow, decay, and death, Aylmer's sombre imagination was not long in rendering the birthmark a frightful object, causing him more trouble and horror than ever Georgiana's beauty, whether of soul or sense, had given him delight.

At all the seasons which should have been their happiest, he invariably and without intending it, nay, in spite of a purpose to the contrary, reverted to this one disastrous topic. Trifling as it at first appeared, it so connected itself with innumerable trains of thought and modes of feeling that it became the central point of all. With the morning twilight Aylmer opened his eyes upon his wife's face and recognized the symbol of imperfection; and when they sat together at the evening hearth his eyes wandered stealthily to her cheek, and beheld, flickering with the blaze of the wood fire, the spectral hand that wrote mortality where he would fain have worshipped. Georgiana soon learned to shudder at his gaze. It needed but a glance with the peculiar expression that his face often wore to change the roses of her cheek into a deathlike paleness, amid which the crimson hand was brought strongly out, like a bas-relief of ruby on the whitest marble.

10   Late one night when the lights were growing dim, so as hardly to betray the stain on the poor wife's cheek, she herself, for the first time, voluntarily took up the subject.

"Do you remember, my dear Aylmer," said she, with a feeble attempt at a smile, "have you any recollection of a dream last night about this odious hand?"

"None! none whatever!" replied Aylmer, starting; but then he added, in a dry, cold tone, affected for the sake of concealing the real depth of his emotion, "I might well dream of it; for before I fell asleep it had taken a pretty firm hold of my fancy."

"And you did dream of it?" continued Georgiana, hastily; for she dreaded lest a gush of tears should interrupt what she had to say. "A terrible dream! I wonder that you can forget it. Is it possible to forget this one expression?—'It is in her heart now; we must have it out!' Reflect, my husband; for by all means I would have you recall that dream."

The mind is in a sad state when Sleep, the all-involving, cannot confine her spectres within the dim region of her sway, but suffers them to break forth, affrighting this actual life with secrets that perchance belong to a deeper one. Aylmer now remembered his dream. He had fancied himself with his servant Aminadab, attempting an operation for the removal of the birthmark; but the deeper went the knife, the deeper sank the hand, until at length its tiny grasp appeared to have caught hold of Georgiana's heart; whence, however, her husband was inexorably resolved to cut or wrench it away.

15   When the dream had shaped itself perfectly in his memory, Aylmer sat in his wife's presence with a guilty feeling. Truth often finds its way to the mind

close muffled in robes of sleep, and then speaks with uncompromising directness of matters in regard to which we practise an unconscious self-deception
during our waking moments. Until now he had not been aware of the tyran-
nizing influence acquired by one idea over his mind, and of the lengths which
he might find in his heart to go for the sake of giving himself peace.

"Aylmer," resumed Georgiana, solemnly, "I know not what may be the
cost to both of us to rid me of this fatal birthmark. Perhaps its removal may
cause cureless deformity; or it may be the stain goes as deep as life itself. Again:
do we know that there is a possibility, on any terms, of unclasping the firm
gripe of this little hand which was laid upon me before I came into the world?"

"Dearest Georgiana, I have spent much thought upon the subject,"
hastily interrupted Aylmer. "I am convinced of the perfect practicability of its
removal."

"If there be the remotest possibility of it," continued Georgiana, "let the
attempt be made at whatever risk. Danger is nothing to me; for life, while this
hateful mark makes me the object of your horror and disgust,—life is a burden which I would fling down with joy. Either remove this dreadful hand, or
take my wretched life! You have deep science. All the world bears witness of it.
You have achieved great wonders. Cannot you remove this little, little mark,
which I cover with the tips of two small fingers? Is this beyond your power,
for the sake of your own peace, and to save your poor wife from madness?"

"Noblest, dearest, tenderest wife," cried Aylmer, rapturously, "doubt not
my power. I have already given this matter the deepest thought—thought which
might almost have enlightened me to create a being less perfect than yourself.
Georgiana, you have led me deeper than ever into the heart of science. I feel
myself fully competent to render this dear cheek as faultless as its fellow; and
then, most beloved, what will be my triumph when I shall have corrected what
Nature left imperfect in her fairest work! Even Pygmalion, when his sculptured
woman assumed life, felt not greater ecstasy than mine will be."

"It is resolved, then," said Georgiana, faintly smiling. "And, Aylmer, spare   *20*
me not, though you should find the birthmark take refuge in my heart at last."

Her husband tenderly kissed her cheek—her right cheek—not that
which bore the impress of the crimson hand.

The next day Aylmer apprised his wife of a plan that he had formed
whereby he might have opportunity for the intense thought and constant
watchfulness which the proposed operation would require; while Georgiana,
likewise, would enjoy the perfect repose essential to its success. They were to
seclude themselves in the extensive apartments occupied by Aylmer as a laboratory, and where, during his toilsome youth, he had made discoveries in the
elemental powers of Nature that had roused the admiration of all the learned
societies in Europe. Seated calmly in this laboratory, the pale philosopher had
investigated the secrets of the highest cloud region and of the profoundest
mines; he had satisfied himself of the causes that kindled and kept alive the

fires of the volcano; and had explained the mystery of fountains, and how it is that they gush forth, some so bright and pure, and others with such rich medicinal virtues, from the dark bosom of the earth. Here, too, at an earlier period, he had studied the wonders of the human frame, and attempted to fathom the very process by which Nature assimilates all her precious influences from earth and air, and from the spiritual world, to create and foster man, her masterpiece. The latter pursuit, however, Aylmer had long laid aside in unwilling recognition of the truth—against which all seekers sooner or later stumble—that our great creative Mother, while she amuses us with apparently working in the broadest sunshine, is yet severely careful to keep her own secrets, and, in spite of her pretended openness, shows us nothing but results. She permits us, indeed, to mar, but seldom to mend, and, like a jealous patentee, on no account to make. Now, however, Aylmer resumed these half-forgotten investigations; not, of course, with such hopes or wishes as first suggested them; but because they involved much physiological truth and lay in the path of his proposed scheme for the treatment of Georgiana.

As he led her over the threshold of the laboratory, Georgiana was cold and tremulous. Aylmer looked cheerfully into her face, with intent to reassure her, but was so startled with the intense glow of the birthmark upon the whiteness of her cheek that he could not restrain a strong convulsive shudder. His wife fainted.

"Aminadab! Aminadab!" shouted Aylmer, stamping violently on the floor.

25   Forthwith there issued from an inner apartment a man of low stature, but bulky frame, with shaggy hair hanging about his visage, which was grimed with the vapors of the furnace. This personage had been Aylmer's underworker during his whole scientific career, and was admirably fitted for that office by his great mechanical readiness, and the skill with which, while incapable of comprehending a single principle, he executed all the details of his master's experiments. With his vast strength, his shaggy hair, his smoky aspect, and the indescribable earthiness that incrusted him, he seemed to represent man's physical nature; while Aylmer's slender figure, and pale, intellectual face, were no less apt a type of the spiritual element.

"Throw open the door of the boudoir, Aminadab," said Aylmer, "and burn a pastil."

"Yes, master," answered Aminadab, looking intently at the lifeless form of Georgiana; and then he muttered to himself, "If she were my wife, I'd never part with that birthmark."

When Georgiana recovered consciousness she found herself breathing an atmosphere of penetrating fragrance, the gentle potency of which had recalled her from her deathlike faintness. The scene around her looked like enchantment. Aylmer had converted those smoky, dingy, sombre rooms, where he had spent his brightest years in recondite pursuits, into a series of beautiful apartments not unfit to be the secluded abode of a lovely woman. The walls were hung with gorgeous curtains, which imparted the combination of grandeur and grace that no other species of adornment can achieve; and as they fell from the ceiling to the floor, their rich and ponderous folds, concealing all angles and straight lines, appeared to shut in the scene from infinite space. For aught Georgiana knew, it might be a pavilion among the clouds. And Aylmer, excluding the sunshine, which would have interfered with his chemical processes, had supplied its place with perfumed lamps, emitting flames of various hue, but all uniting in a soft, impurpled radiance. He now knelt by his wife's side, watching her earnestly, but without alarm; for he was confident in his science, and felt that he could draw a magic circle round her within which no evil might intrude.

"Where am I? Ah, I remember," said Georgiana, faintly; and she placed her hand over her cheek to hide the terrible mark from her husband's eyes.

"Fear not, dearest!" exclaimed he. "Do not shrink from me! Believe me,   *30*
Georgiana, I even rejoice in this single imperfection, since it will be such a rapture to remove it."

"Oh, spare me!" sadly replied his wife. "Pray do not look at it again. I never can forget that convulsive shudder."

In order to soothe Georgiana, and, as it were, to release her mind from the burden of actual things, Aylmer now put in practice some of the light and playful secrets which science had taught him among its profounder lore. Airy figures, absolutely bodiless ideas, and forms of unsubstantial beauty came and danced before her, imprinting their momentary footsteps on beams of light. Though she had some indistinct idea of the method of these optical phenomena, still the illusion was almost perfect enough to warrant the belief that her husband possessed sway over the spiritual world. Then again, when she felt a wish to look forth from her seclusion, immediately, as if her thoughts were answered, the procession of external existence flitted across a screen. The scenery and the figures of actual life were perfectly represented, but with that bewitching, yet indescribable difference which always makes a picture, an image, or a shadow so much more attractive than the original. When wearied of this, Aylmer bade her cast her eyes upon a vessel containing a quantity of earth. She did so, with little interest at first; but was soon startled to perceive the germ of a plant shooting upward from the soil. Then came the slender stalk; the leaves gradually unfolded themselves; and amid them was a perfect and lovely flower.

"It is magical!" cried Georgiana. "I dare not touch it."

"Nay, pluck it," answered Aylmer,—"pluck it, and inhale its brief perfume while you may. The flower will wither in a few moments and leave nothing save its brown seed vessels; but thence may be perpetuated a race as ephemeral as itself."

But Georgiana had no sooner touched the flower than the whole plant   *35*
suffered a blight, its leaves turning coal-black as if by the agency of fire.

"There was too powerful a stimulus," said Aylmer, thoughtfully.

To make up for this abortive experiment, he proposed to take her portrait by a scientific process of his own invention. It was to be effected by rays of light striking upon a polished plate of metal. Georgiana assented; but, on looking at the result, was affrighted to find the features of the portrait blurred and indefinable; while the minute figure of a hand appeared where the cheek should have been. Aylmer snatched the metallic plate and threw it into a jar of corrosive acid.

Soon, however, he forgot these mortifying failures. In the intervals of study and chemical experiment he came to her flushed and exhausted, but seemed invigorated by her presence, and spoke in glowing language of the resources of his art. He gave a history of the long dynasty of the alchemists, who spent so many ages in quest of the universal solvent by which the golden principle might be elicited from all things vile and base. Aylmer appeared to believe that, by the plainest scientific logic, it was altogether within the limits of possibility to discover this long-sought medium; "but," he added, "a philosopher who should go deep enough to acquire the power would attain too lofty a wisdom to stoop to the exercise of it." Not less singular were his opinions in regard to the elixir vitae. He more than intimated that it was at his option to concoct a liquid that should prolong life for years, perhaps interminably; but that it would produce a discord in Nature which all the world, and chiefly the quaffer of the immortal nostrum, would find cause to curse.

"Aylmer, are you in earnest?" asked Georgiana, looking at him with amazement and fear. "It is terrible to possess such power, or even to dream of possessing it."

40   "Oh, do not tremble, my love," said her husband. "I would not wrong either you or myself by working such inharmonious effects upon our lives; but I would have you consider how trifling, in comparison, is the skill requisite to remove this little hand."

At the mention of the birthmark, Georgiana, as usual, shrank as if a red-hot iron had touched her cheek.

Again Aylmer applied himself to his labors. She could hear his voice in the distant furnace room giving directions to Aminadab, whose harsh, uncouth, misshapen tones were audible in response, more like the grunt or growl of a brute than human speech. After hours of absence, Aylmer reappeared and proposed that she should now examine his cabinet of chemical products and natural treasures of the earth. Among the former he showed her a small vial, in which, he remarked, was contained a gentle yet most powerful fragrance, capable of impregnating all the breezes that blow across a kingdom. They were of inestimable value, the contents of that little vial; and, as he said so, he threw some of the perfume into the air and filled the room with piercing and invigorating delight.

"And what is this?" asked Georgiana, pointing to a small crystal globe containing a gold-colored liquid. "It is so beautiful to the eye that I could imagine it the elixir of life."

"In one sense it is," replied Aylmer; "or, rather, the elixir of immortality. It is the most precious poison that ever was concocted in this world. By its aid I could apportion the lifetime of any mortal at whom you might point your finger. The strength of the dose would determine whether he were to linger out years, or drop dead in the midst of a breath. No king on his guarded throne could keep his life if I, in my private station, should deem that the welfare of millions justified me in depriving him of it."

"Why do you keep such a terrific drug?" inquired Georgiana in horror.   *45*

"Do not mistrust me, dearest," said her husband, smiling; "its virtuous potency is yet greater than its harmful one. But see! here is a powerful cosmetic. With a few drops of this in a vase of water, freckles may be washed away as easily as the hands are cleansed. A stronger infusion would take the blood out of the cheek, and leave the rosiest beauty a pale ghost."

"Is it with this lotion that you intend to bathe my cheek?" asked Georgiana, anxiously.

"Oh, no," hastily replied her husband; "this is merely superficial. Your case demands a remedy that shall go deeper."

In his interviews with Georgiana, Aylmer generally made minute inquiries as to her sensations and whether the confinement of the rooms and the temperature of the atmosphere agreed with her. These questions had such a particular drift that Georgiana began to conjecture that she was already subjected to certain physical influences, either breathed in with the fragrant air or taken with her food. She fancied likewise, but it might be altogether fancy, that there was a stirring up of her system—a strange, indefinite sensation creeping through her veins, and tingling, half painfully, half pleasurably, at her heart. Still, whenever she dared to look into the mirror, there she beheld herself pale as a white rose and with the crimson birthmark stamped upon her cheek. Not even Aylmer now hated it so much as she.

To dispel the tedium of the hours which her husband found it necessary   *50* to devote to the processes of combination and analysis, Georgiana turned over the volumes of his scientific library. In many dark old tomes she met with chapters full of romance and poetry. They were the works of philosophers of the middle ages, such as Albertus Magnus, Cornelius Agrippa, Paracelsus, and the famous friar who created the prophetic Brazen Head. All these antique naturalists stood in advance of their centuries, yet were imbued with some of their credulity, and therefore were believed, and perhaps imagined themselves to have acquired from the investigation of Nature a power above Nature, and from physics a sway over the spiritual world. Hardly less curious and imaginative were the early volumes of the Transactions of the Royal Society, in which the members, knowing little of the limits of natural possibility, were continually recording wonders or proposing methods whereby wonders might be wrought.

But to Georgiana the most engrossing volume was a large folio from her husband's own hand, in which he had recorded every experiment of his scientific career, its original aim, the methods adopted for its development, and its final success or failure, with the circumstances to which either event was attributable. The book, in truth, was both the history and emblem of his ardent, ambitious, imaginative, yet practical and laborious life. He handled physical details as if there were nothing beyond them; yet spiritualized them all, and redeemed himself from materialism by his strong and eager aspiration towards the infinite. In his grasp the veriest clod of earth assumed a soul. Georgiana, as she read, reverenced Aylmer and loved him more profoundly than ever, but with a less entire dependence on his judgment than heretofore. Much as he had accomplished, she could not but observe that his most splendid successes were almost invariably failures, if compared with the ideal at which he aimed. His brightest diamonds were the merest pebbles, and felt to be so by himself, in comparison with the inestimable gems which lay hidden beyond his reach. The volume, rich with achievements that had won renown for its author, was yet as melancholy a record as ever mortal hand had penned. It was the sad confession and continual exemplification of the shortcomings of the composite man, the spirit burdened with clay and working in matter, and of the despair that assails the higher nature at finding itself so miserably thwarted by the earthly part. Perhaps every man of genius in whatever sphere might recognize the image of his own experience in Aylmer's journal.

So deeply did these reflections affect Georgiana that she laid her face upon the open volume and burst into tears. In this situation she was found by her husband.

"It is dangerous to read in a sorcerer's books," said he with a smile, though his countenance was uneasy and displeased. "Georgiana, there are pages in that volume which I can scarcely glance over and keep my senses. Take heed lest it prove as detrimental to you."

"It has made me worship you more than ever," said she.

55 "Ah, wait for this one success," rejoined he, "then worship me if you will. I shall deem myself hardly unworthy of it. But come, I have sought you for the luxury of your voice. Sing to me, dearest."

So she poured out the liquid music of her voice to quench the thirst of his spirit. He then took his leave with a boyish exuberance of gayety, assuring her that her seclusion would endure but a little longer, and that the result was already certain. Scarcely had he departed when Georgiana felt irresistibly impelled to follow him. She had forgotten to inform Aylmer of a symptom which for two or three hours past had begun to excite her attention. It was a sensation in the fatal birthmark, not painful, but which induced a restlessness throughout her system. Hastening after her husband, she intruded for the first time into the laboratory.

The first thing that struck her eye was the furnace, that hot and feverish worker, with the intense glow of its fire, which by the quantities of soot clustered above it seemed to have been burning for ages. There was a distilling apparatus in full operation. Around the room were retorts, tubes, cylinders, crucibles, and other apparatus of chemical research. An electrical machine stood ready for immediate use. The atmosphere felt oppressively close, and was tainted with gaseous odors which had been tormented forth by the processes of science. The severe and homely simplicity of the apartment, with its naked walls and brick pavement, looked strange, accustomed as Georgiana had become to the fantastic elegance of her boudoir. But what chiefly, indeed almost solely, drew her attention, was the aspect of Aylmer himself.

He was pale as death, anxious and absorbed, and hung over the furnace as if it depended upon his utmost watchfulness whether the liquid which it was distilling should be the draught of immortal happiness or misery. How different from the sanguine and joyous mien that he had assumed for Georgiana's encouragement!

"Carefully now, Aminadab; carefully, thou human machine; carefully, thou man of clay!" muttered Aylmer, more to himself than his assistant. "Now, if there be a thought too much or too little, it is all over."

"Ho! ho!" mumbled Aminadab. "Look, master! look!"   60

Aylmer raised his eyes hastily, and at first reddened, then grew paler than ever, on beholding Georgiana. He rushed towards her and seized her arm with a gripe that left the print of his fingers upon it.

"Why do you come hither? Have you no trust in your husband?" cried he, impetuously. "Would you throw the blight of that fatal birthmark over my labors? It is not well done. Go, prying woman, go!"

"Nay, Aylmer," said Georgiana with the firmness of which she possessed no stinted endowment, "it is not you that have a right to complain. You mistrust your wife; you have concealed the anxiety with which you watch the development of this experiment. Think not so unworthily of me, my husband. Tell me all the risk we run, and fear not that I shall shrink; for my share in it is far less than your own."

"No, no, Georgiana!" said Aylmer, impatiently; "it must not be."

"I submit," replied she calmly. "And, Aylmer, I shall quaff whatever   65
draught you bring me; but it will be on the same principle that would induce me to take a dose of poison if offered by your hand."

"My noble wife," said Aylmer, deeply moved, "I knew not the height and depth of your nature until now. Nothing shall be concealed. Know, then, that this crimson hand, superficial as it seems, has clutched its grasp into your being with a strength of which I had no previous conception. I have already administered agents powerful enough to do aught except to change your entire physical system. Only one thing remains to be tried. If that fail us we are ruined."

"Why did you hesitate to tell me this?" asked she.

"Because, Georgiana," said Aylmer, in a low voice, "there is danger."

"Danger? There is but one danger—that this horrible stigma shall be left upon my cheek!" cried Georgiana. "Remove it, remove it, whatever be the cost, or we shall both go mad!"

70   "Heaven knows your words are too true," said Aylmer, sadly. "And now, dearest, return to your boudoir. In a little while all will be tested."

He conducted her back and took leave of her with a solemn tenderness which spoke far more than his words how much was now at stake. After his departure Georgiana became rapt in musings. She considered the character of Aylmer, and did it completer justice than at any previous moment. Her heart exulted, while it trembled, at his honorable love—so pure and lofty that it would accept nothing less than perfection nor miserably make itself contented with an earthlier nature than he had dreamed of. She felt how much more precious was such a sentiment than that meaner kind which would have borne with the imperfection for her sake, and have been guilty of treason to holy love by degrading its perfect idea to the level of the actual; and with her whole spirit she prayed that, for a single moment, she might satisfy his highest and deepest conception. Longer than one moment she well knew it could not be; for his spirit was ever on the march, ever ascending, and each instant required something that was beyond the scope of the instant before.

The sound of her husband's footsteps aroused her. He bore a crystal goblet containing a liquor colorless as water, but bright enough to be the draught of immortality. Aylmer was pale; but it seemed rather the consequence of a highly-wrought state of mind and tension of spirit than of fear or doubt.

"The concoction of the draught has been perfect," said he, in answer to Georgiana's look. "Unless all my science have deceived me, it cannot fail."

"Save on your account, my dearest Aylmer," observed his wife, "I might wish to put off this birthmark of mortality by relinquishing mortality itself in preference to any other mode. Life is but a sad possession to those who have attained precisely the degree of moral advancement at which I stand. Were I weaker and blinder it might be happiness. Were I stronger, it might be endured hopefully. But, being where I find myself, methinks I am of all mortals the most fit to die."

75   "You are fit for heaven without tasting death!" replied her husband "But why do we speak of dying? The draught cannot fail. Behold its effect upon this plant."

On the window seat there stood a geranium diseased with yellow blotches, which had overspread all its leaves. Aylmer poured a small quantity of the liquid upon the soil in which it grew. In a little time, when the roots of the plant had taken up the moisture, the unsightly blotches began to be extinguished in a living verdure.

"There needed no proof," said Georgiana, quietly. "Give me the goblet. I joyfully stake all upon your word."

"Drink, then, thou lofty creature!" exclaimed Aylmer, with fervid admiration. "There is no taint of imperfection on thy spirit. Thy sensible frame, too, shall soon be all perfect."

She quaffed the liquid and returned the goblet to his hand.

"It is grateful," said she with a placid smile. "Methinks it is like water   *80* from a heavenly fountain; for it contains I know not what of unobtrusive fragrance and deliciousness. It allays a feverish thirst that had parched me for many days. Now, dearest, let me sleep. My earthly senses are closing over my spirit like the leaves around the heart of a rose at sunset."

She spoke the last words with a gentle reluctance, as if it required almost more energy than she could command to pronounce the faint and lingering syllables. Scarcely had they loitered through her lips ere she was lost in slumber. Aylmer sat by her side, watching her aspect with the emotions proper to a man the whole value of whose existence was involved in the process now to be tested. Mingled with this mood, however, was the philosophic investigation characteristic of the man of science. Not the minutest symptom escaped him. A heightened flush of the cheek, a slight irregularity of breath, a quiver of the eyelid, a hardly perceptible tremor through the frame,—such were the details which, as the moments passed, he wrote down in his folio volume. Intense thought had set its stamp upon every previous page of that volume, but the thoughts of years were all concentrated upon the last.

While thus employed, he failed not to gaze often at the fatal hand, and not without a shudder. Yet once, by a strange and unaccountable impulse, he pressed it with his lips. His spirit recoiled, however, in the very act, and Georgiana, out of the midst of her deep sleep, moved uneasily and murmured as if in remonstrance. Again Aylmer resumed his watch. Nor was it without avail. The crimson hand, which at first had been strongly visible upon the marble paleness of Georgiana's cheek, now grew more faintly outlined. She remained not less pale than ever; but the birthmark with every breath that came and went, lost somewhat of its former distinctness. Its presence had been awful; its departure was more awful still. Watch the stain of the rainbow fading out the sky, and you will know how that mysterious symbol passed away.

"By Heaven! it is well-nigh gone!" said Aylmer to himself, in almost irrepressible ecstasy. "I can scarcely trace it now. Success! success! And now it is like the faintest rose color. The lightest flush of blood across her cheek would overcome it. But she is so pale!"

He drew aside the window curtain and suffered the light of natural day to fall into the room and rest upon her cheek. At the same time he heard a gross, hoarse chuckle, which he had long known as his servant Aminadab's expression of delight.

"Ah, clod! ah, earthly mass!" cried Aylmer, laughing in a sort of frenzy,   *85* "you have served me well! Matter and spirit—earth and heaven—have both done their part in this! Laugh, thing of the senses! You have earned the right to laugh."

These exclamations broke Georgiana's sleep. She slowly unclosed her eyes and gazed into the mirror which her husband had arranged for that purpose. A faint smile flitted over her lips when she recognized how barely perceptible was now that crimson hand which had once blazed forth with such disastrous brilliancy as to scare away all their happiness. But then her eyes sought Aylmer's face with a trouble and anxiety that he could by no means account for.

"My poor Aylmer!" murmured she.

"Poor? Nay, richest, happiest, most favored!" exclaimed he. "My peerless bride, it is successful! You are perfect!"

"My poor Aylmer," she repeated, with a more than human tenderness, "you have aimed loftily; you have done nobly. Do not repent that with so high and pure a feeling, you have rejected the best the earth could offer. Aylmer, dearest Aylmer, I am dying!"

90   Alas! it was too true! The fatal hand had grappled with the mystery of life, and was the bond by which an angelic spirit kept itself in union with a mortal frame. As the last crimson tint of the birthmark—that sole token of human imperfection—faded from her cheek, the parting breath of the now perfect woman passed into the atmosphere, and her soul, lingering a moment near her husband, took its heavenward flight. Then a hoarse, chuckling laugh was heard again! Thus ever does the gross fatality of earth exult in its invariable triumph over the immortal essence which, in this dim sphere of half development, demands the completeness of a higher state. Yet, had Alymer reached a profounder wisdom, he need not thus have flung away the happiness which would have woven his mortal life of the selfsame texture with the celestial. The momentary circumstance was too strong for him; he failed to look beyond the shadowy scope of time, and, living once for all in eternity, to find the perfect future in the present.   *1843*

CONSIDERATIONS

1. What is revealed about Alymer—his personality, his priorities, his aversions, his strengths, his weaknesses—from the opening paragraph alone? What do we not learn about him, and why might this matter to the central conflict?
2. Compare/contrast the ways in which Alymer and Georgiana are described in terms of their physical appearances. Who is described in greater detail, and how does this contribute to the central theme in this story?
3. Tensions exist in this story between a man and his attempt to control nature, and a man and his battle with his own internal nature. Which force do you find more powerful in undermining Alymer: his internal nature or nature as an outside force?

4. Trace the underlying theme of reality versus illusion in "The Birthmark" and explain how it relates to Alymer's central conflict.
5. Trace the changes within both characters as the story progresses. In what ways does Alymer change? How does Georgiana change? How do these changes affect the outcome of this story?
6. Although Alymer, the scientist, sees the birthmark on Georgiana's cheek as a flaw of nature, others have called it a "charm." If Alymer symbolizes science in general and the birthmark symbolizes beauty, what is Hawthorne's message regarding these two forces?

More Resources on
Nathaniel Hawthorne

In *ARIEL*

- Brief biography of Hawthorne
- Complete text of the short story "Young Goodman Brown," with hyperlinked comments
- Video clip of dramatic production of "Young Goodman Brown"
- Bibliography of scholarly works on Hawthorne

KAY BOYLE (1902–1992)
Astronomer's Wife

Kay Boyle grew up in Cincinnati, Ohio. In 1917, she moved to New York City, where she studied architecture and, while helping edit a literary magazine, married French-born engineer Richard Brault. They moved to France in 1923, but three years later, her marriage and her health failing, she moved alone to the south of France and began working on a magazine with Ernest Walsh. The next year Walsh died, and the pregnant Boyle moved to Paris, where she joined the avant-garde community of artists and writers. In 1932, she formally divorced Brault and married Laurence Vail, with whom she had been living since 1929. During the thirties, they lived in France and Austria, and Boyle published several novels and collections of short stories, many of which assert a woman's right to sexual freedom and artistic independence. The selection here comes from The White Horses of Vienna and Other Stories *(1936). In 1936, she also published a novel,* Death of a Man, *that attacked Nazism before most people in the United States were aware that it was becoming a problem in Europe. She returned to the United States in 1941, divorced Vail, and married Baron Joseph von Franckenstein in 1943. Between 1942 and 1946, she wrote a series of novels about the German occupation of France and the French resistance movement. In 1947, she and von Franckenstein moved to Germany, where he had a post with the U.S. Foreign Service, and she became the European correspondent for* The New Yorker. *After her husband's death in 1963, Boyle began teaching at San Francisco State University, a job she held until 1979. She wrote a novel,* The Underground Woman *(1975), about the student protest movement, in which she had participated. Although she won a number of literary awards during her lifetime, she was "so busy writing and acting upon her beliefs," wrote one critic, that she "had little time to cultivate a following. Indeed, seeking literary fame would be contrary to Boyle's beliefs, for she . . . consistently sought to speak for those who could not speak for themselves."*

There is an evil moment on awakening when all things seem to pause. But for women, they only falter and may be set in action by a single move: a lifted hand and the pendulum will swing, or the voice raised and through every room the pulse takes up its beating. The astronomer's wife felt the interval gaping and at once filled it to the brim. She fetched up her gentle voice and sent it warily down the stairs for coffee, swung her feet out upon the oval mat, and hailed the morning with her bare arms quivering flesh drawn taut in rhythmic exercise: left, left, left my wife and fourteen children, right, right, right in the middle of the dusty road.

The day would proceed from this, beat by beat, without reflection, like every other day. The astronomer was still asleep, or feigning it, and she, once out of bed, had come into her own possession. Although scarcely ever out of sight of the impenetrable silence of his brow, she would be absent from him all the day in being clean, busy, kind. He was a man of other things, a dreamer. At times he lay still for hours, at others he sat upon the roof behind his telescope, or wandered down the pathway to the road and out across the mountains. This day, like any other, would go on from the removal of the spot left there from dinner on the astronomer's vest to the severe thrashing of the mayonnaise for lunch. That man might be each time the new arching wave, and woman the undertow that sucked him back, were things she had been told by his silence were so.

In spite of the earliness of the hour, the girl had heard her mistress's voice and was coming up the stairs. At the threshold of the bedroom she paused, and said: "Madame, the plumber is here."

The astronomer's wife put on her white and scarlet smock very quickly and buttoned it at the neck. Then she stepped carefully around the motionless spread of water in the hall.

5   "Tell him to come right up," she said. She laid her hands on the bannisters and stood looking down the wooden stairway. "Ah, I am Mrs. Ames," she

said softly as she saw him mounting. "I am Mrs. Ames," she said softly, softly down the flight of stairs. "I am Mrs. Ames," spoken soft as a willow weeping. "The professor is still sleeping. Just step this way."

The plumber himself looked up and saw Mrs. Ames with her voice hushed, speaking to him. She was a youngish woman, but this she had forgotten. The mystery and silence of her husband's mind lay like a chiding finger on her lips. Her eyes were gray, for the light had been extinguished in them. The strange dim halo of her yellow hair was still uncombed and sideways on her head.

For all of his heavy boots, the plumber quieted the sound of his feet, and together they went down the hall, picking their way around the still lake of water that spread as far as the landing and lay docile there. The plumber was a tough, hardy man; but he took off his hat when he spoke to her and looked her fully, almost insolently in the eye.

"Does it come from the wash-basin," he said, "or from the other . . . ?"

"Oh, from the other," said Mrs. Ames without hesitation.

In this place the villas were scattered out few and primitive, and although   *10*
beauty lay without there was no reflection of her face within. Here all was awkward and unfit; a sense of wrestling with uncouth forces gave everything an austere countenance. Even the plumber, dealing as does a woman with matters under hand, was grave and stately. The mountains round about seemed to have cast them into the shadow of great dignity.

Mrs. Ames began speaking of their arrival that summer in the little villa, mourning each event as it followed on the other.

"Then, just before going to bed last night," she said, "I noticed something was unusual."

The plumber cast down a folded square of sackcloth on the brimming floor and laid his leather apron on it. Then he stepped boldly onto the heart of the island it shaped and looked long into the overflowing bowl.

"The water should be stopped from the meter in the garden," he said at last.

"Oh, I did that," said Mrs. Ames, "the very first thing last night. I turned   *15*
it off at once, in my nightgown, as soon as I saw what was happening. But all this had already run in."

The plumber looked for a moment at her red kid slippers. She was standing just at the edge of the clear, pure-seeming tide.

"It's no doubt the soil lines," he said severely. "It may be that something has stopped them, but my opinion is that the water seals aren't working. That's the trouble often enough in such cases. If you had a valve you wouldn't be caught like this."

Mrs. Ames did not know how to meet this rebuke. She stood, swaying a little, looking into the plumber's blue relentless eye.

"I'm sorry—I'm sorry that my husband," she said, "is still—resting and cannot go into this with you. I'm sure it must be very interesting. . . ."

20   "You'll probably have to have the traps sealed," said the plumber grimly, and at the sound of this Mrs. Ames' hand flew in dismay to the side of her face. The plumber made no move, but the set of his mouth as he looked at her seemed to soften. "Anyway, I'll have a look from the garden end," he said.

"Oh, do," said the astronomer's wife in relief. Here was a man who spoke of action and object as simply as women did! But however hushed her voice had been, it carried clearly to Professor Ames who lay, dreaming and solitary, upon his bed. He heard their footsteps come down the hall, pause, and skip across the pool of overflow.

"Katherine!" said the astronomer in a ringing tone. "There's a problem worthy of your mettle!"

Mrs. Ames did not turn her head, but led the plumber swiftly down the stairs. When the sun in the garden struck her face, he saw there was a wave of color in it, but this may have been anything but shame.

"You see how it is," said the plumber, as if leading her mind away. "The drains run from these houses right down the hill, big enough for a man to stand upright in them, and clean as a whistle too." There they stood in the garden with the vegetation flowering in disorder all about. The plumber looked at the astronomer's wife. "They come out at the torrent on the other side of the forest beyond there," he said.

25   But the words the astronomer had spoken still sounded in her in despair. The mind of man, she knew, made steep and sprightly flights, pursued illusion, took foothold in the nameless things that cannot pass between the thumb and finger. But whenever the astronomer gave voice to the thoughts that soared within him, she returned in gratitude to the long expanses of his silence. Desert-like they stretched behind and before the articulation of his scorn.

Life, life is an open sea, she sought to explain it in sorrow, and to survive women cling to the floating debris on the tide. But the plumber had suddenly fallen upon his knees in the grass and had crooked his fingers through the ring of the drains' trapdoor. When she looked down she saw that he was looking up into her face, and she saw too that his hair was as light as gold.

"Perhaps Mr. Ames," he said rather bitterly, "would like to come down with me and have a look around?"

"Down?" said Mrs. Ames in wonder.

"Into the drains," said the plumber brutally. "They're a study for a man who likes to know what's what."

30   "Oh, Mr. Ames," said Mrs. Ames in confusion. "He's still—still in bed, you see."

The plumber lifted his strong, weathered face and looked curiously at her. Surely it seemed to him strange for a man to linger in bed, with the sun pouring yellow as wine all over the place. The astronomer's wife saw his lean cheeks, his high, rugged bones, and the deep seams in his brow. His flesh was as firm and clean as wood, stained richly tan with the climate's rigor. His fingers were blunt, but comprehensible to her, gripped in the ring and holding

the iron door wide. The backs of his hands were bound round and round with
ripe blue veins of blood.

"At any rate," said the astronomer's wife, and the thought of it moved
her lips to smile a little, "Mr. Ames would never go down there alive. He likes
going up," she said. And she, in her turn, pointed, but impudently, towards the
heavens. "On the roof. Or on the mountains. He's been up on the tops of them
many times."

"It's matter of habit," said the plumber, and suddenly he went down the
trap. Mrs. Ames saw a bright little piece of his hair still shining, like a star, long
after the rest of him had gone. Out of the depths, his voice, hollow and dark
with foreboding, returned to her. "I think something has stopped the elbow,"
was what he said.

This was speech that touched her flesh and bone and made her wonder.
When her husband spoke of height, having no sense of it, she could not picture
it nor hear. Depth or magic passed her by unless a name were given. But madness in a daily shape, as elbow stopped, she saw clearly and well. She sat down
on the grasses, bewildered that it should be a man who had spoken to her so.

She saw the weeds springing up, and she did not move to tear them up   *35*
from life. She sat powerless, her senses veiled, with no action taking shape beneath her hands. In this way some men sat for hours on end, she knew, tracking a single thought back to its origin. The mind of man could balance and
divide, weed out, destroy. She sat on the full, burdened grasses, seeking to think,
and dimly waiting for the plumber to return.

Whereas her husband had always gone up, as the dead go, she knew now
that there were others who went down, like the corporeal being of the dead.
That men were then divided into two bodies now seemed clear to Mrs. Ames.
This knowledge stunned her with its simplicity and took the uneasy motion
from her limbs. She could not stir, but sat facing the mountains' rocky flanks,
and harking in silence to lucidity. Her husband was the mind, this other man
the meat, of all mankind.

After a little, the plumber emerged from the earth: first the light top of
his head, then the burnt brow, and then the blue eyes fringed with whitest
lash. He braced his thick hands flat on the pavings of the garden-path and
swung himself completely from the pit.

"It's the soil lines," he said pleasantly. "The gases," he said as he looked
down upon her lifted face, "are backing up the drains."

"What in the world are we going to do?" said the astronomer's wife
softly. There was a young and strange delight in putting questions to which
true answers would be given. Everything the astronomer had ever said to her
was a continuous query to which there could be no response.

"Ah, come, now," said the plumber, looking down and smiling. "There's   *40*
a remedy for every ill, you know. Sometimes it may be that," he said as if speaking to a child, "or sometimes the other thing. But there's always a help for
everything amiss."

Things come out of herbs and make you young again, he might have been saying to her; or the first good rain will quench any drought; or time of itself will put a broken bone together.

"I'm going to follow the ground pipe out right to the torrent," the plumber was saying. "The trouble's between here and there and I'll find it on the way. There's nothing at all that can't be done over for the caring," he was saying, and his eyes were fastened on her face in insolence, or gentleness, or love.

The astronomer's wife stood up, fixed a pin in her hair, and turned around towards the kitchen. Even while she was calling the servant's name, the plumber began speaking again.

"I once had a cow that lost her cud," the plumber was saying. The girl came out on the kitchen-step and Mrs. Ames stood smiling at her in the sun.

45   "The trouble is very serious, very serious," she said across the garden. "When Mr. Ames gets up, please tell him I've gone down."

She pointed briefly to the open door in the pathway, and the plumber hoisted his kit on his arm and put out his hand to help her down.

"But I made her another in no time," he was saying, "out of flowers and things and what not."

"Oh," said the astronomer's wife in wonder as she stepped into the heart of the earth. She took his arm, knowing that what he said was true.   *1936*

CONSIDERATIONS

1. From the first two paragraphs, what specific words and images foreshadow the different natures—and thus the heart of the conflict—between the astronomer and his wife?
2. Trace the images in this story that have to do with the natural, physical world and those that relate to the lofty world of science and logic. What do the contrasting images reveal about the two men in this piece? What do they reveal about Mrs. Ames?
3. From whose point of view is this story told? When does the narrator's tone shift in this piece? What causes this shift in tone?
4. Some might argue that Mrs. Ames is living in an abusive relationship with a husband who is stolid, cold, and calculating. What details support this position? What might you offer as an opposing argument?
5. In what ways does the presence of water reflect the feelings and perspective of Mrs. Ames?
6. Mrs. Ames comes to the conclusion that men are "divided into two bodies"—one that goes up, as her husband the astronomer does, and one that goes down into the earth, like the plumber. To what extent does your own experience support or refute her reasoning?

B. TRAVEN (1890–1969)

Assembly Line

The details of Traven's life are elusive and mysterious. His first name is some-times given as Bruno and sometimes as Bernard. He apparently spent his early years in Germany, where he wrote under the pen name of Ret Marut. The anar-chist nature of his writings led to death threats, and he was forced to escape from Germany. In addition to writing fiction, he was also a film scriptwriter, well known for his novel The Treasure of the Sierra Madre, *which was later made into a highly regarded movie. Traven's leftist philosophy is evident throughout his work, and the selection included here suggests his view of how corporations and governments can crush the beauty of individual freedom.*

Mr. E. L. Winthrop of New York was on vacation in the Republic of Mexico. It wasn't long before he realized that this strange and really wild country had not yet been fully and satisfactorily explored by Rotarians and Lions, who are for-ever conscious of their glorious mission on earth. Therefore, he considered it his duty as a good American citizen to do his part in correcting this oversight.

In search for opportunities to indulge in his new avocation, he left the beaten track and ventured into regions not especially mentioned, and hence not recommended, by travel agents to foreign tourists. So it happened that one day he found himself in a little, quaint Indian village somewhere in the State of Oaxaca.

Walking along the dusty main street of this pueblocito, which knew nothing of pavements, drainage, plumbing, or of any means of artificial light save candles or pine splinters, he met with an Indian squatting on the earthen-floor front porch of a palm hut, a so-called jacalito.

The Indian was busy making little baskets from bast and from all kinds of fibers gathered by him in the immense tropical bush which surrounded the village on all sides. The material used had not only been well prepared for its purpose but was also richly colored with dyes that the basket-maker himself extracted from various native plants, barks, roots and from certain insects by a process known only to him and the members of his family.

His principal business, however, was not producing baskets. He was a   5
peasant who lived on what the small property he possessed—less than fifteen acres of not too fertile soil—would yield, after much sweat and labor and after constantly worrying over the most wanted and best suited distribution of rain, sunshine, and wind and the changing balance of birds and insects beneficial or harmful to his crops. Baskets he made when there was nothing else for him to do in the fields, because he was unable to dawdle. After all, the sale of his bas-kets, though to a rather limited degree only, added to the small income he re-ceived from his little farm.

In spite of being by profession just a plain peasant, it was clearly seen from the small baskets he made that at heart he was an artist, a true and accomplished artist. Each basket looked as if covered all over with the most beautiful some-times fantastic ornaments, flowers, butterflies, birds, squirrels, antelopes, tigers, and a score of other animals of the wilds. Yet, the most amazing thing was that these decorations, all of them symphonies of color, were not painted on the baskets but were instead actually part of the baskets themselves. Bast and fibers dyed in dozens of different colors were so cleverly—one must actually say in-trinsically—interwoven that those attractive designs appeared on the inner part of the basket as well as on the outside. Not by painting but by weaving were those highly artistic designs achieved. This performance he accomplished with-out ever looking at any sketch or pattern. While working on a basket these de-signs came to light as if by magic, and as long as a basket was not entirely finished one could not perceive what in this case or that the decoration would be like.

People in the market town who bought these baskets would use them for sewing baskets or to decorate tables with or window sills, or to hold little things to keep them from lying around. Women put their jewelery in them or flowers or little dolls. There were in fact a hundred and two ways they might serve certain purposes in a household or in a lady's own room.

Whenever the Indian had finished about twenty of the baskets he took them to town on market day. Sometimes he would already be on his way shortly after midnight because he owned only a burro to ride on, and if the burro had gone astray the day before, as happened frequently, he would have to walk the whole way into town and back again.

At the market he had to pay twenty centavos in taxes to sell his wares. Each basket cost him between twenty and thirty hours of constant work, not counting the time spent gathering bast and fibers, preparing them, making dyes and coloring the bast. All this meant extra time and work. The price he asked for each basket was fifty centavos, the equivalent of about four cents. It seldom happened however that the buyer paid outright the full fifty centavos asked—or four reales as the Indians called that money. The prospective buyer started bargaining, telling the Indian that he ought to be ashamed to ask such a sinful price. "Why the whole dirty thing is nothing but ordinary petate straw which you find in heaps wherever you may look for it; the jungle is packed full of it," the buyer would argue. "Such a little basket, what's it good for any-how? If I paid you, you thief, ten centavitos for it you should be grateful and kiss my hand. Well it's your lucky day, I'll be generous this time, I'll pay you twenty, yet not one green centavo more. Take it or run along."

10   So he sold finally for twenty-five centavos, but then the buyer would say, "Now, what do you think of that? I've got only twenty centavos change on me. What can we do about that? If you can change me a twenty peso bill, all right, you shall have your twenty-five fierros." Of course, the Indian could not change a twenty peso bill and so the basket went for twenty centavos.

He had little if any knowledge of the outside world or he would have known that what happened to him was happening every hour of every day to every artist all over the world. That knowledge would have made him very proud, because he would have realized that he belonged to the little army which is the salt of the earth and which keeps culture, urbanity and beauty for their own sakes from passing away.

Often it was not possible for him to sell all the baskets he had brought to market, for people here as elsewhere in the world preferred things made by the millions and each so much like the other that you were unable, even with the help of a magnifying glass, to tell which was which and where was the difference between two of the same kind.

Yet he, this craftsman, had in his life made several hundreds of those exquisite baskets, but so far no two of them had he ever turned out alike in design. Each was an individual piece of art and as different from the other as a Murillo from a Velásquez.

Naturally he did not want to take those baskets which he could not sell at the market place home with him again if he could help it. In such a case he went peddling his products from door to door where he was treated partly as a beggar and partly as a vagrant apparently looking for an opportunity to steal, and he frequently had to swallow all sorts of insults and nasty remarks.

Then, after a long run, perhaps a woman would finally stop him, take   15
one of the baskets and offer him ten centavos, which price through talks and talks would perhaps go up to fifteen or even to twenty. Nevertheless, in many instances he would actually get no more than just ten centavos, and the buyer, usually a woman, would grasp that little marvel and right before his eyes throw it carelessly on the nearest table as if to say, "Well, I take that piece of nonsense only for charity's sake. I know my money is wasted. But then, after all, I'm a Christian and I can't see a poor Indian die of hunger since he has come such a long way from his village." This would remind her of something better and she would hold him and say, "Where are you at home anyway, Indito? What's your pueblo? So, from Huehuetonoc? Now, listen here, Indito, can't you bring me next Saturday two or three turkeys from Huehuetonoc? But they must be heavy and fat and very, very cheap or I won't even touch them. If I wish to pay the regular price I don't need you to bring them. Understand? Hop along, now, Indito."

The Indian squatted on the earthen floor in the portico of his hut, attended to his work and showed no special interest in the curiosity of Mr. Winthrop watching him. He acted almost as if he ignored the presence of the American altogether.

"How much that little basket, friend?" Mr. Winthrop asked when he felt that he at least had to say something so as not to appear idiotic.

"Fifty centavos, patroncito, my good little lordy, four reales," the Indian answered politely.

"All right, sold," Mr. Winthrop blurted out in a tone and with a gesture as if he had bought a whole railroad. And examining his buy he added, "I know already who I'll give that pretty little thing to. She'll kiss me for it, sure. Wonder what she'll use it for?"

20   He had expected to hear a price of three or even four pesos. The moment he realized that he had judged the value six times too high, he saw right away what great business possibilities this miserable Indian village might offer to a dynamic promoter like himself. Without further delay he started exploring those possibilities. "Suppose, my good friend, I buy ten of these little baskets of yours, which as I might as well admit right here and now, have practically no real use whatsoever. Well, as I was saying, if I buy ten, how much would you then charge me apiece?"

The Indian hesitated for a few seconds as if making calculations. Finally he said, "If you buy ten I can let you have them for forty-five centavos each, señorito gentleman."

"All right, amigo. And now let's suppose I buy from you straightaway one hundred of these absolutely useless baskets, how much will cost me each?"

The Indian, never looking up to the American standing before him and hardly taking his eyes off his work, said politely and without the slightest trace of enthusiasm in his voice, "In such a case I might not be quite unwilling to sell each for forty centavitos."

Mr. Winthrop bought sixteen baskets, which was all the Indian had in stock.

25   After three weeks' stay in the Republic, Mr. Winthrop was convinced that he knew this country perfectly, that he had seen everything and knew all about the inhabitants, their character and their way of life, and that there was nothing left for him to explore. So he returned to good old Nooyorg and felt happy to be once more in a civilized country, as he expressed it to himself.

One day going out for lunch he passed a confectioner's and, looking at the display in the window, he suddenly remembered the little baskets he had bought in that faraway Indian village.

He hurried home and took all the baskets he still had left to one of the best-known candy-makers in the city.

"I can offer you here," Mr. Winthrop said to the confectioner, "one of the most artistic and at the same time the most original of boxes, if you wish to call them that. These little baskets would be just right for the most expensive chocolates meant for elegant and high-priced gifts. Just have a good look at them sir, and let me listen."

The confectioner examined the baskets and found them extraordinarily well suited for a certain line in his business. Never before had there been anything like them for originality, prettiness and good taste. He, however, avoided most carefully showing any sign of enthusiasm, for which there would be time enough once he knew the price and whether he could get a whole load exclusively.

30   He shrugged his shoulders and said, "Well, I don't know. If you asked me I'd say it isn't quite what I'm after. However, we might give it a try. It depends, of course, on the price. In our business the package mustn't cost more than what's in it."

"Do I hear an offer?" Mr. Winthrop asked.

"Why don't you tell me in round figures how much you want for them? I'm no good at guessing."

"Well, I'll tell you, Mr. Kemple: since I'm the smart guy who discovered these baskets and since I'm the only Jack who knows where to lay his hands on more, I'm selling to the highest bidder, on an exclusive basis of course. I'm positive you can see it my way, Mr. Kemple."

"Quite so, and may the best man win," the confectioner said. "I'll talk the matter over with my partners. See me tomorrow same time, please, and I'll let you know how far we might be willing to go."

Next day when both gentlemen met again Mr. Kemple said: "Now, to be frank with you, I know art on seeing it, no getting around that. And these baskets are little works of art, they surely are. However, we are no art dealers, you realize that of course. We've no other use for these pretty little things except as fancy packing for our French pralines made by us. We can't pay for them what we might pay considering them pieces of art. After all to us they're only wrappings. Fine wrappings, perhaps, but nevertheless wrappings. You'll see it our way, I hope, Mr.—oh yes, Mr. Winthrop. So, here is our offer, take it or leave it: a dollar and a quarter apiece and not one cent more."

Mr. Winthrop made a gesture as if he had been struck over the head.

The confectioner, misunderstanding this involutary gesture of Mr. Winthrop, added quickly "All right, all right, no reason to get excited, no reason at all. Perhaps we can do a trifle better. Let's say one-fifty."

"Make it one-seventy-five," Mr. Winthrop snapped, swallowing his breath while wiping his forehead.

"Sold. One-seventy-five apiece free at port of New York. We pay the customs and you pay the shipping. Right?"

"Sold," Mr. Winthrop also said and the deal was closed.

"There is of course, one condition," the confectioner explained just when Mr. Winthrop was to leave. "One or two hundred won't do for us. It wouldn't pay the trouble and the advertising. I won't consider less than ten thousand, or one thousand dozens if that sounds better in your ears. And they must come in no less than twelve different patterns well assorted. How about that?"

"I can make it sixty different patterns or designs."

"So much the better. And you're sure you can deliver ten thousand let's say early October?"

"Absolutely," Mr. Winthrop avowed and signed the contract.

Practically all the way back to Mexico, Mr. Winthrop had a notebook in his left hand and a pencil in his right and he was writing figures, long rows of them, to find out exactly how much richer he would be when this business had been put through.

"Now, let's sum up the whole goddam thing," he muttered to himself. "Damn it, where is that cursed pencil again? I had it right between my fingers. Ah, there it is. Ten thousand he ordered. Well, well, there we got a clean-cut

35

40

45

profit of fifteen thousand four hundred and forty genuine dollars. Sweet smackers. Fifteen grand right into papa's pocket. Come to think of it, that Republic isn't so backward after all."

"Buenas tardes, mi amigo,[1] how are you?" he greeted the Indian whom he found squatting in the porch of his jacalito as if he had never moved from his place since Mr. Winthrop had left for New York.

The Indian rose, took off his hat, bowed politely and said in his soft voice, "Be welcome, patroncito. Thank you, I feel fine, thank you. Muy buenas tardes.[2] This house and all I have is at your kind disposal." He bowed once more, moved his right hand in a gesture of greeting and sat down again. But he excused himself for doing so by saying, "Perdoneme, patroncito, I have to take advantage of the daylight, soon it will be night."

"I've got big business for you, my friend," Mr. Winthrop began.

50   "Good to hear that, señor."

Mr. Winthrop said to himself, "Now, he'll jump up and go wild when he learns what I've got for him." And aloud he said: "Do you think you can make me one thousand of these little baskets?"

"Why not, patroncito? If I can make sixteen, I can make one thousand also."

"That's right, my good man. Can you also make five thousand?"

"Of course, señor. I can make five thousand if I can make one thousand."

55   "Good. Now, if I should ask you to make me ten thousand, what would you say? And what would be the price of each? You can make ten thousand, can't you?"

"Of course I can, señor. I can make as many as you wish. You see I am an expert in this sort of work. No one else in the whole state can make them the way I do."

"That's what I thought and that's exactly why I came to you."

"Thank you for the honor, patroncito."

"Suppose I order you to make me ten thousand of these baskets, how much time do you think you would need to deliver them?"

60   The Indian, without interrupting his work, cocked his head to one side and then to the other as if he were counting the days or weeks it would cost him to make all these baskets.

After a few minutes he said in a slow voice, "It will take a good long time to make so many baskets, patroncito. You see, the bast and the fibers must be very dry before they can be used properly. Then all during the time they are slowly drying they must be worked and handled in a very special way so that while drying they won't lose their softness and their flexibility and their natural brilliance. Even when dry they must look fresh. They must never lose their natural properties or they will look just as lifeless and dull as straw. Then while they are drying up I got to get the plants and roots and barks and insects

[1]Buenas . . . amigo: (Spanish) Good afternoon, friend. [2]Muy buenas tardes: (Spanish) Very good afternoon.

from which I brew the dyes. That takes much time also, believe me. The plants must be gathered when the moon is just right or they won't give the right color. The insects I pick from the plants must also be gathered at the right time and under the right conditions or else they produce no rich colors and are just like dust. But, of course, jefecito,[3] I can make as many of these canastitas[4] as you wish, even as many as three dozens if you want them. Only give me time."

"Three dozens? Three dozens?" Mr. Winthrop yelled, and threw up both arms in desperation. "Three dozens!" he repeated as if he had to say it many times in his own voice so as to understand the real meaning of it, because for a while he thought that he was dreaming. He had expected the Indian to go crazy on hearing that he was to sell ten thousand of his baskets without having to peddle them from door to door and be treated like a dog with a skin disease.

So the American took up the question of price again, by which he hoped to activate the Indian's ambition. "You told me that if I take one hundred baskets you will let me have them for forty centavos apiece. Is that right, my friend?"

"Quite right, jefecito."

"Now," Mr. Winthrop took a deep breath, "now, then, if I ask you to   65
make one thousand, that is, ten times one hundred baskets, how much will they cost me, each basket?"

That figure was too high for the Indian to grasp. He became slightly confused and for the first time since Mr. Winthrop had arrived he interrupted his work and tried to think it out. Several times he shook his head and looked vaguely around as if for help. Finally he said, "Excuse me, jefecito, little chief, that is by far too much for me to count. Tomorrow, if you will do me the honor, come and see me again and I think I shall have my answer ready for you, patroncito."

When on the next morning Mr. Winthrop came to the hut he found the Indian as usual squatting on the floor under the overhanging palm roof working at his baskets.

"Have you got the price for ten thousand?" he asked the Indian the very moment he saw him, without taking the trouble to say "Good morning!"

"Si, patroncito, I have the price ready. You may believe me when I say it has cost me much labor and worry to find out the exact price, because, you see, I do not wish to cheat you out of your honest money."

"Skip that, amigo. Come out with the salad. What's the price?" Mr.   70
Winthrop asked nervously.

"The price is well calculated now without any mistake on my side. If I got to make one thousand canastitas, each will be three pesos. If I must make five thousand, each will cost nine pesos. And if I have to make ten thousand, in such a case I can't make them for less than fifteen pesos each." Immediately he returned to his work as if he were afraid of losing too much time with such idle talk.

---

[3]jefecito: (Spanish) boss. [4]canastitas: (Spanish) little baskets.

Mr. Winthrop thought perhaps that it was his faulty knowledge of this foreign language that had played a trick on him.

"Did I hear you say fifteen pesos each if I eventually would buy ten thousand?"

"That's exactly and without any mistake what I've said, patroncito," the Indian answered in his soft and courteous voice.

75 "But now, see here, my good man, you can't do this to me. I'm your friend and I want help you get on your feet."

"Yes, patroncito, I know this and I don't doubt any of your words."

"Now, let's be patient and talk this over quietly as man to man. Didn't you tell me that if I would buy one hundred you would sell each for forty centavos?"

"Si, jefecito, that's what I said. If you buy one hundred you can have them for forty centavos apiece, provided that I have one hundred, which I don't."

"Yes, yes, I see that." Mr. Winthrop felt as if he would go insane any minute now. "Yes, so you said. Only what I can't comprehend is why you cannot sell at the same price if you make me ten thousand. I certainly don't wish to chisel on the price. I am not that kind. Only, well, let's see now if you can sell for forty centavos at all, be it for twenty or fifty or a hundred, I can't quite get the idea why the price has to jump that high if I buy more than a hundred."

80 "Bueno,[5] patroncito, what is there so difficult to understand? It's all very simple. One thousand canastitas cost me a hundred times more work than a dozen. Ten thousand cost me so much time and labor that I could never finish them, not even in a hundred years. For a thousand canastitas I need more bast than for a hundred, and I need more little red beetles and more plants and roots and bark for the dyes. It isn't that you can just walk into the bush and pick all the things you need at your heart's desire. One root with the true violet blue may cost me four or five days until I can find one in the jungle. And have you thought how much time it costs and how much hard work to prepare the bast and fibers? What is more, if I must make so many baskets, who then will look after my corn and my beans and my goats and chase for me occasionally a rabbit for meat on Sunday? If I have no corn, then I have no tortillas to eat, and if I grow no beans, where do I get my frijoles from?"

"But since you'll get so much money from me for your baskets you can buy all the corn and beans in the world and more than you need."

"That's what you think, señorito, little lordy. But you see, it is only the corn I grow myself that I am sure of. Of the corn which others may or may not grow, I cannot be sure to feast upon."

"Haven't you got some relatives here in this village who might help you to make baskets for me?" Mr. Winthrop asked hopefully.

"Practically the whole village is related to me somehow or other. Fact is, I got lots of close relatives in this here place."

---

[5]Bueno: (Spanish) well, OK.

"Why then can't they cultivate your fields and look after your goats   *85*
while you make baskets for me? Not only this, they might gather for you the
fibers and the colors in the bush and lend you a hand here and there in preparing the material you need for the baskets."

"They might, patroncito, yes, they might. Possible. But then you see who
would take care of their fields and cattle if they work for me? And if they help
me with the baskets it turns out the same. No one would any longer work his
fields properly. In such a case corn and beans would get up so high in price
that none of us could buy any and we all would starve to death. Besides, as the
price of everything would rise and rise higher still how could I make baskets
at forty centavos apiece? A pinch of salt or one green chili would set me back
more than I'd collect for one single basket. Now you'll understand, highly esti-
mated caballero and jefecito, why I can't make the baskets any cheaper than
fifteen pesos each if I got to make that many."

Mr. Winthrop was hard-boiled, no wonder considering the city he came
from. He refused to give up the more than fifteen thousand dollars which at
that moment seemed to slip through his fingers like nothing. Being really desperate now, he talked and bargained with the Indian for almost two full hours,
trying to make him understand how rich he, the Indian, would become if he
would take this greatest opportunity of his life.

The Indian never ceased working on his baskets while he explained his
points of view.

"You know my good man," Mr. Winthrop said, "such a wonderful chance
might never again knock on your door, do you realise that? Let me explain to
you in ice-cold figures what fortune you might miss if you leave me flat on
this deal."

He tore out leaf after leaf from his notebook, covered each with figures   *90*
and still more figures, and while doing so told the peasant he would be the
richest man in the whole district.

The Indian without answering watched with a genuine expression of
awe as Mr. Winthrop wrote down these long figures, executing complicated
multiplications and divisions and subtractions so rapidly that it seemed to him
the greatest miracle he had ever seen.

The American, noting this growing interest in the Indian, misjudged the
real significance of it. "There you are, my friend," he said. "That's exactly how
rich you are going to be. You'll have a bankroll of exactly four thousand pesos.
And to show you that I'm a real friend of yours, I'll throw in a bonus. I'll make
it a round five thousand pesos, and all in silver."

The Indian, however, had not for one moment thought of four thousand
pesos. Such an amount of money had no meaning to him. He had been interested solely in Mr. Winthrop's ability to write figures so rapidly.

"So, what do you say now? Is it a deal or is it? Say yes and you'll get your
advance this very minute."

"As I have explained before, patroncito, the price is fifteen pesos each."   *95*

"But my good man," Mr. Winthrop shouted at the poor Indian in utter despair, "where have you been all this time? On the moon or where? You are still at the same price as before."

"Yes I know that, jefecito, my little chief," the Indian answered, entirely unconcerned. "It must be the same price because I cannot make any other one. Besides, señor, there's still another thing which perhaps you don't know. You see, my good lordy and caballero, I've to make these canastitas my own way and with my song in them and with bits of my soul woven into them. If I were to make them in great numbers there would no longer be my soul in each, or my songs. Each would look like the other with no difference whatever and such a thing would slowly eat up my heart. Each has to be another song which I hear in the morning when the sun rises and when the birds begin to chirp and the butterflies come and sit down on my baskets so that I may see a new beauty, because, you see, the butterflies like my baskets and the pretty colors on them, that's why they come and sit down, and I can make my canastitas after them. And now, señor jefecito, if you will kindly excuse me, I have wasted much time already, although it was a pleasure and a great honor to hear the talk of such a distinguished caballero like you. But I'm afraid I've to attend to my work now, for day after tomorrow is market day in town and I got to take my baskets there. Thank you, señor, for your visit. Adiós."

And in this way it happened that American garbage cans escaped the fate of being turned into receptacles for empty, torn and crumpled little multicolored canastitas into which an Indian of Mexico had woven dreams of his soul, throbs of his heart: his unsung poems.   *1928*

CONSIDERATIONS

1. Describe the narrator's tone in the opening paragraph of this piece. What does it suggest about the narrator's impression of Mr. Winthrop?
2. The Indian is described as a "plain peasant." Consider the Indian and Mr. Winthrop. Who do you think is more content? More balanced? More at peace with himself? To what do you attribute this happy nature?
3. To what extent does the lack of knowledge about the outside world affect the life of the Indian? To what extent does the lack of knowledge about the Indian culture affect Mr. Winthrop?
4. What are the central differences between the culture represented by the Indian and the culture represented by Mr. Winthrop? What, if anything, do these cultures have in common?
5. What does the Indian mean when he says that if each basket looked alike, "such a thing would slowly eat up [his] heart?" Why does he care so much about the baskets he makes? How does this attitude relate to the nature of

any true artist? How does this point of view differ from the view of those who mass produce products?

DON DELILLO (1936–   )

Videotape

Born in New York City to Italian immigrant parents, Don DeLillo grew up in the Bronx. During a summer spent working as a parking attendant, a job that required him to spend many hours of waiting for patrons to claim their cars, he filled the time by reading the works of authors such as James Joyce, Herman Melville, and Ernest Hemingway. By the end of the summer, he had discovered a passion for the English language, and following his graduation from Fordham University in the early 1960's, he began working on his first novel, Americana *(1971). Since that time, he has published thirteen novels, several plays, and numerous short stories. In 1999, he was the first American author to win the Jerusalem Prize, which is given to writers "whose work expresses the theme of the individual in society."*

It shows a man driving a car. It is the simplest sort of family video. You see a man at the wheel of a medium Dodge.

It is just a kid aiming her camera through the rear window of the family car at the windshield of the car behind her.

You know about families and their video cameras. You know how kids get involved, how the camera shows them that every subject is potentially charged, a million things they never see with the unaided eye. They investigate the meaning of inert objects and dumb pets and they poke at family privacy. They learn to see things twice.

It is the kid's own privacy that is being protected here. She is twelve years old and her name is being withheld even though she is neither the victim nor the perpetrator of the crime but only the means of recording it.

It shows a man in a sport shirt at the wheel of his car. There is nothing   5 else to see. The car approaches briefly, then falls back.

You know how children with cameras learn to work the exposed moments that define the family cluster. They break every trust, spy out the undefended space, catching Mom coming out of the bathroom in her cumbrous robe and turbaned towel, looking bloodless and plucked. It is not a joke. They will shoot you sitting on the pot if they can manage a suitable vantage.

The tape has the jostled sort of noneventness that marks the family product. Of course the man in this case is not a member of the family but a stranger in a car, a random figure, someone who has happened along in the slow lane.

It shows a man in his forties wearing a pale shirt open at the throat, the image washed by reflections and sunglint, with many jostled moments.

It is not just another video homicide. It is a homicide recorded by a child who thought she was doing something simple and maybe halfway clever, shooting some tape of a man in a car.

10   He sees the girl and waves briefly, wagging a hand without taking it off the wheel—an underplayed reaction that makes you like him.

It is unrelenting footage that rolls on and on. It has an aimless determination, a persistence that lives outside the subject matter. You are looking into the mind of home video. It is innocent, it is aimless, it is determined, it is real.

He is bald up the middle of his head, a nice guy in his forties whose whole life seems open to the hand-held camera.

But there is also an element of suspense. You keep on looking not because you know something is going to happen—of course you do know something is going to happen and you do look for that reason but you might also keep on looking if you came across this footage for the first time without knowing the outcome. There is a crude power operating here. You keep on looking because things combine to hold you fast—a sense of the random, the amateurish, the accidental, the impending. You don't think of the tape as boring or interesting. It is crude, it is blunt, it is relentless. It is the jostled part of your mind, the film that runs through your hotel brain under all the thoughts you know you're thinking.

The world is lurking in the camera, already framed, waiting for the boy or girl who will come along and take up the device, learn the instrument, shooting old Granddad at breakfast, all stroked out so his nostrils gape, the cereal spoon baby-gripped in his pale fist.

15   It shows a man alone in a medium Dodge. It seems to go on forever.

There's something about the nature of the tape, the grain of the image, the sputtering black-and-white tones, the starkness—you think this is more real, truer-to-life, than anything around you. The things around you have a rehearsed and layered and cosmetic look. The tape is superreal, or maybe underreal is the way you want to put it. It is what lies at the scraped bottom of all the layers you have added. And this is another reason why you keep on looking. The tape has a searing realness.

It shows him giving an abbreviated wave, stiff-palmed, like a signal flag at a siding.

You know how families make up games. This is just another game in which the child invents the rules as she goes along. She likes the idea of videotaping a man in his car. She has probably never done it before and she sees no reason to vary the format or terminate early or pan to another car. This is her game and she is learning it and playing it at the same time. She feels halfway clever and inventive and maybe slightly intrusive as well, a little bit of brazenness that spices any game.

And you keep on looking. You look because this is the nature of the footage, to make a channeled path through time, to give things a shape and a destiny.

Of course if she had panned to another car, the right car at the precise   20
time, she would have caught the gunman as he fired.

The chance quality of the encounter. The victim, the killer, and the child with a camera. Random energies that approach a common point. There's something here that speaks to you directly, saying terrible things about forces beyond your control, lines of intersection that cut through history and logic and every reasonable layer of human expectation.

She wandered into it. The girl got lost and wandered clear-eyed into horror. This is a children's story about straying too far from home. But it isn't the family car that serves as the instrument of the child's curiosity, her inclination to explore. It is the camera that puts her in the tale.

You know about holidays and family celebrations and how somebody shows up with a camcorder and the relatives stand around and barely react because they're numbingly accustomed to the process of being taped and decked and shown on the VCR with the coffee and cake.

He is hit soon after. If you've seen the tape many times you know from the handwave exactly when he will be hit. It is something, naturally, that you wait for. You say to your wife, if you're at home and she is there, Now here is where he gets it. You say, Janet, hurry up, this is where it happens.

Now here is where he gets it. You see him jolted, sort of wire-shocked—   25
then he seizes up and falls toward the door or maybe leans or slides into the door is the proper way to put it. It is awful and unremarkable at the same time. The car stays in the slow lane. It approaches briefly, then falls back.

You don't usually call your wife over to the TV set. She has her programs, you have yours. But there's a certain urgency here. You want her to see how it looks. The tape has been running forever and now the thing is finally going to happen and you want her to be here when he's shot.

Here it comes, all right. He is shot, head-shot, and the camera reacts, the child reacts—there is a jolting movement but she keeps on taping, there is a sympathetic response, a nerve response, her heart is beating faster but she keeps the camera trained on the subject as he slides into the door and even as you see him die you're thinking of the girl. At some level the girl has to be present here, watching what you're watching, unprepared—the girl is seeing this cold and you have to marvel at the fact that she keeps the tape rolling.

It shows something awful and unaccompanied. You want your wife to see it because it is real this time, not fancy movie violence—the realness beneath the layers of cosmetic perception. Hurry up, Janet, here it comes. He dies so fast. There is no accompaniment of any kind. It is very stripped. You want to tell her it is realer than real but then she will ask what that means.

The way the camera reacts to the gunshot—a startled reaction that brings pity and terror into the frame, the girl's own shock, the girl's identification with the victim.

30   You don't see the blood, which is probably trickling behind his ear and down the back of his neck. The way his head is twisted away from the door, the twist of the head gives you only a partial profile and it's the wrong side, it's not the side where he was hit.

And maybe you're being a little aggressive here, practically forcing your wife to watch. Why? What are you telling her? Are you making a little statement? Like I'm going to ruin your day out of ordinary spite. Or a big statement? Like this is the risk of existing. Either way you're rubbing her face in this tape and you don't know why.

It shows the car drifting toward the guardrail and then there's a jostling sense of two other lanes and part of another car, a split-second blur, and the tape ends here, either because the girl stopped shooting or because some central authority, the police or the district attorney or the TV station, decided there was nothing else you had to see.

This is either the tenth or eleventh homicide committed by the Texas Highway Killer. The number is uncertain because the police believe that one of the shootings may have been a copycat crime.

And there is something about videotape, isn't there, and this particular kind of serial crime? This is a crime designed for random taping and immediate playing. You sit there and wonder if this kind of crime became more possible when the means of taping and playing an event—playing it immediately after the taping—became part of the culture. The principal doesn't necessarily commit the sequence of crimes in order to see them taped and played. He commits the crimes as if they were a form of taped-and-played event. The crimes are inseparable from the idea of taping and playing. You sit there thinking that this is a crime that has found its medium, or vice versa—cheap mass production, the sequence of repeated images and victims, stark and glary and more or less unremarkable.

35   It shows very little in the end. It is a famous murder because it is on tape and because the murderer has done it many times and because the crime was recorded by a child. So the child is involved, the Video Kid as she is sometimes called because they have to call her something. The tape is famous and so is she. She is famous in the modern manner of people whose names are strategically withheld. They are famous without names or faces, spirits living apart from their bodies, the victims and witnesses, the underage criminals, out there somewhere at the edges of perception.

Seeing someone at the moment he dies, dying unexpectedly. This is reason alone to stay fixed to the screen. It is instructional, watching a man shot dead as he drives along on a sunny day. It demonstrates an elemental truth, that every breath you take has two possible endings. And that's another thing.

There's a joke locked away here, a note of cruel slapstick that you are completely willing to appreciate. Maybe the victim's a chump, a dope, classically unlucky. He had it coming, in a way, like an innocent fool in a silent movie.

You don't want Janet to give you any crap about it's on all the time, they show it a thousand times a day. They show it because it exists, because they have to show it, because this is why they're out there. The horror freezes your soul but this doesn't mean that you want them to stop.   *1996*

CONSIDERATIONS

1. Describe your reaction to the narrator's casual and off-handed tone in this piece. What are some possible reasons that DeLillo adopted this stance, and what does he gain by having the narrator talk to "you" throughout this piece?
2. Analyze the details the narrator allows you, the reader, to see. What are you not able to see or know, and what difference does that absence of detail make to this story?
3. As you read this selection, what questions do you have that the narrator does not address? What might the answers to these questions be?
4. What does the husband's reaction to the videotape reveal about technology? What does it reveal about his inner nature? In what ways does it reveal differences between the man and his wife? To what extent does this one scene reveal the true nature of their relationship?
5. What is the relationship between violence and technology in this piece? Between death and technology? Between technology and human relationships?

GEORGE SAUNDERS (1958–   )

My Flamboyant Grandson

Born and raised on the south side of Chicago, George Saunders graduated from the Colorado School of Mines. He has worked as a technical writer, a geophysical engineer, a member of an oil exploration crew in Sumatra, a convenience store clerk, and a knuckle-puller in a West Texas slaughterhouse. Saunders admires writers such as Thomas Wolfe, Leo Tolstoy, Joseph Conrad, and Raymond Carver. In addition, he admires the comic talents of Steve Martin and the Monty Python troupe. Currently, Saunders teaches in the Creative Writing Program at Syracuse University. Saunders' lively, direct writing style, laced with satiric humor, often takes an offbeat approach to the serious questions that face American society.

I had brought my grandson to New York to see a show. Because what is he always doing, up here in Oneonta? Singing and dancing, sometimes to my old show-tune records, but more often than not to his favorite CD, "Babar Sings," sometimes even making up his own steps, which I do not mind, or rather I try not to mind it. Although I admit that once, coming into his room and finding him wearing a pink boa while singing, in the voice of the Old Lady, "I Have Never Met a Man Like That Elephant," I had to walk out and give it some deep thought and prayer, as was also the case when he lumbered into the parlor during a recent church couples dinner, singing "Big and Slow, Yet So Very Regal," wearing a tablecloth spray-painted gray, so as to more closely resemble Babar.

Being a man who knows something about grandfatherly disapproval, having had a grandfather who constantly taunted me for having enlarged calves—to the extent that even today, when bathing, I find myself thinking unkind thoughts about Grandfather—what I prayed on both occasions was: Dear Lord, he is what he is, let me love him no matter what. If he is a gay child, God bless him; if he is a non-gay child who simply very much enjoys wearing his grandmother's wig while singing "Edelweiss" to the dog, so be it, and in either case let me communicate my love and acceptance in everything I do.

Because where is a child to go for unconditional love, if not to his grandfather? He has had it tough, in my view, with his mother in Nevada and a father unknown, raised by his grandmother and me in an otherwise childless neighborhood, playing alone in a tiny yard that ends in a graveyard wall. The boys in his school are hard on him, as are the girls, as are the teachers, and recently we found his book bag in the Susquehanna, and recently also found, taped to the back of his jacket, a derogatory note, and the writing on it was not all that childish-looking, and there were rumors that his bus driver had written it.

Then one day I had a revelation. If the lad likes to sing and dance, I thought, why not expose him to the finest singing and dancing there is? So I called 1-800-CULTURE, got our Promissory Voucher in the mail, and on Teddy's birthday we took the train down to New York.

5   As we entered the magnificent lobby of the Eisner Theatre, I was in good spirits, saying to Teddy, The size of this stage will make that little stage I built you behind the garage look pathetic, when suddenly we were stopped by a stern young fellow (a Mr. Ernesti, I believe) who said, We are sorry, sir, but you cannot be admitted on merely a Promissory Voucher, are you kidding us, you must take your Voucher and your Proof of Purchases from at least six of our Major Artistic Sponsors, such as AOL, such as Coke, and go at once to the Redemption Center, on Forty-fourth and Broadway, to get your real actual tickets, and please do not be late, as latecomers cannot be admitted, due to special effects which occur early, and which require total darkness in order to simulate the African jungle at night.

Well, this was news to me, but I was not about to disappoint the boy.

We left the Eisner and started up Broadway, the Everly Readers in the sidewalk reading the Everly Strips in our shoes, the building-mounted miniscreens at eye level showing images reflective of the Personal Preferences we'd stated on our monthly Everly Preference Worksheets, the numerous Cybec Sudden Emergent Screens outthrusting or down-thrusting inches from our faces, and in addition I could very clearly hear the sound-only messages being beamed to me and me alone via various Kakio Aural Focussers, such as one that shouted out to me between Forty-second and Forty-third, "Mr. Petrillo, you chose Burger King eight times last fiscal year but only two times thus far this fiscal year, please do not forsake us now, there is a store one block north!," in the voice of Broadway star Elaine Weston, while at Forty-third a light-pole-mounted Focusser shouted, "Golly, Leonard, remember your childhood on the farm in Oneonta? Why not reclaim those roots with a Starbucks Country Roast?," in a celebrity rural voice I could not identify, possibly Buck Owens, and then, best of all, in the doorway of PLC Electronics, a life-size Gene Kelly hologram suddenly appeared, tap-dancing, saying, "Leonard, my data indicates you're a bit of an old-timer like myself! Gosh, in our day life was simpler, wasn't it, Leonard? Why not come in and let Frankie Z. explain the latest gizmos!" And he looked so real I called out to Teddy, "Teddy, look there, Gene Kelly, do you remember I mentioned him to you as one of the all-time great dancers?" But Teddy of course did not see Gene Kelly, Gene Kelly not being one of his Preferences, but instead saw his hero Babar, swinging a small monkey on his trunk while saying that his data indicated that Teddy did not yet own a Nintendo.

So that was fun, that was very New York, but what was not so fun was, by the time we got through the line at the Redemption Center, it was ten minutes until showtime, and my feet had swollen up the way they do shortly before they begin spontaneously bleeding, which they have done ever since a winter spent in the freezing muck of Cho-Bai, Korea. It is something I have learned to live with. If I can sit, that is helpful. If I can lean against something, also good. Best of all, if I can take my shoes off. Which I did, leaning against a wall.

All around and above us were those towering walls of light, curving across building fronts, embedded in the sidewalks, custom-fitted to light poles: a cartoon lion eating a man in a suit; a rain of gold coins falling into the canoe of a naked rain-forest family; a woman in lingerie running a bottle of Pepsi between her breasts; the Merrill Lynch talking fist asking, "Are you kicking ass or kissing it?"; a perfect human rear, dancing; a fake flock of geese turning into a field of Bebe logos; a dying grandmother's room filled with roses by a FedEx man who then holds up a card saying "No Charge."

And standing beneath all that bounty was our little Teddy, tiny and sad,   *10* whose grandfather could not even manage to get him into one crummy show.

So I said to myself, Get off the wall, old man, blood or no blood, just keep the legs moving and soon enough you'll be there. And off we went, me hobbling, Teddy holding my arm, making decent time, and I think we would have made the curtain. Except suddenly there appeared a Citizen Helper, who asked were we from out of town, and was that why, via removing my shoes, I had caused my Everly Strips to be rendered Inoperative?

I should say here that I am no stranger to innovative approaches to advertising, having pioneered the use of towable signboards in Oneonta back in the Nixon years, when I moved a fleet of thirty around town with a Dodge Dart, wearing a suit that today would be found comic. By which I mean I have no problem with the concept of the Everly Strip. That is not why I had my shoes off. I am as patriotic as the next guy. Rather, as I have said, it was due to my bleeding feet.

I told all this to the Citizen Helper, who asked if I was aware that, by rendering my Strips Inoperative, I was sacrificing a terrific opportunity to Celebrate My Preferences?

And I said yes, yes, I regretted this very much.

15   He said he was sorry about my feet, he himself having a trick elbow, and that he would be happy to forget this unfortunate incident if I would only put my shoes back on and complete the rest of my walk extremely slowly, looking energetically to both left and right, so that the higher density of Messages thus received would compensate for those I had missed.

And I admit, I was a little short with that Helper, and said, Young man, these dark patches here on my socks are blood, do you or do you not see them?

Which was when his face changed and he said, Please do not snap at me, sir, I hope you are aware of the fact that I can write you up?

And then I made a mistake.

Because as I looked at that Citizen Helper—his round face, his pale sideburns, the way his feet turned in—it seemed to me that I knew him. Or rather, it seemed that he could not be so very different from me when I was a young man, not so different from the friends of my youth—from Jeffie DeSoto, say, who once fought a Lithuanian gang that had stuck an M-80 in the ass of a cat, or from Ken Larmer, who had such a sweet tenor voice and died stifling a laugh in the hills above Koi-Jeng.

20   I brought out a twenty and, leaning over, said, Look, please, the kid just really wants to see this show.

Which is when he pulled out his pad and began to write!

Now, even being from Oneonta, I knew that being written up does not take one or two minutes, we would be standing there at least half an hour, after which we would have to go to an Active Complaints Center, where they would check our Strips for Operability and make us watch that corrective video called "Robust Economy, Super Moral Climate!," which I had already been made to watch three times last winter, when I was out of work and we could not afford cable. And we would totally miss "Babar Sings"!

Please, I said, please, we have seen plenty of personalized messages, via both the building-mounted miniscreens at eye level and those suddenly outthrusting Cybec Emergent Screens, we have learned plenty for one day, honest to God we have—

And he said, Sir, since when do you make the call as far as when you have received enough useful information from our Artistic Partners? And just kept writing me up.

Well, there I was, in my socks, there was Teddy, with a scared look in his   25 eyes I hadn't seen since his toddler days, when he had such a fear of chickens that we could never buy Rosemont eggs, due to the cartoon chicken on the carton, or, if we did, had to first cut the chicken off, with scissors we kept in the car for that purpose. So I made a quick decision, and seized that Citizen Helper's ticket pad and flung it into the street, shouting at Teddy, Run! Run!

And run he did. And run I did. And while that Citizen Helper floundered in the street, torn between chasing us and retrieving his pad, we raced down Broadway, and glancing back over my shoulder I saw a hulking young man stick out his foot, and down that Helper went, and soon I was handing our tickets to the same stern Mr. Ernesti, who was now less stern, and in we went, and took our seats, as the stars appeared overhead and the Eisner was transformed into a nighttime jungle.

And suddenly there was Babar, looking with longing toward Paris, where the Old Lady was saying that she had dreamed of someone named Babar, and did any of us know who this Babar was, and where he might be found? And Teddy knew the answer, from the Original Cast CD, which was Babar is within us, in all of our hearts, and he shouted it out with all the other children, as the Old Lady began singing "The King Inside of You."

And let me tell you, from that moment everything changed for Teddy. I am happy to report he has joined the play at school. He wears a scarf everywhere he goes, throwing it over his shoulder with what can only be described as bravado, and says, whenever asked, that he has decided to become an actor. This from a boy too timid to trick-or-treat! This from the boy we once found walking home from school in tears, padlocked to his own bike! There are no more late-night crying episodes, he no longer writes on his arms with permanent marker, he leaps out of bed in the morning, anxious to get to school, and dons his scarf, and is already sitting at the table eating breakfast when we come down.

The other day as he got off the bus I heard him say, to his bus driver, cool as a cucumber, See you at the Oscars.

When an Everly Reader is reading, then suddenly stops, it is not hard to   30 trace, and within a week I received a certified letter setting my fine at one thousand dollars, and stating that, in lieu of the fine, I could elect to return to the originating location of my infraction (they included a map) and, under the supervision of that Citizen Helper, retrace my steps, shoes on, thus reclaiming a significant opportunity to Celebrate My Preferences

This, to me, is not America.

What America is, to me, is a guy doesn't want to buy, you let him not buy, you respect his not buying. A guy has a crazy notion different from your crazy notion, you pat him on the back and say hey, pal, nice crazy notion, let's go have a beer. America to me should be shouting all the time, a bunch of shouting voices, most of them wrong, some of them nuts, but, please, not just one droning glamorous reasonable voice.

But do the math: a day's pay, plus train ticket, plus meals, plus taxis to avoid the bleeding feet, still that is less than one thousand.

So down I went.

35   That Citizen Helper, whose name was Rob, said he was glad about my change of heart. Every time a voice shot into my ear, telling me things about myself I already knew, every time a celebrity hologram walked up like an old friend, Rob checked a box on my Infraction Correction Form and said, Isn't that amazing, Mr. Petrillo, that we can do that, that we can know you so well, that we can help you identify the things you want and need?

And I would say, Yes, Rob, that is amazing, sick in the gut but trying to keep my mind on the five hundred bucks I was saving and on all the dance classes that would buy.

As for Teddy, as I write this it is nearly midnight and he is tapping in the room above. He looks like a bird, our boy, he watches the same musical fifteen times in a row. Walking through the mall he suddenly emits a random line of dialogue and lunges off to the side, doing a dance step that resembles a stumble, spilling his drink, plowing into a group of incredulous, snickering Oneontans. He looks like no one else, acts like no one else, his clothes are increasingly like plumage, late at night he choreographs using plastic Army men, he fits no mold and has no friends, but I believe in my heart that someday something beautiful may come from him.   *2002*

CONSIDERATIONS

1. Respond to the humorous scenes and reactions in this piece. In what ways does humor allow the narrator to deal with what it is, to most people, a very serious issue concerning sexuality and human nature?
2. What details point to the power of technology in this piece, and how does it link to the subject of human sexuality?
3. In what ways do Broadway plays and Disney movies differ? How are they alike? What is the author's point about these two different forms of entertainment, and how does this relate to the theme of this story?
4. What point might the author be making in the final paragraph of this piece when the grandfather says that Teddy "fits no mold and has no friends, but I believe in my heart that someday something beautiful may come from him"? How does this observation reflect the theme of human nature versus technology?

Poetry

EMILY DICKINSON (1830–1886)
I like to see it lap the Miles

For biographical information on Emily Dickinson, see page 1238.

I like to see it lap the Miles—
And lick the Valleys up—
And stop to feed itself at Tanks—
And then—prodigious step

Around a Pile of Mountains—   5
And supercilious peer
In Shanties—by the sides of Roads—
And then a Quarry pare

To fit its Ribs
And crawl between   10
Complaining all the while
In horrid—hooting stanza—
Then chase itself down Hill—

And neigh like Boanerges[1]
Then—punctual as a Star   15
Stop—docile and omnipotent
At its own stable door—   *1862*

CONSIDERATIONS

1. What relationship does the "it" in this poem have with the natural landscape? With the manmade objects that dot the landscape?
2. Dickinson personifies the "it" by giving it both animal and supernatural
   qualities throughout. Discuss the "it" in terms of both sets of qualities. Why
   might Dickinson have chosen this dual personality?
3. What is the "it" in this poem, and how does it relate to the theme in this
   chapter?

---

[1]Boanerges: "Sons of Thunder" (Mark 3:17).

More Resources on
Emily Dickinson

In *ARIEL*

- Brief biography of Dickinson
- Complete texts of additional Dickinson poems with hyperlinked comments
- Video discussion of Dickinson's writing
- Video clip exploring the world of Dickinson's writing
- Video and audio clips of readings of Dickinson poems such as "Because I could not stop for Death"
- Analysis of Dickinson's style
- Bibliography of scholarly works on Dickinson

In the Online Learning Center for *Responding to Literature*

- Brief biography of Dickinson
- List of major works by Dickinson
- Text of Dickinson's "I heard a Fly buzz—when I died—"
- Web links to more resources on Dickinson
- Additional questions for experiencing and interpreting Dickinson's writing

WALT WHITMAN (1819–1892)
When I Heard the Learn'd Astronomer

> *Born on Long Island, New York, Walt Whitman grew up in Brooklyn in a blue-collar neighborhood, where his father worked as a carpenter. After five years of public school, Whitman left to become a printer's assistant. Later, he worked as a newspaper editor and as a volunteer nurse during the Civil War. Following the war, he wrote his most important work, the long poem titled* Leaves of Grass, *which, mainly because of its highly controversial erotic imagery, was not published until many years after it was written.*

When I heard the learn'd astronomer,
When the proofs, the figures, were ranged in columns before me,
When I was shown the charts and diagrams, to add, divide, and measure them,
When I sitting heard the astronomer where he lectured with much applause
5   in the lecture-room,

How soon unaccountable I became tired and sick,
Till rising and gliding out I wandered off by myself,
In the mystical moist night-air, and from time to time,
Looked up in perfect silence at the stars.   *1865*

CONSIDERATIONS

1. Discuss the differences between "hearing" as presented in the first part of this poem and "listening" as suggested by the word "silence" in the last line.
2. Discuss the differences between "being shown" something in the first half of the poem and "looking up" in the last line of the poem.
3. What point is Whitman making about people's relationship with and understanding of the natural world as represented by the two settings in this piece? To what extent do you agree with this central point?

More Resources on
Walt Whitman

In *ARIEL*
- Brief biography of Whitman
- Excerpt from Whitman's "Song of Myself," with hyperlinked comments
- Complete texts of additional Whitman poems
- Video introduction to Whitman's writing
- Analysis of Whitman's style
- Bibliography of scholarly works on Whitman

WILLIAM JAY SMITH (1918–   )
Galileo Galilei[1]

Born in Winnfield, Louisiana, William Jay Smith was educated at Washington University and Columbia University, and was named a Rhodes Scholar to Oxford

[1]Galileo (1564–1642) was an Italian astronomer whose scientific discoveries caused the Catholic Church to persecute him during the Inquisition.

University. From 1968 to 1970, he served in the position now known as Poet Laureate of the United States. He has published 10 volumes of poetry, and the following selection is taken from his collection of poems titled Celebration at Dark (1950).

Comes to knock and knock again
At a small secluded doorway
In the ordinary brain.

Into light the world is turning,
5   And the clocks are set for six;
And the chimney pots are smoking,
And the golden candlesticks.

Apple trees are bent and breaking,
And the heat is not the sun's;
10   And the Minotaur[2] is waking,
And the streets are cattle runs.

Galileo Galilei,
In a flowing, scarlet robe,
While the stars go down the river
15   With the turning, turning globe,

Kneels before a black Madonna
And the angels cluster round
With grave, uplifted faces
Which reflect the shaken ground

20   And the orchard which is burning,
And the hills which take the light;
And the candles which have melted
On the altars of the night.

Galileo Galilei
25   Comes to knock and knock again
At a small secluded doorway
In the ordinary brain.   *1950*

CONSIDERATIONS

1. One of the most influential early proponents of the modern scientific method, Galileo was renowned for his commonsense, direct approach to

[2]Creature in Greek mythology, half man and half bull.

complicated questions relating to the heavens. How does knowing that Galileo studied the properties of light as well as the properties of motion, such as the movement of a pendulum, add meaning to the images in the second stanza?
2. Galileo was imprisoned because his scientific discoveries conflicted with the teachings of the Catholic Church. Given that biographical information, what added significance do the images in the fifth stanza take on?
3. On whose door is Galileo knocking, and what message is he bringing?

ADRIENNE RICH (1929–   )

Power

> *Born in Baltimore, Maryland, Adrienne Rich grew up in a household with two distinct and conflicting religious traditions: her father was Jewish and her mother had a southern Protestant background. She graduated from Radcliffe, and shortly afterward she was awarded the prestigious Yale Younger Poets prize. Although her early poetry followed traditional, formal patterns, her later work breaks away from tradition, both in form and content. The later poems, written after 1960, are noted for their powerful political content, particularly in relation to gender issues.*

Living   in the earth-deposits   of our history

Today a backhoe divulged   out of a crumbling flank of earth
one bottle   amber   perfect   a hundred-year-old
cure for fever   or melancholy   a tonic
for living on this earth   in the winters of this climate   5

Today I was reading about Marie Curie:[1]
she must have known she suffered   from radiation sickness
her body bombarded for years   by the element
she had purified
It seems she denied to the end   10
the source of the cataracts on her eyes
the cracked and suppurating skin   of her finger-ends
till she could no longer hold   a test-tube or a pencil

She died   a famous woman   denying
her wounds   15
denying
her wounds   came   from the same source as her power   *1978*

---

[1]A Polish scientist (1867–1934) who was instrumental in discovering polonium and radium. She was the first person to win two Nobel Prizes.

CONSIDERATIONS

1. Explore the reasons why the lines of this poem are spaced the way they are. Compare the effect of the poem when read silently and when heard out loud.
2. The spaces in poetry are as essential as the words that take their places. What happens to the meaning of the poem if, in the first line, you insert into the space a word opposite to the one before it? For example, if after "Living" you insert "dying." How might this deepen the meaning of the poem?
3. What is the poet's point about the scientist Madame Curie and her experience? What does the poem suggest about science, knowledge, and power?

 MARGARET ATWOOD (1939–   )

The City Planners

> *Margaret Atwood was born in Ottawa, Canada, and attended the University of Toronto, Radcliffe College, and Harvard University. She later taught literature at several universities in Canada, the United States, and Australia. She is best known for her novels exploring power and gender relationships, including* Edible Woman *(1969),* Surfacing *(1972),* The Handmaid's Tale *(1985),* The Robber Bride *(1993),* Alias Grace *(1996), and* The Blind Assassin *(2000), which won the Booker Prize in 2000. However, starting with* Double Persephone *(1961), which she wrote at the age of nineteen, she has also published some 20 volumes of poetry. The poem here is from* Power Politics *(1971), a collection that examines the use and meaning of power in personal relationships. In* Survival: A Thematic Guide to Canadian Literature, *Atwood analyzes the characteristics that distinguish Canadian literature from that of the United States and England; she argues that the dominant theme of Canadian literature is the victim's ability to survive—a theme that many critics have found in Atwood's own works.*

Cruising these residential Sunday
streets in dry August sunlight:
what offends us is
the sanities:
5   the houses in pedantic rows, the planted
sanitary trees, assert
levelness of surface like a rebuke
to the dent in our car door.
No shouting here, or
10   shatter of glass; nothing more abrupt

than the rational whine of a power mower
cutting a straight swath in the discouraged grass.

But though the driveways neatly
sidestep hysteria
by being even, the roofs all display   *15*
the same slant of avoidance to the hot sky,
certain things:
the smell of spilled oil a faint

sickness lingering in the garages,
a splash of paint on brick surprising as a bruise,   *20*
a plastic hose poised in a vicious
coil; even the too-fixed stare of the wide windows

give momentary access to
the landscape behind or under
the future cracks in the plaster   *25*

when the houses, capsized, will slide
obliquely into the clay seas, gradual as glaciers
that right now nobody notices.

That is where the City Planners
with the insane faces of political conspirators   *30*
are scattered over unsurveyed
territories, concealed from each other,
each in his own private blizzard;

guessing directions, they sketch
transitory lines rigid as wooden borders   *35*
on a wall in the white vanishing air

tracing the panic of suburb
order in a bland madness of snows.   *1966*

CONSIDERATIONS

1. Who is the "us" in the first stanza of this poem, and what are they doing in
   this residential neighborhood on a Sunday in August? What differences do
   you notice between "us" and the people who live in the neighborhood?
2. Locate the sensory images that relate to nature in lines 18 through 33, and
   contrast them with the manufactured objects and images in these same
   lines. Based on these sets of images, what might the speaker be saying about
   this city and those who live here?

3. Why are the words "City Planners" capitalized in line 29, and what tone does the speaker adopt when describing these people? Why is this tone appropriate to the theme in this poem?

More Resources on
Margaret Atwood

 In *ARIEL*

- Brief biography of Atwood
- Complete text of Atwood poems with hyperlinked comments
- Audio clip of a reading of the Atwood poem "This Is a Photograph of Me"
- Analysis of the speaker/author split in Atwood's poetry
- Bibliography of scholarly works on Atwood

 In the Online Learning Center for *Responding to Literature*

- Brief biography of Atwood
- List of major works by Atwood
- Web links to more resources on Atwood
- Additional questions for experiencing and interpreting Atwood's writing

CHARLES BUKOWSKI (1920–1994)

maybe we'll see . . .

> *After years of hard living and working at a variety of jobs, from dishwasher to postal worker, Charles Bukowski became a professional writer at the age of thirty-five. He began writing for underground newspapers in Los Angeles and gradually became known for his tough, direct masculine poems and short stories. After his first book of poetry,* Flower, Fist and Bestial Wail, *was published in 1959, he wrote over 40 others. Like his poetry, most of his short stories and his novels are also somewhat autobiographical, dealing with sex, violence, and the absurdities of life. In 1987, he wrote the screenplay for the movie* Barfly, *starring Mickey Rourke and Faye Dunaway; in 1989, he wrote a novel,* Hollywood, *based on his experiences with the making of that film. His last novel,* Pulp, *a parody of the hard-boiled detective novel, was published after he died of leukemia in 1994.*

sometime soon
they are going to shoot a telescope
from the shuttle platform out there
and the boys and girls are going to see
ten percent more outer space,   *5*
things
they have never seen before.

I am for this.

our inventiveness
our poking around   *10*
is pleasurable.

it makes a peanut butter and
jelly sandwich taste
better.

it is having such things to do   *15*
which keeps us
from doing things
to ourselves.

CONSIDERATIONS

1. Discuss the implications of the title of this poem and what you might add
   at the end, replacing the ellipsis. How does this title as well as its structure
   relate to the theme of technology and ethics?
2. Read this poem out loud, and concentrate on the speaker's word choices as
   well as the rhythm (or lack thereof) that emerges. Based on these two elements of poetry, how would you describe the speaker of this poem, and
   how does this persona connect to the general theme of the poem itself?
3. What might the telescope symbolize in this piece? The peanut butter and
   jelly sandwich? How do both images help explain the last four lines of the
   poem?

MARGE PIERCY (1936–   )

The Market Economy

> *Marge Piercy lives near Wellfleet, Cape Cod, in a communal household where
> she writes poetry and novels dedicated to exploring themes of economic, racial,*

and sexual inequality. Her best-known novels include Small Changes *(1973),* Woman on the Edge of Time *(1976), and* Vida *(1979).*

Suppose some peddler offered
you can have a color TV
but your baby will be
born with a crooked spine;
5   you can have polyvinyl cups
and wash and wear
suits but it will cost
you your left lung
rotted with cancer; suppose
10   somebody offered you
a frozen precooked dinner
every night for ten years
but at the end
your colon dies
15   and then you do,
slowly and with much pain.
You get a house in the suburbs
but you work in a new plastics
factory and die at fifty-one
20   when your kidneys turn off.

But where else will you
work? where else can
you rent but Smog City?
The only houses for sale
25   are under the yellow sky.
You've been out of work for
a year and they're hiring
at the plastics factory.
Don't read the fine
30   print, there isn't any.   *1982*

CONSIDERATIONS

1. Discuss the three hypothetical situations that the speaker presents in the first half of this poem. What is your response to each one of these scenarios, and how do you imagine others would respond to these three situations?
2. What reasons does the author have for connecting the matter-of-fact scenario in lines 17–20 with the previous hypothetical situations, which raise questions? What is the irony in the use of the word "get" in line 17?

3. What point is the speaker making about the choices we make, living as we do in a world that is driven by a market economy?

ELLEN WOLFE (1940–   )
Amniocentesis°

Ellen Wolfe frequently draws on her own experiences, including becoming a mother late in life, as subjects for her poetry. Her work has been published in many small press magazines.

for Yona

Lie up under the umbrella of my ribs
my new island
Sleep while the thin throat
samples your lake
First planting in my old body   5
they worry about you

These people who fear monsters
will be looking for monsters
They will be looking for the skewed pattern
the aberrant piece   10
of your chromosome puzzle
Love
they will be listening
Sing for them
your perfect song   *1982*   15

CONSIDERATIONS

1. Respond to the metaphor "umbrella of my ribs" in the first line and explain how it relates to the central conflict within this poem.
2. Why does the narrator refer to the medical technicians as "these people"?
3. Why does the poet place the word "Love" on its own line, and how does this one word change the tone of this piece?

Amniocentesis: Surgical procedure performed on a pregnant woman to determine the presence of disease or genetic defects in the fetus.

MICHAEL RYAN

TV Room at the Children's Hospice

Michael Ryan is the author of four volumes of poetry; an autobiography, Secret Life (1994); *and a collection of essays about poetry and writing,* A Difficult Grace (2000). *He is a professor of English at the University of California, Irvine.*

Red-and-green leather-helmeted
maniacally grinning motorcyclists
crash at all angles
on Lev Smith's pajama top

5   and when his chocolate ice cream
dumps like a mud slide down its front
he smiles, not maniacally, still nauseous
from chemotherapy and bald already.

Lev is six but sat still four hours
10 all afternoon with IVs in his arms,
his grandma tells everyone. Marcie
is nine and was born with no face.

One profile has been built in increments
with surgical plastic and skin grafts
15 and the other looks like fudge.
Tomorrow she's having an eye moved.

She finds a hand-mirror in the toy box
and maybe for the minute I watch
she sees nothing she doesn't expect.
20 Ruth Borthnott's son, Richard,

cracked his second vertebra
at diving practice eight weeks ago,
and as Ruth describes getting the news
by telephone (shampoo suds plopped

25 all over the notepad she tried
to write on) she smiles like Lev Smith
at his ice cream, smiles also saying
Richard's on a breathing machine,

if he makes it he'll be quadriplegic,
30 she's there in intensive care every day
at dawn. The gameshow-shrill details
of a Hawaiian vacation for two

and surf teasing the ankles
of the couple on a moonlit beachwalk
keep drawing her attention   *35*
away from our conversation.

I say it's amazing how life can change
from one second to the next,
and with no apparent disdain
for this dismal platitude,   *40*

she nods yes, and yes again
at the gameshow's svelte assistant
petting a dinette set, and yes
to Lev Smith's grandma

who has appeared beside her   *45*
with microwaved popcorn
blooming like a huge
cauliflower from its tin.

CONSIDERATIONS

1. Discuss the observations that the narrator makes in the first four stanzas of
   this poem. What do these details reveal about the children? What do they
   reveal about the narrator?
2. The poet writes that Ruth Borthnott, whose son Richard has been on a
   breathing machine for eight weeks, "smiles like Lev Smith / at his ice cream."
   How might you describe this type of smile—the facial expression itself—
   and why doesn't the poet provide this description for you?
3. What purpose do the details about technology in this room serve, from the
   television game show to the microwaved popcorn? How do they reveal a
   part of the poem's theme?

Drama

MARGARET EDSON (1961–   )
Wit

> *Born in Washington, D.C., Margaret Edson was encouraged by both parents to
> pursue her talent for drama. While she was active in theater during her high*

school years, she majored in Renaissance history at Smith College, then spent several years traveling and working at such jobs as waiting on tables and selling hot dogs. In addition, she worked as a physical therapy aide and then as a unit clerk at a hospital that is similar to the one depicted in Wit. *The play, which won the Pulitzer Prize in 1999, reflects Edson's observations and experiences during her work at this highly respected medical facility. Currently, Edson works as a kindergarten teacher.*

Characters

VIVIAN BEARING, PH.D., *50; professor of seventeenth-century poetry at the university*
HARVEY KELEKIAN, M.D., *50; chief of medical oncology, University Hospital*
JASON POSNER, M.D., *28; clinical fellow, Medical Oncology Branch*
SUSIE MONAHAN, R.N., B.S.N., *28; primary nurse, Cancer Inpatient Unit*
E. M. ASHFORD, D.PHIL., *80; professor emerita of English literature*
MR. BEARING, *Vivian's father*
LAB TECHNICIANS
CLINICAL FELLOWS
STUDENTS
CODE TEAM

> *The play may be performed with a cast of nine: the four* TECHNICIANS, FELLOWS, STUDENTS, *and* CODE TEAM MEMBERS *should double;* DR. KELEKIAN *and* MR. BEARING *should double.*

Notes

Most of the action, but not all, takes place in a room of the University Hospital Comprehensive Cancer Center. The stage is empty, and furniture is rolled on and off by the technicians.

Jason and Kelekian wear lab coats, but each has a different shirt and tie every time he enters. Susie wears white jeans, white sneakers, and a different blouse each entrance.

Scenes are indicated by a line rule in the script; there is no break in the action between scenes, but there might be a change in lighting. There is no intermission.

Vivian has a central-venous-access catheter over her left breast, so the IV tubing goes there, not into her arm. The IV pole, with a Port-a-Pump attached, rolls easily on wheels. Every time the IV pole reappears, it has a different configuration of bottles.

> (VIVIAN BEARING *walks on the empty stage pushing her IV pole. She is fifty, tall and very thin, barefoot, and completely bald. She wears two hospital gowns—one tied in the front and one tied in the back—a baseball cap, and a*

hospital ID bracelet. The house lights are at half strength. VIVIAN *looks out at the audience, sizing them up.)*

VIVIAN: *(In false familiarity, waving and nodding to the audience)* Hi. How are you feeling today? Great. That's just great. *(In her own professorial tone)* This is not my standard greeting, I assure you.

   I tend toward something a little more formal, a little less inquisitive, such as, say, "Hello."   5

   But it is the standard greeting here.

   There is some debate as to the correct response to this salutation. Should one reply "I feel good," using "feel" as a copulative to link the subject, "I," to its subjective complement, "good"; or "I feel well," modifying with an adverb the subject's state of being?   10

   I don't know. I am a professor of seventeenth-century poetry, specializing in the Holy Sonnets of John Donne.

   So I just say, "Fine."

   Of course it is not very often that I do feel fine.

   I have been asked "How are you feeling today?" while I was throw-   15
ing up into a plastic washbasin. I have been asked as I was emerging from a four-hour operation with a tube in every orifice, "How are you feeling today?"

   I am waiting for the moment when someone asks me this question and I am dead.   20

   I'm a little sorry I'll miss that.

   It is unfortunate that this remarkable line of inquiry has come to me so late in my career. I could have exploited its feigned solicitude to great advantage: as I was distributing the final examination to the graduate course in seventeenth-century textual criticism—"Hi. How are you   25
feeling today?"

   Of course I would not be wearing this costume at the time, so the question's *ironic significance* would not be fully apparent.

   As I trust it is now.

   Irony is a literary device that will necessarily be deployed to great   30
effect.

   I ardently wish this were not so. I would prefer that a play about me be cast in the mythic-heroic-pastoral mode; but the facts, most notably stage-four metastatic ovarian cancer, conspire against that. *The Faerie Queene* this is not.   35

   And I was dismayed to discover that the play would contain elements of . . . *humor.*

   I have been, at best, an *unwitting* accomplice. *(She pauses.)* It is not my intention to give away the plot; but I think I die at the end.

40   They've given me less than two hours.

If I were poetically inclined, I might employ a threadbare metaphor—the sands of time slipping through the hourglass, the two-hour glass.

Now our sands are almost run;
45   More a little, and then dumb.

Shakespeare. I trust the name is familiar.
At the moment, however, I am disinclined to poetry.
I've got less than two hours. Then: curtain.

(She disconnects herself from the IV pole and shoves it to a crossing TECHNICIAN. *The house lights go out.)*

50   VIVIAN: I'll never forget the time I found out I had cancer.

(DR. HARVEY KELEKIAN enters at a big desk piled high with papers.)

KELEKIAN: You have cancer.
VIVIAN: *(To audience)* See? Unforgettable. It was something of a shock. I had to sit down. *(She plops down.)*
KELEKIAN: Please sit down. Miss Bearing, you have advanced metastatic ovar-
55   ian cancer.
VIVIAN: Go on.
KELEKIAN: You are a professor, Miss Bearing.
VIVIAN: Like yourself, Dr. Kelekian.
KELEKIAN: Well, yes. Now then. You present with a growth that, unfortu-
60   nately, went undetected in stages one, two, and three. Now it is an insidi-
ous adenocarcinoma, which has spread from the primary adnexal mass—
VIVIAN: "Insidious"?
KELEKIAN: "Insidious" means undetectable at an—
VIVIAN: "Insidious" *means* treacherous.
65   KELEKIAN: Shall I continue?
VIVIAN: By all means.

KELEKIAN: Good. In invasive epithelial carcinoma, the most
effective treatment modality is
70   a chemotherapeutic agent. We
are developing an experimental
combination of drugs designed
for primary-site ovarian, with a
target specificity of stage three-
75   and-beyond administration.

VIVIAN: Insidious. Hmm. Curious
word choice. Cancer. Cancel.

"By cancer nature's changing
course untrimmed." No—that's
not it.

Am I going too fast?

Good.

You will be hospitalized as an
in-patient for treatment each
cycle. You will be on complete
intake-and-output measurement
for three days after each treatment to monitor kidney function. After the initial eight
cycles, you will have another
battery of tests.

The antineoplastic will inevitably affect some healthy
cells, including those lining the
gastrointestinal tract from the
lips to the anus, and the hair
follicles. We will of course be
relying on your resolve to
withstand some of the more
pernicious side effects.

(To KELEKIAN*)* No.

Must read something about
cancer.

Must get some books, articles.
Assemble a bibliography.

Is anyone doing research on
cancer?
Concentrate.

Antineoplastic. Anti: against.
Neo: new. Plastic. To mold.
Shaping. Antineoplastic. Against
new shaping.

Hair follicles. My resolve.

"Pernicious" That doesn't
seem—

KELEKIAN: Miss Bearing?
VIVIAN: I beg your pardon?
KELEKIAN: Do you have any questions so far?
VIVIAN: Please, go on.
KELEKIAN: Perhaps some of these terms are new. I realize—
VIVIAN: No, no. Ah. You're being very thorough.
KELEKIAN: I make a point of it. And I always emphasize it with my students—
VIVIAN: So do I. "Thoroughness"—I always tell my students, but they are
   constitutionally averse to painstaking work.
KELEKIAN: Yours, too.
VIVIAN: Oh, it's worse every year.
KELEKIAN: And this is not dermatology, it's medical oncology, for Chrissake.
VIVIAN: My students read through a text once—*once!*—and think it's time for
   a break.
KELEKIAN: Mine are blind.
VIVIAN: Well, mine are deaf.
KELEKIAN: *(Resigned, but warmly)* You just have to hope . . .
VIVIAN: *(Not so sure)* I suppose.

(Pause)

KELEKIAN: Where were we, Dr. Bearing?

115   VIVIAN: I believe I was being thoroughly diagnosed.

KELEKIAN: Right. Now. The tumor is spreading very quickly, and this treatment is very aggressive. So far, so good?

VIVIAN: Yes.

KELEKIAN: Better not teach next semester.

120   VIVIAN: *(Indignant)* Out of the question.

KELEKIAN: The first week of each cycle you'll be hospitalized for chemotherapy; the next week you may feel a little tired; the next two weeks'll be
fine, relatively. This cycle will repeat eight times, as I said before.

VIVIAN: Eight months like that?

125   KELEKIAN: This treatment is the strongest thing we have to offer you. And, as
research, it will make a significant contribution to our knowledge.

VIVIAN: Knowledge, yes.

KELEKIAN: *(Giving her a piece of paper)* Here is the informed-consent form.
Should you agree, you sign there, at the bottom. Is there a family mem-

130   ber you want me to explain this to?

VIVIAN: *(Signing)* That won't be necessary.

KELEKIAN: *(Taking back the paper)* Good. The important thing is for you to
take the full dose of chemotherapy. There may be times when you'll wish
for a lesser dose, due to the side effects. But we've got to go full-force.

135   The experimental phase has got to have the maximum dose to be of any
use. Dr. Bearing—

VIVIAN: Yes?

KELEKIAN: You must be very tough. Do you think you can be very tough?

VIVIAN: You needn't worry.

140   KELEKIAN: Good. Excellent.

(KELEKIAN and the desk exit as VIVIAN stands and walks forward.)

VIVIAN: *(Hesitantly)* I should have asked more questions, because I know
there's going to be a test.

I have cancer, insidious cancer, with pernicious side effects—no,
the *treatment* has pernicious side effects.

145   I have stage-four metastatic ovarian cancer. There is no stage five.
Oh, and I have to be very tough. It appears to be a matter, as the saying
goes, of life and death.

I know all about life and death. I am, after all, a scholar of Donne's
Holy Sonnets, which explore mortality in greater depth than any other

150   body of work in the English language.

And I know for a fact that I am tough. A demanding professor. Uncompromising. Never one to turn from a challenge. That is why I chose,
while a student of the great E. M. Ashford, to study Donne.

(PROFESSOR E. M. ASHFORD, fifty-two, enters, seated at the same desk as KELEKIAN was. The scene is twenty-eight years ago. VIVIAN suddenly turns twenty-two, eager and intimidated.)

VIVIAN: Professor Ashford?

E.M.: Do it again.   *155*

VIVIAN: *(To audience)* It was something of a shock. I had to sit down. *(She plops down.)*

E.M.: Please sit down. Your essay on Holy Sonnet Six, Miss Bearing, is a melodrama, with a veneer of scholarship unworthy of you—to say nothing of Donne. Do it again.   *160*

VIVIAN: I, ah . . .

E.M.: You must begin with a text, Miss Bearing, not with a feeling.

Death be not proud, though some have called thee
Mighty and dreadfull, for, thou art not soe.

You have entirely missed the point of the poem, because, I must tell you,   *165*
you have used an edition of the text that is inauthentically punctuated.
In the Gardner edition—

VIVIAN: That edition was checked out of the library—

E.M.: Miss Bearing!

VIVIAN: Sorry.   *170*

E.M.: You take this too lightly, Miss Bearing. This is Metaphysical Poetry, not
The Modern Novel. The standards of scholarship and critical reading
which one would apply to any other text are simply insufficient. The effort must be total for the results to be meaningful. Do you think the punctuation of the last line of this sonnet is merely an insignificant detail? *175*

   The sonnet begins with a valiant struggle with death, calling on all
the forces of intellect and drama to vanquish the enemy. But it is ultimately about overcoming the seemingly insuperable barriers separating
life, death, and eternal life.

   In the edition you chose, this profoundly simple meaning is sacri-   *180*
ficed to hysterical punctuation:

And Death—*capital D*— shall be no more—*semicolon!*
Death—*capital D*—*comma*—thou shalt die—*exclamation point!*

   If you go in for this sort of thing, I suggest you take up Shakespeare.
   Gardner's edition of the Holy Sonnets returns to the Westmore-   *185*
land manuscript source of 1610—not for sentimental reasons, I assure
you, but because Helen Gardner is a *scholar.* It reads:

And death shall be no more, *comma,* Death thou shalt die.

(As she recites this line, she makes a little gesture at the comma.)

Nothing but a breath—a comma—separates life from life everlast-
190 ing. It is very simple really. With the original punctuation restored, death
is no longer something to act out on a stage, with exclamation points.
It's a comma, a pause.

This way, the *uncompromising* way, one learns something from this
poem, wouldn't you say? Life, death. Soul, God. Past, present. Not insu-
195 perable barriers, not semicolons, just a comma.

VIVIAN: Life, death . . . I see. *(Standing)* It's a metaphysical conceit. It's wit! I'll
go back to the library and rewrite the paper—

E.M.: *(Standing, emphatically)* It is *not wit,* Miss Bearing. It is truth. *(Walking
around the desk to her)* The paper's not the point.

200 VIVIAN: It isn't?

E.M.: *(Tenderly)* Vivian. You're a bright young woman. Use your intelligence.
Don't go back to the library. Go out. Enjoy yourself with your friends.
Hmm?

(VIVIAN walks away. E.M. slides off.)

VIVIAN: *(As she gradually returns to the hospital)* I, ah, went outside. The sun was
205 very bright. I, ah, walked around, past the . . . There were students on the
lawn, talking about nothing, laughing. The insuperable barrier between
one thing and another is . . . just a comma? Simple human truth, uncompromising scholarly standards? They're *connected?* I just couldn't . . .

I went back to the library.
210 Anyway.

All right. Significant contribution to knowledge.

Eight cycles of chemotherapy. Give me the full dose, the full dose
every time.

(In a burst of activity, the hospital scene is created.)

215 VIVIAN: The attention was flattering. For the first five minutes. Now I know
how poems feel.

*(SUSIE MONAHAN, VIVIAN's primary nurse, gives VIVIAN her chart, then
puts her in a wheelchair and takes her to her first appointment: chest x-ray. This
and all other diagnostic tests are suggested by light and sound.)*

TECHNICIAN 1: Name.

VIVIAN: My name? Vivian Bearing.

TECHNICIAN 1: Huh?

220 VIVIAN: Bearing. B–E–A–R–I–N–G. Vivian. V–I–V–I–A–N.

TECHNICIAN 1: Doctor.

VIVIAN: Yes, I have a Ph.D.

TECHNICIAN 1: *Your* doctor.

VIVIAN: Oh. Dr. Harvey Kelekian.

(TECHNICIAN 1 *positions her so that she is leaning forward and embracing the metal plate, then steps offstage.*)

VIVIAN: *I* am a doctor of philosophy—   225

TECHNICIAN 1: *(From offstage)* Take a deep breath, and hold it. *(Pause, with light and sound)* Okay.

VIVIAN: —a scholar of seventeenth-century poetry.

TECHNICIAN 1: *(From offstage)* Turn sideways, arms behind your head, and hold it. *(Pause)* Okay.   230

VIVIAN: I have made an immeasurable contribution to the discipline of English literature. (TECHNICIAN 1 *returns and puts her in the wheelchair.*) I am, in short, a force.

(TECHNICIAN 1 *rolls her to upper GI series, where* TECHNICIAN 2 *picks up.*)

TECHNICIAN 2: Name.

VIVIAN: Lucy, Countess of Bedford.   235

TECHNICIAN 2: *(Checking a printout)* I don't see it here.

VIVIAN: My name is Vivian Bearing. B-E-A-R-I-N-G. Dr. Kelekian is my doctor.

TECHNICIAN 2: Okay. Lie down. (TECHNICIAN 2 *positions her on a stretcher and leaves. Light and sound suggest the filming.*)   240

VIVIAN: After an outstanding undergraduate career, I studied with Professor E. M. Ashford for three years, during which time I learned by instruction and example what it means to be a scholar of distinction.

As her research fellow, my principal task was the alphabetizing of index cards for Ashford's monumental critical edition of Donne's *Devo-*   245
tions upon Emergent Occasions.

(During the procedure, another TECHNICIAN *takes the wheelchair away.*)

I am thanked in the preface: "Miss Vivian Bearing for her able assistance."

My dissertation, "Ejaculations in Seventeenth-Century Manuscript and Printed Editions of the Holy Sonnets: A Comparison," was revised for publication in the *Journal of English Texts,* a very prestigious venue for   250
a first appearance.

TECHNICIAN 2: Where's your wheelchair?

VIVIAN: I do not know. I was busy just now.

TECHNICIAN 2: Well, how are you going to get out of here?

VIVIAN: Well, I do not know. Perhaps you would like me to stay.   255

TECHNICIAN 2: I guess I got to go find you a chair.

VIVIAN: *(Sarcastically)* Don't inconvenience yourself on my behalf. (TECHNICIAN 2 *leaves to get a wheelchair.*)

My second article, a classic explication of Donne's sonnet "Death be not proud," was published in *Critical Discourse.*   260

The success of the essay prompted the University Press to solicit a volume on the twelve Holy Sonnets in the 1633 edition, which I produced in the remarkably short span of three years. My book, entitled *Made Cunningly,* remains an immense success, in paper as well as cloth.

265   In it, I devote one chapter to a thorough examination of each sonnet, discussing every word in extensive detail.

(TECHNICIAN 2 returns with a wheelchair.)

TECHNICIAN 2: Here.

VIVIAN: I summarize previous critical interpretations of the text and offer my own analysis. It is exhaustive.

(TECHNICIAN 2 deposits her at CT scan.)

270   Bearing. B–E–A–R–I–N–G. Kelekian.

(TECHNICIAN 3 has VIVIAN lie down on a metal stretcher. Light and sound suggest the procedure.)

TECHNICIAN 3: Here. Hold still.

VIVIAN: For how long?

TECHNICIAN 3: Just a little while. *(TECHNICIAN 3 leaves. Silence)*

VIVIAN: The scholarly study of poetic texts requires a capacity for scrupu-
275   lously detailed examination, particularly the poetry of John Donne.

The salient characteristic of the poems is wit: "Itchy outbreaks of far-fetched wit," as Donne himself said.

To the common reader—that is to say, the undergraduate with a B-plus or better average—wit provides an invaluable exercise for sharp-
280   ening the mental faculties, for stimulating the flash of comprehension that can only follow hours of exacting and seemingly pointless scrutiny.

(TECHNICIAN 3 puts VIVIAN back in the wheelchair and wheels her toward the unit. Partway, TECHNICIAN 3 gives the chair a shove and SUSIE MONAHAN, VIVIAN's primary nurse, takes over. SUSIE rolls VIVIAN to the exam room.)

To the scholar, to the mind comprehensively trained in the sub-tleties of seventeenth-century vocabulary, versification, and theological, historical, geographical, political, and mythological allusions, Donne's wit
285   is . . . a way to see how good you really are.

After twenty years, I can say with confidence, no one is quite as good as I.

(By now, SUSIE has helped VIVIAN sit on the exam table. DR. JASON POSNER, clinical fellow, stands in the doorway.)

JASON: Ah, Susie?

SUSIE: Oh, hi.

JASON: Ready when you are.   290

SUSIE: Okay. Go ahead. Ms. Bearing, this is Jason Posner. He's going to do
your history, ask you a bunch of questions. He's Dr. Kelekian's fellow.

(SUSIE *is busy in the room, setting up for the exam.*)

JASON: Hi, Professor Bearing. I'm Dr. Posner, clinical fellow in the medical
oncology branch, working with Dr. Kelekian.

   Professor Bearing, I, ah, I was an undergraduate at the U. I took   295
your course in seventeenth-century poetry.

VIVIAN: You did?

JASON: Yes. I thought it was excellent.

VIVIAN: Thank you. Were you an English major?

JASON: No. Biochemistry. But you can't get into medical school unless you're   300
well-rounded. And I made a bet with myself that I could get an A in the
three hardest courses on campus.

SUSIE: Howdjya do, Jace?

JASON: Success.

VIVIAN: *(Doubtful)* Really?   305

JASON: A minus. It was a very tough course. *(To* SUSIE*)* I'll call you.

SUSIE: Okay. *(She leaves.)*

JASON: I'll just pull this over. *(He gets a little stool on wheels.)* Get the proxemics
right here. There. *(Nervously)* Good. Now. I'm going to be taking your
history. It's a medical interview, and then I give you an exam.   310

VIVIAN: I believe Dr. Kelekian has already done that.

JASON: Well, I know, but Dr. Kelekian wants *me* to do it, too. Now. I'll be taking a few notes as we go along.

VIVIAN: Very well.

JASON: Okay. Let's get started. How are you feeling today?   315

VIVIAN: Fine, thank you.

JASON: Good. How is your general health?

VIVIAN: Fine.

JASON: Excellent. Okay. We know you are an academic.

VIVIAN: Yes, we've established that.   320

JASON: So we don't need to talk about your interesting work.

VIVIAN: No.

(*The following questions and answers go extremely quickly.*)

JASON: How old are you?

VIVIAN: Fifty.

JASON: Are you married?   325

VIVIAN: No.

JASON: Are your parents living?

VIVIAN: No.

JASON: How and when did they die?

330   VIVIAN: My father, suddenly, when I was twenty, of a heart attack. My mother, slowly, when I was forty-one and forty-two, of cancer. Breast cancer.

JASON: Cancer?

VIVIAN: Breast cancer.

JASON: I see. Any siblings?

335   VIVIAN: No.

JASON: Do you have any questions so far?

VIVIAN: Not so far.

JASON: Well, that about does it for your life history.

VIVIAN: Yes, that's all there is to my life history.

340   JASON: Now I'm going to ask you about your past medical history. Have you ever been hospitalized?

VIVIAN: I had my tonsils out when I was eight.

JASON: Have you ever been pregnant?

VIVIAN: No.

345   JASON: Ever had heart murmurs? High blood pressure?

VIVIAN: No.

JASON: Stomach, liver, kidney problems?

VIVIAN: No.

JASON: Venereal diseases? Uterine infections?

350   VIVIAN: No.

JASON: Thyroid, diabetes, cancer?

VIVIAN: No—cancer, yes.

JASON: When?

VIVIAN: Now.

355   JASON: Well, not including now.

VIVIAN: In that case, no.

JASON: Okay. Clinical depression? Nervous breakdowns? Suicide attempts?

VIVIAN: No.

JASON: Do you smoke?

360   VIVIAN: No.

JASON: Ethanol?

VIVIAN: I'm sorry?

JASON: Alcohol.

VIVIAN: Oh. Ethanol. Yes, I drink wine.

365   JASON: How much? How often?

VIVIAN: A glass with dinner occasionally. And perhaps a Scotch every now and then.

JASON: Do you use substances?

VIVIAN: Such as.

370   JASON: Marijuana, cocaine, crack cocaine, PCP, ecstasy, poppers—

VIVIAN: No.

JASON: Do you drink caffeinated beverages?

VIVIAN: Oh, yes!

JASON: Which ones?

VIVIAN: Coffee. A few cups a day.   *375*

JASON: How many?

VIVIAN: Two . . . to six. But I really don't think that's immoderate—

JASON: How often do you undergo routine medical check-ups?

VIVIAN: Well, not as often as I should, probably, but I've felt fine, I really have.

JASON: So the answer is?   *380*

VIVIAN: Every three to . . . five years.

JASON: What do you do for exercise?

VIVIAN: Pace.

JASON: Are you having sexual relations?

VIVIAN: Not at the moment.   *385*

JASON: Are you pre- or post-menopausal?

VIVIAN: Pre.

JASON: When was the first day of your last period?

VIVIAN: Ah, ten days—two weeks ago.

JASON: Okay. When did you first notice your present complaint?   *390*

VIVIAN: This time, now?

JASON: Yes.

VIVIAN: Oh, about four months ago. I felt a pain in my stomach, in my ab-
    domen, like a cramp, but not the same.

JASON: How did it feel?   *395*

VIVIAN: Like a cramp.

JASON: But not the same?

VIVIAN: No, duller, and stronger. I can't describe it.

JASON: What came next?

VIVIAN: Well, I just, I don't know, I started noticing my body, little things. I   *400*
    would be teaching, and feel a sharp pain.

JASON: What kind of pain?

VIVIAN: Sharp, and sudden. Then it would go away. Or I would be tired. Ex-
    hausted. I was working on a major project, the article on John Donne
    for *The Oxford Encyclopedia of English Literature*. It was a great honor. But   *405*
    I had a very strict deadline.

JASON: So you would say you were under stress?

VIVIAN: It wasn't so much more stress than usual, I just couldn't withstand it
    this time. I don't know.

JASON: So?   *410*

VIVIAN: So I went to Dr. Chin, my gynecologist, after I had turned in the ar-
    ticle, and explained all this. She examined me, and sent me to Jefferson

the internist, and he sent me to Kelekian because he thought I might
have a tumor.

415   JASON: And that's it?

VIVIAN: Till now.

JASON: Hmmm. Well, that's very interesting.

(Nervous pause)

Well, I guess I'll start the examination. It'll only take a few minutes. Why don't you, um, sort of lie back, and—oh—relax.

*(He helps her lie back on the table, raises the stirrups out of the table, raises her
legs and puts them in the stirrups, and puts a paper sheet over her.)*

420   Be very relaxed. This won't hurt. Let me get this sheet. Okay. Just
stay calm. Okay. Put your feet in these stirrups. Okay. Just. There. Okay?
Now. Oh, I have to go get Susie. Got to have a girl here. Some crazy
clinical rule. Um. I'll be right back. Don't move.

*(JASON leaves. Long pause. He is seen walking quickly back and forth in the
hall, and calling SUSIE's name as he goes by.)*

VIVIAN: *(To herself)* I wish I had given him an A. *(Silence)*

425   Two times one is two.
Two times two is four.
Two times three is six.
Um.
Oh.

430   Death be not proud, though some have called thee
Mighty and dreadfull, for, thou art not soe,
For, those, whom thou think'st, thou dost overthrow,
Die not, poore death, nor yet canst thou kill mee . . .

JASON: *(In the hallway)* Has anybody seen Susie?

435   VIVIAN: *(Losing her place for a second)* Ah.

Thou'art slave to Fate, chance, kings, and desperate men,
And dost with poyson, warre, and sicknesse dwell,
And poppie,' or charmes can make us sleepe as well,
And better than thy stroake; why swell'st thou then?

440   JASON: *(In the hallway)* She was here just a minute ago.

VIVIAN:

One short sleepe past, wee wake eternally,
And death shall be no more—*comma*—Death thou shalt die.

(JASON and SUSIE return.)

JASON: Okay. Here's everything. Okay.

SUSIE: What is this? Why did you leave her—   445

JASON: *(To* SUSIE*)* I had to find you. Now, come on. *(To* VIVIAN*)* We're ready, Professor Bearing. *(To himself, as he puts on exam gloves)* Get these on. Okay. Just lift this up. Ooh. Okay. *(As much to himself as to her)* Just relax. *(He begins the pelvic exam, with one hand on her abdomen and the other inside her, looking blankly at the ceiling as he feels around.)* Okay. *(Silence)* Susie, isn't   450 that interesting, that I had Professor Bearing.

SUSIE: Yeah. I wish I had taken some literature. I don't know anything about poetry.

JASON: *(Trying to be casual)* Professor Bearing was very highly regarded on campus. It looked very good on my transcript that I had taken her   455 course. *(Silence)* They even asked me about it in my interview for med school— *(He feels the mass and does a double take.)* Jesus! *(Tense silence. He is amazed and fascinated.)*

SUSIE: What?

VIVIAN: What?   460

JASON: Um. *(He tries for composure.)* Yeah. I survived Bearing's course. No problem. Heh. *(Silence)* Yeah, John Donne, those metaphysical poets, that metaphysical wit. Hardest poetry in the English department. Like to see *them* try biochemistry. *(Silence)* Okay. We're about done. Okay. That's it. Okay, Professor Bearing. Let's take your feet out, there. *(He takes off his   465 gloves and throws them away.)* Okay. I gotta go. I gotta go.

(JASON quickly leaves. VIVIAN slowly gets up from this scene and walks stiffly away. SUSIE cleans up the exam room and exits.)

VIVIAN: *(Walking downstage to audience)* That . . . was . . . hard. That . . . was . . . One thing can be said for an eight-month course of cancer treatment: it is highly educational. I am learning to suffer.   470

Yes, it is mildly uncomfortable to have an electrocardiogram, but the . . . agony . . . of a proctosigmoidoscopy sweeps it from memory. Yes, it was embarrassing to have to wear a nightgown all day long—two nightgowns!—but that seemed like a positive privilege compared to watching myself go bald. Yes, having a former student give me a pelvic   475 exam was thoroughly *degrading*—and I use the term deliberately—but I could not have imagined the depths of humiliation that—

Oh, God— *(VIVIAN runs across the stage to her hospital room, dives onto the bed, and throws up into a large plastic washbasin.)* Oh, God. Oh. Oh. *(She lies slumped on the bed, fastened to the IV, which now includes a small bottle with a   480 bright orange label.)* Oh, God. It can't be. *(Silence)* Oh, God. Please. Steady. Steady. *(Silence)* Oh—Oh, no! *(She throws up again, moans, and retches in agony.)* Oh, God. What's left? I haven't eaten in two days. What's left to puke?

You may remark that my vocabulary has taken a turn for the
485 Anglo-Saxon.

God, I'm going to barf my brains out.

(She begins to relax.) If I actually did barf my brains out, it would be
a great loss to my discipline. Of course, not a few of my colleagues would
be relieved. To say nothing of my students.

490 It's not that I'm controversial. Just uncompromising. Ooh— *(She
lunges for the basin. Nothing)* Oh. *(Silence)* False alarm. If the word went
round that Vivian Bearing had barfed her brains out . . .

Well, first my colleagues, most of whom are my former students,
would scramble madly for my position. Then their consciences would
495 flare up, so to honor *my* memory they would put together a collection
of *their* essays about John Donne. The volume would begin with a warm
introduction, capturing my most endearing qualities. It would be short.
But sweet.

Published *and* perished.

500 Now, watch this. I have to ring the bell *(She presses the button on the
bed)* to get someone to come and measure this emesis, and record the
amount on a chart of my intake and output. This counts as output.

(SUSIE enters.)

SUSIE: *(Brightly)* How you doing, Ms. Bearing? You having some nausea?
VIVIAN: *(Weakly)* Uhh, yes.
505 SUSIE: Why don't I take that? Here.
VIVIAN: It's about 300 cc's.
SUSIE: That all?
VIVIAN: It was very hard work.

(SUSIE takes the basin to the bathroom and rinses it.)

SUSIE: Yup. Three hundred. Good guess. *(She marks the graph.)* Okay. Anything
510 else I can get for you? Some Jell-O or anything?
VIVIAN: Thank you, no.
SUSIE: You okay all by yourself here?
VIVIAN: Yes.
SUSIE: You're not having a lot of visitors, are you?
515 VIVIAN: *(Correcting)* None, to be precise.
SUSIE: Yeah, I didn't think so. Is there somebody you want me to call for you?
VIVIAN: That won't be necessary.
SUSIE: Well, I'll just pop my head in every once in a while to see how you're
coming along. Kelekian and the fellows should be in soon. *(She touches
520 VIVIAN's arm.)* If there's anything you need, you just ring.
VIVIAN: *(Uncomfortable with kindness)* Thank you.
SUSIE: Okay. Just call. *(SUSIE disconnects the IV bottle with the orange label and
takes it with her as she leaves. VIVIAN lies still. Silence)*

VIVIAN: In this dramatic structure you will see the most interesting aspects of   *525*
my tenure as an in-patient receiving experimental chemotherapy for advanced metastatic ovarian cancer.

But as I am a *scholar* before . . . an impresario, I feel obliged to document what it is like here most of the time, between the dramatic cli-
maxes. Between the spectacles.   *530*

In truth, it is like this:

(She ceremoniously lies back and stares at the ceiling.)

You cannot imagine how time . . . can be . . . so still.
It hangs. It weighs. And yet there is so little of it.
It goes so slowly, and yet it is so scarce.
If I were writing this scene, it would last a full fifteen minutes. I   *535*
would lie here, and you would sit there.

(She looks at the audience, daring them.)

Not to worry. Brevity is the soul of wit.
But if you think eight months of cancer treatment is tedious for
the *audience,* consider how it feels to play my part.

All right. All right. It is Friday morning: Grand Rounds. *(Loudly,*   *540*
giving a cue) Action.

(KELEKIAN enters, followed by JASON and four other FELLOWS.)

KELEKIAN: Dr. Bearing.
VIVIAN: Dr. Kelekian.
KELEKIAN: Jason.

(JASON moves to the front of the group.)

JASON: Professor Bearing. How are you feeling today?   *545*
VIVIAN: Fine.
JASON: That's great. That's just great. *(He takes a sheet and carefully covers her legs*
and groin, then pulls up her gown to reveal her entire abdomen. He is barely au-
dible, but his gestures are clear.)

VIVIAN: "Grand Rounds." The term   *550*
is theirs. Not "Grand" in the
traditional sense of sweeping or
magnificent. Not "Rounds" as
in a musical canon, or a *round*
of applause (though either
would be refreshing at this
point). Here, "Rounds" seems
to signify darting *around* the
main issue . . . which I sup-

JASON: Very late detection. Staged
as a four upon admission.
Hexamethophosphacil with
Vinplatin to potentiate. Hex at
300 mg. per meter squared, Vin   *555*
at 100. Today is cycle two, day
three. Both cycles at the *full dose.*
(The FELLOWS are impressed.)
The primary site is—*here (He*

560 pose would be the struggle
for life . . . *my* life . . . with
heated discussions of side effects,
other complaints, additional
treatments.

565

Grand Rounds is not Grand
Opera. But compared to lying
here, it is positively *dramatic*.

570 Full of subservience, hierarchy,
gratuitous displays, sublimated
rivalries—I feel right at home.
It is just like a graduate seminar.

575 With one important difference:
in Grand Rounds, *they* read *me*
like a book. Once I did the
teaching, now I am taught.

580

This is much easier. I just hold
still and look cancerous. It requires less acting every time.

585 Excellent command of details.

*puts his finger on the spot on her
abdomen), behind the left ovary.*
Metastases are suspected in the
peritoneal cavity—here. And—
here. *(He touches those spots.)*

Full lymphatic involve-
ment. *(He moves his hands over
her entire body.)*

At the time of first-look
surgery, a significant part of the
tumor was de-bulked, mostly in
this area—here. *(He points to each
organ, poking her abdomen.)* Left,
right ovaries. Fallopian tubes.
Uterus. All out.

Evidence of primary-site
shrinkage. Shrinking in
metastatic tumors has not been
documented. Primary mass
frankly palpable in pelvic exam,
frankly, all through here—*here*.
(Some FELLOWS *reach and press
where he is pointing.)*

KELEKIAN: Excellent command of details.
VIVIAN: *(To herself)* I taught him, you know—
KELEKIAN: Okay. Problem areas with Hex and Vin. *(He addresses all the* FEL-
590 LOWS, *but* JASON *answers first and they resent him.)*
FELLOW 1: Myelosu—
JASON: *(Interrupting)* Well, first of course is myelosuppression, a lowering of
blood-cell counts. It goes without saying. With this combination of
agents, nephrotoxicity will be next.
595 KELEKIAN: Go on.
JASON: The kidneys are designed to filter out impurities in the bloodstream.
In trying to filter the chemotherapeutic agent out of the bloodstream,
the kidneys shut down.
KELEKIAN: Intervention.
600 JASON: Hydration.
KELEKIAN: Monitoring.

JASON: Full recording of fluid intake and output, as you see here on these graphs, to monitor hydration and kidney function. Totals monitored daily by the clinical fellow, as per the protocol.

KELEKIAN: Anybody else. Side effects.   *605*

FELLOW 1: Nausea and vomiting.

KELEKIAN: Jason.

JASON: Routine.

FELLOW 2: Pain while urinating.

JASON: Routine. *(The* FELLOWS *are trying to catch* JASON.*)*   *610*

FELLOW 3: Psychological depression.

JASON: No way.

(The FELLOWS *are silent.)*

KELEKIAN: *(Standing by* VIVIAN *at the head of the bed)* Anything else. Other complaints with Hexamethophosphacil and Vinplatin. Come on. *(Silence.* KELEKIAN *and* VIVIAN *wait together for the correct answer.)*   *615*

FELLOW 4: Mouth sores.

JASON: Not yet.

FELLOW 2: *(Timidly)* Skin rash?

JASON: Nope.

KELEKIAN: *(Sharing this with* VIVIAN*)* Why do we waste our time, Dr. Bearing?   *620*

VIVIAN: *(Delighted)* I do not know, Dr. Kelekian.

KELEKIAN: *(To the* FELLOWS*)* Use your eyes. *(All* FELLOWS *look closely at* VIVIAN.*)* Jesus God. Hair loss.

FELLOWS: *(All protesting.* VIVIAN *and* KELEKIAN *are amused.)*

—Come on.   *625*

—You can see it.

—It doesn't count.

—No fair.

KELEKIAN: Jason.

JASON: *(Begrudgingly)* Hair loss after first cycle of treatment.   *630*

KELEKIAN: That's better. *(To* VIVIAN*)* Dr. Bearing. Full dose. Excellent. Keep pushing the fluids.

(The FELLOWS *leave.* KELEKIAN *stops* JASON.*)*

KELEKIAN: Jason.

JASON: Huh?

KELEKIAN: Clinical.   *635*

JASON: Oh, right. *(To* VIVIAN*)* Thank you, Professor Bearing. You've been very cooperative. *(They leave her with her stomach uncovered.)*

VIVIAN: Wasn't that . . . Grand? *(She gets up without the IV pole.)* At times, this obsessively detailed examination, this *scrutiny* seems to me to be a nefarious

640   business. On the other hand, what is the alternative? Ignorance? Ignorance
          may be . . . bliss; but it is not a very noble goal.
                So I play my part.
                (Pause)
                I receive chemotherapy, throw up, am subjected to countless indig-
645   nities, feel better, go home. Eight cycles. Eight neat little strophes. Oh,
          there have been the usual variations, subplots, red herrings: hepatotoxic-
          ity (liver poison), neuropathy (nerve death).
                (Righteously) They are medical terms. I look them up.
                It has always been my custom to treat words with respect.
650   I can recall the time—the very hour of the very day—when I knew
          words would be my life's work.

          (A pile of six little white books appears, with MR. BEARING, VIVIAN's *father,
          seated behind an open newspaper.)*

          It was my fifth birthday.

          (VIVIAN, *now a child, flops down to the books.)*

          I liked that one best.
655   MR. BEARING: *(Disinterested but tolerant, never distracted from his newspaper)* Read
          another.
      VIVIAN: I think I'll read . . . *(She takes a book from the stack and reads its spine
          intently) The Tale of the Flopsy Bunnies. (Reading the front cover) The Tale of
          the Flopsy Bunnies.* It has little bunnies on the front.

          (Opening to the title page) The Tale of the Flopsy Bunnies by Beatrix Potter.
          (She turns the page and begins to read.)

660   It is said that the effect of eating too much lettuce is sopor—sop—or—
          what is that word?
      MR. BEARING: Sound it out.
      VIVIAN: Sop—or—fic. Sop—or—i—fic. Soporific. What does that mean?
      MR. BEARING: Soporific. Causing sleep.
665   VIVIAN: Causing sleep.
      MR. BEARING: Makes you sleepy.
      VIVIAN: "Soporific" means "makes you sleepy"?
      MR. BEARING: Correct.
      VIVIAN: "Soporific" means "makes you sleepy." Soporific.
670   MR. BEARING: Now use it in a sentence. What has a soporific effect on *you?*
      VIVIAN: A soporific effect on me.
      MR. BEARING: What makes you sleepy?
      VIVIAN: Aahh—nothing.
      MR. BEARING: Correct.
675   VIVIAN: What about you?

MR. BEARING: What has a soporific effect on me? Let me think: boring conversation, I suppose, after dinner.

VIVIAN: Me too, boring conversation.

MR. BEARING: Carry on.

VIVIAN:

It is said that the effect of eating too much lettuce is soporific. 680
    The little bunnies in the picture are asleep! They're sleeping! Like you said, because of *soporific!*

(She stands up, and MR. BEARING exits.)

The illustration bore out the meaning of the word, just as he had explained it. At the time, it seemed like magic.
    So imagine the effect that the words of John Donne first had on 685
me: ratiocination, concatenation, coruscation, tergiversation.
    Medical terms are less evocative. Still, I want to know what the doctors mean when they . . . anatomize me. And I will grant that in this particular field of endeavor they possess a more potent arsenal of terminology than I. My only defense is the acquisition of vocabulary. 690

(SUSIE enters and puts her arm around VIVIAN's shoulders to hold her up. VIVIAN is shaking, feverish, and weak.)

VIVIAN: *(All at once)* Fever and neutropenia.

SUSIE: When did it start?

VIVIAN: *(Having difficulty speaking)* I—I was at home—reading—and I—felt so bad. I called. Fever and neutropenia. They said to come in. 695

SUSIE: You did the right thing to come. Did somebody drive you?

VIVIAN: Cab. I took a taxi.

SUSIE: *(She grabs a wheelchair and helps VIVIAN sit. As SUSIE speaks, she takes VIVIAN's temperature, pulse, and respiration rate.)* Here, why don't you sit? Just sit there a minute. I'll get Jason. He's on call tonight. We'll get him to 700
give you some meds. I'm glad I was here on nights. I'll make sure you get to bed soon, okay? It'll just be a minute. I'll get you some juice, some nice juice with lots of ice.

(SUSIE leaves quickly. VIVIAN sits there, agitated, confused, and very sick. SUSIE returns with the juice.)

VIVIAN: Lights. I left all the lights on at my house.

SUSIE: Don't you worry. It'll be all right. 705

(JASON enters, roused from his sleep and not fully awake. He wears surgical scrubs and puts on a lab coat as he enters.)

JASON: *(Without looking at VIVIAN)* How are you feeling, Professor Bearing?

VIVIAN: My teeth—are chattering.

JASON: Vitals.

SUSIE: *(Giving* VIVIAN *juice and a straw, without looking at* JASON*)* Temp 39.4.
710   Pulse 120. Respiration 36. Chills and sweating.

JASON: Fever and neutropenia. It's a "shake and bake." Blood cultures and
urine, stat. Admit her. Prepare for reverse isolation. Start with aceta-
minophen. Vitals every four hours. *(He starts to leave.)*

SUSIE: *(Following him)* Jason—I think you need to talk to Kelekian about low-
715   ering the dose for the next cycle. It's too much for her like this.

JASON: Lower the dose? No way. Full dose. She's tough. She can take it. Wake
me up when the counts come from the lab.

(He pads off. SUSIE *wheels* VIVIAN *to her room, and* VIVIAN *collapses on
the bed.* SUSIE *connects* VIVIAN'S *IV, then wets a washcloth and rubs her face
and neck.* VIVIAN *remains delirious.* SUSIE *checks the IV and leaves with the
wheelchair.*

After a while, KELEKIAN *appears in the doorway holding a surgical mask near
his face.* JASON *is with him, now dressed and clean-shaven.)*

KELEKIAN: Good morning, Dr. Bearing. Fifth cycle. Full dose. Definite
progress. Everything okay.

720 VIVIAN: *(Weakly)* Yes.

KELEKIAN: You're doing swell. Isolation is no problem. Couple of days. Think
of it as a vacation.

VIVIAN: Oh.

*(*JASON *starts to enter, holding a mask near his face, just like* KELEKIAN.*)*

KELEKIAN: Jason.

725 JASON: Oh, Jesus. Okay, okay.

(He returns to the doorway, where he puts on a paper gown, mask, and gloves.
KELEKIAN *leaves.)*

VIVIAN: *(To audience)* In isolation, I am isolated. For once I can use a term literally. The chemotherapeutic agents eradicating my cancer have also
eradicated my immune system. In my present condition, every living
thing is a health hazard to me . . .

*(*JASON *comes in to check the intake-and-output.)*

730 JASON: *(Complaining to himself)* I really have not got time for this . . .

VIVIAN: . . . particularly health-care professionals.

JASON: *(Going right to the graph on the wall)* Just to look at the I&O sheets for
one minute, and it takes me half an hour to do precautions. Four, seven,
eleven. Two-fifty twice. Okay. *(Remembering)* Oh, Jeez. Clinical. Professor
735   Bearing. How are you feeling today?

VIVIAN: *(Very sick)* Fine. Just shaking sometimes from the chills.

JASON: IV will kick in anytime now. No problem. Listen, gotta go. Keep pushing the fluids.

(As he exits, he takes off the gown, mask, and gloves.)

VIVIAN: *(Getting up from bed with her IV pole and resuming her explanation)* I am
not in isolation because I have cancer, because I have a tumor the size of   *740*
a grapefruit. No. I am in isolation because I am being treated for cancer.
My treatment imperils my health.

    Herein lies the paradox. John Donne would revel in it. I would
revel in it, if he wrote a poem about it. My students would flounder in
it, because paradox is too difficult to understand. Think of it as a puzzle, I   *745*
would tell them, an intellectual game.

(She is trapped.) Or, I *would have* told them. Were it a game. Which it is not.

(Escaping) If they were here, if I were lecturing: How I would *perplex*
them! I could work my students into a frenzy. Every ambiguity, every
shifting awareness. I could draw so much from the poems.   *750*

    I could be so powerful.

---

*(VIVIAN stands still, as if conjuring a scene. Now at the height of her powers,
she grandly disconnects herself from the IV.* TECHNICIANS *remove the bed and
hand her a pointer.)*

VIVIAN: The poetry of the early seventeenth century, what has been called
the metaphysical school, considers an intractable mental puzzle by exercising the outstanding human faculty of the era, namely *wit*.   *755*

    The greatest wit—the greatest English poet, some would say—was
John Donne. In the Holy Sonnets, Donne applied his capacious, agile
wit to the larger aspects of the human experience: life, death, and God.

    In his poems, metaphysical quandaries are addressed, but never re-
solved. Ingenuity, virtuosity, and a vigorous intellect that jousts with the   *760*
most exalted concepts: these are the tools of wit.

*(The lights dim. A screen lowers, and the sonnet "If poysonous mineralls," from
the Gardner edition, appears on it.* VIVIAN *recites.)*

If poysonous mineralls, and if that tree,
Whose fruit threw death on else immortall us,
If lecherous goats, if serpents envious
Cannot be damn'd; Alas; why should I bee?   *765*
Why should intent or reason, borne in mee,
Make sinnes, else equall, in mee, more heinous?
And mercy being easie, 'and glorious
To God, in his sterne wrath, why threatens hee?

770   But who am I, that dare dispute with thee?
        O God, Oh! of thine onely worthy blood,
        And my teares, make a heavenly Lethean flood,
        And drowne in it my sinnes blacke memorie.
        That thou remember them, some claime as debt,
775   I thinke it mercy, if thou wilt forget.

(VIVIAN occasionally whacks the screen with a pointer for emphasis. She moves around as she lectures.)

Aggressive intellect. Pious melodrama. And a final, fearful point. Donne's Holy Sonnet Five, 1609. From the Ashford edition, based on Gardner.

The speaker of the sonnet has a brilliant mind, and he plays the
780 part convincingly; but in the end he finds God's *forgiveness* hard to believe, so he crawls under a rock to *hide.*

If arsenic and serpents are not damned, then why is he? In asking the question, the speaker turns eternal damnation into an intellectual game. Why would God choose to do what is *hard,* to condemn, rather
785 than what is *easy,* and also *glorious*—to show mercy?
(Several scholars have disputed Ashford's third comma in line six, but none convincingly.)

But. Exception. Limitation. Contrast. The argument shifts from cleverness to melodrama, an unconvincing eruption of piety: "O" "God"
790 "Oh!"

A typical prayer would plead "Remember me, O Lord." (This point is nicely explicated in an article by Richard Strier—a former student of mine who once sat where you do now, although I dare say he was *awake*—in the May 1989 issue of *Modern Philology.*) True believers ask to
795 be *remembered* by God. The speaker of this sonnet asks God to forget. *(VIVIAN moves in front of the screen, and the projection of the poem is cast directly upon her.)* Where is the hyperactive intellect of the first section? Where is the histrionic outpouring of the second? When the speaker considers his own *sins,* and the inevitability of God's *judgment,* he can
800 conceive of but one resolution: to *disappear. (VIVIAN moves away from the screen.)* Doctrine assures us that no sinner is denied *forgiveness,* not even one whose sins are overweening *intellect* or overwrought *dramatics.* The speaker does not need to *hide* from God's *judgment,* only to accept God's *forgiveness.* It is very simple. Suspiciously simple.
805 We want to correct the speaker, to remind him of the assurance of salvation. But it is too late. The poetic encounter is over. We are left to our own consciences. Have we outwitted Donne? Or have we been outwitted?

(SUSIE comes on.)

SUSIE: Ms. Bearing?

VIVIAN: *(Continuing)* Will the po—

SUSIE: Ms. Bearing?   810

VIVIAN: *(Crossly)* What is it?

SUSIE: You have to go down for a test. Jason just called. They want another
     ultrasound. They're concerned about a bowel obstruction—Is it okay if I
     come in?

VIVIAN: No. Not now.   815

SUSIE: I'm sorry, but they want it now.

VIVIAN: Not right now. It's not *supposed* to be now.

SUSIE: Yes, they want to do it now. I've got the chair.

VIVIAN: It should not be now. I am in the middle of—this. I have *this* planned
     for now, not ultrasound. No more tests. We've covered that.   820

SUSIE: I know, I know, but they need for it to be now. It won't take long, and
     it isn't a bad procedure. Why don't you just come along.

VIVIAN: *I do not want to go now!*

SUSIE: Ms. Bearing.

> *(Silence.* VIVIAN *raises the screen, walks away from the scene, hooks herself to
> the IV, and gets in the wheelchair.* SUSIE *wheels* VIVIAN, *and a* TECHNICIAN
> *takes her.)*

TECHNICIAN: Name.   825

VIVIAN: B-E-A-R-I-N-G. Kelekian.

TECHNICIAN: It'll just be a minute.

VIVIAN: Time for your break.

TECHNICIAN: Yup.

> *(The* TECHNICIAN *leaves.)*

VIVIAN: *(Mordantly)* Take a break!   830

> *(*VIVIAN *sits weakly in the wheelchair.)*

VIVIAN:

> This is my playes last scene, here heavens appoint
> My pilgrimages last mile; and my race
> Idly, yet quickly runne, hath this last pace,   835
> My spans last inch, my minutes last point,
> And gluttonous death will instantly unjoynt
> My body, 'and soule

> John Donne. 1609.
>   I have always particularly liked that poem. In the abstract. Now I   840
> find the image of "my minute's last point" a little too, shall we say, *pointed.*
>   I don't mean to complain, but I am becoming very sick. Very, very
> sick. Ultimately sick, as it were.

845

In everything I have done, I have been steadfast, resolute—some would say in the extreme. Now, as you can see, I am distinguishing myself in illness.

850

I have survived eight treatments of Hexamethophosphacil and Vinplatin at the *full* dose, ladies and gentlemen. I have broken the record. I have become something of a celebrity. Kelekian and Jason are simply delighted. I think they foresee celebrity status for themselves upon the appearance of the journal article they will no doubt write about me.

But I flatter myself. The article will not be about *me,* it will be about my ovaries. It will be about my peritoneal cavity, which, despite their best intentions, is now crawling with cancer.

855

What we have come to think of as *me* is, in fact, just the specimen jar, just the dust jacket, just the white piece of paper that bears the little black marks.

My next line is supposed to be something like this:
"It is such a *relief* to get back to my room after those infernal tests."

860

This is hardly true.

It would be *a relief* to be a cheerleader on her way to Daytona Beach for Spring Break.

To get back to my room after those infernal tests is just the next thing that happens.

865

————————————————

(She returns to her bed, which now has a commode next to it. She is very sick.)

Oh, God. It is such a relief to get back to my goddamn room after those goddamn tests.

(JASON enters.)

JASON: Professor Bearing. Just want to check the I&O. Four-fifty, six, five. Okay. How are you feeling today? *(He makes notations on his clipboard*

870

throughout the scene.)

VIVIAN: Fine.

JASON: That's great. Just great.

VIVIAN: How are my fluids?

JASON: Pretty good. No kidney involvement yet. That's pretty amazing, with

875

Hex and Vin.

VIVIAN: How will you know when the kidneys are involved?

JASON: Lots of in, not much out.

VIVIAN: That simple.

JASON: Oh, no way. Compromised kidney function is a highly complex reac-

880

tion. I'm simplifying for you.

VIVIAN: Thank you.

JASON: We're supposed to.

VIVIAN: Bedside manner.

JASON: Yeah, there's a whole course on it in med school. It's required. Colossal waste of time for researchers. *(He turns to go.)*   885
VIVIAN: I can imagine. *(Trying to ask something important)* Jason?
JASON: Huh?
VIVIAN: *(Not sure of herself)* Ah, what . . . *(Quickly)* What were you just saying?
JASON: When?
VIVIAN: Never mind.   890
JASON: Professor Bearing?
VIVIAN: Yes.
JASON: Are you experiencing confusion? Short-term memory loss?
VIVIAN: No.
JASON: Sure?   895
VIVIAN: Yes. *(Pause)* I was just wondering: why cancer?
JASON: Why cancer?
VIVIAN: Why not open-heart surgery?
JASON: Oh yeah, why not *plumbing.* Why not run a *lube rack,* for all the surgeons know about *Homo sapiens sapiens.* No way. Cancer's the only thing   900
I ever wanted.
VIVIAN: *(Intrigued)* Huh.
JASON: No, really. Cancer is . . . *(Searching)*
VIVIAN: *(Helping)* Awesome.
JASON: *(Pause)* Yeah. Yeah, that's right. It is. It is awesome. How does it do it?   905
The intercellular regulatory mechanisms—especially for proliferation
and differentiation—the malignant neoplasia just don't get it. You grow
normal cells in tissue culture in the lab, and they replicate just enough to
make a nice, confluent monolayer. They divide twenty times, or fifty
times, but eventually they conk out. You grow cancer cells, and they never   910
stop. No contact inhibition whatsoever. They just pile up, just keep replicating forever. *(Pause)* That's got a funny name. Know what it is?
VIVIAN: No. What?
JASON: Immortality in culture.
VIVIAN: Sounds like a symposium.   915
JASON: It's an error in judgment, in a molecular way. But *why?* Even on the
protistic level the normal cell–cell interactions are so subtle they'll take
your breath away. Golden-brown algae, for instance, the lowest multicellular life form on earth—they're *idiots*—and it's incredible. It's perfect. So
what's up with the cancer cells? Smartest guys in the world, with the   920
best labs, funding—they don't know what to make of it.
VIVIAN: What about you?
JASON: Me? Oh, I've got a couple of ideas, things I'm kicking around. Wait
till I get a lab of my own. If I can survive this . . . *fellowship.*
VIVIAN: The part with the human beings.   925
JASON: Everybody's got to go through it. All the great researchers. They want
us to be able to converse intelligently with the clinicians. As though

researchers were the impediments. The clinicians are such troglodytes. So smarmy. Like we have to hold hands to discuss creatinine clearance. Just
930   cut the crap, I say.

VIVIAN: Are you going to be sorry when I—Do you ever miss people?

JASON: Everybody asks that. Especially girls.

VIVIAN: What do you tell them?

JASON: I tell them yes.

935 VIVIAN: Are they persuaded?

JASON: Some.

VIVIAN: Some. I see. *(With great difficulty)* And what do you say when a patient is . . . apprehensive . . . frightened.

JASON: Of who?

940 VIVIAN: I just . . . Never mind.

JASON: Professor Bearing, who is the President of the United States?

VIVIAN: I'm fine, really. It's all right.

JASON: You sure? I could order a test—

VIVIAN: No! No, I'm fine. Just a little tired.

945 JASON: Okay. Look. Gotta go. Keep pushing the fluids. Try for 2,000 a day, okay?

VIVIAN: Okay. To use your word. Okay.

    (JASON leaves.)

VIVIAN: *(Getting out of bed, without her IV)* So. The young doctor, like the senior scholar, prefers research to humanity. At the same time the senior
950   scholar, in her pathetic state as a simpering victim, wishes the young doctor would take more interest in personal contact.

    Now I suppose we shall see, through a series of flashbacks, how the senior scholar ruthlessly denied her simpering students the touch of human kindness she now seeks.

955   ————————————————

    (STUDENTS appear, sitting at chairs with writing desks attached to the right arm.)

VIVIAN: *(Commanding attention)* How then would you characterize *(pointing to a student)*—you.

STUDENT 1: Huh?

VIVIAN: How would you characterize the animating force of this sonnet?

960 STUDENT 1: Huh?

VIVIAN: In this sonnet, what is the principal poetic device? I'll give you a hint. It has nothing to do with football. What propels this sonnet?

STUDENT 1: Um.

VIVIAN: *(Speaking to the audience)* Did I say *(tenderly)* "You are nineteen years
965   old. You are so young. You don't know a sonnet from a steak sandwich."
(Pause) By no means.

(Sharply, to STUDENT 1*)* You can come to this class prepared, or you can excuse yourself from this class, this department, and this university. Do not think for a moment that I will tolerate anything in between. 970

(To the audience, defensively) I was teaching him a lesson. *(She walks away from* STUDENT 1, *then turns and addresses the class.)*

So we have another instance of John Donne's agile wit at work: not so much *resolving* the issues of life and God as *reveling* in their complexity.

STUDENT 2: But why? 975

VIVIAN: Why what?

STUDENT 2: Why does Donne make everything so *complicated? (The other* STUDENTS *laugh in agreement.)* No, really, *why?*

VIVIAN: *(To the audience)* You know, someone asked me that every year. And it was always one of the smart ones. What could I say? *(To* STUDENT 2*)* 980 What do you think?

STUDENT 2: I think it's like he's hiding. I think he's really confused, I don't know, maybe he's scared, so he hides behind all this complicated stuff, hides behind this *wit.*

VIVIAN: *Hides* behind *wit?* 985

STUDENT 2: I mean, if it's really something he's sure of, he can say it more simple—simply. He doesn't have to be such a brain, or such a performer. It doesn't have to be such a big deal.

(The other STUDENTS *encourage him.)*

VIVIAN: Perhaps he is suspicious of simplicity.

STUDENT 2: Perhaps, but that's pretty stupid. 990

VIVIAN: *(To the audience)* That observation, despite its infelicitous phrasing, contained the seed of a perspicacious remark. Such an unlikely occurrence left me with two choices. I could draw it out, or I could allow the brain to rest after that heroic effort. If I pursued, there was the chance of great insight, or the risk of undergraduate banality. I could never predict. 995 *(To* STUDENT 2*)* Go on.

STUDENT 2: Well, if he's trying to figure out God, and the meaning of life, and big stuff like that, why does he keep running away, you know?

VIVIAN: *(To the audience, moving closer to* STUDENT 2*)* So far so good, but they can think for themselves only so long before they begin to self-destruct. 1000

STUDENT 2: Um, it's like, the more you hide, the less—no, wait—the more you are getting closer—although you don't know it—and the simple thing is there—you see what I mean?

VIVIAN: *(To the audience, looking at* STUDENT 2, *as suspense collapses)* Lost it.

(She walks away and speaks to the audience.) I distinctly remember an 1005 exchange between two students after my lecture on pronunciation and scansion. I overheard them talking on their way out of class. They were

young and bright, gathering their books and laughing at the expense of seventeenth-century poetry, at *my* expense.

1010

(*To the class*) To scan the line properly, we must take advantage of the contemporary flexibility in "i-o-n" endings, as in "expansion." The quatrain stands:

> Our two souls therefore, which are one,
>> Though I must go, endure not yet
> A breach, but an ex-*pan*-see-on,
>> Like gold to airy thinness beat.

1015

Bear this in mind in your reading. That's all for today.

(The STUDENTS *get up in a chaotic burst.* STUDENT 3 *and* STUDENT 4 *pass by* VIVIAN *on their way out.)*

STUDENT 3: I hope I can get used to this pronuncia-see-on.

STUDENT 4: I know. I hope I can survive this course and make it to gradua-see-on.

1020

(They laugh. VIVIAN *glowers at them. They fall silent, embarrassed.)*

VIVIAN: *(To the audience)* That was a witty little exchange, I must admit. It showed the mental acuity I would praise in a poetic text. But I admired only the studied application of wit, not its spontaneous eruption.

*(*STUDENT 1 *interrupts.)*

STUDENT 1: Professor Bearing? Can I talk to you for a minute?

1025

VIVIAN: You may.

STUDENT 1: I need to ask for an extension on my paper. I'm really sorry, and I know your policy, but see—

VIVIAN: Don't tell me. Your grandmother died.

STUDENT 1: You knew.

1030

VIVIAN: It was a guess.

STUDENT 1: I have to go home.

VIVIAN: Do what you will, but the paper is due when it is due.

(As STUDENT 1 *leaves and the classroom disappears,* VIVIAN *watches. Pause)*

VIVIAN: I don't know. I feel so much—what is the word? I look back, I see these scenes, and I . . .

(Long silence. VIVIAN *walks absently around the stage, trying to think of something. Finally, giving up, she trudges back to bed.)*

1035

————————————

VIVIAN: It was late at night, the graveyard shift. Susie was on. I could hear her in the hall.

I wanted her to come and see me. So I had to create a little emergency. Nothing dramatic.

(VIVIAN *pinches the IV tubing. The pump alarm beeps.*)

It worked.   1040

(SUSIE *enters, concerned.*)

SUSIE: Ms. Bearing? Is that you beeping at four in the morning? (*She checks the tubing and presses buttons on the pump. The alarm stops.*) Did that wake you up? I'm sorry. It just gets occluded sometimes.

VIVIAN: I was awake.

SUSIE: You were? What's the trouble, sweetheart?   1045

VIVIAN: (*To the audience, roused*) Do not think for a minute that anyone calls me "Sweetheart." But then . . . I allowed it. (*To* SUSIE) Oh, I don't know.

SUSIE: You can't sleep?

VIVIAN: No. I just keep thinking.

SUSIE: If you do that too much, you can get kind of confused.   1050

VIVIAN: I know. I can't figure things out. I'm in a . . . *quandary,* having these . . . *doubts.*

SUSIE: What you're doing is very hard.

VIVIAN: Hard things are what I like best.

SUSIE: It's not the same. It's like it's out of control, isn't it?   1055

VIVIAN: (*Crying, in spite of herself*) I'm scared.

SUSIE: (*Stroking her*) Oh, honey, of course you are.

VIVIAN: I want . . .

SUSIE: I know. It's hard.

VIVIAN: I don't feel sure of myself anymore.   1060

SUSIE: And you used to feel sure.

VIVIAN: (*Crying*) Oh, yes, I used to feel sure.

SUSIE: Vivian. It's all right. I know. It hurts. I know. It's all right. Do you want a tissue? It's all right. (*Silence*) Vivian, would you like a Popsicle?

VIVIAN: (*Like a child*) Yes, please.   1065

SUSIE: I'll get it for you. I'll be right back.

VIVIAN: Thank you.

(SUSIE *leaves.*)

VIVIAN: (*Pulling herself together*) The epithelial cells in my GI tract have been killed by the chemo. The cold Popsicle feels good, it's something I can digest, and it helps keep me hydrated. For your information.   1070

(SUSIE *returns with an orange two-stick Popsicle. Vivian unwraps it and breaks it in half.*)

VIVIAN: Here.

SUSIE: Sure?

VIVIAN: Yes.

SUSIE: Thanks. *(SUSIE sits on the commode by the bed. Silence)* When I was a kid, we
1075   used to get these from a truck. The man would come around and ring his
bell and we'd all run over. Then we'd sit on the curb and eat our Popsicles.
Pretty profound, huh?

VIVIAN: It sounds nice.

(Silence)

SUSIE: Vivian, there's something we need to talk about, you need to think
1080   about.

(Silence)

VIVIAN: My cancer is not being cured, is it.

SUSIE: Huh-uh.

VIVIAN: They never expected it to be, did they.

SUSIE: Well, they thought the drugs would make the tumor get smaller, and it
1085   has gotten a lot smaller. But the problem is that it started in new places
too. They've learned a lot for their research. It was the best thing they
had to give you, the strongest drugs. There just isn't a good treatment for
what you have yet, for advanced ovarian. I'm sorry. They should have explained this—

1090 VIVIAN: I knew.

SUSIE: You did.

VIVIAN: I read between the lines.

SUSIE: What you have to think about is your "code status." What you want
them to do if your heart stops.

1095 VIVIAN: Well.

SUSIE: You can be "full code," which means that if your heart stops, they'll
call a Code Blue and the code team will come and resuscitate you and
take you to Intensive Care until you stabilize again. Or you can be "Do
Not Resuscitate," so if your heart stops we'll . . . well, we'll just let it.
1100   You'll be "DNR." You can think about it, but I wanted to present both
choices before Kelekian and Jason talk to you.

VIVIAN: You don't agree about this?

SUSIE: Well, they like to save lives. So anything's okay, as long as life continues. It doesn't matter if you're hooked up to a million machines. Kelekian
1105   is a great researcher and everything. And the fellows, like Jason, they're
really smart. It's really an honor for them to work with him. But they always . . . want to know more things.

VIVIAN: I always want to know more things. I'm a scholar. Or I was when I
had shoes, when I had eyebrows.

SUSIE: Well, okay then. You'll be full code. That's fine.   *1110*

    (Silence)

VIVIAN: No, don't complicate the matter.
SUSIE: It's okay. It's up to you—
VIVIAN: Let it stop.
SUSIE: Really?
VIVIAN: Yes.   *1115*
SUSIE: So if your heart stops beating—
VIVIAN: Just let it stop.
SUSIE: Sure?
VIVIAN: Yes.
SUSIE: Okay. I'll get Kelekian to give the order, and then—   *1120*
VIVIAN: Susie?
SUSIE: Uh-huh?
VIVIAN: You're still going to take care of me, aren't you?
SUSIE: 'Course, sweetheart. Don't you worry.

    (As SUSIE *leaves,* VIVIAN *sits upright, full of energy and rage.)*

VIVIAN: That certainly was a *maudlin* display. Popsicles? "Sweetheart"? I can't   *1125*
believe my life has become so . . . *corny.*
    But it can't be helped. I don't see any other way. We are discussing
life and death, and not in the abstract, either; we are discussing *my* life
and *my* death, and my brain is dulling, and poor Susie's was never very
sharp to begin with, and I can't conceive of any other . . . *tone.*   *1130*
    (Quickly) Now is not the time for verbal swordplay, for unlikely
flights of imagination and wildly shifting perspectives, for metaphysical
conceit, for wit.
    And nothing would be worse than a detailed scholarly analysis.
Erudition. Interpretation. Complication.   *1135*
    (Slowly) Now is a time for simplicity. Now is a time for, dare I say
it, kindness.
    (Searchingly) I thought being extremely smart would take care of it.
But I see that I have been found out. Ooohhh.
    I'm scared. Oh, God. I want . . . I want . . . No. I want to hide. I   *1140*
just want to curl up in a little ball. *(She dives under the covers.)*

    *(*VIVIAN *wakes in horrible pain. She is tense, agitated, fearful. Slowly she calms
down and addresses the audience.)*

VIVIAN: *(Trying extremely hard)* I want to tell you how it feels. I want to explain it, to use *my* words. It's as if . . . I can't . . . There aren't . . . I'm like

1145   a student and this is the final exam and I don't know what to put down
        because I don't understand the question and I'm *running out of time*.
                The time for extreme measures has come. I am in terrible pain.
        Susie says that I need to begin aggressive pain management if I am going
        to stand it.
1150   "It": such a little word. In this case, I think "it" signifies "being
        alive."
                I apologize in advance for what this palliative treatment modality
        does to the dramatic coherence of my play's last scene. It can't be helped.
        They have to do something. I'm in terrible pain.
1155   Say it, Vivian. *It hurts like hell. It really does.*

        (SUSIE *enters.* VIVIAN *is writhing in pain.*)

        Oh, God. Oh, God.
        SUSIE: Sshh. It's okay. Sshh. I paged Kelekian up here, and we'll get you some
            meds.
        VIVIAN: Oh, God, it is so painful. So painful. So much pain. So much pain.
1160   SUSIE: I know, I know, it's okay. Sshh. Just try and clear your mind. It's all right.
            We'll get you a Patient-Controlled Analgesic. It's a little pump, and you
            push a little button, and you decide how much medication you want.
            (Importantly) It's very simple, and it's up to you.

        (KELEKIAN *storms in;* JASON *follows with chart.*)

        KELEKIAN: Dr. Bearing. Susie.
1165   SUSIE: Time for Patient-Controlled Analgesic. The pain is killing her.
        KELEKIAN: Dr. Bearing, are you in pain? (KELEKIAN *holds out his hand for
            chart;* JASON *hands it to him. They read.*)
        VIVIAN: *(Sitting up, unnoticed by the staff)* Am I in pain? I don't believe this. Yes,
            I'm in goddamn pain. *(Furious)* I have a fever of 101 spiking to 104. And
1170   I have bone metastases in my pelvis and both femurs. *(Screaming)* There is
            cancer eating away at my goddamn bones, and I did not know there
            could be such pain on this earth.
                (She flops back on the bed and cries audibly to them.) Oh, God.
        KELEKIAN: *(Looking at* VIVIAN *intently)* I want a morphine drip.
1175   SUSIE: What about Patient-Controlled? She could be more alert—
        KELEKIAN: *(Teaching)* Ordinarily, yes. But in her case, no.
        SUSIE: But—
        KELEKIAN: *(To* SUSIE) She's earned a rest. *(To* JASON) Morphine, ten
            push now, then start at ten an hour. *(To* VIVIAN) Dr. Bearing, try to relax.
1180   We're going to help you through this, don't worry. Dr. Bearing? Excel-
            lent. *(He squeezes* VIVIAN's *shoulder. They all leave.)*
        VIVIAN: *(Weakly, painfully, leaning on her IV pole, she moves to address the
            audience.)* Hi. How are you feeling today?

(Silence)

These are my last coherent lines. I'll have to leave the action to the professionals. 1185

It came so quickly, after taking so long. Not even time for a proper conclusion.

(VIVIAN concentrates with all her might, and she attempts a grand summation, as if trying to conjure her own ending.)

And Death—*capital D*—shall be no more—semicolon.
Death—*capital D*—thou shalt die—*ex-cla-mation point!*

(She looks down at herself, looks out at the audience, and sees that the line doesn't work. She shakes her head and exhales with resignation.)

I'm sorry. 1190

———————————

(She gets back into bed as SUSIE injects morphine into the IV tubing. VIVIAN lies down and, in a final melodramatic gesture, shuts the lids of her own eyes and folds her arms over her chest.)

VIVIAN: I trust this will have a soporific effect.
SUSIE: Well, I don't know about that, but it sure makes you sleepy.

(This strikes VIVIAN as delightfully funny. She starts to giggle, then laughs out loud. SUSIE doesn't get it.)

SUSIE: What's so funny? *(VIVIAN keeps laughing.)* What?
VIVIAN: Oh! It's that—"Soporific" *means* "makes you sleepy." 1195
SUSIE: It does?
VIVIAN: Yes. *(Another fit of laughter)*
SUSIE: *(Giggling)* Well, that was pretty dumb—
VIVIAN: No! No, no! It was *funny!*
SUSIE: *(Starting to catch on)* Yeah, I guess so. *(Laughing)* In a dumb sort of way. 1200
(This sets them both off laughing again) I never would have gotten it. I'm glad you explained it.
VIVIAN: *(Simply)* I'm a teacher.

(They laugh a little together. Slowly the morphine kicks in, and VIVIAN's laughs become long sighs. Finally she falls asleep. SUSIE checks everything out, then leaves. Long silence)

———————————

(JASON and SUSIE chat as they enter to insert a catheter.)

JASON: Oh, yeah. She was a great scholar. Wrote tons of books, articles, was the 1205
head of everything. *(He checks the I&O sheet.)* Two hundred. Seventy-five.

Five-twenty. Let's up the hydration. She won't be drinking anymore. See if we can keep her kidneys from fading. Yeah, I had a lot of respect for her, which is more than I can say for the *entire* biochemistry department.

1210   SUSIE: What do you want? Dextrose?

JASON: Give her saline.

SUSIE: Okay.

JASON: She gave a hell of a lecture. No notes, not a word out of place. It was pretty impressive. A lot of students hated her, though.

1215   SUSIE: Why?

JASON: Well, she wasn't exactly a cupcake.

SUSIE: *(Laughing, fondly)* Well, she hasn't exactly been a cupcake here, either. *(Leaning over* VIVIAN *and talking loudly and slowly in her ear)* Now, Ms. Bearing, Jason and I are here, and we're going to insert a catheter to

1220   collect your urine. It's not going to hurt, don't you worry. *(During the conversation she inserts the catheter.)*

JASON: Like she can hear you.

SUSIE: It's just nice to do.

JASON: Eight cycles of Hex and Vin at the full dose. Kelekian didn't think it

1225   was possible. I wish they could all get through it at full throttle. Then we could really have some data.

SUSIE: She's not what I imagined. I thought somebody who studied poetry would be sort of dreamy, you know?

JASON: Oh, not the way she did it. It felt more like boot camp than English

1230   class. This guy John Donne was incredibly intense. Like your whole brain had to be in knots before you could get it.

SUSIE: He made it hard on purpose?

JASON: Well, it has to do with the subject. The Holy Sonnets we worked on most, they were mostly about Salvation Anxiety. That's a term I made up

1235   in one of my papers, but I think it fits pretty well. Salvation Anxiety. You're this brilliant guy, I mean, brilliant—this guy makes Shakespeare sound like a Hallmark card. And you know you're a sinner. And there's this promise of salvation, the whole religious thing. But you just can't deal with it.

1240   SUSIE: How come?

JASON: It just doesn't stand up to scrutiny. But you can't face life without it either. So you write these screwed-up sonnets. Everything is brilliantly convoluted. Really tricky stuff. Bouncing off the walls. Like a game, to make the puzzle so complicated.

(The catheter is inserted. SUSIE *puts things away.)*

1245   SUSIE: But what happens in the end?

JASON: End of what?

SUSIE: To John Donne. Does he ever get it?

JASON: Get what?

SUSIE: His Salvation Anxiety. Does he ever understand?

JASON: Oh, no way. The puzzle takes over. You're not even trying to solve it *1250* anymore. Fascinating, really. Great training for lab research. Looking at things in increasing levels of complexity.

SUSIE: Until what?

JASON: What do you mean?

SUSIE: Where does it end? Don't you get to solve the puzzle? *1255*

JASON: Nah. When it comes right down to it, research is just trying to quantify the complications of the puzzle.

SUSIE: But you *help* people! You save lives and stuff.

JASON: Oh, yeah, I save some guy's life, and then the poor slob gets hit by a bus! *1260*

SUSIE: *(Confused)* Yeah, I guess so. I just don't think of it that way. Guess you can tell I never took a class in poetry.

JASON: Listen, if there's one thing we learned in Seventeenth-Century Poetry, it's that you can forget about that sentimental stuff. *Enzyme Kinetics* was more poetic than Bearing's class. Besides, you can't think about that *1265* *meaning-of-life* garbage all the time or you'd go nuts.

SUSIE: Do you believe in it?

JASON: In what?

SUSIE: Umm. I don't know, the meaning-of-life garbage. *(She laughs a little.)*

JASON: What do they *teach* you in nursing school? *(Checking* VIVIAN's *pulse)* *1270* She's out of it. Shouldn't be too long. You done here?

SUSIE: Yeah, I'll just . . . tidy up.

JASON: See ya. *(He leaves.)*

SUSIE: Bye, Jace. *(She thinks for a minute, then carefully rubs baby oil on* VIVIAN's *hands. She checks the catheter, then leaves.)* *1275*

(Professor E. M. ASHFORD, *now eighty, enters.)*

E.M.: Vivian? Vivian? It's Evelyn. Vivian?

VIVIAN: *(Waking, slurred)* Oh, God. *(Surprised)* Professor Ashford. Oh, God.

E.M.: I'm in town visiting my great-grandson, who is celebrating his fifth birthday. I went to see you at your office, and they directed me here. *(She* *1280* *lays her jacket, scarf, and parcel on the bed.)* I have been walking all over town. I had forgotten how early it gets chilly here.

VIVIAN: *(Weakly)* I feel so bad.

E.M.: I know you do. I can see. (VIVIAN *cries.)* Oh, dear, there, there. There, there. (VIVIAN *cries more, letting the tears flow.)* Vivian, Vivian. *1285*

*(*E.M. *looks toward the hall, then furtively slips off her shoes and swings up on the bed. She puts her arm around* VIVIAN.)

There, there. There, there, Vivian. *(Silence)*
    It's a windy day. *(Silence)*

Don't worry, dear. *(Silence)*

Let's see. Shall I recite to you? Would you like that? I'll recite some-
1290   thing by Donne.

VIVIAN: *(Moaning)* Nooooooo.

E.M.:   Very well. *(Silence)* Hmmm. *(Silence)* Little Jeffrey is very sweet. Gets into
everything.

*(Silence. E.M. takes a children's book out of the paper bag and begins reading.
VIVIAN nestles in, drifting in and out of sleep.)*

Let's see. *The Runaway Bunny.* By Margaret Wise Brown. Pictures
1295   by Clement Hurd. Copyright 1942. First Harper Trophy Edition, 1972.
Now then.

Once there was a little bunny who wanted to run away.
So he said to his mother, "I am running away."
"If you run away," said his mother, "I will run after you. For you are
1300   my little bunny."

"If you run after me," said the little bunny, "I will become a fish in a
trout stream and I will swim away from you."

"If you become a fish in a trout stream," said his mother, "I will become a fisherman and I will fish for you."

1305   *(Thinking out loud)* Look at that. A little allegory of the soul. No
matter where it hides, God will find it. See, Vivian?

VIVIAN: *(Moaning)* Uhhhhhh.

E.M.:

"If you become a fisherman," said the little bunny, "I will be a bird and
1310   fly away from you."

"If you become a bird and fly away from me," said his mother, "I will be
a tree that you come home to."

(To herself) Very clever.

"Shucks," said the little bunny, "I might just as well stay where I am and
1315   be your little bunny."

And so he did.
"Have a carrot," said the mother bunny.

(To herself) Wonderful.

*(VIVIAN is now fast asleep. E.M. slowly gets down and gathers her things. She
leans over and kisses her.)*

It's time to go. And flights of angels sing thee to thy rest. *(She leaves.)*

(JASON strides in and goes directly to the I&O sheet without looking at VIVIAN.)

JASON: Professor Bearing. How are you feeling today? Three p.m. IV hydra-   *1320*
tion totals. Two thousand in. Thirty out. Uh-oh. That's it. Kidneys gone.
  (He looks at VIVIAN.) *Professor Bearing? Highly unresponsive. Wait
a second— (Puts his head down to her mouth and chest to listen for heartbeat
and breathing)* Wait a sec—Jesus Christ! *(Yelling)* CALL A CODE!

*(JASON throws down the chart, dives over the bed, and lies on top of her body
as he reaches for the phone and punches in the numbers.)*

  (To himself) Code: 4-5-7-5. *(To operator)* Code Blue, room 707.   *1325*
Code Blue, room 707. Dr. Posner—P-O-S-N-E-R. Hurry up!

(He throws down the phone and lowers the head of the bed.)

  Come on, come on, COME ON.

(He begins CPR, kneeling over VIVIAN, *alternately pounding frantically and
giving mouth-to-mouth resuscitation. Over the loudspeaker in the hall, a droning
voice repeats "Code Blue, room 707. Code Blue, room 707.")*

  One! Two! Three! Four! Five! *(He breathes in her mouth.)*

(SUSIE, hearing the announcement, runs into the room.)

SUSIE: WHAT ARE YOU DOING?
JASON: A GODDAMN CODE. GET OVER HERE!   *1330*
SUSIE: She's DNR! *(She grabs him.)*
JASON: *(He pushes her away.)* She's Research!
SUSIE: She's NO CODE!

(SUSIE grabs JASON and hurls him off the bed.)

JASON: Ooowww! Goddamnit, Susie!
SUSIE: She's no code!   *1335*
JASON: Aaargh!
SUSIE: Kelekian put the order in—you saw it! You were right there, Jason!
Oh, God, the code! *(She runs to the phone. He struggles to stand.)* 4-5-7-5.

*(The CODE TEAM swoops in. Everything changes. Frenzy takes over. They
knock* SUSIE *out of the way with their equipment.)*

SUSIE: *(At the phone)* Cancel code, room 707. Sue Monahan, primary nurse.
Cancel code. Dr. Posner is here.   *1340*
JASON: *(In agony)* Oh, God.
CODE TEAM:
  —Get out of the way!

1345

—Unit staff out!

—Get the board!

—Over here!

(They throw VIVIAN's *body up at the waist and stick a board underneath for CPR. In a whirlwind of sterile packaging and barked commands, one team member attaches a respirator, one begins CPR, and one prepares the defibrillator.* SUSIE *and* JASON *try to stop them but are pushed away. The loudspeaker in the hall announces "Cancel code, room 707. Cancel code, room 707.")*

CODE TEAM:

—Bicarb amp!

—I got it! *(To* SUSIE*)* Get out!

1350

—One, two, three, four, five!

—Get ready to shock! *(To* JASON*)* Move it!

SUSIE: *(Running to each person, yelling)* STOP! Patient is DNR!

JASON: *(At the same time, to the* CODE TEAM*)* No, no! Stop doing this. STOP!

CODE TEAM:

1355

—Keep it going!

—What do you get?

—Bicarb amp!

—No pulse!

SUSIE: She's NO CODE! Order was given— *(She dives for the chart and holds it*

1360

up as she cries out) Look! Look at this! DO NOT RESUSCITATE. KELEKIAN.

CODE TEAM: *(As they administer electric shock,* VIVIAN's *body arches and bounces back down.)*

—Almost ready!

1365

—Hit her!

—CLEAR!

—Pulse? Pulse?

JASON: *(Howling)* I MADE A MISTAKE!

(Pause. The CODE TEAM *looks at him. He collapses on the floor.)*

SUSIE: No code! Patient is no code.

1370 CODE TEAM HEAD: Who the hell are you?

SUSIE: Sue Monahan, primary nurse.

CODE TEAM HEAD: Let me see the goddamn chart. CHART!

CODE TEAM: *(Slowing down)*

—What's going on?

1375

—Should we stop?

—What's it say?

SUSIE: *(Pushing them away from the bed)* Patient is no code. Get away from her!

(SUSIE *lifts the blanket.* VIVIAN
steps out of the bed.

*She walks away from the scene,
toward a little light.
She is now attentive and eager,
moving slowly toward the light.*

*She takes off her cap and lets it
drop.*

She slips off her bracelet.

*She loosens the ties and the top
gown slides to the floor. She lets the
second gown fall.*

*The instant she is naked, and
beautiful, reaching for the light—*

Lights out.)

CODE TEAM HEAD: *(Reading)*
Do Not Resuscitate. Kelekian.
Shit.

(The CODE TEAM *stops working.)*

JASON: *(Whispering)* Oh, God.

CODE TEAM HEAD: Order was put
in yesterday.

CODE TEAM:
—It's a doctor fuck-up.
—What is he, a resident?

—Got us up here on a DNR.
—Called a code on a
no-code.
JASON: Oh, God.

(The bedside scene fades.)

CONSIDERATIONS

1. From the opening in which Vivian is alone, talking to the audience, what do we learn about her—as a person, a woman, a professor, and a patient?
2. Dramatic irony is a term used to describe a situation in which there is a contradiction between what appears to be true and what is actually true. With this in mind, discuss the ironic implications of the following, and then find at least five more examples of irony in the play.

   • The title of this play
   • "Hi, how are you feeling?" (repeated throughout the play)
   • Vivian: "I know all about life and death. I am, after all, a scholar of Donne's Holy Sonnets. . . ."
   • Vivian: "One thing can be said for an eight-month course of cancer treatment: it is highly educational. I am learning to suffer."

3. Discuss the tension of opposites at work in this short play as seen in the following:

Characters
Settings
Readings
Emotions
Professions

4. What role does the audience perform in this play, and why is this role especially appropriate given the subject matter and the nature of the conflict?

5. What do you admire most about Vivian? What do you see as her greatest weakness or flaw? Is she a realistic character? Explain.

6. What do we learn about Vivian's life before teaching and before cancer that might help to explain how she became someone who put all of her faith in her mental abilities? Comment on the author's selection of past experiences that help develop Vivian into a whole person.

7. In a flashback to a classroom scene, one of Vivian's students asks, "Why does Donne make everything so complicated?" Then he goes on to say, "I think it's like he's hiding. I think he's really confused, I don't know, maybe he's scared, so he hides behind all this complicated stuff, hides behind this *wit.*" How does Vivian respond to this student's insights, and why does the author include this scene?

8. Explore all of the many ethical issues that this play raises concerning technology and the ethical treatment of patients from diagnosis to the end of life.

9. Among the characters within the medical community, Susie seems to be the one least respected or noticed. What is your impression of Susie and her role in this play?

10. Edson says that while the subject matter of this play may be considered depressing, it is, on a deeper level, about love, grace, and redemption. What scenes and actions in this play support this contention?

11. After reading and studying this play, what conclusions can you draw about what people really need in order to communicate and connect with one another on a meaningful level?

Commentary

LLOYD ROSE
Review of Wit

"Most things never happen," wrote the poet Philip Larkin. "This one will." He was talking about death, and his grim observation accounts for the power of Margaret Edson's Pulitzer Prize–winning "Wit," which opened last night at the Kennedy Center's Eisenhower Theater. It will happen to us all and the odds are strong that it will happen as it happens to Edson's heroine: incurable cancer, treatment worse than the disease, a callous medical establishment, dehumanization, humiliation, and terrible pain.

Having been diagnosed with Stage 4 ovarian cancer ("There is no Stage 5," she notes dryly), Vivian Bearing, PhD (Judith Light), agrees to serve as a subject for advanced chemotherapy research. The program is run by a vast unnamed medical center with a strong resemblance to the National Institutes of Health, where Edson once worked, and Bearing is continually doused with the cold water of her physicians' indifference to her as a person. Late in the play, having astonishingly survived eight months of intense experimental chemo, she muses that she will be famous in the papers her doctors write—then realizes that, in fact, only her ovaries will be famous.

Dr. Bearing is an expert in the 17th-century metaphysical poetry of John Donne. A devout Christian with a strong skeptical bent, Donne wavered between faith in God and doubts about his own spiritual worthiness, between hope of redemption and terror of damnation. The wavering itself became his defense against the fear of death. Similarly, Bearing tries to use Donne's wrestlings with mortality and salvation—particularly in his so-called "Holy Sonnets"—as a shield against her ordeal.

It's against our modern prejudices, however, for a character to triumph through the intellect. That would be somehow . . . repressed. So Bearing cannot find transcendence until she learns to feel—until she looks back at her students and decides she was as callous with them as her doctors are with her (the audience may disagree), until she longs for kindness and comes to understand that there is as much wisdom in the children's story "The Runaway Bunny" as there is in the brilliance of Donne.

This gooey ending seems unworthy of Edson's heroine, a tough, salty   *5* woman who as the play opens informs us curtly, "It is not my intention to give away the plot, but I think I die at the end." For those in the audience who find Dr. Bearing's tough-mindedness heroic, her capitulation to what she herself describes as the "maudlin" and the "corny" is a disappointment and a defeat.

In the first part of the play (which runs only 90 minutes, without an intermission), Light acts on one unvarying note of steely resolve. There's no nuance in her performance, or in Bearing's personality. She's much stronger later, when Bearing is pitifully collapsing into physical helplessness and emotional nakedness. The rest of the actors play their roles strongly but shallowly, making the most obvious choices and staying on the surface of their characters.

Leah C. Gardiner's direction, based on the original direction by the late Derek Anson Jones, is visually spare and efficient, with flimsy hospital curtains zipping back and forth on chrome rods to change and define scenes. But set designer Myung Hee Cho has emphasized the diaphanous lightness of those curtains, which float when they move as if stirred by a breeze, some fresh air blown in from the living world outside the hospital. Michael Chybowski lights those curtains in stark white or clinical green. Still, for all its association with hospital corridors, that green can't help reminding us of spring and rebirth.

Edson's frankness about the clinical awfulness of modern death is what makes "Wit" such a strong theater experience. But if that were all there was to the play, no one could bear to go see it, and it probably wouldn't have won a Pulitzer. Unflinching in its surface details, "Wit" still has the usual soft center: Dr. Bearing learns through suffering to be a better—i.e., "more feeling"—person. No one ever dies meaninglessly on the popular American stage.

ALVIN KLEIN

A Professor's Passions in Life and Death (Review of Wit*)*

The greeting is standard-issue cheery ("Hi. How are you?"), but the tone is caustic and the speaker is known to be forbidding. That's how Vivian Bearing, Ph.D., a professor of 17th-century poetry, specializing in the Holy Sonnets of John Donne, welcomes the audience at the George Street Playhouse here, and she makes sure that we know it is not her standard greeting.

It is forced and fake, laced with bitterness and irony, reinforced by the hospital gown and ID bracelet she wears.

Vivian wastes no time telling us that she knows she is in a play and that she thinks she dies at the end. The play covers eight months of experimental chemotherapy during her battle with metastatic ovarian cancer. Followers of theater that counts, or even just the Pulitzer Prize winners, know that the play is "Wit," a perfectly titled contemplation of the poetry of life and death.

For all its honors, a play that dissects words like "antineoplastic" and talks of invasive epithelial carcinoma is still resisted by many people. Besides, references to metaphysics, critical reading and Donne's explorations of mortality can be as off-putting as death to people who go to shows to be entertained. And this show ends not just with the death of a ravaged woman of 50, but with a medical foul-up about the instruction: Do Not Resuscitate.

Yet, it is imprecise to say that's how "Wit" ends, not when the memory   *5*
can be forever haunted by the play's final vision, and a glorious, affirming vision it is. Say simply that "Wit" has a textual ending and a visual one and no
one is going to remember the words without looking them up, though it must
be emphasized that the last luminous image is dictated by the stage directions
of the playwright, Margaret Edson.

"Wit" is a play of nobility. Funny how some people think it is odd or
surprising that a kindergarten teacher wrote it.

The acclaimed, now historic, production that began life in 1997 at the
Long Wharf Theater in New Haven, Conn., ran successfully off-Broadway,
first in a nonprofit theater, then commercially.

It is not irrelevant to note that Broadway would not take a chance on it,
and that Ms. Edson's script was initially rejected by 60 regional theaters.
George Street, under its former management, was one. Call it artistic justice
that "Wit" is now here.

Like all masterworks, Ms. Edson's play is subject to different valid interpretations, and will go on, fittingly, into eternity. But it would be naive to say
that Ted Sod's staging, at times more didactic than dramatic, is comparable to
the classic one by Doug Hughes. Somehow, the cast can be separated simplisti-
cally: The women in this production are better than the men, who do not transcend stereotype, and that's that.

Start, as one must, with Suzzanne Douglas, a vibrant, defiant Vivian, a life   *10*
force debilitated, truly transmitting a palpable rage against the dying of the
light. If anyone thinks Ms. Douglas looks too good to be playing a dying
woman, it is likely that she is being seen for the first time. Ms. Douglas is simply paying the price of outer beauty, not that she fails to radiate inner beauty
as well. The sight of a bald Vivian, who usually wears a cap, is intended to startle. It does, but not as intended. And, yes, the actress is made up to appear gaunt
and frail.

Ms. Douglas effectively depicts Vivian as a tough lady, demanding and
uncompromising in her scholarly standards, meticulous in her intolerance of a
semicolon when a comma is essential. If Vivian is more passionate about punctuation than about people, that's Vivian. But Ms. Edson's point about an abrasive
woman of intellect making a last-minute human connection is less convincing
than it is supposed to be, though the importance of that point, and the notion
that Vivian was too tough and heartless as a teacher, are arguable. That's just
one aspect of a rich, many-layered play.

Emotion to spare is provided by Helen Gallagher as Vivian's colleague,
immensely moving in a bedside scene, and Jodi Somers, very strong and
poignant as a caring registered nurse.

. . .

No matter how you take it, "Wit" is life-enhancing.

■■■ Film Connection: *Wit*

While film and other genres of literature share certain elements, such as word choice and plot development, there are some elements unique to film. Of course, it is obvious that a film, unlike a written work, offers visual images that can be seen with the eye rather than imagined in the mind. These visual aspects contribute to the viewers' response, to their pleasure, and to their ability to analyze and evaluate the film.

Consider, as an example, the HBO production of *Wit* (2001), directed by Mike Nichols and with Emma Thompson playing the lead role of Vivian Bearing. In this film, the role of technology in healthcare and the ethical issues related to it raise questions that are at the core of this chapter's theme.

Color and Light   In *Wit*, bright, harsh light contributes much to the tone of the main setting, a large teaching hospital. In the hospital, even at night, the patients cannot escape the lights that illuminate their beds, their rooms, and even parts of their bodies for examination and testing by various medical professionals. In addition, the bright light that frequently focuses on Vivian Bearing ironically suggests that she is in the spotlight, forced by her illness to play the central role in a terrifying drama.

> *Exercise*   Notice the color of various objects that are part of the hospital setting. In what ways do these colors contrast with the washed out whites and pastels of the patient's room, her regulation hospital garments, and even the uniforms of the medical staff? How does the emphasis on these objects relate to the theme of the film?

Camera Angles and Movement   In several scenes, the camera pulls away and up, looking straight down on Vivian Bearing as she struggles with various stages of her illness and treatment. The viewer experiences a sense of distance and separation from the character, yet remains acutely aware of the suffering human being at the distant focus of this shot. Through the camera work, Bearing's isolation and loneliness are emphasized, as well as her loss of power. No longer is she in the center of the action, controlling her life, her subject matter, and her students. Now she is at the mercy of the hospital, the medical professionals, and the technology used to pursue the research study to which she has agreed.

> *Exercises*
> 1. Note the extreme close-up shots, and choose one or two to discuss. How do the shots you chose contribute to the development of character, conflict, or theme? For instance, consider the opening shot of Dr. Kelekian when he delivers the diagnosis of advanced ovarian cancer.

2. In many scenes, Vivian Bearing faces directly into the camera and speaks to the audience. Consider what these shots contribute to the development of character, conflict, or theme.

Visual Symbols of Setting   The most prominent symbolic elements of setting in this film are the tools and machines that represent the technology of the medical community. In many scenes, these tools and machines are pointed at or connected to Bearing, the patient. In addition, they often serve to provide a barrier between Bearing and the doctors who attend her. Jason, her former student, seems particularly uncomfortable with the human dimension of a terminal illness and often tinkers with some medical tool or machine as a way of dealing with his patient on a strictly objective level. In the horrifying ending scene, technology moves from being a menacing presence in the background to becoming the symbol of a deeply troubling medical error.

> *Exercise*   Consider some of the other symbolic elements of setting, such as the items people bring to Vivian's bedside. For instance, consider the popsicle the nurse, Susie, shares with her patient, or the book Vivian's former professor reads to her. Consider also the patient's chart, which several characters hold as they talk with Vivian. What do these elements of setting suggest about the characterization, conflicts, or themes of the film?

Essays

STEPHEN JAY GOULD (1941–2002)
The Median Isn't the Message

> *Born in New York City, Stephen Jay Gould worked for much of his life to make science exciting and accessible to as many audiences as possible. Beginning in 1967, he taught biology, geology, and the history of science at Harvard. In addition, he served as an advisor to the* Children's Television Workshop *from 1978 to 1987 and as an advisor to the science series* Nova *from 1980 to 1992. He wrote many books, including* The Panda's Thumb *(1980) and* The Flamingo's Smile *(1985). In March 2002, just two months before his death, he published what is regarded by many as his seminal work,* The Structure of Evolutionary Theory. *The following selection, which first appeared in* Discover *magazine in June 1985, suggests Gould's complex view of science and technology. In*

his own battle with cancer, he saw both the positive effects of the most recent tech-
nological developments and also the questions they raise.

My life has recently intersected, in a most personal way, two of Mark Twain's
famous quips. One I shall defer to the end of this essay. The other (sometimes
attributed to Disraeli), identifies three species of mendacity, each worse than
the one before—lies, damned lies, and statistics.

Consider the standard example of stretching the truth with numbers—a
case quite relevant to my story. Statistics recognizes different measures of an
"average," or central tendency. The *mean* is our usual concept of an overall average—add up the items and divide them by the number of sharers (100 candy
bars collected for five kids next Halloween will yield 20 for each in a just
world). The *median,* a different measure of central tendency, is the half-way
point. If I line up five kids by height, the median child is shorter than two and
taller than the other two (who might have trouble getting their mean share of
the candy). A politician in power might say with pride, "The mean income of
our citizens is $15,000 per year." The leader of the opposition might retort,
"But half our citizens make less than $10,000 per year." Both are right, but
neither cites a statistic with impassive objectivity. The first invokes a mean, the
second a median. (Means are higher than medians in such cases because one
millionaire may outweigh hundreds of poor people in setting a mean; but he
can balance only one mendicant in calculating a median).

The larger issue that creates a common distrust or contempt for statistics
is more troubling. Many people make an unfortunate and invalid separation
between heart and mind, or feeling and intellect. In some contemporary traditions, abetted by attitudes stereotypically centered on Southern California,
feelings are exalted as more "real" and the only proper basis for action—if it
feels good, do it—while intellect gets short shrift as a hang-up of outmoded
elitism. Statistics, in this absurd dichotomy, often become the symbol of the
enemy. As Hilaire Belloc wrote, "Statistics are the triumph of the quantitative
method, and the quantitative method is the victory of sterility and death."

This is a personal story of statistics, properly interpreted, as profoundly
nurturant and life-giving. It declares holy war on the downgrading of intellect
by telling a small story about the utility of dry, academic knowledge about science. Heart and head are focal points of one body, one personality.

5   In July 1982, I learned that I was suffering from abdominal mesothelioma, a rare and serious cancer usually associated with exposure to asbestos.
When I revived after surgery, I asked my first question of my doctor and
chemotherapist: "What is the best technical literature about mesothelioma?"
She replied, with a touch of diplomacy (the only departure she has ever made
from direct frankness), that the medical literature contained nothing really
worth reading.

Of course, trying to keep an intellectual away from literature works about as well as recommending chastity to *Homo sapiens,* the sexiest primate of all. As soon as I could walk, I made a beeline for Harvard's Countway medical library and punched *mesothelioma* into the computer's bibliographic search program. An hour later, surrounded by the latest literature on abdominal mesothelioma, I realized with a gulp why my doctor had offered that humane advice. The literature couldn't have been more brutally clear: mesothelioma is incurable, with a median mortality of only eight months after discovery. I sat stunned for about fifteen minutes, then smiled and said to myself: so that's why they didn't give me anything to read. Then my mind started to work again, thank goodness.

If a little learning could ever be a dangerous thing, I had encountered a classic example. Attitude clearly matters in fighting cancer. We don't know why (from my old-style materialistic perspective, I suspect that mental states feed back upon the immune system). But match people with the same cancer for age, class, health, socioeconomic status, and, in general, those with positive attitudes, with a strong will and purpose for living, with commitment to struggle, with an active response to aiding their own treatment and not just a passive acceptance of anything doctors say, tend to live longer. A few months later I asked Sir Peter Medawar, my personal scientific guru and a Nobelist in immunology, what the best prescription for success against cancer might be. "A sanguine personality," he replied. Fortunately (since one can't reconstruct oneself at short notice and for a definite purpose), I am, if anything, even-tempered and confident in just this manner.

Hence the dilemma for humane doctors: since attitude matters so critically, should such a somber conclusion be advertised, especially since few people have sufficient understanding of statistics to evaluate what the statements really mean? From years of experience with the small-scale evolution of Bahamian land snails treated quantitatively, I have developed this technical knowledge—and I am convinced that it played a major role in saving my life. Knowledge is indeed power, in Bacon's proverb.

The problem may be briefly stated: What does "median mortality of eight months" signify in our vernacular? I suspect that most people, without training in statistics, would read such a statement as "I will probably be dead in eight months"—the very conclusion that must be avoided, since it isn't so, and since attitude matters so much.

I was not, of course, overjoyed, but I didn't read the statement in this vernacular way either. My technical training enjoined a different perspective on "eight months median mortality." The point is a subtle one, but profound—for it embodies the distinctive way of thinking in my own field of evolutionary biology and natural history.

We still carry the historical baggage of a Platonic heritage that seeks sharp essences and definite boundaries. (Thus we hope to find an unambiguous

10

"beginning of life" or "definition of death," although nature often comes to us as irreducible continua.) This Platonic heritage, with its emphasis in clear distinctions and separated immutable entities, leads us to view statistical measures of central tendency wrongly, indeed opposite to the appropriate interpretation in our actual world of variation, shadings, and continua. In short, we view means and medians as the hard "realities," and the variation that permits their calculation as a set of transient and imperfect measurements of this hidden essence. If the median is the reality and variation around the median just a device for its calculation, the "I will probably be dead in eight months" may pass as a reasonable interpretation.

But all evolutionary biologists know that variation itself is nature's only irreducible essence. Variation is the hard reality, not a set of imperfect measures for a central tendency. Means and medians are the abstractions. Therefore, I looked at the mesothelioma statistics quite differently—and not only because I am an optimist who tends to see the doughnut instead of the hole, but primarily because I know that variation itself is the reality. I had to place myself amidst the variation.

When I learned about the eight-month median, my first intellectual reaction was: fine, half the people will live longer; now what are my chances of being in that half. I read for a furious and nervous hour and concluded, with relief: damned good. I possessed every one of the characteristics conferring a probability of longer life: I was young; my disease had been recognized in a relatively early stage; I would receive the nation's best medical treatment; I had the world to live for; I knew how to read the data properly and not despair.

Another technical point then added even more solace. I immediately recognized that the distribution of variation about the eight-month median would almost surely be what statisticians call "right skewed." (In a symmetrical distribution, the profile of variation to the left of the central tendency is a mirror image of variation to the right. In skewed distributions, variation to one side of the central tendency is more stretched out—left skewed if extended to the left, right skewed if stretched out to the right.) The distribution of variation had to be right skewed, I reasoned. After all, the left of the distribution contains an irrevocable lower boundary of zero (since mesothelioma can only be identified at death or before). Thus, there isn't much room for the distribution's lower (or left) half—it must be scrunched up between zero and eight months. But the upper (or right) half can extend out for years and years, even if nobody ultimately survives. The distribution must be right skewed, and I needed to know how long the extended tail ran—for I had already concluded that my favorable profile made me a good candidate for that part of the curve.

15   The distribution was indeed, strongly right skewed, with a long tail (however small) that extended for several years above the eight month median. I saw no reason why I shouldn't be in that small tail, and I breathed a very long sigh of relief. My technical knowledge had helped. I had read the graph

correctly. I had asked the right question and found the answers. I had obtained, in all probability, the most precious of all possible gifts in the circumstances— substantial time. I didn't have to stop and immediately follow Isaiah's injunction to Hezekiah—set thine house in order for thou shalt die, and not live. I would have time to think, to plan, and to fight.

One final point about statistical distributions. They apply only to a prescribed set of circumstances—in this case to survival with mesothelioma under conventional modes of treatment. If circumstances change, the distribution may alter. I was placed on an experimental protocol of treatment and, if fortune holds, will be in the first cohort of a new distribution with high median and a right tail extending to death by natural causes at advanced old age.

It has become, in my view, a bit too trendy to regard the acceptance of death as something tantamount to intrinsic dignity. Of course I agree with the preacher of Ecclesiastes that there is a time to love and a time to die—and when my skein runs out I hope to face the end calmly and in my own way. For most situations, however, I prefer the more martial view that death is the ultimate enemy—and I find nothing reproachable in those who rage mightily against the dying of the light.

The swords of battle are numerous, and none more effective than humor. My death was announced at a meeting of my colleagues in Scotland, and I almost experienced the delicious pleasure of reading my obituary penned by one of my best friends (the so-and-so got suspicious and checked; he too is a statistician, and didn't expect to find me so far out on the right tail). Still, the incident provided my first good laugh after the diagnosis. Just think, I almost got to repeat Mark Twain's most famous line of all: the reports of my death are greatly exaggerated.   *2000*

CONSIDERATIONS

1. What reasons might Gould have for opening and closing this piece with references to Mark Twain and literature instead of to more technical and scientific writing?
2. In what way does the use of statistics correspond to scientific thinking, and what is Gould's point regarding this approach to understanding the truth revealed by research?
3. How does Gould's role as a renowned scientist add deeper significance to his point about the mercurial nature of truth?
4. Poet Muriel Rukeyser has said that "the world is made up of stories, not atoms." How does this quote reinforce what Gould is saying in this piece?
5. Gould admits that his technical knowledge helped him to understand his illness. However, what does he say about the limitations of technology, and

what does he say was most necessary to his survival, more important, even, than all the research he conducted?

6. In addition to research studies, Gould also includes overt and subtle references to literary, biblical, and philosophical authorities. Discuss these references and how they relate to the central conflict in this essay.

REBECCA MEAD
Eggs for Sale

> Rebecca Mead is a British journalist who was previously a contributing editor at New York *magazine and is now a staff writer for the* New Yorker, *where this essay originally appeared on August 9, 1999. Mead has also reviewed several books, including Eileen Boris's* Home to Work *and Lorrie Moore's* A Predilection for the Zinger.

The first time I met Cindy Schiller, at the Hungarian Pastry Shop on Amsterdam Avenue and 111th Street one morning this winter, she told me that she wasn't feeling quite herself, on account of what she called "the whole menopause thing." Her short-term memory was out of whack, she was lethargic, and she'd been finding herself suddenly drenched in sweat. "Hot flashes sound like they're no big deal, but hot flashes kick your ass," she said.

Schiller is a student at Columbia University Law School, and at twenty-six she should be only halfway to menopause. But she had been undergoing an artificially induced change of life over the previous weeks, which was precipitated by an array of drugs and an unusually relaxed attitude about sticking needles into herself. For three weeks, she had injected her stomach with a drug called Lupron, which shut down her ovaries, so that none of her eggs ripened and none of her egg follicles developed that month. Then menopause was suddenly over; she switched medications, and started injecting a combination of Pergonal and Metrodin—follicle-stimulating hormones—into her hip every morning. This kicked her quiescent ovaries into overdrive, swelling them to the size of oranges, and brought a cluster of her eggs to the brink of ripeness. After eight days, Schiller took a final shot of a hormone called human chorionic gonadotropin, or H.C.G., and exactly thirty-six hours later she went to the office of a fertility doctor on Central Park West. There she was put under general sedation, and an ultrasound probe was introduced into her vagina and threaded up through her uterus, so that a needle could be inserted into each of her ovaries and the eggs sucked out, one by one. Twelve eggs were whisked away, to be fertilized in a petri dish with the sperm of a man Schiller wasn't especially fond of, in preparation for transfer to the uterus of a woman she didn't really know, in the hope that at least one would grow into a child whom Schiller would probably never see.

Schiller, whose name has been changed in this article at her request, is a lively young woman with blue eyes, long light-brown hair, and very pale skin, unmarked except for five tattoos—tattoos that her mother, back home in the Southwest, has been begging her to remove with laser surgery. She also has sixteen piercings, including several of the kind that only real intimates or fertility doctors get to see.

If she were your daughter, you, too, would probably want her to have the tattoos removed, because in other respects Schiller is such a nice girl: she doesn't drink, she doesn't smoke, she doesn't take drugs, she's pretty and quick to laugh, and she has a lovely singing voice. . . .

Not long after she arrived at Columbia last fall, Schiller read a notice   5 pinned to a bulletin board in the law school by an infertile couple who were seeking an egg donor. For a woman who is trying to get pregnant and has no viable eggs of her own, donor eggs are a last resort. Schiller had signed up with an egg-donor agency while she was an undergraduate in her home state and had twice donated eggs there. She was now eager to do it again, even though the last time she had "hyperstimulated," which means that she had produced too many eggs (more than thirty, in her case) and had suffered so much abdominal pain and nausea that she could hardly get out of bed for two days. On both occasions, she had been selected as a donor immediately, no doubt because she is fair and blue-eyed and has a good academic record.

Schiller donates her eggs because she thinks that it's a worthy thing to do, and because it's a worthy thing to do for which she can be paid in sums that seem handsome to a heavily indebted student. Schiller's parents, who are divorced, know that she donates eggs, and they are not opposed to her doing it, though they are concerned about its effect on her health. They aren't especially wealthy, and Schiller says she would rather support herself with eggs than ask them to help her out.

She does, however, have . . . political objections to the trade. . . . She thinks it would be "really cool" to donate to a gay couple, say, rather than to the upper-middle-class wives and husbands who are the typical recipients of donor eggs. She also disapproves of the preference for egg donation over adoption. "It's the fact that I'm helping a white-supremacist system work," she told me earnestly. "People are getting these fair, blue-eyed children, and that does bother me philosophically." Still, she had earned twenty-five hundred dollars for each of her earlier donations, and by last fall the going rate in New York was five thousand dollars, so when she saw the ad she called the couple and arranged to meet them at a café on Broadway.

They turned out to be a professional Manhattan couple old enough to be Schiller's parents, and they bought her lunch and quizzed her about her interests and skills. She told them about her expertise in martial arts and music, and about the fact that she was really good at math and science and was also a decent writer. It was a bit like a job interview, she told me, though she hadn't done some of the things that a career counsellor might have advised, like removing her nose ring or the stud in her tongue. The hardest part of the interview came when it was time to negotiate the fee, and the couple asked her to name her price. "The husband wouldn't, like, name a figure, so I had to," she said. "Five thousand was the amount that I needed to make in this period of time, and he jumped at it. I probably could have asked for more and got it."

This past February, in the middle of Schiller's fertility-drug regimen, she heard about an advertisement that had been placed in several Ivy League school newspapers offering fifty thousand dollars to a donor who was athletic, had S.A.T. scores of 1400 or more, and was at least five feet ten inches tall. She was a few inches too short to apply, but it made her think that there might be someone who was willing to pay such a premium for her eggs, thereby making her next year at Columbia a whole lot easier. "I'm only now beginning to realize that I could tap into some cash here," she said.

10   In 1984, a woman gave birth to a child who was genetically unrelated to her for the first time, after a donor's egg had been fertilized in a petri dish in the laboratory of Dr. Alan Trounson, an embryologist at Monash University, in Melbourne, Australia, and transferred to another woman's womb. This year, there will probably be around five thousand egg donations in the United States.

In the early days of egg donation, very few patients could take advantage of the procedure. These recipients were given whatever eggs clinics could lay their hands on: some were leftover eggs donated by women who had undergone in-vitro fertilization, which involves the same kind of ovary-stimulating hormonal regimen as egg donation; a few came from women who were having their tubes tied and agreed to give away the eggs they would no longer be using. Some infertile women were helped by their younger sisters, or by friends. There was little concern about matching donors and recipients beyond the broadest categories of race. One recipient I spoke with, who is dark-haired, olive-skinned, and Jewish, received donor eggs ten years ago from a woman who was tall, blond, and Nordic.

These days, such a match would be unlikely, although if a dark, Jewish recipient wanted to introduce a little Nordic blood into her family stock, she would certainly be able to find an egg-donor agency happy to oblige. Nowadays, donors and recipients are matched with remarkable precision, right down to tanning ability and hair texture. There are around two hundred private egg-donation agencies and clinics in the United States, and they are intensely competitive, offering patients donor data bases that may include as many as three hundred women. Different agencies specialize in different kinds of donors: one bicoastal agency is known for signing up donors who are in their late twenties and early thirties, are married, and have children of their own; a former actress in Los Angeles runs an agency that specializes in donors who are models and actresses; at another Los Angeles agency, the two proprietresses accompany donors to their medical appointments and have had dinner and flowers delivered to them on the night after the surgery.

Marketing strategies are ingenious. A New York egg-donation program advertises in movie theatres, inviting would-be donors to dial 1-877-BABY-MAKERS. A new company in Los Angeles called the Center for Egg Options hired a hip advertising agency to write catchy ad copy. Instead of variations on the usual "give the gift of life" theme, one ad reads simply, "Pay your tuition with eggs." Another, which appeared in the magazine *Backstage*, says, "Get paid $4,000 for a small part." The same company is known for sending fertility doctors promotional giveaways that consist of shrink-wrapped egg cartons filled with chocolate eggs. . . .

The United States is the only country in the world in which the rules of the marketplace govern the trade in gametes and genes. In parts of Europe, and in most of South America, egg donation is illegal, often because of the influence of the Catholic Church, which holds that only intercourse should lead to conception. (Muslim law also forbids egg donation; Judaism generally has a more flexible view toward methods of assisted reproduction.) In other countries, egg donation is legal only under certain circumstances. A recent British law allows patients of in-vitro fertilization to sell their leftover eggs, thereby offsetting the cost of the original I.V.F. procedure, but it is against the law to pay women to undergo voluntary egg retrieval. Many foreigners seeking fertility treatments travel to the United States, which is seen by overseas patients as the place where their prayers may be answered and by their overseas doctors as something of a rogue nation. Robert Jansen, a prominent Australian fertility doctor, characterizes the American egg trade as "a thoroughly commercial activity," and regrets that "people are not even pretending anymore that it is an altruistic act to donate eggs." He adds, "Personally, I am frightened by it."

In the United States, though, the controversy has centered less on   15
whether donors should be paid than on how much they should earn. When Thomas Pinkerton, a San Diego lawyer, placed the fifty-thousand-dollar-egg-donor advertisement earlier this year on behalf of an anonymous client, he was accused of exercising unreasonable influence over students who may be hard-up. Television news magazines grilled him about his ethics, and the Academy of Assisted Reproductive Technology, an organization on whose legal advisory board he sits, was troubled by the controversy. But Pinkerton's clients aren't alone in looking for high-end eggs: last year, a donor in Los Angeles received thirty-five thousand dollars for her eggs.

Escalating fees are causing doctors in this country, somewhat belatedly, to express reservations about the commercial traffic in eggs. At a recent conference on infertility that I attended in Sydney, Australia, Dr. Mark V. Sauer, who is the director of reproductive endocrinology at Columbia Presbyterian Medical Center, in New York, addressed the issue. "First of all, we have to recognize that we have a problem," he said. "It is like saying at A.A. meetings, 'I am an alcoholic.' Well, I am an egg-donor man, and I do pay my donors, and I pay them too much, and I recognize that, so what are we going to do about it?"

Doctors are concerned that high prices are attracting women who aren't mature enough to be able to make the kind of philosophical decision implicit in donating eggs; but they are also worried about the interests of their infertility patients, many of whom are being priced out of the market. Egg donation is generally not covered by insurance, and the price for one retrieval (known as a cycle) in New York City, including donor fees and medications for both participants, is currently twenty thousand dollars, with the chances of success being around fifty per cent. Some patients undergo as many as three cycles in their efforts to become parents.

The ethical quandary that doctors now find themselves in, however, is one of their own making. It has long been accepted that gametes have a monetary value, ever since commercial sperm donation took off in the nineteen-sixties. (Although there are laws against the commodification of body parts, a curious legislative loophole has enabled a market in eggs and sperm to emerge. There is no doubt that if such a loophole existed for the market in, say, kidneys, you would be able to order them on the Internet from donors who would provide detailed accounts of their families' excellent urological history.) The average sperm-donor fee is fifty dollars per deposit, which works out to about 0.00001 cent per spermatozoon. Part of the reason that egg-donor fees are higher than sperm-donor fees is that the effort required is so much greater. Being an egg donor can be inconvenient, because, unlike sperm, eggs cannot easily be frozen, so there are no "egg banks"; instead, the donor takes drugs to synchronize her reproductive system with the recipient's. What's more, as Cindy Schiller found out, the process can be painful, and it can be dangerous as well: hyperstimulation can, in very rare instances, lead to stroke. Donating eggs does not deplete a donor's own reserves, since the eggs that are taken would otherwise have been wasted that month; but it is too early in the history of egg donation to know what the long-term side effects might be. Ovarian scarring may compromise a donor's own fertility, and one medical study, which has since been disputed, has suggested that there might be an association between fertility drugs and ovarian cancer.

All of these factors have led some doctors to argue that egg donors are actually underpaid. Dr. Jamie Grifo, who heads New York University's infertility clinic, says, "If you consider the hourly wage for a sperm donor and the hourly wage for an egg donor—my God, five thousand dollars is about ten times too little."

In its egg-donor guidelines, the American Society for Reproductive   *20*
Medicine stipulates that donors be paid not for the actual eggs but for the "inconvenience, time, discomfort, and for the risk undertaken." Agencies reject
potential donors who say they are doing it just for the money, in part because
most recipients wouldn't want a donor who appears to be mercenary; they
would prefer a donor who has chosen to perform this service out of the goodness of her heart. (In the euphemistic parlance of the industry, eggs are "donated," never "sold.") The ideal egg donor embodies all sorts of paradoxes: she
is compassionate toward an infertile stranger but feels no necessary attachment
to her own genetic kin; she is fecund but can easily divorce the reproductive
from the maternal.

Before Cindy Schiller was allowed to become an egg donor, she underwent psychological counselling and testing. Egg-donor programs generally reject any young women who view their eggs as protochildren. "They always
ask what you are going to do when in eighteen years' time someone comes
knocking at your door," Schiller told me, her tone implying that she thought
the question was a silly one to ask of someone her age. "How would I know
what I'm going to do?". . .
Cindy Schiller was nonchalant when discussing the children who might
result from her donations. "I'm really getting a good bargain, because I don't
have to raise them," she said, half seriously. Schiller had nonetheless become
deeply invested in the pregnancies of the women she was helping. (The agency
back in her home state didn't tell Schiller whether her donations were successful, but she did receive a thank-you card from one couple, telling her that
they now had a son.) "Of course, you are doing it for the money," she said,
"but I always hope it works. I really hope it works."
In the weeks after we first met, Schiller had sent away for an application
form from a large West Coast agency called Options. Most agencies do not
allow women to donate eggs more than four or five times, because of the
health risks, and Schiller was approaching her limit; she hoped that Options
would help her market herself for what might be the last time. She was asked
to provide head shots, and was taken aback by a number of other details that
Options expected. "They even ask whether your grandparents had acne," she
marvelled. "I can see why you would want to know about diseases and stuff,
but acne? *Please.* I know they're paying top dollar here for the genes, but if
acne is your biggest problem you're good to go."
Options is one of the largest egg-brokering agencies in the country: it can
offer around two hundred and fifty donors to recipients worldwide at any given
moment, and it conducts almost all of its business on the Internet. I went to visit
the Options offices, which are located in a nondescript building on an anonymous street in the Los Angeles area; before I was provided with the address,

I was required to sign a nondisclosure agreement stating that I would not reveal it. Teri Royal, who runs the company, said that she kept her address secret in order to preserve the security of her records, some of which deal with high-profile clients in Hollywood and in Washington.

25   The place had the feeling of a cottage industry that needs to move into a mansion: partitions had been set up to divide small spaces into even smaller ones, and there was hardly room to turn around without bumping into another woman with a phone clamped to her ear and a computer screen glowing in front of her. Royal is a stout thirty-nine-year-old woman with strawberry-blond hair. She explained that Options donors are carefully selected for their marketability as well as for their general health; Options does not accept donors older than thirty, for instance, because recipients shy away from them. But when it comes to accepting recipients into the program, Royal practices reproductive free trade.

"We would never turn somebody down," she said. "It is none of my business how someone wants to make her baby, so long as all parties are informed and give their consent. So I'm not going to turn away homosexuals, bisexuals, transracials, single parents, older couples." She showed me a photograph of twins born to a couple who had been rejected by another agency before coming to Options because they were both Asian but wanted a Caucasian donor. "They thought the mix was beautiful," Royal said. The agency's oldest would-be mother had been sixty-eight years old; she and her husband, both of whom already had grown children, recruited an egg donor and also a gestational surrogate to carry the new baby. "Everyone realized that the mother wasn't going to be around for the whole of the child's life," Royal said, "but the rest of the family planned to step in and be there for the parenting of this child, and it was a wonderful thing." Royal sees herself as a service provider, and she cites a higher authority for her policy of nonintervention: "In the Bible, Sarah didn't conceive until she was ninety. So I figure that until I get someone over ninety I am not going to say no to them, because if God thinks it's O.K., then who am I to say it's not?"

Using Options is expensive. The agency charges eighteen hundred and sixty-five dollars for bringing donors and recipients together. Administrative and legal costs are close to another thousand dollars. Then there is the compensation for the donor. Options donors are among the best paid in the country: those who appear on the Internet data base receive between thirty-five hundred and five thousand dollars, and others who are recruited through private advertisements placed for specific couples earn still more. Last year, Options placed a cap of sixty-five hundred dollars on payments, because would-be recipients were trying to outbid one another in the pages of the same college newspapers. "We had recipients saying they wanted to offer ten thousand, fifteen thousand, twenty thousand," Royal said. It turns out that the cap is not screwed on very tightly, however: Options still allows recipients to reward donors with additional "gifts." The *Columbia Daily Spectator* recently featured an Options ad seeking a donor who was "5'5"or taller, Caucasian, slim with dark hair, intelligent and kind"; the ad also stated that "although our gratitude cannot be measured in dollars, if we were in your shoes, the least we would expect is: $6,500 plus expenses (and a gift).". . .

As egg donation has changed from being an experimental procedure to being just one of a range of infertility treatments, consumers have begun to demand more from agencies like Options. They expect to be offered donors who are not just healthy but bright and accomplished and attractive. One recent morning, I attended a matching session at Saint Barnabas Medical Center, in New Jersey, where the members of the egg-donation team were going over the wish lists of various recipients. (Like all the New York-area egg-donation programs, Saint Barnabas practices anonymous donation, in which recipients and donors are matched by nurses and psychologists; the recipients never see a picture of the woman who is chosen for them.) . . .

Egg-donor recipients bridle at the suggestion that they are shopping for genes, but the agencies and the programs provide so much personal information about donors that recipients are invited to view eggs as merchandise. After all, most modern parents do everything they can to give a child its best start in life—from taking folic acid while trying to conceive to not drinking during pregnancy to drilling a toddler with flash cards and sending a ten-year-old to tennis camp. So it is not surprising that egg recipients are particularly choosy before conception even takes place. Lyne Macklin, the administrator of an agency in Beverly Hills, the Center for Surrogate Parenting and Egg Donation, told me that there's a great temptation among recipients to engage in a kind of genetic upgrading. "It's like shopping," she said. "If you have the option between a Volkswagen and a Mercedes, you'll select the Mercedes."

It is impossible to determine just how likely a child is to inherit such characteristics as academic ability or athleticism or musicality. Still, would-be parents can play the odds. Robert Plomin, a behavioral geneticist at the University of London, says that a recipient probably ought to pay attention to such characteristics as cognitive ability, which is about fifty per cent heritable. "I generally try to be a scientist and say, 'These are populations and averages, and we can't make very good predictions for an individual,'" he told me. "But I do let friends know that some of these things are heritable."

Egg-donation specialists tend to tell their patients that they should not worry too much about behavioral genetics. Nonetheless, there is some speculation that paying donors high rates might have an effect on the character of the children produced. Robert Jansen, the Australian fertility doctor, told me, "As the price rises and becomes more and more of a motivating factor, and we also appreciate the genetics of personality and character, you start to ask, 'Do you really want to bring up a little girl whose biological mother was someone who decided to charge ten thousand dollars for eggs?'"

30

Jansen's question suggests a profound anxiety about the new reproductive territory that egg donation has opened up. Egg donation makes it possible, for the first time, for a woman's procreative capacity to be detached from any maternal investment on her part. Though men have always been able to father children they may never meet, the fact that an egg donor might, by semantic equivalence, mother a child she will never know confounds both the dictionary and an ingrained assumption about the maternal instinct. . . .

As the egg-donation industry grows, however, legal changes are expected. "There is currently no controlling federal legislation," Sean Tipton, a spokesman for the American Society for Reproductive Medicine, explains. Donors sign a consent form saying that they are relinquishing any claim to their retrieved eggs. Five states—Florida, North Dakota, Oklahoma, Texas, and Virginia—have passed legislation that releases donors from responsibility for the children born from their eggs. "In most cases, people should be confident that they are giving up those rights," Tipton says. "But it is not clear whether it would survive a court challenge."

Legal scholars expect that, in years to come, lawsuits will be brought by donors who develop regrets about having sold their eggs back in their student days. Karen Synesiou, the co-owner of the Center for Surrogate Parenting and Egg Donation, told me, "If you get an eighteen- or nineteen-year-old who has been stimulated four or five times and her ovaries stop functioning because of all the scarring, she is going to want to sue someone for being infertile." At least one donor has threatened to sue a fertility clinic after being hyperstimulated, but the suit was dropped when the clinic agreed to pay her medical expenses. . . .

35   So far, there has been very little case law in which egg donation plays a role. One notorious case that does involve an egg donor is known as Buzzanca v. Buzzanca. John and Luanne Buzzanca were both infertile, so they obtained an embryo that was left over from an I.V.F. cycle performed on an infertile woman, using a donor egg and her husband's sperm. The embryo was transferred to the womb of a gestational surrogate whom the Buzzancas had hired. During the pregnancy, the Buzzancas separated; shortly after the baby's birth, John claimed that he was exempt from paying child support, because the child was not genetically related to him and had not been born to his wife. A lower court agreed with John Buzzanca that he was not the little girl's parent, but it declined to say who, precisely, was; however, a higher court ruled that John and Luanne were indeed the child's father and mother. The child now lives with Luanne Buzzanca, and she receives child support from John Buzzanca. Some legal scholars have suggested that the original egg donor, who seemed to be unaware that her eggs had been passed on to yet another infertile couple, might have had a claim if she had decided to sue her clinic.

The Buzzanca case has implications not just for the field of assisted reproduction but also for the contemporary cultural definition of parenthood.

According to the Buzzanca ruling, parenthood is not a biological category but a conceptual one: its defining characteristic is that of intent. John and Luanne Buzzanca were the child's parents because at one point they had meant to be her parents. This reasoning—the idea that intent trumps biology—makes for some remarkably slippery values. A woman who bears an egg-donor child is encouraged to believe that carrying the fetus is the crucial component of motherhood. But a woman who hires a surrogate to carry her fertilized egg to term for her is encouraged to believe the opposite: that the important thing is the genetic link to the baby, and not the womb out of which the baby came. Biologically, an egg donor's situation is identical to that of a woman who uses a surrogate. But egg donors are encouraged to believe that what makes a woman into a mother is the wish to be a mother—to be what is known in the infertility business as "the social parent."

The American fertility industry is based upon the conviction that a person is the agent of his or her own destiny—that fate and fortune are fashioned, not inflicted. Effective contraception has made it possible for people to believe that all pregnancies can be planned, and that children are chosen. The corollary of that belief is the conviction that choosing to have a child is a right, and that the desire to have one, even when pregnancy is against the odds, should command the utmost attention and effort and resources. The jargon of the reproductive-services industry, which talks about "nontraditional family-building" and "creating families," illustrates this very American idea: that sleeves-rolled-up diligence is what makes people into parents—rather than anything as unreliable as chance, or fate, or luck, or God. . . .

Schiller had recently heard from Columbia's Financial Aid office that she'd be receiving more funds than she expected this academic year, so she hadn't yet decided whether to go through with a fourth donation. But just in case, she had looked into taking a Mensa test in order to have proof of her intelligence, and she had decided one thing: "If someone offers me something really high, and they are an asshole, I won't do it." In any case, Schiller has no regrets about her adventures in the egg marketplace. "It's almost like a hobby now," she said. "This is weird, isn't it? But it is a very interesting experience. I don't think I would trade it for anything."

CONSIDERATIONS

1. What was your initial response to the idea of a woman selling her eggs in order to make money?
2. Examine the way this essay is organized. How effective do you find it to be? What other choices did the author have? Would they have been as effective? Explain.

1146 TECHNOLOGY AND ETHICS

3. From reading this piece, can you discern the author's opinion on this subject? What does she think about this new technology and the ethical questions it raises?
4. In what ways does the United States differ from the rest of the world as far as the sale of eggs is concerned? What might this say about the values of Americans compared to the rest of the world?
5. What is the most important thing you learned from reading this article? What questions do you now have regarding this topic that you may not have had previously? Explain.

Connections: Technology and Ethics

1. A recurrent theme in literature is the conflict a person faces between opposing aspects of his or her own nature. Compare and contrast the nature of this internal conflict by examining several of the following pieces: "The Birthmark," "Astronomer's Wife," "Videotape," "My Flamboyant Grandson," *Wit,* and "Eggs for Sale."
2. Poets often depend on images to evoke emotional responses from their readers. Choose any three poems from this section and analyze the power of the natural images that the poet employs. Come to some conclusions about the relationship of these images to human nature. Suggestions for selections include the following: "I like to see it lap the Miles," "When I Heard the Learn'd Astronomer," "The Market Economy," "Amniocentesis," "TV Room at the Children's Hospice," and "Power."
3. Create the discussion that might take place among the members of a panel comprised of any three to five characters in this section. The topic of the discussion would be the question "What does it mean to be fully human?" Consider juxtaposing characters who have a scientific point of view with those who have a more humanistic point of view. Suggestions for those representing science and technology include: Alymer, the Astronomer, Mr. Winthrop, a City Planner, Dr. Kelekian, Jason, and Stephen Jay Gould. Suggestions for characters representing the humanistic approach include: Georgiana, the Indian, the speaker in "When I Heard the Learn'd Astronomer," Mrs. Ames, Susie, E. M. Ashford, Vivian Bearing, and Stephen Jay Gould.
4. Examine the theories and philosophies contained in the following pieces: "Astronomer's Wife," "Assembly Line," "My Flamboyant Grandson," *Wit,* and "Eggs for Sale." After considering these selections, how would you fill in this blank: "Human happiness really depends upon ____."
5. Compare and contrast the similarities and differences between males and females and their approaches to technology and its role in their lives. Con-

sider the following selections: "The Birthmark," "Astronomer's Wife," "Videotape," and *Wit*.

SUGGESTIONS FOR EXTENDED CONNECTIONS AMONG CHAPTERS

1. Consider the effect of technology, progress, and power on family life and how these external factors contribute to or detract from a person's quest for her or his own identity:

"Sonny's Blues"	412
"I Stand Here Ironing"	692
"The Management of Grief"	948
"The Red Convertible"	218
"The Yellow Wallpaper"	532
"My Father's Life"	797
Soul Gone Home	792
"The Man Who Was Almost a Man"	402

2. Analyze the extent to which technological advances affect human relationships in these selections:

"Hills like White Elephants"	839
"Cathedral"	437
"The Red Convertible"	218
"The Things They Carried"	934
"The Management of Grief"	948
"A Crime of Compassion"	1230

3. Analyze the tools that a character needs in order to succeed in the world or to survive in a difficult situation. Compare and contrast these "tools" to scientific discoveries and technological advances that were also available at the time of the story but that the character did not use.

"Learning to Read and Write"	520
"Cathedral"	437
"A Jury of Her Peers"	558
"How Far She Went"	717
"Who's Irish?"	724
"The Open Boat"	820
"A Worn Path"	844
"The Management of Grief"	948
"A Rose for Emily"	1170

4. Discuss the hopes, dreams, and faith that a particular character clings to that are directly opposed to scientific theories and technological advances. In

what ways are these people better off? In what ways could their lives improve with the addition of science and technology?

"My People"	517
"The Yellow Wallpaper"	532
"A Jury of Her Peers"	558
A Doll's House	608
"Everyday Use"	709
"A Worn Path"	844
"The Deer at Providencia"	890
"The Management of Grief"	948
"Old Man and Old Woman"	1152

SUGGESTIONS FOR COLLABORATIVE LEARNING

1. As a group, select several poems (not included in this chapter) by Dickinson, Whitman, or Atwood that explore the theme of progress and technology. In addition to discussing and analyzing these new selections as a group, locate primary sources that will establish the poet's philosophy regarding the roles of science and technology, and his or her predictions for the future. Present your findings in a well-developed presentation to the rest of the class.

2. Choose any one of the short stories, essays, or poems in this chapter, and transform it into a one-act play. Collaborate on the lighting, music, setting, props, plot, and characters that are necessary to this new art form, and then with each member of the group playing a part, perform this play for this class.

WEB CONNECTIONS

1. Many of the selections in this chapter deal with the differences between the scientific approach to learning, which is often concerned with that which can be measured in a controlled environment, and the humanities, which often consider human experiences and emotions that cannot be quantified. Doctors, nurses, and medical technicians are increasingly encouraged to explore issues related to the humanities during their studies, giving them new ways of thinking about patients and possible insights into how these patients may see the world of medicine. The Web site "Medical Humanities" (http://endeavor.med.nyu.edu/lit-med/), which is maintained by New York University, has been constructed to put medical students in touch with literature, the arts, and patient narratives. The links on this site are numerous and suggest extensive connections between the study of medicine and the humanities.

2. This chapter asks readers to consider how technology has affected the world
   in which we live. In addition to the questions raised by the selections in
   this chapter, there are many other questions about the possible ways in
   which technology may impact our lives. For example, with the increased
   rate of medical discoveries and with longer life expectancies, will the earth
   be able to support the ever-expanding human population, which is expected to number more than 9 billion by the year 2050? Other questions
   relate to such topics as urbanization, disasters caused by humans, technological advances that affect gender issues, and how to combat the spread of
   AIDS and other infectious diseases. The Web site www.worldwatch.org,
   which is maintained by the Worldwatch Institute, contains an extensive library of online resources related to the way in which technology has affected the natural world as well as the economy.

How does this photograph suggest the fear, hope, and mystery that surround the idea of death?

Death

13

For most people in our society, death is a painful and difficult topic; yet it is one that we all either have faced or will have to face at some time. While each of the selections in this chapter looks at death, the points of view are highly varied. In some, the tone is solemn and sad; in others, ironic and even darkly humorous.

As you read the selections in this chapter, keep in mind the following questions:

1. How do today's attitudes toward death differ from those in the past?
2. Death is often personified as the Grim Reaper: a hollow, hooded character with a large scythe over its shoulder. Create another persona for death, and explain your reasons for creating this characterization.
3. Consider the many ways the dying process, as well as the death itself, affects the survivors.
4. Is there any such thing as "a good death"? Explain your response.
5. List five controversial issues related to death and dying. What are your current opinions and beliefs about these issues?

Fiction

CHEWING BLACKBONES
Old Man and Old Woman
A Blackfoot Indian Myth Retold

RECORDED BY ELLA E. CLARK

> *Chewing Blackbones, a Native American and member of the Blackfoot tribe, was described by writer Ella Clark as "an elderly grandfather [. . . who] could tell the old tales only in the old Blackfoot language." Ella E. Clark, who recorded this tale in 1953, was born in 1896 and became a professor of English at Washington State University in Pullman, Washington. Clark received a B.A. in 1921 and an M.A. in 1927 from Northwestern University; she taught at Washington State from 1927 to 1961, when she retired to become a full-time writer. In 1960, she published* Indian Legends in Canada; *the story presented here is included in her 1966 collection,* Indian Legends from the Northern Rockies, *which was followed by two children's books for the Montana Indian Publication Fund. Clark and co-author Margot Edmonds wrote* Sacagawea of the Lewis and Clark Expedition *in 1979 and* Voices of the Winds: Native American Legends *in 1989.*

Long, long ago, there were only two persons in the world: Old Man and Old Woman. One time when they were traveling about the earth, Old Woman said to Old Man, "Now let us come to an agreement of some kind. Let us decide how the people shall live when they shall be on the earth."

"Well," replied Old Man, "I am to have the first say in everything."

"I agree with you," said Old Woman. "That is—if I may have the second say."

Then Old Man began his plans. "The women will have the duty of tanning the hides. They will rub animals' brains on the hides to make them soft and scrape them with scraping tools. All this they will do very quickly, for it will not be hard work."

5   "No," said Old Woman, "I will not agree to this. They must tan hides in the way you say; but it must be very hard work, so that the good workers may be found out."

"Well," said Old Man, "we will let the people have eyes and mouths, straight up and down in their faces."

"No," replied Old Woman, "let us not have them that way. We will have the eyes and mouths in the faces, as you say, but they shall be set crosswise."

"Well," said Old Man, "the people shall have ten fingers on each hand."

"Oh, no!" replied Old Woman. "That will be too many. They will be in the way. There will be four fingers and one thumb on each hand."

So the two went on until they had provided for everything in the lives   *10*
of the people who were to be.

"What shall we do about life and death?" asked Old Woman. "Should the people live forever, or should they die?"

Old Woman and Old Man had difficulty agreeing about this. Finally Old Man said, "I will tell you what we will do. I will throw a buffalo chip into the water. If it floats, the people will die for four days and then come to life again; if it sinks, they will die forever."

So he threw a buffalo chip into the water, and it floated.

"No," said Old Woman, "we will not decide in that way. I will throw this rock into the water. If it floats, the people will die for four days; if it sinks, they will die forever."

Then Old Woman threw the rock into the water, and it sank to the   *15*
bottom.

"There," said she. "It is better for the people to die forever. If they did not, they would not feel sorry for each other, and there would be no sympathy in the world."

"Well," said Old Man, "let it be that way."

After a time, Old Woman had a daughter, who soon became sick and died. The mother was very sorry, then, that they had agreed that people should die forever. "Let us have our say over again," she said.

"No," replied Old Man. "Let us not change what we have agreed upon."

And so people have died ever since.   *20*

CONSIDERATIONS

1. In the beginning of this story, Old Man and Old Woman agree that Old Man will have the first say and Old Woman will have the second. What are the advantages to going first? What are the advantages to going second? Which one would you prefer? Explain.

2. How does the dialogue reflect certain differences between Old Man and Old Woman?

3. What reasons might Old Woman have for choosing a rock to throw into the water? Could there be some underlying motive in this choice, or is this a wise choice on her part? What do you think?

4. In the end, the roles of Old Man and Old Woman are reversed; Old Woman has the first say and Old Man has the second. What might be the reason for this shift?

EDGAR ALLAN POE (1809–1849)
The Black Cat

> *Born in Boston, Massachusetts, to itinerant actors, Edgar Allan Poe was or-*
> *phaned at the age of three. He was adopted by a young merchant, John Allan,*
> *who lived with his family in Richmond, Virginia. After a stormy adolescence, Poe*
> *attended the University of Virginia, where, in spite of gambling sprees and bouts*
> *of heavy drinking, he did well in his studies. After his freshman year, however, his*
> *gambling debts led to a quarrel with his stepfather, who then refused to support*
> *him. He left school and served in the army from 1827 to 1829. Later, he at-*
> *tended West Point but was expelled for failure to observe military discipline and*
> *academy policies. He then began a career as an editor, reporter, and reviewer while*
> *writing poetry and short stories on his own time. In 1836, he married Virginia*
> *Clemm, his thirteen-year-old cousin; the marriage ended tragically with her death*
> *from tuberculosis in 1837. Known as the father of the American short story, Poe*
> *wrote such works as "The Gold Bug," "The Murders in the Rue Morgue,"*
> *"The Tell-Tale Heart," and "The Fall of the House of Usher." In 1849, he was*
> *found unconscious in a street in Philadelphia and died the next day.*

For the most wild yet most homely narrative which I am about to pen, I neither expect nor solicit belief. Mad indeed would I be to expect it, in a case where my very senses reject their own evidence. Yet, mad am I not—and very surely do I not dream. But to-morrow I die, and to-day I would unburden my soul. My immediate purpose is to place before the world, plainly, succinctly, and without comment, a series of mere household events. In their conse-quences, these events have terrified—have tortured—have destroyed me. Yet I will not attempt to expound them. To me, they have presented little but hor-ror—to many they will seem less terrible than *baroques.*° Hereafter, perhaps, some intellect may be found which will reduce my phantasm to the common-place—some intellect more calm, more logical, and far less excitable than my own, which will perceive, in the circumstances I detail with awe, nothing more than an ordinary succession of very natural causes and effects.

From my infancy I was noted for the docility and humanity of my dis-position. My tenderness of heart was even so conspicuous as to make me the jest of my companions. I was especially fond of animals, and was indulged by my parents with a great variety of pets. With these I spent most of my time, and never was so happy as when feeding and caressing them. This peculiarity of character grew with my growth, and, in my manhood, I derived from it one of my principal sources of pleasure. To those who have cherished an affection

---

baroques: Statues on carvings from the baroque era (Europe 1550–1700), often grotesque or frightening images.

for a faithful and sagacious dog, I need hardly be at the trouble of explaining the nature or the intensity of the gratification thus derivable. There is something in the unselfish and self-sacrificing love of a brute, which goes directly to the heart of him who has had frequent occasion to test the paltry friendship and gossamer fidelity of mere *Man.*

I married early, and was happy to find in my wife a disposition not uncongenial with my own. Observing my partiality for domestic pets, she lost no opportunity of procuring those of the most agreeable kind. We had birds, goldfish, a fine dog, rabbits, a small monkey, and a *cat.*

This latter was a remarkably large and beautiful animal, entirely black, and sagacious to an astonishing degree. In speaking of his intelligence, my wife, who at heart was not a little tinctured with superstition, made frequent allusion to the ancient popular notion, which regarded all black cats as witches in disguise. Not that she was ever *serious* upon this point—and I mention the matter at all for no better reason than that it happens, just now, to be remembered.

Pluto°—this was the cat's name—was my favorite pet and playmate. I alone   5
fed him, and he attended me wherever I went about the house. It was even with difficulty that I could prevent him from following me through the streets.

Our friendship lasted, in this manner, for several years, during which my general temperament and character—through the instrumentality of the Fiend Intemperance—had (I blush to confess it) experienced a radical alteration for the worse. I grew, day by day, more moody, more irritable, more regardless of the feelings of others. I suffered myself to use intemperate language to my wife. At length, I even offered her personal violence. My pets, of course, were made to feel the change in my disposition. I not only neglected, but ill-used them. For Pluto, however, I still retained sufficient regard to restrain me from maltreating him, as I made no scruple of maltreating the rabbits, the monkey, or even the dog, when, by accident, or through affection, they came in my way. But my disease grew upon me—for what disease is like Alcohol!—and at length even Pluto, who was now becoming old, and consequently somewhat peevish—even Pluto began to experience the effects of my ill temper.

One night, returning home, much intoxicated, from one of my haunts about town, I fancied that the cat avoided my presence. I seized him; when, in his fright at my violence, he inflicted a slight wound upon my hand with his teeth. The fury of a demon instantly possessed me. I knew myself no longer. My original soul seemed, at once, to take its flight from my body; and a more than fiendish malevolence, gin-nurtured, thrilled every fibre of my frame. I took from my waistcoat-pocket a penknife, opened it, grasped the poor beast by the throat, and deliberately cut one of its eyes from the socket! I blush, I burn, I shudder, while I pen the damnable atrocity.

Pluto: In Roman mythology, god of the dead and ruler of the underworld.

When reason returned with the morning—when I had slept off the fumes of the night's debauch—I experienced a sentiment half of horror, half of remorse, for the crime of which I had been guilty; but it was, at best, a feeble and equivocal feeling, and the soul remained untouched. I again plunged into excess, and soon drowned in wine all memory of the deed.

In the meantime the cat slowly recovered. The socket of the lost eye presented, it is true, a frightful appearance, but he no longer appeared to suffer any pain. He went about the house as usual, but, as might be expected, fled in extreme terror at my approach. I had so much of my old heart left, as to be at first grieved by this evident dislike on the part of a creature which had once so loved me. But this feeling soon gave place to irritation. And then came, as if to my final and irrevocable overthrow, the spirit of Perverseness. Of this spirit philosophy takes no account. Yet I am not more sure that my soul lives, than I am that perverseness is one of the primitive impulses of the human heart—one of the indivisible primary faculties, or sentiments, which give direction to the character of Man. Who has not, a hundred times, found himself committing a vile or stupid action, for no other reason than because he knows he should *not*? Have we not a perpetual inclination, in the teeth of our best judgment, to violate that which is *Law,* merely because we understand it to be such? This spirit of perverseness, I say, came to my final overthrow. It was this unfathomable longing of the soul *to vex itself*—to offer violence to its own nature—to do wrong for the wrong's sake only—that urged me to continue and finally to consummate the injury I had inflicted upon the unoffending brute. One morning, in cold blood, I slipped a noose about its neck and hung it to the limb of a tree;—hung it with the tears streaming from my eyes, and with the bitterest remorse at my heart;—hung it *because* I knew that it had loved me, and *because* I felt it had given me no reason of offence;—hung it *because* I knew that in so doing I was committing a sin—a deadly sin that would so jeopardize my immortal soul as to place it—if such a thing were possible—even beyond the reach of the infinite mercy of the Most Merciful and Most Terrible God.

10   On the night of the day on which this most cruel deed was done, I was aroused from sleep by the cry of fire. The curtains of my bed were in flames. The whole house was blazing. It was with great difficulty that my wife, a servant, and myself, made our escape from the conflagration. The destruction was complete. My entire worldly wealth was swallowed up, and I resigned myself thenceforward to despair.

I am above the weakness of seeking to establish a sequence of cause and effect, between the disaster and the atrocity. But I am detailing a chain of facts—and wish not to leave even a possible link imperfect. On the day succeeding the fire, I visited the ruins. The walls, with one exception, had fallen in. This exception was found in a compartment wall, not very thick, which stood about the middle of the house, and against which had rested the head of my bed. The plastering had here, in great measure, resisted the action of the fire—a fact which I attributed to its having been recently spread. About this wall a dense crowd were collected, and many persons seemed to be examining a particular portion of it with very minute and eager attention. The words "strange!" "singular!" and other similar expressions, excited my curiosity. I approached and saw, as if graven in *bas-relief* upon the white surface, the figure of a gigantic *cat*. The impression was given with an accuracy truly marvelous. There was a rope about the animal's neck.

When I first beheld this apparition—for I could scarcely regard it as less—my wonder and my terror were extreme. But at length reflection came to my aid. The cat, I remembered, had been hung in a garden adjacent to the house. Upon the alarm of fire, this garden had been immediately filled by the crowd—by some one of whom the animal must have been cut from the tree and thrown, through an open window, into my chamber. This had probably been done with the view of arousing me from sleep. The falling of other walls had compressed the victim of my cruelty into the substance of the freshly-spread plaster, the lime of which, with the flames, and the *ammonia* from the carcass, had then accomplished the portraiture as I saw it.

Although I thus readily accounted to my reason, if not altogether to my conscience, for the startling fact just detailed, it did not the less fail to make a deep impression upon my fancy. For months I could not rid myself of the phantasm of the cat; and, during this period, there came back into my spirit a half-sentiment that seemed, but was not, remorse. I went so far as to regret the loss of the animal, and to look about me, among the vile haunts which I now habitually frequented, for another pet of the same species, and of somewhat similar appearance, with which to supply its place.

One night as I sat, half stupefied, in a den of more than infamy, my attention was suddenly drawn to some black object, reposing upon the head of one of the immense hogsheads of gin, or of rum, which constituted the chief furniture of the apartment. I had been looking steadily at the top of this hogshead for some minutes, and what now caused me surprise was the fact that I had not sooner perceived the object thereupon. I approached it, and touched it with my hand. It was a black cat—a very large one—fully as large as Pluto, and closely resembling him in every respect but one. Pluto had not a white hair upon any portion of his body; but this cat had a large, although indefinite splotch of white, covering nearly the whole region of the breast.

Upon my touching him, he immediately arose, purred loudly, rubbed   15 against my hand, and appeared delighted with my notice. This, then, was the very creature of which I was in search. I at once offered to purchase it of the landlord; but this person made no claim to it—knew nothing of it—had never seen it before.

I continued my caresses, and when I prepared to go home, the animal evinced a disposition to accompany me. I permitted it to do so; occasionally stooping and patting it as I proceeded. When it reached the house it domesticated itself at once, and became immediately a great favorite with my wife.

For my own part, I soon found a dislike to it arising within me. This was just the reverse of what I had anticipated; but—I know not how or why it was—its evident fondness for myself rather disgusted and annoyed me. By slow degrees these feelings of disgust and annoyance rose into the bitterness of hatred. I avoided the creature; a certain sense of shame, and the remembrance of my former deed of cruelty, preventing me from physically abusing it. I did not, for some weeks, strike, or otherwise violently ill use it; but gradually—very gradually—I came to look upon it with unutterable loathing, and to flee silently from its odious presence, as from the breath of a pestilence.

What added, no doubt, to my hatred of the beast, was the discovery on the morning after I brought it home, that like Pluto, it also had been deprived of one of its eyes. This circumstance, however, only endeared it to my wife, who, as I have already said, possessed, in a high degree, that humanity of feeling which had once been my distinguishing trait, and the source of many of my simplest and purest pleasures.

With my aversion to this cat, however, its partiality for myself seemed to increase. It followed my footsteps with a pertinacity which it would be difficult to make the reader comprehend. Whenever I sat, it would crouch beneath my chair, or spring upon my knees, covering me with its loathsome caresses. If I arose to walk it would get between my feet and thus nearly throw me down, or, fastening its long and sharp claws in my dress, clamber, in this manner, to my breast. At such times, although I longed to destroy it with a blow, I was yet withheld from so doing, partly by a memory of my former crime, but chiefly—let me confess it at once—by absolute dread of the beast.

20   This dread was not exactly a dread of physical evil—and yet I should be at a loss how otherwise to define it. I am almost ashamed to own—yes, even in this felon's cell, I am almost ashamed to own—that the terror and horror with which the animal inspired me, had been heightened by one of the merest chimeras it would be possible to conceive. My wife had called my attention, more than once, to the character of the mark of white hair, of which I have spoken, and which constituted the sole visible difference between the strange beast and the one I had destroyed. The reader will remember that this mark, although large, had been originally very indefinite; but, by slow degrees—degrees nearly imperceptible, and which for a long time my reason struggled to reject as fanciful—it had, at length, assumed a rigorous distinctness of outline. It was now the representation of an object that I shudder to name—and for this, above all, I loathed, and dreaded, and would have rid myself of the monster *had I dared*—it was now, I say, the image of a hideous—of a ghastly thing—of the Gallows!—oh, mournful and terrible engine of Horror and of Crime—of Agony and of Death!

And now was I indeed wretched beyond the wretchedness of mere Humanity. And *a brute beast*—whose fellow I had contemptuously destroyed—*a brute beast* to work out for *me*—for me, a man fashioned in the image of the High God—so much of insufferable woe! Alas! neither by day nor by night knew I the blessing of rest any more! During the former the creature left me no moment alone, and in the latter I started hourly from dreams of unutterable fear to find the hot breath of *the thing* upon my face, and its vast weight—an incarnate nightmare that I had not power to shake off—incumbent eternally upon my *heart!*

Beneath the pressure of torments such as these the feeble remnant of the good within me succumbed. Evil thoughts became my sole intimates—the darkest and most evil of thoughts. The moodiness of my usual temper increased to hatred of all things and of all mankind; while from the sudden, frequent, and ungovernable outbursts of a fury to which I now blindly abandoned myself, my uncomplaining wife, alas, was the most usual and the most patient of sufferers.

One day she accompanied me, upon some household errand, into the cellar of the old building which our poverty compelled us to inhabit. The cat followed me down the steep stairs, and, nearly throwing me headlong, exasperated me to madness. Uplifting an axe, and forgetting in my wrath the childish dread which had hitherto stayed my hand, I aimed a blow at the animal, which, of course, would have proved instantly fatal had it descended as I wished. But this blow was arrested by the hand of my wife. Goaded by the interference into a rage more than demoniacal, I withdrew my arm from her grasp and buried the axe in her brain. She fell dead upon the spot without a groan.

This hideous murder accomplished, I set myself forthwith, and with entire deliberation, to the task of concealing the body. I knew that I could not remove it from the house, either by day or by night, without the risk of being observed by the neighbors. Many projects entered my mind. At one period I thought of cutting the corpse into minute fragments, and destroying them by fire. At another, I resolved to dig a grave for it in the floor of the cellar. Again, I deliberated about casting it in the well in the yard—about packing it in a box, as if merchandise, with the usual arrangements, and so getting a porter to take it from the house. Finally I hit upon what I considered a far better expedient than either of these. I determined to wall it up in the cellar, as the monks of the Middle Ages are recorded to have walled up their victims.

For a purpose such as this the cellar was well adapted. Its walls were loosely constructed, and had lately been plastered throughout with a rough plaster, which the dampness of the atmosphere had prevented from hardening. Moreover, in one of the walls was a projection, caused by a false chimney, or fireplace, that had been filled up and made to resemble the rest of the cellar. I made no doubt that I could readily displace the bricks at this point, insert the corpse, and wall the whole up as before, so that no eye could detect anything suspicious.

25

And in this calculation I was not deceived. By means of a crowbar I easily dislodged the bricks, and, having carefully deposited the body against the inner wall, I propped it in that position, while with little trouble I relaid the whole structure as it originally stood. Having procured mortar, sand, and hair, with every possible precaution, I prepared a plaster which could not be distinguished from the old, and with this, I very carefully went over the new brickwork. When I had finished, I felt satisfied that all was right. The wall did not present the slightest appearance of having been disturbed. The rubbish on the floor was picked up with the minutest care. I looked around triumphantly, and said to myself: "Here at least, then, my labor has not been in vain."

My next step was to look for the beast which had been the cause of so much wretchedness; for I had, at length, firmly resolved to put it to death. Had I been able to meet with it at the moment, there could have been no doubt of its fate; but it appeared that the crafty animal had been alarmed at the violence of my previous anger, and forbore to present itself in my present mood. It is impossible to describe or to imagine the deep, blissful sense of relief which the absence of the detested creature occasioned in my bosom. It did not make its appearance during the night; and thus for one night, at least, since its introduction into the house, I soundly and tranquilly slept; aye, slept even with the burden of murder upon my soul.

The second and the third day passed, and still my tormentor came not. Once again I breathed as a freeman. The monster, in terror, had fled the premises for ever! I should behold it no more! My happiness was supreme! The guilt of my dark deed disturbed me but little. Some few inquiries had been made, but these had been readily answered. Even a search had been instituted—but of course nothing was to be discovered. I looked upon my future felicity as secured.

Upon the fourth day of the assassination, a party of the police came, very unexpectedly, into the house, and proceeded again to make a rigorous investigation of the premises. Secure, however, in the inscrutability of my place of concealment, I felt no embarrassment whatever. The officers bade me accompany them in their search. They left no nook or corner unexplored. At length, for the third or fourth time, they descended into the cellar. I quivered not in a muscle. My heart beat calmly as that of one who slumbers in innocence. I walked the cellar from end to end. I folded my arms upon my bosom, and roamed easily to and fro. The police were thoroughly satisfied and prepared to depart. The glee at my heart was too strong to be restrained. I burned to say if but one word, by way of triumph, and to render doubly sure their assurance of my guiltlessness.

30   "Gentlemen," I said at last, as the party ascended the steps, "I delight to have allayed your suspicions. I wish you all health and a little more courtesy. By the bye, gentlemen, this—this is a very well-constructed house," (in the rabid desire to say something easily, I scarcely knew what I uttered at all),—"I

may say an exceptionally well-constructed house. These walls—are you going, gentlemen?—these walls are solidly put together"; and here, through the mere frenzy of bravado, I rapped heavily with a cane which I held in my hand, upon that very portion of the brick-work behind which stood the corpse of the wife of my bosom.

But may God shield and deliver me from the fangs of the Arch-Fiend! No sooner had the reverberation of my blows sunk into silence, than I was answered by a voice from within the tomb—by a cry, at first muffled and broken, like the sobbing of a child, and then quickly swelling into one long, loud, and continuous scream, utterly anomalous and inhuman—a howl—a wailing shriek, half of horror and half of triumph, such as might have arisen only out of hell, conjointly from the throats of the damned in their agony and of the demons that exult in the damnation.

Of my own thoughts it is folly to speak. Swooning, I staggered to the opposite wall. For one instant the party on the stairs remained motionless, through extremity of terror and awe. In the next a dozen stout arms were toiling at the wall. It fell bodily. The corpse, already greatly decayed and clotted with gore, stood erect before the eyes of the spectators. Upon its head, with red extended mouth and solitary eye of fire, sat the hideous beast whose craft had seduced me into murder, and whose informing voice had consigned me to the hangman. I had walled the monster up within the tomb.   *1845*

CONSIDERATIONS

1. Who is to blame for the events in the story? The narrator blames the cat, and early in the story the wife suggests that "all black cats [are] witches in disguise." Is the cat a supernatural being that causes the narrator to go mad? What other motivations can you suggest for his actions?
2. How reliable do you find the narrator's descriptions and explanations? For example, he contends that he is bothered "but little" by his wife's murder and says that he feels no concern when the police arrive at his house. Do you find these claims believable? Explain.
3. What is your response to the narrator's question, "Who has not a hundred times found himself committing a vile or stupid action, for no other reason than because he knows he should *not?* Do you agree? Explain.
4. What is the central irony of this story? How does this irony relate to the crime or crimes that are committed and to the punishment of the perpetrator?
5. To what extent does the black cat function as a symbol? Would the story be equally effective, for example, if the animal involved were a dog or a hamster? Explain.

More Resources on
Edgar Allan Poe

In *ARIEL*
- Brief biography of Poe
- Complete texts of Poe poems such as "The Raven" and the short story "The Cask of Amontillado," with hyperlinked comments
- Video and audio clips of readings of Poe's writing
- Analysis of sound in Poe's "The Raven"
- Bibliography of scholarly works on Poe

In the Online Learning Center for *Responding to Literature*
- Brief biography of Poe
- List of major works by Poe
- Web links to more resources on Poe
- Additional questions for experiencing and interpreting Poe's writing

KATHERINE ANNE PORTER (1890–1980)
The Jilting of Granny Weatherall

> *Born in Indian Creek, Texas, Katherine Anne Porter knew early in her life that she wanted to be a writer. In 1911, she began work as a reporter in Chicago and Denver. Following a nearly fatal bout with influenza in 1918, Porter went to Mexico, where her studies of Aztec and Mayan art motivated her to begin writing short fiction. Her first collection of short stories,* Flowering Judas and Other Stories, *in which "The Jilting of Granny Weatherall" appears, was published in 1930; she went on to write several short novels and her full-length novel,* Ship of Fools *(1962). In 1965, her* Collected Stories *won both the Pulitzer Prize and the National Book Award.*

She flicked her wrist neatly out of Doctor Harry's pudgy careful fingers and pulled the sheet up to her chin. The brat ought to be in knee breeches. Doctoring around the country with spectacles on his nose! "Get along now, take your schoolbooks and go. There's nothing wrong with me."

Doctor Harry spread a warm paw like a cushion on her forehead where the forked green vein danced and made her eyelids twitch. "Now, now, be a good girl, and we'll have you up in no time."

"That's no way to speak to a woman nearly eighty years old just because she's down. I'd have you respect your elders, young man."

"Well, Missy, excuse me." Doctor Harry patted her cheek. "But I've got to warn you, haven't I? You're a marvel, but you must be careful or you're going to be good and sorry."

"Don't tell me what I'm going to be. I'm on my feet now, morally speak-   5
ing. It's Cornelia. I had to go to bed to get rid of her."

Her bones felt loose, and floated around in her skin, and Doctor Harry floated like a balloon around the foot of the bed. He floated and pulled down his waistcoat and swung his glasses on a cord. "Well, stay where you are, it certainly can't hurt you."

"Get along and doctor your sick," said Granny Weatherall. "Leave a well woman alone. I'll call for you when I want you. . . . Where were you forty years ago when I pulled through milk-leg and double pneumonia? You weren't even born. Don't let Cornelia lead you on," she shouted, because Doctor Harry appeared to float up to the ceiling and out. "I pay my own bills, and I don't throw my money away on nonsense!"

She meant to wave good-by, but it was too much trouble. Her eyes closed of themselves, it was like a dark curtain drawn around the bed. The pillow rose and floated under her, pleasant as a hammock in a light wind. She listened to the leaves rustling outside the window. No, somebody was swishing newspapers: no, Cornelia and Doctor Harry were whispering together. She leaped broad awake, thinking they whispered in her ear.

"She was never like this, *never* like this!" "Well, what can we expect?" "Yes, eighty years old. . . ."

Well, and what if she was? She still had ears. It was like Cornelia to whis-   10
per around doors. She always kept things secret in such a public way. She was always being tactful and kind. Cornelia was dutiful; that was the trouble with her. Dutiful and good: "So good and dutiful," said Granny, "that I'd like to spank her." She saw herself spanking Cornelia and making a fine job of it.

"What'd you say, Mother?"

Granny felt her face tying up in hard knots.

"Can't a body think, I'd like to know?"

"I thought you might want something."

"I do. I want a lot of things. First off, go away and don't whisper."   15

She lay and drowsed, hoping in her sleep that the children would keep out and let her rest a minute. It had been a long day. Not that she was tired. It was always pleasant to snatch a minute now and then. There was always so much to be done, let me see: tomorrow.

Tomorrow was far away and there was nothing to trouble about. Things were finished somehow when the time came; thank God there was always a little margin over for peace: then a person could spread out the plan of life and tuck in the edges orderly. It was good to have everything clean and folded away, with the hair brushes and tonic bottles sitting straight on the white embroidered linen: the day started without fuss and the pantry shelves laid out with rows of jelly glasses and brown jugs and white stone-china jars with blue whirligigs and words painted on them: coffee, tea, sugar, ginger, cinnamon, all-spice: and the bronze clock with the lion on top nicely dusted off. The dust that lion could collect in twenty-four hours! The box in the attic with all those letters tied up, well she'd have to go through that tomorrow. All those letters—George's letters and John's letters and her letters to them both—lying around for the children to find afterwards made her uneasy. Yes, that would be tomorrow's business. No use to let them know how silly she had been once.

   While she was rummaging around she found death in her mind and it felt clammy and unfamiliar. She had spent so much time preparing for death there was no need for bringing it up again. Let it take care of itself now. When she was sixty she had felt very old, finished, and went around making farewell trips to see her children and grandchildren, with a secret in her mind: This is the very last of your mother, children! Then she made her will and came down with a long fever. That was all just a notion like a lot of other things, but it was lucky too, for she had once for all got over the idea of dying for a long time. Now she couldn't be worried. She hoped she had better sense now. Her father had lived to be one hundred and two years old and had drunk a noggin of strong hot toddy on his last birthday. He told the reporters it was his daily habit, and he owed his long life to that. He had made quite a scandal and was very pleased about it. She believed she'd just plague Cornelia a little.

   "Cornelia! Cornelia!" No footsteps, but a sudden hand on her cheek. "Bless you, where have you been?"

20   "Here, mother."

   "Well, Cornelia, I want a noggin of hot toddy."

   "Are you cold, darling?"

   "I'm chilly, Cornelia. Lying in bed stops the circulation. I must have told you that a thousand times."

   Well, she could just hear Cornelia telling her husband that Mother was getting childish and they'd have to humor her. The thing that most annoyed her was that Cornelia thought she was deaf, dumb, and blind. Little hasty glances and tiny gestures tossed around her and over her head saying, "Don't cross her, let her have her way, she's eighty years old," and she sitting there as if she lived in a thin glass cage. Sometimes Granny almost made up her mind to pack up and move back to her own house where nobody could remind her every minute that she was old. Wait, wait, Cornelia, till your own children whisper behind your back!

25   In her day she had kept a better house and had got more work done. She wasn't too old yet for Lydia to be driving eighty miles for advice when one of the children jumped the track, and Jimmy still dropped in and talked things over: "Now, Mammy, you've a good business head, I want to know what you think of this? . . ." Old Cornelia couldn't change the furniture around

without asking. Little things, little things! They had been so sweet when they were little. Granny wished the old days were back again with the children young and everything to be done over. It had been a hard pull, but not too much for her. When she thought of all the food she had cooked, and all the clothes she had cut and sewed, and all the gardens she had made—well, the children showed it. There they were, made out of her, and they couldn't get away from that. Sometimes she wanted to see John again and point to them and say, Well, I didn't do so badly, did I? But that would have to wait. That was for tomorrow. She used to think of him as a man, but now all the children were older than their father, and he would be a child beside her if she saw him now. It seemed strange and there was something wrong in the idea. Why, he couldn't possibly recognize her. She had fenced in a hundred acres once, digging the post holes herself and clamping the wires with just a negro boy to help. That changed a woman. John would be looking for a young woman with the peaked Spanish comb in her hair and the painted fan. Digging post holes changed a woman. Riding country roads in the winter when women had their babies was another thing: sitting up nights with sick horses and sick negroes and sick children and hardly ever losing one. John, I hardly ever lost one of them! John would see that in a minute, that would be something he could understand, she wouldn't have to explain anything!

It made her feel like rolling up her sleeves and putting the whole place to rights again. No matter if Cornelia was determined to be everywhere at once, there were a great many things left undone on this place. She would start tomorrow and do them. It was good to be strong enough for everything, even if all you made melted and changed and slipped under your hands, so that by the time you finished you almost forgot what you were working for. What was it I set out to do? she asked herself intently, but she could not remember. A fog rose over the valley, she saw it marching across the creek swallowing the trees and moving up the hill like an army of ghosts. Soon it would be at the near edge of the orchard, and then it was time to go in and light the lamps. Come in, children, don't stay out in the night air.

Lighting the lamps had been beautiful. The children huddled up to her and breathed like little calves waiting at the bars in the twilight. Their eyes followed the match and watched the flame rise and settle in a blue curve, then they moved away from her. The lamp was lit, they didn't have to be scared and hang on to mother any more. Never, never, never more. God, for all my life I thank Thee. Without Thee, my God, I could never have done it. Hail, Mary, full of grace.

I want you to pick all the fruit this year and see that nothing is wasted. There's always someone who can use it. Don't let good things rot for want of using. You waste life when you waste good food. Don't let things get lost. It's bitter to lose things. Now, don't let me get to thinking, not when I am tired and taking a little nap before supper. . . .

The pillow rose about her shoulders and pressed against her heart and the memory was being squeezed out of it: oh, push down the pillow, somebody: it would smother her if she tried to hold it. Such a fresh breeze blowing and such a green day with no threats in it. But he had not come, just the same. What does a woman do when she has put on the white veil and set out the white cake for a man and he doesn't come? She tried to remember. No, I swear he never harmed me but in that. He never harmed me but in that . . . and what if he did? There was the day, the day, but a whirl of dark smoke rose and covered it, crept up and over into the bright field where everything was planted so carefully in orderly rows. That was hell, she knew hell when she saw it. For sixty years she had prayed against remembering him and against losing her soul in the deep pit of hell, and now the two things were mingled in one and the thought of him was a smoky cloud from hell that moved and crept in her head when she had just got rid of Doctor Harry and was trying to rest a minute. Wounded vanity, Ellen, said a sharp voice in the top of her mind. Don't let your wounded vanity get the upper hand of you. Plenty of girls get jilted. You were jilted, weren't you? Then stand up to it. Her eyelids wavered and let in streamers of blue-gray light like tissue paper over her eyes. She must get up and pull the shades down or she'd never sleep. She was in bed again and the shades were not down. How could that happen? Better turn over, hide from the light, sleeping in the light gave you nightmares. "Mother, how do you feel now?" and a stinging wetness on her forehead. But I don't like having my face washed in cold water!

30   Hapsy? George? Lydia? Jimmy? No, Cornelia, and her features were swollen and full of little puddles. "They're coming, darling, they'll all be here soon." Go wash your face, child, you look funny.

Instead of obeying, Cornelia knelt down and put her head on the pillow. She seemed to be talking but there was no sound. "Well, are you tongue-tied? Whose birthday is it? Are you going to give a party?"

Cornelia's mouth moved urgently in strange shapes. "Don't do that, you bother me, daughter."

"Oh, no, Mother, oh, no. . . ."

Nonsense. It was strange about children. They disputed your every word. "No what, Cornelia?"

35   "Here's Doctor Harry."

"I won't see that boy again. He just left five minutes ago."

"That was this morning, Mother. It's night now. Here's the nurse."

"This is Doctor Harry, Mrs. Weatherall. I never saw you look so young and happy!"

"Ah, I'll never be young again—but I'd be happy if they'd let me lie in peace and get rested."

40   She thought she spoke up loudly, but no one answered. A warm weight on her forehead, a warm bracelet on her wrist, and a breeze went on whispering, trying to tell her something. A shuffle of leaves in the everlasting hand of

God. He blew on them and they danced and rattled. "Mother, don't mind, we're going to give you a little hypodermic." "Look here, daughter, how do ants get in this bed? I saw sugar ants yesterday." Did you send for Hapsy too?

It was Hapsy she really wanted. She had to go a long way back through a great many rooms to find Hapsy standing with a baby on her arm. She seemed to herself to be Hapsy also, and the baby on Hapsy's arm was Hapsy and himself and herself, all at once, and there was no surprise in the meeting. Then Hapsy melted from within and turned flimsy as gray gauze and the baby was a gauzy shadow, and Hapsy came up close and said, "I thought you'd never come," and looked at her very searchingly and said, "You haven't changed a bit!" They leaned forward to kiss, when Cornelia began whispering from a long way off, "Oh, is there anything you want to tell me? Is there anything I can do for you?"

Yes, she had changed her mind after sixty years and she would like to see George. I want you to find George. Find him and be sure to tell him I forgot him. I want him to know I had my husband just the same and my children and my house like any other woman. A good house too and a good husband that I loved and fine children out of him. Better than I hoped for even. Tell him I was given back everything he took away and more. Oh, no, oh, God, no, there was something else besides the house and the man and the children. Oh, surely they were not all? What was it? Something not given back. . . . Her breath crowded down under her ribs and grew into a monstrous frightening shape with cutting edges; it bored up into her head, and the agony was unbelievable: Yes, John, get the doctor now, no more talk, my time has come.

When this one was born it should be the last. The last. It should have been born first, for it was the one she had truly wanted. Everything came in good time. Nothing left out, left over. She was strong, in three days she would be as well as ever. Better. A woman needed milk in her to have her full health.

"Mother, do you hear me?"

"I've been telling you—"   45

"Mother, Father Connolly's here."

"I went to Holy Communion only last week. Tell him I'm not so sinful as all that."

"Father just wants to speak to you."

He could speak as much as he pleased. It was like him to drop in and inquire about her soul as if it were a teething baby, and then stay on for a cup of tea and a round of cards and gossip. He always had a funny story of some sort, usually about an Irishman who made his little mistakes and confessed them, and the point lay in some absurd thing he would blurt out in the confessional showing his struggles between native piety and original sin. Granny felt easy about her soul. Cornelia, where are your manners? Give Father Connolly a chair. She had her secret comfortable understanding with a few favorite saints who cleared a straight road to God for her. All as surely signed and sealed as the papers for the new Forty Acres. Forever . . . heirs and assigns forever. Since the day the wedding cake was not cut, but thrown out and wasted. The whole bottom dropped out of the world, and there she was blind and sweating with nothing under her feet and the walls falling away. His hand had caught her under the breast, she had not fallen, there was the freshly polished floor with the green rug on it, just as before. He had cursed like a sailor's parrot and said, "I'll kill him for you." Don't lay a hand on him, for my sake leave something to God. "Now, Ellen, you must believe what I tell you. . . ."

50   So there was nothing, nothing to worry about any more, except sometimes in the night one of the children screamed in a nightmare, and they both hustled out shaking and hunting for the matches and calling, "There, wait a minute, here we are!" John, get the doctor now, Hapsy's time has come. But there was Hapsy standing by the bed in a white cap. "Cornelia, tell Hapsy to take off her cap. I can't see her plain."

Her eyes opened very wide and the room stood out like a picture she had seen somewhere. Dark colors with the shadows rising towards the ceiling in long angles. The tall black dresser gleamed with nothing on it but John's picture, enlarged from a little one, with John's eyes very black when they should have been blue. You never saw him, so how do you know how he looked? But the man insisted the copy was perfect, it was very rich and handsome. For a picture, yes, but it's not my husband. The table by the bed had a linen cover and a candle and a crucifix. The light was blue from Cornelia's silk lampshades. No sort of light at all, just frippery. You had to live forty years with kerosene lamps to appreciate honest electricity. She felt very strong and she saw Doctor Harry with a rosy nimbus around him.

"You look like a saint, Doctor Harry, and I vow that's as near as you'll ever come to it."

"She's saying something."

"I heard you, Cornelia. What's all this carrying-on?"

55   "Father Connolly's saying—"

Cornelia's voice staggered and bumped like a cart in a bad road. It rounded corners and turned back again and arrived nowhere. Granny stepped up in the cart very lightly and reached for the reins, but a man sat beside her and she knew him by his hands, driving the cart. She did not look in his face, for she knew without seeing, but looked instead down the road where the trees leaned over and bowed to each other and a thousand birds were singing a Mass. She felt like singing too, but she put her hand in the bosom of her dress and pulled out a rosary, and Father Connolly murmured Latin in a very solemn voice and tickled her feet. My God, will you stop that nonsense? I'm a married woman. What if he did run away and leave me to face the priest by myself? I found another a whole world better. I wouldn't have exchanged my husband for anybody except St. Michael himself, and you may tell him that for me with a thank you in the bargain.

Light flashed on her closed eyelids, and a deep roaring shook her. Cornelia, is that lightning? I hear thunder. There's going to be a storm. Close all the windows. Call the children in. . . . "Mother, here we are, all of us." "Is that you, Hapsy?" "Oh, no, I'm Lydia. We drove as fast as we could." Their faces drifted above her, drifted away. The rosary fell out of her hands and Lydia put it back. Jimmy tried to help, their hands fumbled together, and Granny closed two fingers around Jimmy's thumb. Beads wouldn't do, it must be something alive. She was so amazed her thoughts ran round and round. So, my dear Lord, this is my death and I wasn't even thinking about it. My children have come to see me die. But I can't, it's not time. Oh, I always hated surprises. I wanted to give Cornelia the amethyst set—Cornelia, you're to have the amethyst set, but Hapsy's to wear it when she wants, and, Doctor Harry, do shut up. Nobody sent for you. Oh, my dear Lord, do wait a minute. I meant to do something about the Forty Acres, Jimmy doesn't need it and Lydia will later on, with that worthless husband of hers. I meant to finish the altar cloth and send six bottles of wine to Sister Borgia for her dyspepsia. I want to send six bottles of wine to Sister Borgia, Father Connolly, now don't let me forget.

Cornelia's voice made short turns and tilted over and crashed. "Oh, Mother, oh, Mother, oh, Mother. . . ."

"I'm not going, Cornelia. I'm taken by surprise. I can't go."

You'll see Hapsy again. What about her? "I thought you'd never come."   *60*
Granny made a long journey outward, looking for Hapsy. What if I don't find her? What then? Her heart sank down and down, there was no bottom to death, she couldn't come to the end of it. The blue light from Cornelia's lampshade drew into a tiny point in the center of her brain, it flickered and winked like an eye, quietly it fluttered and dwindled. Granny lay curled down within herself, amazed and watchful, staring at the point of light that was herself; her body was now only a deeper mass of shadow in an endless darkness and this darkness would curl around the light and swallow it up. God, give a sign!

For the second time there was no sign. Again no bridegroom and the priest in the house. She could not remember any other sorrow because this grief wiped them all away. Oh, no, there's nothing more cruel than this—I'll never forgive it. She stretched herself with a deep breath and blew out the light.   *1929*

CONSIDERATIONS

1. How appropriate is the title? Would you argue that it is more appropriate than, say, "The Death of Granny Weatherall"? Explain.
2. Compare the words Granny uses to describe her state of health to Doctor Harry with the words the author/narrator uses to describe Granny's physical and emotional feelings. Discuss the tone established by the contrast between the two descriptions. What does the discrepancy suggest about Granny's character?
3. Describe Granny's attitude toward death. In what ways does this attitude parallel (or contrast to) her approach to life?

4. Describe the relationships between Granny and her children. What significance do you see in the ways the children respond to their mother's old age and dying?
5. Describe Granny's response to the priest, then consider that response in relation to the final paragraph of the story.

WILLIAM FAULKNER (1879–1962)
A Rose for Emily

William Faulkner was born in New Albany, Mississippi, and lived most of his life in nearby Oxford. An erratic student, Faulkner did not graduate from high school, although he was granted special admission to the University of Mississippi and attended from 1919 to 1921. Faulkner had a profound love for and fascination with his Southern heritage, yet he also questioned and challenged what he learned from his family's history. His forebears had owned slaves, fought in the Civil War, and lived through the difficult years of Reconstruction. In his works, Faulkner creates as his setting the imaginary Yoknapatawpha County, which he positions in northern Mississippi. Most of his short stories and novels examine the lives of people who live in his mythical county. Among his best-known novels are The Sound and the Fury *(1929),* Light in August *(1932), and* Absalom! Absalom! *(1936). "A Rose for Emily" originally appeared in his collection of short stories* These Thirteen *(1931). In 1950, he received the Nobel Prize for literature, declaring in his acceptance speech that it is "the problems of the human heart in conflict with itself which alone can make good writing."*

I

When Miss Emily Grierson died, our whole town went to her funeral: the men through a sort of respectful affection for a fallen monument, the women mostly out of curiosity to see the inside of her house, which no one save an old manservant—a combined gardener and cook—had seen in at least ten years.

It was a big, squarish frame house that had once been white, decorated with cupolas and spires and scrolled balconies in the heavily lightsome style of the seventies, set on what had once been our most select street. But garages and cotton gins had encroached and obliterated even the august names of that neighborhood; only Miss Emily's house was left, lifting its stubborn and coquettish decay above the cotton wagons and the gasoline pumps—an eyesore among eyesores. And now Miss Emily had gone to join the representatives of those august names where they lay in the cedar-bemused cemetery among the ranked and anonymous graves of Union and Confederate soldiers who fell at the battle of Jefferson.

Alive, Miss Emily had been a tradition, a duty, and a care; a sort of hereditary obligation upon the town, dating from that day in 1894 when Colonel Sartoris, the mayor—he who fathered the edict that no Negro woman should appear on the streets without an apron—remitted her taxes, the dispensation dating from the death of her father on into perpetuity. Not that Miss Emily would have accepted charity. Colonel Sartoris invented an involved tale to the effect that Miss Emily's father had loaned money to the town, which the town, as a matter of business, preferred this way of repaying. Only a man of Colonel Sartoris' generation and thought could have invented it, and only a woman could have believed it.

When the next generation, with its more modern ideas, became mayors and aldermen, this arrangement created some little dissatisfaction. On the first of the year they mailed her a tax notice. February came, and there was no reply. They wrote her a formal letter, asking her to call at the sheriff's office at her convenience. A week later the mayor wrote her himself, offering to call or to send his car for her, and received in reply a note on paper of an archaic shape, in a thin, flowing calligraphy in faded ink, to the effect that she no longer went out at all. The tax notice was also enclosed, without comment.

They called a special meeting of the Board of Aldermen. A deputation   5 waited upon her, knocked at the door through which no visitor had passed since she ceased giving china-painting lessons eight or ten years earlier. They were admitted by the old Negro into a dim hall from which a stairway mounted into still more shadow. It smelled of dust and disuse—a close, dank smell. The Negro led them into the parlor. It was furnished in heavy, leather-covered furniture. When the Negro opened the blinds of one window, they could see that the leather was cracked; and when they sat down, a faint dust rose sluggishly about their thighs, spinning with slow motes in the single sun-ray. On a tarnished gilt easel before the fireplace stood a crayon portrait of Miss Emily's father.

They rose when she entered—a small, fat woman in black, with a thin gold chain descending to her waist and vanishing into her belt, leaning on an ebony cane with a tarnished gold head. Her skeleton was small and spare; perhaps that was why what would have been merely plumpness in another was obesity in her. She looked bloated, like a body long submerged in motionless water, and of that pallid hue. Her eyes, lost in the fatty ridges of her face, looked like two small pieces of coal pressed into a lump of dough as they moved from one face to another while the visitors stated their errand.

She did not ask them to sit. She just stood in the door and listened quietly until the spokesman came to a stumbling halt. Then they could hear the invisible watch ticking at the end of the gold chain.

Her voice was dry and cold. "I have no taxes in Jefferson. Colonel Sartoris explained it to me. Perhaps one of you can gain access to the city records and satisfy yourselves."

"But we have. We are the city authorities, Miss Emily. Didn't you get a notice from the sheriff, signed by him?"

10   "I received a paper, yes," Miss Emily said. "Perhaps he considers himself the sheriff . . . I have no taxes in Jefferson."

"But there is nothing on the books to show that, you see. We must go by the—"

"See Colonel Sartoris. I have no taxes in Jefferson."

"But, Miss Emily—"

"See Colonel Sartoris." (Colonel Sartoris had been dead almost ten years.) "I have no taxes in Jefferson. Tobe!" The Negro appeared. "Show these gentlemen out."

II

15   So she vanquished them, horse and foot, just as she had vanquished their fathers thirty years before about the smell. That was two years after her father's death and a short time after her sweetheart—the one we believed would marry her—had deserted her. After her father's death she went out very little; after her sweetheart went away, people hardly saw her at all. A few of the ladies had the temerity to call, but were not received, and the only sign of life about the place was the Negro man—a young man then—going in and out with a market basket.

"Just as if a man—any man—could keep a kitchen properly," the ladies said; so they were not surprised when the smell developed. It was another link between the gross, teeming world and the high and mighty Griersons.

A neighbor, a woman, complained to the mayor, Judge Stevens, eighty years old.

"But what will you have me do about it, madam?" he said.

"Why, send her word to stop it," the woman said. "Isn't there a law?"

20   "I'm sure that won't be necessary," Judge Stevens said. "It's probably just a snake or a rat that nigger of hers killed in the yard. I'll speak to him about it."

The next day he received two more complaints, one from a man who came in diffident deprecation. "We really must do something about it, Judge. I'd be the last one in the world to bother Miss Emily, but we've got to do something." That night the Board of Aldermen met—three gray-beards and one younger man, a member of the rising generation.

"It's simple enough," he said. "Send her word to have her place cleaned up. Give her a certain time to do it in, and if she don't . . ."

"Dammit, sir," Judge Stevens said, "will you accuse a lady to her face of smelling bad?"

So the next night, after midnight, four men crossed Miss Emily's lawn and slunk about the house like burglars, sniffing along the base of the brickwork and at the cellar openings while one of them performed a regular sow-

ing motion with his hand out of a sack slung from his shoulder. They broke
open the cellar door and sprinkled lime there, and in all the outbuildings. As
they recrossed the lawn, a window that had been dark was lighted and Miss
Emily sat in it, the light behind her, and her upright torso motionless as that of
an idol. They crept quietly across the lawn and into the shadow of the locusts
that lined the street. After a week or two the smell went away.

That was when people had begun to feel really sorry for her. People in   25
our town, remembering how old lady Wyatt, her great-aunt, had gone completely crazy at last, believed that the Griersons held themselves a little too
high for what they really were. None of the young men were quite good
enough for Miss Emily and such. We had long thought of them as a tableau,
Miss Emily a slender figure in white in the background, her father a spraddled
silhouette in the foreground, his back to her and clutching a horsewhip, the
two of them framed by the back-flung front door. So when she got to be thirty
and was still single, we were not pleased exactly, but vindicated; even with insanity in the family she wouldn't have turned down all of her chances if they
had really materialized.

When her father died, it got about that the house was all that was left to
her; and in a way, people were glad. At last they could pity Miss Emily. Being
left alone, and a pauper, she had become humanized. Now she too would know
the old thrill and the old despair of a penny more or less.

The day after his death all the ladies prepared to call at the house and
offer condolence and aid, as is our custom. Miss Emily met them at the door,
dressed as usual and with no trace of grief on her face. She told them that her
father was not dead. She did that for three days, with the ministers calling on
her, and the doctors, trying to persuade her to let them dispose of the body.
Just as they were about to resort to law and force, she broke down, and they
buried her father quickly.

We did not say she was crazy then. We believed she had to do that. We
remembered all the young men her father had driven away, and we knew that
with nothing left, she would have to cling to that which had robbed her, as
people will.

III

She was sick for a long time. When we saw her again, her hair was cut
short, making her look like a girl, with a vague resemblance to those angels in
colored church windows—sort of tragic and serene.

The town had just let the contracts for paving the sidewalks, and in the   30
summer after her father's death they began the work. The construction company came with niggers and mules and machinery, and a foreman named Homer
Barron, a Yankee—a big, dark, ready man, with a big voice and eyes lighter than
his face. The little boys would follow in groups to hear him cuss the niggers,

and the niggers singing in time to the rise and fall of picks. Pretty soon he knew everybody in town. Whenever you heard a lot of laughing anywhere about the square, Homer Barron would be in the center of the group. Presently we began to see him and Miss Emily on Sunday afternoons driving in the yellow-wheeled buggy and the matched team of bays from the livery stable.

At first we were glad that Miss Emily would have an interest, because the ladies all said, "Of course a Grierson would not think seriously of a Northerner, a day laborer." But there were still others, older people, who said that even grief could not cause a real lady to forget *noblesse oblige*°—without calling it *noblesse oblige*. They just said, "Poor Emily. Her kinsfolk should come to her." She had some kin in Alabama; but years ago her father had fallen out with them over the estate of old lady Wyatt, the crazy woman, and there was no communication between the two families. They had not even been represented at the funeral.

And as soon as the old people said, "Poor Emily," the whispering began. "Do you suppose it's really so?" they said to one another. "Of course it is. What else could . . ." This behind their hands; rustling of craned silk and satin behind jalousies closed upon the sun of Sunday afternoon as the thin, swift clop-clop-clop of the matched team passed: "Poor Emily."

She carried her head high enough—even when we believed that she was fallen. It was as if she demanded more than ever the recognition of her dignity as the last Grierson; as if it had wanted that touch of earthiness to reaffirm her imperviousness. Like when she bought the rat poison, the arsenic. That was over a year after they had begun to say "Poor Emily," and while the two female cousins were visiting her.

"I want some poison," she said to the druggist. She was over thirty then, still a slight woman, though thinner than usual, with cold, haughty black eyes in a face the flesh of which was strained across the temples and about the eyesockets as you imagine a lighthouse-keeper's face ought to look. "I want some poison," she said.

35   "Yes, Miss Emily. What kind? For rats and such? I'd recom—"

"I want the best you have. I don't care what kind."

The druggist named several. "They'll kill anything up to an elephant. But what you want is—"

"Arsenic," Miss Emily said. "Is that a good one?"

"Is . . . arsenic? Yes, ma'am. But what you want—"

40   "I want arsenic."

The druggist looked down at her. She looked back at him, erect, her face like a strained flag. "Why, of course," the druggist said. "If that's what you want. But the law requires you to tell what you are going to use it for."

---

noblesse oblige: The obligation of those holding high rank or social position to behave generously and courteously toward others.

Miss Emily just stared at him, her head tilted back in order to look him eye for eye, until he looked away and went and got the arsenic and wrapped it up. The Negro delivery boy brought her the package; the druggist didn't come back. When she opened the package at home there was written on the box, under the skull and bones: "For rats."

IV

So the next day we all said, "She will kill herself"; and we said it would be the best thing. When she had first begun to be seen with Homer Barron, we had said, "She will marry him." Then we said, "She will persuade him yet," because Homer himself had remarked—he liked men, and it was known that he drank with the younger men in the Elks' Club—that he was not a marrying man. Later we said, "Poor Emily" behind the jalousies as they passed on Sunday afternoon in the glittering buggy, Miss Emily with her head high and Homer Barron with his hat cocked and a cigar in his teeth, reins and whip in a yellow glove.

Then some of the ladies began to say that it was a disgrace to the town and a bad example to the young people. The men did not want to interfere, but at last the ladies forced the Baptist minister—Miss Emily's people were Episcopal—to call upon her. He would never divulge what happened during that interview, but he refused to go back again. The next Sunday they again drove about the streets, and the following day the minister's wife wrote to Miss Emily's relations in Alabama.

So she had blood-kin under her roof again and we sat back to watch developments. At first nothing happened. Then we were sure that they were to be married. We learned that Miss Emily had been to the jeweler's and ordered a man's toilet set in silver, with the letters H. B. on each piece. Two days later we learned that she had bought a complete outfit of men's clothing, including a nightshirt, and we said, "They are married." We were really glad. We were glad because the two female cousins were even more Grierson than Miss Emily had ever been. 45

So we were not surprised when Homer Barron—the streets had been finished some time since—was gone. We were a little disappointed that there was not a public blowing-off, but we believed that he had gone on to prepare for Miss Emily's coming, or to give her a chance to get rid of the cousins. (By that time it was a cabal, and we were all Miss Emily's allies to help circumvent the cousins.) Sure enough, after another week they departed. And, as we had expected all along, within three days Homer Barron was back in town. A neighbor saw the Negro man admit him at the kitchen door at dusk one evening.

And that was the last we saw of Homer Barron. And of Miss Emily for some time. The Negro man went in and out with the market basket, but the front door remained closed. Now and then we would see her at a window for a moment, as the men did that night when they sprinkled the lime, but for almost six months she did not appear on the streets. Then we knew that this was to be expected too; as if that quality of her father which had thwarted her woman's life so many times had been too virulent and too furious to die.

When we next saw Miss Emily, she had grown fat and her hair was turning gray. During the next few years it grew grayer and grayer until it attained an even pepper-and-salt iron-gray, when it ceased turning. Up to the day of her death at seventy-four it was still that vigorous iron-gray, like the hair of an active man.

From that time on her front door remained closed, save for a period of six or seven years, when she was about forty, during which she gave lessons in china-painting. She fitted up a studio in one of the downstairs rooms, where the daughters and granddaughters of Colonel Sartoris' contemporaries were sent to her with the same regularity and in the same spirit that they were sent to church on Sundays with a twenty-five-cent piece for the collection plate. Meanwhile her taxes had been remitted.

50   Then the newer generation became the backbone and the spirit of the town, and the painting pupils grew up and fell away and did not send their children to her with boxes of color and tedious brushes and pictures cut from the ladies' magazines. The front door closed upon the last one and remained closed for good. When the town got free postal delivery, Miss Emily alone refused to let them fasten the metal numbers above her door and attach a mailbox to it. She would not listen to them.

Daily, monthly, yearly we watched the Negro grow grayer and more stooped, going in and out with the market basket. Each December we sent her a tax notice, which would be returned by the post office a week later, unclaimed. Now and then we would see her in one of the downstairs windows— she had evidently shut up the top floor of the house—like the carven torso of an idol in a niche, looking or not looking at us, we could never tell which. Thus she passed from generation to generation—dear, inescapable, impervious, tranquil, and perverse.

And so she died. Fell ill in the house filled with dust and shadows, with only a doddering Negro man to wait on her. We did not even know she was sick; we had long since given up trying to get any information from the Negro. He talked to no one, probably not even to her, for his voice had grown harsh and rusty, as if from disuse.

She died in one of the downstairs rooms, in a heavy walnut bed with a curtain, her gray head propped on a pillow yellow and moldy with age and lack of sunlight.

V

The Negro met the first of the ladies at the front door and let them in, with their hushed, sibilant voices and their quick, curious glances, and then he disappeared. He walked right through the house and out the back and was not seen again.

The two female cousins came at once. They held the funeral on the sec- *55* ond day, with the town coming to look at Miss Emily beneath a mass of bought flowers, with the crayon face of her father musing profoundly above the bier and the ladies sibilant and macabre; and the very old men—some in their brushed Confederate uniforms—on the porch and the lawn, talking of Miss Emily as if she had been a contemporary of theirs, believing that they had danced with her and courted her perhaps, confusing time with its mathematical progression, as the old do, to whom all the past is not a diminishing road but, instead, a huge meadow which no winter ever quite touches, divided from them now by the narrow bottle-neck of the most recent decade of years.

Already we knew that there was one room in that region above stairs which no one had seen in forty years, and which would have to be forced. They waited until Miss Emily was decently in the ground before they opened it.

The violence of breaking down the door seemed to fill this room with pervading dust. A thin, acrid pall as of the tomb seemed to lie everywhere upon this room decked and furnished as for a bridal: upon the valance curtains of faded rose color, upon the rose-shaded lights, upon the dressing table, upon the delicate array of crystal and the man's toilet things backed with tarnished silver, silver so tarnished that the monogram was obscured. Among them lay collar and tie, as if they had just been removed, which, lifted, left upon the surface a pale crescent in the dust. Upon a chair hung the suit, carefully folded; beneath it the two mute shoes and the discarded socks.

The man himself lay in the bed.

For a long while we just stood there, looking down at the profound and fleshless grin. The body had apparently once lain in the attitude of an embrace, but now the long sleep that outlasts love, that conquers even the grimace of love, had cuckolded him. What was left of him, rotted beneath what was left of the nightshirt, had become inextricable from the bed in which he lay; and upon him and upon the pillow beside him lay that even coating of the patient and biding dust.

Then we noticed that in the second pillow was the indentation of a head. *60* One of us lifted something from it, and leaning forward, that faint and invisible dust dry and acrid in the nostrils, we saw a long strand of iron-gray hair.   *1930*

CONSIDERATIONS

1. Who is the narrator? What is his attitude toward Miss Emily? What values are reflected by his observations about Miss Emily and about the town and its citizens?
2. Reread the story, making note of details that mean more to you or that you had not noticed from your first reading. In addition, make a list of the events

of the story in chronological order. How would the story be different if it were told according to the chronology you have outlined?

3. What is your response to the title? How does it relate to the story's action and themes?

4. What role does Tobe play in the story? Why does he leave when the townspeople enter Miss Emily's house?

5. Read the following commentary and then write your response to it. Does your understanding of or reaction to the story change after reading Faulkner's explanation of his process of writing? Explain.

Commentary

WILLIAM FAULKNER
On the Meaning of "A Rose for Emily"°

Q. What is the meaning of the title "A Rose for Emily"?

A. Oh, it's simply the poor woman had had no life at all. Her father had kept her more or less locked up and then she had a lover who was about to quit her, she had to murder him. It was just "A Rose for Emily"—that's all.

Q. I was wondering, one of your short stories, "A Rose for Emily," what ever inspired you to write this story . . . ?

A. That to me was another sad and tragic manifestation of man's condition in which he dreams and hopes, in which he is in conflict with himself or with his environment or with others. In this case there was the young girl with a young girl's normal aspirations to find love and then a husband and a family, who was brow-beaten and kept down by her father, a selfish man who didn't want her to leave home because he wanted a housekeeper, and it was a natural instinct of—repressed which—you can't repress it—you can mash it down but it comes up somewhere else and very likely in a tragic form, and that was simply another manifestation of man's injustice to man, of the poor tragic human being struggling with its own heart, with others, with its environment, for the simple things which all human beings want. In that case it was a young girl that just wanted to be loved and to love and to have a husband and a family.

Q. And that purely came from your imagination?   *5*

A. Well, the story did but the condition is there. It exists. I didn't invent that condition, I didn't invent the fact that young girls dream of someone to love and children and a home, but the story of what her own particular tragedy was was invented, yes. . . .

Q. Sir, it has been argued that "A Rose for Emily" is a criticism of the North, and others have argued saying that it is a criticism of the South. Now, could this story, shall we say, be more properly classified as a criticism of the times?

A. Now that I don't know, because I was simply trying to write about people. The writer uses environment—what he knows—and if there's a symbolism in which the lover represented the North and the woman who murdered him represents the South, I don't say that's not valid and not there, but it was no intention of the writer to say, Now let's see, I'm going to write a piece

Setting: From 1957 to 1958, William Faulkner served as writer-in-residence at the University of Virginia. The following commentary, which is an excerpt from *Faulkner in the University* (1959), edited by Frederick Gwynn and Joseph Blotner, records a question-and-answer session between Faulkner and University of Virginia students.

in which I will use a symbolism for the North and another symbol for the South, that he was simply writing about people, a story which he thought was tragic and true, because it came out of the human heart, the human aspiration, the human—the conflict of conscience with glands, with the Old Adam. It was a conflict not between the North and the South so much as between, well you might say, God and Satan.

Q. Sir, just a little more on that thing. You say it's a conflict between God and Satan. Well, I don't quite understand what you mean. Who is—did one represent the—

10   A. The conflict was in Miss Emily, that she knew that you do not murder people. She had been trained that you do not take a lover. You marry, you don't take a lover. She had broken all the laws of her tradition, her background, and she had finally broken the law of God too, which says you do not take human life. And she knew she was doing wrong, and that's why her own life was wrecked. Instead of murdering one lover, and then to go and take another and when she used him up to murder him, she was expiating her crime.

Q. Was the "Rose for Emily" an idea or a character? Just how did you go about it?

A. That came from a picture of the strand of hair on the pillow. It was a ghost story. Simply a picture of a strand of hair on the pillow in the abandoned house.

ALICE WALKER (1944–   )

To Hell with Dying

> *"To Hell with Dying" appears in Alice Walker's anthology of short stories* In Love and Trouble: Stories of Black Women *(1967). For biographical information on Walker, see page 1180.*

"To hell with dying," my father would say. "These children want Mr. Sweet!"

Mr. Sweet was a diabetic and an alcoholic and a guitar player and lived down the road from us on a neglected cotton farm. My older brothers and sisters got the most benefit from Mr. Sweet, for when they were growing up he had quite a few years ahead of him and so was capable of being called back from the brink of death any number of times—whenever the voice of my father reached him as he lay expiring. "To hell with dying, man," my father would say, pushing the wife away from the bedside (in tears although she knew the death was not necessarily the last one unless Mr. Sweet really wanted it to be). "These children want Mr. Sweet!" And they did want him, for at a signal from Father they would come crowding around the bed and throw themselves on the covers, and whoever was the smallest at the time would kiss him all over his wrinkled brown face and tickle him so that he would laugh all down in his stomach, and his mustache, which was long and sort of straggly, would shake like Spanish moss and was also that color.

Mr. Sweet had been ambitious as a boy, wanted to be a doctor or lawyer or sailor, only to find that black men fare better if they are not. Since he could become none of these things he turned to fishing as his only earnest career and playing the guitar as his only claim to doing anything extraordinarily well. His son, the only one that he and his wife, Miss Mary, had, was shiftless as the day is long and spent money as if he were trying to see the bottom of the mint, which Mr. Sweet would tell him was the clean brown palm of his hand. Miss Mary loved her "baby," however, and worked hard to get him the "li'l necessaries" of life, which turned out mostly to be women.

Mr. Sweet was a tall, thinnish man with thick kinky hair going dead white. He was dark brown, his eyes were squinty and sort of bluish, and he chewed Brown Mule tobacco. He was constantly on the verge of being blind drunk, for he brewed his own liquor and was not in the least a stingy sort of man, and was always very melancholy and sad, though frequently when he was "feelin' good" he'd dance around the yard with us, usually keeling over just as my mother came to see what the commotion was.

Toward all of us children he was very kind, and had the grace to be shy   5 with us, which is unusual in grown-ups. He had great respect for my mother for she never held his drunkenness against him and would let us play with him even when he was about to fall in the fireplace from drink. Although Mr. Sweet would sometimes lose complete or nearly complete control of his head and neck so that he would loll in his chair, his mind remained strangely acute and his speech not too affected. His ability to be drunk and sober at the same time made him an ideal playmate, for he was as weak as we were and we could usually best him in wrestling, all the while keeping a fairly coherent conversation going.

We never felt anything of Mr. Sweet's age when we played with him. We loved his wrinkles and would draw some on our brows to be like him, and his white hair was my special treasure and he knew it and would never come to visit us just after he had had his hair cut off at the barbershop. Once he came to our house for something, probably to see my father about fertilizer for his crops because, although he never paid the slightest attention to his crops, he liked to know what things would be best to use on them if he ever did. Anyhow, he had not come with his hair since he had just had it shaved off at the barbershop. He wore a huge straw hat to keep off the sun and also to keep his head away from me. But as soon as I saw him I ran up and demanded that he take me up and kiss me with his funny beard which smelled so strongly of tobacco. Looking forward to burying my small fingers into his woolly hair I threw away his hat only to find he had done something to his hair, that it was no longer there! I let out a squall which made my mother think that Mr. Sweet had finally dropped me in the well or something and from that day I've been wary of men in hats. However, not long after, Mr. Sweet showed up with his hair grown out and just as white and kinky and impenetrable as it ever was.

Mr. Sweet used to call me his princess, and I believed it. He made me feel pretty at five and six, and simply outrageously devastating at the blazing age of eight and a half. When he came to our house with his guitar the whole family would stop whatever they were doing to sit around him and listen to him play. He liked to play "Sweet Georgia Brown," that was what he called me sometimes, and also he liked to play "Caldonia" and all sorts of sweet, sad, wonderful songs which he sometimes made up. It was from one of these songs that I heard that he had had to marry Miss Mary when he had in fact loved somebody else (now living in Chi-ca-go, or De-stroy, Michigan). He was not sure that Joe Lee, her "baby," was also his baby. Sometimes he would cry and that was an indication that he was about to die again. And so we would all get prepared, for we were sure to be called upon.

I was seven the first time I remember actually participating in one of Mr. Sweet's "revivals"—my parents told me I had participated before, I had been the one chosen to kiss him and tickle him long before I knew the rite of Mr. Sweet's rehabilitation. He had come to our house, it was a few years after his wife's death, and was very sad, and also, typically, very drunk. He sat on the floor next to me and my older brother, the rest of the children were grown up and lived elsewhere, and began to play his guitar and cry. I held his woolly head in my arms and wished I could have been old enough to have been the woman he loved so much and that I had not been lost years and years ago.

When he was leaving, my mother said to us that we'd better sleep light that night for we'd probably have to go over to Mr. Sweet's before daylight. And we did. For soon after we had gone to bed one of the neighbors knocked on our door and called my father and said that Mr. Sweet was sinking fast and if he wanted to get in a word before the crossover he'd better shake a leg and get over to Mr. Sweet's house. All the neighbors knew to come to our house if something was wrong with Mr. Sweet, but they did not know how we always managed to make him well, or at least stop him from dying, when he was so often near death. As soon as we heard the cry we got up, my brother and I and my mother and father, and put on our clothes. We hurried out of the house and down the road for we were always afraid that we might someday be too late and Mr. Sweet would get tired of dallying.

10　　　When we got to the house, a very poor shack really, we found the front room full of neighbors and relatives and someone met us at the door and said it was all very sad that old Mr. Sweet Little (for Little was his family name, although we mostly ignored it) was about to kick the bucket. My parents were advised not to take my brother and me into the "death room," seeing we were so young and all, but we were so much more accustomed to the death room than he that we ignored him and dashed in without giving his warning a second thought. I was almost in tears, for these deaths upset me fearfully, and the thought of how much depended on me and my brother (who was such a ham most of the time) made me very nervous.

The doctor was bending over the bed and turned back to tell us for at least the tenth time in the history of my family that, alas, old Mr. Sweet Little was dying and that the children had best not see the face of implacable death (I didn't know what "implacable" was, but whatever it was, Mr. Sweet was not!). My father pushed him rather abruptly out of the way saying, as he always did and very loudly for he was saying it to Mr. Sweet, "To hell with dying, man, these children want Mr. Sweet"—which was my cue to throw myself upon the bed and kiss Mr. Sweet all around the whiskers and under the eyes and around the collar of his nightshirt where he smelled so strongly of all sorts of things, mostly liniment.

I was very good at bringing him around, for as soon as I saw that he was struggling to open his eyes I knew he was going to be all right, and so could finish my revival sure of success. As soon as his eyes were open he would begin to smile and that way I knew that I had surely won. Once, though, I got a tremendous scare, for he could not open his eyes and later I learned that he had had a stroke and that one side of his face was stiff and hard to get into motion. When he began to smile I could tickle him in earnest because I was sure that nothing would get in the way of his laughter, although once he began to cough so hard that he almost threw me off his stomach, but that was when I was very small, little more than a baby, and my bushy hair had gotten in his nose.

When we were sure he would listen to us we would ask him why he was in bed and when he was coming to see us again and could we play his guitar, which more than likely would be leaning against the bed. His eyes would get all misty and he would sometimes cry out loud, but we never let it embarrass us, for he knew that we loved him and that we sometimes cried too for no reason. My parents would leave the room to just the three of us; Mr. Sweet, by that time, would be propped up in bed with a number of pillows behind his head and with me sitting and lying on his shoulder and along his chest. Even when he had trouble breathing he would not ask me to get down. Looking into my eyes he would shake his white head and run a scratchy old finger all around my hairline, which was rather low down, nearly to my eyebrows, and made some people say I looked like a baby monkey.

My brother was very generous in all this, he let me do all the revival-   *15* ing—he had done it for years before I was born and so was glad to be able to pass it on to someone new. What he would do while I talked to Mr. Sweet was pretend to play the guitar, in fact pretend that he was a young version of Mr. Sweet, and it always made Mr. Sweet glad to think that someone wanted to be like him—of course, we did not know this then, we played the thing by ear, and whatever he seemed to like, we did. We were desperately afraid that he was just going to take off one day and leave us.

It did not occur to us that we were doing anything special; we had not learned that death was final when it did come. We thought nothing of triumphing over it so many times, and in fact became a trifle contemptuous of people who let themselves be carried away. It did not occur to us that if our father had been dying we could not have stopped it, that Mr. Sweet was the only person over whom we had power.

When Mr. Sweet was in his eighties I was studying in the university many miles from home. I saw him whenever I went home, but he was never on the verge of dying that I could tell and I began to feel that my anxiety for his health and psychological well-being was unnecessary. By this time he not only had a mustache but a long flowing snow-white beard, which I loved and combed and braided for hours. He was very peaceful, fragile, gentle, and the only jarring note about him was his old steel guitar, which he still played in the old sad, sweet, down-home blues way.

On Mr. Sweet's ninetieth birthday I was finishing my doctorate in Massachusetts and had been making arrangements to go home for several weeks' rest. That morning I got a telegram telling me that Mr. Sweet was dying again and could I please drop everything and come home. Of course I could. My dissertation could wait and my teachers would understand when I explained to them when I got back. I ran to the phone, called the airport, and within four hours I was speeding along the dusty road to Mr. Sweet's.

The house was more dilapidated than when I was last there, barely a shack, but it was overgrown with yellow roses which my family had planted many years ago. The air was heavy and sweet and very peaceful. I felt strange walking through the gate and up the old rickety steps. But the strangeness left me as I caught sight of the long white beard I loved so well flowing down the thin body over the familiar quilt coverlet. Mr. Sweet!

20   His eyes were closed tight and his hands, crossed over his stomach, were thin and delicate, no longer scratchy. I remembered how always before I had run and jumped up on him just anywhere; now I knew he would not be able to support my weight. I looked around at my parents, and was surprised to see that my father and mother also looked old and frail. My father, his own hair very gray, leaned over the quietly sleeping old man, who, incidentally, smelled still of wine and tobacco, and said, as he'd done so many times, "To hell with dying, man! My daughter is home to see Mr. Sweet!" My brother had not been able to come as he was in the war in Asia. I bent down and gently stroked the closed eyes and gradually they began to open. The closed, wine-stained lips twitched a little, then parted in a warm, slightly embarrassed smile. Mr. Sweet could see me and he recognized me and his eyes looked very spry and twinkly for a moment. I put my head down on the pillow next to his and we just looked at each other for a long time. Then he began to trace my peculiar hairline with a thin, smooth finger. I closed my eyes when his finger halted above my ear (he used to rejoice at the dirt in my ears when I was little), his hand

stayed cupped around my cheek. When I opened my eyes, sure that I had reached him in time, his were closed.

Even at twenty-four how could I believe that I had failed? That Mr. Sweet was really gone? He had never gone before. But when I looked at my parents I saw that they were holding back tears. They had loved him dearly. He was like a piece of rare and delicate china which was always being saved from breaking and which finally fell. I looked long at the old face, the wrinkled forehead, the red lips, the hands that still reached out to me. Soon I felt my father pushing something cool into my hands. It was Mr. Sweet's guitar. He had asked them months before to give it to me; he had known that even if I came next time he would not be able to respond in the old way. He did not want me to feel that my trip had been for nothing.

The old guitar! I plucked the strings, hummed "Sweet Georgia Brown." The magic of Mr. Sweet lingered still in the cool steel box. Through the window I could catch the fragrant delicate scent of tender yellow roses. The man on the high old-fashioned bed with the quilt coverlet and the flowing white beard had been my first love.   *1967*

CONSIDERATIONS

1. What is your response to Mr. Sweet? The mother and father in the story see him as a fine companion to accompany the growing years of their children. Do you agree? Explain.
2. What reasons does the narrator suggest for Mr. Sweet's life choices (including his many "deaths")? What is your response to these reasons?
3. What do the narrator and her brother learn from the many "rescues" they perform? Do you see these lessons as negative? Positive? A combination? Explain.
4. The narrator leaves her dissertation and her classes behind—assuming that her teachers will understand—to rush to the bedside of Mr. Sweet. If you were one of her professors, listening to her explanation, how would you respond? Explain your reasons.
5. What does the narrator learn from her final encounter with Mr. Sweet? Consider the way she sees her parents as well as the way she sees herself. What insights does she seem to have about the relationship between life and death?

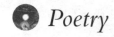 *Poetry*

JOHN DONNE (1572–1631)
Death, be not proud

> *John Donne was forced to leave Oxford University without a degree because he refused to repudiate his Roman Catholic heritage at a time when anti-Catholic sentiment in England ran high. For years, he educated himself and struggled through prayer and reading to decide between the Roman Catholic and Anglican churches. During this time, he also became known as a witty, wise poet whose output varied from secular, erotic poems to holy sonnets. Finally, in 1615, Donne was ordained in the Anglican Church and became known as one of the greatest preachers of his time.*

Death, be not proud, though some have called thee
Mighty and dreadful, for thou are not so;
For those whom thou think'st thou dost overthrow
Die not, poor Death, nor yet canst thou kill me.
5   From rest and sleep, which but thy pictures be,
Much pleasure; then from thee much more must flow,
And soonest our best men with thee do go,
Rest of their bones, and soul's delivery.
Thou art slave to fate, chance, kings, and desperate men,
10 And dost with poison, war, and sickness dwell,
And poppy or charms can make us sleep as well
And better than thy stroke; why swell'st thou then?
One short sleep past, we wake eternally
And death shall be no more; Death, thou shalt die.   *c. 1610*

CONSIDERATIONS

1. In this poem, the speaker directly addresses death. Death becomes personified, rather than remaining an abstract concept. Give a brief description of the character Death as pictured by the speaker.

2. Discuss the paradox (apparent contradiction) in the final line: "Death, thou shalt die." How can death die? What value system is implied by this statement?

3. Using the approach suggested here, plan a speech addressing an abstract concept: Love, Anger, Hope, Envy, Pride (or a concept of your choice).

More Resources on
John Donne and "Death, be not proud"

In *ARIEL*
- Brief biography of Donne
- Text of "Death, be not proud," with hyperlinked comments, in addition to several other hyperlinked Donne poems
- Audio clip of dramatic reading of "Death, be not proud" and of "The Sun Rising"
- Video clip of documentary on the metaphysical peots
- Analysis of figurative language in Donne's writing
- Bibliography of scholarly works on Donne

 EMILY DICKINSON (1830–1886)

For biographical information on Emily Dickinson, see page 1239.

Apparently with no surprise

Apparently with no surprise
To any happy Flower
The Frost beheads it at its play—
In accidental power—
The blonde Assassin passes on—   5
The Sun proceeds unmoved
To measure off another Day
For an Approving God.   *c. 1884*

CONSIDERATIONS

1. Who or what might be represented by the "blonde Assassin"?
2. What is implied by the phrase "an Approving God"? Why not "the Approving God" or "our Approving God"? To what and why does this God give approval?
3. What view of death does the poem suggest?

I heard a Fly buzz—when I died—

I heard a Fly buzz—when I died—
The Stillness in the Room
Was like the Stillness in the Air—
Between the Heaves of Storm—

5   The Eyes around—had wrung them dry—
And Breaths were gathering firm
For the last Onset—when the King
Be witnessed—in the Room—

I willed my Keepsakes—Signed away
10   What portion of me be
Assignable—and then it was
There interposed a Fly—

With Blue—uncertain stumbling Buzz—
Between the light—and me—
15   And then the Windows failed—and then
I could not see to see—   *c. 1862*

CONSIDERATIONS

1. Isolate four significant words that are repeated in this poem. In what ways do these four words represent the tension between dying and living?

2. How would you describe the speaker's attitude toward his or her impending death? Despairing? Peaceful? Accepting? Woeful? Something else?

The Bustle in a House

The Bustle in a House
The Morning after Death
Is solemnest of industries
Enacted upon Earth—

5   The Sweeping up the Heart
And putting Love away
We shall not want to use again
Until Eternity.   *c. 1866*

CONSIDERATIONS

1. What difference would it make if Dickinson had used the homonym "mourning" instead of "morning" in line 2?

2. How would you characterize the speaker's tone in this poem?
3. How realistic is the poem? Are people able to put "Love away" the morning after someone dies? What do you think Dickinson's intention is here?

More Resources on
Emily Dickinson and her poetry

 In *ARIEL*
- Brief biography of Dickinson
- Complete texts of Dickinson poems with hyperlinked comments
- Video discussion of Dickinson's writing
- Video clip exploring the world of Dickinson's writing
- Video clip of a dramatic reading of "Because I could not stop for Death"
- Audio clips of readings of "My life closed twice before its close" and "I taste a liquor never brewed"
- Analysis of Dickinson's style
- Bibliography of scholarly works on Dickinson

 In the Online Learning Center for *Responding to Literature*
- Brief biography of Dickinson
- List of major works by Dickinson
- Text of Dickinson's "I heard a Fly buzz—when I died—"
- Web links to more resources on Dickinson
- Additional questions for experiencing and interpreting Dickinson's writing

---

A. E. HOUSMAN (1859–1936)

To an Athlete Dying Young

For biographical information on A. E. Housman, see page 234.

The time you won your town the race
We chaired you through the market-place;
Man and boy stood cheering by,
And home we brought you shoulder-high.

5   To-day, the road all runners come,
     Shoulder-high we bring you home,
     And set you at your threshold down,
     Townsman of a stiller town.

     Smart lad, to slip betimes away
10   From fields where glory does not stay
     And early though the laurel grows
     It withers quicker than the rose.

     Eyes the shady night has shut
     Cannot see the record cut,
15   And silence sounds no worse than cheers
     After earth has stopped the ears:

     Now you will not swell the rout
     Of lads that wore their honours out,
     Runners whom renown outran
20   And the name died before the man.

     So set, before its echoes fade,
     The fleet foot on the sill of shade,
     And hold to the low lintel up
     The still-defended challenge-cup.

25   And round that early-laurelled head
     Will flock to gaze the strengthless dead,
     And find unwithered on its curls
     The garland briefer than a girl's.   *1896*

CONSIDERATIONS

1. Discuss the differences between the first two stanzas in terms of tone and images. What reasons might Housman have had for adopting a predictable rhythm and rhyme scheme to go with this topic?
2. In one sentence, summarize the speaker's point about youth and glory in the third, fourth, and fifth stanzas? What is your response to this point?
3. The intended audience for this poem is not, of course, the young athlete who has died. Who, then, is its audience, and what might the poet hope this audience would understand as the theme of this poem?

e. e. cummings (1894–1962)
Buffalo Bill's

> *Edward Estlin Cummings was born in Cambridge, Massachusetts, and earned*
> *bachelor's and master's degrees from Harvard University before serving as a vol-*
> *unteer ambulance driver in France during World War I. His experimental punc-*
> *tuation, line division, and capitalization brought him wide attention and acclaim*
> *as an innovative and entertaining poet.*

Buffalo Bill's
defunct
    who used to
    ride a watersmooth-silver
                  stallion   5
and break onetwothreefourfive   pigeonsjustlikethat
                            Jesus
he was a handsome man
               and what i want to know is
how do you like your blueeyed boy   10
Mister Death   *1923*

CONSIDERATIONS

1. Consider the effect of the word "defunct" as opposed to these words:
   "dead," "deceased," "passed on," "gone to his just reward."
2. How would the poem be changed if the lines were printed as traditional
   sentences rather than in the arrangement cummings chose?
3. Three names are capitalized in this poem: Buffalo Bill, Jesus, Mister Death.
   Consider the possible significance of this choice. For example, what relationship among the three might be implied?

More Resources on
e. e. cummings

 In the Online Learning Center for *Responding to Literature*
- Brief biography of cummings
- List of major works by cummings
- Web links to more resources on cummings

LANGSTON HUGHES (1902–1967)

Night Funeral in Harlem

For biographical information on Langston Hughes, see page 382.

Night funeral
In Harlem:

Where did they get
Them two fine cars?

5 Insurance man, he did not pay—
His insurance lapsed the other day—
Yet they got a satin box
For his head to lay.

Night funeral
10 In Harlem:

Who was it sent
That wreath of flowers?

Them flowers came
from that poor boy's friends—
15 They'll want flowers, too,
When they meet their ends.

Night funeral
In Harlem:

Who preached that
20 *Black boy to his grave?*

Old preacher man
Preached that boy away—
Charged Five Dollars
His girl friend had to pay.

25 Night funeral
In Harlem:

When it was all over
And the lid shut on his head
and the organ had done played
30 and the last prayers been said
and six pallbearers
Carried him out for dead
And off down Lenox Avenue

More Resources on
Langston Hughes

In *ARIEL*

- Brief biography of Hughes
- Complete texts of additional Hughes poems, such as "I, Too" and "Dream Deferred"
- Audio clip of a reading of the Hughes poem "Theme for English B"
- Analysis of figurative writing in Hughes's poetry
- Bibliography of scholarly works on Hughes

In the Online Learning Center for *Responding to Literature*

- Brief biography of Hughes
- List of major works by Hughes
- Web links to more resources on Hughes
- Additional questions for experiencing and interpreting Hughes's writing

That long black hearse done sped,
  The street light   *35*
  At his corner
  Shined just like a tear—
That boy that they was mournin'
Was so dear, so dear
To them folks that brought the flowers,   *40*
To that girl who paid the preacher man—
It was all their tears that made
  That poor boy's
  Funeral grand.

Night funeral   *45*
In Harlem.   *1949*

CONSIDERATIONS

1. What is so distinct and unusual about having a funeral at night? In what ways does the night setting affect the mood of this piece?

2. What does the deceased person receive in death that he may not have received in his life?
3. Who is missing from this funeral, and what difference does that make? What does this absence indicate about life in Harlem?
4. What does the speaker mean in the end when he says, "It was all their tears that made/That poor boy's/Funeral grand."

THEODORE ROETHKE (1908–1963)

Elegy for Jane
My Student, Thrown by a Horse

For biographical information on Theodore Roethke, see page 733.

I remember the neckcurls, limp and damp as tendrils;
And her quick look, a sidelong pickerel° smile;
And how, once startled into talk, the light syllables leaped for her,
And she balanced in the delight of her thought,
5   A wren, happy, tail into the wind,
Her song trembling the twigs and small branches.
The shade sang with her;
The leaves, their whispers turned to kissing;
And the mold sang in the bleached valleys under the rose.

10   Oh, when she was sad, she cast herself down into such a pure depth,
Even a father could not find her:
Scraping her cheek against straw;
Stirring the clearest water.
My sparrow, you are not here,
15   Waiting like a fern, making a spiny shadow.
The sides of wet stones cannot console me,
Nor the moss, wound with the last light.

If only I could nudge you from this sleep,
My maimed darling, my skittery pigeon.
20   Over this damp grave I speak the words of my love:
I, with no rights in this matter,
Neither father nor lover.   *1958*

2 *pickerel:* A fish that swims very quickly.

CONSIDERATIONS

1. Describe the emotions that the speaker, Jane's teacher, has for his student. Do you think these are typical emotions for a teacher to have? Explain.
2. Examine the bird imagery that the speaker uses to describe Jane. What do these images reveal about Jane? What do they suggest about the speaker's relationship to Jane?
3. In the last stanza, the speaker says, "I speak the words of love." What words do you find in this poem that connote love? Explain.

DENISE LEVERTOV (1923–1997)

During a Son's Dangerous Illness

> *Denise Levertov, whose life is described in the chapter "War and Power" (page 968), had a son, Nikolai Goodman, in 1949. He is now a poet and a painter.*

You could die before me—
I've known it
always, the
dreaded worst, "unnatural" but
possible   5
in the play
of matter, matter and
growth and
fate.

My sister Philippa died   10
twelve years before I was born—
the perfect, laughing firstborn,
a gift to be cherished as my orphaned mother
had not been cherished. Suddenly:
death, a baby   15

cold and still.

Parent, child—death ignores
protocol, a sweep of its cape brushes
this one or that one at random
into the dust, it was   20
not even looking.
                    What becomes

of the past if the future
snaps off, brittle,
25   the present left as a jagged edge
opening on nothing?

Grief for the menaced world—lost rivers,
poisoned lakes—all creatures, perhaps
to be fireblasted
30   off the
whirling cinder we
love but not enough . . .
The grief I'd know if I
lived into
35   your unthinkable death
is a splinter
of that selfsame grief,
infinitely smaller but
the same in kind:
40   one
stretching the mind's fibers to touch
eternal nothingness,
the other
tasting in fear, the
45   desolation of
survival.   *1987*

CONSIDERATIONS

1. How would you describe the speaker's tone in this piece, and how does this tone relate to the differences between knowing about death and experiencing it firsthand?
2. Find the section in this poem where the speaker sounds as if she is preparing herself for this death. What does she imagine the future to be like without her son?
3. What is "the swirling cinder" (line 31) in this poem, and what point does the author make about death by using this comparison?

SEAMUS HEANEY (1939–   )

Punishment

For biographical information on Seamus Heaney, see page 239.

I can feel the tug
of the halter at the nape
of her neck, the wind
on her naked front.

It blows her nipples   5
to amber beads,
it shakes the frail rigging
of her ribs.

I can see her drowned
body in the bog,   10
the weighing stone,
the floating rods and boughs.

Under which at first
she was a barked sapling
that is dug up   15
oak-bone, brain-firkin:°

her shaved head
like a stubble of black corn,
her blindfold a soiled bandage,
her noose a ring   20

to store
the memories of love.
Little adulteress,
before they punished you

you were flaxen-haired,   25
undernourished, and your
tar-black face was beautiful.
My poor scapegoat,

I almost love you
but would have cast, I know,   30

6 *brain-firkin:* A firkin is a small vessel or cask, here, the skull holding her brain.

the stones of silence.
I am the artful voyeur

of your brain's exposed
and darkened combs,
35   your muscles' webbing
and all your numbered bones:

I who have stood dumb
when your betraying sisters,
cauled in tar,
40   wept by the railings,

who would connive
in civilized outrage
yet understand the exact
and tribal, intimate revenge.   1975

CONSIDERATIONS

1. Where does the speaker see the remains of the woman he describes? What are the details that led you to your answer?
2. Why has the woman been punished and what punishment was she given?
3. What is the speaker's response to his understanding of the woman's crime and means of death? How does he imagine he would have responded had he lived at the time of the woman's death?

WILLIAM TREMBLAY (1940–   )

The Lost Boy

Born in Southbridge, Massachusetts, William Tremblay has taught for more than thirty years in the graduate writing program at Colorado State University. He has published seven volumes of poetry, a screenplay, and a novel, The June Rise. *He is active in ecological programs in the Poudre Valley area in Colorado.*

Across the Poudre river bridge
stands a stone monument to a lost boy.
Carved words fix the mystery. Did
he wander off, or was he carried off
5   by tooth or talon? Family, friends,

searched the mountainside calling his
name. The weather turned. Sleet, wind,
snow in slants across the ponderosas.
He blacked out under the canyon's
Milky Way. I hear his cries in   10
echoing arroyos. Though his bones
mouldered in cold drizzle he comes
crashing through wild plum thickets
clutching at my shirt, asking where I was
in his sagebrush hours. Through his   15
ripped jacket a flash of bone. I dare not
touch his skeletal shoulder. He's forgotten
how to be alive. The climb is no relief,
his weight dogs my knees. Breezes
sough through purple yarrow aspen groves,   20
dry waterfalls. I reach the cloud meadows,
hairpin switchbacks until Mount
Greyrock juts its granite forehead into
one hard thought: what remains unfinished
in the soul keeps doubling back   25
until earth and sky are balanced aches
like the cliff swallow's swift flight.   *2003*

CONSIDERATIONS

1. Why is this poem titled "The Lost Boy" instead of "The Dead Boy?" What
   does the title reveal about the culture as well as the theme of this poem?
2. What are the overriding emotions that the speaker experiences, and what
   images in this poem convey those emotions?
3. Who is the "I" in this poem, and what are the reasons this person is making
   this climb? What is he or she really attempting to reach?

MICHAEL LASSELL (1947–   )

How to Watch Your Brother Die

> *Michael Lassell is a native New Yorker who holds degrees from Colgate University, California Institute of the Arts, and the Yale School of Drama. Currently an editor for* Metropolitan Home, *he has written for the* LA Weekly, *the* Herald Examiner, LA Style, *the* Advocate, Interview, *and the* New York Times.

In addition to two books of prose fiction and three of nonfiction, he has written three books of poetry: Poems for Lost and Un-Lost Boys *(1985), which is the source of the selection here;* Decade Dance: Poems *(1990); and* A Flame for the Touch That Matters *(1998). He has also edited several volumes of poetry; the most recent is* The World in Us: Lesbian and Gay Poetry of the Next Wave *(with Elena Georgiou) for St. Martin's Press.*

When the call comes, be calm.
Say to your wife, "My brother is dying. I have to fly
to California."
Try not to be shocked that he already looks like
5   a cadaver.
Say to the young man sitting by your brother's side,
"I'm his brother."
Try not to be shocked when the young man says,
"I'm his lover. Thanks for coming."

10   Listen to the doctor with a steel face on.
Sign the necessary forms.
Tell the doctor you will take care of everything.
Wonder why doctors are so remote.

Watch the lover's eyes as they stare into
15   your brother's eyes as they stare into
space.
Wonder what they see there.
Remember the time he was jealous and
opened your eyebrow with a sharp stick.
20   Forgive him out loud
even if he can't
understand you.
Realize the scar will be
all that's left of him.

25   Over coffee in the hospital cafeteria
say to the lover, "You're an extremely good-looking
young man."
Hear him say,
"I never thought I was good enough looking to
30   deserve your brother."

Watch the tears well up in his eyes. Say,
"I'm sorry. I don't know what it means to be
the lover of another man."
Hear him say,
35   "It's just like a wife, only the commitment is

deeper because the odds against you are so much
greater."
Say nothing, but
take his hand like a brother's.

Drive to Mexico for unproved drugs that might   40
help him live longer.
Explain what they are to the border guard.
Fill with rage when he informs you,
"You can't bring those across."

Begin to grow loud.   45
Feel the lover's hand on your arm
restraining you. See in the guard's eye
how much a man can hate another man.
Say to the lover, "How can you stand it?"
Hear him say, "You get used to it."   50
Think of one of your children getting used to
another man's hatred.

Call your wife on the telephone. Tell her,
"He hasn't much time.
I'll be home soon." Before you hang up say,   55
"How could anyone's commitment be deeper than
a husband and wife?" Hear her say,
"Please. I don't want to know all the details."

When he slips into an irrevocable coma,
hold his lover in your arms while he sobs,   60
no longer strong. Wonder how much longer
you will be able to be strong.
Feel how it feels to hold a man in your arms
whose arms are used to holding men.
Offer God anything to bring your brother back.   65
Know you have nothing God could possibly want.
Curse God, but do not
abandon Him.

Stare at the face of the funeral director
when he tells you he will not   70
embalm the body for fear of
contamination. Let him see in your eyes
how much a man can hate another man.

Stand beside a casket covered in flowers,
white flowers. Say,   75
"Thank you for coming," to each of several hundred men

who file past in tears, some of them
holding hands. Know that your brother's life
was not what you imagined. Overhear two
80   mourners say, "I wonder who'll be next?" and
"I don't care anymore,
as long as it isn't you."

Arrange to take an early flight home.
His lover will drive you to the airport.
85   When your flight is announced say,
awkwardly, "If I can do anything, please
let me know." Do not flinch when he says,
"Forgive yourself for not wanting to know him
after he told you. He did."
90   Stop and let it soak in. Say,
"He forgave me, or he knew himself?"
"Both," the lover will say, not knowing what else
to do. Hold him like a brother while he
kisses you on the cheek. Think that
95   you haven't been kissed by a man since
your father died. Think.
"This is no moment not to be strong."

Fly first class and drink Scotch. Stroke
your split eyebrow with a finger and
100   think of your brother alive. Smile
at the memory and think
how your children will feel in your arms,
warm and friendly and without challenge.   *1985*

CONSIDERATIONS

1. How would this poem be changed if it were titled, "How to Watch My
   Brother Die"? How does the actual title reflect the central conflict within
   this piece?
2. Trace the pattern of "advice" that the speaker is giving in this poem, beginning with "stay calm" and ending with "think of how your children will
   feel in your arms." Where did the speaker begin, how and when does he
   change, and what is the meaning of his last piece of advice?
3. What scenes reveal the most love? Which ones reveal the most hate? What
   other opposing emotions do you find within this poem, and which ones, in
   the end, win out?

Drama

HARVEY FIERSTEIN (1954–   )
On Tidy Endings

> *Born in Brooklyn to parents who had emigrated from eastern Europe, Harvey*
> *Fierstein began his career in the theater early: at age eleven, he was a founding*
> *actor in the Gallery Players Community Theater in Brooklyn. In addition, he*
> *studied painting at New York's Pratt Institute and acted in several Broadway*
> *plays before writing* Torch Song Trilogy *(1982), which won the Drama Desk*
> *Award, the Theater World Award, and the Tony Award for best play. He also*
> *won the Tony for best actor in the Broadway production of this play and holds*
> *the distinction of being the first person to earn Tonys for both best play and best*
> *actor for the same production. His plays present themes related to the lives of gay*
> *men; Fierstein said of his success with* Torch Song Trilogy *that the play*
> *demonstrated that "you could use a gay context and a gay experience and speak*
> *in universal truths."* On Tidy Endings *appears in* Safe Sex, *a collection of*
> *Fierstein's plays (1987).*

Scene *The curtain rises on a deserted, modern Upper West Side apartment. In the*
bright daylight that pours in through the windows we can see the living room of the
apartment. Far Stage Right is the galley kitchen, next to it the multilocked front door
with intercom. Stage Left reveals a hallway that leads to the two bedrooms and baths.

Though the room is still fully furnished (couch, coffee table, etc.), there are boxes
stacked against the wall and several photographs and paintings are on the floor leaving
shadows on the wall where they once hung. Obviously someone is moving out. From the
way the boxes are neatly labeled and stacked, we know that this is an organized person.

From the hallway just outside the door we hear the rattling of keys and two ar-
guing voices:

JIM *(Offstage)*: I've got to be home by four. I've got practice.
MARION *(Offstage)*: I'll get you to practice, don't worry.
JIM *(Offstage)*: I don't want to go in there.
MARION *(Offstage)*: Jimmy, don't make Mommy crazy, alright? We'll go inside,
   I'll call Aunt Helen and see if you can go down and play with Robbie.

> *(The door opens.* MARION *is a handsome woman of forty. Dressed in a busi-*
> *ness suit, her hair conservatively combed, she appears to be going to a business*
> *meeting.* JIM *is a boy of eleven. His playclothes are typical, but someone has ob-*
> *viously just combed his hair.* MARION *recovers the key from the lock.)*

5   JIM: Why can't I just go down and ring the bell?
    MARION: Because I said so.

> *(As* MARION *steps into the room she is struck by some unexpected emotion. She freezes in her path and stares at the empty apartment.* JIM *lingers by the door.)*

    JIM: I'm going downstairs.
    MARION: Jimmy, please.
    JIM: This place gives me the creeps.
10   MARION: This was your father's apartment. There's nothing creepy about it.
    JIM: Says you.
    MARION: You want to close the door, please?

> *(*JIM *reluctantly obeys.)*

    MARION: Now, why don't you go check your room and make sure you didn't leave anything.
    JIM: It's empty.
15   MARION: Go look.
    JIM: I looked last time.
    MARION *(Trying to be patient)*: Honey, we sold the apartment. You're never going to be here again. Go make sure you have everything you want.
    JIM: But Uncle Arthur packed everything.
    MARION *(Less patiently)*: Go make sure.
20   JIM: There's nothing in there.
    MARION *(Exploding)*: I said make sure!

> *(*JIM *jumps, then realizing that she's not kidding, obeys.)*

    MARION: Everything's an argument with that one. *(She looks around the room and breathes deeply. There is sadness here. Under her breath:)* I can still smell you. *(Suddenly not wanting to be alone)* Jimmy? Are you okay?
    JIM *(Returning)*: Nothing. Told you so.
    MARION: Uncle Arthur must have worked very hard. Make sure you thank him.
25   JIM: What for? Robbie says, *(Fey mannerisms)* "They love to clean up things!"
    MARION: Sometimes you can be a real joy.
    JIM: Did you call Aunt Helen?
    MARION: Do I get a break here? *(Approaching the boy understandingly)* Wouldn't you like to say good-bye?
    JIM: To who?
30   MARION: To the apartment. You and your daddy spent a lot of time here together. Don't you want to take one last look around?
    JIM: Ma, get a real life.
    MARION: "Get a real life." *(Going for the phone)* Nice. Very nice.

JIM: Could you call already?

MARION *(Dialing)*: Jimmy, what does this look like I'm doing?

(JIM kicks at the floor impatiently. Someone answers the phone at the other end.)

MARION *(Into the phone)*: Helen? Hi, we're upstairs. . . . No, we just walked in   35
the door. Jimmy wants to know if he can come down. . . . Oh, thanks.

(Hearing that, JIM breaks for the door.)

MARION *(Yelling after him)*: Don't run in the halls! And don't play with the
elevator buttons!

(The door slams shut behind him.)

MARION *(Back to the phone)*: Hi. . . . No, I'm okay. It's a little weird being
here. . . . No. Not since the funeral, and then there were so many people.
Jimmy told me to get "a real life." I don't think I could handle anything
realer. . . . No, please. Stay where you are. I'm fine. The doorman said
Arthur would be right back and my lawyer should have been here already. . . . Well, we've got the papers to sign and a few other odds and
ends to clean up. Shouldn't take long.

(The intercom buzzer rings.)

MARION: Hang on, that must be her.

(MARION goes to the intercom and speaks.) Yes? . . . Thank you.

(Back to the phone) Helen? Yeah, it's the lawyer. I'd better go. . . . Well, I   40
could use a stiff drink, but I drove down. Listen, I'll stop by on my way
out. Okay? Okay. 'Bye.

*(She hangs up the phone, looks around the room. That uncomfortable feeling re-
turns to her quickly. She gets up and goes to the front door, opens it and looks
out. No one there yet. She closes the door, shakes her head knowing that she's
being silly and starts back into the room. She looks around, can't make it and
retreats to the door. She opens it, looks out, closes it, but stays right there, her
hand on the doorknob.
    The bell rings. She throws open the door.)*

MARION: That was quick.

*(JUNE LOWELL still has her finger on the bell. Her arms are loaded with con-
tracts. MARION'S contemporary, JUNE is less formal in appearance and more
hyper in her manner.)*

JUNE: *That* was quicker. What, were you waiting by the door?

MARION *(Embarrassed)*: No. I was just passing it. Come on in.

JUNE: Have you got your notary seal?

45   MARION: I think so.

JUNE: Great. Then you can witness. I left mine at the office and thanks to gentrification I'm double-parked downstairs. *(Looking for a place to dump her load)* Where?

MARION *(Definitely pointing to the coffee table)*: Anywhere. You mean you're not staying?

JUNE: If you really think you need me I can go down and find a parking lot. I think there's one over on Columbus. So, I can go down, park the car in the lot and take a cab back if you really think you need me.

MARION: Well . . . ?

50   JUNE: But you shouldn't have any problems. The papers are about as straight-forward as papers get. Arthur is giving you power of attorney to sell the apartment and you're giving him a check for half the purchase price. Everything else is just signing papers that state that you know that you signed the other papers. Anyway, he knows the deal, his lawyers have been over it all with him, it's just a matter of signatures.

MARION *(Not fine)*: Oh, fine.

JUNE: Unless you just don't want to be alone with him . . . ?

MARION: With Arthur? Don't be silly.

JUNE *(Laying out the papers)*: Then you'll handle it solo? Great. My car thanks you, the parking lot thanks you, and the cab driver that wouldn't have gotten a tip thanks you. Come have a quick look-see.

55   MARION *(Joining her on the couch)*: There are a lot of papers here.

JUNE: Copies. Not to worry. Start here.

(MARION starts to read.)

JUNE: I ran into Jimmy playing Elevator Operator.

(MARION jumps.)

JUNE: I got him off at the sixth floor. Read on.

MARION: This is definitely not my day for dealing with him.

(JUNE gets up and has a look around.)

60   JUNE: I don't believe what's happening to this neighborhood. You made quite an investment when you bought this place.

MARION: Collin was always very good at figuring out those things.

JUNE: Well, he sure figured this place right. What, have you tripled your money in ten years?

MARION: More.

JUNE: It's a shame to let it go.

65   MARION: We're not ready to be a two-dwelling family.

JUNE: So, sublet it again.

MARION: Arthur needs the money from the sale.

JUNE: Arthur got plenty already. I'm not crying for Arthur.

MARION: I don't hear you starting in again, do I?

JUNE: Your interests and your wishes are my only concern.   70

MARION: Fine.

JUNE: I still say we should contest Collin's will.

MARION: June! . . .

JUNE: You've got a child to support.

MARION: And a great job, and a husband with a great job. Tell me what   75
    Arthur's got.

JUNE: To my thinking, half of everything that should have gone to you. And
    more. All of Collin's personal effects, his record collection . . .

MARION: And I suppose their three years together meant nothing.

JUNE: When you compare them to your sixteen-year marriage? Not nothing,
    but not half of everything.

MARION *(Trying to change the subject)*: June, who gets which copies?

JUNE: Two of each to Arthur. One you keep. The originals and anything else   80
    come back to me. *(Looking around)* I still say you should've sublet the
    apartment for a year and then sold it. You would've gotten an even better
    price. Who wants to buy an apartment when they know someone died
    in it. No one. And certainly no one wants to buy an apartment when
    they know the person died of AIDS.

MARION *(Snapping)*: June. Enough!

JUNE *(Catching herself)*: Sorry. That was out of line. Sometimes my mouth
    does that to me. Hey, that's why I'm a lawyer. If my brain worked as fast
    as my mouth I would have gotten a real job.

MARION *(Holding out a stray paper)*: What's this?

JUNE: I forgot. Arthur's lawyer sent that over yesterday. He found it in Collin's
    safety-deposit box. It's an insurance policy that came along with some con-
    sulting job he did in Japan. He either forgot about it when he made out
    his will or else he wanted you to get the full payment. Either way, it's yours.

MARION: Are you sure we don't split this?   85

JUNE: Positive.

MARION: But everything else . . . ?

JUNE: Hey, Arthur found it, his lawyer sent it to me. Relax, it's all yours. Minus
    my commission, of course. Go out and buy yourself something. Any-
    thing else before I have to use my cut to pay the towing bill?

MARION: I guess not.

JUNE *(Starting to leave)*: Great. Call me when you get home. *(Stopping at the*   90
    door and looking back) Look, I know that I'm attacking this a little coldly. I
    am aware that someone you loved has just died. But there's a time and

place for everything. This is about tidying up loose ends, not holding hands. I hope you'll remember that when Arthur gets here. Call me.

(And she's gone.

MARION looks ill at ease to be alone again. She nervously straightens the papers into neat little piles, looks at them and then remembers:)

MARION: Pens. We're going to need pens.

(At last a chore to be done. She looks in her purse and finds only one. She goes to the kitchen and opens a drawer where she finds two more. She starts back to the table with them but suddenly remembers something else. She returns to the kitchen and begins going through the cabinets until she finds what she's looking for: a blue Art Deco teapot. Excited to find it, she takes it back to the couch.

Guilt strikes. She stops, considers putting it back, wavers, then:)

MARION *(To herself)*: Oh, he won't care. One less thing to pack.

(She takes the teapot and places it on the couch next to her purse. She is happier. Now she searches the room with her eyes for any other treasures she may have overlooked. Nothing here. She wanders off into the bedroom.

We hear keys outside the front door. ARTHUR lets himself into the apartment carrying a load of empty cartons and a large shopping bag.

ARTHUR is in his mid-thirties, pleasant looking though sloppily dressed in work clothes and slightly overweight.

ARTHUR enters the apartment just as MARION comes out of the bedroom carrying a framed watercolor painting. They jump at the sight of each other.)

MARION: Oh, hi, Arthur. I didn't hear the door.

ARTHUR *(Staring at the painting)*: Well hello, Marion.

95　MARION *(Guiltily)*: I was going to ask you if you were thinking of taking this painting because if you're not going to then I'll take it. Unless, of course, you want it.

ARTHUR: No. You can have it.

MARION: I never really liked it, actually. I hate cats. I didn't even like the show. I needed something for my college dorm room. I was never the rock star poster type. I kept it in the back of a closet for years until Collin moved in here and took it. He said he liked it.

ARTHUR: I do too.

MARION: Well, then you keep it.

100　ARTHUR: No. Take it.

MARION: We've really got no room for it. You keep it.

ARTHUR: I don't want it.

MARION: Well, if you're sure.

ARTHUR *(Seeing the teapot)*: You want the teapot?

105　MARION: If you don't mind.

ARTHUR: One less thing to pack.

MARION: Funny, but that's exactly what I thought. One less thing to pack. You know, my mother gave it to Collin and me when we moved in to our first apartment. Silly sentimental piece of junk, but you know.

ARTHUR: That's not the one.

MARION: Sure it is. Hall used to make them for Westinghouse back in the thirties. I see them all the time at antiques shows and I always wanted to buy another, but they ask such a fortune for them.

ARTHUR: We broke the one your mother gave you a couple of years ago.   *110* That's a reproduction. You can get them almost anywhere in the Village for eighteen bucks.

MARION: Really? I'll have to pick one up.

ARTHUR: Take this one. I'll get another.

MARION: No, it's yours. You bought it.

ARTHUR: One less thing to pack.

MARION: Don't be silly. I didn't come here to raid the place.   *115*

ARTHUR: Well, was there anything else of Collin's that you thought you might like to have?

MARION: Now I feel so stupid, but actually I made a list. Not for me. But I started thinking about different people; friends, relatives, you know, that might want to have something of Collin's to remember him by. I wasn't sure just what you were taking and what you were throwing out. Anyway, I brought the list. *(Gets it from her purse)* Of course these are only suggestions. You probably thought of a few of these people yourself. But I figured it couldn't hurt to write it all down. Like I said, I don't know what you are planning on keeping.

ARTHUR *(Taking the list)*: I was planning on keeping it all.

MARION: Oh, I know. But most of these things are silly. Like his high school yearbooks. What would you want with them?

ARTHUR: Sure. I'm only interested in his Gay period.   *120*

MARION: I didn't mean it that way. Anyway, you look it over. They're only suggestions. Whatever you decide to do is fine with me.

ARTHUR *(Folding the list)*: It would have to be, wouldn't it. I mean, it's all mine now. He did leave this all to me.

(MARION is becoming increasingly nervous, but tries to keep a light approach as she takes a small bundle of papers from her bag.)

MARION: While we're on the subject of what's yours. I brought a batch of condolence cards that were sent to you care of me. Relatives mostly.

ARTHUR *(Taking them)*: More cards? I'm going to have to have another printing of thank-you notes done.

MARION: I answered these last week, so you don't have to bother. Unless you   *125* want to.

ARTHUR: Forge my signature?

MARION: Of course not. They were addressed to both of us and they're mostly distant relatives or friends we haven't seen in years. No one important.

ARTHUR: If they've got my name on them, then I'll answer them myself.

MARION: I wasn't telling you not to, I was only saying that you don't have to.

130   ARTHUR: I understand.

(MARION *picks up the teapot and brings it to the kitchen.*)

MARION: Let me put this back.

ARTHUR: I ran into Jimmy in the lobby.

MARION: Tell me you're joking.

ARTHUR: I got him to Helen's.

135   MARION: He's really racking up the points today.

ARTHUR: You know, he still can't look me in the face.

MARION: He's reacting to all of this in strange ways. Give him time. He'll come around. He's really very fond of you.

ARTHUR: I know. But he's at that awkward age: under thirty. I'm sure in twenty years we'll be the best of friends.

MARION: It's not what you think.

140   ARTHUR: What do you mean?

MARION: Well, you know.

ARTHUR: No I don't know. Tell me.

MARION: I thought that you were intimating something about his blaming you for Collin's illness and I was just letting you know that it's not true. (*Foot in mouth, she braves on.*) We discussed it a lot and . . . uh . . . he understands that his father was sick before you two ever met.

ARTHUR: I don't believe this.

145   MARION: I'm just trying to say that he doesn't blame you.

ARTHUR: First of all, who asked you? Second of all, that's between him and me. And third and most importantly, of course he blames me. Marion, he's eleven years old. You can discuss all you want, but the fact is that his father died of a "fag" disease and I'm the only fag around to finger.

MARION: My son doesn't use that kind of language.

ARTHUR: Forget the language. I'm talking about what he's been through. Can you imagine the kind of crap he's taken from his friends? That poor kid's been chased and chastised from one end of town to the other. He's got to have someone to blame just to survive. He can't blame you, you're all he's got. He can't blame his father; he's dead. So, Uncle Arthur gets the shaft. Fine, I can handle it.

MARION: You are so wrong, Arthur. I know my son and that is not the way his mind works.

150   ARTHUR: I don't know what you know. I only know what I know. And all I know is what I hear and see. The snide remarks, the little smirks . . . And

it's not just the illness. He's been looking for a scapegoat since the day you and Collin first split up. Finally he has one.

MARION *(Getting very angry now)*: Wait. Are you saying that if he's going to blame someone it should be me?

ARTHUR: I think you should try to see things from his point of view.

MARION: Where do you get off thinking you're privy to my son's point of view?

ARTHUR: It's not that hard to imagine. Life's rolling right along, he's having a happy little childhood, when suddenly one day his father's moving out. No explanations, no reasons, none of the fights that usually accompany such things. Divorce is hard enough for a kid to understand when he's listened to years of battles, but yours?

MARION: So what should we have done? Faked a few months' worth of fights before Collin moved out? 155

ARTHUR: You could have told him the truth, plain and simple.

MARION: He was seven years old at the time. How the hell do you tell a seven-year-old that his father is leaving his mother to go sleep with other men?

ARTHUR: Well, not like that.

MARION: You know, Arthur, I'm going to say this as nicely as I can: Butt out. You're not his mother and you're not his father.

ARTHUR: Thank you. I wasn't acutely aware of that fact. I will certainly keep that in mind from now on. 160

MARION: There's only so much information a child that age can handle.

ARTHUR: So it's best that he reach his capacity on the street.

MARION: He knew about the two of you. We talked about it.

ARTHUR: Believe me, he knew before you talked about it. He's young, not stupid.

MARION: It's very easy for you to stand here and criticize, but there are aspects that you will just never be able to understand. You weren't there. You have no idea what it was like for me. You're talking to someone who thought that a girl went to college to meet a husband. I went to protest rallies because I liked the music. I bought a guitar because I thought it looked good on the bed! This lifestyle, this knowledge that you take for granted, was all a little out of left field for me. 165

ARTHUR: I can imagine.

MARION: No. I don't think you can. I met Collin in college, married him right after graduation and settled down for a nice quiet life of Kids and Careers. You think I had any idea about this? Talk about life's little surprises. You live with someone for sixteen years, you share your life, your bed, you have a child together, and then you wake up one day and he tells you that to him it's all been a lie. A lie. Try that on for size. Here you are the happiest couple you know, fulfilling your every life fantasy and he tells you he's living a lie.

ARTHUR: I'm sure he never said that.

MARION: Don't be so sure. There was a lot of new ground being broken back
   then and plenty of it was muddy.

170   ARTHUR: You know that he loved you.

MARION: What's that supposed to do, make things easier? It doesn't. I was
   brought up to believe, among other things, that if you had love that was
   enough. So what if I wasn't everything he wanted. Maybe he wasn't exactly everything I wanted either. So, you know what? You count your
   blessings and you settle.

ARTHUR: No one has to settle. Not him. Not you.

MARION: Of course not. You can say, "Up yours!" to everything and everyone who depends on and needs you, and go off to make yourself happy.

ARTHUR: It's not that simple.

175   MARION: No. This is simpler. Death is simpler. *(Yelling out)* Happy now?

   (They stare at each other. MARION *calms the rage and catches her breath.*
   ARTHUR *holds his emotions in check.)*

ARTHUR: How about a nice hot cup of coffee? Tea with lemon? Hot cocoa
   with a marshmallow floating in it?

MARION *(Laughs):* I was wrong. You *are* a mother.

   *(*ARTHUR *goes into the kitchen and starts preparing things.* MARION *loafs by
   the doorway.)*

MARION: I lied before. He *was* everything I ever wanted.

   *(*ARTHUR *stops, looks at her, and then changes the subject as he goes on with
   his work.)*

ARTHUR: When I came into the building and saw Jimmy in the lobby I absolutely freaked for a second. It's amazing how much they look alike. It
   was like seeing a little miniature Collin standing there.

180   MARION: I know. He's like Collin's clone. There's nothing of me in him.

ARTHUR: I always kinda hoped that when he grew up he'd take after me.
   Not much chance, I guess.

MARION: Don't do anything fancy in there.

ARTHUR: Please. Anything we can consume is one less thing to pack.

MARION: So you've said.

185   ARTHUR: So *we've* said.

MARION: I want to keep seeing you and I want you to see Jim. You're still
   part of this family. No one's looking to cut you out.

ARTHUR: Ah, who'd want a kid to grow up looking like me anyway. I had
   enough trouble looking like this. Why pass on the misery?

MARION: You're adorable.

ARTHUR: Is that like saying I have a good personality?

190   MARION: I think you are one of the most naturally handsome men I know.

ARTHUR: Natural is right, and the bloom is fading.

MARION: All you need is a few good nights' sleep to kill those rings under your eyes.

ARTHUR: Forget the rings under my eyes, *(Grabbing his middle)* . . . how about the rings around my moon?

MARION: I like you like this.

ARTHUR: From the time that Collin started using the wheelchair until he   *195*
died, about six months, I lost twenty-three pounds. No gym, no diet. In the last seven weeks I've gained close to fifty.

MARION: You're exaggerating.

ARTHUR: I'd prove it on the bathroom scale, but I sold it in working order.

MARION: You'd never know.

ARTHUR: Marion, *you'd* never know, but ask my belt. Ask my pants. Ask my underwear. Even my stretch socks have stretch marks. I called the ambulance at five A.M., he was gone at nine and by nine-thirty, I was on a first-name basis with Sara Lee. I can quote the business hours of every ice-cream parlor, pizzeria and bakery on the island of Manhattan. I know the location of every twenty-four-hour grocery in the greater New York area, and I have memorized the phone numbers of every Mandarin, Szechuan and Hunan restaurant with free delivery.

MARION: At least you haven't wasted your time on useless hobbies.   *200*

ARTHUR: Are you kidding? I'm opening my own Overeater's Hotline. We'll have to start small, but expansion is guaranteed.

MARION: You're the best, you know that? If I couldn't be everything that Collin wanted then I'm grateful that he found someone like you.

ARTHUR *(Turning on her without missing a beat)*: Keep your goddamned gratitude to yourself. I didn't go through any of this for you. So your thanks are out of line. And he didn't find "someone like" me. It was me.

MARION *(Frightened)*: I didn't mean . . .

ARTHUR: And I wish you'd remember one thing more: He died in my arms,   *205*
not yours.

(MARION *is totally caught off guard. She stares disbelieving, openmouthed.* ARTHUR *walks past her as he leaves the kitchen with place mats. He puts them on the coffee table. As he arranges the papers and place mats he speaks, never looking at her.)*

ARTHUR: Look, I know you were trying to say something supportive. Don't waste your breath. There's nothing you can say that will make any of this easier for me. There's no way for you to help me get through this. And that's your fault. After three years you still have no idea or understanding of who I am. Or maybe you do know but refuse to accept it. I don't know and I don't care. But at least understand, from my point of view, who you are: You are my husband's *ex*-wife. If you like, the mother of *my* stepson. Don't flatter yourself into thinking you're any more than that. And whatever you are, you're certainly not my friend.

(He stops, looks up at her, then passes her again as he goes back to the kitchen. MARION is shaken, working hard to control herself. She moves toward the couch.)

MARION: Why don't we just sign these papers and I'll be out of your way.

ARTHUR: Shouldn't you say *I'll* be out of *your* way? After all, I'm not just signing papers, I'm signing away my home.

MARION *(Resolved not to fight, she gets her purse)*: I'll leave the papers here. Please have them notarized and returned to my lawyer.

210   ARTHUR: Don't forget my painting.

MARION *(Exploding)*: What do you want from me, Arthur?

ARTHUR *(Yelling back)*: I want you the hell out of my apartment! I want you out of my life! And I want you to leave Collin alone!

MARION: The man's dead. I don't know how much more alone I can leave him.

(ARTHUR laughs at the irony, but behind the laughter is something much more desperate.)

ARTHUR: Lots more, Marion. You've got to let him go.

215   MARION: For the life of me, I don't know what I did, or what you think I did, for you to treat me like this. But you're not going to get away with it. You will not take your anger out on me. I will not stand here and be badgered and insulted by you. I know you've been hurt and I know you're hurting but you're not the only one who lost someone here.

ARTHUR *(Topping her)*: Yes I am! You didn't just lose him. I did! You lost him five years ago when he divorced you. This is not your moment of grief and loss, it's mine! *(Picking up the bundle of cards and throwing it toward her)* These condolences do not belong to you, they're mine! *(Tossing her list back to her)* His things are not yours to give away, they're mine! This death does not belong to you, it's mine! Bought and paid for outright. I suffered for it, I bled for it. I was the one who cooked his meals. I was the one who spoon-fed them. I pushed his wheelchair. I carried and bathed him. I wiped his backside and changed his diapers. I breathed life into and wrestled fear out of his heart. I kept him alive for two years longer than any doctor thought possible and when it was time I was the one who prepared him for death.

I paid in full for my place in his life and I will *not* share it with you. We are not the two widows of Collin Redding. Your life was not here. Your husband didn't just die. You've got a son and a life somewhere else. Your husband's sitting, waiting for you at home, wondering, as I am, what the hell you're doing here and why you can't let go.

(MARION *leans back against the couch. She's blown away.* ARTHUR *stands staring at her.*)

ARTHUR *(Quietly)*: Let him go, Marion. He's mine. Dead or alive; mine.

(*The teakettle whistles.* ARTHUR *leaves the room, goes to the kitchen and pours the water as* MARION *pulls herself together.*

   ARTHUR *carries the loaded tray back into the living room and sets it down on the coffee table. He sits and pours a cup.*)

ARTHUR: One marshmallow or two?

(MARION *stares, unsure as to whether the attack is really over or not.*)

ARTHUR *(Placing them in her cup)*: Take three, they're small.   *220*

(MARION *smiles and takes the offered cup.*)

ARTHUR *(Campily)*: Now let me tell you how I *really* feel.

(MARION *jumps slightly, then they share a small laugh. Silence as they each gather themselves and sip their refreshments.*)

MARION *(Calmly)*: Do you think that I sold the apartment just to throw you out?

ARTHUR: I don't care about the apartment . . .

MARION: . . . Because I really didn't. Believe me.

ARTHUR: I know.

MARION: I knew the expenses here were too much for you, and I knew you   *225*
couldn't afford to buy out my half . . . I figured if we sold it, that you'd at least have a nice chunk of money to start over with.

ARTHUR: You could've given me a little more time.

MARION: Maybe. But I thought the sooner you were out of here, the sooner you could go on with your life.

ARTHUR: Or the sooner you could go on with yours.

MARION: Maybe. *(Pauses to gather her thoughts)* Anyway, I'm not going to tell   *230*
you that I have no idea what you're talking about. I'd have to be worse than deaf and blind not to have seen the way you've been treated. Or mistreated. When I read Collin's obituary in the newspaper and saw my name and Jimmy's name and no mention of you . . . *(Shakes her head, not knowing what to say)* You know that his secretary was the one who wrote that up and sent it in. Not me. But I should have done something about it and I didn't. I know.

ARTHUR: Wouldn't have made a difference. I wrote my own obituary for him and sent it to the smaller papers. They edited me out.

MARION: I'm sorry. I remember, at the funeral, I was surrounded by all of Collin's family and business associates while you were left with your friends. I knew it was wrong. I knew I should have said something but it felt good to have them around me and you looked like you were holding up . . . Wrong. But saying that it's all my fault for not letting go? . . . There were other people involved.

ARTHUR: Who took their cue from you.

MARION: Arthur, you don't understand. Most people that we knew as a couple had no idea that Collin was Gay right up to his death. And even those that did know only found out when he got sick and the word leaked out that it was AIDS. I don't think I have to tell you how stupid and ill-informed most people are about homosexuality. And AIDS . . . ? The kinds of insane behavior that word inspires? . . .

235   Those people at the funeral, how many times did they call to see how he was doing over these years? How many of them ever went to see him in the hospital? Did any of them even come here? So, why would you expect them to act any differently after his death?

So, maybe that helps to explain their behavior, but what about mine, right? Well, maybe there is no explanation. Only excuses. And excuse number one is that you're right, I have never really let go of him. And I am jealous of you. Hell, I was jealous of anyone that Collin ever talked to, let alone slept with . . . let alone loved.

The first year, after he moved out, we talked all the time about the different men he was seeing. And I always listened and advised. It was kind of fun. It kept us close. It kept me a part of his intimate life. And the bottom line was always that he wasn't happy with the men he was meeting. So, I was always allowed to hang on to the hope that one day he'd give it all up and come home. Then he got sick.

He called me, told me he was in the hospital and asked if I'd come see him. I ran. When I got to his door there was a sign, INSTRUCTIONS FOR VISITORS OF AN AIDS PATIENT. I nearly died.

ARTHUR: He hadn't told you?

240 MARION: No. And believe me, a sign is not the way to find these things out. I was so angry . . . And he was so sick . . . I was sure that he'd die right then. If not from the illness then from the hospital staff's neglect. No one wanted to go near him and I didn't bother fighting with them because I understood that they were scared. I was scared. That whole month in the hospital I didn't let Jimmy visit him once.

You learn.

Well, as you know, he didn't die. And he asked if he could come stay with me until he was well. And I said yes. Of course, yes. Now, here's something I never thought I'd ever admit to anyone: had he asked to stay with me for a few weeks I would have said no. But he asked to stay with me until he was well and knowing there was no cure I said yes. In my craziness I said yes because to me that meant forever. That he was coming back to me forever. Not that I wanted him to die, but I assumed from everything I'd read . . . And we'd be back together for whatever time he had left. Can you understand that?

(ARTHUR *nods.*)

MARION (*Gathers her thoughts again*): Two weeks later he left. He moved in here. Into this apartment that we had bought as an investment. Never to live in. Certainly never to live apart in. Next thing I knew, the name Arthur starts appearing in every phone call, every dinner conversation.

"Did you see the doctor?"

"Yes. Arthur made sure I kept the appointment."   245

"Are you going to your folks for Thanksgiving?"

"No. Arthur and I are having some friends over."

I don't know which one of us was more of a coward, he for not telling or me for not asking about you. But eventually you became a given. Then, of course, we met and became what I had always thought of as friends.

(ARTHUR *winces in guilt.*)

MARION: I don't care what you say, how could we not be friends with something so great in common: love for one of the most special human beings there ever was. And don't try and tell me there weren't times when you enjoyed my being around as an ally. I can think of a dozen occasions when we ganged up on him, teasing him with our intimate knowledge of his personal habits.

(ARTHUR *has to laugh.*)

MARION: Blanket stealing? Snoring? Excess gas, no less? (*Takes a moment to*   250
enjoy this truce) I don't think that my loving him threatened your relationship. Maybe I'm not being truthful with myself. But I don't. I never tried to step between you. Not that I ever had the opportunity. Talk about being joined at the hip! And that's not to say I wasn't jealous. I was. Terribly. Hatefully. But always lovingly. I was happy for Collin because there was no way to deny that he was happy. With everything he was facing, he was happy. Love did that. You did that.

He lit up with you. He came to life. I envied that and all the time you spent together, but more, I watched you care for him (sometimes *overcare* for him), and I was in awe. I could never have done what you did. I never would have survived. I really don't know how you did.

ARTHUR: Who said I survived?

MARION: Don't tease. You did an absolutely incredible thing. It's not as if you met him before he got sick. You entered a relationship that you knew in all probability would end this way and you never wavered.

ARTHUR: Of course I did. Don't have me sainted, Marion. But sometimes you have no choice. Believe me, if I could've gotten away from him I would've. But I was a prisoner of love.

(He makes a campy gesture and pose.)

255 MARION: Stop.

ARTHUR: And there were lots of pluses. I got to quit a job I hated, stay home all day and watch game shows. I met a lot of doctors and learned a lot of big words. (ARTHUR *jumps up and goes to the pile of boxes where he extracts one and brings it back to the couch.*) And then there was all the exciting traveling I got to do. This box has a souvenir from each one of our trips. Wanna see?

(MARION nods. He opens the box and pulls things out one by one.)

ARTHUR *(Continues) (Holding up an old bottle):* This is from the house we rented in Reno when we went to clear out his lungs. *(Holding handmade potholders)* This is from the hospital in Reno. Collin made them. They had a great arts and crafts program. *(Copper bracelets)* These are from a faith healer in Philly. They don't do much for a fever, but they look great with a green sweater. *(Glass ashtrays)* These are from our first visit to the clinic in France. Such lovely people. *(A Bible)* This is from our second visit to the clinic in France. *(A bead necklace)* A Voodoo doctor in New Orleans. Next time we'll have to get there earlier in the year. I think he sold all the pretty ones at Mardi Gras. *(A tiny piñata)* Then there was Mexico. Black market drugs and empty wallets. *(Now pulling things out at random)* L.A., San Francisco, Houston, Boston . . . We traveled everywhere they offered hope for sale and came home with souvenirs. (ARTHUR *quietly pulls a few more things out and then begins to put them all back into the box slowly. Softly as he works:)*

Marion, I would have done anything, traveled anywhere to avoid . . . or delay . . . Not just because I loved him so desperately, but when you've lived the way we did for three years . . . the battle becomes your life. *(He looks at her and then away.)*

260 His last few hours were beyond any scenario I had imagined. He hadn't walked in nearly six months. He was totally incontinent. If he spoke two words in a week I was thankful. Days went by without his eyes ever focusing on me. He just stared out at I don't know what. Not the meals as I fed him. Not the TV I played constantly for company. Just out. Or maybe in.

It was the middle of the night when I heard his breathing become labored. His lungs were filling with fluid again. I knew the sound. I'd heard it a hundred times before. So, I called the ambulance and got him to the hospital. They hooked him up to the machines, the oxygen, shot him with morphine and told me that they would do what they could to keep him alive.

But, Marion, it wasn't the machines that kept him breathing. He did it himself. It was that incredible will and strength inside him. Whether it came from his love of life or fear of death, who knows. But he'd been counted out a hundred times and a hundred times he fought his way back.

I got a magazine to read him, pulled a chair up to the side of his bed and holding his hand, I wondered whether I should call Helen to let the cleaning lady in or if he'd fall asleep and I could sneak home for an hour. I looked up from the page and he was looking at me. Really looking right into my eyes. I patted his cheek and said, "Don't worry, honey, you're going to be fine."

But there was something else in his eyes. He wasn't satisfied with that. And I don't know why, I have no idea where it came from, I just heard the words coming out of my mouth, "Collin, do you want to die?" His eyes filled and closed, he nodded his head.

I can't tell you what I was thinking, I'm not sure I was. I slipped   265
off my shoes, lifted his blanket and climbed into bed next to him. I helped him to put his arms around me, and mine around him, and whispered as gently as I could into his ear, "It's alright to let go now. It's time to go on." And he did.

Marion, you've got your life and his son. All I have is an intangible place in a man's history. Leave me that. Respect that.

MARION: I understand.

(ARTHUR suddenly comes to life, running to get the shopping bag that he'd left at the front door.)

ARTHUR: Jeez! With all the screamin' and sad storytelling I forget something. *(He extracts a bouquet of flowers from the bag.)* I brung you flowers and everything.

MARION: You brought *me* flowers?

ARTHUR: Well, I knew you'd never think to bring me flowers and I felt that   270
on an occasion such as this somebody oughta get flowers from somebody.

MARION: You know, Arthur, you're really making me feel like a worthless piece of garbage.

ARTHUR: So what else is new? *(He presents the flowers.)* Just promise me one thing: Don't press one in a book. Just stick them in a vase and when they fade just toss them out. No more memorabilia.

MARION: Arthur, I want to do something for you and I don't know what. Tell me what you want.

ARTHUR: I want little things. Not much. I want to be remembered. If you get a Christmas card from Collin's mother, make sure she sent me one too. If his friends call to see how you are, ask if they've called me. Have

me to dinner so I can see Jimmy. Let me take him out now and then. Invite me to his wedding.

(They both laugh.)

275   MARION: You've got it.

ARTHUR *(Clearing the table)*: Let me get all this cold cocoa out of the way. We
still have the deed to do.

MARION *(Checking her watch)*: And I've got to get Jimmy home in time for
practice.

ARTHUR: Band practice?

MARION: Baseball. *(Picking her list off the floor)* About this list, you do what
you want.

280   ARTHUR: Believe me, I will. But I promise to consider your suggestions. Just
don't rush me. I'm not ready to give it all away. *(ARTHUR is off to the
kitchen with his tray and the phone rings. He answers it in the kitchen.)* Hello?
. . . Just a minute. *(Calling out)* It's your eager Little Leaguer.

(MARION picks up the living room extension and ARTHUR hangs his up.)

MARION *(Into the phone)*: Hello, honey. . . . I'll be down in five minutes. No.
You know what? You come up here and get me. . . . No, I said you should
come up here. . . . I said I want you to come up here. . . . Because I said
so. . . . Thank you.

(She hangs up the receiver.)

ARTHUR *(Rushing to the papers)*: Alright, where do we start on these?

MARION *(Getting out her seal)*: I guess you should just start signing everything
and I'll stamp along with you. Keep one of everything on the side for
yourself.

ARTHUR: Now I feel so rushed. What am I signing?

285   MARION: You want to do this another time?

ARTHUR: No. Let's get it over with. I wouldn't survive another session like this.

(He starts to sign and she starts her job.)

MARION: I keep meaning to ask you; how are you?

ARTHUR *(At first puzzled and then)*: Oh, you mean my health? Fine. No, I'm
fine. I've been tested, and nothing. We were very careful. We took many
precautions. Collin used to make jokes about how we should invest in
rubber futures.

MARION: I'll bet.

290   ARTHUR *(Stops what he's doing)*: It never occurred to me until now. How
about you?

MARION *(Not stopping)*: Well, we never had sex after he got sick.

ARTHUR: But before?

MARION *(Stopping but not looking up)*: I have the antibodies in my blood. No signs that it will ever develop into anything else. And it's been five years so my chances are pretty good that I'm just a carrier.

ARTHUR: I'm so sorry. Collin never told me.

MARION: He didn't know. In fact, other than my husband and the doctors,   *295* you're the only one I've told.

ARTHUR: You and your husband . . . ?

MARION: Have invested in rubber futures. There'd only be a problem if we wanted to have a child. Which we do. But we'll wait. Miracles happen every day.

ARTHUR: I don't know what to say.

MARION: Tell me you'll be there if I ever need you.

(ARTHUR gets up, goes to her and puts his arms around her. They hold each other. He gently pushes her away to make a joke.)

ARTHUR: Sure! Take something else that should have been mine.   *300*

MARION: Don't even joke about things like that.

(The doorbell rings. They pull themselves together.)

ARTHUR: You know we'll never get these done today.

MARION: So, tomorrow.

(ARTHUR goes to open the door as MARION gathers her things. He opens the door and JIMMY is standing in the hall.)

JIM: C'mon, Ma. I'm gonna be late.

ARTHUR: Would you like to come inside?   *305*

JIM: We've gotta go.

MARION: Jimmy, come on.

JIM: Ma!

(She glares. He comes in. ARTHUR closes the door.)

MARION *(Holding out the flowers)*: Take these for Mommy.

JIM *(Taking them)*: Can we go?   *310*

MARION *(Picking up the painting)*: Say good-bye to your Uncle Arthur.

JIM: 'Bye, Arthur. Come on.

MARION: Give him a kiss.

ARTHUR: Marion, don't.

MARION: Give your uncle a kiss good-bye.   *315*

JIM: He's not my uncle.

MARION: No. He's a hell of a lot more than your uncle.

ARTHUR *(Offering his hand)*: A handshake will do.

MARION: Tell Uncle Arthur what your daddy told you.

JIM: About what?   *320*

MARION: Stop playing dumb. You know.

ARTHUR: Don't embarrass him.

MARION: Jimmy, please.

JIM *(He regards his mother's softer tone and then speaks)*: He said that after me and Mommy he loved you the most.

325 MARION *(Standing behind him)*: Go on.

JIM: And that I should love you too. And make sure that you're not lonely or very sad.

ARTHUR: Thank you.

> (ARTHUR *reaches down to the boy and they hug.* JIM *gives him a little peck on the cheek and then breaks away.*)

MARION *(Going to open the door)*: Alright, kid, you done good. Now let's blow this joint before you muck it up.

> (JIM *rushes out the door.* MARION *turns to* ARTHUR.)

MARION: A child's kiss is magic. Why else would they be so stingy with them. I'll call you.

> (ARTHUR *nods understanding.* MARION *pulls the door closed behind her.* ARTHUR *stands quietly as the lights fade to black.*)

THE END

NOTE: *If being performed on film, the final image should be of* ARTHUR *leaning his back against the closed door on the inside of the apartment and* MARION *leaning on the outside of the door. A moment of thought and then they both move on.*   *1987*

CONSIDERATIONS

1. Describe the relationship between Jim and Marion. Evaluate the way each responds to Collin's death and to the other's response to Collin's death.
2. June says, "Arthur got plenty already. I'm not crying for Arthur." What does she mean by this? What is your evaluation of Arthur's losses—and gains—from his relationship with Collin and from Collin's death?
3. Think about the title of the play. June warns Marion to "[tidy] up loose ends . . . when Arthur gets here." What is implied by a "tidy" ending or by "tidying up loose ends"? To what extent is the ending described "tidy"? How might the play's title be considered ironic?

4. Describe the relationship between Arthur and Marion. For whom do you have more sympathy? Explain.
5. What do the three main characters in the play (Arthur, Marion, and Jimmy) learn about themselves, about each other, about Collin, and—especially— about facing death (either their own or the death of others)?

Essays

ELISABETH KÜBLER-ROSS (1924–2004)
On the Fear of Death

A Swiss-American psychiatrist, Elisabeth Kübler-Ross did extensive research on the topics of death and dying. Born in Zurich, Switzerland, she earned her doctorate from the University of Zurich and then came to the United States for her internship. Following her years as an intern and resident, she began her work with terminally ill patients while teaching psychiatry at the University of Chicago Medical School. "On the Fear of Death" comes from her first book, On Death and Dying *(1969).*

> Let me not pray to be sheltered from
> dangers but to be fearless in facing
> them.
> Let me not beg for the stilling of
> my pain but for the heart to conquer it.
> Let me not look for allies in life's
> battlefield but to my own strength.
> Let me not crave in anxious fear to
> be saved but hope for the patience to
> win my freedom.
> Grant me that I may not be a
> coward, feeling your mercy in my
> success alone; but let me find the grasp
> of your hand in my failure.
> —RABINDRANATH TAGORE, *Fruit-Gathering*

Epidemics have taken a great toll of lives in past generations. Death in infancy and early childhood was frequent and there were few families who didn't lose a member of the family at an early age. Medicine has changed greatly in the last decades. Widespread vaccinations have practically eradicated many illnesses, at least in western Europe and the United States. The use of chemotherapy, especially the antibiotics, has contributed to an ever-decreasing number of fatalities in infectious diseases. Better child care and education [have] effected a low morbidity and mortality among children. The many diseases that have taken an impressive toll among the young and middle-aged have been conquered. The number of old people is on the rise, and with this fact come the number of people with malignancies and chronic diseases associated more with old age.

Pediatricians have less work with acute and life-threatening situations as they have an ever-increasing number of patients with psychosomatic disturbances and adjustment and behavior problems. Physicians have more people in their waiting rooms with emotional problems than they have ever had before, but they also have more elderly patients who not only try to live with their decreased physical abilities and limitations but who also face loneliness and isolation with all its pains and anguish. The majority of these people are not seen by a psychiatrist. Their needs have to be elicited and gratified by other professional people, for instance, chaplains and social workers. It is for them that I am trying to outline the changes that have taken place in the last few decades, changes that are ultimately responsible for the increased fear of death, the rising number of emotional problems, and the greater need for understanding of and coping with the problems of death and dying.

When we look back in time and study old cultures and people, we are impressed that death has always been distasteful to man and will probably always be. From a psychiatrist's point of view this is very understandable and can perhaps best be explained by our basic knowledge that, in our unconscious, death is never possible in regard to ourselves. It is inconceivable for our unconscious to imagine an actual ending of our own life here on earth, and if this life of ours has to end, the ending is always attributed to a malicious intervention from the outside by someone else. In simple terms, in our unconscious mind we can only be killed; it is inconceivable to die of a natural cause or of old age. Therefore death in itself is associated with a bad act, a frightening happening, something that in itself calls for retribution and punishment.

One is wise to remember these fundamental facts as they are essential in understanding some of the most important, otherwise unintelligible communications of our patients.

5   The second fact that we have to comprehend is that in our unconscious mind we cannot distinguish between a wish and a deed. We are all aware of some of our illogical dreams in which two completely opposite statements can exist side by side—very acceptable in our dreams but unthinkable and illogical in our wakening state. Just as our unconscious mind cannot differentiate between the wish to kill somebody in anger and the act of having done so, the young child is unable to make this distinction. The child who angrily wishes his mother to drop dead for not having gratified his needs will be traumatized greatly by the actual death of his mother—even if this event is not linked

closely in time with his destructive wishes. He will always take part or the whole blame for the loss of his mother. He will always say to himself—rarely to others—"I did it, I am responsible, I was bad, therefore Mommy left me." It is well to remember that the child will react in the same manner if he loses a parent by divorce, separation, or desertion. Death is often seen by a child as an impermanent thing and has therefore little distinction from a divorce in which he may have an opportunity to see a parent again.

Many a parent will remember remarks of their children such as, "I will bury my doggy now and next spring when the flowers come up again, he will get up." Maybe it was the same wish that motivated the ancient Egyptians to supply their dead with food and goods to keep them happy and the old American Indians to bury their relatives with their belongings.

When we grow older and begin to realize that our omnipotence is really not so omnipotent, that our strongest wishes are not powerful enough to make the impossible possible, the fear that we have contributed to the death of a loved one diminishes—and with it the guilt. The fear remains diminished, however, only so long as it is not challenged too strongly. Its vestiges can be seen daily in hospital corridors and in people associated with the bereaved.

A husband and wife may have been fighting for years, but when the partner dies, the survivor will pull his hair, whine and cry louder and beat his chest in regret, fear and anguish, and will hence fear his own death more than before, still believing in the law of talion—an eye for an eye, a tooth for a tooth— "I am responsible for her death, I will have to die a pitiful death in retribution."

Maybe this knowledge will help us understand many of the old customs and rituals which have lasted over the centuries and whose purpose is to diminish the anger of the gods or the people as the case may be, thus decreasing the anticipated punishment. I am thinking of the ashes, the torn clothes, the veil, the *Klage Weiber*° of the old days—they are all means to ask you to take pity on them, the mourners, and are expressions of sorrow, grief, and shame. If someone grieves, beats his chest, tears his hair, or refuses to eat, it is an attempt at self-punishment to avoid or reduce the anticipated punishment for the blame that he takes on the death of a loved one.

This grief, shame, and guilt are not very far removed from feelings of   10
anger and rage. The process of grief always includes some qualities of anger. Since none of us likes to admit anger at a deceased person, these emotions are often disguised or repressed and prolong the period of grief or show up in other ways. It is well to remember that it is not up to us to judge such feelings as bad or shameful but to understand their true meaning and origin as something very human. In order to illustrate this I will again use the example of the child—and the child in us. The five-year-old who loses his mother is both

---

Klage Weiber: Lamenting widows.

blaming himself for her disappearance and being angry at her for having deserted him and for no longer gratifying his needs. The dead person then turns into something the child loves and wants very much but also hates with equal intensity for this severe deprivation.

The ancient Hebrews regarded the body of a dead person as something unclean and not to be touched. The early American Indians talked about the evil spirits and shot arrows in the air to drive the spirits away. Many other cultures have rituals to take care of the "bad" dead person, and they all originate in this feeling of anger which still exists in all of us, though we dislike admitting it. The tradition of the tombstone may originate in the wish to keep the bad spirits deep down in the ground, and the pebbles that many mourners put on the grave are leftover symbols of the same wish. Though we call the firing of guns at military funerals a last salute, it is the same symbolic ritual as the Indian used when he shot his spears and arrows into the skies.

I give these examples to emphasize that man has not basically changed. Death is still a fearful, frightening happening, and the fear of death is a universal fear even if we think we have mastered it on many levels.

What has changed is our way of coping and dealing with death and dying and our dying patients.

Having been raised in a country in Europe where science is not so advanced, where modern techniques have just started to find their way into medicine, and where people still live as they did in this country half a century ago, I may have had an opportunity to study a part of the evolution of mankind in a shorter period.

15   I remember as a child the death of a farmer. He fell from a tree and was not expected to live. He asked simply to die at home, a wish that was granted without question. He called his daughters into the bedroom and spoke with each one of them alone for a few moments. He arranged his affairs quietly, though he was in great pain, and distributed his belongings and his land, none of which was to be split until his wife should follow him in death. He also asked each of his children to share in the work, duties, and tasks that he had carried on until the time of the accident. He asked his friends to visit him once more, to bid goodbye to them. Although I was a small child at the time, he did not exclude me or my siblings. We were allowed to share in the preparations of the family just as we were permitted to grieve with them until he died. When he did die, he was left at home, in his own beloved home which he had built, and among his friends and neighbors who went to take a last look at him where he lay in the midst of flowers in the place he had lived in and loved so much. In that country today there is still no make-believe slumber room, no embalming, no false makeup to pretend sleep. Only the signs of very disfiguring illnesses are covered up with bandages and only infectious cases are removed from the home prior to the burial.

Why do I describe such "old-fashioned" customs? I think they are an indication of our acceptance of a fatal outcome, and they help the dying patient as well as his family to accept the loss of a loved one. If a patient is allowed to terminate his life in the familiar and beloved environment, it requires less adjustment for him. His own family knows him well enough to replace a sedative with a glass of his favorite wine; or the smell of a home-cooked soup may give him the appetite to sip a few spoons of fluid which, I think, is still more enjoyable than an infusion. I will not minimize the need for sedatives and infusions and realize full well from my own experience as a country doctor that they are sometimes life-saving and often unavoidable. But I also know that patience and familiar people and foods could replace many a bottle of intravenous fluids given for the simple reason that it fulfills the physiological need without involving too many people and/or individual nursing care.

The fact that children are allowed to stay at home where a fatality has struck and are included in the talk, discussions, and fears gives them the feeling that they are not alone in their grief and gives them the comfort of shared responsibility and shared mourning. It prepares them gradually and helps them view death as part of life, an experience which may help them grow and mature.

This is in great contrast to a society in which death is viewed as taboo, discussion of it is regarded as morbid, and children are excluded with the presumption and pretext that it would be "too much" for them. They are then sent off to relatives, often accompanied by some unconvincing lies of "Mother has gone on a long trip" or other unbelievable stories. The child senses that something is wrong, and his distrust in adults will only multiply if other relatives add new variations of the story, avoid his questions or suspicions, shower him with gifts as a meager substitute for a loss he is not permitted to deal with. Sooner or later the child will become aware of the changed family situation and, depending on the age and personality of the child, will have an unresolved grief and regard this incident as a frightening, mysterious, in any case very traumatic experience with untrustworthy grownups, which he has no way to cope with.

It is equally unwise to tell a little child who lost her brother that God loved little boys so much that he took little Johnny to heaven. When this little girl grew up to be a woman she never solved her anger at God, which resulted in a psychotic depression when she lost her own little son three decades later.

We would think that our great emancipation, our knowledge of science   20
and of man, has given us better ways and means to prepare ourselves and our families for this inevitable happening. Instead the days are gone when a man was allowed to die in peace and dignity in his own home.

The more we are making advancements in science, the more we seem to fear and deny the reality of death. How is this possible?

We use euphemisms, we make the dead look as if they were asleep, we ship the children off to protect them from the anxiety and turmoil around the house if the patient is fortunate enough to die at home, we don't allow children to visit their dying parents in the hospitals, we have long and controversial discussions about whether patients should be told the truth—a question that rarely arises when the dying person is tended by the family physician who has known him from delivery to death and who knows the weaknesses and strengths of each member of the family.

I think there are many reasons for this flight away from facing death calmly. One of the most important facts is that dying nowadays is more gruesome in many ways, namely, more lonely, mechanical, and dehumanized; at times it is even difficult to determine technically when the time of death has occurred.

Dying becomes lonely and impersonal because the patient is often taken out of his familiar environment and rushed to an emergency room. Whoever has been very sick and has required rest and comfort especially may recall his experience of being put on a stretcher and enduring the noise of the ambulance siren and hectic rush until the hospital gates open. Only those who have lived through this may appreciate the discomfort and cold necessity of such transportation which is only the beginning of a long ordeal—hard to endure when you are well, difficult to express in words when noise, light, pumps, and voices are all too much to put up with. It may well be that we might consider more the patient under the sheets and blankets and perhaps stop our well-meant efficiency and rush in order to hold the patient's hand, to smile, or to listen to a question. I include the trip to the hospital as the first episode in dying, as it is for many. I am putting it exaggeratedly in contrast to the sick man who is left at home—not to say that lives should not be saved if they can be saved by a hospitalization but to keep the focus on the patient's experience, his needs and his reactions.

25   When a patient is severely ill, he is often treated like a person with no right to an opinion. It is often someone else who makes the decision if and when and where a patient should be hospitalized. It would take so little to remember that the sick person too has feelings, has wishes and opinions, and has—most important of all—the right to be heard.

Well, our presumed patient has now reached the emergency room. He will be surrounded by busy nurses, orderlies, interns, residents, a lab technician perhaps who will take some blood, an electrocardiogram technician who takes the cardiogram. He may be moved to X-ray and he will overhear opinions of his condition and discussions and questions to members of the family. He slowly but surely is beginning to be treated like a thing. He is no longer a person. Decisions are made often without his opinion. If he tries to rebel he will be sedated and after hours of waiting and wondering whether he has the strength, he will be wheeled into the operating room or intensive treatment unit and become an object of great concern and great financial investment.

He may cry for rest, peace, and dignity, but he will get infusions, transfusions, a heart machine, or tracheotomy if necessary. He may want one single person to stop for one single minute so that he can ask one single question—but he will get a dozen people around the clock, all busily preoccupied with his heart rate, pulse, electrocardiogram or pulmonary functions, his secretions or excretions but not with him as a human being. He may wish to fight it all but it is going to be a useless fight since all this is done in the fight for his life, and if they can save his life they can consider the person afterwards. Those who consider the person first may lose precious time to save his life! At least this seems to be the rationale or justification behind all this—or is it? Is the reason for this increasingly mechanical, depersonalized approach our own defensiveness? Is this approach our own way to cope with and repress the anxieties that a terminally or critically ill patient evokes in us? Is our concentration on equipment, on blood pressure, our desperate attempt to deny the impending death which is so frightening and discomforting to us that we displace all our knowledge onto machines, since they are less close to us than the suffering face of another human being which would remind us once more of our lack of omnipotence, our own limits and failures, and last but not least perhaps our own mortality?

Maybe the question has to be raised: Are we becoming less human or more human? . . . it is clear that whatever the answer may be, the patient is suffering more—not physically, perhaps, but emotionally. And his needs have not changed over the centuries, only our ability to gratify them.   *1969*

CONSIDERATIONS

1. What relationship do you see between the poem that serves as the introduction and the essay itself?
2. Consider the various examples and explanations the essay provides of children's reactions to death and then give your responses to the points Kübler-Ross makes.
3. Summarize briefly the story of the farmer's death. Evaluate the values and the attitudes toward death suggested by this story.
4. According to Kübler-Ross, why do humans find facing death or talking about death (particularly their own deaths) so difficult? Do you agree with her observations? Explain.
5. In paragraph 2, Kübler-Ross suggests particular readers she hopes to reach. Evaluate the essay, keeping these readers in mind. How successfully do you think she communicates to them? Cite specific passages from the essay to support your analysis.

BARBARA HUTTMANN (1936–   )

A Crime of Compassion

Barbara Huttmann, R.N., has written two books about the rights of patients:
The Patient's Advocate *(1981) and* Code Blue: A Nurse's True-Life
Story *(1982). The following essay originally appeared on the "My Turn" page*
of Newsweek, *August 8, 1983.*

"Murderer," a man shouted. "God help patients who get *you* for a nurse."
"What gives you the right to play God?" another one asked.

It was the Phil Donahue show where the guest is a fatted calf and the
audience a 220-strong flock of vultures hungering to pick at the bones. I had
told them about Mac, one of my favorite cancer patients. "We resuscitated him
52 times in just one month. I refused to resuscitate him again. I simply sat there
and held his hand while he died."

There wasn't time to explain that Mac was a young, witty, macho cop
who walked into the hospital with 32 pounds of attack equipment, looking as
if he could single-handedly protect the whole city, if not the entire state. "Can't
get rid of this cough," he said. Otherwise, he felt great.

5   Before the day was over, tests confirmed that he had lung cancer. And
before the year was over, I loved him, his wife, Maura, and their three kids as if
they were my own. All the nurses loved him. And we all battled his disease for
six months without ever giving death a second thought. Six months isn't such
a long time in the whole scheme of things, but it was long enough to see him
lose his youth, his wit, his macho, his hair, his bowel and bladder control, his
sense of taste and smell, and his ability to do the slightest thing for himself. It
was also long enough to watch Maura's transformation from a young woman
into a haggard, beaten old lady.

When Mac had wasted away to a 60-pound skeleton kept alive by liquid
food we poured down a tube, IV solutions we dripped into his veins, and oxygen we piped to a mask on his face, he begged us: "Mercy . . . for God's sake,
please just let me go."

The first time he stopped breathing, the nurse pushed the button that
calls a "code blue" throughout the hospital and sends a team rushing to resuscitate the patient. Each time he stopped breathing, sometimes two or three times
in one day, the code team came again. The doctors and technicians worked
their miracles and walked away. The nurses stayed to wipe the saliva that drooled
from his mouth, irrigate the big craters of bedsores that covered his hips, suc-
tion the lung fluids that threatened to drown him, clean the feces that burned
his skin like lye, pour the liquid food down the tube attached to his stomach,
put pillows between his knees to ease the bone-on-bone pain, turn him every
hour to keep the bedsores from getting worse, and change his gown and linen
every two hours to keep him from being soaked in perspiration.

At night I went home and tried to scrub away the smell of decaying flesh that seemed woven into the fabric of my uniform. It was in my hair, the upholstery of my car—there was no washing it away. And every night I prayed that Mac would die, that his agonized eyes would never again plead with me to let him die.

Every morning I asked his doctor for a "no-code" order. Without that order, we had to resuscitate every patient who stopped breathing. His doctor was one of several who believe we must extend life as long as we have the means and knowledge to do it. To not do it is to be liable for negligence, at least in the eyes of many people, including some nurses. I thought about what it would be like to stand before a judge, accused of murder, if Mac stopped breathing and I didn't call a code.

And after the fifty-second code, when Mac was still lucid enough to beg for death again, and Maura was crumbled in my arms again, and when no amount of pain medication stilled his moaning and agony, I wondered about a spiritual judge. Was all this misery and suffering supposed to be building character or infusing us all with the sense of humility that comes from impotence?   10

Had we, the whole medical community, become so arrogant that we believed in the illusion of salvation through science? Had we become so self-righteous that we thought meddling in God's work was our duty, our moral imperative and our legal obligation? Did we really believe that we had the right to force "life" on a suffering man who had begged for the right to die?

Such questions haunted me more than ever early one morning when Maura went home to change her clothes and I was bathing Mac. He had been still for so long, I thought he at last had the blessed relief of coma. Then he opened his eyes and moaned, "Pain . . . no more . . . Barbara . . . do something . . . God, let me go."

The desperation in his eyes and voice riddled me with guilt. "I'll stop," I told him as I injected the pain medication.

I sat on the bed and held Mac's hands in mine. He pressed his bony fingers against my hand and muttered, "Thanks." Then there was one soft sigh and I felt his hands go cold in mine. "Mac?" I whispered, as I waited for his chest to rise and fall again.

A clutch of panic banded my chest, drew my finger to the code button,   15
urged me to do something, anything . . . but sit there alone with death. I kept one finger on the button, without pressing it, as a waxen pallor slowly transformed his face from person to empty shell. Nothing I've ever done in my 47 years has taken so much effort as it took *not* to press that code button.

Eventually, when I was as sure as I could be that the code team would fail to bring him back, I entered the legal twilight zone and pushed the button. The team tried. And while they were trying, Maura walked into the room and shrieked, "No . . . don't let them do this to him . . . for God's sake . . . please, no more."

Cradling her in my arms was like cradling myself, Mac, and all those patients and nurses who had been in this place before, who do the best they can in a death-denying society.

So a TV audience accused me of murder. Perhaps I am guilty. If a doctor had written a no-code order, which is the only *legal* alternative, would he have felt any less guilty? Until there is legislation making it a criminal act to code a patient who has requested the right to die, we will all of us risk the same fate as Mac. For whatever reason, we developed the means to prolong life, and now we are forced to use it. We do not have the right to die.   *1983*

CONSIDERATIONS

1. Comment on the introduction to this piece. How does it affect you, the reader? Explain.
2. Would you characterize this essay as one that is mainly informative or one that is persuasive? Explain.
3. What details affect you, the reader, the most? Is there any place where the author exaggerates or understates the problem? Do you find her believable? Why or why not?
4. What is the doctor's main reason for not signing a "no-code" order? Is he acting on moral grounds? What do you think?
5. This essay is more than 20 years old, and today, in many cases, the patient is the one who makes her or his wishes known and gives the orders for continued life support or "Do Not Resuscitate." Discuss how this new law changes or supports the argument that Huttmann puts forth in this piece.

CONNECTIONS: DEATH

1. Several works in this section depict death as an enemy to be faced and fought; others view death as a natural part of the life cycle, to be accepted and even welcomed. Respond to these opposing views of death, considering any or all of the following works: "Old Man and Old Woman," "The Jilting of Granny Weatherall," "To Hell with Dying," "Buffalo's Bill's," "Death, be not proud," the three Dickinson poems, and "On the Fear of Death."
2. Compare the use of humor to address the serious subject of death as demonstrated in the following works: "To Hell with Dying" and *On Tidy Endings.*
3. Consider the relationships suggested between love and death by any or all of the following works: "The Jilting of Granny Weatherall," "A Rose for Emily," and *On Tidy Endings.*
4. Explain the advice you think Elisabeth Kübler-Ross would give any or all of the following people: (1) the parents in "To Hell with Dying" during the

time their young children were called on to act as resurrecting angels; (2) the family, doctor, and priest who wait at Granny Weatherall's bedside; (3) the speaker in "How to Watch Your Brother Die," (4) Arthur in *On Tidy Endings.*

5. If you have faced the death of a loved one, how did your feelings and responses compare with those depicted in several of the works in this chapter?

6. Discuss the responses of—and the roles played by—those who are well as they face the dying and death of those close to them. Consider any number of these works: "The Jilting of Granny Weatherall," "During a Son's Dangerous Illness," "How to Watch Your Brother Die," *On Tidy Endings,* and "A Crime of Compassion."

SUGGESTIONS FOR EXTENDED CONNECTIONS AMONG CHAPTERS

1. Under what circumstances can death be deemed "natural" and "right" as opposed to "unnatural" and "unfair"? Consider the following selections as you think about this question:

"The Red Convertible"	218
"Mid-Term Break"	239
"The Black Cat"	1154
"The Birthmark"	1034
Trifles	666
"An Occurrence at Owl Creek Bridge"	904
"The Things They Carried"	934
Wit	1085
"Soul Gone Home"	792

2. Consider the impact of death on those who witness it or those who survive the death of others. Use the following works to raise possibilities for further research and analysis on this topic:

"The Red Convertible"	218
Hamlet	244
"Mid-Term Break"	239
Wit	1085
"Sonny's Blues"	412
"The Shawl"	929
"The Management of Grief"	948
Riders to the Sea	874

3. Reflect on how the perception of death might change depending on the point of view of a character or narrator in the following works. Suggestions for a new point of view are given for each title, but you can certainly choose another perspective.

"The Red Convertible"	218
(Henry, Jr.)	

SUGGESTIONS FOR COLLABORATIVE LEARNING

1. Working in groups of three or four, individually research the history of euthanasia in a variety of cultures, including the United States. As a group, write a report that explains clearly the data you've uncovered; individually, write a conclusion that addresses the future: Will euthanasia become more prevalent and accepted in years to come? Based on the trends you've examined, what do you think?

2. Working in groups of four, interview two groups of people—medical personnel and laypeople—to discover their feelings about death, dying, and euthanasia. Once the interviews have been conducted, share the information collectively; then, individually, write a report in which you analyze the information you've gathered.

WEB CONNECTIONS

1. Awarded the Times Pick by the *Los Angeles Times,* Ethics Updates, as its founders attest, is "dedicated to promoting the thoughtful discussion of difficult moral issues." Many of the issues addressed on this site echo the conflicts raised by the pieces within this section, including issues related to euthanasia, the death penalty, and war and terrorism. In addition to providing links to videos, lectures, readings, and Supreme Court rulings, this site also provides extensive links to ethics authorities and theories, from those of the Greek philosopher Aristotle to more recent theories on ethical relativism, sexism, and racism. Visitors to this site can also post contributions to thoughtful forums. See http://ethics.sandiego.edu.

2. National Public Radio provides a wealth of diverse and provocative resources on their site Exploring Death in America. Visitors to the site can

browse poems by such writers as John Updike and Alice Walker; essays and interviews with hospice workers who talk about the "work of grief"; excerpts from novels and short stories, including *Moby Dick* and *Charlotte's Web*; a select collection of spiritual and religious texts, from Muslim, Christian and Jewish writers; and excerpts from plays and Broadway scripts, including T. S. Eliot's *Family Reunion* as well as the famous "Chuckles Bites the Dust" episode on *The Mary Tyler Moore Show.* The site also includes stunning photographs and artwork, including "Snow Geese with Reflections of the Snow." See http://www.npr.org/programs/death/readings/index.html.

Four Poets: Then and Now

MAKING CONNECTIONS

Poetry intertwines with the European roots of this nation. The tradition begins with the works of Puritan poets Anne Bradstreet (c. 1612–1672) and Edward Taylor (c. 1642–1729). In the eighteenth century, African-American freed slave Phillis Wheatley (c. 1753–1784) adds a new voice. Emily Dickinson's poetry demonstrates the way that this poetic tradition continued in the nineteenth century. This chapter presents selections from Dickinson and the poetry of Robert Frost, Billy Collins, and Rita Dove, three other noted poets who wrote—or began writing—in the twentieth century. Together, these poems provide a sample of themes that are considered quintessentially American.

By the time Robert Frost, the second poet whose work is represented here, was born in San Francisco in 1874, Emily Dickinson, then 44, had written hundreds of poems. At her death in 1886, Frost was 12 years old, and he had already lost his father and moved across the country to Lawrence, Massachusetts. Many years later, he served as poet in residence at Amherst College, located in Dickinson's home town, Amherst, Massachusetts.

Contemporary poet Billy Collins (b. 1941) started his life during the early years of World War II, a time when Frost was a mature, published writer. Like Collins, Rita Dove (b. 1952) lived her early years while Frost was still alive and writing. Frost, Collins, and Dove all served, at different times, as poet laureate of the United States. Robert Frost served as poet laureate from 1958 to 1959, and brought poetry to the entire nation when he was invited to compose a new poem and read it for the Inauguration of John F. Kennedy in 1960. Because this event was televised, a broad audience of Americans saw the aging poet read his words as the new first lady, Jacqueline Kennedy, held the pages of his manuscript steady in the strong winds of the day. Rita Dove, poet laureate

Timeline: Key Events in the Lives of Four American Poets
Emily Dickinson, Robert Frost, Billy Collins, and Rita Dove

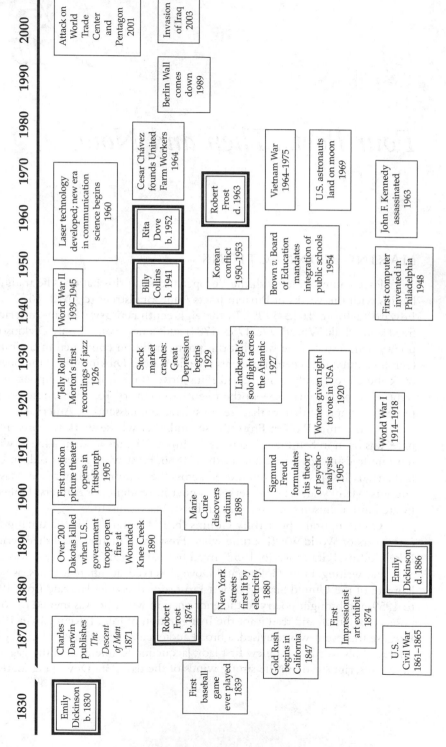

from 1993 to 1995, promoted the work of poets whose themes express the minority experience in America. Many of the events she sponsored paid special attention to children and young adults, including most notably a series of readings by young Crow Indian poets. Billy Collins, laureate from 2001 to 2003, started Poetry 180, a project intended to encourage high school students to read aloud—perhaps over the public address system—one poem on each school day. Collins feels that "poetry is an event for the ear" and believes that hearing poetry every day can lead all of us to "a new relationship with our language"—and new insights into our own lives, the lives of others, and the world in which we live together.

While the poems of Dickinson, Frost, Collins, and Dove were composed at different times in the history of the United States, their works address the themes of loss, isolation, danger, displacement, courage, and survival, which many see as common strands of American culture. The poetry of these four great American writers reflects their diverse cultural backgrounds; each poet also demonstrates a complex understanding of poetic conventions and a canny, almost paradoxical, ability both to work with and to challenge traditional forms. All four poets see the dark side of life, yet write with wit; in their poems, humor and irony often play off violent, ugly, or disturbing images.

The following selections, as well as the brief commentaries on the poets' lives and works, provide the opportunity for a closer look at how each writer sees the world. Their similarities, as well as their differences, open possibilities for thinking about and comparing their visions of the times, people, and places they knew.

EMILY DICKINSON (1830–1886)

Born on December 10, 1830, Emily Dickinson was the daughter of Edward and Emily Norcross Dickinson, a prominent Amherst, Massachusetts, family. Her grandfather was a founder of Amherst College, and her father, who served the college as both treasurer and trustee, was a respected lawyer who later became a member of Congress. Emily Dickinson grew up in a household where her mother apparently bowed to the wishes of her stern and autocratic husband. In addition, Edward Dickinson exercised strong control over his children, and Emily's brother, Austin, gave up his desire to move west in deference to his father. Neither Emily nor her sister, Lavinia, married; however, Austin did defy his father in marrying Susan Gilbert, to whom Edward objected because she was a sophisticated New

Yorker. Despite Emily's father's objections, however, Emily and Susan became fast friends, and Emily found in her sister-in-law the soul mate she had been lacking in the conservative, church-dominated Amherst community. Susan proved a source of mental and emotional nourishment that Emily had not found in her one foray outside the Amherst community when, in 1847, at her father's wishes, she enrolled in the South Hadley Female Seminary (now Mount Holyoke College). During her time at school, Emily's strong independence was severely challenged by the rigorous religious orthodoxy expected of students, and she left after only a year. Following her return to Amherst, she remained in her childhood home for the rest of her life, making only very brief visits to Boston, Washington, and Philadelphia.

Dickinson's reclusiveness contributed to the myths that have grown up around her memory. She is often depicted as an eccentric, retiring maiden lady who spent her time baking her famed "black bread" (probably a molasses gingerbread) and locking herself in her room to write poetry. However, she almost certainly lived a far more lively, engaged life than these images would suggest. Her friendship with her sister-in-law, Susan, led to their reading and discussing books smuggled by Austin into the Dickinson household past the censoring eyes of their father. Also, the Dickinson family was held in great respect throughout the state of Massachusetts, and thus a steady stream of prominent visitors arrived at the Dickinson house and at the neighboring house of Austin and Susan. In addition, Dickinson was a lively and prolific letter writer who kept up an engaged, thoughtful, and witty correspondence with many friends, relatives, and literary figures such as the poet Helen Hunt Jackson. Dickinson enjoyed the friendship and encouragement of at least two male mentors, the Reverend Charles Wadsworth and Thomas Wentworth Higginson, a poetry editor for The Atlantic Monthly.

The Reverend Charles Wadsworth, a charismatic minister whom Dickinson apparently met in Philadelphia in 1855 during one of her few trips away from Amherst, has been identified by some scholars as the tragic and unattainable (because he was married) love of Dickinson's life. However, her most recent biographers question the supposition that Dickinson became a recluse in response to her unrequited love for Wadsworth. Rather than longing for him as a lover, Dickinson seemed to see him, instead, as a "preceptor" and as her "safest friend," a man with great intelligence and knowledge of the world who could read her poetry and give responses that she highly valued.

In 1861, when she was 31, Dickinson submitted several poems to Thomas Wentworth Higginson at The Atlantic Monthly *requesting that he read them and "say if my Verse is alive." Her purpose in sending the poems seems to have been a desire not for publication but rather for the critical response she believed Higginson could give. However, in one of her early letters, she did ask him to help her struggle with the question of how a poet can write for publication and still remain true to her own artistic vision. She continued her correspondence with Higginson throughout her lifetime and respected him as a mentor. It is interesting to note, however, that there is no evidence that she revised any of her poems to the more conventional forms Higginson suggested.*

Although Dickinson scholars differ in reporting the exact number, it appears that no more than twelve, and possibly as few as six, poems were published in her lifetime. When she died, in 1886, she left behind instructions for her sister to destroy the letters she had received from her large circle of correspondents. As Lavinia was gathering these papers, she came across a box that held over 1,100 poems, some already bound into neat packets. Since Dickinson had not specifically required that the poems be destroyed, Lavinia, in consultation with Dickinson's confidante and sister-in-law, Susan, saved the manuscripts and, after various complications, convinced Thomas Higginson and Mabel Loomis Todd° to edit and publish a selection of the poems.

Dickinson's poetry, with its innovative punctuation, capitalization, and line breaks, was indeed unusual for the nineteenth century and today remains arresting in its freshness and lack of conventionality. While the poems contain the occasional comma, period, exclamation mark, or question mark, the dash is by far the most common punctuation. In the original manuscripts, the dashes are far from uniform. Some seem slanted upward, some down. Some are quite short, others long. There has been much scholarly speculation about the meaning of the dashes. A convincing argument can be made for seeing these dashes as the poet's invitation to the reader to slow down and pay particular attention to the words or phrases they surround.

Dickinson's poems confront difficult questions relating to faith, mortality, love, and friendship. Her stunning images reflect a connection to the mystical, transcendent dimension of life yet also express her highly original and witty view of the details of day-to-day living. While some of the poems no doubt reflect the opinions and attitudes of the poet herself, it's important to remember that she understood the concept of the literary persona and spoke about the "self" in her poetry as "a supposed person." In her literary work, as well as in her relationships with her family, friends, and community, Dickinson was a person far ahead of her time, a visionary with a keen understanding of the intricacy of human hearts, minds, and spirits.

If I can stop one Heart from breaking

If I can stop one Heart from breaking
I shall not live in vain
If I can ease one Life the Aching
or cool one Pain

Or help one fainting Robin   5
Unto his Nest again
I shall not live in Vain.   *c. 1864*

Mabel Loomis Todd: A neighbor of the Dickinsons (with whom Emily's brother, Austin, had an extramarital affair).

Wild Nights—Wild Nights!

Wild Nights—Wild Nights!
Were I with thee
Wild Nights should be
Our luxury!

5   Futile—the Winds—
To a Heart in port—
Done with the Compass—
Done with the Chart!

Rowing in Eden—
10   Ah, the Sea!
Might I but moor—Tonight—
In Thee!   *1861*

There's a certain Slant of light

There's a certain Slant of light,
Winter Afternoons—
That oppresses, like the Heft
Of Cathedral Tunes—

5   Heavenly Hurt, it gives us—
We can find no scar,
But internal difference,
Where the Meanings, are—

None may teach it—Any—
10   'Tis the Seal Despair—
An imperial affliction
Sent us of the Air—

When it comes, the Landscape listens—
Shadows—hold their breath—
15   When it goes, 'tis like the Distance
On the look of Death—   c. *1861*

I'm Nobody! Who are you?

I'm Nobody! Who are you?
Are you—Nobody—too?
Then there's a pair of us!
Don't tell! they'd banish us—you know!

How dreary—to be—Somebody!   *5*
How public—like a Frog—
To tell your name—the livelong June—
To an admiring Bog!   *c. 1861*

"Heaven"—is what I cannot reach!

"Heaven"—is what I cannot reach!
The Apple on the Tree—
Provided it do hopeless—hang—
That—"Heaven" is—to Me!

The Color, on the Cruising Cloud—   *5*
The interdicted Land—
Behind the Hill—the House behind—
There—Paradise—is found!

Her teasing Purples—Afternoons—
The credulous—decoy—   *10*
Enamored—of the Conjuror—
That spurned us—Yesterday!   *c. 1861*

After great pain, a formal feeling comes—

After great pain, a formal feeling comes—
The Nerves sit ceremonious, like Tombs—
The stiff Heart questions was it He, that bore,
And Yesterday, or Centuries before?

The Feet, mechanical, go round—   *5*
Of Ground, or Air, or Ought—
A Wooden way
Regardless grown,
A Quartz contentment, like a stone—

This is the Hour of Lead—   *10*
Remembered, if outlived,
As Freezing persons, recollect the Snow—
First—Chill—then Stupor—then the letting go—   *c. 1862*

The Brain—is wider than the Sky—

The Brain—is wider than the Sky—
For—put them side by side—
The one the other will contain
With ease—and You—beside—

5   The Brain is deeper than the sea—
    For—hold them—Blue to Blue—
    The one the other will absorb—
    As Sponges—Buckets—do—

    The Brain is just the weight of God—
10 For—Heft them—Pound for Pound—
    And they will differ—if they do—
    As Syllable from Sound—   *c. 1862*

This is my letter to the World

    This is my letter to the World
    That never wrote to Me—
    The simple News that Nature told—
    With tender Majesty

5   Her Message is committed
    To Hands I cannot see—
    For love of Her—Sweet—countrymen—
    Judge tenderly—of Me   *c. 1862*

The Soul selects her own Society—

    The Soul selects her own Society—
    Then—shuts the Door—
    To her divine Majority—
    Present no more—

5   Unmoved—she notes the Chariots—pausing—
    At her low Gate—
    Unmoved—an Emperor be kneeling
    Upon her Mat—

    I've known her—from an ample nation—
10 Choose One—
    Then—close the Valves of her attention—
    Like Stone—   *c. 1862*

I felt a Cleaving in my Mind—

    I felt a Cleaving in my Mind—
    As if my Brain had split—
    I tried to match it—Seam by Seam—
    But could not make them fit.

More Resources on
Emily Dickinson

 In *ARIEL*
- Brief biography of Dickinson
- Complete texts of Dickinson poems with hyperlinked comments
- Video discussion of Dickinson's writing
- Video clip exploring the world of Dickinson's writing
- Video clip of a dramatic reading of "Because I could not stop for Death"
- Audio clips of readings of "My life closed twice before its close" and "I taste a liquor never brewed"
- Analysis of Dickinson's style
- Bibliography of scholarly works on Dickinson

 In the Online Learning Center for *Responding to Literature*
- Brief biography of Dickinson
- List of major works by Dickinson
- Text of Dickinson's "I heard a Fly buzz—when I died—"
- Web links to more resources on Dickinson
- Additional questions for experiencing and interpreting Dickinson's writing

The thought behind, I strove to join   5
Unto the thought before—
But Sequence ravelled out of Sound
Like Balls—upon a Floor.   *c. 1864*

Tell all the Truth but tell it slant—

Tell all the Truth but tell it slant—
Success in Circuit lies
Too bright for our infirm Delight
The Truth's superb surprise

As Lightning to the Children eased   5
With explanation kind
The Truth must dazzle gradually
Or every man be blind—   c. *1868*

ROBERT FROST (1874–1963)

*Robert Frost's father, William Frost, ventured out
of his native New Hampshire to work as headmaster at a small private school in Pennsylvania.
There he met and married the school's only
teacher, Isabelle Moodie. After their marriage in
1873, William and Isabelle struck out for San
Francisco, where their son Robert was born. Their
marriage was apparently stormy, and Isabelle left
William for a year during Robert's early childhood. During these years, William worked as a
journalist for the* San Francisco Bulletin. *He
died in 1885 of tuberculosis, possibly complicated
by alcoholism. Following her husband's last
wishes, Isabelle and her children returned east with his body so that he might be
buried in Lawrence, Massachusetts.*

*Robert attended high school in Lawrence, proving himself an excellent student
of classics and becoming known as class poet. He shared the honor of being
named class valedictorian with Elinor White, whom he resolved to marry. After
attending Dartmouth for part of a semester, Frost dropped out and attempted to
persuade Elinor to set the wedding date immediately. She, however, insisted on
first completing her studies at St. Lawrence College, graduating in 1895 and
agreeing to the marriage in the same year.*

*After supporting himself and Elinor at a variety of jobs while continuing to
write poetry, Frost decided to return to college and in 1897 persuaded Harvard
to accept him as a special student. In 1899, the Frosts moved to Derry, New
Hampshire, living on a farm purchased for them by Frost's grandfather. The years
in New Hampshire were difficult. By 1905, Elinor had given birth to five children, and the family faced constant economic problems. Frost acknowledged to
friends that he had seriously contemplated suicide during this time. In 1906,
however, his financial circumstances improved when he accepted a teaching position at Pinkerton Academy, where he was inspired to introduce creative innova-
tions to the established curriculum, teaching drama and writing most of the
poems that he eventually published in his first book.*

*Because of his difficulty in finding an American publisher, Frost sold the farm
in 1911 and moved his family to London. There he submitted his poems to the
English publisher Alfred Nutt, who published the collection* A Boy's Will *in
1913. The book won great acclaim in England, and as a result Frost became
acquainted with many poets whose work he had long admired, including Ezra
Pound, William Butler Yeats, and Amy Lowell. In 1915, World War I forced the
Frost family to return to the United States. The success that Frost had enjoyed in
England spread to the United States, and in 1917 he was invited to teach at*

Amherst College, where he remained for many years, occasionally spending time at other colleges and universities as visiting professor or poet-in-residence.

Lawrance Thompson's biography of Frost, published between 1966 and 1976, presents convincing evidence that Frost was not simply the kindly, wise poet-farmer living the idyllic rural life that many of his admirers imagined; he was far more complex. He had suffered many personal tragedies, including the death, at age four, of his first-born son, the mental illness of his sister Jeanie, the death of his daughter Marjorie following childbirth in 1934, the estrangement and death of his wife (who refused to see him during her final illness) in 1938, and the suicide of his only living son in 1940. Thompson's research suggests that these troubles, combined with Frost's ambitions and vanity, often led to mean-spirited and even vindictive actions that alienated many of his friends and family members.

Whatever his personal failings may have been, he traveled widely, serving as a goodwill ambassador to South America and to what was then the Soviet Union. In 1961, he was recognized as one of America's strongest and most distinct voices when John F. Kennedy invited him to read a poem at the inauguration ceremonies. Frost continued to accept speaking engagements until his death, at the age of eighty-eight, on January 29, 1963.

Frost's poems often seem deceptively simple because he draws on familiar subjects, often depicting scenes from the natural world as well as people with easily recognized strengths and failings. His language, while powerful and evocative, is easily accessible to most readers and so it is easy to overlook the way his poems often depend on ambiguity for their impact. His works offer many different possibilities, whether they focus on an image from nature (see, for example, the extended discussion of "The Road Not Taken" in Chapter 1, page 5, as well as "Nothing Gold Can Stay," "Stopping by Woods on a Snowy Evening," and "Desert Places") or on a scene from daily life ("Mending Wall," "Home Burial," and "Out, Out—"). Frost's poetry can never be reduced to a formula; his work often surprises the reader. For example, "Acquainted with the Night" uses city images rather than the rural, country scenes many readers associate with his work. The selections offered here provide merely a glimpse at the variety that characterizes Frost's vast body of work.

Mending Wall

Something there is that doesn't love a wall,
That sends the frozen-ground-swell under it,
And spills the upper boulders in the sun;
And makes gaps even two can pass abreast.
The work of hunters is another thing: 5
I have come after them and made repair
Where they have left not one stone on a stone,
But they would have the rabbit out of hiding,
To please the yelping dogs. The gaps I mean,

10   No one has seen them made or heard them made,
      But at spring mending-time we find them there.
      I let my neighbor know beyond the hill;
      And on a day we meet to walk the line
      And set the wall between us once again.
15   We keep the wall between us as we go.
      To each the boulders that have fallen to each.
      And some are loaves and some so nearly balls
      We have to use a spell to make them balance:
      "Stay where you are until our backs are turned!"
20   We wear our fingers rough with handling them.
      Oh, just another kind of outdoor game,
      One on a side. It comes to little more:
      There where it is we do not need the wall:
      He is all pine and I am apple orchard.
25   My apple trees will never get across
      And eat the cones under his pines, I tell him.
      He only says, "Good fences make good neighbors."
      Spring is the mischief in me, and I wonder
      If I could put a notion in his head:
30   "*Why* do they make good neighbors? Isn't it
      Where there are cows? But here there are no cows.
      Before I built a wall I'd ask to know
      What I was walling in or walling out,
      And to whom I was like to give offense.
35   Something there is that doesn't love a wall,
      That wants it down." I could say "Elves" to him,
      But it's not elves exactly, and I'd rather
      He said it for himself. I see him there
      Bringing a stone grasped firmly by the top
40   In each hand, like an old-stone savage armed.
      He moves in darkness as it seems to me,
      Not of woods only and the shade of trees.
      He will not go behind his father's saying,
      And he likes having thought of it so well
45   He says again, "Good fences make good neighbors."   *1914*

Home Burial°

He saw her from the bottom of the stairs
Before she saw him. She was starting down,

Home Burial: It was the custom until the early twentieth century for remote homes and farms to
have their own family burial ground.

Looking back over her shoulder at some fear.
She took a doubtful step and then undid it
To raise herself and look again. He spoke   5
Advancing toward her: "What is it you see
From up there always—for I want to know."
She turned and sank upon her skirts at that,
And her face changed from terrified to dull.
He said to gain time: "What is it you see,"   10
Mounting until she cowered under him.
"I will find out now—you must tell me, dear."
She, in her place, refused him any help
With the least stiffening of her neck and silence.
She let him look, sure that he wouldn't see,   15
Blind creature; and a while he didn't see.
But at last he murmured, "Oh," and again, "Oh."

"What is it—what?" she said.

                    "Just that I see."

"You don't," she challenged. "Tell me what it is."

"The wonder is I didn't see at once.   20
I never noticed it from here before.
I must be wonted° to it—that's the reason.
The little graveyard where my people are!
So small the window frames the whole of it.
Not so much larger than a bedroom, is it?   25
There are three stones of slate and one of marble,
Broad-shouldered little slabs there in the sunlight
On the sidehill. We haven't to mind *those*.
But I understand: it is not the stones,
But the child's mound—"

              "Don't, don't, don't, don't," she cried.   30

She withdrew, shrinking from beneath his arm
That rested on the banister, and slid downstairs;
And turned on him with such a daunting look,
He said twice over before he knew himself:
"Can't a man speak of his own child he's lost?"   35

"Not you!—Oh, where's my hat? Oh, I don't need it!
I must get out of here. I must get air.—
I don't know rightly whether any man can."

22 *wonted:* Accustomed.

"Amy! Don't go to someone else this time.
40 Listen to me. I won't come down the stairs."
He sat and fixed his chin between his fists.
"There's something I should like to ask you, dear."

"You don't know how to ask it."

                              "Help me, then."
Her fingers moved the latch for all reply.
45 "My words are nearly always an offense.
I don't know how to speak of anything
So as to please you. But I might be taught,
I should suppose. I can't say I see how.
A man must partly give up being a man
50 With womenfolk. We could have some arrangement
By which I'd bind myself to keep hands off
Anything special you're a-mind to name.
Though I don't like such things 'twixt those that love.
Two that don't love can't live together without them.
55 But two that do can't live together with them."
She moved the latch in a little. "Don't—don't go.
Don't carry it to someone else this time.
Tell me about it if it's something human.
Let me into your grief. I'm not so much
60 Unlike other folks as your standing there
Apart would make me out. Give me my chance.
I do think, though, you overdo it a little.
What was it brought you up to think it the thing
To take your mother-loss of a first child
65 So inconsolably—in the face of love.
You'd think his memory might be satisfied—"

"There you go sneering now!"

                              "I'm not, I'm not!
You make me angry. I'll come down to you.
God, what a woman! And it's come to this,
70 A man can't speak of his own child that's dead."

"You can't because you don't know how to speak.
If you had any feelings, you that dug
With your own hand—how could you?—his little grave;
I saw you from that very window there,
75 Making the gravel leap and leap in air,
Leap up, like that, like that, and land so lightly

And roll back down the mound beside the hole.
I thought, Who is that man? I didn't know you.
And I crept down the stairs and up the stairs
To look again, and still your spade kept lifting.   *80*
Then you came in. I heard your rumbling voice
Out in the kitchen, and I don't know why,
But I went near to see with my own eyes.
You could sit there with the stains on your shoes
Of the fresh earth from your own baby's grave   *85*
And talk about your everyday concerns.
You had stood the spade up against the wall
Outside there in the entry, for I saw it."

"I shall laugh the worst laugh I ever laughed.
I'm cursed. God, if I don't believe I'm cursed."   *90*

"I can repeat the very words you were saying.
'Three foggy mornings and one rainy day
Will rot the best birch fence a man can build.'
Think of it, talk like that at such a time!
What had how long it takes a birch to rot   *95*
To do with what was in the darkened parlour.
You *couldn't* care! The nearest friends can go
With anyone to death, comes so far short
They might as well not try to go at all.
No, from the time when one is sick to death,   *100*
One is alone, and he dies more alone.
Friends make pretense of following to the grave,
But before one is in it, their minds are turned
And making the best of their way back to life
And living people, and things they understand.   *105*
But the world's evil. I won't have grief so
If I can change it. Oh, I won't, I won't!"

"There, you have said it all and you feel better.
You won't go now. You're crying. Close the door.
The heart's gone out of it: why keep it up?   *110*
Amy! There's someone coming down the road!"

"*You*—oh, you think the talk is all. I must go—
Somewhere out of this house. How can I make you—"

"If—you—do!" She was opening the door wider.
"Where do you mean to go? First tell me that.   *115*
I'll follow and bring you back by force. I *will!*—"   *1914*

"Out, Out—"

The buzz saw snarled and rattled in the yard
And made dust and dropped stove-length sticks of wood,
Sweet-scented stuff when the breeze drew across it.
And from there those that lifted eyes could count
5   Five mountain ranges one behind the other
Under the sunset far into Vermont.
And the saw snarled and rattled, snarled and rattled,
As it ran light, or had to bear a load.
And nothing happened: day was all but done.
10   Call it a day, I wish they might have said
To please the boy by giving him the half hour
That a boy counts so much when saved from work.
His sister stood beside them in her apron
To tell them "Supper." At the word, the saw,
15   As if to prove saws knew what supper meant,
Leaped out at the boy's hand, or seemed to leap—
He must have given the hand. However it was,
Neither refused the meeting. But the hand!
The boy's first outcry was a rueful laugh,
20   As he swung toward them holding up the hand,
Half in appeal, but half as if to keep
The life from spilling. Then the boy saw all—
Since he was old enough to know, big boy
Doing a man's work, though a child at heart—
25   He saw all spoiled. "Don't let him cut my hand off—
The doctor, when he comes. Don't let him, sister!"
So. But the hand was gone already.
The doctor put him in the dark of ether.
He lay and puffed his lips out with his breath.
30   And then—the watcher at his pulse took fright.
No one believed. They listened at his heart.
Little—less—nothing!—and that ended it.
No more to build on there. And they, since they
Were not the one dead, turned to their affairs.   *1916*

Nothing Gold Can Stay

Nature's first green is gold,
Her hardest hue to hold.
Her early leaf's a flower;
But only so an hour.

Then leaf subsides to leaf.   5
So Eden sank to grief,
So dawn goes down to day.
Nothing gold can stay.   *1923*

Stopping by Woods on a Snowy Evening

Whose woods these are I think I know.
His house is in the village, though;
He will not see me stopping here
To watch his woods fill up with snow.

My little horse must think it queer   5
To stop without a farmhouse near
Between the woods and frozen lake
The darkest evening of the year.

He gives his harness bells a shake
To ask if there is some mistake.   10
The only other sound's the sweep
Of easy wind and downy flake.

The woods are lovely, dark and deep,
But I have promises to keep,
And miles to go before I sleep,   15
And miles to go before I sleep.   *1923*

Acquainted with the Night

I have been one acquainted with the night.
I have walked out in rain—and back in rain.
I have outwalked the furthest city light.

I have looked down the saddest city lane.
I have passed by the watchman on his beat   5
And dropped my eyes, unwilling to explain.

I have stood still and stopped the sound of feet
When far away an interrupted cry
Came over houses from another street,

But not to call me back or say good-by;   10
And further still at an unearthly height
One luminary clock against the sky

Proclaimed the time was neither wrong nor right.
I have been one acquainted with the night.   *1928*

Desert Places

Snow falling and night falling fast, oh, fast
In a field I looked into going past,
And the ground almost covered smooth in snow,
But a few weeds and stubble showing last.

5   The woods around it have it—it is theirs.
All animals are smothered in their lairs.
I am too absent-spirited to count;
The loneliness includes me unawares.

And lonely as it is that loneliness
10 Will be more lonely ere it will be less—
A blanker whiteness of benighted snow
With no expression, nothing to express.

They cannot scare me with their empty spaces
Between stars—on stars where no human race is.
15 I have it in me so much nearer home
To scare myself with my own desert places.   *1936*

More Resources on
Robert Frost

In *ARIEL*

- Brief biography of Frost
- Complete texts of "The Road Not Taken," "Mending Wall," and "Stopping by Woods on a Snowy Evening," all with hyperlinked comments
- Audio clips of readings of "The Road Not Taken" and "Stopping by Woods on a Snowy Evening"
- Analysis of symbol in "The Road Not Taken"
- Bibliography of scholarly works on Frost

In the Online Learning Center for *Responding to Literature*

- Brief biography of Frost
- List of major works by Frost
- Web links to more resources on Frost
- Additional questions for experiencing and interpreting Frost's writing

A Critical Casebook on Robert Frost

DONALD CUNNINGHAM
"Mending Wall"

Perhaps more than any other major American poet of the twentieth century, Robert Frost is considered public property. Despite Lawrance Thompson's biographical revelations, the commonly shared view of Frost, as it has often enough been observed, is that of the crusty old bard with twinkling eyes, white hair and folksy wisdom streaming in the New England air. Even among readers who recognize this public image as something of a pose, the personality of the poet, however it is conceived, often dominates their reading of his poetry.

Among all his poetry, "Mending Wall," with the possible exception of "The Road Not Taken" and "Stopping by Woods on a Snowy Evening," is probably the most widely known, and possibly one of the most suffused with personality. The great mass of Americans who profess little or no interest in poetry usually know at least two lines of "Mending Wall," and probably most of them have at least some idea of what the poem is about. Most also would assume that the first person narrator of the poem is Frost himself. More surprisingly, the prevailing academic view, I suspect, is that the poem's narrative persona grows so directly out of the poet's experience that it is reasonable to refer to it as Frost. Although the voice is not the bitter one of "Forgive, O Lord . . ." or the skeptical one of "Design" and "Desert Places," it is the quintessential Frostian voice that informs so many of his poems, particularly the short, first-person lyric/narratives.

The difficulty with this view arises when one searches for an expression of normative values in the poem. If the narrator is (more-or-less) Frost, and since the tone is not obviously mocking or bitter, then we look for the norms within the narrative of the poem rather than in the tone itself. We expect to find the norms communicated through the confrontation of values which develops between the two characters. Thus, the conventional reading of the poem:

The poet-narrator describes an often repeated scene (often repeated, we assume, from the simple present tense verbs which suggest repetition or habitual action). He and his neighbor meet in spring to repair a stone wall. The wall separates their property, but because neither man owns livestock, it is not really necessary, and the narrator wonders why they must maintain it. Although acknowledging by implication that it isn't really a very important problem here, he states a larger principle: "Something there is that doesn't love a wall." Not just this, but any wall, one supposes, and the narrator tests the idea by questioning the neighbor about the necessity for this one. The neighbor seems to understand neither the question nor the inappropriateness of the aphorism he uses in reply. The theme of the poem seems to concern barriers to communication between human beings. Although the narrator recognizes a powerful urge to break through these barriers ("Something there is that doesn't love a wall"), it is thwarted by a contradictory desire for isolation which is expressed by the neighbor ("Good fences make good neighbors"). Man is left in a rather primitive, unenlightened state ("old stone savage," "he moves in darkness"), isolated and alone ("we keep the wall between us," "to each the boulders that have fallen to each"). The values expressed by the narrator are usually accepted as normative. He is no slave to tradition as the neighbor seems to be. He is witty, analytic, and intelligent. The neighbor is slow-witted, hidebound by tradition, and trapped in the quasi-wisdom of his father's proverb.

5   In spite of its wide acceptance, there is something about this interpretation that leaves many readers a little uneasy. For all his apparent virtues, there is something unattractive about the narrator. His ". . . I'd rather / He said it for himself" (37–38) is condescending, and his humor there ("I could say elves . . .") and in other places is ponderous. His judgments of the neighbors are harsh, and perhaps not justified by the circumstances as he reports them. There is even a note of self-satisfaction and intellectual elitism in his assertion of his own mischievousness (28), and in the "To whom I was like to give offense [a fence?]" pun in line thirty-four. Finally, for all his talk, he never does tell the neighbor (or the reader) what the "something" is. Instead, the poem ends in condemnation not only of the neighbor's understanding, but of his motives as well: "He likes having thought of it so well / He says again . . ." (44–45).

Perhaps the difficulty many readers feel in reconciling these qualities with the normative role they ascribe to the narrator comes from a too ready willingness to identify the narrator with the poet. If the narrator speaks for the poet, and more especially, if he *is* the poet, then we hesitate to find in him the defects that nevertheless seem to be there. This identification, however, obscures the fundamental relationship between the poet and the poem. If we begin an analysis of "Mending Wall" from an assumption that both characters are fictional for the purposes of the poem (whether or not the literal situation was suggested by a real incident in the poet's life is irrelevant) then both characters will be equally subject to our judgments and to the poet's irony. If we recognize the possibility that the narrator is flawed, that his character is not what he seems to think it is, or at least is not what he seems to think he is telling us it is, then our conclusions about the poem will be less presupposed, and more accurate.

The first line of the poem, then, is apparently a thematic statement. It states the principle which we expect the poem will demonstrate, but it is somewhat vague, even mysterious ("Something there is . . ."), and made curiously formal by the inverted structure. And, it is not nearly as strong a statement as one might first suppose. In fact, it is cautious, even hesitant. The narrator does not claim that something "hates a wall," or "abhors a wall," or "cannot tolerate a wall," but only that it "does not love a wall." At this point, of course, we cannot be sure whether it is genuine reticence, or only an ironic understatement, but in either case we cannot be sure that it is really the thematic statement it seems to be at first.

The second line provides a natural explanation for the gaps in the wall. They are the result of successive freezes and thaws. Although it is a literal explanation, it amplifies the statement made in the first line: walls are unnatural, and if nature had her way, people could cross those boundaries. Nature creates "gaps even two can pass abreast" (4). As literal as they are, the lines begin to suggest that human intercommunication is the ultimate theme of the poem.

The next seven lines (5–11) are a curious digression, especially in the light of the apparent approval of nature's wall-breaking in the preceding lines, approval which is reinforced later in the poem. This digression on wall-gap types does not advance the narrative at all, but delays it. It does, however, help to characterize the narrator. First, it appears that he is something of a student of walls; he knows the difference between the gaps made by nature, and those made by hunters. Moreover, his wall-mending activities are apparently not limited just to "spring mending time." He has "made repair" alone (alone one may suppose, since no companion has been mentioned) after hunters have damaged them. When he imagines the scene in which the wall was torn apart, it is clear that his sympathies are with the hiding rabbit, and not with the hunters and their yelping dogs. Perhaps that should be remembered when he asks in line thirty-one if walls aren't useful only "where there are cows." Here he is clearly conscious not just of their usefulness in keeping cattle where they belong, but also of the protection they offer from the forces that will have one out of hiding. Thus we learn that the narrator knows about walls, that he repairs them, and that his sympathies are with the pursued animals that hide among their stones. Lines ten and eleven reemphasize the mysterious nature of the gaps, and bring the reader back to the central narrative.

Lines twelve through sixteen introduce the circumstances surrounding   *10* this particular spring's wall-mending. Line twelve is noteworthy in the contradiction of the narrator's stated values which it suggests: "I let my neighbor know. . . ." The project is initiated by the narrator, not the neighbor. As the work is described in the following lines, another clue that the narrator's claims are not genuine appears: "we meet to walk the line" (13). That is the property line on which the wall stands. But the overtones of the common use of "to walk the line" as synonymous with "to behave correctly" are clear. This could be seen as an ironic thrust by the narrator toward his traditionalist work-partner, but that does not seem to be the tone of the statement. Moreover, twice in the following two lines, the narrator makes it clear that what they are doing is not just mending the wall; they "set the wall between" them (14), and "keep the wall between" them (15). If it were not for the contrary suggestions in the first eleven lines, we could suppose that the narrator did not approve of this walling in and walling out, but there seems to be no judgment expressed in these lines, nor any apparent consciousness of irony.

The next six lines (17–22) characterize the tone of the day's work. It is hard work but not really unpleasant. The stones don't balance easily, but the response of the two men is good-natured, even fanciful in the make believe

1258   FOUR POETS: THEN AND NOW

spell they use. All in all it is like a game, but the extension of that metaphor in line twenty-two is slightly ominous. "One on a side" describes them literally, one on each side of the wall. But it also suggests competition; they don't seem to be on the same team, and the spirit of cooperation which the preceding lines described is partially negated.

The doubt one begins to feel about the narrator continues to grow through the next fourteen lines, which describe the confrontation of the two men. The section begins with a line which, like the first line of the poem, is equivocal. Just as the narrator would not say that something hates walls, here he will not say that they do not need the wall. Rather, he says that it is un-needed "there where it is." The neighbor seems to disagree, but his answer, the first "Good fences make good neighbors" statement, is not really a direct an-swer to the narrator's claim, nor is it the contradiction the narrator seems to think it is. The narrator immediately responds with "mischief": "Why do they make good neighbors?" (30). It is apparently a rhetorical question, however, since he suggests the answer himself. His ironic, almost petulant "Before I built a wall . . ." statement (32–34) does not quite ring true, asked in the midst of wall-building he himself has initiated. Moreover, if we are to understand the literal wall as a symbol for the intangible things which separate people, then we cannot help but wonder if the narrator's condescending attitude here isn't offensive to the neighbor. The narrator says he would ask what he was walling in or walling out if he were to build a wall, and indeed he does ask the neigh-bor the purpose of the wall they are now repairing. But his statements are a kind of walling out of the possibility that the neighbor's saying has a larger meaning than the one the narrator ascribes to it. The passage ends with a rep-etition of the poem's opening line, which in this context sounds a bit senten-tious. As the opening line of the poem, its vagueness and its inversion catch our attention, but we readily accept the line as a formal statement of principle. Here, however, the quotation marks assure us that the line is actually spoken to the neighbor as a part of the conversation, and the formal language sounds wildly out of place.

The last seven-and-a-half lines (38b–45) are the narrator's judgment of the neighbor. He is like "an old stone savage," he "moves in darkness," and he "will not go behind his father's saying," and he repeats the saying because "he likes having thought of it so well." Certainly the narrator may be right; it may be true that the neighbor will not examine the basis for his father's saying. Per-haps he does simply repeat it as a kind of incantation to justify the wall-build-ing. But the narrator's unqualified certainty of the reason for the neighbor's repetition seems rather ironic since the narrator himself has just finished repeat-ing his own aphorism. And the narrator's assertion that one must "go behind" the obvious meaning that good fences prevent disputes over damage caused by roaming livestock rebounds back against him in the reader's mind. Why, indeed, do good fences make good neighbors? In this case it appears that it is only the mutual maintenance of the wall that makes these neighbors "neighborly." Perhaps even where there are no cows, good fences can make good neighbors, for it is the necessity of keeping the wall in good repair that brings these two men together. The poem neither affirms nor denies other contact between the two, but at "spring mending time" at least, they work together.

Nothing in the poem tells the reader what the neighbor means when he repeats the formula. What is clear, however, is that the narrator, for all his talk of going behind, does not. Although we cannot be sure that the neighbor understands more than the narrator says he does, we can be reasonably sure that the narrator understands less than he thinks he does.

The next step is obvious: if we are to go behind the neighbor's saying,   15
we should also go behind the narrator's. What is it, then, that does not love a wall? The narrator implies, especially in lines thirty-seven and thirty-eight, that he knows, but he won't tell. Discounting hunters and elves, the literal destroyer is nature, which sends the frost under the wall. It strains credibility to assume that the implied pun on the poet's name is intentional, but the idea it suggests is useful to contemplate. Even if, as I have suggested, the poet is not within the poem as a character, that does not imply that he remains entirely anonymous. Although the poem is a fiction, and not the re-creation of a real incident in the poet's life, which we are to read as we would read a biographical narrative bemoaning the failure of communication between the poet-narrator and one of his Vermont neighbors, the real subject of the poem is communication. But the story of the wall-mending, and of the meeting of two men who worked to rebuild a wall is the narrator's story. We see his version of the events, and the quotations are his, not the poet's. The poet, on the other hand, communicates with us not through the narrator, but by means of the narrator. The narrator, a creation of the poet, is made not only to tell us his story, but to show us another version inadvertently. The poet asks us to "go behind" the poem, and when we do, we see dramatically, rather than narratively, the inability of the poem's narrator to understand and communicate with the neighbor.

The narrator's rhetoric is so persuasive that he very nearly convinces us to accept his version of the experience. It is only when we examine not only what is said, but what is implied, that we see, perhaps with shock, that the narrator is hollow, vain, and foolish. Perhaps even the poem's title directs the poet's irony toward the narrator. The neighbor's twice repeated proverb doesn't refer to walls, but to fences, and "mending fences" is a common colloquial expression for "making amends," or "re-establishing relationships." Of course the New England physical setting for the poem makes a wall the appropriate property boundary, but the ironic difference between "mending fences" in the metaphorical sense, and building a wall is clear.

No wonder, then, that most casual readers find it hard to remember whether the poem is summed up by "Something there is that doesn't love a wall," or by "Good fences make good neighbors." The essence of the poem is in neither of the two aphorisms, but in the failure to communicate that both of them represent. It is not when we hear only the narrator's story that we find ourselves listening to the poet. That occurs when we discover the narrator's unwittingly ironic self-characterizations which lie behind the literal words of the poem. When we make that discovery we understand that Frost has sent the ground-swell under the wall.

Robert Frost

From *The Figure a Poem Makes*

The figure a poem makes. It begins in delight and ends in wisdom. The figure is the same as for love. No one can really hold that the ecstasy should be static and stand still in one place. It begins in delight, it inclines to the impulse, it assumes direction with the first line laid down, it runs a course of lucky events, and ends in a clarification of life—not necessarily a great clarification, such as sects and cults are founded on, but in a momentary stay against confusion. It has denouement. It has an outcome that though unforeseen was predestined from the first image of the original mood—and indeed from the very mood. It is but a trick poem and no poem at all if the best of it was thought of first and saved for the last. It finds its own name as it goes and discovers the best waiting for it in some final phrase at once wise and sad—the happy-sad blend of the drinking song.

No tears in the writer, no tears in the reader. No surprise for the writer, no surprise for the reader. For me the initial delight is in the surprise of remembering something I didn't know I knew. I am in a place, in a situation, as if I had materialized from cloud or risen out of the ground. There is a glad recognition of the long lost and the rest follows. Step by step the wonder of unexpected supply keeps growing. The impressions most useful to my purpose seem always those I was unaware of and so made no note of at the time when taken, and the conclusion is come to that like giants we are always hurling experience ahead of us to pave the future with against the day when we may want to strike a line of purpose across it for somewhere. The line will have the more charm for not being mechanically straight. We enjoy the straight crookedness of a good walking stick. Modern instruments of precision are being used to make things crooked as if by eye and hand in the old days. . . .

More than once I should have lost my soul to radicalism if it had been the originality it was mistaken for by its young converts. Originality and initiative are what I ask for my country. For myself the originality need be no more than the freshness of a poem run in the way I have described: from delight to wisdom. The figure is the same as for love. Like a piece of ice on a hot stove the poem must ride on its own melting. A poem may be worked over once it is in being, but may not be worried into being. Its most precious quality will remain its having run itself and carried away the poet with it. Read it a hundred times: it will forever keep its freshness as a metal keeps its fragrance. It can never lose its sense of a meaning that once unfolded by surprise as it went.

Donald J. Greiner
From *The Indispensable Robert Frost*

"Home Burial" was first published in *North of Boston* (1914). It is the best of the renowned dialogue poems not only because it movingly details a failing marriage but also because of its dazzling combination of sentence sounds and blank verse. Lawrance Thompson reports that Frost recalled writing the poem in 1912 or 1913 and that his inspiration was the marital estrangement between Nathaniel and Leona Harvey following the death of their first-born child in 1895.[1] Mrs. Harvey was Frost's wife's older sister. But as numerous scholars and Thompson himself point out, the composition of "Home Burial" cannot be totally separated from the death of Frost and Elinor's own first-born child, Elliott, in 1900 at age four. Mrs. Frost could not ease her grief following Elliott's death, and Frost later reported that she knew then that the world was evil. Amy in "Home Burial" makes the same observation. Further evidence that the poem may be partly autobiographical is Thompson's recollection of Frost's once telling him that he could never read "Home Burial" in public because it was "too sad." These biographical particulars are relevant when one remembers the American public's misconception of Frost's forty-three year marriage to Elinor as idyllic and serene.

But even if one dismisses biographical significance, one had to admire the technical virtuosity of "Home Burial." Frost himself did. In a letter (27 July 1914) to John Cournos, he explains both his pleasure with the poem and his innovative technique:

> I also think well of those four "don'ts" in Home Burial. They would be good in prose and they gain something from the way they are placed in the verse. Then there is the threatening

> "If—you—do!" (Last of Home Burial)

[1] Lawrance Thompson, *Robert Frost: The Early Years, 1874–1915* (New York: Holt, Rinehart and Winston, 1966), p. 417. The other two volumes of the Frost biography are Thompson, *Robert Frost: The Years of Triumph, 1915–1938* (New York: Holt, Rinehart and Winston, 1970); and Thompson and R. H. Winnick, *Robert Frost: The Later Years, 1938–1963* (New York: Holt, Rinehart and Winston, 1976). Further references to these three volumes will be noted by volume and page number. All quotations of Frost's poetry are taken from *The Poetry of Robert Frost,* ed. Edward Connery Lathem (New York: Holt, Rinehart and Winston, 1969).

It is that particular kind of imagination that I cultivate rather than the kind that merely sees things, the hearing imagination rather than the seeing imagination though I should not want to be without the latter.

I am not bothered by the question whether anyone will be able to hear or say those three words ("If—you—do!") as I mean them to be said or heard. I should say that they were sufficiently self expressive.[2]

Frost was correct. These words are "sufficiently self expressive," and they illustrate his theory of sentence sounds as well as his letter to John Bartlett of 22 February 1914 explains it. His decision to combine the irregular rhythms of colloquial diction and normal speech patterns with the regularity of iambic pentameter revolutionized blank verse. The revolution was so total, in fact, that not only did such perspicacious critics as Ford Madox Heuffer feel bewildered but also such less perceptive readers as Jessie B. Rittenhouse, then the secretary of the Poetry Society of America, wondered if Frost would not be better off leaving the complexities of poetry for the relative safety of the short story.[3]

The four "don'ts" are a case in point. Frost positions them on the page so that the regularity of the iambic pentameter rhythm gives way to the irregularity of the husband's declaration and the wife's despairing response:

"But the child's mound—"

"Don't, don't don't, don't," she cried.

The stresses fall on "child," "mound," and the first three "don'ts" to make the pentameter line. Frost then leaves incomplete the line of "'don't', she cried" to illustrate the shattered communication between husband and wife that is the theme of "Home Burial."

5   A home is truly buried in this poem. Marital love is so engulfed by the disaster of the baby's death that the husband and wife exchange the effort to discuss their differences for a tense outbreak of accusations. The development of this theme is as important as the innovative technique in making "Home Burial" indispensable. For sexual love—itself a form of communication—also breaks down. Although the sexual allusions are never explicit, they reverberate throughout the poem from the very beginning: Amy cowers under the husband's "mounting," and their bedroom is equated with a graveyard:

The little graveyard where my people are!
So small the window frames the whole of it.
Not so much larger than a bedroom, is it?

In recent years more and more readers have admitted that the difficulties of communication via sex as well as talk were always major considerations in

---

[2] *Selected Letters of Robert Frost,* ed. Lawrance Thompson (New York: Holt, Rinehart and Winston, 1964). [3] Jessie B. Rittenhouse, "*North of Boston:* Robert Frost's Poems of New England Farm Life," *New York Times Book Review,* 16 May 1915, p. 189.

Frost's work. [. . .] Despite Frost's comments to the contrary, it seems certain that at least part of his personal experiences went into the writing of "Home Burial." Death and the threat of insanity were inextricably mixed with sex and love in his long marriage to Elinor, and his poetic rendering of this baffling mixture is one of the highlights of his career. "Home Burial" is a masterpiece, as modern in theme as it is in technique. [. . .]

Jay Parini

From *One Long, Wild Conversation: Robert Frost as Teacher*

Frost was always . . . an eccentric teacher, slightly at odds with the culture of the academy. "I hate academic ways," he told one interviewer. "I fight everything academic. Think of what time we waste in trying to learn academically—and what talent we staunch with academic teaching." Presumably, by "academic teaching" he meant teaching that was dead on its feet, uninformed by the give and take of the minds at play. Frost disliked rote learning, and he was mistrustful of "content" as the goal of education. He did not believe that the specific texts a student was given to study mattered very much; what counted, he wrote in his journal, was that "students are made to think fresh and fine, to stand by themselves, to make a case."

He believed in what he called "teaching by presence," and repeatedly suggested that informal contacts between teachers and students were vastly more important than anything that happened inside the classroom walls. But in the classroom, too, he sought the freedom of informality: "It is the essence of symposium I am after," he said. "Heaps of ideas and the subject matter of books [are] purely incidental." He once told a class at Amherst: "I'm looking for subject matter, for substance, in yourself." In his journal in 1917, he wrote: "What we do in college is to get over our little-mindedness. To get an education you have to hang around till you catch on." . . .

Frost gave his students something they could take with them out into the world: an approach to reading and thinking that was radically skeptical of the text and its rhetoric. He taught them to read closely—to read not only what was in the lines, but what was between the lines. He also gave them a way of being in the world, a way that involved making endless connections, of drawing things into comparison. Most important, he taught them about metaphor, which he believed to lie at the heart of the human intellectual enterprise.

In his famous essay "Education by Poetry," Frost wrote: "Poetry begins in trivial metaphors, pretty metaphors, 'grace' metaphors, and goes on to the profoundest thinking that we have. Poetry provides the one permissible way of saying one thing and meaning another." He cautioned that "unless you have had your proper poetic education in the metaphor, you are not safe anywhere. Because you are not at ease with figurative values: you don't know the metaphor in its strength and its weakness. You don't know how far you may expect to ride it and when it may break down with you. You are not safe in science; you are not safe in history."

5   As both teacher and writer, Frost put an emphasis on metaphor and analogical thinking. In this, his roles converged beautifully. He understood that success in both teaching and writing depends on a visceral sense of metaphor—its limits and its possibilities. We must, as Frost suggested, learn how far we can go with a metaphor as it evolves, how to play with the figure in graceful ways that add to our small but precious pile of understanding. We must take thinking—critical and creative thinking—to the edge, without spilling over it.

          Frost stands before us an example, a challenging one.... we have much to learn from him.

Katherine Kearns

"The Place Is the Asylum": Women and Nature in Robert Frost's Poetry

In Frost's "A Servant to Servants" the speaker describes her mad uncle. He was kept at home with his family, but within the house was another "house" made of hickory-wood bars, a cage to keep him safe, and to keep others safe. He tore to shreds any furniture put inside to make him comfortable; he removed all his clothes and carried them on his arm. He lived, animal-like, in a bed of straw. The man "went mad quite young," and the speaker believes it likely that he was "crossed in love. . . . Anyway all he talked about was love."[1] The other prominent figure in the speaker's memory is the bride, her mother, brought into the madhouse where "She had to lie and hear love things made dreadful / By his shouts in the night." She witnesses the madness, and she is in her role as bride an embodiment of the cause of his madness. The speaker has left this house with her husband,[2] moving from the isolated cabin "ten miles from anywhere" to a place with a lake stretching out beyond her kitchen window like a sheet of glass. Her vistas opened, she feels still a prisoner and has escaped outside to talk with the migrant workers camped on her husband's land. She is torn by conflicting desires, "to live out on ground" and yet to keep "a good roof overhead." She knows the power of place, for she has been sent, once, to the State Asylum, where walls are impregnable and the roof is more than

---

[1] All quotations from Frost's poetry are from *The Poetry of Robert Frost,* ed. Edward Connery Lathem, 2nd ed. (New York: Holt, 1979).   [2] See Floyd G. Watkins, "The Poetry of the Unsaid—Robert Frost's Narrative and Dramatic Poems," *Texas Quarterly,* 15 (1972), 89; Watkins points out that it is never specifically stated that Len is the speaker's husband; it seems, nonetheless, reasonable to assign Len the conventional role of husband rather than brother or lover.

sound. Now trapped in a house filled by her husband's hired men, who come and go readily through doors that remain unlocked, she recognizes an essential truth: "The place," she says, "is the asylum." And of course the statement is the embodiment of paradox, for her "place" is one of "safety" and of potential madness just as surely as was her uncle's cage.

These two figures, the disturbed woman and the love-crossed and naked madman, may be seen as emblematic, for Frost's poetry subtly but persistently reiterates a vision of sexual anarchy. Men and women possess the power to make each other mad, yet it is the man in "A Servant to Servants" who must be locked away. Women are powerful, active, magnetic in their madness, which is manifested in escape from the asylum of households into nature. Men are rendered impotent; they can only pursue unsuccessfully or withdraw into themselves. They have nowhere else to go, because Frost's world is controlled by a powerful femininity. As brides or as keepers, women dominate households. Their houses embody them so that symbolically every threshold is sexually charged; "cellar holes" become pits that represent female sexuality, birth, death, and the grave, and attics are minds filled with the bones of old lovers. Frost's men can no more fulfill their women than they can fill the houses with life and children, and so the women run away and the men follow. Yet the pursuit is dangerous, for it leads into nature that is equally female and thus potentially deadly. While Frost fills his outside world with walls, and with ceilings of dark leaves, and with the bars of birch and hickory trees, nature resists containment and defies control as surely as a woman does. The earth, flowers, trees, and water have almost mythological powers, as if nature were possessed by naiads and dryads and flower maidens, all thriving under the nurture of Mother Earth and waiting, invitingly, for women to discover their kinship. Domesticated sexuality is pale and fruitless compared to nature. The woods in Frost's poetry are indeed "lovely, dark, and deep," and while his households are often left cold and vacant, his nature is enticing, provocative at once of both desire and death.

Men in Frost's poetry are thus potentially circumscribed in their movements. In "The Housekeeper" Frost places a woman, the "housekeeper" of the title, immovably indoors; she is fat, "built in here like a big church organ," she says. Only her fingers work, and she is beading a pair of delicate dancing shoes "for some miss" who will presumably dance away with a man's heart. Her daughter has run away from her lover and married someone else; the forsaken lover stands impotently outside his house, refusing to enter but paralyzed to act. He is caught almost literally between the classic dichotomy of the mother and the "whore," and while the mother fills his house, his ex-lover has abandoned it for the outside world. His idealized version of domesticity lies out in the yard with his prized fifty-dollar imported Langshang cock and its pampered harem of hens. But his own women describe him as a "helpless," "bedeviled" exotic himself, one who needs extra care and who is, ultimately, in the last taunting words of the mother, a "dreadful fool." Women who stay inside might then incite men to murder by their actions, their words, or their

FOUR POETS: THEN AND NOW

mere presence (the witch of Coös says that her husband killed her lover so that he wouldn't have to kill her), but women outside, in real and metaphorical dress, exert an equivalent, dangerous, sexual power.

"Home Burial" may be used to clarify Frost's intimate relationships between sex, death, and madness. The physical iconography is familiar—a stairwell, a window, a doorway, and a grave—elements which Frost reiterates throughout his poetry. The marriage in "Home Burial" has been destroyed by the death of a first and only son. The wife is in the process of leaving the house, crossing the threshold from marital asylum into freedom. The house is suffocating her. Her window view of the graveyard is not enough and is, in fact, a maddening reminder that she could not enter the earth with her son. With its transparent barrier, the window is a mockery of a widened vision throughout Frost's poetry and seems to incite escape rather than quelling it; in "Home Burial" the woman can "see" through the window and into the grave in a way her husband cannot, and the fear is driving her down the steps toward the door—"She was starting down— / Looking back over her shoulder at some fear"—even before she sees her husband. He threatens to follow his wife and bring her back by force, as if he is the cause of her leaving, but his gesture will be futile because it is based on the mistaken assumption that she is escaping him. Pathetically, he is merely an obstacle toward which she reacts at first dully and then with angry impatience. He is an animate part of the embattled household, but her real impetus for movement comes from the grave.

5   The house itself, reduced symbolically and literally to a womblike passageway between the bedroom and the threshold, is a correlative for the sexual tension generated by the man's insistence on his marital rights. He offers to "give up being a man" by binding himself "to keep hands off," but their marriage is already sexually damaged and empty. The man and woman move in an intricate dance, she coming downward and then retracing a step, he "Mounting until she cower[s] under him," she "shrinking from beneath his arm" to slide downstairs. Randall Jarrell examines the image of the woman sinking into "a modest, compact, feminine bundle" upon her skirts;[3] it might be further observed that this childlike posture is also very much a gesture of sexual denial, body bent, knees drawn up protectively against the breasts, all encompassed by voluminous skirts. The two are in profound imbalance, and Frost makes the wife's speech and movements the poetic equivalent of stumbling and resistance; her lines are frequently eleven syllables, and often are punctuated by spondees whose forceful but awkward slowness embodies the woman's vacillations "from terrified to dull," and from frozen and silent immobility to anger. Her egress from the house will be symbolic verification of her husband's impotence, and if she leaves it and does not come back, the house will rot as the best birch fence will rot. Unfilled, without a woman with child, it

[3] "Robert Frost's 'Home Burial,'" in *The Moment of Poetry*, ed. Don Cameron Allen (Baltimore: Johns Hopkins Univ. Press, 1962), p. 104.

will fall into itself, an image that recurs throughout Frost's poetry.[4] Thus the child's grave predicts the dissolution of household, a movement towards the open cellar of "The Generations of Men," almost a literal "home burial."

The husband seems about to learn what the husband learns in "The Hill Wife"—"of finalities / Besides the grave"—but he will learn the lesson *because* of the grave of his son, the once and future rival for his wife's attention. . . . *1987*

BILLY COLLINS (1941–   )

Born in New York City in 1941, Billy Collins developed an early interest in poetry. His father, who was working as an electrician when Collins was born and who later became the vice president of an insurance company, was a vibrant, passionate individual with a wide variety of avocations, ranging from playing golf to reading poetry. As a high school student, Collins worked as a caddy at his father's golf club, where he learned a great deal about himself and about social class in America. In an interview with James Dodson, Collins noted, "When you're a caddie, you're basically invisible. People talk as if you aren't even there . . . [and] you gain a valuable new insight into people." These insights later contributed to an essential aspect of Collins's poetry: The creation of a speaker, whose voice sounds throughout the body of his work. In an interview with Elizabeth Lund, Collins observed, "A novelist invents many characters . . . but the poet's job is to create one character, one distinctive voice." Collins believes that his poetic voice "attempts to blend humor and seriousness, to balance those two realms."

Collins remembers his father commuting to Wall Street, then returning in the evening with reading material such as Poetry *magazine. Intrigued by his father's interest in poetry, Collins began to read widely in the magazines he brought home, and by the time he entered his freshman year at the College of the Holy Cross in Worcester, Massachusetts, he was also writing and publishing his own poems. Reading poetry, however, continued to be central and essential to his life. He remembers, for example, that he and his roommates circumvented the strict 10:00 P.M. lights out policy in his dorm by stuffing the cracks of their door with towels and tin foil so that they could keep their lamps burning—and the pages of books turning—late into the night. The writers he remembers most from that*

---

[4]See, for example, "The Census Taker," where the rotting and abandoned house never held women; "The Black Cottage," where the boards are warping and bees live in the walls; "A Fountain, a Bottle, A Donkey's Ears, and Some Books," where the doors still hold but the broken windows allow easy entry; and "The Thatch," where a hundred-year-old cottage opens itself to the rain at the dissolution of the marriage within.

time are the beats, who challenged traditional ideas about poetry and fiction. Particularly influential to Collins's writing were Allen Ginsberg, Lawrence Ferlinghetti, and Jack Kerouac.

While Collins had begun publishing his poetry in small literary magazines when he was still in high school, he sold his first poems shortly after college graduation to Rolling Stone Magazine, which paid $39 per poem. Since then, he has published eight volumes of poetry, and his works appear regularly in such periodicals as American Scholar, Harper's, The New Yorker, and American Poetry Review. In addition to his work as a professor of English at Lehman College, City University of New York, Collins has won many awards and honors, including being chosen by the New York Public Library in 1992 to serve in the prestigious capacity of "Literary Lion." Most notably, in 2001 he was appointed poet laureate of the United States, serving in this office for two years.

As poet laureate, Collins created Poetry 180, a program designed to encourage high school students to read poems. Through the Library of Congress Web site, Collins provided 180 poems, one for each day of the school year, and urged that teachers, principals, and especially students read one poem aloud each day. He hoped that their voices, reading over the public address systems available in most high schools, would move poems from the written page to ears, and hearts, of faculty, administrators, and students across the country.

Collins' ear for the rhythms of everyday speech, his eye for striking details, and his low-key, yet sharply perceptive wit contribute to the power of his work. The subjects of his poems range from felonious mice, intent on arson, to the pain of a lover's apology, to a history teacher who tries to protect students' innocence by claiming that the Ice Age was really just "the Chilly Age, a period of a million years / when everyone had to wear sweaters."

Because Collins served as poet laureate during the time of the 9/11 terrorist attacks, he was often asked about the relationship between historic events and the writing of poetry. In an interview with Laura Secor in March of 2002, he said, "My poetry was never written for a nation in crisis. . . . But my poems and lots of people's poems are unintentional responses to terrorism, in that they honor life. Poems are a preservative for experience, and there would be no reason to preserve experience if one did not feel that there's something special and even sacred about it." In his poem "The Names," Collins responds to the memorial service for those killed at the World Trade Center. The images and the repetition of names in this poem strongly reflect Collins's sense of the sacred and his belief in the power of words.

The History Teacher

Trying to protect his students' innocence
he told them the Ice Age was really just
the Chilly Age, a period of a million years
when everyone had to wear sweaters.

And the Stone Age became the Gravel Age,   *5*
named after the long driveways of the time.

The Spanish Inquisition was nothing more
than an outbreak of questions such as
"How far is it from here to Madrid?"
"What do you call the matador's hat?"   *10*

The War of the Roses took place in a garden,
and the Enola Gay dropped one tiny atom
on Japan.

The children would leave his classroom
for the playground to torment the weak   *15*
and the smart,
mussing up their hair and breaking their glasses,
while he gathered up his notes and walked home
past flower beds and white picket fences,
wondering if they would believe that soldiers   *20*
in the Boer War told long, rambling stories
designed to make the enemy nod off.   *1991*

Jack

Just when I am about to telephone her
so she can hear me swallowing my pride,
a thing the size of a watermelon,

a giant barges out of a fairy tale,
picks up the house by the chimney   *5*
and carries it off laughing like thunder.
She will never believe this I tell myself.

From the windowsill where I hang on
I can see geysers of plumbing,
the exposed basement embarrassed by its junk,   *10*
snapped telephone wires on the lawn,
and the neighbors looking up with little
apocalypse expressions on their faces.

I realize on the way up the beanstalk
apologizing over the phone was a bad idea.   *15*
A letter provides a more reflective means
of saying hard things, expressing true feelings.

If there is pen and paper in his kingdom,
I plan to write her a long vivid one

20 communicating my ardor, but also describing
the castle floating in high clouds,
the goose, the talking musical instruments,
and the echo of his enormous shoes.

In fact, to convince her of my unwavering love,
25 I will compose it while pacing back and forth
in his palm.   *1991*

Going Out for Cigarettes

It's a story as famous as the three little pigs:
one evening a man says he is going out for cigarettes,
closes the door behind him and is never heard from again,
not one phone call, not even a postcard from Rio.

5 For all anyone knows, he walks straight into the distance
like a line from Euclid's notebooks and vanishes
with the smoke he blows into the soft humid air,
smoke that forms a screen, smoke to calm the bees within.

He has his fresh pack, an overcoat with big pockets.
10 What else does he need as he walks beyond city limits,
past the hedges, porch lights and empty cars of the suburbs
and into a realm no larger than his own hat size?

Alone, he is a solo for piano that never comes to an end,
a small plane that keeps flying away from the earth.
15 He is the last line of a poem that continues off the page
and down to a river to drag there in the cool flow,

questioning the still pools with its silver hook.
Let us say this is the place where the man who goes out
for cigarettes finally comes to rest: on a riverbank
20 above the long, inquisitive wriggling of that line,

sitting content in the quiet picnic of consciousness,
nothing on his mind as he lights up another one,
nothing but the arc of the stone bridge he notices
downstream, and its upturned reflection in the water.   *1991*

My Life

Sometimes I see it as a straight line
drawn with a pencil and a ruler
transecting the circle of the world

or as a finger piercing
a smoke ring, casual, inquisitive,   5

but then the sun will come out
or the phone will ring
and I will cease to wonder

if it is one thing,
a large ball of air and memory,   10
or many things,
a string of small farming towns,
a dark road winding through them.

Let us say it is a field
I have been hoeing every day,   15
hoeing and singing,
then going to sleep in one of its furrows,

or now that it is more than half over,
a partially open door,
rain dripping from the eaves.   20

Like yours, it could be anything,
a nest with one egg,
a hallway that leads to a thousand rooms—
whatever happens to float into view
when I close my eyes   25

or look out a window
for more than a few minutes,
so that some days I think
it must be everything and nothing at once.

But this morning, sitting up in bed,   30
wearing my black sweater and my glasses,
the curtains drawn and the windows up,

I am a lake, my poem is an empty boat,
and my life is the breeze that blows
through the whole scene   35

stirring everything it touches—
the surface of the water, the limp sail,
even the heavy, leafy trees along the shore.   *1998*

The Names

Yesterday, I lay awake in the palm of the night.
A soft rain stole in, unhelped by any breeze,

And when I saw the silver glaze on the windows,
I started with A, with Ackerman, as it happened,
5   Then Baxter and Calabro,
Davis and Eberling, names falling into place
As droplets fell through the dark.
Names printed on the ceiling of the night.
Names slipping around a watery bend.
10   Twenty-six willows on the banks of a stream.
In the morning, I walked out barefoot
Among thousands of flowers
Heavy with dew like the eyes of tears,
And each had a name—
15   Fiori inscribed on a yellow petal
Then Gonzalez and Han, Ishikawa and Jenkins.
Names written in the air
And stitched into the cloth of the day.
A name under a photograph taped to a mailbox.
20   Monogram on a torn shirt,
I see you spelled out on storefront windows
And on the bright unfurled awnings of this city.
I say the syllables as I turn a corner—
Kelly and Lee,
25   Medina, Nardella, and O'Connor.
When I peer into the woods,
I see a thick tangle where letters are hidden
As in a puzzle concocted for children.
Parker and Quigley in the twigs of an ash,
30   Rizzo, Schubert, Torres, and Upton,
Secrets in the boughs of an ancient maple.
Names written in the pale sky.
Names rising in the updraft amid buildings.
Names silent in stone
35   Or cried out behind a door.
Names blown over the earth and out to sea.
In the evening—weakening light, the last swallows.
A boy on a lake lifts his oars.
A woman by a window puts a match to a candle,
40   And the names are outlined on the rose clouds—
Vanacore and Wallace,
(let X stand, if it can, for the ones unfound)
Then Young and Ziminsky, the final jolt of Z.
Names etched on the head of a pin.
45   One name spanning a bridge, another undergoing a tunnel.
A blue name needled into the skin.

Names of citizens, workers, mothers and fathers,
The bright-eyed daughter, the quick son.
Alphabet of names in a green field.
Names in the small tracks of birds.   50
Names lifted from a hat
Or balanced on the tip of the tongue.
Names wheeled into the dim warehouse of memory.
So many names, there is barely room on the walls of the
heart.   *2002*   55

More Resources on
Billy Collins

  In the Online Learning Center for *Responding to Literature*
  • Brief biography of Collins
  • List of major works by Collins
  • Web links to more resources on Collins

 RITA DOVE (1952–   )

*Born in 1952, in Akron, Ohio, Rita Dove is the
daughter of a research scientist, who started his
work life as a janitor for the Goodyear Company
and eventually challenged the race barrier to become
one of the first African-American chemists in the
U.S. tire industry. Dove grew up aware of the
barriers she and other African Americans faced,
but her talents were nurtured by a family that
emphasized the importance of reading, of appreciating music, and of excelling academically. In
1970, as one of the top 100 high school students
in the United States, she was named a Presidential
Scholar, which led to her undergraduate study at Miami University in Ohio.
Following graduation, she became a Fulbright Scholar, studying at Universitat
Tübingen in Germany, and then earning her M.F.A. in 1977 from the University of Iowa, where she was a participant in the prestigious Iowa Writers' Workshop.
    Dove's work has appeared in many poetry magazines, academic journals, and
anthologies, and she has published more than half a dozen volumes of poetry,
several collections of short stories, a novel (*Through the Ivory Gate, 1993*)
and a verse drama (*The Darker Face of the Earth, 1996*). One of her best*

known and most highly acclaimed works is the collection of interrelated poems
Thomas and Beulah *(1986), which in 1987 earned her the Pulitzer Prize. This
collection, Dove said in an interview with Jack E. White, was inspired "by a very
small unassuming moment." After her grandfather died, when she was fourteen
years old, Dove was asked to spend time with her grandmother. During these
hours, intended to help her grandmother through the grief, Dove received the unexpected gift of the stories that made up her grandparents' lives: As Dove visited the
old family home, her grandmother recounted how she and her husband met, describing details of their courtship, their work, their struggles with racism, and their ways
of raising their family. While Thomas and Beulah are fictional characters, their spirits are brought to life by the details and anecdotes Dove heard from her grandmother.*

*In 1993, Dove was appointed poet laureate of the United States, the second
African-American woman to earn this honor (following in the footsteps of Gwendolyn Brooks, who was appointed to the position in 1985). During her time in this
office, from 1993 to 1995, Dove worked especially diligently to incorporate themes
related to African Americans and other minority groups in the events she sponsored.
Many of these events focused on children and young adults, and in a particularly
successful series she presented readings by young Crow Indian poets. In her interview with White, Dove stated that she hoped through the national office of poet
laureate to "re-recreate for the young her own awestruck discovery of poetry's power."*

*In addition to writing poetry and to promoting poetry through her work as
poet laureate, Dove has also brought the love of language to hundreds of students
through her teaching. She has taught creative writing at Arizona State University
and currently serves as Commonwealth Professor of English at the University of
Virginia in Charlottesville. Whether she is writing, giving poetry readings, or
teaching, Dove focuses on the power of language. In an interview with Patrick
Henry Bass, she expresses her conviction that "poetry deals with language at its
most skeletal level, deeper than bone, because poetry pays special attention not
only to the words, but also to the very texture of the words—their history, their
sound, their rhythm, their shadows and highlights." Drawing on the conventions
of Western literature, as well as on the rhythms of everyday speech and on the
oral tradition of storytelling, Dove offers a fresh, clear, and often challenging look
at life in today's complex world.*

Geometry

I prove a theorem and the house expands:
the windows jerk free to hover near the ceiling,
the ceiling floats away with a sigh.

As the walls clear themselves of everything
5   but transparency, the scent of carnations
leaves with them. I am out in the open

and above the windows have hinged into butterflies,
sunlight glinting where they've intersected.
They are going to some point true and unproven.   *1980*

Adolescence—I

In water-heavy nights behind grandmother's porch
We knelt in the tickling grasses and whispered:
Linda's face hung before us, pale as a pecan,
And it grew wise as she said:
    "A boy's lips are soft,   5
      As soft as baby's skin."
The air closed over her words.
A firefly whirred near my ear, and in the distance
I could hear streetlamps ping
Into miniature suns   10
Against a feathery sky.   *1980*

Grape Sherbet

The day? Memorial.
After the grill
Dad appears with his masterpiece—
swirled snow, gelled light.
We cheer. The recipe's   5
a secret and he fights
a smile, his cap turned up
so the bib resembles a duck.

That morning we galloped
through the grassed-over mounds   10
and named each stone
for a lost milk tooth. Each dollop
of sherbet, later,
is a miracle,
like salt on a melon that makes it sweeter.   15

Everyone agrees—it's wonderful!
It's just how we imagined lavender
would taste. The diabetic grandmother
stares from the porch,
a torch   20
of pure refusal.

We thought no one was lying
there under our feet,
we thought it
25   was a joke. I've been trying
to remember the taste,
but it doesn't exist.
Now I see why
you bothered,
30   father.   *1983*

Adolescence—II

Although it is night, I sit in the bathroom, waiting.
Sweat prickles behind my knees, the baby-breasts are alert.
Venetian blinds slice up the moon; the tiles quiver in pale strips.

Then they come, the three seal men with eyes as round
5   As dinner plates and eyelashes like sharpened tines.
They bring the scent of licorice. One sits in the washbowl,

One on the bathtub edge; one leans against the door.
"Can you feel it yet?" they whisper.
I don't know what to say, again. They chuckle,

10   Patting their sleek bodies with their hands.
"Well, maybe next time." And they rise,
Glittering like pools of ink under moonlight,

And vanish. I clutch at the ragged holes
They leave behind, here at the edge of darkness.
15   Night rests like a ball of fur on my tongue.

Daystar

She wanted a little room for thinking:
but she saw diapers steaming on the line,
a doll slumped behind the door.

So she lugged a chair behind the garage
5   to sit out the children's naps.

Sometimes there were things to watch—
the pinched armor of a vanished cricket,

a floating maple leaf. Other days
she stared until she was assured
10   when she closed her eyes
she'd see only her own vivid blood.

She had an hour, at best, before Liza appeared
pouting from the top of the stairs.
And just *what* was mother doing
out back with the field mice? Why,   15
building a palace. Later
that night when Thomas rolled over and
lurched into her, she would open her eyes
and think of the place that was hers
for an hour—where   20
she was nothing,
pure nothing, in the middle of the day.   *1986*

Poem in Which I Refuse Contemplation

A letter from my mother was waiting:
read in standing, one a.m.,
just arrived at my German mother-in-law

six hours from Paris by car.
Our daughter hops on Oma's bed,   5
happy to be back in a language

she knows. *Hello, all! Your postcard
came on the nineth*—familiar misspelled
words, exclamations. I wish my body

wouldn't cramp and leak; I want to—   10
as my daughter says, pretending to be
"Papa"—pull on boots and go for a long walk

alone. *Your cousin Ronnie in D.C.—
remember him?—he was the one
a few months younger than you—*   15

*was strangulated at some chili joint,
your Aunt May is beside herself!*
Mom skips to the garden which is

*producing—onions, swiss chard,
lettuce, lettuce, lettuce, turnip greens and more lettuce*   20
so far! The roses are flurishing.

Haven't I always hated gardening? And German,
with its patient, grunting building blocks,
and for that matter, English, too.

Americanese's chewy twang? *Raccoons*   25
have taken up residence
we were ten *in the crawl space*

but I can't feel his hand *who knows*
anymore *how we'll get them out?*
30 I'm still standing. Bags to unpack.

That's all for now. Take care. *1989*

Missing

I am the daughter who went out with the girls,
never checked back in and nothing marked my "last
known whereabouts," not a single glistening petal.

Horror is partial; it keeps you going. A lost
5 child is a fact hardening around its absence,
a knot in the breast purring *Touch, and I will*

come true. I was "returned," I watched her
watch as I babbled *It could have been worse. . . .*
Who can tell
10 what penetrates? Pity is the brutal
discipline. Now I understand she can never
die, just as nothing can bring me back—

I am the one who comes and goes;
I am the footfall that hovers.   *1995*

Connections: American Poets: Then and Now

1. Each of these poets was born in the United States. How does each poet's
   work represent (or fail to represent) your view of the "American" identity?
   In what ways do these poets' visions of American life affirm each other? In
   what ways do they extend or modify one another? In what ways do they
   contradict one another?
2. Do further research about the lives of one of the poets. Do biographers always agree? To what extent do any of the works included in this chapter
   impress you as autobiographical? How does knowing more about an author's life affect your interpretation of his or her work?
3. Considering the biographical details and the works included, focus on the
   topic of either gender or race as it is addressed (or not addressed) by these
   four poets. What similarities and differences do you observe?
4. Do some research into important social, cultural, or historical events or decisions that occurred during the time these poems were written. (The time-
15 line on page 1238 will provide some ideas.) In what ways do the poems
   reflect the era in which they were written?

More Resources on
Rita Dove

In *ARIEL*

- Brief biography of Dove
- Complete texts of several of Dove's poems: "Dusting," "Testimonial," "Canary," and "Champagne"
- Video clip of an interview with Dove
- Video clip of Dove reading her poem "Canary"
- Analysis of understatement in Dove's writing
- Bibliography of scholarly works on Dove

In the Online Learning Center for *Responding to Literature*

- Brief biography of Dove
- List of major works by Dove
- Web links to more resources on Dove

5. Choose one of the following themes for consideration: loss, isolation, danger, displacement, courage, survival. How does each poet demonstrate in his or her poetry that particular theme? What is your response to the ways that each poet handles the theme? Provide illustrations from poems included in this section or from other poems by these writers.

6. Choose any poem in this book (other than those included in this chapter). Read the poem and write your response. Then do research on the author's life and times. Reread the poem and write your response, keeping in mind what you discovered as you researched. Then compare your initial response with your second response. Comment on the changes (or lack of changes) you observe.

7. Choose a poet from this text (other than the four poets represented in this chapter). Read a wide selection of his or her poems, and then select six you consider to be particularly intriguing, important, or representative of the poet's work. Do research on the poet's life and times, and use the information you find to write an introduction that will interest readers in the six poems you selected.

Glossary of Literary Terms

allegory (p. 60) A story in which each character, action, and setting stands for one specific idea or principle.

alliteration (p. 50, 52) The repetition of identical initial sounds in neighboring words or syllables.

allusion (p. 51, 52) A reference to a person, place, object, or event outside the work itself.

amphitheater (p. 72) A large, semicircular, outdoor theater, seating as many as 15,000 people, where Greek dramas were performed.

antagonist (p. 37, 40) The character with whom the protagonist is in conflict, generally not a sympathetic character.

antistrophe (p. 72) In Greek drama, that part of the ode in which the chorus moves from left to right, singing and dancing.

apostrophe (p. 50, 52) Addressing an inanimate object, a place, or an absent or imaginary person as if it were alive or present.

author/speaker/narrator (p. 38, 40) The *author* is the person who writes the literary work. He or she should not be confused with the *speaker,* the voice that is heard in a poem, or the *narrator,* the voice that tells a work of fiction (or, sometimes, frames a play).

ballad (p. 68) A narrative poem written in four-line, rhymed stanzas, generally involving lively, often violent, action.

belles–lettres (p. 78) Literally, French for "fine letters"; a kind of essay that often pursues a philosophical subject, frequently using figurative language traditionally considered literary.

canon (p. 85) An authoritative list; the literary canon comprises the standard group of works traditionally accepted as great literature.

catastrophe (p. 75) In a tragedy, the downfall of the hero, which generally involves the death of not only the hero, but also other, often innocent, individuals.

catharsis (p. 75) The relief of tension and the subsequent insight experienced by the audience of a tragic drama after viewing the catastrophe and resolution.

characters (p. 34–39) The fictional people who are part of the action of a literary work.

chorus (p. 72) In Greek drama, a group of characters who generally speak with one voice and who usually represent the community.

climax (p. 29, 31) In a literary work, the turning point, often signified by a character's making a significant decision or taking action in an attempt to resolve the conflict.

closed form (p. 67) Any traditional poetic form in which the lines and stanzas must be arranged according to established patterns.

comedy (p. 75–76) A play in which the plots, conflicts, and characters primarily amuse the audience. The problems of the characters are seldom deeply serious and are treated in a lighthearted way. Whereas tragedy moves toward the main characters' downfalls, comedy moves toward the improvement of the main characters' fortunes. Whereas tragedy generally ends with death and the restoration of order, comedy concludes with reconciliation, often through a triumphant wedding scene.

complication (p. 28–29, 31) In a literary work, an event or action that serves to establish the conflict.

conclusion (p. 29, 31) In a literary work, the ending, where the effects of the climactic action or decision are often shown.

conflict (p. 29–30) In a literary work, a struggle between internal or external forces.

couplet (p. 68) Two rhyming lines of poetry.

creative nonfiction (p. 78) Essays that use narration and description to meditate upon, analyze, evaluate, or reflect on various subjects and experiences.

deus ex machina (p. 72) Literally, "god from the machine." In Greek theater, the elaborate mechanisms used to lower actors to the stage to play the role of gods, often meting out punishments to human characters.

dialect (p. 34, 39) A variant of a language that is different from the one generally taught in school; may include distinctive pronunciations of words, original vocabulary, or grammatical constructions that are not considered standard.

dialogue (p. 34, 39) A conversation between two or more characters.

diction (p. 48–49, 52) Choice of words.

dynamic character (p. 36, 40) A character who changes in some significant way during the course of the work.

English sonnet (p. 68) Also called the Shakespearean sonnet, a poem of fourteen lines, falling into three quatrains (four lines each) and a concluding couplet (two lines). The rhyme scheme is abab cdcd efef gg. The first three quatrains develop an idea or image, and the closing couplet comments on it.

enjambment (p. 65–66) In poetry, the carrying over of a sentence from one line or couplet to the next, so that closely related words fall on different lines.

epic (p. 68) A long narrative poem that often tells the story of a god, mythic figure, or national hero.

epiphany, story of (p. 62) A short story depicting a character who faces a conflict that leads him or her to a sudden insight or profound understanding.

exterior setting (p. 44–45, 46) Aspects of setting that occur outside the characters.

fable (p. 61) A form of short fiction usually featuring animals who talk, walk about on their hind legs, and, in general, act just as rationally (and just as irrationally) as humans. Unlike myths, legends, and fairy tales, fables state an explicit lesson.

fairy tale (p. 61) Like myths, a form of short fiction that focuses on supernatural beings and events. Unlike myths, fairy tales contain giants, trolls, fairy godmothers, and talking animals rather than gods and goddesses. They do not attempt to explain the natural world or to affirm civic values, but instead focus on the struggle between clearly defined good and evil.

feminist criticism (p. 85) Feminist criticism posits that our civilization has been predominantly male centered and therefore literature reflects *patriarchal* (male-dominated) themes.

figurative language (p. 50–51, 52) Words or expressions that carry more than their literal meaning.

first-person narrator (p. 38–39, 40) A narrator who is also a character in the work and who uses "I" or "we" to tell the story. First-person narrators can report their own thoughts but not the thoughts of others. They may offer evaluations and judgments of characters and events.

flashback (p. 46) An interruption in the chronological order of a work to describe something that happened previously.

flat character (p. 36, 40) Usually, a character who has only one outstanding trait or feature.

formalist criticism (p. 84) Formalist criticism looks at a text as existing by itself. Formalists pay little attention to biographical or historical information, using instead a process called *close reading* to look at the various parts of the work in detail.

genre (p. 57–60) In literary criticism, a type or form of literature.

groundlings (p. 73) The common folk who could not afford seats and thus stood at the foot of the stage to watch Elizabethan theater productions.

haiku (p. 67) A Japanese poetic form consisting of seventeen syllables, generally divided into three lines (in the original Japanese).

imagery (p. 51, 52) Words that appeal to the five senses: touch, taste, sight, hearing, and smell.

initiation, story of (p. 62) A short story about a person moving from innocence to experience.

interior setting (p. 45, 46) Aspects of setting that occur inside the minds and hearts of the characters.

introduction (p. 28, 31) The beginning of a work; usually establishes the setting (time and place) and introduces one or more of the main characters.

irony of situation (p. 30–31) A discrepancy between what is said and what is done or between what is expected and what actually happens.

Italian sonnet (p. 68) See **Petrarchan sonnet.**

legend (p. 61) Legends recount the amazing achievements of people who are sometimes imagined creations but sometimes based on men and women who actually lived. Legends—which are often combined with the entertaining tall tale—frequently praise and confirm traits that a society particularly values.

limited omniscient narrator (p. 38, 40) A narrator who can report external actions and conversations but can only describe the internal thoughts of one character. A limited omniscient narrator may offer evaluations and judgments of characters and events.

lyric poetry (p. 68) Although it may depict actions, a lyric poem generally focuses on the inward reactions, insights, responses, feelings, musings, or emotions of a single character (often the speaker).

Marxist criticism (p. 85) Marxist readings of literature refer to the theories of social and economic reformer Karl Marx. Literary critics who subscribe to Marx's theories read literary texts to discover the impact of unfair distribution of wealth and power on their themes and characters.

melodrama (p. 73) Plays with stereotyped villains and heroes who represent extremes of good and evil.

memoir (p. 78) A subgenre of creative nonfiction that uses as its subject matter events from the writer's past.

metaphor (p. 50, 52) Relating of two apparently unlike things to each other by means of a common element that isn't obvious.

monologue (p. 34–35, 39) Speech by one character addressed to a silent or absent listener (sometimes the audience).

motivation (p. 35, 40) The factor or factors that cause a character to think, act, or speak in a certain way.

myth (p. 60–61) Myths often tell the stories of ancient deities, sometimes describing their exploits, sometimes explaining how a particular god or goddess came into being. Some myths address the mysteries of nature, including the creation of the universe and its diverse population.

narrative essay (p. 80) An essay that tells a story.

narrative poetry (p. 68) Poems that tell stories, often presenting a significant episode or series of episodes in the life of one or two primary characters.

narrator (p. 38, 40) See **author.**

new historicism (p. 84, 86) New-historicist criticism is related to sociological criticism and reader-response criticism in that its proponents point out the impact of the politics, ideologies, and social customs of the author's world on the themes, images, and characterizations of the work.

nonfiction (p. 78–82) prose works that are based on fact.

objective narrator (p. 39, 41) A narrator who, like a camera, shows only external events and conversations but does not go inside the minds of characters or offer evaluations and judgments.

octave (p. 68) In literature, the first eight lines of a Petrarchan (Italian) sonnet, rhyming abbaabba and usually developing an idea or image on which the final six lines of the poem (the sestet) comment.

ode (p. 72) In Greek drama, the dances and songs of the chorus, which end scenes and sometimes comment on the action of a scene or provide background information clarifying it.

omniscient narrator (p. 38, 40) A narrator who knows everything, can report both external actions and conversations as well as the internal thoughts of all characters, and often provides evaluations and judgments of characters and events.

open form (p. 67–68) The form used in poems that do not follow established patterns for lines, stanzas, or rhymes.

orchestra (p. 72) In ancient Greece, the round area at the foot of the amphitheater where dramas were performed and where the chorus generally danced and sang.

parable (p. 61–62) A form of short fiction that teaches a lesson or explains a complex spiritual concept.

patriarchal (p. 85) Male dominated.

persona (p. 38, 40) The speaker in any literary work that uses the first-person point of view.

personification (p. 51, 52) Attributing to an inanimate object the qualities of a person or animal.

Petrarchan sonnet (p. 68) Also called the Italian sonnet, a lyric poem of fourteen lines divided into two parts: an octave (the first eight lines) with the rhyme scheme abbaabba, and a sestet (the final six lines) with the rhyme scheme cdecde (or some variation).

plot (p. 28, 31) The sequence of events and actions in a literary work.

point of view (p. 37–39, 40) The position from which the details of the work are reported or described.

protagonist (p. 37, 40) The major character, with whom the reader generally sympathizes.

psychoanalytic criticism (p. 84, 85) Psychoanalytic criticism views the themes, conflicts, and characterizations of a work primarily as a reflection of the needs, emotions, states of mind, and subconscious desires of the author.

quatrain (p. 68) A stanza of poetry consisting of four lines.

reader-response criticism (p. 84–85) Reader-response criticism focuses on the meaning that is created when a reader interacts with a text.

realistic drama (p. 73–74) Plays presenting everyday life—crises, conflicts, and emotional responses to which ordinary people can relate.

reliable/unreliable narrator (p. 39, 40–41) A reliable narrator convinces readers that he or she is reporting events, actions, and conversations accurately and without prejudice. An unreliable narrator raises suspicions in the minds of readers that events, actions, and conversations may be reported inaccurately and that evaluations may be made with prejudice, intentional or unintentional.

resolution (p. 75) The conclusion of a tragic drama, in which order is generally restored to the society at large.

rhyme (p. 49–50, 52) The matching of final sounds in two or more words.

rhythm (p. 49–50, 52) Pattern of sound.

romantic comedy (p. 76) A comic drama in which the source of humor is frequently mistaken identity and unexpected discoveries.

round character (p. 36, 40) A character who shows many different facets, often presented in depth and with great detail.

satiric comedy (p. 75) Comic drama that exposes the foibles and shortcomings of humanity.

scenic directions (p. 45, 46) Explanation at the beginning of a play that provides details of the setting.

sestet (p. 68) The final six lines of a Petrarchan (Italian) sonnet, with the rhyme scheme cdecde (or some variation), and which generally comment on an idea or image developed in the first eight lines (octave).

setting (p. 44–45, 46) The time and place of a literary work, including social, political, and economic background as well as geographic and physical location.

Shakespearean sonnet (p. 68) See **English sonnet.**

short story, nonrealistic (p. 62–63) A form of short fiction that began in the nineteenth century and has continued to evolve. The nonrealistic short story has the fully developed characters, settings, and plots of the realistic short story but also includes supernatural or absurd elements. Unbound by realistic dimensions of time and space, unfettered by the laws of physics or even by the conventions of human psychology, authors of nonrealistic short stories tease and push their own imaginations—and those of their readers—in new and sometimes unsettling directions.

short story, realistic (p. 62) A form of short fiction that originated during the nineteenth century and has continued to evolve. The realistic short story differed from earlier forms of fiction in many ways. Nineteenth-century realistic short stories focused on scenes and themes enacted by ordinary people. Characters were developed more fully; rather than representing one primary quality, the central figures of short stories exhibited the complexities and contradictions of real people. Plots, too, were expanded to become more intricate and to suggest the internal working of characters' souls and minds as well as to depict their external actions. Settings became more than briefly sketched backdrops; times and places were described in vivid detail.

Most important, realistic short stories moved away from teaching one particular moral or lesson.

simile (p. 50, 52) Comparison of two apparently unlike things, using the word "like" or "as."

sociological criticism (p. 84, 85) Sociological criticism argues that interpretation of literature is profoundly affected both by the societal forces that surround authors and by the societal forces that surround readers. (See also **feminist criticism** and **Marxist criticism.**)

soliloquy (p. 35, 40) Speech by one character in a play, given while the character is alone on the stage or standing apart from other characters and intended to represent the inner thoughts of the character.

speaker (p. 38, 40) See **author.**

stage directions (p. 35–36, 40) Comments provided by the playwright to give actors (or readers) information about the time(s) and place(s) in which the play is set, actors' actions, and ways of speaking particular lines.

static character (p. 37, 40) A character who does not change in any significant way during the course of a literary work.

strophe (p. 72) In Greek drama, that part of the ode in which the chorus moves from right to left onstage.

structure (p. 28–29, 31) The pattern formed by the events and actions in a literary work.

style (p. 48, 52) The way an author chooses words, arranges them in lines, sentences, paragraphs, or stanzas, and conveys meaning through the use of imagery, rhythm, rhyme, figurative language, irony, and other devices.

symbol (p. 51, 52) In a literary work, an object, action, person, or animal that stands for something more than its literal meaning.

syntax (p. 49, 52, 66–67) The way words are arranged in phrases or sentences and the way phrases or sentences are arranged in paragraphs (fiction), speeches (plays), or lines and stanzas (poetry).

theater of the absurd (p. 74) Plays with actions that lead in no predictable direction and in which the motivations of characters are often contradictory or absent altogether. Conversations and speeches often ramble disjointedly.

theme (p. 55–56) The central idea of a work of literature; a generalization; an idea that can be broadly applied both to the work itself and to situations outside the work.

thesis statement (p. 95) A sentence or group of sentences, usually appearing near the beginning of an essay, indicating what a writer plans to say about his or her topic.

tone (p. 48, 52) The attitude of the author toward the subject of the work.

tragedy (p. 74–75) Drama that focuses on life's sorrows and serious problems. Traditionally, the tragic play looks at the life of a royal figure or highly respected individual who meets his or her downfall.

tragic hero (p. 75) In a tragedy, a character who, having enjoyed high status in society, meets his or her downfall for one (or a combination) of three reasons: fate or coincidence beyond the control of the character, a flaw in the character, or a mistake in judgment.

tragicomedy (p. 76) A play in which elements of comedy and tragedy are mixed.

transition (p. 109) Words, phrases, and sentences that connect one paragraph or section to the next.

verbal irony (p. 51, 52) A discrepancy between what is said and what is meant or between what is said and what the reader knows to be true.

Credits

Text:

Joan Aleshire, "Slipping." Copyright © Joan Aleshire 1985 in *Poetry*; 1987 in *This Far, QRL Poetry Series.* Reprinted by permission.

Sherman Alexie, "Evolution" from *The Business Of Fancy Dancing.* Copyright © 1992 by Sherman Alexie. Used by permission of Hanging Loose Press.

Maya Angelou, "Graduation in Stamps" from *I Know Why The Caged Bird Sings.* Copyright © 1969 and renewed 1997 by Maya Angelou. Used by permission of Random House, Inc.

Jose Armas, "El Tonto del Barrio." Copyright © Jose Armas. First published by Pajarito Publications.

Margaret Atwood, "The City Planners" from *The Circle Game.* Copyright © 1966 by Margaret Atwood. Originally published in Canada by House of Anansi. Reprinted by permission of Houghton Mifflin Company and Phoebe Larmore Agency on behalf of the author. "You Fit into Me" from *Selected Poems, 1965–1975.* Copyright © 1976 by Margaret Atwood. Reprinted by permission of Houghton Mifflin Company and House of Anansi Press, Inc. All rights reserved.

W. H. Auden, "Musee des Beaux Arts" from *W. H. Auden: Collected Poems.* Copyright © 1940 and renewed 1968 by W. H. Auden. Used by permission of Random House, Inc.

James Baldwin, "Sonny's Blues." Originally published in *Partisan Review.* Collected *In Going To Meet The Man.* © 1965 by James Baldwin. Copyright renewed. Published by Vintage Books. Reprinted by arrangement with the James Baldwin Estate.

Toni Cade Bambara, "The Lesson" from *Gorilla, My Love.* Copyright © 1972 by Toni Cade Bambara. Used by permission of Random House, Inc.

Willis Barnstone, "To Me He Seems Like a God" from *Sappho And The Greek Lyric Poets,* translated by Willis Barnstone. Copyright © 1962, 1967, 1988 by Willis Barnstone. Used by permission of Schocken Books, a division of Random House, Inc.

Kristine Batey, "Lot's Wife." Copyright © 1978 by *Jam To-Day.* Reprinted with permission.

Ervin Beck, "Fugard's 'Master Harold . . . and the Boys'" from *Explicator,* Winter 2000, Vol. 58, Issue 2. Copyright © 2001. Reprinted with permission of the Helen Dwight Reid Educational Foundation. Published by Heldref Publications, 1319 18th St., NW, Washington DC 20036-1802.

David Bevington, footnotes from "Hamlet" from *The Complete Works Of Shakespeare,* 4/e, edited by David Bevington. Copyright © 1997 by Addison-Wesley Educational Publishers, Inc. Reprinted by permission of Pearson Education, Inc.

Elizabeth Bishop, "The Fish" from *The Complete Poems: 1927–1979* by Elizabeth Bishop. Copyright © 1979, 1983 by Alice Helen Methfessel. Reprinted by permission of Farrar, Straus and Giroux, LLC.

Chewing Blackbones, "Old Man and Old Woman" from *Indian Legends from The Northern Rockies* by Ella B. Clark. Copyright © 1966 University of Oklahoma Press. Reprinted by permission of the publisher. All rights reserved.

Laura Bohannan, "Shakespeare in the Bush," *Natural History,* Vol 75, 1966, pp. 28–33. Copyright © 1966 Laura Bohannan.

Neal Bowers, "Driving Lessons" from *Out of the South.* Reprinted by permission of the author.

Kay Boyle, "Astronomer's Wife" from *Life Being The Best & Other Stories.* Copyright © 1988 by Kay Boyle. Reprinted by permission of New Directions Publishing Corp.

Gwendolyn Brooks, "The Mother" and "We Real Cool" from *Blacks.* Copyright © 1991 Gwendolyn Brooks. Reprinted by permission of Brooks Permissions.

Index of First Lines (alphabetical)

Index of Authors, Titles, and Subjects